DR. NORMAN A. WIGGINS

Grant Stephenson
Wilmington, Delaware

SCHOOL RECORD

Gallery

AUSTIN WAKEMAN SCOTT
Professor of Law

A Harvard Law S...
al...ni function
... to find
...rs of
...is
...rous
...same

SELECT CASES AND OTHER AUTHORITIES

ON

THE LAW OF TRUSTS

BY

AUSTIN WAKEMAN SCOTT

STORY PROFESSOR OF LAW IN HARVARD UNIVERSITY

Second Edition

LANGDELL HALL, CAMBRIDGE
PUBLISHED BY THE EDITOR
1931

Copyright, 1931
BY AUSTIN WAKEMAN SCOTT

THE · PLIMPTON · PRESS
NORWOOD · MASS · U · S · A

PREFACE

During the dozen years which have elapsed since the first edition of this book was published, the subject of Trusts has been one of increasing importance. The number and kinds of trusts which have been created and the value of the property held in trust have greatly increased. New problems and new applications of old problems have been presented to trustees, lawyers and courts. Many recent cases have been inserted in the present edition and the footnotes have been extensively revised. The editor has attempted to furnish the student with sufficient material to show him the nature of the trust device, what it is today and how it became what it is, what are the functions which it performs and how it performs them.

A. W. S.

LANGDELL HALL,
MARCH, 1931.

TABLE OF CONTENTS

TABLE OF CASES vii
TABLE OF STATUTES ix
BIBLIOGRAPHY x
LIST OF LORD CHANCELLORS AND LORD KEEPERS xii

CHAPTER I.
THE NATURE OF A TRUST 1
   Sec.   I.   A Trust distinguished from a Use 1
   Sec.   II.   A Trust distinguished from a Bailment 14
   Sec.   III. A Trust Obligation distinguished from a Liability for a Tort 16
   Sec.   IV. A Trust distinguished from a Debt or Contract . . 20
            1. In General 20
            2. The Relation Between Banker and Customer . 46
                A. Deposit of Money 46
                B. Deposit of Commercial Paper 69
   Sec.   V.   A Trust distinguished from a Condition 83
   Sec.   VI. A Trust distinguished from a Mortgage or Pledge . 89
   Sec.   VII. A Trust distinguished from an Equitable Charge . 91
   Sec. VIII. A Trust of a Chose in Action distinguished from an Assignment 96
   Sec.   IX. A Trust distinguished from an Executorship 110

CHAPTER II.
THE CREATION OF A TRUST 125
   Sec.   I.   The Intention to Create a Trust 125
   Sec.   II. Consideration 137
   Sec.   III. The Statute of Frauds 172
   Sec.   IV. Statutes of Wills 191

CHAPTER III.
THE ELEMENTS OF A TRUST 206
   Sec.   I.   The Subject-Matter of a Trust 206
   Sec.   II. The Trustee 221
   Sec.   III. The *Cestui Que Trust* 250

CHAPTER IV.
CHARITABLE TRUSTS 287

CHAPTER V.

Resulting and Constructive Trusts 337
    Sec.   I.   Where an Express Trust Fails in Whole or in Part.   337
    Sec.   II.   Where an Express Trust does not Exhaust the Entire Property Transferred to the Trustee 356
    Sec.   III.   Where an Intended Trust is not Expressly or is not Properly Declared 368
    Sec.   IV.   Where the Purchase-Money is Paid by One Person and the Conveyance is Taken in the Name of Another 413
    Sec.   V.   Where a Person Acquires an Interest in Property in Regard to which, by Reason of his Fiduciary Position, he owes a Duty to Another 440
    Sec.   VI.   Where Property is Acquired by One Person by the Wrongful Use of the Property of Another . . . 475

CHAPTER VI.

The Administration of Trusts 517
    Sec.   I.   The Nature of the Remedies of the *Cestui Que Trust* against the Trustee 517
    Sec.   II.   Powers and Duties of the Trustee 528
    Sec.   III.   The Investment of Trust Funds 542
    Sec.   IV.   Successive Beneficiaries 555
    Sec.   V.   Liabilities of the Trustee to the Beneficiary 580

CHAPTER VII.

Liabilities to Third Persons 587

CHAPTER VIII.

The Transfer of the Interest of the Cestui Que Trust 622

CHAPTER IX.

The Persons who are Bound by a Trust 667

CHAPTER X.

The Termination of a Trust 769
Appendix A — Modern Uses of the Trust Device 801
Appendix B — Form of Deed of Trust 805
Appendix C — Form of Unfunded Life Insurance Trust Agreement 810
Index 815

TABLE OF CASES

Adams v. Adams	228
Amherst College v. Ritch	390
Anon. (Bro. Abr.)	3, 8, 138
Anon. (Cary 11)	7
Anon. (Fitz. Abr.)	668
Anon. (Freem. C. C. 261)	320
Anon. (6 Jenk. C. C. pl. 30)	670
Anon. (4 Leon. 2)	83
Anon. (Roll. Abr.)	141
Anon. (3 Swanst. 79n.)	534
Anon. (2 Vent. 361)	413
Anon. (Y. B. 12 & 13 Ed. III.)	14
Anon. (Y. B. 4 Ed. IV.)	523
Anon. (Y. B. 5 Ed. IV.)	623, 625, 667
Anon. (Y. B. 8 Ed. IV.)	668
Anon. (Y. B. 14 Hen. VIII.)	668
Arguello, Re	552
Armstrong v. Wolsey	368
Ashley v. Denton	14
Attorney General v. Downing	319
Attorney General v. Landerfield	222
Aylsworth v. Whitcomb	770
Babbitt v. Fidelity Trust Co.	547
Baker v. Disbrow	585
Baptist Association v. Hart's Exrs.	288
Barker v. Keate	138
Barthrop v. West	633
Bascom v. Albertson	296
Baugh's Exr. v. Walker	442
Beatty v. Guggenheim, etc. Co.	465
Becher v. Contoure Laboratories	467
Belknap v. Belknap	664
Bischoff v. Yorkville Bank	713
Bisel v. Ladner	207
Blackwell v. Blackwell	402
Boggs v. Yates	173
Bottomley v. Fairfax	626
Bovey v. Smith	719
Bowden v. Brown	334
Bowditch v. Attorney General	311
Boyes, Re	394
Brandon v. Robinson	637
British Red Cross, Re	364
Broadway Bank v. Adams	640
Brooks v. Davis	774
Brown, Re	134
Brown v. Burdett	281
Bryant v. Bryant	406
Bryant v. Klatt	183
Bullock, Re	652
Burton v. Boren	251
Butterworth v. Keeler	308
Cable v. St. Louis Ry. Co.	104
Caldwell v. Caldwell	388
Campbell v. Drake	479
Carpenter v. Carpenter	625
Carrington v. Manning's Heirs	111
Cathorpe, Ex parte	542
Cave v. Cave	753
Chace v. Chapin	688
Chace v. Gardner	177
Chambers v. Chambers	16
Chase Nat. Bk. v. Sayles	164
City of Sturgis v. Meade Co. Bk.	46
Claflin v. Claflin	783
Clark's Case	519
Clark v. Campbell	268
Clarke, Re	342
Coggeshall v. Pelton	310
Colonial Trust Co. v. Brown	538
Commissioners v. Pemsel	302
Compton's Case	673
Conybeare's Settlement	241
Cornet v. Cornet	554
Cunnack v. Edwards	366
Curriden v. Chandler	163
Da Costa v. De Pas	318
Dale v. Sollet	520
Daly v. Farrell	769
Danser v. Warwick	175
Dantzler v. McInnis	590
D'Arcy v. Blake	627
Davies v. Otty	370
Davis, Re	423
Davis v. Downer	433
Dean, Re	277
Deare, Re	584
Dearle v. Hall	660
DeLadson v. Crawford	786
Dickinson, App.	544
Digby v. Legard	338
Dixon v. Caldwell	483
Dixon v. Olmius	386
Doe v. Passingham	10
Doily v. Sherratt	530
Downer v. Church	94
Drummond, Re	285
Duncan Townsite Co. v. Lane	758
Eaton v. Boston Trust Co.	649
Edwards v. Edwards	573
Ellenborough, Re	212
Equitable Trust Co. v. First Nat. Bk.	63
Equitable Trust Co. v. Rochling	73
Essex Trust Co. v. Enwright	469
Evansville Bk. v. German-Amer. Bk.	82

vii

TABLE OF CASES

Case	Page
Eyre v. Burmester	720
Farmers Savings Bk. v. Pugh	689
Farrell v. Passaic Co.	152
Farrigan v. Pevear	613
Farrington v. Lee	520
Fidelity Ins. Co. v. Clark	746
Fletcher v. Fletcher	166
Flye v. Hall	521
Fogg v. Middleton	98
Folk v. Hughes	250
Foly's Case	636
Foord, Re	360
Foreman v. Foreman	420
Foster v. Elsley	136
Frost v. Frost	198
Fur & Wool Trading Co. v. Fox	480
Geiger v. Simpson, etc. Church	617
Graham v. King	535
Graves v. Graves	206
Great Berlin Co., Re	348
Green v. Blackwell	238
Green v. Folgham	208
Gregory v. Bowlsby	375
Guidise v. Island Refining Corp.	56
Gurlitz, Re	215
Hamer v. Sidway	27
Hamilton v. Drogo	658
Hammond v. Messenger	96
Harding v. Glyn	125
Harland v. Trigg	127
Harrop v. Cole	462
Hartman v. Hartle	440
Hartzell v. Whitmore	382
Herlihy v. Coney	430
Hickok v. Bunting	34
Hiles v. Garrison	227
Hill v. Peters	761
Holmes v. Holmes	180
Hooper v. Felgner	4
Howells v. Hettrick	685
Hull v. Farmers' Co.	650
Humphrey's Est.	129
Jackson v. Phillips	325
Jacquet v. Jacquet	91
James Roscoe, Ltd. v. Winder	490
Jessup v. Smith	606
Jevon v. Bush	224
Jones v. Old Colony T. Co.	195
Kain v. Gibboney	283
Kansas Pac. Ry. Co. v. Cutter	117
Keech v. Sandford	447
Kellogg, Re	235
Kildare v. Eustace	525
King v. Boys	222
King v. Daccombe	624
King v. Denison	95
Legniti v. Mechanics Nat. Bk.	59
Lensman, Re	776
Lewellin v. Mackworth	674
Lewis v. Switz	587
Lippitt v. Thames Co.	69
London Banking Co. v. Bank	723
Long v. Mechem	419
Lucas, Re	302
Lurie v. Pinanski	448
McAlpine, Re	122
McEvoy v. Boston Bank	191
M'Fadden v. Jenkyns	36
McGowan v. McGowan	435
M'Mahon v. Fetherstonhaugh	503
Magruder v. Drury	443
Mann v. Bank	681
Marshall's Trustee v. Rash	633
Mason v. Pomeroy	592
Matthews v. Thompson	188
Megod's Case	517
Meinhard v. Salmon	450
Melenky v. Melen	630
Merry v. Abney	701
Miller v. Davis	414
Minot v. Baker	320
Molera v. Cooper	39
Moore v. Darton	35
More v. Mayhow	696
Morgan v. Malleson	145
Morice v. Bishop of Durham	258
Morley v. Morley	536
Mortimer v. Ireland	240
Murray v. Lylburn	742
Mussett v. Bingle	275
Newell v. Hadley	728
Newman v. Newman	765
Nirdlinger's Estate	559
Noel v. Jevon	669
Norman v. Prince	265
Northwest Lumber Co. v. Bank	49
Note (Fitz. Abr.)	667
Nowell v. Hudston	138
Oatway, Re	498
O'Brien v. Mass. Catholic Order	216
Olliffe v. Wells	398
Oxley, Re	602
Palmer v. Schribb	125
Parker v. Hall	678
Pegge v. Skynner	225
Pember v. Knighton	304
People v. Meadows	30
Perabo v. Gallagher	646
Philbrick's Settlement	798
Philip Carey Co. v. Pingree	605
Phillips v. Phillips	749
Pimbe's Case	221
Pittsburgh Nat. Bk. v. McMurray	22
Plympton v. Boston Dispensary	555
Poage v. Bell	671

Poff v. Poff	159
Price's Estate	246
Pugh v. Highley	693
Pye, Ex parte	142
Raybould, Re	596
Reichenbach v. Quin	275
Reichert v. Mo. etc. Co.	242
Reminger v. Joblonski	428
Rex v. Williams	623
Rhode Island Co. v. Copeland	609
Richards v. Delbridge	146
Richardson, Re	600
Ringo v. McFarland	680
Robinson v. Robinson	580
Rorebeck v. Benedict Flour Co.	512
St. Nicholas Bk. v. State Nat. Bk.	76
Salmon, Re	543
Salusbury v. Denton	339
Sambach v. Dalston	9
Saunders v. Dehew	699
Saunders v. Vautier	781
Sayer v. Wynkoop	257
Schultz's Appeal	391
Scott v. Jones	110
Sears v. Attorney General	317
Selous, Re	771
Shaler v. Trowbridge	475
Sharington v. Strotton	139, 518
Shaw v. Spencer	701
Sheffield v. Parker	119
Shoemaker v. Hinze	21
Sieger v. Sieger	486
Sinclair v. Purdy	378
Skehill v. Abbott	437
Slater v. Oriental Mills	504
Smith, Re	790
Smith v. Alterly	84
Smith v. Mooney	528
Smithwick v. Bank	144
Sonley v. Clock-Makers Co.	226
Spickernell v. Hotham	44
Spokane County v. Bank	508
Stambaugh's Estate	793
Steele v. Clark	41
Stevens, Re	577
Stewart v. Hamilton	779
Stokes v. Cheek	797
Stout v. Stout	385
Supreme Lodge v. Rutzler	103
Swetland v. Swetland	205
Symson v. Turner	11
Tetley, Re	348
Thetford School, Re	323
Thomas v. Thomas	415
Thomassen v. Van Wyngaarden	101
Thomson, Re	537
Thornton v. Howe	304
Tillman v. Kifer	384
Titcomb v. Morrill	373
Todd v. Meding	107
Toplan v. Hoover	697
Totten, Re	200
Tourville v. Naish	684
Townsend, Re	248
Trinity College v. Browne	587
Trustees of M. E. Church v. Trustees	354
Tucker v. Linn	24
Tyrrel's Case	8
Van Hagan, Re	352
Vidal v. Girard's Exrs.	291
Vincent v. Kelly	219
Walter J. Schmidt & Co., Re	495
Washington Loan Co. v. Bank	79
Watling v. Watling	530
Watts v. Ball	626
Weekes' Settlement	132
Wehrle v. Mercantile Bk.	89
Welch v. Episcopal School	777
Welford v. Stokoe	337
Wetherell v. Langston	237
Wetmore v. Porter	675
Whitehead v. Bishop	149
Whiting v. Hudson Trust Co.	737
Whittemore v. Equitable Trust Co.	254
Williams v. Barton	445
Willys-Overland, Inc. v. Blake	710
Witham's Case	632
Wittmeier v. Heiligenstein	231
Woodbury v. Hayden	357
Woodruff v. Woodruff	226
Woodward v. Walling	86
Wright v. Wilkin	84
Wych v. East India Co.	674

TABLE OF STATUTES

Statute of Uses, 27 Hen. VIII. c. 10	1
Statute of Charitable Uses, 43 Eliz. c. 4	287
Statute of Frauds, 29 Chas. II. c. 3	172
Wills Act, 7 Will. IV. & 1 Vict. c. 26	191
Trustee Act, 1925, sec. 33(1)	657
Mass. G. L., 1920, c. 208, sec. 18	242
N. Y. Real Prop. Law, Consol. Laws, 1909, chap. 50	12

BIBLIOGRAPHY

ABBOTT. Cases on Equity Jurisprudence and Trusts, 1909.

AGNEW. Law of Trusts in British India, 2 ed., 1920.

AMES. Cases on Trusts, 2 ed., 1893 (herein referred to as " Ames ").
  An extensively annotated collection of cases by a pioneer to whom his successors owe a great debt.

AMES. Lectures on Legal History, 1911.
  A posthumous collection of legal articles by a great scholar, most of them on questions of the law of Trusts, to which are added previously unpublished lectures on forms of actions.

ASHBURNER. Principles of Equity, 1902.

BACON. Reading on the Statute of Uses, Rowe's ed., 1804.
  A book which shows the versatility of one who has perhaps inaccurately been called "the wisest, brightest, meanest of mankind."

BEACH. Trusts and Trustees, 1897.

BILLSON. Equity in its Relations to Common Law, 1917.

BIRRELL. Duties and Liabilities of Trustees, 1896.
  A series of lectures delivered by a noted author, editor of Boswell and former Irish Secretary, with a very deft touch.

BISPHAM. Principles of Equity, 10 ed., 1922.

BOGERT. Handbook of the Law of Trusts, 1921.
  An excellent elementary textbook.

BOYLE. Law of Charities, 1837.

BOURCHIER–CHILCOTT. Charities, 3 ed., 1912.

BRACKENRIDGE. Essay on Trusts and Trustees, 1842.

BRIDGMAN. Law of Charitable Uses, 1805.

BRISTOWE. Mortmain and Charitable Uses Act, 1891.

CANFIELD. Cases and Statutes on Trusts and Powers, Perpetuities, Accumulations and Charitable Uses in N. Y., 1914.

CAREY. Cases on Trusts, 1931.

CARLISLE. Origin of Commission on Charities, 1828.

CHAPLIN. Express Trusts and Powers, 1897.

COMPLEAT ATTORNEY. 1656.

CONYNGTON, KNAPP, PEMBERTON. Wills, Estates, and Trusts, 1921.

COSTIGAN. Cases on Trusts, 1925.

COSWAY. Manual of Trust Law, 1928.

CRUISE. Essay on Uses, 1795.

DUKE. Law of Charitable Uses, 1676.

DWIGHT. Argument in Rose Will Case, 1863.

ESCARRA. Les Fondations en Angleterre, 1907.

FINLASON. History of the Laws of Mortmain, 1853.

FLINT. Trusts and Trustees, 1890.

BIBLIOGRAPHY

FONBLANQUE. Equity, Laussat's ed., 1835.

GARROW. Trusts and Trustees, 1919. Supplement, 1930.
> A good book of especial value to students intending to practice in New Zealand.

GILBERT. Uses and Trusts, 3 ed., 1811.
> A very valuable book on the historical side.

GODEFROI. Trusts and Trustees, 5 ed., 1927.
> A good modern English treatise.

GRAY. Restraints on Alienation, 2 ed., 1895.
> A powerful attack upon spendthrift trusts; *vox clamantis in deserto*.

GRAY. Rule against Perpetuities, 3 ed., 1915.
> A classic on the subject with which it deals.

HAMILTON. Law of Charities in Ireland, 2 ed., 1881.

HART. Digest of the Law of Trusts, 1909.
> An excellent English book containing the text of a proposed code drafted by the author, with extensive annotations.

HERNE. Law of Charitable Uses, 2 ed., 1663.

HILL. Trustees, 1845, Am. ed., 1857.
> An excellent treatise though now long out of date.

HOBHOUSE. The Dead Hand, 1880.

HUSTON. Enforcement of Decrees in Equity, 1915.

KELLY AND COLE–HAMILTON. Trusts, 1927.

KENNESON. Cases on the Law of Trusts, 1911.

KENNY. Endowed Charities, 1880.

KERLY. Equitable Jurisdiction of the Court of Chancery, 1890.

LANGDELL. Brief Survey of Equity Jurisdiction, 2 ed., 1908.

LANGDELL. Summary of Equity Pleading, 2 ed., 1883.

LEWIN. Trusts, 13 ed., 1928.
> The leading English textbook. The more recent editions are of less value to American students than the earlier editions, owing to numerous statutory changes of the law in England.

LORING. Trustee's Handbook, 4 ed., 1928.
> A small and very practical work of value to trustees and lawyers.

McKINNEY. Trust Investments, 2 ed., 1927.

MADDEN. Wills, Trusts and Estates, 1927.

MAITLAND. Lectures on Equity and the Forms of Action, 1913.
> A posthumous book by a great English legal historian.

MENZIES. Law of Scotland affecting Trustees, 2 ed., 1913.

MITCHESON. Charity Commission Acts, 1887.

NOBLE. Notes on Charity Trusts under Massachusetts Decisions, 2 ed., 1918.

O'LEARY. Charitable Uses, 1847.

PERRY. Trusts and Trustees, 7 ed., 1929.
> The leading American textbook on the subject. It was originally largely taken from Lewin on Trusts and although a great deal of modern American law has been added in the various editions it still retains in many places an old-world flavor.

POMEROY. Equity Jurisprudence, 4 ed., 1918.
> The leading American treatise on equity, of which the third volume is largely devoted to Trusts.

REMSEN. The Preparation of Wills and Trusts, 2 ed., 1930.

Report from the Select Committee (of the House of Commons) on Trusts Administration, 1895.

Reports from the Select Committee (of the House of Commons) on the Trusts Bill, 1908.

ROBINSON. Saving Taxes in Drafting Wills and Trusts, 1930.

ROTH. Der Trust in seinem Entwicklungsgang vom Feoffee to Uses zur amerikaneschen Trust Company, 1928.

SANDERS. Uses and Trusts, 5 ed., 1844, Am. ed., 1855.
A valuable book chiefly on the historical side.

SHATTUCK. The Living Insurance Trust, 1928.

SHELFORD. Law of Mortmain, 1836.

SMITH. Trust Companies in the United States, 1928.
A valuable account by a layman of the history and the activities of trust companies, with an extensive bibliography.

SMITH. Cases on Trusts, 1928.

SNELL. Principles of Equity, 20 ed., 1929.

SPENCE. Equity Jurisdiction of the Court of Chancery, 1846-9.

STEPHENSON. Living Trusts, 1926.

STEPHENSON. English Executor and Trustee Business, 1930.

STORY. Commentaries on Equity Jurisprudence, 14 ed., 1918.
This book has had a great influence on the development of equity in the United States. The earlier editions are of especial value to the student.

STRAHAN AND KENRICK. Digest of Equity, 5 ed., 1928.

TIFFANY AND BULLARD. Trusts and Trustees, 1862.

TUDOR. Charities and Mortmain, 5 ed., 1919.

TYSSEN. Law of Charitable Bequests, 2 ed., 1921.

UNDERHILL. Trusts and Trustees, 8 ed., 1926.
An excellent modern English treatise.

WHITE AND TUDOR. Leading Cases in Equity, 9 ed., 1928.

WILLOUGHBY. The Legal Estate, 1912.

ZOLLMANN. American Law of Charities, 1924.

LIST OF LORD CHANCELLORS AND LORD KEEPERS

[SINCE THE BEGINNING OF THE REIGN OF HENRY VIII.]

Henry VIII.	Warham, Archbishop of Canterbury	1504
(1509)	Wolsey, Cardinal	1515
	Sir Thomas More	1529
	Sir Thomas Audley	1532
Edward VI.	Wriothesley	1544
(1546-7)	St. John (William Paulet)	1547
	Rich	1547
	Goodrich, Bishop of Ely	1551
Mary	Gardiner, Bishop of Winchester	1553
(1553)	Heath, Archbishop of York	1556
Elizabeth	Sir Nicholas Bacon	1558
(1558)	Sir Thomas Bromley	1579
	Sir Christopher Hatton	1587
	Sir John Puckering	1592

LIST OF LORD CHANCELLORS AND LORD KEEPERS

Monarch	Chancellor/Keeper	Year
James I. (1602–3)	Ellesmere (Thomas Egerton)	1596
	Bacon	1617
Charles I. (1625)	Williams, Bishop of Lincoln	1621
	Coventry	1625
	Finch (John)	1640
	Lyttleton	1641
Charles II. (1648–9)	Clarendon (Edward Hyde)	1658
	Sir Orlando Bridgeman	1667
	Shaftesbury (Anthony Ashley Cooper)	1672
	Nottingham (Heneage Finch)	1673
James II. (1684–5)	Guilford (Francis North)	1682
	Jeffreys	1685
William and Mary (1688–9)	Somers	1693
Anne (1701–2)	Sir Nathan Wright	1700
	Cowper	1705, 1714
	Harcourt	1710
George I. (1714)	Macclesfield (Thomas Parker)	1718
	King	1725
George II. (1727)	Talbot	1733
	Hardwicke (Philip Yorke)	1737
George III. (1760)	Northington (Robert Henley)	1757
	Camden (Charles Pratt)	1766
	Bathurst	1771
	Thurlow	1778
	Loughborough (Alexander Wedderburn)	1793
George IV. (1820)	Eldon (John Scott)	1801, 1807
	Erskine	1806
William IV. (1830)	Lyndhurst (John Singleton Copley)	1827, 1834, 1841
	Brougham	1830
Victoria (1837)	Cottenham (Charles Christopher Pepys)	1836, 1846
	Truro (Thomas Wilde)	1850
	St. Leonards (Edward Sugden)	1851
	Cranworth (Robert Monsey Rolfe)	1852, 1865
	Chelmsford (Frederick Thesiger)	1858, 1866
	Campbell	1859
	Westbury (Richard Bethell)	1861
	Cairns	1868, 1874
	Hatherley (William Page Wood)	1868
	Selborne (Roundell Palmer)	1872, 1880
	Halsbury (Hardinge Stanley Giffard)	1885, 1886, 1895
	Herschell	1886, 1892
Edward VII. (1901)	Loreburn (Robert Threshie Reid)	1905
George V. (1910)	Haldane	1912, 1924
	Buckmaster	1915
	Finlay	1916
	Birkenhead (Frederick Edwin Smith)	1919
	Cave	1922, 1924
	Hailsham (Douglas McGarel Hogg)	1928
	Sankey	1929

For an account of the English Chancellors, see Campbell, Lives of the Chancellors; Atlay, The Victorian Chancellors; Holdsworth, History of English Law, vol. 5, pp. 218–261. For an account of the reports in which their decisions are to be found, see Wallace, Reporters, 4 ed., 457–518; Fox, Hand

Book of English Law Reports; Holdsworth, History of English Law, vol. 5, pp. 274–278; vol. 7, pp. 215–238. See also Winfield, The Chief Sources of English Legal History. See also 15 Harv. L. Rev. 109, 117.

At the beginning of the 19th century there were two judges in the High Court of Chancery, the Chancellor or Lord Keeper (whose authority is the same as that of a Chancellor though the title is of less dignity) and the Master of the Rolls. A dispute as to how far the Master of the Rolls had independent authority was settled by Stat. 3 Geo. II. c. 30 (1730), which provided that all orders and decrees made by him while acting within his authority should be deemed valid orders and decrees of the Court of Chancery, but subject to be revised or modified by the Chancellor. In 1813 a Vice-Chancellor was created, and in 1841 provision was made for two additional Vice-Chancellors. In 1851 two Lords Justices of the Court of Appeal in Chancery were created. Thereafter the three Vice-Chancellors and the Master of the Rolls sat as equity judges of first instance; and the Chancellor might also act as a judge of first instance though he seldom did so. From the decision of any of the three Vice-Chancellors or the Master of the Rolls there lay an appeal to the Court of Appeal in Chancery, in which the Chancellor might sit alone or the two Lords Justices together although in some matters a Lord Justice might sit alone. By the Judicature Act, 1873, the Supreme Court of Judicature was created, composed of the High Court of Justice and the Court of Appeal. The High Court of Justice was composed of five (reduced in 1880 to three) divisions, one of which is the Chancery Division, of which the Chancellor is President. From the latter part of the 17th century an appeal lay from the Court of Chancery, and now lies from the Court of Appeal, to the House of Lords. The Chancellor, unlike the other judges, is a political officer and the office usually changes hands on a change of ministry.

Until 1841 the Court of Exchequer was a court of equity as well as a court of law. An appeal lay from the equity side to the House of Lords. But in 1841 its general equity jurisdiction was transferred to the Court of Chancery.

As to the development of equity jurisdiction in the United States, see Fonblanque, Equity, 4 Am. ed., 12; Pomeroy, Eq. Juris., secs. 40–42, 282–358; Story, Equity Jurisprudence, chap. 2; Wilson, Courts of Chancery in the American Colonies, 2 Select Essays in Anglo-American Legal History, 779, 18 Amer. L. Rev. 226; Woodruff, Chancery in Massachusetts, 5 Law Quar. Rev. 370; Fisher, Administration of Equity through Common Law Forms in Pennsylvania, 2 Select Essays in Anglo-American Legal History, 810, 1 Law Quar. Rev. 455; Keasbey, The Courts of New Jersey, 18 N. J. Law Jour. 69; 19 N. J. Eq. 577 (App.); Proctor, Origin of Chancery Courts in New York, 56 Albany L. Jour. 173.

CASES ON TRUSTS

CHAPTER I.
THE NATURE OF A TRUST.

Section I.
A Trust distinguished from a Use.

AMES, LECTURES ON LEGAL HISTORY, 236–237. We find in the books many references to uses of lands, from the latter part of the twelfth to the beginning of the fifteenth century, but no intimation of any right of the intended beneficiary to proceed in court against the feoffee. But the evidence against such a right is not merely negative. In 1402 a petition to Parliament by the Commons prays for relief against disloyal feoffees to uses because "in such cases there is no remedy unless one be provided by Parliament." The petition was referred to the King's Council, but what further action was taken upon it we do not know. But from about this time bills in equity became frequent. It is a reasonable inference that equity gave relief to *cestuis que use* as early as the reign of Henry V. (1413–1422), although there seems to be no record of any decree in favor of a *cestui que use* before 1446. The first decree for a *cestui que use*, whenever it was given, was the birth of the equitable use in land. Before that first decree there was and could be no doctrine of uses. One might as well talk of the doctrine of gratuitous parol promises in our law of to-day.[1]

THE STATUTE OF USES.

27 Hen. VIII. c. 10 (1535).

WHERE by the common laws of this realm, lands, tenements and hereditaments be not devisable by testament, (2) nor ought to be transferred from one to another, but by solemn livery and seisin, matter of record, writing sufficient made *bona fide*, without covin or

---

[1] For an account of the origin of the law of uses and trusts and its history prior to the Statute of Uses, see Holdsworth, History of English Law, vol. 4, 407–449; Ames, Lect. Leg. Hist., 233–242; 2 Pollock & Maitland, Hist. Eng. Law, 2 ed., 228–239; Maitland, Equity, 23–42; Holmes, Early English Equity, 1 L. Quar. Rev. 162; Turner, Uses before the Statute of Uses, 3 Va. L. Rev. 439; Scott, The Trust as an Instrument of Law Reform, 31 Yale L. Jour. 457.

fraud; (3) yet nevertheless divers and sundry imaginations, subtle inventions and practices have been used, whereby the hereditaments of this realm have been conveyed from one to another by fraudulent feoffments, fines, recoveries and other assurances craftily made to secret uses, intents and trusts; (4) and also by wills and testaments, sometime made by nude parolx and words, sometime by signs and tokens, and sometime by writing, and for the most part made by such persons as be visited with sickness, in their extreme agonies and pains, or at such time as they have scantly had any good memory or remembrance; (5) at which times they being provoked by greedy and covetous persons lying in wait about them, do many times dispose indiscreetly and unadvisedly their lands and inheritances; (6) by reason whereof, and by occasion of which fraudulent feoffments, fines, recoveries and other like assurances to uses, confidences and trusts, divers and many heirs have been unjustly at sundry times disherited, the lords have lost their wards, marriages, reliefs, harriots, escheats, aids *pur fair fils chivalier & pur file marier,* (7) and scantly any person can be certainly assured of any lands by them purchased, nor know surely against whom they shall use their actions or executions for their rights, titles and duties; (8) also men married have lost their tenancies by the curtesy, (9) women their dowers, (10) manifest perjuries by trial of such secret wills and uses have been committed; (11) the King's highness hath lost the profits and advantages of the lands of persons attainted, (12) and of the lands craftily put in feoffments to the uses of aliens born, (13) and also the profits of waste for a year and a day of lands of felons attainted, (14) and the lords their escheats thereof; (15) and many other inconveniences have happened, and daily do increase among the King's subjects, to their great trouble and inquietness, and to the utter subversion of the ancient common laws of this realm; (16) for the extirping and extinguishment of all such subtle practiced feoffments, fines, recoveries, abuses and errors heretofore used and accustomed in this realm, to the subversion of the good and ancient laws of the same, and to the intent that the King's highness, or any other his subjects of this realm, shall not in any wise hereafter by any means or inventions be deceived, damaged or hurt, by reason of such trusts, uses or confidences: (17) it may please the King's most royal majesty, That it may be enacted by his Highness, by the assent of the lords spiritual and temporal, and the commons, in this present parliament assembled, and by the authority of the same, in manner and form following; that is to say,

That where any person or persons stand or be seized, or at any time hereafter shall happen to be seized, of and in any honours, castles, manors, lands, tenements, rents, services, reversions, remainders or other hereditaments, to the use, confidence or trust of any other person or persons, or of any body politick, by reason of any bargain, sale, feoffment, fine, recovery, covenant, contract, agreement, will or otherwise, by any manner means whatsoever it be; that in every such case, all and every such person and persons, and bodies politick, that have or hereafter shall have any such use, confidence or trust, in fee simple, fee tail, for term of life or for years, or otherwise, or any use, confidence or trust, in remainder or reverter, shall from henceforth stand and be seized, deemed and adjudged in lawful seisin, estate and possession of and in the same honours, castles, manors, lands, tenements, rents, services, reversions, remainders and hereditaments, with their appurtenances, to all intents, constructions and purposes in the law, of and in such like estates as they had or shall have in use, trust or confidence of or in the same; (19) and that the estate, title, right and possession that was in such person or persons that were, or hereafter shall be seized of any lands, tenements or hereditaments, to the use, confidence or trust of any such person or persons, or of any body politick, be from henceforth clearly deemed and adjudged to be in him or them that have, or hereafter shall have, such use, confidence or trust, after such quality, manner, form and condition as they had before, in or to the use, confidence or trust that was in them.[1] . . .

ANONYMOUS.

———, 1545.

Bro. Abr. Feoff. al Uses, pl. 52, March's Transl., 94.

A MAN makes a feoffment in fee to his use for term of life, and that after his decease J. N. shall take the profits; this makes a use in J. N. Contrary if he says that after his death his feoffees shall take the profits and deliver them to J. N., this doth not make a use in J. N.: for he hath them not but by the hands of the feoffees.

BACON, READING ON THE STATUTE OF USES, 10. It followeth to consider the parts and properties of an use: wherein by the consent of all books, as it was distinctly delivered by Justice Walmsley in 36 of Elizabeth: That a trust consisteth upon three parts:
  The first, that the feoffee will suffer the feoffor to take the profits.
  The second, that the feoffee upon request of the feoffor, or notice

[1] See Holdsworth, History of English Law, vol. 4, pp. 449–480, 572–581; Holdsworth, The Political Causes which shaped the Statute of Uses, 26 Harv. L. Rev. 108.
  The Statute of Uses was repealed by Law of Property Act, 1925, 15 Geo. V, c. 20, sec. 1. See Bordwell, The Repeal of the Statute of Uses, 39 Harv. L. Rev. 466.
  On the question how far the Statute of Uses is in force in the United States, see Perry, Trusts, sec. 299n.; 16 L. R. A. (N. S.) 1148. See Rood, The Statute of Uses and the Modern Deed, 4 Mich. L. Rev. 109.

of his will, will execute the estates to the feoffor, or his heirs, or any other by his direction.

The third, that if the feoffee be disseised, and so the feoffor disturbed, the feoffee will re-enter, or bring an action to recontinue the possession. So that those three, pernancy of profits, execution of estates, and defence of the land, are the three points of trust.

HOOPER *v.* FELGNER.

Courts of Appeals, Maryland. 1894.

80 Md. 262.

ROBINSON, C. J.[1] . . . After several specific devices and bequests, the testator, by the twelfth clause, directed that all the residue of his estate, real and personal, should be divided into ten equal parts; one equal part thereof he devised and bequeathed to each of his four sons, absolutely. The remaining six parts he devised and bequeathed to his four sons upon trust for his six daughters, in manner following:

" And as to one-tenth part of my said entire residuary estate upon trust to pay the net income thereof as it shall accrue (except as hereinafter provided) unto my daughter, Grace Felgner, during her natural life, and for her sole and separate use, without power of anticipation, or to charge or encumber the trust estate; and from and after her decease, *upon trust* for all and singular the children or child of the said Grace living at her death, and the issue then surviving of any child or children of the said Grace who may be then deceased, equally and *absolutely;* but so that the issue of a deceased child or children, if any, shall take by representation the share or shares only, which their parent or parents, if living, would have taken.

" In case of any one or more of my said six daughters dying without leaving issue surviving, then I give, devise and bequeath the tenth part or tenth parts of my residuary estate devised above in trust for the benefit of such, my daughter or daughters so dying without surviving issue, unto all and every my grandchildren who shall survive such my daughter or daughters so dying, and the then surviving issue of any of my grandchildren who may have previously departed this life leaving such surviving issue, absolutely and equally *per capita* as to such surviving grandchildren, but by representation as to such issue of deceased grandchildren, who are to take by substitution only what their respective parents would have taken had they survived."

Grace Felgner, the life-tenant, died in 1893, leaving two children, Marie Theresa, about nineteen years, and Catharine, about thirteen years of age. These were her only children, and both of them were

[1] The statement of facts and a part of the opinion are omitted.

living at the death of their grandfather, William E. Hooper, the testator.

The plain and obvious intention of the testator was to create and protect a life-estate for his daughter, Grace Felgner, with remainder to her children, if any, and the children of any deceased child *per stirpes;* and in the event of the failure of such children or descendants, then to the other grandchildren of the testator, either nominated by will, or in case of no such nomination, then to his grandchildren generally. The trustees, it is clear, therefore, took a legal *estate* in the trust property, the *equitable life-estate* being in Grace Felgner, the testator's daughter, and the *equitable remainder* being in her two children, then living, subject to the contingency of their death before their mother, and subject in case they survived her, to be diminished by the birth and survival of other children of their mother. And the mother having died, leaving as her only children or descendants Marie Theresa and Catharine, these two children of the life-tenant answer the description of those entitled in remainder; they answer that description at the time of the happening of the contingency, namely, the death of their mother, without other children or descendants, and they are therefore the only persons who could ever have answered it. And this brings us to the real question in this case. Does the trust created by the will continue after the death of Grace Felgner, the life-tenant, or does the property upon her death vest absolutely in her two daughters, both of whom were living at that time? There is nothing, it must be admitted, in the will, providing expressly for the continuance of the trust beyond the life of Grace Felgner, the testator's daughter, nor is there anything from which it can be fairly implied that the testator meant that it should continue after her death. During her life, certain duties are imposed upon the trustees, the language of the will being, "Upon trust to pay the net income thereof, as it shall accrue (except as hereinafter provided), unto my daughter, Grace Felgner, during her natural life, and for her *sole and separate use,* without power of anticipation or to charge or encumber the trust estate, and from and after her decease upon trust for all and singular the children or child of the said Grace living at her death, and the issue *then* surviving of any child or children of the said Grace, who may be then deceased, *equally and absolutely*." The testator does not say that the trustees shall after the death of his daughter receive and pay the net income of the trust property to her children or descendants living at that time, for their sole and separate use, nor does he impose any limitation upon the power of the remaindermen to charge or incumber the estate. After her death they are to hold the property in trust for all and singular the children or child of the said Grace living at her death, *equally and absolutely.* Where an estate is given to trustees and their heirs upon trust to receive and pay the net income thereof to one for life, and upon his death, in trust for all and singular his children and the issue of such children living at the death of the life-tenant, the trust ceases upon the death of such life-tenant, for the reason that it remains no longer an active trust. In such cases the Statute of Uses executes the use in those who are limited to take upon the expiration of the life-estate; or, in other words, the statute transfers the use into possession by converting the estate or interest of the *cestui que trust* into a legal estate, thereby determining the intermediate estate of the trustee. As to the real estate, it is clear, therefore, that upon the death of Grace Felgner, the life-tenant, the trustees, having no longer any active duties to perform, the legal estate was executed under the statute in her two children, and the trust was thereby at an end.

Now, as to the personal property, though it has been said that the object of the statute was to abolish all uses and trusts, yet, as the language of the statute was: "*Whenever any person is seized*," &c., the English Courts, by a strict construction, held that it did not apply to personal property, for the reason that one could [not] be said to be "*seized*" of a mere *chattel interest*. At the same time, however, it may be considered settled, that a trust in regard to personal property will continue so long and no longer, than the purposes of the trust require. And that when all the objects of the trust have been accomplished, the person entitled to the beneficial use is regarded as the absolute owner, and as such, entitled to the possession of the property. Under this will the objects and purposes of the trust, namely, that the trustees should pay the net income to Grace Felgner during her life, and for her sole and separate use, without power of anticipation, &c., were fully accomplished, and upon her death the trustees had no longer any active duty to discharge. And this being so, her two children being entitled to the ultimate use, became the absolute owners of the property.

Nor can we agree with the Court below, that the fact of the minority of one of the *cestui que trusts*, is any reason why the trust should continue until she is *sui juris*. . . .

We find nothing from which it can be inferred that the testator meant the trust to continue after the death of his daughter, the life-tenant.

The purposes of the trust having been accomplished, and the trustees having no longer any active duties to perform, and Marie Theresa Felgner, one of the daughters, being over eighteen years of age, she is entitled in her own right to her share of the personal estate. And as to the other daughter, Catharine Hooper Felgner, she has, the record shows, guardians legally appointed and qualified, and this being so, such guardians are entitled to receive her share of the personal estate. There can be no reason why the trust should continue merely to allow the trustees to receive the income and pay it over to her guardians. In the case of an ordinary bequest to an infant, the guardians are the proper persons to take the property bequeathed and, where a trust has terminated, and one who becomes thereby the absolute owner of the property is a minor, there is no reason why the guardian should not take and hold the property for the benefit of his ward.

Decree reversed and cause remanded in both appeals.[1]

ANONYMOUS.

CHANCERY. ——

Cary 11.

ALTHOUGH [*cestui que use*] of a term for years be not within the Statute of Uses, rather therefore he shall have remedy in Chancery.

BACON, READING ON THE STATUTE OF USES, 42. The second word material is the word *seised:* this excludes chattels. The reason is, that the statute meant to remit the common law, and not but that

[1] In the following cases it was held that an active trust was created which was not executed by the Statute of Uses. Henderson v. Henderson, 210 Ala. 73; Kathman v. Sheehan, 332 Ill. 280; Rosenthal v. Miller, 148 Md. 226; Matthews v. Van Cleve, 282 Mo. 19; Henderson's Estate, 258 Pa. 510; Young v. McNeill, 78 S. C. 143; White v. O'Bryan, 148 Tenn. 18.

In the following cases where no active duties were imposed upon the trustee, it was held that the use was executed and that the legal title vested in the beneficiary. Berry v. Wooddy, 16 Ala. App. 348; Dixon v. Dixon, 123 Me. 470; Woolfitt v. Histed, 208 Mich. 308; Jones v. Jones, 223 Mo. 424; Spann v. Carson, 123 S. C. 371; Welborn v. Holder, 143 S. C. 277.

When all the active duties imposed upon the trustee have been performed, the Statute of Uses will execute the trust. See, in addition to the principal case, Brill v. Green, 316 Ill. 583; Hinds v. Hinds, 126 Me. 521; Jones v. Jones, 223 Mo. 424; Warren v. Warren, 85 N. J. Eq. 346, 589; Zelley v. Zelley, 101 N. J. Eq. 37; Goodgeon v. Stuart, 144 Atl. 670 (R. I. 1929); Lee v. Oates, 171 N. C. 717. See also Lynch v. Swayne, 83 Ill. 336; Springs v. Hopkins, 171 N. C. 486; Wilson v. Heilman, 219 Pa. 237; Holder v. Melvin, 106 S. C. 245; Hudson v. Leathers, 141 S. C. 32. See Perry, Trusts, sec. 309. But see Kales, Estates, sec. 69. See 37 Yale L. Jour. 1099.

In general as to the distinction between active and passive trusts, see Bogert, Trusts, secs. 44–46; 3 Pomeroy, Eq. Juris., sec. 986. For a suggestion as to the reason why the Statute of Uses does not execute active trusts, see 17 Mich. L. Rev. 87.

Testamentary trusts. On the question of the application of the Statute of Uses to wills, see Baker v. White, L. R. 20 Eq. 166; *Re* Tanqueray-Willaume and Landau, 20 Ch. D. 465, 478; *Re* Brooke, [1894] 1 Ch. 43; Gilbert, Uses, 356; Sanders, Uses and Trusts, 260; Challis, Real Property, 3 ed., 387; Perry, Trusts, sec. 320.

Extent of trustee's estate. The trustee ordinarily takes such an estate and only such an estate as is necessary to enable him to perform the trust by the exercise of such powers as are incident to the ownership of the estate. See Perry, Trusts, secs. 298–320; Bogert, Trusts, 291; Kales, Estates, secs. 183–193; 23 Ill. L. Rev. 383; 2 L. R. A. (N.S.) 172.

In England the rule was different in the case of trusts created by deed prior to 1926. See Underhill, Trusts and Trustees, art. 37.

the chattels might ever pass by testament or by parole; therefore the use did not pervert them. It excludes rights, for it is against the rules of the common law to grant or transfer rights; and therefore the statute would not execute them.

COMPLEAT ATTORNEY, ed. 1656, 315. If I be seised of land in fee, and convey it to D. L. and his heirs, to the use of W. S., his executors and administrators, for twenty years, or for any other number of years, in this case the use will be executed within the Statute: But in case where I be possessed of a term of years in being, and grant it to friends to any uses and purposes in trust, this is out of the Statute of Uses, and orderable in Chancery only, where if the trust be broken, I must have remedy.[1]

ANONYMOUS.
COMMON BENCH. 1532.
Bro. Abr. Feoff. al Uses, pl. 40, March's Transl., 90.

THERE is a tenure betwixt the donors and the donees, which is a consideration that the tenant in tail shall be seized to his own use; and the same law of tenant for term of years, and tenant for life, their fealty is due; and where a rent is reserved, there, though a use be expressed to the use of the donor, or lessor; yet this is a consideration that the donee or lessee shall have it to his own use: and the same law where a man sells his land for 20l. by indenture, and executes an estate to his own use; this is a void limitation of the use: for the law by the consideration of money, makes the land to be in the vendee.[2]

TYRREL'S CASE.
COURT OF WARDS. 1557.
2 Dyer 155 a.[3]

JANE TYRREL, widow, for the sum of four hundred pounds paid by G. Tyrrel, her son and heir apparent, by indenture enrolled in chancery in the 4th year of E. VI. bargained, sold, gave, granted, covenanted, and concluded to the said G. Tyrrel all her manors, lands, tenements, &c. to have and to hold the said &c. to the said G. T. and

[1] See Fox's Case, 8 Co. 93 b; Barker v. Keate, 2 Vent. 35, Freem. K. B. 249, 1 Mod. 262, 2 Mod. 249.

[2] "A man cannot sell land to J. S. to the use of the vendor, nor let land to him rendering rent, habend. to the use of the lessor, for this is contrary to law and reason, for he hath recompense for it." Bro. Abr. Feoff. al Uses, pl. 54, (1533).

[3] Benl. (ed. 1669) 61, 1 And. 37, s. c.

his heirs for ever, to the use of the said Jane during her life, without impeachment of waste; and immediately after her decease to the use of the said G. T. and the heirs of his body lawfully begotten; and in default of such issue, to the use of the heirs of the said Jane for ever. *Quaere* well whether the limitation of those uses upon the *habendum* are not void and impertinent, because an use cannot be springing, drawn, or reserved out of an use, as appears *prima facie?* And here it ought to be first an use transferred to the vendee before that any freehold or inheritance in the land can be vested in him by the inrollment, &c. And this case has been doubted in the Common Pleas before now; *ideo quaere legem.* But all the Judges of C. B. and SAUNDERS, Chief Justice, thought that the limitation of uses above is void, &c. for suppose the Statute of Inrollments [cap. 16.] had never been made, but only the Statute of Uses [cap. 10.] in 27 H. VIII. then the case above could not be, because an use cannot be ingendered of an use, &c. See M. 10 & 11 Eliz. fol.

SAMBACH *v.* DALSTON.

CHANCERY. 1634.

Tothill 188.

BECAUSE one use cannot be raised out of another, yet ordered, and the defendant ordered to pass according to the intent.[1]

COMPLEAT ATTORNEY, 314. If I without any consideration bargain and sell my land by indenture, to one and his heirs, to the use of another and his heirs (which is a use upon a use) it seems the court will order this: But if it were in consideration of money by him paid, here it seems the express use is void both in law and equity.

And if a woman in consideration of four hundred pounds paid her by her son, bargain and sell her land by indenture to him and his heirs, to the use of herself for life, and after of the heirs of her son, in which case by law the fee-simple is to the son presently, and the use for life to the mother void; nor is there as it seems any relief for her in this court in a way of equity, because of the consideration paid, but if there were no consideration, on the contrary.

[1] As to the law in regard to a use on a use, see the explanation advanced by Professor Ames in an article on "The Origin of Trusts" in 4 Green Bag 81; 21 Harv. L. Rev. 261; Ames, Lect. Leg. Hist. 243. This explanation is approved in Williams, Real Property, 20 ed., 174, Tiffany, Real Property, 2 ed., 359, and in Maitland, Equity, 42.

DOE ON THE DEMISE OF LLOYD v. PASSINGHAM.

KING'S BENCH. 1827.

6 B. & C. 305.

EJECTMENT for lands in the county of Merioneth. Plea, the general issue. At the trial before Burrough, J., at the last Summer assizes for Salop, it appeared that the lessor of the plaintiff claimed as devisee in tail under the will of Catherine Lloyd, who was coheiress, with her sister Mary, of Giwn Lloyd, who died in 1774. In 1746, by indenture made between himself, G. Lloyd, of the first part, Sarah Hill of the second part, Sir Rowland Hill and John Wynne of the third part, and Sir Watkin Williams Wynne and Edward Lloyd of the fourth part; in consideration of an intended marriage with the said Sarah Hill, and of a sum of 8000*l.*, being the marriage portion of the said Sarah Hill, paid or secured to be paid to him Giwn Lloyd, he, Giwn Lloyd, did grant, release, and confirm unto the said Sir Watkin Williams Wynne and Edward Lloyd in their actual possession then being, by virtue of an indenture of bargain and sale, &c., and to their heirs and assigns, certain premises therein particularly described, and, amongst others, the premises in question; to have and to hold the said premises with their appurtenances, unto the said Sir Watkin Williams Wynne and Edward Lloyd, their heirs and assigns; to the only proper use and behoof of them the said Sir Watkin Williams Wynne and Edward Lloyd, their heirs and assigns for ever, upon trust, nevertheless, and subject to the several uses, intents, and purposes thereinafter mentioned, that is to say, to the use of the said Giwn Lloyd and his heirs.[1] . . .

Giwn Lloyd died in 1774, and Sarah his wife in 1782, intestate, and without having had any issue. Catherine Lloyd, the testatrix, continued in possession of the estate from the death of Sarah Lloyd until the time of her own death, in 1787. For the defendants, it was contended, that the legal estate was vested in Sir W. W. Wynne and Edward Lloyd, by the deed of 1746, and, consequently, that neither Giwn Lloyd nor the testatrix had any legal estate; and, therefore, the lessor of the plaintiff could not derive any such estate from her. The learned Judge reserved the point, and the plaintiff having obtained a verdict, a rule nisi for entering a nonsuit was granted in Michaelmas term.

HOLROYD, J.[2] I agree with my Brother Bayley, that in this case there ought to be a new trial. Upon the first perusal of the deed in question I had no doubt that the legal estate was vested in the trustees, having always understood that an use cannot be limited upon an use; and although I was struck by the ingenuity of the distinction

[1] A part of the statement of facts, setting forth limitations of the equitable interest which did not take effect, is omitted.

[2] Concurring opinions of Bayley and Littledale, JJ., are omitted.

pointed out by Mr. Taunton, yet upon further consideration it appears to me that his argument does not warrant it. The argument is, that as the trustees did not in the first instance take to the use of another, but of themselves, they were in by the common law, and not the statute; that the first use was, therefore, of no effect, and the case was to be considered as if the deed had merely contained the second limitation to uses. But that is not so, for although it be true that the trustees take the seisin by the common law, and not by the statute, yet they take that seisin to the use of themselves, and not to the use of another, in which case alone the use is executed by the statute. They are, therefore, seised in trust for another, and the legal estate remains in them. As to the question of intention, even if it were intended that the deed should operate in a different mode from that pointed out by the law, when the legal estate is given to trustees, that intention cannot countervail the law. But the intention appears to me altogether doubtful; the absence of trustees to preserve contingent remainders affording a strong reason for supposing that the parties meant to give the legal estate to the trustees.

Rule absolute for a new trial.

SYMSON *v.* TURNER.

CHANCERY. 1700.

1 Eq. Ca. Abr. 383n.

NOTWITHSTANDING this statute [the Statute of Uses] there are three ways of creating an use or a trust, which still remains as at common law, and is a creature of the court of equity, and subject only to their controul and direction: 1st, Where a man seised in fee raises a term for years, and limits it in trust for A., &c. for this the statute cannot execute, the termor not being seised. 2dly, Where lands are limited to the use of A. in trust to permit B. to receive the rents and profits; for the statute can only execute the first use. 3dly, Where lands are limited to trustees to receive and pay over the rents and profits to such and such persons; for here the lands must remain in them to answer these purposes; and these points were agreed to.

———

HOLDSWORTH, HISTORY OF ENGLISH LAW, vol. 1, pp. 454–5. Of the history of this branch [uses and trusts] of the jurisdiction of the court [of Chancery] I shall speak at length in later volumes. Here it will be sufficient to say that the Chancellor so developed the duties of the feoffees to uses, that is the persons to whom property had been conveyed on trust, that the interest of the cestui-que use, that is the person for whose benefit the property was conveyed, became a form of equitable ownership of a sort which has no parallel in any other system of law. This branch of equitable jurisdiction was from the first, and has always continued to be, its most important branch. As Maitland has said, in the early days of the court it made its fortune. It imparted a much needed element of elasticity into the mediæval land law, and gave to landowners far wider powers over their property than they possessed at common law. But there is no doubt that the possession of these powers facilitated frauds on purchasers, frauds on creditors, evasions of the mortmain laws, and evasion of the rights of king and lords to the incidents of military tenure. Hence, from the latter part of the fourteenth century onwards, these uses were controlled and regulated by the legislature. These attempts at legislative control culminated in 1535 in the Statute of Uses. That statute adopted the plan of abolishing in certain cases the dual ownership of the feoffees to uses and the cestui-que use, by taking from the feoffees to uses so much of their legal estate as was sufficient to give to the cestui-que use a legal estate corresponding to his equitable interest. One result of the statute, therefore, was to give jurisdiction over the uses which had been thus turned into legal estates to the courts of common law. We shall see that for some time before 1535 the rivalry between the courts of common law and the court of Chancery had been growing acute; and, on that account, the common lawyers assisted the passage of a statute which gave them jurisdiction at the expense of the court of Chancery. But the statute did not apply to all uses. It did not, for instance, apply to cases where the feoffees were possessed of chattels real or personal to the use of others; nor did it apply to cases where they had active duties to perform, for instance if they were given land to the use that they should collect and pay the rents to a beneficiary. Thus the court of Chancery still retained some of its jurisdiction; and it regained much of the jurisdiction of which the statute had deprived it in the latter part of the seventeenth century. The court of Wards and the courts of common law had decided in *Tyrrel's Case*, (1557) Dyer 155a, that if land was conveyed to A to the use of B to the use of C, the statute gave B the legal estate, and that the second use in favour of C was void; but after the Restoration the court of Chancery decided to enforce this second use as a trust. Thus the old distinction between legal and equitable estates in conveyances of property to which the Statute of Uses applied was restored; and so, in another form, the court of Chancery recovered its old jurisdiction.

NEW YORK REAL PROPERTY LAW.[1]

Consol. Laws, 1909, chap. 50.

SEC. 91. Uses and trusts concerning real property, except as authorized and modified by this article, have been abolished; every

[1] These provisions in substantially the same form were adopted in New York in 1830. Rev. Stat. 1830, Pt. 2, chap. 1, tit. 2. See Canfield, New York

estate or interest in real property is deemed a legal right, cognizable as such in the courts, except as otherwise prescribed in this chapter.

SEC. 92. Every person, who, by virtue of any grant, assignment or devise, is entitled both to the actual possession of real property, and to the receipt of the rents and profits thereof, in law or equity, shall be deemed to have a legal estate therein, of the same quality and duration, and subject to the same conditions, as his beneficial interest; but this section does not divest the estate of the trustee in any trust existing on the first day of January, eighteen hundred and thirty, where the title of such trustee is not merely nominal, but is connected with some power of actual disposition or management in relation to the real property which is the subject of the trust.

SEC. 96. An express trust may be created for one or more of the following purposes:

1. To sell real property for the benefit of creditors;
2. To sell, mortgage or lease real property for the benefit of annuitants or other legatees, or for the purpose of satisfying any charge thereon;
3. To receive the rents and profits of real property, and apply them to the use [1] of any person, during the life of that person, or for any shorter term, subject to the provisions of law relating thereto;
4. To receive the rents and profits of real property, and to accumulate the same for the purposes, and within the limits, prescribed by law.

SEC. 99. Where an express trust relating to real property is created for any purpose not specified in the preceding sections of this article, no estate shall vest in the trustees; but the trust, if directing or authorizing the performance of any act which may be lawfully performed under a power, shall be valid as a power in trust, subject to the provisions of this chapter. Where a trust is valid as a power, the real property to which the trust relates shall remain in or descend to the persons otherwise entitled, subject to the execution of the trust as a power.

SEC. 109. When the purpose for which an express trust is created ceases, the estate of the trustee shall also cease

---

Cases and Statutes on Trusts and Powers; Chaplin, Express Trusts and Powers. They do not apply to trusts in personalty. Matter of Carpenter, 131 N. Y. 86.

They were adopted, with some modifications, in California, Michigan, Minnesota, Montana, North Dakota, Oklahoma, South Dakota and Wisconsin. See Bogert, Trusts, sec. 47. In California the restrictions have been repealed. Stats. 1929, p. 282.

[1] The word " use " was substituted for the words " education and support or either " by Laws of 1830, ch. 320, sec. 10.

Section II.

A Trust distinguished from a Bailment.

ANONYMOUS.

Common Pleas. 1339.

Y. B. 12 & 13 Edw. III. 244.

DETINUE of chattels to the value of 100*l.* against an Abbot by a man and his wife, on a bailment, made by the father of the wife when she was under age, of chattels to be delivered to his daughter, when she was of full age, at her will; and they counted that he delivered pots, linen, cloths, and 20*l.* in a bag sealed up, &c. — *Pole.* He demands money, which naturally sounds in an action of Debt or Account; judgment of the count. — *Stouford.* We did not count of a loan which sounds in Debt, nor of a receipt of money for profit, which would give an action of Account, but of money delivered in keeping under seal, etc., which could not be changed; and if your house were burnt, that would be an answer. — SCHARDELOWE. *Answer over.*[1]

ASHLEY'S ADMINISTRATORS AND HEIRS *v.* DENTON.

Court of Appeals, Kentucky. 1822.

1 Littell 86.

PER CURIAM. Thomas Denton and wife exhibited this bill in chancery against the administrators of Thomas Ashley, deceased, charging that said decedent was the son of the female complainant by a former husband; that during her widowhood she became possessed of sundry slaves, which passed to her from the estate of a deceased relative in North Carolina, where she resided, and that she removed with them to Kentucky, in some of the upper counties; that she entrusted the negroes aforesaid with her said son, for the purpose of his going in search of a suitable residence for her, and there making preparations for her family, and then he was to return and move her to it; that the son took possession of the slaves, for the purposes aforesaid, and, to her astonishment, did not return, nor was he heard of for several years, and was then discovered, by a person employed for the purpose of searching for him, to be living, with the slaves

---

[1] A bailment of goods by A to B, to deliver to C, or for use of C, gave C, as in the principal case, the right to maintain detinue against B. See Ames, 52n.

Similarly trover will lie. Flewllin *v.* Rave, 1 Bulst. 68; Jackson *v.* Anderson, 4 Taunt. 24; Jones *v.* Cole, 2 Bail. (S.C.) 330.

aforesaid, in the state of Tennessee. Some time after his discovery, he removed to the now county of Butler in this state, where he resided until his death, in 1817. That, after his return to Kentucky, he refused to surrender them, when demanded; that they were increased, and are in the possession of said administrators and heirs. They allege that they are fully able to substantiate said facts by proof, and pray that the restoration of the slaves may be decreed, with payment of the hire.

The defendants, in their answer, . . . insist that there is no equity in the bill, and that the remedy is at law. . . . The court below decreed . . . the slaves to be restored, and the hire to be paid. From this decree the administrators and heirs of Ashley appealed.[1]

It is now contended that the Chancellor had no jurisdiction of the case, and that the remedy of the appellee is properly at law. On the other side, it is insisted that the claim of the appellants is founded on a trust, and that the son took and held the slaves for the use of his mother, and therefore the Chancellor properly entertained jurisdiction of the case.

It is true that uses and trusts are a favored part of the jurisdiction of the Chancellor, and frequently he will, on that ground, decide in cases where the law may be adequate to give relief. But, notwithstanding this acknowledged authority, it cannot be extended to every case where one party has trusted another, or, in other words, placed a confidence which has been abused. If so, every case of bailment, and every instance of placing chattels by loans or hire, would be swallowed up by courts of equity. Nay, every case where credit was given for debt or duty would soon be drawn into the same vortex. It ought, then, to be confined to cases of controlling legal rights, vested and remaining in trustees, created as such in some proper mode, and not be extended to all cases of abused confidence. If the case, therefore, of the appellee is to be tested by the original bill alone, we have no doubt it makes out no case for the interposition of the Chancellor; that placing the slaves in the possession of her son, for the purpose of preparing and improving her a home, and his right then to cease, was not such a trust as would sustain the bill, and that she had a plain and adequate remedy at law.[2] . . .

---

[1] Only so much of the case is given as relates to the point of jurisdiction.

[2] Young *v.* Mercantile Co., 140 Fed. 61, aff'd 145 Fed. 39; Taylor *v.* Turner, 87 Ill. 296, 301; Tennessee Packing, etc., Co. *v.* Fitzgerald, 140 Ill. App. 430; Thompson *v.* Whitaker Iron Co., 41 W. Va. 574, *accord.*

Wood *v.* Rowcliffe, 2 Ph. 382, 3 Hare 304; Schrafft *v.* Wolters, 61 N. J. Eq. 467, reversed on another ground, 63 N. J. Eq. 793, *contra.*

In Doyle *v.* Burns, 123 Iowa 488, the court said (p. 497): "It [the argument] fails to distinguish between a bailment and a trust. We are aware that some very good text-writers have made the same mistake. Story on Bailments, sec. 2; 2 Kent's Com. 559. A bailment exists whenever the ownership and the possession of specific corporeal chattels are lawfully severed from each other. In a trust of personal property, the legal ownership passes to the trustee, and he has something more than bare possession. In cases of

SECTION III.

A Trust Obligation distinguished from a Liability for a Tort.

CHAMBERS *v.* CHAMBERS.

SUPREME COURT, ALABAMA. 1892.

98 Ala. 454.

McCLELLAN, J. This bill is exhibited by J. W. Chambers and W. H. Chambers, as the administrators of the estate of Isaac H. Chambers, deceased, against George H. Chambers, Mary A. Chambers and Malinda Chambers, who are, as are also the complainants, heirs at law and children of the intestate. The case made by its averments, is this: Isaac H. Chambers, during his last illness, had at his residence, but in a different room from that in which he lay, a fire-proof combination lock safe, in which he kept a considerable sum of money — about four thousand dollars — some account books, and choses in action, a mortgage evidencing and securing an indebtedness amounting to about twelve hundred dollars of said George Chambers to him, being among the latter. On the forenoon of the day preceding his death, said Mary Chambers, being alone in the room with her father, " asked him for the combination of the safe, stating certain reasons for wanting it; he told her that the paper with the combination on it was in his coat pocket, but refused to let her or anyone else have it before he died." Afterwards when he fell asleep, said Mary took some papers from his said coat pocket, and complainants assert their belief that the paper containing the combination was among them. On the afternoon of the same day, the said Mary and her brother George Chambers, " went into the room where the safe was, and locked all the doors by which an entrance

---

bailment the legal ownership is in the bailor, and the bailee simply has possession, which may or may not be for some specific purpose." See McIntyre *v.* Smith, 154 Md. 660; National Cattle Loan Co. *v.* Ward, 113 Tex. 312. See also Maitland, Equity, 45–48.

A safe deposit company or bank is a bailee and not a trustee of securities deposited in a safe deposit box. See National Safe Dep. Co. *v.* Stead, 250 Ill. 584; Roberts *v.* Stuyvesant Safe Dep. Co., 123 N. Y. 57. See also 9 Harv. L. Rev. 131–143; Ann. Cas. 1912B 441.

If the trustee transfers trust property to a purchaser for value and without notice, the interest of the beneficiary is cut off. See Chap. VIII, *post*. On the other hand, a bailee cannot ordinarily cut off the interest of the bailor by such a transfer. By the old Teutonic law, it is true, a bailor's remedy did not extend beyond the bailee and he could not recover against a purchaser or finder or even a thief; but this doctrine became obsolete centuries ago. See Scott, Cases on Trusts, 1 ed., 17.

could be obtained into said room, and, having the combination then in their possession, tried for a long time to unlock the same "; but failing to do so, they requested Dr. Patterson, who was about leaving the premises, to come into the room and then asked him to " see if he could unlock the combination to said safe," assuring him that they had permission to open it. Patterson then unlocked the safe, and the said George and Mary, in his presence, took therefrom said money, books, papers and mortgage, and put the same in a bag, of which said Mary retained possession. Four or five days after this, and three or four days after the death of Isaac H. Chambers, " the said George and Mary Chambers divided said papers and money as follows: giving the said George Chambers a thousand dollars in money, said mortgage and an account book; to the said Mary Chambers fourteen hundred and eighty dollars in money, and to the said Malinda Chambers twelve hundred dollars in money; and the said Mary Chambers kept possession of a paper which the said Isaac H. Chambers had left in the safe directing how his property should be divided after his death." George Chambers is wholly insolvent. Mary Chambers owns nothing except her interest in said estate, which will not amount to more than four or five hundred dollars. And said Malinda is not worth the amount of twelve hundred dollars; and complainant expresses a fear that she will soon be totally insolvent. At the time of filing the bill, Mary Chambers had spent two hundred and thirty dollars of the money apportioned to her, George had expended five hundred dollars of his share, and Malinda had expended a small part — about seventy dollars — of the twelve hundred dollars, which were allotted to her in the division between the three; and complainants aver that " if they are permitted to keep possession of said money, &c., they will waste and squander the entire sum, and it will be wholly lost to the rest of the heirs of the estate." It is further alleged that the respondents " lay pretended claims to the amounts severally held by them, all of which is entirely false and without foundation," and that complainants " have not an adequate remedy at law, for the reason that said property is kept concealed by the defendants so that it can not be levied upon by any means afforded by a court of law." The prayer is for the appointment of a receiver to take charge of said money, account books, mortgage and papers pending the suit, that an order be passed requiring the respondents to immediately deliver said property into the hands of the receiver, &c.; that they be required to set forth an account of what of said property they have disposed of in any way, and a list of the persons to whom they, or either of them have loaned any of said property, and that, upon final hearing, said property be decreed to belong to complainants, as such administrators, as trust funds for the purpose of administration, and that the same be delivered in their hands, &c., &c. Answer on oath was waived.

Respondents demurred to the bill, and assigned the following grounds:

"1. The bill shows a larceny or trespass in taking the money and other things out of the safe of Isaac H. Chambers in his life time, and if complainants had any rights, they have an adequate and complete remedy at law. 2. The bill nowhere alleges any fraud on the part of the defendants whereby a trust might be created. 3. The bill nowhere alleges any confidence or trust reposed in the defendants by Isaac H. Chambers, deceased, to give the complainants, who have no more rights than their intestate would have had, if he had lived, the remedy here invoked. 4. The bill shows on its face that as to the money alleged to have been taken from the iron safe in the life time of Isaac H. Chambers, deceased, if the complainants have any rights as to the money, they had adequate and complete remedy at law. 5. That on the allegations of the bill, it appears that this court has no jurisdiction of the subject-matter about which complaint is made in this bill."

The court overruled this demurrer, and from the decree in that behalf this appeal is prosecuted.

It is insisted for appellees that the facts averred in the bill involve a charge of fraud against the respondents, against which equity will relieve because of the absence of an adequate legal remedy, and also, that on the case made, the respondents are trustees *de son tort* of the money and choses in action in controversy for the estate of Isaac H. Chambers, deceased. Both these contentions are, in our opinion, unsound.

The facts present no case of fraud, but wholly a case of simple trespass or larceny. There was no undue influence resorted to to get possession of the property, no overreaching, no false representations, or fraudulent concealment practised as means of acquiring the possession and control of the money and papers. All that was done as the facts are now stated amounted only to the surreptitious abstraction of the property from Isaac H. Chambers' safe without his knowledge or consent; and surely this can be no more a fraud in legal contemplation than had the respondents been casual strangers to Chambers, and had unlocked his stable and carried away his horse *animo furandi*.

It is equally clear that the transaction involved no element of an express trust. No trust or confidence was reposed in the respondents by Chambers in respect of this property. George and Mary Chambers secured possession of this property in the life time of the owner, not only without his consent, or knowledge even, but against his expressed wish and purpose. He not only did not intend that they should take the property with the understanding that they should dispose of it in a certain way or hold it for certain purposes, but he did not consent to their possession of it at all. Every material element of an express trust is lacking. Does the transaction involve a *constructive* trust? It is too clear for much discussion that considered as between the respondents and Isaac H. Chambers in his life time, no such trust can be evolved out of the premises. Had the respondents acquired the *title* to this property *by fraud*, they would have been constructive trustees for the benefit of Isaac H. Chambers, while he lived, and for his estate now. But they clearly acquired no *title* to the property by *fraud* or otherwise; they have no title to it now, and have, as we have seen, committed no fraud but rather a trespass or larceny. Clearly too, if the property when they intermeddled with and acquired the possession of it was trust property, they would be held to have taken in subject to the trust and thereby to have made themselves trustees *in invitum*. But at that time the property had no semblance of a trust character. It was simply held and owned by Isaac H. Chambers in his own right and to his own beneficial use. To hold that the respondents by depriving him — not of his title, for that of course remained in him, but — of his possession and use became trustees for his benefit would be to convert all wrongful possessions into trust estates and all persons who tortiously acquire the possession of the property of another into trustees for the owner, a result which finds no support in principle or authority. An essential element of all trusts is a use in a person other than the trustee or rather, since the statute of uses, a trust is a use not executed into a legal estate. Not only was this element wholly wanting in the case as it stood between George and Mary Chambers, on the one hand, and Isaac H. Chambers, on the other, they, on the facts averred, holding this property not to the use of another but for their own benefit and behoof as joint tort feasors, but for the further essential element of a *title* in them to feed uses, so to speak, is not at all involved. Very clearly they were not trustees to Isaac H. Chambers by construction or otherwise. They simply held the possession of this property at the time of his death as the result of a purely wrongful caption made for their own benefit, and involving no other duties or obligations upon them than would have rested on any other person who had without pretense of right or suggestion of other than ulterior selfish purposes seized or stolen the property in question. Isaac H. Chambers had a clear right to sue them in trover, or in detinue upon identification, but he had no standing in chancery to invoke the execution of a trust; and it will not be contended that his representatives on the facts as now averred, had any other or different rights or remedies than were his while he lived. Had what occurred taken place after his death, had these respondents then intermeddled with the assets of his estate and assumed to dispose of the same by way of administration on his estate, clearly they could be proceeded against as trustees *de son tort*, for such they would have made themselves because of the *then* trust character of the property which would have continued impressed upon it in their hands; but that is not the case made by the bill. Of course the mere fact that complainants' legal remedies would prove abortive because of the insolvency of the respondents can not impart equity to the bill, there must be some ground of equity jurisdiction stated, and that inadequacy of legal remedies which results from the impotency of process out of courts of law can never be a basis for equitable interposition. And we are constrained to hold it to be without equity, and of consequence that the chancellor erred in overruling the demurrer.

It may be that if George and Mary Chambers took possession of the money and papers in the life time of Isaac H. not for the purpose of conversion to their own use simply, or of making such dispositions of it as they would of their own property, but for the purpose of holding it till after his death as his property, and then dividing and distributing it in accordance with written directions left by him, and if they held it in this way and for this purpose till a time subsequent to his death and then assumed to divide and distribute it as assets of his estate that they and Malinda Chambers would, on these facts, be held to be trustees. We do not decide this, however, and have referred to this possible aspect of the case because there is passing statement in the bill which leads us to infer the property may have been taken and held in this way and for this purpose, but, if so, the facts are not averred.

Reversed and remanded.[1]

Section IV.

A Trust distinguished from a Debt or Contract.

1. *In General.*

THE ACTIONS OF ACCOUNT AND DEBT. The distinction between a trust of money and a debt was to a certain extent developed in early cases involving the question whether the common-law action of account or that of debt was the proper remedy where A paid money to B which was to be repaid to A, or where A paid money to B which was to be paid to C. If the money was lent to B, B being authorized to use the money as he liked, the action of debt could be maintained by A where the amount was to be repaid to him, or by C where the amount was to be paid to him. On the other hand, if money was delivered by A to B and B took it as a

---

[1] See Doyle *v.* Murphy, 22 Ill. 502.

On the question whether if one acquires title to a chattel by a tort equity will compel him to reconvey when the legal remedy is adequate, see Ames, Cas. Eq. Juris., 44n.

On the question whether a converter who receives property in exchange for the property converted is a constructive trustee of the property so received, see Ames, Cas. Eq. Juris., 44n. See also Chap. V, sec. VI, *post*.

fiduciary and not by way of loan, it was held that A or C might maintain an action of account but not an action of debt. Anon., Y. B. 6 Hen. IV., fol. 7, pl. 33, and cases cited in Ames, Cases on Trusts, 1. The scope of the action of debt was later extended, and it was held that either debt or account would lie against a person who received money as a fiduciary. Clark's Case, Godb. 210 (1612), *post*. Although debt lay only if the amount due was liquidated, it was held by Lord Mansfield in Dale *v.* Sollet, 4 Burr, 2133 (1767) *post*, that *indebitatus assumpsit* would lie although the amount due was not liquidated. As has been pointed out (Langdell, Brief Survey of Equity Jurisdiction, 85; Ames, Cases on Trusts, 8), a person receiving money as a fiduciary does not become a debtor although the action of debt or *indebitatus assumpsit* might be maintained against him. The common-law action of account proved too cumbersome for practical use and was superseded by a bill in equity and by the actions of debt and *indebitatus assumpsit*. See Holdsworth, Hist. Eng. Law, vol. 3, 426, 428.

SHOEMAKER *v.* HINZE.

SUPREME COURT, WISCONSIN. 1881.

53 Wis. 116.

APPEAL from the Circuit Court for Waukesha County.

The action is to recover $40, which the complaint alleges "the defendant received from the plaintiff, as his agent, . . . to the use of the plaintiff." Demand of payment thereof before action, and neglect of the defendant to pay the same, are also alleged. The answer, in addition to the general denial, is in substance that the money was received by the defendant as a bailment, without compensation, and that it was stolen from him without his fault or neglect. The case is further stated in the opinion. The plaintiff recovered, and the defendant appealed from the judgment.

LYON, J. The uncontradicted evidence is, that the plaintiff, when at work for the defendant, requested the defendant to take care of $40 in money for him. After some hesitation, the defendant consented to do so, and received the money. The defendant thereupon, presumably in the presence of the plaintiff, placed the money, with other money of his own, in his wallet. The next day the defendant took a small amount of money from the wallet for use, and in the evening of that day added $100 of his own money to that remaining therein. The evidence tends to show that during the same night the wallet and contents were stolen from the defendant's vest pocket, in which he had placed the same. We think the evidence shows conclusively that the parties did not contemplate or understand that the same identical money received by the defendant was to be kept for and returned to the plaintiff on demand, but only that a like sum of money should be repaid by the defendant. The transaction is not, therefore, a bailment or special deposit, but rather what, in commercial language, is termed a general deposit, which is not a bailment, but is in the nature of a loan. Story on Bailments, §§ 41, note 2, 88. So we think the liability of the defendant in this case is precisely the same as the liability of a bank for a general deposit made with it; that is, he is not liable in tort for the money, but is liable in *assumpsit* for a sum equal to the sum deposited. His liability is absolute, and it is immaterial that the money was lost without his fault. The instructions to the jury related solely to the law of bailment. The view we take of the case renders it unnecessary to determine whether the judge gave the law correctly or not; for on the undisputed facts the plaintiff was entitled to recover, and the defendant could not have been injured by any error in the charge. Van Trott *v.* Weise, 36 Wis. 439; Dufresne *v.* Weise, 46 Wis. 290.

By the Court. — *The judgment of the circuit court is affirmed.*[1]

PITTSBURGH NATIONAL BANK OF COMMERCE
v. McMURRAY.

SUPREME COURT, PENNSYLVANIA. 1881.

98 Pa. 538.

Before SHARSWOOD, C. J., MERCUR, GORDON, PAXSON, TRUNKEY and STERRETT, JJ. GREEN, J., absent.

ERROR to the Court of Common Pleas No. 1, of Allegheny county: Of October and November Term 1881, No. 9.

Assumpsit, by George W. and William McMurray against the Pittsburgh National Bank of Commerce, to recover the sum of $1,300.

On the trial, before Collier, J., the following facts appeared: The plaintiffs, who lived in Noblestown, had been in the habit for several years of sending money to S. B. W. Gill, an attorney-at-law in Pittsburgh, as their agent and attorney, for the purpose of investment, on the understanding that Gill was to pay interest on the money from the time he received it until he invested it. On September 17th, 1877, the plaintiffs sent the sum of $1,300 to Gill's office, with a message that it was for investment. Mr. Gill was absent

---

[1] Chiles *v.* Garrison, 32 Mo. 475, *accord.*

But if there is a bailment or trust of money, the depositee is not liable for its loss, unless he is at fault. See Doorman *v.* Jenkins, 2 A. & E. 256; Giblin *v.* McMullin, L. R. 2 C. P. 317; Tracy *v.* Wood, 3 Mas. (U. S.) 132; Foster *v.* Essex Bank, 17 Mass. 479; Furber *v.* Barnes, 32 Minn. 105; First Nat. Bk. *v.* Ocean Nat. Bk., 60 N. Y. 278; Scott *v.* Nat. Bk., 72 Pa. 471; Duncan *v.* Magette, 25 Tex. 245.

from the city, and the money was left with his son and business assistant, who gave the following receipt: —

"Received, Pittsburgh, September 17th, 1877, of George W. and W. McMurray, the sum of thirteen hundred dollars, to be invested by me for them.
S. B. W. GILL,
H. B. GILL."

The standing arrangement that Gill was to pay interest on such funds until invested was not countermanded or alluded to. H. B. Gill, on the same day, deposited this sum in the defendant bank, to the credit of his father's general private account. Subsequently he drew from the bank, on blank checks left with him and signed by his father, sums exceeding $1,300.

Two months afterwards, it being currently rumored that S. B. W. Gill was a defaulter and had absconded, the plaintiffs demanded the sum of $1,300 from the bank, on the ground that it was trust money belonging to them. At this time the balance to Gill's credit was $1,954. The bank refused the demand. On the same day a writ of sequestration, issued from the Orphans' Court, was served upon the bank, and the said balance standing to Gill's credit, was paid to the sheriff, who afterwards, under an order of the Orphans' Court, paid the same to Gill's assignee in bankruptcy. The plaintiffs afterwards brought this suit.

The bank alleged that they had an agreement with Gill that he was to keep a large balance on deposit to secure a line of discounts; that they received the $1,300 as Gill's money, without notice of any trust; and that, in fact, the transaction between the plaintiffs and Gill was a loan and not a trust.

The defendant presented, *inter alia*, the following point: "(5) If the jury find that the money in question was sent to S. B. W. Gill for investment under the same arrangement as he had before that time received other moneys from plaintiffs for investment, to wit, under an arrangement that he (Gill) was to pay interest to the plaintiffs until the money should be invested, then the verdict should be for the defendant. And if the fact was as stated by Wm. McMurray, one of the plaintiffs, that such arrangement was not countermanded when they sent the money claimed in this case to Gill, the presumption would be that the same arrangement was to continue in respect to said money as had been agreed upon before that time in respect to other moneys placed by plaintiffs in Gill's hands for investment." *Refused.* Exception.

Verdict and judgment for the plaintiffs. The defendant took this writ, assigning for error, *inter alia*, the refusal of the above point.

Mr. Justice PAXSON delivered the opinion of the court, October 24th, 1881.

The defendant's fifth point ought to have been affirmed. If, as was alleged, the money was placed in Gill's hands for investment, with an understanding or agreement that until he could find a satisfactory mortgage he should pay interest thereon, the plaintiffs below cannot hold him as a trustee, nor follow his deposit in the bank as trust money. As the court below negatived the point, we must assume the jury would have found the facts as stated therein. The plaintiffs cannot treat Gill in the dual character of trustee and debtor. Undoubtedly the receipt by him of the money for investment, without more, would have made him a trustee. The money would have been trust money, and if misapplied, could have been followed until it reached the hands of an innocent holder for value. But the agreement to pay interest necessarily implied the right to use the money. Interest is the price or consideration for the use of money. It follows that Gill became the mere banker or debtor of the plaintiffs, subject to the duty of investing the money in a mortgage when a suitable opportunity should occur. In the meantime he had the right to use it in any way his convenience or necessities required. When deposited in the bank, it was the money of Gill, not of the plaintiffs, if the facts be as stated in the point.

The remaining assignments are without merit.

Judgment reversed, and a venire facias de novo awarded.[1]

TUCKER *v.* LINN.

COURT OF CHANCERY, NEW JERSEY. 1904.

57 Atl. 1017.

SUIT by Ethel L. Tucker against Clarence Linn, individually and as administrator of John Linn, deceased, and others. Bill dismissed.

STEVENSON, V. C. (orally). The complainant in her bill charges that between and during the years 1895 and 1898 the complainant " placed the sum of $1,840 in the hands of the defendant John Linn for investment in such securities as he might deem safe, and for the care, custody, management, and control for her of such securities after the investment of the said money; that the said John Linn, acting as attorney of and trustee for the complainant, thereupon took the entire charge of said moneys and investments until the death of the said John Linn, which occurred in the year 1898; that at the time of his death the said John Linn had in his possession, as attorney as aforesaid, and held in trust for the complainant, the

---

[1] Wetherell *v.* O'Brien, 140 Ill. 146, *accord.*

The cases are numerous to the effect that an agreement to pay interest indicates a debt and not a trust. Old Colony Trust Co. *v.* Puritan Motors Corp., 244 Mass. 259. On the other hand, where the agreement is to pay such interest as the money may earn, a trust and not a debt is created. Allen *v.* Pollard, 109 Tex. 536; Keller *v.* Washington, 83 W. Va. 659.

said sum of $1,840, or the securities representing the same, together with the accrued interest or dividends thereon." I think that quotation from the bill sufficiently indicates what the cause of action is which the complainant sets forth. She failed to procure any of this trust estate from Mr. Linn in his lifetime. She says that she has failed to procure any of it since his death from his administrator, the defendant Clarence Linn. In my opinion, there is an entire failure of proof of that perfectly plain, simple, correctly stated, equitable cause of action. No doubt the counsel of complainant was disappointed at the rulings of the court with respect to the competency of the complainant to testify herself in this cause in regard to statements by the deceased, John Linn, or personal transactions with the deceased, John Linn. The proof which was presented and allowed to be competent indicated that at some time — probably in the year 1894 — John Linn received $1,000 from the complainant. It was also proved that from 1893 until April, 1898, the time of the death of John Linn, the complainant acted in the capacity of working housekeeper, and that her services as such were not gratuitous. Whether she was paid for those services or not did not appear. That she rendered the services was perfectly plain, and that they were not rendered gratuitously was also plain. But here the proof stops, and the insistment is on the part of the complainant that $840 of those earnings were retained by Mr. Linn, and under an arrangement or understanding that he would pay interest — a better interest for the amount than the complainant could receive from the banks. Now, I am not going to deal with the question whether the fact of the payment of the $1,000 in 1894 or thereabouts was proved, or whether it was proved that any moneys due from Mr. Linn to the complainant as wages were retained by him, and remained unpaid by him at the time of his death. The answer sets up three defenses. The answer insists that the complainant has a complete remedy at law, and that she has no standing in a court of equity to prosecute her claim. The answer, in the next place, pleads the statute of limitations. I may not state the order of these defenses correctly. And then, last of all, denies the existence of the indebtedness. As I recall it, it denies that John Linn ever received the said sum of $1,840, or any sum, from the complainant, and denies that John Linn at the time of his death owed the complainant anything. It seems to me that, if the evidence is to be construed most favorably to the complainant, if it be conceded that John Linn received this $1,000, and also owed the complainant some amount of money for wages earned by her, and which he had not paid at the time of his death, the demand of the complainant is cognizable in a court of law, and not cognizable in equity. In my judgment, there is an entire failure, as I said before, to prove this particular equitable cause of action which is set forth in the bill of complaint. Undoubtedly, the cause of action set forth in the bill is one of which this court has full cognizance. That cause of action involves a perfectly simple and well-settled trust. The charge is that particular money was paid over by the complainant to the defendant's intestate to be invested in securities, and these securities were to be held by the defendant's intestate. No equitable title to the money passes in such a case. No equitable title to the securities in any way exists in the holder. If this bill had been proved to be true, then John Linn received money which he had no right to appropriate to his own use. He did not, by receiving the money, become a debtor to the complainant. He was charged with the duty of expending these moneys for securities or investing them in securities, and when he did so the equitable title to those securities would be in the complainant, and he would be the mere trustee, not having any beneficial ownership.

Now, it seems to me that, even if this bill could be amended so as to make its allegations correspond with the proofs, and the proofs are to be taken most favorably to the complainant, as I am undertaking to do, then we have a transaction, or series of transactions, which resulted in creating the relation of debtor and creditor between these people, pure and simple. The money, whether you take the $1,000 or take any portion of these wages that were earned — the money received or retained by John Linn — according to the bargain between these two persons, was to be appropriated by John Linn; was to become his own property, his own estate. He could expend it, do with it as he pleased. He was not to hold that money in specie as a deposit for the benefit of the complainant, who trusted him with it, in which case one kind of a trust would exist; and he was not to pay it out for her use; and he was not to invest it in securities, and then hold the securities for her, the legal title to which would be in him and the equitable title to which would be in her. He was to appropriate that money, and pay her back, either on demand or at some future time, other money, equivalent to what he had borrowed, presumably, plus interest thereon. Now, whenever you have that kind of a transaction, you have a case of legal indebtedness, and you cannot have any trust. There is a great deal of vague thought, I think, in some of the books arising from overlooking the essential element of a trust. There can be no trust unless you have property held by one person for the benefit of somebody else. You may have confidential or fiduciary relations, as they are called, and you can have situations in which these equitable words are employed which relate to trusts. But in order to the existence of a trust you must have property which is held by one person, as I have said, for the benefit of somebody else. The essential element of the trust is the division of the title between the legal and the equitable title. You have no such situation where you have the relation of debtor and creditor. The man who borrows money appropriates the money, and the lender means that he shall. He does not take that money to hold it in trust for the lender. He takes it for himself. And upon the facts which the complainant may claim in this case a bill in equity, in my judgment, is no more appropriate than it would be for a depositor, so called, of money in a bank, to file a bill in the court of chancery against the bank to recover his debt. . . .

I do not find in this case that the parties did use any terms which indicate anything more than an ordinary contract of borrowing and lending. The employer often says to his employé " Well, let me keep your wages." " Keep " is the word commonly used. " Keep " is the word that is proved here to have been used by Mr. Linn — " Let me keep your wages, and I will pay you interest; better interest than you can get in the bank." That does not indicate any trust relation. It does not indicate that the employer is receiving the fund in trust to invest for the employé. Nothing of the kind. It indicates that the employer is borrowing money. He is enabling his employé to lend him money at a higher rate than he can get at the bank. It is a very common thing. And so with all the other words that were employed. I followed the witnesses very closely, and I have since to some extent reviewed the testimony. I do not find that there is any language that indicates that Mr. Linn at any time assumed any other relation than that of debtor to the complainant. I think, therefore, that on that ground alone the bill should be dismissed — on the ground that the court has no jurisdiction.[1] . . .

HAMER v. SIDWAY.

COURT OF APPEALS, NEW YORK. 1891.

124 N. Y. 538.

PARKER, J. The question which provoked the most discussion by counsel on this appeal, and which lies at the foundation of plaintiff's asserted right of recovery, is whether by virtue of a contract defendant's testator William E. Story became indebted to his nephew William E. Story, 2d, on his twenty-first birthday in the sum of five thousand dollars. The trial court found as a fact that " on the 20th day of March, 1869, . . . William E. Story agreed to and with William E. Story, 2d, that if he would refrain from drinking liquor, using tobacco, swearing, and playing cards or billiards for money until he should become 21 years of age then he, the said William E. Story, would at that time pay him, the said William E. Story, 2d, the sum of $5,000 for such refraining, to which the said

[1] See Kraemer v. World Wide Trading Co., 195 N. Y. App. Div. 305, holding that where the defendant agreed to pay the plaintiff one-half of commissions received on the sale of ships, the defendant held the commissions upon trust and the plaintiff was entitled to maintain a suit in equity for an accounting.

William E. Story, 2d, agreed," and that he " in all things fully performed his part of said agreement."

The defendant contends that the contract was without consideration to support it, and, therefore, invalid.[1] . . .

In further consideration of the questions presented, then, it must be deemed established for the purposes of this appeal, that on the 31st day of January, 1875, defendant's testator was indebted to William E. Story, 2d, in the sum of $5,000, and if this action were founded on that contract it would be barred by the Statute of Limitations which has been pleaded, but on that date the nephew wrote to his uncle as follows:

" DEAR UNCLE — I am now 21 years old to-day, and I am now my own boss, and I believe, according to agreement, that there is due me $5,000. I have lived up to the contract to the letter in every sense of the word."

A few days later, and on February sixth, the uncle replied, and, so far as it is material to this controversy, the reply is as follows:

" DEAR NEPHEW — Your letter of the 31st ult. came to hand all right saying that you had lived up to the promise made to me several years ago. I have no doubt but you have, for which you shall have $5,000 as I promised you. I had the money in the bank the day you was 21 years old that I intended for you, and you shall have the money certain. Now, Willie, I don't intend to interfere with this money in any way until I think you are capable of taking care of it, and the sooner that time comes the better it will please me. I would hate very much to have you start out in some adventure that you thought all right and lose this money in one year. . . . This money you have earned much easier than I did, besides acquiring good habits at the same time, and you are quite welcome to the money. Hope you will make good use of it. . . .

W. E. STORY.

" P. S. — You can consider this money on interest."

The trial court found as a fact that " said letter was received by said William E. Story, 2d, who thereafter consented that said money should remain with the said William E. Story in accordance with the terms and conditions of said letter." And further, " That afterwards, on the first day of March, 1877, with the knowledge and consent of his said uncle, he duly sold, transferred and assigned all his right, title and interest in and to said sum of $5,000, to his wife Libbie H. Story, who thereafter duly sold, transferred and assigned the same to the plaintiff in this action."

We must now consider the effect of the letter, and the nephew's assent thereto. Were the relations of the parties thereafter that

[1] A part of the opinion holding the contract to be valid is omitted. The statement of facts is also omitted. See Williston, Cases on Contracts, 2 ed., 233; Corbin, Cases on Contracts, 252.

of debtor and creditor simply, or that of trustee and *cestui que trust?* If the former, then this action is not maintainable, because barred by lapse of time. If the latter, the result must be otherwise. No particular expressions are necessary to create a trust. Any language clearly showing the settler's intention is sufficient if the property and disposition of it are definitely stated. (Lewin on Trusts, 55.)

A person in the legal possession of money or property acknowledging a trust with the assent of the *cestui que trust,* becomes from that time a trustee if the acknowledgment be founded on a valuable consideration. His antecedent relation to the subject, whatever it may have been, no longer controls. (2 Story's Eq. § 972.) If before a declaration of trust a party be a mere debtor, a subsequent agreement recognizing the fund as already in his hands and stipulating for its investment on the creditor's account will have the effect to create a trust. (Day *v.* Roth, 18 N. Y. 448.)

It is essential that the letter interpreted in the light of surrounding circumstances must show an intention on the part of the uncle to become a trustee before he will be held to have become such; but in an effort to ascertain the construction which should be given to it, we are also to observe the rule that the language of the promisor is to be interpreted in the sense in which he had reason to suppose it was understood by the promisee. (White *v.* Hoyt, 73 N. Y. 505, 511.) At the time the uncle wrote the letter he was indebted to his nephew in the sum of $5,000, and payment had been requested. The uncle, recognizing the indebtedness, wrote the nephew that he would keep the money until he deemed him capable of taking care of it. He did not say "I will pay you at some other time," or use language that would indicate that the relation of debtor and creditor would continue. On the contrary, his language indicated that he had set apart the money the nephew had "earned" for him so that when he should be capable of taking care of it he should receive it with interest. He said: "I had the money in the bank the day you were 21 years old that I intended for you and you shall have the money certain." That he had set apart the money is further evidenced by the next sentence: "Now, Willie, I don't intend to interfere with this money in any way until I think you are capable of taking care of it." Certainly, the uncle must have intended that his nephew should understand that the promise not "to interfere with this money" referred to the money in the bank which he declared was not only there when the nephew became 21 years old, but was intended for him. True, he did not use the word "trust," or state that the money was deposited in the name of William E. Story, 2d, or in his own name in trust for him, but the language used must have been intended to assure the nephew that his money had been set apart for him, to be kept without interference until he should be capable of taking care of it, for the uncle said in substance and in effect: " This money you have earned much easier than I did . . . you are quite welcome to. I had it in the bank the day you were 21 years old and don't intend to interfere with it in any way until I think you are capable of taking care of it and the sooner that time comes the better it will please me." In this declaration there is not lacking a single element necessary for the creation of a valid trust, and to that declaration the nephew assented.

The learned judge who wrote the opinion of the General Term, seems to have taken the view that the trust was executed during the life-time of defendant's testator by payment to the nephew, but as it does not appear from the order that the judgment was reversed on the facts, we must assume the facts to be as found by the trial court, and those facts support its judgment.

The order appealed from should be reversed and the judgment of the Special Term affirmed, with costs payable out of the estate.

All concur.

Order reversed and judgment of Special Term affirmed.[1]

PEOPLE v. MEADOWS.

COURT OF APPEALS, NEW YORK. 1910.

199 N. Y. 1.

GRAY, J. The defendant was indicted for the crime of grand larceny in the first degree. The charge in the indictment, in substance, was that, on the 22nd day of May, 1908, at the city of Buffalo, the defendant, as the servant, bailee, or agent, of one William E. Silverthorne, had in his possession and custody $72,012.50, the property of said Silverthorne, and that he, thereafter, with the intent to deprive and defraud the said Silverthorne of the said moneys, did, feloniously, steal the same. Upon being brought to trial, the defendant was found guilty by the jury and the judgment of conviction has been affirmed at the Appellate Division. The indictment was found under subdivision 2 of section 528 of the Penal Code; which includes, under the offense of larceny, the offense, formerly, known as embezzlement. That form of larceny required that the People, to support a conviction, should establish, in this case, that the moneys were delivered to the defendant as the bailee, or agent, of their owner and that he had, intentionally, appropriated the same to his own use, or to that of any other person than the owner.

[1] See *Re* Tidd, [1893] 3 Ch. 154; Wright *v.* Paine, 62 Ala. 340; Greenfield Sav. Bank *v.* Abercrombie, 211 Mass. 252, 259; Schmidt *v.* Schmidt, 216 Mass. 572; Keller *v.* Washington, 83 W. Va. 659.

A claim against a constructive trustee or trustee who has openly repudiated or disavowed the trust may be barred by laches or by the Statute of Limitations. Perry, Trusts, chap. 28; Wood, Limitations, 4 ed., chap. 20; 13 Ann. Cas. 1165; Ann. Cas. 1917C 1018.

The evidence upon the trial was such as to justify the verdict rendered by the jurors and by that verdict the following facts must be deemed to have been established. The defendant was a member of the firm of Meadows, Williams & Company, a firm engaged in a general brokerage business in the city of Buffalo, and, at the time of the transaction in question, was the active member in charge of the business. The complainant, Silverthorne, had been a customer of the office and, upon several occasions, had made investment purchases of securities. On May 20th, 1908, he came to the office and ordered the defendant to purchase 700 shares of the preferred stock of the United States Steel Corporation, at the price of $102\frac{3}{4}$. He told the defendant that he was buying for investment and that he wished the stock to be placed in his, Silverthorne's, name. He knew that the stock was to be purchased on the New York market. Defendant's correspondents in that city were Post & Flagg and a private wire connected the two offices; but the relation between the two firms was no other than that of a correspondence for the doing of business for the one, or the other, as the case might be. The quotations, upon which Silverthorne gave his order, were procured from Post & Flagg and they were given the order by the defendant to buy the stock. The next day the defendant sent Silverthorne a "memorandum," to the effect that his firm had " bought 700 U. S. Steel pfd. at $102\frac{3}{4}$ " and showing the cost, with commissions, to be the sum of $72,012.50. Accompanying the memorandum was a letter from the firm, which, after stating the purchase, further, stated as follows: " This account received by telegraph from New York. Names of parties from whom purchase was made will be given if desired as soon as advices are received by mail." The next day, upon receiving this letter and memorandum of account, Silverthorne mailed to the defendant his check for the $72,012.50; the receipt of which the defendant acknowledged by the return of the memorandum receipted. This check was deposited to the general account of the firm in their bank. Upon occasions, during the next few days, when Silverthorne called to know if his stock had arrived, he was told, in explanation of its non-arrival, that the delay was caused through the transfer office being closed. Silverthorne, being then on the eve of his departure for Europe, requested the defendant, as the stock was to be in his name, to keep it for him until his return; which the defendant agreed to do. When Silverthorne's check was received, the firm's bank account showed a credit of only $1,500 and the same day, and on days following, the defendant drew upon it, as so increased by the funds received from Silverthorne, in payment of the demands of creditors; individual as well as firm. Payment was never made by defendant to Post & Flagg for the stock; no payment was ever, specifically, made upon account of its purchase and the shares of stock were never taken up from Post & Flagg. The course of dealings between that firm and the defendant's appears to have been for the former concern, upon executing orders given by the latter, to carry all securities upon marginal account, and these 700 shares of stock were bought, and were being carried, for the defendant's firm in that way. They knew no one in the transactions but defendant's firm; which, alone, was their customer. Payments were made to Post & Flagg, subsequently to the execution of Silverthorne's order, to which, largely, the proceeds of Silverthorne's check contributed; but they were made upon the general marginal account, which the New York firm was carrying. Within three months of this transaction, the members of defendant's firm were adjudged bankrupts, with liabilities very greatly in excess of their assets, and that was the situation which Silverthorne found, upon returning from Europe in September. Neither defendant's firm, nor the trustee in bankruptcy, had received the shares of stock, for the purchase of which Silverthorne had furnished the former the moneys in question.

It seems to me that this was as plain a case, as could be imagined, of embezzlement within the statutory definition of that form of larceny. The defendant's firm, in his transaction with Silverthorne, acted as his agent and, as such, their duty was to use the money intrusted to them in payment for the stock purchased on his order. They had no discretionary power over the fund whatever. Silverthorne had no general account with them. Brokers are but agents for those who employ their services and the terms of the agency define and govern the nature and scope of the agent's powers. The terms of the agency undertaken by the defendant, neither directly, nor by implication, authorized the doing of any acts, beyond such as were necessary to effect the purchase of, and the payment for, the particular kind and number of shares of stock. For the effectuation of the purpose of the agency, these moneys were delivered to the defendant's firm. There was no other purpose, which Silverthorne had to subserve in sending them this sum of money.

Of course, the moneys came lawfully into defendant's possession and therein lies the distinction between the embezzlement, of which the defendant was guilty, and the common-law form of larceny; in which latter offense, the intent to misappropriate must have existed at the inception of the transaction, in which the property was obtained. Where the offense consists in the appropriation by an agent, a bailee, a trustee, or an attorney, of the property of the owner, the felonious intent need only exist at the time of the appropriation; for, in such a case, the property stolen would have been properly in the possession of the defendant. (People *v.* Moore, 37 Hun 84.) The criminal act in this case was committed, and the criminal intent evidenced, when, departing from his duty to use the moneys in paying for the stock, the defendant diverted it to other purposes. Evidence of a criminal intent to defraud Silverthorne of his property was not wanting. The firm was heavily involved, the pressure of debt very great and the bank balance very low. The jurors were warranted in inferring that the defendant yielded to the temptation of relieving the pressure by diverting the funds received from Silverthorne to his own purposes; hoping, if not believing, that, during the latter's absence from the country, an opportunity might be afforded for restoration. A deliberate diversion of the moneys being shown, it required but slight evidence in the facts and circumstances to satisfy the jurors as to the existence of the felonious, or criminal, intent. His expectation, or intention, of restoring the moneys so diverted, of course, was of no avail. (Penal Code, section 549.)

The argument that the relation of debtor and creditor existed is quite untenable. Not only did the defendant's firm have no funds to the credit of Silverthorne in general account, at the time; but the verdict establishes the truth of his evidence that he intrusted the moneys in question to them for the specific purpose of paying for the stocks he had ordered to be bought and of causing their transfer into his name.

The answer to the appellant's argument, that the title to the stocks was in Silverthorne and that the relation of pledgor and pledgee existed between him and appellant's firm, is that the verdict has established the fact to be that, immediately upon being notified of his order having been executed, he remitted the amount representing the cost of the stocks. He had no general account with the firm. His check went to discharge his whole liability and if the moneys had been faithfully forwarded to New York, as the defendant was bound to do, the title to the stocks would have been perfected in him.

The dissent below is based upon a mistaken view of the effect of the defendant's acts, if not of the facts themselves. The criminal act charged was not in depositing the check to the credit of the firm account in the bank; it was in the misapplication, thereafter, of the funds, with which Silverthorne had provided defendant's firm through the check, by appropriating them to other uses than in payment for the stocks. In this form of larceny, it is assumed that the property stolen comes properly into the possession of the party appropriating it. When the check went to swell the bank account of defendant's firm, the fact that the relation of debtor and creditor then arose between the bank and its depositor in no wise changes the fact that the firm was in possession of Silverthorne's property as his agent for a particular purpose. They were not obliged to segregate it by a separate deposit; they were obliged, having it in their possession, to at once appropriate it to the purpose for which received. . . .

CULLEN, Ch. J., VANN, WERNER, WILLARD BARTLETT, HISCOCK and CHASE, JJ., concur.

Judgment of conviction affirmed.[1]

[1] The defendant being allowed, in the following cases, to use as his own the money received, and becoming thereby a debtor, was not an embezzler: Kribs v. People, 82 Ill. 425 (borrower); Mulford v. People, 139 Ill. 586 (bor-

HICKOK *v.* BUNTING, 67 N. Y. App. Div. 560 (1902): The defendant signed and delivered to the plaintiff, Gerardine H. Hickok, an instrument reading as follows: "Having been cause of a money loss to my friend Gerardine H. Hickok, I have given her three thousand dollars. I hold this amount in trust for her, and one year after date or thereafter on demand I promise to pay to the order of Gerardine H. Hickok, her heirs or assigns, three thousand dollars, with interest." It was held that no trust was created, and that the instru-

rower); Comm. *v.* Stearns, 2 Met. 343 (auctioneer or factor); Comm. *v.* Libbey, 11 Met. 64 (general collection agent); [State *v.* Karri, 51 Mont. 157, L. R. A. 1916F 90]; Miller *v.* State, 16 Neb. 179 (selling agent, special agreement); Webb *v.* State, 8 Tex. App. 310 (selling agent, special agreement); State *v.* Covert, 14 Wash. 652 (agent for a laundry).

In the following cases the defendant, not being allowed to use as his own the money received, was guilty of embezzlement: Wallis *v.* State, 54 Ark. 611 (attorney); Haupt *v.* State, 108 Ga. 64; Comm. *v.* Tuckerman, 10 Gray, 173 (treasurer of corporation); Comm. *v.* Smith, 129 Mass. 104 (special agent for collection); Comm. *v.* Moore, 166 Mass. 513 (treasurer of corporation); People *v.* Converse, 74 Mich. 478 (attorney); People *v.* Karste, 132 Mich. 455 (stockbroker); People *v.* Birnbaum, 114 N. Y. App. Div. 480 (attorney); State *v.* Maines, 26 Wash. 160 (agent to sell). — AMES.

In United States *v.* Johnston, 268 U. S. 220, it was held that the promoter of a boxing-match who failed to pay to the government the tax on admission fees was not guilty of embezzlement.

Liability to arrest. In many jurisdictions one who receives property as a fiduciary and appropriates it to his own use, is liable to arrest in a civil action. A factor, auctioneer, agent to sell or buy or collect or the like, is so liable, in the absence of an agreement with his principal allowing him to appropriate. See Ames, 27n.

Discharge in bankruptcy. Under various bankruptcy statutes, including the present Bankruptcy Act of the United States, it is held that a defaulting factor, auctioneer or agent does not come within a clause denying a discharge in the case of a "defalcation while acting . . . in any fiduciary capacity." Crawford *v.* Burke, 195 U. S. 176; American etc. Co. *v.* Berry, 110 Me. 528, Ann. Cas. 1915A 1295; 1 Collier, Bankruptcy, 12 ed., 444–8; Ames, 28n.

A similarly narrow construction has been given to some other statutes relating to trustees. Tiedeman *v.* Imperial etc. Co., 109 Ga. 661. See also Southern etc. Co. *v.* Cleghorn, 59 Ga. 782.

Relation between stockbroker and customer. In Webb *v.* Newhall, 274 Pa. 135, it was held that where a broker received shares to sell for a customer and deposited the proceeds in his general bank account and sent the customer a check, the customer is entitled to priority although the broker failed before the check was presented.

By the weight of authority stock purchased by a broker for a customer is held by the broker as trustee or pledgee. Richardson *v.* Shaw, 209 U. S. 365; Thomas *v.* Taggart, 209 U. S. 385; Gorman *v.* Littlefield, 229 U. S. 19; Duel *v.* Hollins, 241 U. S. 523; Cashman *v.* Root, 89 Cal. 373; Skiff *v.* Stoddard, 63 Conn. 198; Brewster *v.* Van Liew, 119 Ill. 554; Markham *v.* Jaudon, 41 N. Y. 235; Wynkoop *v.* Seal, 64 Pa. 361. But see *contra*, Furber *v.* Dane, 204 Mass. 412. See Smith, Margin Stocks, 35 Harv. L. Rev. 485; Hagar, The Bankruptcy Law as Applied to Stockbrokerage Transactions, 30 Yale L. Jour. 488; Oppenheimer, Rights and Obligations of Customers in Stockbrokerage Bankruptcies, 37 Harv. L. Rev. 860; Tillinghast, Problems of Distribution in Bankruptcies of Stockbrokers, 44 Harv. L. Rev. 65. See 7 Minn. L. Rev. 398; 32 Yale L. Jour. 286.

ment was not enforceable as a promissory note in the absence of consideration. HATCH, J., said (p. 562):

"The language following contains what would be a good declaration of trust, assuming that there was a *res* to which it could attach. It is not claimed by the plaintiff, nor does the evidence establish that the deceased had at the time of the execution of the instrument, assuming that she executed it, $3,000 or any other sum of money, or other property representing it, which was set apart or in any manner placed so that it could become the subject of a trust. In order to constitute a trust there must be a *res* to which it can attach, and where that does not exist there is nothing which can be made the subject of a trust. (Hamer *v.* Sidway, 124 N. Y. 538; Curry *v.* Powers, 70 *id.* 212.) It is, therefore, evident that this instrument did not constitute the deceased a trustee of the plaintiff for the $3,000 or of any other sum or property, and no liability attached to her estate in such capacity." [1]

MOORE *v.* DARTON.

CHANCERY. 1851.

4 De G. & Sm. 517.

THIS was an administration suit, which now came on to be heard upon exceptions to the report of the Master; and the question was, whether the delivery of two documents constituted a donatio mortis causâ. The testatrix had advanced to William Moore, one of the plaintiffs, 600*l.*, and had taken from him upon that occasion the two documents in question signed by him, and which were as follows:

"Received the 22nd of October, 1843, of Miss Darton Five Hundred Pounds, to bear interest at 4 per cent. per annum, but not to be withdrawn at less than six months' notice.

"£500. "WILLIAM MOORE."

"Received the 22nd of October, 1843, of Miss Darton, for the use of Ann Dye, One Hundred Pounds, to be paid to her at Miss Dar-

[1] In Marble *v.* Marble, 304 Ill. 229, the court said: "A debtor cannot create a trust out of a debt which he owes without providing a fund to be applied to the payment of the debt. The relation continues to be merely that of debtor and creditor so long as he merely owes the debt and has provided no fund for its payment. The relation may be changed to that of trustee and *cestui que trust,* but in order to effect the change there must be some particular property or certain fund held for the benefit of the *cestui que trust.*"

In Day *v.* Roth, 18 N. Y. 448, it was held that where a debtor by an agreement with his creditor sets aside the amount owed and agrees to hold it upon trust, the debtor becomes trustee.

ton's decease, but the interest at 4 per cent. to be paid to Miss Darton.

"£100.   "WILLIAM MOORE."

"(I approve of the above) BETTY DARTON."

The transactions relied upon as constituting the donatio mortis causâ took place on June the 28th, 1845, between Miss Darton and Ann Dye, who was mentioned in the second memorandum, and who was Miss Darton's lady's maid.[1] . . .

Miss Darton died ten days afterwards.

The Master found, that the 600*l.* was an outstanding debt from the plaintiff William Moore, who now excepted to that finding.

The VICE-CHANCELLOR [KNIGHT BRUCE]. The case as to the 100*l.* is, I think, beyond the influence of the question, whether there was a donatio mortis causâ; for, in my opinion, an effectual trust was declared, *inter vivos*, in favour of the servant maid. The document relating to this sum appears to have been written contemporaneously with the creation of the debt. It is thus: [His Honour read it]. Now, although this was not then signed by Miss Darton, yet it is probable, that, as she so intended the transaction, and as she received the document, she would be deemed to have assented to it, even without signing it. But, in fact, she afterwards signed it. Mr. Moore therefore became a trustee of the amount for Miss Darton during her life, and for Ann Dye after Miss Darton's death. . . .

M'FADDEN *v.* JENKYNS.

CHANCERY. 1842.

1 Phil. 153.

IN the month of February 1841, Thomas Warry lent the sum of 500*l.* to the Defendant Jenkyns. In the month of December following Thomas Warry died, and the Defendant George Warry having shortly afterwards, as his personal representative, brought an action against Jenkyns to recover the 500*l.*, this bill was filed, alleging that the money was originally intended to be repaid in a short time, but that soon after the loan had been made, Thomas Warry sent a verbal message to Jenkyns by one Bartholomew, a common friend of theirs, desiring him no longer to consider the money as due to him, Thomas Warry, but to hold it " upon trust for the Plaintiff, to be at her absolute disposal, for her own use and benefit." That Bartholomew delivered the message, and Jenkyns accepted the trust; and that the

[1] So much of the case as relates to the *donatio mortis causa* is omitted. It appeared that both documents were given by Miss Darton, when on her death-bed, to Ann Dye, to be delivered at her death to William Moore in forgiveness of the debt. The gift was held effective as to the document for 500*l.*

transaction was communicated to the Plaintiff both by Thomas Warry and by Jenkyns, and that Jenkyns, afterwards, during the lifetime of Warry, and with his knowledge, paid to the Plaintiff the sum of 10*l*. in part execution of the trust; and that Thomas Warry had never afterwards demanded payment of the money or any part of it.

The bill prayed, that it might be declared that, under those circumstances, Jenkyns became and was a trustee of the 500*l*. for the Plaintiff, and that he might be decreed to pay the 490*l*. residue thereof, to the Plaintiff, and that the Defendant George Warry might be restrained from further proceeding in his action against Jenkyns.

The case made by the bill was verified by the affidavits of the Plaintiff, Bartholomew, and Jenkyns, and upon those affidavits Vice-Chancellor Wigram granted an injunction to restrain the prosecution of the action until the hearing of the cause, the Plaintiff submitting to pay the 500*l*. into Court.

The Defendant George Warry now moved, by way of appeal, before the Lord Chancellor, that the Vice-Chancellor's order might be discharged.

The LORD CHANCELLOR [LYNDHURST]. This was an appeal from a judgment of Vice-Chancellor Wigram (reported 1 Hare 458), upon a motion for an injunction to stay proceedings at law. The facts stated in support of the motion were shortly these. The testator Thomas Warry had lent a sum of 500*l*. to the Defendant Jenkyns, to be returned within a short period. Some time afterwards Warry sent a verbal direction to Jenkyns to hold the 500*l*. in trust for Mrs. M'Fadden. This he assented to, and, upon her application, paid her a small sum, 10*l*., in respect of this trust. The main question was, whether, assuming the facts to be as stated, this transaction was binding upon the estate of Thomas Warry. The executor had brought an action to recover the 500*l*. so lent to Jenkyns. It is obvious that the rights of the parties could not, with reference to this claim, be finally settled in a court of law; and, if the trust were completed and binding, an injunction ought to be granted.

Some points were disposed of by the Vice-Chancellor in this case, which are indeed free from doubt, and appear not to have been contested in this Court, viz. that a declaration by parol is sufficient to create a trust of personal property; and that if the testator Thomas Warry had, in his lifetime, declared himself a trustee of the debt for the Plaintiff, that, in equity, would perfect the gift to the Plaintiff, as against Thomas Warry and his estate. The distinctions upon this subject are undoubtedly refined, but it does not appear to me that there is any substantial difference between such a case and the present. The testator, in directing Jenkyns to hold the money in trust for the Plaintiff, which was assented to and acted upon by Jenkyns, impressed, I think, a trust upon the money which was complete and irrevocable. It was equivalent to a declaration by the testator that the debt was a trust for the Plaintiff.

The transaction bears no resemblance to an undertaking or agreement to assign. It was in terms a trust, and the aid of the Court was not necessary to complete it. Such being the strong inclination of my opinion, and corresponding, as it appears to do, with that of the learned Judge in the Court below, and with the decision of the Master of the Rolls in the case to which he refers [Wheatley v. Purr, 1 Keen 551], I cannot do otherwise upon this motion, and in this stage of the cause, than refuse the application.

I must not, however, be understood as pronouncing any conclusive opinion upon the facts of the case. The witness Bartholomew, a professional gentleman, I believe, swears distinctly and in positive terms as to the direction given by the testator; but there are some improbabilities in the case, and it is difficult to say, as the Vice-Chancellor justly observes, what may be the result at the hearing of the cause. As the appeal appears to have been encouraged, if not suggested by the Vice-Chancellor, the motion must be refused without costs.[1]

[1] In the following cases the court was of the opinion that a direction given by a creditor to his debtor to pay a third person, when assented to by the debtor, made the debtor a trustee for the third person: Paterson v. Murphy, 11 Hare 88; Parker v. Stones, 38 L. J. Ch. 46; Eaton v. Cook, 25 N. J. Eq. 55. But see Morgan v. Larivière, L. R. 7 H. L. 423.

In Rycroft v. Christy, 3 Beav. 238; Meert v. Moessard, 1 Moo. & P. 8; and Lambe v. Orton, 1 Dr. & Sm. 125, a *cestui que trust* directed his trustee to pay the trust fund to a third person, and the trustee assented. It was held that a valid trust for the third person was created.

Obligee as trustee. In the following cases it was held that the *obligee* was trustee of the obligation for the intended beneficiary: Vandenberg v. Palmer, 4 K. & J. 204; Lamb v. Vice, 6 M. & W. 467; Robertson v. Wait, 8 Ex. 299; Lloyd's v. Harper, 16 Ch. D. 290; Re Flavell, 25 Ch. D. 89; Gandy v. Gandy, 30 Ch. D. 57; Leopold Walford Ltd. v. Les Affréteurs etc. Société, [1918] 2 K. B. 498, aff'd [1919] A. C. 801; Horseshoe Pier etc. Co. v. Sibley, 157 Cal. 442; Grime v. Borden, 166 Mass. 198. See also the numerous cases where, as in Wheatley v. Purr, 1 Keen 551, and in Matter of Totten, 179 N. Y. 112, *post*, one makes a deposit in a bank in trust for another.

In the following cases, on the other hand, it was held that there was merely a contract to pay a third party: Re Empress Engineering Co., 16 Ch. D. 125; Colyear v. Countess of Mulgrave, 2 Keen 81; Re D'Angibau, 15 Ch. D. 228, 241; M'Coubray v. Thomson, I. R. 2 C. L. 226.

In Leopold Walford Ltd. v. Les Affreteurs etc. Société, [1918] 2 K. B. 498, Pickford, L. J., said (p. 501): "If A. agrees with B. that he will pay a certain sum of money to B. for the benefit of C., B., as trustee for C., can sue A."

In *Re* Empress Engineering Co., 16 Ch. D. 125, Jessel, M. R., said (pp. 127, 129): "A. being liable to B., C. agrees with A. to pay B. That does not make B. a *cestui que trust*. . . . I am far from saying that there may not be agreements which may make [B.] a *cestui que trust*. . . . It is quite possible that one of the parties to the agreement may be the nominee or trustee of the third person. . . . A married woman may nominate somebody to contract on her behalf, but then the person makes the contract really as trustee for somebody else, and it is because he contracts in that character that the *cestui que trust* can take the benefit of the contract."

MOLERA v. COOPER.

Supreme Court, California. 1916.

173 Cal. 259.

Shaw, J.— The plaintiff [as executor of the will of Ana M. Wohler] sued upon a promissory note for one thousand dollars executed to the testatrix, Ana M. Wohler, by the defendant. A demurrer to the third amended answer was sustained and judgment was thereupon given for the plaintiff. From this judgment the defendant appeals.

The note sued on was dated July 2, 1909, and was payable two years after date. The first count of said answer alleges that on April 10, 1911, it was agreed between the defendant and Mrs. Wohler that in consideration of the extinguishment of said note by Mrs. Wohler and the release by her of all obligation of the defendant upon said note, the defendant would thereupon hold said amount of one thousand dollars and interest from the date of said note, in trust, and would thenceforth apply and pay the same to the joint use and benefit of Isabel Ellsworth Cooper and Gladys Greene Cooper, in equal shares; that during the minority of said two beneficiaries the defendant would apply said moneys according to the discretion of her, said defendant; that said Ana M. Wohler accepted said agreement and declaration of trust of the defendant in full satisfaction and extinction of said note and then and there verbally released the defendant from the obligation thereof, and that the defendant has ever since April 10, 1911, held said amount of money upon the said trust, and that said Isabel and Gladys own the entire beneficial interest in said sum of money, subject to the trust stated.

It is not alleged that the defendant then had in her possession or under her control the money owing upon said note, or that she has at any time since procured the same and devoted the same to said trust, or that she was then or has been since, solvent and able to do so. One ground of demurrer was that the answer was uncertain in that it cannot be ascertained therefrom what particular moneys the defendant held in trust as set forth therein, or whether or not any specific amount of money was held in trust. In view of this ground of demurrer the allegation that the defendant has ever since April 10, 1911, " held and does now hold said amount of money upon the trust proposed " is not to be construed as meaning that the defendant then had the money in hand, or has at any time since then possessed the same and devoted it to said trust. If she had desired to allege these facts she should have done so more specifically. The agreement is to be taken as a conclusion of the pleader upon the facts previously stated in the endeavor to allege a valid trust. The case must be considered upon the theory that all she did in regard to the creation of a trust was to agree that she would thenceforth hold the sum of money specified in the note in trust for the two children mentioned. It is alleged that these two children were minors then of the age of eight and four years, respectively, and that the defendant and their father were joint guardians of the estates of said minors, and it is not alleged that either of them as guardian has agreed to the said arrangement with Mrs. Wohler.

It is clear that no trust was created by the aforesaid arrangement. There never was any property in existence which could be the subject of the trust. The debt owing from the defendant to Mrs. Wohler was a property right vested in Mrs. Wohler, but no property or estate therein was vested in the defendant which could be the subject of any trust. A mere promise to obtain money and thereupon hold it in trust does not create a trust until it is at least so far executed that the money has been obtained in accordance with the promise. Considered in that light the agreement between the payer and the payee was ineffectual to alter or extinguish the note, since it was an attempt to alter a written agreement by an unexecuted parol agreement. (Civ. Code, sec. 1698.)

The decision in Booth *v.* Oakland Bank of Savings, 122 Cal. 19, [54 Pac. 370], is not authority for the proposition that a trust can be created by the mere promise of a debtor to the creditor to obtain money and hold it in trust for a third person. The subject matter involved in that case was money on deposit in the bank. It is clear from a reading of the decision that the money was considered by the court as money actually in possession of the bank belonging to the depositor, and that the effect of the transaction was that the bank thereupon agreed to hold the money so on deposit in trust for the benefit of sisters of the depositor. In the present case, as we have said, there is no sufficient allegation that there was anything on hand to be made the subject of a trust.

Considered as a novation, it was ineffectual for the reason that the persons to whom the obligation was to run, the two children, did not accept the same or agree thereto. Under section 1531 of the Civil Code a novation is made.

"1. By the substitution of a new obligation between the same parties, with intent to extinguish the old obligation;

"2. By the substitution of a new debtor in place of the old one, with intent to release the latter; or,

"3. By the substitution of a new creditor in place of the old one, with intent to transfer the rights of the latter to the former."

The second mode is not involved. It is not claimed that any new debtor was substituted. It was ineffectual as a novation under the first mode and under the third mode because no new obligation was created and no new creditor was substituted. The proposal was to create a new obligation in favor of the two children. A novation whereby a new obligation to a third party is substituted cannot be made unless all agree. As is said in 3 Elliott on Contracts, section 1867: " All must agree, for it requires the consent of the original parties to change the old contract or their relations to it and extinguish the liability, and of the parties to the new contract to create it." The following cases announce the same doctrine: McKinney *v.* Alvis, 14 Ill. 33; Reid *v.* Degener, 82 Ill. 508; Commercial Bank *v.* Kirkwood, 172 Ill. 568, [50 N. E. 219]; Kirchman *v.* Standard Coal Co., 112 Iowa, 673, [52 Am. St. Rep. 318, 84 N. W. 939]; Darling *v.* Rutherford, 112 Mich. 70, [83 N. W. 999]; Hanson *v.* Nelson, 82 Minn. 220, [84 N. W. 742]. There was no new obligation created to the children for neither they nor their guardians consented to it or accepted it. For the same reason there was no transfer to them of the rights of the original obligee. The arrangement lacked these essential elements of a novation. . . .

[The judgment for the plaintiff, modified to include interest, was affirmed.] [1]

STEELE *v.* CLARK.

SUPREME COURT, ILLINOIS. 1875.

77 Ill. 471.

Mr. JUSTICE BREESE delivered the opinion of the Court.

This proceeding was commenced before the county court of Clinton county, and taken by appeal to the circuit court, wherein a judgment was rendered for the plaintiffs for four hundred and forty-four dollars, and costs, from which judgment this appeal is prosecuted by the defendants. It is a case in which the administrator of one Thomas Moore, deceased, presented a claim for allowance against the estate of John Brewster, deceased, for one thousand dollars. The county court allowed the claim to the extent of seven hundred and seventy-seven dollars, and, on appeal to the circuit court, the same was reduced to the above sum of four hundred and forty-four dollars.

[1] In *Re* Caplen's Estate, 45 L. J. Ch. 280 (1876), the testatrix holding a promissory note for 300*l* told the maker that she wanted him to hold the 300*l* for the benefit of one Mrs. Bulbeck and her daughters, directing him after her own death to pay the interest to Mrs. Bulbeck during her life, and to divide the principal among her daughters after her death. The testatrix never surrendered the note. It was held that no trust was created, that her executors and not Mrs. Bulbeck and her daughters were entitled to the 300*l*. Jessel, M. R., said that " there is nothing to shew that the owner of the note intended to part with her legal title to the money." It would seem that the result reached in this case is sound. The maker of the note was clearly not a trustee, and the testatrix did not intend to declare herself trustee of the note, and since she did not surrender the note she probably did not intend to effect a novation, substituting a contract for the benefit of third parties for her claim on the note, nor did she intend to assign her interest in the note. As to the validity of a gratuitous assignment, see Chapter II, sec. III, *post*.

A brief statement of the facts will show that this judgment ought not to stand.

It appears that Thomas Moore, the father of Thomas Moore in behalf of whose estate this claim is prosecuted, died in 1852 or 1853, leaving an estate in land, which descended to his son, Robert Moore, this Thomas Moore, and a granddaughter, Mary Stephens; that, in 1850, Thomas Moore, the younger, then about twenty years of age, left this State for California, and has not been heard from since 1866. In 1853, proceedings were instituted for a partition of the estate of Thomas Moore, senior, and one Alfred Tucker was appointed a commissioner to make partition and pay over the proceeds to these several heirs, each share amounting to four hundred and forty-four dollars, which the commissioner received in money, and paid to John Brewster, deceased, the guardian of Mary Stephens, her share, to Robert Moore his share, and, without any authority whatever, as appears, paid to Robert his brother Thomas' share. In 1859 or 1860, Robert Moore, being in debt to his brother Thomas in this sum of four hundred and forty-four dollars, and also to other parties, agreed to sell his farm to Brewster, to pay his debts, and among them this debt to his brother Thomas. For what price the farm was sold, does not appear. Brewster's administrator proved one payment of more than two hundred dollars to one Fouke, a creditor of Robert, and offered to show for what the farm was sold by Robert Moore to him. This evidence the court refused to admit. The defense was, the Statute of Frauds and Perjuries and the Statute of Limitations.

To sustain the recovery, it is urged by appellee that this was a trust fund, and the recovery not barred by the Statute of Limitations. It is claimed and argued by appellee that Brewster, in his lifetime, had become security for the payment of the money received by Robert Moore, belonging to his brother Thomas, which fact, they insist, gives it the character of trust money, and not barred by the Statute of Limitations. A careful examination of the record betrays the existence of no such fact. Neither Dougherty, Dill, the Clarks, nor Mrs. Pratt, called for appellee, state anything of the kind. The simple fact is, that Brewster, on the purchase of Robert Moore's farm, undertook to pay this debt Robert then owed his brother Thomas. As Dougherty states it, Brewster told his brother he had bought Robert Moore's farm, and had become paymaster to Thomas for Robert Moore. This was in 1860. At this time, the relation of these parties was that of debtor and creditor.

It has been settled, by repeated decisions of this court, that, in case of simple contracts, the person for whose benefit a promise is made may maintain an action in his own name upon it, although the consideration does not move from him. Eddy *v.* Roberts, 17 Ill. 505; Brown *v.* Strait, 19 ib. 89; Bristow *et al. v.* Lane *et al.*, 21 ib. 194, where the English and American authorities are considered.

In 1860, when this promise was made by Brewster to Robert Moore, admitting it was made, Thomas Moore had a clear right of action against Brewster to recover the amount, had he chosen to accept Brewster as his creditor [debtor?], and, if dead, his administrator had a right of action for five years thereafter. These proceedings were instituted more than thirteen years thereafter, and some years after the death of Brewster.

Under this state of fact, we are at a loss to perceive why the claim was not barred by the Statute of Limitations. We fail to see in the transaction any indication of a trust, to any greater extent than any ordinary assumpsit by one person, for a valuable consideration, to pay a debt he owes, to a third party, instead of paying to the party with whom he contracted.

A court of equity has jurisdiction in all cases of strict trust, but where a mere confidence is reposed, or a credit given, it will not exercise such jurisdiction. As this court said, in Doyle *et al. v.* Murphy *et al.*, 22 Ill. 502, the various affairs of life, in almost every act between individuals in trade and commerce, involve the reposing of confidence or trust in each other, and yet it has never been supposed that because such confidence or trust in the integrity of another has been extended and abused, therefore a court of equity would, in all such cases, assume jurisdiction.

It is true, as there said, when property is conveyed or given by one person to another, to hold for the use of a third person, such a trust would thereby be created as would give equity jurisdiction to compel the application to the purposes of the trust. But such is not this case. Here was the sale of a farm by the owner, to pay his debts, among which was this debt due his brother Thomas, and which Brewster assumed to pay. It is an ordinary case of debtor and creditor, and the Statute of Limitations was a bar to a recovery.

This money, when in the hands of Tucker, the commissioner, was a trust fund, from which he had no right, of his own mere motion, to part, and place in the hands of Robert Moore, who is not shown to have had any authority to receive it. There can be no doubt the estate of Thomas Moore has a right of action against Tucker, to recover this money, with interest. . . .

For the errors above discussed, the judgment is reversed and the cause remanded.

Judgment reversed.[1]

---

[1] If A conveys property to B in consideration of B's promise to pay or support A or C, B does not hold the property in trust, but at most only a personal obligation is created. M'Coubray *v.* Thomson, I. R. 2 C. L. 226 (personal obligation held invalid because consideration did not move from promisee); Clitheroe *v.* Simpson, 4 L. R. Ir. 59 (land conveyed by deed in

SPICKERNELL v. HOTHAM.

CHANCERY. 1854.

Kay 669, 673.

THOMAS PRICE, Harry Stephen Thompson, James Croft, and Stephen Croft, as trustees, claimed to be specialty creditors of the testator [George V. Drury] in the cause, under and by virtue of an indenture, dated the 26th of September, 1828, and made between the testator of the first part, the Rev. Thomas Hatton Croft of the second part, Eliza Thompson, spinster, of the third part, and the said trustees of the fourth part, whereby, after reciting that a marriage was intended between the said Thomas Hatton Croft and Eliza Thompson; and that the said testator, being desirous of making some provision, after the decease of the survivor of himself and Charlotte his wife, for the said Eliza Thompson and the issue of the said marriage, had agreed to transfer 962*l.* New 4*l.* per cent. Annuities belonging to him unto the said trustees, upon the trusts and for the purposes thereinafter expressed or referred to, the said

---

consideration of agreement to pay 100*l* to a third party, action by the third party dismissed on the ground that he was not a party to the contract); Maxwell *v.* Wood, 133 Iowa 721 (transferee of property not bound); Fellows *v.* Fellows, 69 N. H. 339 (held revocable); Faust *v.* Faust, 144 N. C. 383. But see Ahrens *v.* Jones, 169 N. Y. 555. See 12 Harv. L. Rev. 564.

If A conveys property to B, who agrees to pay C out of the property or its proceeds, a trust arises. Kelly *v.* Larkin, [1910] 2 I. R. 550. See Sayer *v.* Wynkoop, 248 N. Y. 54, *post.*

The distinction between a trust and a purely personal obligation in the nature of a debt is illustrated by cases of assignment of partnership assets to a partner. If the assignment is upon trust to pay the firm creditors out of the assets, they will be preferred to the separate creditors of the assignee partner as to the assets so transferred. If, on the other hand, the assignment to the partner is absolute, the assignors being content to take the assignee's personal agreement to pay the firm liabilities, and if the assignment is not fraudulent, the firm creditors will have no greater rights against the firm assets so transferred than against any other assets of the assignee partner; and if that partner becomes insolvent, the firm creditors will either get nothing until the separate creditors are paid in full. See Scott, Cases on Trusts, 1 ed., 53.

If B is indebted to A, and B conveys property to C, who agrees to pay B's debt to A out of that property, a trust is created, and C's promise is not required by the Statute of Frauds to be in writing as a "special promise to answer for the debt, default or miscarriage of another." Dock *v.* Boyd & Co., 93 Pa. 92. See Ames, Cas. Suretyship, 42n.

In Attorney General *v.* American Legion of Honor, 206 Mass. 158, it was held that there is no fiduciary relation between the beneficiary of a contract and the promisor, and that a release given by the beneficiary cannot be set aside for failure of the promisor to communicate facts affecting the value of the beneficiary's claim.

As to the distinction between trusts and contracts for the benefit of third persons, see Anson, Contracts, 3 Am. ed., secs. 277, 285; Williston, Contracts, secs. 348, 355, 360; Corbin, Contracts for Third Persons, 46 L. Quar. Rev. 12.

testator, for himself, his heirs, executors, administrators, and assigns, covenanted with the said trustees, that he the said testator, his executors or administrators, would, immediately after the solemnisation of the said intended marriage, transfer into their names in the books of the Governor and Company of the Bank of England the said 962*l*. New 4*l*. per cent. Bank Annuities, and it was thereby declared, that the said trustees should permit the said testator to receive the dividends of the said 962*l*. New 4*l*. per cent. Annuities for his own use during his life, and after his decease should permit the said Charlotte Drury his wife to receive the said dividends during her life, and after the decease of the survivor of them should hold the said 962*l*. New 4*l*. per cent. Annuities, and the dividends thereof, upon the trusts therein declared for the benefit of the said Eliza Thompson and the issue of the said then intended marriage.

The marriage between the said Thomas Hatton Croft and Eliza Thompson was duly solemnised, but the said testator did not during his lifetime transfer the said 962*l*. New 4*l*. per cent. Annuities to the trustees, pursuant to his said covenant.

Mr. *J. H. Palmer* for the trustees. This debt is a specialty debt, and is not barred by the statute, because time did not run against the claim during the lifetime of the testator to whom the interest was payable for life, upon the doctrine laid down in Burrell *v.* The Earl of Egremont, 7 Beav. 205, where it was held, that, if the owner of a charge upon an estate be also tenant for life of the estate, as he is bound to apply the rents in payment of the interest of the charge, he will be assumed to have done so, and thus time will not run against the charge during his life. And it was decided in Megginson *v.* Harper, 2 Cr. & M. 322, that part payment to a *cestui que trust* would prevent the operation of the statute. But further, this is not a mere debt, but a trust; for the testator covenanted to transfer a certain sum of stock then belonging to him; and therefore he was a trustee of this stock until he should transfer it according to his covenant.

VICE-CHANCELLOR SIR W. PAGE WOOD. This is like many other cases which occur upon the Statute of Limitations, a case of considerable hardship; but the legislature having enacted, that the lapse of a certain period shall bar the right to recover a debt, I can see nothing in this case to take it out of the operation of the statute. The debt in question is a legal debt, which accrued in 1828 in respect of a breach of covenant by the omission to transfer a sum of stock into the names of trustees which ought then to have been done.

I think that the principle of Burrell *v.* The Earl of Egremont can have no application to this case. It was there decided, that, when there is a charge on real estate, and it is the duty of the person entitled to the charge to keep down the interest, it is assumed that he, being in possession of the estate, has done his duty, and that the interest has been paid to himself. But here the sum of stock which ought to have been brought into existence as a trust fund never had any such existence, and I cannot assume that a person has been paying himself the interest of a non-existing fund.

The *cestuis que trust* could not get at the fund in any other way than by an action to be brought by the trustees; therefore, it is not in any sense a trust on the part of the testator and the action upon the covenant is now barred by the statute.[1] . . .

2. The Relation Between Banker and Customer.[2]

A. Deposit of Money.

CITY OF STURGIS v. MEADE COUNTY BANK.

SUPREME COURT, SOUTH DAKOTA. 1917.

38 S. D. 317.

ACTION by the City of Sturgis, a municipal corporation, against the Meade County Bank, a banking corporation, and J. L. Wingfield, as Public Examiner of the State of South Dakota, [to] establish a preferential claim against defendant bank in favor of plaintiff. From a judgment for defendants, and from an order denying a new trial, plaintiff appeals. Judgment and order affirmed.

POLLEY, J. The defendant Meade County Bank failed, and was taken in charge by the public examiner, who proceeded to collect the assets and pay the debts. At the time of the failure of the bank, there was on deposit therein a considerable sum of money belonging to the plaintiff, the city of Sturgis. This money had been deposited therein by the city treasurer, and it had been the practice of the city treasurer, for several years prior to the time of the failure, to keep the funds of the city on deposit in said bank, subject to check, and pay the same out by check as needed. This was done with knowledge of the city authorities; and the bank, through its managing officers, knew that the money so

---

[1] *Re* Plumptre's Marriage Settlement, [1910] 1 Ch. 609, *accord.* Compare Fogg v. Middleton, 2 Hill Ch. (S. C.) 591, *post;* Fletcher v. Fletcher, 4 Hare 67, *post.*

[2] If a separate course is given on the law of Banks and Banking, the cases in this topic can be omitted. Since such a course is not given in many law schools, the editor has thought it wise to insert these cases in order that the students may become familiar with some of the problems which arise with reference to the duties of banks with respect to money or commercial paper deposited with them. The question dealt with in this topic is whether a bank with respect to money or commercial paper deposited with it is a trustee, bailee or agent on the one hand, or is merely a debtor or under a contractual liability. The question of following the money or paper into its product and acquiring priority over other claimants against the bank is treated in Chapter V, section VI.

deposited by the city treasurer belonged to the city. After the failure of the bank, the city presented its claim for payment, and demanded that it be paid in full in preference to the claims of the other creditors. It is conceded that the assets of the bank were not sufficient to pay its debts in full, but the city claimed that its money constituted a trust fund. The public examiner allowed the amount of the claim, but refused to give it preference over the claims of other creditors. The city brought this action for the purpose of establishing a preference, but the trial court sustained the public examiner, and the city brings the case here on appeal.

When a bank becomes insolvent and is taken over by the public examiner, the assets of the bank become a fund for the payment of the claims of the various creditors, and, unless there is some reason, recognized by law, that entitles one creditor to a preference over the others, they should all be treated alike. If the assets are sufficient in amount, the creditors can all be paid in full; but, where there are not sufficient funds to pay the just claims of all the creditors in full, then such fund as there is should be proportioned among such creditors according to the amount of their respective claims. As between the creditors of an insolvent bank, equality is equity. Cavin v. Gleason, 105 N. Y. 256, 11 N. E. 504. This rule applies to all bank depositors.

As a rule, when money is deposited in a bank, title to such money passes to the bank. The bank becomes the debtor of the depositor to the extent of the deposit, and, to that extent, the depositor becomes the creditor of the bank. Allibone v. Ames et al., 9 S. D. 74, 68 N. W. 165, 33 L. R. A. 585. Such deposit then constitutes a part of the assets of the bank, and, in case of insolvency, belongs to the creditors of the bank in proportion to the amount of their respective claims. Exceptions to this rule are: First, where money or other thing is deposited with the understanding that that particular money or thing is to be returned to the depositor; second, where the money or thing deposited is to be used for a specifically designated purpose; and, third, where the deposit itself was wrongful or unlawful.

The money involved in this case was deposited by the city treasurer subject to his check, and without any understanding that the identical money deposited should be returned to him, or that it should be used for any specific purpose. Therefore it falls within neither of the first two of the above classes. But it is contended by the appellant that the treasurer was without authority to deposit the city funds in the Meade County Bank, or in any other bank; that the law made him custodian of the city funds, and that it was unlawful for him to deposit such funds in any bank, and for that reason the title thereto did not pass to the bank; but that the bank took and held the same as trustee only, and is now in duty bound to return the same in full regardless of the claims of the other creditors.

While the law makes the city treasurer the custodian of the city funds, it does not, either in terms or by implication, require him to maintain the actual or physical possession thereof, nor that he shall keep the same in a private safe or vault. It is customary and altogether proper, in the absence of a law to the contrary, that such funds should be deposited for safe-keeping in some reputable bank, and that they be paid out by check when needed, just as was done by the city treasurer in this case. Where the law prohibits the deposit of specific public funds in banks, it is held by the courts that it is unlawful for the bank to accept the same; that the title to such deposits does not pass to the bank; and, in case of the insolvency of the bank, such deposits shall be allowed as preferred claims and paid in full by the receiver. [Cases cited.] But in this state there is no law that prohibits a city treasurer from keeping the city funds in a bank; and, where such funds are deposited by the treasurer to be paid out on check, the transaction constitutes a general deposit. The relation of debtor and creditor arises in the same manner as in case of the deposit of individual funds. Allibone v. Ames, *supra*. And, in case of insolvency of the bank, the claim of the city, based on a deposit of public funds, is in no wise superior to, or entitled to a preference over, a claim based on a deposit of individual funds. [Cases cited.] We believe this is a proper case for the application of the above rule, and we hold accordingly that the deposits involved, made by the city treasurer of the plaintiff city, constitute a general deposit only, and that the city should be treated as a general creditor and be paid ratably from the assets of the bank that are applicable to the payment of the claims of the general creditors.

The judgment and order appealed from are affirmed.[1]

[1] *General deposit in a bank.* A general deposit in a commercial bank creates a relation of debtor and creditor between the bank and the depositor. Foley v. Hill, 2 H. L. C. 28; Manhattan Co. v. Blake, 148 U. S. 412; Collins v. State, 33 Fla. 429; Bayor v. American T. & S. Bank, 157 Ill. 62; State v. Bartley, 39 Neb. 353; Bank v. Brewing Co., 50 Oh. St. 151; Leaphart v. Commercial Bank, 45 S. C. 563.

If the bank refuses to honor the checks of the depositor, it may be held liable for damages. Wildenberger v. Ridgewood Nat. Bank, 230 N. Y. 425. See Brady, Bank Checks, 2 ed., secs. 209–213; 22 Col. L. Rev. 175. As to the distinction between a deposit and a loan, see 27 Col. L. Rev. 88.

The bank is merely a debtor although it issues its certificate of deposit, its cashier's check (21 A. L. R. 680), or certifies a check (51 A. L. R. 1034).

General deposit by a trustee. If a general deposit is properly made by a trustee or other fiduciary, the bank does not become a trustee of the money but a debtor to the trustee. Hawkins v. Cleveland, etc. Ry. Co., 89 Fed. 266; Thompson v. Bank, 76 Colo. 20 (administrator); Officer v. Officer, 120 Iowa 389 (executor); Leach v. Beazley, 201 Iowa 337 (executor, *semble*); Phillips v. Yates Center Nat. Bank, 98 Kan. 383; Kendall v. Fidelity Trust

NORTHWEST LUMBER COMPANY v. SCANDINAVIAN AMERICAN BANK.

SUPREME COURT, WASHINGTON. 1924.

130 Wash. 33.

APPEAL from a judgment of the superior court for King county, Ronald, J., entered January 18, 1923, in favor of the plaintiff, in an action to enforce a claim against an insolvent bank, tried to the court. Affirmed.

FULLERTON, J. — On August 16, 1911, the respondent, Northwest Lumber Company, issued a number of its obligations payable over a period of years. The interest on the obligations was made payable on the first days of January and July of each year. To secure

---

Co., 230 Mass. 238; Paul v. Draper, 158 Mo. 197 (guardian); Pethybridge v. First State Bank, 75 Mont. 173 (guardian); Providence Institution for Savings v. Dailey, 22 R. I. 239; Valentine v. Duke, 128 Wash. 128 (administrator); United States F. & G. Co. v. Home Bank, 77 W. Va. 665; Henry v. Martin, 88 Wis. 367; Gray v. Elliott, 36 Wyo. 361 (administrator). See 37 A. L. R. 120; 53 A. L. R. 564.

Deposit of public funds. Similarly a debt is created by a deposit of public funds properly made in a bank. Re Nichols, 166 Fed. 603; Warren v. Nix, 97 Ark. 374; Otis v. Gross, 96 Ill. 612; Brown v. Sheldon State Bank, 139 Iowa 83; Leach v. Castana Sav. Bank, 201 Iowa 346; Kuhl v. Farmers Bank, 203 Iowa 71; Retan v. Union Trust Co., 134 Mich. 1; Board of Education v. Union Trust Co., 136 Mich. 454; Campion v. Big Stone County Bank, 177 Minn. 51; Yellowstone County v. First Trust & Sav. Bank, 46 Mont. 439; City of Missoula v. Dick, 76 Mont. 502; State v. Madison State Bank, 77 Mont. 498; County Court v. Mathews, 99 W. Va. 483.

In some states by statute or decision a state or county or municipality is entitled, on the failure of the bank of deposit, to priority over other creditors. See United States v. Brock, 5 F.(2d) 265; People v. Farmers State Bank, 335 Ill. 617, Re Marathon Sav. Bank, 198 Iowa 692 (statute later repealed, see Kuhl v. Farmers Bank, 203 Iowa 71); Fogg v. Bank, 80 Miss. 750; Lockwood v. Lockwood, 68 S. C. 328. See 24 A. L. R. 1495; 36 A. L. R. 640; 42 A. L. R. 1296; 51 A. L. R. 1336, 1355; 52 A. L. R. 755; 65 A. L. R. 690, 1331; 40 Harv. L. Rev. 322; 42 Harv. L. Rev. 442; 2 So. Cal. L. Rev. 298.

As to the priority of the United States, see U. S. v. Oklahoma, 261 U. S. 253.

Deposit made in breach of trust. If a trustee or other fiduciary wrongfully makes a deposit in a bank, the bank becomes a constructive trustee of the money so deposited, unless the bank is a purchaser for value and without notice. Thus the bank becomes constructive trustee of public funds deposited in violation of law. San Diego County v. California Nat. Bank, 52 Fed. 59; Board of Commissioners v. Strawn, 157 Fed. 49; City of Centralia v. U. S. Nat. Bank, 221 Fed. 755; State v. Bruce, 17 Idaho 1; Brown v. Sheldon State Bank, 139 Iowa 83 (*semble*); City of New Hampton v. Leach, 201 Iowa 316; Leach v. Farmers Sav. Bank, 204 Iowa 1083, 76 U. Pa. L. Rev. 864; Myers v. Board of Education, 51 Kan. 87; Brogan v. Kriepe, 116 Kan. 506; Fogg v. Bank, 80 Miss. 750; Special Road Dist. v. Cantley, 8 S. W.(2d) 944 (Mo. App., 1928); Yellowstone County v. First Trust & Sav. Bank, 46 Mont. 439; State v. Midland State Bank, 52 Neb. 1; City of Lincoln v.

the payment of the principal and interest as the same fell due, the lumber company executed to the Scandinavian American Bank, of Seattle, a mortgage deed covering certain described real and personal property owned by it. The deed described the bank as trustee, and provided that the bank should hold the property in trust for the benefit of the purchasers of the obligations, which obligations were made payable at the banking house of the bank. The deed also provided that the lumber company should, prior to each due day of the principal and interest, deposit with the bank sufficient funds to pay the principal and interest then maturing.

From the time of the execution of the instrument to the time of the circumstances subsequently to be mentioned, the terms of the instrument were carried out by the parties. Prior to each maturing date of principal or interest on the obligations, the lumber company furnished the bank with funds necessary to make the payments, and the bank, in the performance of the trust it had assumed, made the payments out of the fund so provided.

On June 24, 1921, the lumber company had on deposit with the

Morrison, 64 Neb. 822; County of Grand Forks *v.* Baird, 54 N. D. 315; Watts *v.* Board of Commissioners, 21 Okla. 231.

On the question of notice to the bank that the deposit is wrongful, see Chap. VIII, and particularly Bischoff *v.* Yorkville Bank, 218 N. Y. 106, *post*.

On the question whether the bank is a purchaser for value, see Chap. VIII, and particularly Mann *v.* Second Nat. Bank, 30 Kan. 412, *post*.

Deposit induced by fraud of bank. A bank receiving a deposit when it knows that it is insolvent is not privileged to use the money as its own. It is to be treated therefore not merely as a debtor but as a constructive trustee. See Scott, Cases on Trusts, 1 ed., 68–69. See also Steele *v.* Commissioner of Banks, 240 Mass. 394; St. Louis-San Francisco Ry. Co. *v.* Millspaugh, 220 Mo. App. 110; Lunenburg County *v.* Prince Edward-Lunenburg County Bank, 138 Va. 333. See 20 A. L. R. 1206; 25 A. L. R. 728; 37 A. L. R. 620.

If, however, the bank has no knowledge of its insolvency, the rule is otherwise. Scott, Cases on Trusts, 1 ed., 69. See also Fidelity & Deposit Co. *v.* Kelso State Bank, 287 Fed. 828; United States Nat. Bank *v.* Glanton, 146 Ga. 786; Union Nat. Bank *v.* Citizens Bank, 153 Ind. 44; Steele *v.* Commissioner of Banks, 240 Mass. 394; Beehive Marketeria *v.* Citizens Bank, 126 Wash. 526 (where the deposits were kept in separate envelopes).

So also a constructive trust arises if the bank is guilty of other fraudulent acts in procuring a deposit; as for example in giving a draft on another bank in which it has no funds. Leach *v.* Central Trust Co., 203 Iowa 1060; Union State Bank *v.* Peoples State Bank, 192 Wis. 28. The bank is a constructive trustee if it receives money in payment of a note of which it purports to be the holder but which it has transferred. Massey *v.* Fisher, 62 Fed. 958; People *v.* City Bank, 96 N. Y. 32. See also Smith *v.* Mottley, 150 Fed. 266, where a bank obtained payment of a note by fraudulently representing that it had authority to collect the note. Compare Millett *v.* Omaha Nat. Bank, 30 F.(2d) 665, where it was held that the bank was liable to the transferee of the note and that the transferee could set off his claim against his indebtedness to the bank which was insolvent.

So also a bank is constructive trustee of the proceeds of securities converted by it. See 51 A. L. R. 914.

bank, subject to its general checking account, a sum in excess of $85,000. On that day it forwarded to the bank its check for $5,220, to meet the payments on the outstanding obligations maturing on July 1, 1921. With the check it sent a letter, explaining the purpose of the check, in the following form:

" We hand you herewith check No. 5970 for $5,220.00 in payment of six months interest on Northwest Lumber Company's outstanding bonds of $174,000.00."

The bank was authorized by its charter to do a general trust business, and had as one of its employees a person whose duty it was to attend to its general business relating to trusts of this character. On receipt of the check, the cashier of the bank forwarded the check to the person having charge of its trust department. It was by him received, but for some reason, not explained in the record, was not marked as paid or cancelled, nor was the amount thereof charged to the lumber company's general account. On June 30, 1921, prior to the due day of the interest obligation, the bank was taken over by the state supervisor of banking, who since that time has proceeded with its liquidation as an insolvent institution. The undertaking on the part of the bank to meet the interest payments was not recognized by the supervisor, and the lumber company was compelled to make payment through other channels.

Between the time of the delivery of the check to the bank and the time the bank was taken over by the supervisor, the lumber company's general deposit account with the bank remained unchanged, and the bank, during the same period and at the time it was so taken over by the supervisor, had in its vaults cash largely in excess of the amount of the check.

Later on the lumber company presented a claim to the supervisor for the amount of the check, claiming a preferential payment from the assets of the bank. The supervisor refused to allow it other than as a general claim, and the present action was instituted to enforce it as a preferred claim. Judgment went in favor of the lumber company in the court below, and the supervisor of banking appeals.

The question presented by the record is a narrow one, although we have not found it free from difficulty. Before discussing the particular question, it may be well to notice certain of the applicable general principles. All deposits of money made with a banker may be divided into two classes, namely, general deposits and special deposits. The former character of deposit is the more common one in which the depositor leaves his money with the banker for his own convenience. In effect the depositor thereby loans his money to the banker, and the relation of debtor and creditor is created between them. The banker has the right to use the money deposited for his own purposes; his only obligation being to return the amount thereof to the depositor either in partial payments or as a whole, as the depositor demands it. A special deposit, on the other hand, is where the depositor leaves his money with the banker for a particular purpose or for a particular use. It does not create the relation of debtor and creditor, but rather that of trustee and *cestui que trust*. The banker obtains no title to the money, and may not use it for his own purposes; his obligation being to apply it to the uses and purposes for which he receives it. The distinction between the two forms of deposit is a wide one, not only as it affects the immediate parties thereto, but as it affects other creditors of the banker.

On the insolvency of the banker, all of his general depositors have an equal lien on his general assets and can have a return of no more than their proportionate share; while the special depositor may reclaim his entire deposit if it is found intact, or, under the modern modification of the rule, may reclaim it from the general mass with which it has been commingled, if it appears that the banker has not, subsequent to the time of the intermingling, reduced the mass to an amount less than the amount of the special deposit. These principles, we think, are well established by the authorities. [Citing cases.]

Tested by the rules above stated, it is at once apparent that had the lumber company, instead of sending its check to the bank for the amount to become due on the interest payment, sent to the bank the cash for the amount due, it would, under the circumstances shown, have constituted a special deposit which it could have reclaimed in its entirety after the bank passed into the hands of the supervisor of banking, and this notwithstanding the bank might have intermingled the money with its general cash deposits. A like result would have followed had the lumber company required its messenger carrying the check to the bank to exact payment of the check and, after payment, leave the money so received with the bank as a deposit to pay the maturing interest obligation when it became due. The difference between transactions such as these and the transaction in question, it seems clear, is one of manner rather than one of legal effect. By presenting the check to the bank and directing what disposition should be made of the fund represented by it, the lumber company sought to collect this part of the debt due it from the bank and deposit the fund for a special purpose. In other words, it sought thereby to change a part of its general deposit into a special deposit. The bank, by accepting the check with knowledge of the purposes of the lumber company, consented to the change. It thereby lost its right of general lien on the fund, its right of offset against it, its title thereto, its right to use it for its own purposes, and had no right with respect to it other than to pay it out in accordance with the directions of the lumber company. While the lumber company could have changed its directions with respect to the fund prior to its actual disposition in accordance with the directions given, the bank had no such right. Its sole right and duty was to carry out the instructions given it by the lumber company. It follows from these considerations, we think, that the relation of the parties with respect to the fund were changed by the transaction between them; that their relation thereafter with respect to it was not that of debtor and creditor, but that of trustee and *cestui que trust*. As between the immediate parties thereto, we conclude that it cannot be successfully contended that the lumber company was not entitled to claim the fund as a special deposit.

What reason is there for contending that the fund is not a special deposit as between the lumber company and the general creditors of the bank? The first of the reasons suggested by the supervisor, he states in the following language:

"The bank, of course, may be indebted to the plaintiff, but what is the property, the title to which is in the plaintiff? Nothing except the unused check with the letter. To the return of these the plaintiff is entitled. The letter and check were to serve a specific purpose, which, of course, was frustrated by the closing of the bank prior to July 1, 1921. The check coming into the hands of the liquidator of the bank in the same condition as delivered by the plaintiff to the bank and the check not having been cashed and no funds substituted in lieu of the check, the plaintiff, of course, cannot prevail except as to the return of its check."

But this reasoning, in our opinion, overlooks the substance of the transaction. The check, it is true, was not marked as paid, nor did the bank set apart from its general funds the amount of money called for by the check into a special fund. But these acts, had they been carried out, would have been here nothing more than evidence of the transaction. The check and the letter did not, as between the parties, represent value. They were mere directions from the one party to the other as to property which in itself alone had value. The subsequent insolvency of the bank in no way changed the original nature of the check and letter, and they do not now have value. To allow a recovery of them only, would be to allow a recovery of the shadow and not the substance. But the argument mistakes the real question at issue. That question is, was there such a segregation of this particular fund from the moneys of the bank as to withdraw it from the general lien of the general creditors. If there was such a segregation, it matters little what means were taken for its accomplishment. Nor do we think it accurate to say that the check was not cashed. Plainly it was cashed as between the parties, as to all intents and purposes, by the mere issuance and acceptance of the check with that understanding. The pertinent matter in the objection is the fact that there was no actual segregation of the fund; no separation of it from the bank's general fund. But this objection is answered by the rule with respect to the intermingling of funds. Since there can be a recovery where the bank intermingles its special funds with its general fund, so, on the like principle, can there be a recovery where the bank leaves a special fund intermingled with its general fund after it becomes its duty to segregate it.

The case of Raynor v. Scandinavian American Bank, 122 Wash. 150, 210 Pac. 499, 25 A. L. R. 716, cited in support of the proposition that nothing but the check and letter can be recovered, lends no support to the proposition. In that case the checks under consideration were checks drawn on a solvent bank and deposited by the drawee in the insolvent bank. They represented a solvent fund and had value in the hands of the holder, and a recovery of the checks was equivalent to a recovery of the fund, which is not so in the present instance.

The second reason urged is that the situation of the lumber company is not different from the situation of other creditors of the bank who held uncashed checks at the time it was closed by the supervisor. But we think there is a difference between the situations. The lumber company presented its check at a time when the bank was a going concern, when it was open for the transaction of business, and its check was accepted and (in legal effect) cashed by the bank. In the other instances, there was no presentation during the business life of the bank, and no cashing of the checks. The holders of the checks were mere general creditors of the bank, and are not in positions such as to entitle them to claim that there was a withdrawal of the sums represented by the checks from the general funds of the bank and deposited as special funds.

As a final reason, against a recovery, it is urged that there was by the transaction no augmentation of the assets of the bank. The fact here assumed is undoubtedly true as applied to the general assets of the bank; that is to say, it is true in the sense that the bank held no greater assets at the completion of the transaction than it held at its beginning. But it is not our understanding that this is the principle upon which the doctrine of augmentation rests. The equitable right to follow misapplied property into the hands of the parties receiving it depends upon the ability of identifying it in specie, or the ability of identifying the property with which it has been confused, or into which it has been converted. If this cannot be done there can be no recovery, even though it be shown that the general assets of the estate have been increased to the amount and value of the property. The rule as applied to money which has been intermingled with other money thus means that it must be shown that the mass of money from which it must be taken has been increased by the amount of money which has been misapplied, not that it must be shown that the general assets of the possessor of the money have been increased. In the instant case,

SECT. IV.] NORTHWEST LUMBER CO. *v.* SCANDINAVIAN AM. BK. 55

there is a showing that the money which came into the hands of the supervisor on the insolvency of the bank was greater by the amount of the check than it would have been had the bank performed its duty and made the actual segregation, and in consequence an augmentation of that mass. . . .

The trial court allowed interest on the claim from the date the bank was taken over by the supervisor, at the statutory rate. This is assigned as error, but the ruling is supported by the case of Hitt Fireworks Co. *v.* Scandinavian American Bank, 121 Wash. 261, 209 Pac. 680, and that case can be consulted for the reasons supporting the rule.

The judgment is affirmed.[1]

MAIN, C. J., PEMBERTON, MITCHELL, and BRIDGES, JJ., concur.

[1] On rehearing the court held that the plaintiff was not entitled to interest out of the general funds of the bank. 132 Wash. 449.

Special deposit and general deposit for a special purpose. In the following cases it was held that where money was deposited with a bank for a special purpose but without any agreement that the money should be kept separate and applied specifically to the purpose, and the bank failed, the depositor was not entitled to priority over the other creditors of the bank. *Re* Hosie, 7 N. B. R. 601, Fed. Cas. No. 6711 (to pay note); Minard *v.* Watts, 186 Fed. 245 (to be paid to successful party in lawsuit); Fallgatter *v.* Citizens' Nat. Bank, 11 F.(2d) 383 (deposit by stockholders of bank to make good impairment of capital); Northern Sugar Corp. *v.* Thompson, 13 F.(2d) 829 (to pay on check a particular class of creditors); Schofield M'f'g Co. *v.* Cochran, 119 Ga. 901 (to pay pledgee); Mutual Accident Ass'n *v.* Jacobs, 141 Ill. 261 (to indemnify depositee from liability on appeal bond); Kuehne *v.* Union Trust Co., 133 Mich. 602 (to indemnify depositee from liability on letter of credit); Butcher *v.* Butler, 134 Mo. App. 61 (to pay third person on certain conditions); Taussig *v.* Carnegie Trust Co., 156 App. Div. 519, *aff'd* 213 N. Y. 627 (deposit of salary to secure letter of credit); Bank of Blackwell *v.* Dean, 9 Okla. 626 (to meet draft).

In the following cases, however, it was held that where money was deposited with a bank for a special purpose, the deposit was special, and upon the failure of the bank the depositor was entitled to receive the amount of his deposit in priority to other creditors of the bank. Titlow *v.* Sundquist, 234 Fed. 613 (to pay note); Anderson *v.* Pacific Bank, 112 Cal. 598 (to indemnify third person against liability as bail); Smith *v.* Ringelman, 79 Colo. 333 (deposit in "sales account" not subject to check); City of Miami *v.* Shutts, 59 Fla. 462 (as security for performance of contract); Woodhouse *v.* Crandall, 197 Ill. 104 (as security for performance of covenants in lease); Star Cutter Co. *v.* Smith, 37 Ill. App. 212 (to pay a check); Shopert *v.* Indiana Nat. Bank, 41 Ind. App. 474 (to be paid to third person on delivery of goods); Hudspeth *v.* Union Trust & Sav. Bank, 196 Iowa 706, 197 Iowa 913 (to be paid on completion of contract); Peak *v.* Ellicott, 30 Kan. 156 (to pay note); Ellicott *v.* Barnes, 31 Kan. 170 (to pay note); Secrest *v.* Ladd, 112 Kan. 23 (to pay for shares of stock of depositee); Ryan *v.* Phillips, 3 Kan. App. 704 (to pay note); Stein *v.* Kemp, 132 Minn. 44 (to pay vendor on deposit of title deeds); Blummer *v.* Scandinavian Amer. St. Bank, 169 Minn. 89 (to pay mortgage, interest payable in meantime); Blythe *v.* Kujawa, 175 Minn. 88 (to pay vendor on deposit of title deeds); Mitchell *v.* Bank of Indianola, 98 Miss. 658 (to pay vendor on deposit of title deeds); Sawyers *v.* Conner, 114 Miss. 363 (to pay debt to third person); Harrison *v.* Smith, 83

GUIDISE v. ISLAND REFINING CORPORATION.

DISTRICT COURT, S. D. NEW YORK. 1923.

291 Fed. 922.

In Equity. Suit by Edward A. Guidise against the Island Refining Corporation. On motion by Charles B. Hill and another, as receivers of the defendant, to compel payment to them of certain funds. Petition granted.

Motion on petition by a general receiver on sequestration to compel the trustee under a mortgage to pay over certain funds. The Island Refining Corporation executed a mortgage and a series of coupon bonds in conventional form in which the Metropolitan Trust Company was named as trustee. Each coupon was payable at the office of the trustee, and it was the mortgagor's custom to remit to the trustee, which was a bank, the necessary funds to meet the coupons a little before they fell due. These remittances were credited to accounts in the bank, entitled "Island Refining Corporation Coupon Account"; a separate account being set up for each installment of semiannual interest. As the coupons were presented, the bank's cashier paid them out of the proper "Coupon Account" by cashier's check.

The receiver claims against the bank the balance in each of the

---

Mo. 210 (to invest on a particular mortgage); Stoller v. Coates, 88 Mo. 514 (to pay another bank to the credit of a third person); Marshall v. Farmers & Merchants Bank, 215 Mo. App. 365 (to indemnify surety); Kimmel v. Dickson, 5 S. D. 221 (to pay vendor on deposit of title deeds); Carlson v. Kies, 75 Wash. 171 (to forward by draft when receipts received); Central Bank & Trust Co. v. Ritchie, 120 Wash. 160 (to pay note); Pacific Building & Loan Ass'n v. Central Bank, 127 Wash. 524 (collection on commission of assessments for building and loan association).

See 31 A. L. R. 472; 39 A. L. R. 930; 57 A. L. R. 386; 60 A. L. R. 336. See also 24 A. L. R. 1111; 39 A. L. R. 1138; 2 So. Cal. L. Rev. 64; 77 U. Pa. L. Rev. 280.

Specific directions with respect to money already on general deposit. In the following cases where money was already on general deposit and was never segregated, it was held that no trust was created. Mechanics & Metals National Bank v. Buchanan, 12 F.(2d) 891; Phoenix Title & Trust Co. v. Central Bank, 30 Ariz. 431; Border v. State Sav. Bank, 202 Iowa 27; State v. Banking Corporation, 77 Mont. 134. See 75 U. Pa. L. Rev. 69; 36 Yale L. Jour. 682; 14 Minn. L. Rev. 407.

In the following cases the opposite result was reached. Titlow v. Sundquist, 234 Fed. 613; Leach v. Farmers & Mechanics Sav. Bank, 202 Iowa 881; State v. McKinley County Bank, 32 N. Mex. 147; People v. City Bank, 96 N. Y. 32; Central Bank & Trust Co. v. Ritchie, 120 Wash. 160. See also State v. Grills, 35 R. I. 70.

Tracing the product. On the question of tracing the product, see Chapter V, Section VI, and particularly Spokane County v. First Nat. Bank, 68 Fed. 979, and Rorebeck v. Benedict Flour & Feed Co., 26 F.(2d) 440, *post*.

"Coupon Accounts" arising from the failure of some of the holders to present their coupons.

LEARNED HAND, District Judge (after stating the facts as above). I cannot conceive any legal distinction between a fund deposited in a bank to meet a declared dividend, and called a "Dividend Account," and a similar fund deposited to meet coupons and called a "Coupon Account." A declared dividend is universally regarded as a debt, and a coupon is, of course, no more than a secured debt. How it can be thought, ceteris paribus, that one account should be a trust fund, and another not, passes the limit of my discrimination. But this case concerns coupons, and however the law be written I must try to spell it out.

[1] The fact that the fund remains subject only to the obligor's order has usually been deemed enough to rebut the inference of a trust. There must be some intention to give the beneficiary irrevocable rights in the res, and that scarcely comports with the obligor's sole right to draw. That was the case in Re Interborough Consol. Co. (Ex parte Gustave Porges) 288 Fed. 334 (C. C. A. 2, January 16, 1923), and it is authoritative on me even if I did not agree with it, which (though that makes no difference) I do.

In the case at bar the funds when deposited were plainly enough earmarked for their purpose and the bank disbursed them directly upon presentation of the coupons. That method of paying the debts might, I should think, be interpreted either way. I do not mean that it is of any moment that the bank was also the trustee under the mortgage. What seems to me of consequence is that each remittance was sent on with the understanding that the obligor should not have anything more to do with it, and that the bank should distribute it to those who were entitled. That, I should think, might well have been treated as an irrevocable release of control, and so a valid declaration of trust. At least, in such a case, where the whole thing turns on how you will interpret papers whose meaning is entirely indeterminate, I should incline to think that the obligor showed by its practice that it was permanently done with the funds. Of course, that does not mean that the debt was paid. Adams v. Hackensack Improvement Commission, 44 N. J. Law, 638, 43 Am. Rep. 406.

[2] But the whole thing is very tenebrous at best, and it is more important that the law should be certain than that ideal justice should be done, whatever that may mean. In Noyes v. First National Bank, 180 App. Div. 162, 167 N. Y. Supp. 288, the bank paid the coupons out of the fund by its own checks, and still no trust arose. The Court of Appeals accepted Mr. Justice Scott's opinion as its own (224 N. Y. 542, 120 N. E. 870), and that settles the law there against my supposed test. Of course, this is a matter of general commercial law, and federal judges are free to follow their own notions; but it is undesirable to do so, unless one's convictions

are firmer than my own. Anyway this case, along with Staten Island Cricket & Baseball Club *v.* Farmers' L. & T. Co., 41 App. Div. 321, 58 N. Y. Supp. 460, on which it stood, was approved in Re Interborough Consol. Co. (Ex parte Gustave Porges) *supra*, and indeed appears to have been the basis of that decision. The distinction which I have ventured to suggest as possibly critical was ignored, and I have no doubt that it would be overruled, if now made a point of departure. There is no distinction between the state law and the case at bar.

Petition granted.[1]

[1] *Re* Interborough Consolidated Corp., 288 Fed. 334; Noyes *v.* First Nat. Bank, 180 App. Div. 162, *aff'd* 224 N. Y. 542, *accord*. See Grinnell, Status of Funds Deposited for Payment of Interest on Bonds, 19 Ill. L. Rev. 429. See also 28 Col. L. Rev. 477; 32 A. L. R. 950.

In the following cases it was held that where a corporation deposited money in a bank with a direction to pay dividends which had been declared by the corporation and the corporation failed before all the dividends had been paid, the stockholders who had not received their dividends were entitled to recover in priority to the general creditors of the corporation on the ground that the corporation had become a trustee. *Re* Interborough Consolidated Corp., 267 Fed. 914; Ford *v.* Easthampton Rubber Thread Co., 158 Mass. 84 (*semble*); LeRoy *v.* Globe Ins. Co., 2 Edw. Ch. (N. Y.) 657; Matter of LeBlanc, 14 Hun 8, *aff'd* 75 N. Y. 598; Searles *v.* Gebbie, 115 App. Div. 778, *aff'd* 190 N. Y. 533.

If money is deposited in a bank to the credit of a creditor of the depositor in accordance with an agreement between the depositor and the creditor, a novation is effected whereby the creditor obtains a direct right against the bank. Stradley *v.* Union Trust Co., 41 Cal. App. 17; Elk Point I. C. School Dist. *v.* Bennett Bank, 168 N. W. 292 (Iowa, 1918); Heath *v.* New Bedford Safe Dep. & T. Co., 184 Mass. 481; Andrews *v.* State Bank, 9 N. D. 325; Neador *v.* Rudolph, 218 S. W. 520 (Tex. Civ. App., 1920).

In Steel Cities Chemical Co. *v.* Virginia-Carolina Chemical Co., 7 F.(2d) 280, it was held that where a deposit by a corporation with a bank for the purpose of paying coupons on bonds of the depositor was made in pursuance of an agreement with the bondholders, and the corporation failed, the bondholders were entitled to payment in priority to other creditors of the corporation. Hand, J., dissented.

In Rogers Locomotive & Machine Works *v.* Kelley, 88 N. Y. 234, it was held that where money was deposited with a bank to pay coupons on bonds of the depositor and it appeared that the corporation intended an irrevocable release of control, the bondholders were entitled to be paid by the bank ahead of an attaching creditor of the corporation.

In the following cases it was held that where money was deposited in a bank which agreed to pay a creditor of the depositor, and the depositor revoked the authority of the bank, the creditor could not recover against the bank. Brockmeyer *v.* Nat. Bank, 40 Kan. 744; Pierson *v.* Swift County Bank, 163 Minn. 344; McDonald *v.* American Nat. Bank, 25 Mont. 456; New England Water Works Co. *v.* Farmers' Loan & T. Co., 54 N. Y. App. Div. 309; First Nat. Bank *v.* Higbee, 109 Pa. 130. Compare Gellert *v.* Bank of California, 107 Ore. 162, where the depositor purchased a draft payable to a third person intending to make a gift but died before transmitting the draft to the donee.

If the depositor is not insolvent and has not revoked the authority of the bank, it would seem that the bondholder or other creditor whom the bank

LEGNITI v. MECHANICS & METALS NATIONAL BANK.

COURT OF APPEALS, NEW YORK. 1921.

230 N. Y. 415.

APPEAL from a judgment, entered July 24, 1919, upon an order of the Appellate Division of the Supreme Court in the first judicial department, reversing a judgment in favor of defendants entered upon a dismissal of the complaint by the court on trial at Special Term and directing judgment in favor of plaintiff and against defendant, appellant, upon new findings.

The nature of the action and the facts, so far as material, are stated in the opinion.

CRANE, J. It has long been an established custom among banks and financial institutions to sell credit usually represented by draft or check. Thus a bank having a credit with a correspondent in a foreign country will sell its draft or check, drawn upon such correspondent, to a purchaser who desires to make a foreign payment. The draft is not the credit but represents the credit, or in other words, it is a notification to the correspondent or foreign representative to pay the money as directed. The draft is a direction to pay. It is not, itself, money or credit. It is simply used as such. The money paid the bank by the purchaser of the draft becomes the bank's money. The transaction is that of purchase and sale. No trust relationship is established. (Taussig v. Carnegie Trust Company, 213 N. Y. 627.)

This practice of selling credit by means of drafts or checks grew up among merchants and bankers with the expansion of trade and the necessities of commerce. With the increase of foreign trade and the development of international relationships, communication by cable and wireless met the insistent demands for haste and dispatch. Thus the custom has developed of selling credit to be established by cable or wireless. A purchaser does not receive a draft or check which is to be transmitted by mail, but pays for a credit, which will be given him in the foreign country by an immediate cable or wireless from the seller to his correspondent at the foreign

---

agreed to pay can as beneficiary of a contract maintain a suit against the bank. Kirby v. Wait, 120 Kan. 400; Scott, Cases on Trusts, 1 ed., 80. But in the following cases it was held that such a suit could not be maintained against the bank by the bondholder or other creditor, either because the beneficiary of a contract is not allowed to maintain an action, or because there was no contract by the bank to make the payment but merely a direction by the depositor. Pike v. Anglo-South American Trust Co., 166 N. E. 553 (Mass., 1929); Staten I. C. & B. B. Club v. Farmers' Loan & T. Co., 41 N. Y. App. Div. 321; Erb v. Banco di Napoli, 243 N. Y. 45. See Murray v. North Liberty Sav. Bank, 196 Iowa 734. See Scott, Cases on Trusts, 1 ed., 80.

point. The thing sold is the same in the case of the cable or wireless transaction as in the case of the draft or check. It is the credit of the bank or seller. The means of establishing or transmitting the credit is simply an incident of the transaction. In the one case, it is a formal paper drawn up and signed by the seller directing his foreign correspondent to make payment of the amount and to the person therein stated. In the other case, it is a similar direction transmitted by cable or wireless. Cable transfers, therefore, mean a method of transmitting money by cable wherein the seller engages that he has the balance at the point on which the payment is ordered and that on receipt of the cable directing the transfer his correspondent at such point will make payment to the beneficiary described in the cable. All these transactions are matters of purchase and sale and create no trust relationships. (Strohmeyer & Arpe Co. v. Guaranty Trust Co., 172 App. Div. 16; Katcher v. American Express Company, 109 Atl. Rep. 741; A. C. Whitaker on Foreign Exchange, section 26, p. 89.)

In some of the cases this purchase of a cable transfer is referred to as a contract. (Bank of British North America v. Cooper, 137 U. S. 473; Bank of China, Japan, and the Straits, Limited v. American Trading Company, Law Reports A. C. 1894, page 266; Atlantic Communication Co. v. Zimmermann, 182 App. Div. 862.) The terms of the contract are in such a case that the banker agrees to send a cablegram establishing a credit with his foreign correspondent. The contract, it is said, is executory until the credit has been established and that upon failure to send the message the customer may rescind the contract and sue to get back his money or else sue for breach of contract. Whether the transaction be considered a purchase or an executory contract, we need not now determine. So far as this case is concerned, it is a mere matter of nomenclature. In either case, the money paid by the customer to the banker becomes the latter's property and does not establish a trust relationship; the banker does not hold the money as agent or trustee until the foreign credit is established.

There is a marked distinction between these transactions which I have just described and a direction to a bank or other person to transmit a certain specific sum of money to a person abroad. In such cases the bank or transmitter is the agent of the person paying the money, and until the money is sent holds it as agent or trustee for the owner. Such were the cases of Musco v. United Surety Company (132 App. Div. 300) and People *ex rel.* Zotti v. Flynn (135 App. Div. 276). In these latter transactions the intention of the payer is that the money he gives to his agent shall be sent abroad. It is the amount which he gives that is to be transmitted. How it is sent may be immaterial to him. If there be time, currency might be purchased and sent. If not, it may be transmitted in any form recognized in financial circles. It is not at all necessary that the sender or agent have credit in the place to which the money is to be sent. On the other hand, in the contract for credit it is not a specific sum which is to be sent but rather a specific credit which is to be purchased. The amount paid varies with the market. The actual thing that is done by the sender in both of these cases may or may not be the same, but the practice of the merchants and banks has recognized a difference; so have the courts. In the case now before us was the transaction between Angelo Legniti and A. Bolognesi & Co. a purchase of credit or the direction to transmit, as the plaintiff's agent, a specific sum of money? It is frankly conceded by the attorney for the respondent that if it be the former, the plaintiff has no right of recovery. The facts, therefore, must be briefly stated to determine this question.

In February of 1914 Alessandro Bolognesi and Aldo Bolognesi were copartners doing business in the city of New York under the firm name of A. Bolognesi & Co. The plaintiff was a banker at 64 Mulberry street in the city of New York who was in arrears in Naples on account of the failure of one Caesari Conti, and needed to transfer some money to that place at once. He applied to several banking houses in New York to obtain the best rate for the transfer of 18,000 lire to Naples, Italy. On the afternoon of February 10th, 1914, he made his arrangements for this purpose with A. Bolognesi & Co. He said to their representatives: " I give you the order to cable this money for me to Italy, on condition that you send the cable immediately, tonight because as you know, on account of the failure of Caesari Conti, I am overdrawn. I need this money to reach Naples tomorrow." A few minutes before six o'clock on that day a boy from Bolognesi & Co. brought to the plaintiff's office a bill which reads as follows:

" NEW YORK, *February* 10, 1914.

" Mr. ANGELO LEGNITI,
 " Bought of A. BOLOGNESI & Co.,
  " 52 Wall Street.

" Cable Transfer to Italy to pay by cable to Banca Commerciale Italiana, Napoli, advice to be forwarded by Cable from New York.

" Lire 18,000 at 5:19 7 8	$3,462.37
" Cabling	1.24
" Paid ck 3450	$3,463.61
" (cash 13.61)	
" Bolognesi & Co.	
" Maselli	

" Payments required in cash or certified cheques, otherwise order if accepted, will be executed after collection of cheque.

" It is fully understood and agreed that no liability shall attach to us nor to our correspondent for any loss or damage in consequence of any delay or mistake in transmitting this message or for any other cause beyond our control."

Thereupon the plaintiff delivered to the messenger a certified check for $3,450 indorsed to A. Bolognesi & Co. and $13.61 in cash. This check was deposited the next day by A. Bolognesi & Co. in its account in the Mechanics and Metals National Bank of New York, collected and credited to the account of the depositor. The cable credit was never transmitted, as on the 11th day of February A. Bolognesi & Co. made a general assignment for the benefit of creditors. Later, in March of 1914, a petition in bankruptcy was filed against them, resulting in the election on the 14th day of August, 1915, of the trustees, parties to this litigation. On the 10th day of February, 1914, the firm of A. Bolognesi & Co. was indebted to the defendant, the Mechanics and Metals National Bank of New York, in the sum of $51,329.90 for moneys advanced, secured by discounts, acceptances and notes. There was a balance on deposit with the defendant, the Mechanics and Metals National Bank of New York, to the credit of A. Bolognesi & Co. of $18,985.05 which was increased by the deposit of the check delivered by the plaintiff to A. Bolognesi & Co. and $6,241.65 in addition thereto. This amount was reduced by three checks aggregating $732.94. As against this balance due to its depositor, the defendant bank claims the right to offset under the Bankruptcy Law the indebtedness of A. Bolognesi & Co. as above stated.

This action has been brought by Angelo Legniti upon the theory that A. Bolognesi & Co. became his agents for the sending of 18,000 lire to Naples, Italy, and that as the money was not sent, he may recover it from the bank into whose possession it can be traced. The bank, he claims, holds it, charged with a trust to pay it to him; it is his money, he says, as he never lost title to it. We do not think there is evidence here of any trust. It was stated by Alessandro Bolognesi in his examination as follows: " Q. As I understand it, you sold for a given number of American dollars a certain number of lire to be delivered in Italy to somebody else? A. To be transferred from my account. Q. That was the transaction in this particular matter? A. That was the regular transaction. Q. What is the difference between that and the sale of a draft for so many lire credit in Italy? A. Only that the draft is advised by mail and this is advised by cable."

It will be noted that the bill presented to the plaintiff late in the afternoon of February 10th, above quoted, upon which the plaintiff parted with his money, stated that he, Mr. Angelo Legniti, *bought* of A. Bolognesi & Co. cable transfer to Italy — to pay by cable to Banca Commerciale Italiana. This was not the case of a specific sum of American money being sent to Naples after being exchanged for lire. It was a case of 18,000 lire being needed in Naples and the purchase of A. Bolognesi & Company's credit with the Banca Commerciale Italiana for this amount which credit was to be used by and for the benefit of Legniti. The money was not to be sent to the Banca Commerciale Italiana for Legniti. It was A. Bolognesi & Co. who on February 10, 1914, had either money or credit at the Banca Commerciale Italiana of Naples, the use of which for compensation was sold and transferred to the plaintiff.

We are naturally impressed, as any one must be, with the fact that the plaintiff gave his money to establish a relative value or worth in Naples and that the receiver kept the money and did not deliver the value, and that this money the bank now holds. Why should not the plaintiff get it back? Upon the failure of A. Bolognesi & Co. many claims sprang into existence beside this of the plaintiff and it is the duty of the courts as far as possible to adjust these relationships according to well-established principles, usages and customs.

The Mechanics and Metals National Bank of New York also had given money or money value to A. Bolognesi & Co. and has a claim for $51,329.90. There were also many other claimants to the assets. To establish a rule that in a case like this the plaintiff becomes a preferred creditor; that the transaction is in the nature of a trust, and that checks deposited with banks upon the purchase of credit are trust funds held for certain and specified purposes, is apt to lead to much confusion, especially when those who have developed this method of doing business into a well-established custom have never treated them as such.

The judgment of the Appellate Division must, therefore, be reversed and that of the trial court affirmed, with costs in this court and in the Appellate Division.

HISCOCK, Ch. J., HOGAN, CARDOZO, POUND, MCLAUGHLIN and ANDREWS, JJ., concur.

Judgment accordingly.[1]

EQUITABLE TRUST COMPANY v. FIRST NATIONAL BANK.

SUPREME COURT OF THE UNITED STATES. 1928.

275 U. S. 359.

MR. JUSTICE HOLMES delivered the opinion of the Court.

Knauth, Nachod and Kuhne being in bankruptcy, the respondent, The First National Bank of Trinidad, Colorado, claimed priority in respect of certain funds collected by the trustee in bankruptcy, the petitioner, from the Banca Commerciale Italiana; the ground of the

[1] Morandi v. Italian-American Bank, 80 Colo. 332; American Express Co. v. Cosmopolitan Trust Co., 239 Mass. 249; Spiroplos v. Scandinavian American Bank, 116 Wash. 491, *accord.* See Carmen v. Higginson, 245

claim being that these funds were charged with a trust in the hands of the Italian bank. The respondent prevailed in the Circuit Court of Appeals. 13 F. (2d) 732. A writ of certiorari was granted by this Court. 273 U. S. 684.

The facts are as follows. The bankrupts had credit with many foreign banks and to enable small banks in this country to issue drafts upon such banks in their own name offered these terms: " Upon receipt of advice of draft, accompanied by adequate funds payable at par in New York, we shall promptly forward our advice of the same and provide the drawee with funds sufficient for the payment of the draft abroad, by a transfer of credit from our balance, or otherwise, provided the draft is drawn on a bank named in our latest list of correspondents." It was added that the drawing banks act as principals and draw in their own name, the bankrupts being employed merely " as agents of the drawers for the purpose of advising the issue of their drafts and providing the drawee banks with sufficient funds to cover their payment." The bankrupts sent out lists of their foreign correspondents and also daily rate cards fixing the rate for the various foreign currencies, including their own compensation, good only for the day of the date. In accordance with this plan the Trinidad bank drew a draft on a branch of the Banca Commerciale Italiana for 24360 lire, sent notice to the bankrupts that they had sold it " and shall thank you to protect same upon presentation," and remitted therewith a check for $1,191.20, which the bankrupts received on May 22, 1923, and deposited to their general account. On the same day the bankrupts sent to the Italian bank and to its branch a list and description of the drafts issued by inland banks and by the bankrupts and requested it to " honor the above listed drafts charging same to our account." The list was received on or before June 4, 1923; the account of the bankrupts was debited with the total amount and to that extent ceased to draw interest, the bank getting its compensation in this way. At the same time an account termed " Drafts Payable " was credited with the same amount, this account being credited in the same way with drafts from other dealers with the bank and the bankrupts themselves. In accordance with the practice in international banking, the bankrupts when they saw fit to do so cancelled their advices and were recredited in their general account; and although in fact they did not cancel the advice of inland drafts except when requested by the inland banks, the Italian bank did not know or inquire into reasons and so far as appears the Trinidad bank, or at all events the holder of the draft, knew nothing of the mode of bookkeeping described.

Mass. 511; Katcher *v.* American Express Co., 94 N. J. L. 165; Gellert *v.* Bank of California, 107 Ore. 162. See Stone, Some Legal Problems Involved in the Transmission of Funds, 21 Col. L. Rev. 507. See also 33 Yale L. Jour. 177; 16 A. L. R. 190; 57 A. L. R. 1168.

The draft was presented after the petition in bankruptcy had been filed and was dishonored; the petitioner as drawer had to take it up and now claims on the two grounds that the sum paid by it was paid upon trust to be applied to the draft, and that as holder of the draft it is, by subrogation, an equitable assignee of the bankrupts' deposit with the drawee. The first of these need not detain us. Beecher *v.* Cosmopolitan Trust Co., 239 Mass. 48. Legniti *v.* The Mechanics & Metals National Bank, 230 N. Y. 415. The identity of the fund was not maintained and no one expected it to be. See National City Bank *v.* Hotchkiss, 231 U. S. 50, 56, 57. The bankrupts undertook to 'forward' advice but only to 'provide' the drawee with funds. The second contention was that which prevailed below. Of course there is room for difference if the parties did not express very clearly what they wanted or meant, but we are led to a different conclusion whether the reliance be upon the rights of the holder or upon the original contract between the respondent and the bankrupts. In the first place the ignorance of the whole affair on the part of the holder and the general understanding that the party dealing immediately with the bank having the 'Bills Payable' account is master of it, as between himself and the bank, are quite inconsistent with the notion that an entry on that account is the appropriation of a fund to the holder's use. The respondent tries to give a different turn to the evidence but the master's finding and our own conclusion from the testimony leave no doubt in our minds. It is true that after such an entry the interest allowed to the depositor stops but that is only a convenient way of giving compensation to the bank. It is not uncommon in commercial transactions to see some of the elements of an earlier or a half imitated transaction appear, although the essentials of the transaction are not there. Whether a fund was appropriated or not depended wholly on the dealings between the bankrupts and the Italian bank; and both of them dealt with the account as subject to the bankrupt's control. The cessation of interest was for the benefit of the bank because the account was only with its general funds, and did not have any assets especially set aside and appropriated to it — in short was a bookkeeping device for the convenience of the bank.

Again, the terms offered by the bankrupts to their correspondents seem to us to promise the appropriation of a specified fund to the draft as little as they promise to apply the money received by them to that end. They are to provide the drawee banks with sufficient funds for the payment of the drafts by transfer of credit 'from our balance or otherwise.' They are to provide, that is, as convenient to themselves, for payment by the drawee banks, not to give them an earmark corpus to be handed over. They are requested by their correspondents to protect the drafts, which again means merely to see that they are paid. Wabash, St. Louis & Pacific Ry. Co. *v.* Ham, 114 U. S. 587, 596. People dealing with large banks do not ordinarily seek the ambiguous security of an identified fund, they are satisfied if the bank gives them credit. We see no indications that the Trinidad bank was not perfectly content to know that it would have credit with the Banca Commerciale, and that in the usual course of things its drafts would be paid. Evidently with this conception of their duties the bankrupts asked the Italian bank " to protect to the debit of our account the drafts " in question and others, and the branch bank to " honor the above listed drafts." That such a letter of advice is not an assignment is clearly explained in Eastman Kodak Co. *v.* National Park Bank, 231 Fed. Rep. 320, 323; (affirmed, 247 Fed. Rep. 1002.)

We have called the instrument under which the respondent claims as assignee, a draft. But on its face it is called ' check.' The form was a general form furnished by the bankrupts and the purpose is said to have been that in continental Europe or some parts of it checks are not subject to the same stamp tax as drafts. It is said in a reputable work that the fact that the instrument purports to be drawn upon a deposit is what constitutes it a check. Daniels, Negotiable Instruments, 6th ed., § 1569. The existence of this opinion sufficiently explains the words of the document before us ' Pay from balance against this check.' They no more purport to assign a fraction of a fund than does an ordinary check. They would not naturally take that shape as the respondent, the drawer of the check, had no fund in the hands of the drawee.

The decision of this case depends more upon the general import of the transaction and upon what the parties were likely to want than upon the phrases that can be picked out from the several steps. We repeat that in our opinion what the parties meant to establish and what the respondent got was the assurance of a credit abroad to the extent of its check as in the case of a letter of credit, not an attenuated property right in an account to which no special funds were attached and the particulars of which neither the respondent nor the purchaser of the check could know.

Order reversed.

Mr. Justice Stone, dissenting

The agreement of the bankrupts, on the faith of which petitioner sold its draft, did more than stipulate that the draft should be paid on presentation. It provided specifically the method of payment; that the bankrupts should " promptly," on notice of the draft, " provide the drawee with funds sufficient for the payment of the draft abroad, by a transfer of credit or otherwise." It plainly contemplated the course of business, actually followed, in which a credit, to be established with the drawee, was to be set apart and specifically appropriated to the payment of the draft. The draft was by its terms made payable from " balance against this Check."

We need not discuss what the petitioner's rights would have been

SECT. IV.]   EQUITABLE TRUST CO. *v.* FIRST NAT. BK.   67

if no such credit had been established, for here the bankrupts had performed their contract fully and to the letter. They set apart the stipulated credit. Withdrawal of it by them would have been a violation of their contract with petitioner, for the contract contained no intimation of a right to revoke it, and if the receiver had not done what they had no right to do the draft would have been paid. Nor does it appear to me that the real question is whether the Italian bank was charged with a trust with respect to funds lodged with it by the bankrupts. It may be assumed that it was not a trustee, but only a debtor to the bankrupts for the funds thus received, with power to discharge the debt *pro tanto* by payment of the draft when presented.

Stated with precision the question seems rather to be whether, since the bankrupts had performed their agreement by specifically designating and setting apart enough of their credit with the Italian bank to meet the draft, the credit thus set apart is to be treated in equity as security for the payment of the draft. If subject to that equitable obligation, neither the bankrupts nor the receiver could convert the credit, so set apart, into cash and turn the proceeds over to general creditors freed of that obligation.

Since Holroyd *v.* Marshall, 10 H. L. Cas. 191, it has been generally accepted doctrine, the recording acts permitting, that an agreement to hold property which the promisor may afterward acquire as security for the payment of a debt, operates in equity once the property is acquired, to give the stipulated security to the promisee in preference to general creditors. Such is the rule in this Court. Sexton *v.* Kessler, 225 U. S. 90. I had supposed it to be equally well settled that the agreement need not mention the word "security" to accomplish that result, if its plain purpose is to provide for the satisfaction of a debt or obligation out of identifiable property. Compare Walker *v.* Brown, 165 U. S. 654; Ingersoll *v.* Coram, 211 U. S. 335; Hurley *v.* Atchison, Topeka & Santa Fe Ry., 213 U. S. 126; Ketchum *v.* St. Louis, 101 U. S. 306; Parlin & Orendorff Implement Co. *v.* Moulden, 228 Fed. 111; Curtis *v.* Walpole Tire & Rubber Co., 218 Fed. 145. There has been no dissent from the view that an agreement to apply a designated credit or account to the payment of a check or draft drawn upon it creates security in the credit enforcible in equity as against general creditors. Fourth Street Bank *v.* Yardley, 165 U. S. 634; Farley *v.* Turner, 35 L. J. Ch. 710; Coates *v.* First National Bank, 91 N. Y. 20; Muller *v.* Kling, 209 N. Y. 239; *In re* Hollins, 215 Fed. 41. Equity, in making such agreements effective, does no more than it habitually does in compelling the performance of an agreement to give a mortgage to secure advances made on the faith of the agreement.

Both parties to this transaction knew that American drafts drawn on European banks would be worthless unless definite arrangement for their payment by the drawee was made in advance of their presentation, and that where, as here, a particular credit was set apart for that purpose the utility of such drafts would be seriously impaired if the credit, once established, could be cancelled at will. No intelligent banker would sell such drafts if the establishment of such a credit were not contemplated. A bank here, drawing and selling such drafts against a credit to be established abroad by others, pledges its own credit to the payee and is secured against loss and the dishonor of its drafts only in so far as it may insure the creation of the appropriate credit and retain the benefit of it once it is created. The stipulation that the bankrupts should promptly set apart a credit for that purpose upon receipt of advice of the draft and advise the drawee of it was a material inducement to petitioner to pledge its own credit by the sale of its draft. Once performed it is valuable security to both payee and drawer, if it is permitted to have the legal sanctions which ordinarily attach to agreements of this character.

The evidence in this case appears to me, as it did to the court below, to fall far short of establishing a practice or custom, or any rule of Italian law, permitting the depositor, while the drafts are outstanding, to cancel or control for his own purposes the credit set apart for their payment. Our own rule is that a bank of deposit may not, with impunity, ignore the known equitable rights of others to the credit established by its depositor, National Bank v. Insurance Co., 104 U. S. 54, and it would seem that that rule should be applied here in determining the rights of the parties in the absence of proof of any other. But in any case, such control, if retained by the bankrupts as between themselves and the Italian bank, could not be rightfully exercised in violation of their contract with petitioner.

The case would therefore seem to be a proper one for the application of the rule announced by this Court in Fourth Street Bank v. Yardley, *supra*, that a court of equity will lend its aid to carry into effect an agreement that an obligation shall be satisfied out of a specified credit. Applied here that rule would make effective the intention of the parties and give stability to a large and important class of banking transactions. The judgment should be affirmed.

MR. JUSTICE MCREYNOLDS joins in this dissent.[1]

[1] See 8 B. U. L. Rev. 127; 2 U. Cinn. L. Rev. 317; 40 Harv. L. Rev. 481; 28 Mich. L. Rev. 96; 76 U. Pa. L. Rev. 735; 14 Va. L. Rev. 658; 37 Yale L. Jour. 626. See also 26 Col. L. Rev. 777; 27 Col. L. Rev. 601.

If the initial bank remits money or its equivalent to another bank with directions to pay the depositor or a third person, and the initial bank fails, it has been held that the depositor does not lose. Farley v. Turner, 26 L. J. Ch. 710; City of St. Louis v. Johnson, 5 Dill. (U. S.) 241. Compare Johnson v. Robarts, L. R. 10 Ch. 505.

If after the remittance the *correspondent* bank fails, it would seem that the depositor cannot hold the initial bank liable. See Drovers' Bank v. O'Hare, 119 Ill. 646. Compare Shrewsbury v. Dupont Nat. Bank, 10 F.(2d)

B. *Deposit of Commercial Paper.*

LIPPITT v. THAMES LOAN & TRUST COMPANY.

SUPREME COURT OF ERRORS, CONNECTICUT. 1914.

88 Conn. 185.

APPLICATION by a receiver of the defendant company for advice in the discharge of his official duties. . . .

WHEELER, J. . . . On April 7th, 1913, the National Reserve Bank of New York sent the Thames Company, " for collection and remittance," items of $523.29 and $647.84. The second of these items was collected and credited to the bank on April 15th, 1913, and the first on April 25th, 1913. The Thames Company was restrained by order of court from paying out moneys on April 16th, 1913, and the receiver appointed on June 27th, and qualified on July 1st, 1913. Upon the letter accompanying these items, and beneath the signature, appeared the following: " For collection only. Please do not credit until paid." On April 14th, 1913, the Reserve Bank sent the Thames Company, " for collection and remittance," an item of $27.15, which was collected and credited the bank on the next day. All three items were collected and credited the bank on collection account, but no moneys were set apart for their payment. The bank at the time of the collections was indebted to the Thames Company in the sum of $294.30, on general account.

There was an agreement between the bank and the Thames Company that the bank should pay the company a fee for collecting items. The bank was the agent to collect these items for the owners; it has since paid their face value, which amounts have never been repaid it. The bank claims that these items so collected constitute a trust fund for it, and as to them it is a preferred creditor and entitled to immediate payment. An adjudication of these questions is asked, and also as to whether the Thames Company can set off the $294.30 due it on general account against the sum due the bank, if this be found to be a trust fund.

The indorsement of these items " for collection and remittance " was a restrictive indorsement. Freeman's National Bank *v.* National Tube Works Co., 151 Mass. 413, 418, 24 N. E. 779. It created, between the sending and receiving bank, the relation of prin-

---

632; Basila *v.* Western Union Tel. Co., 24 F.(2d) 569; Nicoletti *v.* Bank of Los Banos, 190 Cal. 637; Katz *v.* Western Union Tel. Co., 119 N. Y. Misc. 489.

If before the initial bank remits to the correspondent bank, the latter fails, the depositor can recover in full from the initial bank. American Exch. Bank *v.* Mining Co., 165 Ill. 103; Cutler *v.* American Exch. Nat. Bank, 113 N. Y. 593.

cipal and agent. So long as the items remained uncollected, the principal could control their disposition. The agent had received the items for a specific purpose, and stood toward its principal as a trustee charged with an active duty toward the purpose of the agency, which was the subject of the trust. Dale *v.* Gear, 38 Conn. 15, 18. After the collections were made, the agent or trustee might have continued the trust relation, or, by its conduct toward the collections, have changed the relation to that of debtor and creditor. For example, the agent would change the relation to that of debtor and creditor were it to mingle the funds collected with its own funds, and credit the collections to the sending bank under its arrangement with it to make remittances at specified times. If, on the other hand, it held the funds collected, intending under its agreement to make immediate remittance, and for a very brief period, for business convenience, keeping the funds set apart or on special deposit for its principal, there would be no change in the relation, the trust would continue, and, on failure of the agent pending transmission of the funds, the principal would be entitled to them. Commercial Bank *v.* Armstrong, 148 U. S. 50, 56, 13 Sup. Ct. Rep. 533.

Some of the courts hold the test is found in the ability to trace the fund; if this can be done the trust continues; if it cannot, the trust ceases, and the principal must share with other creditors of the insolvent. While other courts hold the test to be whether the relation of principal and agent has ceased and that of debtor and creditor begun. We agree with the Supreme Court of the United States (Commercial Bank *v.* Armstrong, 148 U. S. 50, 13 Sup. Ct. Rep. 533) that the latter test furnishes the more satisfactory reason. Whether or not the fund can be traced is, as it seems to us, evidence of the existence or non-existence of this relation.

But whatever the ground of recovery adopted, the claimant to the fund must assume the burden of proving the existence of this trust relation. Bank Commissioners *v.* Security Trust Co., 70 N. H. 536, 550, 49 Atl. 113. The insolvency of the Thames Company terminated its authority to collect. The receiver of the company could not inventory uncollected items, for they never became part of the assets of the company. If the company collected in spite of the termination of its agency to collect, it held the proceeds as an agent for the sending bank, and they became impressed with a trust from which they cannot be disassociated. Freeman's National Bank *v.* National Tube Works Co., 151 Mass. 413, 418, 24 N. E. 779; Manufacturers' National Bank *v.* Continental Bank, 148 Mass. 553, 559, 20 N. E. 193; 5 Cyc. 512. The order of court of April 16th restrained the Thames Company from paying out any of its funds, or declaring or paying dividends on its deposits or capital stock. The order did not in terms purport to prevent the company from making collections of items in its hands. But when the power of the company to remit the proceeds of its collections was taken from it, its power to fulfil the purposes of the agency committed to it by the Reserve Bank was taken away. The bank would not have authorized the collection had it known that the proceeds could not be remitted to it. It would not have converted a practically cash asset into a general claim against the company. When the company lost its power to carry out the terms of its agency, the agency ceased. The claim collected after the order of court of April 16th is in the same position as the claim collected after an adjudication in insolvency. The proceeds are impressed with a trust; the relation of principal and agent has never been transformed to that of debtor and creditor.

As to the two items collected before the order was passed, the facts stipulated do not indicate that the bank intended that the sums collected on these items should be a trust fund, or be forthwith remitted to it. The letter of April 7th, forwarded with the two largest items, did state that the enclosure was " for collection and remittance." There is nothing in the facts presented, and no legal inference to be drawn from the use of these words, which compel the conclusion that immediate remittance was intended. The letter also said: " Please do not credit until paid." This undoubtedly had reference to the custom between banks holding business relations to credit items unless otherwise directed; and it implied that credit might be made upon collection. We think the custom of the banking business is so universal that we may take judicial notice of it, that items collected for another bank are in fact credited, whether the provision " for collection and remittance " be among the printed directions of the letter of the forwarding bank to its correspondent or not. We must presume that by a well-known custom among banks, moneys of its correspondents, when collected, are mingled with the funds of the collecting bank. Freeman's National Bank v. National Tube Works Co., 151 Mass. 413, 418, 24 N. E. 779. When this is done, the forwarding bank will get a like sum of money, but not the specific fund collected. If the payment of a fee for the collections indicates, as the Reserve Bank asserts, a custom that immediate remittance of the items collected should be made, we could not so hold without a finding of the custom. Until the case is presented of such custom, it will not be necessary to consider the effect of the violation of its contract by the agent by crediting the collections made.

We should have preferred that the record should show more fully all of the facts surrounding this transaction: the relation and course of business between the Reserve Bank and the Thames Company; their mutual custom in making collections; all of their communications with each other; their intention to impress these items with a trust or otherwise; and the customs of banks in similar transactions. Upon the case as presented by this record, we are of opinion that the Reserve Bank, as to these two items, is a general creditor of the Thames Company, and that the proceeds of these items are not impressed with a trust. Against these items the Reserve Bank is entitled to set off the $294.30 due from it to the Thames Company.

Against the $523.29 item, impressed as it is with a trust, the amount due the receiver from the Reserve Bank cannot be set off, since these are neither mutual credits nor mutual debts. The Thames Company held the amount due the Reserve Bank as trustee, while the bank owed the Thames Company in its corporate capacity. Libby v. Hopkins, 104 U. S. 303, 309; General Statutes, § 649.[1] . . .

[1] *Relation before collection.* In the decisions a bank to which commercial paper is indorsed for collection is referred to sometimes as an agent, sometimes as a bailee, sometimes as a trustee. It seems not inaccurate to refer to the bank as a trustee, although the trust is not a formal trust. See Mechanics & Metals Nat. Bank v. Termini, 117 N. Y. Misc. 309. It is true that the depositor has sometimes been allowed to maintain an action of trover against the bank, but this action has not infrequently been allowed as a substitute for a bill in equity. See Scott, Cases on Trusts, 1 ed., 65. Although the indorsement to the bank is for collection the bank can maintain an action upon the paper in its own name, both at common law and under the Negotiable Instruments Law, sec. 37. See Scott, Cases on Trusts, 1 ed., 65. In Moore v. Hall, 48 Mich. 143, it was held that the authority of the indorsee for collection was not terminated by the death of the indorser, since the indorsement and delivery for the purpose of collection passed the legal title in trust.

The rights of the parties depend upon the intention of the parties, as determined in the light of business usage, rather than upon the application of the ordinary principles and rules of the law of trusts. See Turner, Deposits of Demand Paper as "Purchases," 37 Yale L. Jour. 874; Baker, Bank Deposits and Collections, 11 Mich. L. Rev. 122, 210.

If matured or demand paper is indorsed to a bank "for collection," the bank is presumptively not a debtor until the paper is paid, although the depositor is credited at once with the amount of the deposit. The same result has been generally reached in the case of other restrictive indorsements, such as "for deposit" or "for deposit to the credit of" the depositor. See Morse, Banks and Banking, 6 ed., chaps. 16, 36; Dec. Dig., Banks and Banking, secs. 156–159; 7 C. J. 600; Scott, Cases on Trusts, 1 ed., 64–67; 7 L. R. A. (N. S.) 694; 47 L. R. A. (N. S.) 552; 11 A. L. R. 1043; 16 A. L. R. 1084; 42 A. L. R. 492.

Relation after collection. Whether after collection the bank becomes a debtor depends upon the intention of the parties as determined in the light of business usage. In a great many cases it is held that presumptively the bank becomes a debtor from the moment of collection. In some cases, however, particularly those in which the paper is deposited for "collection and remittance," it has been held that presumptively the bank does not become a debtor, although there is considerable authority the other way. See Scott, Cases on Trusts, 1 ed., 67, 68. Bryan, Trust Nature of Collection Items, 13 Va. L. Reg. (N. S.) 1; Harris, Credit Nature of Collection Items, *ibid.* 296; 14 St. Louis L. Rev. 406.

A bank collecting paper when it knows that it is insolvent, has no right to use the proceeds as its own, and is to be treated not as a debtor but as a constructive trustee of the proceeds. Scott, 68.

On the question of following the proceeds of the collection where the bank is not a debtor, see Chapter V, section VI, and particularly Spokane County v. First Nat. Bank, 68 Fed. 979, and Rorebeck v. Benedict Flour & Feed Co., 26 F.(2d) 440, *post.*

EQUITABLE TRUST COMPANY v. ROCHLING.
SUPREME COURT OF THE UNITED STATES. 1927.
275 U. S. 248.

MR. JUSTICE STONE delivered the opinion of the Court.

Respondents, bankers of Frankfort-on-Main, maintained a general deposit account with the bankrupts, who were private bankers in New York City. On instruction of Lloyds Bank, Ltd., London, which was requested by respondents " to procure this amount for us " on June 15, 1923, " at Knauth, Nachod & Kuhne, New York," the National Bank of Commerce in New York on that day delivered to Knauth, Nachod & Kuhne, the bankrupts, its cashier's check for $30,000 payable to their order " for account of Rochling Bank, Gebt. Frankfort-on-Main," and took from them their receipt for the check " for account of Rochling Bank." On instruction of the Swiss Bank, London, the National City Bank, New York, on the same date delivered its cashier's check for $30,000, payable to the order of Knauth, Nachod & Kuhne, " A/C Gebr. Rochling, Frankfort A/M," taking from them a receipt in like form. On that day, too, the bankrupts credited the account of respondents with the two checks and made an entry on their books indicating that respondents were entitled to interest on the amount of the checks from that date. The checks were deposited by Knauth, Nachod & Kuhne in their own deposit accounts in other banks and were there credited to those accounts. On the following day, June 16, 1923, before the collection of the checks, the petition in bankruptcy was filed.

In receiving these checks, forthwith crediting respondents with them, and in crediting interest from the date of their receipt, the bankrupts followed the established course of their business with respondent which had extended over a period of more than two years. Periodic statements of the account rendered to respondents showed that interest was credited from the day of deposit, and that on occasion drafts were made against deposits before they had been collected.

Respondents' petition, filed in the district court for southern New York, for reclamation of the proceeds of the checks, was dismissed. The order of the district court was reversed by the circuit court of appeals for the second circuit, 10 Fed. (2d) 935. This Court granted certiorari. 271 U. S. 653.

The proceeds of the two checks concededly have come into the hands of the petitioner, the bankrupts' trustee, and the sole question presented is whether the bankrupts, on receipt of the checks and before the filing of the petition in bankruptcy, became the owners of them, or whether as the court of appeals held, Knauth, Nachod &

Kuhne were respondents' agents to collect them. If the former, respondents were creditors of the bankrupts, Douglas v. Federal Reserve Bank, 271 U. S. 489; Burton v. United States, 196 U. S. 283, entitled to share only on an equal footing with other creditors. If the latter, respondents were entitled to reclamation from the petitioner since the checks had not been collected at the time of the petition in bankruptcy. St. Louis & San Francisco Ry. v. Johnston, 133 U. S. 566; White v. Stump, 266 U. S. 310, 313; Bankruptcy Act, § 70 (a), c. 541, 30 Stat. 544, 565, as amended, § 16, c. 487, 32 Stat. 797, 800.

Ordinarily, where paper is indorsed without restriction by a depositor and is at once placed to his credit by the bank, the inference is that the bank has become the purchaser of the paper and in making the collection is not acting as the agent of the depositor. Douglas v. Federal Reserve Bank, *supra;* Burton v. United States, *supra; In re* Jarmulowsky, 249 Fed. 319, 321. But the court below thought, and respondents argue here, that the form of the check directing payment to be made to the bankrupts " for account of " the respondents operated to make them agents to collect the paper. The point is made that this is the effect of these or equivalent words where the payee of negotiable paper indorses it " for account of " the indorser. It may be conceded that such an indorsement indicates that the transaction is not a purchase and sale of the paper and, at least when not otherwise explained or limited, may fairly be taken to mean that the interest gained by the indorsee is that of an agent for collection. White v. National Bank, 102 U. S. 658; Evansville Bank v. German-American Bank, 155 U. S. 556; Commercial Bank of Penn. v. Armstrong, 148 U. S. 50, 57.

Here, however, the words were used not by a payee in his indorsement, but by a third person making a deposit for respondents' benefit. They are thus of much less significance than in the usual case as data in determining the relation between respondents and the bankrupts, and the course of conduct of the parties becomes correspondingly more important. Moreover, the words themselves, despite their wide commercial use and the importance of giving them, as far as practicable, a uniform effect, have no rigid and unchangeable significance. Their purpose is to express intention. They are not an incantation which unfailingly invokes an agency. And the circumstances in this case indicate that they were here used with a different object.

The dominant purpose of the entire transaction, as far as respondents were concerned, was to arrange that a credit with the bankrupts should be available on June 15, and this they accomplished as soon as the checks were delivered to the bankrupts. While we need not stress the point, the added facts that respondents were international bankers requiring the credit, in the course of their business, and that the credit was effected by the deposit of cashier's checks, which pass among bankers as current funds, are not without their significance. Nothing in the previous course of dealing or in the actions of respondents indicates that they intended or had any reason for intending that Knauth, Nachod & Kuhne should take the paper as their agents for collection, or that any restriction should be placed on the use of the checks by Knauth, Nachod & Kuhne once they had credited respondents.

Nor was there anything in the relationship to the transaction of the New York banks whose checks established the credit to suggest any reason or purpose so to restrict it. The duty of these banks was performed and their interest in the paper, apart from their liability to pay it, ceased as soon as they had delivered it to the bankrupts. But it was indispensable to the completion of the transaction that the bankrupts should be advised to what account the checks were to be credited. And it was apparently the function of the words in question to tell them. That alone, we think, was their purpose. To assign them any other would be to ignore the course of business followed here and banking usage in general, and to give them a strained and unnatural construction. We think the district court was right, and the judgment of the court of appeals is *Reversed.*[1]

LIABILITY OF COLLECTING BANK. *Sending paper directly to the drawee.* It is generally held that in the absence of an agreement or custom to the contrary a bank which receives commercial paper for collection is liable for negligence if it forwards the paper by mail to the bank on which it is drawn. Morse, Banks and Banking,

[1] See also Latzko *v.* Equitable Trust Co., 275 U. S. 254, where a correspondent of the claimants deposited with the bankrupt bankers a cashier's check payable to the bankrupt's order "favor" the claimants, and another correspondent deposited its check drawn on a third bank payable to the bankrupt's order "for account of" the claimants. It was held, following the principal case, that the claimants were not entitled to priority over other creditors. See 37 Yale L. Jour. 874; 28 Col. L. Rev. 377; 76 U. Pa. L. Rev. 455; 6 Tex. L. Rev. 381; 8 B. U. L. Rev. 130.

The cases are divided on the question whether the bank acquires the beneficial interest in matured or demand paper indorsed without words indicating the purpose of the deposit if the depositor is immediately credited with the amount of the deposit. It is held by the Supreme Court of the United States and by a majority of the state courts that the bank presumptively becomes a debtor. Burton *v.* United States, 196 U. S. 283; Douglas *v.* Federal Reserve Bank, 271 U. S. 489. See also Salem Elevator Works *v.* Com'r of Banks, 252 Mass. 366, 370; Carson *v.* Federal Reserve Bank, 226 N. Y. App. Div. 225, 231. See Scott, Cases on Trusts, 1 ed., 66, 67; Townsend, Bank Deposits of Commercial Paper, 7 N. Y. U. L. Quar. Rev. 293, 618; 27 Col. L. Rev. 73; 11 A. L. R. 1043, 1054; 16 A. L. R. 1084; 42 A. L. R. 492, 495.

By the terms of the Bank Collection Code which has been adopted in several states, the bank is an agent and not a purchaser, although the indorsement is not restrictive. See 43 Harv. L. Rev. 307.

6 ed., sec. 236; Dec. Dig., Banks and Banking, sec. 171(3). See Turner, Bank Collections — The Direct Routing Practice, 39 Yale L. Jour. 468, 471. See 12 Minn. L. Rev. 744. The rule has been changed in many states by statute authorizing the practice of direct forwarding.

Accepting in payment anything other than money. It is generally held that in the absence of an agreement or custom to the contrary a bank which receives commercial paper for collection is liable for negligence if it accepts in payment anything else than money and surrenders the paper. Morse, Banks and Banking, 6 ed., sec. 247; Dec. Dig., Banks and Banking, sec. 171(7); 39 Yale L. Jour. 468, 483, 577; 61 A. L. R. 739. See Federal Reserve Bank *v.* Malloy, 264 U. S. 160; Hommerberg *v.* State Bank, 170 Minn. 15. *Cf.* United States F. &. G. Co. *v.* Forest County State Bank, 199 Wis. 560. The rule has been changed in many states by statute.

As to the rules regulating collections by Federal Reserve Banks, see Federal Reserve Bank *v.* Malloy, 264 U. S. 160; Farmers & Merchants Bank v. Federal Reserve Bank, 262 U. S. 649; Transcontinental Oil Co. *v.* Federal Reserve Bank, 172 Minn. 58. See 30 A. L. R. 647; 31 A. L. R. 1269; 61 A. L. R. 481.

As to the Bank Collection Code adopted in a number of states, see 43 Harv. L. Rev. 307.

SAINT NICHOLAS BANK *v.* STATE NATIONAL BANK.

Court of Appeals, New York. 1891.

128 N. Y. 26.

Appeal from order of the General Term of the Supreme Court in the first judicial department, made January 13, 1891, which reversed a judgment in favor of plaintiff entered upon a verdict directed by the court and granted a new trial.

This action was brought to recover the proceeds of a draft for $473.57 sent for collection by the plaintiff to the defendant, and paid to the defendant's correspondents. The trial resulted in the direction of a verdict for the plaintiff for the amount demanded upon appeal to the General Term, the judgment entered upon the verdict was reversed and a new trial ordered. From the order of reversal the plaintiff appeals to this court.

There is no controversy as to the facts, which for the most part were set forth in a stipulation read upon the trial. They may be summarized as follows:

The plaintiff is a corporation organized under the laws of the state of New York, and engaged in the business of banking in the city of New York; and the defendant is a corporation organized under the National Banking Act, and doing business in the city of Memphis.

For two years prior to the 18th day of November, 1884, the plaintiff had been accustomed to send checks, notes and drafts to the defendant for collection, including such as were drawn upon persons residing at a distance, in the state of Texas and elsewhere. The commercial paper was enclosed in letters, consisting of printed forms, filled out by the insertion in writing of the date, the name of the defendant's cashier, and a description of the enclosure. The checks and drafts were collected by the defendant, and the proceeds were remitted to the plaintiff, less one-fourth of one per cent, the defendant's commission, and the expense incurred in making distant collections.

On November 10, 1884, the plaintiff was the owner and holder of a check for $473.57, dated November 6, 1884, drawn upon the City National Bank of Dallas, Texas, by A. D. Aldridge & Co., and payable to the order of Henry Levy & Son. This check was indorsed by the plaintiff to the defendant for collection, and was sent to the latter in the usual course of business.

The defendant received the check on November 13, 1884, and on that day indorsed it for collection and forwarded it by mail to the firm of Adams & Leonard, at Dallas, Texas. They were at the time, and had been for many years bankers in good standing at Dallas, and the correspondents of the defendant. They received the check on November 17, 1884, and on that day duly presented it for payment to the bank upon which it was drawn, and it was immediately paid, and the proceeds were received by them. They then remitted to the defendant a sight draft for the amount collected, drawn by them upon Jemison & Co. of the city of New York. This draft was sent by the defendant for collection to the First National Bank of New York, and on November 24, 1884, was presented to Jemison & Co., who, in the meantime, had suspended payment. The draft was accordingly protested and returned to the defendant; thereupon, the defendant, on November 28, 1884, mailed the protested draft to the plaintiff and the plaintiff refused to accept it. Adams & Leonard had failed in business before the draft on Jemison & Co. was presented for payment.

The only evidence offered by the defendant in opposition to these facts was proof of a decision of the Supreme Court of Tennessee, in the case of Bank of Louisville v. First National Bank of Knoxville, which is referred to in the opinion.[1] . . .

EARL, J. The rule has long been established in this state that a bank receiving commercial paper for collection, in the absence of a special agreement, is liable for a loss occasioned by the default of

[1] A part of the opinion in which it was held that the transaction was not governed by the law of Tennessee is omitted.

its correspondents or other agents selected by it to effect the collection. (Allen *v.* Merchants' Bank, 22 Wend. 215; Montgomery County Bank *v.* Albany City Bank, 7 N. Y. 459; Commercial Bank *v.* Union Bank, 11 id. 203; Ayrault *v.* Pacific Bank, 47 id. 570; Naser *v.* First National Bank, 116 id. 498). And the same rule prevails in some of the other states, in the United States Supreme Court and in England. (Titus *v.* Mechanics' National Bank, 35 N. J. L. 588; Wingate *v.* Mechanics' Bank, 10 Pa. St. 104; Reeves *v.* State Bank, 8 Ohio St. 465; Tyson *v.* State Bank, 6 Blackf. 225; Simpson *v.* Waldry, 30 N. W. Rep. [Mich.] 199; Mackersy *v.* Ramsays, 9 Cl. & Fin. 818). In such a case the collecting bank assumes the obligation to collect and pay over, or remit the money due upon the paper, and the agents it employs to effect the collection, whether they be in its own banking house or at some distant place, are its agents, and in no sense the agents of the owner of the paper. Because they are its agents it is responsible for their misconduct, neglect or other default.

Here when this money was received by Adams & Leonard, the defendant's agent, it was, in fact, received by it, and it became absolutely bound to pay or remit the same to the plaintiff. It is difficult to see upon what principle the defendant could be held liable if Adams & Leonard, its agents, had carelessly failed to collect the draft, or had collected it and then purposely misappropriated the proceeds thereof, and yet not be liable for their failure to pay over the proceeds in consequence of their unexplained insolvency. Upon what principle can the defendant be held liable for one default of their agents and not for every default. That the insolvency of the sub-agent in such a case does not shield the collecting agent from responsibility for the loss has been decided in several cases quite analogous to this. (Reeves *v.* State Bank; Simpson *v.* Waldry; Mackersy *v.* Ramsays, *supra;* Bradstreet *v.* Everson, 72 Pa. St. 124.) It is not needful now to vindicate the principle upon which these cases rest, as that has been sufficiently done by learned judges writing the opinions therein. They are well supported by many analogous cases in other branches of the law, and it is believed they lay down the best and safest rule and subserve the wisest commercial policy. . . .

Our conclusion, therefore, is that the order of the General Term should be reversed and the judgment entered upon the verdict affirmed, with costs.

All concur.

Judgment accordingly.[1]

---

[1] The rule stated in the principal case, frequently called "the New York rule," is followed in England, in the federal courts and in a large number of states. The opposite rule, frequently called "the Massachusetts rule," is followed in other states. The rule is applicable where the correspondent bank is negligent as well as where it becomes insolvent. For a collection of cases,

WASHINGTON LOAN & BANKING CO. v. FOURTH NATIONAL BANK.

CIRCUIT COURT OF APPEALS, FIFTH CIRCUIT. 1930.

38 F.(2d) 772.

Appeal from the District Court of the United States for the Middle District of Georgia; Bascom S. Deaver, Judge.

Suit by the Washington Loan & Banking Company against the Fourth National Bank of Macon and Herbert Pearson, receiver. From a decree dismissing the bill, plaintiff appeals.

Reversed and remanded.

Before BRYAN and FOSTER, Circuit Judges, and SIBLEY, District Judge.

SIBLEY, District Judge.

The bill of Washington Loan & Banking Company of Washington, Ga., against the receiver of Fourth National Bank of Macon, Ga., sought to impress a trust on the funds of the latter bank upon the ground that at the time of the failure, November 26, 1928, there were identifiable funds in the hands of the Macon bank, which equitably belonged to the Washington bank, and which passed into the hands of the receiver. The bill was dismissed as without equity upon its face. The facts alleged, generally stated, are these: For a long time before the failure of the Macon bank, the Washington bank had sent to it checks and drafts indorsed in blank, and inclosed in a form letter as follows: "Enclosed find for collection and credit items enumerated below. . . . Return promptly if unpaid." The form of the Macon bank's acknowledgment is not stated. The items so sent were at once entered by the Macon bank to the credit of the Washington bank, no separate collection register apparently being kept; but the Washington bank did not check against them until sufficient time had elapsed for the drafts to be collected and the funds or the uncollected drafts to be actually returned to the Macon bank by its correspondents. Uncollected items were, when returned, charged to the Washington bank without previous notice to or consent by it. Just prior to the failure,

---

see Morse, Banks and Banking, 6 ed., chap. 17; Scott, Cases on Trusts, 1 ed., 72; Dec. Dig., Banks and Banking, sec. 171(6); 14 Va. L. Rev. 473; 36 A. L. R. 1308; 44 A. L. R. 1430. As to the right of the depositor to sue the correspondent bank, see Douglas v. Federal Reserve Bank, 271 U. S. 489; 58 A. L. R. 764.

It is very common for a bank receiving commercial paper for collection to stipulate that it shall not be liable for the negligence or insolvency of its correspondents if selected by it with due care. See 27 Col. L. Rev. 294. By statute in many states, including those which have adopted the Bank Collection Code, the Massachusetts rule is adopted. See 43 Harv. L. Rev. 307.

a number of drafts on points in Massachusetts, Pennsylvania, and New Jersey were thus sent by the Washington bank to the Macon bank. Those on Pennsylvania and New Jersey were by the Macon bank sent to the First National Bank of Philadelphia, where the Macon bank had a general deposit account. What special instructions were given the Philadelphia bank do not appear, but the proceeds of these drafts so far as collected were all put to the general credit of the Macon bank on or before November 24, 1928, two days before the failure, but were not checked out by the Macon bank. The drafts on Massachusetts were sent by the Macon bank to the Federal Reserve Bank of Atlanta, no special instructions appearing, and by it forwarded to the Federal Reserve Bank of Boston for collection for the account of the Macon bank. The Macon bank had no account with the Federal Reserve Bank of Boston, so that collections made by it were customarily remitted to the Federal Reserve Bank of Atlanta and credited there to the general account of the Macon bank. Some drafts were collected in Boston the very day of the failure of the Macon bank, and their total of $856.48 was on that date in the hands of the Federal Reserve Bank of Boston, not yet remitted to Atlanta. The Macon bank, after its failure, had large balances both at the First National Bank of Philadelphia and the Federal Reserve Bank of Atlanta, and its receiver received also the funds in the hands of the Federal Reserve Bank of Boston. All drafts remaining uncollected have been returned to the Washington Bank as its property by the receiver. The controlling question is whether any of the collected funds which came to his hands were then the legal or equitable property of the Washington bank, and can be traced as such.

There is really no problem of tracing. Identifying coin or currency is impossible, for no coin or currency was probably ever handled in the transactions. Tracing credits under modern doctrine is sufficient. Richardson *v.* New Orleans Coffee Co. (C. C. A.) 102 F. 780, 52 L. R. A. 67. The Macon bank's general accounts with the Atlanta and Philadelphia banks were equivalent to separate vaults or drawers in which some of its funds were kept, and if funds of the Washington bank are shown to have gone into one of them and no withdrawal has since been made which must have taken these funds out, equity concludes that the fund which the Macon bank did not withdraw was that which it ought not to have used. If therefore any of the collections at the time of the failure still rightly belonged to the Washington bank, it is plain that the receiver got them, and must account for them. Monticello Hardware Co. *v.* Weston (C. C. A.) 28 F.(2d) 673.

The relationship of a bank to a draft or check turned over to it by a customer depends on their contract respecting it. This contract may appear in the form of the indorsement, or otherwise. If in the form of indorsement, notice is carried to all persons dealing with the paper. Otherwise not. Evansville Bank v. German-American Bank, 155 U. S. 556, 15 S. Ct. 221, 39 L. Ed. 259. Statutes and local and general banking customs may influence or control the contract. No statute is referred to as important here unless Georgia Code of 1910, § 2362, is such. It converts into statute the decision in Bailie v. Augusta Savings Bank, 95 Ga. 277, 21 S. E. 717, 51 Am. St. Rep. 74, and, in the absence of a contrary expressed or implied contract, makes of force in Georgia the New York rule that a collecting bank is liable to the customer for defaults of its correspondents. Federal Reserve Bank v. Malloy, 264 U. S. 160, 44 S. Ct. 296, 68 L. Ed. 617, 31 A. L. R. 1261.

No question of default by a correspondent of the Macon bank is here in question, and the statute is immaterial. No custom, general or local, is set up. This case, therefore, rests on the contract interpreted by the conduct of the Macon and Washington banks. We think it plain that notwithstanding the blank indorsement of the draft (which is of no great consequence where the original parties only are involved, Richardson v. New Orleans Coffee Co. [C. C. A.] 102 F. 788), and the immediate entry of a credit to the Washington bank (even the right to check against the credit would not be conclusive, Bailie v. Augusta Savings Bank, 95 Ga. 277, 21 S. E. 717, 51 Am. St. Rep. 74), that it was not their understanding that the Macon bank had at once bought the drafts and credited the proceeds on general deposit. The letter of transmittal expressly stated that each draft was indorsed for collection first, and for credit after its collection, or prompt return if unpaid. Until collection the ownership of the draft remained in the Washington bank, the Macon bank and its correspondents being only agents for the collection, and after collection the proceeds remained the property of the Washington bank until finally passed to the latter's checking account by the Macon bank. See Freeman v. Exchange Bank, 87 Ga. 45, 13 S. E. 160. The immediate posting of the amount of the draft to the general deposit account of the Washington bank obscures but does not defeat the truth. It is as though the entry of the credit had read expressly as of a draft instead as of cash. The former form of credit imports a collection only. Bailie v. Augusta Savings Bank, 95 Ga. 277, 21 S. E. 717, 51 Am. St. Rep. 74. The facts alleged authorize the conclusion that the agency was to cease and the relationship of general depositor, that is, general creditor, to begin only when the collection having been made, the proceeds became available to the Macon bank, and it in turn made them available to the Washington bank. Had the banking customs involved remittances of collected funds by correspondents, or even notice of their collection, no doubt would exist of the precise time that each draft became so available, but no such custom appears except between the Federal Reserve Bank of Boston and Federal Reserve Bank of Atlanta. A collection made by the former did not become available to the

Macon bank until remittance or notice to the Federal Reserve Bank of Atlanta under the bill's allegations, and by fair inference was not to be considered an effected collection subject to check at the Macon bank until that time. On the other hand, the collections which went to the general credit of the Macon bank at Philadelphia were thereafter subject to its check, and the Macon bank, if it did not choose to be certainly informed by notice, was bound, after a reasonable time for notice of the draft's collection or its return in default of collection, to assume that collection had been made and permit checking by the Washington bank.

It follows that collections in Boston unremitted and unnoticed to the Federal Reserve Bank of Atlanta on November 26, 1928, were uncompleted collections, and were still the property of the Washington bank. Of those made through the Philadelphia bank the collections made in New Jersey on November 21 and November 23 may be recoverable, remembering that November 25 was Sunday. The evidence will more certainly show whether these collections reached Philadelphia in time to be available in Macon on November 26. The previous collections were all completed in sufficient time for notice to have been given the Macon bank before its failure, and became general deposits of the Washington bank, unless by an earlier knowledge of the Macon bank's insolvency on the part of its officers they were precluded from honestly accepting them as such. Commercial Nat. Bank v. Armstrong, 148 U. S. 50, 13 S. Ct. 533, 37 L. Ed. 363; People's National Bank v. Moore (C. C. A.) 25 F.(2d) 599.

Reversed and remanded for further proceedings not inconsistent with this opinion.[1]

EVANSVILLE BANK v. GERMAN-AMERICAN BANK, 155 U. S. 556 (1895): On June 14, 1887, the A bank deposited with the B bank a draft payable to the order of the A bank. The draft was indorsed by the A bank "Pay [the B bank] or order, for collection for [the A bank]." On June 16, the B bank forwarded the draft to the C bank with the additional indorsement "Pay [the C bank] or order, for collection." On June 18, the C bank forwarded the draft to the D bank which received and collected it from the drawee on June 20, and immediately notified the C bank of the collection by letter stating that the amount had been credited to the account of the C bank. On June 21, before banking hours, the C bank received the letter and credited the B bank and sent a letter to the B bank notifying it of the payment and the entry of the credit.

On June 20 and for ten days prior thereto, the B bank was in-

[1] Matter of Bank of Cuba, 198 N. Y. App. Div. 733, *accord*.

solvent, but none of the other banks knew this until the failure of the B bank at 8:30 A.M., June 21.

Subsequently the C bank and the D bank made a settlement of their collection accounts up to and including the entries representing the draft. The mutual collection accounts between the C bank and the B bank were not settled because of the failure of the B bank.

It appeared that the B bank was indebted to the C bank in a considerable sum in excess of the amount of the draft.

It was held that the A bank was entitled to recover the amount of the draft from the C bank. At the time when the C bank credited the B bank the B bank was insolvent and in the custody of the officers of the law. The court said that it was unnecessary to consider what would be the rights of the parties if a settlement between the C bank and the B bank had been consummated while the latter was actually engaged in business although in fact insolvent. The B bank had in fact closed its doors before the C bank credited or notified the B bank. The mere fact that the C bank did not know of the failure of the B bank at the time it made its entry was held immaterial.[1]

Section V.

A Trust distinguished from a Condition.

ANONYMOUS.

———. 1581.

4 Leon. 2.

A MAN made a feoffment in fee *sub conditione, ea intentione,* that his wife should have the land for her life, the remainder to his

[1] If the paper is indorsed by the depositor "for collection" or otherwise so as to indicate his interest in the paper and before collection the initial bank fails, the depositor is entitled to reclaim the paper or the amount of the proceeds from the correspondent bank, although the initial bank was indebted to the correspondent bank. Scott, Cases on Trusts, 1 ed., 77.

If the initial bank fails after collection by the correspondent bank, but before the latter has paid the amount of the proceeds to the initial bank or settled with it, the claim of the initial bank against the correspondent bank does not form part of the assets of the initial bank, but is held by it for the benefit of the depositor. Scott, 77.

If the paper is not so indorsed by the depositor as to indicate his interest in it and the paper is forwarded to the correspondent bank to be credited to the initial bank, and then the initial bank fails, being indebted to the correspondent bank, the correspondent bank, being a purchaser for value, is entitled to a lien upon the paper before collection and to a set off after collection. See Scott, Cases on Trusts, 1 ed., 78–79. But see Gamble *v.* Sioux Falls Nat. Bank, 51 S. D. 331.

younger son in fee; the feoffee died without making such an estate; the heir of the feoffor entered. It was resolved, that it was not a condition, but an estate, which was executed presently accordingly to the intent.[1]

SMITH v. ALTERLY.

CHANCERY. 1672.

Freem. C. C. 136.

A. DEVISETH his lands to his wife, and after to his eldest son, with condition that if his wife should be with child, 80*l.* should be paid by his eldest son and heir at law to the child after the mother's death; the wife had a child, and [there]after her eldest son conveys away the land to a purchaser. And on proof that the purchaser had notice of the will, a decree was for the daughter for her money devised, and declared it was a trust to go with the lands; and yet this will was void in law, as to the legacy, seeing he who was to have the benefit of the breach of the condition was the heir, who was to pay the legacy.

WRIGHT v. WILKIN.

EXCHEQUER CHAMBER. 1862.

31 L. J. Q. B. 196.

THIS was an action of ejectment brought by the heir-at-law of one Mary Mann, to recover certain lands and tenements in the county of Norfolk.

The defendant appeared and defended as landlord for the whole.

At the trial, which took place before Cockburn, C. J., at the Norwich Lent Assizes for 1860, it appeared that the defendant claimed as devisee in fee under the last will and testament of one Mary Mann above mentioned, which bore date the 15th of May 1854. By this will the testatrix made several bequests of goods and chattels and sums of money to different persons, amongst others to the vicar

---

[1] "*Per plures,* if a man make a feoffment in fee *ad intentionem* to perform his will, this is no condition, but a declaration of the purpose and will of the feoffor, and the heir cannot enter for non-performance. 31 H. 8." Bro. Abr. Conditions, pl. 191.

"If, indeed, a feoffment to uses was subject to a condition that the land should revest in the feoffor if the feoffee failed to perform the trust, the feoffor or his heir, upon the breach of this condition subsequent, might enter, or bring an action at common law for the recovery of the land. Only the feoffor or his heir could take advantage of the breach of the condition (Y. B. 10 Hen. IV. f. 3, pl. 3), and the enforcement of the condition was not the enforcement of the use, but of a forfeiture for its non-performance. Moreover, such conditions seem not to have been common in feoffments to uses, the feoffors trusting rather to the fidelity of the feoffees." — Ames, Lect. Leg. Hist., 236.

and chapelwardens of Tilney St. Lawrence, in the county of Norfolk, for charitable purposes. The will then proceeded as follows: " And I give, devise and bequeath unto Thomas Martin Wilkin, of " &c., " all my real estates, both freehold and copyhold, in " &c., " and all the residue of my personal estate and effects, to hold to him the said T. M. Wilkin, his heirs, executors, administrators and assigns for ever, upon this express condition, that if my personal estate should be insufficient for the purpose, that he or they do and shall, within twelve months after my decease, pay and discharge all and every the legacies hereinbefore bequeathed, and I feel confident that he will comply with my wish, it being my particular desire that all the above legacies shall be paid. And I do hereby charge and make chargeable all my said real and personal estate with the payment of the aforesaid several legacies and bequests."

It appeared that Mr. Wilkin, the defendant, had not paid any of the legacies within the period of twelve months, and it was contended that the estate left to him was forfeited in consequence of his not having done so. The jury found a verdict for the defendant; and the learned Judge gave leave to the plaintiff to move to enter the verdict for him.

A rule was accordingly obtained, which, after argument, was discharged. 2 B. & S. 232.

WILLIAMS, J.[1] I cannot find sufficient upon the face of this will to shew that the testatrix intended this devise to operate by way of condition. With regard to the passage from Sugden on Powers, 122, which has been here referred to, all that Lord St. Leonards means to say is, I take it, this — That the remedy given by the Court of Chancery to carry out the testator's intention was not in old times regarded by the Courts of common law; and that the Courts of common law held words in a will to constitute a condition on the consideration that if they did not, there would be no remedy at all; that that reason has long ago ceased, and that therefore a different view has been taken and ought to be taken as to whether particular words constitute a condition. Looking at the whole will in this case, it seems to me more convenient to construe this as a trust than as a condition.

The other Judges concurred.

Judgment affirmed.[2]

[1] Concurring opinions of Erle, C. J., and Pollock, C. B., are omitted.
[2] Merchant Taylors' Co. v. Attorney General, L. R. 6 Ch. 512; Attorney General v. Wax Chandlers' Co., L. R. 6 H. L. 1; Goodman v. Mayor of Saltash, 7 App. Cas. 633; Stanley v. Colt, 5 Wall. (U. S.) 119; Jones v. Habersham, 107 U. S. 174; Amory v. Amherst College, 229 Mass. 374, 383; Rolphe etc. Asylum v. Lefebre, 69 N. H. 238; Ashuelot Nat. Bk. v. City of Keene, 74 N. H. 148; Mills v. Davison, 54 N. J. Eq. 659; MacKenzie v. Trustees of Presbytery, 67 N. J. Eq. 652; Van De Bogert v. Reformed Dutch Church, 219 N. Y. App. Div. 220; Greene v. O'Connor, 18 R. I. 56, *accord.*

On the other hand it was held in the following cases that a condition

WOODWARD v. WALLING.

Supreme Court, Iowa. 1871.
31 Iowa 533.

Action at law to recover the possession of certain lands. Both plaintiff and defendants claim title under a will of Esther Walling in the following words: " I give and bequeath to my son, Elisha Jennings (describing the lands devised), during his natural life, and after his decease to revert to his heirs, provided, however, that the said Elisha Jennings shall provide a home for his sister, Oriel Zerna, till her marriage, and then to give her an outfit equal to what her sisters have received at their marriage, provided, however, that if the said Elisha Jennings does not accept of the provisions of this will within eighteen months from the date of this, then said property to revert to his sister, Oriel Zerna."

"Second. I give and bequeath to my daughter, Oriel Zerna, all my personal property and money except what is needed to bear the expenses of the said Elisha Jennings to this place, which shall not exceed $100." Plaintiff is the daughter named in the will, and defendant, Elisha J. Walling, is the son. Verdict and judgment for defendants; plaintiff appeals.

Beck, J. — The question here presented for our determination involves the construction of and the force and effect to be given to the conditions contained in the will. It was specially found by the jury that defendant, Elisha J. Walling, took possession of the lands under the will. This fact is not controverted, and no question is made of his right to the land so far as the last condition is concerned. The plaintiff's counsel contend that, by a failure to perform the first condition, defendant's title to the land was defeated, and thereby became vested in plaintiff. In their view, the language of the will is such that plaintiff would become entitled to the property, not only upon defendant failing to accept under the will, but also upon his failure to perform the first condition prescribed. This question becomes important in its bearing upon the ultimate decision of the case, as it will serve to introduce for consideration and application another doctrine of the law, namely: If in a devise a condition

---

and not a trust or charge was created. Bennett v. Baltimore etc. Society, 91 Md. 10; Clarke v. Society of the Holy Child Jesus, 82 Neb. 85; Re Estate of Douglass, 94 Neb. 280; Upington v. Corrigan, 151 N. Y. 143; Norton v. Valentine, 151 N. Y. App. Div. 392; Trustees of Calvary Presbyterian Church v. Putnam, 221 N. Y. App. Div. 502, 37 Yale L. Jour. 530 (release by heirs).

On the difference between a trust and a condition, see Gray, Rule ag. Perp., sec. 282; Kales, Estates, secs. 219–227; Underhill, Trusts, art. 7.

On the difference between a trust and an equitable charge, see sec. VII, *post*.

is annexed to an estate thereby created, upon the breach or non-performance of which the estate is devised over to another, the condition operates as a limitation upon the estate of the first devisee which, upon the breach or performance of the condition, determines, without entry of the second devisee, who becomes seized and has an immediate right to the estate. 1 Greenleaf's Cruise, tit. 16, ch. 2, § 30. Applying this doctrine to the case, plaintiff insists that, by the terms of the will, an estate is devised over to plaintiff upon the non-performance of the first condition to provide a home and outfit for her, as well as upon a failure to comply with the second condition — acceptance under the will. It will be necessary for us to determine whether the devise can bear such a construction.

There are two distinct and separate conditions embodied in the instrument; the first imposing upon defendant the obligation to furnish to plaintiff a home and outfit; the second, that he accept the provisions of the will in eighteen months. The language under which plaintiff claims a devise over to her in case of non-performance of the condition is so intimately and entirely coupled with the words of the last condition, that it would be a great violence to the rules of our language to make it extend to the first condition. The second condition, with the devise over, make one sentence full and complete. We know of no rule of construction or principle of our language which will permit us to make the adjunct of this sentence which declares the devise over to plaintiff, qualify, limit, or in any manner affect the preceding sentence, containing the devise to defendant and the first condition. The devise over to plaintiff is only on condition of the failure of defendant to accept under the will. That this is the effect of the language there can be no ground on which to build a doubt; that such was the intention of the devisor cannot be questioned, for the language and structure of the will can express nothing else.

We come now to consider the first condition. Under the rule just stated, the forfeiture of this condition, if there were a devise over dependent thereon, would divest defendant of the title. But as we have seen there is no devise over coupled with this condition, we must then inquire whether the non-performance of the condition produces the same effect, namely, divests defendants of the title conferred by the will.

When there is no limitation over, in a devise upon a condition, raising an estate in another upon its breach, the condition or proviso is not always construed as a limitation whereby the first estate devised may be defeated. Greenleaf's Cruise, tit. 16, ch. 2, § 34. As the intention of the testator must be followed, the estate devised upon condition will be defeated or upheld after the condition broken, as such intention may be discovered in the language and construction of the will. It appears quite plain to us, that the testator in the will before us did not intend that the estate devised to the defendant should terminate upon his failure to perform the condition first expressed. The language of the instrument fails to convey any such intention. That such intention existed we cannot presume, for the law does not favor forfeitures, and will not, by implication or construction, create them. That the intention did not exist in the mind of the testator appears quite certain, from the fact that the question was before her, and contemplated by her, and yet no such intention is expressed. The question of forfeiture of the estate on account of the non-performance of the condition we know was contemplated by the testator, because she provided for a forfeiture upon the failure of the devisee to perform another condition subsequently expressed. Here are two conditions distinctly and separately prescribed. The non-performance of one, it is declared, shall defeat the estate. But it is not so expressed as to the other. The subject of the forfeiture of the estate upon breach of conditions being in the mind of the devisor, we must presume that it was the intention of the devisor that forfeiture should extend only to the case wherein it is prescribed. Such would be the construction applied to all written instruments containing like expressions. A limitation, too, whereby an estate may be determined, must be clearly expressed in order to be enforced as such. 2 Redf. on Wills, 668, § 18. It certainly ought not to rest upon construction, which will do violence to the rules of our language, and is not in accord with the usual manner of expressing our intentions.

The condition under consideration being for the benefit of plaintiff, without any expressed intention that its breach shall work a forfeiture of the estate, should be regarded as creating a trust or charge upon the land in her favor, to be enforced as other trusts and charges, and not as a limitation upon the estate devised. This is the doctrine announced in many cases arising under similar conditions. An extended review of these cases is not called for; a simple citation of those which have come under our observation is deemed sufficient. Fox v. Phelps, 17 Wend. 393; Woods v. Woods, 1 Busbee (N. C.), 290; Taft v. Morse, 4 Metc. 523; Hanna's Appeal, 31 Penn. St. 53; Luckett v. White, 10 Gill. and Johns. 480; Sands v. Champlin, 1 Story, 376; Ward v. Ward, 15 Pick. 511; Sheldon v. Purple, id. 528; Veasey v. Whitehouse, 10 N. H. 409; Jennings v. Jennings, 27 Ill. 518.

It is our opinion that the first condition expressed in the will does not operate as a limitation upon the estate therein devised to defendant and his heirs; and, therefore, that a breach or non-performance of such condition does not operate to divest the title held under the will. Other questions presented in argument by counsel need not be considered, as the foregoing ruling is decisive of the case.

Affirmed.

Section VI.

A Trust distinguished from a Mortgage or Pledge.

WEHRLE *v.* MERCANTILE NATIONAL BANK.

Supreme Judicial Court, Massachusetts. 1915.

221 Mass. 585.

Rugg, C. J. This case comes before us on appeal from a decree dismissing the bill after an order sustaining a demurrer. The material averments are that, in 1878, Rebekah K. Jacobs indorsed and delivered to the firm of James O. Safford and Company twenty-six shares of stock of the defendant bank as collateral security for notes made by her for the accommodation of her son. The stock subsequently was transferred to the name of the firm and has been held by them. In 1881, one Choate was appointed assignee of the estate of Mrs. Jacobs, who had been adjudged insolvent. In 1884, Safford and Company executed and delivered a full release of all claims against the son, and a year later the surviving partner acknowledged full settlement of all claims against Mrs. Jacobs in the insolvency proceedings against her, and that the indebtedness as security for which the stock had been transferred was paid in full in 1884 or 1885. Choate, the assignee in insolvency of the estate of Mrs. Jacobs, died in 1890 and there was no assignee of her estate until the plaintiff was appointed in his stead in 1912. This suit in equity is brought to recover the twenty-six shares of bank stock and the dividends which have accrued thereon. The bill was filed in March, 1913, twenty-eight years after it is averred that the debt for which the stock was deposited as collateral was paid.

The parties defendant are the bank whose shares of stock are sought to be recovered, the surviving partner of Safford and Company, who has deceased since the bringing of the suit and whose administrators defend, and the administrator of the estate of the other partner. The demurrer sets up the statute of limitations, laches, and staleness of the plaintiff's demand.

It is not necessary to determine whether the right of action of a pledgor to recover the pledge accrues without demand and at once upon the satisfaction of the claim to secure which the pledge was deposited. See Hancock *v.* Franklin Ins. Co., 114 Mass. 155, 156, and Currier *v.* Studley, 159 Mass. 17. If it be assumed in favor of the plaintiff, without so deciding, that a demand sometimes may be necessary, the delay in making the demand and in bringing the action in the case at bar is so great that he cannot prevail. The right to make the demand, if one was necessary, came into existence at latest in 1885. The subsequent death of the assignee of Mrs. Jacobs and a considerable interval before the appointment of his successor did not suspend the effect of the efflux of time. In this respect the rule of the statute of limitations must apply. If time begins to run when competent parties are in existence to represent both sides of the controversy, it continues to run notwithstanding the death or disability of the person whose rights may be barred. Ballard v. Demmon, 156 Mass. 449, 453. Hogan v. Kurtz, 94 U. S. 773, 779. Bower v. Chetwynd, [1914] 2 Ch. 68, 76.

It was said by Mr. Justice Sheldon, speaking for the court, in Whitney v. Cheshire Railroad, 210 Mass. 263, at page 268, with ample citation of authorities, " The rule has been laid down that where a demand is necessary to fix the legal rights of a party and give a complete cause of action, the demand ordinarily must be made within the time limited for bringing an action at law." The plaintiff contends that this rule is confined in its operation to cases where an executory contract calls for the performance of some act upon demand. But while many instances where it has been invoked are of that nature, the rule is general in its scope and applies commonly where no fiduciary relation exists. An indeterminate bailment is distinguishable. Wilkinson v. Verity, L. R. 6 C. P. 206.

That principle governs the present case. While a pledge sometimes has been spoken of as in the nature of a trust, Newton v. Fay, 10 Allen, 505, 507, strictly it has not the legal characteristics of a trust and a transaction like that here shown is a pledge with the incidents attaching to that well recognized relation. Gamson v. Pritchard, 210 Mass. 296. Shaw v. Silloway, 145 Mass. 503. The lapse of twenty-eight years without any excuse other than appears upon the face of this bill is fatal to the maintenance of this suit. There is nothing to indicate fault on the part of the defendants in this respect or any conduct by deception or otherwise to prevent seasonable action by the plaintiff. It is not the province even of equity to afford relief against the natural consequences of such protracted slumber upon rights of the character here alleged. Kase v. Burnham, 206 Penn. St. 330. Gilmer v. Morris, 80 Ala. 78, 83. Mackall v. Casilear, 137 U. S. 556, 566. Waterman v. Brown, 31 Penn. St. 161. See Brown v. Bronson, 93 App. Div. (N. Y.) 312. The case has been ably presented in behalf of the plaintiff, but the best argument is unavailing upon these facts.

Decree affirmed with costs.[1]

[1] See Colantuoni v. Balene, 95 N. J. Eq. 748; State v. Channer, 115 Oh. St. 350. But see Green v. Turner, 38 Iowa 112.

There is not a fiduciary relationship existing between a mortgagee and mortgagor such as exists between a trustee and *cestui que trust*. See Dobson v. Land, 8 Hare 216; Shaw v. Foster, L. R. 5 H. L. 321; Field v. Debenture Corporation, 12 T. L. R. 469; King v. State Mut. Fire Ins. Co., 7 Cush. (Mass.) 1, 7; Dennett v. Tilton, 227 Mass. 299.

In Dobson v. Land, 8 Hare 216, the court said (p. 220): " Now, that a mortgagee is in some sense a trustee for the mortgagor, may be admitted; for every person in whom the legal estate is vested, with a beneficial interest

Section VII.
A Trust distinguished from an Equitable Charge.
JACQUET *v.* JACQUET.
Chancery. 1859.
27 Beav. 332.

The testator was resident in Jamaica. He had two plantations, called "Content" and "Epsom." By his will, dated in 1832, the testator requested his executors to "pay and discharge his funeral

---

for another person, in a sense, is a trustee for that person. . . . A trustee can never make a benefit to himself by any dealing with the trust property; but if a second mortgagee should buy in the first mortgage for half its amount, or even obtain an assignment without consideration from the first mortgagee, I can have no doubt he would be entitled to charge the mortgagor with the full amount of the first mortgage in addition to his own."

In Taylor *v.* Russell, [1892] A. C. 244, Lord Herschell said (p. 255) : "No authority was cited for the proposition that a mortgagee is, subject to his security, a trustee of the legal title for the mortgagor. The rights of a mortgagor are no doubt well established in a court of equity. He may redeem the mortgage, and no dealings with the property by the mortgagee, save a conveyance under the power of sale, can deprive him of this right. But it is quite a different proposition and one which I think is wholly untenable to assert that a mortgagee is trustee for the mortgagor. It is admitted that a mortgagee may create such estates as he pleases, he may convey, by way of sub-mortgage, to whom and in as many parcels as he pleases."

In Willett *v.* Herrick, 258 Mass. 585, the court said that a pledgee is not a trustee and a purchase by him from the pledgor of the subject matter of the pledge cannot be set aside on the ground that the pledgee did not make full disclosure to the pledgor. The court said (p. 599) : "As pledgees they were required to use good faith in dealing with the property pledged or in conducting a sale, but this did not impose on them the additional duties of a fiduciary in matters unrelated to the pledge. A pledge is not a trust and the defendants were not trustees in the true sense of the term. . . . Even if the contract were a mortgage, the relation of mortgagor and mortgagee is not of a fiduciary character."

If one lends money and takes a mortgage in the name of a trustee, there is no fiduciary relation between the trustee and the mortgagor. Dennett *v.* Tilton, 227 Mass. 299. But a trustee under a deed of trust in the nature of a mortgage (*e.g.* one securing a bond issue) stands in a fiduciary relation to the debtor as well as to the creditors. 42 Harv. L. Rev. 198, 200.

Vendor and purchaser. In the case of a contract for the sale of land, although the vendor is sometimes spoken of as trustee for the purchaser (Green *v.* Smith, 1 Atk. 572; Lysaght *v.* Edwards, 2 Ch. D. 499; Phillips *v.* Silvester, L. R. 8 Ch. 173), he is not really a trustee, for there is no fiduciary relationship between the parties. Shaw *v.* Foster, *supra; Re* Lynders, [1910] 1 I. R. 231. See Raynor *v.* Preston, 18 Ch. D. 1, 10; 9 Harv. L. Rev. 117n. And of course the purchaser, though sometimes said to be trustee of the purchase-money (Green *v.* Smith, 1 Atk. 572), is not a trustee in any sense. See Pound, Progress of the Law, 33 Harv. L. Rev. 813, 830; Stone, Equitable Conversion by Contract, 13 Col. L. Rev. 369, 372.

expenses and all just and legal demands that might be against him," " with the payment of which (he said) I do charge and make liable all my property in Jamaica both real and personal," &c. " It is my desire, and I do hereby direct, that my executors hereinafter named, or such of them as shall qualify under this my will, do dispose of the freehold of Content plantation, with the buildings thereon," &c., " the moneys arising from the sale thereof to be applied to the liquidation of my debts, and the overplus (if any) to fall into the residue of my estate. All the rest, residue and remainder of my property in Jamaica, but subject to the payment of my debts and legacies comprised of Epsom plantation " &c., " and everything else on the plantation or elsewhere in Jamaica, of whatsoever nature and kind," he gave, devised, and bequeathed to certain persons whom he named.

The testator died in 1834, and in 1843 the plantations were sold to Philip Jacquet and the money was in court. The Chief Clerk found that a debt of 318*l*. was still due to Spicer, and that he had a claim to that amount on the trust funds. The question was, whether the real estate was charged with the debt, and whether his remedy against the estate and the produce was or [was] not barred by the Statute of Limitations.

The plaintiff took out a summons to vary the certificate by finding that he had no claim on the trust funds.

THE MASTER OF THE ROLLS [ROMILLY.] I think that this will created a trust for the payment of debts as regards the Content plantation; but with respect to the other plantation there is a mere charge of debts. I am of opinion that the statute does not apply as regards the Content estate; but I wish to consider whether the transaction of 1843 amounted to a sale to Mr. Philip Jacquet, in consideration of his paying a sum of money into court; because, if it did, I am of opinion that the fund is affected by the trusts specified by the will, and is now applicable to the payment of the debts.

I came to the conclusion that the debts were charged on the whole of the property, but the trust was limited to the Content estate, which the testator directed to be sold by his executors, and the produce applied in payment of his debts. The testator died in 1834, and, under the Statute of Limitations, passed in 1837, the lapse of twenty years bars any power of recovery in respect of the charge, but it does not bar the right of recovery as regards the Content estate, as to which a trust was created.

I think the result of the transaction in 1843 is, that Philip Jacquet is the purchaser for value of the Content estate, and from that time the statute begins to run in his favor under the 25th section of 3 & 4 Will. IV. c. 27; but as against the produce of the Content estate, the statute does not apply, and it remains liable for the payment of the testator's debts. I cannot make out how much of the fund in court is attributable to the Content estate, and that must be ascertained by an inquiry.

I will, however, make this declaration: that so much of the money now in court as is properly attributable to the purchase of the Content estate, under the deed of 1843, is applicable to the payment of Mr. Spicer's debt.[1]

PERSONAL LIABILITY OF DEVISEE. Where land is devised to A, "he paying," or "on condition that he pay," a certain sum of money to B, B acquires a twofold right, the one an equitable charge upon the land, the other a money claim against A. And this claim against A is enforced at common law by an action of Debt, or *Indebitatus Assumpsit*, although B was a stranger to the transaction. See Ames, Cases on Trusts, 3; Scott, Cases on Trusts, 1 ed., 91; Williston, Contracts, sec. 370; Dec. Dig., Wills, secs. 819-826.

In Zimmer v. Sennott, 134 Ill. 505, and in Miltenberger v. Schlegel, 7 Pa. 241, there was said to be a claim against the devisee, but no equitable charge upon the land.

If the testator shows an intention merely to charge the land and not to impose a personal liability upon the devisee, as where the devise is simply "subject to" a payment, the devisee is not personally liable. Jillard v. Edgar, 3 DeG. & S. 502; *Re* Cowley, 53 L. T. 494; Den v. Small, 20 N. J. L. 151.

On the question whether a subsequent transferee is liable, see Houck v. Herrick, 179 Ill. App. 274; Swasey v. Little, 7 Pick. (Mass.) 296; Sheldon v. Purple, 15 Pick. (Mass.) 528; Jordan v. Donahue, 12 R. I. 199; and especially Hodges v. Phelps, 65 Vt. 303.

In Millington v. Hill, 47 Ark. 301, Loder v. Hatfield, 71 N. Y. 92, and Yearly v. Long, 40 Oh. St. 27, a devise of land charged with an annuity was so worded as to impose upon the devisee a personal liability in the nature of a debt. It was held that, as soon as the statute barred the personal claim, the right to enforce the equitable charge was also barred. But see *contra*, Stringer v. Gamble, 155 Mich. 295, in which the court said, (p. 299): "There is no undertaking of the devisee to pay the annuity although he became liable to do so by accepting the devise. The lien did not exist to secure the liability thus arising, but it did exist to secure, out of the land itself, the benefit intended for the [equitable encumbrancer]." See Balz v. Kircher, 192 Pa. 63.

---

[1] Francis v. Grover, 5 Hare 39; Proud v. Proud, 32 Beav. 234; Dickenson v. Teasdale, 1 De G. J. & S. 52; Cunningham v. Foot, 3 App. Cas. 974; *Re* Oliver, 62 L. T. 533; *Re* Barker, [1892] 2 Ch. 491; *Re* Lacy, [1899] 2 Ch. 149; Dundas v. Blake, 11 Ir. Eq. 138; *Re* Hazlette, [1915] 1 I. R. 285; *Re* Mitchell, 182 Pa. 530, *accord*.

For cases in which it was held that a trust was created and that the claimant was not barred by the Statute of Limitations, see Ames 57n.

The testator may charge simply the rents and profits of the land. Nudd v. Powers, 136 Mass. 273 (and cases cited). In that event the devisee is not personally liable, nor will the land be sold to pay the amount charged thereon.

DOWNER v. CHURCH.

Court of Appeals, New York. 1871.
44 N. Y. 647.

This action was brought to compel the specific performance of a contract between the plaintiff and the defendant Loren Church. It appears from the facts found by the referee that Roswell Downer died in January, 1857, leaving a widow but no child. By his will he devised all his property to Church, charging it with the support and maintenance of his widow during her life. The plaintiff, a nephew and one of the heirs of the deceased, informed the defendant Church that the heirs of the deceased claimed the estate and would contest his title. The plaintiff and the defendant Church thereupon entered into the agreement in writing involved in this action, whereby in order to settle the controversy without resort to law, the plaintiff agreed on behalf of himself and the other heirs to accept from Church a deed of the five acres of land occupied by Roswell Downer at his death, and certain other property which Church agreed to convey to the plaintiff. The plaintiff agreed to procure from all the heirs a release of all their claims to the estate of the deceased. He was not to be required to procure any release from the widow of Roswell Downer, and her rights and interests were not to be affected, but to remain the same; except that she was not to have any right or claim to the property so to be conveyed to the plaintiff. Church executed and delivered in escrow to one Symonds a deed to the property. The plaintiff procured the releases as agreed, but the defendant refused to order Symonds to give the deed to the plaintiff.

The referee found, as conclusion of law, that the defendant had violated his contract in the particulars above mentioned, and adjudged a specific performance with costs. The defendants, Church and wife, duly excepted; and on appeal to the General Term of the Supreme Court, the facts and conclusions of law to which exceptions had been taken were fully reviewed and affirmed, with cost.

The defendants, Church and wife, thereupon appealed to the Court of Appeals.[1]

Leonard, C. There can be no doubt of the validity of the agreement to compromise the hostile and conflicting claims of the plain-

[1] The statement of facts is abridged and a part of the opinion is omitted.

tiff and defendant, as between themselves. The defendant Church argues that the property devised to him is charged with a trust for the maintenance of the widow of Roswell Downer, the deceased testator, and hence that he cannot legally convey it as he had agreed. The provision of the will, as stated in the case, is that the property is devised to Loren Church, subject to the support and maintenance of the widow. This language does not create a trust, it creates an encumbrance. The title to the property devised is vested in Church, charged with the support of the widow, as an encumbrance. There is no difficulty in his conveying such title as he has. The plaintiff takes it subject to the charge contained in the instrument creating the title in the defendant. The facts, as they are found by the referee, show no hardship or injustice in requiring the defendant to deliver the papers deposited in escrow with Mr. Symonds. The plaintiff has fully performed his part of the agreement, at some expense and loss of time, and there is no hardship or injustice in requiring the defendant to complete the performance of it on his part. The hardship and injustice would be the other way, if the defendant is not held to his contract, in damages or by its due performance. The facts do not support the defendant's position. There is no trust as to the property. . . .

All concurred.

Judgment affirmed, with costs.[1]

IN KING *v.* DENISON, 1 Ves. & B. 260, LORD ELDON said (pp. 272, 276): "I will here point out the nicety of distinction, as it appears to me, upon which this court has gone. If I give to A. and his heirs all my real estate, charged with my debts, that is a devise to him for a particular purpose, but not for that purpose only. If the devise is upon trust to pay my debts, that is a

---

[1] Jillard *v.* Edgar, 3 DeG. & S. 502, *accord.* See Neikerk *v.* Lamaster, 261 Pa. 571. But if the devisee sells to a purchaser for value without notice of the charge, the devisee is liable to the equitable encumbrancer. Jillard *v.* Edgar, *supra* (*semble*).

A transferee who is not a purchaser for value and without notice takes subject to the charge. Low *v.* Ramsey, 135 Ky. 333. So do the heirs of the devisee. Ellis *v.* Dumond, 259 Ill. 483; Sullivan *v.* Sullivan, 242 Ill. App. 501.

If the owner of land and a building thereon charged with the payment of a legacy insures the building, which is subsequently destroyed, and collects the insurance money, the charge does not attach to the insurance money. Whitehouse *v.* Cargill, 88 Me. 479.

A devisee of land subject to an annuity in favor of A, unlike a trustee for A, may buy the annuity of A as freely as any one else. Powell *v.* Murray, 2 Edw. (N. Y.) 636, 644–645.

An equitable charge is not within the exemption in favor of beneficiaries under the so-called spendthrift trusts. DeGraw *v.* Clason, 11 Paige (N. Y.) 136. See also Matthews *v.* Studley, 17 N. Y. App. Div. 303.

devise for a particular purpose, and nothing more; and the effect of those two modes admits just this difference. The former is a devise of an estate of inheritance for the purpose of giving the devisee the beneficial interest, subject to a particular purpose; the latter is a devise for a particular purpose, with no intention to give him any beneficial interest. Where therefore the whole legal interest is given for the purpose of satisfying trusts expressed, and those trusts do not in their execution exhaust the whole, so much of the beneficial interest as is not exhausted belongs to the heir; but, where the whole legal interest is given for a particular purpose, with an intention to give to the devisee of the legal estate the beneficial interest, if the whole is not exhausted by that particular purpose, the surplus goes to the devisee, as it is intended to be given to him. . . . There is a great difference here between a devise upon trust and a devise subject to a charge; but the object is effected much in the same way, compelling the party to make good the charge, or trust, by very similar operations, as applied in this court." See Chap. V, sec. II, *post*.

SECTION VIII.

A Trust of a Chose in Action distinguished from an Assignment.

HAMMOND *v.* MESSENGER.

CHANCERY. 1838.

9 Sim. 327.

THE VICE CHANCELLOR [SHADWELL].[1] If this case were stripped of all special circumstances, it would be simply a bill filed by a plaintiff who had obtained from certain persons to whom a debt was due a right to sue in their names for the debt. It is quite new to me that, in such a simple case as that, this Court allows, in the first instance, a bill to be filed, against the debtor, by the person who has become the assignee of the debt. I admit that, if special circumstances are stated, and it is represented that, notwithstanding the right which the party has obtained to sue in the name of the creditor, the creditor will interfere and prevent the exercise of that right, this Court will interpose for the purpose of preventing that species of wrong being done; and, if the creditor will not allow the matter to be tried at law in his name, this Court has a jurisdiction, in the first instance, to compel the debtor to pay the debt to the plaintiff; especially in a case where the act done by the creditor is done in collusion with the debtor.

If bills of this kind were allowable, it is obvious that they would

[1] The statement of facts and a portion of the opinion are omitted.

be pretty frequent; but I never remember any instance of such a bill as this being filed, unaccompanied by special circumstances.

The only question then is, whether, on this record, there are any special circumstances which create a ground for a court of equity to entertain the bill against the debtor.

The bill sets out with a statement that a partnership was carried on between Wilks and Wooler; and a variety of instruments and transactions are stated, the result of which was, that the partnership was to be dissolved, that the plaintiff was to pay the debts due from the partnership, and to be entitled to the partnership assets. Then it represents that Messenger, the demurring party, at the time of the agreement for the dissolution of the partnership, was justly indebted to the firm in the sum of 80*l.* for coal and coke sold and delivered to him by the firm, and that Messenger is now indebted to the plaintiff in the said sum of 80*l.* as the assignee of such debt. Therefore the debt in question was, purely, a debt recoverable at law. Then the bill states a notice given to Messenger by the plaintiff to pay the debt to him. It then states that on the 2d of October the plaintiff called on Messenger, and applied to him for payment of the sum of 80*l.*, and fully apprised him of the plaintiff's right and title to demand and receive payment of it from him; that Messenger, for the first time, pretended that the plaintiff was not entitled to receive the debt, but that he was bound to pay it to Wilks and Wooler. That, of itself, creates no equitable ground.

The bill then alleges, in the usual manner, that the plaintiff had applied to Messenger for the payment of the debt, and that Messenger, combining and confederating with Wilks, had refused so to do, and pretended that there was no such debt: that, however, gives no equity. Then it charges that Messenger, on receiving notice of the plaintiff's right and title to the debt, became and still was a trustee of it for the plaintiff. That again does not make him a trustee, that is to say, such a trustee as the plaintiff has a right to sue in equity, unless the whole circumstances of the case taken together, do show that the plaintiff has a right to sue in equity. . . .

When I come to the prayer, I find that it, first of all, prays, " that Messenger may be decreed to pay to the plaintiff the sum of 80*l.*, so due to the firm of Wilks and Wooler as aforesaid, or, if necessary, that an account may be taken." Now no case whatever is stated to show the necessity for an account, and therefore it must, of necessity, stand as a mere prayer that Messenger may be decreed to pay the debt. It then proceeds as follows: " or that the plaintiff may be at liberty to use the name of the defendants, Wilks and Wooler, in an action at law to be brought by him against Messenger." There is, however, no case stated which shows that Wilks & Wooler have at all interfered to prevent, or that they intend to prevent the plaintiff from using their names at law. . . .

It seems to me that this case is altogether denuded of those special circumstances, the existence of which is the only ground for this Court to lend its aid to a party who, like the plaintiff, has taken an assignment of a debt; and, consequently, the demurrer must be allowed.[1]

Demurrer allowed, with liberty to the plaintiff to amend his bill.

FOGG v. MIDDLETON.

COURT OF APPEALS, SOUTH CAROLINA. 1837.

2 Hill Ch. 591.

MRS. MARY MIDDLETON, in her lifetime, conveyed by deed to her second son, Mr. J. I. Middleton, her large real estate; and by a will, purporting to be her last will and testament, disposing of her personal estate, bequeathed the greater part thereof between her two sons, and gave considerable pecuniary legacies (as is alleged, and which does not seem to be contradicted) to each of her daughters (except Mrs. Manigault, who was dead). Afterwards, she executed another will, and died in 1814, leaving the same in full force, by which she disposed of the bulk of her personal estate to her two sons, subject to certain legacies, and particularly a legacy to each of her daughters of 100*l*. sterling, which was greatly below the legacies under the former will.

The personal estate of Mrs. Middleton was appraised at upwards of seventy-one thousand dollars.

Some discontents naturally arose in the minds of daughters so slightly provided for by a wealthy parent, who bestowed so large a fortune on her sons. . . . These discontents reached the ears of

---

[1] Western Union Tel. Co. *v.* Ryan, 126 Ga. 191; Fultz *v.* Walters, 2 Mont. 165, *accord*. See also Ames, 60n.; 5 C. J. 997, 998.

In the code states the assignee is allowed to sue in his own name, as a result of the general provision that actions shall be brought in the name of the real party in interest. Clark, Code Pleading, sec. 23.

In many other states it is expressly provided by statute that an assignee of a *chose* in action may sue in his own name. See 30 Harv. L. Rev. 105; Williston, Contracts, sec. 446. *Cf.* Judicature Act, 1873, 36 & 37 Vict. c. 66, sec. 25 (6); Law of Property Act, 1925, 5 Geo. V, c. 20, sec. 136.

In special cases where an action at law in the name of the assignor is not an available or adequate remedy, the assignee may sue the obligor in equity. This is true where the assignor is a corporation which has ceased to exist (Lenox *v.* Roberts, 2 Wheat. (U. S.) 373; Person *v.* Barlow, 35 Miss. 174); or where the obligor is executor of the assignor (Hodge *v.* Cole, 140 Mass. 116); or where the assignor is dead and no domestic administrator has been appointed (Cobb *v.* Thompson, 1 A. K. Marsh. (Ky.) 507); or where the assignor is threatening to collect the claim or release the obligor. See French *v.* Peters, 177 Mass. 568. As to the effect of a marriage between the obligor and assignor, see MacKeoun *v.* Lacey, 200 Mass. 437.

Mr. J. I. Middleton, with the exaggerated report that the use or the abuse of his personal influence over an aged mother had produced the effect of diminishing her bounty to her daughters, by her last will and testament, to his benefit. . . . [Being disturbed by these reports he determined to relinquish the amount to which his sisters would have been entitled under the former will of their mother, and accordingly] executed bonds in trust to his brother, Mr. Henry Middleton, with conditions for the payment of certain sums for the eldest daughter of each of his sisters, and placed them in the possession of his brother, Mr. Henry Middleton. He then went to Europe, about 1817, and has remained there ever since, leaving his estate, including the personal estate, the slaves derived from his mother's will, in the hands of his brother, Henry, as his attorney and agent; and to apply the income of the estate to the payment of the debts of her estate, and the legacies under her will. The debts have been paid, and the bond to Mr. Izard's family has been paid, but no payment has been made on the bond for the obligor's niece, Miss Mary Rutledge, now the wife of Mr. Fogg, the plaintiff. After many years, applications were made, by letters to Mr. Henry Middleton, as the agent and attorney of Mr. J. I. Middleton, for payment, which applications, being unattended to, the bill was filed in this Court, which makes this case. . . .

[CHANCELLOR DE SAUSSURE made a decree for the plaintiffs, from which the defendants appeal.]

CHANCELLOR JOHNSTON. Under the decided cases, the delivery of the bond would have been established upon even less evidence than was furnished on the trial. As it is, the proof fully sustains the Chancellor's conclusion on the fact.

The law of the case seems to admit of little doubt.

Cases have been quoted to show that equity will not aid a mere volunteer, where no legal right has passed, or where the action of this Court is necessary to constitute the relation of trustee and *cestui que trust*.

But the delivery and acceptance of the bond, *ipso facto*, constituted Mr. Henry Middleton trustee. The bond contained his commission, and set forth his duties.

It also vested in him the debt of which it was evidence; and if that debt should be detained, he had a legal remedy to recover it.

Wherever a trustee has accepted a trust, he is bound to a diligent discharge of his duties. If he holds choses in action, with a clear remedy on them, it is unfaithful in him not to endeavor to enforce them. If he holds a bond, even although that bond is a free gift, he has no right to remit it.[1]

It never was the law that a trustee was not as amenable to a volunteer *cestui que trust* as to one who is not a volunteer. If

[1] Gordon *v.* Small, 53 Md. 550. See Fletcher *v.* Fletcher, 4 Hare 67, *post;* Spickernell *v.* Hotham, Kay 669, *ante.*

that were the law, no executor would be accountable to collateral legatees.

So that, without going further than Mr. H. Middleton, the plaintiffs have a right to come here to compel him to perform his trusts.

But if he is liable, it results that he may be compelled also to surrender to his *cestui que trusts* all the legal remedies he possesses. And this puts the plaintiffs in possession of the bond, to all intents, as if it had been drawn to them as obligee, or assigned to them.

If it had been drawn to the plaintiffs by Mr. John Izard Middleton, or assigned to them by Mr. Henry Middleton, will it be pretended that the plaintiffs could not recover from the obligor, even if it was given on no consideration? If it had been given on a consideration, which failed, that would be a good defence. But the original want of consideration would be none. . . .

If the Court, in this case, travels beyond the case of the *trustee* and *cestui que trusts*, and takes cognizance of the liabilities of the obligor, it is at the instance of the defendants, who insisted on his being made a party. Being here at his own instance, the Court will, to prevent circuity of action, decree against him what he would have been liable to pay the defaulting trustee or what the plaintiffs could recover if the bond had been assigned to them.[1] . . .

The motion is dismissed.

Chancellors JOHNSON and HARPER concurred.

Chancellor DE SAUSSURE absent, from indisposition.

[1] The right of a *cestui que trust* of an obligation to have a subpœna against his trustee, who refused to enforce the claim, has been recognized from very early times: (1391) 3 Rot. Parl. 297; Y. B. 2 Ed. IV. 2–6; Rose v. Clarke, 1 Y. & C. C. C. 534, 548; *Re* Uruguay Co., 11 Ch. D. 372 (*semble*); Thompson v. R. R. Co., 6 Wall. 134; N. Y. Co. v. Memphis Co., 107 U. S. 205; Morgan v. Kansas Co., 21 Blatchf. 134; Doggett v. Hart, 5 Fla. 215; Mason v. Mason, 33 Ga. 435; Forrest v. O'Donnell, 42 Mich. 556; Western Co. v. Nolan, 48 N. Y. 513; Wetmore v. Porter, 92 N. Y. 76 (*semble*); Crosby v. Bowery Bank, 50 N. Y. Sup'r Ct. 453; Phœbe v. Black, 76 N. C. 379. See also Sandford v. Jodreu, 2 Sm. & G. 176.

But for some time the *cestui que trust* could proceed only against his trustee: Dhegetoft v. London Co., Mosely 83, affirmed in 4 Bro. P. C. (Toml. ed.) 436; Fall v. Chambers, Mosely 193; Motteux v. London Co., 1 Atk. 545, 547.

Now, however, the beneficiary is allowed, on the principle of avoiding multiplicity of actions, to join the obligor as a defendant with the recusant trustee: Fletcher v. Fletcher, 4 Hare 67; Gandy v. Gandy, 30 Ch. Div. 57; [Kelly v. Larkin, [1910] 2 I. R. 550;] Alexander v. Central R. R., 3 Dill. 487; Owens v. Ohio Co., 20 Fed. 10; Billings v. Aspen etc. Co., 52 Fed. 250; Mangels v. Donau Brewing Co., 53 Fed. 513; Reinach v. Atlantic etc. Co., 58 Fed. 33 (if neither trustee nor obligor is a citizen of the same state as the *cestui que trust*, the suit may be brought in a federal court); Mason v. Mason, 33 Ga. 435 (*semble*); Wright v. Mack, 95 Ind. 332; Hale v. Nashua Co., 60 N. H. 333; De Kay v. Hackensack Co., 38 N. J. Eq. 158; O'Beirne v. Alleghany etc. Co., 151 N. Y. 372; Davies v. N. Y. Co., 41 Hun 492. See, further, the analogous cases of proceedings in equity against an executor and a debtor of the testator: Barker v. Birch, 1 DeG. & Sm. 376; or against a guardian

THOMASSEN v. VAN WYNGAARDEN.

SUPREME COURT, IOWA. 1885.

65 Iowa 687.

ACTION in equity to foreclose two mortgages. From the decree the plaintiff appeals.

SEEVERS, J. The defendant Wyngaarden executed the following promissory note:

"$1,400. Pella, Iowa, November 11, 1878.

"Six years after date, for value received, I promise to pay to Jantie Van Wyngaarden, in trust for Gertruda Geradina Thomassen, Jana Thomassen, Wilhemina Thomassen, Johannes Thomassen, and Jan Thomassen, heirs of Maarke Thomassen, deceased, or order, the sum of fourteen hundred dollars, payable at the First National Bank, Pella, Iowa, with interest, payable annually, at the rate of six per cent per annum from date until paid. Interest when due to become principal and draw ten per cent, and an attorney fee of ten per cent if suit is commenced on this note."

The mortgages were given to Jantie Van Wyngaarden in trust for the beneficiaries named in the note. . . . It was pleaded as a defence that the interest up to that time had been paid. The mortgages provided that, in the event the interest was not paid as therein provided, then the whole debt became due. The beneficiaries are grandchildren of Jantie Van Wyngaarden, and are minors, and the plaintiff is their guardian. This suit was commenced in March, 1882, and the court found that there was nothing due at that time. . . .

I. Counsel for the appellant insist that there is no sufficient evidence showing that the interest due on the note up to January, 1882, has been paid. . . .

The defendants introduced in evidence a receipt in the following words, and proved that it was executed by the trustee:

---

and a debtor to the ward's estate: Mesmer v. Jenkins, 61 Cal. 151; Frost v. Libby, 79 Me. 56. — AMES.

A suit cannot ordinarily be maintained by the beneficiary against the obligor without joining the obligee-trustee as a party. Cope v. Parry, 2 J. & W. 538. See Head v. Ld. Teynham, 1 Cox 57; Wood v. Williams, 4 Madd. 136.

When a life insurance policy is payable to the insured or his executors for the benefit of the wife and children of the insured, the executor is the proper party to sue. Mass. Mut. Life Ins. Co. v. Robinson, 98 Ill. 324.

As to the rights of the *cestui que trust* when the trustee is not subject to the jurisdiction of the court, see Amparo Mining Co. v. Fidelity Trust Co., 75 N. J. Eq. 555; Ettlinger v. Persian Rug etc. Co., 142 N. Y. 189, *post*.

"Pella, Iowa, December 22, 1880.

"Received of Jan Van Wyngaarden the sum of one hundred and forty-seven dollars, as interest on a certain note, secured by mortgage, to me given by the said Jan Van Wyngaarden in trust (for the beneficiaries above named); this being in full up to January 1, 1882.

"JANTIE VAN WYNGAARDEN."

Counsel for the plaintiff insist that the receipt is signed by the trustee as an individual, and therefore the beneficiaries are not bound thereby. But we think it fairly appears from the receipt itself that the money was received by the trustee as such. It was paid to and received by the person to whom it was payable by the terms of the note, and she will be charged as having received it in her capacity as trustee. . . .

II. Counsel for the appellant insist that the trust created by the execution of the notes and mortgages is a simple or dry trust, and that the trustee in such a trust does not have the power to manage and dispose of the trust estate, and therefore the beneficiaries are not bound by what the trustee did. A simple or dry trust is defined to be one "where property is vested in one person in trust for another, and the nature of the trust, not being prescribed by the donor, is left to the construction of the law." Perry, Trusts, § 520. "There can be but few of these dry trusts; for, when there is no control, and no duty to be performed by the trustee, it becomes a simple use, which the statute of uses executes in the *cestui que trust*, and he thus unites both the legal and beneficial estate in himself."

The trust under consideration is materially different; for it is so far declared as to cast on the trustee a duty for the performance of which she will be held accountable. It is made the duty of the trustee to receive and collect the interest and the principal when it becomes due. The legal title to the note and mortgages is vested in the trustee. It is her duty to preserve and protect the interest of the beneficiaries. But, in the absence of fraud or collusion, the trustee could satisfy the mortgages and acknowledge satisfaction of the debt, which would be binding on the beneficiaries. It is said that any one dealing with the trustee must see that money paid in the discharge of the trust was properly appropriated; but we do not think this is so, for the simple reason that the trustee was the legal owner of the note, and authorized to receive payment of both the principal and interest. An administrator in one sense is a trustee for the estate he represents; and yet he is the legal owner of the notes and mortgages belonging thereto. A person making him a payment is not bound to see that the money is properly accounted for.

The rule, it seems to us, should be the same in the case under consideration.

The decree of the Circuit Court must be affirmed.[1]

SUPREME LODGE, KNIGHTS OF PYTHIAS v. RUTZLER, TRUSTEE.

COURT OF ERRORS AND APPEALS, NEW JERSEY. 1917.

87 N. J. Eq. 342.

PARKER, J. The suit would be essentially one of interpleader except for the fact that complainant before filing its bill had already paid over the fund to one of the claimants and sought by the bill to be protected in that course, and to secure an injunction against the further prosecution of a suit at law by the other claimant.

The fund was the proceeds of a death benefit certificate issued by the complainant to Henry B. Lupton in his lifetime. At the time of his death it was payable to " his daughter Lillian M. Rutzler as trustee for his daughter Florence S. Lupton." Florence survived her father, but died before the money was paid, and this raised the question whether Lillian, as " trustee," was entitled to the money, or Florence's mother, Anna, who had taken out letters of administration of Florence's estate. The complainant finally paid the money to Anna, as administratrix, and, upon Lillian bringing an action at law against complainant on the certificate, filed this bill for an injunction, making the administratrix also a party. On final hearing an injunction was awarded and Lillian appeals.

We are of opinion that the court of chancery properly enjoined the suit at law. On the face of the certificate the trust was a " dry " or passive one. The characteristics of such a trust are so elementary that in all the range of our reported equity decisions I do not find, and counsel do not appear to have found, any direct adjudication of them. In Cooper v. Cooper, 36 N. J. Eq. 121, 123, they are described incidentally by Chancellor Runyon, quoting from Lew. Trusts (8th ed. § 18) 21. In Rosenbaum v. Garrett, 57 N. J. Eq. 186, the disposition of the fund turned on whether the trust was to be held active or passive; and Vice-Chancellor Reed (on p. 194) held that if the trust was passive (*i.e.*, if the trustee had no active duties to perform in respect to the trust estate) he could be called

---

[1] Sayre v. Weil, 94 Ala. 466 (*semble*); Rhodes v. Gauladett, 40 Ga. 212; Munnerlyn v. Augusta Sav. Bk., 88 Ga. 333; Austin v. Thorp, 30 Iowa 376, (*semble*); Sherburne v. Goodwin, 44 N. H. 271; Boone v. Bank, 84 N. Y. 83, 21 Hun 235; Schluter v. Bowery Sav. Bk., 117 N. Y. 125; Knoch v. Van Bernuth, 145 N. Y. 643, *accord*.

But if the obligor pays the obligee-trustee knowing that he intends to commit a breach of trust he is liable as a confederate in the breach of trust. See Bischoff v. Yorkville Bank, 218 N. Y. 106, *post*.

on to convey it to the *cestui que trust* or her appointee. See, also, Perry, Trusts § 18; sections 520 *et seq.,* and 39 Cyc. 30, where the classification of trusts into "simple" and "special" is dealt with as synonymous with passive (or dry) and active. As the trustee of a passive trust, the sole duty of Lillian after her father's death and in the lifetime of the sister was to act as a conduit of the money from the complainant to Florence or her appointee. Upon the death of Florence, her personal representative became vested with the same *jus habendi* that Florence had in her life-time; and, as the vice-chancellor very properly said, if the complainant had paid the money over to the trustee, there was nothing for the trustee to do but to turn it over to the administratrix. As the complainant wished to settle the question who was the beneficial owner of the fund as distinct from the purely legal owner, the litigation was properly transferred into the court of chancery by filing the bill, and properly retained there for the settlement of this equitable question; and the award of an injunction against proceeding further with the action at law was a remedy incidental to the nature of the case and the jurisdiction of the court.[1] . . .

CABLE *v.* THE ST. LOUIS MARINE RAILWAY & DOCK CO.

SUPREME COURT, MISSOURI. 1885.

21 Mo. 133.

THIS was an action by the owners of the steamboat James Hewitt, to recover damages for the sinking of said boat by the negligence of the defendant.

At the trial, there was evidence tending to show that, at the time

---

[1] In Day *v.* Old Colony Trust Co., 232 Mass. 207, an obligor of a *chose* in action held by a conservator for an incompetent was held liable for a payment made to the executor of the incompetent instead of to the conservator. See 2 A. L. R. 1557.

If a *chose* in action is assigned by the trustee in the proper exercise of a power of sale, and the obligor thereafter pays the *cestui que trust* without notice of the assignment, the obligor is not discharged. Seymour *v.* Smith, 114 N. Y. 481.

As to the effect of a payment by the obligor to the assignor with knowledge of the assignment, see Jones *v.* Farrell, 1 DeG. & J. 208; Kitzinger *v.* Beck, 4 Colo. App. 206; Chicago etc. Co. *v.* Smith, 158 Ill. 417; Ames, 63n. As to the effect of a payment without such knowledge, see Hellen *v.* Boston, 194 Mass. 579. See Williston, Contracts, secs. 432–3; 5 C. J. 960; Dec. Dig., Assignments, 93.

In Roberts *v.* Lloyd, 2 Beav. 376, the obligee of a *chose* in action assigned it to one as trustee for others. The obligor made a partial payment to the *cestuis que trust,* another partial payment on the trustee's order, and a third partial payment to the executrix of the obligee after having received notice of the assignment. It was held that the obligor was liable for the amount of the third payment, but not for the other amounts.

of the loss, there was an insurance upon three-fourths of the boat, and that immediately afterwards, and before the commencement of this suit, the interest insured was by the plaintiffs abandoned to and accepted by the underwriters.

The defendant asked the court to instruct the jury that, in respect to the interest abandoned, the right of action was in the underwriters alone, and that they should have been joined as plaintiffs; and that, in any event, the plaintiffs could not recover more than one-fourth of the value of the boat. These instructions were refused, and after a verdict and judgment for the plaintiffs for the value of the boat, the defendant appealed to this court.

T. T. Gantt, for plaintiff in error. 1. The abandonment operated as an assignment to the underwriters of all the interest of the plaintiffs in the subject insured. (2 Phillips on Ins. (3d ed. of 1853), §§ 1711, 1712, and cases there cited.) 2. It cannot be presumed that the plaintiffs are trustees for the underwriters, and besides, there is no allegation of such a trust in the petition.

John A. Kasson, for defendants in error, insisted that the provision in the code of 1849 that suits shall be brought in the name of the real party in interest did not apply to a case like this, where the cause of action had become divided; that the legal title or claim to the damages was still in the plaintiffs, and a part of the equitable claim, and that therefore the whole action might be sustained in their names.

SCOTT, J. All other questions in this cause have been abandoned except that in relation to the right of the plaintiffs to maintain this action for the entire value of the boat.

There can be no doubt but that the plaintiffs would have been the proper parties to institute this action for the entire sum claimed, had it been brought under our former system of practice. Though there had been an abandonment of the subject insured, and that abandonment accepted by the underwriters, yet the action would have been properly brought for the full value of the boat in their names.

It remains, then, to be seen, whether, under the circumstances of this case, the action is not properly brought in the name of the present plaintiffs, notwithstanding the present practice act. It is not controverted, but is admitted, that a right of action for a portion of the damages arising from the injury to the subject insured, is in the plaintiffs, and that they have a right to recover the value of one-fourth part of the boat, which was lost through the alleged negligence of the defendant.

Now, is there any thing in the present practice act which affects or in any way impairs the rule of the common law against dividing a cause of action, or making two causes of action out of one contract or injury by a division of it. The endorsee of a bill of exchange is the legal owner of it, and regularly a suit upon such an instrument must be brought in his own name. But if the holder of a bill assign by way of endorsement one half of its amount, would not the action, notwithstanding the assignment, still have to be brought in the name of the holder? By our law, the assignee of a bond is the legal owner of it, and suit thereon must be brought in his name. If the obligee of a bond assign one half of the sum of it, could the assignee, although the legal owner, maintain an action in his own name for his portion of the debt? In such a case, would not the suit necessarily be brought in the name of the obligee, who would recover the full amount due on the instrument?

A cause of action arising *ex maleficio*, cannot be used as an illustration of this principle, because neither by the common law nor statute was it assignable, so as to enable an assignee to maintain a suit for the damages in his own name.

We do not consider that the provision in the present practice act, which requires actions to be brought in the name of the real party in interest, affects this principle of the common law. Under the former practice, and even now, the legal owner of an instrument transferred by assignment must sue in his own name, yet we have seen that the legal owner of a part of a debt secured by a bond, could not maintain an action upon it. It could only be done when he was the assignee of the entire debt. So the statute requiring the real party in interest to sue, should be construed in reference to the principle of the common law above stated, and must be limited to those cases in which the real party in interest possesses the entire cause of action. The original owner of a cause of action cannot, by parting with a portion of his interest in it, give a right of action to his assignee, neither by the common law nor by any thing contained in the present act regulating practice in the courts of justice.

We do not wish to be understood as expressing any opinion as to the manner in which the suit should have been brought had the entire boat been insured by the owners, and they indemnified by their policy.

The other judges concurring, the judgment will be affirmed.[1]

[1] Although the partial assignee of a *chose* in action could not in the absence of a statute sue at law either alone or by joining the assignor, he might sue in equity, joining the assignor either as plaintiff or defendant. Under the code procedure it is generally held that the partial assignee can bring an action joining the assignor as plaintiff or defendant. See Clark, Code Pleading, 103.

As to the validity of a gratuitous partial assignment of a *chose* in action, see Chap. II, sec. II, and particularly Chase Nat. Bank *v.* Sayles, 11 F.(2d) 948, *post.*

In general as to the rights of a partial assignee, see Ames, 63n.; Williston, Contracts, secs. 441–4; 5 C. J. 894–7, 999–1000; Dec. Dig., Assignments, 30.

TODD v. MEDING.

COURT OF CHANCERY, NEW JERSEY. 1897.

56 N. J. Eq. 83.

IN MAY, 1893, the Butler Silk Manufacturing Company was indebted to the defendant Madeline A. Roe in the sum of about $10,000 (witnessed in part by four promissory notes) for money loaned by her to the company. On the 7th of August, 1893, the company being insolvent, the defendant Meding was appointed receiver. At that time the complainant Todd held a promissory note of the company for $5000, endorsed by Miss Roe, and, in order to secure him, Miss Roe, on the same 7th day of August, executed to him an assignment of a one-half interest of her claim against the company, and Todd agreed that in case the note for $5000 held by him were paid he would re-assign the one-half interest to her. In September, 1893, the receiver obtained an order calling on the creditors to present their claims. Todd presented a claim based upon the promissory note for $5000 above mentioned. Miss Roe presented a claim based upon the four promissory notes above mentioned. Both claims were in typewriting with the exception of a special clause in Miss Roe's claim, which was in the handwriting of Mr. (now Governor) Griggs who acted as solicitor for Todd and for Miss Roe, and is in these words:

"Deponent further says that an interest to the extent of $5000 in said claim has been assigned by her to J. C. Todd as collateral security, and this claim is presented on behalf of the said Todd as well as on her own behalf."

A dividend of twenty per cent. was declared, and the receiver paid Todd $1,000.37 and Miss Roe $2,071. The object of the bill is to compel the receiver Meding to make good to the complainant Todd the alleged mispayment to Miss Roe, who is insolvent.[1]

PITNEY, V. C. The first question raised at the argument was to whom was the dividend upon the claim of $10,000, verified by Miss Roe, properly due and payable. It was argued that it was due and payable to Miss Roe because the debt was originally due to her; that the affidavit was made by her, and the receiver was not bound to notice or act upon any partial assignment of the debt, or, at least, that the notice of the assignment contained in the sworn claim amounted to no more than a mere declaration of trust by Miss Roe which reserved to her the right to receive the dividend as trustee for Mr. Todd and pay it over to him.

The point is thus put in the remarkably able brief of defendant's counsel: "*First.* Treating this as a case of notice from the as-

[1] The statement of facts is abridged.

signee of a debt to the debtor, Meding is not charged under the circumstances with notice of Todd's right to receive the money instead of Miss Roe."

I am unable to adopt that view. The claim was, on its face, plainly made in favor of Todd to the extent of $5,000 — just one-half — and in favor of Miss Roe for the remainder. The language used — "this claim is presented on behalf of the said Todd as well as on her own behalf" — will admit of no other interpretation. The express declaration " that an interest in the said claim has been assigned by her to J. C. Todd as collateral," is in and of itself an assignment of so much of the debt; quite independent of the previous formal deed of assignment duly made and executed by her, of which Meding and his counsel had full notice.

An ingenious argument was made to the effect that an assignment as collateral did not vest in the assignee any right to the immediate receipt of the money, and that Todd's right to receive the money from the receiver depended upon the question whether or not the state of the indebtedness, as collateral to which the assignment was made, was such as to entitle him to receive the money as between him and Miss Roe.

But I do not understand such to be the law. Take a simple illustration. If A wishes to borrow money from B, and holds a bond and mortgage of C, which is due, but upon which he cannot immediately realize, and gives his promissory note to B for a sum of money payable at a future day, and assigns the mortgage of C to B as collateral to that note, and before the maturity of the note, C wishes to pay his mortgage, and has notice of the assignment to B as collateral, he cannot, with safety, pay the money to A, the mortgagee. B is entitled to receive the money, although the debt which it is assigned to secure is not yet due. The assignment vests the title to the money in the assignee. The mere fact that it is assigned as collateral, does not alter the situation of the parties. Any other rule would destroy the value of such an assignment. The fact that the assignment is merely as collateral to a certain debt, does not affect the intrinsic character of the transaction or disentitle the assignee to demand the money, so long as the debt which it is assigned to secure still exists.

The circumstance that only a part of the claim was assigned, does not affect the result. It is too late to dispute the proposition that a part of a debt may be effectually assigned in equity. The qualifying rule that such an assignment cannot be enforced by action at law without the acceptance or assent of the debtor does not vary the result. The qualifying rule avails the debtor only to the extent that if he wishes to dispute the existence of the debt, he is entitled to make his defence in a single suit, and cannot be subjected to several suits at law. But it does not justify him in ignoring the partial assignment, after he has notice of it, and in paying the whole sum to the original creditor. To so hold would be to nullify the doctrine which sanctions partial assignments. The rule is well settled that the payment of the whole debt to the original creditor, after notice of an assignment of part of it, will not avail the debtor when sued in equity by the assignee. If the debtor is in any doubt as to the right of the person claiming to be an assignee, as against the assignor, he has an easy remedy. He can inquire of the original creditor and alleged assignor, and if he denies the assignment the debtor may file his bill of interpleader.

I can find no solid basis for the notion that Miss Roe occupied the position of trustee of a part of this fund for Mr. Todd, with power, as such, to receive the money without his consent. In one sense no doubt she was a trustee, but not in the sense which would give her a legal right to handle the money for his use and benefit and without his consent.

By the old common-law practice the assignee of a negotiable chose in action was obliged to bring suit thereon in the name of the original contractee as nominal plaintiff to his use. But the necessity to use the name of the original contractee as nominal plaintiff did not authorize the payment by the debtor of the amount due to such plaintiff in person, after notice of the assignment. . . .

An examination of the numerous authorities cited by counsel for defendant fails to disclose any which covers the case in hand. And I am unable to find any ground upon which the receiver in this case can be relieved and credited with the overpayment to Miss Roe.[1] . . .

[1] The decision of the Vice Chancellor was reversed in 56 N. J. Eq. 820, on the ground that Todd had not given proper notice to the receiver or made a proper sworn claim in regard to his interest in Miss Roe's claim.

See Brice v. Bannister, 3 Q. B. D. 569; Palmer v. Palmer, 112 Me. 149; Williston, Contracts, sec. 444; 28 Yale L. Jour. 395; 5 C. J. 896. But see Shearer v. Shearer, 137 Ga. 51; Henry Clay Fire Ins. Co. v. Denker's Executrix, 218 Ky. 68.

If the partial assignor collects the whole amount he is constructive trustee *pro tanto* for the assignee. See Hinkle Iron Co. v. Kohn, 229 N. Y. 179.

In *Re* Steele Wing Co., [1921] 1 Ch. 349, it was held that a partial assignee of a *chose* in action may present a petition to wind up the obligor company since he is in equity a creditor of the obligor.

The interest of a partial assignee of a *chose* in action is not cut off by the subsequent bankruptcy of the assignor. Andrews Elec. Inc. v. St. Alphonse etc. Society, 233 Mass. 20; nor by a subsequent garnishment by a creditor of the assignor. National Exchange Bank v. McLoon, 73 Me. 498.

Section IX.
A Trust distinguished from an Executorship.

SCOTT *v.* JONES.
House of Lords. 1838.
4 Cl. & Fin. 382.

Lord Lyndhurst.[1] The facts of the case are extremely simple, and the question resolves itself into a mere question of law. It appears that, in 1815, Messrs. Evans & Jelf carried on business in partnership, as bankers, at Gloucester. In that year they became bankrupts, and their effects were assigned under their commission to assignees in the usual manner. Mr. R. Donovan had a running account with the bank, and there was a balance against him at the time of the bankruptcy to the amount of 262*l.* 4*s.* 3*d.* R. Donovan in the same year made his will, and by that will he disposed of the personal estate he possessed to trustees, for the payment of his debts; and he also devised to the same trustees, what he considered to be his real estate at Tibberton-court; and he directed that in the event of the personal estate not being sufficient to discharge the debts, a sum should be added for that purpose, to be raised by the sale or mortgage of the real estate of Tibberton. He died in the following year; one of the trustees alone proved the will, the other renounced. The trustee who proved the will administered part of the assets and soon afterwards died, and the ultimate administration *de bonis non* was granted to one of the Appellants, the daughter of R. Donovan. . . . The assignees commenced an action against Mrs. Scott, one of the Appellants, and her husband. To this action the defendants pleaded the Statute of Limitations, and there were then no further proceedings taken in the action. There cannot be a doubt, that that was because the Statute of Limitations was a sufficient bar to the action. . . . In consequence of that, the present bill was filed, demanding an application of the trust funds in payment of the debts of the testator. The defendants, in their answer to this suit, insist on the Statute of Limitations, and the only question is, whether the trust was of such a nature as to prevent the setting up of such a defence. I have mentioned that the testator considered the estate at Tibberton to be real estate. When sold, however, it turned out to be mere leasehold, and to form part of the personalty. Had it been real estate, in that case the plaintiff would have been entitled to recover, but though part of the personalty, it is said to be taken subject to the trust, and the question is, whether a trust of

---

[1] The statement of facts and a small part of the opinion are omitted.

this description declared of the personal estate, prevents the Statute of Limitations being set up by way of defence, and I am clearly of opinion that it does not, because it does not at all vary the legal liability of the parties, or make any difference with respect to the effect and operation of the statute itself. The executors take the estate subject to the claim of the creditors: they are, in point of law, the trustees for the creditors; the trust is a legal trust, and there is nothing whatever added to their legal liabilities from the mere circumstance of the testator himself declaring in express terms, that the estate shall be subject to the payment of his debts. I conceive therefore, that the circumstance of there being an express trust in this case, does not make any alteration with respect to the question. And if in ordinary circumstances, as to personalty, where there was a mere legal liability, the existence of a mere legal trust would not have been an answer to a plea of the Statute of Limitations; so I conceive that in the present case no alteration can take place, from the existence of an express trust, and that that trust cannot under these circumstances be considered as an answer to the statute. I am of opinion, therefore, that the judgment of the Master of the Rolls was the correct judgment, and that the judgment of the late Lord Chancellor, reversing it, ought to be set aside. As, however, two learned judges have entertained different opinions on this point, the decree of the Court below must be set aside without costs.

Judgment reversed without costs.[1]

CARRINGTON & CO. v. MANNING'S HEIRS.

SUPREME COURT, ALABAMA. 1848.

13 Ala. 611.

Error to the Chancery Court sitting at Huntsville. Before the Hon. D. G. Ligon, Chancellor.

THE bill was filed by the plaintiffs in error, who alledge, that they are creditors of B. M. Lowe, upon four several bonds of $6,000 each, and that one James Manning was a co-obligor, and surety upon said bonds. That judgments have been obtained against said Lowe on the bonds, and execution returned no property found. That Manning has departed this life, having on the 26th September,

---

[1] Freake v. Cranefeldt, 3 Myl. & Cr. 499; Evans v. Tweedy, 1 Beav. 55; Re Hepburn, 14 Q. B. D. 394 (*semble*); Re Stephens, 43 Ch. D. 39; Hines v. Spruill, 2 Dev. & B. Eq. (N. C.) 93; Man v. Warner, 4 Whart. (Pa.) 455, *accord.*

As to the history of the distinction between an executorship and a trust, see Holdsworth, History of English Law, vol. 3, 534-5, 585-595; vol. 5, 316-320; vol. 6, 632, 652. See also Woerner, Law of Administration, 3 ed., 517. See also Chase Nat. Bank v. Sayles, 11 F.(2d) 948, *post.*

1837, made his will duly attested, &c. which, among other clauses, contains the following:

"It is my will, that the interest which I have in a house and lot in the town of Huntsville, jointly with Thomas Bibb, Esq. of Limestone county, together with my lots lying in the towns of Triana and Florence, be sold, and the proceeds applied to the payment of legacies hereafter bequeathed, and the discharge of my debts. I hereby direct, and require my executors hereinafter named, to keep my estate in the county of Marengo, Alabama, together, until all my debts and legacies are paid off and discharged, and out of the proceeds of my said estate in Marengo county, to pay annually to my beloved wife, Sophia, one thousand dollars, for her support and maintenance during the time that said estate shall remain undivided." The testator further expressed his intention, that his estate in Marengo should not be divided, until all his debts and the legacies given by the will were satisfied. The testator died first March, 1841, his widow and all his children surviving him, and B. M. Lowe and James Manning qualified as his executors, and entered upon the execution of their trust. That the wife of said Lowe was the daughter of said Manning, and has also departed this life, leaving certain children who are described.

It is admitted in the bill, that the bonds were not presented to the executors for payment, being with the obligee in the State of Connecticut; but that Lowe being the principal obligor in the bond, as well as one of the executors in the will, knew of their existence, and that they were unpaid, and had repeatedly by letter recognized them, but charges, and expressly relies upon the will of the testator, as having charged his real estate, with the payment of all his debts, &c.

The chancellor dismissed the bill for want of equity, which is the matter now assigned for error.

COLLIER, C. J.[1] — We do not deem it necessary elaborately to consider the doctrine, that a trust for the benefit of creditors, attaches to a devise of real estate, where the words "after my debts are paid," or other equivalent terms are used by the testator. This doctrine owes its introduction into British jurisprudence to the exclusion of simple-contract-creditors from the lands of their deceased debtors, as the means of satisfying their demands, and has often been carried to an extent not contemplated by the testators. Treating of this subject, an elementary writer of great respectability says, "it seems to be generally admitted, that the courts have allowed their anxiety to prevent moral injustice, and that men should not sin in their graves, to carry them beyond the limits prescribed by established general principles of construction." 2 Jarm. on Wills,

[1] A part of the opinion and the concurring opinion of Chilton, J., are omitted.

520. The trust being ascertained, the debts were considered as withdrawn from the influence of the statute of limitations, where the bar was not complete before the testator's death. See the learned judgment of Sir William Plumer, in Burke *v.* Jones, 2 Ves. & B. Rep. 275, and cases there cited; 2 Story's Eq. § 1245, 1246–7.

It is natural enough that terms not the most significant and direct, should be seized upon to create a trust upon the real estate of a testator for the payment of his debts, where the creditor, according to the law, could not otherwise subject it to liability. There are few men who do not cherish an innate sense of justice, and are pleased to see it accorded to others; no matter how unwilling they may be to render it, where it costs a sacrifice of interest or feeling. Judges are but men, and, with the most honest intentions, sometimes unconsciously yield to the extraneous influences which operate on others. Hence we have no difficulty in accounting for the implication of a trust upon grounds often unwarrantable, in cases analogous in point of fact to the one now before us. But in this State, where all distinction in dignity as it respects the debts of a deceased person, is abolished, and a debt by simple contract is placed on the footing with one which is evidenced by a record, if the latter is not a lien on the debtor's estate, it cannot be expected that the courts should be astute in creating trusts by construction.

According to the common law, if a testator devotes his land to the payment of his debts, without particularizing or distinguishing them, it is regarded but a fair construction of his will, to suppose that he intended to embrace all the debts which were recoverable at the time of his death: But is it allowable to deduce this inference from the same terms, applied to the same description of property, where by statute it is already charged with the payment of the decedent's estate? Is there not great danger under such a state of the law, of making that which the testator intended as a direction to his executor, when his devisee should be let into the enjoyment of his bounty, a condition precedent to the enjoyment? In England, personal estate in the hands of the executor is a fund for the payment of the debts, and words which would create a trust upon the realty of the testator, will have the effect of modifying the duties of the executor as the personal representative. True, in Jones *v.* Scott, 1 R. & Mylne's Rep. 255, Lord Brougham decided, in opposition to the master of the rolls, that there was no difference " between a charge upon the real and charge upon the personal estate." It was admitted that the point had never received a judicial decision, and the Lord Chancellor advised that it should be reconsidered elsewhere. An appeal was accordingly taken to the House of Lords, where, after great consideration, the decree was reversed. . . .

It is enacted, by a statute passed in 1806, that the lands, tenements and hereditaments of the testator or intestate, shall stand chargeable with all the debts of the deceased, over and above what the personal estate shall be sufficient to pay. In 1803, 1818, 1820, and 1822, acts were passed authorizing the sale of the lands belonging to the estate of a deceased person, upon application to the orphans' court, either upon a deficiency of personal property, or where it would be more beneficial to the estate to sell the lands than the slaves, &c. See Wyman, et al. *v.* Campbell, et al. 6 Port. Rep. 219. It is also provided, that whenever an executor, &c. shall fail to apply to the orphans' court for the sale of real estate, for the purpose of paying debts of the deceased, the judgment creditor may proceed by *scire facias*, and subject the lands to the payment of his demand; and if an executor, &c., shall fail to apply for leave to sell real estate, three months after reporting the estate insolvent, he shall be deemed guilty of a *devastavit*, and himself and sureties may be sued on his bond. Clay's Dig. 197. So it is made lawful for executors, &c., to rent at public outcry, the real estate of any decedent until he makes a final settlement of his accounts; and the proceeds shall be assets in his hands. Id. 199. And by a statute subsequent to the testator's death, the orphans' court granting letters testamentary, &c., is required to take into the estimated value of the estate, the real estate of which the testator, &c., may have died siezed or possessed of, and shall require of the executor, &c., a bond with security under such penalty as the law previously required. Id. 229.

These several legislative provisions may suffice to show that lands in this State are subjected to the payment of the debts of a deceased person, where the personal assets are insufficient, and that in such case it is not only competent for, but the duty of the executor to take proper measures to make them available. It must be conceded that the important modifications they make in the common law, when connected with the equalization of debts in point of dignity, should indispose us to extend the doctrine of implied trusts, such as we are considering. We will not deny that it is within the power of a testator so to provide by will that his real estate shall be charged beyond what the terms of our statutes direct; though the authorities cited are conclusive to show that the course of administration in respect to the personalty cannot be thus controlled. . . .

The statute of non-claim differs in its effect and consequences from the statute of limitations, technically so called — it must be insisted on by the personal representative, and cannot be safely waived. It requires claims against the estates of deceased persons to be presented to the executor or administrator within eighteen months, &c. " and all claims not so presented within the time aforesaid, shall be forever barred from a recovery: *Provided*, that the provisions of this section shall not extend to persons under age, *femes covert*, persons insane or *non compos mentis*, to debts contracted out of the State, nor to claims of heirs or legatees, claiming as such." Clay's Dig. 195, § 17. This enactment was not designed merely as a security for the estate against neglected and dormant claims, but was intended for the benefit of heirs, distributees and devisees, whom the policy of the law requires should be placed in a condition in which they may safely act with property apparently their own. . . .

Such being the object and policy of the statute of non-claim, we are inclined to think that its effect is to throw upon the creditors the necessity of presenting their demands to the executor, or administrator, before any trust by implication can become operative against the heir or devisee. Have not the legislature very significantly indicated that the heir or devisee shall take the estate freed from all implied trusts for the payment of the testator's debts, if they are not presented to the personal representative within the time prescribed? If this be so, it is an indispensable duty of the courts to sustain — not to defeat the legislative will.

Such is the authority and duty of an executor in respect to the real estate of his testator, that no disposition could be made of it by will, which would withdraw it from liability to pay the testator's debts, if its appropriation should become necessary. If devised, the devisee takes it *cum onere* — subject to the provisional duty and authority of the executor. It may well be questioned whether by any other than express terms, or language most significant and direct, a testator in this State can throw upon his heirs or devisees, the burthen of paying claims, other than those excepted from the influence of the statute, where the creditor omits to present and enforce them against the personal representative.

The construction contended for by the plaintiffs' counsel would make it difficult, if not impossible, for an heir or devisee, or a purchaser from either, where the will, according to the common law, made the real estate subject to the testator's debts, to act with safety in the sale or improvement of the estates received by them under the will; lest debts of which they had no means of ascertaining, and of which the negligence of the creditor has prevented the payment, should afterwards be enforced. If, in the present case, a trust can be established, it would be hazardous for a testator to give any directions in respect to his land in connection with his debts, if he did not intend to take them out of the course of administration which the legislature has prescribed, or to arrest the operation of the act of limitations, and dispense with the statute of non-claim. Under, perhaps, a majority of wills in this country, the administration would be disturbed — trusts would be created involving responsibilities and consequences which testators never contemplated, and procrastinating to the prejudice of heirs and devisees, the settlement of estates to an indefinite period. The duties of an executor, instead of being controlled by the statutes which apply to the estates of deceased persons, would be regulated by principles recognized by the English chancery, under a state of the law altogether different from ours — and when, too, we have studiously endeavored to avoid the very evils that superinduced them. Our policy is decidedly adverse to the origination of trusts by implication for the payment of debts, not only because it is unnecessary, but because the character of the executor is changed to a mere equitable trustee, not accountable to the orphans' court, and whose default in that character, perhaps his administration bond would not cover. In Cook v. Fountain, 3 Swanst. Ch. Rep. 592, it was said by Lord Chief Justice Raynsford, that "the law never implies, the court never presumes a trust, but in case of absolute necessity. The reason of this rule is sacred; for if the chancery do once take liberty to construe a trust by implication of law, or to presume a trust unnecessarily, a way is opened to the Lord Chancellor to construe or presume any man in England out of his estate; and so at last every case in court will become *casus pro amico*."

Whatever construction might be placed by an English chancellor upon the different clauses of the will from which it is attempted to deduce a trust, in view of our statute law, which has effected such important modifications as to the powers and duties of an executor, they can be regarded as nothing more than mere directions by the testator as to the mode of fulfilling his intentions — as an expression of his wishes, how, and from what portion of his estate, the means of paying his debts, and some of his legacies, should be raised. The direction to keep his Marengo estate together, until his debts, and the legacies he had given, should be "paid off and discharged," could not operate to the prejudice of his creditors; for if their demands were not extinguished before judgments were recovered, they could coerce a sale.

It is a matter not unworthy of consideration in a proper case, that in this country, where land is so abundant, it is much less appreciated than at least one description of personal property; and as it can be so easily obtained, it is often most beneficial for a testator's estate, that it should furnish by a sale the means of paying his debts. Besides, considerations of humanity and benevolence may make it desirable, and even a duty, to provide for retaining the slaves in his family. Under such circumstances, would it not be unjust to raise a trust which would render inoperative the statutes of *non-claim* and *limitations*, from the mere fact that the will made the lands primarily liable for the payment of the testator's debt, when he never could have contemplated such a consequence. . . .

Having determined that the testator did not create a devise by implication for the payment of his debts, so as to arrest the operation of the statutes of *limitations* and *non-claim* and give to a court of chancery, jurisdiction to subject his real estate to the payment of a debt at the suit of a creditor, it is unnecessary to consider the effect of the allegations in the bill as to the presentation of the complainant's demand. The decisions of this court as to what will constitute a presentment within the meaning of the statute, furnish rules by which, in almost every case that occurs, it may be determined whether the claim has been duly presented to the executor or administrator. It remains but to add, that the decree of the court of chancery is affirmed.[1]

KANSAS PACIFIC RAILWAY CO. v. CUTTER.

SUPREME COURT, KANSAS. 1876.

16 Kan. 568.

ACTION by Mrs. Cutter as administratrix, to recover damages sustained by the next of kin of one Joseph Stewart, deceased. The petition alleged the death of said Stewart by the wrongful acts, negligence and mismanagement of the Railway Company while he was a passenger in the cars of said company between Manhattan and Ogden, in Riley county, in this state, in August 1872. It named the heirs and next of kin of said Stewart, and alleged that in September 1872, " letters of administration upon the estate of the said Joseph Stewart were duly issued by the probate court of Arrapahoe county, Territory of Colorado, to Lydia H. Harvey, who since the issuance of said letters of administration, has intermarried with

---

[1] In England it is held that if land is devised upon trust to sell it and out of the proceeds to pay the testator's debts, a trust is created and the claims of the creditors are not barred by the Statute of Limitations, although creditors are allowed under the Land Transfer Act, 1897, to reach the land of a deceased debtor. *Re* Balls, [1909] 1 Ch. 791. See 2 Williams, Executors, 11 ed., 1637.

In the United States it is held that a mere direction by the testator to his executors to pay debts does not create a trust, and the claims of creditors are barred by the Statute of Limitations or statutes of non-claim. Starke v. Wilson, 65 Ala. 576; Kaufman v. Redwine, 97 Ark. 546; Bidwell v. Beckwith, 86 Conn. 462; Cohn v. McClintock, 107 Miss. 831; Stevens v. Dunlap Mercantile Co., 108 Miss. 690; Trinity Church v. Watson, 50 Pa. 518; Hurlburt Brothers v. Hinde, 86 Vt. 517; Foley v. McDonnell, 48 Wash. 272; Estate of Kleinschmidt, 167 Wis. 450. See 24 C. J. 322; Perry, Trusts, sec. 559.

A testator may, however, create a trust of land or personalty for the payment of his debts, and if he does so the creditors are not barred by the Statute of Limitations or statutes of non-claim from enforcing their rights as beneficiaries of the trust. Gordon v. McDougall, 84 Miss. 715. In that case the testator was insolvent and he hoped by postponing the final settlement of his estate to increase its value. Although the creditors cannot be precluded from enforcing their claims as creditors without their consent, they may by the terms of the will be given rights as beneficiaries of a trust, either in addition to or, if they consent, in substitution for their rights as creditors. *Cf. Re* Oxley, [1914] 1 Ch. 604, *post.*

Relation between executor and legatees and next of kin. Although an executor or administrator as such is not a trustee for legatees or next of kin, there is a diversity of opinion on the question whether and when the claim of the legatee or next of kin is barred by the Statute of Limitations. See Woerner, Law of Administration, 3 ed., 1950–1958.

Benjamin P. Cutter, by which the said Lydia H. Harvey, (now Lydia H. Cutter,) was appointed administratrix of all the goods and credits belonging to the said Joseph Stewart at the time of his death, and that she thereupon qualified and entered upon the duties of said administration." The Railway Company demurred, assigning the following grounds: " 1st, The plaintiff has no capacity to sue, not having been appointed administratrix of the estate of Joseph Stewart within the state of Kansas; 2d, There is a defect of parties plaintiff, inasmuch as Benjamin P. Cutter, husband of the plaintiff in the petition mentioned, is not joined as plaintiff in the action; 3d, The petition does not state facts sufficient to constitute a cause of action." [1] The district court, at the September Term 1874, overruled the demurrer, and the Railway Company brings the case here on error.

BREWER, J. The first question in this case is, whether a foreign administrator can maintain an action under § 422 of the code of civil procedure. We think he can. The section provides that, " When the death of one is caused by the wrongful act or omission of another, the personal representatives of the former may maintain an action therefor against the latter, if the former might have maintained an action had he lived, against the latter for an injury, for the same act or omission." Now the language is general, purports to give the cause of action in every such case happening within this state, whether the deceased be a resident or nonresident, whether death ensues here, or elsewhere. All that it nominates as the condition of a right of recovery is, the wrongful act, and the resulting death. Nor do the proceeds of the recovery become assets in the hand of the administrator for payment of the debts of the intestate. They are appropriated by the same section which gives the right of action, to the " exclusive benefit of the widow and children, if any, or next of kin," and the recovery by a foreign administrator does not at all conflict with those provisions of our law which attempt to secure the appropriation of the property of the decedent within this state to the payment of his debts due here, in preference to those due elsewhere. It, so to speak, creates a fund for the exclusive use of certain relatives of the deceased, and names the personal representatives as the trustees of that fund, and authorizes suit in their names. Any one else might have been named as the proper party plaintiff. Authority might have been given to the widow, and for the benefit of herself and children. This question has been before the supreme court of Indiana in the case of J. M. & I. Rld. Co. v. Hendricks, 41 Ind. 49, and the right of action sustained. This is the only authority counsel have cited that is apparently exactly in point, and to that we refer for a fuller discussion of the question. There is a slight difference between the section of the Indiana statute and ours con-

[1] The part of the opinion in which the last two grounds of objection were overruled is omitted.

cerning the right of foreign administrators to sue, but we do not think it affects the question materially. See also, Hartford Rld. Co. v. Andrews, 36 Conn. 213. . . .

The judgment will be affirmed.[1]

SHEFFIELD v. PARKER.

SUPREME JUDICIAL COURT, MASSACHUSETTS. 1893.

158 Mass. 330.

TWO APPEALS, the first by the children, and the second by the executors of the will, of Joel Parker, from a decree of the Probate Court, dated September 9, 1890, upon the first account of the executors. The cases were heard together by Holmes, J., and, at the request of the executors, reported by him for the consideration of the full court. The facts material to the points decided appear in the opinion.

KNOWLTON, J. This case comes before us on a report containing findings of fact of a single justice, and the evidence taken at the hearing. So far as the decision depends on the findings of fact, the conclusions of the single justice must be sustained, unless they are clearly erroneous. Francis v. Daley, 150 Mass. 381.

The most important question involved is whether the executors can be allowed in their account for an investment of $10,000 in the stock of the Equitable Trust Company, which they made in their names as executors. They were authorized and directed to set apart the sum of $12,000 from the general estate of the testator, and invest it for the benefit of his son, Edmund M. Parker, during his life, the fund to be paid over at his death to his lineal descendants, or, if he should leave no descendants, to the trustees of Dartmouth College. They were also authorized, under certain contingencies, to sell the testator's homestead, and invest and hold the proceeds as a trust fund. This sale, however, has not been made. The executors contend that their investment in the stock referred to was made for Edmund M. Parker, and that the stock has been held by them ever since as a part of the trust fund of $12,000 which it was their duty to create. The evidence produced failed to prove, to the satisfaction of the judge who heard it, that at the time of the purchase

---

[1] Wilson v. Tootle, 55 Fed. 211; Pearson v. Norfolk & W. Ry. Co., 286 Fed. 429; Reilly v. Antonio Pepe Co., 108 Conn. 436; Knight v. Ry. Co., 160 Iowa 160; McCullough v. Powell Lumber Co., 205 Mo. App. 15, 25; Ghilain v. Couture, 146 Atl. 395 (N. H., 1929); Wooden v. Western etc. R. R. Co., 126 N. Y. 10; Hamilton v. Erie R. R. Co., 219 N. Y. 343, 350; Boulden v. Pa. R. R. Co., 205 Pa. 264; Connor v. N. Y. etc. Co., 28 R. I. 560, *accord*. But compare Metrakos v. Ry. Co., 91 Kan. 342; Battese v. R. R. Co., 102 Kan. 468, 31 Harv. L. Rev. 1161; Hall v. Southern R. R. Co., 149 N. C. 108.

Money paid on a policy of insurance payable to the administrator of the decedent in trust for his widow is not a part of the assets of his estate. Cincinnati etc. Co. v. Thiebaud, 114 Fed. 918; Nickals v. Stanley, 146 Cal. 724.

the stock was appropriated to this trust " in such a sense as to give Edmund M. Parker the right at and from that moment to have it accounted for as his, or to prevent them from making a different disposition of it thereafter, if for any reason they should be so minded." There is no evidence to show the subsequent appropriation of it to this trust, until after it had so far depreciated in value as to deprive them of the right so to appropriate it. It was conceded that they had no right to make such an investment for the general purposes of the estate, and the justice therefore found that the decree of the Probate Court was correct in disallowing this item in their account. The issue is narrowed to the simple question whether the judge should have found an appropriation to this trust by the executors when they took the stock.

It was held in Miller v. Congdon, 14 Gray, 114, and in Collins v. Collins, 140 Mass. 502, 506, 507, that, when a trust fund is to be created by an executor out of the assets of an estate, something more must be done by the executor in order to impress the trust on particular property than to hold the property with an intention that it shall constitute the trust fund. There must be some act of appropriation which transfers it to the trust fund and gives the beneficiaries the right to have it held for them. Doubtless the purchase of property by itself expressly to be held under the trust would be a sufficient act of appropriation; and there was evidence in this case from which a finding might have been made in favor of the executors. On the other hand, there was evidence which, without any imputation on the honesty or good faith of the executors, well warranted the finding that they had failed to sustain the burden of proving an appropriation of the stock to this trust. In the first place, the letter of February 27, 1878, from H. R. Bond, secretary, to the executors, which mentions the issuing of a certificate, refers to the subscription as made by " the estate of Joel Parker "; the certificate under which they held the stock was in the name of " Horatio G. Parker and Francis J. Parker, executors of will of Joel Parker," with no reference to the trust; the evidence tends to show that not until January, 1890, nearly twelve years after the stock was subscribed for, did either of the executors inform Edmund M. Parker, or any one else, that the stock was held as part of the trust fund; a statement of account made by one of the executors in 1882 treated the legacy of $12,000 which was to constitute the trust fund as a liability against the estate, and included the stock subscribed for among the assets of the estate, and put upon it the valuation of $60 per share; until the making of the probate account there was never anything on the books of the executors, either in their accounts with Edmund M. Parker or elsewhere, to identify the investment as made on account of the trust fund, and there was evidence of a conversation in which one of the executors offered to convey to Edmund M. Parker and his sister, Mrs. Sheffield, the other legatee, interested in the general assets disposed of under the second clause of the will, other stock which belonged to the executors to make good the loss from this investment. We cannot say that the court was wrong in finding against the executors on the question whether the stock subscribed for was appropriated by them to the trust for the benefit of Edmund M. Parker and his descendants. For the purposes of the discussion, we have assumed without deciding that, if they had so appropriated it, the investment would have been one which they had a right to make.[1] . . .

[1] Although the same person is named in the will as executor and trustee, his duties as executor are distinct from his duties as trustee. Williams v. Hund, 302 Mo. 451; Strite v. Wolf, 268 Pa. 221.

If a person is named as executor and trustee, the revocation of his appointment as executor will not necessarily revoke his appointment as trustee; but where by the terms of the will his duties as executor and as trustee are blended together, the revocation of his appointment as executor revokes his power to act as trustee. Tuckerman v. Currier, 54 Colo. 25; Mullanny v. Nangle, 212 Ill. 247. Similarly, a person named as executor and trustee may accept one office and disclaim the other, unless by the will the duties are blended together. West v. Bailey, 196 Mo. 517; Murphy v. Reed, 180 N. C. 624.

Where a person is named in the will as executor and trustee, the sureties on his bond as executor are not liable for his failure to perform his duties as trustee. Freeman v. Brown, 115 Ga. 23; Hinds v. Hinds, 85 Ind. 312; Givens v. Flannery, 105 Ky. 451; Re Quimby, 84 N. J. Eq. 1; Ruffin v. Harrison, 81 N. C. 208; Joy v. Elton, 9 N. D. 428. But if as executor he turns over property to himself as trustee without having filed a bond as trustee where such a bond is required, he is liable for breach of duty as executor in so doing and the sureties on his bond as executor are liable. Newcomb v. Williams, 9 Met. (Mass.) 525. See also Coates v. Lunt, 213 Mass. 401; Lannin v. Buckley, 256 Mass. 78; Bellinger v. Thompson, 26 Ore. 320; Karel v. Pereles, 161 Wis. 598.

On the question when a person named as executor and trustee ceases to act as executor and begins to act as trustee, see the cases cited above, and see Massachusetts Institute v. A. G., 235 Mass. 288; Olcott v. Baldwin, 190 N. Y. 99; Matter of McDowell, 178 N. Y. App. Div. 243; Probate Court v. Angell, 14 R. I. 495; Story's Adm'r v. Hall, 86 Vt. 31.

One of several executors has power to transfer or otherwise to deal with the personal property of the estate. Oldham's Trustee v. Boston Ins. Co., 189 Ky. 844; George v. Baker, 3 Allen (Mass.) 326; Mutual Life Ins. Co. v. Sturges, 33 N. J. Eq. 328; Geyer v. Snyder, 140 N. Y. 394; Pearse v. National Lead Co., 162 N. Y. App. Div. 766; Fesmire v. Shannon, 143 Pa. 201. One of several trustees has not power alone to transfer or otherwise to deal with the trust property. Astbury v. Astbury, [1898] 2 Ch. 111; Attenborough v. Solomon, [1913] A. C. 76; Ham v. Ham, 58 N. H. 70; DeHaven v. Williams, 80 Pa. 480; Fesmire v. Shannon, 143 Pa. 201; Angell v. Moni, 45 R. I. 186.

If the executor who is also named as trustee sets aside a sum of money to be held in trust in accordance with the terms of the will and the fund diminishes in value, the deficiency cannot be supplied out of the residue of the estate. Hubbard v. Lloyd, 6 Cush. (Mass.) 522; Scott, Cases on Trusts, 1 ed., 119. Similarly, if shares of national bank stock are transferred by the executor to himself as trustee, the general assets of the estate are not liable for a subsequent assessment on the stock. Williams v. Cobb, 242 U. S. 307.

The remedies of the legatee against the executor are generally in the probate court, but those of the beneficiary of a trust against the trustee are in

MATTER OF McALPINE.

COURT OF APPEALS, NEW YORK. 1891.

126 N. Y. 285.

CROSS-APPEALS from judgment of the General Term of the Supreme Court in the fifth judicial department, entered upon an order made the first Tuesday of January, 1891, which modified, and affirmed as modified, a decree of the surrogate of the county of Monroe upon an accounting of the petitioners, as executors of the last will and testament of Henry S. Potter, deceased.

The opening clauses of the will of Henry S. Potter, are as follows:

"I give, devise and bequeath to my trustees hereinafter named, excepted as otherwise provided, all my real and personal estate of which I shall die seized or possessed, in trust, nevertheless, for the uses and purposes, that is to say:

"I direct my executors and trustees hereinafter named, or those that shall be such at my decease, to retain my estate entire and undivided until and except as hereinafter directed.

"*First.* Pay my funeral expenses and my just debts and all taxes legally assessed on my estate, and all necessary repairs and reasonable insurance."

The will then directed the payment of an annuity of $200 to a beneficiary named during her life, and the payment of one-sixth of the net annual income to each of six beneficiaries during his or her life, the annuities, however, to cease upon the death of the survivor of two persons named. Upon the decease of the surviving child of the testator, if all died before the survivor of said two persons named, or upon the death of such survivor, the executors were directed to close and distribute the estate as directed. Then followed this clause:

"*Twenty-first.* I do hereby give, devise and bequeath to my trustees hereinafter named, all and every part of my property and estate of whatever name, nature or description, and wheresoever situate, to have and to hold the same in trust for the uses and purposes in this my will expressed, with power to lease, sell, assign, transfer and convey the same, collect, invest and reinvest the proceeds thereof as they shall deem best for the interest of my estate, excepting only as otherwise herein provided."

---

equity. DeLadson *v.* Crawford, 93 Conn. 402; Scott, 119. In many states, however, the probate court is given jurisdiction over testamentary trusts and in some states over trusts created *inter vivos*.

Different rules as to the payment of taxes are frequently applicable to executors from those applicable to trustees. See *Re* Claremont, [1923] 2 K. B. 718; Cornwall *v.* Todd, 38 Conn. 443; State *v.* Beardsley, 77 Fla. 803, 29 Yale L. Jour. 467.

FINCH, J. The principal question which is presented by this appeal is whether the commissions to be allowed are to be governed by the doctrine of Johnson *v.* Lawrence, 95 N. Y. 154, or Laytin *v.* Davidson, 95 id. 263. Both cases agree in the rule that double commissions to the same persons, first in the character of executors and then in that of trustees, are to be awarded only when the will contemplates a several and separable action in each capacity, not at the same but different stages of the administration, and that they are not to be allowed where the will makes no such separation, but blends the two duties and commingles them without a severance. To the ordinary duties of an executor may be added the performance of a trust in such a manner that the two functions run on together. It is the duty of an executor as such to pay to a legatee the amount of the legacy in the manner and at the time provided by the testator, and it does not change that duty that the payment of the principal is postponed and the income made payable annually in the meantime. A trust duty may thus be imposed upon an executor which thereby becomes and is made a function of his office. A will must go further than that to admit of double commissions, and must clearly and definitely indicate an intention of the testator to end the executor's duty at some point of time, and require him thereupon to constitute and set up one or more several trusts, to be held and managed as such for the interest of the beneficiary. This will manifests no purpose of that character, for, while it creates a trust and speaks of the executors sometimes as trustees, there is no provision in it which requires or contemplates a holding of any part of the estate by trustees as distinguished from executors. At its very outset it makes the executors either wholly and continuously such, or wholly and continuously trustees, for in its first sentences it gives the entire estate in trust, and directs the " executors and trustees hereinafter named " to retain it undivided till the period of distribution, and meanwhile to pay funeral expenses, debts, accruing taxes, repairs, reasonable insurance, one fixed and definite annuity, and aliquot parts of the net accruing income until the final distribution. There is no provision requiring any share or trust fund to be severed from the body of the estate, or to be ascertained as a residue of principal to be kept invested for its specific income payable to a beneficiary, but all duties without separation, whether imposed by the law or by the will, run on together mingled and blended to the end. An examination of the cases in which double commissions have been allowed will show that they were exceptional in their nature and contained provisions distinctly and definitely pointing to a holding by trustees as such after the duties of the executors were completed and ended. This is not such a case, and double commissions were properly withheld.[1] . . .

---

[1] Double commissions were denied in Matter of Ziegler, 218 N. Y. 544. They were allowed in Hurlburt *v.* Durant, 88 N. Y. 121; Matter of Willets,

112 N. Y. 289. See Abbott, N. Y. Digest, Executors and Administrators, sec. 495(2).

For decisions in other states, see Bemmerly *v.* Woodard, 136 Cal. 326; Lamar *v.* Harris, 121 Ga. 285; Arnold *v.* Alden, 173 Ill. 229, 237; Dunne *v.* Cooke, 197 Ill. App. 422, 441; Estate of Gloyd, 93 Iowa 303; Albro *v.* Robinson, 93 Ky. 195, 199; Mitchell *v.* Holmes, 1 Md. Ch. 287; Sanderson *v.* Pearson, 45 Md. 483; Abell *v.* Brady, 79 Md. 94, 100; Judson *v.* Bennett, 233 Mo. 607, 647; Johnston *v.* Grice, 272 Mo. 423; Baker *v.* Johnston, 39 N. J. Eq. 493; Pitney *v.* Everson, 42 N. J. Eq. 361; Hibbler's Estate, 78 N. J. Eq. 217; Lyon *v.* Bird, 79 N. J. Eq. 157; Steelman's Estate, 87 N. J. Eq. 270; *Re* Larrabee, 98 N. J. Eq. 655; Parker *v.* Wright, 143 Atl. 870 (N. J. Ch., 1928); Riter's Estate, 260 Pa. 168; Von Storch's Estate, 88 Pa. Super. Ct. 43. *Cf. Ex parte* Witherspoon, 3 Rich. Eq. (S. C.) 13.

CHAPTER II.
THE CREATION OF A TRUST.

SECTION I.
The Intention to Create a Trust.

PALMER v. SCHRIBB.
CHANCERY. 1713.

2 Eq. Ca. Abr. 291, pl. 9.

J. S. devises the residue of his estate to his wife, and desires her to give all her estate at her death to his and her relations. *Quære*, If this does amount to a devise on a trust in the wife for all the estate which the husband gave her by his will. HARCOURT, C. thought these words too general to amount to a devise over of his estate after the death of the wife; nor can it be taken as a trust, because the words extend to all the estate which she shall be possessed of at the time of her death, which the husband has not any power over, and therefore it must be taken over as a recommendation, and not as a devise or trust. But if the testator had desired his wife by his will to give at her death all the estate which he had devised to her, to his and her relations, there the estate devised to her ought to go after her death to his and her relations, according to the statute of distributions.

Bill dismissed.[1]

HARDING v. GLYN.
CHANCERY. 1739.

1 Atk. 469.

NICHOLAS HARDING in 1701 made his will, and thereby gave "to Elizabeth, his wife, all his estate, leases, and interest in his house

[1] Anon., 2 Eq. Ca. Abr. 291, pl. 8; Eade v. Eade, 5 Madd. 118; Lechmere v. Lavie, 2 M. & K. 197; Hood v. Oglander, 34 Beav. 513; Parnall v. Parnall, 9 Ch. D. 96; *Re* Williams, [1897] 2 Ch. 12; Trustees of Hillsdale College v. Wood, 145 Mich. 257; Springs v. Springs, 182 N. C. 484; Hopkins v. Glunt, 111 Pa. 287, *accord*.

Although the testator cannot impose any trust upon other property than that bequeathed by him, yet he may attach to the bequest a condition that the legatee declare himself trustee of his own property or bequeath his own property to another. In *Re* Williams, *supra*, one judge found sufficient evidence of such an intent, but the majority of the court held that the testator did not intend to attach any condition to the bequest.

in Hatton Garden, and all the goods, furniture, and chattels therein at the time of his death, and also all his plate, linen, jewels, and other wearing-apparel, but did desire her at or before her death to give such leases, house, furniture, goods and chattels, plate and jewels, unto and amongst such of his own relations as she should think most deserving and approve of," and made his wife executrix, and died the 23d of January, 1736, without issue.

Elizabeth, his widow, made her will on the 12th of June, 1737, " and thereby gave all her estate, right, title, and interest to Henry Swindell in the house in Hatton Garden, which her husband had bequeathed to her in manner aforesaid; and after giving several legacies, bequeathed the residue of her personal estate to the defendant Glyn and two other persons, and made them executors," and soon after died, without having given at or before her death the goods in the said house, or without having disposed of any of her husband's jewels, to his relations.

The plaintiffs insisting that Elizabeth Harding had no property in the said furniture and jewels but for life, with a limited power of disposing of the same to her husband's relations, which she has not done, brought their bill in order that they might be distributed amongst his relations, according to the rule of distribution of intestates' effects.

MASTER OF THE ROLLS [VERNEY]. The first question is, If this is vested absolutely in the wife? And the second, If it is to be considered as undisposed of, after her death, who are entitled to it?

As to the first, it is clear the wife was intended to take only beneficially during her life; there are not technical words in a will, but the manifest intent of the testator is to take place, and the words " willing " or " desiring " have been frequently construed to amount to a trust, Eacles *et ux. v.* England *et ux.*, 2 Vern. 466; and the only doubt arises upon the persons who are to take after her.

Where the uncertainty is such that it is impossible for the court to determine what persons are meant, it is very strong for the court to construe it only as a recommendation to the first devisee, and make it absolute as to him; but here the word " relations " is a legal description, and this is a devise to such relations, and operates as a trust in the wife, by way of power of naming and apportioning, and her non-performance of the power shall not make the devise void, but the power shall devolve on the court; and though this is not to pass by virtue of the statute of distributions, yet that is a good rule for the court to go by. And therefore I think it ought to be divided among such of the relations of the testator Nicholas Harding, who were his next of kin at her death; and do order that so much of the said household goods in Hatton Garden, and other personal estate of the said testator Nicholas Harding, devised by his will to the said Elizabeth Harding, his wife, which she did not dispose of according to the power given her thereby, in case the same remains in specie, or the value thereof, be delivered to the next of kin of the said testator Nicholas Harding, to be divided equally amongst them, to take place from the time of the death of the said Elizabeth Harding.[1]

HARLAND v. TRIGG.

CHANCERY. 1782.

1 Bro. C. C. 142.

RICHARD HARLAND, being seised in fee of the manor of Sutton, in the county of York, and having four sons, Philip, John, Richard (the plaintiff), and Francis, by his will in 1747 devised the said manor (with other lands) to Philip, the eldest son, for life, with remainder to his first and other sons in tail male, remainder to John, the second son, for life, remainder to the plaintiff for life, remainder to Richard for life, with like remainders to their several first and other sons, and with further remainders over. Richard, the father, died in 1750; Philip entered, and, being himself also possessed of leasehold estates in Sutton, some for lives and others for years, by his will, made in the year 1764, gave his leasehold estate for lives to the trustees of his father's will, to the same uses to which the lands devised by the father's will were limited, so far as by law he could; and then followed this clause: "And all other my leasehold estates in the parish or township of Sutton I give to my brother John Harland, forever, hoping he will continue them in the family." Philip died in 1766. John entered on the estate; and died in 1772, having made his will and given these leasehold estates to his widow, whom he made executrix, and who since married the defendant Trigg. Richard, the third son, filed this bill, insisting the devise in Philip's will subjected these estates to the same uses as those declared by the father's will; that he was, therefore, entitled to the next estate in remainder, and praying that it might be so declared.

Mr. Attorney General, Mr. Madocks, Mr. Ainge, and *Mr. Spranger* contended that John had an estate only for life. . . .

LORD CHANCELLOR [THURLOW]. I have no doubt but a requisition made with a clear object will amount to a trust. In the case of the Duchess of Buckingham's will, the words were very gentle, but had a distinct object. But where the words are not clear as to their object, they cannot raise a trust. Where this testator had a leasehold estate, which he meant should go to the family, he has used apt words; therefore, where he has not used such words, he had a different intent.

Mr. Mansfield and *Mr. Lloyd,* for the defendant. . . .

[1] See Salusbury v. Denton, 3 K. & J. 529, *post;* 25 Harv. L. Rev. 26–28. For cases where the class is definite, *e.g.* the children of X, see Ames, 99–103; 25 Harv. L. Rev. 19–26.

LORD CHANCELLOR. I think every will ought to be construed according to the intent of the testator, where it can be collected. In order to make a title, the plaintiff states that the father had settled his estates in strict settlement, and insists that I shall understand this devise as giving the leasehold estates to the same uses, as nearly as their nature will admit. The testator gives other estates to trustees, subject to charges, to the uses in that settlement; he therefore understood how to make his estates liable to those uses, and intended something different here. The argument is, that there will be part of the will ineffectual, the words, "hoping that he will continue them in the family": the answer is, that the words are precatory, not imperative. Another argument made use of is, that, if this was furniture, the devise would carry it: but, if so, it would be on this ground, that he recollected that the house would pass and meant the furniture should remain attached to it under all its limitations. That case has peculiarities that do not occur here. It would be a great deal too much to tie this up as a strict settlement. I had a doubt whether the family could not claim some interest in the subject, but when I come to consider, I take the rule of law to be this: that two things must concur to constitute these devises, — the terms and the object. Hoping is in contradistinction to a direct devise; but whenever there are annexed to such words precise and direct objects, the law has collected the whole together, and held the words sufficient to raise a trust; but then the objects must be distinct; where there is a choice, it must be in the power of the devisee to dispose of it either way. If he had sold these leaseholds, the family could not have taken them from the vendee, or if he had given them to any one part of the family, the others could have no remedy. The will does not import a devise, as the words do not clearly demonstrate an object. I am therefore of opinion that the bill must be dismissed.[1]

[1] See *Re* Hill, [1923] 2 Ch. 259 (to testator's brothers and sisters "for the benefit of themselves and their respective families"; held, no trust). As to the meaning of "family," see 25 Harv. L. Rev. 26; Lewin, Trusts, 95.

Indefinite objects. In Stead *v.* Mellor, 5 Ch. D. 225, the testatrix bequeathed the residue of her property in trust for her two nieces, "my desire being that they shall distribute such residue as they think will be most agreeable to my wishes." It was held that the nieces took the residue beneficially. Jessel, M. R., said, "I am not aware of any case in which words so vague and so indefinite have been held to create a trust." For other cases where the object was indefinite and the words were held to be precatory merely, see Ames, 93n. For cases in which although the object was indefinite the words were held to be mandatory with the result that the devisee or legatee became a constructive trustee for the heirs or next of kin, see Ames, 94n.

In re HUMPHREY'S ESTATE.

HIGH COURT OF JUSTICE, CHANCERY DIVISION, IRELAND. 1915.

[1916] 1 I. R. 21.

MOTION.

John Edmund Longfield, of Kilcoleman, Enniskeane, Co. Cork, died on the 12th June, 1913, having made his will, dated the 1st March, 1912, in the following terms: — " I John Edmund Longfield, of Kilcoleman, Enniskeane, Co. Cork, do hereby make this my last will and testament. I revoke all former wills. All my property, real and personal of every kind, I leave to my wife, Elinor Mary Augusta, and I appoint her the sole executrix of this my last will and testament. I express the wish that she should leave by her will, or transfer during her life, as she shall think fit, my house and demesne of Kilcoleman to my son John Foster, with sufficient money for his and its maintenance, but not before he has reached the age of twenty-five years. The remainder of my property I wish to be left, or transferred, to my daughters, Elinor Frances Beatrice and Margaret Lilian, in such way as the said Elinor Mary Augusta shall see fit."

John Edmund Longfield died on the 12th June, 1913, and probate of his will was granted to his executrix, Elinor Mary Augusta Longfield.

The testator left issue, one son and three daughters, viz., John Foster Longfield, Elinor Frances Beatrice Longfield, and Margaret Lilian Longfield, who were living at the date of the execution of his will, and Frances Emily Lydia Longfield, who was born after the date of the will.

The property left by the testator included a fee-farm rent of £37 8s. 9d. per annum, payable out of the lands of East Ballyspillane, sold in the present matter, which rent was redeemed for the sum of £900. When the matter came before the examiner, he required that the questions arising out of the testator's will should be judicially determined. Accordingly, the present application was made to the Court by Mrs. Elinor Mary Augusta Longfield, asking for a declaration that, upon the true construction of the will, she was absolutely entitled to all assets, real and personal, of the said testator.

Ross, J. [His lordship having stated the facts and read the will, proceeded as follows: —]

The earlier words in the will confer an absolute interest on the wife. The question is whether the later clauses cut down this interest to an estate for life. In the latter event the daughter who was born after the date of the will is altogether excluded from participation. To the ordinary man of intelligence, uninstructed in the doctrine of what are called precatory trusts, it would, no doubt, cause astonishment that there could be any doubt about the true meaning of this will.

The testator in clear words gives all his property to his wife, and appoints her executrix. He then expresses a wish that she should dispose of it for the benefit of his children in a certain way. I am sure the testator himself would have been amazed if the mere expression of his wish for the guidance of his wife should have the effect of creating a legal obligation of the strictest character, tying up all the property and preventing her from providing for any children that might be born after the making of the will. After a devise and bequest in clear and explicit terms, if a trust is intended to be created one would expect that this would be done in terms equally clear and explicit. When we come to consider the innumerable decisions in which the Courts of equity have displayed their benevolent astuteness in imposing an obligatory meaning upon words merely expressive of desire, the mind is reduced to a condition of perplexity and confusion. Trusts have been held to be created by the following expressions: — " I desire him to give," " I advise him to settle," " It is my dying request," " It is my will and desire," " I recommend," " Well knowing," and such like. All these one would think impose at most a moral obligation. On the other hand, an expression of hope that the devisee would continue the estate in the family has been held to create no trust. I think it is quite impossible to reconcile the cases. However that may be, there is no doubt that the tide has turned and is running strong against precatory trusts.

In Lambe v. Eames, L. R. 6 Ch. 597, at p. 599, Lord Justice James said: — " In hearing case after case cited, I could not help feeling that the officious kindness of the Court of Chancery, in interposing trusts where in many cases the father of the family never meant to create trusts, must have been a very cruel kindness indeed." These words are approved of by Lopes L. J. in Hill v. Hill, [1897] 1 Q. B. 483, at p. 488, who further says: " It is inconceivable to me that a testator who really meant his hope, recommendation, confidence, or request to be imperative should not express his intention in a mandatory form. I agree with Mr. Farwell in his book on Powers, when he says at p. 480, ' It would not be a very strained inference to regard all such expressions as stating the motive that induced the absolute gift rather than as a fetter imposed upon it.' " He adds, " It is in every case a question of intention, and the whole document with the surrounding circumstances must be considered."

Lord Lindley says in In re Hamilton, [1895] 2 Ch. 370, at p. 373: — " You must take the will which you have to construe and see what it means, and if you come to the conclusion that no trust was intended, you say so, although previous judges have said the contrary on some wills more or less similar to the one which you have to construe."

Lord St. Leonards, in his work on the Law of Property, published in 1849, wrote as follows (p. 375): — " The law as to the operation of words of recommendation, confidence, request, or the like, attached to an absolute gift, has in late times varied from the earlier authorities. In nearly every recent case the gift has been held to be uncontrolled by the request or recommendation made or confidence expressed. This undoubtedly simplifies the law, and it is not an unwholesome rule that, if a testator really mean his recommendation to be imperative, he should express his intention in a mandatory form; but this conclusion was not arrived at without a considerable struggle."

In *In re* Diggles, 39 Ch. D. 253, the Court held that in considering whether on the whole will the testator's intention was to create a trust, regard may be had to any embarrassment and difficulty which would arise from a trust. Applying this to the case before me, surely the possibility that children might be born to the testator after making his will, for whom his wife could not provide, is such an embarrassment and difficulty.

In Wright *v.* Atkyns, Turn. & R. 143, which was much relied on in the contention in favour of a trust, it was laid down (at p. 157) that three things are required to create such a trust: — (1) the words must be imperative; (2) the subject must be certain; (3) the object must be certain. Assuming certainty in the subject and object indicated in this will, am I obliged to hold the words used imperative? I think not.

The outcome of the cases is simply this, that the words are to be interpreted in their ordinary sense, unless there is something in the terms of the will operating upon the property disposed of, from which a Court ought to infer that a trust is intended or a condition imposed. In this will there is not a trust, in language, from the beginning to the end of it, or anything in the will from which a trust can be legitimately inferred.

I therefore hold that Elinor Mary Augusta Longfield took the property absolutely uncontrolled by any legal obligation, and I make a declaration accordingly in respect of the £900 now in Court.[1]

[1] See the following cases exemplifying the modern rule: *Re* Williams, [1897] 2 Ch. 12; Hill *v.* Hill, [1897] 1 Q. B. 483; Comiskey *v.* Bowring-Hanbury, [1905] A. C. 84; *Re* Conolly, [1910] 1 Ch. 219; *Re* Atkinson, 80 L. J. Ch. 370; Est. of Browne, 175 Cal. 361; Loomis Inst. *v.* Healy, 98 Conn. 102; Aldrich *v.* Aldrich, 172 Mass. 101; McCurdy *v.* McCallum, 186 Mass. 464; Lemp *v.* Lemp, 264 Mo. 533; Clay *v.* Wood, 153 N. Y. 134; Tillman *v.* Ogren, 227 N. Y. 495, 228 N. Y. 559; Carter *v.* Strickland, 165 N. C. 69; Smith *v.* Bloomington Coal Co., 282 Pa. 248; Will of Jansen, 181 Wis. 83.

In the following cases it was thought that the testator intended to create a trust or charge. *Re* Burley, [1910] 1 Ch. 215; M'Cabe *v.* Campbell, [1918]

In re WEEKES' SETTLEMENT.

HIGH COURT OF JUSTICE, CHANCERY DIVISION. 1897.

[1897] 1 Ch. 289.

SUMMONS for payment out of court of a sum of Consols standing to the credit of ex parte the London, Brighton and South Coast Railway Company, the account of the persons interested in Brookside Farm under the settlement referred to in the summons.

By a settlement dated April 27, 1857, made on the marriage of Emily Mary Weekes with James Slade, certain real property to which Emily Mary Weekes was entitled, which included the remainder in fee of Brookside Farm expectant on the death of her mother, was settled to uses in favour of the intended wife for life, and upon her death as she should, whether covert or sole, by will appoint, and in default of appointment to the use of the person or persons who at the decease of E. M. Weekes would have been entitled thereto by descent in case she had died seised thereof by purchase intestate and a widow.

By a settlement of even date certain personal property therein described was settled in favour of James Slade and his wife during their lives and the life of the survivor, and after the decease of the survivor in trust for the issue of the marriage as the husband and wife should by deed jointly appoint, and in default as the survivor should by deed or will appoint, and in default of appointment for all the children who being a son or sons should attain twenty-one, or being a daughter or daughters should attain that age or marry, and if more than one in equal shares.

Pursuant to the powers given to them by their Acts the London, Brighton and South Coast Railway Company took certain parts of the Brookside Farm and paid the purchase-money into Court, and the Consols in court represented such purchase-money.

Emily Mary Slade died in May, 1885, having made her will, dated April 15, 1885, which so far as is material was in the following words: "I bequeath to my husband James Slade a life interest in all property real or personal which may come to me in accordance with the will of my late father Richard Weekes and also in the house which I took under the will of my late cousin George Weekes and I give to him power to dispose of all such property by

---

1 I. R. 429; Moseley *v.* Bolster, 201 Mass. 135; Temple *v.* Russell, 251 Mass. 231; Phillips *v.* Phillips, 112 N. Y. 197; Turrill *v.* Davenport, 173 N. Y. App. Div. 543; *Re* Dewey's Est., 45 Utah 98.

In New Jersey the courts still seem to cling to the older view. Deacon *v.* Cobson, 83 N. J. Eq. 122. See *Re* Hochbrunn's Est., 138 Wash. 415.

There is a full citation of authorities on precatory trusts in 49 A. L. R. 10. See also 37 L. R. A. (N. s.) 646; Ann. Cas. 1915D 418.

will amongst our children in accordance with the power granted to him as regards the other property which I have under my marriage settlements. I also bequeath unto him the said James Slade all my effects clothes jewellery and other articles to be at his entire will and disposal." The will contained no gift over in default of appointment.

James Slade died in February, 1893, intestate and without having exercised the power of disposition given him by the will of his wife, Emily Mary Slade.

There were fourteen children of the marriage, eight of whom survived their mother and were living.

The tenant for life having recently died, this was an application for payment out of the Consols in court in eighths on the ground that the will of Emily Mary Slade gave to James Slade a life interest in the Brookside Farm with a power to appoint among the children of the marriage, and that this power not having been exercised the children were entitled equally. The respondent, the eldest son, claimed the Consols as heir-at-law of Emily Mary Weekes.

ROMER, J. By the settlement of April 27, 1857, the property now represented by the Consols in court was settled on Emily Mary Slade for life with remainder as she should by will appoint, and with a gift over in default of appointment.

By her will, dated April 15, 1885, Mrs. Slade bequeathed the property in the following terms: [His Lordship read the will as above set out.]

The husband did not exercise the power of appointment, and the question is whether the children take in default of appointment.

Now, apart from the authorities, I should gather from the terms of the will that it was a mere power that was conferred on the husband, and not one coupled with a trust that he was bound to exercise. I see no words in the will to justify me in holding that the testatrix intended that the children should take if her husband did not execute the power.

This is not a case of a gift to the children with power to the husband to select, or to such of the children as the husband should select by exercising the power.

If in this case the testatrix really intended to give a life interest to her husband and a mere power to appoint if he chose, and intended if he did not think fit to appoint that the property should go as in default of appointment according to the settlement, why should she be bound to say more than she has said in this will?

I come to the conclusion on the words of this will that the testatrix only intended to give a life interest and a power to her husband — certainly she has not said more than that.

Am I then bound by the authorities to hold otherwise? I think I am not. The authorities do not shew, in my opinion, that there is a hard and fast rule that a gift to A for life with a power to A to appoint among a class and nothing more must, if there is no gift over in the will, be held a gift by implication to the class in default of the power being exercised. In my opinion the cases shew (though there may be found here and there certain remarks of a few learned judges which, if not interpreted by the facts of the particular case before them, might seem to have a more extended operation) that you must find in the will an indication that the testatrix did intend the class or some of the class to take — intended in fact that the power should be regarded in the nature of a trust — only a power of selection being given, as, for example, a gift to A for life with a gift over to such of a class as A shall appoint.

I will now examine the authorities which have been cited, and shew that this is so, though I may remark that the case before me is peculiar in this, that there is a gift over in default of appointment by the husband by force of the settlement, so that this will need not in any case come within the general proposition above stated. . . .

I have now shewn that none of the cases relied on by the applicants establish the general proposition; and I hold that in this case there was no gift by implication to the children of Emily Mary Slade in default of appointment by her husband.[1]

MATTER OF BROWN, 252 N. Y. 366 (1930): A father signed instruments certifying that certain land was the property of his son, that he had given it to his son, that part of the land stood in the name of a certain corporation, and that it was to be conveyed to the son at any time the son might request. The corporation was a

---

[1] *Re* Combe, [1925] Ch. 210, 35 Yale L. Jour. 505; *Re* Hall, [1899] 1 I. R. 308, *accord*.

If the donee of a power to appoint among a class is by the will directed and not merely authorized to appoint and he fails to make an appointment, a constructive trust arises in favor of the members of the class, unless there was an express or implied gift over upon default of appointment. Wetmore *v.* Henry, 259 Ill. 80; Gorin *v.* Gordon, 38 Miss. 205; Millikin *v.* Welliver, 37 Oh. St. 460; Hazard *v.* Bacon, 42 R. I. 415; Cathey *v.* Cathey, 9 Humph. (Tenn.) 470; Jones *v.* Roberts, 84 Wis. 465. See also Waterman *v.* N. Y. Life Ins. & Trust Co., 204 N. Y. App. Div. 12 (statutory).

Although the donee is not directed to exercise the power, there may be circumstances from which the court will imply a gift to the class upon the failure to exercise the power. In such a case, the members of the class will take equally. McGaughey's Adm'r *v.* Henry, 15 B. Mon. (Ky.) 383; Loosing *v.* Loosing, 85 Neb. 66; Withers *v.* Yeadon, 1 Rich. Eq. (S. C.) 324; Rogers *v.* Rogers, 2 Head (Tenn.) 660; Milhollen's Adm'r *v.* Rice, 13 W. Va. 510. See Gray, Powers in Trust and Gifts Implied in Default of Appointment, 25 Harv. L. Rev. 1; Simes, Powers in Trust and Termination of Powers by the Donee, 37 Yale L. Jour. 63, 211; Rood, Unexercised Powers, 15 Mich. L. Rev. 386, 399; Kales, Estates, secs. 634–7; Underhill, Trusts, art. 7; 152 Law Times 343.

dummy wholly owned and controlled by the father and used by him in his real estate transactions. The father later executed a deed transferring the rest of the land to the corporation, and thereafter died. It was held that a valid trust was created in favor of the son. It was not clearly proved that the instruments were delivered by the father to the son, but this was held to be immaterial. CRANE, J., said (p. 275):

" But while there is evidence to support the inference that these written trust declarations were delivered to Elliott [the son], yet delivery is not necessary to constitute a valid trust. While a transfer of the property to a trustee for the purposes of the settlement may be the surest way to create a trust, yet the same result will be accomplished if the owner declare that he himself holds the property in trust for the person designated, and this trust may be created either in writing or, if relating to personal property, by parol. The declaration need not be made to the beneficiary, nor the writing given to him; in fact, his ignorance of the trust is immaterial. There must be proof of a *declaration of trust* in writing to pass real property (Real Prop. Law, § 242; Cons. Laws, ch. 50), but the declaration varies with the circumstances of each case; it may be contained in a letter (Percy v. Huyck, 252 N. Y. 168; McKenna v. Meehan, 248 N. Y. 206), or as here by formal witnessed statement. A declaration implies an announcement of an act performed, not a mere intention, and in most instances to another party. However, a writing formally creating a trust, kept by the donor without delivery to any one, under such circumstances and conditions as to show that a trust was declared, created and intended, will be given effect as such by the courts. (Martin v. Funk, 75 N. Y. 134.) " [1]

[1] It is well settled that no particular form of words is necessary for the creation of a trust *inter vivos,* whether the settlor declares himself trustee or transfers the property to another person as trustee. It is sufficient if his intention to create a trust appears. McCaffrey v. North Adams Sav. Bank, 244 Mass. 396. See Dec. Dig., Trusts, secs. 24–29.

It is not essential that his intention should be communicated to the beneficiary nor to anyone. Stoehr v. Miller, 296 Fed. 414; Janes v. Falk, 50 N. J. Eq. 468, 472; Irving Bank-Columbia Trust Co. v. Rowe, 213 N. Y. App. Div. 281; Smith's Estate, 144 Pa. 428; Estabrook's Estate, 197 Pa. 153. See 33 Yale L. Jour. 789. In Massachusetts, however, it has been held that even though there is other evidence of an intention by the settlor to declare himself trustee, no trust is created unless he communicates his intention to the beneficiary. Clark v. Clark, 108 Mass. 522; Boynton v. Gale, 194 Mass. 320.

The absence of such communication may be strong evidence, however, against the intention to create a trust. *Re* Cozens, [1913] 2 Ch. 478, 482; Ambrosius v. Ambrosius, 239 Fed. 474.

As to the distinction between a declaration of trust and a gift, see section II, and particularly Richards v. Delbridge, L. R. 18 Eq. 11, *post*.

FOSTER v. ELSLEY.

HIGH COURT OF JUSTICE, CHANCERY DIVISION. 1881.

19 Ch. D. 518.

GEORGE MAY UPFIELD, by his will, dated the 31st of October, 1879, after appointing the defendants his executors and trustees, devised and bequeathed to them all his real and personal estate upon the trusts therein set forth, and the will contained the following clause: " And I declare that my solicitor, William Edward Foster " (the plaintiff), " shall be the solicitor to my estate and to my said trustees in the management and carrying out the provisions of this my will."

The testator died on the 3d of November, 1879, and his will was subsequently proved by the defendants, who, in pursuance of the directions contained in the will, employed the plaintiff as their solicitor in the management of the trust estate up to the 13th of October, 1881, when he received a letter from certain solicitors at Oldham stating that they were instructed by the defendants to ask for the immediate delivery of all deeds, documents, and securities in his possession, relating to the estate of the testator, and also an account of costs due to the plaintiff, and also for an appointment for them to attend at the plaintiff's office and pay such costs, and receive the documents.

This was a motion by the plaintiff to restrain the defendants from employing any person other than the plaintiff as solicitor to the estate of the testator, or in any business relating to the management or carrying out of the provisions of his will.

CHITTY, J. The testator in this case has inserted a clause in his will that " my solicitor, W. E. Foster, shall be the solicitor to my estate and to my said trustees in the management and carrying out the provisions of this my will," and this motion is founded on the proposition that this clause imposes on his trustees the duty of employing this gentleman (the plaintiff) as their solicitor. In Finden v. Stephens, to which I have been referred, the direction was that a certain person should be employed as agent and manager of the testator's estates whenever his trustees should have occasion for the services of a person in that capacity, and it was held that the direction did not create a trust which such person could enforce. The case of Shaw v. Lawless, in the House of Lords, had previously decided the question. I am told that no case is to be found in the books like the one before me where a testator has appointed a particular person as solicitor to his estate, but in analogy to the cases to which I have referred I decide that the direction in this will imposes no trust or duty on the trustees to continue the plaintiff as their solicitor, and that being my decision I refuse this motion with costs.[1]

Section II.
Consideration.

DOCTOR AND STUDENT (1523).
Dialogue II, Chapter 22.

Doctor. May not a use be assigned to a stranger, as well as to be reserved to the feoffor, if the feoffor so appointed it upon his feoffment?

Student. Yes, as well, and in like wise to the feoffee, and that upon a free gift, without any bargain or recompence, if the feoffor so will.[2]

Doct. What if no feoffment be made, but that a man grant to his feoffee, that from henceforth he shall stand seised to his own use? Is not that use changed, though there be no recompence?

Stud. I think yes, for there was an use in esse before the gift, which he might as lawfully give away, as he might the land if he had it in possession.[3]

---

[1] Shaw *v.* Lawless, 5 Cl. & F. 129 (agent to collect rents); Finden *v.* Stephens, 2 Phil. 142 (manager of estate); *Re* Ogier, 101 Cal. 381 (attorney); Colonial Trust Co. *v.* Brown, 105 Conn. 261 (office manager and janitor); Jewell *v.* Barnes' Adm'r, 110 Ky. 329 (business employee); Matter of Caldwell, 188 N. Y. 115, 120 (attorney); *Re* Wallach, 164 N. Y. App. Div. 600, aff'd 215 N. Y. 622 (attorney); *Re* Thistlethwaite, 104 N. Y. Supp. 264 (attorney); Hughes *v.* Hiscox, 110 N. Y. Misc. 141 (business employee); *Re* Pickett's Will, 49 Ore. 127 (attorney); *Re* Pittock, 102 Ore. 159 (manager and editor of newspaper); Young *v.* Alexander, 84 Tenn. 108 (attorney), *accord.* See Ramsdell *v.* O'Connell, 168 N. E. 793 (Mass., 1929) (business employee).

Williams *v.* Corbet, 8 Sim. 349 (auditor of accounts); Hibbert *v.* Hibbert, 3 Meriv. 681 (receiver of property); Consett *v.* Bell, 1 Y. & C. Ch. 569 (receiver of property); Rivet *v.* Battistella, 167 La. 766, 43 Harv. L. Rev. 148 (attorney); Hughes *v.* Hiscox, 105 N. Y. Misc. 21 (business employee), *contra.*

See Scott, Testamentary Directions to Employ, 41 Harv. L. Rev. 709.

[2] "When the estate was by legal conveyance transferred to a person to uses, equity made no scruple in enforcing the trustee to observe the uses. The estate being actually divested out of the owner, it was not necessary to exercise the power of the court over him, and as the feoffee, &c. was a mere trustee, he was considered bound under all circumstances to observe the will of his donor, although the uses were unsupported by any consideration. Therefore a feoffment to A to the use of B, a mere friend of the feoffor's, who paid no consideration whatever for the estate, was binding, and A was compellable to permit B to receive the profits." Gilbert, Uses, Introd. xlv.

[3] "I say there is no doubt but that if I sell you my use, the use is changed from my person to you: so I understand that if I say to you, 'I give you my

Doct. And what if a man being seised of land in fee, grant to another of his mere motion without bargain or recompence, that he from thenceforth shall be seised to the use of the other; is not that grant good?

Stud. I suppose that it is not good; for, as I take the law, a man cannot commence an use but by livery of seisin, or upon a bargain, as [or?] some other recompence.[1]

ANONYMOUS.

———. 1545.

Bro. Abr., Feoff. al Uses, pl. 54, March's Transl., 95.

HALES, J. A man cannot change a use by a covenant which is executed before, as to covenant to bee seised to the use of W. S. because that W. S. is his cosin; or because that W. S. before gave to him twenty pound, except the twenty pound was given to have the same land. But otherwise of a consideration, present or future, for the same purpose, as for one hundred pounds paid for the land *tempore conventionis,* or to bee paid at a future day, or for to marry his daughter, or the like.

NOWELL *v.* HUDSTON.

———. 1595.

2 Roll. Abr. Uses, 790, pl. 3.

IF ONE bargains and sells to J. S. to the use of J. S. and his heirs, without mention of any consideration, particular or general, and without such general words as by divers good considerations, still a consideration may be averred.

BARKER *v.* KEATE.

COMMON PLEAS. 1677.

2 Vent. 35.[2]

IN AN ejectment upon a special verdict the sole point was, whether a lease for a year, upon no other consideration than re-

---

use in certain lands,' you have the use by such words; for the use does not pass as the land does; for land cannot pass except by livery, but a use passes by bare words." — *Per* York, Y. B. 27 H. VIII. fol. 8, pl. 22.

[1] "*Cestui que use* may grant his use without consideration, as he may his horse or other chattel; but he cannot raise a use without good consideration. And this consideration must bee some cause or occasion meritorious, amounting to a mutuall recompence in deed or in law." Finch, Law (ed. 1636), 34.

[2] 1 Freem. K. B. 249, 1 Mod. 262, 2 Mod. 249. s. c.

serving a pepper-corn, if it be demanded, shall work as a bargain and sale, and so to make the lessee capable of a release?

And it was resolved that it should, and that the reservation made a sufficient consideration to raise an use, as by bargain and sale. *Vide* 10 Co. in the case of Sutton's Hospital.

GILBERT, USES, 98, 96. — If a man, in consideration of so much money, to be paid at a day to come, bargains and sells, the use passes presently, and after the day the party has an action for the money; for 'tis a sale, be the money paid presently or hereafter.

If there be a consideration of money expressed in the deed, no averment or evidence can be admitted against it; for the affirmative is proved by the deed, and 'tis impossible in law or equity the negative should ever be proved.[1]

SHARINGTON *v.* STROTTON.

QUEEN'S BENCH. 1565.

Plowd. 298.

TRESPASS *quare clausum fregit*. The defendants justified as servants of Edward and Agnes Baynton, whose title was founded upon an indenture between Edward and his brother Andrew Baynton, whereby Andrew, being seised of the close in question, by an indenture reciting his intent that the land might continue and remain to such of the blood and name of Baynton as in the indenture should be named, for the said cause, and for the good will, brotherly love, and favor which he bore to Edward his brother and his other brothers named, covenanted and granted that he and his heirs should stand seised thereof to the use of himself for life, and after his death to the use of Edward and Agnes his wife for their lives, with divers remainders over. Andrew died. Edward and Agnes claimed as legal tenants for life under the indenture and the Statute of Uses. The plaintiffs demurred upon the defendant's plea.

The case was argued at Michaelmas Term, 1565 [2] . . .

And after these arguments the court took time to deliberate until Hilary Term, and from thence until Easter Term, and from thence until this present Trinity Term, in the eighth year of the reign of the present Queen, and the defendants now prayed judgment. And

---

[1] See Fisher *v.* Smith, Moore 569; Wilkes *v.* Leuson, Dy. 169 *a;* Jackson *v.* Alexander, 3 Johns. (N. Y.) 484 ("for value received"); Fuller *v.* Missroon, 35 S. C. 314.

[2] This short statement of the case is taken from Ames, 109, and is substituted for the very lengthy statement in the report.

CORBET, Justice, said, that he and all his companions had resolved that judgment should be given against the plaintiffs. For it seemed to them that the considerations of the continuance of the land in the name and blood, and of brotherly love, were sufficient to raise the uses limited. But, he said, as my Lord Chief Justice is not now present, you must move it again when he is present, and you shall have judgment. And afterwards, at another day, CATLINE, Chief Justice, being present, the apprentice prayed judgment. And CATLINE and the court were agreed that judgment should be entered against the plaintiffs, and he ordered Haywood, the Prothonotary, to enter it. And the apprentice said, May it please your lordship to shew us, for our learning, the causes of your judgment. And CATLINE said, It seems to us that the affection of the said Andrew for the provision of the heirs males which he should beget, and his desire that the land should continue in the blood and name of Baynton, and the brotherly love which he bore to his brothers, are sufficient considerations to raise the uses in the land. And where you said in your argument *Naturae vis maxima*, I say *Natura bis maxima*, and it is the greatest consideration that can be to raise a use. But as to the other consideration moved in the argument, viz. of the marriage had between Edward Baynton and Agnes, the record does not prove this, nor is it so averred, and it shall not be so intended, and therefore I don't regard it, but the other causes and considerations are effectual, and those which moved us to our judgment. . . .

BACON, READING ON THE STATUTE OF USES, 13, 14. — I would have one case shewed by men learned in the law where there is a deed and yet there needs a consideration. As for parole, the law adjudgeth it too light to give action without consideration; but a deed ever in law imports a consideration, because of the deliberation and ceremony in the confection of it; and therefore in 8 Reginae (Sharington *v.* Strotton, Plowd. 298, 309) it is solemnly argued that a deed should raise an use without any other consideration. . . . And yet they say that an use is but a nimble and light thing; and now contrariwise, it seemeth to be weightier than anything else; for you cannot weigh it up to raise it, neither by deed nor deed inrolled, without the weight of a consideration. But you shall never find a reason of this to the world's end in the law, but it is a reason of Chancery and it is this: that no court of conscience will enforce *donum gratuitum*, tho' the intent appear never so clearly, where it is not executed or sufficiently passed by law; but if money had been paid, and so a person damnified, or that it was for the establishment of his house, then it is a good matter in the Chancery.

AMES, THE HISTORY OF ASSUMPSIT.[1] — Not only was the consideration of the common-law action of assumpsit not borrowed from equity, but on the contrary, the consideration which gave validity to parol uses by bargain and agreement was borrowed from the common law. The bargain and sale of a use, as well as the agreement to stand seised, were not executory contracts but conveyances. No action at law could ever be brought against a bargainor or covenantor. Sharington v. Strotton, Plow. 298, 308; Buckley v. Simonds, Winch, 35–37, 59, 61; Hore v. Dix, 1 Sid. 25, 27; Pybus v. Mitford, 2 Lev. 75, 77. The absolute owner of land was conceived of as having in himself two distinct things, the seisin and the use. As he might make livery of seisin and retain the use, so he was permitted, at last, to grant away the use and keep the seisin. The grant of the use was furthermore assimilated to the grant of a chattel or money. A *quid pro quo*, or a deed, being essential to the transfer of a chattel or the grant of a debt, it was required also in the grant of a use. Equity might conceivably have enforced uses wherever the grant was by deed. But the chancellors declined to carry the innovation so far as this. They enforced only those gratuitous covenants which tended to "the establishment of the house" of the covenantor; in other words, covenants made in consideration of blood or marriage.

ANONYMOUS.

2 Roll. Abr. Uses, 784 (I), pl. 5, 6, 7.

IF a man in consideration that B. will marry his daughter covenants to stand seised to the use of B. and his daughter, remainder to C., this is a void remainder to C., for he is a stranger to the consideration.

In consideration of certain money given by B. a man may covenant to stand seised to the use of A. for life, remainder to C. in fee; for here it is apparent that the money was given for both estates; and although A. and C. are strangers to the giving of the money, still they are sufficiently privy since it was given for them.

So, in consideration of certain moneys given by B., a man may covenant to stand seised to the use of B. for life, remainder to C. in fee, or with divers mesne remainders, for the money was given for all the estates. Cit. Plow. 307b.[2]

[1] 2 Harv. L. Rev. 18, 19; Ames, Lect. Leg. Hist., 148. See also 21 Harv. L. Rev. 266; Ames, Lect. Leg. Hist. 241.

[2] As to the character of the relationship necessary and sufficient to support a covenant to stand seised, see Scott, Cases on Trusts, 1 ed., 142.

PYE,
DUBOST, } Ex Parte.

Chancery. 1811.

18 Ves. 140.

WILLIAM MOWBRAY, by his will dated the 10th of April, 1806, giving his wife the residue of his property after payment of his debts, except the sums after mentioned, among other legacies, gave as follows: " I give and bequeath the sum of 4,000*l*. sterling to Louisa Hortensia Garos, daughter of John Louis Garos, formerly of Berwick Street, Westminster; the like sum of 4,000*l*. to Emily Garos, her sister, and 4,000*l*. to Julia Garos, her other sister; and in case of the death of one of the three, I desire that the legacy may be divided equally betwixt the two surviving sisters; and in case of the death of two of them, I desire the whole 12,000*l*. may be paid to the surviving sister."

The testator also gave to John Louis Garos 600*l*.; and " to Marie Genevieve Garos, his wife, the sum of 2,500*l*. sterling for her own use, and over which her husband is not to have any power: he having lived abroad for many years, and she in this country, and no correspondence having passed between them during that time. Her own receipt shall be a sufficient authority to my executors for paying her the above legacy."

The testator died on the 8th of June, 1809. His widow became a lunatic; the petitioner, Pye, was the committee under the commission, and, upon her death, took out administration to her, and administration *de bonis non* to the testator.

The Master's report stated . . . that, by a letter written by the testator to Christopher Dubost, in Paris, on the 25th of November, 1807, the testator authorized him to purchase in France an annuity of 100*l*. for the benefit of the said Marie Genevieve Garos for her life, and to draw on him for 1,500*l*. on account of such purchase; and under that authority Dubost purchased an annuity of that value; but that, as she was married at the time, and also deranged, the annuity was purchased in the name of the testator; and the testator sent to Dubost, by his desire, a power of attorney, authorizing him to transfer to Marie Genevieve Garos the said annuity, dated the 10th of June, 1808.

The report further found, upon the affidavit of Dubost and the copy of the deed, that the first intimation he received of the death of the testator, who died in June, 1809, was in November, 1809; and that, in ignorance of such death, Dubost, on the 21st of October, 1809, exercised the power vested in him, by executing to Marie Genevieve Garos, her late husband being then dead, and she of sound mind, a deed of gift of the said annuity; and the

Master found that, by the law of France, if an attorney be ignorant of the death of the party who has given the power of attorney, whatever he has done while ignorant of such death is valid. The Master, therefore, stated his opinion that the annuity was no part of the personal estate of William Mowbray.

The first petition prayed that so much of the report as certifies the French annuity to be no part of the testator's personal estate may be set aside; and that it may be declared that the said annuity is part of his personal estate. . . .

Sir Arthur Piggott, Mr. *Richards,* Mr. *Wingfield,* Mr. *Horne,* and Mr. *Wear,* for different parties, in support of the first petition. The French annuity being purchased in the testator's name, and no third person interposed as a trustee, the interest could not be transferred from him without certain acts, which were not done at the time of his death. It was therefore competent to him, during his life, to change his purpose, and to make some other provision for this lady by funds in this country; conceiving, perhaps, that she might return here. The authority given to purchase this annuity could not have been enforced against him during his life by a person claiming as a volunteer; nor can it be established against his estate after his death, the act which would have given the benefit of it against the personal representative not having been completed. Cotton *v.* Missing, 1 Madd. 176. See 2 Ves. Jr. 120, note. Where a question is to be decided by a foreign law, the first step is an inquiry by the Master to ascertain what is the law of that country. . . .

Sir Samuel Romilly and *Mr. Bell, contra.* . . .

THE LORD CHANCELLOR [ELDON]. . . . The other question involves not only the construction of the French law, and the point whether that has been sufficiently investigated, but further, whether the power of attorney amounts here to a declaration of trust. It is clear that this court will not assist a volunteer; yet, if the act is completed, though voluntary the court will act upon it. It has been decided that, upon an agreement to transfer stock, this court will not interpose; but if the party had declared himself to be the trustee of that stock, it becomes the property of the *cestui que trust* without more; and the court will act upon it.

June 13th. THE LORD CHANCELLOR. These petitions call for the decision of points of more importance and difficulty than I should wish to decide in this way, if the case was not pressed upon the court. With regard to the French annuity, the Master has stated his opinion as to the French law, perhaps without sufficient authority, or sufficient inquiry into the effect of it, as applicable to the precise circumstances of this case; but it is not necessary to pursue that, as upon the documents before me it does appear that, though in one sense this may be represented as the testator's personal estate, yet he has committed to writing what seems to me a sufficient declaration that he held this part of the estate in trust for the annuitant.[1] . . .

Under this judgment, the order was pronounced dismissing the first petition. . . .

SMITHWICK v. BANK OF CORNING.

Supreme Court, Arkansas. 1910.

95 Ark. 463.

Battle, J. On the 27th day of January, 1901, J. J. Smithwick departed this life, intestate, leaving C. A. Smithwick, his widow, and W. R. Smithwick his only heir. At the time of his death he was the owner of considerable real estate, and two thousand dollars in cash and notes, and about forty head of cattle. After his death the widow and heir by a written contract divided the estate of the deceased between themselves. In the division some money was set apart to the widow. She deposited it in a bank to her credit. She often referred to it as W. R. Smithwick's money, but never relinquished control over it, and always controlled it, collecting interest on it.

Mrs. Smithwick died on the 16th day of July, 1908, leaving a last will and testament. She left nothing to W. R. Smithwick. G. B. Oliver became administrator of her estate. W. R. Smithwick brought a suit against the bank, claiming the money deposited in the bank as held in trust for him. Oliver, as administrator, was made a defendant.

The court, after hearing the evidence, dismissed the complaint for want of equity; and plaintiff appealed.

The money received by the widow in the division of the estate of her husband was her absolute property. Her frequent declara-

---

[1] In Forrest v. Forrest, 34 L. J. Ch. 428, Stuart, V. C., remarked (p. 432): "In some cases this court has gone extremely far, and particularly in that of *Ex parte* Pye, *Ex parte* Dubost, where Lord Eldon went extraordinarily far certainly, to hold a gift valid which was very imperfect. But Lord Eldon found his way, with that extraordinary power which he possessed, to satisfy his mind that a power of attorney by the donor to receive the dividends could be construed to amount to a declaration of trust."

The validity of a gratuitous declaration of trust is now generally admitted, Smith's Est., 144 Pa. 428; Ames, 125n.; Lewin, Trusts, 71; Perry, Trusts, sec. 96; Pomeroy, Eq. Juris., sec. 996; 14 Cal. L. Rev. 188.

In the following cases a gratuitous declaration of trust of *land* was upheld: Steele v. Waller, 28 Beav. 466 (copyhold); Lynch v. Rooney, 112 Cal. 279 (decided under a statute); Schumacher v. Dolan, 154 Iowa 207; Morgan v. Hayward, 115 Miss. 354; Neal v. Bryant, 291 Mo. 81; Estate of Brown, 252 N. Y. 366, *ante*. But see Pittman v. Pittman, 107 N. C. 159, *contra*. *Cf.* Rood, The Statute of Uses and the Modern Deed, 4 Mich. L. Rev. 109, 121; Parks, Declarations of Trusts and the Statute of Uses, 23 Law Ser. Mo. Bull. 3.

tions that it was the appellant's money did not convert it into a trust fund. They manifested an intention to give the same to appellant at some time. But they were not based on any consideration, and were not binding on her. Intention without acts is of no effect.

Decree affirmed.[1]

MORGAN *v.* MALLESON.

CHANCERY. 1870.

L. R. 10 Eq. 475.

THE following memorandum was given by John Saunders, the testator in the cause, to his medical attendant, Dr. Morris: —

"I hereby give and make over to Dr. Morris an India bond, No. D., 506, value 1,000*l.*, as some token for all his very kind attention to me during illness.

"Witness my hand, this 1st day of August, 1868,
(Signed) "JOHN SAUNDERS."

The signature was attested by two witnesses, and the memorandum was handed over to Dr. Morris, but the bond, which was transferable by delivery, remained in the possession of Saunders. There was no consideration for it.

Saunders died more than a year afterwards, having by his will bequeathed the residue of his personal estate to charities. A suit was instituted for the administration of his estate, and a summons was taken out by the Attorney General on behalf of absent charities for the direction of the court on the question whether this memorandum was or was not a valid declaration of trust in favor of Dr. Morris.

LORD ROMILLY, M. R. I am of opinion that the paper-writing signed by Saunders is equivalent to a declaration of trust in favor

---

[1] In the following cases it was held that a promise or mere expression of intention to make a gift or to create a trust did not amount to a declaration of trust. Bayley *v.* Boulcott, 4 Russ. 345; Dipple *v.* Corles, 11 Hare 183; Jones *v.* Lock, L. R. 1 Ch. App. 25; Estate of Webb, 49 Cal. 541; Lanterman *v.* Abernathy, 47 Ill. 437; Hamilton *v.* Hall's Estate, 111 Mich. 291; Farmers' Loan & Trust Co. *v.* Winthrop, 238 N. Y. 477; Foley *v.* Peters, 5 Oh. Dec. (Reprint) 517; Allen *v.* Hendrick, 104 Ore. 202, 223; Wolff's Appeal, 123 Pa. 438, *accord. Cf.* Sell *v.* West, 125 Mo. 621. See Perry, Trusts, sec. 97; 12 L. R. A. (N. S.) 547.

In Farmers' Loan & Trust Co. *v.* Winthrop, 238 N. Y. 477, the beneficiary of a trust gave a power of attorney to the trustee under another trust previously created by her authorizing him to receive certain securities from the trustee of the estate of which she was beneficiary, intending that he should hold the securities upon the trust theretofore created by her. She died, however, before the securities were received. The court held that the beneficiary had not made an effective assignment of her interest since there was no expression of a purpose to effectuate a present gift.

of Dr. Morris. If he had said, " I undertake to hold the bond for you," or if he had said, " I hereby give and make over the bond in the hands of A.," that would have been a declaration of trust, though there had been no delivery. This amounts to the same thing; and Dr. Morris is entitled to the bond, and to all interest accrued due thereon.[1]

RICHARDS v. DELBRIDGE.

CHANCERY. 1874.

L. R. 18 Eq. 11.

DEMURRER. The bill, filed by Edward Bennetto Richards, an infant, by his next friend, stated that John Delbridge, deceased, was possessed of a mill, with the plant, machinery, and stock in trade thereto belonging, in which he carried on the business of a bone manure merchant, and which was held under a lease dated the 24th of June, 1863.

That on the 7th of March, 1873, John Delbridge indorsed upon the lease and signed the following memorandum: —

" 7th March, 1873. This deed and all thereto belonging I give to Edward Bennetto Richards from this time forth, with all the stock in trade.

" JOHN DELBRIDGE."

That the plaintiff was the person named in the memorandum, and the grandson of John Delbridge, and had then for some time assisted him in the business; that John Delbridge, shortly after signing the memorandum, delivered the lease on his behalf to Elizabeth Ann Richards, the plaintiff's mother, who was still in possession thereof.

That John Delbridge died in April, 1873, having executed several testamentary instruments which did not refer specifically to the

---

[1] Richardson v. Richardson, L. R. 3 Eq. 686, *accord*.

A gift of a chattel is imperfect if there is neither delivery of the chattel nor of a deed of gift. Irons v. Smallpiece, 2 B. & A. 551; Cochrane v. Moore, 25 Q. B. D. 57. A deed of gift of a chattel vests the title in the donee without delivery. Ames, 130n. See also Y. B. 42 Ed. III, f. 1 pl. 7; Foster v. Mitchell, 15 Ala. 571; Hope v. Hutchins, 9 Gill & J. (Md.) 77; McWillie v. Van Vachter, 35 Miss. 428; Gordon v. Wilson, 4 Jones (N. C.) 64; McEwen v. Troost, 1 Sneed (Tenn.) 186. And see Warren, Cas. Prop., 198–214; Bigelow, Cas. Pers. Prop., 260–263; Stone, Delivery in Gifts of Personal Property, 20 Col. L. Rev. 196; Pound, Juristic Science and Law, 31 Harv. L. Rev. 1047, 1053–57; Graves, Gifts of Personalty, 1 Va. L. Reg. 871, Roberts, Necessity of Delivery in Making Gifts, 32 W. Va. L. Quar. 313; Mechem, Requirement of Delivery in Gifts of Chattels and of Choses in Action Evidenced by Commercial Instruments, 21 Ill. L. Rev. 341, 457, 568.

As to the effect of the delivery of a written but unsealed instrument of gift, see Matter of Cohn, 187 N. Y. App. Div. 392; Hawkins v. Union Trust Co., 187 N. Y. App. Div. 472; 20 Col. L. Rev. 196.

said mill and premises, but gave his furniture and effects, after his wife's death, to be divided among his family.

That the testator's widow, Elizabeth Richards, took out administration to his estate, with the testamentary papers annexed.

The bill, which was filed against the defendants, Elizabeth Delbridge, Elizabeth Ann Richards, and the testator's two sons, who claimed under the said testamentary instruments, prayed a declaration that the indorsement upon the lease by John Delbridge and the delivery of the lease to Elizabeth Ann Richards created a valid trust in favor of the plaintiff of the lease [1] and of the estate and interest of John Delbridge in the property therein comprised, and in the good will of the business carried on there, and in the implements and stock in trade belonging to the business.

The defendants demurred to the bill for want of equity.

SIR G. JESSEL, M. R. This bill is warranted by the decisions in Richardson v. Richardson, L. R. 3 Eq. 686, and Morgan v. Malleson, L. R. 10 Eq. 475; but, on the other hand, we have the case of Milroy v. Lord, 4 De G. F. & J. 264, before the Court of Appeal, and the more recent case of Warriner v. Rogers, L. R. 16 Eq. 340, 348, in which Vice-Chancellor Bacon said: " The rule of law upon this subject I take to be very clear, and with the exception of two cases which have been referred to" (Richardson v. Richardson and Morgan v. Malleson), "the decisions are all perfectly consistent with that rule. The one thing necessary to give validity to a declaration of trust — the indispensable thing — I take to be, that the donor, or grantor, or whatever he may be called, should have absolutely parted with that interest which had been his up to the time of the declaration, should have effectually changed his right in that respect, and put the property out of his power, at least in the way of interest."

The two first mentioned cases are wholly opposed to the two last. That being so, I am not at liberty to decide the case otherwise than in accordance with the decision of the Court of Appeal. It is true the judges appear to have taken different views of the construction of certain expressions, but I am not bound by another judge's view of the construction of particular words; and there is no case in which a different principle is stated from that laid down by the Court of Appeal. Moreover, if it were my duty to decide the matter for the first time, I should lay down the law in the same way.

The principle is a very simple one. A man may transfer his property, without valuable consideration, in one of two ways: he may either do such acts as amount in law to a conveyance or assignment of the property, and thus completely divest himself of the legal ownership, in which case the person who by those acts

---

[1] The assignment of the term, not being by deed, was void under Stat. 8 & 9 Vict. c. 106, sec. 3.

acquires the property takes it beneficially, or on trust, as the case may be; or the legal owner of the property may, by one or other of the modes recognized as amounting to a valid declaration of trust, constitute himself a trustee, and, without an actual transfer of the legal title, may so deal with the property as to deprive himself of its beneficial ownership, and declare that he will hold it from that time forward on trust for the other person. It is true he need not use the words, "I declare myself a trustee," but he must do something which is equivalent to it, and use expressions which have that meaning; for, however anxious the court may be to carry out a man's intention, it is not at liberty to construe words otherwise than according to their proper meaning.

The cases in which the question has arisen are nearly all cases in which a man, by documents insufficient to pass a legal interest, has said, "I give or grant certain property to A. B." Thus, in Morgan v. Malleson the words were, "I hereby give and make over to Dr. Morris an India bond"; and in Richardson v. Richardson the words were, "grant, convey, and assign." In both cases the judges held that the words were effectual declarations of trust. In the former case, Lord Romilly considered that the words were the same as these: "I undertake to hold the bond for you"; which would undoubtedly have amounted to a declaration of trust.

The true distinction appears to me to be plain, and beyond dispute; for a man to make himself a trustee, there must be an expression of intention to become a trustee, whereas words of present gift shew an intention to give over property to another, and not retain it in the donor's own hands for any purpose, fiduciary or otherwise.

In Milroy v. Lord, Lord Justice Turner, after referring to the two modes of making a voluntary settlement valid and effectual, adds these words: "The cases, I think, go further, to this extent, that if the settlement is intended to be effectuated by one of the modes to which I have referred, the court will not give effect to it by applying another of those modes. If it is intended to take effect by transfer, the court will not hold the intended transfer to operate as a declaration of trust, for then every imperfect instrument would be made effectual by being converted into a perfect trust."

It appears to me that that sentence contains the whole law on the subject. If the decisions of Lord Romilly and of Vice-Chancellor Wood were right, there never could be a case where an expression of a present gift would not amount to an effectual declaration of trust, which would be carrying the doctrine on that subject too far. It appears to me that these cases of voluntary gifts should not be confounded with another class of cases in which words of present transfer for valuable consideration are held to be evidence of a contract which the court will enforce. Applying that reasoning to cases of this kind, you only make the imperfect instrument evidence of a contract of a voluntary nature, which this court will not enforce; so that, following out the principle even of those cases, you come to the same conclusion.

I must, therefore, allow the demurrer, and, though I feel some hesitation, owing to the conflict of the authorities, I think the costs must follow the result.[1]

MERITORIOUS CONSIDERATION. — It has been held in many cases that a meritorious consideration is sufficient to turn an imperfect gift into a perfect trust. Thus, an attempted gift made by a husband to a wife, imperfect because a husband could not transfer title to his wife, has been enforced in equity as a trust. Ames, Cases on Trusts, 164–175. See also Thomas *v.* Hornbrook, 259 Ill. 156; Dayton etc. Co. *v.* Sloan, 47 Neb. 622; Estate of Wise, 182 Pa. 168. In England after some vacillation the courts finally rejected this doctrine. *Re* Breton's Estate, 17 Ch. D. 416. Today it is possible for a husband to make a gift directly to his wife.

WHITEHEAD *v.* BISHOP.

COURT OF APPEALS, OHIO, LICKING COUNTY. 1925.

23 Ohio App. 315.

HOUCK, P. J. The plaintiff, Gwennie Whitehead, brought suit to set aside an alleged trust contract wherein Thomas Harris, the father of plaintiff, in his lifetime attempted by a paper writing to transfer to the defendants herein, as trustees, $17,000 in bonds, notes, mortgages and money, the purpose of said purported transfer, as set forth in the paper writing, being that such trustees should turn over such trust fund, together with any accumulations thereon, to the village of Alexandria, Ohio, for the establishment and mainte-

---

[1] The cases holding that an imperfect gift will not be upheld as a trust are numerous. Milroy *v.* Lord, 4 DeG. F. & J. 264; West *v.* West, L. R. 9 Ir. 121; Eschen *v.* Steers, 10 F.(2d) 739); Pratt *v.* Griffin, 184 Ill. 514; Clay *v.* Layton, 134 Mich. 317; Young *v.* Young, 80 N. Y. 422; Beaver *v.* Beaver, 117 N. Y. 421, 137 N. Y. 59; Wadd *v.* Hazelton, 137 N. Y. 215; Farmers' Loan & Trust Co. *v.* Winthrop, 238 N. Y. 477; Govin *v.* DeMiranda, 76 Hun (N. Y.) 414, 79 Hun 286; Smith's Estate, 144 Pa. 428 (*semble*); Ashman's Estate, 223 Pa. 543. See Perry, Trusts, sec. 96; Ames, 130n., 133n.; 24 Col. L. Rev. 767; 37 Yale L. Jour. 836; 16 Ann. Cas. 373. In Young *v.* Young, 80 N. Y. 422, 437, the court said: "It is established as unquestionable law that a court of equity cannot by its authority render that gift perfect which the donor has left imperfect, and cannot convert an imperfect gift into a declaration of trust, merely on account of that imperfection."

But if the owner of land intends to make a common-law conveyance which is ineffective as such, it will be upheld if possible as a bargain and sale or as a covenant to stand seised. Roe *v.* Tranmer, 2 Wils. 75; Warren, Cas. Prop. 534; Gray, Rule ag. Perp., sec. 65n.; 4 Mich. L. Rev. 111n.

nance of a public library to be known as the Harris Memorial Library. However, if the village refused to accept the fund for said purpose, then and in that event the trustees were authorized and directed to turn over the fund to the board of education of the village of Alexandria. Plaintiff in her petition alleged that said claimed or so-called trust was never in fact and law executed, by reason of the fact that the property was never delivered to the trustees in the lifetime of Thomas Harris, but he continued to and did have control of same during his entire lifetime, and said property never was in fact and law in possession of the trustees.

The answer of defendants denied all of the material allegations set forth in the petition of plaintiff. Upon the issues thus raised by the pleadings, the cause was submitted to this court upon a transcript of the testimony, taken in the trial in the common pleas court, together with oral testimony offered in the trial in this court. The cause was ably presented in oral argument by counsel for plaintiff and defendants, and we have examined all of the authorities cited, together with many others obtained by our own research. We think that, under the pleadings and evidence, but one question is presented to this court for determination, to wit: Was there a delivery of the property in question by Thomas Harris during his lifetime to the defendants, his trustees named in said paper writing? The evidence offered upon this question is undisputed, and is that, during the lifetime of Thomas Harris, he received the interest on some of the notes alleged to have been turned over by him to said trustees, that at times he had access to some of the mortgages and securities alleged to have been absolutely turned over by him to said trustees, and that in other ways he had such control of them or at least a part of them as would clearly indicate that he had not divested himself of the ownership therein.

Therefore we are fully satisfied from the evidence that the bonds, notes, mortgages, and property of Thomas Harris were not in fact and law delivered to the trustees by said Thomas Harris in his lifetime. It, no doubt, was the intention of Thomas Harris to create the trust in question, and to give the property described in the paper writing to either the village of Alexandria, for the purpose of establishing a Thomas Harris Memorial Library, or to the board of education of the village of Alexandria, upon the terms and conditions stated in said paper writing. But one of the essential elements necessary to carry out the gift was lacking, namely, delivery of the property sought or intended to be given. In other words, it is the opinion of this court that under the facts as established by the evidence, there being no delivery of the property in question during the lifetime of the donor to either the trustees or donee, it necessarily follows that there is or was an unexecuted gift.

We think the rule is well settled that a voluntary trust is an equitable gift, and like a legal gift *inter vivos* must be complete. Since delivery is essential to the consummation of a gift, it follows that, whenever the donor undertakes to divest himself of the entire ownership, either by direct transfer to the donee or conveyance to the trustees to hold for the donee's benefit, the transaction will not be complete unless there is actual delivery of the thing given or of the instrument by which the donor signifies his intention of parting with the control of it. If the donor selects a third person to act as trustee, the subject of the trust must be transferred to him in such mode as will be effectual to pass the legal title.

It seems to us that applying this rule of law to the facts as disclosed by the testimony offered in the trial this court is bound to and must reach the conclusion that there was no delivery in fact and law of the property which said Thomas Harris attempted to place in trust with the defendants.

Before a trust can be established in law, it must be clearly proven that there was a delivery of the property sought to be placed in trust. We are fully satisfied that the evidence in this case does not show a delivery of the property sought to be placed in trust by that degree of proof required in law. In our opinion the rule of law stated in the case of Worthington, Admr., *v.* Redkey, Exr., 86 Ohio St., 128, 99 N. E., 211, when applied to the facts in the present case is decisive in favor of the plaintiff and against the defendants upon the issue here raised. The syllabus of above case is:

"Where property is claimed as a gift by way of a trust which is not testamentary, it devolves upon the donees to prove an express and certain trust for their benefit, either assumed by the donor himself or imposed upon a third person, and in the latter case that the property or the legal title thereto passed beyond the dominion or control of the donor in his lifetime, to the donees or to the person designated as a trustee for them."

It therefore follows that the plaintiff is entitled to all the relief prayed for in her petition, and judgment is accordingly entered in favor of the plaintiff and against the defendants.

SHIELDS, J., concurs.

Decree for plaintiff.[1]

[1] If a conveyance upon trust is ineffective for want of delivery, no trust arises. Milroy *v.* Lord, 4 DeG. F. & J. 264; Barnum *v.* Reed, 136 Ill. 388; McCartney *v.* Ridgway, 160 Ill. 129, 156; Stokes *v.* Sprague, 110 Iowa 89; Loring *v.* Hildreth, 170 Mass. 328; Brannock *v.* Magoon, 141 Mo. App. 316; Worthington *v.* Redkey, 86 Oh. St. 128; Cameron *v.* Cameron, 96 Okla. 98.

FARRELL v. THE PASSAIC WATER CO.

COURT OF CHANCERY, NEW JERSEY. 1913.

82 N. J. Eq. 97.

STEVENS, V. C. This is a bill filed by the administratrix of Catherine Farrell against the Passaic Water Company and the executors of James Atkinson. It is alleged that Mr. Atkinson was engaged to be married to Miss Farrell, and that about the year 1905 [1895?], and while so engaged, he handed her a coupon bond of the Passaic Water Company for $1,000, intending to make her a gift of it. The bond was, at the time of the alleged gift, and still is, registered, as to principal, in the name of Atkinson. The principal sum is payable in July, 1937. Miss Farrell drew the interest coupons during her life and died in 1909. Atkinson died in 1902. Since the death of Miss Farrell, the bond has been in the possession of either her next of kin or her administratrix. On its face it provides that it is payable to the bearer or registered holder thereof and that it " may at any time be registered in the name of the owner on the books of the company; . . . after which this bond shall be transferable only upon the books of the company, until it shall, at the request of the holder, be registered as payable to bearer, which shall restore transferability by delivery."

The bill prays that the bond may be declared to be a part of the estate of Catherine Farrell, and that the company may be decreed to register it in the name of her administratrix.

The defence is, first, that no gift is proven, and second, that if an intention to give has been shown, such gift was imperfect without registry and a court of equity will not lend its aid to perfect it.

Nothing is better settled than that there is no equity to perfect an imperfect gift. Says Sir George Jessel, M. R., in Richards v. Delbridge, L. R. 18 Eq. 11: " The principle is a very simple one. A man may transfer his property without valuable consideration in one of two ways: he may either do such acts as amount in law to a conveyance or assignment of the property and thus completely divest himself of the legal ownership in which case the person who by those acts acquires the property takes it beneficially or on trust, as the case may be; or the legal owner of the property may by one or other of the modes recognized as amounting to a valid declaration of trust constitute himself a trustee and without an actual transfer of the legal title may so deal with the property as to deprive himself of its beneficial ownership and declare that he will hold it from that time forward in trust for the other person."

There is nothing in this case to indicate that Atkinson declared that he held the bond in controversy as trustee for Miss Farrell. What he did was not to set it aside among his own papers and to declare in any way that from that time forth, he held it for her benefit, but to give her the possession of it, and, as far as appears, concern himself no further about it. If, says the master of the rolls, in the case cited, the gift is intended to take effect by transfer, the court will not hold the intended transfer to operate as a declaration of trust, for then every imperfect instrument would be made effectual by being converted into a perfect trust.

If, then, the complainant has a valid title, it must be because Atkinson completely divested himself of all title.

I think considerable confusion has resulted from the use, in some of the later cases, of the term "equitable" in connection with the title of the assignee to a chose in action. If by "equitable" is meant such a title as only a court of equity can give effect to, the assumption is manifestly erroneous. If a right is recognized, and protected by a court of law (of course, I am speaking of those jurisdictions in which the courts of law and equity are still constitutionally distinct), and if such a court has come to be the proper tribunal in which to enforce it, it is a misuse of terms to call the right equitable in contradistinction to legal.

The history of the law on this subject is somewhat curious. In the time of Coke, the property in the paper on which an obligation was written and in the wax with which it was sealed could be divorced from the property in the debt which the paper manifested. He says (Fol. 232b § 377): "it is implied that if a man hath an obligation, though he cannot grant the thing in action, yet he may give or grant the deed, viz., the parchment and wax, to another who may cancel and use the same at his pleasure."

This distinction constituted the basis of decision by the Lords-Justices in Rummens v. Hare, 1 Ex. D. 169, as late as 1876.

Property in the debt evidenced by the paper stood on a different footing. As the advantages arising from commerce began to be felt, the custom of merchants whereby a foreign bill of exchange was assignable by the payee to a third person so as to vest in him the *legal* as well as the equitable title, was recognized and supported by the English law courts as early as the fourteenth century, and a like custom rendering an inland bill transferable was established in the seventeenth century. Chit. Bills *10. Promissory notes were put upon the footing of inland bills by the statute of 7 Anne. Other choses in action long stood upon a different footing. Lord Coke (214a) says that it is one of the maxims of the common law that no right of action can be transferred, "because under color thereof pretended titles might be granted to great men, whereby right might be trodden down and the weak oppressed, which the common law forbiddeth."

But the necessities of trade and commerce were too strong for this maxim, and courts of equity at an early period began to recognize the interest of the assignee. During this period the title of the assignee was equitable, and equitable only. Then the law courts began, indirectly at first, to recognize his right. In Winch *v.* Keeley, 1 T. R. 619 (A.D. 1787), they did so for the first time explicitly. There a suit was brought in the name of the assignor for the use of the assignee. The defence was that the assignor had become bankrupt and that his title had passed to his assignee in bankruptcy. It was held that the title had not passed and that the suit would lie. Having recognized and protected the assignee's right, it became, at least to some extent, a mere question of procedure whether the suit should be brought in the one name or the other. This was the view of Mr. Justice Buller in Master *v.* Miller, 4 T. R. 341 (A.D. 1791). He says: "It must be admitted that though the courts of law have gone the length of taking notice of choses in action and acting upon them, yet in many cases they have adhered to the formal objection that the action shall be brought in the name of the assignor and not in the name of the assignee. I see no use or convenience in preserving that shadow when the substance is gone, and that it is merely a shadow is apparent from the later cases in which the courts have taken care that it shall never work injustice." Still, in England, the action continued for many years to be brought in the name of the assignor. But it became mere form, for, said Chief-Justice Hornblower, in Allen *v.* Pancoast, 20 N. J. Law (Spenc.) 68: "It has long since been held that an assignment of a chose in action carries with it by implication a right to use the name of the assignor even against his consent and in opposition to his release or defeasance of the debt or security assigned."

It is going pretty far to call the right of such an assignee, so protected, an *equitable* in contradistinction to a *legal* right. But when our legislature in 1797 enacted that the "assignment of bills, bonds and other writings obligatory for the payment of money shall be good and effectual in law and an assignee of any such may thereupon maintain an action of debt in his own name," the only excuse for calling the assignee's title equitable vanished. Reed *v.* Bambridge, 4 N. J. Law (1 South.) 358. The legal title to the wax and paper had always been in the assignee, the legal title to the debt was now also in the assignee.

It thus conclusively appears that the aid of a court of equity to perfect the title of an assignee to a sealed bond for the payment of money is unnecessary, for the right is perfect already. Agreements to assign stand upon quite another footing. If based upon valuable consideration, equity may sometimes enforce them; if not so based, it will not.

Then a perfectly distinct question arises. By what formalities may title be vested in an assignee? At first it was held that an instrument under seal could only be assigned by an instrument of equal dignity (Wood *v.* Partridge, 11 Mass. 488); but this view has been abandoned, and it is now held that instruments such as bonds, mortgages and policies of insurance may be assigned by writing without seal, or even by parol accompanied by delivery. Vreeland *v.* Van Horn, 17 N. J. Eq. (2 C. E. Gr.) 137; Travelers Insurance Co. *v.* Grant, 54 N. J. Eq. (9 Dick.) 208; Allen *v.* Pancoast, 20 N. J. Law (Spenc.) 71. The effect of the assignment is precisely the same in any of these forms — it vests the legal title in the assignee. The proof of it may be more difficult in the case of an assignment by parol, but in any mode the debt theretofore owing to the obligee passes to the assignee; he is the creditor, and the only creditor.

These several modes of assignment are as applicable to the case of gifts as to those of transfers for value. The gift is just as completely vested by the one mode as by the other, and it is settled law that the fact that the bond is not payable to bearer or that the instrument is not negotiable does not prevent a valid gift of it by manual tradition without writing. Executors of Egerton *v.* Egerton, 17 N. J. Eq. (2 C. E. Gr.) 421; Corle *v.* Monkhouse, 50 N. J. Eq. (5 Dick.) 537; Travelers Insurance Co. *v.* Grant, 54 N. J. Eq. (9 Dick.) 208; Thompson *v.* West, 56 N. J. Eq. (11 Dick.) 660. Proof of delivery, coupled with proof of intent to pass a present interest by way of gift, has precisely the same effect as a formal written transfer A moment's consideration will show that this is necessarily so. The instrument given remains, in either case, unchanged. If payable by A to B it remains so payable on the face of it, whether transferred by writing or not; but by the effect of the transfer, what theretofore was payable to B has in law become payable to C, the transferee. In the case of Green *v.* Tulane, 52 N. J. Eq. (7 Dick.) 169, the question was not before the court. I do not think it can be fairly gathered from what Vice-Chancellor Pitney said that he thought that a writing was necessary, but if he there so expressed himself, when the point came squarely before him, in the Insurance Case, he held otherwise. The question then is, did Atkinson make a gift — that is, a perfect gift? Two objections are made — *first*, it is said that the proof fails to show delivery accompanied with a declaration of intent, and *secondly*, that the instrument itself forbids the making of a gift in the manner in which it is alleged to have been made.

As to the first objection: The evidence is that Atkinson, a business man of mature years, possessed of considerable property, while engaged to be married to Miss Farrell, parted with the bond in question; how or when does not appear. Although he lived for six or seven years after it came into Miss Farrell's possession, he did not reclaim it; reclamation being all the more easy because of the fact that the bond stood registered in his name. He told a friend that he had made Miss Farrell a present of a bond of that description. She took the interest accruing upon it for ten or twelve years before her death. It was natural that, situated as they were, he should have made a gift, and there is no evidence against it. Under these circumstances, I think the inference that a gift was actually made is the only fair inference from the proofs.

But counsel argues that, conceding that an intention to give is proved, the gift remains incomplete because of the clauses in the bond, which provide that it is payable to the bearer or registered holder, and that if registered, it shall be transferable only on the books of the company, until it shall, at the request of the holder, be registered payable to bearer, "*which shall restore transferability by delivery.*"

There are two kinds of corporation bonds in common use today — those that are negotiable and those that are merely assignable. It seems quite apparent that the object of the clause in question was to give the owner the option of having either the one form of obligation or the other, at his pleasure. It is hardly to be supposed that the company was endeavoring to put upon the market a new kind of obligation, viz., one, *title* to which would not pass from one man to another unless or until there was an actual transfer on the books. The implied prohibition against transfer would be just as effective in the case of a written assignment, even an assignment under seal, as in the case of a verbal one. There might indeed be a question whether such a limitation could be made effective; but here, I do not think it was intended to impose it. The clause was probably suggested by the similar one put in the ordinary stock certificate, as to which Chancellor Green said: " The title of the holder is in nowise affected by a provision in the charter or by-laws of the corporation that the stock is transferable only on the books of the corporation. Such a provision is intended merely for the protection and benefit of the corporation." The fact that in the one case the provision is intended chiefly to protect the company and in the other the bondholder, can make no difference, so far as the point under consideration is concerned. It is well settled that as between the transferrer and transferee, title to the stock certificate is completely vested without transfer on the books. Matthews *v.* Hoagland, 48 N. J. Eq. (3 Dick.) 486.

But it is said that the failure to direct the company to make a transfer on its books is evidence that Atkinson did not intend his gift to be irrevocable. If the facts justify the inference that he did so intend, proof that he failed to authorize the company by power of attorney to make a transfer is immaterial. He had, I have shown, the option of making the gift with or without writing. Such failure might indeed be a circumstance militating against the gift, if coupled with other circumstances throwing doubt upon it. Standing by itself, it is without significance as long as it is the doctrine of this court that a valid gift may be made by parol. Proof of failure to make in one way is no proof of failure to make in another.

Considering, as I do, that the question as between the administratrix of Miss Farrell and the executor of Mr. Atkinson is one of legal title — title of which the law courts take cognizance — it would seem to follow that if there were a real doubt as to who was legal owner, that doubt would have to be, under our system, settled by the law courts. There is, however, no dispute as to the material facts and no reasonable doubt as to the inference to be drawn from them. The case seems really to be one between the administratrix and the water company; Atkinson's executors being proper parties because their testator stands upon the company's books as registered owner. There is proof that a request to register was made by the administratrix and that such request was refused. If a court of equity has jurisdiction to decree a registry of stock (Archer v. American Water Co., 50 N. J. Eq. (5 Dick.) 50; Reilly v. Absecon Land Co., 75 N. J. Eq. (5 Buch.) 71), I see no good reason why it may not compel performance of the company's agreement to register the bond. A suit for damages, based on a refusal to do so, would not be a complete or satisfactory remedy.

Under the peculiar circumstances of the case neither party should have costs.

ASSIGNMENT OF SPECIALTY CHOSES IN ACTION. A gift of a *chose* in action represented by a specialty is valid if, but only if, the specialty is delivered or the gift is evidenced by a deed, or in some states a writing, evidencing the gift.

Bonds. By the weight of authority the delivery of a bond or of a deed of gift of a bond is sufficient to effect a gift of the bond.[1] The opposite result was reached in Edwards v. Jones, 1 Myl. & Cr. 226; but this case is probably overruled by *Re* Patrick, [1891] 1 Ch. 82.

Shares of stock. A gift of shares of stock is valid and irrevocable where there has been delivery of the certificate, either with or without an express power of attorney to transfer the shares on the company's books. It has also been held that a deed of transfer, with or without an express power of attorney, is sufficient. In the

[1] *Re* Richards, [1921] 1 Ch. 513 (*mortis causa*); Conlon v. Turley, 10 F.(2d) 890; Mangan v. Howard, 238 Mass. 1; Tarbox v. Grant, 56 N. J. Eq. 199 (deed of gift); Miller v. Silverman, 247 N. Y. 447; Funston v. Twining, 202 Pa. 88. See Ames, 145n.

absence of delivery of the certificate or of a deed or other instrument of transfer, the gift is incomplete.[1]

Life insurance policies. A parol gift of a life insurance policy is valid if the policy is delivered.[2] So also a gift by deed is sufficient although the policy itself is not delivered.[3]

Savings bank deposits. The gift of a deposit in a savings bank is valid and irrevocable if the bank book is delivered, with or without an express power of attorney or written assignment or order. It has been held that a deed of transfer without delivery of the bank book is sufficient. In the absence of delivery of the bank book or of a deed or other instrument of transfer, the gift is incomplete.[4]

Bills and notes. The gift of a non-negotiable bill of exchange or promissory note, or of a negotiable bill or note, is valid without indorsement if the note is delivered or if the gift is evidenced by a deed of gift.[5] If a note is secured by mortgage, a delivery of the note by way of gift will give the donee the equitable interest in the security.[6] A delivery of the mortgage deed without the note would seem to be insufficient.[7]

[1] Grissom *v.* Sternberger, 10 F.(2d) 764; Herbert *v.* Simson, 220 Mass. 480; Miller *v.* Silverman, 247 N. Y. 447; Talbot *v.* Talbot, 32 R. I. 72. See also Ames, 155n.; Scott, Cases on Trusts, 1 ed., 155–6; Mechem, Gifts of Corporation Shares, 20 Ill. L. Rev. 9; 27 Yale L. Jour. 956; 30 Yale L. Jour. 767; 4 Minn. L. Rev. 70; 24 Harv. L. Rev. 481; Lowell, Transfer of Stock, secs. 43–4; 2 L. R. A. (N. S.) 806; 29 L. R. A. (N. S.) 166; L. R. A. 1915D 733; Ann. Cas. 1912C 1235; 38 A. L. R. 1366. See Uniform Stock Transfer Act, sec. 9.

[2] Knowles *v.* Knowles, 205 Mass. 290; Gledhill *v.* McCoombs, 110 Me. 341; Chapman *v.* McIlwrath, 77 Mo. 38; Travellers' Ins. Co. *v.* Grant, 54 N. J. Eq. 208; McGlynn *v.* Curry, 82 N. Y. App. Div. 431 (in spite of provisions in the policy requiring written evidence of the assignment, which were held to be designed only for the protection of the company); Hani *v.* Germania etc. Co., 197 Pa. 276; Barron *v.* Williams, 58 S. C. 280; Opitz *v.* Karel, 118 Wis. 527.

[3] Fortescue *v.* Barnett, 3 Myl. & K. 36; Pearson *v.* Amicable Co., 27 Beav. 229; Hurlbut *v.* Hurlbut, 49 Hun (N. Y.) 189; Kulp *v.* March, 181 Pa. 627; Northwestern Mut. Life Ins. Co. *v.* Wright, 153 Wis. 252. See Ames, 139n.; Ann. Cas. 1914D 297; 47 A. L. R. 738.

[4] Hill *v.* Stevenson, 63 Me. 364; Almont Sav. Bank *v.* Warner, 228 Mich. 130. See Ames, 155n.; Scott, Cases on Trusts, 1 ed., 165; Dec. Dig., Gifts, 30, 66; 40 A. L. R. 1249.

For cases involving deposits by A " in trust for B," see Chap. III, sec. IV, and particularly *Re* Totten, 179 N. Y. 112, *post*.

[5] Duffield *v.* Elwes, 1 Bligh (N. S.) 497; Wright *v.* Bragg, 106 Fed. 25; Walker *v.* Crews, 73 Ala. 412 (deed of gift); Edwards *v.* Wagner, 121 Cal. 376; Burkett *v.* Doty, 176 Cal. 89 (written assignment); Grover *v.* Grover, 24 Pick. (Mass.) 261; MacKeown *v.* Lacey, 200 Mass. 437; Hoyt *v.* Gillen, 181 Mich. 509; Meyer *v.* Koehring, 129 Mo. 15; Egerton *v.* Carr, 94 N. C. 648. See Ames, 162n.; Warren, Cas. Wills, 829, 830; 25 A. L. R. 642; 40 A. L. R. 508.

[6] O'Connor *v.* McHugh, 89 Ala. 531; Druke *v.* Heiken, 61 Cal. 346 (*mortis causa*); Brown *v.* Brown, 18 Conn. 410 (*mortis causa*); Kiff *v.* Weaver, 94 N. C. 276 (*mortis causa*). But see *contra,* Tiffany *v.* Clarke, 6 Grant Ch. (Upper Can.) 474, 481.

[7] McHugh *v.* O'Connor, 91 Ala. 243. But see Caufield *v.* Davenport, 75 Hun (N. Y.) 541.

On the other hand, a gift of the donor's own note is not effective, since he is not attempting to transfer property but is merely making a gratuitous promise.[1]

So also, a gift of the donor's own check is not effective, since he is not attempting to transfer property but is merely making a gratuitous promise.[2] It would be possible for him to make a total or partial assignment of his claim against the bank, but it is well settled that the delivery of a check is not of itself such an assignment.[3] If the check is paid by the bank before the donor has died or revoked the gift, the gift is of course complete.[4] If the bank pays a check after the death of the drawer but without knowledge of his death, it is not liable to the estate of the drawer;[5] but a donee cannot keep the proceeds of the check paid after the death of the donor.[6]

Other specialties. The courts have upheld gifts of bank deposit receipts,[7] lottery tickets[8] and exchequer tallies.[9]

POFF v. POFF.

Supreme Court of Appeals, Virginia. 1920.

128 Va. 62.

[This is a suit in equity. It appeared that the decedent, J. W. Poff, purchased land for his four younger sons who agreed to pay him $4000. When they offered to pay him he told them to pay the money to his two married daughters. No payment was made prior to his death. The Circuit Court decreed that the daughters were not entitled to the money which they claimed as a gift from their father, but that the younger sons were indebted to his estate to the

---

[1] *Re* Leaper, [1916] 1 Ch. 579; Parish *v.* Stone, 14 Pick. (Mass.) 198; Sanborn *v.* Sanborn, 65 N. H. 172; Executors of Egerton *v.* Egerton, 17 N. J. Eq. 419; Starr *v.* Starr, 9 Oh. St. 74. See 7 L. R. A. (N. S.) 156; 27 L. R. A. (N. S.) 308; Ann. Cas. 1914C 1139.

If the note is paid by the donor or is negotiated before the donor's death or revocation, the donee may keep the proceeds. Armstrong *v.* Armstrong, 142 Ill. App. 507.

[2] Burrows *v.* Burrows, 240 Mass. 485; Simmons *v.* Cincinnati Sav. Society, 31 Oh. St. 457. See also Scott, Cases on Trusts, 1 ed., 183; L. R. A. 1918C 340; 20 A. L. R. 177; 44 A. L. R. 625; 53 A. L. R. 1119.

[3] Negotiable Instruments Law, sec. 189. See also Williston, Contracts, secs. 425–6; Scott, Cases on Trusts, 1 ed., 183.

[4] Boutts *v.* Ellis, 4 DeG., M. & G. 249; Frantz *v.* Porter, 132 Cal. 49; Conners *v.* Murphy, 100 N. J. Eq. 280; Pickslay *v.* Starr, 149 N. Y. 432.

[5] Glennan *v.* Rochester Trust & S. D. Co., 209 N. Y. 12.

[6] Burrows *v.* Burrows, 240 Mass. 485.

[7] Porter *v.* Walsh, [1895] 1 I. R. 284; *Re* Griffin, [1899] 1 Ch. 408; *Re* Westerton, [1919] 2 Ch. 104. See Ames, 156n.; Warren, Cas. Wills, 841n.

[8] See Ames, 162n.

[9] Ames, 163n. See *Re* Lee, [1918] 2 Ch. 320.

amount of such money paid for them by him in his lifetime. From the decree the daughters appealed.] [1]

SIMS, J. . . . We come now to the sole remaining question for our decision, and that is this:

Was the parol gift, made by J. W. Poff in his lifetime to his two married daughters, Mrs. Nolley and Mrs. Pritchett, of the $4,000 debt of the four younger sons to the donor, a valid gift?

We are of opinion that this question must be answered in the negative.

The payment of the money in question by J. W. Poff for the younger sons unquestionably created the relationship of creditor and debtor between them. The presumption of gift to the younger sons, which might have arisen from the bare fact of the payment, is rebutted by the express evidence in the case that J. W. Poff told such sons that they owed him the amount of the money so paid, and that they admitted the existence of such obligation.

The transaction was not a deposit of money, or other thing, by J. W. Poff into the hands of such sons in trust for the daughters, where the act of the donor in making the deposit accompanied the creation of a trust, so that there was a complete assignment or transfer of the subject of the gift in trust, as was true in the case of Russell's Ex'rs v. Passmore, 127 Va. 475, 103 S. E. 652. In such a case as that just cited, the act of making the deposit into the hands, not of a mere agent of the donor, but of a trustee who accepts the trust, is equivalent to the act of a donor in delivering the possession of tangible personal property, which is indispensable to the validity of a gift thereof *causa mortis*, and also of a gift thereof *inter vivos*, except that in the case of the latter character of gift of personal chattels, the acquiescence of a donor in a previously acquired possession of the donee has been held to be sufficient evidence from which to imply delivery of the possession. Shankle v. Spahr, 121 Va. 598, at pp. 607-8, 93 S. E. 605; Wood v. Treadway, 111 Va. 526, 69 S. E. 445, and authorities there cited; Russell's Ex'rs v. Passmore, *supra*. Besides the last mentioned exception to the rule that some act of the donor making, or held to be equivalent to the making of the transfer of the possession of the subject of the gift from himself to the donee, or to some one in trust for the latter, is essential to the execution, and, hence, to the validity of a gift *inter vivos*, as well as *causa mortis*, there is one other exception, and only one, namely, in the case of a gift by way of a declaration of trust. In such case, " the donor does not part with the possession of the subject of the gift, but retaining it, declares that he holds it *in* trust for the donee." See Gifts of Personalty, by Prof. Graves, 1 Va. Law Reg., at p. 878.

But the gift to the daughters in the case before us comes within none of the exceptions above mentioned, and is plainly an at-

---

[1] The statement of facts is abridged and a part of the opinion relating to other questions involved in the suit is omitted.

tempted equitable assignment of a chose in action, *i.e.*, of the debt due the donor by the younger sons.

The doctrine of equitable assignments as applied to the gift of a chose in action has been long well settled. Although it is an equitable gift, it must be executed in order to be valid. " The delivery of some instrument, by using which the chose is to be reduced into possession, as a bond or a receipt or the like," is absolutely essential to the validity of the gift. Miller *v.* Jeffress, 4 Gratt. (45 Va.) 472; Gifts of Personalty, by Prof. Graves, *supra* (1 Va. Law Reg. 877–8). The delivery of such instrument need not be actual. It may be symbolical. But one or the other is essential to the validity of a gift of a chose in action. Where a previously existing debt is sought to be given of which there is no documentary evidence — as where there is but an implied promise of the debtor to pay the creditor, as is true of the case before us — " there is nothing of which even a symbolical delivery can be made, and therefore there can be no valid, binding and executed gift." Ross *v.* Milne, 12 Leigh (39 Va.) at p. 222, 37 Am. Dec. 646.

It may seem that since gifts by way of a declaration of trust are upheld as executed gifts, which is in direct violation of the rule aforesaid as to the necessity of delivery of possession of the subject of the gift, actual or symbolical, that the rule should be relaxed in the cases of attempted gifts of choses in action which are not effectual because of a lack of symbolic delivery; and that, since in such case the donor occupies the position of continued owner of the chose in action, he should, in equity, be held to have, by the declaration of gift, made a gift by way of a declaration of a trust; but the authorities are to the contrary. As said by Prof. Graves in his article on Gifts of Personalty, *supra* (1 Va. Law Reg. at pp. 879–880): " * * * it sometimes happens that a donor, with a gift intent, neither declares himself trustee nor makes an *effectual* equitable assignment, though his *purpose* is evidently to *assign,* and not to create a trust. The question then arises, can the defective assignment be treated as tantamount to a declaration of trust, and the gift sustained on that theory? Some of the earliest English cases are in favor of this view, but they are now discredited, and the doctrine is that an abortive assignment will not (contrary to the intent of the donor) be converted into an implied declaration of trust, in order to save the gift from failure. It is said by Jessel, M. R., in Richards *v.* Delbridge, L. R. 18 Eq. 11: ' However anxious the court may be to carry out a man's intention (*i.e.*, to make a gift), it is not at liberty to construe words otherwise than according to their proper meaning.' And in Moore *v.* Moore, L. R. 18 Eq. 474, it is said by Hall, V. C.: ' I do think it very important to keep a clear and definite distinction between cases of imperfect gift and cases of declaration of trust; and that we should not extend, beyond what the authorities have already established, declarations of trust so as to supplement and supply what, according to decisions of the highest authority, would otherwise be imperfect gifts.' In other words, a donor is legally put to his election whether he will *assign* or *declare a trust;* and if he elects the former, as is shown by his attempted assignment, the gift must stand or fall as the donor designed to make it; and if ineffectual as an assignment, it can derive no assistance from the doctrine of declarations of trust. Otherwise, it has been said, ' there would never be a case where an expression of a present gift would not amount to a declaration of trust, which would be carrying the doctrine too far.' Per Jessel, M. R., 18 Eq. Cas. 15."

Therefore, while we have every disposition to uphold the attempted gift to the daughters, in question in the case before us, as a valid gift, we cannot do so without relaxing the rules aforesaid on the subject which have been long settled, and this, we feel, should not be done. The rules may appear to be technical, and they undoubtedly work grave hardships in some cases; but, as to gifts *inter vivos*, they are based upon the very same foundation as is the rule that no mere executory promise is enforceable, unless it is supported by a valuable consideration, a *locus penitentiae* being, in the wisdom of the common law, left attached to every matter of mere voluntary intention, until the intention is executed by an unequivocal act; they have been the subject of consideration and approval of many eminent judges and authorities; and contrary rules might result in a yet greater miscarriage of justice. At any rate, the courts are powerless to change rules so long and so firmly established.

We conclude, therefore, that there is no error in the holding of the decree under review on the question last disposed of, and it will be affirmed.

Affirmed.[1]

---

[1] If a *chose* in action is not in the form of a common-law or mercantile specialty, so that there is no document to pass by delivery or deed, a gift of it by the obligee is so far operative as a power of attorney that the obligor cannot set up the gratuitous character of the assignment against the donee. See Scott, Cases on Trusts, 1 ed., 168. It is generally held, however, that the donor may revoke the power of attorney and that his death revokes it. Cook *v.* Lum, 55 N. J. L. 373; Scott, Cases on Trusts, 1 ed., 168; Dec. Dig., Assignments, 53–55, 59; 3 A. L. R. 933; 14 A. L. R. 707. Thus, it has been held that a deposit in a commercial bank is not gratuitously assignable by delivery of the depositor's passbook. Simpkins *v.* Old Colony Trust Co., 254 Mass. 576; Brophy *v.* Haeberle, 220 N. Y. App. Div. 511. See Scott, 169; 9 Minn. L. Rev. 484.

An assignment by deed of a parol *chose* in action is valid. Hambleton *v.* Brown, [1917] 2 K. B. 93. See Williston, Contracts, sec. 440.

On the general question of gratuitous assignments of *choses* in action, see Jenks, Consideration and the Assignment of Choses in Action, 16 L. Quar. Rev. 241; Anson, Assignment of Choses in Action, 17 L. Quar. Rev. 90; Costigan, Gifts Inter Vivos of Choses in Action, 27 L. Quar. Rev. 326; Mechem, The Requirement of Delivery in Gifts of Chattels and Choses in Action Evidenced by Commercial Instruments, 21 Ill. L. Rev. 341, 457, 568; Bruton, The Requirement of Delivery as Applied to Gifts of Choses in Action, 39

[SECT. II.]

EXTINGUISHMENT OF A CHOSE IN ACTION. A creditor may gratuitously extinguish his claim, either by a release under seal or, in the case of a common-law or mercantile specialty, by a surrender or destruction of the instrument. A parol and gratuitous forgiveness of a debt, however, is ordinarily inoperative both at law and in equity. Williston, Contracts, secs. 694, 1830–1; Scott, Cases on Trusts, 1 ed., 192. If a creditor gratuitously and orally declares himself trustee of his claim for the debtor, it is possible that under the doctrine of *Ex parte* Pye the declaration of trust is effective to give the debtor an equitable defense to the claim. See Flower *v.* Marten, 2 Myl. & C. 459. But see Cross *v.* Sprigg, 6 Hare 552. At any rate a gratuitous oral forgiveness of a debt will not be upheld as a declaration of trust. Cardoza *v.* Leveroni, 233 Mass. 310.

CURRIDEN *v.* CHANDLER, 79 N. H. 269 (1919): John P. H. Chandler, one of the beneficiaries of a trust created by deed of trust on the marriage of his parents, executed and delivered to his wife, Madeleine V. Chandler, a sealed instrument purporting to convey to his wife and their son and any future children all his interest under the trust. The trustees were notified of the conveyance which was gratuitous. The court held that the conveyance by the beneficiary of his interest was valid. PLUMMER, J., said:

" The conveyance by John P. H. Chandler to his wife and children is valid. The fact that there was no delivery of the property conveyed does not render the transfer invalid. The property was trust funds, and was in the possession of trustees. It was not in the power of the grantor to make a manual delivery of the property. He did all that it was possible for him to do in making and delivering to Madeleine V. Chandler a conveyance under seal, and that was sufficient. The deed under seal took the place of a physical transfer of the property. It was the best transfer that the grantor could make under the circumstances. The delivery of a deed under seal is deemed to be a delivery of the property conveyed. [Citing cases.]

" It is sought to set the conveyance aside because it was not supported by a valuable consideration. No consideration is required to

---

Yale L. Jour. 837; Cook, The Alienability of Choses in Action, 29 Harv. L. Rev. 816, 30 Harv. L. Rev. 449; Williston, Is the Right of an Assignee of a Chose in Action Legal or Equitable?, 30 Harv. L. Rev. 97; Williston, Gifts of Rights under Contracts in Writing by Delivery of the Writing, 40 Yale L. Jour. 1; Maitland, Equity, 68–75.

In England by Law of Property Act, 1925, 15 Geo. V. c. 20, sec. 136, it is provided that any absolute assignment by writing of a debt, of which notice in writing is given to the debtor, is effectual in law to transfer the legal right to such debt and all legal and other remedies for the same and the power to discharge the debt. This section supersedes Judicature Act, 1873, sec. 25(6).

render this transaction valid. The conveyance was a voluntary gift. . . . A gift perfected by delivery of a deed of gift is complete, although made without consideration." [1]

CHASE NATIONAL BANK *v.* SAYLES, 11 F.(2d) 948 (C. C. A. 1, 1926): A testator bequeathed the sum of $4,000,000 to his widow, Mary D. A. Sayles. The widow executed and delivered to one Rupprecht an instrument under seal assigning to him an interest in the legacy to the extent of $1,500,000, of which assignment the executors were notified. There was no consideration for the assignment. Rupprecht subsequently for value assigned his interest in the legacy to the Chase National Bank. The bank brought a suit in equity in the United States District Court in Rhode Island, joining Rupprecht as plaintiff, against the executors and the widow to recover the part of the legacy so assigned. The District Court dismissed the bill. On appeal the decree was reversed. The court was of the opinion that the interest of a legatee is an equitable *chose* in action and that a gratuitous partial assignment by deed of an equitable *chose* in action is valid; but that even if it be assumed that the legatee has a legal *chose* in action the assignment was valid. BINGHAM, J., said (p. 954):

"These decisions disclose the idea that a legatee has, in equity, in addition to a right in personam against the executor, an equitable interest in the property of the estate to the extent of his legacy, even though his interest may be subject to abatement in case the assets remaining after payment of the debts and expenses of administration may be less than enough to pay his legacy in full. . . .

"It has long been recognized that equitable interests in property may be assigned by way of gift, that the assignment may be of the whole or a part of the assignor's interest, and that the only material question is whether the circumstances show a completed transaction — an intention to pass a present interest and such delivery of

---

[1] Villers *v.* Beaumont, 1 Vern. 100; Ellison *v.* Ellison, 6 Ves. 656; Bentley *v.* Mackay, 15 Beav. 12; Voyle *v.* Hughes, 2 Sm. & G. 18; Lambe *v.* Orton, 1 Dr. & Sm. 125; Gilbert *v.* Overton, 2 Hem. & M. 110; *Re* Way's Trusts, 2 D. J. & S. 365; [Kekewich *v.* Manning, 1 DeG. M. & G. 176; Donaldson *v.* Donaldson, Kay, 711;] Nanney *v.* Morgan, 37 Ch. D. 346; *Re* Lucan, 45 Ch. D. 470 (*semble*); Gannon *v.* White, 2 Ir. Eq. 207; Ensign *v.* Kellogg, 4 Pick. 1; Stone *v.* Hackett, 12 Gray 227; Henderson *v.* Sherman, 47 Mich. 267; Tarbox *v.* Grant, 56 N. J. Eq. 199; Johnson *v.* Williams, 63 How. Pr. 233; Ham *v.* Van Orden, 84 N. Y. 257; [Matson *v.* Abbey, 141 N. Y. 179 (deed); Heise *v.* Wells, 211 N. Y. 1 (deed);] Patton *v.* Clendenin, 3 Murph. (N. C.) 68 (*semble*); Chasteen *v.* Martin, 84 N. C. 391, *accord*.

Bridge *v.* Bridge, 16 Beav. 315 (said in *Re* King, 14 Ch. D. 184, to have been decided on a wrong ground); Meek *v.* Kettlewell, 1 Hare 464, 1 Ph. 342 (said in Penfold *v.* Mould, 4 Eq. 562, and Sullivan *v.* Sullivan, Brunner 645, to be in effect overruled), *contra*. — AMES.

the subject-matter as its nature permits, and that if they do, the gift is irrevocable. [Citing cases.]

"While we are of the opinion that a legatee's right is an equitable interest in property, nevertheless, if it be assumed, as the defendants contend, that his right is a legal chose in action, we are further of the opinion that, according to the weight of authority, he may make a valid and irrevocable gift of his right or interest, which equity will uphold. . . .

"The theory upon which the decisions have proceeded is that the assignment, on being completed, vests in the assignee an equitable interest in the debt or deposit with a power to sue and collect the same; that the power to sue and collect, being coupled with an equitable interest in the debt or deposit, cannot be revoked by the assignor in his lifetime, and is not revoked by his death. The theory of these decisions — that the assignment vests in the assignee an equitable interest in the debt or fund — whether anomalous or not, is unquestionably the one upon which the decisions proceed, and is the only theory upon which many of them can be sustained, whether the assignment is by way of gift or of sale. For instance, it has been held that the assignee of a nonnegotiable note, or one payable to order unindorsed, whether the assignment be for value or not, might maintain an action after the death of the assignor in the name of the executor or administrator of the assignor and collect the claim. If this can be done, it must be upon the theory that an equitable interest in the debt passed to the assignee, and rendered the implied power to sue and collect in the name of the assignor irrevocable; for, if no interest passes by the assignment and the assignor dies, a consideration will not render the power irrevocable. His death will revoke it. . . .

"Equity is not hampered, as is the law, in the enforcement of an assignment of a part of a debt or demand. Such an assignment may be enforced in equity against the debtor, whether he accepts and assents to it or not, and by joining the assignor the interests of all parties can be determined in a single suit. This being so, the division of the debt or demand does not subject the debtor to burdens which his contract does not require him to bear. [Citing cases.]"[1]

---

[1] *Certiorari* refused, 273 U. S. 708. For comments on this decision, see 27 Col. L. Rev. 86; 39 Harv. L. Rev. 368; 40 Harv. L. Rev. 129; 24 Mich. L. Rev. 826; 25 Mich. L. Rev. 802; 36 Yale L. Jour. 272. See *accord,* Young v. Gnichtel, 28 F.(2d) 789; Commissioner v. Field, 42 F.(2d) 820.

In Alger v. Scott, 54 N. Y. 14, it was held that a gratuitous partial assignment of a legal *chose* in action by a written order on the obligor is revocable. See *Re* Lucan, 45 Ch. D. 470 (gratuitous equitable charge by deed held invalid). See Dickinson, Gratuitous Partial Assignments, 31 Yale L. Jour. 1.

FLETCHER v. FLETCHER.

Chancery. 1844.

4 Hare 67.

The bill was filed by Jacob, a natural son of the testator, Ellis Fletcher, for the payment, by the defendants, his executors, out of the assets, of a sum of 60,000*l*., with interest thereon, from the expiration of twelve months from the decease of the testator. The claim was founded upon a voluntary deed, executed by the testator, between four and five years before his death, which was thenceforward retained by the testator in his own possession, without having been communicated either to the trustees appointed in the deed, or, so far as it appeared to the plaintiff or the other parties interested under it, and which was ultimately discovered some years after the death of the testator, by a person the executors employed to make a schedule of his papers, by whom it was found, wrapped together with an examined copy of the same deed, in a brown paper parcel.

The indenture in question was expressed to be made the 1st day of September, 1829, between Ellis Fletcher of the one part, and five trustees therein named of the other part; and it recited that Ellis Fletcher, being desirous of making provision for his two natural sons, John, then of the age of eleven years, and Jacob (the plaintiff), then of the age of six years, had proposed and agreed to enter into the covenant and declaration of trust thereinafter contained; and it was thereby witnessed, that, in consideration of the premises and of the natural love and affection which Ellis Fletcher bore towards his said sons John and Jacob, he the said Ellis Fletcher did, for himself, his heirs, executors, and administrators, covenant and agree with and to the said trustees, their heirs, executors, administrators, and assigns, that, in case the said John and Jacob, or either of them, should survive the said Ellis Fletcher, then and in such case the heirs, executors, or administrators of him the said Ellis Fletcher, should and would, within twelve calendar months next after his decease, well and fully pay, or cause to be paid, unto the said trustees, their executors, administrators, and assigns, the sum of 60,000*l*. And it was thereby expressed to be agreed and declared, and particularly the said Ellis Fletcher did thereby declare, that the said trustees, and the survivor of them, and the executors, administrators, and assigns of such survivor, should stand and be possessed of and interested in the said sum of 60,000*l*. when and as the same should come to their or his hands, upon trust for the said John and Jacob, or such one of them as should attain the age of twenty-one years and should be living at the decease of the said Ellis Fletcher, and their or his executors, administrators, and assigns; and, if both of them should attain that age, and be then living, then the same to be divided between them in equal shares as tenants in common. And it was thereby expressed to be further agreed and declared, that in case neither of them, the said John and Jacob, having survived the said Ellis Fletcher, should attain the age of twenty-one years, then the said sum of 60,000*l.* should remain and be in trust for Ellis Fletcher, his executors, administrators, and assigns, and be deemed part of his personal estate. And it was declared that, if, on the decease of the said Ellis Fletcher, the said John and Jacob, or either of them, should be under the age of twenty-one years, then the trustees or trustee for the time being should invest, in their or his names or name, the said sum of 60,000*l.*, or so much thereof as should not be absolutely vested or payable under the trust therein-mentioned, and should stand and be possessed of the said stocks, funds, and securities upon trust to pay and apply the whole or a competent part of the interest or dividends of the said sum of 60,-000*l.* unto or for the maintenance or education of the said John and Jacob during their minorities, with power to raise and apply sums, not exceeding 10,000*l.* each, for their preferment or advancement. And it was further agreed and declared, that, after the decease of the said Ellis Fletcher, the trustees or trustee for the time being, until the said trust monies should vest absolutely in some person or persons, under the trusts thereinbefore expressed, should receive and accumulate the interest, dividends, and annual produce thereof, or so much thereof as should be unapplied and undisposed of under the said trusts; and that the said interest, dividends, and accumulations should belong to and be in trust for the person or persons who, under the trusts thereinbefore declared, should ultimately become entitled to the fund or funds from which such accumulations should have proceeded. And the deed contained the usual clauses enabling the trustees to give receipts and for indemnifying them.

The testator, by his will, dated the 11th of January, 1834, after revoking all previous testamentary dispositions which he might have made, gave and devised all his real and personal estate to the trustees and executors therein named, upon certain trusts, for the benefit of his wife, his said sons John and Jacob, and his three legitimate children, who were infants.

The testator died on the 26th of April, 1834. John, one of his said sons, died in 1836, an infant. The plaintiff, Jacob, the other son, attained twenty-one, in September, 1843.

The plaintiff, by his bill, claimed to have become solely entitled to the 60,000*l.* and interest, under the indenture of covenant of September, 1829, upon the death of John, his brother, under twenty-one; and the bill prayed that the said indenture might, if necessary, be established; and that it might be declared that by virtue thereof the plaintiff was entitled to have the sum of 60,000*l.* and interest, in addition to any benefit given to him by the testator's will; and that the defendants, the executors, might be decreed to pay to the plaintiff what should be due to him in respect of the same.

The executors admitted assets. The surviving trustees named in the indenture of covenant of September, 1829, by their answer, said, that they had not accepted or acted in the trusts of the indenture; and they declined to accept or act in such trusts, unless the Court should be of opinion that they were bound so to act; they also declined to take proceedings either at law or in equity, or to permit their names to be used for the purpose of recovering the said sum of 60,000*l.*, except under the order and upon being indemnified by the decree of the Court; and they declined to receive the said sum, or to hold it upon the trusts of the indenture unless under such decree; but they stated that they were willing to act as the Court should direct.

VICE-CHANCELLOR [SIR JAMES WIGRAM]. It is not denied, that if the plaintiff in this case had brought an action in the name of the trustees, he might have recovered the money; and it is not suggested, that if the trustees had simply allowed their name to be used in the action, their conduct could have been impeached. There are two classes of cases, one of which is in favour of, and the other, if applicable, against, the plaintiff's claim. The question is, to which of the two classes it belongs.

In trying the equitable question, I shall assume the validity of the instrument at law. If there was any doubt of that, it would be reasonable to allow the plaintiff to try the right by suing in the name of the surviving trustee. The first proposition relied upon against the claim in equity was, that equity will not interfere in favour of a volunteer. That proposition, though true in many cases, has been too largely stated. A court of equity, for example, will not, in favour of a volunteer, enforce the performance of a contract in specie. That it will, however, sometimes act in favour of a volunteer, is proved by the common case of a volunteer on a bond who may prove his bond against the assets. Again, where the relation of trustee and cestui que trust is constituted, as where property is transferred from the author of the trust into the name of a trustee, so that he has lost all power of disposition over it, and the transaction is complete as regards him, the trustee, having accepted the trust, cannot say he holds it, except for the purposes of the trust; and the Court will enforce the trust at the suit of a volunteer. According to the authorities, I cannot, I admit, do anything to perfect the liability of the author of the trust, if it is not already perfect. This covenant, however, is already perfect. The covenantor is liable at law, and the Court is not called upon to do any act to perfect it. One question made in argument has been, whether there can be a trust of a covenant the benefit of which shall belong to a third party; but I cannot think there is any difficulty in that. Suppose, in the case of a personal covenant to pay a certain annual sum for the benefit of a third person, the trustee were to bring an action against the covenantor; would he be afterwards allowed to say he was not a trustee? If he cannot do so after once acknowledging the trust, then there is a case in which there is a trust of a covenant for another. In the case of Clough v. Lambert, 10 Sim. 174, the question arose; the point does not appear to have been taken during the argument, but the Vice-Chancellor of England was of opinion that the covenant bound the party; that the cestui que trust was entitled to the benefit of it; and that the mere intervention of a trustee made no difference. The proposition, therefore, that in no case can there be a trust of a covenant, is clearly too large, and the real question is, whether the relation of trustee and cestui que trust is established in the present case.

There is another class of cases: — Brackenbury v. Brackenbury, 2 J. & W. 391, Cecil v. Batcher, Id. 565, and others, in which it was doubted whether, if the author of a voluntary deed retains it in his possession, the Court will interfere in favour of the volunteer to have it delivered up; but these are cases which I think hardly affect the present question.

It was then said that this was an agreement by A. and B. for the benefit of C., a stranger to both; and, that, according to the cases, of which Colyear v. Lady Mulgrave, 2 Keen, 81, is an example, C., the stranger, could not enforce the agreement. But where the transaction is of such a nature that there is no doubt of the intention of A., while dealing with his own property, to constitute B. a trustee for C., and B. has accepted the trust, may not C. be in a condition to compel B. to enforce the legal right which the trust-deed confers upon him? If the trustees have in this case accepted the trust, I think the decision in Clough v. Lambert applies; and if they have not accepted the trust, I scarcely think that fact can make a difference. It is an extraordinary proposition, that nothing being wanted to perfect the liability of the estate to pay the debt, the plaintiff has no right in equity to obtain the benefit of the trust.

VICE-CHANCELLOR. The objections made to the relief sought by the plaintiff under the covenant in the trust-deed of September, 1829, were three: first, that the covenant was voluntary; secondly, that it was executory; and, thirdly, that it was testamentary, and had not been proved as a will. For the purpose of considering these objections I shall first assume, that the surviving trustee of the deed of September, 1829, might recover upon the covenant at law; and upon that assumption the only questions will be, first, whether I shall assist the plaintiff in this suit so far as to allow him the use of the name of the surviving trustee, upon the latter being indemnified, a course which the trustee does not object to if the Court shall direct it; and, secondly, whether I shall further facilitate the plaintiff's proceeding at law by ordering the production of the deed of covenant for the purposes of the trial.

Now, with regard to the first objection, for the reasons which I mentioned at the close of the argument, I think the proposition insisted upon, that because the covenant was voluntary, therefore the plaintiff could not recover in equity, was too broadly stated. I referred to the case of a volunteer by specialty claiming payment out of assets, and to the case of one claiming under a voluntary trust, where a fund has been transferred. The rule against relief to volunteers cannot, I conceive, in a case like that before me, be stated higher than this, — that a court of equity will not, in favour of a volunteer, give to a deed any effect beyond what the law will give to it. But if the author of the deed has subjected himself to a liability at law, and the legal liability comes regularly to be enforced in equity, as in the cases before referred to, the observation that the claimant is a volunteer is of no value in favour of those who represent the author of the deed. If, therefore, the plaintiff himself were the covenantee, so that he could bring the action in his own name, it follows, from what I have said, that, in my opinion, he might enforce payment out of the assets of the covenantor in this case. Then, does the interposition of the trustees of this covenant make any difference? I think it does not. Upon this part of the case I have asked myself the question proposed by Vice-Chancellor Knight Bruce, in Davenport *v.* Bishopp, 2 Y. & C. C. C. 451, whether, if the surviving trustee chose to sue, there would be any equity on the part of the estate to restrain him from doing so; or, which is the same question, in principle, whether, in a case in which the author of the deed has conferred no discretion on the trustees (upon which supposition the estate is liable at law) the right of the plaintiff is to depend upon the caprice of the trustee, and to be kept in suspense until the Statute of Limitations might become a bar to an action by the trustee? Or, in the case of new trustees being appointed, (perhaps by the plaintiff himself, there being a power to appoint new trustees) supposing his own nominees to be willing to sue, the other trustees might refuse to sue? I think the answer to these and like questions must be in the negative. The testator has bound himself absolutely. There is a debt created and existing. I give no assistance against the testator. I only deal with him as he has dealt by himself, and if in such a case the trustee will not sue without the sanction of the Court, I think it is right to allow the *cestui que* trust to sue for himself, in the name of the trustee, either at law, or in this court, as the case may require. The rights of the parties cannot depend upon mere accident and caprice. Having come to this conclusion upon abstract reasoning, it was satisfactory to me to find, that this view of the case is not only consistent with, but is supported by, the cases of Clough *v.* Lambert, 10 Sim. 174, and Williamson *v.* Codrington, 1 Ves. sen. 511. If the case, therefore, depended simply upon the covenant being voluntary, my opinion is, that the plaintiff would be entitled to use the name of the trustee at law, or to recover the money in this court, if it were unnecessary to have the right decided at law, and, where the legal right is clear, to have the use of the deed, if that use is material.

The second question is, whether, taking the covenant to be executory, the title of the plaintiff to relief is affected by that circumstance? The question is answered by what I have already said. Its being executory makes no difference, whether the party seeks to recover at law in the name of the trustee, or against the assets in this court.

The third question is, whether the plaintiff is precluded from relief in this court, on the ground suggested, that this is a testamentary paper. I may observe, that this objection goes also to the right to sue at law — a right which I have assumed in the observations I have already made. I have read the cases cited by Mr. Follett, as to the instrument being testamentary, and I have also referred to many other cases upon the same point. See 1 Williams Tr. on Executors, p. 75, ed. 3. I certainly was not prepared to find that the cases had gone so far as they have upon the subject. Those cases, however, are very distinguishable from the one before me. This is not a case where there is a general power of revocation reserved — a general power to dispose by will notwithstanding the execution of the instrument. In the cases referred to there has been a general reservation — or something like a reservation — of the party's right to deal with the property, notwithstanding the instrument; and the courts have held, that in such cases the instrument being one which was not to have effect until the death of the party — or rather, I would say, to use the language of Sir John Nicholl in one of the cases in which, until the death of the party, the instrument itself was not consummated — until then no conclusive effect could be given to it. If that does not occur, the instrument is not to be considered as testamentary. In this case the party clearly was bound, and there is, therefore, no ground for the argument that the interest is testamentary.

The only other question arises from the circumstance of the instrument having been kept in the possession of the party, — does that affect its legal validity? In the case of Dillon *v.* Coppin, (see 4 Myl. & Cr. 660), I had occasion to consider that subject, and I took pains to collect the cases upon it. The case of Doe *v.* Knight (Doe d. Garnons *v.* Knight, 5 B. &. C. 671) shews, that if an instrument is sealed and delivered, the retainer of it by the party in his possession does not prevent it from taking effect. No doubt the intention of the parties is often disappointed by holding them to be bound by deeds which they have kept back, but such unquestionably is the law.

As to taking the deed out of the possession of the trustees of the testator's will, I was referred to Cecil *v.* Butcher, 2 J. & W. 565, and Brackenbury *v.* Brackenbury, Id. 391, where a doubt is suggested, whether the Court would take the deed out of the possession of the party. The doubt in those cases was founded on the fact, that the instrument was for illegal purposes, concerted by both parties; but, where the instrument is free from all objection in that respect, the cases are clear that such instrument is binding at law, and, if binding, it ought to be produced. Unless, therefore, there is some reason for trying the case at law, I think the decree must be for payment upon the admission of assets.

Declare that the deed of the 1st September, 1829, constitutes a debt at law, and decree payment of the principal and interest on the same to the plaintiff out of the assets of the testator, deducting thereout as in part payment thereof any sums which have been applied for his maintenance during his minority.[1]

SECTION III.

The Statute of Frauds.

THE STATUTE OF FRAUDS.

29 Chas. II. c. 3 (1676).

VII. And be it further enacted by the authority aforesaid, That from and after the said four and twentieth day of June [1677] all declarations or creations of trusts or confidences of any lands, tenements, or hereditaments, shall be manifested and proved by some writing signed by the party who is by law enabled to declare such trust, or by his last will in writing, or else they shall be utterly void and of none effect.

VIII. Provided always, That where any conveyance shall be made of any lands or tenements by which a trust or confidence shall or may arise or result by the implication or construction of law, or be transferred or extinguished by an act or operation of law, then and in every such case such trust or confidence shall be of the like force and effect as the same would have been if this statute had not been made; anything hereinbefore contained to the contrary notwithstanding.

IX. And be it further enacted, That all grants and assignments of any trust or confidence shall likewise be in writing, signed by the

---

[1] See Gordon *v.* Small, 53 Md. 550; Fogg *v.* Middleton, 2 Hill Ch. (S. C.) 451, *ante;* Lewin, Trusts, 70, note (*a*).

In Landon *v.* Hutton, 50 N. J. Eq. 500, it was held that where A gratuitously credits B in trust for C, no debt is created and consequently no trust arises; nor is meritorious consideration in such case sufficient to create a valid debt.

On the question of the invalidity of a trust on the ground that it is a testamentary disposition made without proper formalities, see sec. IV, *post.*

party granting or assigning the same, or by such last will or devise, or else shall likewise be wholly void and of none effect.[1]

BOGGS v. YATES, 101 W. Va. 407 (1926): The plaintiff in her bill alleged that her husband by an absolute deed conveyed certain land to the defendant, their daughter, who promised to convey the land

[1] These sections of the Statute of Frauds are re-enacted in somewhat different language in Law of Property Act, 1925, 15 Geo. V. c. 20, sec. 53.

They have been adopted in many states with substantially the same phraseology. In some states the statute provides that trusts of land must be " created or declared " in writing or by deed or conveyance in writing. See Bogert, Trusts, 56.

In the following states there is no statute expressly making a writing essential to the validity of a trust: Arizona, Connecticut, Delaware, Kentucky, Louisiana, New Mexico, North Carolina, Ohio, Tennessee, Texas, Virginia, Washington, West Virginia, Wyoming. In some of these states, however, it is held that the provisions requiring a writing in the case of conveyances of and contracts concerning interests in land forbid oral trusts of land. In some of them it is held that if the owner of land orally declares himself trustee the trust is unenforceable, but that a trust created on a transfer is enforceable though oral. In West Virginia an oral trust is enforceable if in favor of a third person, but is unenforceable if in favor of the grantor. In some of the states oral trusts of land are upheld in any case. See Bogert, Trusts, 54–58; Ames, 177; Scott, Cases on Trusts, 1 ed., 193; Lord and Van Hecke, Parol Trusts in North Carolina, 8 N. C. L. Rev. 152; Madden, Trusts and the Statute of Frauds, 31 W. Va. L. Quar. 166; Benson, Parol Trusts in Real Estate, 1 Va. L. Reg. (N. s.) 81; 61 U. Pa. L. Rev. 687; 5 Tex. L. Rev. 186.

Sufficiency of memorandum. A memorandum to satisfy the Statute of Frauds must set forth with reasonable certainty the trust property, the beneficiaries, and the purposes of the trust. Blodgett v. Hildreth, 103 Mass. 484, 486; Ranney v. Byers, 219 Pa. 332. See also Snyder v. Snyder, 280 Ill. 467; Osborn v. Rearick, 325 Ill. 529; Kintner v. Jones, 122 Ind. 148, 151; Nesbitt v. Stevens, 161 Ind. 519; McClellan v. McClellan, 65 Me. 500; Renz v. Stoll, 94 Mich. 377; Illinois Steel Co. v. Konkel, 146 Wis. 556; Ann. Cas. 1913B 1024.

A writing may be sufficient as a memorandum even though it was not made for that purpose, whether the statute provides that a trust must be "manifested and proved" by a writing or that a trust must be "created or declared" in writing. Kellogg v. Peddicord, 181 Ill. 22; Urann v. Coates, 109 Mass. 581. See Ames, 178; Scott, Cases on Trusts, 1 ed., 201; Perry, Trusts, secs. 80, 81.

A signed letter may serve as a memorandum. Childers v. Childers, 1 DeG. & J. 482; Forster v. Hale, 3 Ves. Jr. 696, 5 Ves. Jr. 308; Howisohn v. Baird, 40 So. 94 (Ala. 1906); Brackenbury v. Hodgkin, 116 Me. 399; Barrell v. Joy, 16 Mass. 221; Woolfitt v. Histed, 208 Mich. 308; Neal v. Bryant, 291 Mo. 81; Smith v. Hainline, 253 S. W. 1049 (Mo., 1923); Sinclair v. Purdy, 235 N. Y. 245. See Ann. Cas. 1913B 1026.

A will may serve as a memorandum. Hiss v. Hiss, 228 Ill. 414; Wehe v. Wehe, 44 N. D. 280.

A pleading may serve as a memorandum. Myers v. Myers, 167 Ill. 52, 64; Bridgman v. McIntyre, 150 Mich. 78; McVay v. McVay, 43 N. J. Eq. 47; Schumacher v. Draeger, 137 Wis. 618. See 22 A. L. R. 735.

A memorandum may consist of several writings. Loring v. Palmer, 118 U. S. 321; Tenney v. Simpson, 37 Kan. 579; Smith v. Hainline, 253 S. W. 1049

to the plaintiff; that although the deed was absolute and recited consideration, no consideration ever passed; and that after the death of the husband the daughter refused to convey the land to the plaintiff. The defendant demurred on the ground that the alleged oral trust could not be enforced because of the Statute of Frauds and the parol evidence rule. The lower court sustained the demurrer. This ruling was reversed by the Supreme Court of Appeals. The latter court held that the Statute of Frauds was not a bar in West Virginia, and that the parol evidence rule did not prevent a recovery by the plaintiff. WOODS, J., said (p. 409):

"As to the second ground of demurrer, it is a general rule of evidence that parol testimony cannot be admitted to vary or add to a written contract, and especially a contract or deed conveying lands. There are some cases which are sometimes called exceptions to this general rule, but which are really not exceptions; they being cases to which the rule is not properly applicable. Thus, a deed absolute on its face may be shown by parol evidence to have been given as security for a loan. The real office of the parol evidence in such a case is not to vary the contract in writing, but to establish the existence of a collateral fact which when established controls the deed. So as here, if a party obtained a deed without any consideration, upon a parol assurance by the grantee that she would make a particular disposition of it, a court of equity will enforce the specific performance of such an agreement, even though the deed recites that it was made for a valuable consideration, if in point of fact no consideration was really paid by the grantee. Onson v. Cown, 22 Wis. 329; Miller v. Pearce, 6 Watts & S. (Pa.) 97; Hoge v. Hoge, 1 Watts (Pa.) 163; Thompson et ux. v. White, 1 Dall. (Pa.) 447; Kennedy's Heirs v. Kennedy's Heirs, 2 Ala. 571. In such case the deed is not added to or altered by the parol evidence; but this evidence fastens on the individual who got the title without consideration the personal obligation of fulfilling her agreement whereby she procured

---

(Mo. 1923); Hutchins v. Van Vechten, 140 N. Y. 115; Gates v. Paul, 117 Wis. 170. See Smith v. Matthews, 3 DeG. F. & J. 138; McCandless v. Warner, 26 W. Va. 754, 780; Ann. Cas. 1913B 1026.

Part performance. In the following cases it was held that the trust was enforceable because of "part performance." Rundell v. McDonald, 62 Cal. App. 721; Hayden v. Denslow, 27 Conn. 335; Gallagher v. Northrup, 215 Ill. 563; Chantland v. Sherman, 148 Iowa 352; Goff v. Goff, 98 Kan. 201; Thierry v. Thierry, 298 Mo. 25; Jeremiah v. Pitcher, 26 App. Div. 402, *aff'd* 163 N. Y. 574; McKinley v. Hessen, 202 N. Y. 24; Foreman v. Foreman, 251 N. Y. 237, *post;* Waters v. Hall, 218 N. Y. App. Div. 149. See 32 Yale L. Jour. 509; Perry, Trusts, sec. 82.

In the following cases it was held that there was not such "part performance" as to make the trust enforceable. Feeney v. Howard, 79 Cal. 525; Verzier v. Convard, 75 Conn. 1; McCartney v. Fletcher, 11 App. D. C. 1, 18; Wentworth v. Wentworth, 2 Minn. 277; Pillsbury-Washburn Flour-Mills Co. v. Kistler, 53 Minn. 123; Rathbun v. Rathbun, 6 Barb. (N. Y.) 98; Cooley v. Lobdell, 153 N. Y. 596; Spaulding v. Collins, 51 Wash. 488.

the title, as without its enforcement by a court of equity the grantee would be allowed to avail herself of a fraud in so obtaining the deed."[1]

DANSER v. WARWICK.

CHANCERY, NEW JERSEY. 1880.

33 N. J. Eq. 133.

THE VICE-CHANCELLOR [VAN FLEET]. The complainant is the widow of David C. Danser. She seeks to have a parol trust established and enforced against the defendant. She alleges that her husband, some months before his death, assigned the bond and mortgage in controversy to the defendant, upon a parol trust or understanding that he would forthwith, or by a short day, transfer them to her. The transfer to the defendant was intended to be merely a step in vesting her with title. The assignment to the defendant bears date February 1st, 1875, and Danser died on the 13th day of the following September. The bond and mortgage were in Danser's possession at the time of his death, and have since then been constantly in the possession of the complainant. The defendant has never asked for them, nor attempted to get possession of them. A month or six weeks prior to Danser's death, the defendant directed an assignment to be drawn to the complainant, stating to the person to whom he gave the direction that he must draw it for Danser, who would pay him. He, at the same time, said it was right that the old lady — referring to the complainant — should have the bond and mortgage. Danser, at this time, was prostrated by the disease which shortly afterwards caused his death. The defendant did not remain to execute the assignment, but said

---

[1] It is generally held that the parol evidence rule does not forbid engrafting a trust upon a conveyance made by deed absolute on its face. Minchin v. Minchin, 157 Mass. 265 (personalty); Harvey v. Gardner, 41 Oh. St. 642; Russell v. Bruer, 64 Oh. St. 1; Mee v. Mee, 113 Tenn. 454 (*semble*); Young v. Brown, 136 Tenn. 184; Young v. Holland, 117 Va. 433. But see *contra,* Kelly v. McNeill, 118 N. C. 349; Gaylord v. Gaylord, 150 N. C. 222; Walters v. Walters, 172 N. C. 328.

Where the instrument clearly negatives any trust, parol evidence of the intention to create a trust is inadmissible. Mee v. Mee, 113 Tenn. 454. Where a trust is clearly declared in the instrument, a different trust cannot be shown by parol evidence. Earl of Worcester v. Finch, 4 Inst. 85, 86; Walton v. Follansbee, 165 Ill. 480; Supreme Lodge v. Rutzler, 87 N. J. Eq. 342. The mere fact that the word " trustee " is inserted after the name of the grantee does not prevent the introduction of extrinsic evidence to the effect that no trust was intended. See Taylor, Effect of " Trustee " in Deed, 16 Lawyer & Banker 138. Where a deposit is made in a savings bank in the name of the depositor " as trustee " for another, parol evidence is admissible to show that no trust was intended. Schauberger v. Tafel, 202 Ky. 9. See 43 Harv. L. Rev. 541.

As to the parol evidence rule, see Perry, Trusts, sec. 75; 5 Wigmore, Evidence, 2 ed., sec. 2437; L. R. A. 1916B 169; 35 A. L. R. 280, 284; 45 A. L. R. 851, 852.

he would return soon and do so. He did not return that day. He was subsequently informed, on two or three different occasions, while Danser was living, that the assignment had been drawn and was ready for execution. On each occasion he said he had forgotten or neglected to execute it, but would call soon and do so. He never fulfilled his promise. Two or three weeks after Danser's death, he called for the assignment Danser had made to him, and which he had left when he gave direction for the draft of the one to the complainant, and stated that he meant to do what was right about the matter, but he would not execute the assignment to the complainant until things were fixed up; Danser owed him. He took both papers and has never executed the assignment to the complainant. . . .

The trust, it will be observed, affects personal property, and not lands. The subject of it is a debt. That part of the statute of frauds which enacts that all declarations and creations of trusts shall be manifested by writing and signed by the party creating the same, or else shall be void and of no effect, applies only to trusts of lands, and has no application to trusts of personal property. A valid trust of personalty may be created verbally, and proved by parol evidence. A trust of personal property, almost precisely like the one under consideration, and which had been created by mere spoken words, and was supported by only parol evidence, was upheld by Chancellor Williamson in Hooper v. Holmes, 3 Stock. 122; also Kimball v. Morton, 1 Hal. Ch. 26; Sayre v. Fredericks, 1 C. E. Gr. 205; Eaton v. Cook, 10 C. E. Gr. 55; 2 Story's Eq. Jur. § 972; 1 Perry on Trusts § 86. A valid trust of a mortgage debt may be created by parol; for, though a trust thus created cannot embrace the land held in pledge, yet it is good as to the debt, and will entitle the *cestui que trust* to sufficient of the proceeds of sale, when the land is converted into money, to pay the debt. Sayre v. Fredericks, supra; Benbow v. Townsend, 1 M. & K. 506; Childs v. Jordan, 106 Mass. 321.

It must be held, then, that the trust alleged in this case is valid, and if it has been sufficiently proved, the complainant is entitled to have it established and enforced. . . .

There must be a decree establishing the trust and requiring the defendant to execute it. The defendant must pay costs.[1]

[1] Bellasis v. Compton, 2 Vern. 294; Benbow v. Townsend, 1 Myl. & K. 506 (*semble*); Patterson v. Mills, 69 Iowa 755; Sturtevant v. Jacques, 14 Allen (Mass.) 523; Childs v. Jordan, 106 Mass. 321; [Thacher v. Churchill, 118 Mass. 108;] Rice v. Rice, 107 Mich. 241; Bucklin v. Bucklin, 1 Abb. App. (N. Y.) 242, 1 Keyes 141; Bunn v. Vaughan, 1 Abb. App. (N. Y.) 253; Robbins v. Robbins, 89 N. Y. 251, accord. — AMES.

Under the English and almost all the American statutes, a trust of personalty may be created by parol. Ames, 187; 51 L. R. A. (N. S.) 1208; 39 Cyc. 51. But see Oglesby v. Wilmerding, 149 Ga. 45. In a few jurisdictions an *assignment* of a trust of personal property must be in writing, for example, in

CHACE v. GARDNER.

SUPREME JUDICIAL COURT, MASSACHUSETTS. 1917.

228 Mass. 533.

BILL IN EQUITY, inserted in a common law writ dated July 21, 1914, against the executor of the will of Katherine F. Gardner, late of Swansea, the aunt of the plaintiff, praying that a trust in favor of the plaintiff be established in a fund of $2,500 in the hands of the defendant as executor, which constituted the proceeds from the sale of certain real estate in Swansea, as described in the opinion.

In the Superior Court the case was heard by Dubuque, J., who made findings of fact, which are stated in substance in the opinion, and ruled that upon the facts found the plaintiff was entitled to recover the amount of the proceeds from the land sales, namely, $2,224.75 with interest from the date of the writ. Later by order of the judge a final decree was entered for the plaintiff; and the defendant appealed.

R. L. c. 147, § 1, is as follows: " No trust concerning land, except such as may arise or result by implication of law, shall be created or declared unless by an instrument in writing signed by the party or by the attorney of the party creating or declaring the trust."

CARROLL, J. It was found by the judge who heard this suit in equity that the plaintiff's father, Charles F. Chace, and Katherine F. Gardner (brother and sister) owned two tracts of land in Swansea; that by partition proceedings one tract was set off to Charles and one to Katherine; that on September 18, 1880, Charles conveyed to his sister the parcel owned by him, by warranty deed in the usual form, without consideration being paid by the grantee to the grantor, upon the oral agreement that she should hold the land in trust for her own benefit during her life, and after her death it was to become the property of the plaintiff; that, if said real estate was converted into money, the proceeds of the sale were to be held by the grantee to enjoy the income thereof during her life, the plaintiff to be the sole " beneficiary and owner of the principal of said proceeds after his aunt's death "; and that this agreement was made known to the plaintiff by his father and by the grantee. He further found that Mrs. Gardner sold the land in

---

California, Minnesota, Montana, Nebraska, New York, North Dakota, Wisconsin.

Chattels real are within the Statute of Frauds. See Skett v. Whitmore, Freem. C. C. 280; Riddle v. Emerson, 1 Vern. 108; Hutchins v. Lee, 1 Atk. 447; Forster v. Hale, 3 Ves. Jr. 696, 5 Ves. 308; Gardner v. Rowe, 2 Sim. & St. 346, 5 Russ. 258.

As to the amount of evidence necessary to establish an oral trust, see 51 L. R. A. (N. S.) 1210; 23 A. L. R. 1500.

1907 and 1909, for the sum of $2,245.75, and deposited the proceeds in several banks in Fall River " (without mention of any trust) where the same are traceable now; but mingled with other money of hers."

Mrs. Gardner died in 1914. The defendant is the executor of her will. The presiding judge states that " The statute of frauds does not appear to have been pleaded," but it was agreed that the case might be heard as though it had been pleaded. A decree was entered in the Superior Court declaring that the plaintiff was entitled to the proceeds arising from the sale of the real estate, amounting to $2,245.75 and ordering the defendant to pay that sum of money to the plaintiff. The defendant appealed.

If the oral agreement concerned the real estate alone the statute would apply, the trust could not be enforced and no constructive trust would arise. R. L. c. 147, § 1. Campbell *v.* Brown, 129 Mass. 23. Tourtillotte *v.* Tourtillotte, 205 Mass. 547. The statute requiring an instrument in writing for the creation or declaration of a trust applies to a trust concerning land only; an oral trust in personal property is valid. Chase *v.* Perley, 148 Mass. 289. Taft *v.* Stow, 167 Mass. 363.

The judge found that the grantee converted the real estate into money and the fund arising from the sale was in existence at the time of her death; he also found, and there was sufficient evidence to support the finding, that when Mrs. Gardner received the deed of real estate she agreed, if the real estate was converted into money, to hold the proceeds, the income to be hers during her life, the principal to be payable to the plaintiff on her death.

That part of the agreement relating to the proceeds of the sale is separate and distinct from the part relating to the land. When the real estate was converted into money Mrs. Gardner held it as she agreed to hold it when the trust was created; and this trust in personal property did not require a memorandum in writing. The bill is not brought to enforce an oral trust in land; it is brought to enforce a trust in personal property which the defendant has in his possession, and where nothing remains to be done except the payment by the defendant of the amount which he holds as the executor of the trustee.

The rule governing cases of this kind was stated by Mr. Justice Metcalf in Rand *v.* Mather, 11 Cush. 1, 7, as follows: " The true doctrine is this: If any part of an agreement is valid, it will avail *pro tanto*, though another part of it may be prohibited by statute; provided the statute does not, either expressly or by necessary implication, render the whole void; and provided, furthermore, that the sound part can be separated from the unsound, and be enforced without injustice to the defendant."

In Trowbridge *v.* Wetherbee, 11 Allen, 361, 364, Chapman, J., speaking of the statute of frauds, said: "If some of the stipulations in a contract are within the statute and others are not, and those which are within it have been performed, an action lies upon the other stipulations, if they are separate." The plaintiff in Zwicker v. Gardner, 213 Mass. 95, a mortgagor of real estate, was allowed to recover on an oral agreement made with the mortgagee that if the plaintiff would not bid at the foreclosure proceedings, the mortgagee would pay to him the balance that remained after deducting the mortgage, interest and expenses. It was there held that the action was not to enforce an oral contract for the sale of land; that the land had been sold and a part of the contract relating to it had been executed and it was separable from the part of the contract which concerned the excess. The same principle applies in the case at bar: Mrs. Gardner's executor holds the proceeds of the sale by reason of an agreement made by his testatrix that this money was to belong to the plaintiff after her death. This section of the agreement is separable from the part relating to the real estate, to which part alone the statute applies, and which has been fully performed. See Page v. Monks, 5 Gray, 492; Wetherbee v. Potter, 99 Mass. 354, 361; Lyman v. Lyman, 133 Mass. 414; Graffam v. Pierce, 143 Mass. 386.

Accordingly, where land has been conveyed on a parol trust to hold the proceeds for a certain purpose, if that event has taken place and the land is converted into money, the statute of frauds is not a defence. The trust will be enforced although there was no declaration of trust subsequent to the conversion. Lasley v. Delano, 139 Mich. 602. Bork v. Martin, 132 N.Y. 280. Logan v. Brown, 20 Okla. 334. And see Bailey v. Wood, 211 Mass. 37.

There are some decisions at variance with what is here decided. See 39 Cyc. 52, where the cases are collected. But we think the conclusion which we have reached is supported by both principle and authority. In view of what has been said it is unnecessary to consider the other questions which have been discussed.

Decree affirmed with costs.[1]

---

[1] The same result was reached in Miller v. Kendig, 55 Iowa 174 (and see Allen v. Rees, 136 Iowa 423); Youngs v. Read, 246 Mich. 219; Michael v. Foil, 100 N. C. 178; and Kickland v. Menasha etc. Co., 68 Wis. 34, where there was no agreement to sell the land but only to pay over the proceeds if the land were sold.

The same result was reached in the following cases where the grantee orally agreed to sell the land and to pay over the proceeds. Mohn v. Mohn, 112 Ind. 285; Thomas v. Merry, 113 Ind. 83; Talbot v. Barber, 11 Ind. App. 1; Hall v. Hall, 8 N. H. 129; Graves v. Graves, 45 N. H. 323; Bork v. Martin, 132 N. Y. 280; Logan v. Brown, 20 Okla. 334. See also Rosenberg v. Drooker, 229 Mass. 205; Fencer v. Wills, 259 Mass. 546. But see *contra*, McGinness v. Barton, 71 Iowa 644; Rapley v. McKinney's Est., 143 Mich. 508; White v. McKenzie, 193 Mich. 189; Marvel v. Marvel, 70 Neb. 498; Johnson v. Mc-

HOLMES v. HOLMES.

SUPREME COURT, WASHINGTON. 1911.

65 Wash. 572.

APPEAL from a judgment of the superior court for King county, Gilliam, J., entered November 22, 1910, upon findings in favor of the defendants, after a trial on the merits before the court without a jury, in an action for specific performance. Affirmed.

GOSE, J. — The plaintiff conveyed certain property in the city of Seattle to his brother, the defendant Edward B. Holmes, on the 7th day of June, 1909, by a deed absolute in form. On the same day he assigned to him a contract which he had for the purchase of ten acres of land in Benton county. Both instruments of conveyance recite a consideration of five dollars. The complaint alleges, in substance, that the conveyances were made without consideration and upon condition that the property should be reconveyed upon demand. A demand for a reconveyance proving unavailing, this action was brought to compel it. The defendant answered that he holds the property under the terms of an express trust, evidenced by his declaration executed upon the day the deed and assignment were executed and delivered, and which is as follows:

"June 7th, 1909.

"I hereby acknowledge that I hold in trust the following property transferred to me by Thomas Holmes, that is the house and lot in block B, Brooklyn Sup'l Addition, and ten acres near Prosser, in Benton county, for the following purposes: 1st; to collect the rents and apply them to paying any indebtedness to Holmes Lumber Company of Seattle, or in paying for the Benton land. 2d. After that to use the income in investments for Thomas Holmes, or to pay

---

Kenzie, 80 Ore. 160; Kinsey v. Bennett, 37 S. C. 319. *Cf.* National etc. Bank v. Lindsell, [1922] 1 K. B. 21. For conflicting decisions, see 1 Tiffany, Real Property, 2 ed., sec. 106(c); 39 Cyc. 52.

If the grantee of land orally agrees to hold it upon trust for the grantor and there is no agreement with reference to the proceeds of the land if it should be sold, and the grantee subsequently sells the land, there is no enforceable trust of the proceeds.

If the grantee after converting the land into money orally admits that he holds the money in trust, the trust is enforceable. Mills v. Thomas, 194 Ind. 648; Calder v. Moran, 49 Mich. 14; Tracy v. Tracy, 3 Bradf. (N. Y.) 57; Maffitt v. Rynd, 69 Pa. 380; Everhart's App., 106 Pa. 349; Hess' App., 112 Pa. 168. See Aynesworth v. Haldeman, 2 Duv. (Ky.) 565.

But if the grantee of land orally agrees to sell it and to pay the proceeds to the *cestui que trust*, and refuses to sell it, the *cestui que trust* cannot reach the land or compel a sale. Gee v. Thrailkill, 45 Kan. 173; Pearson v. Pearson, 125 Ind. 341; Grantham v. Conner, 97 Kan. 150; Walters v. Walters, 172 N. C. 328.

See 8 L. R. A. (N. S.) 1137; 20 L. R. A. (N. S.) 298; Perry, Trusts, secs. 79, 86.

them to him, if necessary for his support. 3rd. When he dies to deed it, or any investments of it to his sisters and brother James.

(Signed) Edward B. Holmes."

The court found that the plaintiff conveyed the property to Edward B. Holmes " of his own free will and accord," in consideration of the latter's promise to hold the property in trust. It further found that, at the same time and as a part of the transaction, the defendant Edward B. Holmes executed the declaration of trust which we have set forth; that it was shown to plaintiff, and delivered to defendant Joseph Holmes for safe keeping. These findings are supported by the evidence. The court deduced as a conclusion of law, "that said trust agreement, being made as a part and parcel of the same transaction in which the deeds were executed and delivered, is to be considered with said deeds as an express trust." There was a judgment for the defendants. The plaintiff has appealed.

The appellant's contention is that the property having been conveyed without consideration, an implied or resulting trust arose, and that he was entitled to revoke the trust at his pleasure and compel a reconveyance. The respondent Edward B. Holmes, who will hereafter be spoken of as the respondent, contends that he holds the property subject to an express trust, the terms of which are stated in his declaration, and that it is irrevocable. The appellant meets this contention with the argument that no one but the beneficial owner can declare the trust, or execute a declaration which will take the transaction out of the statute of frauds.

The rule in this state is that a resulting trust can, and an express trust cannot, be proven by parol testimony. Spaulding v. Collins, 51 Wash. 488, 99 Pac. 306. The important and decisive question in the case is, can an express trust be proven by a writing signed by the trustee. We think the question must receive an affirmative answer. In vol. 3, Pomeroy's Equity Jurisprudence (3d ed.), § 1007, this view is announced in the following language:

" The written evidence of the trust which will satisfy the statute *may* come from the grantor, — the one who intends that a trust shall be created for a certain beneficiary, — or from the trustee, — the grantee to whom the land is conveyed for the purposes of the trust, but not from the *cestui que trust*. The grantor may declare the trust in the will or the deed by which the land is conveyed or devised, or in an instrument separate and distinct from the conveyance; or he may declare himself a trustee, and that he holds the land in trust, without conveying the legal title. When the trust is not created in and by the instrument of conveyance, it may be sufficiently declared and evidenced by the trustee to whom the land is conveyed, or who becomes holder of the legal title; and this may be done by a writing executed simultaneously with or subsequent to the conveyance, and such writing may be of a most informal nature." . . .

Where a trust has been properly created, with an intelligent understanding of the nature of the act, it is irrevocable even though it be voluntary. 28 Am. & Eng. Ency. Law (2d ed.), 899.

The judgment is affirmed.[1]

DUNBAR, C. J., FULLERTON, PARKER, and MOUNT, JJ., concur.

[1] 1. *Declaration of trust.* If one declares himself trustee he is of course the proper party to execute the memorandum, whether at the time of the creation of the trust or subsequently. As to the sufficiency of a declaration of trust made prior to the creation of the trust, see Brackenbury v. Hodgkin, 116 Me. 399; Compo v. Jackson Iron Co., 49 Mich. 39.

2. *Transfer upon trust.* a. *For the transferor.* It is of course sufficient if the trust is declared in the instrument by which the estate is transferred. As to the sufficiency of a prior or contemporaneous memorandum signed by the transferor, see Childers v. Childers, 1 DeG. & J. 482 (prior to transfer); Patterson v. McClenathan, 296 Ill. 475; Ellison v. Ganiard, 167 Ind. 471; Rogers v. Rogers, 52 Wis. 36 (not known to grantee). As to the sufficiency of a memorandum signed by the transferee, see Forster v. Hall, 3 Ves. Jr. 696, 5 Ves. Jr. 308; Nesbitt v. Stevens, 161 Ind. 519 (prior to transfer); Barrell v. Joy, 16 Mass. 221; Urann v. Coates, 109 Mass. 581; McVay v. McVay, 43 N. J. Eq. 47; McCandless v. Warner, 26 W. Va. 754. On the question whether there is a constructive trust if no memorandum is executed, see *post*, Chap. V, sec. III.

b. *For a third person.* It is of course sufficient if the trust is declared in the instrument by which the estate is transferred. As to the sufficiency of a contemporaneous memorandum signed by the transferor, see Gaylord v. La-Fayette, 115 Ind. 423, 428. As to the sufficiency of a contemporaneous memorandum signed by the transferee, see Kintner v. Jones, 122 Ind. 148; Holmes v. Holmes, 65 Wash. 572, Ann. Cas. 1913B 1023. As to the sufficiency of a subsequent memorandum signed by the transferor, see Phillips v. South Park Commissioners, 119 Ill. 626, 639. As to the sufficiency of a subsequent memorandum signed by the transferee, see Union etc. Co. v. Campbell, 95 Ill. 267; Myers v. Myers, 167 Ill. 52; Bates v. Hurd, 65 Me. 180; M'Clellan v. M'Clellan, 65 Me. 500; Geddis v. Congdon, 262 Mass. 294; Clark v. Kinnaugh, 133 Atl. 381 (N. J. 1926); Baldwin v. Humphrey, 44 N. Y. 609; Sinclair v. Purdy, 235 N. Y. 245; 3 Pomeroy, Eq. Juris., sec. 1007. On the question whether there is a constructive trust if no memorandum is executed and if the transferee refuses to carry out the trust, see *post*, Chap. V, sec. III.

3. *Purchase in the name of another.* If A purchases property but takes title in the name of B, a memorandum signed by B showing the actual terms on which he took title is sufficient. Quackenbush v. Leonard, 9 Paige (N. Y.) 334 (contemporaneous memorandum); Bragg v. Paulk, 42 Me. 502 (subsequent memorandum). But if such memorandum shows different terms from those agreed upon it will not bind A. Kronheim v. Johnson, 7 Ch. D. 60; Adams v. Carey, 53 N. J. Eq. 334; Griffith v. Eisenberg, 215 Pa. 182. See Dale v. Hamilton, 2 Phil. 266. On the question whether there is a resulting trust if no memorandum is executed, see *post*, Chap. V, sec. IV.

4. *Assignment by the cestui que trust.* When the *cestui que trust* assigns his interest, the memorandum whether executed contemporaneously with or subsequently to the assignment should be signed by the assignor. Tierney v. Wood, 19 Beav. 330.

BRYANT v. KLATT.

DISTRICT COURT OF THE UNITED STATES, S. D. N. Y. 1924.

2 F.(2d) 167.

IN EQUITY. Suit by Walter L. Bryant, trustee in bankruptcy of Fred. H. Ruggles and August O. Klatt, individually and as partners comprising the firm of the R. & K. Bakery, against August O. Klatt and others. Decree for complainant establishing lien.

Final hearing on bill in equity to set aside a conveyance of real estate by a bankrupt on the eve of the filing of the petition. It was agreed that, if the property belonged to the bankrupt at that time, the conveyance was void. The circumstances were as follows:

The bankrupts were a firm, consisting of August O. Klatt and his sister's husband, one Ruggles. August J. Klatt was the father of August O., and had as children besides him and his sister, Mrs. Ruggles, another son, Charles. The father had fallen into enmity with his son-in-law, Ruggles, who he feared might take some action against him. He was seized in fee of a tenement in the city of New York on which he lived with August O. and the Ruggleses. Unknown to the grantees, August J. Klatt, on June 1, 1923, executed a deed, recorded June 3, 1923, of this parcel of land to his sons, Charles and August O., supposing that thus he could defeat any possible machinations of his son-in-law, Ruggles.

The grantees learned nothing of the deed until June 27th, when they were asked to sign a notice to Ruggles that he must vacate on August 1st. At that time the father told the sons, as the reason why he had conveyed the property to them, that it was to be held in trust for him by them, he paying taxes and the interest upon a mortgage. The sons signed the notice to vacate and collected one month's rent, after which August O., finding himself on the verge of bankruptcy, conveyed his interest to Charles.

LEARNED HAND, District Judge (after stating the facts as above). [1] I am satisfied that this old gentleman had no intention of conveying the beneficial interest in his property from himself to his sons, but that the deed was a device of an incompetent lawyer to protect him against his son-in-law. It is true that, in the nature of things, the evidence could not be disputed, but it is antecedently probable in itself. It is not likely that he meant to strip himself of his life's earnings, and put his property out of his hands, for no reason at all. It so happens that, if the trust which he attempted so to create had been expressed in the deed, or in any adequate writing, it would have been void in New York under section 93 of the Real Property Law (Consol. Laws, c. 50), which vests all " dry " trusts at once in the cestui que trust, just as the statute of uses executed uses. The trust attempted not being one of those allowed under section 96, and the cestui que trust being the settlor himself, the deed would have been a nullity.

However, the trust was not in writing, and was therefore void under section 242. It is therefore the plaintiff's position that August O. Klatt took a fee as tenant in common with his brother, free and clear of all equitable interest, and leviable in the interests of his creditors. The conveyance on the eve of bankruptcy was, they claim, as much a fraud on them as though the land had been bought with their money. Perhaps this ought to be the law, but in fact it is not. While as against the grantee the cestui que trust has no rights which he can enforce, still if the grantee chooses to recognize his "moral" obligation, as it is called, his creditors may not complain. The courts seem to have been able to endure the spectacle of a man who in his own interest defrauds a confiding fellow, but to stick at allowing the same privilege to his creditors. Whatever may be thought of the logic of the distinction, it is well settled. Gardner v. Rowe, 2 Sim. & Stu. 346, affirmed by Lord Lyndhurst 5 Russ. 258; Silvers v. Potter, 48 N. J. Eq. 539, 22 A. 584; Iauch v. De Socarras, 56 N. J. Eq. 538, 39 A. 370; Desmond v. Myers, 113 Mich. 437, 71 N. W. 877; Hays v. Reger, 102 Ind. 524, 1 N. E. 386; Cresswell v. McCaig, 11 Neb. 222, 9 N. W. 52; Brisco v. Norris, 112 N. C. 671, 16 S. E. 850. The same rule was laid down in Davis v. Graves, 29 Barb. (N. Y.) 480, Lowry v. Smith, 9 Hun (N. Y.) 514, and Dunn v. Whalen, 66 Hun, 634, 21 N. Y. S. 869. The only exception I have found is an early Massachusetts case. Smith v. Lane, 3 Pick. 205. Therefore I hold that August O. Klatt's conveyance to his brother in recognition of the fiduciary origin of his estate was not a fraud upon his creditors, even though the trust rested in parol, and though August J. could not have enforced it against him.

The plaintiff further argues that he may win by estoppel. This rests upon a talk between Lang, the agent of a creditor, Coulter, and August O. Klatt, in which Klatt is supposed to have said that he had a one-half interest in the house he lived in, which was the locus in quo. This talk Lang places some time before June 9th, and the theory is that the goods sold after it were sold on the faith of August O.'s supposed title. These goods amounted in all to $943.10. Of them only $300 were sold after August O. Klatt says that his father told him of the deed. Assuming that the trustee is vested by section 70e (Comp. St. § 9654) with the rights of Coulter to avoid the deed, I think that the circumstances do not justify the relief. It may be that the sons learned of the deed earlier than August O. admits. Indeed Charles J. says that it was early in June, though he also says it was after he signed the notice to quit. But the date makes no difference, I think, because I do not see why the equity arising from Klatt's declaration to Lang should be superior to that arising on the parol trust. If the trust had been enforceable, no one would say that any declaration of the trustee could affect the rights of the cestui que trust.

But in cases of this kind apparently the law treats the trust as valid so long as the trustee does not choose to insist upon the absence of any writing. Foote *v.* Bryant, 47 N. Y. 544. Perhaps a creditor who has been deceived by him has a greater complaint than a creditor who is merely as such entitled to pursue his assets, but at most it is a case of two conflicting equities, the creditor's and the beneficiary's, and there is no reason to prefer the creditor. In such situations it is always the practice of the courts to let the legal title prevail. Certainly there can be no propriety in saying that the beneficiary, even though he be also the grantor, is privy to the representation. Indeed, I have much doubt whether, at the time when August O. Klatt made the statement, he knew of the deed, or whether it could be said to have been then accepted. If so, under no principle of estoppel could the lien have been for more than $300, the price of the last parcel of goods. But I do not stand upon that distinction; I place my decision on the doctrine I have mentioned.

Bill dismissed, but without costs.

On Reargument.

The first point is the distinction between the New York statute of frauds and those in many other jurisdictions. The New York statute provides that no trusts shall be created without writing; the others, that they shall not be enforced. The distinction is thoroughly casuistical. If the trustee cannot be legally compelled to recognize the trust, his recognition is as voluntary as though no trust was created at all. In either case it is really a question of how far the courts will consider the moral obligation of the trustee as binding on his creditors. The whole doctrine is, strictly speaking, anomalous, and it seems to me a mistaken notion to graft upon it purely verbal and sophistical distinctions which ignore the real reason of it; i.e., the unwillingness of the courts to allow a man's creditors to profit by what was truly never his at all. Therefore I decline to change my ruling as to this point.

[2] The second point rests upon a case in New York, Fritz *v.* Worden, 20 App. Div. 241, 46 N. Y. S. 1040, and two in New Jersey, Budd *v.* Atkinson, 30 N. J. Eq. 530, and Besson *v.* Eveland, 26 N. J. Eq. 468, which recognize a superior equity in the creditor, who has acted on the faith of the trustee's ownership over the equity of the beneficiary by parol. I really fail to see any principle on which this can be established, though, as I have said, the whole doctrine is so anomalous that one may be prepared for anything. For the reasons I gave originally, I am disposed to treat the equities as equal, but here are three authorities which hold otherwise, and although Hegstedt *v.* Wysiecki, 178 App. Div. 733, 165 N. Y. S. 898, is readily

distinguishable, it recognizes the rule. While these decisions are not authoritative on me, I think I ought to take them as binding. In passing, I may add that Fritz v. Worden, supra, appears to recognize the validity of the parol trust in general as against creditors who can claim no estoppel.

Hence it becomes necessary to take a more positive position upon the evidence than I did in my first opinion. Did August O. Klatt, while he held title, tell Lang that he owned half the house, and did Coulter sell him the three last bills of goods on the faith of that representation? Unless this took place after August O. Klatt had title, and knew he had title, it would not be an estoppel. August J. could not be bound by a declaration made before he had given any color for the making of it. Lang's memory was naturally hazy about dates, but he is sure that he had the talk before the bill of goods of June 9th was delivered. By implication it was after May 26th, because it was the bill of that day which, added to the rest, caused his concern. Now it seems to me rather curious that August O. Klatt should have told Lang that he owned one-half, and not the whole, property as an inducement to give him credit, if he merely intended a fraud upon Lang. He did own one-half between June 3d and June 9th in a sense which he might well have claimed it, without supposing himself to be cheating Lang, though he did in good morals owe a duty to his father to guard it for him.

Klatt denies that he knew of the deed till June 27th, and he is in some measure borne out by the fact that on June 7th it was Weiss, and not Charles J. and August O. Klatt, who collected the rent, something more consonant with the Klatts' story than with Lang's. Further, while Klatt's denial is not as categorical as one might wish, he does deny that he ever told any one in June that he had a half interest in the property.

On the whole, I believe that Lang's story is the more credible, and that Klatt knew of the deed before June 9th, perhaps only a day or two. I cannot account otherwise for the curious compatibility between Lang's story and the truth. Hence I hold that to the extent of $943.10 the trustee has established his lien.

A decree may therefore pass, declaring a lien upon a one-half interest in the tenement to the extent of $943.10, with interest from the several dates of delivery.[1]

---

[1] *Effect of Subsequent Memorandum or Performance.* If land is transferred upon an oral trust and the trustee thereafter signs a memorandum or performs the trust, it has been held that the trust is enforceable or the performance effective not only as against the trustee but as against the claims of third persons.

1. *As against creditors of the trustee.* If the trustee of land under an oral trust conveys to the *cestui que trust,* the conveyance cannot be impeached by the trustee's general creditors. Moran v. Morgan, 252 Fed. 719; Smith v. Ellison, 80 Ark. 447; Fraser v. Churchman, 43 Ind. App. 200; Mc-

Cormick H. M. Co. *v.* Griffin, 116 Iowa 397; Bailey *v.* Wood, 211 Mass. 37; Ferguson *v.* Winchester Trust Co., 166 N. E. 709 (Mass. 1929); Patton *v.* Chamberlain, 44 Mich. 5; Desmond *v.* Myers, 113 Mich. 437; Silvers *v.* Potter, 48 N. J. Eq. 539; Iauch *v.* de Socarras, 56 N. J. Eq. 538; Davis *v.* Graves, 29 Barb. (N. Y.) 480; Lockren *v.* Rustan, 9 N. D. 43 (breach of promise of marriage); Richmond *v.* Bloch, 36 Ore. 590; Gottstein *v.* Wist, 22 Wash. 581; Martin *v.* Remington, 100 Wis. 540. See also Karr *v.* Washburn, 56 Wis. 303. But see Hegstad *v.* Wysiecki, 178 N. Y. App. Div. 733 (tort creditor). See Ames, 181; 64 A. L. R. 576.

In the following cases the conveyance was allowed to stand although made after a creditor of the trustee had obtained a judgment lien upon the land. Hays *v.* Reger, 102 Ind. 524; Hurt *v.* Drew, 122 Kan. 357; Wilmere *v.* Dunn, 133 Md. 354; Siemon *v.* Schurck, 29 N. Y. 598, *aff'g* 33 Barb. 9; Arntson *v.* First Nat. Bank, 39 N. D. 408; Kauffman *v.* Kauffman, 266 Pa. 270; Pinney *v.* Fellows, 15 Vt. 525; Main *v.* Bosworth, 77 Wis. 660; Blaha *v.* Borgman, 142 Wis. 43. But see *contra,* Connor *v.* Follansbee, 59 N. H. 124; Dewey *v.* Dewey, 35 Vt. 555, 560 (*semble*).

In some cases the same result has been reached in the case of an oral ante-nuptial settlement. *Re* Holland, [1902] 2 Ch. 360. But there are cases in which the opposite view is taken; seemingly because of the peculiar danger of fraud against creditors. Ames, 181.

In accordance with the decision in the principal case, creditors who extended credit in reliance upon the trustee's apparent ownership were protected on the ground of estoppel in the following cases. Pierce *v.* Hower, 142 Ind. 626; Roy *v.* McPherson, 11 Neb. 197; Besson *v.* Eveland, 26 N. J. Eq. 468; Budd *v.* Atkinson, 30 N. J. Eq. 530; Fritz *v.* Worden, 20 N. Y. App. Div. 241; Van Dusen *v.* Hinz, 108 Wis. 178. *Cf.* Farmers Sav. Bank *v.* Pugh, 204 Iowa 580, *post* (resulting trust).

2. *As against the trustee in bankruptcy of the trustee.* See in addition to the principal case: Ambrose *v.* Ambrose, 1 P. Wms. 321; Gardner *v.* Rowe, 2 Sim. & St. 346, *aff'd* 5 Russ. 258; *Re* Holland, [1902] 2 Ch. 360; *Re* Davies, [1921] 3 K. B. 628; *Re* Farmer, 18 N. B. R. 207, 216 (*semble*); Moran *v.* Morgan, 252 Fed. 719. See also Smith *v.* Howell, 3 Stockt. (N. J.) 349; 24 Col. L. Rev. 68.

3. *As against the wife of the trustee.* An oral contract by a bachelor to convey land, if performed after his marriage, deprives his wife of dower. Jones *v.* Jones, 281 Ill. 595; Johnston *v.* Jickling, 141 Iowa 444; Oldham *v.* Sale, 1 B. Mon. (Ky.) 76. See King *v.* Bushnell, 121 Ill. 656 (curtesy). *Cf.* Ambrose *v.* Ambrose, 1 P. Wms. 321. But see Bartlett *v.* Tinsley, 175 Mo. 319; Pruitt *v.* Pruitt, 57 S. C. 155.

4. *As against one who has contracted to purchase from the trustee.* If A contracts orally to convey certain land to B, and then contracts in writing to convey the same land to C, and finally conveys to B, who has notice of the written contract in favor of C, it is held that B may keep the land. Dawson *v.* Ellis, 1 J. & W. 524 (*semble*); Clark's Adm'r. *v.* Rucker, 7 B. Mon. (Ky.) 583, 585 (*semble*); Maguire *v.* Heraty, 163 Pa. 381. See Atlanta etc. Co. *v.* Southern etc. Co., 131 Fed. 657. Query, if A simply made a memorandum of the contract with B, without conveying to B. See Hunter *v.* Bales, 24 Ind. 299.

5. *As against a purchaser from the trustee.* But a *cestui que trust* under an oral trust is cut out by a sale by the trustee, although the purchaser has notice of the oral trust. See Pickerell *v.* Morss, 97 Ill. 220; Van Clooostere *v.* Logan, 149 Ill. 588; Wright *v.* Raftree, 181 Ill. 464; Koenig *v.* Dohm, 209 Ill. 468; Stubbings *v.* Stubbings, 248 Ill. 406; Asher *v.* Brock, 95 Ky. 270. But see *contra,* Eisler *v.* Halperin, 89 N. J. L. 278 (*semble*).

MATTHEWS v. THOMPSON.

Supreme Judicial Court, Massachusetts. 1904.

186 Mass. 14.

Knowlton, C. J.[1] Edward Thompson, the testator of the plaintiff in the first suit, became indebted from time to time in a considerable sum to his unmarried sisters, Elizabeth B. Thompson and Frances M. Thompson, who were old ladies unfamiliar with business. Of his own motion, he made to them, as security, a mortgage of the real estate in question, subject to other mortgages which together amounted to about $37,000, and afterwards he caused them to foreclose this mortgage. A conveyance of the property, subject to the prior mortgages, was made to his son, who held it as agent of these sisters of the testator. Subsequently the testator caused his son to convey the property to the testator's nephew, one Eldridge, who executed a declaration of trust for the benefit of the old ladies, to secure them for their previous mortgage debts, and also for the benefit of their brother, Henry Thompson, to secure him for any advancements that he might make to Edward Thompson, and any other claims that he might hold against Edward. The declaration of trust also provided that after the payment of these debts the trustee should pay the balance, if any, to Edward Thompson. This declaration was not acknowledged nor recorded. It was understood that Edward Thompson was to have the entire management of the property, and these arrangements for security were made at his suggestion. At the end of about a year and a half, at his request, a paper was signed by the beneficiaries and sent to Eldridge, as follows:

"September 16, 1896.

Mr. William T. Eldridge,

Dear Sir, — We hereby request and authorize you to convey to Edward Thompson the real estate in Boston conveyed to you by Frederick P. Thompson.

          Henry Thompson
          Elizabeth B. Thompson
          Frances Mary Thompson."

The testator enclosed this paper to Eldridge and asked him for a conveyance of the real estate. Thereupon, on October 6, 1896, Eldridge conveyed the land to Edward Thompson by a deed which was duly recorded, and which contained no reference to a trust. The deed was in the form of an ordinary quitclaim, purporting

---

[1] The statement of facts and a part of the opinion are omitted.

to be for a consideration of $1 paid by Edward Thompson, not describing him as trustee, and it contained a warranty that the premises were free from all incumbrances made or suffered by Eldridge, and a warranty against the lawful claims and demands of all persons claiming by, through or under him. This deed was delivered by Eldridge to Edward Thompson and was duly recorded. After this conveyance Edward Thompson held the land as if it were his own, mortgaged it several times for his own debts, had repeated negotiations for the sale of it, and treated it in all respects as if he were the absolute owner of it. The first question in the cases is whether he held it charged with a trust in favor of his brother and sisters, so that it still remains subject to this trust in the hands of his widow, to whom it was afterwards conveyed in his lifetime.

In reference to the transfer from Eldridge to the intestate, the presiding justice found " as a fact that the intention of all parties interested, including that of the retiring trustee, Mr. Eldridge, was not that Mr. Edward Thompson should hold as trustee." He found, " that the intention of his brother and sisters and of the retiring trustee was that the title should go back to him, Edward Thompson, and that the brother and sisters relied upon his saying what he would do in regard to their debts, not because he was a trustee, but because he was their brother and they were willing to trust him."

As all the parties were of full age, and as the trust was created by an arrangement to which the trustee and the *cestuis que trust* were the only parties, there is no doubt that they could terminate it at any time. Smith v. Harrington, 4 Allen, 566. South Scituate Savings Bank v. Ross, 11 Allen, 442. Sears v. Choate, 146 Mass. 395. Brown v. Cowell, 116 Mass. 461. Upon the findings of the judge, it is plain that they undertook to terminate it and supposed that they had terminated it. The plaintiffs in the second suit, the former *cestuis que trust*, rely upon the Pub. Sts. c. 120, § 3, (R. L. c. 127, § 3,) which provides that " No estate or interest in land shall be assigned, granted, or surrendered unless by such writing [an instrument in writing signed by the grantor or by his attorney] or by operation of law." The kind of instrument in writing required under this section depends upon the nature of the interest to be assigned or surrendered. In the present case, not only the legal estate, but by the record title an absolute estate in fee, including equitable interests as well as legal, was in Eldridge. This title was affected only by an unacknowledged and unrecorded paper. By his deed to Edward Thompson, Eldridge assigned and conveyed, according to the record, a perfect title subject to prior mortgages. This deed was an instrument in writing. The only additional instrument required by the statute was a writing which would relieve the grantor from the consequences of what would have been a breach of trust if he had acted without authority from the *cestuis que trust*. Nothing more was needed to pass a title which was free from equities. As applied to conditions like the present, we are of opinion that the assignment of the equitable rights of the plaintiffs in the second suit, made by a deed of one who held of record a perfect title and who acted under their authority given in writing, was a compliance with the statute. If we consider it as a surrender of equitable rights, we are of opinion that the paper which they signed was all the instrument required by the statute, it being given as an authority to be acted upon, and which was in fact acted upon, by the trustee who held of record an absolute title. The principle is analogous to that which has been applied to the surrender and cancellation of an unrecorded deed of defeasance, given in connection with an absolute deed to constitute a mortgage. When this is done in good faith, and is subsequently acted upon by the person to whom the surrender is made, the original holder is estopped from setting up the surrendered instrument against the existing title. Trull *v.* Skinner, 17 Pick. 213. Falis *v.* Conway Ins. Co., 7 Allen, 46, 49. See also as to parol waiver by *cestuis que trust* under the statute of frauds, Kline's appeal, 39 Penn. St. 463; Miller *v.* Pierce, 104 N. C. 389; Gorrell *v.* Alspaugh, 120 N. C. 362, 368. The action of the parties, taken in good faith, makes it impossible in equity for the *cestuis que trust* to hold the trustee for a violation of his duty in making the conveyance, or to charge the conscience of the grantee having knowledge of the previous trust, with a duty to hold subject to the trust.

The suggestion that the trust could not be discharged without the action of the prior mortgagees is not well founded. They are not *cestuis que trust* under the declaration, but the reference to the mortgagees and the payment of their debts is only a recognition of the prior incumbrances subject to which the trust must be executed, and the payment of which would be a necessary preliminary to the payments to the sisters and brother.

We are of opinion that Edward Thompson took the property discharged from the trust, and that the second bill must be dismissed.[1] . . .

[1] See Scott, Parol Extinguishment of Trusts in Land, 42 Harv. L. Rev. 849.

Section IV.

Statutes of Wills.

THE WILLS ACT.
7 Will. IV. & 1 Vict. c. 26 (1837).[1]

IX. AND be it further enacted, That no will shall be valid unless it shall be in writing and executed in manner hereinafter mentioned; (that is to say) it shall be signed at the foot or end thereof by the testator, or by some other person in his presence and by his direction; and such signature shall be made or acknowledged by the testator in the presence of two or more witnesses present at the same time, and such witnesses shall attest and shall subscribe the will in the presence of the testator, but no form of attestation shall be necessary.

McEVOY v. BOSTON FIVE CENTS SAVINGS BANK.
SUPREME JUDICIAL COURT, MASSACHUSETTS. 1909.

201 Mass. 50.

CONTRACT, by a trustee under an instrument in writing executed by Jane Lever of Boston during her lifetime, against the Boston Five Cents Savings Bank, for $1,017.50, the amount of a deposit standing in the name of Jane Lever, who died in April, 1902. Writ in the Municipal Court of the City of Boston, dated November 22, 1902.

Andreas Blume was appointed administrator of the estate of Jane Lever, and thereafter was admitted as a claimant in the action.

On appeal to the Superior Court the case was tried before *Aiken*, C. J. The following facts appeared in evidence: On April 9, 1902, Jane Lever executed and delivered to the plaintiff the following two instruments in writing:

" Commonwealth of Massachusetts.

"I, Jane Lever of Boston in the County of Suffolk and Commonwealth of Massachusetts in consideration of the love and affection that I have for my relatives herein named hereby give, transfer and convey to John J. McEvoy all my personal property consisting of six hundred and fifty one dollars and seventy cents in the Elliott Five Cent Savings Bank of Boston, two hundred and sixty dollars in the Institution for Savings of Roxbury, Boston, one thousand

[1] For the earlier English statutes and some typical American statutes relating to wills, see Warren, Cas. Wills, 27–42.

and fifty three dollars and forty one cents in the Boston Five Cent Savings Bank of Boston in trust for the following uses:

" (1) Said trustee shall pay to me such moneys as I may demand of him at any time during my life until I have used the amount conveyed to him by me by this deed.

" (2) Upon my death said trustee shall pay my funeral expenses. And the sum of fifty dollars to my nurse Mary M. Wilson for services rendered as nurse.

" (3) After my death said trustee shall pay to my husband, Joseph Lever, if he survives me, the sum of three dollars per week during his life or as long as said trust funds shall last.

" (4) If upon the death of my husband and myself there are any funds remaining in the hands of said trustee said trustee shall divide said balance of said trustee funds in equal parts and give said parts to my second cousin, Jane Anne Harrison of Bolton, Lancastershire, England, to my second cousin Thomas Wilson, of Bolton, Lancastershire, England, to the two children of my second cousin, Edward Wilson late of Bolton, Lancastershire, England, to my second cousin Mary Wilson of Bolton, Lancastershire, England. I hereby reserve to myself the right to revoke this deed at any time during my life.

" Witness my hand and seal at Boston this ninth day of April, 1902.

her
Jane × Lever (Seal)
mark."

" Witnessed by
 " William W. Clarke.
  Mary A. McTighe.
  Mary M. Wilson."

" April 9, 1902.

" To the Treasurer of the Boston Five Cents Savings Bank.
  Boston, Mass.

" Sir: — Please pay to John J. McEvoy all the moneys that have been and may be deposited, together with the interest that has and may become due on account of Book No. 17722.

her

" William Burns.
Jane × Lever
mark."

Under the second of the instruments printed above, the plaintiff drew interest on the deposit in the defendant bank during the lifetime of Jane Lever. Jane Lever died in the latter part of April, 1902. The plaintiff testified that the doctor who attended Jane Lever in her last sickness had a bill for his services and the nurse had a bill; that there were funeral and other bills; that at the time of the execution of the trust deed and until the time of her death Jane Lever was living with her husband, Joseph Lever; that the plaintiff knew of no property which she possessed other than that which he had taken possession of under the instruments printed above; that he had one bank book of a bank in Roxbury transferred to him; that the amount was about two hundred and thirty or two hundred and forty dollars; that he presented the assignment to the bank and got the book and put the money right back in his name; that there was also the bank account which is the subject of this action and also an account in the Eliot Five Cents Savings Bank that he had not transferred; that he was the executor of the will of Joseph Lever, the husband of Jane; that Joseph died twelve weeks after his wife and left $530 that was deposited in the defendant bank; that the amount left by Jane Lever in the Eliot Five Cents Savings Bank was about $600 and the amount left by her in the defendant bank was about $1,000; that she left a little less than $2,000 all told; that during her lifetime the plaintiff drew $70 in interest on the account in the defendant bank; that there were outstanding unpaid bills of the doctor for $30 and one or two other small bills; that she told him to pay all legitimate bills; that there was an undertaker's bill; that part of it had been paid; that he also sent for a person in England that Mrs. Lever wanted to come over here; that he sent her $30; that he paid the minister and bought Mr. Lever a suit of clothes; that he paid Mr. Lever $3 per week during his lifetime; that he did not know of any bills other than the undertaker's, the doctor's and the nurse's; that he paid out $125; that there were bills of $250 outstanding, the doctor's, nurse's and undertaker's bills and a milk bill; and that what he paid out included what he paid the undertaker. He further testified as follows: " Q. And you understood that she intended by this instrument to dispose of the property after she was dead as well as while she was living? That is what you understood, was it not? A. Yes, that is what she told me. — Q. You understood that was what she intended at the time? A. Yes. — Q. That she intended this instrument in place of any will she might leave? A. She did."

The above was all the material evidence in the case. The plaintiff asked the judge to rule that upon all the evidence the claimant was not entitled to recover. The judge refused to make this ruling, and found for the claimant in the sum of $1,017.50, that being the amount represented by the book in the defendant bank, standing in the name of Jane Lever at the time of the service of the plaintiff's writ, together with whatever interest might have accrued since on that account, less the costs of the defendant taxed at $34.55 and without costs to the claimant. The plaintiff alleged exceptions.

The case was submitted on briefs.

KNOWLTON, C. J. The question in this case is whether the assignment to a trustee, made by Jane Lever, was a transfer of her property which divested her of her ownership and control during her lifetime, or whether it was in intention and legal effect an attempted testamentary disposition of such of her money as should remain at her decease. The property included in the conveyance was merely the deposits in certain savings banks. The trustee testified that she told him she intended to dispose of the property after she was dead as well as while she was living, and that she intended the instrument in place of any will she might leave. There was in the deed an express reservation of a power of revocation. This in itself would not render it invalid if the instrument otherwise seemed intended to divest her of her absolute control of the property, as owner or as *cestui que trust* during her life, and to deprive her of the rights of a beneficiary who has a perfect power of disposition under the trust.

The trust in this case may be considered first in reference to its effect on the property during her life, and then in reference to its effect upon what might remain after her death. The first statement of the trust by the assignor in the assignment is in these words: " Said trustee shall pay to me such moneys as I may demand of him at any time during my life until I have used the amount conveyed to him by me by this deed." This gave her the right to demand any part or the whole of the money at any time, for any use that she chose to make of it. It left her the sole beneficial owner of it, with an absolute power of disposition as long as she lived. As against her, therefore, the only practical effect of the instrument during her lifetime was to give the trustee a right to collect and hold the property until she should ask for it. Her rights as beneficial owner during her life were not limited in any material way. She could revoke the trust at any time, or she could demand and receive from the trustee all the money, at any time, under the trust, and then do with it what she chose.

The assignment is very different from that in Kelley *v.* Snow, 185 Mass. 288, in which the only right in the property reserved to the assignor for herself during her life was a right to use the income. While she had a power by the writing to change the disposition of what remained after her death, she could not diminish the property which necessarily would pass to others under the trust.

The other part of the trust created by the instrument in the present case relates solely to the disposition of the property after the assignor's death. It follows that the only material effect of the instrument was testamentary, and that it cannot be given effect under our statutes, which permit a testamentary disposition of property only by a duly executed will. See Nutt *v.* Morse, 142 Mass. 1; Sherman *v.* New Bedford Five Cents Savings Bank, 138 Mass. 581; Brownell *v.* Briggs, 173 Mass. 529; Welch *v.* Henshaw,

170 Mass. 409; Bailey *v.* New Bedford Institution for Savings, 192 Mass. 564.

But, if it be thought that this view of the construction and necessary legal effect of the instrument is too favorable to the claimant, the exceptions must be overruled on the ground that the evidence justified a finding by the trial judge that the paper was intended as a mere testamentary disposition of property, and not as a creation of a trust for any other purpose, and that therefore there was no error of law in the finding.

No question has been raised by either party in regard to the finding and order as to costs, and we do not consider it.

Exceptions overruled.

JONES *v.* OLD COLONY TRUST COMPANY.

SUPREME JUDICIAL COURT, MASSACHUSETTS. 1925.

251 Mass. 309.

BILL IN EQUITY, filed in the Superior Court on March 20, 1924, and afterwards amended, by the administrator of the estate of Olivia LeBosquet Endicott, late of Haverhill, to require the defendant Old Colony Trust Company to deliver to the plaintiff certain securities delivered by the intestate to that trust company under the terms of an instrument denominated a trust, of which The Cathedral Church of the Diocese of Massachusetts, admitted as a defendant by amendment, was one beneficiary.

The instrument referred to was dated August 13, 1917, and was executed by the intestate under seal. It was acknowledged before a notary public, but was not witnessed. By its provisions, the intestate purported to "sell, transfer and deliver to Old Colony Trust Company, the securities" referred to "in trust nevertheless, for the following uses and purposes: To hold, manage, invest or reinvest same and any additions thereto which I may make at any time in accordance with its sole discretion, and to pay over the net income therefrom to me or upon my order, upon my request or in accordance with my instructions at any time or from time to time as long as I shall live, and upon my decease to liquidate the trust fund and pay over the following sums: "

[Here followed twenty-eight paragraphs directing the disposition of designated sums and specific securities to sundry persons. There then followed these paragraphs:]

"Twenty-ninth: I give to Old Colony Trust Company all powers with reference to the management, sale and conversion, investment and reinvestment of the trust estate which I should have if personally present and acting, together with full power to hold the estate, or any part thereof, invested as it receives it, without liability for so doing; and I direct that no person or corporation buying from or dealing with said Trustee shall be under any obligation to see to the application of the purchase money or otherwise to inquire into the reasons or authority for any action taken by said Trustee; and the Trustee shall have full power of determining all questions whether any money or things are to be treated as capital or income and of determining the mode in which the expense of management or other expense incident to or connected with the execution of the trusts hereof shall be borne as between capital and income and every such determination shall be conclusive on all parties interested.

"Thirtieth: Notwithstanding anything hereinbefore contained to the contrary, the right is hereby reserved to alter or amend this instrument by a writing setting forth such alteration or amendment executed by me and delivered to the Trustee hereunder and upon my request in writing, the Trustee hereunder shall pay over to me at one time or from time to time such portion or all of the principal of the trust fund as may be requested in such writing."

On the bottom of the instrument was indorsed a receipt of the securities by Old Colony Trust Company and an acceptance of "the foregoing trust."

There were six amendments in writing, each executed by the intestate under seal and none of them either acknowledged or witnessed. They all related to some of the paragraphs whereby specific disposition of portions of the trust property were made.

The defendants demurred to the bill for want of equity. The demurrers were heard by *Morton*, J., by whose order an interlocutory decree was entered overruling them. The judge, being of the opinion that the interlocutory decree so affected the merits of the controversy that, before further proceedings, the matter ought to be determined by this court, reported the question to this court under G. L. c. 214, § 30, for that purpose.

RUGG, C. J. This is a suit in equity brought by an administrator for the recovery of property alleged to belong to the estate of his intestate. She transferred to the Old Colony Trust Company, hereafter called the defendant, deposits in banks and other securities. The transfer was made by instrument in writing and under seal in terms selling the legal title and delivering possession of all the property, described in detail in a schedule annexed, but upon specified trusts. Those trusts were to hold, manage, invest and reinvest in its sole discretion, with the widest powers in this respect, to pay the income during her life to the intestate or in accordance with her directions, and at her decease to liquidate the fund and distribute it among numerous named beneficiaries. Power was reserved to alter or amend the trust instrument in writing and to require the trustee to pay over to the settlor "at one time or from time to time such portion or all of the principal of the trust fund as may be requested" by her in writing.

The validity of this trust is established by Stone *v.* Hackett, 12 Gray, 227. The instrument of trust there assailed, while slightly less explicit than the one in the case at bar, contained unequivocal power of modification and revocation with requirement for payment of income to the donor during his life. The power of management and control conferred upon the trustee in that case was less ample and unrestrained than in the case at bar. That case was decided more than sixty years ago. It has been cited many times, always with respect. It must be regarded as an unshaken authority. Doubtless many trusts have been declared in reliance upon the principle there established. It may be treated as a rule of property.

The validity of such a trust instrument, being under seal and accompanied by actual delivery of the property, is not open to successful attack because of want of consideration. This was a fully executed trust *inter vivos*. A purely voluntary trust will be upheld in such circumstances. Reservation of income to the settlor for life does not impair the validity of the trust. Viney *v.* Abbott, 109 Mass. 300. Gerrish *v.* New Bedford Institution for Savings, 128 Mass. 159. Chippendale *v.* North Adams Savings Bank, 222 Mass. 499, 502.

The power to change the terms of the trust does not affect the validity of the trust. Kelley *v.* Snow, 185 Mass. 288.

The right in the donor to withdraw the principal of the trust does not defeat the trust. Stone *v.* Hackett, 12 Gray, 227. Davis *v.* Ney, 125 Mass. 590. Such unqualified right in reason stands on the same footing as the right to withdraw as and when required for the support of the donor, which has been upheld. Lovett *v.* Farnham, 169 Mass. 1. The soundness of the decision in Stone *v.* Hackett is either affirmed or recognized in numerous cases where not absolutely essential to the judgment. Kendrick *v.* Ray, 173 Mass. 305, 310. Seaman *v.* Harmon, 192 Mass. 5, 8. Bone *v.* Holmes, 195 Mass. 495, 505. Mackernan *v.* Fox, 220 Mass. 197, 200.

The case of McEvoy *v.* Boston Five Cents Savings Bank, 201 Mass. 50, is distinguishable. There the nominal trustee had none of the ordinary powers of a trustee and was in substance and effect only an agent of the donor. In many cases upon which the plaintiff relies the attempted creation of a trust or gift was held to be the equivalent of an agency or bailment. Hale *v.* Joslin, 134 Mass. 310. Nutt *v.* Morse, 142 Mass. 1. Stratton *v.* Athol Savings Bank, 213 Mass. 46. Russell *v.* Webster, 213 Mass. 491.

The gifts to take effect after the death of the settlor, while in some aspects having a testamentary appearance, became operative immediately upon the execution of the trust subject to the contingencies created by the trust instrument itself. There is nothing in that instrument which manifests a purpose to circumvent the statute of wills. The case on this point is within the authority of numerous decisions. Stone v. Hackett, 12 Gray, 227. Davis v. Ney, 125 Mass. 590, 592. Krell v. Codman, 154 Mass. 454. Bromley v. Mitchell, 155 Mass. 509, 511. Eaton v. Eaton, 233 Mass. 351, 370, 372.

The class of cases illustrated by Williams v. Milton, 215 Mass. 1, Frost v. Thompson, 219 Mass. 360, Flint v. Codman, 247 Mass. 463, 469, 470, and cases there collected, where elaborate instruments for the purpose of carrying on the business of managing estates and properties through the medium of trustees have been held to create partnerships, has no relevancy to the issues here raised. Trust instruments of that nature are essentially designed for the conduct of commercial enterprises. They are not to be confused through analogies or otherwise with a strict trust like that created by the trust instrument here under examination.

The interlocutory decree is reversed and a decree is to be entered sustaining the demurrers.

So ordered.[1]

FROST v. FROST.

SUPREME JUDICIAL COURT, MASSACHUSETTS. 1909.

202 Mass. 100.

BILL IN EQUITY, filed in the Supreme Judicial Court by the widow of Albert G. Frost, late of Boston, who died on October 24, 1907, and whose will was admitted to probate, the defendants being named therein as trustees and executors and having qualified by giving bonds as required by law, praying to have the defendants declared to be trustees for the plaintiff's sole benefit under assignments of five life insurance policies alleged to have been made by her husband on May 17 and August 4, 1898, and that the defendants be ordered to pay to her the amounts of life insurance received by them as executors and trustees under the policies in question.

The case was referred to William H. H. Emmons, Esquire, as master.

[1] See Scott, Trusts and the Statute of Wills, 43 Harv. L. Rev. 521; Leaphart, The Trust as a Substitute for a Will, 78 U. Pa. L. Rev. 626; Rowley, Living Testamentary Dispositions, 3 U. of Cinn. L. Rev. 361; Seftenberg, Border Lines of Agency, Living Trusts, and Testamentary Disposition, 5 Wis. L. Rev. 321; 26 Mich. L. Rev. 834; 28 Mich. L. Rev. 603; 38 Yale L. Jour. 1135; 39 Yale L. Jour. 438; 10 B. U. L. Rev. 113; 15 St. Louis L. Rev. 204; 25 Ill. L. Rev. 178.

In *Re* Koss, 106 N. J. Eq. 323, a corporation established a stock-purchase plan whereby its employees contributed a certain sum and the corporation a like sum, the contributions to be held and invested by trustees in stock of the corporation. It was provided that on the death of the employee the trustees were to convey the stock to such person as the employee might designate in writing at any time. It was held that such a designation by the employee was not a testamentary disposition. *Cf.* Siter v. Hall, 220 Ky. 43. But see Tensfield v. Magnolia Petroleum Co., 134 Okla. 38.

[It appeared that two of the policies in question were payable to the executors, administrators and assigns of the insured, the other three being payable to his legal representatives. He made an assignment purporting to transfer all his right, title and interest in the several policies to " the trustees to be named in my will " for the sole use and benefit of the plaintiff, his wife. The plaintiff was informed of the assignments and assented thereto although she never saw any of the policies or any of the assignments until after her husband's death.[1]]

HAMMOND, J. One of the questions is whether the assignments were valid. The plaintiff does not contend that there was a gift, but insists first that the assignments were operative as a perfected trust, and second, that there was a " statutory investiture " under St. 1894, c. 120, which was in force when the policies were taken out and assigned.

1. Was the trust perfected during the lifetime of the assignor? . . .

Who were the assignees? They were to be named in his will. What will? Was it to be the first testamentary document he should thereafter make, whether or not revoked before his death, or was it to be the one which should finally be admitted to probate as his will? The assignor actually made three wills after the assignments were executed and " the trustees named in the different wills were not exactly the same." There can only be one sensible interpretation of the phrase " my will." It must be held to mean the document finally admitted to probate as the will of the assignor. It is certain, therefore, that the trustees could not be finally ascertained until after his death. The assignment could not be delivered to the assignees until after his death. There is nothing to indicate that he intended to make any delivery to any third person to hold for the trustees until they were finally ascertained, nor is it shown upon the facts in the case that he intended to hold the policies himself as trustee. While it is true, as contended by the plaintiff, that the trustees when finally ascertained would derive their appointment under the assignment and not under the will, still it remains equally true that they could not be appointed, nor even ascertained, until after the death of the assignor. It is to be noted that the papers were all retained by the assignor.

Here then is a case where no assignments are delivered to the assignees, nor can they be delivered until after the assignor's death, where also there is no delivery to any one for them and where it does not appear that the assignor intends to hold for them. The language of the assignments seems to point to a testamentary intention, and the whole scheme is manifestly not to take effect as an operative assignment during the lifetime of the testator. The

[1] The statement of facts is abridged, and a part of the opinion is omitted. The court held that the provisions of St. 1894, c. 120, were not applicable.

assignments were of a testamentary nature, and, not being witnessed as required by the statutes concerning wills, were inoperative after his death.

Nor is the defect cured by the assent of the *cestui que trust* to the assignments. While such an assent might have a bearing upon the validity of the trust if there was any question as to notice or acceptance, still it has no effect upon the validity of the assignments upon which the trust depends. The question is not simply whether, assuming the validity of the assignments, the trust was good, but is much deeper, and is whether the assignments upon which alone the trust depends ever became operative in law. The case is plainly distinguishable from Kendrick *v.* Ray, 173 Mass. 305, upon which the plaintiff relies. There the trustee was the beneficiary named in the policy; and the question was as to the terms of the oral trust upon which he received the insurance, and not as to the validity of the appointment of the trustee. See also Gould *v.* Emerson, 99 Mass. 154.

Upon the facts in the case these assignments never took effect within the lifetime of the assignor, for want of assignees, and never took effect after his death for want of proper attestation. There was therefore nothing upon which to base the contemplated trust, and it never was perfected. . . .

Bill dismissed.[1]

MATTER OF TOTTEN.

COURT OF APPEALS, NEW YORK. 1904.

179 N. Y. 112.

APPEAL from an order of the Appellate Division of the Supreme Court in the second judicial department, entered December 30, 1903, which reversed a decree of the Kings County Surrogate's Court rejecting certain claims of the respondent herein against the estate of Fanny Amelia Lattan, deceased.

This is a controversy between the administrator of Fanny Amelia Lattan, deceased, and Emile R. Lattan, who presented a claim against the estate of said decedent which was duly rejected by the representative thereof. The claim was for the sum of $1,775.03, besides interest, alleged to be due "by reason of certain deposits made by" the decedent "in the Irving Savings Institution, as trustee for the said Emile R. Lattan, the moneys so deposited having been subsequently withdrawn by the said decedent." Upon the final accounting of the administrator the justice of said claim, in ac-

---

[1] If the owner of property executes an instrument, not properly attested as a will, purporting to convey to another as trustee such property as he might own at his death, the intended trust fails. Roth *v.* Michalis, 125 Ill. 325. See 43 Harv. L. Rev. 521-523.

cordance with the stipulation of all concerned, was determined by the surrogate after a referee had reported the evidence, the facts and his conclusion. The surrogate confirmed the report and dismissed the claim upon the merits, but the decree entered accordingly was reversed by the Appellate Division " upon the law and the facts " and the claim was allowed with costs. The administrator and certain heirs and next of kin of the decedent appealed to this court.

VANN, J. . . . Beginning in 1886 the decedent and her sister Angelica each had numerous accounts in the Irving Savings Institution, the greater part in the name of the former individually, or as trustee. At various times there were sixteen of the latter class. While no single account in the name of the decedent ever exceeded $3,000 the aggregate amount of all her accounts always exceeded that sum and occasionally by several thousand dollars. At the same time many accounts were kept by her in other savings institutions, some in her own name simply and others with the addition of " trustee for " or " in trust for " some person named. It was her practice to draw from all these accounts at will, whether they were kept in her name as trustee or otherwise, and to close them and open others as she saw fit. She kept the pass books and no beneficiary named in any account ever drew therefrom except upon drafts signed by her. When she died intestate in March, 1900, accounts were outstanding in her name as trustee in favor of Emile R. Lattan and three other persons and they had the benefit thereof without controversy.

On the 2nd of January, 1886, the decedent opened an account in the Irving Savings Institution by depositing the sum of $355. A rule of the bank required the depositor to give the name of the person for whom he wished to place the money in trust, but the one making the deposit had absolute control of the account so long as he retained possession of the pass book. The pass book was numbered 42,728 and the deposit was entered thereon as well as on the books of the bank as an account with Fanny A. Lattan, trustee for Emile R. Lattan, depositor. At some time, but it does not appear when except that it was prior to May, 1893, the words " Trustee for Emile R. Lattan " were canceled by rulings in red ink. As at first entered in the ledger of the bank the account stood as at first entered on the pass book, but when carried forward to a new ledger in 1892 it stood as an account with the decedent individually. When she opened this account she had between $6,000 and $7,000 standing in her name individually and as trustee on the books of the same bank. Two other deposits were made in this account, the first of $5.10 on July 1st, 1886, and the second of $740, September 21st, 1886. Twelve drafts were drawn against it at various times. The first, dated January 27th, 1886, for $100 in favor of Lewis H. Lattan, was signed by the decedent as trustee, but all the rest, commencing with September 19th, 1890, were signed by her individually. July 8th, 1898, the account was closed by her individual draft for $1,104.06 and the pass book was surrendered. With the amount thus drawn she opened two new accounts in the same bank, the first No. 66,807 in favor of Fanny A. Lattan in trust for Rosalie M. Beam for the sum of $552.03, and the other No. 66,808 in favor of Fanny A. Lattan in trust for Emile R. Lattan for the same amount. Both of these accounts remained open at the time of the decedent's death and the pass books were delivered by her administrator to the parties named who drew the money accordingly. During the existence of account No. 42,728 the decedent at all times had possession of the pass book and Emile R. Lattan received no part of the moneys deposited to the credit of that account except as already mentioned.

On the 19th of September, 1890, the decedent had ten accounts amounting to between $8,000 and $9,000 standing in her name, individually or as trustee, on the books of the Irving Savings Institution. On that day she opened account No. 51,556 in that bank by depositing $462.03 in her name as trustee for Emile R. Lattan. Said amount was largely made up of sums drawn from other accounts in her name as trustee. She retained possession of the pass book, and no one, except herself and the officers of the bank, appears to have known of the existence of the account until after her death. September 19th, 1892, she deposited $100 in that account and September 13th, 1893, the further sum of $80.60. When it was closed on the 15th of November, 1894, it amounted with interest to $733.30, which she drew out and deposited in another account, in her name as trustee for Lewis H. Lattan, who after her death drew the amount thereof.

Emile R. Lattan was the son of Lewis H. Lattan, a spendthrift, who in 1884 turned over to his sisters Angelica Lattan and the decedent all his property, worth about $20,000, for their management, but without instructions as to their course in managing the same. No accounting was ever made to him with reference thereto, although he survived them both.

There was no evidence that the decedent ever spoke to any one about any of these accounts or stated what her intention was in opening them. The accounts in question were opened with her own money and no part thereof came from her brother Lewis. Out of thirty-one accounts in seven savings banks she paid over to the alleged beneficiaries the balance left when two thereof were closed, but in both of these instances, as well as in all other cases, she treated the accounts as her own, drawing against them and making new deposits from time to time as she thought best. All the pass books with a trust heading, containing accounts which had not been closed when the decedent died, were delivered to the respective beneficiaries who drew the balance on hand. Emile R. Lattan did not know of the existence of any accounts on which he relies in this proceeding until more than a year after the decedent died. Angelica Lattan, who was appointed and qualified as administratrix, died on the 10th of April, 1901, leaving the administrator as the sole representative of the estate. The personal property of Fanny A. Lattan was inventoried at the sum of $32,950.08, but owing to increase in values the amount on hand at the date of the final decree of distribution was more than $40,000.

The most favorable view of these facts and others of like character not mentioned does not permit the inference as matter of fact that the decedent in making the deposits in question intended to establish an irrevocable trust in favor of the respondent. Aside from what took place when the deposits were made, every act of the decedent, with one exception, is opposed to the theory of a trust. That exception is the closing of one account after the words of trust had been canceled and the deposit of part of the proceeds in the same form as the original. This is not enough when considered with the other facts to establish an irrevocable trust. (Cunningham v. Davenport, 147 N. Y. 43.) No connection was shown between any deposit and the sum held in trust by the decedent and her sister Angelica for Lewis H. Lattan, who is still living and was sworn as a witness at the trial. A deposit in favor of the son would not have satisfied the claim of the father in the absence of a request from the latter, of which there was no evidence. In view of the practice of the decedent in doing business with savings banks, the custom of many other persons in that regard, the various objects which people have in making deposits in the form of a trust, the retention of the pass book with the corresponding control of the deposits according to the rules of the bank, the subsequent history of the various accounts with the frequent withdrawals and changes, we think that the form of the deposits as they appear upon the books was not strengthened by the other evidence. There was no question of fact in the case and the Appellate Division had no power to reverse upon the facts. We find no exception in the record warranting a reversal upon the law, unless the exception to the conclusion of the referee and surrogate that the claim should be dismissed upon the merits raises reversible error. This involves the question whether upon the conceded facts, as matter of law, an irrevocable trust was established.

Savings bank trusts, as they are sometimes called, have frequently been before the courts during the past few years. When we considered the pioneer case but few instances of deposits in trust were known and a liberal rule was laid down without the limitations which later cases required. After a while when it became a common practice for persons to make deposits in that form, in order to evade restrictions upon the amount one could deposit in his own name and for other reasons, the courts became more conservative and sought to avoid unjust results by adapting the law to the customs of the people. A brief review of the cases will show how the subject has been gradually developed so as to accord with the methods of the multitude of persons who make deposits in these banks.

The case of Martin v. Funk (75 N. Y. 134) arose more than a quarter of a century ago when savings bank trusts were in their infancy. A lady had made a deposit of her own money to the amount of $500 in a savings bank, declaring that she wished the account opened in trust for the plaintiff, a distant relative. Entry was made accordingly on the books of the bank and on the pass book, which was delivered to the depositor and retained by her until her death. At the same time she deposited a like amount in the same manner in trust for a sister of the plaintiff. No change was made in either account except that the depositor drew out the interest for one year and no other act or declaration bearing on her intention was shown. Neither the plaintiff nor her sister knew anything of either deposit until the depositor died nine years after the account was opened. It was held that a trust was created and that the plaintiff was entitled to the money standing to the credit of the account. . . .

While we have considered we do not cite the numerous cases decided by the Supreme Court bearing upon the question, owing to the conflict in the opinions of learned justices in different appellate divisions. It is necessary for us to settle the conflict by laying down such a rule as will best promote the interests of all the people in the state. After much reflection upon the subject, guided by the principles established by our former decisions, we announce the following as our conclusion: A deposit by one person of his own money, in his own name as trustee for another, standing alone, does not establish an irrevocable trust during the lifetime of the depositor. It is a tentative trust merely, revocable at will, until the depositor dies or completes the gift in his lifetime by some unequivocal act or declaration, such as delivery of the pass book or notice to the beneficiary. In case the depositor dies before the beneficiary without revocation, or some decisive act or declaration of disaffirmance, the presumption arises that an absolute trust was created as to the balance on hand at the death of the depositor. This rule requires us to reverse the order of the Appellate Division and to affirm the decree of the surrogate, with costs to the appellants in all courts.

PARKER, Ch. J., O'BRIEN, BARTLETT, MARTIN, CULLEN and WERNER, JJ., concur.

Order reversed, etc.[1]

INHERITANCE TAX. Although a trust may not be invalid for failure of the settlor to comply with the requirements of the Statute of Wills, the disposition may nevertheless be subject to an inheritance tax. The statutes imposing such a tax are usually broad enough to include dispositions which take effect in possession or

[1] There are numerous cases in New York upholding the doctrine of tentative trusts. See also Littig v. Mt. Calvary Church, 101 Md. 494; Sturgis v.

enjoyment on the death of the person making the disposition, even though irrevocable, and dispositions taking effect during his lifetime but subject to a power of revocation.[1] The problems of taxation are usually treated in a separate course.

SWETLAND *v.* SWETLAND, 102 N. J. Eq. 294 (1928): A testator bequeathed property to his son as trustee " under the trust agreement heretofore mentioned and created by me under date of July 14, 1917, for the purposes therein provided." By the trust agreement referred to, the testator had transferred a large number of shares of stock to his son in trust for the son's wife and children, the testator reserving power at any time during his life to terminate the trust. After the death of the testator his executors brought a bill for instructions. The Vice Chancellor upheld the trust created by the will and the decree was affirmed by the Court of Errors and Appeals. The court said that it was doubtful whether the doctrine of incorporation by reference prevails in New Jersey, but that the trust was valid since the trust agreement, not being testamentary, might be referred to in order to ascertain the terms of the testamentary trust. In reference to the bequest the court said (p. 297):

" By it the testator merely added additional property to a trust fund established by him years before the execution of his will under a valid, active trust and to which he had, from time to time during his lifetime, added securities. The trust to which this bequest is added is not theoretical, nebulous, intangible or incapable of identification, but exists in fact, and the trustee-legatee is as distinct and definite an entity as would have been an individual or corporation legatee." [2]

Citizens' National Bank, 152 Md. 654; Walso *v.* Latterner, 140 Minn. 455, 143 Minn. 364; Dyste *v.* Farmers & Mechanics Sav. Bank, 179 Minn. 430.

In New Jersey the doctrine is condemned as violating the Statute of Wills. Nicklas *v.* Parker, 69 N. J. Eq. 743, 71 N. J. Eq. 777. See Fiocchi *v.* Smith, 97 Atl. 283 (N. J. Ch. 1916).

See Scott, Trusts and the Statute of Wills, 43 Harv. L. Rev. 521, 540; 14 Yale L. Jour. 315; 37 Yale L. Jour. 1133; 14 Minn. L. Rev. 701; 16 Va. L. Rev. 67; 59 A. L. R. 979.

[1] See Bullen *v.* Wisconsin, 240 U. S. 625; Saltonstall *v.* Saltonstall, 276 U. S. 260; Reinecke *v.* Northern Trust Co., 278 U. S. 339. But see May *v.* Heiner, 281 U. S. 238, 44 Harv. L. Rev. 131. See Stimson, When Revocable Trusts are Subject to an Inheritance Tax, 25 Mich. L. Rev. 839; Rottschaefer, Taxation of Transfers Intended to Take Effect in Possession or Enjoyment at Grantor's Death, 14 Minn. L. Rev. 453, 613; Leaphart, The Use of the Trust to Escape the Imposition of Federal Income and Estate Taxes, 15 Cornell L. Quar. 587. See 35 Yale L. Jour. 601; 38 Yale L. Jour. 657; 43 Harv. L. Rev. 530; 49 A. L. R. 864; 67 A. L. R. 1247.

[2] Estate of Willey, 128 Cal. 1, *accord.* Atwood *v.* Rhode Island Hospital Trust Co., 275 Fed. 513, *certiorari* denied 257 U. S. 661, *contra.* See 43 Harv. L. Rev. 521, 547; 37 Yale L. Jour. 1002; Evans, Incorporation by Reference, Integration and Non-Testamentary Acts, 25 Col. L. Rev. 879, 898.

As to the effect of a devise or bequest upon a trust not properly declared, see Chap. V, sec. III, *post.*

CHAPTER III.
THE ELEMENTS OF A TRUST.

SECTION I.
The Subject-Matter of a Trust.

GRAVES *v.* GRAVES.

CHANCERY, IRELAND. 1862.

13 Ir. Ch. 182.

WILLIAM GRAVES, by his will, devised certain real and personal property to trustees upon trust, amongst other things, to pay to his wife an annuity of 100*l*. a-year for life, in addition to her jointure; and also to pay to his sister an annuity of 50*l*. a-year for life. The will then contained the following passage. " And I do hereby declare it to be my earnest wish that my said sister shall reside at Gravesend with my dear wife, during her life." The testator devised his house at Gravesend, with the household furniture, &c., to his wife for life. Mr. Graves died in 1853. Misunderstandings having arisen between Mrs. and Miss Graves, they, in 1853, ceased to live together; and the petition in this cause was filed by Miss Graves, praying a declaration of her right to reside at Gravesend during her life, and to be boarded by Mrs. Graves.

THE LORD CHANCELLOR [BRADY]. There can be no doubt that an expression of the testator's wish may attach on the property devised by him, and may be enforced by this court; but we are always bound to consider the subject-matter to be effected, and to see what the testator really intended to be done.

Had this expression of wish been attached on any property, as upon a house, it would be one thing; as, if he had said " I wish that my sister should reside in my house at Gravesend," it might be said that this gave her a right to have a portion of the house allotted to her. Those, however, are not the words of the present will, which says, " I declare it to be my earnest wish that my said sister shall reside at Gravesend with my dear wife during her life." What does that mean? It means, if anything, that they should reside together. He intends, with respect to both, for the sake of mutual society and comfort, that they should pass their lives together. I should hesitate long before saying that this was a trust which this court would enforce. The right of maintenance is given up; but if it were not, could this court be called on to say which was right and which was wrong, in their misunderstanding, or to say that they were to be compelled to spend their time together? The will, however, in my opinion, does not point to residence as property in the house, but to residence with Mrs. Graves as a member of her family. I cannot give an equivalent. An equivalent would destroy a part of the bequest, the intention of which was to give to each from the other the benefit of society and intercourse. I cannot say that a residence, or payment for one, would be an equivalent; and if these ladies cannot agree to live together on friendly terms, I cannot compel them.[1]

BISEL v. LADNER.

CIRCUIT COURT OF APPEALS, THIRD CIRCUIT. 1924.

1 F.(2d) 436.

Appeal from the District Court of the United States for the Eastern District of Pennsylvania; Oliver B. Dickinson, Judge.

Suit in equity by Grover Cleveland Ladner against George T. Bisel, trading as the George T. Bisel Company. Decree for complainant, and defendant appeals. Affirmed.

Before WOOLLEY and DAVIS, Circuit Judges, and BODINE, District Judge.

BODINE, District Judge. Grover Cleveland Ladner, a lawyer and author of a book on the Law of Conveyancing in Pennsylvania, is the complainant. George T. Bisel, trading as the George T. Bisel Company, who published Mr. Ladner's book in 1913, is one of the defendants. Louis W. Robey, a member of the Pennsylvania bar, who revised the book, is also a defendant. The copyright for the book was taken out in the publisher's name.

[1] The trial judge found that the copyright was legally issued to the Bisel Company and subsequently assigned to George T. Bisel individually, but that in equity the copyright was the property of Mr. Ladner, and that Mr. Robey, in revising the book, had not acted improperly, but that the revised edition ought to be published and distributed upon the payment of royalties to Mr. Ladner. "The legal title to a copyright vests in the person in whose name the copyright is taken out. It may, however, be held by him in trust for the true owner, and the question of true ownership is one

---

[1] In the following cases it was held that a trust or charge was created. Wolfe v. Croft, 46 Nova Scotia 106, 26 Harv. L. Rev. 559 (devisee to support third person and reserve a room and bedroom for his use); Woodward v. Walling, 31 Iowa 533, *ante* (devisee to provide a home for his sister till her marriage); Hammel v. Barrett, 79 N. J. Eq. 96 (devisee to look after his sister and see that she has a home); Lyon v. Lyon, 65 N. Y. 339 (direction that the testator's house, devised to his sons, should be a home for his daughters free of expense as long as they should remain single); Connly v. McElroy, 46 R. I. 93 (trustees to permit testatrix's son and her friend to occupy her house as a residence free from rent). See Estate of Goodrich, 38 Wis. 492.

of fact, dependent upon the circumstances of the case. Press Publishing Co. *v.* Falk (C. C.) 59 Fed. 324 (1894); Black *v.* Henry G. Allen Co. (C. C.) 42 Fed. 618, 9 L. R. A. 432 (1890); Lawrence *v.* Dana, Fed. Cas. No. 8136; 9 Cyc. 930." Harms et al. *v.* Stern et al., 229 Fed. 42, 46, 145 C. C. A. 2, 6.

[2] It is not controverted that, when the negotiations were pending for the publication of the book, Mr. Bisel said, " We don't buy books." The work was a completed work, and Mr. Ladner brought it to Mr. Bisel for publication. It is not controverted that Bisel said, " I will attend to the copyrighting for you," to which Mr. Ladner assented.

[3] The trial judge properly found that the beneficial interest in the copyright was retained by Mr. Ladner. Complainant has the right to sue in equity. He acted promptly, and his rights were infringed and he is not a mere licensee, but the equitable owner of the copyright. " It is the general rule that a mere licensee cannot in its own name sue strangers who infringe. Birdsell *v.* Shaliol, 112 U. S. 485, 5 Sup. Ct. 244, 28 L. Ed. 768. Here, however, the complainant is not a mere licensee, but has the full equitable title, and Wooster, who has the legal title, is one of the infringers and occupies a position altogether hostile to the complainant. Its right in this situation to sue in equity in its own name is plain in principle and well established by authority. [Citing Cases.] "

The judgment below will be affirmed.[1]

GREEN *v.* FOLGHAM.

CHANCERY. 1823.

1 Sim. & St. 398.

IN 1791 William Singleton was possessed of a recipe for making an ointment called " Dr. Johnson's Ointment for the Eyes," the contents of which were known only to himself; and in the month of September in that year, upon the treaty for the marriage of his daughter Selina with Timothy Folgham, it was agreed that the ownership of the ointment, and the recipe, should be settled, after the decease of Singleton and his wife, for the benefit of Folgham and his intended wife, and their issue, in the manner after mentioned. Accordingly, by an indenture dated the 12th of September 1794, and

---

[1] *Patents.* A patent may be held in trust. The letters may be originally issued to a person as trustee for another. *Re* Russell's Patent, 2 DeG. & J. 130; Whiting *v.* Graves, Fed. Cas. No. 17,577 (C. C. Mass.). See Davis etc. Wheel Co. *v.* Davis etc. Wagon Co., 20 Fed. 699 (C. C. N. Y.).

A patent may be assigned in trust. Campbell *v.* James, Fed. Cas. No. 2361, 17 Blatch. 42 (C. C. N. Y.), rev'd on other grounds in James *v.* Campbell, 104 U. S. 356; Jonathan Mills Mfg. Co. *v.* Whitehurst, 56 Fed. 589 (C. C. Ohio).

A patent may be the subject of a constructive trust. Becher *v.* Contoure Laboratories, 279 U. S. 388.

made between Mr. and Mrs. Singleton of the first part, Mr. and Mrs. Folgham of the second part, and three trustees, of whom the defendant Church was the survivor, of the third part, in pursuance of the agreement, and in consideration of the marriage which had then lately taken place, Singleton assigned to the trustees the proprietorship of the medicine, upon trust for Singleton and his wife, during their lives, and the life of the survivor of them; and after the survivor's decease, upon trust for Selina Folgham, for her life, for her separate use; and after her decease, upon trust for Folgham for his life; and it was declared, that if at the decease of the survivor of these four persons there should be more than one child of Folgham and his wife, the trustees should sell the ownership of the ointment, and the money arising from the sale should be laid out by the trustees in their names, on government or real securities, for the benefit of such children, in equal shares, and to be transferred to them at the usual periods. And Mr. and Mrs. Folgham covenanted, that if any of their children should survive them, they should discover to one or more of them the method of making the ointment.

Mr. Singleton survived his wife and Mr. Folgham; and on his death the recipe was delivered to Mrs. Folgham. She, assisted by the defendant, William Singleton Folgham, one of her sons, made and vended the ointment until about six months before her death; when, having previously communicated to him verbally the secret of making the ointment, she retired into the country, and left him in the entire management of the concern. In Jan. 1816 Mrs. Folgham died, leaving issue the plaintiff, Selina Elizabeth Green, (who afterwards married the plaintiff Stephen Green), the defendant William Singleton Folgham, and three other children, all of whom were then infants. The recipe was not found after Mrs. Folgham's death, and it was therefore believed that she had destroyed it. In March 1816, William Singleton Folgham came of age; when Church, the surviving trustee, conceiving that it would be more beneficial to the parties interested, that W. S. Folgham should make up and vend the ointment according to his mother's instructions, for the benefit of himself and his brothers and sisters, than that the secret should be sold, an indenture, dated the 22d day of June 1816, was made between W. S. Folgham of the one part, and Church, and one Hall, of the other part; by which, after reciting that the secret of making the ointment had been communicated to W. S. Folgham by his mother, for the benefit of himself and his brothers and sisters, W. S. Folgham covenanted to make up and sell the ointment, and twice in every year to pay to Church and Hall four fifths of the clear profits, after deducting 25*l.* per cent. yearly from the gross amount of the sales, for his trouble. And it was declared that Church and Hall should stand possessed of the four fifths of the profits, in trust for Mr. and Mrs. Folgham's other children.

W. S. Folgham made up and sold the ointment, and disposed of the profits according to the provisions of this deed. In March 1817, Mrs. Green came of age; and on the 17th of September in that year, she, at W. S. Folgham's request, signed an agreement to transfer to him all her interest in the ointment, in consideration of his paying an annuity of 100*l*. to her, and to the plaintiff Stephen Green (to whom she was then about to be married) for their lives; and on the 22d of the same month she also, at W. S. Folgham's request, executed a deed-poll confirming the indenture of the 22d of June 1816.

The bill did not take any notice of the recital before mentioned in the indenture of June 1816; but it charged that the provisions made by that indenture for the plaintiff Mrs. Green, and the other younger children whilst they were under age, was very disadvantageous to them: That Church and Hall acted in concert together, and had imposed upon them in respect of the provisions of that deed: That Mrs. Green was imposed upon by W. S. Folgham in respect of the deed-poll of September 1817: That she was ignorant of its contents when she executed it: That it was obtained from her by fraud: That the annuity of 100*l*. a year was a grossly inadequate consideration for the share of the profits of the ointment to which she was entitled under the settlement: That W. S. Folgham held the proprietorship of the ointment subject to the trusts to the settlement: That those trusts ought to be performed, and the ownership of the ointment sold, as directed by that instrument.

The bill prayed, that the deeds of June 1816, and September 1817, and the agreement, might be declared fraudulent and void, and be delivered up to be cancelled: That the trusts of the settlement of September 1794 might be performed: That an account might be taken of the quantities of the ointment sold since Mrs. Folgham's death, and of the monies produced by the sale: That one fifth of the profits might be paid to the trustees of Mr. and Mrs. Green's marriage settlement, and three fifths be placed out at interest for the benefit of the three other younger children: That the ownership of the ointment might be sold, and the proceeds applied according to the trusts of the settlement; and that W. S. Folgham might be restrained from divulging the method of preparing the ointment.

W. S. Folgham, by his answer, said, that the existence of the settlement was not known to him until long after he had been in possession of the secret of preparing the ointment: That his mother communicated the secret to him without imposing any conditions on him, or stating that any other person was to partake of the profits of the ointment; and he submitted whether, under these circumstances, his brothers and sisters took any interest in the ownership of the ointment under the trusts of the settlement, and whether he was bound by the provisions thereof. He admitted that he came of age on the 20th of March 1816; and that, having become acquainted with the contents of the settlement, he was desirous that his brothers and sisters should partake of the profits of the ointment; and that he accordingly executed the indenture of June 1816; and he submitted that that deed, having been made for the interest of all the infants, ought not to be disturbed. He said that he had devoted his whole time and attention to the conduct of the business, and was brought up with the full expectation of having the profits for his provision; and that, in order to assist his mother in the business, he had given up a situation which he had filled for five years; and that, in the course of conducting the business, he had been obliged to forego many advantageous opportunities of advancement in other pursuits; and he denied all the allegations in the bill as to the deed-poll and agreement having been obtained from Mrs. Green by fraud or surprise, and as to the annuity of 100*l.* being an inadequate consideration for her share of the profits of the ointment.

The cause now came on to be heard on the bill and answer.

THE VICE-CHANCELLOR [SIR JOHN LEACH]. It was stated, at the bar, that the defendant, W. S. Folgham, was a purchaser of this secret for a valuable consideration, without notice of the settlement; but no such case is made in his answer. And, after the admission made by him in his answer that he voluntarily considered himself as a trustee for the marriage settlement, and after the execution of the deed of June 1816, which is not impeached, he cannot successfully assert a personal title to this secret.

By the terms of the marriage settlement the trustees were directed to sell this secret upon the death of Selina Folgham; and, having no authority to deal with this subject as they have in fact dealt with it by the deed of June 1816, that deed is merely void against the younger children, who were all then infants. The subsequent agreement of September 1817, by which Selina Green engaged to assign her interest in the secret to the defendant for the annuity therein stated, being abandoned at the bar, is now out of the question. The defendant, W. S. Folgham, being to be considered therefore as a trustee of this secret under the settlement, the first relief to which the plaintiffs are entitled is, that he should come to an account for the profits actually made by him since the death of his mother, from the sale of the ointment, having a reasonable allowance made to him for his time and trouble in preparing and vending the same. If this secret could be made a subject of sale, the plaintiffs would be next entitled to ask from the court that a sale should be directed accordingly. But, inasmuch as the court has no possible means either to communicate this secret to a purchaser with certainty, or to protect him in the enjoyment of it, a sale becomes impracticable. But although the court cannot direct a sale, it has the power of taking a course which, in point of advantage, will be equivalent to the plaintiffs. It can inquire what would be the value of this secret to sell, provided it could be made the subject of sale; and the annual profits whch have actually been made by the sale of the ointment from the death of the mother will be a fair criterion by which that value may be estimated. I think that this value is more fit for the consideration of a jury than of the Master; and, after decreeing the account of the profits from the death of the mother, in the manner which I have stated, I shall direct the parties to proceed to an issue at law, in order to try what, at the date of this decree, was the pecuniary value of the secret for the preparation of the ointment in the pleadings mentioned, called, " Dr. Johnson's Ointment for the Eyes, or the Golden Ointment." The circumstances, that the plaintiff Selina Green's interest in the secret is made the subject of her marriage settlement, and that one or more of Mrs. Folgham's children are still infants, are not material for present consideration.

Let further directions and costs be reserved.[1]

In re ELLENBOROUGH.
TOWRY LAW *v.* BURNE.

HIGH COURT OF JUSTICE, CHANCERY DIVISION. 1903.

[1903] 1 Ch. 697.

THIS was an originating summons taken out by the Hon. Emily Julia Towry Law in the matter of the estate of the late Lord Ellenborough and of a settlement dated December 22, 1893.

The settlement in question was a voluntary settlement by deed, executed by Miss E. J. Towry Law, by which she granted to trustees the real estate and assigned the personal estate to which she, in the event of the deaths of her brother and sister respectively in her lifetime, might become entitled under their respective wills or intestacies. At that time she had no property in the real or personal estate of her brother or sister, but she had an expectation that, owing to the state of their health, she might become entitled to their

---

[1] See Vulcan Detinning Co. *v.* American Can Co., 72 N. J. Eq. 387. But see Rosenthal *v.* Goldstein, 112 N. Y. Misc. 606. In *Re* Keene, [1922] 2 Ch. 475, 36 Harv. L. Rev. 878, 8 Cornell L. Quar. 174, it was held that a bankrupt manufacturer of proprietary articles made according to a secret formula may be compelled to disclose the formula to his trustee in bankruptcy.

As to the protection afforded to trade secrets, see 23 Col. L. Rev. 164; 42 Harv. L. Rev. 254; 30 Yale L. Jour. 197; 37 Yale L. Jour. 1154; 69 U. Pa. L. Rev. 65.

Business good will. The good will of a business together with the business itself can be held in trust. See Farey *v.* Cooper, [1927] 2 K. B. 384. The good will, however, cannot be assigned in trust or otherwise apart from the business. Bailly *v.* Betti, 241 N. Y. 22, 35 Yale L. Jour. 496.

An unlawful business cannot be held in trust. Joe Guoy Shong *v.* Joe Chew Shee, 254 Mass. 366 (illegal practice of medicine).

Equitable interest. An equitable interest such as the interest of the beneficiary of a trust may be the subject matter of a trust. Gilbert *v.* Overton, 2 H. & M. 110; Durant *v.* Hospital Life Ins. Co., 2 Lowell (U. S.) 575; Chase *v.* Chase, 2 Allen (Mass.) 101.

property. The sister died in 1895, and the settlor, Miss E. J. Towry Law, became entitled to and received a share of her estate, and handed it over to the trustees. The brother, Lord Ellenborough, died in 1902. Miss E. J. Towry Law became entitled to all his property; this she did not desire to transfer to the trustees, and she took out a summons to decide the question whether she could refuse to do so.

BUCKLEY, J. On December 22, 1893, there were living Charles, Lord Ellenborough, and Gertrude Edith Towry Law, brother and sister of the applicant upon this summons. They were entitled respectively to certain property absolutely. In their property the applicant had no property or interest of any kind. She had an expectation arising from the fact that, owing to the relationship between them and herself and to their state of health, she might be (as was subsequently the case) the survivor, and might under their respective wills or intestacies become entitled to their property. She had neither a future interest nor a possibility coupled with an interest capable of being disposed of under s. 6 of 8 & 9 Vict. c. 106. She had only a *spes successionis*, and that is not a title to property by English law: *In re* Parsons, 45 Ch. D. 51. In that state of facts the applicant, on December 22, 1893, executed a voluntary settlement by deed by which she granted to the trustees, who are the respondents on this summons, the real estate, and assigned the personal estate to which the applicant, in the event of the death of her brother and sister respectively in her lifetime, might become entitled under their respective wills or intestacies. That deed could not operate by way of grant, but could in a Court of Equity operate as an agreement on the part of the applicant to grant and assign that which in fact could not by the deed be granted or assigned. The brother and sister are now dead, intestate, and the applicant has become entitled by devolution. The property coming to the applicant from her sister has been handed over to the trustees, and the applicant does not say that she can get it back. The property of the brother has not so been handed over, and the applicant does not desire to hand it over unless she is compelled to do so. The question to be determined upon this summons is whether she can be called upon by the trustees to assign and hand over to them that which has come to her by devolution from the late Lord Ellenborough, or whether she can refuse to do anything further to perfect that which was a mere voluntary deed. In order to raise the question in proper form a writ has been, or will be, issued by the trustees against the applicant seeking to recover the funds, and the order will be drawn up on this summons and in that action. The deed was purely voluntary. The question is whether a volunteer can enforce a contract made by deed to dispose of an expectancy. It cannot be and is not disputed that if the deed had been for value the trustees could have enforced it. If value be given, it is immaterial what is the form of assurance by which the disposition is made, or whether the subject of the disposition is capable of being thereby disposed of or not. An assignment for value binds the conscience of the assignor. A Court of Equity as against him will compel him to do that which *ex hypothesi* he has not yet effectually done. Future property, possibilities, and expectancies are all assignable in equity for value: Tailby *v.* Official Receiver, 13 App. Cas. 523. But when the assurance is not for value, a Court of Equity will not assist a volunteer. In Meek *v.* Kettlewell, 1 Hare 464, affirmed by Lord Lyndhurst, 1 Ph. 342, the exact point arose which I have here to decide, and it was held that a voluntary assignment of an expectancy, even though under seal, would not be enforced by a Court of Equity. " The assignment of an expectancy," says Lord Lyndhurst, " such as this is, cannot be supported unless made for a valuable consideration." It is however suggested that that decision was overruled or affected by the decision of the Court of Appeal in Kekewich *v.* Manning, 1 D. M. & G. 176, and a passage in White and Tudor's Leading Cases in Equity, 7th ed. vol. ii. p. 851, was referred to upon the point. In my opinion Kekewich *v.* Manning has no bearing upon that which was decided in Meek *v.* Kettlewell. The assignment in Kekewich *v.* Manning was not of an expectancy, but of property. " It is on legal and equitable principles," said Knight Bruce, L. J., " we apprehend, clear that a person *sui juris*, acting freely, fairly, and with sufficient knowledge, ought to have and has it in his power to make, in a binding and effectual manner, a voluntary gift of any part of his property, whether capable or incapable of manual delivery, whether in possession or reversionary, and howsoever circumstanced." The important words there are " of his property." The point of Meek *v.* Kettlewell and of the case before me is that the assignment was not of property, but of a mere expectancy. On December 22, 1893, that with which the grantor was dealing was not her property in any sense. She had nothing more than an expectancy. In *Re* Tilt, 74 L. T. 163, there was again a voluntary assignment of an expectancy, and the point was not regarded as arguable. " It was rightly admitted," said Chitty, J., " that as, when this plaintiff executed the deed of 1880, she had no interest whatever in the fund in question, which was a mere expectancy, the deed was wholly inoperative both at law and in equity, being entirely voluntary." By "wholly inoperative" there the learned judge of course did not mean that if the voluntary settlor had handed over the funds the trustees would not have held them upon the trusts, but that the grantees under the deed could not enforce it as against the settlor in a Court of Equity or elsewhere. In my judgment the interest of the plaintiff as sole heiress-at-law and next of kin of the late Lord Ellenborough was not effectually assigned to the trustees by the deed, and the trustees cannot call upon her to grant, assign, transfer, or pay over to them his residuary real and personal estate.[1]

MATTER OF GURLITZ, 105 N. Y. Misc. 30 (1918), modified *sub nom.* IN RE LYNDE'S ESTATE, 175 N. Y. Supp. 289, aff'd, 190 App. Div. 907: Rollin H. Lynde executed an instrument under seal whereby he purported to assign to a trust company as trustee for Elsie S. Dodge Pattee his interest under a trust created by his grandfather, Joseph W. Harper. The assignment was gratuitous. His mother was a beneficiary under the trust but he was not. His mother subsequently died bequeathing all her property to him. The court held that nothing passed under the assignment. FOWLER, S., said:

"When Rollin H. Lynde assigned he had no interest vested or contingent in the estate of Joseph W. Harper. His interest was not assignable. . . . I have before stated that as an assignment of legal title the instrument is inoperative because there is no interest considered assignable. Viewed as an engagement that the property in question was to belong to the assignee when received, the instrument would be promissory only. The absence of consideration recognized at law or equity as valuable consideration prevents its enforcement. [Citations.] Under the authorities just cited an imperfect gift cannot be enforced where there is no consideration, nor can it be enforced as a declaration of a trust. To convert an imperfect gift into a declaration of trust, where such was not the intention, is not within the realm of even so benign a system of jurisprudence as equity.

"But the absence of consideration will not stop a court of equity

---

[1] Lenning's Est., 182 Pa. 485, *accord.*

An assignment by an heir of his expectancy even if made for value is invalid if it is a hard bargain. In a few jurisdictions it has been held invalid unless communicated to the ancestor. McClure v. Raben, 133 Ind. 507 (but see McAdams v. Bailey, 169 Ind. 518); McCall v. Hampton, 98 Ky. 166; Boynton v. Hubbard, 7 Mass. 112. But the weight of authority is the other way. See Hale v. Hollon, 90 Tex. 427; 33 L. R. A. 266; 56 Am. St. Rep. 339.

As to the nature and effect of an assignment for value of an expectancy, see *Re* Lind, [1915] 2 Ch. 345; Bridge v. Kedon, 163 Cal. 493; Fidelity Union Trust Co. v. Reeves, 96 N. J. Eq. 490, *aff'd* 98 N. J. Eq. 412; Dec. Dig., Assignments, 6–9; 17 A. L. R. 597; 44 A. L. R. 1465.

In *Re* Baker, 13 F.(2d) 707, a woman who owned a valuable farm had seven children. Two of the children for value assigned to another of them their expectant interests in the estate of their mother. Some years later the latter child was adjudicated a bankrupt, and six days after the adjudication the mother died. It was held that the trustee in bankruptcy was not entitled to the two-sevenths share of the mother's estate which the bankrupt had purchased from his brothers. See 27 Col. L. Rev. 87; 36 Yale L. Jour. 272. Compare *Re* Lage, 19 F.(2d) 153, 41 Harv. L. Rev. 106. Property inherited by the bankrupt after the adjudication cannot of course be reached by the trustee in bankruptcy. Bank of Elberton v. Swift, 268 Fed. 305; *Re* Seal, 261 Fed. 112; Matter of Beinhauer, 118 Misc. 527, *aff'd* 202 N. Y. App. Div. 747.

from carefully scrutinizing the language of an instrument, apparently purporting to be one of assignment, in order to ascertain whether or not there was a real intention to declare a trust. In the case before me, even if we deem the instrument not one of assignment to third parties as trustees for the benefit of Elsie S. Dodge Pattee, and should come to the conclusion that Rollin H. Lynde declared that the beneficial ownership in the property which might be derived directly or indirectly from his grandfather's estate should belong to his assignee, then we are met with an insuperable obstacle. No *res* would come into existence upon which to predicate the trust. Even considering Rollin H. Lynde as the trustee of a trust declared by him, the trust could not be deemed to have come into existence until the property was received. It would be at most a voluntary promise to declare a trust — an obligation unenforcible either at law or in equity." [1]

O'BRIEN *v.* MASSACHUSETTS CATHOLIC ORDER OF FORESTERS.

SUPREME JUDICIAL COURT, MASSACHUSETTS. 1915.

220 Mass. 79.

BILL IN EQUITY, filed in the Superior Court on October 15, 1912, by the surviving children of John F. O'Brien, late of Boston, who constituted his sole next of kin, against the Massachusetts Catholic Order of Foresters, a Massachusetts fraternal beneficiary corporation of which John F. O'Brien at the time of his death was a member and a holder of a death benefit certificate, and one Augustine A. Donovan, a cousin of John F. O'Brien, whom O'Brien after the death of his wife had designated as his sole beneficiary. The plaintiffs alleged that the designation of Donovan as beneficiary was procured through fraud and undue influence on his part and on the part of one Ellen F. Beals and brought this suit to enjoin the payment of the death benefit to Donovan.

The suit was heard by *Jenney*, J., who filed a memorandum of facts found and rulings made by him. Among other facts, he

---

[1] There cannot be a trust unless there is property held in trust. A *chose* in action may be held in trust by the obligee but not by the obligor. See Chap. I, sec. IV, and particularly Molera *v.* Cooper, 173 Cal. 259, *ante;* Chap. II, sec. II, and particularly Fletcher *v.* Fletcher, 4 Hare 67, *ante.*

Property not yet in existence or not yet owned by the settlor or not yet identified cannot be the subject matter of a trust. 42 Harv. L. Rev. 559.

In National City Bank *v.* Hotchkiss, 231 U. S. 50, it was held that a debt and not a trust is created where no specific property is held for another. Mr. Justice Holmes said (p. 57): "A trust cannot be established in an aliquot share of a man's whole property, as distinguished from a particular fund, by showing that trust monies have gone into it." See also *Re* Imperial Textile Co., 255 Fed. 199.

found that the designation of Donovan as beneficiary was not procured by the fraud or undue influence of Donovan or of Beals, but was the free and voluntary act of O'Brien.

Other material facts found by the judge are stated in the opinion.

The plaintiffs asked for the following rulings among others:

" 2. The designation of a beneficiary of the death benefit fund in the defendant association, to be valid, must be of a person within the classes prescribed by statute and the by-laws of the association, and the limitation of beneficiaries to said classes cannot be evaded by the designation of an eligible person who secretly agrees to take the fund as trustee for the benefit of a person or persons ineligible.

" 3. The facts and evidence in this case warrant a finding that the designation of the respondent Donovan as beneficiary was made, not because he was in any sense a 'dependent' or 'relative' of the deceased, but for the express purpose of having said Donovan pay certain creditors of the deceased out of the death benefit fund with perhaps a balance over for himself and said Mrs. Beals or his children. In other words: that said designation was simply an attempt to circumvent the constitution and by-laws of the association and defeat the very purpose for which said mortuary fund was established and one of the principal objects for which the association itself was organized, viz.: 'making suitable provision for the widows, orphans, relatives, and dependents of deceased members' and if the court so finds then said designation is void."

" 9. The deceased had no power or authority to dispose of the death benefit fund of the order for the benefit of his creditors directly or indirectly, by will or otherwise, and if the Court finds that the defendant Donovan was named as beneficiary, not that he should have the death fund, or any part of it, for his own benefit, but simply as a subterfuge and under a secret agreement, so that he, being a 'relative' could draw the money for the benefit of certain creditors of the deceased including Mrs. Beals with the remainder if any for the children, then said designation is void so far as the creditors are concerned, and the whole fund in equity belongs to the children."

The judge refused to rule as requested; and the plaintiffs alleged exceptions.

LORING, J. In contemplation of law the only interest in the death benefit which the deceased (John F. O'Brien) had was a power of appointment and the power of appointment which he had was a limited one. He was limited in making the appointment to his widow, children, relatives or dependents.

If the deceased had undertaken to make an appointment of the death benefit to and among his creditors it would have been an appointment outside the class to which he was limited and void. The appointment to Donovan (who was within the class) on

Donovan's agreeing to apply the amount of the death benefit so far as it might be necessary to the payment of his (O'Brien's) debts, was an attempt on O'Brien's part to do by indirection what he could not do by direct appointment in favor of his creditors and was equally void.

By the terms of the agreement between O'Brien and Donovan, Donovan was to hold the balance left after paying O'Brien's debts in trust for the plaintiffs. It is not necessary therefore to decide whether the appointment to Donovan was wholly void or was void only so far as O'Brien sought to secure payment of his debts out of the fund. And decisions to each proposition are equally in point. *In re* Cohen, [1911] 1 Ch. 37. Duke of Portland *v.* Topham, 11 H. L. Cas. 32. *In re* Perkins, [1893] 1 Ch. 283. *In re* Kirwan's Trusts, 25 Ch. D. 373. Sadler *v.* Pratt, 5 Sim. 632. Bruce *v.* Bruce, L. R. 11 Eq. 371. Pryor *v.* Pryor, 2 DeG., J. & S. 205. Carver *v.* Richards, 1 DeG., F. & J. 548. *In re* Marsden's Trust, 4 Drew. 594. Daubeny *v.* Cockburn, 1 Meriv. 626.

The defendant Donovan has based his contention to the contrary upon the decision in Kerr *v.* Crane, 212 Mass. 224. But the question here presented was not before the court in that case. In that case, as in the case at bar, there was an appointment to one within the class for the benefit of one outside the class. In that respect the two cases are alike. But when that has been stated the similarity between the two cases is at an end. In Kerr *v.* Crane the person who was entitled to the death benefit in case no legal designation was made agreed to the designation made by the deceased outside the class when that designation was made. In addition to that she intervened in the suit of Kerr *v.* Crane and asked to have that agreement carried into effect. That suit was a suit brought to prevent one within the class (who had been designated as a beneficiary for the benefit of one without the class) keeping the money for himself when the person entitled in the absence of the legal designation intervened in the suit and asked to have the designation outside the class carried into effect. But the suit now before us is a suit by those entitled in case no legal designation is made to secure for themselves the death benefit which under the arrangement with Donovan was a fraud upon their rights. The case of Kerr *v.* Crane, *ubi supra,* is not fully reported; for some of the facts to which we have referred above resort must be had to the original papers.

The finding of the judge " that said O'Brien had no intent to evade the laws of the Commonwealth or the constitution and by-laws of the defendant corporation, and that in making said designation he acted under advice of counsel," is of no consequence. His act was an evasion of the laws of the Commonwealth and of the constitution and by-laws of the defendant corporation. The fact that counsel wrongly advised him to the contrary and the fact that he believed that counsel's advice was right did not change the character of the designation or appointment made by him. See in this connection Ulman *v.* Ritter, 72 Fed. Rep. 1,000; Rodgers *v.* Pitt, 89 Fed. Rep. 424; Royal Trust Co. *v.* Washburn, Bayfield & Iron River Railway, 113 Fed. Rep. 531; Green *v.* Griffin, 95 N. C. 50; McKillop *v.* Taylor, 10 C. E. Green, 139. The second, third and ninth rulings asked for should have been given and the exceptions must be sustained.

It appears from the bill of exceptions that the findings which have been made dispose of the whole controversy. We are therefore of opinion that acting under St. 1913, c. 716, § 3, we should now direct that a final decree be entered. It has been agreed among the parties that the $1,000 (the amount of the death benefit certificate) should be paid without costs or interest and that the defendant corporation should not claim its costs. The decree to be entered should declare that no legal designation in favor of his creditors was made by the deceased during his lifetime and should direct the defendant corporation to pay the $1,000 to the plaintiffs. It is

So ordered.[1]

VINCENT *v.* KELLY.

SUPREME COURT, NEW YORK. 1922.

118 Misc. Rep. 591.

FINCH, J. This is an action to impress a trust upon the proceeds of a policy of insurance issued by the United States to one John J. Kelly, deceased, under the provisions of the War Risk Insurance Act. The purpose of said act appears to be to provide protection for relatives of soldiers and sailors within prescribed limits, to the exclusion of all other persons. This is shown particularly by the act of December 24, 1919, sections 15 and 16, amending section 402 of said War Risk Insurance Act.

The defendant is a brother of the said John J. Kelly, and at the time of the application for the insurance was the only relative of the deceased then residing in the United States who came within the class of persons permitted by the War Risk Insurance Act to be named as beneficiaries and to receive such insurance. It was shown at the trial that the said John J. Kelly at about the time he procured the insurance gave to the defendant the names of certain persons who were to share proportionately in the proceeds of the policy. Some of these persons were not within the class prescribed

[1] Gillam *v.* Dale, 69 Kan. 362; Fisher *v.* Donovan, 57 Neb. 361, *accord.* But see Peek's Ex'r *v.* Peek's Ex'r, 101 Ky. 423; Cowin *v.* Hurst, 124 Mich. 545; Grand Lodge *v.* Beath, 150 Mich. 657; Hurd *v.* Doty, 86 Wis. 1. See *Re* Reid's Estate, 170 Mich. 476; Steller *v.* Sell, 55 N. J. Eq. 530.

For conflicting views as to who is entitled to the proceeds of a policy issued by a benefit society if the beneficiary predeceases the insured, see 31 A. L. R. 762.

by the act. It was also shown that the defendant had recognized the claims of these persons to share in the proceeds of the policy in the proportions indicated by the deceased. In other words, it appears that the deceased had sought to evade the provisions of the War Risk Insurance Act by creating a trust for the benefit of persons not within the class prescribed by the act and in violation of its purpose. It necessarily follows that such trust is illegal and cannot be enforced. As was said by Mr. Justice Bartlett in Fairchild v. Edson, 154 N. Y. 199, 219, in considering an analogous statute: " It needs no argument to demonstrate that a secret trust, having for its object the circumvention of this statute, is void." This being so, a court of equity will not permit the defendant to retain the proceeds of the policy, the subject of the attempted trust, but will declare a trust in favor of those legally entitled to receive such proceeds. Fairchild v. Edson, *supra;* O'Hara v. Dudley, 95 N. Y. 403. Settle all proposed findings and decree accordingly on notice, and if either party objects to any finding proposed by opponent, kindly so state, giving reasons therefor.

Decreed accordingly.[1]

NON-TRANSFERABLE PROPERTY. Purely personal interests such as a peerage or an office are not transferable and cannot be held in trust. Buckhurst Peerage, 2 App. Cas. 1, 27.

On grounds of public policy the salary attached to a public office is not assignable, at least before it is due. Cooper v. Reilly, 2 Sim. 560 (Parliamentary Counsel to the Treasury); Grenfell v. Dean & Canons of Windsor, 2 Beav. 544, 549; M'Creery v. Bennett, [1904] 2 I. R. 69 (clerk of court); Stewart v. Sample, 168 Ala. 270 (tax assessor); Schmitt v. Dooling, 145 Ky. 240 (fireman). But see State Bank v. Hastings, 15 Wis. 75 (salary of judge). *Cf.* Re Mirams, [1891] 1 Q. B. 594 (salary of chaplain to work-house assignable because not a public office).

Pensions from the government are not transferable and cannot be held in trust. Davis v. Duke of Marlborough, 1 Swanst. 74.

It has been held that where a lessee covenants not to assign the lease he cannot effectively declare himself trustee of the lease. Weintraub v. Weingart, 98 Cal. App. 690, 18 Cal. L. Rev. 90. See also Ellis v. Small, 209 Mass. 147.

It would seem that a cause of action for a tort which is not assignable cannot be held in trust.

---

[1] See Cessna v. Adams, 93 N. J. Eq. 276.

A trust may be created in favor of a member of the class designated by the statute. See Ambrose v. United States, 15 F.(2d) 52, 40 Harv. L. Rev. 785. But see Staples v. Murray, 124 Kan. 730, 28 Col. L. Rev. 506.

Section II.
The Trustee.

PIMBE'S CASE.
——. 1585.

Moore 196.— Translated in Cruise, Uses, 47.

THROCKMORTON committed high treason, 18 Eliz., for which in 26 Eliz. he was attainted by trial. Between the treason and the attainder a fine was levied to him by Scudamore of certain lands to the use of Scudamore and his wife (who was sister to Throckmorton); and of the heirs of the said Scudamore. Afterwards Scudamore and his wife bargained and sold the lands to Pimbe for money. Upon discovery of the treason and the attainder of Throckmorton, the purchaser Pimbe was advised by Plowden, Popham, and many others, that the estate of the land was in the Queen, because the Queen is entitled to all the lands that traitors had at the time of the treason, or after. So the use which was declared to Scudamore and his wife upon the fine was void, by the relation of the right of the Queen under the attainder, and the Queen must hold the land, discharged of the use, because the Crown cannot be seised to a use.[1]

[1] Similarly, the King could not make a conveyance by bargain and sale. Atkins *v.* Longvile, Cro. Jac. 50; [Bacon, Uses, 56.]

The common statement that the crown or a state cannot be a trustee means simply that the *cestui que trust* cannot file a bill in equity against the sovereign. Dillon *v.* Fraine, Poph. 70; Wike's Case, Lane 54, 2 Roll. Ab. 780 [C] 1 s. c.; Paulett *v.* Atty. Gen., Hardres 465, 467; Kildare *v.* Eustace, 1 Vern. 437, 439; Reeve *v.* Atty. Gen., 2 Atk. 223, 1 Ves. 446 (cited), s. c.; Penn *v.* Baltimore, 1 Ves. Sr. 444, 453; Burgess *v.* Wheate, 1 Eden 177, 255; Hodge *v.* Atty. Gen., 3 Y. & C. 342; People *v.* Ashburner, 55 Cal. 517; Shoemaker *v.* Board, 36 Ind. 175; Briggs *v.* Light-Boats, 11 All. 157, 170–173; Pinson *v.* Ivey, 1 Yerg. 296, 332. In Farmers' Co. *v.* The People, 1 Sandf. Ch. 139, the difficulty of procedure seems to have been overlooked.

If the beneficiary sues by petition, the sovereign will, as a matter of course, recognize the just claim of the petitioner. Pimbe's Case, *supra;* Scounden *v.* Hawley, Comb. 172; Briggs *v.* Light-Boats, *supra.* See Rustomjee *v.* Queen, 2 Q. B. Div. 69. [For an instance of a private act whereby the state released its title to an equitable claimant, see Laws N. J., 1912, c. 230.]

The validity of the trust is recognized also in legal proceedings in which the sovereign is not made a defendant. *E.g.:* A grantee of the sovereign takes the title subject to the trust. Winona *v.* St. Paul Co., 26 Minn. 179; Pinson *v.* Ivey, *supra;* Marshall *v.* Lovelass, Cam. & Nor. (N. C.) 217. And if the sovereign obtains the title to trust property, his title will be barred and with it the claim of the *cestui que trust* by the same lapse of time which would have protected the adverse possession if a private individual had been trustee. Miller *v.* State, 38 Ala. 600; Molton *v.* Henderson, 62 Ala. 426. — AMES.

To the effect that the United States may take and hold property in trust,

It is but justice to mention that, the case being represented to Queen Elizabeth, she, much to her honor, granted the land to the *cestui que use* by patent.

KING *v.* BOYS.

——. 1569.

Dyer 283 b.

ONE T. King enfeoffed one Jasper Boys, an alien, and Forcet of Gray's Inn, to the use of himself and his wife in tail, remainder to his right heirs. Whether the Queen be entitled to a moiety of the land immediately, or not, was the question. And it seems that if an office be found of it, the Queen shall have the moiety by her prerogative to her own use, and the other use in this moiety is gone forever.[1]

ATTORNEY GENERAL *v.* LANDERFIELD.

CHANCERY. 1743.

9 Mod. 286.

NOTE. In this case the Attorney General argued, that as corporations could not be seised to an use at law, no more could they be trustees, but should have the lands to their own use, divested and freed from the trust.[2]

---

see U. S. *v.* Jackson, 280 U. S. 183; Briggs *v.* Light-Boats, 11 Allen (Mass.) 157; President of the U. S. *v.* Drummond, cited in 7 H. L. C. 124, 155. In U. S. *v.* Fox, 94 U. S. 315, *aff'g* 52 N. Y. 530, a devise of land in New York to the government of the United States was held void on the ground that under the law of New York land could be devised only to natural persons and New York corporations. See also Levy *v.* Levy, 33 N. Y. 97, where the trust failed for want of a definite beneficiary.

To the effect that a state may take and hold property in trust, see Appeal of Yale College, 67 Conn. 237; Bedford *v.* Bedford's Adm'rs, 99 Ky. 273, 289; Pinson *v.* Ivey, 1 Yerg. (Tenn.) 296.

In Catt *v.* Catt, 118 N. Y. App. Div. 742, a devise of land in New York to another state was held invalid since under the law of New York the state is not qualified to take and hold land in New York.

[1] Fish *v.* Klein, 2 Mer. 431; Marshall *v.* Lovelass, Cam. & Nor. 217 (*semble*) accord. [See Sanders, Uses, 85.]

An alien grantee upon trust acquired title defeasible only by the sovereign. Com. Dig. Alien, C. 4; Ferguson *v.* Franklins, 6 Munf. 305.

The alien's disability was removed in England by St. 33 Vict. c. 14, § 2; and by similar statutes an alien may at the present day in almost all jurisdictions hold property as freely as a subject, and may therefore be a trustee. In *Re* Hill, W. N. (1874), 228, the court appointed an alien as trustee of English property for beneficiaries in France. — AMES.

As to the capacity of aliens to take or hold land, see Tiffany, Domestic Relations, 3 ed., 560; Dec. Dig., Aliens, secs. 5–13; 14 Iowa L. Rev. 183.

[2] Chudleigh's Case, 1 Co. 122*a*. See, *accord*, Bro. Ab. Feff. al Uses, 60;

But the CHANCELLOR [LORD HARDWICKE] would not let him go on, nothing being clearer than that corporations might be trustees.[1]

Bury v. Bokenham, Dy. 7b; Bacon, Uses, 57. But see, *contra*, Holland's Case, 2 Leon. 121, 3 Leon. 175, [holding that a corporation may make a conveyance by bargain and sale. See also Gilbert, Uses, 7]. The reason for the ancient doctrine is thus quaintly expressed in Popham, 72: "Yet every feoffee is not bound although he hath knowledge of the confidence, as an alien person, attaint, and the like; nor the King, he shall not be seised to another's use, because he is not compellable to perform the confidence; nor a corporation, because it is a dead body, although it consist of natural persons: and in this dead body a confidence cannot be put, but in bodies naturall." — AMES.

"Bodies politik are not capable of a use or trust, because they are bodies framed at the will of the king, and are no further capable than he wills them: and it is his will that they should purchase for the common benefit, and for the ends of their creation, and not that they should take any thing in trust for others. Besides, being incorporate, the Chancery had no process on the persons to compel them to discharge their trust." 7 Bac. Abr., 6 ed., 94.

[1] As to the powers and liabilities of trust companies, see Sears, Trust Company Law; Smith, Trust Companies in the United States. This matter is regulated by statute in the several states. By the act of Congress establishing the Federal Reserve Board, that board is given authority "to grant by special permit to national banks applying therefor, when not in contravention of state or local law, the right to act as trustee, executor, administrator, or registrar of stocks and bonds under such rules and regulations as the said board may prescribe." 38 Stat. L. 251, 262, c. 6, sec. 11(k). This provision is constitutional. First Nat. Bk. v. Fellows, 244 U. S. 416; State of Missouri v. Duncan, 265 U. S. 17. See 15 Col. L. Rev. 386; 32 Harv. L. Rev. 689. See Lévitt, The Trust Powers of National Banks, 77 U. Pa. L. Rev. 835.

A trust company or other corporation, however, cannot lawfully engage in the practice of law. *Re* Eastern Idaho Loan & Trust Co., 288 Pac. 157 (Idaho, 1930).

As to the power of other private corporations to act as trustees, see Ames, 216n., 1 Machen, Corporations, sec. 57.

As to the power of municipal corporations to act as trustees, see Gloucester v. Osborn, 1 H. L. C. 272, 285; Vidal v. Girard's Executors, 2 How. (U. S.) 127, 189; Girard v. Philadelphia, 7 Wall. (U. S.) 1, 14; Webb v. Neal, 5 Allen (Mass.) 575; Boston v. Doyle, 184 Mass. 373; *Re* Franklin's Est., 150 Pa. 437; 3 McQuillan, Municipal Corps., secs. 1128–1139; Dec. Dig., Corps., 434; 6 Harv. L. Rev. 202; 19 Mich. L. Rev. 757.

Merger and consolidation. As to the effect of merger or consolidation of corporate trustees, see *Ex parte* Worcester National Bank, 279 U. S. 347, aff'g Petition of Worcester County National Bank, 263 Mass. 444; Chicago Title & Trust Co. v. Zinser, 264 Ill. 31; Commonwealth National Bank, Petitioner, 249 Mass. 440; Atlantic National Bank, Petitioner, 261 Mass. 217; Petition of Worcester County National Bank, 263 Mass. 394. See Bogert, Some Recent Developments in the Law of Trusts, 23 Ill. L. Rev. 749, 757. See 61 A. L. R. 994.

Foreign corporations. As to the power of a trust company of another state to act as trustee, see Estate of Wellings, 192 Cal. 506; Guaranty Trust Co., petitioner, 248 Mass. 319; Bank of New York & Trust Co. v. Tilton, 82 N. H. 81. See 24 Col. L. Rev. 649; 65 A. L. R. 1237.

As to the power of a charitable corporation of another state, see Gould v. Board of Home Missions, 102 Neb. 526.

JEVON v. BUSH.

Chancery. 1685.

1 Vern. 342.

Lord Bellamount in 1647 lent 600*l*. to one Gardiner on a recognizance of 1,000*l*., which he took in the name of the defendant Bush, and intended it as a provision for the plaintiff, his infant daughter, then but two years old; and Bush at the same time executed a declaration of the trust. Gardiner being about to sell his estate, and the purchaser having notice of the recognizance, Bush is prevailed upon in 1654 to acknowledge satisfaction; and in 1657, and not before, the plaintiff had notice of this declaration of trust, and, understanding that Bush had acknowledged satisfaction on this recognizance, brings her bill to be relieved against this breach of trust.

The defendant by answer insisted and it was so proved in the cause, that he was but 18 years old when he made this declaration of trust; and insisted likewise, that he never had one penny for his acknowledging satisfaction on that recognizance, but that Lord Bellamount's widow, as he believes, received the moneys due thereon.[1]

The counsel for the defendant insisted, that the plaintiff ought to prove some fraud in the trustee, or that he received to his own use part of the money.

Lord Chancellor [Jeffreys]. The proof lies on the defendant's side; he ought to discharge himself, and it is not sufficient for him to say he never received any of this money for his own use: there is no doubt but an infant may be a trustee; and the breach of trust was committed in 1654, after he was of full age; and therefore decreed him to pay the principal money, with damages not exceeding 1,000*l*., being the penalty of the recognizance; and cited my Lord Hobart, who says that *cestui que trust* in an action of the case against his trustee shall recover for a breach of trust in damages.[2]

---

[1] The statement of facts has been abridged. See Ames, 217.

[2] Although an infant may be a trustee, no judicious person and no court would appoint an infant as trustee.

(1) There was formerly no mode of divesting the infant trustee of his title to the trust property. An equity judge could make no other decree against the infant than that which was made in Anonymous, 3 P. Wms. 389, n. [A]; namely, "to convey when of age, unless he should shew cause to the contrary within six months after he should come of age." See also Perry *v.* Perry, 65 Me. 399; [McClellan *v.* McClellan, 65 Me. 500;] Whitney *v.* Stearns, 11 Met. 319; and compare King *v.* Bellord, 1 H. & M. 343.

[By statute in England and in the various states, the court has power to remove an infant trustee and to vest the title in a new trustee.]

Independently of these statutes, if an infant trustee actually conveyed

PEGGE v. SKYNNER AND RICHARDSON.

CHANCERY. 1784.

1 Cox. Eq. Cas. 23.

BILL for specific performance of an agreement for a lease from plaintiff to defendants. It was objected that the defendant Richardson had since become incapable of doing any act in consequence of a paralytic stroke. It was ordered that the defendant Skynner should execute a counterpart of a lease, and also the defendant Richardson, when he should be capable of so doing.[1]

LORD THURLOW refused to give plaintiff costs.

MARRIED WOMEN. A married woman may be a trustee. Curran v. Green, 18 R. I. 329. At common law, however, she could not convey the title to the trust property without the co-operation of her husband. But by statute both in England and almost everywhere in this country a *feme covert* is independent of her husband in her dealings with trust property. At common law liability for any breach of trust falls not upon her but upon her husband. This also has been largely changed by statute.

As to the powers and liabilities of married women as trustees, see Ames 220n.; Perry, Trusts, secs. 49–51; 30 C. J. 722.

---

to the *cestui que trust,* or according to his directions, he could not, on attaining majority, disaffirm the conveyance. —— v. Handcock, 17 Ves. 383; Elliott v. Horn, 10 Ala. 348; Starr v. Wright, 20 Oh. St. 97; Thompson v. Dulles, 5 Rich. Eq. 370. [See 17 Col. L. Rev. 61. In Levin v. Ritz, 17 N. Y. Misc. 737, where an infant held a *chose* in action in trust, it was held that the *cestui que trust* could compel the obligor to make payment directly to him. See Williston, Contracts, sec. 228, n.4.]

(2) An infant, it is obvious, has not the discretion requisite to the due administration of a trust, and cannot be held accountable for its maladministration. Russel's Case, 5 Rep. 27a; Whitmore v. Weld, 1 Vern. 326; Hindmarsh v. Southgate, 3 Russ. 324; Stott v. Meanock, 31 L. J. Ch. 746; in which cases it was adjudged that an infant executor was not liable for a *devastavit.*

Although an infant is not liable for a breach of trust, he is chargeable *ex delicto* as a constructive trustee for any property acquired by his misconduct. Anon., 2 Eq. Ab. 489, n.(a); Esron v. Nicholas, 1 DeG. & Sm. 118n.; Clare v. Watts, 9 Vin. Ab. 415; Anon., 2 Eden, 71, 72; Overton v. Banister, 3 Hare 503; Lemprière v. Lange, 12 Ch. D. 675. [See Cory v. Gertchen, 2 Madd. 40.] — AMES.

An infant who embezzles money is liable in an action for money had and received. Briston v. Eastman, 1 Esp. 172.

[1] Owen v. Davies, 1 Ves. 82; Hall v. Warren, 9 Ves. 605, *accord.* See Ames, Cas. Eq. Juris., 6.

Apart from statutes, the only decree that could be made against a trustee *non compos mentis* was in the form indicated in the principal case. The difficulty has been removed by statute in England and in the several states.

In general as to capacity to be trustee, see Perry, Trusts, secs. 38–59; 3 Pomeroy, Eq. Juris., sec. 987; Bogert, Trusts, 253–258.

WOODRUFF v. WOODRUFF.

COURT OF CHANCERY, NEW JERSEY. 1888.

44 N. J. Eq. 349.

PATRICK WOODRUFF died in December, 1886, leaving a daughter, Louisa C. Woodruff, his only child, him surviving. He died testate, having by his will appointed his daughter, Louisa, and one Charles P. Stratton, the executrix and executor thereof, and having also by it devised to Charles P. Stratton, in fee, the farm "Oaklands," and bequeathed to him other property upon trust. . . . The trustee, Charles P. Stratton, died during the life of the testator. . . . The bills prays (1) that a trustee may be appointed in the place of Charles P. Stratton, to execute the trust.[1] . . .

THE CHANCELLOR [MCGILL]. . . . As Mr. Stratton, to whom the lands were devised in trust, died before the testator, the title to the farm descended to Louisa C. Woodruff as heir-at-law of her father, Patrick, but charged with the trust established by the will. Lewin on Trusts (8th ed.) 833; Perry on Trusts, § 38. From the character of that trust, it seems to me that a trustee should now be appointed in the place of Mr. Stratton. I will order a reference to a Master, to ascertain who will be a fit and proper person to receive the appointment, and what security the person selected should be required to give. I will appoint a new trustee. . . .

SONLEY v. THE MASTER, &c., OF THE CLOCK–MAKERS COMPANY.

CHANCERY. 1780.

1 Bro. Ch. 81.

CONYERS DUNLOP devised freehold estates to his wife for life, remainder to his brother Charles in tail male, remainder to the Clock-makers Company, in trust that they should, as soon as conveniently might be after the decease of his wife and brother Charles without issue male, or after the death of such issue under the age of twenty-one years, sell the premises, and that the money to arise from such sale, and the receipts and profits from the decease &c. till the sale, should be divided among all and every the testator's nephews and nieces already born, or to be born, and their child or children begotten, or to be begotten, to wit, &c. The testator's wife and brother both died in his life-time. The question therefore was, whether the devise to the corporation being void [by Stat. 34 & 35

---

[1] The statement of facts is taken from the opinion of the Chancellor, and a large part of the opinion is omitted.

Hen. VIII, c. 5], the heir at law took beneficially, or subject to the trust.

Mr. Baron Eyre. Although the devise to the corporation be void at law, yet the trust is sufficiently created to fasten itself upon any estate the law may raise. This is the ground upon which courts of equity have decreed, in cases where no trustee is named.

Decreed that the heir at law is a trustee to the uses of the will.[1]

HILES v. GARRISON.

Court of Chancery, New Jersey. 1906.

70 N. J. Eq. 605.

Bergen, V. C. The bill in this case is filed by the complainant, widow of Richard Hiles, deceased, for the construction of his last will and testament, and the appointment of a trustee to execute such trusts as may be determined are established by such will. As the relief sought is the appointment of a trustee, and the necessity for such appointment requires the construction of the will as an incident to the relief sought for, the complainant is properly here.

The pertinent part of the will is the second clause, which reads as follows:

" I do devise that all my property and bonds and morgages be put in a trust, and the income be devided equally between my brother, Biddle Hiles, and sister, Caroline Garrison, and my wife, as long as she remains my widow, in case of her marring or deth her share to gowe to my brother Biddle Hiles, and my sister Caroline Garrison."

The testator died possessed of considerable estate, the personal having been appraised at the sum of $54,039.88. His real property consisted of an undivided interest in certain real estate in the county of Salem, in this state, such interest being estimated by the parties in interest at something over $20,000. At the time of his death the only next of kin of the testator was his brother, Biddle, and his sister, Caroline. The will was prepared by the testator, and does not clearly express his desires, and the purpose of this cause is to ascertain whether a trust has been established by the

---

[1] Anon., 2 Vent. 349; Farmers' Co. v. Chicago Co., 27 Fed. Rep. 146; Vidal v. Girard, 2 How. 127; Walker v. Walker, 25 Ga. 420; Hoeffer v. Clogan, 171 Ill. 462; Byers v. McCartney, 62 Iowa 339; [Amer. Bible Soc. v. Amer. Tract Soc., 62 N. J. Eq. 219;] Jackson v. Hartwell, 8 Johns. 422; Sheldon v. Chappell, 47 Hun 59; Frazier v. St. Luke's Church, 147 Pa. 256; White v. Baylor, 10 Ir. Eq. R. 43, 53–54. — Ames.

In Olson v. Larson, 320 Ill. 50, property was devised to a bank upon certain trusts. A stockholder of the bank was one of the witnesses to the will. By statute it was provided that if a devise is made to a witness, the devise should be void. It was held that the bank could not take as trustee, but that the trust should not fail. See Re Wiese, 98 Neb. 463.

terms of such will, and if so, that a trustee be appointed to carry out such trust.

While this will is very inartistically drawn, I think the clear intention of the testator was to create a trust, by the terms of which the income of his estate was to be divided equally between his widow, brother and sister, and that this trust shall continue as long as his widow lives or remains unmarried, and on the happening of either of such events the trust terminates.

As the testator has made no disposition of the *corpus* of the fund after the expiration of the trust estate, he died intestate as to the residue of his property, and it will go to his next of kin. That the testator named no trustee will not prevent the execution of the trust, for the court will always appoint a trustee wherever necessary to sustain the trust, and a trustee will be appointed. The will contains no power of sale, and therefore the trustee cannot dispose of the land by virtue of any authority contained in the will. It is, in my judgment, however, included in the trust, and subject to that will vest in the heirs-at-law of the testator.

I will advise a decree in accordance with the above.[1]

ADAMS *v.* ADAMS.

Supreme Court of the United States. 1874.

21 Wall. 185.

Appeal from the Supreme Court of the District of Columbia. The case was thus.

Adams, a government clerk in Washington, owning a house and lot there, on the 13th of August, 1861, executed, with his wife, a deed of the premises to one Appleton, in fee, as trustee for the wife. The deed by appropriate words *in præsenti* conveyed, so far as its terms were concerned, the property for the sole and separate use of the wife for life, with power to lease and to take the rents for her own use, as if she was a feme sole; the trustee having power, on request of the wife, to sell and convey the premises in fee and pay the proceeds to her or as she might direct; and after her death (no sale having been made), the trust being that the trustee should hold the property for the children of the marriage as tenants in common, and in default of issue living at the death of the wife, then for Adams, the husband, his heirs and assigns.

The deed was signed by the grantors, and the husband acknowledged it before two justices "to be his act and deed." The wife

---

[1] See Dodkin *v.* Brunt, L. R. 6 Eq. 580; Goffe *v.* Goffe, 37 R. I. 542; Ames, 227n.; Ann. Cas. 1916B 246.

Where the testator has named an executor but no trustee, the executor is allowed to act as trustee if such was the expressed or presumed intention of the testator. Bean *v.* Comm., 186 Mass. 348.

did the same; being separately examined. The instrument purported to be " signed, sealed, and delivered " in the presence of the same justices, and they signed it as attesting witnesses. The husband put it himself on record in the registry of deeds for the county of Washington, D. C., which was the appropriate place of record for it.

Subsequent to this, that is to say in September, 1870, the husband and wife were divorced by judicial decree.

And subsequently to this again, that is to say, in December, 1871, — the husband being in possession of the deed, and denying that any trust was ever created and executed, and Appleton, on the wife's [husband's?] request, declining to assert the trust, or to act as trustee, — Mrs. Adams filed a bill in the court below against them both, to establish the deed as a settlement made upon her by her husband, to compel a delivery of it to her; to remove Appleton, the trustee named in it, and to have some suitable person appointed trustee in his place. . . .

The court below declared the trust valid and effective in equity as between the parties; appointed a new trustee; required the husband to deliver up the deed to the wife or to the new trustee; and to deliver also to him possession of the premises described in the deed of trust, and to account before the master for the rents and profits of it which had accrued since the filing of the bill, receiving credit for any payment made to the complainant in the mean time, and to pay the complainant's costs of the suit.

From a decree accordingly, the husband appealed.

HUNT, J. The first question in this case is whether there was a delivery of the deed of August 13th, 1861. If not a formal ceremonious delivery, was there a transaction which, between such parties and for such purposes as exist in the present case, the law deems to be sufficient to create a title? The bill avers that the deed was delivered by the parties and put on record in the way which it states.

The answer is responsive to the allegations in the plaintiff's bill, that the deed, after being signed, sealed, and delivered, was recorded at the request of the defendant, Adams, and at his expense.

The burden is thus imposed upon the plaintiff of maintaining her allegation by the proof required where a material allegation in the bill is denied by the answer.

It is evident, however, that the apparent issues of fact and seeming contradictions of statement become less marked by looking at what the parties may suppose to constitute a delivery. That the defendant signed and sealed the deed he admits. That with his wife, the present plaintiff, he acknowledged its execution before two justices of the peace, and that the deed thus acknowledged by him not only purported by words *in præsenti* to grant, bargain, and convey the premises mentioned, but declared that the same was signed, sealed, and delivered, and that this deed, with these declarations in it, he himself put upon the record, is not denied. If these facts constitute a delivery under circumstances like the present, then the defendant, when he denies that a delivery was made, denies the law simply.

Mrs. Adams and two other witnesses were examined. None of Mrs. Adams's statements are denied by Mr. Adams. He was as competent to testify as she was. So, although time, place, and circumstances are pointed out in the testimony of one of the other witnesses, the defendant makes no denial of the statement; nor does he deny the statement of the other witness, giving her conversation with him in detail, in which she says that he admitted the trust.

The deed corresponded substantially with the intention which these witnesses state that Adams expressed. Should the property be sold by the order of Mrs. Adams, the money received would be subject to the same trusts as the land, to wit, for the use of Mrs. Adams during her lifetime and her children after her death. It would not by such transmutation become the absolute property of Mrs. Adams.

Upon the evidence before us we have no doubt that the deed was executed, acknowledged, and recorded by the defendant with the intent to make provision for his wife and children; that he took the deed into his own possession with the understanding, and upon the belief on his part, that he had accomplished that purpose by acknowledging and procuring the record of the deed, by showing the same to his wife, informing her of its contents, and placing the same in the house therein conveyed in a place equally accessible to her and to himself.

The defendant now seeks to repudiate what he then intended, and to overthrow what he then asserted and believed he had then accomplished.

It may be conceded, as a general rule, that delivery is essential, both in law and in equity, to the validity of a gift, whether of real or personal estate. Antrobus *v.* Smith, 12 Vesey, 39 and note. What constitutes a delivery is a subject of great difference of opinion, some holding that a parting with a deed, even for the purpose of recording, is in itself a delivery. Cloud *v.* Calhoun, 10 Rich. Eq. 362.

It may be conceded also to have been held many times that courts of equity will not enforce a merely gratuitous gift or mere moral obligation. *Ib.*

These concessions do not, however, dispose of the present case.

1st. We are of opinion that the refusal of Appleton, in 1870, to accept the deed, or to act as trustee, is not a controlling circumstance.

Although a trustee may never have heard of the deed, the title vests in him, subject to a disclaimer on his part.[1] Such disclaimer will not, however, defeat the conveyance as a transfer of the equitable interest to a third person. Lewin, Trusts, 152; King v. Donnelly, 5 Paige, 46. A trust cannot fail for want of a trustee, or by the refusal of all the trustees to accept the trust. The court of chancery will appoint new trustees. . . .

We think that the decree of the court below was well made, and that it should be

Affirmed.[2]

WITTMEIER v. HEILIGENSTEIN.

SUPREME COURT, ILLINOIS. 1923.

308 Ill. 434.

MR. JUSTICE CARTER delivered the opinion of the court:

Certain issues in this case were decided in Heiligenstein v. Schlotterbeck, 300 Ill. 206. The issue here relates to rights claimed to arise under an invalid deed executed by Josephine Wittmeier to the

---

[1] See Ames 229n.

[2] Mallott v. Wilson, [1903] 2 Ch. 494; Smith v. Davis, 90 Cal. 25; Wells v. Ins. Co., 128 Iowa 649; Minot v. Tilton, 64 N. H. 371, 375 (*semble*); King v. Donnelly, 5 Paige (N. Y.) 46 (*semble*); Talbot v. Talbot, 32 R. I. 72; Cloud v. Calhoun, 10 Rich. Eq. (S. C.) 358, *accord*. See Ames, 230n.; Dec. Dig., Trusts, 38.

In Mallott v. Wilson, [1903] 2 Ch. 494, Byrne, J., said (p. 501): "Mr. Preston, in his edition (7th) of Sheppard's Touchstone, says, at p. 285: 'The law presumes that every grant, etc., is for the benefit of the grantee, etc.; and therefore till the contrary is shewn, supposes an agreement to the grant. From the moment there is evidence of disagreement, then in construction of law the grant is void *ab initio*, as if no grant had been made; and in intendment of law the freehold never passed from the grantor.' And there is a passage to somewhat similar effect in Preston's Abstracts, vol. ii, p. 226: 'In the first place if a grant be made by one man to another, the estate will, in intendment of law, vest immediately in the grantee; but by refusal or disagreement the grant will be void *ab initio*. This point was fully discussed, and received a determination in the case of Thompson v. Leach, 2 Vent. 198.' I felt somewhat embarrassed by the use of the expression 'void *ab initio*,' but I am satisfied now that the true meaning is that, not in regard to all persons and for all purposes is the case to be treated as though the legal estate had never passed, but that as regards the trustee and the person to whom the grant was made, he is, in respect of his liabilities, his burdens, and his rights, in exactly the same position as though no conveyance had ever been made to him." See further as to the general effect of a disclaimer, 32 L. Quar. Rev. 83, 392; 33 *ibid.* 132, 254.

The execution and recording of a deed of trust, though *prima facie* evidence of delivery (Chilvers v. Race, 196 Ill. 71), is not conclusive evidence; and if there is no sufficient delivery no trust is created. Loring v. Hildreth, 170 Mass. 328.

If the purpose of the trust cannot be carried out unless the person named as trustee acts as trustee, the trust fails unless he accepts the trust. See Beekman v. Bonsor, 23 N. Y. 298; Rogers v. Rea, 98 Oh. St. 315; *Re* Chellew's Est., 127 Wash. 382. *Cf.* Security Co. v. Snow, 70 Conn. 288.

St. Clare's Roman Catholic Church of Altamont, seeking to convey to that church a 60-acre farm and part of two lots in Altamont. The deed was for the consideration of one dollar, and contained a provision that the church " shall pay to Charles Wittmeier the sum of $50 per month, beginning one month after my death, for and during his life, and shall pay the doctor's and hospital bill, if any, and upon his death provide him with a Christian burial and pay his funeral expenses and inter his body on the lot owned by me in the cemetery at Altamont, Illinois." Wittmeier was married to Josephine in 1880, but they separated in 1895 and she subsequently obtained a divorce.

We have already held in Heiligenstein *v.* Schlotterbeck, *supra*, that the deed made to the St. Clare's Roman Catholic Church of Altamont is void because an unincorporated religious society is incapable, in law, of taking by deed, and if the church is unincorporated the deed is in violation of the statute. In that case we said as to the rights of Charles Wittmeier (p. 213) : " Charles Wittmeier contends that the fact that the deed is void for want of a grantee does not defeat his rights under the instrument, and that the lands descended to the grantor's heirs impressed with the trust declared in the instrument in his favor. He has not filed a cross-bill, and no affirmative relief can be granted him in the present state of the record. On remandment he may amend his answer and file a cross-bill asking for such relief, if so advised. What we have said is not to be considered as in any way passing upon the soundness of his claims." Upon further proceedings in the trial court Wittmeier amended his answer and filed an amended cross-bill, setting out that the deed to the St. Clare's Church constitutes a trust in his favor, impressed upon the property descending to Josephine's heirs. The cross-bill further alleges that the property had been largely acquired through the efforts of Wittmeier, and that his former wife out of sympathy and affection desired to make provision for his support in old age. By decree of the circuit court the amended cross-bill was dismissed for want of equity, the deed to the St. Clare's Roman Catholic Church was ordered canceled and partition of the property among the heirs was ordered. From that decree Charles Wittmeier has appealed to this court.

The single issue here involved is whether the deed to the St. Clare's Church, void for want of a lawful grantee, can have the effect of impressing a trust upon the property in favor of Charles Wittmeier. Although void as a deed, does the instrument create a valid trust? Had the church been competent to take the property, words were used adequate to establish his rights. Does the incapacity of the church to take the property destroy the rights sought to be created in favor of Wittmeier? It is held by the standard works on trusts that no particular form of words to create a trust need be used in the instrument; that the word " trust " need not be used. It is a rule of equitable construction that there is no magic in particular words. Any expression which shows unequivocally the intention to create a trust will have that effect. (1 Perry on Trusts, — 5th ed. — sec. 82; Hill on Trustees, 65; 2 Spence on Eq. Jur. 52.) "Any agreement or contract in writing made by a person having the power of disposal over property, whereby such person agrees or directs that a particular parcel of property or a certain fund shall be held or dealt with in a particular manner for the benefit of another, in a court of equity raises a trust in favor of such other person against the person making such agreement, or any other person claiming under him voluntarily or with notice." (1 Perry on Trusts, — 5th ed. — sec. 82.) "Nor does the rule that a conveyance without a grantee capable of receiving the grant is void apply to equitable rights growing out of such a conveyance." (18 Corpus Juris, sec. 36.) The inability of the trustee to take will not invalidate a deed where the settlor and the *cestui que trust* are both competent and the property is of such a nature that it can be legally placed in trust. 1 Perry on Trusts, sec. 240; Willis *v.* Alvey; 30 Tex. Civ. App. 96; Smith *v.* Davis, 90 Cal. 25.

Clearly, Josephine Wittmeier did everything necessary under the law to create a trust in favor of Charles Wittmeier except to choose a competent grantee. The deed was executed by the grantor with the intention to part with the title, subject to provision made for Charles. There were words sufficient to accomplish her purpose. There was a beneficiary capable of taking but no lawful grantee. The void deed did not transfer title to the property from Josephine, and title remained in her, notwithstanding the deed, from the date of its execution, August 21, 1919, until the date of her death, August 25, 1919. If the void deed impresses a trust upon the property in the hands of her heirs it must have had the effect to impress a trust from the date of its execution. It is true, as often said, that equity does not allow a trust to fail for want of a lawful grantee; and this statement applies even though the grantor fails in one of her purposes — that of devoting the property to religious uses.

Somewhat related to the issue here involved was that in Childs *v.* Waite, 102 Me. 451, which involved a will leaving certain property to a school district for the purpose of building and supporting a church. The school district had no legal power to act and it was held not to succeed to the title of the trust fund, but the court ordered the appointment of a trustee. In that case, however, the property was to be devoted to a single purpose, and the preservation of the trust completely carried out that purpose. While this is not exactly the situation here, the principle involved in that case is identical with the one involved here.

A similar issue presented itself in the case of Vidal *v.* Mayor of Philadelphia, 2 How. 127. In that case it was urged that a trust created by the will of Stephen Girard failed because of the incompetency of the city to execute the trust. The United States Supreme Court, through Mr. Justice Story, said (p. 188): " It is true that if the trust be repugnant to or inconsistent with the proper purposes for which the corporation was created, that may furnish a ground why it may not be compellable to execute it. But that will furnish no ground to declare the trust itself void if otherwise unexceptionable, but it will simply require a new trustee to be substituted by the proper court, possessing equity jurisdiction to enforce and perfect the objects of the trust. This will be sufficiently obvious upon an examination of the authorities, but a single case may suffice. In Sonley v. Clockmakers' Co., 1 Bro. Ch. 81, there was a devise of freehold estate to the testator's wife for life with remainder to his brother C in tail male, with remainder to the Clockmakers' Company in trust to sell for the benefit of the testator's nephews and nieces. The devise being to a corporation was by the English Statute of Wills void, that statute prohibiting devises to corporations, and the question was whether, the devise being so void, the heir-at-law took beneficially or subject to the trust. Mr. Baron Eyre in his judgment said that although the devise to the corporation be void at law, yet the trust is sufficiently created to fasten itself upon any estate the law may raise. This is the ground upon which the courts of equity have decreed in cases where no trustee is named." In the Clockmakers' Co. case, again, there was a single purpose of the trust, fully accomplished by the decision of the court.

In the present case the purpose of the grantor is clearly manifested and the trust in favor of Charles Wittmeier clearly created. The trust is fully and finally declared in the instrument creating it. With a competent grantee of the deed no further act was necessary to give it effect. (Massey v. Huntington, 118 Ill. 80.) Viewing the trust as we think it should be properly held here, we do not discuss the issue of the consideration of the trust. The grantor intended the deed to establish a trust in favor of Wittmeier. Although the deed did not, in fact, transfer title from her, we think it sufficient to impress the trust upon the property in the hands of the grantor and of the heirs to whom it descended. We are of the opinion that the incapacity of the church to take the property does not defeat the purpose of the grantor, and that the heirs take the property impressed with a trust in favor of Wittmeier. The fact that the grantor had two purposes in mind, one of which must fail, is no reason why the other should fail when it is expressed with sufficient definiteness and can be legally carried out.

It is suggested it would be possible to take the view that Josephine Wittmeier, while making her purpose clear, did not make it effective because of the incompetent grantee, and that therefore the property descends to her heirs free from all obligations sought to be impressed upon it in favor of Charles Wittmeier, as in Meyer *v.* Holle, 83 Tex. 623; but such a conclusion, in our judgment, by weight of authority, is not required and would unreasonably and unnecessarily defeat the purpose of the grantor.

The decree is reversed and the cause remanded to the circuit court of Effingham county for further proceedings in harmony with the views herein expressed.

Reversed and remanded.[1]

MATTER OF KELLOGG.

COURT OF APPEALS, NEW YORK. 1915.

214 N. Y. 460.

MILLER, J. . . . By the will and codicil thereto the testator appointed the respondent Kellogg and his two sons, the appellant and the respondent Junius S. Morgan, as executors and trustees. The two sons renounced as executors, and the respondent Kellogg qualified as sole executor. Thereafter and on the 10th day of September, 1912, the appellant signed and acknowledged a renunciation as trustee and delivered it to the respondent Kellogg. On the hearing before the referee it was introduced in evidence without objection. On the 1st of December, 1913, the appellant executed a retraction of said renunciation as trustee. A copy thereof was delivered to the respondent Kellogg on the 4th day of December, 1913, and it was filed with the surrogate on January 12th, 1914, and prior to the decree on the accounting of the executor. It appears by the affidavit of said Kellogg that prior to the attempted withdrawal of said renunciation, the other trustees had entered upon their duties as trustees, had set apart for the several trusts securities of the estate amounting to one million dollars and had purchased in their joint names as trustees a real estate mortgage

---

[1] See Dominy *v.* Stanley, 162 Ga. 211 (charity, no trustee named); Visitors M. E. Church *v.* Town, 47 N. J. Eq. 400 (charity, "heirs" of trustees omitted). But *cf.* Frost *v.* Frost, 202 Mass. 100, *ante.*

If the conveyance to the trustee is ineffective for want of delivery, no trust arises. See Chap. II, sec. II, and particularly Whitehead *v.* Bishop, 23 Oh. App. 315, *ante.*

Where a donor makes a conveyance of property which by mistake is not effective to transfer the property, the donee cannot compel the donor to transfer the property. Patterson *v.* McClenathan, 296 Ill. 475; Eaton *v.* Eaton, 15 Wis. 259; 2 Ames, Cas. Eq. Juris., 244; Williston, Contracts, sec. 1556. There is authority, however, to the effect that if the donor has died before the mistake was discovered a court of equity will reform the deed and compel the heir of the donee to transfer the property, where the donee was a wife or child or creditor of the donor. See 43 Harv. L. Rev. 968; 14 Minn. L. Rev. 425; 2 Pomeroy, Eq. Juris., sec. 588. Similarly, it has been held that equity will aid the defective execution of a power in behalf of a wife, child or creditor. 2 Ames, Cas. Eq. Juris., 306; 2 Pomeroy, Eq. Juris., sec. 589.

amounting to seventy thousand dollars and corporate stock of the city of New York amounting to forty thousand dollars. After the payment of his debts and certain specific legacies, the testator gave $200,000 to his executors and trustees in trust for the benefit of his wife, and he directed that the residue be divided into three equal parts, which he gave to his executors and trustees in trust, one of each for the benefit of each of his three children. The decree of the surrogate adjudged that the attempted revocation of the renunciation by the appellant as trustee was without force and effect and that the other trustees having entered upon their duties " they continue as such trustees and execute said trusts in accordance with the provisions of said will."

The appellant insists that the trustees had no duty to perform until the executor accounted and was directed to turn over the estate to the trustees, and that, therefore, the renunciation, which was a mere waiver of a right, was effectually withdrawn. The statute provides for the resignation of a testamentary trustee (see Code of Civil Procedure, section 2814), but not for a renunciation. Section 2639 of the Code of Civil Procedure provides how an executor may renounce, and how such a renunciation may be retracted. The provision for the retraction seems to be but declaratory of the rule at common law. (See Codding *v.* Newman, 3 T. & C. 364; Robertson *v.* McGeoch, 11 Paige, 640.) A testamentary trustee derives his authority from the will. Of course, he may refuse to accept the trust, but if he does any act indicative of his acceptance, he may not thereafter resign without the consent of the *cestui que trust* or the court. (Shepherd *v.* M'Evers, 4 Johns. Ch. 136; Brennan *v.* Willson, 71 N. Y. 502; Earle *v.* Earle, 16 J. & S. 18; 93 N. Y. 104.) Where one of two or more trustees refuses to accept and execute the trust the estate vests in the others the same as though the trustee refusing to act were dead or had not been named. (Matter of Stevenson, 3 Paige, 420; King *v.* Donnelly, 5 Paige, 46; Matter of Van Schoonhoven, Id. 559.) The appellant seeks to distinguish the cases last cited on the ground that they involved devises of real estate to trustees. The estate in this case consisted entirely of personalty, and it may be that until the remaining trustees had done some act indicating their acceptance of the trust, and possibly until they had actually received, as trustees, some part of the trust estate, the appellant could have retracted his renunciation or refusal to accept the trust. It is not the law, however, that trustees may not receive any part of the trust estate, consisting of personalty, until the executor has accounted and been directed to pay it over. Whilst in case the same person is both executor and trustee, a decree of the court is the most satisfactory evidence of a separation of his duties, it is not indispensable. (Hurlburt *v.* Durant, 88 N. Y. 121, 127.) And even with respect to the residuary estate, the trustee may enter upon his duties as such even before his accounting and discharge as executor. (Olcott *v.* Baldwin, 190 N. Y. 99.) Cases dealing with the liability of a person as executor, such as Matter of Hood (98 N. Y. 363) are not decisive of the point involved in this case; but in that case it was recognized that there might be a severance of the trust fund by the executor without a judicial decree.

The trustees were not bound to wait until the final accounting of the executor before investing the money belonging to the trust funds in the manner directed by the testator. Certainly the investment of such moneys was an act of the trustees, who thereupon held the securities purchased as joint tenants. It was then too late for the appellant to withdraw his refusal to serve as trustee. If a person named as trustee were permitted to retract his refusal to accept the trust after the others have entered upon their trust duties, complications might arise which cannot now be foreseen. The only safe rule is to hold a person to his refusal or renunciation unless, at least, it is withdrawn before the others have acted. An executor cannot retract after letters have been issued except by reason of revocation of letters or death there is no other acting executor or administrator. Code of Civil Procedure, section 2639.[1] . . .

In WETHERELL *v.* LANGSTON, 1 Exch. 634 (1847), it was held that if a covenant is executed to two obligees upon trust, and one of them disclaims, the other cannot enforce the covenant in an action at law. The court said (p. 646):

" There were also some authorities cited in the argument on the part of the plaintiff, which, it was contended, shewed that by the disclaimer of Lord Glenelg the plaintiff became solely entitled to the right of action, which, but for that disclaimer would have belonged to him jointly with Lord Glenelg. They were cases in which

---

[1] A trustee may disclaim either by deed — Doe *v.* Harris, 16 M. & W. 517; Peppercorn *v.* Wayman, 5 DeG. & Sm. 230 — or by parol. Townson *v.* Tickell, 3 B. & Al. 31; Stacey *v.* Elph, 1 M. & K. 195; Foster *v.* Dawber, 1 Dr. & Sm. 172; Birchall *v.* Birchall, 40 Ch. Div. 436; [*Re* Clout and Frewer's Contract, [1924] 2 Ch. 230 (non-action for 30 years)]; Adams *v.* Adams, 64 N. H. 224; Barritt *v.* Silliman, 13 N. Y. 93; Beekman *v.* Bonsor, 23 N. Y. 298, 305; *Re* Robinson, 37 N. Y. 261; Green *v.* Green, 4 Redf. 357; Read *v.* Robinson, 6 W. & S. 329.

Disclaimer comes too late after conduct indicating acceptance. Conyngham *v.* Conyngham, 1 Ves. 522; Bence *v.* Gilpin, L. R. 3 Ex. 76; Kennedy *v.* Winn, 80 Ala. 165. In Crewe *v.* Dicken, 4 Ves. 97, Lord Loughborough held that a release by a trustee to a co-trustee by way of disclaimer was ineffectual, because the release implied an acceptance of the trust. But Lord Eldon, in Nicholson *v.* Wordsworth, 2 Sw. 365, declined to follow this doctrine. See, in confirmation of Lord Eldon, Hussey *v.* Markham, Finch 258. — AMES.

On the question whether an heir can disclaim when his ancestor was named as trustee and neither accepted nor disclaimed, see Goodson *v.* Ellisson, 3 Russ. 583; Wise *v.* Wise, 2 Jo. & Lat. 403, 412; King *v.* Phillips, 16 Jur. 1080. Certainly such heir cannot be compelled to administer the trust.

a devise or conveyance to two persons jointly, one of whom disclaimed, has been held to vest the whole estate in the other.[1] But the analogy of those cases is inapplicable, because the subject dealt with was not a mere personal contract, but an interest in land. Now, joint obligees or covenantees in personal contracts differ materially from joint-tenants of estates in land, in respect of their power of dealing with their rights. An interest in land, whether joint or several, may be transferred by the act of the party; and the conveyance by a joint-tenant, by release or otherwise, operates on his moiety only; he may convey it to his co-tenant, or to a stranger; whereas a right to sue on a contract cannot be conveyed, though it may be extinguished, and a release by one of the joint parties extinguishes the right of both. It was upon a similar reason, that, in real actions, a nonsuit of one demandant or plaintiff was not the nonsuit of both, but he that made default should be summoned and severed; but in personal actions the nonsuit of one is generally the nonsuit of both: Co. Lit. 139a. To allow a joint devisee or grantee &c. of land to vest the whole interest in his co-devisee or grantee, &c. by refusing to accept the estate, is allowing him to do no more than he could have done by a release immediately *after* acceptance; but if a joint covenantee could, by refusal, enable his co-covenantee to sue alone, he would do that before acceptance, which he could by no means do after acceptance.

"Since, then, the defendant has not incurred any liability to be sued on a separate contract, and since the plaintiff has not acquired the right to enforce in a separate action any liability to which the defendant might be subject in a joint action, it follows, that whether the defendant's original liability be or be not put an end to, this declaration is bad, and the judgment for the plaintiff ought to be reversed." [2]

GREEN *v.* BLACKWELL.

CHANCERY, NEW JERSEY. 1879.

31 N. J. Eq. 37.

THE CHANCELLOR [RUNYON]. The complainant is one of the two trustees under the marriage settlement of Mrs. Blackwell. He applies, by his bill, to be discharged from that trust on his account-

---

[1] See Shep. Touch. 82; Humphrey *v.* Tayleur, 1 Amb. 136; Adams *v.* Taunton, 5 Madd. 435; Kingdon *v.* Castleman, 46 L. J. Ch. 448; Matter of Stevenson, 3 Paige (N. Y.) 420. The result is the same where one of the grantees is dead or otherwise incapable of taking. McCord *v.* Bright, 44 Ind. App. 275; Ball *v.* Deas, 2 Strob. Eq. (S. C.) 24.

If the conveyance is upon trust, and some of the grantees disclaim, the others may execute the trust. Ames, 230n.

[2] But if some or all of the obligees upon trust disclaim, equity will give relief. Fletcher *v.* Fletcher, 4 Hare 67, *ante.*

ing (due allowance to be made to him for his disbursements and commissions) and paying and delivering over the money and securities of the trust estate which shall be found to be in his hands. The *corpus* of the trust estate under the marriage settlement (which was made in 1863) was $20,000. That estate the complainant took into his hands and has managed up to this time. By the will of the settlor, Henry W. Green, who died in 1876, a very large addition was made to the trust estate. The complainant, under the circumstances and in view of that addition, declines to act further as trustee thereof. He has not assumed, but has renounced, the trusts under the will. The defendants oppose his discharge, insisting that he shows no sufficient reason therefor. But he is undoubtedly at liberty to apply to this court for his release on the sole ground of unwillingness to act further in the trust. Perry on Trusts § 274; Lewin on Trusts 582; Matter of Jones, 4 Sandf. Ch. 614. And the greatly increased amount of the estate devolved upon the trustee by the will, and which it will be incumbent on him to manage if he continues in the office, is a sufficient ground for relieving him if he desires it. Greenwood *v.* Wakeford, 1 Beav. 576; Coventry *v.* Coventry, 1 Keen 758. He undertook, by the marriage settlement, to manage an estate of $20,000. It is not unreasonable in him to decline to continue the management of it, in view of the addition under the will, which was not contemplated in the settlement, by which it is to become ten times greater. Besides, the trust is not in the hands of the complainant alone. His co-trustee remains.

The marriage settlement, indeed, provides that in case of the death of one of the trustees thereunder, before the trust shall be fully executed or otherwise determined, the surviving trustee shall nominate, and, with the consent and approbation of the other parties to the settlement or the survivors or survivor of them, appoint a new trustee in the stead of the one dying, and it is urged that this provision for the exercise of personal judgment and discretion in the successor in the trust, should induce this court to refuse to relieve the complainant. But no difficulty will be experienced on that score, for this court will supply the place of the complainant. Hill on Trustees 190. The complainant will be permitted to account, and, in the account, will be allowed all proper disbursements made by him for the estate, and also proper commissions; and he will be required to pay or deliver over the trust estate which will, on the accounting, be found remaining in his hands, and thereupon he will be discharged. Under the circumstances, he will be entitled to costs. Greenwood *v.* Wakeford, Coventry *v.* Coventry, *ubi supra;* Perry on Trusts § 901.[1]

---

[1] See Forshaw *v.* Higginson, 20 Beav. 485.

If by the trust instrument the trustee is allowed to select a new trustee and resign his office, he may of course do so. And he may resign if all the *cestuis que trust* are *sui juris* and consent. See Williams *v.* Hund, 302 Mo.

MORTIMER v. IRELAND.

CHANCERY. 1847.

11 Jur. 721.

ONE T. B. Mortimer by his will named T. Griffiths and E. Pruen (without mentioning their heirs or executors) as his executors and trustees. Griffiths died without having proved the will or acted in the trusts. Pruen proved the will and acted and later died, leaving a will in which R. Ireland and H. Pruen were named executors, and a codicil whereby he devised and bequeathed the trust property to Ireland to hold on the trusts of the Mortimer will. A bill was filed by persons interested under the will of T. B. Mortimer to determine whether Ireland had been duly appointed trustee and, if not, to appoint a new trustee and to direct a conveyance by Ireland to such trustee. The Vice-Chancellor referred it to a Master to appoint two trustees. Ireland appealed.[1]

LORD CHANCELLOR [COTTENHAM]. The argument amounts to this, that the executor of a trustee is of right a trustee. Whether the property is real or personal estate is no matter, for suppose a man appoints a trustee of real and personal estate *simpliciter*, adding nothing more, this cannot make his representative a trustee. The case before the Master of the Rolls [Titley v. Wolstenholme, 7 Beav. 425] was quite different, for there the court proceeded on the intention manifested, that the trust should be performed by the assigns of the survivor. The property may vest in the representative, but that is quite another question from his being trustee. The testator may select the heir to succeed to the trust, but he only can do so. Here there are two persons appointed trustees; both die; thus there is no trustee, and it is for the court to appoint new ones. The testator having given no indication of intention, the court must refer it to the Master. The decree of the Vice-Chancellor is right in its form. The appeal must be dismissed with costs.[2]

451, 471; Perry, Trusts, sec. 285. But except with the consent of the *cestuis que trust* or in accordance with the provisions of the trust instrument, a trustee cannot resign without the approval of the court. Wilkinson v. Parry, 4 Russ. 272; Spengler v. Kuhn, 212 Ill. 186; Cruger v. Halliday, 11 Paige (N. Y.) 314.

[1] The statement of facts is abridged. See 6 Hare 196.

[2] If there are several trustees and one of them dies, the legal title survives to the others who may continue to administer the trust. Doily v. Sherratt, 2 Eq. Cas. Abr. 742; Perry, Trusts, sec. 343. The court will add new trustees to replace those who died if it was the intention of the creator of the trust that the number should be kept up or if it appears to the court that such a course will be conducive to the benefit of the trust. Perry, Trusts, sec. 286.

At common law a sole trustee has power on his death to devise or bequeath the legal title to the trust property. Whether the devisee or legatee may administer the trust depends upon the intention of the creator of the trust.

Ex parte CONYBEARE'S SETTLEMENT.
CHANCERY. 1853.
1 W. R. 458.

CONYBEARE moved for the appointment as trustee of one of the *cestui que trusts* of an estate in the place of a trustee incapacitated from acting, in consequence of insanity. All parties were desirous that the appointment of the gentleman proposed should be made, and there were special circumstances in the case not necessary to be referred to for the purposes of the report. The Master of the Rolls had declined to make the order asked, on the ground that the Court ought not to appoint a *cestui que trust* as the trustee, even though there was not any other objection to his appointment.

TURNER, L. J. Under ordinary circumstances, no doubt, the Court will not appoint a trustee who is also one of the *cestui que trusts;* but the rule is not imperative, and when there are special circumstances, the Court will exercise its discretion in judging whether the case is one in which the rule may be departed from. Here I think, under the special circumstances, we may make the appointment asked.[1]

KNIGHT BRUCE, L. J., concurred.

See Cook *v.* Crawford, 13 Sim. 91; Titley *v.* Wolstenholme, 7 Beav. 425; Osborne to Rowlett, 13 Ch. D. 774; Lewin, Trusts, 12 ed., 255. On the question how far trust property is included in a general devise by a trustee, see Ames, 316; Lewin, Trusts, 12 ed., 255.

At common law on the death of a sole trustee the legal title to land held in trust and not devised passes to his heir and the legal title to personalty held in trust and not bequeathed passes to his personal representatives. Whether the heir or personal representative of the trustee may administer the trust depends upon the intention of the creator of the trust. Mortimer *v.* Ireland, 11 Jur. 721, 6 Hare 196; *Re* Morton, 15 Ch. D. 143; *Re* Pixton, 46 W. R. 187; *Re* Waidanis, [1908] 1 Ch. 123; *Re* Crunden, [1909] 1 Ch. 690; *Re* Ingleby etc. Co., 13 L. R. Ir. 326; State *v.* Miss. Valley T. Co., 209 Mo. 472; Woodruff *v.* Woodruff, 44 N. J. Eq. 349; 2 Woerner, Law of Administration, secs. 321 (executor of trustee), 350 (executor of executor); Ames, 510n.

In a few states the law of primogeniture determines who shall, as heir of the trustee, take the legal title to land held in trust. Boston Franklinite Co. *v.* Condit, 19 N. J. Eq. 394; Cone *v.* Cone, 61 S. C. 512.

By the Conveyancing Act, 1881 (44 & 45 Vict. c. 41), sec. 30, it was provided that on the death of the trustee, real estate held in trust should, notwithstanding any testamentary disposition, vest in the personal representatives or representative from time to time of the trustee who should be deemed his heirs and assigns within the meaning of all trusts and powers. See Underhill, Trusts, art. 72.

In the United States it is frequently provided by statute that the title to trust property shall be in abeyance or vest in the court until a new trustee is appointed by the court, and that when such trustee is appointed title shall immediately vest in him. See Perry, Trusts, secs. 269, 341; Bogert, Trusts, 281.

[1] The court may select any fit person to act as trustee. In making the

MASSACHUSETTS, GENERAL LAWS, 1920, c. 208.

SEC. 18. If a person who is seized or possessed of real or personal property or of an interest therein upon a trust, express or implied, is a minor, insane, out of the commonwealth or not amenable to the process of any court therein having equity powers, and if in the opinion of the supreme judicial court, the superior court or the probate court a sale should be made of such property or of an interest therein, or a conveyance or transfer should be made thereof in order to carry into effect the objects of the trust, the court may order such sale, conveyance or transfer made and may appoint a suitable person in the place of such trustee to sell, convey or transfer the same in such manner as it may require. If a person so seized or possessed of an estate or entitled thereto upon a trust is within the jurisdiction of the court, he or his guardian may be ordered to make such conveyances as the court orders.[1]

REICHERT v. THE MISSOURI AND ILLINOIS COAL COMPANY.

SUPREME COURT, ILLINOIS. 1907.

231 Ill. 238.

CARTWRIGHT, J. The Appellate Court for the Fourth District affirmed the judgment for $1500 and costs recovered by appellees,

---

selection regard will usually be paid to (1) the wishes of the settlor; (2) the various interests of the *cestuis que trust;* and (3) the promotion of the due execution of the trust. *Re* Tempest, L. R. 1 Ch. 485.

Except in unusual cases therefore the court will not appoint one of the beneficiaries, or a relative of one of the beneficiaries, or even a relative of a sole beneficiary.

Where a testator appoints a sole trustee, the court will not usually add a new trustee. *Re* Badger, 84 L. J. Ch. 567.

The Public Trustee Act, 1906 (6 Edw. VII. c. 55) provides for a Public Trustee who may be appointed to act alone or with other trustees. *Cf.* 2 Mills Ann. Stat. Colo., secs. 7577 *et seq.* See also Judicial Trustees Act, 1896 (59 & 60 Vict. c. 35) providing for the appointment of an official of the court to act as trustee.

In England by the Trustee Act, 1925 (15 Geo. V. c. 19) sec. 36, it is provided that where a trustee is dead or remains out of the realm for more than 12 months or desires to resign or is unfit or incapable, the surviving or continuing trustees or the personal representatives of the last surviving or continuing trustee may by writing appoint new trustees, unless the trust instrument provides otherwise.

[1] For a history and summary of statutes allowing the equity courts either directly by decree or by a conveyance by a master or other officer of the court, to vest title in the *cestui que trust* or in a new trustee, without a conveyance by the old trustee, see Huston, Decrees in Equity, chap. II and Appendix.

against appellant, in the circuit court of St. Clair county, in a suit brought under a mining lease or contract. From the judgment of the Appellate Court the case is brought to this court by appeal.

It is first contended on behalf of appellant that the suit was not brought in the names of the parties in whom the legal interest in the contract was vested. The facts, so far as they relate to that question, are as follows: On May 7, 1891, Joseph Reichert and Maria Reichert, his wife, executed a lease of certain lands in St. Clair county to Crittenden McKinley and William S. Scott, giving to them the right to take coal from under said lands. The lease was for a term of fifty years from its date, unless the coal should be sooner exhausted, and the lessees agreed to pay one-eighth of one cent for every bushel of coal mined and taken out which would pass over a screen with spaces measuring one and one-half inches between the bars, the amount to be determined by the railroad freight bills or weightmaster's certificates or tickets, or upon any other good and sufficient evidence that would satisfy the lessors. The lessees also agreed to mine the coal and do the work in a proper, workmanlike and skillful manner, regularly, properly and effectually, without waste or destruction to the coal. The lease was assigned by the lessees to the appellant, a corporation of the State of Missouri, and it entered into possession under the lease and began mining the coal. On August 22, 1893, Joseph Reichert died, leaving said Maria Reichert, his widow, and eight children, his only heirs-at-law. On September 25, 1893, the widow and heirs, together with the wives and husbands of the said heirs, respectively, executed a trust deed to said Maria Reichert and August Barthel, conveying said lands, subject to the lease, to said trustees, " their successors and assigns." The trust deed provided that the trustees and their successors in trust should have a right to enter into and upon the premises and receive all rents and royalties, issues and profits thereof. The trust deed further provided that if the trustees, or either of them, should die or go abroad to reside, desire to be discharged from, renounce, decline or become incapable or unfit to act in the trusts, then, in every and any such case, it should be lawful for a majority of the heirs mentioned in the trust deed, or a majority of the survivors thereof, by any writing or writings under their hands, attested by two or more witnesses, to nominate and substitute any person or persons to be trustee or trustees in place of the trustee or trustees so dying, going to reside abroad, desiring to be discharged, renouncing, declining or becoming incapable or unfit to act as trustee. The next provision was, that so often as any new trustee or trustees should be appointed, all the real estate which should then be holden upon the trusts should thereupon be conveyed, assigned and transferred, respectively, in such manner that the same might become legally and effectually vested in the acting trustees for the time being, to and for the same uses and upon the same trusts and with and subject to the same powers and provisions as were therein declared and contained of and concerning the real estate. It also provided that every new trustee so appointed should, from the time of filing his bond, be competent, in all things, to act in the execution of the trusts as fully and effectually and with all the same powers and authorities, to all purposes whatsoever, as if he had been thereby originally appointed the trustee in the place of the trustee whom he should, whether immediately or otherwise, succeed. Maria Reichert died, and on May 18, 1896, August Barthel resigned as trustee. The remaining heirs appointed William J. Reichert and Charles Becker, the appellees, successors in trust to Maria Reichert and August Barthel, in the manner specified in the trust deed, and the trustees so appointed accepted the trust and proceeded to act. The appellant rendered accounts and statements to William J. Reichert and sent checks to him at different times. This suit was brought to the September term, 1903, of the court by the appellees, the new trustees, and the original declaration declared for the rent stipulated in the lease. An additional count charged the appellant with failing to properly work and mine the coal in accordance with its agreement and with wasting and destroying coal, whereby appellees were deprived of a large amount of rents which they otherwise would and ought to have received.

The argument that appellees could not maintain the suit is based on the proposition that they did not have the legal title to the reversion, and in support of that claim counsel present two propositions: First, that upon the death of Maria Reichert the legal title which she held descended to her heirs-at-law; and second, that upon the resignation of August Barthel the legal title conveyed to him remained in him, and it would be necessary for him to execute a deed and convey whatever title was vested in him to the newly appointed trustees before they would be authorized to execute the trust.

The grantee of a reversion may or may not be entitled to the rent reserved in a lease. In this case the conveyance is subject to the lease and there is no reservation of rent, but the trust deed expressly provides that the trustees shall collect the rent and apply it to the trusts therein declared. If the appellees were lawfully appointed trustees and vested with the care, control and management of the trust estate they were entitled to maintain the suit. The first proposition above stated is not the law. Trustees are excepted from the provision of the statute requiring a declaration in a conveyance that the estate is in joint tenancy, and unless there is a provision to the contrary they hold as joint tenants. Upon the death of one the administration of the trust devolves upon the survivor and nothing passes to the heir or personal representative of the deceased trustee. Golder *v.* Bressler, 105 Ill. 419.

Whether the second proposition is correct depends upon a consideration of the law and the provisions of the trust deed. A trustee takes precisely that quantum of legal estate which is necessary to the discharge of the declared powers and duties of such trustee, regardless of technical terms ordinarily required for a conveyance. Walton v. Follansbee, 131 Ill. 147; Lawrence v. Lawrence, 181 id. 248. The estate will inure to the trustee until the active trusts are accomplished, when the Statute of Uses will execute the use, and the entire title, both legal and equitable, will be in the one beneficially interested. The decision in Glover v. Condell, 163 Ill. 566, relied upon by counsel for appellant, clearly recognized that doctrine, but held that a conveyance or transfer of personal property was necessary because personal property is not within the Statute of Uses. Barthel had such an estate as would continue until the active trusts were executed and he resigned before that time was reached, when successors in trust to him and Maria Reichert were appointed, as the trust deed provided. One who creates a trust has a right to provide a method for filling vacancies and for the appointment of successors in trust. The trust deed in this case conveyed the estate to the trustees therein named, " their successors and assigns," and it provided for the appointment of successors in trust to whom the estate should go.

Much stress is laid in argument upon the provision of the trust deed that upon the appointment of a new trustee the real estate should thereupon be conveyed, assigned and transferred in such manner as to legally and effectually vest the same in the acting trustee, but we do not interpret that provision as meaning that a conveyance shall be executed by any one. The heirs-at-law of the deceased trustee might be incapable of making a deed, or the beneficiary would have no method of compelling a conveyance except at the end of legal proceedings. The trust deed provides that the trustees and their successors in trust shall have a right to enter upon the premises and collect the rents and royalties, and that every new trustee, from the time of filing his bond, shall be competent, in all things, to act in the execution of the trusts, and we regard the provision in question as meaning that upon the appointment of a new trustee the estate shall thereupon be deemed to be conveyed and transferred to him. That is the only interpretation which is consistent with the conveyance to the trustees and their successors and with the other provisions of the trust deed. The appellees were the proper parties to maintain the suit. . . .

Judgment affirmed.[1]

[1] The donee of a power to appoint new trustees has wide discretion in selecting a trustee. Forster v. Abraham, L. R. 17 Eq. 351 (life beneficiary appointed one of several trustees); Re Coode, 108 L. T. N. s. 94 (husband of life beneficiary); Stearns v. Fraleigh, 39 Fla. 603 (husband of *cestui que trust* appointed by her); Tweedy v. Urquhart, 30 Ga. 446 (like preceding case);

PRICE'S ESTATE.

Supreme Court, Pennsylvania. 1904.

209 Pa. 210.

Petition for removal of trustee.

From the record it appeared that the petition was filed by Mary Kemper, a daughter of testator, and by Austin W. Bennett, guardian of Jesse C. Clagett, a grandson of testator, and a son of Mary Kemper. The petition set forth various proceedings in the orphans' court wherein the petitioners sought to surcharge the trustees in their third and fourth accounts, and to open the first and second accounts by bills of review. It was averred that in the answers to the bills of review, the trustees charged that Jesse C. Clagett was an illegitimate son of Mary Kemper. The petitioners averred that such charge was scandalous and groundless, and that in proceedings before an examiner the trustees were compelled to abandon the charge. The petition further averred that Mary Kemper, and Jesse C. Clagett, through his guardian, had instituted against Thomas R. Fort, Jr., civil suits for damages for libel, and that these suits were still pending. The trustees filed an answer responsive to the petition, and the case was heard on bill and answer.

The court in an opinion by Penrose, J., dismissed the petition.

Per Curiam. Mere differences of opinion or judgment between trustee and cestui que trust are not enough to justify the removal of the former. To deprive the beneficiary of unrestrained control over his estate was the very object of the creation of the trust. The fundamental purpose of the creator of the trust was to protect his beneficiary from some anticipated danger, from creditors, from risks of business, from his or her own improvidence or other like cause, or to protect ultimate beneficiaries from waste or spoliation of the estate by the immediate one. For this reason he substituted

---

Montefiore v. Guedalla, [1903] 2 Ch. 723 (donee appointed himself one of several trustees).

But there are limits to the power of the donee. In Bowditch v. Banuelos, 1 Gray (Mass.) 220, the court said (p. 231): "But when we say, that she had a power at her pleasure to appoint, we do not mean to say that this was an arbitrary power, to appoint a person unfit or unsuitable to execute such a trust; as a minor, an idiot, a pauper, or person incapable of performing the duties. It must be a person of full age, sufficient mental and legal capacity, and in all respects capable of performing the required duties."

In Yates v. Yates, 255 Ill. 66, the court removed a trustee appointed by the donee of a power on the ground that he was a contingent remainderman. If he had been named by the testator, the court would not have removed him. Lorenz v. Weller, 267 Ill. 230.

the judgment and control of the trustee for that of the cestui que trust, or of the courts.

The act of 1868 was intended to facilitate the exercise of the powers of the court over the removal of trustees, and to enlarge the influence and authority in that respect of the cestui que trust. But it was not intended to subject the office of trustee and the discretion of the court to a mandatory whim of the cestui que trust. The court still retains the authority to require that a valid and sufficient cause shall be shown for the removal. This was the construction of the act adopted in Stevenson's Appeal, 68 Pa. 101, and after some departures, more apparent than real, as said by our Brother Mestrezat in Neafie's Estate, 199 Pa. 307, finally settled in the case last named.

The petition for removal in the present case is founded on averments of inharmonious relations amounting to hostile litigation, overcharges and bad management on the part of the trustees, and insecurity of the trust funds. The case was argued on petition and answer. The answer being full and responsive, except in one particular that will be noticed, the court would have been warranted in dismissing the petition without more.

One matter only appears to require special notice. While inharmonious relations between trustee and cestui que trust not altogether the fault of the former, will not generally be considered a sufficient cause for removal, yet where they have reached so acrimonious a condition as to make any personal intercourse impossible and to hinder the proper transaction of business between the parties, a due regard for the interests of the estate and the rights of the cestui que trust may require a change of trustee. "If his management of the trust justly subjects him to criticism and to a lack of confidence by the cestui que trust, he should not be continued in control of the estate:" Neafie's Est., supra. In the present case when the trustees were cited to file an account they set up in answer that Jesse C. Clagett one of the petitioners (by his guardian) and son of the other petitioner, was not legitimate, and therefore had no interest that entitled him to an account. No attempt was made to sustain this averment, except the statement that it was made upon information and belief and as it was admitted that the son was born in wedlock and bore the name of his mother's husband and his legitimacy therefore not legally open to question, it is not easy to perceive the relevancy of the averment, or why it should have been made. As this matter is the subject of litigation still pending, we refrain from further comment, but should the litigation show no sufficient justification for the averment of illegitimacy the court below would be well warranted in entertaining a new petition for removal based on the conclusion that the answer was a gratuitous insult warranting an inference that the conduct and management of the estate by the trustees were governed by other motives than a *bona fide* desire for the best interests of the petitioners.

Decree affirmed.[1]

MATTER OF TOWNSEND.

SURROGATE'S COURT, NEW YORK. 1911.

73 Misc. Rep. 481.

DAVIE, S. William A. Townsend, a resident of the town of Olean, died May 22, 1911, leaving him surviving no widow or descendants. His heirs at law and next of kin are two brothers, Zachariah and Stanley, and one nephew, Henry, the son of a deceased brother. He died possessed of real estate of the value of $11,000 and personal property, $13,000. He left a will bearing date July 6, 1906, and a codicil thereto dated May 16, 1911. . . .

The second paragraph of the codicil is as follows: "I desire to, and do hereby change the fourth paragraph of my said will so that it shall read as follows: All the rest, residue and remainder of my estate, both real and personal, of every kind nature and description I give, devise and bequeath equally, one-third to my brother Stanley C. Townsend of Lancaster, Ohio; one-third to Mrs. Mittie Townsend, widow of my deceased brother, J. E. Townsend of Bridgton, New Jersey; and one-third to my nephew Henry Townsend of Bridgton, New Jersey; the share and third hereby devised and bequeathed to my said nephew Henry Townsend is in trust however for the following uses and purposes: to keep the same invested and to pay over the income therefrom at least annually to my brother Z. A. Townsend of Tuckahoe, New Jersey, during the term of his natural life and if, in the judgment of my said nephew my said brother shall require any part of said principal sum so devised and bequeathed in trust for his comfort and support during

---

[1] See Wylie *v.* Bushnell, 277 Ill. 484. But *cf.* Maydwell *v.* Maydwell, 135 Tenn. 1, Ann. Cas. 1918B 1043.

A court may in its discretion remove a trustee for any cause which renders him an unfit person to administer the trust. Among the numerous grounds for removal may be mentioned embezzlement of the trust property, or other serious breach of trust; commission of felony; incompetency due to old age, habitual drunkenness, lunacy, infancy, etc.; holding views at variance with the object of the trust, in the case of a religious trust; adverse interest; permanent residence abroad; the showing of favoritism to one or more of the *cestuis que trust;* unreasonable or corrupt failure to co-operate with co-trustees. See Ames, 223n., 249n.; Loring, Trustees' Handbook, 24–26; Perry, Trusts, secs. 275 *et seq.*

The insolvency or bankruptcy of the trustee may be but is not necessarily a ground for removal. In Carrier *v.* Carrier, 226 N. Y. 114, it was held that when the trustee became bankrupt and threatened to use the trust fund unwisely, the court might require him to give security instead of removing him.

his life time, I direct my said trustee to pay the same over to him at such time and in such amounts as in his judgment is proper."

The third item of the codicil provides that "Upon the death of my said brother, Z. A. Townsend, I give and devise and bequeath the remainder of the sum herein devised and bequeathed to my said nephew Henry Townsend in trust, to my said nephew Henry Townsend absolutely."

The nephew, Henry, is named as executor. . . .

The trust created by the codicil for the support and maintenance of the brother of decedent during his lifetime is a legal and commendable one, but his selection of trustee is unfortunate. In Rathbone v. Hooney, 58 N. Y. 463, S. died siezed of certain real estate, leaving a will by which she devised the same to P. in trust to receive the rents and profits and apply the same to the benefit of R. during her lifetime, with the remainder to P. in fee. The court sustained this trust and the designation of the trustee. That case, however, differs very materially in principle from the one now under consideration. There the trustee was clothed with no discretion; the line of demarcation between the interests of the *cestui que trust* and the remainderman was clearly defined by the instrument creating the trust. Here it is entirely apparent that the income derived from the one-third of the residue may not be sufficient to comfortably support and maintain the beneficiary during his lifetime and, in consequence, resort to the principal may become necessary. The more of the principal which may in this manner be exhausted, the smaller the interest passing to the remainderman. He is given, by the terms of the codicil, a discretion as to how much of the principal shall be used for that purpose. In that particular his interests and those of the *cestui que trust* are absolutely antagonistic. The trustee not only occupies a dual capacity but, in the performance of the duties of his trust, his personal interests conflict directly with the rights and interests of the beneficiary. . . .

In view of the complications which are very likely to arise in case the trustee designated by the terms of the codicil enters upon the discharge of his duties as such trustee, I am of the opinion that the ordinary letters testamentary should issue to him as executor and, after the amount of the trust estate is established by his judicial settlement as executor, another trustee should be appointed for the purpose of managing and controlling the trust estate during the life of the beneficiary.

Decreed accordingly.[1]

---

[1] But see Rogers v. Rogers, 258 Mass. 228; Boston Safe Dep. & T. Co. v. Taylor, 262 Mass. 287. The mere fact that the person selected is one of the beneficiaries or is related to one or more of the beneficiaries or is a person who for any reason would not be appointed by the court, will not disqualify him. Story v. Palmer, 46 N. J. Eq. 1; Curran v. Green, 18 R. I. 329.

A statute providing that only residents may act as trustees has been held

Section III.

The Cestui Que Trust.

FOLK v. HUGHES.

Supreme Court, South Carolina. 1915.

100 S. C. 220.

This is an action to foreclose a mortgage given to C. Ehrhardt & Sons by G. W. Hughes and now owned by plaintiff. The children of the mortgagor claim an interest in the mortgaged property.

On September 22, 1890, J. W. Hughes conveyed the land to his son, G. W. Hughes, " to have and to hold the said described tract of land with all privileges and appurtenances thereof to the said G. W. Hughes for his uses and benefits, and for the maintenance and support of the children of the said G. W. Hughes during the term of his natural life."

On November 10, 1892, G. W. Hughes reconveyed it to his father by warranty deed " to have and to hold the same unto him, the said J. W. Hughes, and assigns forever."

On April 15, 1899, J. W. Hughes conveyed it back to G. W. Hughes, his heirs and assigns, with full covenants of warranty.

On October 22, 1901, G. W. Hughes executed the mortgage herein sought to be foreclosed.

At date of the first deed to him, in 1890, G. W. Hughes was married, but had no child, and was still childless at the date of his reconveyance to his father in 1892. His first wife died March 2, 1894, having borne him one child, the defendant, Robert, the date of whose birth is not stated in the record. The defendants, Ruth and Grace, are his children by his last wife, the defendant, Lottie Hughes. He died some time before the commencement of the action.

The Circuit Court decreed foreclosure of the mortgage. The defendants appeal.[1]

Hydrick, J. . . . The life estate given him [G. W. Hughes] was not absolute, but, by the terms of the deed, it was given to him " for his uses and benefits and *for the maintenance and support of the children of the said G. W. Hughes during the term of his natural life.*" It was, therefore, partially in trust for the benefit

---

to violate the provisions of the Federal Constitution (Art. 4, sec. 2, and the 14th Amendment) in regard to the privileges and immunities of citizens. Shirk v. LaFayette, 52 Fed. 857; Roby v. Smith, 131 Ind. 342. But see as to executors, Petition of Mulford, 217 Ill. 242. *Cf.* Breen v. Kehoe, 142 Mich. 58.

[1] The statement of facts is taken from the opinion. A part of the opinion in which it was held that the children had a contingent remainder is omitted.

of his after-born children. In Hunter *v.* Hunter, 58 S. C. 382, 36 S. E. 734, a devise to the testator's widow " for and during her lifetime, to support herself and my children and to educate my children," was construed to give the widow a trust estate for life for the benefit of the children, and it was held that the widow had no power to sell even her life estate, no such power having been given her in the will.

It is not necessary to the creation of a trust estate that the *cestui que trust* should be in existence at the time of its creation. 1 Perry on Trusts, sec. 66; Tiffany & Bullard on Trusts 3; Carson *v.* Carson, 1 Winston Ch. (N. C.) 24; Ashurst *v.* Given, 5 Watts & S. (Pa.) 329. In the case last cited, a devise to a father in trust for his children at the time of his death was held to be good, although the father had no children at the time of the vesting of the estate in him as trustee.

A trustee will not be allowed by his own act to defeat or destroy his trust, and those who deal with him in respect of the trust estate, with knowledge of the trust, are bound by the terms of the trust, and if they purchase the trust estate they take it encumbered with the trust. . . .

Judgment reversed.[1]

BURTON *v.* BOREN.

SUPREME COURT, ILLINOIS. 1923.

308 Ill. 440.

Mr. CHIEF JUSTICE FARMER delivered the opinion of the court:

Edward B. Boren prior to October, 1913, owned in fee simple the undivided one-fourth of 350 acres of farm land in Logan county. The other three-fourths were owned by Boren's brother and two sisters. On the first day of October, 1913, Boren conveyed by a deed of trust to his sister, Hannah E. Burton, his undivided one-fourth interest in the land, subject to the conditions specified that the trustee should pay the grantor all the net income received from the land. The trust deed gave the trustee or her successor power to lease or sell the property and convey the same by proper deed and re-invest the funds in other income-producing real estate or loans and pay the net income to the grantor. The deed provided that the trust created by it should continue in force during the life of the grantor and should terminate at his death. Power was given the trustee to appoint a successor in trust, and in case she did not exercise the power a successor was to be appointed by a court having jurisdiction to do so. The fourth provision of the trust deed

[1] A covenant to stand seised to the use of an unborn relative is valid. Gray, Rule ag. Perp., sec. 62. On the question of the validity of a bargain and sale to a person not in *esse*, see *ibid.*, secs. 61–66.

is as follows: " Upon the death of the said Edward B. Boren, *cestui que trust,* the trust herein created shall cease and terminate, and when said trust is terminated the trust property, as the same may exist at the death of the said Edward B. Boren, whether consisting of real or personal property, shall immediately vest in and become the property of the heirs-at-law of the said Edward B. Boren, *cestui que trust* herein, and said heirs-at-law shall be entitled to said property under the laws of descent of the State of Illinois then in force." The trustee named in the deed accepted the trust and acted as trustee until January, 1922, when she filed the bill in this case for an accounting, tendering her resignation as trustee, asking that her report as such trustee be approved and that she be discharged and her successor appointed. Boren answered the bill, admitting the correctness of the account of the trustee, consenting to her resignation, and alleging that the reversion in fee to the undivided one-fourth of the land conveyed to the trustee is in him; that the only interest conveyed by the trust deed was an estate during his life, and that no person other than the trustee and himself has any interest in the trust property. The answer avers the trustee has never exercised the power to appoint her successor and that he is competent and able to efficiently manage the property. Boren also filed a cross-bill, in which he alleged that the only title conveyed by him by the trust deed to Hannah E. Burton was an estate for and during the life of the grantor; that he is the owner of the reversion in fee, and no other person except himself and the trustee has any right, title or interest in the trust property. The cross-bill admits the correctness of the trustee's account filed, consents to her resignation, and prays the trust be decreed terminated and the trustee required to convey the property to cross-complainant and deliver to him all property shown by her report and statement to belong to him. Boren had two children, and both were living when these proceedings were had. They were daughters, Marie Richards and Irene Hagedorn, and were made defendants to the cross-bill. They disclaimed any interest in the subject matter of the litigation, and Hannah E. Burton, the trustee, demurred to the cross-bill. The court overruled the demurrer, and she elected to abide by the demurrer. A decree was entered as prayed in the cross-bill. From that decree Hannah E. Burton has prosecuted this appeal.

Counsel for appellant argue that appellee parted with all his title and interest in the trust property by the deed to the trustee except a beneficial equitable interest during his life and that the trust cannot be terminated until his death, and when so terminated his heirs, to be then determined under the laws of descent, will become seized of the title to the trust property as purchasers under the deed of trust and not as heirs of appellee under the laws of descent. Appellee contends that the trust deed conveyed an estate to the trustee for and during the life of the grantor but the reversion in fee is in him, and that no other person than himself and the trustee have any interest in the trust property, and it was proper for the court to terminate the trust by its decree.

There can be no question that under the decisions in Akers *v.* Clark, 184 Ill. 136, Biwer *v.* Martin, 294 id. 488, and Hobbie *v.* Ogden, 178 id. 357, the provision in clause 4 that on the death of appellee the property should immediately vest in and become the property of his heirs entitled to it under the laws of descent conferred no estate in remainder or of any other character on the heirs of appellee, or those who would be his heirs upon his death. In the Akers and Biwer cases it was held that where a grantor conveys a life estate with a remainder over to his heirs, the heirs do not take a remainder at all. The word "heirs" will be regarded as defining or limiting the estate which the first taker has. In such case the heirs would take as reversioners by descent from the grantor and not under the deed. (1 Tiffany on Real Prop. sec. 130; 2 id. sec. 487.) The children of appellee disclaimed any interest in the property, but it is clear from the decisions they had no interest, and never will have except as reversioners by descent from appellee. No other persons being interested in the trust except appellant and appellee, the question for decision appears to be narrowed to whether the court erred in terminating the trust.

This court has held that where all the parties are capable of acting and desire a trust terminated, a court of equity may decree its determination. Appellant, the trustee in this case, does not wish to longer act in that capacity, tendered and requested the court to accept her resignation, and asked to be relieved from any further duties or responsibilities and that someone else be selected to act in her place. Appellee consents to the acceptance of appellant's resignation as trustee. So far as the interests of the children or heirs of appellee are concerned there is no obstacle in the way of a termination of the trust. Appellant contends appellee parted with all his interest by his deed to the trustee except the beneficial use of it during his life and for that reason the trust cannot be terminated. Under the decisions of this court referred to, he still has the reversion in fee, with right to grant it away. The trustee has no beneficial interest in the continuance of the trust.

This case is unlike Lawrence *v.* Lawrence, 181 Ill. 248, where the trust deed directed the trustee to convey the property to the heirs of the creator of the trust. The court in that case held the trustee took whatever estate was necessary to enable him to carry out the trust — even a fee simple, if required. In the case here under consideration the trustee was not directed to convey to the heirs. Whatever estate the heirs of appellee received would be by inheritance. The trustee was not required to sell the land and distribute the proceeds, but she was given authority to sell and hold the money received in trust or re-invest it in other property on the same terms and conditions, but it was left to the judgment and discretion of the trustee whether to sell or not. Except a small tract sold by the trustee, and as to which no question is raised, the trustee has never exercised the power to sell. She is the sister of appellee and has appealed from the decree. In her brief she says she has no pecuniary interest in continuing the trust and desires to be released from its duties. She says her appeal is prosecuted solely for the purpose of defending the trust and for the protection of herself and her estate from any possible action of the heirs-at-law of appellee after his death.

Under the admitted facts in this case we are of opinion the court did not err in rendering the decree appealed from.

Appellant asks that in case the decree is affirmed the costs be ordered paid out of the trust property. The costs in the court below were so ordered paid, and we are of opinion it is right and equitable that they be so paid here. The order is that the costs of this appeal be paid out of the trust property.

The decree of the circuit court is affirmed.

Decree affirmed.[1]

WHITTEMORE v. EQUITABLE TRUST COMPANY.

COURT OF APPEALS, NEW YORK. 1929.

250 N. Y. 298.

APPEAL, by permission, from an unanimous judgment of the Appellate Division of the Supreme Court in the first judicial department, entered June 21, 1928, in favor of plaintiff upon the submission of a controversy under sections 546–548 of the Civil Practice Act.

CRANE, J. The plaintiffs have had judgment on a submitted controversy revoking a deed of trust. The defendant trustee has appealed, insisting that there are vested interests which have not consented to the revocation. Section 23 of the Personal Property Law (Cons. Laws, ch. 41) states when a trust in personal property may be revoked. It reads:

"Upon the written consent of all the persons beneficially interested in a trust in personal property or any part thereof heretofore or hereafter created, the creator of such trust may revoke the same as to the whole or such part thereof, and thereupon the estate of the trustee shall cease in the whole or such part thereof."

---

[1] Johns v. Birmingham Trust & Sav. Co., 205 Ala. 535; Stephens v. Moore, 298 Mo. 215; Doctor v. Hughes, 225 N. Y. 305; Stella v. New York Trust Co., 224 N. Y. App. Div. 50; Cagliardi v. Bank of New York & T. Co., 230 N. Y. App. Div. 192; Kuhn v. Jackman, 32 Oh. App. 164, *accord.* See Livingston v. Ward, 247 N. Y. 97.

All the adult parties to the deed of trust have consented to the revocation; the children of the settlors, however, being minors, have not and could not consent. The trustee claims that these children are beneficially interested in the trust and that it, therefore, cannot be revoked as has been attempted in this case.

The trust deed, dated December 27, 1921, by Elizabeth L. Wilson, Carolyn W. Quarles and Henry Whittemore, Jr., transferred certain bonds to the Equitable Trust Company to hold and to collect and pay the income to Carolyn G. Whittemore during her natural life, and at her death to her husband, Henry Whittemore, during his life. Upon the death of these two life beneficiaries, the trust estate is to be returned to the settlors in equal shares. If this was the end of the trust agreement, there would be no difficulty. The creators of the trust would simply have transferred a life interest, reserving all other interest in themselves, which could be disposed of by them at any time. Under such conditions, Henry Whittemore, one of the life beneficiaries, having died, the revocation in this case would be perfectly good, as it was executed by the three settlors of the trust and the remaining life beneficiary, Carolyn G. Whittemore.

The interest, if any, of the infant children, however, arises because of other provisions in the trust agreement. Henry Whittemore, Jr., one of the three settlors, is a bachelor. Elizabeth L. Wilson has a husband and three minor children; Carolyn W. Quarles has a husband and two minor children. The trust instrument refers to the children. On the death of the remaining life beneficiary the property, as above stated, is to be returned to the settlors in equal shares. But if one of the settlors has died before the life beneficiary, then the settlor's interest is disposed of as follows:

"Provided, however, that if any of them be then dead, the part of the net principal of the Trust Estate which would have been paid over and delivered to him or her if he or she had survived shall be paid over and delivered to such person or persons, and in such shares, interests and proportions, as such deceased Settlor, by his or her last will and testament, shall have appointed, or, in default of such appointment, to such person or persons, and in such shares, interests and proportions, as the same would have been distributable if such deceased Settlor had been the owner thereof at the time of his or her death and had died intestate."

To be perspicuous I shall refer to the creators of the trust as the settlor, one person.

Taking this agreement in its simplest form, we have a trust created in personal property for the life of the beneficiary. At the death of the life beneficiary, the trustee is directed to do one of three things: pay the principal of the estate to the settlor, if he be alive; or, if he be dead, to pay it as directed in the settlor's last will and testament; or, if the settlor leave no will, to pay it to the persons who would then take under the Statute of Distributions. No provision is made to pay the principal of the trust estate to the grantee or assignee of the settlor.

Why should not this trust agreement be interpreted as it reads? What reason is there for giving it a legal construction just the opposite to its natural meaning? The settlor, in case of death without a will, gives the principal of the trust estate to his next of kin. In this case, if one of the married settlors should presently die, the trust deed directs the trustee upon the death of the life beneficiary, to pay one-third of the trust estate to the husband of the settlor and her children. Reading the instrument as a whole, it is apparent that the settlor intended to make a complete disposition of all the estate at the time of the making of the instrument, and did so in the way indicated. The children or next of kin were given a vested remainder, which might be divested by the last will and testament of the settlor; it could not be divested by the deed or assignment of the settlor. In other words, if the settlor, believing he had not conveyed away all of his interests in the property, had attempted to assign or transfer in his lifetime that which he thought he still possessed, and which in law we call a reversion, the deed or transfer would be ineffectual as against his children. Their interest as next of kin could only be divested or cut off by a last will and testament. That such an uncertain or variable interest of the next of kin is alienable, see Campbell *v.* Stokes (142 N. Y. 23); Moore v. Littel (41 N. Y. 66).

If the provision in the deed of trust by the use of the same words had given the principal to the next of kin of the life beneficiary instead of to the next of kin of the settlor, such persons would have taken a remainder by purchase. (Real Property Law [Cons. Laws, ch. 50], section 54; Personal Property Law, section 11.) Even without these statutes such has been held to be the case. (Sands *v.* Old Colony Trust Co., 195 Mass. 575.) The same rule, in my judgment, should apply in the one case as in the other. In such circumstances, where it fairly appears that intention would be promoted by that construction, words which create a remainder in the next of kin of the life beneficiary should also create a remainder in the next of kin of the settlor of the trust when the provision is for them. This is all a matter of intention. The creator of a trust can do as he pleases with his property and the courts look to his words to guide them in decisions. The directions come from the owner of the property and not from the law, unless there be some specific statute to be enforced. To determine, therefore, whether the settlor of the trust in this case simply created a life interest and nothing more, reserving to himself the balance of the interest in the property, we looked to his intention, as expressed in the instrument. If the trust deed had said that upon the death of the life beneficiary the net principal of the trust estate was to be paid over and delivered to the settlor or his next of kin in equal shares, the addition in this place of the words "next of kin," would not have been sufficient in all probability to create a remainder. Rather it would indicate that the settlor intended all above a life interest to remain with him as a reversion to be disposed of in any way he pleased. The words would indicate a limitation, not a gift. (Whittemore v. Equitable Trust Co., 162 App. Div. 607; Doctor v. Hughes, 225 N. Y. 305.) But that is not this case. Here we have something more. The settlor, as above stated, makes rather full and formal disposition of the principal of the trust estate in case he dies before the life beneficiary. The words used, as already explained, indicate an intention to give a remainder to the spouse and children, as the case may be, subject to change by the settlor's will. The creator of the trust reserves power of disposition only by will; he does something more than merely set up a trust for a life beneficiary; he disposes of the property at the termination of the life interests in case of his previous death. This case is similar to Crackanthorpe v. Sickles (156 App. Div. 753) and Court v. Bankers' Trust Co. (160 N. Y. Supp. 477). (See, also, Gray v. Union Trust Co. of San Francisco, 171 Cal. 637; Mercer v. Safe Deposit & Trust Co., 91 Md. 102.)

The judgment below should, therefore, be reversed, and judgment directed for the defendant, with costs in this court.

CARDOZO, Ch. J., POUND, LEHMAN, KELLOGG, O'BRIEN and HUBBS, JJ., concur.

Judgment reversed, etc.[1]

SAYER v. WYNKOOP, 248 N. Y. 54 (1928): A corporation sent money to the defendant, an insurance broker, with directions to pay premiums on insurance in the State Insurance Fund insuring it against liability under the Workmen's Compensation Law. The State Industrial Commissioner who was in charge of the insurance fund brought suit against the defendant. It was held that the plaintiff was entitled to recover. KELLOGG, J., said (p. 57):

"It is obvious that a person, who delivers property or moneys to another with instructions to pay them to a third person, may intend, upon the one hand, to make the receiver a mere custodian or agent for himself; or, upon the other, to constitute him a trustee for the third person. If the former intention be his, the third person will have no right of action to recover the moneys; if the lat-

---

[1] Gray v. Union Trust Co., 171 Cal. 637; Guaranty Trust Co. v. Halsted, 245 N. Y. 447; Gage v. Irving Bank & Trust Co., 248 N. Y. 554 (*mem.*), *aff'g* 222 App. Div. 92, *accord.* See Hubbard v. Buddemeier, 328 Ill. 76.

In Corbett v. Bank of New York & T. Co., 229 N. Y. App. Div. 570, it was held that the principal case did not prevent revocation with the consent of those who were next of kin at the time of the revocation.

ter be his intention, a cause of action for money had and received will arise against the receiver of the moneys and in favor of such third person. It will thus arise, not because of the express promise of the receiver to pay, but because of property rights acquired by the third person, to enforce which the law will imply a promise on the part of the receiver to pay over. (Williston on Contracts, sections 348, 349). . . . Moreover, a third situation may arise. The receiver of the moneys may be, or pretend to be, the agent of the third person, to receive them. In that event, when the moneys are received, the legal as well as the equitable title thereto will pass to the third person, who may then bring suit to recover the amount paid. Williston on Contracts, sec. 352. These general principles are well settled and readily understood. Difficulty arises only when application of the principles to a given state of facts is sought to be made.

"Manifestly, if the owner of moneys employs another as a mere messenger to carry them to a designated consignee, no trust is created, and no right of action accrues. (Bigelow v. Davis, 16 Barbour, 561). Again, the owner may deposit the moneys with a banker with instructions to apply them in satisfaction of the debt of a third person. In that event, the conventional relationship of debtor and creditor between the banker and the depositor is created, coupled with an agency on the part of the banker to pay the debt, which is revocable at the will of the depositor. [Citing cases.] Where, however, the owner delivers the moneys to another upon an agreement that they will be paid to a third person, such third person acquires an equitable interest entitling him to have a recovery in an action for money had and received." [1]

MORICE v. THE BISHOP OF DURHAM.

Chancery. 1805.

10 Ves. 521.

This cause came on upon an appeal by the defendant, the Bishop of Durham, from the decree of the Master of the Rolls.

Ann Cracherode, by her will, dated the 16th of April, 1801, and duly executed to pass real estate, after giving several legacies to her next of kin and others, some of which she directed to be paid out of the produce of her real estate, directed to be sold, bequeathed all her personal estate to the Bishop of Durham, his executors, &c., upon trust to pay her debts and legacies, &c.; and to dispose of the ultimate residue to such objects of benevolence and liberality as the Bishop of Durham in his own discretion shall most approve of; and she appointed the Bishop her sole executor.

[1] See Chap. I, sec. IV, and particularly Steele v. Clark, 77 Ill. 471, and Guidise v. Island Refining Corp., 291 Fed. 922, *ante.*

The bill was filed by the next of kin to have the will established except as to the residuary bequest, and that such bequest may be declared void. The Attorney General was made a defendant. The Bishop, by his answer, expressly disclaimed any beneficial interest in himself personally.[1]

THE LORD CHANCELLOR [ELDON]. This, with the single exception of Brown *v.* Yeall, 7 Ves. 50, n., is a new case. The questions are, 1st, Whether a trust was intended to be created at all? 2dly, Whether it was effectually created? 3dly, If ineffectually created, whether the defendant, the Bishop of Durham, can, according to the decisions, and upon the authority of those decisions, take this property for his own use and benefit. As to the last, I understand a doubt has been raised in the discussion of some question bearing analogy to this in another court, — how far it is competent to a testator to give to his friend his personal estate, to apply it to such purposes of bounty not arising to trust as the testator himself would have been likely to apply it to. That question, as far as this court has to do with it, depends altogether upon this: if the testator meant to create a trust, and not to make an absolute gift, but the trust is ineffectually created, is not expressed at all, or fails, the next of kin take. On the other hand, if the party is to take himself, it must be upon this ground, according to the authorities, — that the testator did not mean to create a trust, but intended a gift to that person for his own use and benefit; for if he was intended to have it entirely in his own power and discretion whether to make the application or not, it is absolutely given, and it is the effect of his own will and not the obligation imposed by the testament: the one inclining, the other compelling, him to execute the purpose. But if he cannot, or was not intended to, be compelled, the question is not then upon a trust that has failed, or the intent to create a trust; but the will must be read as if no such intention was expressed or to be discovered in it.

Pierson *v.* Garnett, 2 Bro. C. C. 38, 226, and the other cases of that class, do not bear upon this in any degree; for the question, whether a trust was intended, arose from two or three circumstances, which must all concur where there is no express trust. *Primâ facie* an absolute interest was given, and the question was, whether precatory, not mandatory, words imposed a trust upon that person; and the court has said, before those words of request or accommodation create a trust, it must be shewn that the object and the subject are certain; and it is not immaterial to this case that it must be shewn that the objects are certain. If neither the objects nor the subject are certain, then the recommendation or request does not create a trust; for of necessity the alleged trustee is to execute the trust, and, the property being so uncertain and indefinite, it may be conceived the testator meant to leave it entirely to the will and pleasure of the legatee, whether he would take upon himself that which is tech-

[1] The statement of facts is taken from the report of the case in 9 Ves. 399.

nically called a trust. Wherever the subject to be administered as trust property, and the objects for whose benefit it is to be administered are to be found in a will, not expressly creating trust, the indefinite nature and *quantum* of the subject, and the indefinite nature of the objects, are always used by the court as evidence that the mind of the testator was not to create a trust; and the difficulty that would be imposed upon the court to say what should be so applied, or to what objects, has been the foundation of the argument that no trust was intended.

But the principle of those cases has never been held in this court applicable to a case where the testator himself has expressly said he gives his property upon trust. If he gives upon trust, hereafter to be declared, it might perhaps originally have been as well to have held that, if he did not declare any trust, the person to whom the property was given should take it. If he says he gives in trust and stops there, meaning to make a codicil or an addition to his will, or, where he gives upon trusts which fail, or are ineffectually expressed, in all those cases the court has said, if upon the face of the will there is declaration plain that the person to whom the property is given is to take it in trust; and, though the trust is not declared, or is ineffectually declared, or becomes incapable of taking effect, the party taking shall be a trustee; if not for those who were to take by the will, for those who take under the disposition of the law. It is impossible, therefore, to contend that, if this is a trust ineffectually expressed, the Bishop of Durham can hold for his own benefit. I do not advert to what appears upon the record of his intention to the contrary, and his disposition to make the application; for I must look only to the will, without any bias from the nature of the disposition, or the temper and quality of the person who is to execute the trust.

The next consideration is, whether this is a trust effectually declared; and, if not as to the whole, as to part. I put it so; as it is said, if the word "benevolence" means charity, and "liberality" means something different from that idea, which in a court of justice we are obliged to apply to that word "charity" (and, I admit, we are obliged to apply to it many senses not falling within its ordinary signification), there is a ground for an application in this case partially, if it cannot be wholly, to charity. It does not seem to me upon the authorities, particularly the Attorney General *v.* Whorwood, 1 Ves. 534, that the argument for a proportionate division, or a division of some sort, would be displaced. I take the result of that case to be that the substratum of that charity failed, and all those partial dispositions that would have been good charity if not connected with that, failed together with it. It has been decided upon that principle, that, though money may be given to an infirmary or a school, yet, if that bequest is connected with a purpose of building an infirmary or school, and the money is then to be laid out upon it so built, the purpose, which is the foundation, failing, the superstructure must fail with it. The Attorney General *v.* Doyley, 4 Vin. 485, 2 Eq. Ca. Ab. 194, is almost the only case that has been cited for a proportional division. The testator expressly directed the trustees to dispose of his estate to such of his relations, of his mother's side, who were most deserving, and in such manner and proportions as they should think fit, to such charitable use as they should think most proper and convenient; and the court, which has taken strong liberties upon this subject of charity, though the manner and proportion were left to certain individuals, held that equality is equity, and there should be an equal division; but it is expressly declared that those who took were persons who could take under a bequest to charitable uses; and there was no difficulty in that case in saying, those words must be construed according to the habit and allowed authorities of the court.

The only case decided upon any principle that can govern this is Brown *v.* Yeall, which applies strongly. I do not trust myself with the question whether the principle was well applied in that instance, but the decision furnishes a principle which the court must endeavor well to apply in cases that occur. I do not hesitate to say I entertain doubt, not of the principle upon which that case was decided, but whether it was well applied in that instance. Mr. Bradley was a very able lawyer; yet he mistook his way, as Serjeant Aspinall had not long before. Mr. Bradley gave a great portion of his fortune to accumulate for many years; and, meaning that it should be disposed of to charitable purposes, constituted a fund, expressly stating that his purpose was a charitable purpose, and confirming that by directing that charitable purpose to be carried on, as to the mode of executing it, by that court which, according to the constitution of the country, ordinarily administers property given to charitable uses. In his opinion, therefore, independent of particular authority, there was a principle, suggested by all other cases of trust, that if a trust was declared in such terms that this court could not execute it, that trust was ill-declared, and must fail, for the benefit of the next of kin. The principle upon which that trust was ill-declared is this. As it is a maxim that the execution of a trust shall be under the control of the court, it must be of such a nature that it can be under that control, so that the administration of it can be reviewed by the court; or, if the trustee dies, the court itself can execute the trust; a trust, therefore, which, in the case of mal-administration, could be reformed, and a due administration directed, and then, unless the subject and the objects can be ascertained upon principles familiar in other cases, it must be decided that the court can neither reform mal-administration nor direct a due administration. That is the principle of that case. Upon the question whether that principle was well applied in that instance, different minds will reason differently. I should have been disposed to say that, where such a purpose was expressed, it was not a strained construction to hold that the happiness of mankind intended was that which was to be promoted by the circulation of religious and virtuous learning; and, the testator having stated that to be the charitable purpose, which unquestionably was so, the distribution of books for the promotion of religion, the court might have so understood him; and the testator having not only called it a charitable purpose, but delegated the execution to this court, ought to be taken to have meant that.

Upon these grounds in a subsequent case, The Attorney General *v.* Stepney, 10 Ves. 22, as to the Welch charities, it appeared to me too much, considering the Society in this country for the Propagation of the Gospel, &c., to say a trust for the circulation of bibles, prayer-books, and other religious books was not good. Then, looking back to the history of the law upon this subject, I say, with the Master of the Rolls, that a case has not been yet decided in which the court has executed a charitable purpose, unless the will contains a description of that which the law acknowledges to be a charitable purpose, or devotes the property to purposes of charity in general. Upon those cases in which the will devotes the property to charitable purposes, described, observation is unnecessary. With reference to those in which the court takes upon itself to say it is a disposition to charity, where in some the mode is left to individuals, in others individuals cannot select either the mode or the objects, but it falls upon the king, as *parens patriæ,* to apply the property, it is enough at this day to say, the court, by long habitual construction of those general words, has fixed the sense; and, where there is a gift to charity in general, whether it is to be executed by individuals selected by the testator himself, or the king, as *parens patriæ,* is to execute it, (and I allude to the case in Levinz, The Attorney General *v.* Matthews, 2 Lev. 167,) it is the duty of such trustees on the one hand, and of the crown upon the other, to apply the money to charity in the sense which the determinations have affixed to that word in this court; viz. either such charitable purposes as are expressed in the statute (43 Eliz. c. 4), or to purposes having analogy to those. I believe the expression " charitable purposes," as used in this court, has been applied to many acts described in that statute, and analogous to those, not because they can with propriety be called charitable, but as that denomination is by the statute given to all the purposes described.

The question, then, is entirely whether this is according to the intention a gift to purposes of charity in general as understood in this court; such that this court would have held the Bishop bound, and would have compelled him to apply the surplus to such charitable purposes as can be answered only in obedience to decrees where the gift is to charity in general; or is it, or may it be according to the intention, to such purposes, going beyond those partially or altogether which the court understands by " charitable purposes";

and, if that is the intention, is the gift too indefinite to create an effectual trust to be here executed? The argument has not denied, nor is it necessary, in order to support this decree, that the person created the trustee might give the property to such charitable uses as this court holds charitable uses within the ordinary meaning. It is not contended, and it is not necessary, to support this decree, to contend, that the trustee might not consistently with the intention have devoted every shilling to uses in that sense charitable, and of course a part of the property. But the true question is, whether, if upon the one hand he might have devoted the whole to purposes in this sense charitable, he might not equally according to the intention have devoted the whole to purposes benevolent and liberal, and yet not within the meaning of charitable purposes as this court construes those words; and, if according to the intention it was competent to him to do so, I do not apprehend that under any authority upon such words the court could have charged him with maladministration, if he had applied the whole to purposes, which, according to the meaning of the testator, are benevolent and liberal, though not acts of that species of benevolence and liberality which this court in the construction of a will calls charitable acts.

The question, therefore, resolves itself entirely into that; for I agree there is no magic in words, and if the real meaning of these words is charity or charitable purposes, according to the technical sense in which those words are used in this court, all the consequences follow; if, on the other hand, the intention was to describe anything beyond that, then the testator meant to repose in the Bishop a discretion, not to apply the property for his own benefit, but that would enable him to apply it to purposes more indefinite than those to which we must look, considering them purposes creating a trust; for, if there is as much of indefinite nature in the purposes intended to be expressed, as in the cases to which I first alluded, where the objects are too uncertain to make recommendation amount to trust by analogy, the trust is as ineffectual, — the only difference being, that in the one case no trust is declared, and the recommendation fails, the objects being too indefinite; in the other the testator has expressly said it is a trust, and the trustee consequently takes, not for his own benefit, but for purposes not sufficiently defined to be controlled and managed by this court. Upon these words much criticism may be used. But the question is, whether, according to the ordinary sense, not the sense of the passages and authors alluded to, treating upon the great and extensive sense of the word "charity," in the Christian religion, this testatrix meant by these words to confine the defendant to such acts of charity or charitable purposes as this court would have enforced by decree, and reference to a master. I do not think that was the intention; and, if not, the intention is too indefinite to create a trust. But it was the intention to create a trust, and the object being too indefinite has failed. The consequence of law is, that the Bishop takes the property upon trust to dispose of it as the law will dispose of it, not for his own benefit or any purpose this court can effectuate. I think, therefore, this decree is right.

The decree was affirmed.[1]

[1] In the following cases it was held that the purpose of the testator was not confined to charities and the intended trust failed. A. G. v. Nat. Provincial Bank, [1924] A. C. 262, aff'g Re Tetley, [1923] 1 Ch. 258, *post* (political purposes and charitable objects); Re Eades, [1920] 2 Ch. 353 (religious, charitable and philanthropic objects, " and " read as " or "); Re Davis, [1923] 1 Ch. 225 (charitable or public institutions in Wales); Re Clarke, [1923] 2 Ch. 407, *post* (such other funds, charities and institutions as my executors in their absolute discretion shall think fit); Smith v. Pond, 90 N. J. Eq. 445, 29 Yale L. Jour. 242 (for support of a church or such benevolent purposes as the trustees of the church shall direct); Matter of Shattuck, 193 N. Y. 446 (religious, educational or eleemosynary institutions).

The same result was formerly reached in the case of charitable trusts in states which did not then allow trusts for charitable purposes. Baptist Ass'n v. Hart's Ex'rs, 4 Wheat. (U. S.) 1, *post;* Levy v. Levy, 33 N. Y. 97; Tilden v. Green, 130 N. Y. 29.

In the following cases trusts were upheld as charitable. Re Bennett, [1920] 1 Ch. 305 (for the benefit of schools and poor and other objects of charity or any other public objects in the parish of X; " or " interpreted as meaning " and "); Re Baron Ludlow, [1923] W. N. 126, 314 (for hospital or other charitable or benevolent institution, held charitable under principle of *ejusdem generis*); Clark v. Cummings, 83 N. H. 27 (to dispose among charitable, fraternal, benevolent and educational uses, purposes, societies, institutions, associations and corporations, public or private, in New Hampshire).

For numerous additional cases, see Scott, Cases on Trusts, 1 ed., 275–7; 3 A. L. R. 297; 45 A. L. R. 1440.

In Re Gibbon, [1917] 1 I. R. 448, a bequest was made by a Catholic clergyman to his executors, also clergymen, to dispose of " to my best spiritual advantage, as conscience and sense of duty may direct." It was held that although this was not a charitable trust nor a beneficial gift to the executors, yet the executors might perform if willing. " It is true that there is no living *cestui que trust* who can enforce it. . . . The Court is not asked to compel the enforcement of this trust and the executors are willing to carry it out; and I can see no sufficient ground for refusing to allow them to effectuate, as they propose to do, the expressed intentions of the testator."

In a few cases it has been held that a *power* to appoint for general non-charitable purposes is invalid. Bannerman's Trustees v. Bannerman, [1915] S. C. 398, p. 409 (" A proprietary power cannot be too general, whereas a fiduciary power is invalid unless the description of the class to be benefited is 'sufficiently certain to enable men of common sense to carry out the expressed wishes of the testator' or other creator of the power."); Norris v. Thomson, 19 N. J. Eq. 307, 20 N. J. Eq. 489; Tilden v. Green, 130 N. Y. 29; Heiss v. Murphey, 40 Wis. 276. But see 5 Harv. L. Rev. 395; 15 Harv. L. Rev. 512. In Re Clarke, [1923] 2 Ch. 407, *post*, Romer, J., said, " a power to appoint to charitable and non-charitable indefinite objects is just as invalid as a direct gift to such objects."

On the general subject of non-charitable trusts without definite beneficiaries, see Ames, Failure of the Tilden Trust, 5 Harv. L. Rev. 389; Lect. Leg. Hist., 285; Gray, Gifts for a Non-charitable Purpose, 15 Harv. L. Rev. 509; Gray, Rule ag. Perp., App. H. See also 33 L. Quar. Rev. 356–360.

NORMAN v. PRINCE.

Supreme Court, Rhode Island. 1917.

40 R. I. 402.

Sweetland, J. This is a suit in equity brought by the trustees under the will of George H. Norman, late of Newport, for the construction of said will and for instructions.

The questions involved relate to the construction of the provisions contained in the twelfth clause of said will. By said clause the testator devises and bequeaths his residuary estate to his son George H. Norman, Jr., and his heirs in trust. By the terms of the trust the trustee is directed to dispose of the net income of the trust estate as follows: (1) To pay from said net income the sum of $20,000 annually to the testator's wife, Abby D. K. Norman, in equal quarter yearly installments; (2) to divide the residue of said net income into nine equal shares, and as often as once in six months to pay one of said shares to each of eight of the testator's nine children, excluding from said provision the testator's son Hugh K. Norman, and upon the decease of each of said eight children to pay the share of income to which said child would have been entitled as said child shall by will appoint, in default of appointment, to the lawful issue of said child, and in default of appointment and issue, to the testator's then next of kin, omitting and excluding, however, the testator's son Hugh and his descendants, if any; and (3) to pay the remaining or ninth share of income in whole or in part at such time or times as the trustee shall select to testator's said son Hugh or to Hugh's wife or to any child or children of Hugh or to any other person or persons whomsoever, as the trustee for the time being in the uncontrolled absolute discretion or pleasure of said trustee shall see fit.

In said will the testator directs that upon the decease of the survivor or his widow and all of his nine children and when the youngest living grandchild shall have reached 21 the whole principal of said trust shall be divided by the trustee into eight equal shares, said shares to be set apart so that they shall appertain or relate to said eight children, one share to each child, each share so appertaining to each child to be paid absolutely and in fee simple, free from every trust, as said child may by will appoint, in default of appointment, to the lawful issue of said child, and in default of appointment and issue, to the testator's then next of kin; the descendants of said Hugh, however, being specifically excepted.

It was further provided in said will that said George H. Norman, Jr., might at any time or times appoint one or two persons to act as trustee or trustees under said will, both with him and after he should have ceased to act as trustee by death or otherwise, and they and the survivor of them and every other person appointed under the provisions of said will should have every right, power, privilege, and authority conferred by said will on George H. Norman, Jr., as trustee.

George H. Norman, Jr., duly qualified and acted as sole trustee under said will until February 13, 1908, upon which date, in accordance with the provision of the will, he duly appointed his brothers Guy Norman and Maxwell Norman as trustees to carry out said trust. On said February 13, 1908, the said George H. Norman, Jr., died, and since that date the said Guy and Maxwell Norman, the complainants here, have acted and are now acting as trustees. On October 30, 1900, the said Hugh K. Norman died, leaving no issue. His widow, who was the sole beneficiary under his will, and who was duly appointed administratrix with the will annexed of his estate, individually and as such administratrix has executed a release of all claims to the estate of the testator, George H. Norman. Abby D. K. Norman, widow of George H. Norman, the testator, died on September 6, 1915. Certain of the grandchildren of the testator have not yet reached the age of 21 years.

The present trustees and their predecessor as trustee, said George H. Norman, Jr., up to the time of the decease of the testator's widow made the annual payments from income to her in accordance with the provisions of the will, and also, as directed, paid the share of income to each of the eight children of the testator named in his will as aforesaid, the share of income of George H. Norman, Jr., being paid after his death to the appointees under his will; also said trustees distributed said ninth share of income from time to time in varying amounts and proportions with the knowledge, consent, and acquiescence of the defendants to the widow and children of the testator, including Hugh K. Norman and said George H. Norman, Jr., during their respective lives, and after their respective deaths to the widow and surviving children of the testator, to the widow of Hugh K. Norman, and to the appointees of income of said George H. Norman, Jr.[1] . . .

As to the second question presented by the bill, we are of the opinion that the provision relating to the disposition of the ninth share of income is valid and amounts to the creation of an absolute power of disposition. The will provides for the payment of said ninth share of the residuary income " as the trustee hereof for the time being in the uncontrolled absolute discretion or pleasure of said trustee shall see fit." Said provision imposes no trust or obligation with respect to the disposition of said ninth share of income. By the twelfth clause of said will the testator's residuary estate is given to his son George H. Norman, Jr., in trust. As trustee the said George H. Norman, Jr., or the trustees for the time being, are

[1] A part of the opinion in which it was held that on the death of the widow her annuity should go with the residuary income is omitted.

directed to pay $20,000 of the net income of said trust estate annually to the widow, to make division of the residue of said income into nine shares, and to pay eight of said shares to persons definitely designated. From the very broad language of the provision as to the disposition of the said ninth share of net income the testator's intent can readily be found not to bequeath said share in trust for indefinite beneficiaries; but the provision should be regarded rather as a bequest of said share to the trustees with an arbitrary power of disposition. The use of the words "trustee" and "trustees" in this clause of the will is not controlling as to his or their character in the disposition of said ninth share, but said words must be regarded as descriptive. In Gibbs v. Rumsey, 2 Ves. & B. 294, the testatrix bequeathed certain estate, real and personal, to two persons named upon trust to sell; and, after making certain bequests out of the money derived from such sale the testatrix, "proceeded thus, 'I give and bequeath all the rest and residue of the moneys arising from the sale of my estate and all the residue of my personal estate after payment of my debts, legacies and funeral expenses and the expenses of proving this my will unto my said trustees and executors (the said Henry Rumsey and James Rumsey) to be disposed of unto such person and persons and in such manner and form and in such sum and sums of money as they in their discretion shall think proper and expedient.'" The Master of the Rolls held that this provision created a purely arbitrary power of disposition according to a discretion which no court can either direct or control, and not a trust for an indefinite purpose. Although the testator in the case at bar has coupled this power of disposition of a portion of the income of the trust estate with certain trust provisions, we feel warranted in construing this provision as we have in accordance with the testator's obvious intent. See 5 Harvard Law Review, 389.

We accordingly approve the action of George H. Norman, Jr., and of the complainant trustees in the disposition which he and they have made of said ninth share of income. We instruct said trustees that the net income of the trust estate arising after the death of the testator's widow shall be divided into nine equal shares, that eight of said shares are to be disposed of in accordance with the provisions of said twelfth clause of the will, and that the remaining share is held by the trustees to be disposed of by them in their discretion in accordance with the power of disposition given to them by the testator. We also find that the provision relating to said power of disposition is valid.

On July 2d the parties may present to us a form of decree in accordance with this opinion.[1]

[1] Gibbs v. Rumsey, 2 V. & B. 294 (to executors to be disposed of unto such person and persons and in such manner and form and in such sum and sums of money as they in their discretion shall think proper and expedient); Robinson v. Dusgate, 2 Vern. 181 (to be at the disposal of wife by will to

CLARK v. CAMPBELL.

Supreme Court, New Hampshire. 1926.

82 N. H. 281.

Petition for instructions, by the trustees under the will of Charles H. Cummings. Questions, which appear in the opinion, were reserved without ruling by *Sawyer*, J.

Snow, J. 1. The ninth clause of the will of deceased reads: " My estate will comprise so many and such a variety of articles of personal property such as books, photographic albums, pictures, statuary, bronzes, bric-a-brac, hunting and fishing equipment, antiques, rugs, scrapbooks, canes and masonic jewels, that probably I shall not distribute all, and perhaps no great part thereof during my life by gift among my friends. Each of my trustees is competent by reason of familiarity with the property, my wishes and friendships, to wisely distribute some portion at least of said property. I therefore give and bequeath to my trustees all my property embraced within the classification aforesaid in trust to make disposal by the way of

---

whom she shall think fit); *Re* Howell, [1915] 1 Ch. 241 (residue shall be at the discretion of the executor and at his own disposal); Higginson *v.* Kerr, 30 Ont. L. Rep. 62 (I desire that my executors shall have full power to dispose of the residue as they in their judgment may deem best); Harvey *v.* Griggs, 12 Del. Ch. 232, 19 Mich. L. Rev. 455 (the executor and another to divide and distribute according to their best judgment); McElwain *v.* A. G., 241 Mass. 112 (to trustees who are authorized to appropriate and dispose of at their discretion); Beals *v.* Villard, 167 N. E. 264 (Mass. 1929), 14 Minn. L. Rev. 310 (to enable the legatee to devote himself more effectively to the service of humanity); *Re* Perkins, 68 N. Y. Misc. 255; Ralston *v.* Telfair, 2 Dev. Eq. (N. C.) 255 (to executors to dispose of as they may think fit); Will of Dever, 173 Wis. 208 (to certain persons in trust to use their best judgment), *accord*.

In the following cases a resulting trust was imposed: Fowler *v.* Garlike, 1 Russ. & Myl. 232 (to executors upon trust to dispose of for such uses and purposes as they shall think fit); Ellis *v.* Selby, 1 Myl. & Cr. 286 (to executors for such charitable or other purposes as they shall think fit, without being accountable to any person); Buckle *v.* Bristow, 10 Jur. (N. S.) 1095; Yeap Cheah Neo *v.* Ong Cheng Neo, L. R. 6 P. C. 381 (to executors in trust that they, their heirs, successors, etc., may apply in such manner and to such parties as to them may appear just); *Re* Chapman, [1922] 2 Ch. 479, 8 Cornell L. Quar. 179 (to executor to be applied for charitable purposes as the testatrix should in writing direct, or to be retained by him for such objects and such purposes as he might in his discretion select, and to be at his own disposal; no such directions given); Fenton *v.* Nevin, Ir. L. R. 31 Ch. 478 (to executors to apply as they think fit); Anderson v. Smoke, 25 Ses. Cas. 493 (to A and B to dispose of in any way they should think proper); Haskell *v.* Staples, 116 Me. 103 (to A in trust to be distributed as he pleases); Davison *v.* Wyman, 214 Mass. 192 (to A to dispose of in his absolute discretion and according to his own judgment). See 37 L. R. A. (N. S.) 400; L. R. A. 1917D 821; 31 Harv. L. Rev. 661.

a memento from myself, of such articles to such of my friends as they, my trustees, shall select. All of said property, not so disposed of by them, my trustees are directed to sell and the proceeds of such sale or sales to become and be disposed of as a part of the residue of my estate." The question here reserved is whether or not the enumeration of chattels in this clause was intended to be restrictive or merely indicative of the variety of the personal property bequeathed. The question is immaterial if the bequest for the benefit of the testator's "friends" must fail for the want of certainty of the beneficiaries.

By the common law there cannot be a valid bequest to an indefinite person. There must be a beneficiary or a class of beneficiaries indicated in the will capable of coming into court and claiming the benefit of the bequest. Adve v. Smith, 44 Conn. 60. This principle applies to private but not to public trusts and charities. Harrington v. Pier, 105 Wis. 485; 28 R. C. L. 339, 340; Morice v. Bishop of Durham, 9 Ves. 399, 10 Ves. 521. The basis assigned for this distinction is the difference in the enforcibility of the two classes of trusts. In the former there being no definite *cestui que trust* to assert his right, there is no one who can compel performance, with the consequent unjust enrichment of the trustee; while in the case of the latter, performance is considered to be sufficiently secured by the authority of the attorney-general to invoke the power of the courts. The soundness of this distinction and the grounds upon which it rests, as applied to cases where the trustee is willing to act, has been questioned by distinguished authorities (5 Harv. L. Rev. 390, 394, 395; 65 Univ. Pa. L. Rev. 538, 540; 37 Harv. L. Rev. 687–8) and has been supported by other authorities of equal note (15 Harv. L. Rev. 510, 513–515, 530). It is, however, conceded by the former that, since the doctrine was first stated in Morice v. Bishop of Durham, *supra*, more than a century ago, it has remained unchallenged and has been followed by the courts in a practically unbroken line of decisions. 5 Harv. L. Rev. 392, 397; 65 Univ. Pa. L. Rev. 539; 37 Harv. L. Rev. 688; 26 R. C. L. 1189. Although it be conceded that the doctrine is not a legal necessity (15 Harv. L. Rev. 515) the fact that it has never been impeached affords strong evidence that in its practical application it has been generally found just and reasonable. This is a sufficient ground for continued adherence to the rule.

Nor is the force of the precedents impaired by the fact that, of necessity, some exceptions to the application of the doctrine have been recognized, as in the case of bequests to an executor to pay funeral expenses, which have been permitted to take effect notwithstanding the want of a beneficiary capable of invoking judicial power for their enforcement. 15 Harv. L. Rev. 515, 530; Gafney v. Kenison, 64 N. H. 354, 356. See Smart v. Durham, 77 N. H. 56, 58–60.

A more liberal rule as to what constitutes a charitable as distinguished from a private trust prevails here than that which obtained at the time the opinion in Morice v. Bishop of Durham, *supra*, was rendered. It would seem clear that it is in this respect only that Dean Ames treats Goodale v. Mooney, 60 N. H. 528, as drawing away from the earlier case. 5 Harv. L. Rev. 392. " An examination of the authorities generally will show that in modern times instances of testamentary gifts being rendered void for uncertainty have been of much less frequent occurrence than formerly, and that courts are now quite uniformly reluctant to admit uncertainty as a ground for avoiding the formal disposition of property." Gafney v. Kenison, 64 N. H. 354, 356. The court was there construing a bequest in trust for the relief of the most destitute of the testator's relatives, and the language above quoted had reference more particularly to testamentary provisions establishing charitable trusts as they are interpreted in this jurisdiction. Haynes v. Carr, 70 N. H. 463, 481; Carter v. Whitcomb, 74 N. H. 482, 487, and cases cited. The more liberal construction of charitable uses existing here is due in part to the facts that our courts of equity have original and inherent jurisdiction over charities independently of St. 43 Eliz., c. 4 (Goodale v. Mooney, *supra*, 533, 534; Webster v. Sughrow, 69 N. H. 380, 381), and are unrestrained by local statutes which in some states have " reduced charitable bequests to the level of legacies for private purposes." Haynes v. Carr, *supra*, 481, 482, 483; Glover v. Baker, 76 N. H. 393, 414, 417. The general object of a charitable use having been defined, or a means of fixing it having been provided by the testator, indefiniteness of the beneficiaries, if not an essential element of such a trust, at most does not render it void. Haynes v. Carr, *supra*, 481, 482, 484. In the case of purely private trusts, however, the common law rule that there must be a definite or ascertainable beneficiary has always prevailed in this jurisdiction.

" A gift to trustees to dispose of the same as they think fit is too uncertain to be carried out by the court." Theobald on Wills, 7th ed., 495; Fowler v. Garlike (1830), 1 R. & M. 232, 235; Ellis v. Selby (1836), 1 M. & Cr. 286, 298; Buckle v. Briston (1864), 10 Jur. N. S. 1095; Yeap Cheap Neo v. Ong Ching Neo (1875), L. R. 6 P. C. 381, 392; Fenton v. Nevin (1893), 31 L. R. Ir. 478; Olliffe v. Wells (1881), 130 Mass. 221, 223; Davison v. Wyman (1913), 214 Mass. 192; Blunt v. Taylor (1918), 230 Mass. 303.

That the foregoing is the established doctrine seems to be conceded, but it is contended in argument that it was not the intention of the testator by the ninth clause to create a trust, at least as respects the selected articles, but to make an absolute gift thereof to the trustees individually. It is suggested that the recital of the qualifications of the trustees may be considered as investing them with a personal and non-official character and that the word " trustees " is merely descriptive of the persons who had been earlier named as trustees and was not intended to limit the capacity in which they were to act here. Assuming this construction, the petitioners rely upon Gibbs *v.* Rumsey, 35 Eng. Rep. 311; Wells *v.* Doane, 3 Gray 201; Davison *v.* Wyman, 214 Mass. 192, 194; Norman *v.* Prince, 40 R. I. 402; Noane *v.* Larkine, 1 L. R. Ir. 103; Walter *v.* Walter, 113 N. Y. S. 465; Harvey *v.* Griggs, 12 Del. Ch. 232. It is a sufficient answer to this contention that the language of the ninth clause does not warrant the assumed construction. The assertion of the competency of the trustees wisely to distribute the articles in question by reason of their familiarity with the testator's property, wishes and friendships seems quite as consistent with a design to clothe them with a trusteeship as with an intention to impose upon them a moral obligation only. Blunt *v.* Taylor, 230 Mass. 303, 305. If, however, the recited qualifications had the significance ascribed to them, the language of the bequest is too plain to admit of the assumed construction. When the clause is elided of unnecessary verbiage the testator is made to say: " I give to my trustees my property (of the described class) in trust to make disposal of to such of my friends as they shall select." It is difficult to conceive of language more clearly disclosing an intention to create a trust. However, if the trust idea introduced by the words " trustees " and " in trust " were not controlling, all the evidence within the will confirms such idea. In the first clause of the will the testator nominates three trustees and an alternate in case of vacancy. Throughout the will these nominees are repeatedly and invariably referred to as " my trustees " whenever the testator is dealing with their trust duties. Whenever rights are conferred upon them individually, as happens in the fifth, sixth and eighth clauses, they are as invariably severally referred to solely by their individual names. The clause under consideration (ninth) expressly provides for the disposal of only a portion of the classified articles and imposes upon the trustees the duty of selling the balance thereof and adding the proceeds to the residue which they are to continue to hold and administer in their capacity as trustees. The proceeds thus accruing under this clause are expressly referred to in the eleventh clause in the enumeration of the ultimate funds to be distributed by them as trustees " in and among such charitable . . . institutions " as they shall select and designate. The conclusion is inescapable that there was no intention to bestow any part of the property enumerated in the ninth clause upon the trustees for their own benefit. This necessarily follows since the direction to make disposal is clearly as broad as the gift.

It is further sought to sustain the bequest as a power. The distinction apparently relied upon is that a power, unlike a trust (Goodale *v.* Mooney, 60 N. H. 528, 534), is not imperative and leaves the act to be done at the will of the donee of the power. 21 R. C. L. 773; 26 R. C. L. 1169. But the ninth clause by its terms imposes upon the trustees the imperative duty to dispose of the selected articles among the testator's friends. If, therefore, the authority bestowed by the testator by the use of a loose terminology may be called a power, it is not an optional power but a power coupled with a trust to which the principles incident to a trust so far as here involved clearly apply. People v. Kaiser, 306 Ill. 313, 137 N. E. 827, 828; 1 Tiffany, Real Property, s. 317; Greenough v. Wells, 10 Cush. 571; 576; Sweeney v. Warren, 127 N. Y. 426; Read v. Williams, 125 N. Y. 560; 26 R. C. L. 1169.

We must, therefore, conclude that this clause presents the case of an attempt to create a private trust and clearly falls within the principle of well-considered authorities. Nichols v. Allen, 130 Mass. 211, 212; Blunt v. Taylor, 230 Mass. 303, 305. In so far as the cases cited by the petitioners upon this phase of the case are not readily distinguishable from the case at bar they are in conflict with the great weight of authority.

The question presented, therefore, is whether or not the ninth clause provides for definite and ascertainable beneficiaries so that the bequest therein can be sustained as a private trust. In this state the identity of a beneficiary is a question of fact to be found from the language of the will construed in the light of all the competent evidence rather than by the application of arbitrary rules of law. It is believed that in no other jurisdiction is there greater liberality shown in seeking the intention of the testator in this, as in other particulars. Trustees v. Peaslee, 15 N. H. 317; Goodhue v. Clark, 37 N. H. 525, 532; Goodale v. Mooney, *supra;* Harriman v. Harriman, 59 N. H. 135; Galloway v. Babb, 77 N. H. 259, 260; Remick v. Merrill, 80 N. H. 225, 227; Adams v. Hospital, *ante*, 260. We find, however, no case in which our courts have sustained a gift where the testator has attempted to delegate to a trustee the arbitrary selection of the beneficiaries of his bounty through means of a private trust.

Like the direct legatees in a will, the beneficiaries under a trust may be designated by class. But in such case the class must be capable of delimitation, as " brothers and sisters," " children," " issue," " nephews and nieces." A bequest giving the executor authority to distribute his property " among his relatives and for benevolent objects in such sums as in their judgment shall be for the best " was sustained upon evidence within the will that by " relatives " the testator intended such of his relatives within the statute of distributions as were needy, and thus brought the bequest within the line of charitable gifts and excluded all others as individuals. Goodale v. Mooney, 60 N. H. 528, 536. See Portsmouth v. Shackford, 46 N. H. 423, 425; Gafney v. Kenison, 64 N. H. 354, 356. Where a testator bequeathed his stocks to be apportioned to his " relations " according to the discretion of the trustee, to be enjoyed by them after his decease, it was held to be a power to appoint amongst his relations who were next of kin under the statute of distribution. Varrell *v.* Wendell, 20 N. H. 431, 436. Likewise where a devise over after a particular estate was to the testator's "next of kin" *simpliciter*. Pinkham *v.* Blair, 57 N. H. 226, 243. See Snow *v.* Durgin, 70 N. H. 121, 122. Unless the will discloses a plain purpose to the contrary, the words "relatives" or "relations," to prevent gifts from being void for uncertainty, are commonly construed to mean those who would take under statutes of distribution or descent. 2 Schouler, Wills, *s.* 1008; Thompson, Wills, *s.* 181; Thompson *v.* Thornton, 197 Mass. 273; Drew *v.* Wakefield, 54 Me. 291, 298.

In the case now under consideration the *cestuis que trustent* are designated as the "friends" of the testator. The word "friends" unlike "relations" has no accepted statutory or other controlling limitations, and in fact has no precise sense at all. Friendship is a word of broad and varied application. It is commonly used to describe the undefinable relationships which exist not only between those connected by ties of kinship or marriage, but as well between strangers in blood, and which vary in degree from the greatest intimacy to an acquaintance more or less casual. "Friend" is sometimes used in contradistinction to "enemy." "A friendless man is an outlaw." Cowell, Bouvier. Although the word was formerly sometimes used as synonymous with relatives (5 Com. Dig. 336; Sugden on Powers (1823), 519), there is no evidence that it was so used here. The inference is to the contrary. The testator in the will refers to eight different persons, some of them already deceased, by the title of "friends." He never uses the appellation concurrently with "nephew" or "niece," which words occur several times in describing legatees. Nor is there anything to indicate that the word "friends" in the ninth clause was intended to apply only to those who had been thus referred to in the will. See Hall *v.* Wiggin, 67 N. H. 89, 90. There is no express evidence that the word is used in any restricted sense. The only implied limitation of the class is that fixed by the boundaries of the familiarity of the testator's trustees with his friendships. If such familiarity could be held to constitute such a line of demarcation as to define an ascertainable group, it is to be noted that the gift is not to such group as a class, the members of which are to take in some definite proposition (1 Jarman, Wills, 534; 1 Schouler, Wills, *s.* 1011) or according to their needs, but the disposition is to "such of my friends as they, my trustees, may select." No sufficient criterion is furnished to govern the selection of the individuals from the class. The assertion of the testator's confidence in the competency of his trustees " to wisely distribute some portion " of the enumerated articles " by reason of familiarity with the property, my wishes and friendships," does not furnish such a criterion. Where, after expressing confidence in the discretion of his executors and trustees, the testator gave the remainder of his estate to them " for certain purposes which I have made known to them " and authorized them to " make such distribution and division of my estate as I have indicated to them, and as they shall deem proper for the fulfillment of my wishes so well known to them," it was held that the trust created was not sufficiently definite for execution. Blunt v. Taylor, 230 Mass. 303, 305. A bequest to executors " particularly for the purpose of giving to any relatives of mine who without apparent reason I may have overlooked, such sum as may seem to them or him, under all the circumstances, fitting, suitable and proper," was held void for indefiniteness notwithstanding the aid of the statute of distributions. Minot v. Parker, 189 Mass. 176. A limitation over, after the death of the testatrix's son without heirs, " to whoever has been his best friend " was held to be " too indefinite for anyone to determine who was intended as the object of the testatrix's bounty." Early v. Arnold, 119 Va. 500. Where an executor was given direction to distribute in a manner calculated to carry out "wishes which I have expressed to him or may express to him " and such wishes had been orally communicated to the executor by the testator, the devise could not be given effect as against the next of kin. Olliffe v. Wells, 130 Mass. 221, 224, 225. Much less can effect be given to the uncommunicated wishes of the testator here.

It was the evident purpose of the testator to invest his trustees with the power after his death to make disposition of the enumerated articles among an undefined class with practically the same freedom and irresponsibility that he himself would have exercised if living; that is, to substitute for the will of the testator the will and discretion of the trustees. Such a purpose is in contravention of the policy of the statute which provides that " no will shall be effectual to pass any real or personal estate . . . unless made by a person . . . in writing, signed by the testator or by some one in his presence and by his direction, and attested and subscribed in his presence by three or more credible witnesses." P. L., c. 297, s. 2.

Where a gift is impressed with a trust ineffectively declared and incapable of taking effect because of the indefiniteness of the *cestui que trust*, the donee will hold the property in trust for the next taker under the will, or for the next of kin by way of a resulting trust. Varrell v. Wendell, 20 N. H. 431, 438; Lyford v. Laconia, 75 N. H. 220, 223; Sheedy v. Roach, 124 Mass. 472, 476; Nichols v. Allen, 130 Mass. 211, 212; Blunt v. Taylor, *supra;* Drew v. Wakefield, 54 Me. 291, 295. The trustees therefore hold title to the property enumerated in the paragraph under consideration, to be disposed of as a part of the residue, and the trustees are so advised. This conclusion makes it unnecessary to answer the question reserved, and it has not been considered. . . .

Case discharged.

All concurred.

MUSSETT v. BINGLE.

HIGH COURT OF JUSTICE, CHANCERY DIVISION. 1876.

W. N. (1876) 170.

IN this cause, which now came on upon further consideration, the testator had by his will directed his executors to apply 300*l*. in erecting a monument to his wife's first husband, and also to invest 200*l*. and apply the interest in keeping up the monument. It was admitted that the latter direction was bad, and the question argued was whether the former direction was good.

The trustees were ready to carry out the testator's wishes, but some of the beneficiaries contended that the first direction was void as purely " honorary."

THE VICE CHANCELLOR [HALL] said that the direction to the executors was a perfectly good one, and one which they were ready to perform, and it must be performed accordingly.[1]

REICHENBACH v. QUIN.

HIGH COURT OF JUSTICE, CHANCERY DIVISION, IRELAND. 1888.

21 L. R. Ir. 138.

JANE COWLEY, by her will, dated the 30th October, 1881, devised and bequeathed all her property to the defendants, upon the trusts therein declared; and, after giving certain other directions in respect thereof, proceeded: " And whatever interest I have in the lands of Newcastle, County Dublin, and in the premises in Bridge-

---

[1] Bequests for the erection of tombstones for third persons, as well as for the testator himself, have been upheld. In the absence of a statute, however, a bequest for the upkeep of a grave or tomb is invalid if for a period longer than the period of perpetuities. See Smith, Honorary Trusts and the Rule against Perpetuities, 30 Col. L. Rev. 60. A gift over from one charity to another on failure to keep a grave or tomb in repair has been upheld. *Re* Tyler, [1891] 3 Ch. 253; Roche *v.* M'Dermott, [1904] 1 I. R. 394. See *Re* Davies, [1915] 1 Ch. 543.

In *Re* Chardon, [1928] Ch. 464, a bequest to trustees to pay the income to a cemetery company as long as a grave is kept in repair was upheld.

A bequest for the upkeep of a public cemetery or one attached to a church or to erect headstones for graves of poor persons is charitable.

A trust to erect and maintain a monument to a public character may be charitable. Lawrence *v.* Prosser, 89 N. J. Eq. 248.

By statute in many states, trusts for the perpetual upkeep of graves or tombs are permitted. Under some of these statutes the bequest is valid only if made to a cemetery corporation. The amount is usually limited to a fixed sum or to a reasonable amount.

For a collection of cases, see Ames, 201n.; Scott, Cases on Trusts, 1 ed., 281-2; 1 Brit. Rul. Cas., 931; 11 C. J. 324; 4 A. L. R. 1124; 14 A. L. R. 118; 5 Ill. L. Rev. 379; 14 Ill. L. Rev. 531; 29 Yale L. Jour. 729; 30 Yale L. Jour. 96.

foot Street, Dublin, now forming a portion of Darcy's Brewery, I direct that the same shall be sold after my decease, if not previously disposed of, and out of the amount realized thereby, after payment of the expenses of such sale, I direct my trustees to apply 100*l*. towards having masses offered up in public in Ireland for the repose of my soul and the souls of my father, mother, brother, and sisters, and of my servant Anne Hagarty, and apply the balance towards such charitable purposes in Ireland as my trustees shall select." And the testatrix appointed the defendants executors of her said will.

The testatrix died on the 16th June, 1882, and on the 24th July, 1882, probate of her will was granted to the defendants.

Anne Hagarty survived the testatrix.

An action was brought by certain legatees under the said will, for the purpose of having the trusts thereof carried out and the personal estate of the testatrix administered, and a decree was, on the 4th March, 1885, made to that effect.

The case now came before the Court on further consideration of the Chief Clerk's certificate, and a question arose as to the validity of the bequest for masses.

THE VICE CHANCELLOR [CHATTERTON]. I am of opinion that there is no attempt to create a perpetuity by the trust in reference to the 100*l*. for masses. There is a direction in the will that the lands of Newcastle and the testatrix's premises in Bridgefoot Street should be sold, and that out of the amount realized her trustees should apply 100*l*. towards having masses offered up in public in Ireland for the repose of her soul and the souls of the other persons mentioned.

I do not consider that there is any attempt here to create a perpetuity, and on that ground — and I wish it to be understood that on that point only I give a decision — I shall declare that the gift is valid.[1]

[1] In many states it is held that a trust for the saying of masses is charitable. See Estate of Hamilton, 181 Cal. 758; Obrecht *v.* Pujos, 206 Ky. 751; Matter of Morris, 227 N. Y. 141. In England it was formerly held that a trust for the saying of masses is illegal as a superstitious use, but these decisions were reversed by the House of Lords in Bourne *v.* Keane, [1919] A. C. 815, 36 L. Quar. Rev. 152. As to the nature of the mass, see A. G. *v.* Delaney, I. R. 10 C. L. 104, 107.

In states in which a trust for the saying of masses is not held to be charitable, there is a difference of opinion whether a bequest for the saying of masses is valid.

For a collection of cases, see Ames, 210n.; Scott, Cases on Trusts, 1 ed., 283–4; 14 Ann. Cas. 1025; Ann. Cas. 1915D 1122; 14 L. R. A. (N. S.) 96.

In re DEAN.
COOPER–DEAN *v.* STEVENS.

HIGH COURT OF JUSTICE, CHANCERY DIVISION. 1889.

41 Ch. D. 552.

WILLIAM CLAPCOTT DEAN, by his will dated the 12th of November, 1887, devised all his freehold estates, subject to and charged with certain annuities, and with an annuity of 750*l.* thereinafter mentioned to his trustees, and to a term of fifty years thereinafter granted to his trustees, to the use of his trustees, for the term of one year from the day preceding his death, upon certain trusts, and, subject thereto, to the use of James Cooper (the plaintiff) for his life, with remainder to the use of the plaintiff's first and other sons, successively in tail male, with remainders over. The will continued: " I give to my trustees my eight horses and ponies (excluding cart horses) at Littledown, and also my hounds in the kennels there. And I charge my said freehold estates hereinbefore demised and devised, in priority to all other charges created by this my will, with the payment to my trustees for the term of fifty years commencing from my death, if any of the said horses and hounds shall so long live, of an annual sum of 750*l.* And I declare that my trustees shall apply the said annual sum payable to them under this clause in the maintenance of the said horses and hounds for the time being living, and in maintaining the stables, kennels, and buildings now inhabited by the said animals in such condition of repair as my trustees may deem fit; but this condition shall not imply any obligaton on my trustees to leave the said stables, kennels, and buildings in a state of repair at the determination of the said term; but I declare that my trustees shall not be bound to render any account of the application or expenditure of the said sum of 750*l.*, and any part thereof remaining unapplied shall be dealt with by them at their sole discretion." . . .

The testator died on the 3d of December, 1887. This was an originating summons by James Cooper, who had assumed the name of Dean, as plaintiff, against the trustees of the will, asking a declaration that the gift of the 750*l.* a year to the defendants for the purposes mentioned in the will was invalid, or, in the alternative, a declaration that the plaintiff was entitled under the trusts of the will to the balance from time to time in any year, commencing from the testator's death, of the 750*l.*, after making provision for the maintenance of the testator's horses, hounds, stables, kennels and buildings mentioned in his will.

NORTH, J. The first question is as to the validity of the provision made by the testator in favour of his horses and dogs. It is said that it is not valid; because (for this is the principal ground upon which it is put) neither a horse nor a dog could enforce the trust; and there is no person who could enforce it. It is obviously not a charity, because it is intended for the benefit of the particular animals mentioned and not for the benefit of animals generally, and it is quite distinguishable from the gift made in a subsequent part of the will to the Royal Society for the Prevention of Cruelty to Animals, which may well be a charity. In my opinion this provision for the particular horses and hounds referred to in the will is not, in any sense, a charity, and, if it were, of course the whole gift would fail, because it is a gift of an annuity arising out of land alone. But, in my opinion, as it is not a charity, there is nothing in the fact that the annuity arises out of land to prevent its being a good gift.

Then it is said, that there is no *cestui que trust* who can enforce the trust, and that the Court will not recognize a trust unless it is capable of being enforced by some one. I do not assent to that view. There is not the least doubt that a man may, if he pleases, give a legacy to trustees, upon trust to apply it in erecting a monument to himself, either in a church or in a churchyard, or even in unconsecrated ground, and I am not aware that such a trust is in any way invalid, although it is difficult to say who would be the *cestui que trust* of the monument. In the same way, I know of nothing to prevent a gift of a sum of money to trustees, upon trust to apply it for the repair of such a monument. In my opinion such a trust would be good, although the testator must be careful to limit the time for which it is to last, because, as it is not a charitable trust, unless it is to come to an end within the limits fixed by the rule against perpetuities, it would be illegal. But a trust to lay out a certain sum in building a monument, and the gift of another sum in trust to apply the same to keeping that monument in repair, say for ten years, is, in my opinion, a perfectly good trust, although I do not see who could ask the Court to enforce it. If persons beneficially interested in the estate could do so, then the present plaintiff can do so; but if such persons could not enforce the trust, still it cannot be said that the trust must fail because there is no one who can actively enforce it.

Is there then anything illegal or obnoxious to the law in the nature of the provision, that is, in the fact that it is not for human beings, but for horses and dogs? It is clearly settled by authority that a charity may be established for the benefit of horses and dogs, and therefore the making of a provision for horses and dogs, which is not a charity, cannot of itself be obnoxious to the law, provided, of course, that it is not to last for too long a period. Then there is what I consider an express authority upon this point in Mitford *v.* Reynolds, 16 Sim. 105. . . . I think I may treat that case as a decision by very high authority that such a provision is good, and, if I had felt any doubt about the point myself, I should have considered that authority as settling it, so far as I am concerned. There is nothing, therefore, in my opinion, to make the provision for the testator's horses and dogs void.

Then the next question is this: the gift is of an annuity of 750*l.*, during the lives and life (to put it shortly) of the horses and dogs, and the survivors or suvivor of them, and of course a time would arrive when the provision which the testator thought right to make for all the animals would be much more than sufficient for the three or the two or the one which might survive. The annuity is to cease entirely when the last survivor dies, and it is obvious that nothing like that sum could or would be applied for the benefit of the animals when they became greatly reduced in number. The question is, whether the annuity was given to the trustees beneficially. In my opinion it was not given to them beneficially. They are from beginning to end called "the trustees," and beyond all question the principal trust to be discharged by them under the will is that relating to the horses and dogs. There was, no doubt, the management trust, and that was a serious trust while it lasted, but it came to an end at the close of a year after the testator's death. These persons are described throughout as "trustees," and the annuity is given to them as trustees, and in my opinion they took it only as trustees, for the purpose of giving effect to the trust declared of it, and they did not themselves take any beneficial interest in it. The trust is for payment to the trustees. Then there is a declaration that the trustees shall apply the annual sum payable to them in the maintenance of the horses and dogs. They have a discretion as to the repair of the buildings, but they are not under any obligation to leave the buildings in a state of repair at the end of the term. Then come the words: "Any part thereof remaining unapplied shall be dealt with by them at their sole discretion." If the testator had meant them to take beneficially, it would have been very easy to say that "any surplus, after satisfying the aforesaid purposes, shall be divided among them for their own use." But the testator does nothing of that sort. He treats them as having a joint interest. The annuity is to be applied by them, it is to be subject to a discretion to be exercised by them, and, in my opinion, looking at the whole of the will, it was not intended to vest the annuity in them beneficially, but only to give them a discretion with respect to it as trustees. I have omitted to read these words, which form part of the sentence: "I declare that my trustees shall not be bound to render any account of the application or expenditure of the said sum of 750*l.*, and any part thereof remaining unapplied shall be dealt with by them at their sole discretion." In my opinion the testator intended by these words to give them complete latitude as to the keeping up of the stables and kennels for the horses and dogs, and as to the provision to be made for them; in other words, he intended that it should not be open to any one to say that the trustees had spent more than was reasonable for the purpose, or that the animals could have been very well maintained for a much less sum than had been actually spent upon them, and that the trustees must account for the surplus on that footing. In my opinion he intended to give them an absolute discretion as to how much of the annuity was to be applied in that way. His object was to make them absolute masters of the application of the money for the benefit of the horses and dogs, without their being liable to account for having spent more than a reasonable sum upon that object.

Then the final words of the will throw great light upon the testator's intention. It must be remembered that the trust is to come to an end when the last surviving horse or dog has died. It is clear, therefore, that he was considering the benefit of the animals which are the object of the trust, and, *primâ facie*, it was not his intention to benefit the trustees, as distinguished from the animals which they were to maintain, and the final words, I think, shew this very clearly. It is clear that he was not leaving to the trustees a discretion as to the way in which they were to deal with the animals, but he was himself giving directions as to what was to be done about them, and lastly, if a time should arrive at which the trustees should think that any of them should be killed, he gives specific directions as to the mode by which that end is to be accomplished, thus shewing that he was giving directions which they were bound to follow, and not merely giving them an absolute discretion to apply the money to those purposes or to any other purposes they pleased. Then, coming to the final words of the will, why does he give his personal estate not otherwise disposed of to the tenant for life of the real estate? For this reason: "In consideration of the maintenance of my horses, ponies, and hounds being a charge upon my said estates as aforesaid." Not in consideration of there being this charge of 750*l.* a year on the estates, but in consideration of the maintenance of the animals being a charge upon the estates. I have no doubt he was expressing his intention that the charge was to be for carrying out that purpose, and that he did not intend to confer any benefit upon the trustees.

I think it is not necessary to comment upon the cases which have been cited on this point, for there is no conflict between them; the only question is within which class of them the present case falls. In my opinion, upon this will, especially having regard to the last clause, it is clear that the testator is only making a provision for the maintenance of the animals, and that he does not intend to confer any benefit on the trustees.

I must, therefore, declare that the trustees do not take the surplus beneficially, but, upon the question whether the surplus belongs to the heir-at-law or to the devisee of the real estate, by reason of its not being raisable out of the estate, I say nothing in the absence of the heir-at-law.[1]

[1] Mitford *v.* Reynolds, 16 Sim. 105; Pettingall *v.* Pettingall, 11 L. J. Ch. 176; Skrine *v.* Walker, 3 Rich. Eq. (S. C.) 262, 269 (*semble*), *accord.* See 10 Mich. L. Rev. 31, 39.

SLAVES. A bequest of a slave for the purpose of emancipating him in a slave state was held to be against public policy. If the slave was to be taken to a free state and there emancipated, the bequest was not against public policy. In some states such a bequest was held to be charitable. In other states the direction of the testator was held to be enforceable by the slave. In other states it was held that although the direction was not enforceable (a corollary to the general rule that a slave could not be a *cestui que trust*, Ames 214), the legatee had power nevertheless to carry out the direction of the testator. See Ross *v*. Duncan, Freem. Ch. (Miss.) 587, *aff'd* 6 Miss. 305; Ames, 213n.; 15 Harv. L. Rev. 522.

BROWN *v*. BURDETT.

High Court of Justice, Chancery Division. 1882.

W. N. (1882) 134.[1]

TESTATRIX by a codicil, dated the 26th of September, 1868, to her will (dated the 22d of May, 1868), revoked a devise of a messuage, garden, orchard, and out-buildings at Gilmorton, Leicestershire, and gave and devised the same, and the furniture therein, to three trustees upon trust, immediately after her funeral, and upon the

---

In Willett *v*. Willett, 197 Ky. 663, 31 A. L. R. 426, a bequest for the support of a particular dog was held to be good although not charitable under a Kentucky statute permitting trusts for "humane" purposes.

In India it would seem that a trust for the maintenance of an idol is valid. See Pramatha Nath Mullick *v*. Pradyumna Kumar Mullick, L. R. 52 Ind. App. 245 (1925). See Duff, The Personality of an Idol, 3 Camb. L. Jour. 42.

In the following cases bequests for the benefit of animals were held to be charitable: *Re* Foveaux, [1895] 2 Ch. 501 (suppression of vivisection); *Re* Douglas, 35 Ch. D. 472 (to the Royal Society for the protection of animals liable to vivisection and to a home for lost dogs); University of London *v*. Yarrow, 1 DeG. & J. 72 (to found an institution for studying and curing maladies of quadrupeds or other animals useful to man); *Re* Wedgwood, [1915] 1 Ch. 113 (protection and benefit of animals); Armstrong *v*. Reeves, 25 L. R. Ir. 325 (suppression of vivisection); Swifte *v*. A. G., [1912] 1 I. R. 133 (home for starving and forsaken cats); Glasgow Society for Prevention of Cruelty to Animals *v*. National Anti-Vivisection Society, [1915] S. C. 757 (suppression of vivisection); *Re* Coleman's Estate, 167 Cal. 212 (bequest of $30,000 for the erection of a fountain for the benefit of thirsty animals); *Re* Graves' Estate, 242 Ill. 23 (drinking fountain for horses); Minns *v*. Billings, 183 Mass. 126 (society for prevention of cruelty to animals).

In A. G. *v*. Whorwood, 1 Ves. Sr. 534, a trust to feed sparrows was said not to be charitable. In *Re* Grove-Grady, [1929] 1 Ch. 557, a testatrix left money to establish and maintain an institution as a refuge to preserve from molestation or destruction by man "animals birds or other creatures not human," with a further provision that the institution should be controlled by antivivisectionists and opponents of sport involving the pursuit or death of animals. A majority of the Court of Appeal thought that the institution would not afford any advantage to animals that are useful to mankind or any protection from cruelty, and held that the trust failed.

[1] 21 Ch. D. 667, s. c.

same day, to cause the windows and doors of each room in the house (except the kitchen, back kitchen, middle attic, and hall), and of the coach-house, to be well and effectually bricked up from the outside, with every article of whatever kind that might be therein (including testatrix's clock), and cause the same to be repaired and renewed as occasion should require, and so bricked up to continue for the term of twenty years next after her decease; and subject to the trusts aforesaid, upon trust, to place in and remove at pleasure some respectable married couple in the occupation of the rooms excepted as above, and allow them to live therein, and occupy the same place and premises rent-free, in consideration of their taking care of the messuage and premises, and particularly the blockade to the doors and windows, and to see that the same were in no wise tampered or meddled with. From and after the expiration of the term of twenty years, testatrix devised the house and premises to a devisee for life, with remainder to another person in fee. By another codicil, dated the 22d of May, 1871, testatrix gave a number of other minute directions as to how the outside and inside doors, windows, and chimney tops were to be blocked up and covered in; and directed that the married couple should pay a nominal rent of one halfpenny a week.

Testatrix died on the 16th of January, 1872.

THE VICE-CHANCELLOR [BACON] held that there was an intestacy as to the term of twenty years in the house, garden, out-buildings, and furniture.[1]

[1] In Kelly v. Nichols, 17 R. I. 306, a bequest of a favorite clock of the testator to trustees with a direction that it should be kept in repair "so long as they might think it proper and practical" was held invalid.

In M'Caig v. University of Glasgow, [1907] S. C. 231, the court held invalid a trust for the purpose of erecting and maintaining forever artistic towers and monuments and statutes of the testator and various members of his family on land devised by him. A similar bequest was held invalid in M'Caig's Trustees v. Kirk-Session, [1915] S. C. 426. In the former case, Lord Kyllachy said (p. 242): "I consider that if it is not unlawful, it ought to be unlawful, to dedicate by testamentary disposition, for all time, or for a length of time, the whole income of a large estate — real and personal — to objects of no utility, private or public, objects which benefit nobody, and which have no other purpose or use than that of perpetuating at great cost, and in an absurd manner, the idiosyncrasies of an eccentric testator. I doubt much whether a bequest of that character is a lawful exercise of the *testamenti factio*. Indeed, I suppose it would be hardly contended to be so if the purposes, say of the trust here, were to be slightly varied, and the trustees were, for instance, directed to lay the truster's estate waste, and to keep it so; or to turn the income of the estate into money, and throw the money yearly into the sea; or to expend the income in annual or monthly funeral services in the testator's memory; or to expend it in discharging from prominent points upon the estate, salvoes of artillery upon the birthdays of the testator, and his brothers and sisters. Such purposes would hardly, I think, be alleged to be consistent with public policy; and I am by no means satisfied that the purposes which we have here before us are in a better position."

Compare Kennedy v. Kennedy, [1914] A. C. 215, where a devise in trust

KAIN v. GIBBONEY.

SUPREME COURT OF THE UNITED STATES. 1879.

101 U. S. 362.

APPEAL from the Circuit Court of the United States for the Western District of Virginia.

Eliza Matthews made a will, dated Dec. 9, 1854, which contained the following provision: —

"In the event that I may hereafter become a member of any of the religious communities attached to the Roman Catholic Church, and am such at the time of my death, then it is my will that all the foregoing bequests and legacies be void, and that my executors hereinafter named shall pay over the whole of the property or other thing, after disposing of the same for money, to the aforesaid Richard V. Wheelan, bishop as aforesaid, or his successor in said dignity, who is hereby constituted a trustee for the benefit of the community of which I may be a member, the said property or money to be expended by the said trustee for the use and benefit of said community."

After making her will, she became a member of an unincorporated religious community attached to the Roman Catholic Church, known as the "Sisters of Saint Joseph," and was such at the time of her death.

The will was admitted to probate in 1861.

Thereafter Wheelan brought this suit, in the court below, against said Elizabeth, to recover the residue of that estate, and alleged that said Robert had never invested the fund which he received as the trustee of Eliza, but had converted it to his own use, except the bond of Johnson.

Wheelan died, and John J. Kain having been duly appointed Bishop of Wheeling, the suit was revived in his name.

The bill was, on demurrer, dismissed, and Kain appealed to this court.[1]

STRONG, J. The bequest which the complainant seeks to enforce by this bill was an attempted testamentary disposition under the law of Virginia, and the matter now to be determined is whether by that law it can be sustained. It may be conceded that, notwithstanding its uncertainty, a legacy given in the words of this will, if for a charity, would be held valid in England, and in most of the States of the Union. But we have now to inquire, What is the law of Virginia? The gift was made to "Richard V. Wheelan, Bishop of

---

to maintain the testator's residence "in the manner in which it has been heretofore maintained" was held invalid as infringing the rule against perpetuities.

[1] The statement of facts is abridged.

Wheeling, or to his successor in said dignity." It was, therefore, in effect, a gift to the office of the Bishop of Wheeling. Neither Bishop Wheelan, nor any bishop succeeding him, was intended to derive any private advantage from it. Nothing was intended to vest in him but the trust, and that was required to be executed by whomsoever should fill the office of bishop, only so long as he should fill it, and executed in his character of bishop, not as an individual. The bequest was practically to a bishopric, and as a bishop is not a corporation sole, it may be doubted whether, at the decease of the testatrix, there was any person capable of taking it. True it is, that generally a trust will not be allowed to fail for want of a trustee: courts of equity will supply one. But if it could be conceded that Wheelan was, in his lifetime, capable of taking the bequest, and that Bishop Kain is capable of taking and holding after the death of his predecessor, a greater difficulty is found in the uncertainty of the beneficiaries for whose use the trust was created. In the words of the will, they are a religious community, of which the testatrix contemplated she might die a member. She died a member of a religious community attached to the Roman Catholic Church, known as the "Sisters of St. Joseph." That is an unincorporated association, and it is the association as such, and not the individual members who composed it, when the testatrix died, which is declared to be the beneficiary. Nor is it the community attached to any local church which is designated, but a community attached to the Roman Catholic Church, wherever that church may exist. Its members must be constantly changing, and it must always be uncertain who may be its members at any given time. No member can ever claim any individual benefit from the bequest, or assert that she is a *cestui que trust;* and the community having no legal existence, can never have a standing in court to call the trustees to account. This bequest is, therefore, plainly invalid, unless it can be supported as a charity. And it is far from evident that it is a gift for charitable uses. It looks more like private bounty. Charity is generally defined as a gift for a public use. Such is its legal meaning. Here the beneficial interest is given to a religious community, but not declared to be for religious uses. There is nothing in the will to show that aid to the poor, or aid to learning, or aid to religion, or to any humane object was intended.[1] . . .

Decree affirmed.[2]

[1] A part of the opinion of the court is omitted in which it is held that even if the bequest were charitable, it nevertheless failed because under the law of Virginia charities were not upheld to a greater extent than ordinary trusts. The Virginia law on this point has now been changed by statute. Acts 1914, 414.

[2] A trust for an unincorporated non-charitable association is invalid if it is to continue for a longer period than twenty-one years after the expiration of lives in being at its creation. *Re* Amos, [1891] 3 Ch. 159 (trade union); *Re* Clifford, 28 T. L. R. 57, 81 L. J. Ch. 220 (society to preserve and improve

In re DRUMMOND.
ASHWORTH v. DRUMMOND.
HIGH COURT OF JUSTICE, CHANCERY DIVISION. 1914.
[1914] 2 Ch. 90.

By his will, dated November 24, 1911, James Drummond . . . devised and bequeathed all his real and personal estate not thereby otherwise disposed of unto his trustees upon trust for sale and conversion, and, subject to the payments therein mentioned, to stand possessed of the residue of the moneys produced by such sale and conversion upon trust for the Old Bradfordians' Club, London (being a club instituted by Bradford Grammar School old boys), the receipt of the treasurer for the time being of the club to be a sufficient discharge to his trustees.

By a codicil to his will, dated December 2, 1911, the testator, after reciting, *inter alia*, the residuary devise and bequest, thereby declared that he desired that the said moneys should be utilized by the club for such purpose as the committee for the time being might determine, the object and intent of the bequest being to benefit old boys of the Bradford Grammar School residing in London or members of the club, and to enable the committee, if possible, to acquire premises to be used as a club-house for the use of the members, being old boys of the Bradford Grammar School, with power to the committee to make rules and regulations as to residence in or use of the same, and further that it was the object of the bequest that the moneys should be utilized in founding scholarships or otherwise in such manner as the committee for the time being should think best in the interests of the club, or the school.

The testator died on December 6, 1911, and his will with the codicil thereto was duly proved by the plaintiffs as the executors thereof, the other executor having renounced probate. . . .

Questions having arisen as to the true construction of the will and codicil in reference to . . . the effect of the gift of the residuary real and personal estate, an originating summons was taken out on December 3, 1913, by the trustees of the will for the determination of the questions. . . . The Old Bradfordians' Club was founded

---

angling facilities for the benefit of its members); Stewart v. Greene, I. R. 5 Eq. 470 (religious society); Morrow v. M'Conville, 11 L. R. Ir. 236 (religious society), *accord*. But see the explanation of these cases in Gray, Rule ag. Perp., App. H.

In the following cases also the trust was held invalid: Carne v. Long, 2 DeG. F. & J. 75 (library association); *Re* Dutton, 4 Ex. D. 54 (Atheneum and Mechanics Institute); Thomson v. Shakespear, 1 DeG. F. & J. 399 (trust to preserve as a museum Shakespeare's house which was privately owned); Browne v. King, 17 L. R. Ir. 488 (trust for the benefit of tenantry of donor).

in 1899 to encourage social intercourse amongst the old boys of the Grammar School and had been managed by a committee elected by members of the club. On January 3, 1913, the defendant company the Old Bradfordians' Club (London), Limited, was registered under the Companies Act, 1908, to take over the assets and property of the club, and the objects were precisely similar, the management of the club being vested in the committee.[1]

EVE, J., said that he could not hold, as the result of the will and codicil together, that the residuary gift of realty and personalty for the Old Bradfordians' Club was a gift to the members individually. There was, in his opinion, a trust, but there was abundant authority for holding that it was not such a trust as would render the legacy void as tending to a perpetuity: *In re* Clarke, [1901] 2 Ch. 110. The legacy was not subject to any trust which would prevent the committee of the club from spending it in any manner they might decide for the benefit of the class intended. In his opinion, therefore, there was a valid gift to the club for such purposes as the committee should determine for the benefit of the old boys or members of the club.[2]

[1] The statement of facts is abridged and a part of the opinion is omitted.
[2] *Re* Clarke [1901] 2 Ch. 110 (association of veterans of the Crimean War); *Re* Prevost, [1930] 2 Ch. 383 (library association); Bancroft *v.* Cook, 264 Mass. 343 (college fraternity), *accord.* See Ruddick *v.* Albertson, 154 Cal. 640 (Indian tribe).

In *Re* Clarke, *supra,* the court said (p. 114): " It is, I think, established by the authorities that a gift to a perpetual institution not charitable is not necessarily bad. The test, or one test, appears to be, will the legacy when paid be subject to any trust which will prevent the existing members of the association from spending it as they please? If not, the gift is good. So also if the gift is to be construed as a gift to or for the benefit of the individual members of the association. On the other hand, if it appears that the legacy is one which by the terms of the gift, or which by reason of the constitution of the association in whose favour it is made, tends to a perpetuity, the gift is bad."

A bequest for the individual members of a religious or other charitable organization as constituted at the time of the testator's death is valid but is not charitable. Cocks *v.* Manners, 12 Eq. 574; *Re* Smith, [1914] 1 Ch. 937; Stewart *v.* Green, I. R. 5 Eq. 470; *Re* Delany's Estate, 9 L. R. Ir. 226; Morrow *v.* M'Conville, 11 L. R. Ir. 236; *Re* Wilkinson's Trusts, 19 L. R. Ir. 531; Bradshaw *v.* Jackman, 21 L. R. Ir. 12.

In England many clubs and similar associations have been registered under the provisions of Companies Act, 1867 (30 & 31 Vict. c. 131) sec. 23; Companies Consolidation Act, 1908 (8 Edw. VII c. 69) sec. 20. See 33 L. Quar. Rev. 356. See also Friendly Societies Act, 1875 (38 & 39 Vict. c. 60); Friendly Societies Act, 1896 (59 & 60 Vict. c. 25). In the United States there are usually general laws under which such associations may incorporate.

As to trusts for unincorporated associations, see further 3 Maitland, Collected Papers, 271–284, 321–404; Carr, Corporations, chap. 17; Wrightington, Unincorporated Associations; Smith, Law of Associations; Wertheimer, Law of Clubs; Laski, Personality of Associations, 29 Harv. L. Rev. 404. See 41 Harv. L. Rev. 898; 42 Harv. L. Rev. 813.

CHAPTER IV.
CHARITABLE TRUSTS.

STATUTE OF CHARITABLE USES.
43 Eliz. c. 4 (1601).

AN act to redress the mis-employment of lands, goods and stocks of money heretofore given to certain charitable uses.

Whereas lands, tenements, rents, annuities, profits, hereditaments, goods, chattels, money and stocks of money, have been heretofore given, limited, appointed and assigned, as well by the Queen's most excellent Majesty, and her most noble progenitors, as by sundry other well-disposed persons; some for relief of aged, impotent and poor people, some for maintenance of sick and maimed soldiers and mariners, schools of learning, free schools, and scholars in universities, some for repair of bridges, ports, havens, causeways, churches, sea-banks and highways, some for education and preferment of orphans, some for or towards relief, stock or maintenance for houses of correction, some for marriages of poor maids, some for supportation, aid and help of young tradesmen, handicraftsmen and persons decayed, and others for relief or redemption of prisoners or captives, and for aid or ease of any poor inhabitants concerning payments of fifteens, setting out of soldiers and other taxes; which lands, tenements, rents, annuities, profits, hereditaments, goods, chattels, money and stocks of money, nevertheless have not been employed according to the charitable intent of the givers and founders thereof, by reason of frauds, breaches of trust, and negligence in those that should pay, deliver and employ the same: for redress and remedy whereof,

Be it enacted by authority of this present parliament, That it shall and may be lawful to and for the Lord Chancellor . . . from time to time to award commissions under the Great Seal of England, . . . to the bishop of every several diocese . . . and to other persons of good and sound behaviour, authorizing them . . . to enquire . . . of all and singular such gifts, . . . and of the abuses, breaches of trusts, . . . or mis-government of any lands, . . . goods, chattels, money or stocks of money, heretofore given, . . . or which hereafter shall be given, . . . for any of the charitable and godly uses before rehearsed: . . . and upon such enquiry . . . set down such orders, judgments and decrees, as the said lands, . . . goods, chattels, money and stocks of money, may be duly and faithfully employed, to and for such of the charitable uses and intents before rehearsed respectively, for which they were given . . . by the donors and founders thereof: which orders, judgments and decrees, not being contrary or repugnant to the orders, statutes or decrees of the donors or founders, shall by the authority of this present parliament stand firm and good, . . . and shall be executed accordingly, until the same shall be undone or altered by the Lord Chancellor . . . upon complaint by any party grieved to be made to them.[1] . . .

THE TRUSTEES OF THE PHILADELPHIA BAPTIST ASSOCIATION *v.* HART'S EXECUTORS.

Supreme Court of the United States. 1819.

4 Wheat. 1.

In the year 1790, Silas Hart, a citizen and resident of Virginia, made his last will in writing, which contains the following bequest. " Item, what shall remain of my military certificates at the time of my decease, both principal and interest, I give and bequeath to the Baptist association that for ordinary meets at Philadelphia annually, which I allow to be a perpetual fund for the education of youths of the Baptist denomination, who shall appear promising for the ministry, always giving a preference to the descendants of my father's family." In 1792 the legislature of Virginia passed an act, repealing all English statutes, including that of the 43 Eliz. c. 4. In the year 1795 the testator died. The Baptist Association, which met annually at Philadelphia, had existed as a regularly organized body for many years before the date of this will, and was composed of the clergy of several Baptist churches of different States, and of an annual deputation of laymen from the same churches. It was not incorporated until the year 1797, when it received a charter from the legislature of Pennsylvania, incorporating it by the name of " The Trustees of the Philadelphia Baptist Association." The executors having refused to pay the legacy, this suit was instituted in the Circuit Court for the district of Virginia, by the corporation, and by those individuals who were members of the Association at the death of the testator. On the trial of the cause, the judges of that Court were divided in opinion on the question, whether the plaintiffs were capable of taking under this will? Which point was, therefore, certified to this Court.

Marshall, C. J. It was obviously the intention of the testator that the Association should take in its character as an Association; and should, in that character, perform the trust created by the will. The members composing it must be perpetually changing; but, however they might change, it is " The Baptist Association that for

[1] The provisions of this statute, *except the preamble,* were repealed by Mortmain and Charitable Uses Act, 1888 (51 & 52 Vict. c. 42).

ordinary meets at Philadelphia annually," which is to take and manage the "perpetual fund" intended to be created by this will. This Association is described with sufficient accuracy to be clearly understood; but, not being incorporated, is incapable of taking this trust as a society. Can the bequest be taken by the individuals who composed the Association at the death of the testator?

The Court is decidedly of opinion that it cannot. No private advantage is intended for them. Nothing was intended to pass to them but the trust; and that they are not authorized to execute as individuals. It is the Association for ever, not the individuals, who, at the time of his death, might compose the Association, and their representatives, who are to manage this "perpetual fund."

At the death of the testator, then, there were no persons in existence who were capable of taking this bequest. Does the subsequent incorporation of the Association give it this capacity?

The rules of law compel the Court to answer this question in the negative. The bequest was intended for a society which was not at the time, and might never be, capable of taking it. According to law, it is gone for ever. The legacy is void; and the property vests, if not otherwise disposed of by the will, in the next of kin. A body corporate afterwards created, had it even fitted the description of the will, cannot devest this interest, and claim it for their corporation.

There being no persons who can claim the right to execute this trust, are there any who, upon the general principles of equity, can entitle themselves to its benefits? Are there any to whom this legacy, were it not a charity, could be decreed?

This question will not admit of discussion. Those for whose ultimate benefit the legacy was intended, are to be designated and selected by the trustees. It could not be intended for the education of all the youths of the Baptist denomination who were designed for the ministry; nor for those who were the descendants of his father, unless, in the opinion of the trustees, they should appear promising. These trustees being incapable of executing this trust, or even of taking it on themselves, the selection can never be made, nor the persons designated who might take beneficially.

Though this question be answered in the negative, we must still inquire, whether the character of this legacy, as a charity, will entitle it to the protection of this Court?

That such a legacy would be sustained in England, is admitted. But it is contended for the executors that it would be sustained in virtue of the statute of the 43d of Elizabeth, or of the prerogative of the crown, or of both; and not in virtue of those rules by which a Court of Equity, exercising its ordinary powers, is governed. Should these propositions be true, it is farther contended, that the statute of Elizabeth does not extend to the case, and that the equitable jurisdiction of the Courts of the Union does not extend to cases not within the ordinary powers of a Court of Equity.

On the part of the plaintiffs, it is contended, that the peculiar law of charities does not originate in the statute of Elizabeth. Had lands been conveyed in trust, previous to the statute, for such purposes as are expressed in this will, the devise, it is said, would have been good at law; and, of consequence, a Court of Chancery would have enforced the trust in virtue of its general powers. In support of this proposition, it has been said, that the statute of Elizabeth does not even profess to give any validity to devises or legacies, of any description, not before good, but only furnishes a new and more convenient mode for discovering and enforcing them; and that the royal prerogative applies to those cases only where the objects of the trusts are entirely indefinite; as a bequest generally to charity, or to the poor.

It is certainly true, that the statute does not, in terms, profess to give validity to bequests acknowledged not before to have been valid. It is also true, that it seems to proceed on the idea that the trusts it is intended to enforce, ought, in conscience, independent of the statute, to be carried into execution. It is, however, not to be denied, that if, at the time, no remedy existed in any of the cases described, the statute gives one. A brief analysis of the act will support this proposition. . . .

The general principle, that a vague legacy, the object of which is indefinite, cannot be established in a court of equity, is admitted. It follows, that he who contends that charities formed originally an exception to the rule, must prove the proposition. There being no reported cases on the point anterior to the statute, recourse is had to elementary writers, or to the opinions given by judges of modern times.

No elementary writers sustain this exception as a part of the law of England. . . .

If, before the statute of Elizabeth, legacies like that under consideration would have been established, on information filed in the name of the Attorney General, it would furnish a strong argument for the opinion, that some principle was recognised prior to that statute, which gave validity to such legacies.

But although we find *dicta* of Judges, asserting that it was usual before the statute of Elizabeth, to establish charities, by means of an information filed by the Attorney General; we find no *dictum*, that charities could be established on such information, where the conveyance was defective, or the donation was so vaguely expressed, that the donee, if not a charity, would be incapable of taking; and the thing given would vest in the heir or next of kin. All the cases which have been cited, where charities have been established, under the statute, that were deemed invalid independent of it, contradict this position.

In construing that statute, in a preceding part of this opinion, it was shown that its enactments are sufficient to establish charities not previously valid. It affords, then, a broad foundation for the superstructure which has been erected on it. And, although many of the cases go, perhaps, too far; yet, on a review of the authorities, we think they are to be considered as constructions of the statute not entirely to be justified, rather than as proving the existence of some other principle concealed in a dark and remote antiquity, and giving a rule in cases of charity which forms an exception to the general principles of our law. . . .

CERTIFICATE. This cause came on to be heard on the transcript of the record of the Court of the United States, for the Fifth Circuit, and the District of Virginia, and on the question therein stated, on which the Judges of that Court were divided in opinion, and which was adjourned to this Court, and was argued by counsel: On consideration whereof, this Court is of opinion, that the plaintiffs are incapable of taking the legacy for which this suit was instituted; which opinion is ordered to be certified to the said Circuit Court.[1]

VIDAL v. GIRARD'S EXECUTORS.

SUPREME COURT OF THE UNITED STATES. 1844.

2 How. 127.

THIS case came up by appeal from the Circuit Court of the United States, sitting as a court of equity, for the eastern district of Pennsylvania.

The object of the bill filed in the court below was to set aside a part of the will of the late Stephen Girard, under the following circumstances: —

Girard, a native of France, was born about the middle of the last century. Shortly before the declaration of independence he came to the United States, and before the peace of 1783 was a resident of the city of Philadelphia, where he died, in December, 1831, a widower and without issue. Besides some real estate of small value near Bordeaux, he was, at his death, the owner of real estate in this country which had cost him upwards of $1,700,000, and of personal property worth not less than $5,000,000. His nearest collateral relations were, a brother, one of the original complainants, a niece, the other complainant, who was the only issue of a deceased sister, and three nieces who were defendants, the daughters of a deceased brother.

The will of Mr. Girard, with two codicils, was proved at Philadelphia on 31st of December, 1831.

After sundry legacies and devises of real property to various persons and corporations, the will proceeds thus: —

[1] See the concurring opinion of Story, J., 3 Pet. (U. S.) 481.

"XX. And, whereas, I have been for a long time impressed with the importance of educating the poor, and of placing them, by the early cultivation of their minds and the developments of their moral principles, above the many temptations, to which, through poverty and ignorance, they are exposed; and I am particularly desirous to provide for such a number of poor male white orphan children, as can be trained in one institution, a better education, as well as a more comfortable maintenance, than they usually receive from the application of the public funds: . . . Now, I do give, devise and bequeath all the residue and remainder of my real and personal estate of every sort and kind wheresoever situate, (the real estate in Pennsylvania charged aforesaid,) unto 'the Mayor, Aldermen, and Citizens of Philadelphia,' their successors and assigns, in trust, to and for the several uses, intents, and purposes hereinafter mentioned and declared of and concerning the same. . . .

"XXI. And so far as regards the residue of my personal estate, in trust, as to two millions of dollars, part thereof, to apply and expend so much of that sum as may be necessary, in erecting, as soon as practicably may be, in the centre of my square of ground between High and Chestnut streets, and Eleventh and Twelfth streets, in the city of Philadelphia, (which square of ground I hereby devote for the purposes hereinafter stated, and for no other, for ever), a permanent college, with suitable out-buildings, sufficiently spacious for the residence and accommodation of at least three hundred scholars, and the requisite teachers and other persons necessary in such an institution as I direct to be established, and in supplying the said college and out-buildings with decent and suitable furniture, as well as books and all things needful to carry into effect my general design. . . .

"When the college and appurtenances shall have been constructed, and supplied with plain and suitable furniture and books, philosophical and experimental instruments and apparatus, and all other matters needful to carry my general design into execution, the income, issues, and profits of so much of the said sum of two millions of dollars as shall remain unexpended, shall be applied to maintain the said college according to my directions. . . .

"As many poor white male orphans, between the ages of six and ten years, as the said income shall be adequate to maintain, shall be introduced into the college as soon as possible; and from time to time as there may be vacancies, or as increased ability from income may warrant, others shall be introduced. . . .

"I enjoin and require that no ecclesiastic, missionary, or minister of any sect whatsoever, shall ever hold or exercise any station or duty whatever in the said college; nor shall any such person ever be admitted for any purpose, or as a visitor, within the premises appropriated to the purposes of the said college.

"In making this restriction, I do not mean to cast any reflection upon any sect or person whatsoever; but, as there is such a multitude of sects, and such a diversity of opinion amongst them, I desire to keep the tender minds of the orphans, who are to derive advantage from this bequest, free from the excitement which clashing doctrines and sectarian controversy are so apt to produce; my desire is, that all the instructors and teachers in the college shall take pains to instil into the minds of the scholars the purest principles of morality, so that, on their entrance into active life, they may, from inclination and habit, evince benevolence towards their fellow-creatures, and a love of truth, sobriety, and industry, adopting at the same time such religious tenets as their matured reason may enable them to prefer. . . ." . . .

By an act, passed on the 4th of April, 1832, entitled " A supplement to the act entitled ' An act to enable the Mayor, Aldermen, and Citizens of Philadelphia, to carry into effect certain improvements, and to execute certain trusts,' " the Select and Common Council of the city of Philadelphia, are authorized to provide by ordinance, or otherwise, for the election or appointment of such officers or agents as they may deem essential to the due execution of the duties and trusts enjoined and created by the will of the late Stephen Girard. . . .

Under the act of 1832, the corporation of Philadelphia passed an ordinance providing for the building of the college, and the board of trustees created thereby was organized in March, 1833. The building was commenced and carried on from year to year under the direction of the authorities appointed in this ordinance.

On the 28th April, 1841, the cause came on for hearing in the Circuit Court upon the bill, amended bill, and bill of revivor, answers, replications, depositions, and exhibits, when, after argument of counsel, it was ordered, adjudged, and decreed, that the complainants' bill be dismissed with costs.

The complainants appealed to this court.

STORY, J.[1] . . . We are, then, led directly to the consideration of the question which has been so elaborately argued at the bar, as to the validity of the trusts for the erection of the college, according to the requirements and regulations of the will of the testator. That the trusts are of an eleemosynary nature and charitable uses in a judicial sense, we entertain no doubt. Not only are charities for the maintenance and relief of the poor, sick, and impotent, chari-

[1] A part of the statement of facts and the exhaustive and learned arguments of Jones and Webster for the complainants and Binney and Sergeant for the defendants and a large part of the opinion of the court are omitted.

For interesting sidelights on the principal case which excited great interest at the time on account of the amount involved and the eminence of counsel, as well as the importance of the questions of law involved, see Binney, Life of Horace Binney, 213–234. For the arguments of the defendants' counsel in the principal case, see Girard Will Case, published in 1854 by order of the commissioners of the Girard estates.

ties in the sense of the common law, but also donations given for the establishment of colleges, schools and seminaries of learning, and especially such as are for the education of orphans and poor scholars.

The statute of the 43 of Elizabeth, ch. 4, has been adjudged by the Supreme Court of Pennsylvania not to be in force in that state. But then it has been solemnly and recently adjudged by the same court, in the case of Zimmerman v. Andres, 6 W. & S. 218, that " it is so considered rather on account of the inapplicability of its regulations as to the modes of proceeding, than in reference to its conservative provisions." " These have been in force here by common usage and constitutional recognition; and not only these, but the more extensive range of charitable uses which chancery supported before that statute and beyond it." Nor is this any new doctrine in that court; for it was formally promulgated in the case of Witman v. Lex, 17 Serg. & Rawle, 88, at a much earlier period (1827).

Several objections have been taken to the present bequest to extract it from the reach of these decisions. In the first place, that the corporation of the city is incapable by law of taking the donation for such trusts. This objection has been already sufficiently considered. In the next place, it is said, that the beneficiaries who are to receive the benefit of the charity are too uncertain and indefinite to allow the bequest to have any legal effect, and hence the donation is void, and the property results to the heirs. And in support of this argument we are pressed by the argument that charities of such an indefinite nature are not good at the common law, (which is admitted on all sides to be the law of Pennsylvania, so far as it is applicable to its institutions and constitutional organization and civil rights and privileges) and hence the charity fails; and the decision of this court in the case of the trustees of the Philadelphia Baptist Association v. Hart's Executors, 4 Wheat. 1, is strongly relied on as fully in point. There are two circumstances which materially distinguish that case from the one now before the court. The first is, that that case arose under the law of Virginia, in which state the statute of 43 Elizabeth, ch. 4, had been expressly and entirely abolished by the legislature, so that no aid whatsoever could be derived from its provisions to sustain the bequest. The second is, that the donees (the trustees) were an unincorporated association, which had no legal capacity to take and hold the donation in succession for the purposes of the trust, and the beneficiaries also were uncertain and indefinite. Both circumstances, therefore, concurred; a donation to trustees incapable of taking, and beneficiaries uncertain and indefinite. The court, upon that occasion, went into an elaborate examination of the doctrine of the common law on the subject of charities, antecedent to and independent of the statute of 43 Elizabeth, ch. 4, for that was still the common law of Virginia. Upon a thorough examination of all the authorities and all the lights, (certainly in no small degree shadowy, obscure, and flickering,) the court came to the conclusion that, at the common law, no donation to charity could be enforced in chancery, where both of these circumstances, or rather, where both of these defects occurred. . . .

But very strong additional light has been thrown upon this subject by the recent publications of the Commissioners on the public Records in England, which contain a very curious and interesting collection of the chancery records in the reign of Queen Elizabeth, and in the earlier reigns. Among these are found many cases in which the Court of Chancery entertained jurisdiction over charities long before the statute of 43 Elizabeth; and some fifty of these cases, extracted from the printed calendars, have been laid before us. They establish in the most satisfactory and conclusive manner that cases of charities where there were trustees appointed for general and indefinite charities, as well as for specific charities, were familiarly known to, and acted upon, and enforced in the Court of Chancery. In some of these cases the charities were not only of an uncertain and indefinite nature, but, as far as we can gather from the imperfect statement in the printed records, they were also cases where there were either no trustees appointed, or the trustees were not competent to take. These records, therefore, do in a remarkable manner, confirm the opinions of Sir Joseph Jekyll, Lord Northington, Lord Chief Justice Wilmot, Lord Redesdale, and Lord Chancellor Sugden. Whatever doubts, therefore, might properly be entertained upon the subject when the case of the Trustees of the Philadelphia Baptist Association *v.* Hart's Executors, 4 Wheat. 1, was before this court (1819), those doubts are entirely removed by the late and more satisfactory sources of information to which we have alluded.

If, then, this be the true state of the common law on the subject of charities, it would, upon the general principle already suggested, be a part of the common law of Pennsylvania. It would be no answer to say, that if so it was dormant, and that no court possessing equity powers now exists, or has existed in Pennsylvania, capable of enforcing such trusts. The trusts would nevertheless be valid in point of law; and remedies may from time to time be applied by the legislature to supply the defects. It is no proof of the non-existence of equitable rights, that there exists no adequate legal remedy to enforce them. They may during the time slumber, but they are not dead.[1]

But the very point of the positive existence of the law of charities in Pennsylvania, has been (as already stated) fully recognized and enforced in the state courts of Pennsylvania, as far as their remedial process would enable these courts to act. This is abundantly established in the cases cited at the bar, and especially by the case of Witman *v.* Lex, 17 Serg. & Rawle, 88, and that of Sarah Zane's will, before Mr. Justice Baldwin and Judge Hopkinson. [Magill *v.*

[1] See Bartlet *v.* King, 12 Mass. 537.

Brown, Fed. Cas. No. 8952.] In the former case, the court said
" that it is immaterial whether the person to take be *in esse* or not,
or whether the legatee were at the time of the bequest a corporation
capable of taking or not, or how uncertain the objects may be, provided there be a discretionary power vested anywhere over the
application of the testator's bounty to those objects; or whether
their corporate designation be mistaken. If the intention sufficiently
appears in the bequest, it would be valid." In the latter case certain bequests given by the will of Mrs. Zane to the Yearly Meeting
of Friends in Philadelphia, an unincorporated association, for purposes of general and indefinite charity, were, as well as other bequests of a kindred nature, held to be good and valid; and were enforced accordingly. The case, then, according to our judgment, is
completely closed in by the principles and authorities already mentioned, and is that of a valid charity in Pennsylvania, unless it is
rendered void by the remaining objection which has been taken
to it.[1] . . .

Upon the whole, it is the unanimous opinion of the court, that the
decree of the Circuit Court of Pennsylvania dismissing the bill,
ought to be affirmed, and it is accordingly affirmed with costs.[2]

BASCOM *v.* ALBERTSON, 34 N. Y. 584 (1866): A testator devised
and bequeathed the residue of his property to five persons to be
named as trustees by the Supreme Court of Vermont, to found and
establish an institution for the education of females, to be located
in Middlebury, Vt. The Court held the devise and bequest invalid.
PORTER, J., said (p. 615):

" If it be true that charitable uses and trusts were not intended to
be embraced in the broad and comprehensive language of these
statutes,[3] the omission to except them from the general terms of the
prohibition would be inexplicable on any other theory, than that
Benjamin F. Butler, John Duer and John C. Spencer, the commissioners charged with the duty of revision, were unmindful of an important branch of the law, with which professional labor and research had made them probably more familiar than any other
three gentlemen who could have been selected among the leading
jurists of their day; and who were dealing with a question on which
the experience of centuries had poured its light. The statutory provisions they introduced were essentially organic. Their design was

[1] The court held that the objection founded on the exclusion from the
college of all ecclesiastics, missionaries and ministers of any sect was without
merit.

[2] See Perin *v.* Carey, 24 How. (U. S.) 465; Ould *v.* Washington Hospital,
95 U. S. 303; Russell *v.* Allen, 107 U. S. 163; Jones *v.* Habersham, 107 U. S.
174; Taylor *v.* Columbian University, 226 U. S. 126.

[3] Rev. Stat., 1830, Pt. 2, c. 1, tit. 2, *ante*.

to limit the bounds within which trusts might be created, and to prohibit all perpetuities unauthorized by law, and deriving their sole sanction from individual will. The question was considered in the Williams case, [8 N. Y. 525], where the alternative presented was, whether the statute should bend to the bequest, or the bequest bend to the statute; and the practical effect of the ruling was, that the statute was made to bend, by holding that, for this purpose, a trust for a charitable use is neither a use nor a trust.

" This doctrine, if it can be upheld, would render practically nugatory the restraints which the law has imposed upon testators, and the restrictions inserted by the legislature in special charters, and in general laws for the incorporation of charitable societies. Its effect is to divert donations from institutions, incorporated for purposes of philanthropic and Christian benevolence, and to invite evasion of State regulation and avoidance of public scrutiny, by tendering to every private citizen the right to create a perpetuity for such purpose as to him may seem good, and to endue it with more than corporate powers and more than corporate immunity. It holds out to every testator the assurance that though he cannot withdraw his property from the operation of general laws by gifts to societies organized under State authority, which would vest at once in the donees for purposes of charity, he can thus withdraw it from statutory regulation and restrictions, by giving the legal title to trustees of his own appointment, and that he can exercise over the so-called charity and the trustees in perpetual succession, the authority of a supreme legislature, unrestrained by the general statutes regulating the creation and division of estates, limiting uses and trusts, and forbidding perpetuities unauthorized by law. It assures him that though he is prohibited by statute from making an effectual bequest to a chartered charitable society, unless the will containing it be executed at least two months before his decease, he may make it to a private trustee for like purposes on the day of his death; that though he is precluded from making to any existing charitable institution a posthumous donation yielding an income of over ten thousand dollars a year, he may by will create a private institution, bearing his name and free from visitation or inspection, and bestow an endowment yielding an income of ten times that amount; that though he may not, if he has a wife, parent or child, give more than one-quarter or one-half of his estate to any charitable organization sanctioned by law, he may give the whole to a charity which has no sanction but his own. . . .

" The re-examination of the rulings in that case on the principal question involved, has led us to the clear conclusion, that in the light of antecedent and subsequent decisions, they cannot be upheld without subverting what we believe to be the law. We think the English system of indefinite charitable uses, if it ever existed in this State, fell with the repeal of the statute of Elizabeth and the mortmain acts; and we are also of opinion that gifts of this nature are within the scope and meaning, as well as the terms, of our statutes, forbidding perpetuities unauthorized by law."

AMES, THE FAILURE OF THE "TILDEN TRUST."[1] The prominence of the testator, and the magnitude of the "Tilden Trust," which has recently miscarried, have aroused so general an interest that this seems a peculiarly fit time to consider the legal reasons for the failure of that and similar charitable bequests in New York.

Governor Tilden's will is summarized by the majority of the court in Tilden *v.* Green, 130 N. Y. 29, as follows: " I request you (the executors) to cause to be incorporated an institution to be called the 'Tilden Trust,' with capacity to maintain a free library and reading-room in the city of New York, and such other educational and scientific objects as you shall designate; and if you deem it expedient — that is, if you think it advisable and the fit and proper thing to do — convey to that institution all or such part of my residuary estate as you choose; and if you do not think that course advisable, then apply it to such charitable, educational, and scientific purposes as, in your judgment, will most substantially benefit mankind." The trustees procured the incorporation of the "Tilden Trust," and elected to convey the entire residue to that institution. An admirable will and willing trustees — and yet the bequest was not sustained. If the trustees had not elected to give the property to the "Tilden Trust," that institution would have had no claim, nor would there have been, under the law of New York, any means of compelling them to apply it to the alternative charitable purposes. Therefore, the Court of Appeals decided, the trustees could not dispose of the property in either of the two modes indicated in the will, and the entire residue, amounting to some $5,000,000, must be distributed among the heirs and next of kin.

The question of the proper interpretation of the will apart, the failure of the "Tilden Trust" is due to a combination of two causes: the one legislative, the other judicial. Had the Tilden case arisen in England, or in any of our States, except New York, Michigan, Minnesota, Maryland, Virginia, and West Virginia, the trust would have been established. The precise nature of the legislation in New York will be best appreciated by contrasting a private trust with a charitable trust.

A trust, being an obligation of one person to deal with a specific *res* for the benefit of another, cannot be enforced unless there is a definite obligee, that is, a *cestui que trust,* who can file a bill for its specific performance. Furthermore, as equity follows the law, the rule of perpetuities must apply to trusts as well as to legal estates. By the English and general American law, neither of these doc-

[1] 5 Harv. L. Rev. 289, Lect. Leg. Hist., 285.

trines, which are of universal application to private trusts, is extended to charitable trusts. On the one hand, the considerations of public policy, which lie at the foundation of the rule of perpetuities in the case of private property, are obviously inapplicable to property devoted to charity; and, on the other, the specific performance of the charitable trust is abundantly secured through the attorney-general acting in behalf of the State.

In New York, however, the English law of charitable trusts has been abolished by statute, and charitable trusts are thereby put upon the same footing as private trusts, with the single exception that property may be given directly to corporations authorized to receive and hold permanently bequests for specified charitable purposes. This exceptional New York legislation seems to the writer an unmixed evil. Any one who follows the reported cases, to say nothing of the unreported instances, for the last fifty years, will be startled at the number of testators whose reasonable wishes have been needlessly disappointed, and at the amount of property which has been diverted from the community at large for the benefit of unscrupulous relatives.

Nor has New York, whose legislation in general has been widely copied, made any recent converts to her doctrine of charities. On the contrary, Wisconsin, which at one time followed the New York rule, by the revision of 1878 adopted the English practice with the exception of the so-called *cy-pres* doctrine. Virginia, too, which at one time ignored the distinction between private and charitable trusts, has, by statute, sanctioned to a limited extent indefinite charitable trusts.[1]

RESTRICTIONS ON GIFTS FOR CHARITABLE PURPOSES. "Under the feudal system, when land was given to a corporation, the chief lords of whom the land was held, and the king as ultimate chief lord, lost their chances of escheat, and various other rights and incidents of military tenure. During the middle ages, the accumulation of land in the ecclesiastical corporations was so great as to be thought a na-

[1] In 1893 soon after the decision in the Tilden case, the rule in New York was changed by statute. Real Prop. Law, sec. 12; Pers. Prop. Law, sec. 113. The rule was changed in Michigan in 1907; in Minnesota in 1927; and in Virginia in 1914. See Thurston, Charitable Gifts and the Minnesota Statute of Uses and Trusts, 1 Minn. L. Rev. 201; Dwan, Minnesota's Statute of Charitable Trusts, 14 Minn. L. Rev. 587. See 35 W. Va. L. Quar. 370.

Even in states in which charitable trusts fail unless there is a definite beneficiary, a devise or bequest to an existing charitable corporation, or to a charitable corporation to be created within the period allowed by the Rule against Perpetuities, for any or all of its corporate purposes, is valid.

For a discussion of questions of public policy in regard to charitable trusts, see Hobhouse, The Dead Hand; Kenney, Endowed Charities. On methods of supervising charitable trusts in England, see Mitcheson, Charity Commission Acts; Tudor, Charities; Escarra, *Les Fondations en Angleterre*.

tional grievance. Hence the English mortmain acts, which go back for their origin to Magna Charta, St. 9 Hen. III. c. 36, and which have continued with various modifications to this day. . . . Under these acts the alienations were not void, so as to let in the grantors and their heirs; but they merely operated as a forfeiture which gave a right to the mesne lord and the king to enter after due inquest. This right to enter was often waived by a license in mortmain. . . . In form these licenses commonly authorized a holding of property 'not exceeding' a certain value. In later years this authority sometimes has been inserted in the charter, and this limited power of purchase has, it is said, been exceeded by almost all corporations." Hubbard v. Worcester Art Museum, 194 Mass. 280, 283.

In some states there are restrictions on the amount of property which may be held by a charitable corporation. For conflicting decisions as to the effect of a devise or bequest in excess of the statutory amount, see Hubbard v. Worcester Art Museum, 194 Mass. 280; Matter of McGraw, 111 N. Y. 66. See Warren, Cas. Corp., 2 ed., 699–711.

The Statute of Wills, 32 Hen. VIII. c. 1 (1540), as explained in 34 Hen. VIII. c. 5 (1542), in authorizing devises of land, expressly excepted devises to bodies politic or corporate. It has been held, however, that the Stat. 43 Eliz. c. 4 rendered a devise to a corporation for charitable uses valid in equity. Flood's Case, Hob. 136; Collison's Case, Hob. 136. See also Bennet College v. Bishop of London, 2 Wm. Bl. 1182; Incorporated Society v. Richards, 1 Dr. & W. 258, 303. In the present English Wills Act, 7 Will. IV. & 1 Vict. c. 26 (1837), the exception as to bodies politic or corporate was omitted.

In California, Montana, New York, North Dakota, Oklahoma, South Dakota and Utah, statutes provide that no corporation shall take land by devise unless the corporation is especially authorized to do so by its charter or by statute. See N. Y. Consol. Laws, 1909, Decedent Estate Law, sec. 12. In some of these states the statutes apply to bequests as well as to devises. See 14 Iowa L. Rev. 198–9.

In the Georgian Statute of Mortmain, 9 Geo. II. c. 36 (1736), the preamble recited that "Whereas gifts or alienations of land, tenements or hereditaments, in mortmain, are prohibited or restrained by Magna Charta, and divers other wholesome laws, as prejudicial to and against the common utility; nevertheless this public mischief has of late greatly increased by many large and improvident alienations or dispositions made by languishing or dying persons, or by other persons, to uses called charitable uses, to take place after their deaths, to the disherison of their lawful heirs"; and for remedy thereof it was provided that no lands or personalty to be laid out in the purchase of lands should be given to any person or corporation in trust for or for the benefit of any charitable uses, except "by deed indented, sealed and delivered in the presence of two or more credible witnesses twelve calendar months at least before the death of such donor or grantor (including the days of the execution and death) and inrolled in his Majesty's high court of Chancery, within six calendar months next after the execution thereof; . . . and unless the same be made to take effect in possession for the charitable use intended, immediately from the making thereof, and be without any power of revocation, reservation, trust, condition, limitation, clause, or agreement whatsoever, for the benefit of the donor or grantor, or of any person or persons claiming under him. . . ."

The English law as to assurances to corporations and assurances for charitable purposes was consolidated in the Mortmain and Charitable Uses Act, 1888 (51 & 52 Vict. c. 42). A sweeping change in the law was effected by the Mortmain and Charitable Uses Act, 1891 (54 & 55 Vict. c. 73). By this Act land may be given by will to or for the benefit of any charitable use, but it is required that the land be sold within one year from the death of the testator unless the High Court or a Judge thereof or the Charity Commissioners extend the time or sanction the retention of the land when it is required for actual occupation for the purposes of the charity and not as an investment. This Act, however, leaves unchanged the restrictions on the acquisition of land by corporations contained in the Mortmain and Charitable Uses Act, 1888, which restrictions apply to charitable as well as other corporations. See Bristowe, Mortmain and Charitable Uses, 1891; Tudor, Charities, 8–13, 427–506.

In the United States, except in Mississippi, there is no such drastic legislation as that contained in the Georgian Statute of Mortmain. It is provided in some states, however, that no devise or bequest for a charitable purpose shall be good if the will is executed within a certain time before the death of the testator, and limiting the proportion of the testator's estate which can be devised or bequeathed for charitable purposes, if the testator leaves a wife or children or parents. There are statutes imposing one or both of these restrictions in California, Georgia, Idaho, Iowa, Montana, New York, Ohio, and Pennsylvania. See 14 Iowa L. Rev. 196–7. These statutes impose limitations on the power of the testator to dispose of his property, and only his wife, children or parents can take advantage of them. Trustees of State University *v.* Folsom, 56 Oh. St. 701. They have no applicability to bequests by a resident of a state which has no such statute to a charitable corporation of a state which has such a statute. Healy *v.* Reed, 153 Mass. 197.

See Boyle, Law of Charities; Bristowe, Mortmain and Charitable Uses Act, 1891; Finlason, History of the Laws of Mortmain; Shelford, Mortmain; Tudor, Charities; Tyssen, Charitable Bequests; Reports of the Select Committee on the Law of Mortmain; 27 L. Quar. Rev. 204; Woerner, Law of Administration, 3 ed., chap. 47. For a summary of the various English Mortmain Acts, see 73 Sol. J. 83 (1929). See also Zollmann, Charities, chap. 12.

In COMMISSIONERS FOR SPECIAL PURPOSES OF INCOME TAX *v.* PEMSEL, [1891] A. C. 531, LORD MACNAGHTEN said (p. 583) : " ' Charity ' in its legal sense comprises four principal divisions: trusts for the relief of poverty; trusts for the advancement of education; trusts for the advancement of religion; and trusts for other purposes beneficial to the community, not falling under any of the preceding heads. The trusts last referred to are not the less charitable in the eye of the law, because incidentally they benefit the rich as well as the poor, as indeed, every charity that deserves the name must do either directly or indirectly."

In re LUCAS.
RHYS *v.* ATTORNEY GENERAL.
HIGH COURT OF JUSTICE, CHANCERY DIVISION. 1922.

[1922] 2 Ch. 52.

ADJOURNED SUMMONS.

By his will, dated September 17, 1915, the testator directed that after the decease of his wife, who predeceased him, the income derived from all his securities should go to his niece, the defendant, Agnes Eliza Yeatman, during her life, and from and after her decease, he directed that seven trustees should be appointed, in the first place, by the trustees of his will, as he desired that all the income derived from the investments should be given to " the oldest respectable inhabitants in Gunville to the amount of five shillings per week each," and he also requested that a tablet should be prepared at his decease, and placed in or on the outside of the church at Gunville, stating that at the decease of his niece, the income derived from all his investments would be given to the oldest respectable inhabitants in Gunville to be selected by his trustees.

The testator died on October 12, 1920, leaving A. E. Yeatman his sole next to kin and heiress at law.

This summons was taken out by the trustees of the will, and it asked whether the gift in favour of the oldest respectable inhabitants in Gunville was a good charitable bequest, or was wholly or partially void.

RUSSELL, J. In this case the point I have to determine is whether a particular gift contained in the will of Edwin Lucas is or is not a good charitable gift. The gift is in these terms. [His Lordship read the provisions of the will, and continued:] This is a gift of income in perpetuity in favour of the persons above mentioned, and, of course, if the bequest is not a good charitable bequest it would fail, and, as the tenant for life under the will is sole next of kin and sole heiress at law, she would be entitled to the whole of the testator's estate. I confess that when the will was first read to me it did not strike me as being capable of being construed as a good charitable bequest, because the beneficiaries are to be " the oldest respectable inhabitants," words which, by themselves, do not in any way connote poverty. But Mr. Dighton Pollock has referred me to various authorities, and he puts his case in this way: " In the first instance," he says, " I can claim it as a good charitable bequest, it being for the benefit of aged persons and coming within the statute of Elizabeth, or alternatively I can read out of this gift in the will the element of poverty, in which case the gift would then equally be a good charitable gift." Speaking for myself, I am not satisfied that the requirement of old age would of itself be sufficient to constitute the gift a good charitable bequest, although there are several dicta to that effect in the books. I can find no case, and none has been cited to me, where the decision has been based upon age and nothing but age. . . .

Now, turning to this will, we find the words " the oldest respectable inhabitants," and it was suggested that that means not old as regards the number of years the person has spent upon this planet, but only old in regard to the number of years he or she has spent in Gunville, that is to say, the oldest inhabitant. I think the testator here, when he says " oldest " meant very old, just as in the case of Attorney-General *v.* Duke of Northumberland, 7 Ch. D. 745, where the testator said " poor " he meant very poor. Here the testator directs that these old people shall receive five shillings a week and no more. That, to my mind, indicates quite clearly that the class of persons who were to be benefited were persons to whom the receipt of that sum would be of importance and a benefit. In my view, he had in his mind the benefiting of old people who were in straitened circumstances, and to whom five shillings a week would bring comfort and relief. To my mind, the gift here is singularly like the gift in *In re* Dudgeon, 74 L. T. 613, where Stirling J. was able to read into the will the element of poverty, owing to the smallness of the sum contemplated in that case. There it was four shillings, and in this case the amount is five shillings.

Upon these authorities I am prepared to hold, and I do hold, that this gift is a good charitable gift.[1]

[1] Trusts for the relief of poverty take various forms, including doles of money or articles such as coal, blankets and the like; the establishment of orphanages, homes for old people and the like; loan funds for the needy. *Re* Monk, [1927] 2 Ch. 197 (coal fund and loan fund for the poor); Boston *v.* Doyle, 184 Mass. 373 (loan fund under will of Benjamin Franklin).

A trust to provide a pennyworth of sweets each for all boys and girls under fourteen within a certain parish is not charitable. *Re* Pleasants, 39 T. L. R. 675. Nor is a trust to apply the income in providing annually knickers for

PEMBER v. INHABITANTS OF KNIGHTON.

BEFORE LORD FINCH. 1639.

Duke 82.

MONEY was given to maintain a preaching minister; this is no charitable use named in the statute, yet by the Lord Keeper and two Judges, it was decreed to be good, and the use a charitable use, within the equity of that statute; and the executor was ordered to pay that money to the charitable use, for maintenance of it.[1]

THORNTON v. HOWE.

CHANCERY. 1862.

31 Beav. 14.

THE testatrix, Ann Essam, by her will dated in 1843, bequeathed as follows: —

"And as to all the rest, residue and remainder of my estate, both real and personal, whatsoever and wheresoever, that I may be possessed of, after the payment of all my just debts, funeral and testamentary expenses, I give, devise and bequeath the same unto Benjamin Howe, of No. 107, Old Street, St. Luke's, London, engineer, to hold to him, his heirs and assigns for ever. But it is my express wish and desire, that the produce of all my said real and personal estate, so devised and bequeathed to him and his heirs, shall be applied for and towards the printing, publishing and propagation of the sacred writings of the late Joanna Southcote; and I hereby constitute and appoint the said John Spencer sole executor of this my will."

The testatrix died in 1844.

The heiress-at-law of the testatrix filed this bill in 1861 against Howe and the Attorney-General, and it charged as follows: —

---

boys between ten and fifteen in a particular district, not being limited to poor boys. *Re* Gwyon, [1930] 1 Ch. 255.

As to trusts for the relief of poverty, see Zollmann, Charities, chap. 6; Dec. Dig., Charities, sec. 11.

For a criticism of the dole system, see Kenney, Endowed Charities, 50–52.

[1] "A gift of lands, etc., to maintain a chaplain or minister, to celebrate divine service, is neither within the letter nor meaning of this statute; for it was of purpose omitted in the penning of the act, lest the gifts intended to be employed upon purposes grounded upon charity might, in change of times (contrary to the minds of the givers) be confiscate into the King's treasury. For religion being variable, according to the pleasure of succeeding princes, that which at one time is held for orthodox may at another be accounted superstitious, and then such lands are confiscate." Moore, Readings upon the Statute of 43 Elizabeth, Duke 131.

"The plaintiff charges that the trust for the printing and publishing and propagation of the sacred writings of the late Joanna Southcote is either void in law, on the ground that the writings in question are of a blasphemous and profane character, or that the trust so declared is a trust for the propagation of doctrines subversive or contrary to the Christian religion or as being a trust for a charitable purpose within the act of 9 Geo. 2, c. 36.

"The plaintiff charges that the writings of Joanna Southcote, which are referred to in the will of the testatrix, purport to declare, maintain or reveal that she was with child by the Holy Ghost, and that a second Shiloh or Messiah was about to be born of her body, and in other parts thereof purport to be or contain revelations made to her by the Holy Ghost or by Divine inspiration, and to maintain or declare that she was moved or inspired by the Holy Spirit to write the same, and that in other parts they are of a blasphemous and profane character."

The bill prayed, amongst other things, a declaration "that the trust declared by the testatrix's will of her real estate, so far as it directed that the produce thereof should be applied for and towards the printing, publishing and propagation of the sacred writings of the late Joanna Southcote, was void in law, and that there was a resulting trust of her real estate in favor of her heir-at-law, so far as her real estate was subjected to such void trust."

THE MASTER OF THE ROLLS [SIR JOHN ROMILLY] said he must examine the printed works of the founder of this sect before he gave judgment.

THE MASTER OF THE ROLLS. The question is, whether the following is a good devise of real estate: — "It is my express wish," &c. [see *ante*].

In the first place, it is said that this, if a lawful and legitimate purpose, is a charity and therefore void, so far as the real estate is concerned, by reason of the Statute of Mortmain, and, secondly, it is also said, that this is wholly void, both as to realty and personalty, by reason of the immorality and irreligious tendency of the writings of Joanna Southcote, which, by this disposition of her property, the testatrix intended to circulate and make more extensively known.

On the latter point, being unacquainted with the writings of Joanna Southcote, it became my duty to look into them, for the purpose of satisfying myself on this point, and the result of my investigation is, that there is nothing to be found in them which, in my opinion, is likely to corrupt the morals of her followers, or make her readers irreligious.

She was, in my opinion, a foolish ignorant woman, of an enthusiastic turn of mind, who had long wished to become an instrument in the hands of God to promote some great good on earth. By constantly thinking of this it becomes in her mind an engrossing and immovable idea, till at last she came to believe that her wish was accomplished, and that she had been selected by the Almighty for this purpose. Of course she had, during her life, many followers, and probably has some now, as every person will have who has attained to such a pitch of self-confidence as sincerely to believe himself to be the organ of communication with mankind specially selected for that purpose by the Divine Author of his being.

In the history of her life, her personal disputations and conversations with the devil, her prophecies and her inter-communings with the spiritual world, I have found much that, in my opinion, is very foolish, but nothing which is likely to make persons who read them either immoral or irreligious. I cannot, therefore, say that this devise of the testatrix is invalid by reason of the tendency of the writings of Joanna Southcote.

On the other hand, the contention raised, that this is a gift to promote objects which are within the meaning of what this Court, for shortness, terms " charitable objects," and that, consequently, it is within the provisions of the Statute of Mortmain, presents a more serious objection to this devise.

The 43 Eliz. c. 4 is usually referred to for the purpose of testing the enumeration of the various subject-matters which are there considered to be charitable uses, and what testamentary dispositions come within the Statute of Mortmain. The preamble of this statute clearly points out an object within which this would fall. I am of opinion, that if a bequest of money be made for the purpose of printing and circulating works of a religious tendency, or for the purpose of extending the knowledge of the Christian religion, that this is a charitable bequest, and this Court will, upon a proper application being made to it, sanction and settle a scheme for this purpose, and, in truth, it is but lately that I have had in Chambers to settle and approve of a scheme of this description. In this respect, I am of opinion that the Court of Chancery makes no distinction between one sort of religion and another. They are equally bequests which are included in the general term of charitable bequests.

Neither does the Court, in this respect, make any distinction between one sect and another. It may be, that the tenets of a particular sect inculcate doctrines adverse to the very foundations of all religion, and that they are subversive of all morality. In such a case, if it should arise, the Court will not assist the execution of the bequest, but will declare it to be void; but the character of the bequest, so far as regards the Statute of Mortmain, would not be altered by this circumstance. The general immoral tendency of the bequest would make it void, whether it was to be paid out of pure personalty or out of real estate. But if the tendency were not immoral, and although this Court might consider the opinions sought to be propagated foolish or even devoid of foundation, it would not, on that account, declare it void, or take it out of the class of legacies which are included in the general terms charitable bequests.

The words of the bequests here are, " to propagate the sacred writings of Joanna Southcote." The testatrix, it is clear, was a disciple or believer in Joanna Southcote, who, from her writings, it is clear, was a very sincere Christian; but she laboured under the delusion that she was to be made the medium of the miraculous birth of a child at an advanced period of her life, and that thereby the advancement of the Christian religion on earth would be occasioned. But her works, as far as I have looked at them, contain but little upon this subject, and nothing which could shake the faith of any sincere Christian. In truth, though her works are in a great measure incoherent and confused, they are written obviously with a view to extend the influence of Christianity.

I cannot say that the bequest of a testator to publish and propagate works in support of the Christian religion is a charitable bequest, and, at the same time, say that if another testator should select for this purpose some three or four authors, whose works will, in his opinion, produce that effect, such a bequest thereupon ceases to be charitable.

Neither can I do so if a testator should select one single author whose works he thinks will produce that result. If a testator were to leave a fund for the purpose of propagating, at a very reduced price, the religious writings of Dr. Paley or Dr. Butler, I should be of opinion that the bequest was charitable in its character, and I must hold the same in respect of what the testatrix has called " the sacred writings of the late Joanna Southcote."

Had it been given out of pure personalty, or rather if there had been any pure personalty in this case, this Court would, in my opinion, have enforced the bequest and regulated the application of it as well as it could. But, as it is given out of land, it is void, by reason of the prohibition contained in the Statute of Mortmain (9 Geo. 2, c. 36); and at the proper time, which this is not, as this is only an application from chambers, I will make a declaration to that effect.[1]

[1] In Bowman v. Secular Society, [1917] A. C. 406, the House of Lords upheld a bequest upon trust for the Secular Society Ltd., a registered company, the objects of which were *inter alia* " to promote the principle that human conduct should be based upon natural knowledge and not upon supernatural belief, and that human welfare in this world is the proper end of all thought and action." The question whether the objects of the society were charitable was not involved and was not passed upon, although Lord Parker was of the opinion that they were not charitable. See *Re* Jones, [1907] S. Aust. L. R. 190; Kinsey v. Kinsey, 26 Ont. L. R. 99; Pringle v. Napanee, 43 U. C. Q. B. 285; Zeisweiss v. James, 63 Pa. 465; Manners v. Phila. Library Co., 93 Pa. 165. In Mormon Church v. U. S., 136 U. S. 1, it was held that Congress might constitutionally dissolve a church corporation, which advocated the practice of polygamy as one of its fundamental tenets.

In the following cases trusts were upheld as charitable: Shore v. Wilson, 9 Cl. & F. 355 (Unitarianism); *Re* Orr, 40 Ont. L. R. 567 (Christian Science); Chase v. Dickey, 212 Mass. 555 (Christian Science); Glover v. Baker, 76

BUTTERWORTH v. KEELER.

COURT OF APPEALS, NEW YORK. 1916.

219 N. Y. 446.

CARDOZO, J. This action is brought to construe the will of Cornelia Storrs, who died in April, 1912. She directed that her residuary estate be divided into two parts. One of these parts she gave to the New York Skin and Cancer Hospital. The other she gave to her executors " George F. Butterworth and Henry J. Storrs, in trust, nevertheless, to be used and devoted by them to the establishment of a school for girls in the town of North Salem, Westchester County, New York." The question is whether this latter gift is a valid charitable trust.

That it is valid if it is charitable, is not disputed. (Matter of MacDowell, 217 N. Y. 454.) The claim is made, however, by some of the next of kin that in truth it is not charitable. We think the claim is without merit. It is established law in this state that a gift for the promotion of education or learning is a gift for charitable uses. . . . There is no conflict of opinion anywhere. The rule, of course, is different where the school or other institution is maintained for the profit of its owners. The purpose must be the promotion, not of private profit, but of public learning. (Matter of MacDowell, *supra*.) It is not charity to aid a business enterprise. But the fact that fees are charged is not controlling. (Parks *v.* Northwestern University, 218 Ill. 381; Matter of MacDowell, *supra*, at p. 464.) Most of our universities and hospitals would be excluded by such a test, yet universities and hospitals are unquestionably public charities. (Parks *v.* Northwestern University, *supra*; Schloendorff *v.* Society of the N. Y. Hospital, 211 N. Y. 125, 127.) What controls is not the receipt of income, but its purpose. Income added to the endowment helps to make it possible for the work to go on. It is only when income may be applied to the profit of the founders that business has a beginning and charity an end. The line of division is the same whether the gift is devoted to education or to the

---

N. H. 393 (Christian Science); Jones *v.* Watford, 62 N. J. Eq. 339, 64 N. J. Eq. 785 (Spiritualism); Vineland T. Co. *v.* Westendorf, 86 N. J. Eq. 343. See 31 Harv. L. Rev. 289.

As to trusts for masses, see Reichenbach *v.* Quin, 21 L. R. Ir. 138, *ante*.

For cases holding that bequests for objects connected with a church are limited to charitable purposes, see *Re* Bain, [1930] 1 Ch. 224, 78 U. Pa. L. Rev. 1034; *Re* Williams, [1927] 2 Ch. 283. But see Dunne *v.* Byrne, [1912] A. C. 407; *Re* Moore, [1919] 1 I. R. 316; *Re* How, [1930] 1 Ch. 66; *Re* Jackson, [1930] 2 Ch. 389.

As to trusts for the promotion of religion, see Zollmann, Charities, chap. 5; Dec. Dig., Charities, secs. 13, 16; 22 A. L. R. 697.

relief of the poor, the halt and the blind. Charity ministers to the mind as well as to the body.

Our decision in Matter of Shattuck (193 N. Y. 446) is said by the appellants to have revolutionized these ancient principles; but it did nothing of the kind. The trust in that case was not to found a new institution of learning. It was to pay the income to existing institutions, either religious or educational or eleemosynary. This left the trustees free to select any educational institution, whether eleemosynary or not. They were, therefore, free to select institutions organized for private profit. The decisive consideration was the contrast which the court discerned in the mind of the testatrix between purposes that were educational and purposes that were eleemosynary. If the trust had been for the advancement of education, and nothing more, a different conclusion might have followed. The Shattuck case lays down no principle of large and general application. It defines the meaning of a particular will, and later cases have held that it must be limited to its special facts. (Matter of Robinson, 203 N. Y. 380; Matter of Cunningham, 206 N. Y. 601.)

Different altogether is the will before us. No such latitude of choice is given to these trustees. They are not to distribute a fund among existing institutions, whether eleemosynary or not. They are to organize a new school; and unless we can say that they are to organize it for profit, the school will be a charity. But plainly there was no intent that they should organize it for profit. They are at liberty, if they wish, to make the tuition free, but even though it is not free, the conclusion must be the same. If profit was the purpose, the will would have told us to whom the profits were to go. The trustees are certainly not to use the surplus revenue for themselves. They are not to apply it to the use of other legatees, for the subject of the gift is half of the residuary estate, and no other legatees are named. The testatrix did not intend to die intestate, and establish a trust for the benefit of her next of kin. There is significance also in the gift with which the one in controversy is associated. The other half of the residuary estate is given to a corporation unmistakably charitable, the Skin and Cancer Hospital. It is plain that profit is not contemplated; that revenue not expended is to be added to the endowment; and that the purpose of the gift is charity. Extrinsic evidence is not needed to make this purpose clear. It may, however, reinforce the conclusion to which we should be led without it. The finding is that for many years the testatrix had evinced a charitable interest in the young men and women of the town of North Salem, where she resided, and in the public school facilities of the town, which she knew to be inadequate. The purpose perpetuated in her will is thus revealed as the same purpose cherished during life. It cannot be misread, and ought not to be nullified.

The judgment should be affirmed, with costs payable out of the estate.

WILLARD BARTLETT, Ch. J., COLLIN, CUDDLEBACK, HOGAN and POUND, JJ., concur; HISCOCK, J., absent.

Judgment affirmed.[1]

COGGESHALL v. PELTON.

COURT OF CHANCERY, NEW YORK. 1823.

7 Johns. Ch. 292.

WILLIAM HENDERSON, by his last will, dated January 16, 1812, among other legacies to individuals and for charitable purposes, bequeathed as follows: " I give and bequeath unto the town of New-Rochelle 1200 dollars, for the express purpose of building or erecting a town house in said town, for transacting town business, which sum I direct my executors to pay unto such persons as said town shall appoint to receive it, at a legal town meeting; they first giving my executors security, that the said sum shall be appropriated immediately, agreeably to the intention of my will; and until such security is given, I direct my executors not to pay the said sum." And he appointed the defendants his executors. At a legal town meeting of the freeholders and inhabitants of New-Rochelle, on the 2d of April, 1816, the plaintiffs were appointed commissioners to build a town house for the town; and, to remove the doubts entertained by the defendants, as to the safety of paying the plaintiffs the legacy, the plaintiffs were empowered to petition the Legislature for an act authorizing them to receive it. On the petition of the plaintiffs, an act was passed, April 11, 1817, authorizing the plaintiffs, naming them as trustees duly elected and appointed by the town of New-Rochelle, to receive from the executors of William Henderson, de-

---

[1] Trusts for the promotion of education include trusts to establish or endow schools and colleges; to establish professorships and scholarships; to establish or maintain public libraries; to provide for the publication of books and pamphlets or the delivery of lectures; to promote scientific research.

In *Re* Shakespeare Memorial Trust, [1923] 2 Ch. 398, a trust to provide a national theater as a memorial to Shakespeare was upheld as a trust for educational purposes or for purposes generally beneficial to the community.

A gift to an educational institution conducted for private profit is not charitable. Stratton *v.* Physio-Medical College, 149 Mass. 505; Carteret Academy *v.* State Board, 102 N. J. L. 525, 25 Mich. L. Rev. 204 (school, taxable). See Green *v.* Biggs, 167 N. C. 417 (private sanitarium, liable for tort).

A gift is not non-charitable merely because the institution charges fees. Scott, Cases on Trusts, 1 ed., 324. *Cf.* Morgan *v.* Nat. Trust Bank, 331 Ill. 183 (loan fund to students, interest charged); Matter of Davidge, 200 N. Y. App. Div. 437 (like preceding case).

As to trusts for the promotion of education, see Zollmann; Charities, chap. 7; Dec. Dig., Charities, sec. 12; 48 A. L. R. 1126, 1142; 39 Yale L. Jour. 437; 24 Ill. L. Rev. 687.

ceased, such sum or sums of money, as by the last will of the said W. H. is given and bequeathed to the town of N. R. Adequate security was offered to the executors, who, under the advice of counsel, declined paying the legacy to the plaintiffs, except under the direction of this Court. An amicable bill was accordingly filed, and an answer put in, submitting the question to the Court.

THE CHANCELLOR [KENT]. The pecuniary legacy, in this case, to the town of New-Rochelle, for the purpose of erecting a town house for transacting town business, is valid as a charitable bequest. The cases of the Attorney General *v.* Clarke, Amb. 422, and of Jones *v.* Williams, Amb. 651, show that bequests with descriptions and purposes as general as this, have been held good as charities. The object of this legacy, was a general public use, as convenient for the poor and the rich.

The defendants are accordingly directed to pay the legacy to the plaintiffs, who are authorized, by statute, to receive it, provided security is given, as required by the will, to be approved of by a master.

Decree accordingly.[1]

BOWDITCH *v.* ATTORNEY GENERAL.

SUPREME JUDICIAL COURT, MASSACHUSETTS. 1922.

241 Mass. 168.

BILL IN EQUITY, filed in the Supreme Judicial Court on February 1, 1921, by the trustee under the will of James Jackson, late of Boston, for instructions.

The material portions of the will are described in the opinion. The instructions asked for by the plaintiff were as follows:

"1. Whether he may legally make the payments which he has been heretofore making for the promotion of women's rights, and, if not, whether he is justified in making any payments of any kind in any way for the promotion of women's rights.

"2. Whether he may legally make the payments which he has been heretofore making for the promotion of temperance, and, if not, whether he is justified in making any payments of any kind in any way for the promotion of temperance.

"3. Whether he may legally make the payments which he has been heretofore making for the promotion of the best interests of sewing girls in Boston, and, if not, whether he is justified in making any

[1] There are numerous cases upholding, as charitable, gifts for the erection or maintenance of public buildings, highways, parks, museums, water works and other utilities and for other municipal purposes. See Scott, Cases on Trusts, 1 ed., 316–17; Zollmann, Charities, chap. 8; Dec. Dig., Charities, sec. 14; Ann. Cas. 1914A 1215; 50 A. L. R. 593; 52 A. L. R. 980.

payments of any kind in any way for the promotion of the best interests of sewing girls in Boston.

" 4. How, if he is not legally justified in making any further payments for the causes of 'women's rights, temperance and the best interests of sewing girls in Boston,' or any of them, he shall distribute the income from the property in his hands which is not needed for the purpose of paying the four hundred dollars per annum to the last surviving annuitant."

The suit was reserved by *Braley*, J., upon the bill and answer, for determination by the full court.

CROSBY, J. This is a bill for instructions brought by the plaintiff as trustee under the will of James Jackson who died January 31, 1890. The will was executed in 1873, and was admitted to probate in Suffolk County on February 24, 1890. The residue of the estate is given to William I. Bowditch in trust, and, after the payment of certain annuities, the balance of the income is to be divided by the trustee as follows: " into three equal parts and expended by him or given away by him in such manner as will in his judgment best promote the causes (1) of womens rights (2) of temperance and (3) the best interests of Sewing Girls in Boston — and if for any reason the Courts have held or shall hold that a devise, bequest or a trust for either of these causes is invalid, I give the share of the balance of the net income of my estate which would otherwise be paid or expended for such cause to my friends Wm. I. Bowditch, Wendell Phillips and Mrs. Lucy Stone and the survivors and last survivor of them, to his, her or their sole use and behoof wholly free from all trusts and so that he, she or they may keep to his, her or their own use or expend or give away said sums as he, she or they shall think expedient." On the death of the last annuitant the residue of the estate is given to the above named William I. Bowditch, Wendell Phillips and Lucy Stone and the survivors and last survivor of them in trust " to divide the same among such charitable and reformatory institutions and movements as he, she or they shall think most judicious and in accordance with my wishes. And if he, she or they shall deem it wise to aid the cause of woman's rights or any other similar reformatory movement which has not as yet received the sympathy of the Courts, and any objection shall be made by any person or persons to such disposition of my estate, so that the Court may hold or be likely to hold such appropriation of my estate to be invalid, I give the whole residue of my estate to said Bowditch, Phillips and Stone and the survivors and last survivor of them in fee simple wholly free of all trusts whatever. . . ."

Wendell Phillips pre-deceased the testator. At the time of the testator's death Lucy Stone was married to Henry B. Blackwell; she died October 18, 1893, and the defendant Alice Stone Blackwell was appointed executrix of her will. William I. Bowditch was appointed trustee under the will of James Jackson on March 17, 1890, and died in January, 1909. The plaintiff, Frederick C. Bowditch, was appointed his successor as such trustee, and was also appointed executor of the will of William I. Bowditch and as such executor is a defendant. All the annuitants have died except Grace, the daughter of Abby Copeland.

The bill alleges that the trustee has until recently divided the balance of the income of the trust into thirds and distributed it among certain persons and corporations to be used in the furtherance of woman's rights, temperance and the best interests of sewing girls in Boston.

1. The first bequest in question is that which directs that one third of the balance of the net income be distributed by the trustee to promote the cause of "women's rights." The words "women's rights" must be construed in the usual and ordinary sense in which those words were intended to be used by the testator at the time of his death when his will took effect. Jackson v. Phillips, 14 Allen, 539, 560. It is to be observed that the will is silent as to the manner and means by which "women's rights" are to be promoted or secured. The question therefore of the lawfulness of the gift must be determined from the words themselves unaided by any other provision of the will. When the testator executed his will in 1873 no right of suffrage had been extended to women in this Commonwealth. The following year by St. 1874, c. 389, it was provided that "No person shall be deemed to be ineligible to serve upon a school committee by reason of sex." And by St. 1879, c. 223, it was provided that every woman who is a citizen of this Commonwealth of twenty-one years and upwards who has the educational qualifications required by the Twentieth Article of the Amendments to the Constitution, with certain exceptions, and upon stated conditions, was given the right to vote for members of school committees; the right of women to vote in this Commonwealth was so limited until the Nineteenth Amendment to the Federal Constitution was ratified in 1920. The amendment declares that "The right of citizens of the United States to vote shall not be denied or abridged by the United States or by any State on account of sex."

For many years before and after the testator's death in 1890 the phrase "woman's rights" had a definite and well defined meaning. In common parlance it was understood as being the right of women to vote, to hold office and be placed upon an equality with men in a political sense by appropriate legislation. The will does not in express terms provide that the trust is created for the advancement or betterment of the social, business, industrial or economic condition or status of women, nor can it be inferred from the words used. So to hold manifestly would be contrary to the intention of the testator, in view of the language which he employed in creating the trust. This conclusion is strengthened by the circumstance that he undoubtedly had in mind the decision in Jackson v. Phillips, *supra,* which construed the will of his father and held that a bequest " to secure the passage of laws granting women, whether married or unmarried, the right to vote, to hold office, to hold, manage and devise property, and all other civil rights enjoyed by men " cannot be sustained as a charity. In that case, with reference to the bequest above quoted, it was said by this court, speaking through Mr. Justice Gray, at page 571: " This bequest differs from the others in aiming directly and exclusively to change the laws; and its object cannot be accomplished without changing the Constitution also. Whether such an alteration of the existing laws and frame of government would be wise and desirable is a question upon which we cannot, sitting in a judicial capacity, properly express any opinion. Our duty is limited to expounding the laws as they stand. And those laws do not recognize the purpose of overthrowing or changing them, in whole or in part, as a charitable use. This bequest therefore, not being for a charitable purpose, nor for the benefit of any particular persons, and being unrestricted in point of time, is inoperative and void." And at page 555: " Gifts for purposes prohibited by or opposed to the existing laws cannot be upheld as charitable, even if for objects which would otherwise be deemed such. The bounty must, in the words of Sir Francis Moore, be ' according to the laws, not against the law,' and ' not given to do some act against the law.' Duke, 126, 169. . . . In a free republic, it is the right of every citizen to strive in a peaceable manner by vote, speech or writing, to cause the laws, or even the Constitution, under which he lives, to be reformed or altered by the Legislature or the people. But it is the duty of the judicial department to expound and administer the laws as they exist. And trusts whose expressed purpose is to bring about changes in the laws or the political institutions of the country are not charitable in such a sense as to be entitled to peculiar favor, protection and perpetuation from the ministers of those laws which they are designed to modify or subvert."

The gift under consideration cannot be distinguished from that which was held to be invalid in Jackson *v.* Phillips, *supra.* The principles enunciated in that case have been for more than half a century the settled law of the Commonwealth. It has been widely recognized in other jurisdictions as a leading case. As it was unlawful and invalid *ab initio*, and as the testator has provided that if the court should hold that the trust for woman's rights was invalid the entire estate so divided should vest in said Bowditch, Phillips and Stone and the survivors and last survivor of them in fee simple free from the trust, the *cy pres* doctrine is not applicable. [Citing cases.]

Nor can it be sustained as a private trust. The persons to be benefited are not determined: after the death of the last annuitant, the third article of the will provides as follows: " I give to each of my heirs at law the sum of One dollar if demanded and I direct the payments under the second article to cease, and I give all the rest and residue of my estate . . . to . . . William I. Bowditch, Wendell Phillips and Mrs. Lucy Stone and the survivors and last survivor of them in trust to divide the same among such charitable and reformatory institutions and movements as he, she or they shall think most judicious and in accordance with my wishes." It is plain from this provision that the beneficiaries of the trust are undetermined. There is no certainty that any portion of the residue will be distributed to any institutions or movements for the cause of " woman's rights." The selection of the recipients of such residue rests solely in the discretion of the trustees. Neither the objects to which the trust is to be applied nor the persons who are to take it are capable of ascertainment. Jackson *v.* Phillips, *supra*, at page 550. Minot *v.* Attorney General, 189 Mass. 176, 180.

The contention of the defendant Alice Stone Blackwell, that, if any of the trusts in the will are held to be void, she as executrix of the will of Lucy Stone Blackwell takes a vested interest in one half of the residue as her testatrix, and William I. Bowditch survived the testator, is untenable; because the testator devised the whole of the residue " to said Bowditch, Phillips and Stone and the survivors and last survivor of them in fee simple wholly free of all trusts whatever. . . ." The three persons named were joint tenants: Wendell Phillips deceased before the testator, who was survived by Lucy Stone and William I. Bowditch. As the latter survived Mrs. Stone, one third of the income of the residue of the estate subject to the annuity to Grace Copeland is to be paid to the defendant Frederick C. Bowditch as executor of his will. G. L. c. 184, § 7. Simonds *v.* Simonds, 168 Mass. 144. The residuary clause created a joint tenancy and related to a contingent interest which became vested in the last survivor, and he having deceased, it passed to the executor of his will. Cummings *v.* Stearns, 161 Mass. 506. See Dingley *v.* Dingley, 5 Mass. 535; Emerson *v.* Cutler, 14 Pick. 108, 115, 116; Minot *v.* Purrington, 190 Mass. 336.

2. The bequest to promote the cause of temperance is a valid charitable trust. The adoption of the Eighteenth Amendment to the Federal Constitution does not affect its validity. It is not a gift for a political purpose; the adoption of the amendment has not fully accomplished the purpose of the testator, which was to better the condition of people who suffer from the injurious consequences of intemperance caused by the use of intoxicating liquors. Jackson *v.* Phillips, *supra*, at page 595.

3. The trust to promote " the best interests of Sewing Girls in Boston " is for a charitable purpose. It applies to an indefinite number of a particular class and the purpose of the testator is sufficiently certain and defined: manifestly it is a valid charity. Sewing girls are handicraftsmen, and the word " girls " implies youth. The clause " best interests " includes not only the relief of poverty and dis-

tress, but has a broader signification, and well may comprehend within its spirit and intendment whatever adds to their welfare and advancement and enables them to establish themselves in life. " A gift dictated by a general benevolent purpose is to be liberally construed and, if reasonably possible, upheld as a valid charity." Thorp v. Lund, 227 Mass. 474, 477. Charitable uses are favorites with courts of equity. The construction of all instruments where they are concerned is liberal in their behalf. Saltonstall v. Sanders, 11 Allen, 446. Ould v. Washington Hospital for Foundlings, 95 U. S. 303, 313. Jones v. Habersham, 107 U. S. 174, 185. " Such uses had indeed been previously recognized as charitable, and entitled to peculiar favor, by many acts of Parliament, as well as in the courts of justice." Jackson v. Phillips, supra, 552. Re Dudgeon, 74 Law Times (N. S.) 613. Attorney General v. Comber, 2 Sim. & Stu. 93. Loscombe v. Wintringham, 13 Beav. 87. Thompson v. Corby, 27 Beav. 649.

A gift to a public use is not unlawful as a charity because it is not for the purpose of relieving poverty. Such gifts may extend to the rich as well as to the poor; it was said in New England Sanitarium v. Stoneham, 205 Mass. 335, 342: " It is not confined to mere almsgiving or the relief of poverty and distress, but has a wider signification, which embraces the improvement and promotion of the happiness of man." [Citing cases.]

The trustee is instructed that as the gift for the promotion of " woman's rights " is invalid, he cannot hereafter make any payments out of the fund for that purpose, but is required to pay over to the executor of the will of William I. Bowditch one third of the income of the residuary estate, subject to the annuity to Grace Copeland. He is further instructed that the gifts to promote temperance and the best interests of sewing girls in Boston are valid charities and he may expend for each, one third of the income of the residuary estate subject to the annuity to Grace Copeland.

The terms of the decree, including all questions of costs as between solicitor and client, may be settled by a single justice.

Ordered accordingly.[1]

[1] In the following cases trusts to promote various causes were upheld as charitable:

Temperance. People v. Dashaway Ass'n, 84 Cal. 114; Haines v. Allen, 78 Ind. 100; Harrington v. Pier, 105 Wis. 485; Farewell v. Farewell, 22 Ont. Rep. 573. See Re Hood, 74 Sol. J. 154.

Woman's suffrage. Garrison v. Little, 75 Ill. App. 402. But see Jackson v. Phillips, 14 Allen (Mass.) 539. See 28 A. L. R. 720.

Promotion of peace. Tappan v. Deblois, 45 Me. 122; Parkhurst v. Treasurer, 228 Mass. 196.

Vegetarianism. Re Cranston, [1898] 1 I. R. 431; Re Slatter, 21 T. L. R. 295.

Protection of animals. Tatham v. Drummond, 4 DeG. J. & S. 484; Re Foveaux, [1895] 2 Ch. 501 (suppression of vivisection); Re Wedgwood, [1915] 1 Ch. 113; McCran v. Kay, 93 N. J. Eq. 352; Pitney v. Bugbee, 98 N. J. L. 116,

SEARS v. ATTORNEY GENERAL, 193 Mass. 551 (1907): A fund was created by subscription " for the benefit of the widows and orphan children that may be left by the future ministers of " Trinity Church in Boston. It was held that this was a charitable trust, although the class of persons to be directly benefited was narrow. KNOWLTON, C. J., said (p. 553):

"As a general proposition, a gift made for the support of needy widows and orphans of a particular class is an eleemosynary public charity. . . .

"The gift in the present case is primarily to persons of a class, and not to designated individuals. The members of this class, for all time, are to take. The class, considered strictly, is very small, and the only question is whether the object is so general and indefinite as to be deemed of common and public benefit, and so a public charity. It includes the families of deceased clergymen of the Protestant Episcopal Church, and the selection of them is limited to those in which the husband or father was a rector or assistant minister of Trinity Church. In the course of many years the number benefited might be large, and while the number ultimately receiving a direct benefit is limited to those connected with this religious society, the larger class of clergymen of the same religious faith are indirectly helped by the chance that they may be chosen

---

892. But see *Re* Grove-Grady, [1929] 1 Ch. 557, 4 Camb. L. J. 82, 45 L. Quar. Rev. 426. See note to *Re* Dean, 41 Ch. D. 552, *ante*.

Prizes for best kept gardens and cottages. *Re* Pleasants, 39 T. L. R. 675.

Various patriotic or public purposes. *Re* Lord Stratheden, [1894] 3 Ch. 265 (for the benefit of a volunteer military corps); *Re* Good, [1905] 2 Ch. 60 (for books and plates for officers' mess of a certain regiment); *Re* Pardoe, [1906] 2 Ch. 184 (to ring peal of bells on the anniversary of the restoration of the monarchy); *Re* Donald, [1909] 2 Ch. 410 (for the benefit of a mess of a regiment); *Re* Gray, [1925] Ch. 362 (promotion of shooting, fishing, cricket and polo in a regiment); George *v.* Braddock, 45 N. J. Eq. 757 (to publish the works of Henry George); Taylor *v.* Hoag, 273 Pa. 194 (to promote improvements in structure and the methods of government with special reference to the initiative, referendum and recall, etc.); Sargent *v.* Cornish, 54 N. H. 18 (display of the United States flag); Peth *v.* Spear, 63 Wash. 291 (to provide a place where the doctrines of socialism can be taught by example as well as by precept).

As to the validity of trusts to promote changes in the law, see 16 Cal. L. Rev. 468; 21 A. L. R. 951.

Non-charitable purposes. On the other hand, it has been held that trusts for the purpose of promoting sports are not charitable. *Re* Nottage, [1895] 2 Ch. 649 (yacht racing); *Re* Clifford, 81 L. J. Ch. 220 (angling). Such trusts, however, have been held charitable where they are educational, *Re* Mariette, [1915] 2 Ch. 284; or tend to promote the national defence, as in the case of sports for soldiers, *Re* Gray, *supra,* or such sports as rifle shooting, *Re* Stephens, 8 T. L. R. 792.

In the following cases it was held that the trust was invalid. Habershon *v.* Vardon, 4 DeG. & S. 467 (to restore the Jews to Jerusalem, then under Turkish rule; but see *Re* Rosenblum, (1924) 131 L. T. 21); Thrupp *v.* Collet, 26 Beav. 125 (to pay fines of poachers).

to one of these places and their families receive assistance from this fund. . . .

"We think that there are strong reasons for holding that the fund, in the present case is a public charity, viewed solely in its eleemosynary aspect; but we do not decide this, for we think the plaintiff's other contention, that it is good as a religious charity, should be sustained.

"When the different provisions of the vote of the subscribers are considered, it becomes plain that their principal object was religious. They were providing for the encouragement and support of the rector by establishing a fund which would ensure the proper maintenance of his wife and minor children if he died and left them without property." [1]

DA COSTA *v.* DE PAS.

CHANCERY. 1754.

1 Amb. 228.

ELIAS DE PAS, a Jew, by will, dated the 4th of November, 1739, established a fund of 1200*l*. to be appropriated in order to apply and dedicate the revenue of that sum towards establishing a Jesuba, or assembly for reading the law, and instructing people in our holy religion.

Qu. To whom the said sum should belong? whether the next of kin, or as a charity for the crown to dispose of?

A distinction was taken by LORD HARDWICKE, Chancellor, that when the devise is to a superstitious use, and made void by statute, or to a charity, and made void by statute of mortmain, there it should belong to the heir at law or next of kin; but where it is in itself a charity, but the mode in which it is to be disposed, is such

---

[1] For numerous cases holding that a trust is charitable although the beneficiaries are limited to residents of a particular locality, or persons of a particular trade, or members of a particular sect or church, or employees of a particular organization, see Scott, Cases on Trusts, 1 ed., 327–8.

By the weight of authority a gift to a friendly society or other fraternal organization for its general purposes is not charitable, although a gift for poor members or relatives of members of such an organization is charitable. See Scott, 328–9; 1 So. Cal. L. Rev. 180, 303; 5 A. L. R. 1175.

A trust to establish a scholarship is charitable, although preference is given to descendants of the settlor or other designated persons. There is a dispute on the question whether a trust for the education of such descendants, or to support such descendants if poor, is charitable. See Scott, 329. If the trust is for the benefit generally of such descendants and is not conditioned on poverty or for purposes of education, it is not charitable. Amory *v.* Amherst College, 229 Mass. 374. *Cf. Re* Zeagman, 37 Ont. Rep. 536 (masses); Laverty *v.* Laverty, [1907] 1 I. R. 9 (support and education of boys of the name of Laverty). But see *Re* Rosenblum, 131 L. T. 21 (trust to enable members of testator's family and descendants to settle in Palestine). See Hobhouse, The Dead Hand, 6; Bogert, Trusts, 193; Gray, Rule ag. Perp., App. A.

that by the law of England it cannot take effect, as in the present case, it promoting a religion contrary to the established one; there the crown, by sign manual directed to the Attorney-General, may give orders in what charitable manner it shall be disposed.[1]

NOTE. — I was afterwards informed that 1000*l.* of the money was directed by sign manual to be disposed of to the Foundling Hospital.[2]

In ATTORNEY GENERAL *v.* DOWNING, Wilm. 1 (1767), WILMOT, C. J., said (p. 32) : " But where property is given to mistaken charitable uses, this Court distinguishes between the charity and the use; and seeing a charitable bequest in the intention of the testator, they execute the intention, varying the use, as the King, who is the Curator of all charities, and the constitutional Trustee for the performance of them, pleases to direct and appoint.

" If it were *res integra,* much might be said for the heir at law; because in every other case, if the testator's intention in specie cannot take place, the heir at law takes the estate. And as the motive inducing the disinherison in a charitable devise, is a passion for that particular charity which he has named, if that particular charity cannot take place, *cessante causâ cessaret effectus.*

" The right of the heir at law seems to arise as naturally in this case as in any other. But instead of favoring him as in all other cases, the testator is made to disinherit him for a charity he never thought of, perhaps for a charity repugnant to the testator's intention, and which directly opposes and encounters the charity he meant to establish. But this doctrine is now so fully settled that it cannot be departed from; and the reason upon which it is founded seems to be this: The donation was considered as proceeding from a general principle of piety in the testator. Charity was an expiation of sin and to be rewarded in another state; and therefore, if political reasons negatived the particular charity given, this Court thought the merits of the charity ought not to be lost to the testator nor to the public, and that they were carrying on his general pious intention; and they proceeded upon a presumption that the principle which produced one charity would have been equally active in producing another, in case the testator had been told that the particular charity he meditated could not take place. The court thought one kind of charity would embalm his memory as well as another and being equally meritorious would entitle him to the same reward."

[1] See the comments of Lord Eldon in Moggridge *v.* Thackwell, 7 Ves. 36, 76. And see Cary *v.* Abbott, 7 Ves. 940; West *v.* Shuttleworth, 2 Myl. & K. 684; Sims *v.* Quineau, L. R. 16 Ir. 191.

[2] It appears from the Reporter's note that the King by his sign manual directed the application of 1000*l.* to the support of a preacher in the Foundling Hospital and to instruct the children in the Christian religion.

ANONYMOUS.

CHANCERY. 1702.

Freem. C. C. 261.

IT WAS said, and not denied, that if a man deviseth a sum of money to such charitable uses, as he shall direct by a codicil to be annexed to his will, or by a note in writing; and afterwards leaves no direction, neither by note nor codicil, the Court of Chancery hath power to dispose of it to such charitable uses as the court shall think fit: and so it was held in the case of Mr. Sidrofen's will, 1 Vern. 224, and the case of one Jones; but if the will points at any particular charity, as for maintenance of a schoolmaster or poor widows, then the Court of Chancery ought not to direct it to any other purpose but such as is pointed at by the will; as if the devise should be for such school as he should appoint, and appoints none, the court may apply it for what school they please, but for no other purpose than a school, although it may be for what school the court thinks fit.[1]

MINOT v. BAKER.

SUPREME JUDICIAL COURT, MASSACHUSETTS. 1888.

147 Mass. 348.

HOLMES, J. This is a bill for instructions, brought by the administrator *de bonis non*, with the will annexed, of Captain John Percival. The will appointed John P. Healy executor, and gave the residue to Healy, "to be disposed of by him for such charitable purposes as he shall think proper." Healy died, having disposed of only a small portion of the residuary estate in his hands for charitable purposes. The first question raised by the report is, "Whether the sum of $14,503.75, received by the plaintiff from the suit upon the bond of Healy, as executor of Percival's estate, and from the suit against Healy's administrator, should be paid to the next of kin of John Percival, by reason of the failure of said Healy to dispose of the fund in his lifetime for the purposes specified in the residuary clause of the will of said Percival, or should be applied to charitable purposes, according to a scheme under the direction of the court."

It is settled that the gift to Healy was a good charitable trust. [Citing cases.] There was no resulting trust on account of the vagueness of the objects, as there is in cases where the objects are

---

[1] See Attorney General *v.* Syderfen, 1 Vern. 224, 7 Ves. 43n.; Mills *v.* Farmer, 1 Mer. 55, 19 Ves. 482; *Re* White, [1893] 2 Ch. 41; *Re* Pyne, [1903] 1 Ch. 83. See 8 Cornell L. Quar. 179.

not confined to charities. Nichols *v.* Allen, 130 Mass. 211. The first point to be determined, therefore, as a matter of construction, whether the limitation to charities was conditional upon Healy's making an appointment, or whether it should be construed as a gift to charitable uses out and out, with a superadded power to Healy to specify them if he saw fit. And on this part of the question we are of opinion that the gift is an unconditional gift to charitable purposes.

There can be little doubt that such would be the construction adopted by the English courts. [Citing cases.] Although a different opinion has been intimated in some American cases, at least, where there is a naked power not coupled with a trust. Fontain *v.* Ravenel, 17 How. 369, 388, 399 (explained and limited by Russell *v.* Allen, 107 U. S. 163, 169). The question must be kept distinct from other questions which do not bear upon the meaning of the words, such as whether a trust for charity generally is valid, or whether a court of equity can and will exercise so general a discretion as is necessary to carry out the trust, etc. If the meaning of the words alone is considered, it appears to be tolerably plain that the English construction is right. The nature of the gift shows that an application of the funds to charity is the dominant object, and that the selection by the trustee is subordinate, or means to an end. It is not like a gift to a particular charity which fails; there the specific object of bounty or end of the trust may well have furnished the main motive of the testator for giving to charity at all. But to give a power of selection to a party who takes no interest in the fund cannot be supposed to be the main motive of such a trust as we are considering, and the motive of charity goes no further than charity generally, because the testator leaves the rest to his trustee. The testator in such a case says, in effect, I give the fund in trust for charitable purposes, and, to save application to the court, I authorize the trustee to determine the scheme.

In the ordinary case of trusts for such persons of a class as the trustee shall select, when a duty to select is imposed upon the trustee by implication, a general intention to benefit the class is recognized, and the trust will not fail if the trustee accepts it and then fails to make a selection. [Citing cases.]

Here there is a trust, not a mere power, and it was recognized in White *v.* Ditson, 140 Mass. 351, that a duty was imposed upon Healy to act, which is a strong circumstance in favor of the construction that the benefit is not intended to be made dependent upon his acting. Brown *v.* Higgs, 8 Ves. 561, 571, 574. Cole *v.* Wade, 16 Ves. 27. Moggridge *v.* Thackwell, 7 Ves. 36, 82. And it being settled that in some cases you can separate the general intent from the mode of execution, the nature of the gift in the particulars to which we have adverted already seems to us to make the case a stronger one for doing so than where the selection is to be made from relations or the like, as in the decisions cited. At all events, this case is nearer to those than to a gift to such persons as A. may appoint. Mills v. Farmer, 1 Meriv. 55. For there the limitation is as wide as the world, and if A. does not take the beneficial interest it is impossible to suppose that a gift is intended unless he exercises the power confided to him. But charitable purposes constitute a well-defined class, to which it is entirely conceivable that a testator should make a gift. We shall consider the validity of such a gift in a moment.

The construction of the will being what we have declared, the question arises whether a trust originally valid is to fail for want of a trustee, contrary to the general doctrine of equity. There is no doubt that, if there were a very slight indication of the direction which the testator meant his bounty to take, a court of equity would find itself able to carry out the will. In Schouler, petitioner, 134 Mass. 426, the gift was for " charitable purposes, masses, etc.," and the court appointed a new trustee. See also Copinger v. Crehane, Ir. Rep. 11 Eq. 429. But it is argued that when the gift originally is, or through the failure of the first trustee to exercise his discretion afterwards becomes, a gift to charitable uses *simpliciter,* then the disposition of the fund in England was in the king as *parens patriæ,* by the sign manual, and that a court of equity as such has no jurisdiction.

It is to be observed, that the objections to the exercise of the power to frame a scheme in the case supposed are not at all similar to those which apply to a diversion by the sign manual to wholly different uses of property devoted to a specific purpose which fails, because contrary to the policy of the law for instance, as in the well-known case of Da Costa v. De Pas, 1 Ambler, 228, s. c. 2 Swanst. 487, note, where a legacy to establish a Jesuba, or assembly for reading the law and instructing people in the Jewish religion, was devoted to the Foundling Hospital for the instruction of the children in the Christian religion. In such a case there is no pretence, or only a pretence, of carrying out the directions of the testator. His will is arbitrarily over-ridden. Moggridge v. Thackwell, 7 Ves. 36, 81. But in a case like the present, whether the machinery used is the sign manual or a scheme prepared under the direction of the court, the testator's wishes are carried out as he has expressed them, just as they might be by the appointment of a trustee, or by the framing of a scheme in those cases where the jurisdiction of the court is admitted.

The only objection on the ground of policy to the court's entertaining jurisdiction which has occurred to us is, that it must choose from too wide a field when there is nothing more specific to guide it than a general direction to apply the fund to charitable purposes. If the objection in this general form were sound, a trust for charitable purposes generally ought to have been held void, whereas all the English cases imply, and express decisions establish, that it is valid.[1] . . .

We are of opinion that the above mentioned sum of $14,503.75 should be applied to charitable purposes according to a scheme under the direction of the court. . . .

Decree accordingly.[2]

THE CASE OF THETFORD SCHOOL.

OPINION OF THE JUDGES. 1609.

8 Rep. 130 *b.*

UPON a private bill exhibited in the parliament for erection of a free-school, maintenance of a preacher, and of four poor people, *scil.* two poor men and two poor women, according to the will of Sir Thomas Fulmerston, Kt., a question was moved by the Lords, and was such: land of the value of 35*l. anno* 9 *Eliz. Reginae,* was devised by will in writing to certain persons and their heirs, for the maintenance of a preacher four days in the year, of a master and usher of a free grammar-school, and of certain poor people; and a

---

[1] The court examined the cases and held that the generality of the purposes of the trust is not fatal to its validity. *Cf. Re* Pyne, [1903] 1 Ch. 83, in which property was bequeathed to trustees for charitable purposes to be set forth in a codicil and no codicil was executed, and it was held that the trust was valid and the disposition should be under a scheme and not by sign manual.

[2] Ordinarily equity will not allow a charitable trust to fail for want of a trustee. Even though by the terms of the trust the trustee is given discretion in the choice of the charitable objects, and the trustee named declines to act or resigns or dies or fails or ceases to serve for some other reason, the trust will not usually fail. *Re* Willis, [1921] 2 Ch. 44; Thompson's Estate, 282 Pa. 30, 73 U. Pa. L. Rev. 322. See Scott, Cases on Trusts, 1 ed., 339–340. If, however, it appears that the exercise of discretion by the trustee named was an essential part of the testator's scheme, the trust fails if the trustee named is unwilling or unable to act as trustee. Rogers *v.* Rea, 98 Oh. St. 315; Chellew *v.* White, 127 Wash. 382. See 5 A. L. R. 315, 339; 78 U. Pa. L. Rev. 573.

In some states it is held that where the trustee is given wide discretion the trust fails for indefiniteness even though the trustee named is ready and willing to act. Scott, 340–1.

The mere fact that the trustee named is an unincorporated association and incapable of acting as trustee does not cause the trust to fail. American Bible Society *v.* American Tract Society, 62 N. J. Eq. 219. See Dec. Dig., Charities, sec. 20(3). In New York, however, it is held that a devise or bequest directed to an unincorporated charitable association for its general purposes does not create a trust and is invalid. Mount *v.* Tuttle, 183 N. Y. 358, 367; Ely *v.* Megie, 219 N. Y. 112, 143; Fisher *v.* Lister, 130 N. Y. Misc. 1, 37 Yale L. Jour. 258.

In Robinson *v.* Crutcher, 277 Mo. 1, it was held that a bequest to the "capital" of a public school fund failed for want of a trustee and could not be upheld as a bequest to the trustees of the fund.

On the question of indefiniteness of the charitable purpose, see Zollmann, Charities, chap. 9; Dec. Dig., Charities, secs. 21, 22.

special distribution was made by the testator himself, in the same will, amongst them, of the revenues, *scil.* to the preacher a certain sum, and certain sums to the schoolmaster and usher, and to the poor people, amounting in the whole to 35*l. per annum, which was the yearly profit of the land at that time; and afterwards the land became of greater value,* viz. *of the value of* 100*l. per ann.* Now two questions were moved: 1. Whether the preacher, schoolmaster, usher, and poor, should have only the said certain sums appointed to them by the founder, or that the revenue and profit of the land should be employed to the increase of the stipend of the preacher, schoolmaster, usher, and poor? 2. If any surplusage remained, how it should be employed? And it was resolved, on hearing of counsel learned on both parts, several days at Serjeant's Inn, by the two Chief Justices, and Walmsley, Justice (to whom the Lords referred the consideration of the case) that the revenue and profit of the said land should be employed to the increase of the stipend of the preacher, schoolmaster, &c. and poor; and if any surplusage remained, it should be expended for the maintenance of a greater number of poor, &c., and nothing should be converted by the devisees to their own uses. So in the case in question, where lands in Croxton; in the county of Norfolk, were devised by Sir Richard Fulmerston, to his executors, to find the said works of piety and charity, with such certain distribution as is aforesaid; and now the value of the manor was greatly increased, that it shall be employed in performance and increase of the said works of piety and charity instituted and erected by the founder: for it appears by his distribution of the profits, that he intended the whole should be employed in works of piety and charity, and nothing should be converted to the private use of the executors or their heirs. And this resolution is grounded on evident and apparent reason; for, as if the lands had decreased in value, the preacher, schoolmaster &c. and poor people, should lose; so when the lands increase in value, *pari ratione* they shall gain. And they said, that this case concerned the colleges in the universities of Cambridge and Oxford, and other colleges, &c. For in ancient time, when lands were of small yearly value, (victuals then being cheap) and were given for the maintenance of poor scholars, &c. and that every scholar, &c. should have 1*d.* or 1*d. ob.* a day, that then such small allowance was competent in respect of the price of victuals, and the yearly value of the land; and now the price of victuals being increased, and with them the annual value of the lands, it would be now injurious to allow a poor scholar 1*d.* or 1*d. ob.* a day, which cannot keep him, and to convert the residue to private uses, where, in right, the whole ought to be employed to the maintenance or increase (if it may be) of such works of piety and charity which the founder has expressed, and nothing to any private use; for every college is seised *in jure collegii, scilicet,* to the intent that the members of the college, according to the intent of the founder, should take the benefit, and that nothing should be converted to private uses. *Panis egentium vita pauperum, et qui defraudat eos homo sanguinis est.* And afterwards, upon conference had with the other Justices, they were of the same opinion; and according to their opinions, the bill passed in both houses of Parliament, and afterwards was confirmed by the King's royal assent. *Note*, reader, there is a good rule in the act of Parliament called *Statutum Templariorum: ita semper quod pia et celeberrima voluntas donatorum in omnibus teneatur et expleatur, et perpetuo sanctissime perseveret.*[1]

JACKSON v. PHILLIPS.

SUPREME JUDICIAL COURT, MASSACHUSETTS. 1867.

14 Allen 539.

BILL in equity by the executor of the will of Francis Jackson of Boston (who died in 1861) for instructions as to the validity and effect of various bequests and devises.

[1] In some cases the courts have found an intention shown by the testator to allow the trustee to keep the surplus. A. G. v. Dean and Canons of Windsor, 8 H. L. C. 369 (will of Hen. VIII and letters patent of Ed. VI; trustee a charitable corporation); A. G. v. Rector, etc., of Trinity Church, 9 Allen (Mass.) 422 (trustee a charitable corporation). If there is no general charitable purpose and no intent to give the trustee any beneficial interest, there will be a resulting trust of the surplus. See A. G. v. Mayor of Bristol, 2 Jac. & W. 294, 308; *Re* Stanford, [1924] 1 Ch. 73.

"With respect to the application of surplus rents: — When a testator has devised his estate to charitable uses, and has pointed out the particular objects of his bounty, the court construe his intention imperatively to be, not only in exclusion of his next of kin, but to the disinheriting of his heir at law; and they uniformly decree the surplus rents and profits to the augmentation of the charities, upon the ground, that, as the charity must have borne the loss if the value of the thing devised had decreased, it shall enjoy the benefit of its increase (Case of Thetford School, 8 Co. 130; Arnold v. A. G., Show. P. C. 22; A. G. v. Mayor of Coventry, Colles's P. C. 280, 2 Bro. P. C. 236, 2 Vern. 397; A. G. v. Price, 3 Atk. 109; A. G. v. Smart, 1 Ves. 72; A. G. v. Johnson, Amb. 190; A. G. v. Sparks, Amb. 201; Shepherd v. Corporation of Bristol, 3 Mad. Rep. 320); and the court will either increase the bounty limited to the objects (A. G. v. Minshull, 4 Ves. 11), or if the fund is very considerable in proportion to the objects it will apply the surplus upon the principle of *cy pres* for the benefit of the same objects to purposes not expressly pointed out by the will (The Bishop of Hereford v. Adams, 7 Ves. 324); or, after providing for the maintenance of those already established, will extend the bounty by increasing the number of objects of the same description with those pointed out by the testator. A. G. v. Earl of Winchelsea, 3 Bro. C. C. 373; A. G. v. Haberdashers' Company or Turner, 2 Ves. Jun. 1, 4 Bro. C. C. 103; A. G. v. Hurst, 2 Cox 365; A. G. v. Wansey, 15 Ves. 231; A. G. v. The Coopers' Company, 19 Ves. 187." Porter's Case, 1 Rep. 22a, b, note W 1. See also A. G. v. Mayor of Bristol, 2 Jac. & W. 294; Merchant Taylors' Co. v. A. G., L. R. 6 Ch. 512; A. G. v. Wax Chandlers' Co., L. R. 6 H. L. 1; McElwain v. A. G., 241 Mass. 112; Tudor, Charities, 110–117.

In Article 4th the testator bequeathed to trustees $10,000 "in trust, nevertheless, for them to use and expend at their discretion, without any responsibility to any one, in such sums, at such times and such places, as they deem best, for the preparation and circulation of books, newspapers, the delivery of speeches, lectures, and such other means, as, in their judgment will create a public sentiment that will put an end to negro slavery in this country. . . . I hope and trust that they will receive the services and sympathy, the donations and bequests, of the friends of the slave."

In Article 5th the testator bequeathed to the same trustees $2000 "in trust, nevertheless, to be expended by them at their discretion, without any responsibility to any one, for the benefit of fugitive slaves who may escape from the slaveholding states of this infamous Union from time to time."

One argument was had in March 1863, after which the court ordered the attorney general to be made a party, which was done, and he submitted the case without argument, and a second argument by the other counsel was had in November 1865. While the case was under advisement, the thirteenth article of amendment of the Constitution of the United States was adopted, and the effect of this amendment upon the case was argued in March 1866.

GRAY, J.[1] . . . By the thirteenth amendment of the Constitution of the United States, adopted since the earlier arguments of this case, it is declared that "neither slavery nor involuntary servitude, except as a punishment for crime whereof the party shall have been duly convicted, shall exist within the United States or any place subject to their jurisdiction." The effect of this amendment upon the charitable bequests of Francis Jackson is the remaining question to be determined; and this requires a consideration of the nature and proper limits of the doctrine of *cy pres*.

It is contended for the heirs at law, that the power of the English chancellor, when a charitable trust cannot be administered according to its terms, to execute it so as to carry out the donor's intention as nearly as possible — *cy pres* — is derived from the royal prerogative or the St. of 43 Eliz. and is not an exercise of judicial authority; that, whether this power is prerogative or judicial, it cannot, or, if it can, should not, be exercised by this court; and that the doctrine of *cy pres*, even as administered in the English chancery, would not sustain these charitable bequests since slavery has been abolished.

Much confusion of ideas has arisen from the use of the term *cy pres* in the books to describe two distinct powers exercised by the English chancellor in charity cases, the one under the sign manual of the crown, the other under the general jurisdiction in equity; as well as to designate the rule of construction which has sometimes been applied to executory devises or powers of appointment to indi-

[1] The statement of facts is abridged and a part of the opinion is omitted.

viduals, in order to avoid the objection of remoteness. It was of this last, and not of any doctrine peculiar to charities, that Lord Kenyon said, " The doctrine of *cy pres* goes to the utmost verge of the law, and we must take care that it does not run wild;" and Lord Eldon, " It is not proper to go one step farther." Brudenell *v.* Elwes, 1 East, 451; s. c. 7 Ves. 390. 1 Jarman on Wills, 261–263. Sugden on Powers, *c.* 9, sect. 9. Coster *v.* Lorillard, 14 Wend. 309, 348.

The principal, if not the only, cases in which the disposition of a charity is held to be in the crown by sign manual, are of two classes; the first, of bequests to particular uses charitable in their nature, but illegal, as for a form of religion not tolerated by law; and the second, of gifts of property to charity generally, without any trust interposed, and in which either no appointment is provided for, or the power of appointment is delegated to persons who die without exercising it.

It is by the sign manual and in cases of the first class, that the arbitrary dispositions have been made, which were so justly condemned by Lord Thurlow in Moggridge *v.* Thackwell, 1 Ves. Jr. 469, and Sir William Grant in Cary *v.* Abbot, 7 Ves. 494, 495; and which, through want of due discrimination, have brought so much discredit upon the whole doctrine of *cy pres*. Such was the case of Attorney General *v.* Baxter, in which a bequest to Mr. Baxter to be distributed by him among sixty pious ejected ministers, (not, as the testator declared, for the sake of their nonconformity, but because he knew many of them to be pious and good men and in great want), was held to be void, and given under the sign manual to Chelsea College; but the decree was afterward reversed, upon the ground that this was really a legacy to sixty individuals to be named. 1 Vern. 248; 2 Vern. 105; 1 Eq. Cas. Ab. 96; 7 Ves. 76. Such also was the case of Da Costa *v.* De Pas, in which a gift for establishing a jesuba or assembly for reading the Jewish law was applied to the support of a Christian chapel at a foundling hospital. Ambl. 228; 2 Swanst. 489 note; 1 Dick. 258; 7 Ves. 76, 81.

This power of disposal by the sign manual of the crown in direct opposition to the declared intention of the testator, whether it is to be deemed to have belonged to the king as head of the church as well as of the state, " intrusted and empowered to see that nothing be done to the disherison of the crown or the propagation of a false religion;" Rex *v.* Portington, 1 Salk. 162; s. c. 1 Eq. Cas. Ab. 96; or to have been derived from the power exercised by the Roman emperor, who was sovereign legislator as well as supreme interpreter of the laws; Dig. 33, 2, 17; 50, 8, 4; Code, *lib.* 1, *tit.* 2, *c.* 19; *tit.* 14, *c.* 12; is clearly a prerogative and not a judicial power, and could not be exercised by this court; and it is difficult to see how it could be held to exist at all in a republic, in which charitable bequests have never been forfeited to the use or submitted to the disposition of the government, because superstitious or illegal. 4 Dane Ab. 239. Gass *v.* Wilhite, 2 Dana, 176. Methodist Church *v.* Remington, 1 Watts, 226.

The second class of bequests which are disposed of by the king's sign manual is of gifts to charity generally, with no uses specified, no trust interposed, and either no provision made for an appointment, or the power of appointment delegated to particular persons who die without exercising it. Boyle on Charities, 238, 239. Attorney General *v.* Syderfen, 1 Vern. 224; s. c. 1 Eq. Cas. Ab. 96. Attorney General *v.* Fletcher, 5 Law Journal (N. S.) Ch. 75. This too is not a judicial power of expounding and carrying out the testator's intention, but a prerogative power of ordaining what the testator has failed to express. No instance is reported, or has been discovered in the thorough investigations of the subject, of an exercise of this power in England before the reign of Charles II. Moggridge *v.* Thackwell, 7 Ves. 69–81. Dwight's Argument in the Rose Will Case, 272. It has never, so far as we know, been introduced into the practice of any court in this country; and, if it exists anywhere here, it is in the legislature of the Commonwealth as succeeding to the powers of the king as *parens patriæ*. 4 Kent Com. 508, *note*. Fontain *v.* Ravenel, 17 How. 369, 384. Moore *v.* Moore, 4 Dana, 365, 366. Witman *v.* Lex, 17 S. & R. 93. Attorney General *v.* Jolly, 1 Rich. Eq. 108. Dickson *v.* Montgomery, 1 Swan, 348. Lepage *v.* Macnamara, 5 Iowa, 146. Bartlet *v.* King, 12 Mass. 545. Sohier *v.* Massachusetts General Hospital, 3 Cush. 496, 497. It certainly cannot be exercised by the judiciary of a state whose constitution declares that " the judicial department shall never exercise the legislative and executive powers, or either of them: to the end it may be a government of laws and not of men." Declaration of Rights, art. 30.

The jurisdiction of the court of chancery to superintend the administration and decree the performance of gifts to trustees for charitable uses of a kind stated in the gift stands upon different grounds; and is part of its equity jurisdiction over trusts, which is shown by abundant evidence to have existed before the passage of the Statute of Charitable Uses. . . .

A charity, being a trust in the support and execution of which the whole public is concerned, and which is therefore allowed by the law to be perpetual, deserves and often requires the exercise of a larger discretion by the court of chancery than a mere private trust; for without a large discretionary power, in carrying out the general intent of the donor, to vary the details of administration, and even the mode of application, many charities would fail by change of circumstances and the happening of contingencies which no human foresight could provide against; and the probabilities of such failure would increase with the lapse of time and the remoteness of the heirs from the original donor who had in a clear and lawful manner manifested his will to divert his estate from his heirs for the benefit of public charities.

It is accordingly well settled by decisions of the highest authority, that when a gift is made to trustees for a charitable purpose, the general nature of which is pointed out, and which is lawful and valid at the time of the death of the testator, and no intention is expressed to limit it to a particular institution or mode of application, and afterwards, either by change of circumstances the scheme of the testator becomes impracticable, or by change of law becomes illegal, the fund, having once vested in the charity, does not go to the heirs at law as a resulting trust, but is to be applied by the court of chancery, in the exercise of its jurisdiction in equity, as near the testator's particular directions as possible, to carry out his general charitable intent. In all the cases of charities which have been administered in the English courts of chancery without the aid of the sign manual, the prerogative of the king acting through the chancellor has not been alluded to, except for the purpose of distinguishing it from the power exercised by the court in its inherent equitable jurisdiction with the assistance of its masters in chancery. . . .

The intention of the testator is the guide, or, in the phrase of Lord Coke, the lodestone, of the court; and therefore, whenever a charitable gift can be administered according to his express directions, this court, like the court of chancery in England, is not at liberty to modify it upon considerations of policy or convenience. Harvard College v. Society for Promoting Theological Education, 3 Gray, 280. Baker v. Smith, 13 Met. 34. Trustees of Smith Charities v. Northampton, 10 Allen, 498. But there are several cases, where the charitable trust could not be executed as directed in the will, in which the testator's scheme has been varied by this court in such a way and to such an extent as could not be done in the case of a private trust. Thus bequests to a particular bible society by name, whether a corporation established by law or a voluntary association, which had ceased to exist before the death of the testator, have been sustained, and applied to the distribution of bibles through a trustee appointed by the court for the purpose. Winslow v. Cummings, 3 Cush. 358. Bliss v. American Bible Society, 2 Allen, 334. . . .

In all the cases cited at the argument, in which a charitable bequest, which might have been lawfully carried out under the circumstances existing at the death of the testator, has been held, upon a change of circumstances, to result to the heirs at law or residuary legatees, the gift was distinctly limited to particular persons or establishments. Such was Russell v. Kellett, 3 Sm. & Giff. 264, in which the gift was of five pounds outright to each poor person of a particular description in certain parishes, and Vice Chancellor Stuart held that the shares of those who died before receiving them went to the residuary legatees. Such also was Clark *v.* Taylor, 1 Drewry, 642, in which it was held that a legacy to a certain orphan school by name, which ceased to exist after the death of the testator, failed and fell into the residue of the estate; and which can hardly be reconciled with the decisions in Incorporated Society *v.* Price, 1 Jones & Lat. 498; s. c. 7 Irish Eq. 260; *In re* Clergy Society, 2 Kay & Johns. 615; Marsh *v.* Attorney General, 2 Johns. & Hem. 61; Winslow *v.* Cummings, 3 Cush. 358, and Bliss *v.* American Bible Society, 2 Allen, 334. So in Easterbrooks *v.* Tillinghast, 5 Gray, 17, the trust was expressly limited, not only in object, but in duration, to the maintenance of the pastor of a certain church of a specified faith and practice in a particular town, " so long as they or their successors shall maintain the visibility of a church in said faith and order;" and could not have been held to have terminated, had it not been so limited. Attorney General *v.* Columbine, Boyle on Charities, 204, 205. Potter *v.* Thurston, 7 R. I. 25. Dexter *v.* Gardner, 7 Allen, 243.

The charitable bequests of Francis Jackson cannot, in the opinion of the court, be regarded as so restricted in their objects, or so limited in point of time, as to have been terminated and destroyed by the abolition of slavery in the United States. They are to a board of trustees for whose continuance careful provision is made in the will, and which the testator expresses a wish may become a permanent organization and may receive the services and sympathy, the donations and bequests, of the friends of the slave. Their duration is not in terms limited, like that of the trust sought to be established in the sixth article of the will, by the accomplishment of the end specified. They take effect from the time of the testator's death, and might then have been lawfully applied in exact conformity with his expressed intentions. The retaining of the funds in the custody of the court while this case has been under advisement cannot affect the question. The gifts being lawful and charitable, and having once vested, the subsequent change of circumstances before the funds have been actually paid over is of no more weight than if they had been paid to the trustees and been administered by them for a century before slavery was extinguished.

Neither the immediate purpose of the testator — the moral education of the people; nor his ultimate object — to better the condition of the African race in this country; has been fully accomplished by the abolition of slavery.

Negro slavery was recognized by our law as an infraction of the rights inseparable from human nature; and tended to promote idleness, selfishness and tyranny in one part of the community, a destruction of the domestic relations and utter debasement in the other part. The sentiment which would put an end to it is the sentiment of justice, humanity and charity, based upon moral duty, inspired by the most familiar precepts of the Christian religion, and approved by the Constitution of the Commonwealth. The teaching and diffusion of such a sentiment are not of temporary benefit or necessity, but of perpetual obligation. Slavery may be abolished; but to strengthen and confirm the sentiment which opposed it will continue to be useful and desirable so long as selfishness, cruelty, the lust of dominion, and indifference to the rights of the weak, the poor and the ignorant, have a place in the hearts of men. Looking at the trust established by the fourth article of this will as one for the moral education of the people only, the case is within the principle of those, already cited, in which charities for the relief of leprosy and the plague were held not to end with the disappearance of those diseases; and is not essentially different from that of Baliol College, in which a trust for the education at Oxford of Scotch youths, to be sent into Scotland to preach Episcopalianism in the established church there, was applied by Lords Somers and Hardwicke and their successors to educate such youths, although, by the change of faith and practice of the Church of Scotland, the donor's ultimate object could no longer be accomplished.

The intention of Francis Jackson to benefit the negro race appears not only in the leading clause of the fourth article, and in his expression of a hope that his trustees might receive the aid and the gifts of the friends of the slave, but in the trust for the benefit of fugitive slaves in the fifth article of the will, to which, according to the principle established by the house of lords in the case of Betton's Charity, resort may be had to ascertain his intent and the fittest mode of carrying it out. The negroes, although emancipated, still stand in great need of assistance and education. Charities for the relief of the poor have been often held to be well applied to educate them and their children. Bishop of Hereford v. Adams, 7 Ves. 324. Wilkinson v. Malin, 2 Cr. & Jerv. 636; s. c. 2 Tyrwh. 544. Anderson v. Wrights of Glasgow, 12 Law Times, (N. S.) 807. The case of the Mico Charity is directly to the point that a gift for the redemption of poor slaves may be appropriated, after they have been emancipated by law, to educate them; and the reasons given by Lord Cottenham for that decision apply with no less force to those set free by the recent amendment of the Constitution in the United States, than to those who were emancipated by act of parliament in the West Indies.

The mode in which the funds bequeathed by the fourth and fifth articles of the will may be best applied to carry out in a lawful manner the charitable intents and purposes of the testator as nearly as possible must be settled by a scheme to be framed by a master and confirmed by the court before the funds are paid over to the trustees. In doing this, the court does not take the charity out of the hands of the trustees, but only declares the law which must be their guide in its administration. Shelford on Mortmain, 651–654. Boyle on Charities, 214–218. The case is therefore to be referred to a master, with liberty to the attorney general and the trustees to submit schemes for his approval; and all further directions are reserved until the coming in of his report.

Case referred to a master.

The case was then referred to John Codman, Esquire, a master in chancery for this county, who, after notice to the trustees and the attorney general, and hearing the parties, made his report, the results of which were approved by the attorney general; and upon exceptions to which the case was argued by W. Phillips for himself and other excepting trustees, and by J. A. Andrew in support of the master's report, before Gray, J. with the agreement that he should consult the whole court before entering a final decree. No account was asked by any party to sums already expended by the trustees.

As to the bequest in the fifth article, the master reported that the unexpended balance (amounting to $1049.90) was so small that it was reasonable that it should be confined to a limited territory; and that it should therefore be applied by the trustees, in accordance with their unanimous recommendation, to the use of necessitous persons of African descent in the city of Boston and its vicinity. This scheme was approved and confirmed by the court, with this addition: " Preference being given to such as have escaped from slavery."

As to the sum bequeathed in the fourth article of the will, the master reported that a portion had been expended by the trustees before any question arose as to its validity; and that but two schemes had been suggested to him for the appropriation of the residue, namely, first, (which was approved by four of the seven trustees who had accepted the trust,) in part to the support of the Anti-Slavery Standard, and in part to the New England Branch of the American Freedmen's Union Commission; or, second, (which was approved by the remaining trustees,) that the whole should be applied to the last named object.

The master disapproved of the first of these schemes; and reported that the Anti-Slavery Standard was a weekly newspaper published in the city of New York with a circulation of not more than three thousand copies, which was established nearly thirty years ago for the purpose of acting upon public opinion in favor of the abolition of slavery that in his opinion, since the abolition of slavery, and the passage of the reconstruction acts of congress, " the support of a paper of such limited circulation as hardly to be self-sustaining would do very little for the benefit of the colored people in their present *status*, and its direct influence would be almost imperceptible on the welfare of that class most nearly corresponding to those whom the testator had in view in making this bequest;" and that the argument, that it was evidently the intention of the testator to accomplish the object indicated in the fourth article of his will by means of which a newspaper like this might be considered an example, was answered by the fact that the object for which these means were to be used had been already accomplished without them. The master returned with his report a few numbers of the Anti-Slavery Standard, (taken without selection as they were given to him by the chairman of the trustees,) by which it appeared that it was in large part devoted to urging the passage of laws securing to the freedman equal political rights with the whites, the keeping of the southern states under military government, the impeachment of the president, and other political measures.

The master reported that he was unable to devise any better plan than the second scheme suggested; that this mode of appropriation was in his opinion most in accordance with the intention of the testator as expressed in the fourth article of the will, because the intention nearest to that of emancipating the slaves was by educating the emancipated slaves to render them capable of self-government, and this could best be done by an organized society, expressly intended and exactly fitted for this function, and which, if the whole or any part of this fund was to be applied to the direct education and support of the freedmen, was admitted at the hearing before him to be the fittest channel for the appropriation. The master returned with his report printed documents by which it appeared that the object of the American Freedmen's Union Commission, as stated in its constitution, was "the relief, education and elevation of the freedmen of the United States, and to aid and coöperate with the people of the south, without distinction of race or color, in the improvement of their condition, upon the basis of industry, education, freedom and Christian morality;" and that the New England and other branches of the commission were now maintaining large numbers of teachers and schools for this purpose throughout the southern states.

The master accordingly reported that what remained of the fund bequeathed by the fourth article of the will should be "ordered to be paid over to the New England Branch of the Freedmen's Union Commission, to be employed and expended by them in promoting the education, support and interests generally of the freedmen (late slaves) in the States of this Union recently in rebellion." And this scheme was by the opinion of the whole court accepted and confirmed, modified only by directing the executor to pay the fund to the trustees, to be by them paid over at such times and in such sums as they in their discretion might think fit to the treasurer of the branch commission; and by substituting for the words "recently in rebellion" the words "in which slavery has been abolished, either by the proclamation of the late President Lincoln or the amendment of the Constitution."

Final decree accordingly.[1]

[1] For a collection of cases involving the exercise of the *cy pres* power, see Scott, Cases on Trusts, 1 ed., 353.

BOWDEN v. BROWN.

SUPREME JUDICIAL COURT, MASSACHUSETTS. 1908.

200 Mass. 269.

BILL IN EQUITY, filed in the Probate Court for the county of Essex on October 2, 1908, by the trustees under the will of Sarah E. Goodwin, late of Lynn, for instructions as to the construction of the residuary clause of that will, which is quoted in the opinion.

In the Probate Court Harmon, J., made a decree that the plaintiffs should invest the residue of the estate and hold it so invested with its accumulations for the purposes named in the will, instead of paying it over to the next of kin of the testatrix. The defendants Annie S. Brown and others, claiming as the next of kin of the testatrix, appealed.

The case came on to be heard before Hammond, J., who, at the request of the parties, reserved it upon the bill and the answers of the several defendants for determination by the full court, such decree to be entered as law and justice might require.

KNOWLTON, C. J. Sarah E. Goodwin, late of Marblehead, deceased, after giving certain legacies in her will, provided as follows: "The remainder shall . . . be given to the town of Marblehead toward the erection of a building that should be for the sick and poor, those without homes. I leave this in the hands of William S. Bowden, Mary G. Brown and William Reynolds of Marblehead." This gift constitutes a public charity. Richardson v. Mullery, *ante*, 247, and cases cited. But by the terms of the will, it is to go to a designated donee, to be used for a specified purpose, for the benefit of a certain class of sick and poor. The donee, the town of Marblehead, at a meeting of the voters has declined to accept the legacy. It was given " toward the erection of a building " by the town. The action of the town is equivalent to a refusal to erect such a building. It appears that the charity cannot be administered in the way stated in the will. It therefore must fail altogether, unless it can be administered under the doctrine of *cy pres*. The question arises whether the purpose of the testatrix was to give her property for this specific charity, or whether her charitable purpose was general, so that the court is authorized to apply the money to some other charity, similar to that mentioned in the will, under a scheme to be devised for that purpose. It is manifest that the amount of the property, which is only about $8,000, is insufficient for the erection and maintenance of such a building as the testatrix contemplated. She expected that the building would be erected and maintained by the town, with such aid as would be derived from the use of her gift. The trust was not for the erection of a building by trustees under her will, entirely from the proceeds of her property. It being impossible to do that which the testatrix had in mind, can we discover a purpose to do something else of a similar character? We think not. There is nothing to indicate that she intended to make provision generally for the sick and poor of the town, or particularly for those without homes, unless they could be provided with a home in a building to be erected for their use. General provision for the sick and poor would seem to include a charity much broader than anything in her contemplation. The case seems to fall within the class where no intent to use the gift for other charitable purposes can be discovered, if it is impossible to execute the particular charity for which provision is made. In such cases the charity fails altogether. [Citing cases.]

We are of opinion that the gift fails and that the residuary estate must go to the next of kin.

So ordered.[1]

[1] For cases in which the court refused to allow an application *cy pres,* see Scott, Cases on Trusts, 1 ed., 355.

As to the *cy pres* doctrine, see Zollmann, Charities, chap. 3; Dec. Dig., Charities, sec. 37; 13 Cornell L. Quar. 310; 1 N. C. L. Rev. 41; 6 Iowa L. Bull. 177.

If it is possible and practicable to carry out the intention of the testator, there is no room for the application of the *cy pres* doctrine. *Re* Weir Hospital, [1910] 2 Ch. 124; Harvard College *v.* A. G., 228 Mass. 396; Eliot *v.* Trinity Church, 232 Mass. 517. But see *Re* Queen's School, [1910] 1 Ch. 796.

It has been said that even the legislature has no power to authorize the use of trust funds for other purposes than those designated by the testator, if it is possible and practicable to carry out the testator's purpose. Cary Library *v.* Bliss, 151 Mass. 364; Crawford *v.* Nies, 220 Mass. 61, 224 Mass. 474. It is clear that the legislature has no power to modify the charter of a charitable corporation without its consent. Trustees of Dartmouth College *v.* Woodward, 4 Wheat. (U. S.) 518. In State *v.* Adams, 44 Mo. 570, it was held such modification was unconstitutional even with the consent of the corporation. But see Univ. of Maryland *v.* Williams, 9 G. & J. (Md.) 365; St. John's College *v.* Comptroller, 23 Md. 629; *Re* St. Mary's Church, 7 S. & R. (Pa.) 517. See Scott, Education and the Dead Hand, 34 Harv. L. Rev. 1.

A court of equity may authorize alienation of the trust property although alienation is expressly forbidden by the testator. Stanley *v.* Colt, 5 Wall. (U. S.) 119; Odell *v.* Odell, 10 Allen (Mass.) 1; Lackland *v.* Walker, 151 Mo. 210; Rolfe etc. Asylum *v.* Lefebre, 69 N. H. 238; Smart *v.* Town of Durham, 77 N. H. 56; Grace Church *v.* Ange, 161 N. C. 314; Trustees of Sailors' Snug Harbor *v.* Carmody, 211 N. Y. 286; Brown *v.* Meeting Street Baptist Society, 9 R. I. 177. See Gray, Rule ag. Perp., sec. 590, n. 3; Tudor, Charities, 270. In these cases the Attorney General must be a party to the suit. Bernardsville M. E. Church *v.* Seney, 85 N. J. Eq. 271; Trustees of Sailors' Snug Harbor *v.* Carmody, 211 N. Y. 286.

If the trustees are not by the trust instrument given a power to sell land, they have no right to sell without the permission of the court. Seif *v.* Krebs, 239 Pa. 423.

As to the power of the legislature to authorize an alienation of trust property, see Stanley *v.* Colt, 5 Wall. (U. S.) 119; Bridgeport Public Library *v.* Burroughs Home, 85 Conn. 309; Tharp *v.* Fleming, 1 Houst. (Del.) 580; Trustees *v.* Laird, 10 Del. Ch. 118.

Upon a breach of trust by a misuser or by a nonuser, the trust property does not revert to the testator or donor in the absence of an express condition or limitation, if it is still possible to apply the property for the purposes of the trust or to apply it *cy pres*. Barnard *v.* Adams, 58 Fed. 313; Stuart *v.* City of Easton, 74 Fed. 854; Bridgeport Public Library *v.* Burroughs Home, 85 Conn. 309; Huger *v.* Protestant Episcopal Church, 137 Ga. 205; Carroll County Academy *v.* Gallatin Academy, 104 Ky. 621; Mott *v.* Morris, 240 Mo. 137; Goode *v.* McPherson, 51 Mo. 126; Borchers *v.* Taylor, 145 Atl. 666 (N. H., 1929); Green *v.* Blackwell (N. J. Eq.), 37 Atl. 375; Mills *v.* Davison, 54 N. J. Eq. 659; Associate Alumni *v.* Theological Seminary, 163 N. Y. 417; Barr *v.* Weld, 24 Pa. 84; Petition of Sellers Church, 139 Pa. 61; Strong *v.* Doty, 32 Wis. 381. See Perry, Trusts, sec. 744; 11 C. J. 372; Dec. Dig., Charities, sec. 29; 63 A. L. R. 880.

But such a condition or limitation attached to the legal or equitable interest is valid. Porter's Case, 1 Rep. 22*a, b; Re* Estate of Douglas, 94 Neb. 280; Norton *v.* Valentine, 151 N. Y. App. Div. 392. Dec. Dig., Charities, sec. 38. See Gray, Rule ag. Perp., secs. 30, 299–311*a* (right of entry for breach of condition); secs. 31–42, 312, 313 (possibility of reverter after determinable fee); 327*a*, 603*i* (resulting trust after equitable interest).

As to the effect of a taking of the property on eminent domain, see Lyford *v.* Laconia, 75 N. H. 220.

The proper person to enforce a charitable trust is the Attorney General. On the question whether anyone other than the Attorney General, for example the donor or his heirs, or a beneficiary, can institute a proceeding, see Gray, Rule ag. Perp., secs. 680–685; Gray, The Rights of the Donors in Trusts for Charitable Purposes, 14 Mass. L. Quar. 50; 62 A. L. R. 881.

CHAPTER V.

RESULTING AND CONSTRUCTIVE TRUSTS.[1]

SECTION I.

Where an Express Trust Fails in Whole or in Part.

WELFORD *v.* STOKOE.

CHANCERY. 1867.

(1867) W. N. 208.

THIS WAS a suit for the execution of the trusts of the will of George Simpson, made in 1861, whereby, after making several specific devises, he devised and bequeathed the residue of his real estate to " his trustees and executors thereinafter named, the survivor or survivors of them, upon trust to sell and convert into money the whole thereof, and invest the produce in their joint names in the public

---

[1] " In order to understand resulting trusts one must recall the law of resulting uses prior to the Statute of Uses. Before that statute there were three kinds of uses called resulting:

" (1) The typical resulting use was the one held to exist where A., a fee-simple owner, made a feoffment to B. and his heirs; but B. gave no consideration, and A. declared no use in favor of B. or of any one else.

" (2) Another kind of resulting use was that which existed where A. paid the purchase money for a conveyance of land by B. and had B. make a feoffment in fee of the land to C., who was legally a stranger to A.

" (3) Closely akin to the first kind of resulting use was the use found to exist where A. made the feoffment to B. and his heirs to the use of or in trust for C. for life, or on some other use which did not purport to dispose of the whole beneficial interest, or on a use which failed for some reason to take effect, and B. gave no consideration.

" In case (1) the beneficial interest in fee resulted to A., but in case (3) only the undisposed of or ineffectually given part of the fee of the use belonged to A." Costigan, The Classification of Trusts, 27 Harv. L. Rev. 439.

" A group of cases involving constructive trusts invite consideration of what such a 'trust' really is. An express trust is a substantive institution. Constructive trust, on the other hand, is purely a remedial institution. As the chancellor acted *in personam,* one of the most effective remedial expedients at his command was to treat a defendant as if he were a trustee and put pressure upon his person to compel him to act accordingly. Thus constructive trust could be used in a variety of situations, sometimes to provide a remedy better suited to the circumstances of the particular case, where the suit was founded on another theory, as in cases of reformation, of specific performance, of fraudulent conveyance, and of what the civilian would call exclusion of unworthy heirs, and sometimes to develop a new field of equitable interposition, as in what we have come to think the typical case of constructive trust, namely, specific restitution of a received benefit in order to prevent unjust enrichment." Pound, The Progress of the Law, Equity, 33 Harv. L. Rev. 420.

funds, receive the interest and dividends, and divide the same in the following proportions for an equal benefit," and he appointed T. W. Welford and B. Walker, trustees and executors.

Glasse, Q. C., and *C. Hall,* for the plaintiff, T. W. Welford, and *Whitehouse,* for B. Walker, contended, that the trustees and executors took the beneficial interest in the residuary estate.

Faber, for the next of kin, and *Chitty,* for the heir-at-law, contended that there was an intestacy as to the beneficial interest.

The VICE-CHANCELLOR [SIR R. MALINS] held that the testator had affixed a trust upon the residuary estate, without specifying the objects of the trust, and consequently there was a resulting trust, as to the real estate for the heir, and as to the personalty for the next of kin.[1]

DIGBY *v.* LEGARD.

CHANCERY. 1774.

3 P. Wms. 22n.

E. B. devised her real and personal estate to trustees, in trust, to sell, to pay debts and legacies, and to pay the residue to five persons to be equally divided between them, share and share alike; one of the residuary legatees died in the lifetime of the testatrix: the court

[1] See Ackroyd *v.* Smithson, 1 Bro. C. C. 503 (lapse); *Re* Tilt, 74 L. T. 163 (conveyance by deed in trust for one who was dead at the time of the conveyance); *Re* Scott, [1911] 2 Ch. 374 (disclaimer by beneficiary). See Bogert, Trusts, sec. 32; Perry, Trusts, secs. 150–160a; 3 Pomeroy, Eq. Juris., secs. 1032–3; Dec. Dig., Trusts, secs. 64–68.

If personal property is bequeathed upon trusts which fail and the testator leaves no next of kin, the beneficial interest passes to the Crown or to the State. Taylor *v.* Haygarth, 14 Sim. 8. If real property is devised upon trusts which fail and the testator leaves no heir, in England at common law the trustee was allowed to keep the property. Taylor *v.* Haygarth, *supra. Cf.* Burgess *v.* Wheate, 1 W. Bl. 123. But by the Intestates Estates Act, 1884, (47 & 48 Vict. c. 71, sec. 4), in England, and generally by statute or at common law in this country, the beneficial interest in realty as in personalty passes to the Crown or the State. See Johnston *v.* Spicer, 107 N. Y. 185; Commonwealth *v.* Naile, 88 Pa. 429.

If the will or deed of settlement shows an intention to give the beneficial interest to the trustee in the event of the failure of the trusts declared, there will of course be no resulting trust. Wright *v.* Row, 1 Bro. C. C. 60. Similarly where a testator devises a term for years to trustees for a particular purpose and the land *subject thereto* is devised over to another, and the purpose fails, the latter is entitled to the beneficial interest in the term. Sidney *v.* Shelley, 19 Ves. 352, G. Coop. 206; Jarman, Wills, 6th ed., 723. See Randall *v.* Randall, 85 Md. 430; Hall *v.* Smith, 61 N. H. 144. Compare Carrick *v.* Errington, 2 P. Wms. 361; *Re* Scott, [1911] 2 Ch. 374; *Re* Young, [1913] 1 Ch. 272, 26 Harv. L. Rev. 660; *Re* Brooke, [1923] 2 Ch. 265.

Equitable conversion. As to conflicting claims of the next of kin and the heir of a testator who has directed a conversion of the property bequeathed or devised, see Roy *v.* Monroe, 47 N. J. Eq. 356; 3 Pomeroy, Eq. Juris., secs. 1169–74; Perry, Trusts, sec. 448; 6 Gray, Cas. Prop., 2d ed., 382 *et seq.*

[LORD BATHURST, C.] at the hearing, and afterwards upon a rehearing held that this was a resulting trust, as to the share in the real estate of the residuary legatee who died in the testatrix's lifetime, for the benefit of the heir at law.[1]

SALUSBURY v. DENTON.
CHANCERY. 1857.
3 Kay & J. 529.

LYNCH BURROUGHS, by his will in 1835, referring to a policy of insurance which he had settled upon his marriage, upon trust as to 2000*l.*, part of the proceeds, for his wife absolutely, and, as to the residue, upon certain trusts under which, in the event of her surviving him, she was entitled to a life interest therein, with remainder to himself absolutely, proceeded to dispose of his interest as follows: " Now with reference to my policy in the Equitable, No. ——, as settled by my marriage settlement on my dear wife, with absolute disposal of 2000*l.* thereof if she survive me, I leave the same, on her decease, to be divided (whatever may have proved the amount of the claim) one moiety thereof to my daughter," the plaintiff, " (if living) for her life therewith, and the other moiety to be at the disposal, by her will, of my dear wife therewith to apply a part to the foundation of a charity school, or such other charitable endowment for the benefit of the poor of Offley as she may prefer, and under such regulations as she may prescribe herself; and the remainder of said moiety to be at her disposal among my relatives, in such proportions as she may be pleased to direct." The testator bequeathed his residuary personalty to his wife as his sole residuary legatee.

By a codicil to his will the testator gave the first mentioned moiety to Sir Charles Salusbury absolutely, subject to the plaintiff's life interest therein.

The testator died in 1837, leaving the plaintiff his only child.

His widow died in 1856, without having made any will or any disposition of the second moiety; and administration of her estate and effects was granted to the defendant Maria Newberry.

The proceeds of the policy were now represented by 11,619*l.* 16*s.* 2*d.*, 3 per cent. Consols.

The bill prayed that the trusts of the will, so far as related to this sum, might be carried into execution under the direction of the Court.

VICE-CHANCELLOR SIR W. PAGE WOOD: The question in this case

[1] As to the conflicting claims of the next of kin or heir and the residuary legatee or devisee to lapsed shares of the residue, see Rood, Wills, 2 ed., secs. 671–2; Warren, Cas. Wills, 329–332; 4 Gray, Cas. Prop., 2 ed., 362–371; 28 A. L. R. 1237.

arises upon the will of Lynch Burroughs, who having, upon his marriage, settled a certain policy of insurance upon trust, as to 2000*l.*, part of the proceeds for his wife absolutely; and as to the residue upon certain trusts under which, in the event of her surviving him, she would be entitled to a life interest therein, with remainder to himself absolutely, by his will disposed of his interest as follows: — [His Honour read the passage from the will set out above.] Then by a codicil the testator bequeathed the moiety, in which his daughter has a life interest, to Sir Charles Salusbury, subject to the life interest of his daughter, so that the only question is as to the second moiety.

As regards this second moiety, he directs it to be at his wife's disposal by her will " *to apply* a part to the foundation of a charity-school or such other charitable endowment for the benefit of the poor of Offley as she may prefer, and under such regulations as she may prescribe herself, and the remainder to be at her disposal among his relatives in such proportions as she may be pleased to direct."

The first question that was argued was, whether as to the part intended by the testator for charitable purposes, the gift was or was not void; and as to this part of the case I have no doubt, as I said at the close of the argument, that it was not void, because under the terms of the will the widow had an option, — she was at liberty to apply that part " to the foundation of a charity-school, *or* such other charitable endowment," as in the will mentioned. And whatever may be the effect of the words " foundation of a charity-school," occurring in the first branch of that alternative, it is clear as to the second, — the foundation of a charitable endowment, — that a bequest for such a purpose would be a lawful bequest, and not void under the stat. 9 Geo. 2, c. 36.

The gift, therefore, amounts to a bequest of the fund in question to be at his wife's disposal by her will, therewith " *to* apply " a part to the foundation of such charitable endowment for the benefit of the poor of Offley as she may prefer, and under such regulations as she may prescribe, and the remainder " to be at her disposal among " the testator's relatives in such proportions as she may direct.

Now, if either of these purposes had been mentioned alone, the case would be disposed of at once. The words " *to* apply," " to be at her disposal among," are much stronger in favour of construing this as a trust than those in Brown *v.* Higgs, 4 Ves. 708, 5 *Id*. 495, 8 *Id*. 561, where the words, " I authorise and empower," might have been said to create a mere authority, and not a trust. And this is clearly the view which Lord St. Leonards takes of a will like the present, in his treatise on " Powers," where he is discussing the case of the Duke of Marlborough *v.* Lord Godolphin, 2 Ves., sen. 61, and that of Harding *v.* Glyn, 1 Atk. 469, S. C. 5 Ves. 501. Admitting that there was a distinction between the two cases, he says, in effect, that where there is a power of selection among certain objects, and an intention manifested that the objects should not be disappointed, — for instance, where there is a bequest to the testator's wife for life, and after her decease *to be divided or distributed* amongst such of his children as she should appoint, — as the right to exclude some, does not prevent the class from taking in default of appointment, it would now be held, notwithstanding the decision in the Duke of Marlborough *v.* Lord Godolphin, that the children take in default of appointment, either by implication, or because the power is coupled with a trust, 2 Sug. Pow. 163.

Here, I can have no doubt that the words " to apply " and " to be at her disposal among," are clearly sufficient to create a trust; and that if this had been simply a bequest of the whole, to be at the widow's disposal among the testator's relatives in such proportions as she might direct, the widow dying without having so disposed of it, the whole would go to the plaintiff, as the testator's only child, and the only one of his relatives capable of taking within the Statutes of Distribution, (see 2 Sug. Pow. 237); although, having this power of disposal among his " relatives," the widow might have exercised it, had she been so minded, in such manner as to include persons more distantly related to the testator. See Harding *v.* Glyn, *ubi supra.*

Then the question arises, whether the bequest in this case is void for uncertainty, it being only to be at the disposal of the widow " as to a part " (without saying what part) for one set of objects, and " as to the remainder " for another. . . .

Here there is a plain direction to the widow to give a part to the charitable purposes referred to in the will as she may think fit, and the remainder among the testator's relatives as she may direct. And the widow having died without exercising that discretion, the moiety in question must be divided equally.

There will be a declaration, that, as to one moiety, Sir Charles Salusbury is entitled absolutely, subject to the Plaintiff's life interest therein, and that the other moiety is divisible in equal parts, one of such parts to be for charitable purposes, and the other for the Plaintiff absolutely, as the only person entitled under the Statutes of Distribution. There must also be a reference to chambers to settle the scheme for the application of the part devoted to charitable purposes.[1]

[1] In *Re* Kieran, [1916] 1 I. R. 289, property was devised to a trustee upon trust for such son of A as A should appoint. A died without appointing, leaving three sons. It was held that the three sons were entitled as tenants in common. The court said: " To hold that the three sons took equally would be at all events carrying out to a certain extent his [the testator's] declared desire. It might be argued that this would amount to an extension of the doctrine of cy-pres to trusts, but I do not so regard it. I am inclined to think that the Court, without doing any violence to the canons of interpretation, may infer from the words used that the desire of the testa-

In re CLARKE.

BRACEY *v.* ROYAL NATIONAL LIFEBOAT INSTITUTION.

HIGH COURT OF JUSTICE, CHANCERY DIVISION. 1923.

[1923] 2 Ch. 407.

ADJOURNED SUMMONS.

The testator disposed of his residuary estate in the following terms: "I give and bequeath all the residue and remainder of my estate not otherwise disposed of by this my will to (*a*) such institution society or nursing home or nursing homes or similar institutions as assist or provide for persons of moderate means such as clerks governesses and others who may not be able or eligible to benefit under the National Health Insurance Act Old Age Pensions or other Act of a like character to have either surgical operations performed together with medical treatment or medical treatment alone on payment of some moderate contribution (*b*) the Royal National Lifeboat Institution (*c*) the Lister Institute of Preventive Medicine (*d*) and such other funds charities and institutions as my executors in their absolute discretion shall think fit. And I direct that such residue shall be divided amongst the legatees named in the paragraphs (*a*) (*b*) (*c*) and (*d*) lastly hereinbefore contained in such shares and proportions as my trustees shall determine."

This was a summons by the executors to determine (inter alia) whether the residuary estate was validly disposed of by the will or whether the above gifts failed in whole or in part for uncertainty.

ROMER, J., stated the gift of the testator's residuary estate as above set out, and continued: It is admitted that if all the objects referred to under the headings (*a*), (*b*), (*c*) and (*d*) are charitable objects the residue is validly disposed of. But, while admitting that the Royal National Lifeboat Institution and the Lister Institute of Preventive Medicine are charitable objects, it is contended on the part of the next of kin that the objects referred to under the headings (*a*) and (*d*) are not exclusively charitable. Whether this contention is well founded or not is the first question that I have to determine. It was contended on behalf of the next of kin that the objects designated under heading (*a*) are not charitable, because the persons to be benefited by the institution, society or nursing homes are not poor persons but persons of modern means, and because such persons

---

tor was that the three sons should take equally if for any reason the power were not exercised."

If a bequest is made in trust for such of the relatives of a designated person as the trustee may select, the trustee is not confined to the nearest relatives but may select among any relatives. If, however, the trustee fails to make a selection, it is held that the next of kin of the designated person are entitled to the property in equal shares. See Chap. II, sec. 1, *ante*.

can only benefit on payment by themselves of some moderate contribution. . . .

I therefore hold that the objects under heading (a) are charitable objects. On the other hand I am of opinion that the objects under heading (d) are not exclusively charitable. I can find nothing in the will to prevent the executors from selecting under this heading non-charitable funds and institutions. In a later part of his will the testator no doubt refers to certain charitable institutions as " funds charities or institutions," but I cannot infer from this or any other words of the will that the testator contemplated this expression as one that excluded non-charitable objects.

If I am right so far the testator has therefore given his residue to: (a) Indefinite charitable objects; (b) A definite charitable object; (c) Another definite charitable object; (d) Such indefinite charitable and non-charitable objects as his executors think fit, and has directed that the residue shall be divided amongst these legatees in such shares and proportions as his trustees (by which presumably he meant his executors) should determine. It is contended on behalf of the next of kin that such a disposition of the residue fails for uncertainty in accordance with the principle enunciated and applied in Morice v. Bishop of Durham, 9 Ves. 399, and many other similar cases. That principle is stated by Lord Davey in Hunter v. Attorney-General, [1899] A. C. 309, 323, in these words: " There is a long series of cases extending from Morice v. Bishop of Durham, decided by Sir William Grant and Lord Eldon, to In re Macduff, [1896] 2 Ch. 451, decided by the Court of Appeal in 1896, and including two decisions of Lord Cottenham. In these cases it has been held that where charitable purposes are mixed up with other purposes of such a shadowy and indefinite nature that the Court cannot execute them (such as ' charitable or benevolent,' or ' charitable or philanthropic,' or ' charitable or pious ' purposes), or where the description includes purposes which may or may not be charitable (such as ' undertakings of public utility '), and a discretion is vested in the trustees, the whole gift fails for uncertainty. In Vezey v. Jamson, (1822) 1 S. & S. 69, the trust was to dispose of the residue in such charitable or public purposes as the laws of the land would admit, or to any persons as the trustees in their discretion should think fit, or as they should think would have been agreeable to him, if living, and as the laws of the land did not prohibit. Sir John Leach said: ' The testator has not fixed upon any part of this property a trust for a charitable use; I cannot therefore devote any part of it to charity. . . . The necessary consequence is, that the purposes of the trust being so general and undefined that they cannot be executed by this Court, they must fail altogether, and the next of kin become entitled to the property.' "

But as I understand this principle it only applies to cases where, upon the words of the will, the executors in the exercise of their discretion could apply the whole fund to non-charitable indefinite objects. In such cases the testator has not, in the words of Sir John Leach, " fixed upon any part of his property a trust for a charitable use." It is of course obvious that if a testator gives a definite proportion of his property to such charitable objects as his executors may select, and the rest of his property to such non-charitable indefinite objects as his executors may select, the gift of the definite proportion would be a valid charitable gift and it would only be the gift of the rest of his property that would fail. But suppose that instead of himself fixing the definite proportion to be applied for charitable objects the testator should give to charity a part of his property without saying what part and the rest to non-charitable indefinite objects. In such a case the executors could not, I apprehend, devote the whole of the property to the non-charitable objects, and if once the Court can ascertain what is the part to be devoted to charity, I see no reason why the gift of such part should be invalid.

Now, in Salusbury v. Denton, 3 K. & J. 529, 538, there was a bequest of a fund to be at the disposal of the testator's widow, by her will, therewith to apply a part to the foundation of a charity school, or such other charitable endowment for the benefit of certain poor as she might prefer; and the remainder to be at her disposal among the testator's relatives as she might direct. It was held that, although the fund was to be applied as to a part, without saying what part, for one set of objects and as to the remainder for another, and the widow died without exercising her power of determining the proportions in which each were to take, the bequest was not void for uncertainty, but the Court would divide the fund in equal moieties, and give one of such moieties to charitable purposes and the other to the testator's relatives. In giving judgment Wood V.-C. clearly recognizes the distinction between such a case and one where the trustee could give the whole of the fund to non-charitable objects. Referring to a case of Down v. Worrall, (1833) 1 My. & K. 561, he says: " In Down v. Worrall the testator left part of his residuary personal estate to his trustees to settle it either to or for charitable or pious purposes, at their discretion, or otherwise for the separate benefit of his sister and all or any of her children, in such manner as his trustees should think fit. And there it was held, that a sum which remained at the decease of the surviving trustee, and which had not been applied either to charitable purposes or for the benefit of the testator's sister and her children, was undisposed of, and belonged to the testator's next of kin. Now, whether that case can or cannot be reconciled with all the others on this subject, it is very clearly distinguished from the present: for it is one thing to direct a trustee to give *a part* of a fund to one set of objects, *and the remainder* to another, and it is a distinct thing to direct him to give ' either ' to one set of objects ' *or* ' to another. Down v.

Worrall was a case of the latter description. There the trustees could give all to either of the objects. This is a case of the former description. Here the trustee was bound to give a part to each. I am therefore of opinion, that, even if the case of Down v. Worrall can be reconciled with the other authorities on this subject, it cannot affect my decision in the case before me. Here there is a plain direction to the widow to give a part to the charitable purposes referred to in the will as she may think fit, and the remainder among the testator's relatives as she may direct. And the widow having died without exercising that direction, the moiety in question must be divided equally."

If therefore in any case the executors cannot refuse to allocate a part of the fund to charitable purposes they must either fix the part to be given to those purposes, or, if they do not exercise their discretion, the Court would itself divide the fund between the charitable and the non-charitable objects. The Court is therefore able either through the exercise by the executor of his discretion, or by itself dividing the fund, to ascertain the proportion of the fund to be devoted to charitable purposes, and, when once that has been done, it appears to me that there is no difficulty in the Court giving effect to the trusts affecting the parts so allocated to charitable objects. It is true that in Hunter v. Attorney-General, [1899] A. C. 309, Lord Davey, in referring to the case of Salusbury v. Denton, 3 K. & J. 529, and Attorney-General v. Doyley, (1735) 7 Ves. 58n, referred to them as authorities for the proposition that where trustees have a discretion to apportion between charitable objects and definite and ascertainable objects non-charitable the trust does not fail. I think, however, that Lord Davey was merely contrasting cases where the trustees have an option to apply the whole fund to charitable or non-charitable indefinite objects as they think fit and cases where they have a discretion to apply the whole fund to charitable or definite and ascertainable non-charitable objects, and that he did not intend to intimate that the distinction drawn by Wood V.-C. in the passage to which I have referred was only applicable to cases where the non-charitable objects were definite and ascertainable.

The principle of the matter appears to me to be this. Where a fund is directed to be held upon trust for charitable and non-charitable indefinite purposes indiscriminately the trust fails by reason of the uncertainty as to the non-charitable objects of the trust and the consequent inability of the Court to control its administration. In Morice v. Bishop of Durham, 9 Ves. 399, 404, where a fund was given upon trust for such objects of benevolence and liberality as the Bishop of Durham should approve of, Sir William Grant in holding the gift to be invalid expressed himself as follows: "That it is a trust, unless it be of a charitable nature, too indefinite to be executed by this Court, has not been, and cannot be, denied. There can be no trust, over the exercise of which this Court will not assume a control; for an uncontrollable power of disposition would be ownership, and not trust. If there be a clear trust, but for uncertain objects, the property, that is the subject of the trust, is undisposed of; and the benefit of such trust must result to those, to whom the law gives the ownership in default of disposition by the former owner. But this doctrine does not hold good with regard to trusts for charity. Every other trust must have a definite object. There must be somebody, in whose favour the Court can decree performance. But it is now settled, upon authority, which it is too late to controvert, that, where a charitable purpose is expressed, however general, the bequest shall not fail on account of the uncertainty of the object: but the particular mode of application will be directed by the King in some cases, in others by this Court." Where on the other hand a fund is to be held upon trust for charitable and for non-charitable definite purposes there is no uncertainty as to the non-charitable objects of the trust and the trust is a valid one. In both these cases the question that has to be considered is whether the objects of the trust can or cannot be ascertained by the Court. But in a case where a part of a fund is given for charitable purposes and the other part is given for non-charitable purposes, the first question that has to be considered is whether the Court can ascertain what are the two parts. In such a case the Court finds no difficulty where the non-charitable purposes are definite, as appears from Salusbury v. Denton, 3 K. & J. 529, and I cannot see that there is any greater difficulty where the non-charitable purposes are indefinite. It is true, of course, that where such purposes are indefinite it is impossible to say how much is required for those purposes since the purposes cannot be ascertained. But the same impossibility occurred in the case of Hoare v. Osborne, L. R. 1 Eq. 585, where a fund was given upon trust out of the income thereof to keep in repair a monument in a church, a vault in the churchyard and an ornamental window in the church. It was held that the trust for the repair of the vault was not charitable and was void, but that the trusts for the repair of the monument and window were valid as being charitable. The question then arose as to how the fund should be divided, and the Court directed the fund to be equally divided into three parts on the ground of the impracticability from the nature of the gift of ascertaining the proportions that would be required for the three objects respectively. If the difficulty of ascertaining how much is required for any particular object does not deter the Court from dividing the fund, it appears to me to be immaterial whether that object is a definite or an indefinite one. It is moreover to be observed that, though for the purpose of the rule as to uncertainty of the objects of a trust, the Court treats charitable indefinite objects as being certain, owing to the favour always extended by the Court to charities, the impossibility of ascertaining how much of a fund is required for indefinite objects is just as great a practical difficulty where the objects are charitable as where they are non-charitable. And yet, both in Salusbury *v.* Denton and Attorney-General *v.* Doyley the Court was able to make a division of the fund between charitable indefinite objects and definite non-charitable objects.

It only remains to apply these principles to the present case.

Now the effect of the residuary gift appears to me to be that the testator has given his residue to the four objects or sets of objects (*a*), (*b*), (*c*) and (*d*) with power to his executors to determine in what shares and proportions the residue is to be divided between the four. There is no express gift in default of the executors so determining, but the rule of the Court in such a case has been laid down as follows: " If the instrument itself gives the property to a class, but gives a power to A. to appoint in what shares and in what manner the members of that class shall take, the property vests, until the power is exercised, in all the members of the class, and they will all take in default of appointment ": see Lambert *v.* Thwaites, (1866) L. R. 2 Eq. 151, 155.

Now it is said on behalf of the next of kin that the executors in this case have a power of appointment amongst the four objects or sets of objects. I think that they are right in this contention. Although it is in terms a power of distribution and not of selection, it is what used to be called a " non-exclusive " power of appointment. The next of kin then contend that, having regard to Lord Selborne's Act (37 & 38 Vict. c. 37) the executors can, in exercise of such power, appoint the whole fund to the set of objects (*d*). Again, I think that they are right, assuming that such power is a valid one. But if the power be one that enables the executors to appoint the whole fund to those objects such a power must be invalid on the principles already referred to. For a power to appoint to charitable and non-charitable indefinite objects is just as invalid as a direct gift to such objects. There is therefore a gift to the four objects or sets of objects with a super-added power of appointment that I hold to be invalid. The property accordingly remains vested in all the four without the executors having any power to divest it. I therefore arrive at the conclusion that each one of the four objects or sets of objects takes a share in the residue, and in accordance with the principle that equality is equity (of which Salusbury *v.* Denton is an example) they take it in equal shares. The result is that one-fourth of the residue is held upon trust for the charitable objects specified in heading (*a*), one-fourth each for the Royal National Lifeboat Institution and the Lister Institute of Preventive Medicine and the remaining one-fourth in trust for the persons entitled to the testator's estate as upon an intestacy.[1]

[1] See 37 Harv. L. Rev. 277.

In *Re* Porter, [1925] Ch. 746, a testator bequeathed 10,000*l.* to the trustees of a Masonic Temple to apply the income to the maintenance of the temple

IN RE TETLEY, [1923] 1 Ch. 258, aff'd *sub nom.* ATTORNEY-GENERAL *v.* NATIONAL PROVINCIAL BANK, [1924] A. C. 262: A testator bequeathed one-fifth of his residuary estate in trust " for such patriotic purposes or objects and such charitable institution or institutions or charitable object or objects in the British Empire as my trustees may in their absolute discretion select in such shares and proportions as they shall think proper." The court held that the trust failed since "patriotic" purposes were not necessarily charitable. LORD STERNDALE, M. R., said:

"Then the third and last resort was that, at any rate, assuming patriotic purposes and objects to be outside the definition of charity, and therefore bad in law, the fund can be divided between patriotic objects which are not charitable, and patriotic objects which are charitable. I do not see how that can be done. There is no distribution at all between the different objects. The trustees are to apply the fund either to one or to the other, or to one and the other in quite undefined proportions, and it is therefore open to them, on the wording of the will, to apply the whole of the fund to purposes which are not charitable, and have nothing left for charity, and, in those circumstances, it seems to me an apportionment such as is suggested, whether in equal or in other proportions, is impossible." [1]

In re GREAT BERLIN STEAMBOAT COMPANY.

COURT OF APPEAL. 1884.

26 Ch. D. 616.

THE company was formed on the 21st of April, 1882, for the acquisition and working of a concession from the German Government for the running a line of steamers on the River Spree and the ship canal from Berlin to Spandau. The nominal capital was £50,000, in 10,000 shares of £5 each, but no allotment of shares was ever made, and no shares were subscribed for except the seven shares agreed to be taken by the seven subscribers to the memorandum, which they had not paid for.

---

in their sole discretion, the balance if any to be applied annually in favor of any masonic charity which the trustees might select. It was held that the trust for the maintenance of the temple was not charitable and was invalid as a perpetuity, and that since the trustees might have applied all of the income to the maintenance of the temple, the trust as to the balance also failed. The court distinguished cases in which it was held that where the income is to be applied to the maintenance of a tomb and the balance to be applied for charitable purposes, the trust as to the tomb fails but the trust of the surplus over what would be necessary to maintain the tomb is valid. See Fisk *v.* A. G., L. R. 4 Eq. 521; Todd *v.* St. Mary's Church, 45 R. I. 282. But see Van Syckel *v.* Johnson, 80 N. J. Eq. 117.

[1] See Morice *v.* Bishop of Durham, 10 Ves. 521, *ante,* and the cases cited thereunder.

The Appellant, J. P. Bowden, deposed that about the 21st of March, 1883, he was applied to through his solicitors by the directors of the company to transfer a sum of £1000 to the credit of the company at their bankers, Messrs. Glyn, Mills, & Co., so that they might have a creditable balance in case of inquiries from certain Berlin bankers with whom they were endeavouring to place a number of the shares of the company, it being agreed that the sum was not to be used for the general purposes of the company, and that the company were merely to hold the sum as trustees for him.

The Appellant further deposed that on the 21st of March, 1883, the following resolution was passed by the board: —

" Resolved to accept £1000 for a period of one month from Mr. J. P. Bowden for the purpose of having it placed at Messrs. Glyn, Mills, Currie, & Co. to the credit of the company, for the purpose of having a creditable balance in case of inquiries from Berlin bankers, but not for the general purposes of the company, such money to be returned intact at the expiration of one month. No cheque to be drawn by the company unless countersigned by the financial secretary *pro tem.*, the company merely holding such sum as trustee for the said J. P. Bowden. Further, to appoint Mr. A. E. Bunn financial secretary *pro tem.* for two months certain without salary, or until the £1000 is repaid, but with power for the said A. E. Bunn to resign at seven days' notice within that period."

The £1000 was paid by Bowden to the credit of the company.

Subsequently the Appellant was applied to by the directors to allow sums to be drawn out from the above £1000 for the purposes of the company, and he assented to this. The greater part of it was accordingly drawn out by cheques countersigned by the above-named Mr. A. E. Bunn, who was one of the Appellant's solicitors, and applied for purposes not alleged to be improper, leaving a balance of £99 15s. It appeared that the company never had any other money to its credit than Bowden's £1000.

It appeared that no Berlin banker ever made any inquiry as to the funds of the company, and in November, 1883, a letter was received from Berlin which shewed that no application by any Berlin banker was to be expected.

On the 12th of January, 1884, an order was made for the compulsory winding-up of the company. The £99 15s. was then standing to the credit of the company. Bowden made an affidavit in opposition, in which he stated himself to be a creditor for £1350, but did not say anything as to his claim to the £99 15s.

Bowden claimed to prove against the company for £1350, which appeared not to include the £99 15s.

On the 21st of February, 1884, Bowden took out a summons in the winding-up to have the £99 15s. paid to him. The application was adjourned into Court, and on the 7th of March, 1884, Vice-Chancellor Bacon dismissed it with costs.

Bowden appealed, and the appeal was heard on the 7th of May, 1884.

Upjohn, for the Appellant. It is alleged that the deposit was made for a fraudulent purpose and therefore cannot be recovered. But the purpose for which the money was deposited failed, so as the fraud (if any) was only inchoate, I have a right to revoke the arrangement and have my money back so far as it has not been applied: Symes *v.* Hughes (Law Rep. 9 Eq. 475); Taylor *v.* Bowers (1 Q. B. D. 291). The drawings out must be attributed in my favour, Knatchbull *v.* Hallett (13 Ch. D. 696), if any other moneys have been paid in, this being trust money; but on the evidence it does not appear that the company ever had any other money to its account.

Marten, Q. C., and *Ryland, contra*. The Vice-Chancellor said that if a man puts money into the hands of the company to give it a fictitious credit, that is a fraud, and he cannot then turn round and say that the money is his. As to Symes *v.* Hughes, nothing had occurred to prevent repudiation of the illegal agreement. Here nothing was done to repudiate it till after the commencement of the winding-up. Taylor *v.* Bowers is inapplicable for the same reason. Knatchbull *v.* Hallett does not apply, for this is a case of a fraudulent loan, not of trust. There was a fraudulent intent to deceive not only the Berlin bankers but the public, and this intention continued till the commencement of the winding-up which fixes the rights of the parties. The present is an attempt by a lender to be paid in full.

Upjohn, in reply. The commencement of the winding-up prevents any subsequent alteration in rights of property, but I say that this was my property all along. The commencement of the winding-up puts an end to the purpose for which the money was advanced, and so takes the case out of the objection that the fraud continues.

BAGGALLAY, L. J. In my opinion this appeal fails. On the 21st of March, 1883, a resolution was passed by the directors in these terms. [His Lordship read the resolution.] It is not disputed that the £1000 was placed by the Appellant to the credit of the company at the bank of Glyn & Co. for a fraudulent purpose. But the Appellant says that the money was never applied for any fraudulent purpose, that the purpose came to an end, and that he is entitled to have the money back as being impressed with a trust in his favour. What happened was, that about £900 was drawn out pursuant to resolutions of the directors with the consent of the Appellant, for purposes which were not fraudulent, and was applied accordingly. In November last a communication was received by the directors from a person who was negotiating for them at Berlin, from which it appeared that no applications had been made by any Berlin bankers, and that none were to be expected. In the view I take of the case I think it was then open to the Appellant to say at once, "The purpose for which this money was advanced cannot be carried into effect; pay me back the balance." But the Appellant did not recall his money. It was possible, though not probable, that applications might still be received from Berlin bankers, and that the scheme might be carried out. The Appellant, however, did nothing to repudiate the arrangement, and so matters remained till the presentation of the petition to wind up. Then, after a winding-up order has been made, he brings forward this claim. There have been cases in which a party who has parted with his property under a fraudulent arrangement, has nevertheless been allowed to recover the property, but this case differs from them in many respects, especially in this, that there was no repudiation till after the commencement of the winding-up.

COTTON, L. J. I am of opinion that the decision of the Vice-Chancellor is right. I think it the just result of the evidence that the balance now in dispute is ear-marked as part of the money which the Appellant advanced. Then the Appellant says that the company were to hold this sum in trust for him, and the resolution no doubt says that they shall. But that declaration of trust is coupled with a statement that the advance is made in order that the company may appear to have a creditable balance at their bankers if inquiries are made — a purpose which is admitted to be fraudulent. The money was to be represented to be the money of the company, but by a private arrangement it was not to be their money. Then it is said that a person who parts with his property for a fraudulent purpose may repudiate the bargain and get his property back. I give no opinion whether in November last the Appellant could have done so. He did not attempt to do so, but waited till the event happened which put an end to the purpose for which the money was deposited. He left the money at the bank as long as the possibility of carrying out the illegal purpose continued, and it is now too late for him to reclaim it. Assuming that he had the right to repudiate the bargain, he has, in my opinion, lost that right.

LINDLEY, L. J. I also am of opinion that the decision of the Vice-Chancellor is correct. I am not satisfied that this was not a case of loan as distinguished from trust, and if that is the true view it is fatal to the Appellant's case. But if it was a case of trust, the Appellant must shew what the trust was. He does so, and shews an illegal trust, since the purpose of the advance was to give a fictitious credit to the company. The trust at first was to last only for a month. The sum was drawn upon, and the residue was left in the hands of the company to get them credit. If the case is one of debt the Appellant is not entitled to be paid in full. Whether it was loan or trust, I think that the Appellant might have recalled the money at the end of the month. He did not do so, but left it where it was till the commencement of the winding-up. The object for which the advance was made was attained as the company continued to have a fictitious credit till the commencement of the winding-up. After that I think it is too late for the Appellant to repudiate the bargain and claim the money.[1]

In re VAN HAGAN.
SPERLING *v.* ROCHFORT.
COURT OF APPEAL. 1880.
16 Ch. D. 18.

HENRY VAN HAGAN, by his will, dated in 1826, gave to his mother a general power of appointment over certain real estate, provided always that should his mother die without any will, then he gave the said real estate to Edward Clarke, subject to the payment of certain legacies. The mother of the testator many years afterwards made her will, containing a direction to this effect, — " and as to and concerning all the real estate whatsoever and wheresoever, of or to which I or any person or persons in trust for me am, is, or are seised or in any way entitled, or over which I have (either under or by virtue of the will of my deceased son), or over which I shall have any power to dispose, I give, limit, direct, and appoint the same unto and to the use of J. Sperling, F. Wollaston, and G. Sperling, their heirs and assigns, in trust for George R. Green, his heirs and assigns, forever." George R. Green died in the lifetime of the testatrix, and a question was now raised whether the property went as in default of appointment, under the will of Henry Van Hagan, or whether it went as part of the real estate of the testatrix.[2]

[1] See Ward *v.* Lant, Prec. Ch. 182 (conveyance to escape taxes); Birch *v.* Blagrave, 1 Amb. 264 (conveyance to avoid being sheriff); Dent *v.* Ferguson, 132 U. S. 50 (conveyance in fraud of creditors); Baird *v.* Howison, 154 Ala. 359 (like preceding case); Verne *v.* Shute, 232 Mass. 397 (conveyance in fraud of creditors, purpose accomplished); Caines *v.* Sawyer, 248 Mass. 368 (conveyance in fraud of wife). See 1 Pomeroy, Eq. Juris., secs. 401–4. Compare Keener, Quasi-Contracts, 258 *et seq.;* Woodward, Quasi Contracts, secs. 132 *et seq.;* Bump, Fraudulent Conveyances, 4th ed., secs. 432 *et seq.* See 25 Am. L. Rev. 712n.; 23 Col. L. Rev. 665.

In the following cases a resulting trust arose. Carrick *v.* Errington, 2 P. Wms. 361 (devise in trust for papist); Attorney General *v.* Weymouth, 1 Amb. 20 (devise in trust for charity); Jones *v.* Mitchell, 1 S. & S. 290 (like preceding case); West *v.* Shuttleworth, 2 Myl. & K. 684 (bequest for superstitious use); De Themmines *v.* De Bonneval, 5 Russ. 288 (transfer *inter vivos* for superstitious use); *Re* Blundell's Trusts, 30 Beav. 360 (like preceding case); Tregonwell *v.* Sydenham, 3 Dow 194 (devise on trust void for remoteness); Dorrian *v.* Gilmore, L. R. 15 Ir. 69 (like preceding case); Symes *v.* Hughes, L. R. 9 Eq. 475 (conveyance in fraud of creditors, debtor repentant); Carll *v.* Emery, 148 Mass. 32 (like preceding case); Schmidt *v.* Schmidt, 216 Mass. 572 (like preceding case); Amory *v.* Amherst College, 229 Mass. 374 (conveyance on trust partially void for remoteness); Lemmond *v.* Peoples, 6 Ired. Eq. (N. C.) 137 (transfer of slaves for purpose of emancipation). Compare Taylor *v.* Bowers, 1 Q. B. D. 291; Herman *v.* Jeuchner, 15 Q. B. D. 560.

[2] The statement of facts is taken from a report of the case in (1880) W. N. 159. Concurring opinions of James and Cotton, L. JJ., are omitted.

JESSEL, M. R. This case has been decided by the Vice-Chancellor, not on any general ground of law applicable to the exercise of all general powers of appointment, but on the ground that there is a distinction between real and personal estate as regards the exercise of such powers. Now I wish to say, in the first place, that I think there are quite sufficient distinctions in our law between real and personal estate without introducing a new one for the first time, and if in the case of personal estate the exercise of a general power of appointment in favour of a trustee for a legatee who dies in the lifetime of the testator takes effect so as to make the property in substance the testator's own, I see no reason why the same rule should not apply to an appointment of real estate. In fact, to a slight extent, it appears to me that the case of real estate is the stronger of the two, because in the case of an appointment of real estate there is an actual legal estate carrying with it the right of possession which must be disturbed by those who claim the property under the limitations in default of appointment. The Vice-Chancellor does not suggest that, taking the law to be the same as regards both real and personal estate, the Appellant is not entitled to succeed.

Having thus disposed of the only reason for that decision, I will consider in a very few words (for it has been considered so often by myself and by the Lord Justice James, and by other Judges, that it is not right to go through all the cases) what the effect is of a testamentary appointment under a general power to a trustee in trust for a person who dies in the life of the testator, and therefore cannot take. In the first place, I will consider the intention. The intention of the testator is that the person whom I will call the beneficial legatee or devisee, shall take, and there being nothing in the will to shew that the case of dying in the lifetime, or lapse, was contemplated by the testator, the rule has always been that the testator did not contemplate it, but expected that the devisee or legatee would survive him and take accordingly. So that we have to deal with a case as to which there is in some sense no expressed intention, though there is an intention expressed that nobody shall take under the limitations in default of appointment contained in the settlement creating the power, the testator having, according to his belief, disposed of the property, both legally and beneficially, as against the persons claiming under those limitations.

Then the only question remaining is what is to become of the property in case the intention that the beneficial legatee or devisee shall take cannot have effect. That is a mere question of resulting trust. Resulting trust for whom? As already pointed out by Lord Justice James when Vice-Chancellor, it must either be for the original settlor or for the appointor, and, considering that a general power is for almost all purposes equivalent to property, and is so dealt with by the Legislature in the Wills Act as regards testamentary appointments, the fair and proper result, in my opinion, is to treat the trust as resulting to the appointor, so as to carry the property to the person or persons who would take his real or personal estate, as the case may be, or, to put it in the words of Vice-Chancellor Wickens in the case of *In re* Davies' Trusts, Law Rep. 13 Eq. 166. " It seems settled by the cases of Chamberlain *v.* Hutchinson, 22 Beav. 444, and Wilkinson *v.* Schneider, Law Rep. 9 Eq. 423, authorities which are binding on me, that a testamentary appointment under a general power to A in trust for B, which lapses as to the beneficial interest by B's death before the appointor, operates as a good appointment in favour of A, who holds on the same trusts as if it had been the appointor's own property." There is this also to be said, that the gift to trustees is rational, if the testator knew that it would make the property part of his assets and liable to the payment of his debts. But there does not seem to be any sufficient motive for interposing a trustee when the beneficiary takes absolutely in the case of real estate. I do not, however, rely on that. I prefer to rest my judgment on the general principle which I have already stated.

A declaration was made that the property belonged to the surviving appointee, subject to a resulting trust for the heir-at-law, if any, of the testatrix.[1]

THE TRUSTEES OF THE METHODIST EPISCOPAL CHURCH IN THE EAST BALTIMORE STATION *v.* THE TRUSTEES OF THE JACKSON SQUARE EVANGELICAL LUTHERAN CHURCH.

COURT OF APPEALS, MARYLAND. 1896.

84 Md. 173.

BRISCOE, J., delivered the opinion of the Court. The bill in this case is filed for the specific performance of a contract of sale of church property situate in Baltimore City. The case was submitted to the Circuit Court of Baltimore City upon an agreed statement of facts, and from the *pro forma* decree dismissing the bill, this appeal has been taken.

By a lease of the 5th day of December, 1866, Thomas F. Johnson and others, for the consideration of the yearly rent of two hun-

---

[1] *Re* Scott, [1891] 1 Ch. 298, *accord. Cf.* Coxen *v.* Rowland, [1894] 1 Ch. 406; *Re* Boyd, [1897] 2 Ch. 232.

"By a series of English cases the following doctrine has been established. When, under a general power, property is appointed on trusts which do not take effect, either because the share of a *cestui que trust* has lapsed, or because no trusts are declared, or because they do not exhaust the fund, property unappointed goes as part of the donee's property to his residuary legatees or next of kin, and does not pass under the gift in default of appointment. And the doctrine has been extended to cases where the donee has shown an intention to make the property under the power a part of his estate, as by putting it into a mass with his own property." Gray, Rule ag. Perp. sec. 540a.

dred and eighty dollars, conveyed for ninety-nine years, to Wm. F. Pentz and seven others and to their successors, lessees in trust, certain property situate in Baltimore City, upon the following trust: " In trust that the said premises shall be used, kept, maintained and disposed of as a place of divine worship for the use of the white ministry and white membership of the Methodist Episcopal Church in the United States of America, subject to the usages and ministerial appointments of said church as from time to time authorized and declared by the General Conference of said church and the Annual Conference in whose bounds the said premises are situate."

On the 20th day of the same month and year, the Jackson Square Centenary Methodist Episcopal Church was duly incorporated under Art. 23 of the Code, and by the act of incorporation, Wm. F. Pentz and the other lessees in trust, named in the lease of the 5th of December, 1866, were constituted trustees of the church. Subsequently, on the 31st of July, 1876, Alexander Ray and four others, the survivors of the trustees named in the lease of the 5th of December, 1866, conveyed absolutely this property to the Jackson Square Centenary M. E. Church, a body corporate, " unto and to the use of the church (by its corporate name) and its assigns, for all the residue of the term yet to come and unexpired therein, with the benefit of renewal forever." And on the 9th day of February, 1889, the Jackson Square Methodist Church granted and assigned the same property to the appellants, the trustees of the Methodist Episcopal Church in the East Baltimore Station, a body corporate. Afterwards, on the 5th day of April, 1892, the appellants agreed in writing to sell the property to the appellees.

The only question here presented is whether the appellant has a good and marketable title to the property which the appellee has agreed to buy upon the terms set forth in the contract of sale. Now it is very clear, that the trust expressed and contained in the lease from Johnson *et al.* to Pentz *et al.* is void and must fail. In Isaac *et al.*, trustees, *v.* Emory *et al.*, 64 Md. 337, it was held, in construing a similar trust, that " this designation of beneficiaries is too vague and indefinite to be sustained by the Courts. According to the uniform course of decisions in this State, a trust cannot be upheld unless it be of such a nature that the *cestuis que trust* are defined and capable of enforcing its execution by proceedings in a Court of Chancery. Church Extension of M. E. Church *v.* Smith, 56 Md. 397."

But while the trust is void, it does not follow that the lessees failed to acquire any title or that there was a resulting trust in favor of the lessors. The lease was not a voluntary conveyance but was made upon a valuable consideration, the payment of the annual rent of $280. When there is a consideration for the conveyance and it is made upon a trust which is void for uncertainty or otherwise fails, then the grantee takes the beneficial interest. 2

Pomeroy Eq. 1033; Perry on Trusts, sec. 151. A resulting trust will not be raised in opposition to the obvious design of the transaction. Perry on Trusts, sec. 159; Walsh *v.* McBride *et al.*, 72 Md. 45. In the case now under consideration the trust appears to have been set forth in the lease only to show the purpose for which the property was bought and not to limit the right of alienation. Newbold *v.* Glenn, 67 Md. 491. The lease consequently is valid and the lessees took the same free from the trust therein set forth. When, therefore, they assigned this property on the 1st of July, 1876, to the Jackson Square Church, by which it had already been improved and used, they conveyed the legal title to the party for whose benefit the lease had been made. This assignment operated to vest both the legal and equitable ownership in the Jackson Square Church, provided the assignment is otherwise free from objection.

Now both the assignment from the original lessees to the Jackson Square Church, and the assignment of that church to the appellant are conveyances of land to " religious societies or denominations," within the Declaration of Rights, Art. 38. While it appears that legislative assent was given to the assignment of the property from the Jackson Square Centenary M. E. Church to the appellants, no such assent appears to have been given to the deed from Alexander Ray *et als.*, trustees, to the Jackson Square Centenary M. E. Church. Even if this be so, we think the legislative sanction on the 7th of April, 1892 (Act of 1892, ch. 430), to the purchase by the appellants from the Jackson Square Centenary M. E. Church, was necessarily a legislative assent to the validity of the grant by Alexander Ray *et als.*, trustees, to the Jackson Square M. E. Church, and a legislative ratification thereof. And this is so, because the subsequent sanction would be nugatory and of no avail, without a ratification of the former grant.

For these reasons, we think the appellant can give a good and valid title to this property, so the *pro forma* decree in this case will be reversed and the cause remanded to the end that proceedings may be had in accordance with this opinion.

Decree reversed, and cause remanded with costs.[1]

Section II.

Where an Express Trust does not Exhaust the Entire Property Transferred to the Trustee.

Sanders, Uses and Trusts, 5 ed., 101: The law equally favours a resulting use upon a conveyance, where only part of it is limited,

[1] Compare Gibson *v.* Armstrong, 7 B. Mon. (Ky.) 481; Kerlin *v.* Campbell, 15 Pa. 500; Heiskell *v.* Trout, 31 W. Va. 810, where the purchase money was paid by a third person. See also *Re* Davis, 112 Fed. 129, *post*.

and the remainder left undisposed of; it being a rule, that so much of the use as the grantor does not dispose of, remains in him. Thus, if a feoffment in fee be made to the use of the heirs of the body of the feoffor, the use is undisposed of during his life; it will therefore result, and then he will have an estate tail executed in him. So, if the use upon a feoffment in fee be declared to the feoffee for life, and no further declaration be made, the remainder of it will result to the feoffor: or if the use in the first instance be limited to the feoffor in tail without any further declaration, the use in reversion will result to him; but not so, if the use be limited to the feoffor for *life* or for *years;* because if it did, the feoffor could not have an estate for life or years, as he intended.[1]

WOODBURY *v.* HAYDEN.

SUPREME JUDICIAL COURT, MASSACHUSETTS. 1912.

211 Mass. 202.

BILL IN EQUITY, filed in the Probate Court for the County of Middlesex on August 3, 1909, and amended on May 15, 1911, by the administrator with the will annexed of the estate of Lennette A. Woodbury, late of Cambridge, for instructions.

The bill was filed as such administrator by George E. Woodbury, the father of the testatrix. He died on March 17, 1910, and Frederick G. Roby was appointed administrator with the will annexed in his place. On May 15, 1911, an amendment to the bill was allowed by the Probate Court substituting Frederick G. Roby as plaintiff and making the administrator of the estate of George E. Woodbury a defendant, also making Joseph O. Hayden a defendant as trustee under the will of Lennette A. Woodbury, he previously having been a defendant only personally.

In the Probate Court *McIntire,* J., made a decree that the defendant " Joseph O. Hayden took the residue of the property and estate of said deceased upon a trust, to use and apply the same as far as necessary for the support and maintenance of Almira Augusta Woodbury, during her life; that said Almira Augusta Woodbury, the beneficiary under said trust, has deceased, leaving an unexpended balance of the trust fund so created; and that such unexpended balance remaining after the termination of the life estate

[1] In *Re* Fayle, [1918] I. R. 13, land was conveyed by way of mortgage to " M. & Co., their heirs successors and assigns, to hold unto and to the use of M. & Co., their successors and assigns." M. & Co. was a firm of three solicitors. It was held that although the word " heirs " was omitted from the *habendum,* the members of the firm took a fee and not merely a life estate. The court held that there was no resulting use after the use limited to the members of the firm for their lives, since it was apparent that they were intended to take in fee. A resulting use depends upon intention and it would be contrary to the intention of the parties to raise a resulting use.

was not disposed of by said will but devolves, under a resulting trust, upon the heir at law and next of kin of the said testatrix."

Joseph O. Hayden individually and as trustee appealed.

The appeal came on to be heard before *Sheldon*, J., who reserved the case upon the pleadings and an agreed statement of facts for determination by the full court.

The facts are stated in the opinion. The will was as follows:

" Know all men by these presents that I, Lennette A. Woodbury of Cambridge in the County of Middlesex and Commonwealth of Massachusetts, being of sound and disposing mind make this my last will and testament. After the payment of my just debts and funeral charges I give devise and bequeath to Maude Mary Barnes of Somerville County and State aforesaid, lot number 3019 Willow Path Cambridge Cemetery. The balance of my estate both real and personal I bequeath to Joseph O. Hayden, of Somerville County and State aforesaid. The same to be used as far as necessary for the support and maintenance of my Aunt Almira Augusta Woodbury of Cambridge County and State aforesaid

" In testimony whereof I hereunto set my hand and seal this fifth day of February A. D. 1907."

HAMMOND, J. The sole question is whether Hayden took the residue upon a trust, or subject to a trust. If upon a trust, then he took no beneficial interest, and the purposes of the trust having been accomplished, the remainder stands as intestate property; if subject to a trust, the beneficial interest was in him subject to a legal duty to use the same so far as necessary for the support and maintenance of Mrs. Woodbury the aunt of the testatrix, and that duty having been performed he holds the remainder absolutely.

The case is before us upon the pleadings and agreed facts. The testatrix was born in Cambridge in this Commonwealth about 1865. When she was three years old her mother died and the care of her was reposed in her aunt Mrs. Woodbury, but her father and her uncle (the husband of Mrs. Woodbury) and the testatrix had a common home for some years. Her father married in 1875 and for seven years thereafter did not see or communicate with her. The wife died, however, " some twenty years ago " and ever afterwards the father and daughter were on friendly terms, he living in California and she in Cambridge. They saw each other very seldom, she visiting him however once in California. He did not support her after she was ten years old, although after the death of his second wife he at her own solicitation made her several presents.

For many years she worked in the office of Mr. Hayden, the treasurer of Middlesex County, as a typewriter and general assistant, and was much relied on for general efficiency. She had knowledge of many business affairs of Mr. Hayden, and he had known of her investments. She inherited from her mother about $5,000, and she left an estate of about $6,000. She had a home with her aunt Mrs.

Woodbury, the aunt conducting the domestic affairs and she providing the funds.

At the time of making the will she was about forty years of age, in ill health and on the eve of a visit to her father in California. She expected to return soon, and her purpose in going there was not only to visit her father, but also to obtain from him about $10,000 to invest in an apartment house in Massachusetts.

On February 5, 1907, she sat down apparently unaided to make this will. She seems to have been a capable and self reliant woman. She had no blank form. It is apparent from the opening sentence as well as from the other parts of the will, that she had some knowledge of testamentary phrases. After disposing of a cemetery lot she proceeds as follows: " The balance of my estate both real and personal I bequeath to Joseph O. Hayden, of Somerville County and State aforesaid. The same to be used as far as necessary for the support and maintenance of my Aunt Almira Augusta Woodbury of Cambridge County and State aforesaid." And there she stops. She apparently thinks she has done all she set out to do. What did she set out to do? Was it her intent simply to provide for her aunt, then seventy-two years of age, so far as the property should be needed for that purpose, or was it her intent to give all she had to Mr. Hayden subject only to the needs of her aunt? The question although narrow is close and difficult. Without reciting the considerations urged by the respective counsel it is sufficient to say that the arguments appear very evenly balanced, and whichever direction is taken the path is not entirely smooth.

It is plain that while she wanted to have her property used so far as necessary for the support and maintenance of her aunt, she was not willing to let her aunt have the control of it, but desired that it should be in the hands of a trustee. The aunt's comfort was the one thing to which all else should be subordinate, but she was not to have control. There was occasion therefore for the appointment of some one to take care of the property and to pay it out as occasion required for the aunt's necessities, and the testatrix knew all this. She thought of Hayden as a proper man to do this and she appointed him at least for that purpose. Did she mean anything more? She knew that Hayden held a responsible official position and she was familiar with his business methods and he with hers. There were excellent reasons why she should trust him to manage the property, but no reason appears why she should make him her residuary legatee. He was a stranger in blood; she does not appear to have been assisted by him at any time, and there are no ties, either of affection or otherwise, suggested, except those naturally arising out of the relation of employer and employee continued for years. We do not regard the fact that there was a period between the words of gift to Hayden and the clause in favor of the aunt as of very much significance. It is plain that the clause relating to the aunt is elliptical and cannot be understood except by reference to the preceding sentence. And we think that they should be read in substance as one sentence.

Upon the whole, we think that the will, read in the light of all the circumstances, indicates that the sole purpose of the testatrix in placing the residue in the hands of Hayden was that as trustee he should see to it that so far as necessary it should be used for the support and maintenance of her aunt, and that she did not intend that he should have any personal interest in it. The trust having ended, whatever remains of the trust fund should be disposed of as intestate property. For a discussion of some aspects of the law on this general subject see Buffinton v. Maxam, 140 Mass. 557; Buffinton v. Maxam, 152 Mass. 477; McElroy v. McElroy, 113 Mass. 509.

Decree of the Probate Court affirmed.[1]

In re FOORD.

FOORD *v.* CONDER.

HIGH COURT OF JUSTICE, CHANCERY DIVISION. 1922.

[1922] 2 Ch. 519.

ADJOURNED SUMMONS.

A testator Herbert Taynton Foord made his will dated May 26, 1919, in the following terms (omitting formal parts): " I will and bequeath to Selim Awad Khim $2000 as well as all my effects and furniture in China but all the valuable things are to be sent to my sister Miss Foord and $500 is to be allowed from my estate for the cost of packing and sending them home. Selim knows what things are to be sent home. All my effects including rubber and all other shares I leave absolutely to my sister Margaret Juliet on trust to pay to my wife per annum (three hundred pounds) with income tax, 100*l.* (one hundred pounds) to be free of income tax."

The testator was an engineer and had been for many years in China. He made his will on the day before his death by dictating it, as he lay ill, to his servant Selim. The bequest to the testator's sister Margaret Juliet Foord was more than sufficient to satisfy the wife's annuity. This summons was taken out by the sister, who was administratrix with the will annexed, asking (inter alia) whether upon the true construction of the will the gift to her was for her own benefit subject to and charged with payment of

---

[1] Ellcock *v.* Mapp, 3 H. L. Cas. 492; *Re* West, [1900] 1 Ch. 84; *Re* Donnelly's Estate, [1913] 1 I. R. 177, *accord.*

As to the general rule that a resulting trust presumptively arises where the trust is fully performed without exhausting the trust property, see 3 Pomeroy, Eq. Juris., sec. 1034; Dec. Dig., Trusts, sec. 67.

the annuity, or was given her, subject to the annuity, upon trust for the testator's next of kin.

SARGANT J. This is a difficult case and on the border line. The question is whether the gift to the testator's sister is a gift merely for the particular purpose of providing an annuity for the testator's wife, in which case there is a resulting trust of the balance of the estate for the testator's next of kin, or is not merely for that purpose, and as regards any balance belongs to the testator's sister beneficially. [His Lordship stated the facts and continued:] The principles applicable to the decision of this question are stated in what Bowen L.J. called the classic judgment of Lord Eldon in King v. Denison, 1 V. & B. 272, in these terms: " The principles applicable to this case are very well settled. I adopt those expressed in Hill v. Bishop of London, (1738) 1 Atk. 618, as affording the grounds upon which Lord Hardwicke proceeded; but I will here point out the nicety of distinction, as it appears to me, upon which this Court has gone. If I give to A. and his heirs all my real estate, charged with my debts, that is a devise to him for a particular purpose, but not for that purpose only. If the devise is upon trust to pay my debts, that is a devise for a particular purpose, and nothing more; and the effect of those two modes admits just this difference. The former is a devise of an estate of inheritance for the purpose of giving the devisee the beneficial interest, subject to a particular purpose: the latter is a devise for a particular purpose; with no intention to give him any beneficial interest." And according as the one view or the other is adopted of the construction of each particular bequest, the legatee takes or does not take the surplus for his own benefit.

I have felt some doubt as to the effect of the direction to send " the valuable things " to the testator's sister; and the question arises on the construction of the will whether that is a mere direction that they are to be sent to her by the attendant Selim, leaving the beneficial ownership to be determined by the subsequent clause, or is in itself a gift to the sister Miss Foord. At first I thought it was more than a mere direction and that it was intended as a gift, and the only gift, of these valuable things. On the whole I have come to the conclusion that this is not so and that the subsequent gift of " all my effects including rubber and all other shares " operates upon the valuable part of the Chinese effects which were to be sent to the testator's sister.

That being so I have to deal with the main question of the effect of the gift to the sister on trust to pay the wife's annuity. While a gift to A. upon trust for the provision of a certain interest for B., without more, must, I think, be construed as a gift to A. merely to fulfill the beneficial interest of B. and must not be construed as a gift to A. of all that is not required to satisfy B.'s interest, yet looking at the case of Croome v. Croome, 59 L. T. 582, which I employ for the purpose of seeing the general spirit in which the Court deals with cases of this character, I find that the Court is prepared to hold that there is a beneficial gift to the first taker on slight expressions and indications of intention. The indications there were so slight that the judges of the Court of Appeal confessed that it was difficult to state in words reasons for the impression produced on their minds by the language of the testator's will.

Here there are several indications which tend to show that the gift to Margaret Juliet the testator's sister was not a mere gift upon trust. First, there is the use of the word "absolutely." No doubt it might, especially if used by some one acquainted with legal language, be construed as describing the extent of the interest in the property given — namely, the fee simple in freehold property and the absolute interest in personal property. But I think in this extremely untechnical will the testator must have used it to mean "out and out," and that it therefore carried not merely the full legal interest but the beneficial interest also. Another indication is that the beneficiary is described by the testator as "my sister," so that the testator was recognizing the relationship existing between them and was probably founding his generosity on the existence of that relationship. There was no particular reason to describe her as his sister if he was only going to make her a bare trustee. Moreover he refers to her as "my sister Margaret Juliet" and not as Miss Foord, as he did in the earlier part of the will. Thirdly some indication is to be drawn from the words by which he commences the gift "All my effects including rubber and all other shares." That gift includes the testator's effects, so that he was giving property some of which would and some of which would not produce income. That is some indication that the trust only applies to a portion of the property given out and out to the testator's sister. No doubt the effects could be sold in case of need and the proceeds invested and the income so increased. But I do not think that is the sort of thing a testator making his will at the last moment in a foreign land would have in contemplation.

I feel here the difficulty expressed by Bowen and Fry L.JJ. in Croome v. Croome, 59 L. T. 582, 585, 586. As Fry L.J. said: "It is difficult, no doubt, to express in words the exact impression which the language of a testator often produces on the mind; but the result of the language of the testator in this case is to convince me that he had given the real estate to his brother for a purpose which he does not contemplate as exhausting the whole." Here also I find it difficult to express in words the general effect produced on my mind by the language of the testator; but I have become convinced as the argument went on, contrary to the view I took at first, that the beneficial interest was given to the sister, and I will so declare.[1]

[1] Rogers v. Rogers, 3 P. Wms. 193; Re Howell, [1915] 1 Ch. 241, *accord*.

PAROL EVIDENCE TO REBUT RESULTING TRUST. If property is devised or bequeathed upon a trust which fails in whole or in part or which is fully performed without exhausting the property devised or bequeathed to the trustee, the resulting trust which would otherwise arise is rebutted if it appears from the will, as construed in the light of surrounding circumstances, that the trustee was intended to keep the property in the event that the trust should fail or that there should remain a surplus after the performance of the trust. The testator's extrinsic declarations of his intention, however, are not admissible to rebut the resulting trust.

In England at common law when a testator did not dispose of all his personal estate, the executor was allowed to keep the surplus after paying debts and legacies, unless it appeared from the will that the testator intended or presumably intended that he should not keep it, in which case he held the surplus for the next of kin. Thus, if a gift was made to the executor by the will, there was a presumption that he was not to keep the surplus. If on the face of the will it was clear either that the executor was to keep or was not to keep the surplus, evidence of declarations of intention of the settlor was not admissible. Langham v. Sanford, 19 Ves. 641. If, however, on the face of the will it was doubtful whether the testator intended that the executor should or should not take the beneficial interest, as for example where a gift was made in the will to the executor, his declarations of intention were admissible to rebut the equity in favor of the next of kin and to show that the executor was intended to keep the surplus; and his declarations of intention were also admissible to show the contrary. Gladding v. Yapp, 5 Madd. 56. See Thayer, Evidence, 437–439. This rule, however, has been changed in England by Executors Act, 1830 (11 Geo. IV. & 1 Will. IV. c. 4), which provides that the executor shall be trustee of any surplus for the next of kin unless it appears by the will that he was intended to take beneficially. See *Re* Jones, [1925] Ch. 340. The early English rule has not been followed in the United States.

If land is conveyed by deed upon an express trust, parol evidence is not admissible to show that it was intended that the grantee should keep the land if the trust should fail or if a surplus should remain after performance of the trust. See McDermith v. Voorhees, 16 Colo. 402, in which the court said, quoting Perry, Trusts, sec. 150, "Where a trust results by force of the written instrument, it cannot be controlled, rebutted or defeated by parol evidence of any kind." But see Walrath v. Roberts, 12 F.(2d) 443, 23 F.(2d) 32.

In re BRITISH RED CROSS BALKAN FUND.
BRITISH RED CROSS SOCIETY *v.* JOHNSON.

HIGH COURT OF JUSTICE, CHANCERY DIVISION. 1914.

[1914] 2 Ch. 419.

ORIGINATING SUMMONS. In October, 1912, the plaintiffs issued an appeal to the public for subscriptions to a special fund for assisting the sick and wounded in the Balkan war.

Large sums amounting to 28,682*l.* were subscribed from time to time and the fund was duly applied by the plaintiffs from time to time during the war. At the end of the war there was an unexpended balance of 12,655*l.* 19*s.* 6*d.* in the plaintiffs' hands which admittedly belonged to some or all of the subscribers by way of resulting trust.

In July, 1913, the plaintiffs circularized the subscribers asking whether the unexpended balance might be devoted to the general purposes of the society. In the result 2310 subscribers of 23,279*l.* consented, 21 subscribers of 295*l.* dissented, and 923 subscribers of 5108*l.* sent no reply. Some of the dissenting subscribers wished their money returned, others that it should be given to some other fund.

The question arose whether the rule in Clayton's Case (1 Mer. 572, 608) was applicable. If so the accounts shewed that the balance in hand must be treated as derived from subscriptions coming in on or after November 8, 1912, and would belong to the subscribers who had subscribed on or after that date, so that they could get their subscriptions back in full if they so desired. On the other hand, if the rule was not applicable, the expenditure would be treated as made rateably out of all the subscriptions irrespective of their date, and the unexpended balance would belong to all the subscribers rateably in proportion to their subscriptions.

On May 22, 1914, the plaintiffs issued this summons to determine this and other points.

Howard Wright, for the plaintiffs. There is no direct authority on the point, but *prima facie* the presumption is that the subscribers gave their subscriptions to the entire fund *en bloc,* in which case the unexpended balance would belong to them rateably as in *In re* Abbot Fund Trusts, [1900] 2 Ch. 326.

Roger Turnbull, for subscribers who had subscribed before November 8, 1912, adopted this argument.

H. O. Danckwerts, for subscribers who had subscribed on or after November 8, 1912. The rule in Clayton's Case, 1 Mer. 572, 608, is applicable.

[ASTBURY, J. That rule applies to an account current kept as a banking account between two parties: The Mecca, [1897] A. C.

286, 290. Has it ever been applied to a number of subscribers to a fund?]

There is no reported case on the point. But there is no reason why the rule should not be applied. The subscriptions were paid to the plaintiffs. The plaintiffs paid them into their bank and presumably paid them in as and when received. They had obviously no intention of making any appropriation, so that as between them and the bank the rule in Clayton's Case, 1 Mer. 572, 608, is applicable. That being so it is applicable in favour of third parties — Deeley *v.* Lloyds Bank, [1912] A. C. 756, — and the later subscribers are entitled to claim the benefit of the rule.

ASTBURY, J. The rule in Clayton's Case, 1 Mer. 572, 608, as restated by Lord Halsbury L. C. in The Mecca, [1897] A. C. 286, 290, is that " where an account current is kept between parties as a banking account, ' there is no room for any other appropriation than that which arises from the order in which the receipts and payments take place and are carried into the account. Presumably, it is the sum first paid in that is first drawn out. It is the first item on the debit side of the account that is discharged or reduced by the first item on the credit side; the appropriation is made by the very act of setting the two items against each other.' "

It is a mere rule of evidence and not an invariable rule of law, and the circumstances of any particular case may or may not afford ground for inferring that the transactions of the parties were not intended to come under the general rule.

In the present case the rule is obviously inapplicable. At the outbreak of the Balkan war a public appeal was made for subscriptions for a special fund for assisting the sick and wounded. Subscriptions were obtained and duly applied, and at the close of the war there was an unexpended balance of 12,655*l*. 19*s*. 6*d*. That balance belongs to all the subscribers rateably in proportion to their subscriptions, and subscribers who wish their money returned and are unwilling to leave it for the general purposes of the society are entitled to such proportion of their subscriptions as the total amount unexpended bears to the total amount subscribed.[1]

---

[1] See *Re* Randell, 38 Ch. D. 213; Easterbrooks *v.* Tillinghast, 5 Gray (Mass.) 17; Come *v.* Wold, 85 Minn. 302 (contribution by city to benevolent association of police department, held on dissolution resulting trust to city).

It would seem that the court in the principal case should have ordered an application *cy pres* if such a suggestion had been made. See *Re* Welsh Hospital Fund, [1921] 1 Ch. 655.

On the question as to the disposition of property of a charitable corporation on its dissolution, see Mott *v.* Danville Seminary, 129 Ill. 403; Danville Seminary *v.* Mott, 136 Ill. 289; Jacoway *v.* Board of Police, Freem. Ch. (Miss.) 59; Jenkins *v.* Jenkins University, 17 Wash. 160, holding that the donors were entitled to it. See Gray, Rule ag. Perp., secs. 44–51a; Kales, Estates, 2 ed., sec. 302; 18 Mich. L. Rev. 144. If the charitable corporation paid for the property, the vendor is not entitled to it on the dissolution of the

CUNNACK v. EDWARDS.

COURT OF APPEAL. 1896.

[1896] 2 Ch. 679.

APPEAL by the Crown from the decision of Chitty, J. [1895] 1 Ch. 489.

The facts are sufficiently stated in the report of the case in the Court below.

The appeal was heard on November 4, 1895.

On the appeal the defendant Edwards, the legal personal representative of T. H. Edwards, the last surviving ordinary member of the society, abandoned his exclusive claim to the unexpended fund, and he and the other defendant Clarke, who, as is stated in the report in the Court below, had been added as defendant to represent the legal personal representatives of the deceased ordinary members as a body, now appeared by the same counsel.

LORD HALSBURY, L. C.[1] In the year 1810 a certain number of persons associated themselves together for the purpose of providing for their widows. They were not incorporated, and though they obtained some of the advantages which are involved in incorporation — inasmuch as they came under the protection of the Friendly Societies Acts — I do not think, for the purpose of this inquiry, those facts are important. The question which the Court has to determine would, I think, have remained the same if they had been simply an associated body of persons for the purpose which I have described. The society has lasted to a very recent period, but is now extinct. All the members are dead, but a remnant of the common fund, amounting to something over 1200*l.*, now remains.

Chitty, J., has held that there is a resulting trust in favour of the personal representatives of those who contributed to the fund. I think we are all of opinion that that view cannot be maintained. The entire beneficial interest has been exhausted in respect of each contributor. It was, as I shall have to repeat in another view of the case, a perfectly businesslike arrangement: each man contributed a certain sum of money to a common fund upon the bargain that his widow was to receive, upon terms definitely settled, a certain annuity proportionate to the time during which the husband had contributed to the common fund. There never was and there never could be any interest remaining in the contributor other than the right that his wife, if she survived him, should become entitled to a widow's portion thus provided. This was the final and

---

corporation. People *v.* Braucher, 258 Ill. 604; County of Franklin *v.* Blake, 283 Ill. 292.

[1] Concurring opinions of A. L. Smith and Rigby, L. JJ., are omitted.

exhaustive destination of all the sums contributed to the common fund. Under these circumstances, I am at a loss to see what room there is for the contention that there is any resulting trust.

It is contended, however, that this association may be regarded as a charity. Wide as has been the meaning given to the word "charity" in the Court of Chancery, and, indeed, in one case by the House of Lords, a width of interpretation which I confess has seemed to me in some cases extravagant, I do not think that a perfectly businesslike arrangement like this, in which a number of persons associate together and contribute funds to provide for their own widows, has ever been regarded as charity. I think the observations of Hall, V.-C., in *In re* Clark's Trust, 1 Ch. D. 497, are entitled to great weight. His observations were directed to a society whose members were to provide by subscriptions and fines a fund to be distributed for their mutual benefit in cases of sickness, lameness, or old age. In Pease *v.* Pattison, 32 Ch. D. 154, and Spiller *v.* Maude, 32 Ch. D. 158, n., it was assumed by the learned judges in those cases, whether rightly or wrongly it is immaterial to consider, that the relief of poverty and suffering formed one of the elements of the associations therein discussed. Here no such question can possibly arise; it cannot be pretended that a wealthy widow would not be entitled to claim her annuity equally with a poor one. If this be a charitable institution it would be difficult to contend that every life insurance company did not fall under the same category.

I am therefore of opinion that this was not a charitable institution. The only other alternative remaining is that which I adopt, namely, that these funds are *bona vacantia*, and belong to the Crown in that character.[1]

[1] Braithwaite *v.* A. G., [1909] 1 Ch. 510 (friendly society, no resulting trust either to honorary members or to benefited members), *accord.*

In the following cases it was held that there was a resulting trust for the donors. *Re* Trusts of Abbott Fund, [1900] 2 Ch. 326 (fund collected for support of two ladies who subsequently died, held resulting trusts of surplus to contributors *pro rata*); Hopkins *v.* Grimshaw, 165 U. S. 342 (land conveyed in trust for aid and burial of members of a society, held on dissolution resulting trust to donor's heirs); Schlessinger *v.* Mallard, 70 Cal. 326 (like preceding case); Coe *v.* Washington Mills, 149 Mass. 543 (owners and employees of mill contributed to a fund to aid sick and disabled members of association of employees, held on dissolution resulting trust to owners in proportion to their contributions); Walters *v.* Pittsburgh etc. Iron Co., 201 Mich. 379 (like preceding case).

In the following cases it was held that the trust property should be divided among the beneficiaries. *Re* Printers etc. Society, [1899] 2 Ch. 184 (trade union, division among members in proportion to amounts subscribed); *Re* Andrew's Trust, [1905] 2 Ch. 48 (fund for education of children of deceased clergyman, balance on their reaching maturity divided among them); *Re* Trusts of Grand Canal etc. Funds, [1914] 1 I. R. 142 (benefit society, on dissolution division among members in proportion to their contributions, no resulting trust to company which also contributed); *Re* Customs etc. Fund,

Section III.

Where an Intended Trust is not Expressly or is not Properly Declared.

ARMSTRONG v. WOLSEY.

Common Pleas. 1755.

2 Wils. 19.

EJECTMENT, tried at Norwich before Parker, Ch. Baron, who reserved this short case for the opinion of the court. A. B. being in possession of the lands in question, levied a fine *sur conusans de droit come ceo,* etc., with proclamations to the conusee and his heirs, in the 6th year of the present King, without any consideration expressed, and without declaring any use thereof; nor was it proved that the conusee was ever in possession.

So that the single question is, Whether the fine shall enure to the use of the conusor or the conusee? And after two arguments, the court was unanimous, and gave judgment for the plaintiff, who claimed as heir of the conusor.

CURIA. In the case of a fine *come ceo*, etc., where no uses are declared, whether the conusor be in possession, or the fine be of a reversion, it shall enure to the old uses, and the conusor shall be in of the old use; and although it passes nothing, yet after five years and non-claim it will operate as a bar.

And in the case of a recovery suffered, the same shall enure to the use of him who suffers it, (who is commonly the vouchee,) if no uses be declared; but he gains a new estate to him and his heirs

---

[1917] 2 Ch. 18, 27 Yale L. Jour. 418 (benevolent fund, distribution among contributors at time of dissolution in proportion to contributions, no resulting trust to past contributors).

In 1805 the Harmony Society, a religious and communistic association, was formed in Pennsylvania, and property was contributed by the founder to be held by trustees for the members. In 1902 when the society had only eight members left the heirs of the founder sought to reach the property, but it was held that the society had not yet dissolved and they could not reach it. Schwartz *v.* Duss, 187 U. S. 8. In 1905 the society was dissolved and the heirs again sought to reach it. It was held that the surviving members were entitled to the property. Everitt *v.* Duss, 197 Fed. 401. The decision was affirmed on the ground that the claimant was not the true heir. s. c. 206 Fed. 590.

In Easum *v.* Bohon, 180 Ky. 451, it was held that where the members of a communistic society contributed property in return for an agreement to support them, their heirs were not entitled by way of resulting trust on the dissolution of the society, since the members had received value in being supported. It was not decided who was entitled to the property.

See Gray, Rule ag. Perp., secs. 44–51*a*, 327*a*, 603*i*; 41 Harv. L. Rev. 898.

general; and although before the recovery he was siesed *ex parte maternâ,* yet afterwards the estate will descend to his heirs *ex parte paternâ,* as was determined in Martin *v.* Strachan, 1 Wils. 2, 66. *Sed vide* that case, 2 Stra. 1179.

In the case at bar, the ancient use was in the conusor at the time of levying the fine; and it seems to have been long settled before this case, that a fine without any consideration, or uses thereof declared, shall enure to the ancient use in whomsoever it was at the time of levying the fine; and as it was here in the conusor at that time, the judgment must be for the plaintiff.[1]

[1] *Resulting uses.* Before the Statute of Uses, on a feoffment a use resulted to the feoffor unless to raise such a use would violate his expressed or presumed intention. No resulting use was raised so far as the use was expressly declared to be in a third person or in the feoffee. No resulting use was raised when to raise it would defeat the presumed intent of the feoffor, as where there was consideration for the feoffment, actual or recited; or where there was tenure between the feoffor and feoffee; or where a part of the use was expressly reserved to the feoffor and to raise a resulting use of the residue would, by the doctrine of merger, give the feoffor a different equitable estate from that reserved. See Leake, Law of Property in Land, 2d ed., 83-84.

A use resulted on a conveyance by fine or recovery or grant under the same circumstances as on a conveyance by feoffment; but there is some doubt as to whether a use resulted on a release. See Shortridge *v.* Lamplugh, 2 Ld. Raym. 798; Lloyd *v.* Spillet, 2 Atk. 148; 2 Sanders, Uses and Trusts 73.

On the question whether a use resulted on a conveyance by feoffment, fine or recovery after the Statute of Uses, see, in addition to the principal case, Beckwith's Case, 2 Rep. 580; Shortridge *v.* Lamplugh, *supra;* Lloyd *v.* Spillet, *supra.*

Before the Statute of Frauds parol evidence was admissible to show the intent to give the beneficial interest to the feoffee or even to a third person (see Dowman's Case, 9 Rep. 7 *c;* Gilbert, Uses and Trusts, 54; Perry, Trusts, sec. 75); and even after the Statute of Frauds, parol evidence was admissible to show the intent of the feoffor to give the beneficial interest to the feoffee. Bellasis *v.* Compton, 2 Vern. 294; Altham *v.* Anglesey, Gilb. Rep. 16; Roe *v.* Popham, Doug. 25. See 6 Col. L. Rev. 329, n. 3.

Resulting trusts. These doctrines as to raising a resulting use upon a gratuitous conveyance have not been applied to modern trusts. See Leake, Law of Property in Land, 2 ed., 103; 3 Pomeroy, Eq. Juris., secs. 1035, 1036; Ames, Cases on Trusts, 1 ed., 262; Costigan, The Classification of Trusts, 26 Harv. L. Rev. 437, 516; Stone, Resulting Trusts and the Statute of Frauds, 6 Col. L. Rev. 326, 331; Scott, Conveyances Upon Trusts Not Properly Declared, 37 Harv. L. Rev. 653, 655. But see Lewin, Trusts, 158; Maitland, Equity, 63. See Lloyd *v.* Spillet, 2 Atk. 148; Feeney *v.* Howard, 79 Cal. 525; Philbrook *v.* Delano, 29 Me. 410; Blodgett *v.* Hildreth, 103 Mass. 484; Gould *v.* Lynde, 114 Mass. 366; Jackson *v.* Cleveland, 15 Mich. 94; Lovett *v.* Taylor, 54 N. J. Eq. 311; Down *v.* Down, 80 N. J. Eq. 68. In some of the cases just cited the court draws attention to the fact that there was a recital of consideration or a declaration of use.

Where personal property is gratuitously transferred, it depends upon the intention of the transferor whether a trust is created. In the absence of evidence to the contrary, the transferor presumably intends to make a gift and not to create a trust.

DAVIES v. OTTY.
CHANCERY. 1865.

35 Beav. 208.

THIS case, which is reported 33 Beav. 540, on a demurrer, now came on for hearing, but upon allegations of a different state of facts, which the Plaintiff had introduced by amendment. The following statement is founded on the conclusions arrived at by the Court, upon the evidence in the cause.

It appeared that, in 1860, the Plaintiff Davies was entitled to three-and-a-half shares in a building society and to a piece of land and some houses, which he had mortgaged to the society, in the usual way in such cases, for securing to the society an advance of money made to him.

By an indenture dated the 17th of January, 1860, made between the Plaintiff Davies of the one part and the Defendant Otty (his step-son) of the other part. This indenture recited the Plaintiff's title, and proceeded as follows: —

"And whereas Matthew Otty has taken from Thomas Davies all his shares in the said benefit building society, and has contracted and agreed with Thomas Davies for the absolute purchase of the said piece of land, messuages," etc. " (subject to the payment by Matthew Otty, his heirs, executors, administrators or assigns, of all the payments which, from the 6th day of January instant, shall become payable for or in respect of the shares in the said society so taken by the said Matthew Otty from the said Thomas Davies as aforesaid) for the sum of 20*l*." It then witnessed, that the Plaintiff, in consideration of 20*l*. paid by the Defendant to the Plaintiff and of the Defendant's covenant, conveyed to the Defendant and his heirs the land and houses, subject to the mortgage and to the payments to the building society. And the Defendant covenanted to make the several payments to the building society, and to indemnify the Plaintiff therefrom.

The circumstances under which this deed was executed appeared to be as follows: — In 1844, the Plaintiff's wife deserted him, and left the place with her paramour. In 1854, the Plaintiff (who had never heard of his wife since her elopement, and believed her to be dead) married a second wife. Five or six years afterwards (1860) the Plaintiff was informed that his first wife was still living, and fearing a prosecution for bigamy, an arrangement was come to, between the Plaintiff and Defendant, that the Plaintiff should transfer the above property until the "difficulty" in which the Plaintiff was had passed over. It was proved by two witnesses that the "distinct understanding" between them was, that the transfer "was to be a nominal one, and was to be done away with when the unpleasantness was over." The Plaintiff afterwards discovered that the lapse of seven years from the time he knew that his first wife was alive protected him against any proceedings for bigamy, and, in 1863, he called on the Defendant to reconvey the property to him. This the Defendant refused to do, and he claimed it beneficially as his own.

It was proved, that the Plaintiff had, in the meantime, been allowed to remain in possession of the property, and that the Plaintiff had himself made the several payments to the society. The consideration of 20*l.* was not paid in money on the execution of the deed; but the Defendant, who, at that time, held the bill of the Plaintiff for that amount, alleged that the non-payment of this bill was the real consideration. But it was also proved that the amount of this bill had been paid by the Plaintiff to the Defendant since the execution of the deed.

The Defendant denied the trust, and insisted on the Statute of Frauds. . . .

Mr. *Baggallay* and Mr. *H. M. Jackson,* for the Plaintiff, argued, first, that the Plaintiff was entitled to a reconveyance, the deed having been executed under a misapprehension and mistake, and also on the express undertaking of the Defendant to reconvey. That there was no illegality in the nature of the transaction to prevent the Plaintiff from obtaining equitable relief, there being no crime in his second marriage after the disappearance for so long a time of the first wife. Secondly, that the 7th section of the Statute of Frauds was inapplicable, there being a part performance and a fraud, and that these were sufficient grounds for taking the case out of the statute, for Courts of Equity never allow the Statute of Frauds to cover a fraud. But that if the case were within the statute, it came within the 8th section, there being a constructive trust in favour of the Plaintiff, who had never received the alleged purchase-money. [Cases cited.]

Mr. *Hobhouse* and Mr. *W. W. Cooper* for the Defendant. The evidence and the nature of the transaction shew that an absolute conveyance was contemplated and was essential for the object, and the alleged agreement is expressly denied by the Defendant. The case is one intended to be met by the statute, the 7th section of which is express: — that all creations of trusts shall be in writing or else be utterly void. No parol evidence is, therefore, admissible of such a trust. There is no constructive trust or part performance. If the denial of a parol trust is to be considered a fraud, this section of the statute would be inoperative, the object of it being to prevent perjury by excluding parol evidence, and by not allowing a trust of land to be proved by anything but by some writing. [Cases cited.]

Mr. *Baggallay* in reply.

THE MASTER OF THE ROLLS [SIR JOHN ROMILLY]. Upon considering this case, and looking at the various authorities on the subject, and after referring again to the evidence, I am of opinion that the Statute of Frauds can have no application to this case.

Assuming (which I do for the present) that there was nothing whatever illegal in the transaction (the existence of which would, of course, alter the case), I consider it is proved, by the evidence, that the Plaintiff, apparently in a difficulty, or afraid of getting into one, transferred this property to the Defendant, who thereupon agreed that he would retransfer it to the Plaintiff when required; but when the time for the retransfer arrived, the Defendant refused to re-transfer it. Such being the facts, I am of opinion that it is not a case to which the Statute of Frauds applies. There was no consideration paid by the Defendant, the 20*l.* mentioned in the deed never having been paid; for the Plaintiff's bill of exchange held by the Defendant, and which he states to be the consideration for the deed, appears, by the evidence, to have been afterwards repaid by the Plaintiff by instalments in various sums. This being so, I am of opinion that " it is not honest to keep the land." If so, this is a case in which, in my opinion, the Statute of Frauds does not apply. I think that the subsequent course of dealing confirms this view; for the Plaintiff has ever since been allowed to remain in possession of the property, and he has paid all the instalments to the benefit building society. In my opinion, therefore, this case comes within the 8th section of the Statute of Frauds, and is excepted from the operation of the prior section. Therefore, the case is not such as entitles the Defendant to set up the Statute of Frauds as a ground for allowing him to retain the property.

I am also clearly of opinion there was no illegality in the transaction, and that the Plaintiff was quite justified, morally and legally, in marrying the second wife, although the effect of it may have been, that she did not become his wife. The long absence of his first wife was sufficient to justify the Plaintiff in coming to the conclusion that she was dead, and would have induced this Court to have come to the same conclusion, and, possibly, to have acted on it, by paying money out of Court on that footing. That being so, I am of opinion that the Plaintiff is entitled to a decree.

The costs of the conveyance were paid for by the Defendant, and I am of opinion that the Plaintiff ought to repay them; and, upon the Plaintiff's undertaking to repay them, I shall order a reconveyance at the expense of the Plaintiff. Cancelling the deed would not be sufficient, unless it was originally void, and I do not think it was. The Plaintiff must have his costs of suit.[1]

[1] Hutchins *v.* Lee, 1 Atk. 447; Haigh *v.* Kaye, L. R. 7 Ch. App. 469; Booth *v.* Turle, L. R. 16 Eq. 182; *Re* Duke of Marlborough, [1894] 2 Ch. 133; Clarke *v.* Eby, 13 Grant Ch. (U. C.) 371; Breitenstein *v.* Munson, 19 Brit. Col. R. 495; Schuerman *v.* Schuerman, 7 Alberta 380, *accord*. See also Rochefoucauld *v.* Boustead, [1897] 1 Ch. 196; Moore *v.* Oates, 143 Ark. 328; Hall *v.*

TITCOMB v. MORRILL.

SUPREME JUDICIAL COURT, MASSACHUSETTS. 1865.

10 Allen 15.

CHAPMAN, J. The bill alleges that the female plaintiffs are the children and sole heirs of David Morrill, deceased; that in the year 1839 said David made a quitclaim deed of the house and land described in the bill to Timothy P. Morrill, his brother; that there was no valuable consideration paid for said deed; that the land was conveyed in trust, for the benefit of said David and his heirs, on account of his intemperate habits at that time, said David having been prevailed upon to make such conveyance partly by promises and partly by threats. The bill then states the value of the property, the occupation of it by David during his lifetime, and by his heirs since his death, without payment of rent; that it was not the intention of said Timothy P. to avail himself of his legal title against said David or his heirs; and that he held it and meant to hold it in trust for their benefit. It then alleges the pendency of an action at law by the defendants to recover possession of the property, and prays for an injunction against the prosecution of the action at law, and a decree that the defendants shall give up and renounce the trust, and convey the premises to the plaintiffs; that an account may be stated between the parties, with an offer to pay whatever may be due from the plaintiffs, and concludes with a prayer for general relief.

The defendants' answer denies the trust, the want of consideration and the threats, and claims an absolute title under the deed to Morrill, their ancestor; and under the 28th rule, authorizing a defendant in his answer to insist on any special matter and have the same benefit as if he had pleaded or demurred to the bill, it states as special matter: 1. That the bill is founded upon an alleged trust, and the trust is not stated or described with such distinctness that the court can ascertain it or enforce it; 2. That the trust is not alleged to arise or result by implication of law, nor to have been created or declared by any instrument in writing signed by the party declaring or creating the same, as required by the statute; 3. They plead the statute of frauds in bar, and allege

---

Linn, 8 Colo. 264; Todd v. Munson, 53 Conn. 579; Craft v. Craft, 74 Fla. 262; Hunnicutt v. Oren, 84 Kan. 460; Huff v. Fuller, 197 Ky. 119; Peacock v. Nelson, 50 Mo. 256; O'Day v. Annex Realty Co., 191 S. W. 41 (Mo. App., 1917); Miller v. Belville, 98 Vt. 243, 34 Yale L. Jour. 682.

As to the effect of the illegality of the purpose for which the property is transferred, see Haigh v. Kaye, *supra;* Rosenbaum v. Huebner, 277 Ill. 360; Rossow v. Peters, 277 Ill. 436; Doughty v. Miller, 50 N. J. Eq. 529; Hornbeck v. Crawford, 130 Ore. 230.

that the trust was not created or declared by any instrument in writing.

In a plea in bar subsequently filed, they allege that judgment has been recovered by them against the plaintiffs in the action at law. But it is not material to consider the validity or propriety of this plea.

The bill alleges a trust concerning lands. By Gen. Sts. c. 100, sec. 19, " no trust concerning lands, except such as may arise or result by implication of law, shall be created or declared, unless by an instrument in writing signed by the party creating or declaring the same, or his attorney." This is different from the English statute, which does not require the trust to be declared in writing, but only manifested and proved in writing. It is not necessary in this case to decide whether this difference of phraseology is material. Nor is it necessary to decide whether a bill brought to enforce an express trust concerning lands must aver that it was created or declared in writing. The authorities on that point are somewhat conflicting. If it had been intended by the plaintiffs' solicitor that the bill should allege an express trust, it would be defective on another ground. By Rule 4, it is required that the bill shall contain a clear and explicit statement of the plaintiffs' case. This bill does not contain a clear and explicit statement of an express trust. But though its language is loose and general, it is apparently intended to contain a statement of an implied trust. It alleges that the deed of conveyance was a quitclaim, which without further description implies an absolute and unconditional deed. It does not set forth any agreement of the grantee. The promises connected with the threats of which it speaks must be understood as verbal and general, and not as constituting an express trust. The prayer for a decree that the defendants shall give up and renounce the trust and convey the land to the plaintiffs seems to regard it as a trust arising or resulting by implication of law. The plaintiffs' counsel has argued the case upon the ground that the bill sets forth such a trust, and has not contended that there was an express trust within the statute.

Regarding the bill, then, as setting forth a trust arising or resulting by implication of law, the plaintiffs' position is, that the conveyance without consideration, aided perhaps by a parol agreement, raises a trust by implication of law in favor of the grantor such as this court can enforce. No authority is produced to sustain this position; and the case of Bartlett *v.* Bartlett, 14 Gray, 278, is a recent authority to the contrary. It is unlike the cases referred to in Adams on Equity, cited by the plaintiffs' counsel. The most numerous class of these cases is where a purchase is made in the name of one person, and the purchase money is paid by another. None of these are cases where a grantor has been held to be *cestui que trust* on the ground that the consideration was not paid, or that there was a parol understanding that the grantee should hold the land in trust for him.

Demurrer sustained; bill dismissed with costs.[1]

GREGORY v. BOWLSBY.

SUPREME COURT, IOWA. 1902.

115 Iowa 327.[2]

SUIT in equity for the cancellation of a deed made by plaintiffs to defendant, and to declare and enforce a trust in certain real estate. The trial court sustained a demurrer to the petition as amended, the plaintiffs appeal. — *Reversed.*

DEEMER, J. It appears from the amended and substituted petition, which, under the record, must be treated as presenting the facts, that plaintiffs are the children and heirs at law of defendant Benjamin Bowlsby and of Catherine S. Bowlsby, now deceased, and that the defendant M. J. Bowlsby is the second wife of her co-defendant; that Catherine S. Bowlsby died intestate, seised of the real estate in dispute; that at the request of defendant Benjamin Bowlsby certain of the plaintiffs met the father at the home of Frank Davidson, a son-in-law, and that the father then and there requested them to deed to him their interest in the real estate left by his deceased wife, in order that he might use and farm the land to better advantage, and that he then and there verbally agreed that he would hold the land, would not sell or dispose of the same, and that the net proceeds and accumulations thereof should and would at his death descend to the children of Catherine Bowlsby, as provided by law; that, believing in said promises, and that such an arrangement was valid, they executed a deed of bargain and sale to their father of their interest in the real estate thereto-

---

[1] For numerous cases in accord with the principal case, see 6 Col. L. Rev. 326; 20 Harv. L. Rev. 549; 37 Harv. L. Rev. 553, 558; 12 Mich. L. Rev. 423, 515; 39 L. R. A. (N.S.) 906; 35 A. L. R. 280; 45 A. L. R. 851.

In Massachusetts the grantor, although he cannot reach the land conveyed, may recover its value in an action at law. Twomey v. Crowley, 137 Mass. 184; O'Grady v. O'Grady, 162 Mass. 290; Cromwell v. Norton, 193 Mass. 291; Kemp v. Kemp, 248 Mass. 354. But see Sturtevant v. Sturtevant, 20 N. Y. 39.

If land is conveyed to one who orally agrees but later refuses to give other land in exchange therefor, it has been held that the land conveyed may be recovered. Jarboe v. Severin, 85 Ind. 496; Ramey v. Slone, 23 Ky. L. Rep. 301; Dickerson v. Mays, 60 Miss. 388. *Cf.* Keener, Quasi-Contracts, 277 *et seq.*, Woodward, Quasi Contracts, sec. 95.

If a deed, absolute in form, is intended merely as a security, the Statute of Frauds does not preclude redemption. Linkemann v. Knepper, 226 Ill. 473; Vanderpool v. Vanderpool, 163 Ky. 742; Campbell v. Dearborn, 109 Mass. 130; Alexander v. Grover, 190 Mass. 462; Campbell, Cases on Mortgages, 80; 63 U. Pa. L. Rev. 815.

As to the effect of part performance, see Chap. II, sec. III, *ante*.

[2] For the same case on a subsequent appeal, see 126 Iowa 588.

fore owned by their mother, which deed recited a consideration of $1, the receipt whereof was acknowledged by the grantors; that by reason of the relations existing between them and their father these plaintiffs accepted his statements and promises without taking legal advice, and relied on him to advise them as to their rights and protect them in the premises; that neither defendant nor his attorney, who was present with him, advised them that the arrangement could not be enforced. It further appears from the allegations of this petition that the conveyance was procured by mistake on the part of these plaintiffs, induced by the representations made to them by said defendant; that said defendant paid nothing for the conveyance, and that the sole consideration therefor was his agreement as aforesaid. It is further alleged that said defendant did not intend to carry out the arrangement or agreement on his part, but made the representations and agreement aforesaid for the sole purpose of cheating and defrauding plaintiffs out of their interest in the land of their deceased mother; that after his marriage to his co-defendant he conveyed to her an undivided one-third interest in the property received from plaintiffs, but that this conveyance was without consideration, and was made with the intent to cheat and defraud these plaintiffs; that his co-defendant, when she took the conveyance, knew of the terms and conditions under which her husband received his deed from these plaintiffs. The prayer is that these deeds be canceled, that plaintiffs be adjudged to be the owners of an interest in the property, that their title be quieted, and that an accounting be had of the rents and profits of the real estate. The demurrer was the general equitable one, and as further grounds therefor it is claimed that the alleged oral agreement is within the statute of frauds.

It will be observed from this statement that the deed from plaintiffs to defendant was absolute on its face, and recited a consideration, the receipt whereof was acknowledged by the grantors; and that the agreement on which plaintiffs rely was in parol. The conveyance was directly from these plaintiffs to the defendant Benjamin Bowlsby, their father; hence the doctrine of resulting trust does not apply. That plaintiffs, in the first instance, are seeking to establish an express trust is too clear for argument; and it is equally clear that such a trust cannot rest in parol. Code, sections 2918, 4625; Ratliff v. Ellis, 2 Iowa, 59; McGinness v. Barton, 71 Iowa, 644; Hain v. Robinson, 72 Iowa, 735; Dunn v. Zwilling, 94 Iowa, 233; Maroney v. Maroney, 97 Iowa, 711; Hemstreet v. Wheeler, 100 Iowa, 290; Acker v. Priest, 92 Iowa, 610. We need not quote from these cases in support of the rule announced. They fully cover the ground, and need no amplification. That there was no resulting trust clearly appears from the opinion in Acker v. Priest, *supra*. See, also, McClain v. McClain, 57 Iowa, 167, which is directly in point. As the deed was absolute on its face, and recited the payment of a valuable consideration, plaintiffs will not be permitted to establish a trust by showing that there was in fact no consideration but a parol agreement to hold the title in trust. Acker *v.* Priest, *supra,* and cases cited at page 617, 92 Iowa.

As an express trust cannot be shown by parol, and as there was no resulting trust, we have one question left, and that is, was there such a fraud perpetrated by defendant Benjamin Bowlsby as entitled plaintiffs to the relief asked? That relief is not a reformation of the contract, but its cancellation; not a judgment at law as for fraud, but a decree quieting title, and for an accounting. If there is any cause of action stated, it is for the declaration and establishment of a constructive trust, growing out of the alleged fraud of the defendants. While some facts are recited for the purpose of showing fiduciary relations between the parties, we apprehend they are insufficient for that purpose. A father bears no such confidential or fiduciary relations to his adult children as to bring transactions between them relating to the land of either under suspicion. He may deal with them as with strangers, and no presumption of fraud or undue influence obtains. It is charged, however, that, with intent to cheat and defraud, defendant made the representations charged, fully intending at the time he made them not to carry them out, but to obtain the title to the land, and thus defraud the grantors. Does this make such a case of fraud as that a court will declare a constructive trust in the land in favor of the grantors? The instrument was in the exact form agreed upon by the parties, and there was no promise to execute defeasances or other instruments to witness the trust. The sole claim is that defendant made the promises and agreements with intent to cheat and defraud the plaintiffs. Mere denial that there was a parol agreement as claimed will not constitute a fraud. Acker *v.* Priest and McClain *v.* McClain, *supra.* If it did, the statute would be useless. Nor will a refusal to perform the contract be sufficient to create a constructive trust. McClain *v.* McClain, Dunn *v.* Zwilling, *supra.* But the statute was not enacted as a means for perpetrating a fraud; and, if fraud in the original transaction is clearly shown, the grantor will be held to be a trustee *ex maleficio.* If, then, there was fraudulent intent in procuring the deed without intention to hold the land as agreed, and pursuant to that intent the grantee disposed of the property, or otherwise repudiated his agreement, equity will take from the wrongdoer the fruit of his deceit by declaring a constructive trust. Acker *v.* Priest, *supra,* and cases cited. Mere breach or denial of the oral agreement does not, as we have said, constitute a fraud. "It seems to be requisite," says Chief Justice Gibson in Hoge *v.* Hoge, 1 Watts, 163 (26 Am. Dec. 52), "that there should have been an agency, active or passive, on the part of the grantee, in procuring the deed." Or, as said by Mr. Pomeroy, in his work on Equity Jurisprudence (section 1055); "There must be an element of positive fraud accompanying the promise, and by means of which the acquisition of the legal title is wrongfully consummated." Breach of the agreement may, of course, be considered, but it is not alone sufficient. There must be also some clear and explicit evidence of fraud or imposition at the time of the making of the conveyance to constitute the purchaser a trustee *ex maleficio*. The instant case, however, does not present the question of the quantity of proof required, for, as has been stated, it was decided upon demurrer to the petition, which pleads fraud in the inception of the transaction, and specifically alleges that the deed was made through defendant's agency, and upon his promise and representations, with the specific intent to cheat and defraud. Our observations regarding the character of the evidence required will perhaps prevent misapprehension of the rule in the future. The authorities are not harmonious on the questions discussed, although the points of difference seem to relate more to the *quantum* of proof in addition to the mere breach of promise than to the rule itself. [Citing cases.] This seems to be the first time the question has arisen in this court, although the rule announced has been recognized in the Acker and McClain Cases, *supra*, and in Burden *v.* Sheridan, 36 Iowa, 125.

We think the petition on its face recites facts showing a constructive trust, and that the demurrer should have been overruled.

Reversed.[1]

SINCLAIR *v.* PURDY.

Court of Appeals, New York. 1923.

235 N. Y. 245.

Appeal from a judgment of the Appellate Division of the Supreme Court in the first judicial department, entered July 3, 1922, which affirmed a judgment of Special Term dismissing upon the merits the counterclaim of the defendant Mapes and excluding her from any interest in the real property to be partitioned in this action.

Cardozo, J. The action is partition. Elijah F. Purdy succeeded upon his father's death in or about 1868 to the ownership of an un-

[1] Ford *v.* Ford, 44 Cal. App. 415; Kohn *v.* Kempner, 59 Cal. App. 621; Brown *v.* Doane, 86 Ga. 32; Jenkins *v.* Lane, 154 Ga. 454; Henschel *v.* Mamero, 120 Ill. 660; Griffith *v.* Orrill, 214 Ill. App. 228; Revel *v.* Albert, 162 N. W. 595 (Ia., 1917) (*semble*); Meek *v.* Meek, 79 Ore. 579; Johnson *v.* Johnson, 122 Wash. 117, *accord*.

The failure of the transferee to perform his promise is some evidence, though not conclusive evidence, that he did not originally intend to perform. Brock *v.* Brock, 90 Ala. 86; Mussey *v.* Shaw, 274 Ill. 351.

In Dillfelder *v.* Winterling, 150 Md. 626, it was held that the fact that the transferee suggested the arrangement is some evidence, though not conclusive evidence, that he did not originally intend to perform.

divided seventh interest in real estate in the city of New York. An equal interest passed to his sister Elvira, and like interests to other brothers and sisters, whose rights are not involved. Elijah was a clerk of what was then known as the Fifth District Court. His ownership of real estate subjected him to constant importunities to go bail for those in trouble. The desire to escape these importunities led him to execute a deed conveying his undivided half interest to his sister Elvira. The conveyance was made during the pendency of an action for the partition of the estate. The judgment in that action, dated February 21, 1871, directed a sale of the property and the payment to Elvira of two-sevenths of the proceeds. By arrangement with Elijah, she bought in two parcels, 337 and 339 East Twenty-third street, paying the purchase price by offsetting it against her share in the proceeds of partition, for she had not a dollar besides. The record does not make it plain whether at this time brother and sister made their home together. The relation between them in any event was one of harmony and affection, and so continued till the end. Advancing years brought illness and infirmity to the man, and the need of unremitting care. To procure the comforts of a home, he went to live in 1898 with Mrs. Mapes, a niece. An arrangement was made that in return for her care during the rest of his life, he would devise to her his interest in the Twenty-third street property. There is evidence of repeated declarations by Elvira that though the title was in her name, a half interest was his. A letter confirmatory of his rights, to which there will be fuller reference later, was excluded upon the trial. Elijah died at the age of eighty in 1914. He left a will, but gave nothing to his niece. Elvira died in 1917. In this action, brought to partition the Twenty-third street parcels, the niece, Mrs. Mapes, has set up an equitable counterclaim. She asks the judgment of the court establishing a trust in favor of Elijah to the extent of an undivided half, and specific performance of his contract to devise his half to her.

There was a separate trial of the counterclaim upon issues framed by the court for determination by a jury. The jury found by consent of all parties that an agreement had been made between Elijah Purdy and Mrs. Mapes to the effect that in consideration of her care of him, she would receive upon his death his interest in the land in suit. It found performance of the agreement on her part, and fixed the value of her services at $12,000. It found, however, under the direction of the court that Elijah had in fact no interest, legal or equitable, to devise; that Elvira was the sole owner; and that she had not estopped herself either by representations to Mrs. Mapes or otherwise from the assertion of her ownership. The judgment entered upon this verdict was a final adjudication adverse to the appellant's title (Brown *v.* Feek, 204 N. Y. 238; Albany Hospital *v.* Albany Guardian Society, 214 N. Y.

435). The Appellate Division affirmed. An appeal to this court followed.[1] . . .

We hold, therefore, that the letter should have been received, and that its interpretation was for the jury in the light of the surroundings (Lamb v. Norcross Bros. Co., 208 N. Y. 427; Utica City Nat. Bank v. Gunn, 222 N. Y. 204, 208). But even if the memorandum were found to be inadequate, a question would still remain, and would call for answer by the jury, whether there had been such an abuse of a confidential relation as to lead without a writing to the implication of a trust. The sister's deposition shows that her brother disclosed his plan to her before the making of the deed. Some one, he said, had advised him to place his share of the property in her name. He told her that he intended to follow the advice. It was an expedient adopted to save him the bother of going upon bonds. She does not remember that she made any promise in return. He trusted, as she puts it, to her sense of honor. A little later she learned that the title was in her name.

We think a confidential relation was the procuring cause of the conveyance. The grantor could not disclose the trust upon the face of the deed. If he had done so, he would have defeated the purpose of the transfer, which required that title, to outward appearance, be vested in another. He found, as he thought, in the bond of kinship a protection as potent as any that could be assured to him by covenants of title. It was "the case of a confidence induced, not by the bare promise of another, but by the promise and the confidential relation conjoined" (Wood v. Rabe, 96 N. Y. 414, 426). "The absence of a formal writing grew out of that very confidence and trust, and was occasioned by it" (Goldsmith v. Goldsmith, 145 N. Y. 313, 318.) In such conditions, the rule in this state is settled that equity will grant relief (Wood v. Rabe, supra; Goldsmith v. Goldsmith, supra; Gallagher v. Gallagher, 135 App. Div. 457; 202 N. Y. 572; Allen v. Arkenburgh, 2 App. Div. 458; 158 N. Y. 697). Distinctions are, indeed, to be drawn between cases where property is parted with on the faith of an oral promise, and cases where one without an interest in property before obtains a promise that an interest will be given to him thereafter (Leary v. Corvin, 181 N. Y. 222, 229; cf. Amherst College v. Ritch, 151 N. Y. 282). It is not the promise only, nor the breach only, but unjust enrichment under cover of the relation of confidence, which puts the court in motion.

The argument is made that the transfer was intended as a gift. True it is, we are told, that the motive of the grantor was to avoid the embarrassments incidental to notoriety of ownership. The purpose, none the less, was the creation of a title unaffected by a trust. We think a jury would be permitted to draw another in-

[1] A part of the opinion in which it was held that the letter referred to was a memorandum sufficient to satisfy the Statute of Frauds is omitted.

ference. Here was a man transferring to his sister the only property he had in the world. He was transferring it in obedience to advice that embarrassment would be avoided if he put it in her name. He was doing this, as she admits, in reliance upon her honor. Even if we were to accept her statement that there was no distinct promise to hold it for his benefit, the exaction of such a promise, in view of the relation, might well have seemed to be superfluous. The proof of the conveyance, so far as it rests upon Elvira's testimony, was wrung from an unwilling witness. Though a promise in words was lacking, the whole transaction, it might be found, was "instinct with an obligation" imperfectly expressed (Wood v. Duff-Gordon, 222 N. Y. 88, 91). It was to be interpreted, not literally or irrespective of its setting, but sensibly and broadly with all its human implications. Even the denial of an express promise might not unfairly be discredited. There is evidence that in later years Elvira stated again and again that she and her brother were equal owners of the property. There are the significant admissions of the letter which have at least a corroborative value, if they serve no other purpose. When all these circumstances are viewed collectively, we think the triers of the facts might say that the conveyance from brother to sister was made as a form, that both so understood it, and that the transaction was consummated in confidence that the holder would keep the faith.

Some point is made as to the pleadings. So far as the contract between Elijah and Mrs. Mapes is concerned, the Statute of Frauds is irrelevant, since its provisions, in their application to that contract, are not pleaded. So far, however, as the action involves the declaration of a trust relation between Elijah Purdy and his sister, we think the defense of the statute is presented by the answer.

The judgment of the Appellate Division and that of the Special Term should be reversed and a new trial granted, with costs to abide the event.

HISCOCK, Ch. J., HOGAN, POUND, MCLAUGHLIN, CRANE and ANDREWS, JJ., concur.

Judgments reversed, etc.[1]

[1] Jones v. Jones, 140 Cal. 587; Miller v. Miller, 266 Ill. 522; Housewright v. Steinke, 326 Ill. 398; Catalani v. Catalani, 124 Ind. 54; Dillfelder v. Winterling, 150 Md. 626; Wood v. Rabe, 96 N. Y. 414; Cardiff v. Marquis, 17 N. D. 110; Hatcher v. Hatcher, 264 Pa. 105, *accord.*

For numerous other cases holding that a constructive trust will be imposed where the transferee was in a confidential relationship to the transferor, see 37 Harv. L. Rev. 661.

HARTZELL v. WHITMORE.

SUPREME COURT, PENNSYLVANIA. 1922.

271 Pa. 575.

BILLS IN EQUITY to declare a trust and to compel a reconveyance, and an accounting. Before Sloan, P. J.

The opinion of the Supreme Court states the facts.

The court entered a decree in accordance with the prayers of the bills. Defendants appealed.

OPINION BY MR. JUSTICE SCHAFFER, January 3, 1922:

Judgments had been recovered against plaintiffs, Lena Hartzell and John H. Hartzell, mother and son. These judgments were assigned to defendants, who caused executions to issue on them. Two farms, one belonging to the mother and the other to the son, with the personal property thereon, were sold at the resulting sheriff's sales and purchased by defendants. Subsequently these proceedings in equity were instituted by plaintiffs, the object of which was to have defendants declared trustees for complainants of the properties purchased at the sheriff's sales, to compel them to reconvey and to account for any property sold. The chancellor who heard the cases, which were tried together, found a trust existed in favor of each plaintiff and entered decrees as prayed for; from these decrees defendants appealed.

The facts shown on the trial fully warranted the conclusions of the chancellor and the remedial decrees resulting therefrom. It was established that, following the execution, another of Mrs. Hartzell's sons arranged with a bank to lend him the money necessary to liquidate the judgments against his mother and brother; when this was made known to defendant Whitmore, he advised that the arrangement should not be consummated, that he and defendant Kahle would buy in the property and hold it for the benefit of plaintiffs until they could raise the money to pay the indebtedness, — they, defendants, in the meantime, applying the proceeds of any property sold by them to the reduction of their claims.

On the day of, and preceding the first of, the sheriff's sales, both defendants were at Mrs. Hartzell's farm, and Whitmore told her that he would purchase all the property, real and personal, at the sheriff's sales for her and her son John, that the personal property would remain on the farms and, when he and Kahle were paid with interest, the farms and other property would be returned to her and her son. Whitmore made similar statements to John prior to the sale and the arrangement was repeated in the presence of the other defendant, Kahle. It was proven that at the sheriff's sales Whitmore dissuaded other persons from bidding, stating he was buying for the benefit of the defendants in the executions, and, as a consequence, he purchased everything sold at prices greatly below real values, except some of John's articles, which were bid in by one of his brothers, who, in conformity with the understanding, turned them over to defendants, without paying anything on his bid. It was shown that the method of selling the personal property was not such as to command the best price, that in many instances, it was put up in lump, that the cattle were sold as a lot in a field a considerable distance from where the sale was taking place, and that the entire conduct of the sale was not such as would have taken place had not the defendants in the execution been lulled to sleep in protecting their interests. It also appeared that prior to the sale Whitmore learned that other sons of Mrs. Hartzell had labor claims against her and John; these he persuaded them to release, on the representation that he would buy in the property for the benefit of their mother and brother; for these releases no other consideration was received than this promise. Following the sale, John Hartzell continued to pay the taxes on the property and he and his mother stayed in possession. When demand was made on defendants for a reconveyance, they refused to comply.

Under the facts here appearing it would be manifestly unjust and inequitable to permit defendants, by deception, through which they procured appellee's property at a sum far below its real value, to covinously profit. They must now make good their undertaking to return it upon being paid their debt and interest. So long ago as 1829, in a case tried before Chief Justice GIBSON at nisi prius (Brown *v.* Dysinger, 1 Rawle *408), we laid down the rule that parol declarations, made by a purchaser at sheriff's sale, that he was bidding for another, are admissible to establish a trust for the person for whom the purchaser declared he was bidding. It was there said, " To . . . allow him to hold the land under such circumstances would be supporting a breach of trust and a fraud in law." In Cook *v.* Cook, 69 Pa. 443, we said, " Now it is perfectly clear that Phillip purchased [at sheriff's sale] for John and his conduct at the sale preventing bidders and getting the property at a low price, far below its real value, would be a wilful and deliberate fraud, if he did not fulfil his agreement . . . publicly acknowledged at the very moment of the purchase "; and in Faust *v.* Haas, 73 Pa. 295, we declared that where artifice or trick is resorted to to procure property at sheriff's sale at an under-value, the purchaser there takes as trustee for the person misled.

The learned chancellor who heard these cases correctly determined them and his decree in each is affirmed at the cost of appellants.[1]

[1] Rochefoucauld *v.* Boustead, [1897] 1 Ch. 196; Thomas *v.* Goodbread, 78 Fla. 278; Broadwell *v.* Smith, 152 Ga. 161; Judd *v.* Moseley, 30 Ia. 423; McKibben *v.* Diltz, 138 Ky. 684; Stone *v.* Middleton, 144 Ky. 284; Day *v.* Amburgey, 147 Ky. 123 (*semble*); Turner *v.* Weaver, 126 Miss. 496; Johnson

TILLMAN v. KIFER.

SUPREME COURT, ALABAMA. 1910.

166 Ala. 403.

SAYRE, J. In 1891 Robert J. Tillman, being on the eve of a failure in business and a general assignment for the benefit of his creditors, made a deed to his sister, Mrs. Lucy E. Kifer, of certain lots in Tillman's addition to the city of Bessemer on a recited consideration of $600. Now this bill is filed by the children of Robert J., averring that the lots were conveyed on the trust and confidence that the grantee would hold them for complainants, and would at a later time execute a deed to the alleged beneficial owners. There is no semblance of trust shown on the face of the deed. No facts are alleged, as that the consideration, or any part of it, moved from the complainants, with an understanding that the beneficial ownership was to be in them, from which a trust would result by operation of law, without express words of creation. Nor is there averment of undue influence arising out of confidential relation, or other circumstances of fraud between the parties, to constitute the grantee a trustee *ex maleficio*, as was the case in Kyle v. Perdue, 95 Ala. 579, 10 South. 103, and Noble v. Moses, 81 Ala. 530, 1 South. 217, 60 Am. Rep. 175, cited by appellants. The bill shows nothing more than an effort to enforce a trust according to the alleged agreement of the parties to the deed; that agreement having been expressed by parol, and not otherwise. The defendants have denied the agreement, have averred that the transaction was of a character entirely different from that set up in the bill, and it may be said that the weight of the evidence is with them.

But, apart from defendants' version, the case made by the bill,

---

v. Jameson, 209 S. W. 919 (Mo., 1919) (*semble*); State v. Ellison, 282 Mo. 660; Laughlin v. Laughlin, 291 Mo. 472; Robinson v. Cruzen, 202 S. W. 449 (Mo. App., 1918); Thierry v. Thierry, 298 Mo. 25 (*semble*); Moore v. De Bernardi, 47 Nev. 33; Prescott v. Jenness, 77 N. H. 84; Ryan v. Dox, 34 N. Y. 307; Coyle v. Stahl, 42 Okla. 651 (*semble*); Cameron v. Townsend, 286 Pa. 393; Jarrot v. Kuker, 78 S. C. 510; Chandler v. Riley, 210 S. W. 716 (Tex. Civ. App., 1919); Chadwick v. Arnold, 34 Utah 48, *accord*. But see *contra*, Southwick v. Spevak, 252 Mass. 354. See 5 Ann. Cas. 173; 12 Ann. Cas. 542; Ann. Cas. 1918E 309; 42 A. L. R. 10; 54 A. L. R. 1195.

A constructive trust will of course be imposed if the purchaser never intended to perform his promise. Butler v. Watrous, 185 Ala. 130.

If it appears that the owner did not rely upon the promise of the purchaser, no constructive trust will be imposed. Miller v. Kyle, 107 Kan. 388. See Peppard Realty Co. v. Emdon, 204 N. Y. App. Div. 8.

As to the effect of a fiduciary relation between the purchaser and the promisee, see sec. V, and particularly Harrop v. Cole, 85 N. J. Eq. 32, *post*.

As to the effect of a loan of the purchase money by the purchaser to the promisee, see sec. IV, and particularly Herlihy v. Cooney, 99 Me. 469, *post*.

and sustained by complainants' theory of the proof, must fall under the condemnation of the statute which provides that no trust concerning lands, except such as results by implication or construction of law, or which may be transferred or extinguished by operation of law, can be created, unless by instrument in writing, signed by the party creating or declaring the same. — Code, sec. 3412. All questions in this case were settled in Patton v. Beecher, 62 Ala. 579, to which nothing can be added. McCarty v. McCarty, 74 Ala. 552, and Cresswell v. Jones, 68 Ala. 420, cited by appellants, were cases in which the trusts involved were expressed in writing.

The decree of the court below must be affirmed.

Affirmed.[1]

DOWDELL, C. J., and SIMPSON and MCCLELLAN, JJ., concur.

STOUT v. STOUT, 165 Iowa 552 (1914): A husband conveyed land to his second wife who induced him to make the conveyance by an oral promise that on his death she would make certain payments to his children by a former marriage. It was alleged and found as a fact that she never intended to carry out her promise. The husband having died, this suit was brought by his children to establish a constructive trust. It was held for the plaintiffs. GAYNOR, J., said (p. 558):

"The ground and essence of the fraud is the existence of the intent, at the time of the promise, not to perform it, and we gather from this record not only that Margaret made the promises alleged to have been made by her, as an inducing cause to the conveyance, but also that she made them for the purpose of procuring this conveyance to her, with the intent in her mind at the time not to per-

---

[1] Lantry v. Lantry, 51 Ill. 458; Ryder v. Ryder, 244 Ill. 297; Braidwood v. Charles, 327 Ill. 500; Keller v. Joseph, 329 Ill. 148; Westphal v. Heckman, 185 Ind. 88; Willis v. Robertson, 121 Ia. 380; Perkins v. Perkins, 181 Mass. 401; Mugan v. Wheeler, 241 Mo. 376; Thomson v. Thomson, 211 S. W. 52 (Mo. App., 1919); Apgar v. Connell, 160 N. Y. App. Div. 743; Howard v. Foskett, 96 Ore. 446; Salter v. Bird, 103 Pa. 436; Crawford v. Workman, 64 W. Va. 19; Felz v. Felz's Estate, 170 Wis. 550, *accord*. See Ames, Lect. Leg. Hist. 429; 37 Harv. L. Rev. 664.

In Becker v. Neurath, 149 Ky. 421, Androscoggin County Sav. Bank v. Tracy, 115 Me. 433, and Huffine v. Lincoln, 52 Mont. 585, a constructive trust was raised in favor of the intended beneficiary. In these cases there was a confidential relationship between the grantor and grantee, but the courts did not lay any emphasis on that fact. See also Langille v. Nass, 51 Nova Scotia 429. See Costigan, Trusts Based on Oral Promises, 12 Mich. L. Rev. 423, 434.

The intended beneficiary is protected if the trustee transfers the trust property to him or signs a memorandum acknowledging the trust. See Chap. II, sec. III, *ante*. The same result has been reached where the conveyance is to the transferee as "trustee," the terms of the trust not appearing in the deed but there being an oral agreement to hold in trust for a third person. Straw v. Mower, 99 Vt. 56.

form the promises, but to repudiate them, and thereby cut off and defeat the rights of these plaintiffs in their father's property.

"A mere failure to perform a promise, honestly made, will not constitute such fraud as will justify a court in decreeing a constructive trust. It is a fact, though, to be considered by the court in reaching its final conclusion. The gravamen of the offense is the intent to deceive, the bad faith, the securing of an advantage under a false promise, made without intent to perform; made to secure the performance of the act, the performance of which results in benefit to the promisee, with intent to repudiate the obligation upon which the promise rests, to the prejudice of another." [1]

DIXON v. OLMIUS.

CHANCERY. 1787.

1 Cox Eq. 414.

THE BILL was filed by some of the specialty and simple contract creditors of the late Lord Waltham on behalf of themselves and the other creditors, and also by some of the legatees under his will on behalf of themselves and the other legatees, praying that the

[1] McDonald v. Tyner, 84 Ark. 189; McKinney v. Burns, 31 Ga. 295; Reardon v. Reardon, 219 Mass. 594, 225 Mass. 255; Cipperly v. Cipperly, 4 Thomp. & C. (N. Y.) 342; Moyer v. Moyer, 21 Hun (N. Y.) 67, accord. Compare Scholefield v. Templer, Johns. 155, where the fraud was that of a third party.

In Jasinski v. Stankowski, 145 Md. 58, it was held that the fact that the transferee was active in procuring the conveyance is evidence of a fraudulent intent at the outset. See Fischbeck v. Gross, 112 Ill. 208.

Confidential relation. In the following cases it was held that the intended beneficiary was entitled to the property because the transferee abused a confidential relationship existing between himself and the transferor. Kennedy's Heirs & Ex'rs v. Kennedy's Heirs, 2 Ala. 571 (brother to brother); Dieckmann v. Merkh, 20 Cal. App. 655 (father to daughter); Hillyer v. Hynes, 33 Cal. App. 506 (wife to husband); Willats v. Bosworth, 33 Cal. App. 710 (*semble* mother to son); Fisk's Appeal, 81 Conn. 433 (wife to husband); Stahl v. Stahl, 214 Ill. 131 (mother to son); Crossman v. Keister, 223 Ill. 69 (father to daughter); Hilt v. Simpson, 230 Ill. 170 (father to sons); Stout v. Stout, 165 Ia. 552 (husband to wife); Becker v. Neurath, 149 Ky. 421 (husband to wife); Crinkley v. Rogers, 100 Neb. 647 (wife to husband); Walters v. Walters, 26 N. Mex. 22 (father to son); Goldsmith v. Goldsmith, 145 N. Y. 313 (mother to son); Hanson v. Svarverud, 18 N. D. 550 (parents to children); Hughes v. Fargo Loan Agency, 46 N. D. 26 (father to son).

In the following cases it was held that there was no such abuse of a confidential relationship as to justify giving the property to the intended beneficiary. Westphal v. Heckman, 185 Ind. 88 (father to son); Thomson v. Thomson, 211 S. W. 52 (Mo. App., 1919) (husband to wife); Apgar v. Connell, 160 N. Y. App. Div. 743 (children to mother); Howard v. Foskett, 96 Ore. 446 (husband to wife); Felz v. Felz's Estate, 170 Wis. 550 (husband to wife).

Disposition in contemplation of death. In the following cases where the transfer although *inter vivos* was made in contemplation of the settlor's death, it was held that the intended beneficiary was entitled to the property. Simons will might be established, and the trusts thereof performed and carried into execution; that the personal estate might be applied in payment of debts and legacies, and if not sufficient, that a competent part of the real estate might be sold for that purpose.

It stated that on 2d February, 1787, Lord Waltham made his will, and thereby charged his real estates with the payment of his debts in the manner there mentioned, and died on the 10th February following, leaving the defendant Elizabeth, the wife of the defendant Olmius, his sister and heir at law; that the defendants pretended that this will had been revoked by a fine levied and recovery suffered of the real estates charged by the will with payment of the debts, subsequent to the said will. The bill then charged, that if such fine and recovery did operate as a revocation of the will, yet that Lord Waltham only intended such fine and recovery to answer some particular purposes, and that he meant and intended to republish his said will, but was prevented from so doing by several acts of fraud and violence on the part of the defendant, who would not permit the attorney sent for by Lord Waltham to go into his bed-room, together with several circumstances of fraud very fully charged by the bill.

To this bill the defendants put in a demurrer, and a plea and an answer. The demurrer was as to so much of the said bill as required from the defendants a discovery whether the said Lord Waltham did not mean or intend to republish his said will. The plea was to such parts of the bill as prayed any relief in respect of the real estate, and the plea was the fine and recovery, with an averment that Lord Waltham died intestate. The plea was argued at the same time with the demurrer, but was overruled on a point of form.

By the answer the defendants gave explicit denials to the several charges of fraud and obstructing the republication of the will.

Mr. Recorder and *Mansfield* in support of the demurrer argued that the discovery sought was wholly immaterial, which was in itself a good ground of demurrer; it could be of no consequence what the defendant thought to be the intention of Lord Waltham, nor indeed what he did in fact intend, for if the fine and recovery have in law operated a revocation of this will, there must be an actual republication of it in order to give it any effect, and the intentions of Lord Waltham could never get rid of the requisites imposed on a will of real estate. But if such a discovery were material, and could have any operation in giving new effect to this will, then it would be calling upon the heir at law to make discovery of

---

v. Bedell, 122 Cal. 341; Lauricella *v.* Lauricella, 161 Cal. 61; Dieckmann *v.* Merkh, 20 Cal. App. 655; Hillyer *v.* Hynes, 33 Cal. App. 506; Willats *v.* Bosworth, 33 Cal. App. 710 (*semble*); Becker *v.* Neurath, 149 Ky. 421; Schneringer *v.* Schneringer, 81 Neb. 661; Moyer *v.* Moyer, 21 Hun (N. Y.) 67; Ahrens *v.* Jones, 169 N. Y. 555. *Cf.* Pollard *v.* McKenney, 69 Neb. 742.

an adverse title; that this was what the Court would never compel an heir at law to do, who always stood in a favoured light in a Court of Equity; that this had been frequently determined in the case of a purchaser for a valuable consideration, and the same principle would extend to the case of an heir, who was entitled to an equal protection from the Court.

LORD CHANCELLOR [THURLOW]. The charge of the bill is, that Lord Waltham had an intention to republish his will, and that such intention was frustrated by the fraud of the heir at law, or at least of her husband. I think it impossible to separate the fact of Lord Waltham's intention, from the facts of fraud imputed. The defendants must answer the former as well as the latter.

The demurrer was overruled.[1]

CALDWELL *v.* CALDWELL.

COURT OF APPEALS, KENTUCKY. 1871.

7 Bush 515.

CHIEF JUSTICE ROBERTSON delivered the opinion of the Court. In the year 1863 Alexander Caldwell, a citizen of Campbell County, Kentucky, shortly before his death, published his last will, whereby he contemplated a proximate equality in the distribution of his estate among his six children, one of whom, James Caldwell, was then a soldier in the Confederate army. The testator, sympathizing with that son and the cause he had espoused, indicated a desire to secure to him "the home place" of nearly three hundred acres of land, which would not have exceeded the value of the devises to each of his other five children then near him. But apprehending that James, if he should even survive the war, might by his rebellion against the Government of the United States forfeit his estate, he devised the legal title of the "*home* place" to his

---

[1] See Thynn *v.* Thynn, 1 Vern. 296 (fraud); Mestaer *v.* Gillespie, 11 Ves. 621, 638 (force); Bulkley *v.* Wilford, 2 Cl. & Fin. 102, 177 (confidential relation, attorney); Barron *v.* Stuart, 136 Ark. 481 (confidential relation, wife); Brazil *v.* Silva, 181 Cal. 490 (fraud); Dowd *v.* Tucker, 41 Conn. 197 (fraud). See also Gains *v.* Gains, 2 A. K. Marsh. (Ky.) 190; Clingan *v.* Mitcheltree, 31 Pa. 25; Blanchard *v.* Blanchard, 32 Vt. 62. But see Kent *v.* Mahaffey, 10 Oh. St. 204.

If by fraud, duress or undue influence the testator is induced to make a devise or bequest to an innocent third person, it has been held that the latter can be held as a constructive trustee. Bridgeman *v.* Green, 2 Ves. Sr. 627, Wilm. 58 (transfer *inter vivos*, undue influence); Huguenin *v.* Baseley, 14 Ves. 273 (undue influence of clergyman); Powell *v.* Yearance, 73 N. J. Eq. 117 (fraud). See Scholefield *v.* Templer, Johns. 155. But see Dye *v.* Parker, 108 Kan. 304 (provision fraudulently omitted from will).

On the question of the jurisdiction of courts of probate and courts of equity, see Warren, Fraud, Undue Influence, and Mistake in Wills, 41 Harv. L. Rev. 309.

other five children, on a latent trust that if James should ever return, and be capable of holding the title, they should convey it to him. And this, according to satisfactory oral testimony, they understood and tacitly agreed to fulfill.

On his return, about the close of the war, there being no danger of forfeiture, two of those devisees, Daniel and William Caldwell, true to the trust, each conveyed to him one fifth of the land, of the whole of which he thereupon took possession with the apparent acquiescence of the other three devisees of the home tract; and this possession he appears to have retained without disturbance or complaint for more than three years, when the three recusant devisees and the husband of one of them refusing to convey their interests to him, he on the 10th of September, 1869, brought this suit against them for enforcing their obligation under a resulting trust. His petition charging the trust was denied by their answer; and on that issue the circuit court decreed a release to James of their title, and by this appeal they seek to reverse that decree.

Implied trusts being excepted from the statute of frauds and perjuries, if the facts establish such a trust in this case, no written memorial of it was necessary for enforcing it, nor was the oral testimony incompetent on the alleged ground that it contradicts the will.

Extraneous testimony is incompetent to supply an unintentional omission or to contradict an expressed intention in a will. But the facts established by extrinsic evidence in this case have no such aim or effect. They are consistent with the testator's intention, and with the concession that the will is just what he intended it to be, and they supply nothing which he unintentionally omitted. He intended to pretermit his son James as an express devisee of the land, and to rely for his benefit on the plighted honor of the express devisees. Might he not have done so securely on a promise that the five devisees would pay to James ten thousand dollars? And would proof of such agreement contradict the will, or supply any unintentional omission in it, without which omission his purpose of making James a co-equal beneficiary might have been frustrated by impending forfeiture?

The competency of oral testimony for establishing and enforcing such trusts as that claimed in this case is prescriptively recognized by undeviating authorities, among a great multitude of which we only cite the following: Drakeford *v.* Weeks, 3 Atkins, 639; Barrow *v.* Greenhough, 3 Vesey, 152; Stickland *v.* Aldridge, 9 Vesey, 519; Maislar *v.* Gillespie, 11 Vesey, 639; 2 Powell on Devises, 415. To these citations we might, if deemed needful, add many others in England and America, and even in this court, illustrative of the same principles.

On the like principles the most familiar class of resulting trusts is upheld. Why else, where an unqualified title to land is conveyed to one, the law has adjudged that he holds it in trust for another on oral proof that the latter paid the consideration, in the absence of any fact authorizing a countervailing presumption? In such a case there is no sale of land by the one to the other requiring writing, and the extraneous fact is admitted not to contradict the deed, but to prevent a fraud.

So here, had not the actual devisees been understood by the testator as accepting the devise in trust for James, an essentially different will would have been made, excluding their power over the land as devised; and consequently their refusal to execute the trust is a constructive fraud on the testator as well as on their brother James.

The proof of the trust is corroborated by the conduct of Daniel and William, by the testator's purpose of equality, and by the apparent recognition of it by the acquiescence in the claim and possession by James for years since his return.

We are satisfied that the will was made as it is, with the mutual understanding of the trust as claimed.

Wherefore we conclude that the judgment of the circuit court is right, and therefore affirm it.[1]

AMHERST COLLEGE *v.* RITCH, 151 N. Y. 282 (1897): A testator left the residue of his estate to his three executors. Although the bequest was absolute it appeared that it was made upon a secret trust for certain colleges to which the residuary legatees agreed to convey it. By statute (L. 1860, c. 360) it was provided that no person having a husband, wife, child or parent should devise or bequeath to any charitable corporation more than one-half of his estate. The court held that the trust was enforceable to the extent of one-half of the testator's estate, that as to the balance there would be a resulting trust for the widow and next of kin, but that they having waived their rights the whole trust was enforceable. VANN, J., said (p. 332):

[1] For numerous cases in accordance with the principal case and a few cases *contra*, see 37 Harv. L. Rev. 671, n.57; Ames, Cases on Trusts, 1 ed., 297; 20 L. R. A. 465; 8 L. R. A. (N. S.) 698; 31 L. R. A. (N. S.) 176; 21 Ann. Cas. 1384; 66 A. L. R. 156.

The same result has been reached in cases where the promise is made by the heir or next of kin of the decedent. 37 Harv. L. Rev. 677, n.65.

In People *v.* Schaefer, 266 Ill. 337, it was held that the devise was taxable as a devise to the intended beneficiary. But see Cullen *v.* A. G., L. R. 1 H. L. 190 (secret trust for charitable purposes, no exemption); Matter of Edson, 38 App. Div. 19, aff'd 159 N. Y. 568. *Cf.* Estate of Holt, 61 Cal. App. 464 (intention not communicated to devisee).

In *Re* Fleetwood, 15 Ch. Div. 594, it was held that the intended beneficiary cannot take if he is a witness to the will. But see *contra*, O'Brien *v.* Condon, [1905] 1 I. R. 51.

"There are authorities which hold that the rights arising from such a secret trust as we have been discussing are not testamentary in character, because the trust does not act upon the will, but on the fund after it reaches the hands of the legatees. [Citing cases.] Founded on these authorities, the argument is made by some of the respondents that the statute does not apply to this case, because the colleges do not claim under the will, or anything found in it, but on facts wholly outside of it. They insist that the same reason that takes a secret trust away from the Statute of Wills and of Frauds takes it away from the act of 1860, and that their rights do not spring from the mode of changing title, but out of the duty of those who hold the title. They illustrate their argument by saying that if A. wills B. $100,000, and writes him a letter saying that the legacy is in trust for C., but the letter is not delivered until after A.'s death, there is no trust; but if the letter is delivered before A. dies and B. promises to perform, there is a trust. Although the will is the same in both cases, in the one B. takes and in the other C., because the former takes from the will and the latter from the trust. The argument is not without force when applied to a trust that does not run foul of a statute. When, however, as in this case, the trust is a manifest evasion of a statute, sound public policy forbids that the testator should be permitted to effect indirectly that which he could not effect directly, at least until all intervening rights derived from the statute have been lawfully cleared away.[1] We think that the act of 1860 applies, but to what extent and how it was affected by the releases, we will proceed to consider."

The court then said that the act of 1860 does not impose a limitation upon the power of charitable corporations to take or hold property but limits the power of the testator in the interest of the designated relatives and that the latter alone can object to the disposition. A release by them of their claims is therefore effective to make the trust enforceable.

SCHULTZ'S APPEAL.

SUPREME COURT, PENNSYLVANIA. 1876.

80 Pa. 396.

MR. JUSTICE SHARSWOOD [2] delivered the opinion of the court, January 31, 1876. The very able and exhaustive opinions, as well of the auditor as of the learned court below, have relieved us from an examination of the English decisions upon the Mortmain Act of

[1] Stickland v. Aldridge, 9 Ves. 516; Russell v. Jackson, 10 Hare 204; Tee v. Ferris, 2 Kay & J. 357; Moss v. Cooper, 1 J. & H. 352; Sweeting v. Sweeting, 10 Jur. N. S. 31; Re Spencer's Will, 57 L. T. 519; Geddis v. Semple, [1903] 1 I. R. 73; Kenrick v. Cole, 61 Mo. 572; Matter of O'Hara, 95 N. Y. 403; Edson v. Bartow, 154 N. Y. 199; Stirk's Estate, 232 Pa. 98, *accord*.

that country. They undoubtedly throw a clear and strong light upon the question presented upon this record. They establish two positions: 1. That if an absolute estate is devised, but upon a secret trust assented to by the devisee, either expressly or impliedly, by knowledge and silence before the death of the testator, a court of equity will fasten a trust on him on the ground of fraud, and consequently the Statute of Mortmain will avoid the devise if the trust is in favor of a charity. But 2. If the devisee have no part in the devise, and no knowledge of it until after the death of the testator, there is no ground upon which equity can fasten such a trust on him, even though, after it comes to his knowledge, he should express an intention of conforming to the wishes of the testator. The latter proposition applies directly to the case now before us. Reuben Yeakle, the legatee named in the will, was not present when the instrument was executed. He had no communication with the testator, directly or indirectly, upon the subject. The testator had long intended to leave his estate for charitable purposes. On his death-bed he sent for a scrivener, and expressed to him his wish to have his property so disposed of after his death. He was informed that if he should die within thirty days, such a disposition would be ineffectual, but that he might make an absolute bequest to some individual, upon the confidence and belief that when he should be informed of his wishes, he would, of his own accord, carry them out. This plan was adopted, and upon the suggestion of one of the bystanders, Reuben Yeakle, the bishop of the church to which the decedent belonged, was chosen by him. It is clear, not only from the evidence, but from the verdict of the jury in the issue of *devisavit vel non*, that no undue influence was exercised to procure the will. It was the testator's own free and voluntary act, and he was told " that he could dispose of his property to a particular person unconditionally, and if that man would do it, then he could put it to those places where he wanted it; but that would be entirely at his option; he could do it or not." Reuben Yeakle was not informed of the will until some time after the death of the testator. When informed of it he declared his intention to appropriate the money as the testator wished it to be. He said, when examined as a witness before the auditor: " I have not seen the will, but if it gives me the absolute right to the property without condition, I should consider that I had the legal right to do with the property as I pleased. I draw a distinction in this case between the legal and moral right."

But if the testator does not intend to impose a legal obligation on the devisee or legatee, no resulting trust will be raised. O'Donnell *v.* Murphy, 17 Cal. App. 625.

See Ragland, Devise upon Oral Trust for Illegal Object, 16 Ky. L. Jour. 333.

[2] Only the opinion of the court is here given.

We are unshackled by authority upon this question. The English precedents upon the construction of their Statute of Mortmain are not binding upon this court, and with us the question is an entirely new one. By the 11th section of the Act of Assembly of April 26th 1855, Pamph. L. 332, it is provided, "that no estate, real or personal, shall hereafter be bequeathed, devised or conveyed to any body politic, or to any person, in trust for religious or charitable uses, except the same be done by deed or will, attested by two credible and at the time disinterested witnesses, at least one calendar month before the death of the testator or alienor, and all dispositions of property contrary hereto shall be void, and go to the residuary legatee or devisee, next of kin or heirs according to law."

It seems very clear that the bequest in the will of Frederick Schultz to Reuben Yeakle is not within the words of the statute. There is nothing in the circumstances to fasten a trust upon him. The statute out of the way, the charities intended to be benefited would have had no claim, legal or equitable, to enforce payment by him to them. He would, in the eye of the law, be guilty of no fraud, legal or equitable, either against them or the testator, if he should, even at this day, change his intentions and apply the money to some other use. Being the absolute owner, under the will, the declaration of his intention would not be binding upon him. It is not, therefore, in the words of the statute, a bequest "to a body politic or to any person in trust for religious or charitable uses." Had Reuben Yeakle been present when the will was executed, or the objects of the bequest been communicated to him before the testator's death, and he had held his peace, there would have been some ground for fastening a trust upon him *ex maleficio,* as in Hoge *v.* Hoge, 1 Watts 163. But nothing of that kind can be pretended here.

It has been contended, however, very strenuously, that as Edward Schultz proposed Reuben Yeakle to the testator as the man, the acceptance of Reuben Yeakle of the bequest recognised Edward Schultz as his attorney, and ratified whatever he had said and done. They urge the maxim, *omnis ratihabitio retrotrahitur et mandato æquiparatur.* It is a very ingenious contention, but unfortunately for the appellants, there is nothing in the evidence upon which it can be built. Edward Schultz did not undertake for Reuben Yeakle; he gave the testator no assurance that he would accept and carry out his intentions when made known to him. He says: "I proposed Reuben Yeakle, so far as I remember, for the man. Frederick then agreed to Reuben Yeakle. Reuben Yeakle was considered to be an honest man, and it was for this reason he was taken, and because he was acquainted with these societies mentioned." "As far as I can recollect, I said that through Yeakle his desire could be carried out in the distribution of his property."

"The object was to carry out the wish of Frederick in that way. There was a chance to carry it out in that way if the legatee was willing, and Reuben Yeakle was selected because it was thought he would agree to it." There is nothing in all this which indicates any promise or assurance by Edward Schultz to the testator that Reuben Yeakle would accept the bequest in trust for the charities. There was the mere expression of an opinion, concurred in by the testator, that when the legatee came to understand the object and purpose of the bequest to him, as an honest man he would carry out the intention of the testator.

It is urged, however, that this whole plan is nothing but a contrivance to evade the statute. No doubt such was the intention of the testator. It is said that it is a fraud upon the law, and that the bequest ought therefore to be declared void. But that overlooks the fact that the absolute property in the subject of this bequest has vested in the legatee, and that he is entirely innocent of any complicity in the fraud of the testator. If the statute is practically repealed by this construction it is evident that it must be for the legislature to devise and apply a remedy, not the judiciary, whose province is not *jus dare* but *jus dicere*.

Decree affirmed and appeal dismissed at the cost of the appellants.[1]

In re BOYES.
BOYES *v.* CARRITT.

HIGH COURT OF JUSTICE, CHANCERY DIVISION. 1884

26 Ch. D. 531.

THE will of the testator in this cause, dated the 1st of June, 1880, was in these words: " This is the last will and testament of me, George Edmund Boyes, of . . . I direct the payment of my

[1] Adlington *v.* Cann, 3 Atk. 141; Stickland *v.* Aldridge, 9 Ves. 516 (*semble*); Wallgrave *v.* Tebbs, 2 Kay & J. 313; Moss *v.* Cooper, 1 J. & H. 352, 365 (*semble*); Jones *v.* Badley, L. R. 3 Ch. App. 362; Juniper *v.* Batchelor, (1868) W. N. 197; Geddis *v.* Semple, [1903] 1 I. R. 73; Estate of Holt, 61 Cal. App. 464; Boynton *v.* Gale, 194 Mass. 320; Nash *v.* Bremner, 84 N. J. Eq. 131; Flood *v.* Ryan, 220 Pa. 450; Bickley's Estate, 270 Pa. 101 (following the principal case with reluctance), *accord*. But see *contra* Gore *v.* Clarke, 37 S. C. 537 (bequest for uncommunicated purpose of giving testator's mistress and illegitimate children more than one-fourth of his estate in violation of a statute).

For cases where the trust was agreed to by one only of several joint tenants or tenants in common, see Burney *v.* Macdonald, 15 Sim. 6; Russell *v.* Jackson, 10 Hare 204; Tee *v.* Ferris, 2 Kay & J. 357; Moss *v.* Cooper, 1 J. & H. 352; *Re* Stead, [1900] 1 Ch. 237; Hooker *v.* Axford, 33 Mich. 453; Powell *v.* Yearance, 73 N. J. Eq. 117; Amherst College *v.* Ritch, 151 N. Y. 282; Edson *v.* Bartow, 154 N. Y. 199, 215; Winder *v.* Scholey, 83 Oh. St. 204.

just debts and funeral and testamentary expenses as soon as conveniently may be after my decease by my executor hereinafter named, and subject thereto I give, devise, and bequeath all my real and personal estate whatsoever and wheresoever unto Frederick Blasson Carritt absolutely. And I appoint the said Frederick Blasson Carritt sole executor of this my will."

The testator died in April, 1882, at Ghent, leaving personal property only. Immediately after his death probate was granted to Mr. Carritt. Thereupon the Plaintiff, John F. Boyes, one of the brothers and next of kin of the testator, instituted proceedings in the Probate Division of the High Court to recall probate. Mr. Carritt, who was the Defendant in that action, was the solicitor and a private friend of the testator, and had himself prepared the will, and in answer to interrogatories administered to him in the probate action, Mr. Carritt stated as follows: That the testator communicated his intentions to him at the time when he made his will (which was made in London), and that such intentions were that the Defendant should take the property as trustee upon trust to deal with it according to further directions, which the testator was to give by letter after his arrival on the Continent, whither he was then going within a day or two; and that he (Mr. Carritt) accepted the trust. That the deceased did go to the Continent within a day or two, but never gave any further directions in his lifetime. Upon receiving this answer the validity of the will was admitted, and the action to recall probate was discontinued.

This action was shortly afterwards brought by the next of kin of the testator against Mr. Carritt in order to obtain a declaration that they were beneficially entitled to his personal estate.

In his defence, Mr. Carritt said that in giving the instructions the testator expressed to him verbally his desire to provide for a certain lady and child, whose names he did not wish to appear in his will, and he therefore desired to leave the whole of his property to the Defendant as trustee to act with respect thereto according to any further written directions which might be given to him.

In his oral evidence in this action the Defendant confirmed these statements as accurately representing what he believed at the time, and said: "I gathered that I was to dispose of the estate as Mr. Boyes would direct me — the word 'trustee' was never used — the understanding was that he was to write to me, and I was to comply with his directions."

No such directions were ever in fact given by the testator to

---

For cases in which the testator or intestate communicated to one other than the devisee, legatee or heir his intention to create a trust, see Simons v. Bedell, 122 Cal. 341; Mead v. Robertson, 131 Mo. App. 185; Stirk's Estate, 232 Pa. 98.

Mr. Carritt in his lifetime, but after his death there were found among his papers two letters, one dated the 10th of February, 1880 (which was proved to be a mistake for 1881), written at Antwerp, and which was in these words: —

"F. B. Carritt, Esq.

"I wish you to have five and twenty pounds of any property of which I may die possessed for the purchase of any trinket *in memoriam*, everything else I give to Nell Brown, formerly Sears, and I appoint you sole trustee to act at your discretion.

"G. E. Boyes."

The other letter was in these terms: —

"4th June, 1881.

"F. B. Carritt, Esq.

"Dear Sir, — In case of my death I wish Nell Brown to have all except twenty-five pounds in my memory.

"G. E. Boyes."

Neither of these letters was executed as a testamentary instrument.

Mrs. Brown was examined in this action, and she stated that the testator told her that he had written two letters to Mr. Carritt, one in case the other was lost. He directed her in case of his death to send immediately for Mr. Carritt. She did so, and having found these two letters among his papers, she placed them in Mr. Carritt's hands shortly after the testator's death.

KAY, J. (after stating the facts of the case, continued). The result of this is that Mr. Carritt admits that he is a trustee of all the property given to him by the will. He desires to carry out the wishes of the testator as expressed in the two letters, but of course he can only do so if they constitute a binding trust as against the next of kin.

If it had been expressed on the face of the will that the Defendant was a trustee, but the trusts were not thereby declared, it is quite clear that no trust afterwards declared by a paper not executed as a will could be binding: Johnson *v.* Ball, 5 De G. & Sm. 85; Briggs *v.* Penny, 3 Mac. & G. 546; Singleton *v.* Tomlinson, 3 App. Cas. 404. In such a case the legatee would be trustee for the next of kin.

There is another well-known class of cases where no trust appears on the face of the will, but the testator has been induced to make the will, or, having made it, has been induced not to revoke it by a promise on the part of the devisee or legatee to deal with the property, or some part of it in a specified manner. In these cases the Court has compelled discovery and performance of the promise, treating it as a trust binding the conscience of the donee, on the ground that otherwise a fraud would be committed, because it is to be presumed that if it had not been for such promise the testator would not have made or would have revoked the gift.

The principle of these decisions is precisely the same as in the case of an heir who has induced a testator not to make a will devising the estate away from him by a promise that if the estate were allowed to descend he would make a certain provision out of it for a named person: Stickland *v.* Aldridge, 9 Ves. 516; Wallgrave *v.* Tebbs, 2 K. & J. 313; McCormick *v.* Grogan, Law Rep. 4 H. L. 82. But no case has ever yet decided that a testator can by imposing a trust upon his devisee or legatee, the objects of which he does not communicate to him, enable himself to evade the Statute of Wills by declaring those objects in an unattested paper found after his death.

The essence of all those decisions is that the devisee or legatee accepts a particular trust which thereupon becomes binding upon him, and which it would be a fraud in him not to carry into effect.

If the trust was not declared when the will was made, it is essential in order to make it binding, that it should be communicated to the devisee or legatee in the testator's lifetime and that he should accept that particular trust. It may possibly be that he would be bound if the trust had been put in writing and placed in his hands in a sealed envelope, and he had engaged that he would hold the property given to him by the will upon the trust so declared although he did not know the actual terms of the trust: McCormick *v.* Grogan. But the reason is that it must be assumed if he had not so accepted the will would be revoked. Suppose the case of an engagement to hold the property not upon the terms of any paper communicated to the legatee or put into his hands, but of any paper that might be found after the testator's death.

The evidence in this case does not amount to that, but if it did the rule of law would intervene, which prevents a testator from declaring trusts in such a manner by a paper which was not executed as a will or codicil. The legatee might be a trustee, but the trust declared by such an unattested paper would not be good. For this purpose there is no difference whether the devisee or legatee is declared to be a trustee on the face of the will, or by an engagement with the testator not appearing on the will. The devisee or legatee cannot by accepting an indefinite trust enable the testator to make an unattested codicil.

I cannot help regretting that the testator's intention of bounty should fail by reason of an informality of this kind, but in my opinion it would be a serious innovation upon the law relating to testamentary instruments if this were to be established as a trust in her favour.

The Defendant, however, having admitted that he is only a trustee, I must hold, on the authority of Muckleston *v.* Brown, 6 Ves. 52; Briggs *v.* Penny, 3 Mac. & G. 546; and Johnson *v.* Ball, 5 De G. & Sm. 85, that he is a trustee of this property for the next of kin of the testator. I can only hope they will consider the claim which this lady has upon their generosity.[1]

OLLIFFE v. WELLS.

SUPREME JUDICIAL COURT, MASSACHUSETTS. 1881.

130 Mass. 221.

BILL IN EQUITY, filed December 11, 1877, alleging that the plaintiffs were the heirs at law and next of kin of Ellen Donovan, who died in Boston on May 23, 1877, and whose will, which was duly admitted to probate, after giving various legacies, contained the following clause: "13th. To the Rev. Eleazer M. P. Wells, all the rest and residue of my estate, to distribute the same in such manner as in his discretion shall appear best calculated to carry out wishes which I have expressed to him or may express to him;" and nominated said Wells to be the executor.

The bill further alleged that Wells, who had been appointed executor by the Probate Court, claimed the right, after payment of the legacies, to dispose of the residue of the estate according to his own pleasure and discretion, and contended that he had received directions from Ellen Donovan as to the disposition of said residue; whereas, as the bill charged, the legacy of the residue of the estate had lapsed, and said residue should be distributed among the heirs at law and next of kin of the testatrix.

The bill prayed for a discovery, an account, an order for payment of the residue to the plaintiffs, a temporary injunction against distributing the residue of the estate, and for further relief.

The answer admitted the making of the will and the appointment of the defendant as executor; left the plaintiffs to prove whether they were the heirs at law and next of kin of the testatrix; and averred that the testatrix, before and at the time of and after the execution of the will, orally expressed and made known to the defendant her wish and intention that the rest and residue of her estate should be disposed of and distributed by the defendant, as executor of her will, for charitable purposes and uses, according to his discretion and judgment, and directed the defendant so to dispose of and distribute the said rest and residue;

[1] The agreement need not be made at the time the will is made; if the agreement induces the testator not to revoke his will previously made, that is sufficient. Reech v. Kennegal, 1 Ves. Sr. 123; Barrow v. Greenough, 3 Ves. Jr. 151; Moss v. Cooper, 1 J. & H. 352; McCormick v. Grogan, L. R. 4 H. L. 82 (*semble*); Norris v. Fraser, L. R. 15 Eq. 318; *Re* Stead, [1900] 1 Ch. 237; French v. French, [1902] 1 I. R. 172, 230; Shields v. McAuley, 37 Fed. 302; Dowd v. Tucker, 41 Conn. 197; Ragsdale v. Ragsdale, 68 Miss. 92; Belknap v. Tillotson, 82 N. J. Eq. 271; Rutherfurd v. Carpenter, 134 N. Y. App. Div. 881; Hoffner's Estate, 161 Pa. 331; Brook v. Chappell, 34 Wis. 405. But see Fox v. Fox, 88 Pa. 19.

especially expressing to the defendant her desire that the poor, aged and infirm, and the children and others in need, and worthy of charity and assistance, under the care of or connected with Saint Stephen's Mission, of Boston, and other deserving friends and deserving poor, should be aided and assisted out of said rest and residue, if the defendant in his discretion should see fit so to do; that the defendant desired and intended, unless otherwise ordered by the court, to dispose of and distribute the said rest and residue for charitable purposes and uses, according to his discretion, and especially for the benefit of the deserving poor, aged and infirm, and the children and others in need and worthy of charity and assistance, under the care of or connected with said Saint Stephen's Mission, and other deserving friends and deserving poor, as requested and directed by the testatrix; and that the testatrix, except by her will, gave to the defendant no written direction, wish or order as to the distribution of the residue of her estate remaining after the payment of the legacies.

The case was heard by *Colt*, J., and reserved for the consideration of the full court, on the bill and answer, and an agreement of the parties that the facts alleged in the answer should be taken as true. If these facts did not show a defence to the bill, the case was to be sent to a master, to determine whether the plaintiffs were the heirs and next of kin of the testatrix, and the amount of the residue of the estate; otherwise, the bill to be dismissed.

GRAY, C. J. Upon the face of this will the residuary bequest to the defendant gives him no beneficial interest. It expressly requires him to distribute all the property bequeathed to him, giving him no discretion upon the question whether he shall or shall not distribute it, or shall or shall not carry out the intentions of the testatrix, but allowing him a discretionary authority as to the manner only in which the property shall be distributed pursuant to her intentions. The will declares a trust too indefinite to be carried out, and the next of kin of the testatrix must take by way of resulting trust, unless the facts agreed show such a trust for the benefit of others as the court can execute. Nichols *v.* Allen, *ante*, 211. No other written instrument was signed by the testatrix, and made part of the will by reference, as in Newton *v.* Seaman's Friend Society, *ante*, 91.

The decision of the case therefore depends upon the effect of the fact, stated in the defendant's answer, and admitted by the plaintiffs to be true, that the testatrix, before and at the time of and after the execution of the will, orally made known to the defendant her wish and intention that the residue should be disposed of and distributed by him as executor of her will for charitable uses and purposes, according to his discretion and judgment, and directed him so to dispose of and distribute it, especially expressing her desire as to the objects to be preferred, all which objects, taking the whole direction together, may be assumed to be charitable in the legal sense.

In any view of the authorities it is quite clear, and is hardly denied by the defendant's counsel, that intentions not formed by the testatrix and communicated to the defendant before the making of the will could not have any effect against her next of kin. Thayer *v.* Wellington, 9 Allen, 283. Johnson *v.* Ball, 5 De Gex & Sm. 85. Moss *v.* Cooper, 1 Johns. & Hem. 352. But assuming, as the defendant contends, that all the directions of the testatrix set forth in the answer are to be taken as having been orally communicated to the defendant and assented to by him before the execution of the will, we are of opinion that the result must be the same.

It has been held in England and in other States, although the question has never arisen in this Commonwealth, that, if a person procures an absolute devise or bequest to himself by orally promising the testator that he will convey the property to or hold it for the benefit of third persons, and afterwards refuses to perform his promise, a trust arises out of the confidence reposed in him by the testator and of his own fraud, which a court of equity, upon clear and satisfactory proof of the facts, will enforce against him at the suit of such third persons. [Citing cases.]

Upon like grounds, it has been held in England that, if a testator devises or bequeaths property to his executors upon trusts not defined in the will, but which, as he states in the will, he has communicated to them before its execution, such trusts, if for lawful purposes, may be proved by the admission of the executors, or by oral evidence, and enforced against them. Crook *v.* Brooking, 2 Vern. 50, 106. Pring *v.* Pring, 2 Vern. 99. Smith *v.* Attersoll, 1 Russ. 266. And in two or three comparatively recent cases it has been held that such trusts may be enforced against the heirs or next of kin of the testator, as well as against the devisee. Shadwell, V. C., in Podmore *v.* Gunning, 5 Sim. 485, and 7 Sim. 644. Chatterton, V. C., in Riordan *v.* Banon, Ir. R. 10 Eq. 469. Hall, V. C., in Fleetwood's case, 15 Ch. D. 594. But these cases appear to us to have overlooked or disregarded a fundamental distinction.

Where a trust not declared in the will is established by a court of chancery against the devisee, it is by reason of the obligation resting upon the conscience of the devisee, and not as a valid testamentary disposition by the deceased. Cullen *v.* Attorney General, L. R. 1 H. L. 190. Where the bequest is outright upon its face, the setting up of a trust, while it diminishes the right of the devisee, does not impair any right of the heirs or next of kin, in any aspect of the case; for if the trust were not set up, the whole property would go to the devisee by force of the devise; if the trust set up is a lawful one, it enures to the benefit of the *cestuis que trust;* and if the trust set up is unlawful, the heirs or next of kin take by way of resulting trust. Boson v. Statham, 1 Eden, 508; S. C. 1 Cox Ch. 16. Russell v. Jackson, 10 Hare, 204. Wallgrave v. Tebbs, 2 K. & J. 313.

Where the bequest is declared upon its face to be upon such trusts as the testator has otherwise signified to the devisee, it is equally clear that the devisee takes no beneficial interest; and, as between him and the beneficiaries intended, there is as much ground for establishing the trust as if the bequest to him were absolute on its face. But as between the devisee and the heirs or next of kin, the case stands differently. They are not excluded by the will itself. The will upon its face showing that the devisee takes the legal title only and not the beneficial interest, and the trust not being sufficiently defined by the will to take effect, the equitable interest goes, by way of resulting trust, to the heirs or next of kin, as property of the deceased, not disposed of by his will. Sears v. Hardy, 120 Mass. 524, 541, 542. They cannot be deprived of that equitable interest, which accrues to them directly from the deceased, by any conduct of the devisee; nor by any intention of the deceased, unless signified in those forms which the law makes essential to every testamentary disposition. A trust not sufficiently declared on the face of the will cannot therefore be set up by extrinsic evidence to defeat the rights of the heirs at law or next of kin. See Lewin on Trusts (3d ed.) 75.

By the statutes of the Commonwealth, no will (with certain exceptions not material to be here stated) " shall be effectual to pass any estate, whether real or personal, nor to charge or in any way affect the same," unless signed by the testator and attested by three witnesses. Rev. Sts. c. 62, sec. 6. Gen. Sts. c. 92, sec. 6.

In Thayer v. Wellington, 9 Allen, 283, the testator by his will bequeathed to Hastings and Wellington $15,000 " in trust to appropriate the same in such manner as I may by any instrument under my hand direct and appoint," and nominated Hastings executor, and made a residuary bequest to him in trust for the benefit of certain persons named. The testator also signed a paper, dated the same day as the will, referring to it, and addressed to Hastings and Wellington, directing them to pay over the $15,000 to the city of Cambridge for the support of a public library; and they, after the death of the testator, signified in writing to the city their intention of so paying it when they should receive it from the executor. After the death of Hastings, upon a bill in equity by the administrator *de bonis non* for instructions, to which Wellington, the city, the *cestuis que trust*, and the heirs at law of the testator, were made parties, the court held that the clause in the will, the paper signed by the testator but not attested as required by the statute of wills, and the assent in writing of the trustees, gave the city no right to the fund; and that the heirs at law or next of kin would have been entitled to it, but for its being included in the residuary bequest.

It appears in the report on file, upon which that case was reserved for the determination of the full court, that an attorney at law testified that he drew up both the will and the paper at the request of Hastings, and delivered both drafts to him; and that Wellington testified that the paper was handed to him by Hastings after the testator's death. Those facts would, according to the cases of Crook v. Brooking and Smith v. Attersoll, above cited, and which were relied on in the argument for the city of Cambridge, have been sufficient evidence of an assent by Hastings before the execution of the will, and, according to the decision of Vice Chancellor Wood in Tee v. Ferris, 2 K. & J. 357, would have entitled the city to enforce the trust against both trustees. Yet the court did not treat them as of any weight as between the surviving trustee and the city on the one hand, and the next of kin or the residuary legatees on the other, but merely observed that it did not appear at what time the paper was placed by the testator in the hands of Hastings. 9 Allen, 288.

Decree for the plaintiffs.[1]

BLACKWELL v. BLACKWELL.

House of Lords. 1929.

[1929] A. C. 318.

APPEAL from an order of the Court of Appeal, [1928] Ch. 614, affirming a judgment of Eve J.

The action was brought by the appellants, the widow and son of John Duncan Blackwell, the elder (hereinafter called "the testator"), as residuary legatees under his will and codicils, for a declaration that no valid trusts of a legacy of 12,000*l.* bequeathed to the respondents Mark Oliver, Arthur Ernest Harrison, Fred Wettern, Edward Watson Barnett and William Percy Cowley by a fourth codicil to the testator's will were ever declared by the testator in favour of two other respondents, a lady and her son, an infant sixteen years of age, who were the beneficiaries under the trust legacy, or either of them, and that the legacy ought to be held upon the trusts declared by the said will and codicils of and concerning the testator's residuary estate.

[1] Atwood v. Rhode Island Hosp. T. Co., 275 Fed. 513; Fitzsimmons v. Harmon, 108 Me. 456; Thayer v. Wellington, 9 Allen (Mass.) 283; Wilcox v. A. G., 207 Mass. 198; Blunt v. Taylor, 230 Mass. 303; Dunbar v. Hammond, 234 Mass. 554; Moore v. O'Leary, 180 Mich. 261; Reynolds v. Reynolds, 224 N. Y. 429; Matter of Billings, 137 N. Y. Misc. 758; Heidenheimer v. Bauman, 84 Tex. 174; Sims v. Sims, 94 Va. 580, *accord.* See Thomas v. Anderson, 245 Fed. 642. *Cf. Re* Hetley, [1902] 2 Ch. 866. Compare Chap. II, sec. IV, and particularly Swetland v. Swetland, 102 N. J. Eq. 294, *ante.*

The facts are fully stated in the report of the case before the Court of Appeal and sufficiently appear from the opinion of Lord Buckmaster, and they are summarized in the headnote.

Eve J. held on the authority of *In re* Fleetwood, 15 Ch. D. 594, that the parol evidence adduced to prove the testator's declarations of the trusts of the legacy of 12,000*l.* was admissible, and that the codicil and a memorandum of even date of the respondent Cowley disclosed a complete valid and consistent trust of the legacy, and he dismissed the action; and the Court of Appeal (Lord Hanworth M.R., Lawrence and Russell L.JJ.) affirmed his decision.

LORD BUCKMASTER.[1] My Lords, the Lord Chancellor desires me to say that he agrees with the judgment that I am about to read.

The question raised on this appeal is one which in various forms has for over 200 years been the subject of vexed controversy. It may be stated by asking to what extent is it possible to give effect to testamentary intentions that are not contained in a written document duly executed as a will. That to some extent such intentions can be established even when orally expressed is not disputed.

If a testator in his will makes a gift to a named legatee who at the time of making the will has promised he will hold the benefit of the gift for certain defined and lawful purposes, the Court will enforce against the legatee the trust in promised obedience to which he received the gift: McCormick *v.* Grogan, L. R. 4 H. L. 82.

This, however, does not directly govern the present case, as the following facts will show. The testator at the time of his death had a son of sixteen years, the child of a woman, also living, who was not his wife. He was ill for many weeks before he died, and was much concerned as to how he should make provision for this woman and her child without disclosing all the circumstances in his will.

He expressed his anxiety and his wish to the respondents Barnett and Wettern, who were his personal friends, and they agreed to act as trustees. What took place between them is best described in the words of Mr. Barnett, who said: " He was urgently desirous of effecting at once, or as soon as possible, what he had talked about to me for the preceding two years or so. He mentioned the two beneficiaries, the mother and the son, and the sum of 12,000*l.*, and he also mentioned that it was his desire, if we would accept service, for my friend Wettern and myself, Mark Oliver, and Harrison, to act as trustees in a secret trust which he had proposed to effect, the legal side of which would be carried out by Mr. Percy Cowley of the Isle of Man. I agreed to act as a trustee." The testator, therefore, caused the respondent, W. P. Cowley, who had

[1] Concurring opinions of Viscount Sumner and Lord Warrington of Clyffe are omitted.

for some time acted as his solicitor, to be summoned. He arrived on February 13 and saw the testator alone, who gave him instructions to the above effect. These instructions he incorporated in a fourth codicil to the will. At his instance a Mr. Oliver was added to the trustees, and the codicil was then signed. It is in the following terms: "This is a codicil to the last will of me, John Duncan Blackwell. I give and bequeath to my friends, Mark Oliver, Arthur Ernest Harrison, Fred Wettern, Edward Watson Barnett, and William Percy Cowley the sum of twelve thousand pounds free of all duties upon trust to invest the same as they in their uncontrolled discretion shall think fit and to apply the income and interest arising therefrom yearly and every year for the purposes indicated by me to them with full power at any time to pay over the capital sum of eight thousand pounds to such person or persons indicated by me as they think fit, and to pay the balance of four thousand pounds to my trustees as part of my residuary estate, and upon the same trusts as are declared in my will and previous codicils."

Mr. Cowley then made a memorandum of the terms of the trust which has been accepted by Eve J. and the Court of Appeal as accurate. It is as follows: —

"Re Mr. J. D. Blackwell.

Memorandum of verbal instructions given to me at execution of codicil 13/2/25.

Income of 12,000*l*. to be paid to

(then there followed the name and address of the woman)

or applied at discretion of trustees for benefit of herself and her son (mentioning him by name).

At any time trustees may pay over 8000*l*. of capital either to her or [her son] or both of them. In such event 4000*l*. is to go back to testator's trustees on same trusts as his residuary estate.

W. Percy Cowley."

The testator died on June 3, 1925, and his will and four codicils were duly proved. The named trustees in the fourth codicil are ready and willing to carry out the trust evidenced by the memorandum, but the testator's widow and her son object that the trusts fail and contend that the trustees hold the 12,000*l*. as part of the residue. It is first argued that Mr. Cowley's memory is faulty so that his recollection cannot be accepted as to the actual terms of the trust, and further that if the terms in the memorandum are the true record, they are too vague to be enforced.

It is, in my opinion, unnecessary to add anything on these points to the judgment of Eve J. and the Court of Appeal. There can be no reasonable doubt about the accuracy of the memorandum, and none about its efficacy if it can be admitted in evidence.

The real difficulty lies in considering whether the fact that in the will itself it is made plain that the gift is fiduciary destroys the principle upon which verbal evidence has been admitted to show the nature of a gift purporting to be absolute and beneficial.

The argument in favour of the appellants on this point cannot be put more forcibly than in Lewin on Trusts, 13th ed., p. 60, and its strength lies in this — that while in a beneficial gift the imposition of a trust does not contradict the terms of the will but merely adds to them, where the gift is made on trust and no beneficiaries are specified the trust operates either for the residuary legatees or the next of kin and heir at law, so that the admission of verbal evidence showing the trusts contradicts the will. It must be observed, however, that this reasoning in strictness applies to a case where land is devised to trustees on trust and nothing more is said, so that on the will there is a complete trust for the heir at law, but that is not the case here where the intention to benefit persons outside the will is manifest, and further a will is in fact contradicted when a gift complete made to a beneficiary without the hint of a trust is converted into a fiduciary gift for the benefit of some one never mentioned in the will. It is also urged that the underlying principle admitting extraneous evidence is that the legatee cannot profit by his own fraud, a principle that does not apply where, on the face of the will, his interest is fiduciary.

This principle is easily understood and may be also stated by saying that he cannot defraud beneficiaries for whom he has consented to act by keeping the money for himself. Apart, however, from the personal benefit accruing to the trustee, the real beneficiaries are equally defrauded in both cases, and the faith on which the testator relied is equally betrayed. Further, if the trustee was the heir or one of the next of kin or a residuary legatee, the fraud would be just the same. The counsel for the appellants seemed at one time to argue that in such a case and to such an extent as to defeat the beneficial interest of the trustee the outside evidence might be admitted, but it is difficult to see on what principle of reasoning the evidence can be admitted in the one case and rejected in the other, when in both cases the fact of the trust appears in the will itself. Again, in the case where no trusts are mentioned the legatee might defeat the whole purpose by renouncing the legacy and the breach of trust would not in that case enure to his own benefit, but I entertain no doubt that the Court, having once admitted the evidence of the trust, would interfere to prevent its defeat. If this be so the personal benefit of the legatee cannot be the sole determining factor in considering the admissibility of the evidence.

It is, I think, more accurate to say that a testator having been induced to make a gift on trust in his will in reliance on the clear promise by the trustee that such trust will be executed in favour of certain named persons, the trustee is not at liberty to suppress the evidence of the trust and thus destroy the whole object of its creation, in fraud of the beneficiaries. . . .

Order of the Court of Appeal affirmed and appeal dismissed with costs.[1]

BRYANT v. BRYANT.

SUPREME COURT, NORTH CAROLINA. 1927.

193 N. C. 372.

APPEAL by defendant from a final judgment signed by *Cranmer, J.*, in Johnston County, in an action pending in the county of HARNETT. The parties consented that the judge should find the facts upon the pleadings and the admissions of the parties and render a final judgment in the cause out of term and outside the county in which the action was pending. The facts are as follows:

1. The plaintiffs are the children of the defendant, Wash Bryant, and his late wife, Ida Bryant, who died on 12 January, 1920.

[1] Crooke *v.* Brookeing, 2 Vern. 106; Smith *v.* Attersoll, 1 Russ. 266; Podmore *v.* Gunning, 5 Sim. 485, 7 Sim. 644; *Re* Fleetwood, 15 Ch. Div. 594; In the Goods of Marchant, [1893] P. 254; *Re* Huxtable, [1902] 2 Ch. 793; *Re* Gardom, [1914] 1 Ch. 662 (reversed by the Court of Appeal for failure of proof, appeal dismissed by the House of Lords, LePage *v.* Gardom, 84 L. J. (Ch.) 749); Riordan *v.* Banon, 10 I. R. Eq. 469; Morrison *v.* M'Ferran, [1901] 1 I. R. 360; Curdy *v.* Berton, 79 Cal. 420; Cagney *v.* O'Brien, 83 Ill. 72; Hughes *v.* Bent, 118 Ky. 609, *accord.*

For comments on the principal case, see 45 Law Quar. Rev. 4, 282; 3 Camb. L. Jour. 302, 459; 6 Can. Bar Rev. 627; 67 A. L. R. 349.

In the following cases where the intention to create a trust was, but its terms were not, disclosed on the face of the will, and no communication was made to the devisee or legatee in the lifetime of the testator, the devisee or legatee was compelled to hold on a constructive trust for the residuary devisee or legatee or heir or next of kin. Bryan *v.* Bigelow, 77 Conn. 604, 616; Saylor *v.* Plaine, 31 Md. 158.

In the following cases where the intention to create a trust was, but its terms were not, disclosed on the face of the will, and the intention to create a trust was, but its terms were not, communicated to the devisee or legatee in the lifetime of the testator, a constructive trust for the residuary devisee or legatee or heir or next of kin was imposed. *Re* King's Estate, 21 L. R. Ir. 273; Balfe *v.* Halpenny, [1904] 1 I. R. 486. But in Morrison *v.* M'Ferran, [1901] 1 I. R. 360, it was held enough to prevent such a trust that the legatee agreed to hold for the objects named in a paper, then existent and signed by the legatee, although its contents were not known to the legatee.

In Johnson *v.* Ball, 5 De G. & Sm. 85, and in Scott *v.* Brownrigg, 9 L. R. Ir. 246, it was held that a communication to the devisee or legatee of the terms of the trust after the making of the will is insufficient. See *Re* Gardner, [1923] 2 Ch. 230. But compare the cases in which the devise or bequest was absolute on its face.

On the subject of the incorporation in a will of an unattested instrument by reference in the will to the instrument, see Magnus *v.* Magnus, 80 N. J. Eq. 346; 4 Gray, Cas. Prop., 2d ed., 99–145; Warren, Cas. Wills, 105–142.

See Scott, Conveyances upon Trusts Not Properly Declared, 37 Harv. L. Rev. 653.

2. On 14 February, 1913, W. W. Scott and wife conveyed to Wash Bryant and wife, Ida Bryant, one hundred and thirteen acres of land located in Harnett County, North Carolina, by deed which has been duly registered in Book 177, page 506, which deed and the said record thereof are made a part of this finding of fact for full description of the land so conveyed and under said deed. The land was held by said husband and wife as tenants by entireties up to the date of the death of said Ida Bryant.

3. Said Ida Bryant was feloniously murdered and slain on 12 January, 1920, by her husband, Wash Bryant, defendant herein.

4. Said Wash Bryant was convicted of the murder of his wife at the September Term, 1923, of Harnett Superior Court, being convicted of murder in the second degree, and is now serving a term in the State prison on account of same.

5. At the time of the death of said Ida Bryant she was in good health, was younger than her husband, was free from dissipation, while her husband was addicted to the use of strong drink, and under the mortuary table she had a longer expectancy of life than her husband.

6. The defendant, Wash Bryant, at the institution of this action and the granting of the temporary restraining order herein had employed an auction company and was offering said tract of land for sale, claiming to be seized thereof in fee simple.

Upon these facts it was adjudged that the defendant holds the legal title to the land conveyed to him and his wife in trust for the benefit of the plaintiffs, his heirs at law, and that they are the equitable owners and entitled to the actual possession thereof freed and discharged from the claims of the defendant; that the defendant convey the land to the plaintiffs, and upon failure to do so that the judgment should be registered in the office of the register of deeds of Hartnett County, and should operate as such conveyance; and that the defendant account to the plaintiffs for the rents and profits received by him. The cause was retained for a statement of the account. The defendant, assigning error, excepted and appealed. Modified and affirmed.

ADAMS, J. The deed executed by W. W. Scott and his wife on 14 February, 1913, conveyed to the defendant and his wife an estate by entireties. When the defendant put his wife to death, to what extent did his felonious act affect his interest in the land? This is the question proposed for solution.

A review of the cases involving the legal effect of felonious homicide upon the title claimed by the slayer to the property of the deceased discloses three lines of argument: (1) The legal title does not pass to the murderer as heir or devisee; (2) the legal title passes to the murderer and may be retained by him in spite of his crime; (3) the legal title passes to the murderer, but equity will treat him as a constructive trustee of the title because of the unconscionable mode of its acquisition, and compel him to convey it to the heirs of the deceased, exclusive of the murderer. Ames, Lectures on Legal History, 311.

The first of these positions was maintained in Riggs v. Palmer, 115 N. Y., 506, and in Shellenberger v. Ransom, 31 Nebraska, 61. In the Riggs case the facts were that Francis B. Palmer made his will in which he gave small legacies to his two daughters, the plaintiffs in the action, and the remainder to his grandson, the defendant, subject to the support of his mother, with a gift over to the two daughters, subject to the support of the mother, in case the grandson should die under age, unmarried, and without issue. The grandson, sixteen years of age, lived with the testator as a member of his family, and to prevent a revocation of the will took the life of the testator by means of poison. The Court held that the legal title did not pass to the defendant; that by reason of his crime he was deprived of any interest in the devise, and that he should be enjoined from using any part of the estate left him by the testator. The holding that no legal title passed and that the defendant had no interest in the devise was criticized; and a few years afterwards in Ellerson v. Westcott, 148 N. Y., 149, the Court of Appeals said that Riggs v. Palmer must not be interpreted as holding that the will was revoked; that instead of being revoked and made inoperative by reason of the crime the devise took effect and transferred the legal title, the relief to which the plaintiffs were entitled being equitable and injunctive. In the exercise of its equitable jurisdiction the court declared that the devisee should not retain and enjoy his ill-acquired title.

In Shellenberger v. Ransom, *supra*, the question was whether Leander Shellenberger, who wilfully took the life of his daughter for the purpose of getting her property, acquired title to her estate, the facts being that she died intestate and that except for his crime he would have taken her estate by inheritance. The Court, following Riggs v. Palmer, *supra*, said that Leander Shellenberger took no estate from his daughter and that her title passed to her brother. Upon a rehearing this decision was reversed, and it was held that the title to the daughter's estate vested in the criminal by operation of law and was dependent upon no condition, not even his acceptance. Shellenberger v. Ransom, 41 Neb., 631. Referring to these two cases it has been said: "Unfortunately the second opinion was more unsatisfactory than the first. For, although both disregarded legal principles, the first was against, while the second was in favor of the murderer." Ames, *supra*, 312, note.

Among the cases which sustain the position that the legal title vests in the murderer and may be retained by him despite his crime, are Shellenberger v. Ransom, *supra*, decided on the rehearing; Deem v. Milliken, 6 Ohio, C. C., 357; and *In re* Carpenter's Estate, 170 Pa., 203, 32 At., 637. In the case last cited it was shown that James Carpenter was murdered by his son so that the son might get immediate possession of the father's estate under the statute of distributions. After the commission of the crime the son and the widow, who had become an accessory after the fact, conveyed their interest in the property to the attorney who defended them in the prosecution for murder. The collateral heirs of the decedent contended that neither the mother nor the son under these circumstances had a beneficial interest in the estate.

The Supreme Court, disallowing the claim of the collateral heirs, arrived at its conclusion upon the following reasoning: " The Legislature has never imposed any penalty of corruption of blood or forfeiture of estate for the crime of murder, and therefore no such penalty has any legal existence. In the case now under consideration it is asked by the appellant that this Court shall decree that in case of the murder of a father by his son the inheritable quality of the son's blood shall be taken from him, and that his estate, under the statute of distributions, shall be forfeited to others. We are unwilling to make any such decree, for the plain reason that we have no lawful power so to do. The intestate law in the plainest words designates the persons who shall succeed to the estates of deceased intestates. It is impossible for the courts to designate any different persons to take such estates without violating the law. . . . It is argued, however, that it would be contrary to public policy to allow a parricide to inherit his father's estate. Where is the authority for such a contention? How can such a proposition be maintained when there is a positive statute which disposes of the whole subject? How can there be a public policy leading to one conclusion when there is a positive statute which disposes of the whole subject? How can there be a public policy leading to one conclusion when there is a positive statute directing a precisely opposite conclusion? In other words, when the imperative language of a statute prescribes that upon the death of a person his estate shall vest in his children, in the absence of a will, how can any doctrine, or principle, or other thing, called ' public policy,' take away the estate of a child, and give it to some other person? The intestate law casts the estate upon certain designated persons, and this is absolute and peremptory; and the estate cannot be diverted from those persons, and given to other persons, without violating the statute. There can be no public policy which contravenes the positive language of a statute."

In the opinion the Court cites Owens *v.* Owens, 100 N. C., 242, to which we shall hereafter refer, Shellenberger *v.* Ransom, *supra,* Riggs *v.* Palmer, *supra,* and noting a distinction between descent and a devise, which involves the operation of a private grant, differentiates Insurance Co. *v.* Armstrong, 117 U. S., 591, 29 Law Ed., 997, and Cleaver *v.* Association, 1 Q. B., 147, as decisions based entirely upon the ground of fraud perpetrated in breach of contract rights.

But if we concede as a matter of law that the doctrine of public policy cannot affect the imperative language of a statute which directs the course of descent, we are confronted with the question whether this or any other doctrine prevents the application of the familiar equitable principle that, when the legal title passes in case of descent or devise, the wrongdoer may be treated as a constructive trustee of the title he has unlawfully acquired. To this question, in our opinion, a negative answer must be given.

The scope of constructive trusts is thus outlined by Pomeroy: "Constructive trusts include all those instances in which a trust is raised by the doctrines of equity for the purpose of working out justice in the most efficient manner where there is no intention of the parties to create such a relation, and in most cases contrary to the intention of the one holding the legal title, and where there is no express or implied, written or verbal, declaration of the trust. They arise when the legal title to property is obtained by a person in violation, expressed or implied, of some duty owed to the one who is equitably entitled, and when the property thus obtained is held in hostility to his beneficial rights of ownership. As the trusts of this class are imposed by equity, contrary to the trustee's intention and will, upon property in his hands, they are often termed trusts *in invitum;* and this phrase furnishes a criterion generally accurate and sufficient for determining what trusts are truly 'constructive.' An exhaustive analysis would show, I think, that all instances of constructive trusts properly so called may be referred to what equity denominates fraud, either actual or constructive, as an essential element, and as their final source. . . . This notion of fraud enters into the conception in all its possible degrees. Certain species of the constructive trusts arise from actual fraud; many others spring from the violation of some positive fiduciary obligation; in all the remaining instances there is, latent perhaps, but none the less real, the necessary element of that unconscientious conduct which equity calls constructive fraud." 3 Pomeroy's Eq. Jurisprudence, sec. 1044.

After saying that if the legal title to property has been obtained through actual fraud, undue influence, or duress, or under any other similar circumstances which render it unconscientious for the holder of the legal title to retain and enjoy the beneficial interest, equity impresses a constructive trust on the property thus acquired in favor of the one who is truly and equitably entitled to it, although he may never have had the legal estate, the author proceeds: "The forms and varieties of these trusts, which are termed *ex maleficio* or *ex delicto,* are practically without limit. The principle is applied wherever it is necessary for the obtaining of complete justice, although the law may also give the remedy of damages against the wrongdoer." *Ibid.,* sec. 1053. And with respect to a devise or bequest procured by fraud it is said: "It is astonishing that the numerous cases holding that no exception can be made to the statutes of wills or of descent for the case where the testator or ancestor is murdered by his devisee, legatee or heir, have overlooked the plain analogy to the principle of the above paragraph. Unfortunately, the opinions in most of those cases show no evidence that this analogy was considered by the court, or even brought to the court's attention. That the principle should be applied in this class of cases, and the criminal held a constructive trustee of the fruits of his crime seems too plain for argument. See Wellner *v.* Eckstein, 105 Minn., 444, 117 N. W., 830 (opinion by Elliott, J.); Perry *v.* Strawbridge, 209 Mo., 621, 123 A. S. R., 510, 14 Ann. Cas., 92, 16 L. R. A. (N. S.), 244, 108 S. W., 641. For a typical case ignoring the equitable view, see McAllister *v.* Fair, 72 Kan., 533, 115 A. S. R., 233, 7 Ann. Cas., 973, 3 L. R. A. (N. S.), 726, and note, 84 Pac., 112." *Ibid.*, sec. 1054, note b, p. 2411. Several of the " typical cases " were cited and reviewed in 34 Am. Law Register, page 636.

The equitable doctrine is this: As a question of common law the homicide does not prevent the legal title from passing to the criminal as the heir or devisee of his victim, but equity, acting *in personam*, compels the wrongdoer who has acquired the *res*, to hold it as a constructive trustee of the person wronged, or of his representatives, if he be dead; and this result follows although the homicide may not have been committed for the express purpose of acquiring title, if by reason of the homicide the title would have passed to the criminal under the common law. This, we think, is the principle which should be applied in the case before us; it not only makes unnecessary the attempted distinction between cases of devise or bequest and cases of descent; it obviates the reproach of permitting an atrocious criminal to profit by his perfidy. See 30 A. L. Review, 130; 4 Harvard L. Review, 394.

It is altogether reasonable that the appellant should rely upon the decision in Owens *v.* Owens, 100 N. C., 240; for it was cited by the Supreme Court of Pennsylvania in support of the conclusion reached in the Carpenter case. *In re* Carpenter's Estate, *supra.* In the Owens case the question was whether the criminal act of participating in the murder of her husband deprived the widow of her right to have dower allotted in the estate of which he had died seized, and it was held that it did not. It is apparent, however, that the appeal was treated as presenting nothing more than a question of law, in reference to which the Court said as the law gives dower and makes no provision for its forfeiture for crime, adultery being the only bar (The Code, sec. 1844), no obstacle stood in the way of the widow's seeking what the law had given. There is an intimation that she was entitled to share in the personal estate of her husband as a distributee; but this also was dealt with as a question of law. The Court remarked, " We have searched in vain for an authority or ruling on the question and we find no adjudged case." It does not appear what the decision would have been if the equitable jurisdiction of the court had been invoked for the administration of the doctrine to which we have adverted; for as suggested by Pomeroy, this is one of those cases in which the equitable principle was not brought to the attention of the Court.

If the doctrine is applicable, how does it affect the appellant's title? The answer depends upon the nature of an estate by entireties. In such case by a legal fiction the husband and wife hold the title as one person. Whenever the fictitious unity of person is severed by the death of either the survivor has the title, the deceased leaving no interest which is descendible or devisable. During its continuance neither the husband nor the wife can convey or encumber the estate so as to destroy the right of the survivor, but the husband has the control and use of the property and is entitled to the possession, income, and usufruct thereof during their joint lives. Bruce *v.* Nicholson, 109 N. C., 204; Bank *v.* McEwen, 160 N. C., 414; Dorsey *v.* Kirkland, 177 N. C., 520; Davis *v.* Bass, 188 N. C., 200. It is therefore manifest that if the deceased wife were now living the appellant could not be deprived of his interest in the estate by an arbitrary judgment of the court. None the less is he entitled to the enjoyment of such interest after her death; but for the benefit of her heirs at law a court of equity will interpose its protecting shield. This principle is illustrated by Ames, *supra*, 321: "Similar reasoning would be applicable if land bought by B. and C. had been conveyed to them as joint tenants in fee simple, and C. were then to murder B. Each joint tenant has a vested interest in a moiety of the land so long as he lives, and a contingent right to the whole upon surviving his fellow. The vested interest of C., the murderer, cannot be taken from him even by a court of equity. But C. having by his crime taken away B.'s vested interest must hold that as a constructive trustee for the heir of B."

In the application of this principle a court of equity will not deprive the appellant of his interest in the estate, but the appellant by his crime took away his wife's interest, and as to this he must be held a constructive trustee for the benefit of her heirs, the judge in effect having found as a fact that the deceased would have survived him. Even in the absence of such finding, equity would probably give the victim's representatives the benefit of the doubt. Ames, *supra*, 321.

Our conclusion is that the appellant holds the interest of his deceased wife in the property as a trustee for her heirs at law; that he should be perpetually enjoined from conveying the property in fee; that the plaintiffs should be adjudged the sole owners, upon the appellant's death, of the entire property as the heirs of their deceased mother; and that the judgment as thus modified should be affirmed.

As our decision is based upon equitable principles, it is not necessary to determine whether the provisions of C. S., 2522, in reference to the felonious slaying of the husband or wife, which was enacted after the decision in Owens *v.* Owens, *supra*, embraces estates held by entireties. Laws 1889, ch. 499.

Modified and affirmed.[1]

Section IV.

Where the Purchase Money is Paid by One Person and the Conveyance is Taken in the Name of Another.

ANONYMOUS.

Chancery. 1683.

2 Vent. 361.

Where a man buys land in another's name, and pays money, it will be in trust for him that pays the money, tho' no deed declaring the trust, for the Statute of 29 Car. 2. called the Statute of Frauds, doth not extend to trusts, raised by operation of the law.[2]

[1] For a collection of cases on the question of imposing a constructive trust upon an heir who murders the ancestor or a beneficiary under a will who murders the testator, see 3 L. R. A. (N. S.) 726; 39 L. R. A. (N. S.) 1088; L. R. A. 1915C 328; 51 A. L. R. 1096, 1106, 1113; 5 N. C. L. Rev. 373 (note to principal case). See Ames, Lect. Leg. Hist., 310; 30 L. Quar. Rev. 211; 44 Harv. L. Rev. 125.

There is legislation on the matter in California, Colorado, Indiana, Iowa, Kansas, Louisiana, Minnesota, Mississippi, Nebraska, North Carolina, North Dakota, Oklahoma, Pennsylvania, South Carolina, Tennessee, Utah, Virginia, Wyoming, and the District of Columbia. See 14 Iowa L. Rev. 304.

Compare the cases where the claimant under a life insurance policy kills the insured. Cleaver *v.* Mutual Reserve Fund Life Ass'n, [1892] 1 Q. B. 147; Supreme Lodge *v.* Menkhausen, 209 Ill. 277; Schmidt *v.* Northern Life Ass'n, 112 Iowa 45; Sharpless *v.* Grand Lodge, 135 Minn. 35; Equitable Life Assur. Soc. *v.* Weightman, 61 Okla. 106; Johnston *v.* Metropolitan Life Ins. Co., 85 W. Va. 70; Grossman, Liability and Rights of the Insurer when the Death of the Insured is Caused by the Beneficiary or by an Assignee, 10 B. U. L. Rev. 281; 20 Col. L. Rev. 465; 18 Mich. L. Rev. 430; 68 U. Pa. L. Rev. 298. See L. R. A. 1917B 671.

[2] See cases cited Ames, Cases on Trusts, 1 ed., 270, 292; Perry, Trusts, sec 126; 3 Pomeroy, Eq. Juris., sec. 1037; Dec. Dig., Trusts, secs. 71 *et seq.*

In Froemke *v.* Marks, 259 Ill. 146, it was held that a resulting trust arose although the person in whose name land was purchased had no knowledge of the purchase.

The doctrine of purchase-money resulting trusts is applicable to personal property. James *v.* Holmes, 4 DeG. F. & J. 470; *Re* Policy No. 6402, [1902] 1 Ch. 282; Briggs *v.* Sanford, 219 Mass. 572.

Effect of recitals in the deed of conveyance. A resulting trust may arise although the deed recites that the consideration was paid by the grantee. Milner *v.* Freeman, 40 Ark. 62; Brooks *v.* Union Trust and Realty Co., 146 Cal. 134; Elliott *v.* Armstrong, 2 Blackf. (Ind.) 198 (*semble*); Livermore *v.* Aldrich, 5 Cush. (Mass.) 431; Lynch *v.* Lynch, 249 Mass. 543; Chicago B. & Q.

MILLER v. DAVIS.

SUPREME COURT, MISSOURI. 1872.

50 Mo. 572.

ADAMS, J. delivered the opinion of the court. . . .

The facts stated in this petition are, substantially, that the defendant's father, under the laws of Congress, had entered all the forty-acre tracts of land he was entitled to enter, and, not being able to enter the forty acres in dispute in his own name, made the entry in the name of his infant son, the defendant. The petition then alleges that the father sold and conveyed this forty acres to the plaintiff, and asks a decree for the title to be divested out of the infant and invested in the plaintiffs.

It is a well-settled principle of equity jurisprudence that in general, when one person pays the purchase-money for land and the title is conveyed to another, a trust results in favor of the party who paid for the land. But where such purchase is made in fraud of an existing statute and in evasion of its express provisions, no trust can result in favor of the party who is guilty of the fraud. There is no pretense here that the plaintiffs are innocent purchasers. They make no such allegation in the petition. They occupy the precise relation to the defendant that was held by their assignor, and boldly assert that he, in order to obtain this tract of land from the United States, used the name of his infant son, because he could not make the entry in his own name, having already entered as many forty-acre tracts as he was entitled to by the laws of the United States. His act in making this entry was against public policy. Under the facts as stated in the petition, no trust resulted to the father; and as between him and his assignees and the son, a court of equity cannot disturb the title.

The judgment will therefore be reversed and the cause remanded.[1]
Judge WAGNER concurs. Judge BLISS absent.

R. R. Co. v. First Nat. Bank, 58 Neb. 548, 59 Neb. 348; Pinney v. Fellows, 15 Vt. 525. It was once held otherwise in England. Sanders, Uses & Trusts, 5 ed., 353. But the English rule now seems to be like that in the United States. Lench v. Lench, 10 Ves. 511, 517.

So also a resulting trust may arise although the deed states that the conveyance is made to the use of the grantee. Cotton v. Wood, 25 Iowa 43; Stratton v. Dialogue, 16 N. J. Eq. 70.

[1] In the following cases in which property was purchased by one person in the name of another in order to avoid payment of debts it was held that the payor could not recover against the transferee. Gascoigne v. Gascoigne, [1918] 1 K. B. 223; Ford's Ex'rs v. Lewis, 10 B. Mon. (Ky.) 127; Pollock v. Pollock, 223 Mass. 382; Sell v. West, 125 Mo. 621; Keener v. Williams, 307 Mo. 682; Baldwin v. Campfield, 8 N. J. Eq. 600, 891; Sayre v. Lemberger, 92 N. J. Eq. 656; Proseus v. McIntyre, 5 Barb. (N. Y.) 424; McClintock v. Loisseau, 31 W. Va. 865; Scheuerman v. Scheuerman, 52 Can. S. C. 625. But

THOMAS v. THOMAS.

COURT OF CHANCERY, NEW JERSEY. 1911.

79 N. J. Eq. 461.

FINAL hearing on bill, answer, replication and proofs.

LEAMING, V. C. My views in this case are entirely defined; the arguments which have been made, and the references to authorities during the progress of the case, have sufficiently refreshed my memory of adjudications in cases of this class, to enable me, I think, to correctly dispose of the matter at this time without taking it under advisement.

There is no doubt touching the facts of the case. Under the evidence which has been received the facts are clearly and indubitably established. The only possible ground of opposition that can be made to the decree sought is necessarily based upon the claim that some of the evidence which has been received is not competent by reason of our statutes.

---

see *contra,* Perkins *v.* Nichols, 11 Allen (Mass.) 542. See the cases collected in Ann. Cas. 1915C 1091 (purchase in name of wife).

In several states, *e.g.* Kentucky, Michigan, Minnesota, New York, and Wisconsin, by statute it is provided that a purchase in the name of another is presumptively in fraud of creditors.

In the following cases also where the payor's purpose was unlawful the same result was reached. Gascoigne *v.* Thwing, 1 Vern. 366 (to erect nunnery); *Ex parte* Yallop, 15 Ves. 60 (to avoid ship registry laws); *Ex parte* Houghton, 17 Ves. 251 (to avoid ship registry laws); Groves *v.* Groves, 3 Y. & J. 163 (to enable grantee to vote or to sit in Parliament, *semble*); Keely *v.* Gregg, 33 Mont. 216, 227 (to avoid requirements as to entry on public lands, *semble*). But see *contra,* Monahan *v.* Monahan, 77 Vt. 133 (to avoid taxation). See 14 Minn. L. Rev. 103.

If in a jurisdiction where aliens cannot hold land, an alien pays the purchase price for land and the conveyance is made to a citizen, it would seem that a resulting trust will arise in favor of the alien but that the state may reach his equitable estate by inquest of office. Leggett *v.* Dubois, 5 Paige (N. Y.) 114. See Isaacs *v.* De Hon, 11 F.(2d) 943. In Hubbard *v.* Goodwin, 3 Leigh (Va.) 492, the court doubted whether a resulting trust should be raised. In Anstice *v.* Brown, 6 Paige (N. Y.) 448, it was held that where the land was to be sold the trust was, under the doctrine of equitable conversion, one of personalty, and the state would not take. In Marx *v.* McGlynn, 88 N. Y. 357, it was held that under the New York statutes the beneficiary of a trust to receive the income of land had not an interest in land and was entitled to the income although he was an alien.

In Cockrill *v.* California, 268 U. S. 258, the court upheld as constitutional a statute which provided that if land is transferred upon trust for an alien not eligible to citizenship, the land should escheat to the state if the transfer was made with the intention to prevent escheat, and which further provided that a *prima facie* presumption that the conveyance is made with such intent shall arise upon proof that the property was taken in the name of one other than such alien if the consideration was paid or agreed to be paid by such alien.

The evidence which has been offered and received under my rulings establishes beyond all doubt the fact that Mr. Thomas, Sr., purchased the land in question for his own benefit at sheriff's sale, paying $21,400 for it with his own money. He took the title, however, in the name of his three sons, causing the sheriff to make a deed to them instead of to himself. By prior arrangements with his sons, he had procured from them their assent that he should do so, and their promise that at such time as he desired the property conveyed by them to him, they would execute the deeds. He accepted their assurance to that effect without any writing being executed, and trusted them with the legal title to the property, which, as already stated, he purchased for himself, and for his own use and benefit and paid for with his own funds. The evidence clearly discloses that no money was contributed by either of these sons, and that neither understood that the purchase was for their benefit, but that all three understood that the purchase was for the sole benefit of the father. The fact is that a reason existed, which Mr. Thomas, Sr., thought was a good reason, for putting the title in the names of his sons. He was living separate from his wife at the time, under an agreement of separation, and was expecting at the time that he would soon have occasion to sell a portion of the property to an anticipated purchaser, and thought that by putting the title in the names of his sons, he would avoid any possibility of difficulty in getting his wife to sign the deed. Unfortunately, one of the sons has since died, leaving the legal title in his name, which legal title has descended to the son of that son, who is now a minor and a defendant in this suit. These facts, I say, are clearly established if the evidence which has been introduced is entitled to be considered. Under this testimony but one conclusion can result, and that is that the complainant is entitled to a decree establishing his title in this land. He is entitled to such decree as may be necessary to fully confirm his title, as he is undoubtedly the equitable owner, and is entitled to be restored to the status of a legal owner.

The objections to the admissibility of the testimony to which I have already referred, have been considered during the progress of the trial, and need not be here restated at any length. . . .

The first objection is that the testimony of complainant touching conversations with his deceased son is incompetent because of the fact that there is before the court a defendant in a representative capacity. As stated, during the hearing, the case of Cowdrey *v.* Cowdrey, reported in 71 N. J. Eq. (1 Buch.) 353, fully meets that objection. There is no defendant before this court in a representative capacity within the meaning of the statute. The present suit is essentially a suit *in rem*, a suit purely for the restoration of legal title, and seeks no relief *in personam*. If it were true, however, that the complainant should be excluded from testifying to conversations between himself and his deceased son, the evidence would yet be ample to establish the facts which I have stated to exist, because the two remaining sons who are still alive have both testified to substantially the same conversations to which the father testified and have fully established the fact, and no objection can arise, so far as their testimony is concerned, based on the ground of a suit against a defendant in a representative capacity.

The other objection on which defendant relies is that the effect of the decree sought is to establish a trust in the deceased defendant, and that the statute of frauds prohibits the establishment of a trust in lands by parol testimony.

An examination of the statute of frauds will disclose that it is not so broad as the statement which I have just made. The statute of frauds will not permit an express trust to be established by parol testimony, but, by its very terms, it excepts resulting trusts. The language of the statute is, as I recall it, that there is excepted from its operation trusts which arise from implications or construction of law. That may not be the language of the statute, but it is substantially the language. Such trusts are not within the statute, and the courts have uniformly held that parol testimony is competent to aid in their ascertainment. Therefore, if this case were a case in which Mr. Thomas, Sr., had caused a deed to be made to a stranger, the consideration having been supplied by Mr. Thomas, the presumption of law would be that the person who supplied the money had supplied it for his own benefit, and not for the benefit of the stranger, that the title follows the consideration, and in such a case the law creates and determines the existence of a resulting trust. That is what the statute refers to as a trust which results from implication or construction of the law, and is therefore one of the trusts which is excepted by the terms of statute. It follows in consequence that where money is supplied by one person to pay for property, the title to which is taken in the name of another, the law permits the person who supplies the money to testify that he supplied the money, and the trust results as a matter of law.

An additional element arises, however, when the conveyance, the consideration for which is paid for a father, is made to a son, daughter, wife or other near relative or dependent; the mere fact of supplying the consideration, in such a case, does not create a presumption of ownership in the person who supplies the consideration. On the contrary, the presumption is the reverse. The presumption in such a case is that the father supplies the consideration not for his own benefit but for the benefit of the relative; therefore, standing alone, the mere testimony on the part of the father or any other witness that the father supplied the money will not be sufficient to create a resulting trust, but, on the contrary, such testimony will create a presumptive gift, settlement or advancement. That presumption, however, is a rebuttable presumption; if the presumption of gift, settlement or advancement can be dispelled or overcome by competent evidence then the conveyance to the son stands exactly on the same plane as a conveyance to a stranger. So, the only real question here now is, whether or not the presumption of gift has been dispelled or overcome by competent evidence. The courts have uniformly held that this presumption of gift, advancement or settlement is not only rebuttable, but it may be rebutted by any circumstance precedent to the transaction, or contemporaneous with the transaction, or so nearly contemporaneous with the transaction as to form part of the *res gestæ*, but that it cannot be rebutted by circumstances other than admission of the parties, subsequent thereto.

When conversations between the party who supplies the consideration, the father, and the party who receives the conveyance, the son, are sought to be introduced into evidence for the purpose of repelling the presumption of gift, the thought necessarily suggests itself that the effect of such testimony is to establish a trust. As such it would be incompetent, but it is competent to establish that it was not a gift, settlement or advancement. In other words, it is competent to repel or rebut the presumption of gift which the law has created, and it will be received for that purpose and for that purpose alone, and if, when received, it is adequate to fully dispel the presumption of settlement or advancement or gift, then the case stands exactly as it would stand in the case already suggested of a conveyance made to a stranger. In other words, the testimony in this case is competent for the purpose of establishing, and is ample in quality to establish, the fact that this conveyance was not by the father ordered made to these children as a gift, and the presumption of gift which arose from the relationship is dispelled by that evidence. That brings the case upon the same plane as a conveyance made to a stranger, by money supplied by the complainant, and in such case the law creates or presumes the trusts.

It follows that in this case, under the circumstances named, there is no course that can be properly adopted but to reach the conclusion, and make that conclusion effective through whatever decree is found necessary to answer the needs of the complainant, that this legal title, now in the name of the heirs of John Thomas, Jr., is held under a trust to reconvey, upon request, to John Thomas, Sr., and that the entire equitable title to the property is in John Thomas, Sr., and that he is entitled to have the legal title fully restored to him. I will advise a decree of that nature.[1]

[1] The cases are numerous to the effect that presumptively no resulting trust is created where property is purchased in the name of the purchaser's wife or child or one to whom the purchaser otherwise stands *in loco parentis*. See Ames, Cases on Trusts, 1 ed., 268, 294; Perry, Trusts, sec. 144; Ann. Cas. 1915C 1082; 26 A. L. R. 1126; Dec. Dig., Trusts, sec. 81; 40 Harv. L. Rev. 682.

Parol evidence is admissible, however, of the intention of the purchaser to create a trust. Stock *v.* McAvoy, L. R. 15 Eq. 55; Smithsonian Institution *v.* Meech, 169 U. S. 398; Wilson *v.* Warner, 89 Conn. 243; McKey *v.* Cochran,

LONG v. MECHEM.

SUPREME COURT, ALABAMA. 1904.

142 Ala. 405.

SIMPSON, J. This is an appeal from an interlocutory decree, overruling demurrers and a plea. The original bill was filed, to remove a cloud from the title of complainant, and was afterwards amended by adding a section, setting up a resulting trust, but making no additional prayer.

The first assignment of error is based on the overruling of the plea, the substance of the plea being that the trust set up in the amended bill was not in writing and consequently void under section 1041 of the Code of Alabama (1896).

The allegations of the amended bill show that the land, in question, was bought and paid for by the complainant, and the title taken in the name of one Duncan, under an agreement that Duncan was to hold the legal title for complainant, and to convey the land, whenever desired under complainant's direction.

The contention of the respondent is that the fact that there was a parol agreement in regard to said trust takes it out of the category of resulting trusts, and it is therefore void.

If the complainant had a resulting trust in the lands, from having paid the purchase money, and placed the title in the name of another, the mere fact that the party, in whom the legal title was vested recognized, by parol, the obligation to hold the land in trust, certainly could not destroy the resulting trust held by the complainant, by operation of law. In addition to this, the section of the Code provides that no trust in lands, not in writing is valid "*except such as result by implication or construction of law, or which may be* transferred or extinguished by operation of law."

The inevitable result from the grammatical construction of the sentence is that this class of trusts is excepted entirely from the operation of the section, and parol declarations of the parties regarding the same are admissible.

The distinction between this case and such cases as Patton v. Beecher, *et al.*, 62 Ala. 579, and Brock v. Brock, 90 Ala. 86, is that these cases correctly hold that the "*mere* verbal promise, by the grantee of a deed for lands, absolute on its face" will not take it out of the requirements of the statute, while this case comes under another principle of law, equally well established, and recognized

---

262 Ill. 376; Dodge v. Thomas, 266 Ill. 76 (*semble*); Link v. Emrich, 336 Ill. 337; Yetman v. Hedgeman, 82 N. J. Eq. 221. But see *contra*, Kinley v. Kinley, 37 Colo. 35; Mullong v. Schneider, 155 Iowa 12. See also Dyer v. Dyer, 2 Cox 92; Dumper v. Dumper, 3 Giff. 583; Mercier v. Mercier, [1903] 2 Ch. 98; Ann. Cas. 1915C 1082. See 40 Harv. L. Rev. 683

in the exception contained in the statute under consideration, to wit; that "if the purchaser of lands, paying the purchase money, takes the conveyance in the name of another, the trust of the lands results, by construction to him from whom the purchase money moves." — Lehman, *et al. v.* Lewis, 62 Ala. 129, 131; Tillman *v.* Murrell, *et al.*, 120 Ala. 239.

It is true that in the last named case, as counsel for appellant say, the lands had been conveyed in accordance with the parol agreement, but the case was decided distinctly on the principle that Murrell held the legal title in trust for the party who paid the money for it, " not by virtue of the parol agreement, but because of their having paid the consideration."

There was no error in the decree of the court as to said plea.[1] . . .

FOREMAN *v.* FOREMAN.

COURT OF APPEALS, NEW YORK. 1929.

251 N. Y. 237.

APPEAL from a judgment of the Appellate Division of the Supreme Court in the second judicial department, entered March 30, 1928, affirming a judgment in favor of defendant, entered upon a dismissal of the complaint by the court on trial at Special Term.

CARDOZO, Ch. J. A house and lot in the city of New York was conveyed to Edith Foreman in January, 1924. The purchase price, $25,500, was paid by her husband, the plaintiff. There is testimony that he asked her to take the contract and conveyance in her name because he wished to keep his real estate separate from the property that was used in his business. There is testimony that she promised to give him a deed upon demand and to dispose of the land or the proceeds in accordance with his wishes. After the purchase had been made, he collected the rents and used them as his own. He paid the taxes, the insurance premiums, the interest on the mortgages, and the cost of improvements and repairs. The dominion that goes with ownership was continuously his.

The wife died intestate in 1925, leaving as her sole heir an infant son, the defendant, to whom the legal title has descended, subject to a life estate in the plaintiff as tenant by the curtesy. This action is brought to compel a conveyance to the plaintiff in fulfillment of the oral trust. Judgment has gone for the defendant on the ground that the trust is unenforcible under the Statute of Frauds (Real Prop. Law [Cons. Laws, ch. 50], § 242).

The rule is now settled by repeated judgments of this court that the statute does not obstruct the recognition of a constructive trust

[1] Murrell *v.* Peterson, 59 Fla. 566; Brennaman *v.* Schell, 212 Ill. 356; Mercury Club *v.* Keillen, 323 Ill. 24; Geraghty *v.* Geraghty, 335 Ill. 494; Linnel *v.* Hudson, 59 S. C. 283, *accord.* See 42 A. L. R. 55.

affecting an interest in land where a confidential relation would be abused if there were repudiation, without redress, of a trust orally declared (Sinclair v. Purdy, 235 N. Y. 245, 253; Gallagher v. Gallagher, 135 App. Div. 457; 202 N. Y. 572; Leary v. Corvin, 181 N. Y. 222, 229; Goldsmith v. Goldsmith, 145 N. Y. 313; Wood v. Rabe, 96 N. Y. 414; cf. Scott, Conveyance upon Trusts not Properly Declared, 37 Harv. L. Rev. 653, 661, 669; Scott, Resulting Trusts, 40 Harv. L. Rev. 669; Costigan, Constructive Trusts, 28 Harv. L. Rev. 237, 256, 266, 374; Ames Lectures on Legal History, 425, 432). Criticism of the rule as involving a partial repeal of the prohibition of the statute is heard from time to time in commentary and treatise. Whatever force the criticism may have had while the rule was in the making, has vanished with the years. By long acquiescence, the exception, if such it be, has wrought itself by construction into the body of the statute as if written there from the beginning. "It is not the promise only, nor the breach only, but unjust enrichment under cover of the relation of confidence, which puts the court in motion" (Sinclair v. Purdy, supra).

The husband paid for her land and managed and improved it. The wife, far from attempting to rid herself of the trust because orally declared, submitted to it as completely as if seals and parchments had perfected the evidence of duty (cf. Bork v. Martin, 132 N. Y. 280). No objection was heard from her, or none that has been disclosed, when the husband gathered in the rents and used them for himself. In its origin the trust was dependent for proof of its existence on nothing better than word of mouth. In the end, at her death, what was oral in its beginnings, had been confirmed by part performance, with the result that conduct as well as words had become the signs of its creation (Jeremiah v. Pitcher, 26 App. Div. 402; aff'd., 163 N. Y. 574; McKinley v. Hessen, 202 N. Y. 24; Burns v. McCormick, 233 N. Y. 230). The wife would have been guilty of an abuse of confidence by disclaimer during life. Her heir will not be suffered to nullify her submission to the call of equity and honor by disclaimer after death.

Nothing in the statute as to the implication of resulting trusts is at war with this conclusion (Real Prop. Law, § 94). The statute has put an end to the rule at common law that where a grant is made to one for a consideration paid by another a trust results inevitably and always, by force merely of the payment, irrespective of intention (Garfield v. Hatmaker, 15 N. Y. 475, 477; Scott, Resulting Trusts in Purchase of Land, 40 Harv. L. Rev. 675). The conveyance is operative according to its terms if nothing else is proved. The statute has no effect, however, on trusts constructively imposed as a consequence not of payment alone, but of payment in combination with other or extrinsic equities. As to this the decisions are uniform and ample. "It is only the common-law trust for the benefit of an individual from whom the consideration for a grant issues, and resulting from the fact of payment of the consideration, and having no other foundation, that the statute abolishes " (Carr v. Carr, 52 N. Y. 251, 260; Gage v. Gage, 83 Hun, 362; Jeremiah v. Pitcher, *supra;* Leary v. Corvin, *supra;* Wood v. Rabe, *supra;* Scott, Conveyances upon Trusts not Properly Declared, 37 Harv. L. Rev. 653, 661, 669; Costigan, The Classification of Trusts, 27 Harv. L. Rev. 437; cf. as to resulting trusts, Perry on Trusts, § 124, and as to constructive trusts, the same author, § 166).

Enough and ample there is here to put the case for the plaintiff in the field uncovered by the statute. His equity does not grow out of payment and nothing more. It is reinforced by words of promise, by the relation of man and wife, and by unequivocal acts of confirmation and performance. In such circumstances, the plastic remedies of the chancery are moulded to the needs of justice. Where, as in Leary v. Corvin (*supra*), the one whose confidence has been abused, has paid part of the consideration, and part only, a lien proportioned to the value thus contributed will be charged upon the land. Where, as in the case at hand, the full price has been paid by the victim of the wrong, unjust enrichment will ensue if the holder of the legal title retains for his own use any portion of the purchase, and the trust will reach the whole. (Scott, 40 Harv. L. Rev. 673).

What has been written assumes that the testimony of the plaintiff's witnesses is truthful and accurate. As to this there is a question of credibility which the trier of the facts, and not this court, must resolve. True, the testimony is uncontradicted, and to some extent, besides, has corroboration in the circumstances, yet in view of the death of the wife, with direct contradiction difficult, if not impossible, a question of fact remains (Tousey v. Hastings, 194 N. Y. 79; McKeon v. Van Slyck, 223 N. Y. 392, 398). The trial judge did not decide it either one way or the other (Galle v. Tode, 148 N. Y. 270, 277; Morehouse v. B. H. R. Co., 185 N. Y. 520, 527, 528; Alcock v. Davitt, 179 N. Y. 9). He placed his ruling on the ground that the trust, if declared, was void under the statute. There is need of a new trial.

The judgment of the Appellate Division and that of the Special Term should be reversed and a new trial granted, with costs to abide the event.

POUND, CRANE, LEHMAN, KELLOGG, O'BRIEN and HUBBS, JJ., concur.

Judgments reversed, etc.[1]

[1] The New York statute (Real Property Law, sec. 94) provides:

"A grant of real property for a valuable consideration, to one person, the consideration being paid by another, is presumed fraudulent as against the creditors, at that time, of the person paying the consideration, and, unless a fraudulent intent is disproved, a trust results in favor of such creditors, to an extent necessary to satisfy their just demands, but the title vests in the

In re DAVIS.

DISTRICT COURT OF THE U. S., MASSACHUSETTS. 1901.

112 Fed. 129.[1]

IN Bankruptcy. On petition for an order requiring the trustee to convey to the petitioner property claimed to have been held by the bankrupt in trust.

LOWELL, District Judge. I find the facts in this case to be as follows: Mrs. Sullivan paid the entire original consideration for the property, and since the purchase has paid off mortgages thereon to the amount of $1,600. She never intended to take by the conveyance any title to the property, legal or equitable. Had she so intended, there was nothing to prevent her from substituting her name for her daughter's in the deed as prepared, which could have been done without expense. She intended the entire equitable estate for her grandchildren's benefit, especially for their education. She never intended her daughter to take any beneficial interest in the property, and had no distinct intention that she should take any legal interest. As to the legal interest, she never had any clear intention. Mrs. Davis did not know about the conveyance until shortly after it was made, when she was informed generally of Mrs. Sullivan's intention. She neither repudiated nor expressly accepted the trust. Some time afterwards she mortgaged the property as her own, and still later inserted the same in her bankruptcy

---

grantee, and no use or trust results from the payment to the person paying the consideration, or in his favor, unless the grantee either,

"1. Takes the same as an absolute conveyance, in his own name, without the consent or knowledge of the person paying the consideration; or,

"2. In violation of some trust, purchases the property so conveyed with money or property belonging to another."

There are similar statutes in Kentucky, Michigan, Minnesota and Wisconsin.

In Indiana and Kansas a third exception is added: "Where it shall be made to appear that, by agreement and without any fraudulent intent, the party to whom the conveyance was made, or in whom the title shall vest, was to hold the land or some interest therein in trust for the party paying the purchase-money or some part thereof."

See, in accordance with the principal case, Carr v. Carr, 52 N. Y. 251; Waters v. Hall, 218 N. Y. App. Div. 149, 36 Yale L. Jour. 715; Benedict v. Benedict, 242 N. Y. 597. But see *contra*, Chapman v. Chapman, 114 Mich. 144; Sherwood v. Davis, 168 Mich. 398; Hoar v. Hoar, 48 Hun (N. Y.) 314, *aff'd* 125 N. Y. 735. In Kentucky it has been held that the purchaser may recover the purchase price from the grantee if a trust was intended and the grantee refuses to perform. Martin v. Martin, 5 Bush (Ky.) 47; Deposit Bank v. Rose, 113 Ky. 946 (*semble*); Brooks v. Brooks, 31 Ky. L. Rep. 969.

For comments on the principal case, see 15 Cornell L. Quar. 319.

[1] The decision was affirmed by the Circuit Court of Appeals *sub nom.* Re Peabody, 118 Fed. 266.

schedules. These acts were unknown to Mrs. Sullivan, until after bankruptcy and after the bankruptcy Mrs. Sullivan, while not clear as to her precise legal rights, did nothing to waive them. I have to determine whether a trust results in favor of the person paying the consideration when that person distinctly intended that the entire beneficial interest in the property should vest in another not the grantee, and intended that no interest, legal or beneficial, should vest in herself. Where one pays the consideration for real estate, and the title is taken in another, a trust in favor of the one paying the consideration is presumed to result. If the grantee is a child, a counter presumption arises. But none of these presumptions are conclusive, and all are controlled by the circumstances of the particular case. As it appears here by evidence not objected to that the bankrupt grantee was not intended to take any beneficial interest in the property conveyed, she is to be deemed a trustee for some one, whether for her children, as Mrs. Sullivan intended, or for Mrs. Sullivan, because the trust for the children was not sufficiently declared, this court cannot determine for want of necessary parties. That a trust does sometimes result in favor of the person paying the consideration where an intended trust has failed is settled law. Perry, Trusts, 157. One who has taken the legal title to land upon a trust which cannot be enforced cannot retain the beneficial interest in it against the person who has failed to establish the trust, whether a former beneficial owner or one who has paid the purchase money. If the petitioner will make her grandchildren parties to this proceeding, this court will pass upon her claims and theirs. As things stand, no resulting trust in her favor is shown, and, unless the grandchildren are brought in, the petition must be dismissed.

(December 6, 1901.)

Mrs. Sullivan's grandchildren have now been made parties defendant to the petition, and a stipulation has been entered into between their guardian *ad litem* and Mrs. Sullivan, whereby Mrs. Sullivan agrees to convey the real estate in question outright to them if this court shall direct a conveyance to her by the trustee. By their guardian *ad litem* the grandchildren have withdrawn opposition to Mrs. Sullivan's petition. Counsel for the trustee has objected to this phrase in the earlier opinion: " She [Mrs. Sullivan] intended the entire equitable estate for her grandchildren's benefit." If the phrase be taken to imply that Mrs. Sullivan conceived of an equitable estate in all its technical meaning passing to her grandchildren, doubtless it was inaccurate, since she had no conception of the technical meaning of the words " equitable estate"; but the statement is accurate if it be taken to mean that she intended the property altogether for her grandchildren's benefit, and not at all for the benefit of Mrs. Davis. A trust is ordinarily presumed to result in favor of one paying the purchase money of land as against the grantee named in the deed. In this case, as has been said, no beneficial interest was intended, either in purchaser or grantee. Admitting this, at least for the sake of the argument, the trustee here contends that, where the person paying the purchase money intends neither a beneficial interest in himself nor in the grantee, but exclusively in a third person, and where the trust in favor of that third person is not so declared as to be enforceable against the trustee, the grantee there takes the entire beneficial interest. In other words, he contends that a resulting trust may be defeated by an unsuccessful attempt to create a trust in favor of a third person; that in such case, though the intended beneficiary is remediless, yet, as between the person paying the purchase money and the grantee, the entire beneficial interest will pass to the latter. . . .

The trust is presumed to result from the circumstance of payment alone. It results, even if the grantee had no notice of the conveyance, and though he made no agreement, oral or written, to hold the estate in trust. To create the trust, there need be nothing savoring of fraud or misrepresentation or mistake. The trust is not fastened upon the conscience of the legal owner by any action or inaction of his. It arises, as is said in the statute of frauds, by operation of law. The trust may arise in an aliquot part of the property conveyed, or in an estate therein less than a fee simple. The nature and extent of the beneficial interest which passes to the person paying the purchase money may be shown by parol. The trust in favor of the purchaser which is presumed to result may itself be rebutted by parol.

The trust in favor of the grandchildren which was intended by Mrs. Sullivan is enforceable against Mrs. Davis or it is not. Let us suppose that it cannot be enforced. From the payment of the purchase money by Mrs. Sullivan a trust is presumed to result in her favor. How does the trustee in bankruptcy of Mrs. Davis seek to rebut this presumption? Mrs. Davis is Mrs. Sullivan's daughter, and from some relations a rebutting counter presumption arises in favor of the grantee. It is doubtful, however, if this counter presumption arises from the relation of mother and daughter. See Murphy *v.* Nathans, 46 Pa. 508; Sayre *v.* Hughes, L. R. 5 Eq. 376; Johnson *v.* Wyatt, 2 De Gex, J. & S. 18; Bennet *v.* Bennet, 10 Ch. Div. 474; *In re* Orme, 50 Law T. (N. S.) 51. In any case the counter presumption in favor of a grantee who is the child of the purchaser, even where it exists, " is not a presumption of law, but of fact, and can be overthrown by proof of the real intent of the parties." Institution *v.* Meech, 169 U. S. 398, 407, 18 Sup. Ct. 396, 400, 42 L. Ed. 793, 798. . . . As it is abundantly clear that Mrs. Davis was intended to take no beneficial interest in the estate, her relation to Mrs. Sullivan is unimportant, and the case must be decided as if she were a stranger in blood. The trustee thus stands in the place of a grantee who seeks to rebut the presumption that the trust results to the purchaser, and seeks to do so by showing that a trust was intended in favor of a third person, which trust is not enforceable against the grantee. The grantee thus claims the entire beneficial interest in the estate, of which she would otherwise have taken nothing, by showing that a beneficial interest was intended in some one else. She claims a beneficial interest in property because of the expressed intent that she should take no beneficial interest therein. If the purchaser had said nothing, the grantee would have taken nothing. Because the purchaser has said that the grantee is to take nothing, the grantee claims to take everything. This does not appear to be equitable. The intended beneficiaries, the grandchildren, are excluded by the terms of the supposition. As between the grantee and the purchaser, neither of whom was intended to benefit, the equity of the purchaser is the better. It is true that there are cases in which it has been asserted that, where there is an express trust, there can be no resulting trust. But if by "express trust" is meant an attempt to create a trust by parol, the statement is clearly too broad. Institution $v.$ Meech, 169 U. S. 398, 18 Sup. Ct. 396, 42 L. Ed. 793; Hall $v.$ Congdon, 56 N. H. 279; Harrold $v.$ Lane, 53 Pa. 268. These cases and others established that an attempted parol trust identical with the resulting trust will not defeat the latter. Why should an attempted parol trust, which differs from the resulting trust, have a more destructive effect, so long as it is invalid, and cannot itself be established? Again, if a difference between the intended parol trust, which has failed, and the trust which would otherwise have resulted, will defeat the latter, and defeat it altogether, how great must be the difference to bring this about? Will a trust in the half of an estate, which results from paying half the purchase money, be defeated by an invalid oral agreement to hold $\frac{11}{20}$ or $\frac{9}{20}$ of the estate for the person paying half the money?

Again, it is settled that, upon an oral declaration by the purchaser that the grantee is to take the beneficial interest in part of the estate, he will do so, and the beneficial interest in the remaining part will pass by way of resulting trust to the purchaser. The expression by the purchaser of an intention that the grantee shall take only a part, causes a trust in the rest of the estate to result. Rider $v.$ Kidder, 10 Ves. 360; Cook $v.$ Patrick, 135 Ill. 499, 26 N. E. 658, 11 L. R. A. 573. Why should a declaration that a grantee is to take nothing defeat the resulting trust, and cause him to take everything? Still again, it is settled that, where a trust is validly declared in only a part of the estate conveyed, the rest of the estate will result to the purchaser; and the like happens where a trust is declared in the whole estate, but fails in part. It is hard to say why the failure of a valid trust, once created, should inure to the benefit of the purchaser, while a failure to create a valid trust inures to the benefit of the grantee. Furthermore, if an attempted trust under a will fails because contrary to the statutes of mortmain, a trust results to the heir. See Boson *v.* Statham, 1 Eden, 508; Russell *v.* Jackson, 10 Hare, 204. It should seem that a trust results to the purchaser in the case of a deed where the intended trust fails because contrary to the statute of frauds. . . . In Emmons *v.* Moore, 85 Ill. 304, A. bought land, and had the conveyance made to B., his son. At the time of the purchase he expressed an intention to make by the purchase provision for another son, C. This intention was not communicated to B. until some time afterwards. The court held that B. took no beneficial interest, but held in trust for A. or C., it is not quite clear which. In Titcomb *v.* Morrill, 10 Allen, 15, it was held that a voluntary conveyance, absolute in form, though aided by an oral agreement to hold for the benefit of the grantor, raises no trust in his favor. This decision does not express the law of all the states. But the attempt of the grantor in Titcomb *v.* Morrill to set up a resulting trust in the case of his own voluntary conveyance was there expressly distinguished from the case " where a purchase is made in the name of one person, and the purchase money is paid by another." 10 Allen, 18. In the somewhat analogous case of a will, it has been held that, if property is devised in trust for purposes expressed by parol, and the intended beneficiary cannot take because the statute of wills has not been complied with, yet the devisee does not take the beneficial interest, but there results a trust in favor of the testator's representatives. Olliffe *v.* Wells, 130 Mass. 221, and cases cited. It is true that, upon an unqualified devise to A. no trust was held to result, though the testator, by a letter communicated after his death to A., requested A. to apply the devise to a particular purpose. Wallgrave *v.* Tebbs, 2 Kay & J. 313. But in that case the court reached the conclusion that the testator intended A. to take the entire beneficial interest, and to leave the application of the devise to his mere honor, uncontrolled by any court. That is not this case, for here Mrs. Sullivan intended to control Mrs. Davis' discretion. Let us put the hardest possible case to test the theory just stated. Let us suppose that Mrs. Sullivan had become bankrupt, instead of Mrs. Davis, and that the trustee of Mrs. Sullivan sought to recover the property from Mrs. Davis, while the latter was trying to carry out the intention of Mrs. Sullivan for the benefit of the grandchildren. Even in that case, it must still be said that Mrs. Sullivan's intention was not to rely upon Mrs. Davis' honor, but to impose on her a binding trust. If that intention failed, and if the trust did not bind the grantee, the person paying the purchase money would naturally prefer to take into her disposition the property for which she had paid, rather than to leave it altogether in the disposition of the nominal grantee. If, therefore, the trust in favor of the grandchildren was not validly declared, there was a resulting trust in favor of Mrs. Sullivan. Even if there be a possibility that Mrs. Davis so agreed to hold the property in question as to create a valid trust for the grandchildren, the result is the same. After the stipulation entered into by Mrs. Sullivan, the guardian of the children has practically withdrawn opposition to the petition of the bill. By that stipulation the grandchildren have practically ceased to be interested in the establishment of the trust. They are to have the entire beneficial interest, even if a resulting trust is declared. Therefore the court is justified, considering the stipulation and the action of the guardian *ad litem*, in granting the prayer of the petition, even if there be a possibility that the trust was validly declared. The grandchildren cannot alienate the real estate without the consent of their guardian, duly appointed, and substantial justice is done to them and to all. The prayer of the petition is granted.

Decree for complainant, without costs.[1]

REMINGER *v.* JOBLONSKI.

SUPREME COURT, ILLINOIS. 1915.

271 Ill. 71.

Mr. JUSTICE CARTWRIGHT delivered the opinion of the court:

This is an appeal by Branislaw Joblonski from a decree of the county court of Washington county entered in a proceeding by the administrator of the estate of John Joblonski, deceased, to sell real estate to pay debts of the estate, setting aside a deed made to the

---

[1] In Kronheim *v.* Johnson, 7 Ch. Div. 60, it was held that where the grantee refused to perform the intended trust, the purchaser could recover the property. See also Martin *v.* Lincoln, 4 Lea (Tenn.) 289, 334.

On the other hand, the grantee was allowed to keep the property in Spradling *v.* Spradling, 101 Ark. 451; Betsner *v.* Betsner, 84 Ind. App. 319; and Bender *v.* Bender, 281 Mo. 473.

In the following cases it was held that a resulting trust arose in favor of the intended beneficiary. Siemon *v.* Schurck, 29 N. Y. 595; Matter of Steel, 68 N. Y. Misc. 579; Freeland *v.* Williamson, 220 Mo. 217; Lewis *v.* Lewis, 225 S. W. 974 (Mo. 1920). See Jarrett *v.* Manini, 2 Hawaii 667. But see Connelly *v.* Sheridan, 41 Minn. 18. These cases proceed upon the theory that the purchase price although not paid by the intended beneficiary is paid for him.

If the grantee is willing to convey the land to the intended beneficiary, the grantor cannot prevent his doing so. Sherman *v.* Citizens' Right of Way Co., 37 Idaho 528; Riesenberger *v.* Shelden, 86 N. J. Eq. 436.

In People *v.* Tombaugh, 303 Ill. 591, a man purchased land in the name of his wife who orally agreed to devise it to his children by a former marriage, and she did devise it to them. It was held that the children derived their interest from their father, not from their stepmother, and did not have to pay an inheritance tax which would have been payable had they derived their interest from their stepmother.

If by fraud or by an abuse of a confidential relationship, the grantee prevented the purchaser from making a gift to the intended beneficiary, the latter can recover the property from the grantee. See Kern *v.* Beatty, 267 Ill. 127.

SECT. IV.] REMINGER v. JOBLONSKI 429

appellant by his father, John Joblonski, and ordering a sale of the premises described in the deed.

The appellant interposed three defenses to the petition of the administrator: First, that he was the owner by virtue of a deed executed by his father to him; second, that the beneficial title was in him on account of his having furnished the purchase price of the premises; and third, that the premises were the homestead of his father and of his widow, and for that reason could not be sold to pay debts of the estate.[1] . . .

The next defense was that the property was bought with the money of the appellant and therefore a resulting trust arose at the time of the purchase. He was a witness and was objected to as not being competent to testify. He was disqualified, but if he had been a competent witness his testimony would not have established a resulting trust. It went no farther than to show a loan of the purchase money to his father. The competent testimony in behalf of the appellant showed that John Joblonski wanted to purchase the property for himself but did not have the means, and appellant borrowed $350 (which was the purchase price) and let his father have it. An intention that the grantee of a deed is not to receive and hold the legal title as the beneficial owner, not expressed but inferred by the courts of equity from the payment of the consideration, is an essential element to the creation of a resulting trust. That intention could not be inferred in this case, both because the evidence tended to show a loan of the money, and for the reason that the deed, made more than five years afterward, reserving a life estate to the father, tended to negative such an intention. The court was right in deciding that the premises were the property of the estate. . . .

Decree affirmed.[2]

[1] So much of the opinion as relates to the first and third defenses is omitted. The deed was held ineffective because the premises were the father's homestead and his wife did not join therein. It was held that the fact that the premises were the father's homestead did not prevent the court from ordering a sale after his death, the widow consenting and receiving a share of the proceeds.

[2] Whaley v. Whaley, 71 Ala. 159; Holmes v. Holmes, 153 Ga. 790; Meredith v. Citizens Nat. Bank, 92 Ind. 343; Fike v. Ott, 76 Neb. 439; Phillips v. Phillips, 81 N. J. Eq. 459, *aff'd* 83 N. J. Eq. 345; Smith v. Wildman, 194 Pa. 294; Cornman's Estate, 197 Pa. 125 (loan by wife to husband), *accord.*

The result is the same where the grantee borrows a part of the purchase price and pays the balance. Botsford v. Burr, 2 Johns. Ch. (N. Y.) 405; Sayre v. Lemberger, 92 N. J. Eq. 656.

The result is the same where the purchase price was paid at the grantee's request in discharge of an indebtedness of the payor to him. Jackson v. Morse, 16 Johns. (N. Y.) 197; King v. King, 281 Pa. 511; Harris v. Elliott, 45 W. Va. 245.

On the question whether the payor acquires an equitable lien to secure his claim for the repayment of the purchase price advanced by him, when there is an agreement between him and the grantee that he shall have such a lien,

HERLIHY v. CONEY.

SUPREME JUDICIAL COURT, MAINE. 1905.

99 Me. 469.

SAVAGE, J. Bill in equity to enforce a resulting trust in an undivided half interest in the Hotel Brewer property at Bar Harbor. The case comes here on the defendants' appeal. The plaintiff claims that as the result of certain negotiations to which he was a party, the Hotel Brewer was purchased for $9,000; that $6,000 of the purchase money was raised on the notes of the defendants secured by a mortgage of the property; that of the remaining $3,000, he and John J. Coney each paid one-half, and that in accordance with an arrangement between himself and John J. Coney the deed was taken in the name of defendant Catherine Coney, wife of John J. Coney, and sister of the plaintiff. From all this the plaintiff claims that an implied trust arose for his benefit in one-half of the property subject to the mortgage. He claims indeed that it was expressly agreed that he should have half of the property. But the express agreement was not in writing and so not enforceable. The testimony of the plaintiff in one aspect is to the effect that when they were arranging for the payment of the $3,000 in addition to the amount to be raised by the notes and mortgage, the plaintiff informed John J. Coney that he had only $400, that the latter offered to loan him the balance to make their contributions equal, and the offer was accepted. The plaintiff put in his $400 and John J. Coney put in $2600, but $1100 of this the plaintiff claims was advanced on his account, and was in fact a loan to him by Coney, although the money did not pass through the plaintiff's hands. According to plaintiff's evidence it was agreed that Coney should have the entire management of the property.

The defendants deny that plaintiff had anything to do with the negotiations leading up to the purchase. They deny all except that the plaintiff did contribute $400 of the purchase money under such circumstances as to raise a resulting trust in the property to that

---

or in the absence of such an agreement, see 40 Harv. L. Rev. 681; 18 A. L. R. 1098; 60 A. L. R. 1240.

Intention to make a gift. Parol evidence of the intention of the purchaser to make a gift to the grantee is admissible to rebut the presumption of a resulting trust. Fowkes v. Pascoe, L. R. 10 Ch. 343 (personalty); Wolters v. Shraft, 69 N. J. Eq. 215, 70 N. J. Eq. 807; Carter v. Montgomery, 2 Tenn. Ch. 216. *Cf.* Ward v. Ward, 59 Conn. 188. See Ames, Cases on Trusts, 1 ed., 270; 3 Pomeroy, Eq. Juris., sec. 1040; Perry, Trusts, 139.

The resulting trust may be rebutted by parol evidence as to a part of the interest in the property; for instance, it may be shown that after the death of the purchaser the grantee was to have the beneficial interest. Benbow v. Townsend, 1 Myl. & K. 506; Larisey v. Larisey, 93 S. C. 450.

extent. And the defendants further say that the plaintiff's own evidence shows that even if the $1100 was advanced for the plaintiff, no indebtedness was thereby created, that the plaintiff did not become debtor and Coney creditor, as to the $1100, that the plaintiff in no way became obligated to repay it to Coney, but that Coney was to repay himself out of the rents when received by him, and that he was to look not to the plaintiff for repayment, but to the property only. And, hence it is claimed that the $1100 was not the plaintiff's, was not loaned to him, was not paid by him or for him, and that under such circumstances a resulting trust would not arise. This presents the one important question of fact argued before us. There is no dispute or uncertainty about the law.

A resulting trust arises by implication of law when the purchase money is paid by one person out of his own money, and the land is conveyed to another. Baker *v.* Vining, 30 Maine, 121; Stevens *v.* Stevens, 70 Maine, 92. It may be paid by the cestui que trust himself. It may be paid by another for him. It may be paid for him by the trustee. Page *v.* Page, 8 N. H. 187; Boyd *v.* McLean, 1 Johns. Ch. 542; Kendall *v.* Mann, 11 Allen, 15. But the money must belong to the cestui que trust in specie, or by its payment by the hands of another he must incur an obligation to repay, so that the consideration actually moves from him at the time. He may take money from his purse, or he may borrow it, and he may borrow it from the trustee. And if the lender pays the money borrowed for the borrower, the borrower pays it. The test is whose money pays the consideration for the purchase. The trust arises from the circumstance that the money of the real purchaser and not that of the grantee in the deed formed the consideration of the purchase. The plaintiff says the money was a loan to him. If by force of the loan the borrower became bound by law to repay, then a resulting trust arose, even if the money did not pass through the plaintiff's hands. And from the use of the term "loan," in its ordinary signification, the law implies a promise to repay. And if the cestui que trust is bound to repay, it matters not whether it is by implied or by express promise.

If, on the other hand, as the defendants claim, it appears, assuming the evidence of the plaintiff as a whole to be true, that John J. Coney advanced the $1100 for the plaintiff, with the understanding that it should be paid back out of the rents, and without any obligation on the part of the plaintiff to repay, and with the agreement that one-half of the property should belong to the plaintiff when the advance was repaid, no trust of any kind arose. No express trust, because not in writing. No implied trust, because the plaintiff paid nothing.

Now what was the fact? The question was submitted to a jury who found for the plaintiff. The presiding justice found and decreed for the plaintiff. All this gives the plaintiff a strong advantage. The question now is, — Is the decision of the presiding justice as to the facts clearly wrong? If not it must be affirmed. Young v. Witham, 75 Maine, 536; Paul v. Frye, 80 Maine, 26; Gilpatrick v. Glidden, 81 Maine, 137. There was sufficient evidence to support the finding that the transaction was a loan, and that the plaintiff was bound to repay, unless its effect is destroyed by the evidence given by plaintiff and one or more witnesses that Coney said " he would take it (the $1100) out of the rents." Whether, in view of this and the other language used by the parties, it was mutually understood by the parties that Coney was to take the money out of the rents alone, without any obligation of the plaintiff to pay, or whether it was understood that it was a loan and the plaintiff was bound to pay, and the words used were simply expressive of the expectation that plaintiff's part of the rents which would be received by Coney would be enough to pay the plaintiff's debt to him, is the question here. The language is susceptible of either construction. The mutual understanding of the parties at the time must control.

It would serve no useful purpose to comment at length upon the evidence. But after a careful examination of the whole record, we are of opinion that the evidence warrants the conclusion that the decree should be sustained.

Decree below affirmed, with additional costs.[1]

[1] See Kauffman v. Kauffman, 266 Pa. 270.

See also the following cases in which the purchase price was advanced by the grantee as a loan. Pollak v. Millsap, 219 Ala. 273; Murchison v. Murchison, 156 Ark. 403; Breitenbucher v. Oppenheim, 160 Cal. 98; Scott v. Beach, 172 Ill. 273; Hansen v. Hall Mfg. Co., 196 Iowa 1; Miller v. Miller, 101 Md. 600; McDonough v. O'Neil, 113 Mass. 92; Fagen v. Falvey, 96 N. J. Eq. 461, 98 N. J. Eq. 411; Boyd v. M'Lean, 1 Johns. Ch. (N. Y.) 582; Gates v. Keichline, 282 Pa. 584; Raines v. Raines, 96 W. Va. 65.

The same result has been reached where the grantee pays part of the purchase price by way of loan and the borrower pays the balance. Parks v. Parks, 179 Cal. 472; Stern v. Howell, 160 Ga. 261; Wallace v. Carpenter, 85 Ill. 590; Levy v. Ryland, 32 Nev. 460; Cutler v. Tuttle, 19 N. J. Eq. 549; Raines v. Raines, 96 W. Va. 65.

Where the grantee pays the whole purchase price, partly by way of loan and partly on his own account, there is a resulting trust *pro tanto*. Towle v. Wadsworth, 147 Ill. 80; Holliday v. Perry, 38 Ind. App. 588.

The grantee cannot be compelled to convey the property until the loan is paid. He holds upon "a resulting trust in the nature of a mortgage." Pollak v. Millsap, 219 Ala. 273. See Miller v. Miller, 101 Md. 600.

See 42 A. L. R. 10, 21; 54 A. L. R. 1195.

Contract to re-sell. If the grantee does not lend the purchase price but merely makes an oral contract to re-sell the land, the oral agreement is unenforceable under the Statute of Frauds. Pumphrey v. Furlow, 144 Ark. 219; Walter v. Klock, 55 Ill. 362; Farnham v. Clements, 51 Me. 426; Southwick v. Spevak, 252 Mass. 354; McDonald v. Conway, 254 Mass. 429; Longdon v. Clouse, 1 Atl. 600 (Pa. 1885); Fogel v. Schall, 4 Atl. 339 (Pa. 1886); Pinnock v. Clough, 16 Vt. 500. See 42 A. L. R. 13.

Intention of grantee to make a gift. If the grantee pays the purchase price intending to make a gift to a third person, it has been held that no resulting trust arises. Crawford v. Manson, 82 Ga. 118; Thorne v. Thorne, 18 Ind. 462; Carson v. Potter, 18 Pa. 457; Fidelity Ins. Trust & Safe Deposit Co. v.

DAVIS v. DOWNER.

SUPREME JUDICIAL COURT, MASSACHUSETTS. 1912.

210 Mass. 573.

BILL IN EQUITY, filed in the Superior Court on August 4, 1908, by Henry O. Davis of Gloucester against Flora Downer, the plaintiff's sister, Iretta Davis, the plaintiff's mother, and Oscar S. Davis, the plaintiff's brother and former partner, with a prayer for a decree that the two lots of land mentioned in the opinion, which were conveyed to the defendant Downer by the defendant Iretta Davis, were held by the defendant Downer for the use and benefit of the partnership consisting of the plaintiff and the defendant Oscar S. Davis, and that the defendant Downer be ordered to convey to the plaintiff one undivided half of said lots subject to any existing incumbrances thereon.

The answers of the defendants, as amended, set up the statute of frauds.

In the Superior Court the case was referred to William Perry, Esquire, as master, and later was heard by *Schofield*, J., who overruled exceptions to the master's report and made a final decree confirming the master's report as to all matters of fact contained therein and ordering that the bill be dismissed. The plaintiff appealed. The material facts found by the master are stated in substance in the opinion.

RUGG, C. J. This is a suit in equity by which the plaintiff seeks to establish the right of a partnership, composed of himself and his brother Oscar, to the conveyance of two parcels of real estate. The two parcels are known respectively as the "factory lot" and the "home lot." The master's findings of facts must be taken as final, the evidence not being reported.

The title to the "factory lot" was taken in the name of Iretta Davis in 1897. The purchase price was $250, of which $50 was paid in cash by the partnership, and the balance by two mortgages, each for $100, executed by Iretta Davis. It was the oral understanding that she held title in trust for the benefit of the firm, and would convey it to the firm at any time on demand. In March,

---

Moore, 194 Pa. 617. But see *contra,* Dudley v. Bachelder, 53 Me. 403; Hughes v. McDougall, 142 Md. 1; Getman v. Getman, 1 Barb. Ch. (N. Y.) 499 (*semble*); Beck's Ex'rs v. Graybill, 28 Pa. 66.

On the question of imposing a constructive trust upon the purchaser of property who orally promises the owner of the property that he will reconvey it, see Hartzell v. Whitmore, 271 Pa. 575, *ante.*

As to the effect of a fiduciary relationship between the grantee and the person for whom he agrees to hold the property, see Harrop v. Cole, 85 N. J. Eq. 32, *post.*

1901, the mortgages were paid by the firm. A factory was built upon the land by the firm wholly with its money, with an exception so trifling as to be negligible. These facts are sufficient to establish a resulting trust under the well recognized equitable principle, that where one pays for real estate but the conveyance is to another, a resulting trust arises in favor of the one who pays the purchase price against the grantee named in the deed, the latter being treated as subject to all the obligations of a trustee, notwithstanding the statute of frauds. . . .

The application of the principle just stated is not affected by the circumstance that at the time of the original purchase the grantee executed mortgages for a part of the purchase price. This was done upon the understanding that the mortgages should be paid by the partnership, an agreement which was carried out, and the grantee was thereby exonerated from all liability, and the entire consideration really was paid by the partners. It was the equivalent of a loan of credit by the grantee for the benefit of persons paying for the purchase. It can stand on no different ground from a loan of money. McDonough v. O'Niel, 113 Mass. 92. It follows that the rule of McGowan v. McGowan, 14 Gray, 119, Dudley v. Dudley, 176 Mass. 34, Kennerson v. Nash, 208 Mass. 393, and other like decisions, to the effect that, where two or more persons contribute indiscriminately to the purchase price without agreement as to the proportion of interest to be held by each and the title is taken by one, no trust results in favor of the others, does not govern the case at bar. . . .

The decree dismissing the bill is reversed, and the form of the remedial decree to be entered in accordance with this opinion may be fixed in the Superior Court.

So ordered.[1]

[1] If the grantee gives his note for the purchase price with the understanding that the note shall be paid by a third person, the grantee holds upon a resulting trust for the third person. Kronheim v. Johnson, 7 Ch. D. 60; Haliday v. Haliday, 11 F.(2d) 565; Breitenbucher v. Oppenheim, 160 Cal. 98; Fleming v. McHale, 47 Ill. 282; Skahen v. Irving, 206 Ill. 597; Dudley v. Bachelder, 53 Me. 403; Miller v. Miller, 101 Md. 600; Crowley v. Crowley, 72 N. H. 241; Cleavenger v. Felton, 46 W. Va. 249. *Contra:* Lincoln v. Chamberlain, 61 Cal. App. 399.

If the third person agreed to contribute in part to the payment of the note, a resulting trust *pro tanto* arises. Heflin v. Heflin, 208 Ala. 69 (1/2); Gerety v. O'Sheehan, 9 Cal. App. 447 (3/10); Fox v. Shanley, 94 Conn. 350 (39/55); Towle v. Wadsworth, 147 Ill. 80; Burleigh v. White, 64 Me. 23; Wood v. White, 123 Me. 139 (1/2); Rose v. Hegeman, 2 Edw. Ch. (N. Y.) 373 (1/2); Kernkamp v. Schulz, 44 N. D. 20 (1/2).

The mere fact that a third person subsequently paid the grantee's note is insufficient to raise a resulting trust in his favor. Olcott v. Bynum, 17 Wall. (U. S.) 44, 59; Ducie v. Ford, 138 U. S. 587, *aff'g* 9 Mont. 233; Allen v. Caylor, 120 Ala. 251; Reeves v. Reeves, 165 Ark. 505; Gales v. Stokeley, 151 Ga. 718; Pickler v. Pickler, 180 Ill. 168; Westerfield v. Kimmer, 82 Ind. 365; Wallaces v. Marshall, 9 B. Mon. (Ky.) 148; Buck v. Swazey, 35 Me. 41; Bush v. Bush,

McGOWAN v. McGOWAN.

SUPREME JUDICIAL COURT, MASSACHUSETTS. 1859.

14 Gray 119.

ACTION of contract, by the heirs of John McGowan, praying for relief in equity, to enforce a resulting trust. The plaintiff alleged that on the 15th of December 1851 John McGowan purchased certain real estate of Duncan McKendrick; that "the consideration paid was three hundred and twenty dollars, and also twenty four dollars more agreed at the time to be paid and paid by said John to McKendrick; that said John did not take the deed in his own name, but had it conveyed from said McKendrick to said John's brother, James McGowan, who took the said property in trust to hold the same to the use of said John and his heirs and assigns, though it did not appear in the deed that said James took said property in trust as aforesaid, but the deed showed an absolute conveyance to said James in fee;" that on the 19th of said December said James, at John's request, made a note for $320, secured by mortgage of the premises, to Samuel B. King of Taunton, payable in five years, with interest annually; "that at the time of the purchase of the property, and at the time of said mortgage, it was agreed and understood by James and John that said John was to proceed and erect a dwelling-house on said premises, and whatever other buildings he chose for his residence, and that said James should hold the same in trust for said John as aforesaid;" that John, within two years, proceeded to erect a dwelling-house on the premises at an expense of $1100, and from the time of the completion of the house until his death in June 1858 occupied the premises with his family, and leased a part of the house and received the rents to his own use, and " also paid the annual interest on said mortgage to King as aforesaid, furnishing his brother James with the money for that purchase;" that on the 7th of June 1852 James conveyed most of his real estate, including this land, with notice of the trust, to his brother Patrick, who, on the next day, conveyed the same to Catharine McGowan, wife of James, with like notice; that Catharine and James, at the request of John, made a note of $400 and interest, secured by mortgage on the premises, to Abiathar K. Williams, in payment for lumber furnished by him and used in building the dwelling-house; that John regularly paid the interest on this note during his lifetime, and that all the labor and materials for the house were furnished at John's

---

134 Miss. 523; Sayre v. Townsends, 15 Wend. (N. Y.) 647; De Roboam v Schmidtlin, 50 Ore. 388; Allen v. Allen, 101 Tex. 362; Wilder's Executrix v Wilder, 75 Vt. 178; Moss v. Moss, 88 W. Va. 135.

request and charge, and paid for by him; " and the said James and Catharine and Patrick never, during the lifetime of said John, paid from their or either of their own proper funds, any part or portion of the interest on said mortgage, or of the sums expended for the labor and materials aforesaid; nor did they expend anything except moneys furnished by said John; and during the lifetime of said John, by their acts and admissions, always acknowledged that they held said premises upon the trust aforesaid, to wit, as trustee and trustees of said John McGowan; but that since the decease of said John, said Catharine claims and pretends that the whole of said property belongs to her absolutely, and that she does not hold it in trust as aforesaid; and she and her said husband threatened and have attempted to eject the plaintiffs from said premises, and do claim to receive the rents and profits of the premises, and have received a portion of them."

The defendants demurred generally.

HOAR, J. The plaintiffs seek, by their bill, to enforce the execution of a resulting trust. The case made by the bill is undoubtedly one of considerable hardship; but we are unable, upon careful examination, to perceive that it admits of any relief from a court of equity, consistently with a due regard to the well settled principles of law. The whole consideration for the purchase of the estate was three hundred and forty four dollars, of which three hundred and twenty dollars was paid by the note of James McGowan, under whom the defendants claim, and to whom the conveyance was made; and twenty four dollars agreed to be paid in labor by John McGowan, the father of the plaintiffs, which was afterward paid by him. The subsequent transactions between the parties, and the improvements made upon the estate, being all proved by parol evidence, and proceeding from contracts not in writing, do not change their original relation to the title.

There is no doubt of the correctness of the doctrine, that where the purchase money is paid by one person, and the conveyance taken by another, there is a resulting trust created by implication of law in favor of the former. And where a part of the purchase money is paid by one, and the whole title is taken by the other, a resulting trust *pro tanto* may in like manner, under some circumstances, be created.

But in the latter case we believe it to be well settled that the part of the purchase money paid by him in whose favor the resulting trust is sought to be enforced, must be shown to have been paid for some specific part, or distinct interest in the estate; for " some aliquot part," as it is sometimes expressed; that is, for a specific share, as a tenancy in common or joint tenancy of one half, one quarter, or other particular fraction of the whole; or for a particular interest, as a life estate, or tenancy for years, or remainder, in the whole; and that a general contribution of a sum of money toward the entire purchase is not sufficient. Crop *v.* Norton, 2 Atk. 74. Sayre *v.* Townsends, 15 Wend. 647. White *v.* Carpenter, 2 Paige, 217. Perry *v.* McHenry, 13 Ill. 227. Baker *v.* Vining, 30 Maine, 121.

The case of Jenkins *v.* Eldredge, 3 Story, 181, might be considered a conflicting authority; but, beside the question how far the doctrines of that case can be reconciled with the general current of decisions in this commonwealth, the ground upon which Mr. Justice Story proceeded with the most confidence in his elaborate judgment in that cause seems undoubtedly to have been, that the agreement of Eldredge to make and preserve as evidence a written declaration of trust, which he afterwards neglected and refused to make, would constitute a case of constructive fraud, against which equity would relieve.

In the case at bar, there is no allegation that any division of the property was contemplated by the parties; or that the work done by John McGowan in part payment for the conveyance was intended as anything but a small contribution toward the entire purchase.

Demurrer sustained and bill dismissed.[1]

SKEHILL *v.* ABBOTT.

SUPREME JUDICIAL COURT, MASSACHUSETTS. 1903.

184 Mass. 145.

BILL IN EQUITY, filed July 24, 1902, by the widow of Patrick Skehill, against the children of her late husband by a former marriage, to establish a resulting trust in certain real estate in Watertown.

In the Superior Court *Hardy,* J., found that a resulting trust had been established, and made a decree that two fifths of the property on Royal Street in Watertown standing in the name of the late Patrick Skehill should be set apart for the sole use and benefit of the plaintiff by partition, or, if partition should not be practicable, that the whole property should be sold and two fifths of the proceeds paid to the plaintiff.

The defendants appealed. The judge made a finding of facts,

[1] Olcott *v.* Bynum, 17 Wall. (U. S.) 44; Lane *v.* Lane, 149 Ga. 581; Brooks *v.* Gretz, 323 Ill. 161; Stelling *v.* Stelling, 323 Ill. 122 (intended trust for third person); Andrew *v.* Andrew, 114 Iowa 524; Hinkle *v.* Hinkle, 236 S. W. 30 (Mo. 1921); Reynolds *v.* Morris, 17 Ohio St. 510; Barger *v.* Barger, 30 Ore. 268; McDonald *v.* McClarren, 280 Pa. 243; O'Donnell *v.* White, 18 R. I. 659; Billings *v.* Clinton, 6 S. C. 90; Watts Bros. & Co. *v.* Frith, 79 W. Va. 89, *accord.*

In some of these cases parents and adult children have pooled their earnings and the fund is ultimately used in buying land, title usually being taken in the name of the father. See as typical, Onasch *v.* Zinkel, 213 Ill. 119.

called memorandum for decree, and there also was a report of evidence by a commissioner appointed under Chancery Rule 35.

LORING, J. This is a bill in equity by a widow who claims an undivided two fifths interest in a parcel of land by way of a resulting trust. The title to the land was taken in the name of her husband, now deceased, but she contributed $1,000 of the $2,500 which was paid for it. The judge who tried the case found these facts: The plaintiff was sixty years old, was not able to read or write, and was ignorant of business methods and the meaning of legal instruments. It was understood between the plaintiff and her husband that she should have the benefit of the $1,000 contributed by her to provide for her old age, and it was at first suggested that this should be effected by the husband's taking the title and giving a mortgage to secure the payment of the $1,000. This was abandoned on the husband's reporting that a lawyer who was consulted by him had said that there could be no mortgage between husband and wife. The plaintiff then said that she wanted her name to be in the deed, and this was agreed to by the husband. In addition to these facts found by the judge there was evidence that the plaintiff not only stipulated that her name should appear in the deed, but what she insisted on was that it should appear in the deed for her interest in the property. The judge further found that in place of keeping his agreement the husband took the whole title in his own name, and the title remained in him until he died; and that although the plaintiff did not stipulate for an undivided two fifths interest in terms, yet that was what was understood between the plaintiff and her husband, and it was on that understanding that she parted with her money. We are of opinion that this brings the case within Hayward v. Cain, 110 Mass. 273, and takes it out of McGowan v. McGowan, 14 Gray, 119, Snow v. Paine, 114 Mass. 520, Bourke v. Callanan, 160 Mass. 195, and Dudley v. Dudley, 176 Mass. 34. See also Bancroft v. Curtis, 108 Mass. 47; McDonough v. O'Niel, 113 Mass. 92.

The defendants contend that unless a plaintiff has stipulated for such a fraction as is contained in the whole without a remainder no resulting trust can be created, that is to say, if one person contributes $500 where the purchase money is $2,500, stipulating for an undivided fifth interest, a resulting trust is raised in his favor, but if he has parted with $1,000 for the same purchase, stipulating for an undivided two fifths interest, he would not be entitled to anything by way of a resulting trust. They arrive at this extraordinary conclusion by finding first that the court in some of the cases cited above has said that it is not enough for a plaintiff to have contributed to the purchase money, but he must have stipulated for an aliquot interest in the property; and then by finding that it is laid down in the dictionaries that the word "aliquot" means something contained in another a certain number of times without leaving a remainder.

Whatever definition may be given in the dictionaries, the word " aliquot " was used in these opinions to mean a " particular fraction of the whole," as distinguished from a general contribution to the purchase money. To that effect see McGowan v. McGowan, 14 Gray, 119, 121.

The other point made by the defendants is that the judge was wrong in his findings of fact. There was a direct conflict between the witnesses on the question whether the plaintiff's $1000 was lent to the husband or was contributed for an interest in the property. The judge saw the witnesses and heard the testimony of the plaintiff. It is enough that his decision was not plainly wrong. Dickinson v. Todd, 172 Mass. 183, and cases cited.

Decree affirmed.[1]

[1] In the following cases where there was an express oral agreement that the contributor was to have an interest in the land proportional to his contribution, it was held that a resulting trust *pro tanto* arose. Breitenbucher v. Oppenheim, 160 Cal. 98 (85/1000); Gerety v. O'Sheehan, 9 Cal. App. 447 (3/10); Madsen v. Madsen, 35 Cal. App. 487 (12/27); Neathery v. Neathery, 114 Va. 650 (252/588).

In the following cases where the contributor paid an aliquot part of the purchase price but no express agreement as to his share was shown, it was held that a resulting trust *pro tanto* arose. Beadle v. Seat, 102 Ala. 532; Case v. Codding, 38 Cal. 191 (1/2); Hayward v. Cain, 110 Mass. 273; Baumgartner v. Gussfeld, 38 Mo. 36 (1/2); Collins v. Corson, 30 Atl. 862 (N. J. Ch. 1894) (1/2); Hopkinson v. Dumas, 42 N. H. 296 (1/5 to each of 5); O'Donnell v. McCool, 89 Wash. 537 (1/2).

The same result was reached in the following cases where the contribution was not strictly an aliquot part but it appeared that no loan or gift was intended. Lindley v. Blumberg, 7 Cal. App. 140 (16/35); Fox v. Shanley, 94 Conn. 350 (39/55); Latham v. Henderson, 47 Ill. 185 (12/25); Harris v. McIntyre, 118 Ill. 275 (16/21); Derry v. Derry, 98 Ind. 319 (apparently 53/225); Clark v. Clark, 43 Vt. 685 (3/7); Currence v. Ward, 43 W. Va. 367. See also Stark's Heirs v. Cannady, 3 Litt. (Ky.) 399.

In the following cases it was said that there was a resulting trust in proportion to the amount contributed, nothing being said as to any agreement or as to what the contributed amount was. Tebbetts v. Tilton, 31 N. H. 273; Hall v. Young, 37 N. H. 134 (contributions by others than the grantee); McGee v. Wells, 52 S. C. 472; Penman v. Blount, 264 S. W. 169 (Tex. Civ. App. 1924).

In the following cases the same result was reached although there was no evidence as to the intention of the parties other than the fact of payment. The Venture, [1908] P. 218 (11/21) (ship); Camden v. Bennett, 64 Ark. 155 (7/10); Crawford v. Manson, 82 Ga. 118 (17/35); Hinshaw v. Russell, 280 Ill. 235 (29/124); Crawford v. Hurst, 299 Ill. 503, 307 Ill. 243 (47/52); Lowell v. Lowell, 185 Iowa 508 (18/29); Stevenson v. Smith, 189 Mo. 447 (5/16); Larrick v. Heatham, 288 Mo. 370 (63/88) (*semble*); Baylor v. Hopf, 81 Tex. 637 (48/169) (*semble*).

If a fund owned by two or more persons in common is paid for land, and title is taken in the name of one of them with the consent of the others, presumptively a resulting trust arises in favor of the others *pro tanto,* so that each will have a beneficial interest in the land purchased corresponding to his interest in the fund. Jones v. Jenkinson, 316 Ill. 264; O'Brien v. O'Brien,

Section V.

Where a Person Acquires an Interest in Property in Regard to which, by Reason of his Fiduciary Position, he owes a Duty to Another.

HARTMAN v. HARTLE.

COURT OF CHANCERY, NEW JERSEY. 1923.

95 N. J. Eq. 123.

FOSTER, V. C. Mrs. Dorothea Geick died testate on April 8th, 1921, leaving five children, one of them being the complainant. She named her two sons-in-law executors and they qualified. Among other matters the will expressly directed her executors to sell her real estate and to divide the proceeds equally among her children.

On February 9th, 1922, the executors sold part of the real estate known as the farm, at public auction, for $3,900, to one of the testatrix's sons, Lewis Geick, who actually bought the property for his sister, Josephine Dieker, who is the wife of one of the executors.

On April 11th, 1922, Mrs. Dieker sold the property to the defendant Mike Contra (and another who is not a party to the action) for $5,500, part cash and part on mortgage.

The executors settled their final accounts on April 21st, 1922, and at or about that time complainant expressed to the deputy surrogate her dissatisfaction with the price realized from the sale of the farm.

About March 21st, 1923, she filed her bill in this cause, charging the sale of the farm to have been improperly and fraudulently made by the executors, to Mrs. Dieker, and further charging that Mrs. Dieker and the other heirs of the testatrix had agreed at the sale, because of slow bidding and inadequate price, to have the farm bid in for the benefit of all the heirs.

At the hearing each and every one of these allegations were shown to be untrue by the great weight of the testimony; and this proof was so conclusive that it left complainant with but one contention to sustain her case, viz., that under the law the sale of the property by the executors and trustees to Mrs. Dieker, the wife of one of them, without previous authority from the court, was illegal and void, and that it should be set aside and the farm resold, or if that be found impossible because of the sale made by Mrs. Dieker to Contra, an innocent purchaser, then that complainant should have paid to her one-fifth of the $1,600 profits realized by Mrs. Dieker from the sale of the property.

---

256 Mass. 308; Wilson v. Wilson, 64 Mont. 533; Stutzman v. Gearhart, 112 Neb. 827; Fay v. Fay, 50 N. J. Eq. 260; Speer v. Burns, 173 Pa. 77; Addison v. Ball, 262 S. W. 877 (Tex. Civ. App. 1924).

It is the settled law of this state that a trustee cannot purchase from himself at his own sale, and that his wife is subject to the same disability, unless leave so to do has been previously obtained under an order of the court. Scott *v.* Gamble, 9 N. J. Eq. 218; Bassett *v.* Shoemaker, 46 N. J. Eq. 538; Bechtold *v.* Read, 49 N. J. Eq. 111. And under the circumstances of the case complainant cannot be charged with laches under the view expressed in Bechtold *v.* Read, *supra.*

In view of the fact that the property is now owned by innocent purchasers a resale cannot be ordered, but as an alternative Mrs. Dieker and the executors will be held to account for complainant's one-fifth share of the profits made on the resale of the property under the authority of Marshall *v.* Carson, 38 N. J. Eq. 250, and a decree will be advised to that effect.[1]

[1] As to the purchase of trust property by the trustee from himself or his co-trustee, see Fox *v.* Mackreth, 2 Bro. C. C. 400, 2 Cox 320; Whichcote *v.* Lawrence, 3 Ves. 740; Campbell *v.* Walker, 5 Ves. 678; *Ex parte* Lacey, 6 Ves. 625; Delves *v.* Gray, [1902] 2 Ch. 606; Wright *v.* Morgan, [1926] A. C. 788; Andrews *v.* Hobson's Adm'r, 23 Ala. 219, 235; Broder *v.* Conklin, 121 Cal. 282; Bennett *v.* Weber, 323 Ill. 283; Clay *v.* Thomas, 178 Ky. 199; Hayes *v.* Hall, 188 Mass. 510.

The principle is applicable to other fiduciaries as well as to trustees. *Re* B. Solomon & Co., 268 Fed. 108, 112 (stockbroker); Hall *v.* Paine, 224 Mass. 62 (stockbroker); Witherington *v.* Nickerson, 256 Mass. 351 (guardian); Dixmoor Golf Club *v.* Evans, 325 Ill. 612 (corporate director).

As to a sale to the trustee's wife, see Hayes *v.* Hall, 188 Mass. 510; Bassett *v.* Shoemaker, 46 N. J. Eq. 538; Davoue *v.* Fanning, 2 Johns. Ch. (N. Y.) 252; Scottish-American Mtg. Co. *v.* Clowney, 70 S. C. 229; Perry, Trusts, sec. 195.

"The *cestuis que trust,* if they represent the whole beneficial interest, can insist upon a reconveyance of the property from the purchasing trustee, or from any person who purchased from him with notice or knowledge that he has purchased from himself; but the purchase money must be repaid with interest, and, when there has been no actual fraud, permanent improvements must be paid for; and the purchaser must account for rents, profits, and waste. If the *cestuis que trust* do not wish a reconveyance, the property can be put up for sale either absolutely or at a minimum price. If the purchasing trustee has sold the property, he can be held to account as trustee for the price he has received; or if the property remains unsold in his hands, the *cestuis que trust,* if they so elect, can compel him to account for its actual value, at the time of the purchase." Morse *v.* Hill, 136 Mass. 60, 64. See Hayes *v.* Hall, 188 Mass. 510; *Ex parte* Lacey, 6 Ves. 625.

The trustee may purchase the trust property by permission of the court. Corbin *v.* Baker, 167 N. Y. 128.

The trustee may purchase the trust property if authorized by the terms of the trust to do so. *Re* Sykes, [1909] 2 Ch. 241.

On the question whether the trustee may properly purchase the trust property after he has ceased to be trustee, see Wright *v.* Morgan, [1926] A. C. 788; Clark *v.* Delano, 205 Mass. 224.

For further cases, see Perry, Trusts, sec. 195; Underhill, Trusts, art. 58; 1 A. L. R. 747.

Effect of beneficiary's consent. If with the consent of the *cestui que trust* the trustee acquires an interest in the trust property, the transaction is voidable by the *cestui que trust* if, but only if, the trustee failed to disclose material facts or the transaction was unfair to the *cestui que trust.* Coles *v.* Tre-

CORNET v. CORNET, 269 Mo. 298 (1916): The defendant trustee was in the habit of purchasing securities in his own name, paying the purchase price out of his own funds, and afterward distributing the securities at cost to various estates held by him in trust or to his own account as seemed to him desirable. It was held that this practice was wrongful and that the defendant was liable for the loss where the securities depreciated. BROWN, C., said (p. 322):

"In making this investment the defendant violated various rules by which equity seeks to secure trust funds from mismanagement and waste. One of these rules is that the trustee who invests such funds in his own name becomes personally responsible. This is only a corollary of the rule that if he deals with the estate on his own account it must be at his own risk. Were he permitted to do otherwise it would place before him the constant temptation to make the trust fund a dumping ground for his own unsatisfactory ventures." [1]

BAUGH'S EXECUTOR v. WALKER.

SUPREME COURT OF APPEALS, VIRGINIA. 1883.

77 Va. 99.

LACY, J. . . . In this case the trustee paid $900.87 to lift a lien from the trust estate, but he paid it at a time when Confederate money was the sole currency of the country, and if it did effect the raising of a gold debt of that amount from the trust estate, which is admitted, such an advantage cannot enure to him personally, but must be credited to the trust estate with which he was dealing; but he is entitled to receive back, upon the rule of compensation, the value of what he paid. It is not perfectly clear when he paid it, as to the precise time; the deed for his benefit was written and dated November 5, 1862. Delivered by intendment of law on the 22d of

---

cothick, 9 Ves. 234; Mills v. Mills, 63 Fed. 511; Cole v. Stokes, 113 N. C. 270. See Hodge v. Mackintosh, 248 Mass. 181 (specific performance denied).

The *cestui que trust* may at his option ratify a sale by the trustee to himself. If there are several beneficiaries, any one of them may avoid the transaction although the others are willing to ratify it. Morse v. Hill, 136 Mass. 60.

In Colburn v. Hodgdon, 241 Mass. 183, 191, it was held that there is no fiduciary relationship between the trustee and the settlor prior to the creation of the trust; and that if a person induces another person to convey property to him upon trust for the transferor, the transfer cannot be set aside merely because the transferee did not make full disclosure of facts known to him.

[1] In Kelly v. First Minneapolis Trust Co., 178 Minn. 215, 14 Minn. L. Rev. 308, a trust company purchased for a trust of which it was trustee certain securities owned by it. It was held that the company was accountable for the amount of the trust funds invested in these securities, although a statute authorized a trust company to invest trust funds in securities "then held by it or specially procured by it." See Larson v. Security Bank & Trust Co., 178 Minn. 209; Matter of Union Trust Co., 219 N. Y. 514; Matter of Thomson, 135 N. Y. Misc. 62. See New York Banking Law, sec. 188.

August, 1863, it might be contended that he did not pay this money until this deed was delivered, but the court below has fixed the date of its payment at the date of the deed, and it cannot be presumed to have been paid before that time. But there is one circumstance in this record which fixes beyond all question the fact that it was paid in Confederate money. It was paid to take in John Baugh's note to Wilson, but was not paid to Wilson. Wilson had sold the note, and the trustee bought from the assignee of Wilson, and evidence in the cause shows what this assignee paid Wilson, the principal of the note being about $800. Wilson received $200 in money, and a horse which he allowed $600 for. It is very improbable that this transaction was on a gold basis, and this was antecedent to the purchase by the trustee, and it would be most inequitable to allow this trustee, by the payment of so small a value, to raise so large a claim against his *cestui que trust*. The court scaled this debt at three for one, and under the circumstances of this case, that action ought not to be disturbed.[1] . . .

MAGRUDER v. DRURY.

Supreme Court of the United States. 1914.

235 U. S. 106.

Mr. Justice Day delivered the opinion of the court. . . .

The next exception involves the allowance of commissions on the notes purchased from Mr. Drury's firm. The contention before the auditor was that one trustee had received compensation in connection with the handling of these investments, and that that should be taken into account. As to this exception, the auditor finds that "the fact clearly appears from the testimony that Arms & Drury as real estate brokers, made loans on trust notes, upon which loans they were paid by the borrowers a commission ranging from one to two per cent., according to the circumstances of the case, many being building loans; that subsequently as notes of the trust estate were paid off Mr. Drury would reinvest the monies of the estate in trust notes held by Arms & Drury, paying the face value and accrued interest on the notes so purchased." As a matter of law, the auditor concluded: "No profit was made by the firm of Arms & Drury on the sales of the notes to the trustees. . . . The transactions of Arms & Drury with the trustees were in the regular course of their business, in which they had their own monies invested. They cost the estate not a penny more than if the transactions had been with some other firm or individual. If the firm of Arms & Drury, out of their

---

[1] See M'Clanahan's Heirs v. Henderson's Heirs, 2 A. K. Marsh. (Ky.) 388; Baker v. Springfield, etc., Ry. Co., 86 Mo. 75. Compare Fulton v. Whitney, 66 N. Y. 548; Kimball v. Ranney, 122 Mich. 160; Haight v. Pearson, 11 Utah 51. See Perry, Trusts, sec. 428.

own monies, made loans on promissory notes, upon which loans were paid by the borrower the customary brokerages, those were profits on their own funds, in which this estate could have no interest, and in which it could acquire no interest by reason of the subsequent purchase of those notes by the trustees for their real value, any more than could any of the purchasers of such notes from Arms & Drury claim such an interest. No charge of malfeasance or misfeasance is made against the trustees or that by reason of these transactions the trustees benefited in any manner out of the money of this estate. On the contrary, the relation of the firm of Arms & Drury to Drury and Maddox, trustees, benefited the estate, by enabling the trustees at all times to make immediate reinvestment of its funds, without loss of income, and by enabling the trustees to at all times readily procure re-investments without payment of brokerage, a brokerage not uncommonly charged the lender for placing his money, as well as the borrower for procuring his loan in times of stringency. The application of the well known rule in equity should rather, therefore, be in favor of the trustees than against them with respect to these transactions. The objection narrows itself to a claim that Drury by reason of his position as trustee, should in addition to the benefit of his valuable services, commercial knowledge, and business acumen, make the estate a gift of profits on his individual monies, to which the estate is in no wise entitled, and to which it could not make a semblance of reasonable claim, had the trustees been other than Drury or the agents of the estate been other than Arms and Drury." This view seems to have met with the approval of the Supreme Court, and a like view was taken by the Court of Appeals of the District of Columbia, 37 D. C. App. 519, *supra*.

It is a well settled rule that a trustee can make no profit out of his trust. The rule in such cases springs from his duty to protect the interests of the estate, and not to permit his personal interest to in any wise conflict with his duty in that respect. The intention is to provide against any possible selfish interest exercising an influence which can interfere with the faithful discharge of the duty which is owing in a fiduciary capacity. "It therefore prohibits a party from purchasing on his own account that which his duty or trust requires him to sell on account of another, and from purchasing on account of another that which he sells on his own account. In effect, he is not allowed to unite the two opposite characters of buyer and seller, because his interests, when he is the seller or buyer on his own account, are directly conflicting with those of the person on whose account he buys or sells." Michoud *v.* Girod, 4 How. 503, 555.

It makes no difference that the estate was not a loser in the transaction or that the commission was no more than the services were reasonably worth. It is the relation of the trustee to the estate which prevents his dealing in such way as to make a personal profit for himself. The findings show that the firm of which Mr. Drury was a member, in making the loans evidenced by these notes, was allowed a commission of one to two per cent. This profit was in fact realized when the notes were turned over to the estate at face value and accrued interest. The value of the notes when they were turned over depended on the responsibility and security back of them. When the notes were sold to the estate it took the risk of payment without loss. While no wrong was intended, and none was in fact done to the estate, we think nevertheless that upon the principles governing the duty of a trustee, the contention that this profit could not be taken by Mr. Drury owing to his relation to the estate, should have been sustained.

We find no other error in the proceedings of the Court of Appeals, but for the reason last stated, its decision must be reversed, and the cause remanded to that court with directions to remand the cause to the Supreme Court of the District of Columbia for further proceedings in accordance with this opinion.

Reversed.[1]

WILLIAMS *v.* BARTON.

HIGH COURT OF JUSTICE, CHANCERY DIVISION. 1927.

[1927] 2 Ch. 9.

WITNESS ACTION.

The facts were stated in the judgment as follows: —

" This is an action by one of the two trustees of a will against his co-trustee, by which it is sought to make the defendant accountable to the trust estate for moneys received by him from a firm of stockbrokers. The basis of the claim is that in retaining such moneys the defendant is making a profit out of his trusteeship.

The defendant was formerly a stockbroker, but ceased to be a member of the Stock Exchange in 1919. In 1920 he entered the employ of a firm of stockbrokers, George Burnand & Co., and has continued in such employment to the present time. The terms of his employment are that, on his side, he is bound to give the firm his services in connection with Bank of England transfer work; on the firm's side, they agree to pay him half the commission earned by the firm on all such work introduced by him to the firm as the firm is willing to carry out.

On the death of the testator, Sir John Roper Parkington, in 1924 it became necessary to have his securities valued, and it was at first proposed to employ for this purpose a firm of stockbrokers who had usually acted for the testator, but at the instigation of the defendant George Burnand & Co. were in fact employed to do the work. On the subsequent death of the tenant for life a similar valuation became necessary and was in fact done by George Burnand & Co.

[1] See St. Paul Trust Co. *v.* Strong, 85 Minn. 1. *Cf.* Re Sykes, [1909] 2 Ch. 241.

For the work so done the stockbrokers charged fees which were paid to them out of the testator's estate, and, in accordance with their contract with the defendant, they paid over to him one-half of the fees so earned and paid to them. The defendant took no part in making the valuations or in fixing the fees to be charged. It is claimed by the plaintiff that the moneys so paid over to the defendant and any half commission which may have been paid to him in respect of sales and purchases of trust investments must be paid to the estate."

RUSSELL, J. [after stating the facts]. It is a well established and salutary rule of equity that a trustee may not make a profit out of his trust. A person who has the management of property as a trustee is not permitted to gain any profit by availing himself of his position, and will be a constructive trustee of any such profit for the benefit of the persons equitably entitled to the property. On the same principle a trustee has no right to charge for his time and trouble. The rule is thus stated by Lord Herschell in Bray v. Ford, [1896] A. C. 44, 51: "It is an inflexible rule of a Court of Equity that a person in a fiduciary position . . . is not, unless otherwise expressly provided, entitled to make a profit; he is not allowed to put himself in a position where his interest and duty conflict." It was argued on behalf of the defendant that the case was altogether outside that rule of equity, because the sums received by the defendant were merely parts of his salary paid to him by his employers under the contract of service and were not of a character for which he was liable to account.

The point is not an easy one and there is little, if any, authority to assist in its determination. The situation is an unusual one and the contract of service presents the following peculiar features. The remuneration has no relation to the services, which the defendant has to render to his employers. The defendant, while bound to render the services, might get no remuneration at all if he introduced no work, or introduced none which was acceptable to his employers. The amount of his remuneration depends (subject to his employers' acceptance of orders) upon his own efforts, but upon efforts not in relation to the work which he is engaged to do. Any increase of his remuneration rests with him.

From this it seems to me evident that the case falls within the mischief which is sought to be prevented by the rule. The case is clearly one where his duty as trustee and his interest in an increased remuneration are in direct conflict. As a trustee it is his duty to give the estate the benefit of his unfettered advice in choosing the stockbrokers to act for the estate; as the recipient of half the fees to be earned by George Burnand & Co. on work introduced by him his obvious interest is to choose or recommend them for the job.

In the event that has happened they have been chosen, and

chosen because the defendant was a trustee, with the result that half of what the estate pays must necessarily pass through them to the defendant as part of his remuneration for other services rendered, but as an addition to the remuneration which he would otherwise have received for those self-same services. The services rendered remain unchanged, but the remuneration for them has been increased. He has increased his remuneration by virtue of his trusteeship. In my opinion this increase of remuneration is a profit made by the defendant out of and by reason of his trusteeship, which he would not have made but for his position as trustee.

Much reliance was properly placed on the decision of the Court of Appeal in *In re* Dover Coalfield Extension, Ld., [1908] 1 Ch. 65, but that case seems to me very different. At the request of the Dover company Mr. Cousins had entered into a contract with the Kent company to serve them as a director, the Kent company paying him remuneration for his services. The necessary qualification shares were provided by the Dover company, and in respect of those shares he became a trustee for the Dover company. He had not, however, used his position as a trustee for the purpose of acquiring his directorship. He had, in fact, been appointed a director before he became a trustee of the shares. The profit which he gained was not procured by him by the use of his position as trustee, but was a profit earned by reason of work which he did for the Kent company and which would not have been earned by him had he not been willing to do the work for which it was the remuneration. It was not (as in the present case) a profit acquired solely by reason of his use of his position as trustee and a profit in respect of which no extra services were rendered.

The plaintiff is entitled to the declaration asked for. If necessary, an inquiry must be directed, but if the amount can be agreed it may be inserted in the order and an order made for the payment of the agreed amount.[1]

KEECH *v.* SANDFORD.

Chancery. 1726.

Sel. Cas. Ch. 61.

A PERSON being possessed of a lease of the profits of a market devised his estate to a trustee in trust for the infant. *Before* the expiration of the term the trustee applied to the lessor for a renewal, for the benefit of the infant, which he refused, in regard that, it being

---

[1] See *Re* Francis, 74 L. J. Ch. 198; White *v.* Sherman, 168 Ill. 589 (trustee receiving commission on insurance premiums); Matter of Hirsch, 116 App. Div. 367, *aff'd* 188 N. Y. 584 (trustee of stock causing himself to be elected president and counsel). But see *Re* Dover Coalfield Extension, [1907] 2 Ch. 76, [1908] 1 Ch. 65. See Perry, Trusts, sec. 427.

only of the profits of a market, there could be no distress, and must rest singly in covenant, which the infant could not enter into.

There was clear proof of the refusal to renew for the benefit of the infant, on which the trustee gets a lease made to himself.

Bill is now brought [by the infant] to have the lease assigned to him, and for an account of the profits, on this principle, that wherever a lease is renewed by a trustee or executor, it shall be for the benefit of *cestui que use*, which principle was agreed on the other side, though endeavoured to be differenced on account of the express proof of refusal to renew to the infant.

LORD CHANCELLOR KING. I must consider this as a trust for the infant, for I very well see, if a trustee, on the refusal to renew, might have a lease to himself, few trust estates would be renewed to *cestui que use*. Though I do not say there is a fraud in this case, yet he [the trustee] should rather have let it run out than to have had the lease to himself. This may seem hard, that the trustee is the only person of all mankind who might not have the lease; but it is very proper that rule should be strictly pursued, and not in the least relaxed; for it is very obvious what would be the consequences of letting trustees have the lease on refusal to renew to *cestui que use*.

So decreed, that the lease should be assigned to the infant, and that the trustee should be indemnified from any covenants comprised in the lease, and an account of the profits made since the renewal.[1]

LURIE *v.* PINANSKI.

SUPREME JUDICIAL COURT, MASSACHUSETTS. 1913.

215 Mass. 229.

MORTON, J. This is a bill in equity for an accounting in respect of a partnership, consisting of the plaintiff, the defendant and one Silverman, in relation to certain leasehold interests. The case was sent to a master who made a report in favor of the plaintiff. A decree was entered confirming the report and ordering the defendant to pay to the plaintiff the sum of $1,041.60, with costs of suit. The defendant appealed.

The principal contention of the defendant is that the plaintiff is not entitled to relief because he himself at one time, according to the findings of the master, " asked the lessor," " without the knowledge or consent of the defendant or Silverman," " for a new lease of the Brooks' estate in his own name at an increased rent." In other words, the defendant contends that the plaintiff does not come into court with clean hands. But, to quote from Dering *v.* Winchelsea, 1 Cox, 318, 319, though a man must come into equity

[1] See *Re* Biss, [1903] 2 Ch. 40; Smyth *v.* Byrne, [1914] 1 I. R. 53; 21 L. Quar. Rev. 258.

with clean hands, " when this is said, it does not mean a general depravity; it must have an immediate and necessary relation to the equity sued for." In the present case, there was no such immediate and necessary relation between what the plaintiff did or attempted to do and what the defendant did as to render the principle applicable. If the plaintiff and the defendant had confederated together to have the defendant obtain a renewal of the lease in his own name without the knowledge of and to the exclusion of Silverman, with the agreement that any profits resulting therefrom should be divided between the plaintiff and the defendant, and the defendant for some reason had concluded to pay Silverman what would have been his share of the profits and had refused to pay the plaintiff and the plaintiff had brought a bill for an accounting, a case would have been presented for the application of the principle. But the present is not such a case. What the plaintiff did was to attempt without success to get a lease for himself without the knowledge of his copartners. And though his conduct shows a readiness on his part to circumvent his copartners if he could, that does not bring the case within the principle referred to. See Lawton v. Estes, 167 Mass. 181; Snow v. Blount, 182 Mass. 489.

Amongst other things on which the defendant relies is the statute of frauds. It is manifest that that has nothing to do with the case. Besides, it is not pleaded. The master having found that the plaintiff and defendant were partners, the defendant stood in a fiduciary relation to the plaintiff and could not clandestinely take (as the master has in effect found that he did take) a renewal of the lease for his own benefit. Leach v. Leach, 18 Pick. 68, 76. The option was clearly impressed with a trust in favor of the plaintiff. In addition to the trust arising out of the fiduciary relation created by the partnership, a part of the consideration for the option was furnished by the plaintiff under and pursuant to an understanding between the lessor and lessees, as the master has found that the lessees should have an extension of the lease. Under such circumstances, for the defendant to take the option in his own name and attempt to appropriate the profits thereof to his own use constituted not only a breach of trust but a fraud upon his copartners.

Decree affirmed with costs.[1]

[1] See Acker v. McGaw, 106 Md. 536; Pikes Peak Co. v. Pfuntner, 158 Mich. 412; Paw Paw Sav. Bank v. Free, 205 Mich. 52 (president of corporation); Knapp v. Reed, 88 Neb. 754; Mitchell v. Reed, 61 N. Y. 123, 84 N. Y. 556. See Perry, Trust, sec. 196.

In Dunfee v. Terwilliger, 15 F.(2d) 523, it was held that although one holding a lease in a fiduciary character cannot renew the lease for himself, he may do so if the lease had expired before he took the renewal and he was no longer in a fiduciary position.

To the effect that if a partner or other fiduciary buys the reversion with his own funds, he is not a constructive trustee, see Bevan v. Webb, [1905] 1 Ch. 620 (lease not renewable by custom or contract); Thanos v. Thanos, 313 Ill. 499; Anderson v. Lemon, 8 N. Y. 236 (*semble*). But see Griffith v.

MEINHARD v. SALMON.

COURT OF APPEALS, NEW YORK. 1928.

249 N. Y. 458.

APPEAL from a judgment of the Appellate Division of the Supreme Court in the first judicial department, entered June 28, 1928, modifying and affirming as modified a judgment in favor of plaintiff entered upon the report of a referee.

CARDOZO, Ch. J. On April 10, 1902, Louisa M. Gerry leased to the defendant Walter J. Salmon the premises known as the Hotel Bristol at the northwest corner of Forty-second street and Fifth avenue in the city of New York. The lease was for a term of twenty years, commencing May 1, 1902, and ending April 30, 1922. The lessee undertook to change the hotel building for use as shops and offices at a cost of $200,000. Alterations and additions were to be accretions to the land.

Salmon, while in course of treaty with the lessor as to the execution of the lease, was in course of treaty with Meinhard, the plaintiff, for the necessary funds. The result was a joint venture with terms embodied in a writing. Meinhard was to pay to Salmon half of the moneys requisite to reconstruct, alter, manage and operate the property. Salmon was to pay to Meinhard 40 per cent of the net profits for the first five years of the lease and 50 per cent for the years thereafter. If there were losses, each party was to bear them equally. Salmon, however, was to have sole power to " manage, lease, underlet and operate " the building. There were to be certain pre-emptive rights for each in the contingency of death.

The two were coadventurers, subject to fiduciary duties akin to those of partners (King v. Barnes, 109 N. Y. 267). As to this we are all agreed. The heavier weight of duty rested, however, upon Salmon. He was a coadventurer with Meinhard, but he was manager as well. During the early years of the enterprise, the building, reconstructed, was operated at a loss. If the relation had then ended, Meinhard as well as Salmon would have carried a heavy burden. Later the profits became large with the result that for each of the investors there came a rich return. For each, the venture had its phases of fair weather and of foul. The two were in it jointly, for better or for worse.

When the lease was near its end, Elbridge T. Gerry had become the owner of the reversion. He owned much other property in the neighborhood, one lot adjoining the Bristol Building on Fifth avenue and four lots on Forty-second street. He had a plan to lease the

---

Owen, [1907] 1 Ch. 195, 20 Harv. L. Rev. 639; Maas v. Goldman, 122 N. Y. Misc. 221, aff'd 210 App. Div. 845, 33 Yale L. Jour. 885.

entire tract for a long term to some one who would destroy the buildings then existing, and put up another in their place. In the latter part of 1921, he submitted such a project to several capitalists and dealers. He was unable to carry it through with any of them. Then, in January, 1922, with less than four months of the lease to run, he approached the defendant Salmon. The result was a new lease to the Midpoint Realty Company, which is owned and controlled by Salmon, a lease covering the whole tract, and involving a huge outlay. The term is to be twenty years, but successive covenants for renewal will extend it to a maximum of eighty years at the will of either party. The existing buildings may remain unchanged for seven years. They are then to be torn down, and a new building to cost $3,000,000 is to be placed upon the site. The rental, which under the Bristol lease was only $55,000, is to be from $350,000 to $475,000 for the properties so combined. Salmon personally guaranteed the performance by the lessee of the covenants of the new lease until such time as the new building had been completed and fully paid for.

The lease between Gerry and the Midpoint Realty Company was signed and delivered on January 25, 1922. Salmon had not told Meinhard anything about it. Whatever his motive may have been, he had kept the negotiations to himself. Meinhard was not informed even of the bare existence of a project. The first that he knew of it was in February when the lease was an accomplished fact. He then made demand on the defendants that the lease be held in trust as an asset of the venture, making offer upon the trial to share the personal obligations incidental to the guaranty. The demand was followed by refusal, and later by this suit. A referee gave judgment for the plaintiff, limiting the plaintiff's interest in the lease, however, to 25 per cent. The limitation was on the theory that the plaintiff's equity was to be restricted to one-half of so much of the value of the lease as was contributed or represented by the occupation of the Bristol site. Upon cross-appeals to the Appellate Division, the judgment was modified so as to enlarge the equitable interest to one-half of the whole lease. With this enlargement of plaintiff's interest, there went, of course, a corresponding enlargement of his attendant obligations. The case is now here on an appeal by the defendants.

Joint adventurers, like copartners, owe to one another, while the enterprise continues, the duty of the finest loyalty. Many forms of conduct permissible in a workaday world for those acting at arm's length, are forbidden to those bound by fiduciary ties. A trustee is held to something stricter than the morals of the market place. Not honesty alone, but the punctilio of an honor the most sensitive, is then the standard of behavior. As to this there has developed a tradition that is unbending and inveterate. Uncompromising rigidity has been the attitude of courts of equity when petitioned to undermine the rule of undivided loyalty by the "disintegrating erosion" of particular exceptions (Wendt *v.* Fischer, 243 N. Y. 439, 444). Only thus has the level of conduct for fiduciaries been kept at a level higher than that trodden by the crowd. It will not consciously be lowered by any judgment of this court.

The owner of the reversion, Mr. Gerry, had vainly striven to find a tenant who would favor his ambitious scheme of demolition and construction. Baffled in the search, he turned to the defendant Salmon in possession of the Bristol, the keystone of the project. He figured to himself beyond a doubt that the man in possession would prove a likely customer. To the eye of an observer, Salmon held the lease as owner in his own right, for himself and no one else. In fact he held it as a fiduciary, for himself and another, sharers in a common venture. If this fact had been proclaimed, if the lease by its terms had run in favor of a partnership, Mr. Gerry, we may fairly assume, would have laid before the partners, and not merely before one of them, his plan of reconstruction. The pre-emptive privilege, or, better, the pre-emptive opportunity, that was thus an incident of the enterprise, Salmon appropriated to himself in secrecy and silence. He might have warned Meinhard that the plan had been submitted, and that either would be free to compete for the award. If he had done this, we do not need to say whether he would have been under a duty, if successful in the competition, to hold the lease so acquired for the benefit of a venture then about to end, and thus prolong by indirection its responsibilities and duties. The trouble about his conduct is that he excluded his coadventurer from any chance to compete, from any chance to enjoy the opportunity for benefit that had come to him alone by virtue of his agency. This chance, if nothing more, he was under a duty to concede. The price of its denial is an extension of the trust at the option and for the benefit of the one whom he excluded.

No answer is it to say that the chance would have been of little value even if seasonably offered. Such a calculus of probabilities is beyond the science of the chancery. Salmon, the real estate operator, might have been preferred to Meinhard, the woolen merchant. On the other hand, Meinhard might have offered better terms, or reinforced his offer by alliance with the wealth of others. Perhaps he might even have persuaded the lessor to renew the Bristol lease alone, postponing for a time, in return for higher rentals, the improvement of adjoining lots. We know that even under the lease as made the time for the enlargement of the building was delayed for seven years. All these opportunities were cut away from him through another's intervention. He knew that Salmon was the manager. As the time drew near for the expiration of the lease, he would naturally assume from silence, if from nothing else, that the lessor was willing to extend it for a term of years, or at least to let it stand as a lease from year to year. Not impossibly the lessor would have done so, whatever his protestations of unwillingness, if Salmon had not given assent to a project more attractive. At all events, notice of termination, even if not necessary, might seem, not unreasonably, to be something to be looked for, if the business was over and another tenant was to enter. In the absence of such notice, the matter of an extension was one that would naturally be attended to by the manager of the enterprise, and not neglected altogether. At least, there was nothing in the situation to give warning to any one that while the lease was still in being, there had come to the manager an offer of extension which he had locked within his breast to be utilized by himself alone. The very fact that Salmon was in control with exclusive powers of direction charged him the more obviously with the duty of disclosure, since only through disclosure could opportunity be equalized. If he might cut off renewal by a purchase for his own benefit when four months were to pass before the lease would have an end, he might do so with equal right while there remained as many years (cf. Mitchell v. Reed, 61 N. Y. 123, 127). He might steal a march on his comrade under cover of the darkness, and then hold the captured ground. Loyalty and comradeship are not so easily abjured.

Little profit will come from a dissection of the precedents. None precisely similar is cited in the briefs of counsel. What is similar in many, or so it seems to us, is the animating principle. Authority is, of course, abundant that one partner may not appropriate to his own use a renewal of a lease, though its term is to begin at the expiration of the partnership (Mitchell v. Reed, 61 N. Y. 123; 84 N. Y. 556). The lease at hand with its many changes is not strictly a renewal. Even so, the standard of loyalty for those in trust relations is without the fixed divisions of a graduated scale. There is indeed a dictum in one of our decisions that a partner, though he may not renew a lease, may purchase the reversion if he acts openly and fairly (Anderson v. Lemon, 8 N. Y. 236; cf. White & Tudor, Leading Cases in Equity [9th ed.], vol. 2, p. 642; Bevan v. Webb, 1905, 1 Ch. 620; Griffith v. Owen, 1907, 1 Ch. 195, 204, 205). It is a dictum, and no more, for on the ground that he had acted slyly he was charged as a trustee. The holding is thus in favor of the conclusion that a purchase as well as a lease will succumb to the infection of secrecy and silence. Against the dictum in that case, moreover, may be set the opinion of DWIGHT, C., in Mitchell v. Read, where there is a dictum to the contrary (61 N. Y. at p. 143). To say that a partner is free without restriction to buy in the reversion of the property where the business is conducted is to say in effect that he may strip the good will of its chief element of value, since good will is largely dependent upon continuity of possession (Matter of Brown, 242 N. Y. 1, 7). Equity refuses to confine within the bounds of classified transactions its precept of a loyalty that is undivided and unselfish. Certain at least it is that a " man obtaining his *locus standi,* and his opportunity for making such arrangements, by the position he occupies as a partner, is bound by his obligation to his co-partners in such dealings not to separate his interest from theirs, but, if he acquires any benefit, to communicate it to them" (Cassels v. Stewart, 6 App. Cas. 64, 73). Certain it is also that there may be no abuse of special opportunities growing out of a special trust as manager or agent (Matter of Biss, 1903, 2 Ch. 40; Clegg v. Edmondson, 8 D. M. & G. 787, 807). If conflicting inferences are possible as to abuse or opportunity, the trier of the facts must make the choice between them. There can be no revision in this court unless the choice is clearly wrong. It is no answer for the fiduciary to say "that he was not bound to risk his money as he did, or to go into the enterprise at all" (Beatty v. Guggenheim Exploration Co., 225 N. Y. 380, 385). "He might have kept out of it altogether, but if he went in, he could not withhold from his employer the benefit of the bargain" (Beatty v. Guggenheim Exploration Co., *supra*). A constructive trust is then the remedial device through which preference of self is made subordinate to loyalty to others (Beatty v. Guggenheim Exploration Co., *supra*). Many and varied are its phases and occasions (Selwyn & Co. v. Waller, 212 N. Y. 507, 512; Robinson v. Jewett, 116 N. Y. 40; cf. Tournier v. Nat. Prov. & Union Bank, 1924, 1 K. B. 461).

We have no thought to hold that Salmon was guilty of a conscious purpose to defraud. Very likely he assumed in all good faith that with the approaching end of the venture he might ignore his coadventurer and take the extension for himself. He had given to the enterprise time and labor as well as money. He had made it a success. Meinhard, who had given money, but neither time nor labor, had already been richly paid. There might seem to be something grasping in his insistence upon more. Such recriminations are not unusual when coadventurers fall out. They are not without their force if conduct is to be judged by the common standards of competitors. That is not to say that they have pertinency here. Salmon had put himself in a position in which thought of self was to be renounced, however hard the abnegation. He was much more than a coadventurer. He was a managing coadventurer (Clegg v. Edmondson, 8 D. M. & G. 787, 807). For him and for those like him, the rule of undivided loyalty is relentless and supreme (Wendt v. Fischer, *supra;* Munson v. Syracuse, etc., R. R. Co., 103 N. Y. 58, 74). A different question would be here if there were lacking any nexus of relation between the business conducted by the manager and the opportunity brought to him as an incident of management (Dean v. MacDowell, 8 Ch. D. 345, 354; Aas v. Benham, 1891, 2 Ch. 244, 258; Latta v. Kilbourn, 150 U. S. 524). For this problem, as for most, there are distinctions of degree. If Salmon had received from Gerry a proposition to lease a building at a location far removed, he might have held for himself the privilege thus acquired, or so we shall assume. Here the subject-matter of the new lease was an extension and enlargement of the subject-matter of the old one. A managing coadventurer appropriating the benefit of such a lease without warning to his partner might fairly expect to be reproached with conduct that was underhand, or lacking, to say the least, in reasonable candor, if the partner were to surprise him in the act of signing the new instrument. Conduct subject to that reproach does not receive from equity a healing benediction.

A question remains as to the form and extent of the equitable interest to be allotted to the plaintiff. The trust as declared has been held to attach to the lease which was in the name of the defendant corporation. We think it ought to attach at the option of the defendant Salmon to the shares of stock which were owned by him or were under his control. The difference may be important if the lessee shall wish to execute an assignment of the lease, as it ought to be free to do with the consent of the lessor. On the other hand, an equal division of the shares might lead to other hardships. It might take away from Salmon the power of control and management which under the plan of the joint venture he was to have from first to last. The number of shares to be allotted to the plaintiff should, therefore, be reduced to such an extent as may be necessary to preserve to the defendant Salmon the expected measure of dominion. To that end an extra share should be added to his half.

Subject to this adjustment, we agree with the Appellate Division that the plaintiff's equitable interest is to be measured by the value of half of the entire lease, and not merely by half of some undivided part. A single building covers the whole area. Physical division is impracticable along the lines of the Bristol site, the keystone of the whole. Division of interests and burdens is equally impracticable. Salmon, as tenant under the new lease, or as guarantor of the performance of the tenant's obligations, might well protest if Meinhard, claiming an equitable interest, had offered to assume a liability not equal to Salmon's, but only half as great. He might justly insist that the lease must be accepted by his coadventurer in such form as it had been given, and not constructively divided into imaginary fragments. What must be yielded to the one may be demanded by the other. The lease as it has been executed is single and entire. If confusion has resulted from the union of adjoining parcels, the trustee who consented to the union must bear the inconvenience (Hart v. Ten Eyck, 2 Johns. Ch. 62).

Thus far, the case has been considered on the assumption that the interest in the joint venture acquired by the plaintiff in 1902 has been continuously his. The fact is, however, that in 1917 he assigned to his wife all his " right, title and interest in and to " the agreement with his coadventurer. The coadventurer did not object, but thereafter made his payments directly to the wife. There was a reassignment by the wife before this action was begun.

We do not need to determine what the effect of the assignment would have been in 1917 if either coadventurer had then chosen to treat the venture as dissolved. We do not even need to determine what the effect would have been if the enterprise had been a partnership in the strict sense with active duties of agency laid on each of the two adventurers. The form of the enterprise made Salmon the sole manager. The only active duty laid upon the other was one wholly ministerial, the duty of contributing his share of the expense. This he could still do with equal readiness, and still was bound to do, after the assignment to his wife. Neither by word nor by act did either partner manifest a choice to view the enterprise as ended. There is no inflexible rule in such conditions that dissolution shall ensue against the concurring wish of all that the venture shall continue. The effect of the assignment is then a question of intention (Durkee v. Gunn, 41 Kan. 496, 500; Taft v. Buffum, 14 Pick. 322; cf. 69 A. S. R. 417, and cases there cited).

Partnership Law (Cons. Laws, ch. 39), section 53, subdivision 1, is to the effect that " a conveyance by a partner of his interest in the partnership does not of itself dissolve the partnership, nor, as against the other partners in the absence of agreement, entitle the assignee, during the continuance of the partnership, to interfere in the management or administration of the partnership business or affairs, or to require any information or account of partnership transactions, or to inspect the partnership books; but it merely entitles the assignee to receive in accordance with his contract the profits to which the assigning partner would otherwise be entitled." This statute, which took effect October 1, 1919, did not indeed revive the enterprise if automatically on the execution of the assignment a dissolution had resulted in 1917. It sums up with precision, however, the effect of the assignment as the parties meant to shape it. We are to interpret their relation in the revealing light of conduct. The rule of the statute, even if it has modified the rule as to partnerships in general (as to this see Pollock, Partnership, p. 99, § 31; Lindley, Partnership [9th ed.], 695; Marquand v. N. Y. M. Co., 17 Johns. 525), is an accurate statement of the rule at common law when applied to these adventurers. The purpose of the assignment, understood by every one concerned, was to lower the plaintiff's tax by taking income out of his return and adding it to the return to be made by his wife. She was the appointee of the profits, to whom checks were to be remitted. Beyond that, the relation was to be the same as it had been. No one dreamed for a moment that the enterprise was to be wound up, or that Meinhard was relieved of his continuing obligation to contribute to its expenses if contribution became needful. Coadventurers and assignee, and most of all the defendant Salmon, as appears by his own letters, went forward on that basis. For more than five years Salmon dealt with Meinhard on the assumption that the enterprise was a subsisting one with mutual rights and duties, or so at least the triers of the facts, weighing the circumstantial evidence, might not unreasonably infer. By tacit, if not express approval, he continued and preserved it. We think it is too late now, when charged as a trustee, to come forward with the claim that it had been disrupted and dissolved.

The judgment should be modified by providing that at the option of the defendant Salmon there may be substituted for a trust attaching to the lease a trust attaching to the shares of stock, with the result that one-half of such shares together with one additional share will in that event be allotted to the defendant Salmon and the other shares to the plaintiff, and as so modified the judgment should be affirmed with costs.

ANDREWS, J. (dissenting). A tenant's expectancy of the renewal of a lease is a thing, tenuous, yet often having a real value. It represents the probability that a landlord will prefer to relet his premises to one already in possession rather than to strangers. Less tangible than "good will" it is never included in the tenant's assets, yet equity will not permit one standing in a relation of trust and confidence toward the tenant unfairly to take the benefit to himself. At times the principle is rigidly enforced. Given the relation between the parties, a certain result follows. No question as to good faith, or injury, or as to other circumstances is material. Such is the rule as between trustee and *cestui* (Keich *v.* Sanford, Select Cas. in Ch. 61); as between executor and estate (Matter of Brown, 18 Ch. Div. 61); as between guardian and ward (Milner *v.* Harewood, 18 Ves. 259, 274).

At other times some inquiry is allowed as to the facts involved. Fair dealing and a scrupulous regard for honesty is required. But nothing more. It may be stated generally that a partner may not for his own benefit secretly take a renewal of a firm lease to himself. (Mitchell *v.* Reed, 61 N. Y. 123.) Yet under very exceptional circumstances this may not be wholly true. (W. & T. Leading Cas. in Equity [9th ed.], p. 657; Clegg *v.* Edmondson, 8 D. M. & G. 787, 807.) In the case of tenants in common there is still greater liberty. There is said to be a distinction between those holding under a will or through descent and those holding under independent conveyance. But even in the former situation the bare relationship is not conclusive. (Matter of Biss, 1903, 2 Ch. 40.) In Burrell *v.* Bull (3 Sand. Ch. 15) there was actual fraud. In short, as we once said, "the elements of actual fraud — of the betrayal by secret action of confidence reposed, or assumed to be reposed, grows in importance as the relation between the parties falls from an express to an implied or a quasi trust, and on to those cases where good faith alone is involved." (Thayer *v.* Leggett, 229 N. Y. 152.)

Where the trustee, or the partner or the tenant in common, takes no new lease but buys the reversion in good faith a somewhat different question arises. Here is no direct appropriation of the expectancy of renewal. Here is no offshoot of the original lease. We so held in Anderson *v.* Lemon (8 N. Y. 236), and although Judge DWIGHT casts some doubt on the rule in Mitchell *v.* Reed, it seems to have the support of authority. (W. & T. Leading Cas. in Equity, p. 650; Lindley on Partnership [9th ed.], p. 396; Bevan *v.* Webb, 1905, 1 Ch. 620.) The issue then is whether actual fraud, dishonesty, unfairness is present in the transaction. If so, the purchaser may well be held as a trustee. (Anderson *v.* Lemon, cited above.)

With this view of the law I am of the opinion that the issue here is simple. Was the transaction in view of all the circumstances surrounding it unfair and inequitable? I reach this conclusion for two reasons. There was no general partnership, merely a joint venture for a limited object, to end at a fixed time. The new lease, covering additional property, containing many new and unusual terms and conditions, with a possible duration of eighty years, was more nearly the purchase of the reversion than the ordinary renewal with which the authorities are concerned.

The findings of the referee are to the effect that before 1902, Mrs. Louisa M. Gerry was the owner of a plot on the corner of Fifth avenue and Forty-second street, New York, containing 9,312 square feet. On it had been built the old Bristol Hotel. Walter J. Salmon was in the real estate business, renting, managing and operating buildings. On April 10th of that year Mrs. Gerry leased the property to him for a term extending from May 1, 1902, to April 30, 1922. The property was to be used for offices and business, and the design was that the lessee should so remodel the hotel at his own expense as to fit it for such purposes, all alterations and additions, however, at once to become the property of the lessor. The lease might not be assigned without written consent.

Morton H. Meinhard was a woolen merchant. At some period during the negotiations between Mr. Salmon and Mrs. Gerry, so far as the findings show without the latter's knowledge, he became interested in the transaction. Before the lease was executed he advanced $5,000 toward the cost of the proposed alterations. Finally, on May 19th he and Salmon entered into a written agreement. " During the period of twenty years from the 1st day of May, 1902," the parties agree to share equally in the expense needed " to reconstruct, alter, manage and operate the Bristol Hotel property; " and in all payments required by the lease, and in all losses incurred " during the full term of the lease, *i. e.*, from the first day of May, 1902, to the 1st day of May, 1922." During the same term net profits are to be divided. Mr. Salmon has sole power to " manage, lease, underlet and operate " the premises. If he dies, Mr. Meinhard shall be consulted before any disposition is made of the lease, and if Mr. Salmon' representatives decide to dispose of it, and the decision is theirs, Mr. Meinhard is to be given the first chance to take the unexpired term upon the same conditions they could obtain from others.

The referee finds that this arrangement did not create a partnership between Mr. Salmon and Mr. Meinhard. In this he is clearly right. He is equally right in holding that while no general partnership existed the two men had entered into a joint adventure and that while the legal title to the lease was in Mr. Salmon, Mr. Meinhard had some sort of an equitable interest therein. Mr. Salmon was to manage the property for their joint benefit. He was bound to use good faith. He could not willfully destroy the lease, the object of the adventure, to the detriment of Mr. Meinhard.

Mr. Salmon went into possession and control of the property. The alterations were made. At first came losses. Then large profits which were duly distributed. At all times Mr. Salmon has acted as manager.

Some time before 1922 Mr. Elbridge T. Gerry became the owner of the reversion. He was already the owner of an adjoining lot on Fifth avenue and of four lots adjoining on Forty-second street, in all 11,587 square feet, covered by five separate buildings. Obviously all this property together was more valuable than the sum of the value of the separate parcels. Some plan to develop the property as a whole seems to have occurred to Mr. Gerry. He arranged that all leases on his five lots should expire on the same day as the Bristol Hotel lease. Then in 1921 he negotiated with various persons and corporations seeking to obtain a desirable tenant who would put up a building to cover the entire tract, for this was the policy he had adopted. These negotiations lasted for some months. They failed. About January 1, 1922, Mr. Gerry's agent approached Mr. Salmon and began to negotiate with him for the lease of the entire tract. Upon this he insisted as he did upon the erection of a new and expensive building covering the whole. He would not consent to the renewal of the Bristol lease on any terms. This effort resulted in a lease to the Midpoint Realty Company, a corporation entirely owned and controlled by Mr. Salmon. For our purposes the paper may be treated as if the agreement was made with Mr. Salmon himself.

In many respects, besides the increase in the land demised, the new lease differs from the old. Instead of an annual rent of $55,000 it is now from $350,000 to $475,000. Instead of a fixed term of twenty years it may now be, at the lessee's option, eighty. Instead of alterations in an existing structure costing about $200,000 a new building is contemplated costing $3,000,000. Of this sum $1,500,000 is to be advanced by the lessor to the lessee, " but not to its successors or assigns," and is to be repaid in installments. Again no assignment or sale of the lease may be made without the consent of the lessor.

This lease is valuable. In making it Mr. Gerry acted in good faith without any collusion with Mr. Salmon and with no purpose to deprive Mr. Meinhard of any equities he might have. But as to the negotiations leading to it or as to the execution of the lease itself Mr. Meinhard knew nothing. Mr. Salmon acted for himself to acquire the lease for his own benefit.

Under these circumstances the referee has found and the Appellate Division agrees with him, that Mr. Meinhard is entitled to an interest in the second lease, he having promptly elected to assume his share of the liabilities imposed thereby. This conclusion is based upon the proposition that under the original contract between the two men "the enterprise was a joint venture, the relation between the parties was fiduciary and governed by principles applicable to partnerships," therefore, as the new lease is a graft upon the old, Mr. Salmon might not acquire its benefits for himself alone.

Were this a general partnership between Mr. Salmon and Mr. Meinhard I should have little doubt as to the correctness of this result assuming the new lease to be an offshoot of the old. Such a situation involves questions of trust and confidence to a high degree; it involves questions of good will; many other considerations. As has been said, rarely if ever may one partner without the knowledge of the other acquire for himself the renewal of a lease held by the firm, even if the new lease is to begin after the firm is dissolved. Warning of such an intent, if he is managing partner, may not be sufficient to prevent the application of this rule.

We have here a different situation governed by less drastic principles. I assume that where parties engage in a joint enterprise each owes to the other the duty of the utmost good faith in all that relates to their common venture. Within its scope they stand in a fiduciary relationship. I assume *prima facie* that even as between joint adventures one may not secretly obtain a renewal of the lease of property actually used in the joint adventure where the possibility of renewal is expressly or impliedly involved in the enterprise. I assume also that Mr. Meinhard had an equitable interest in the Bristol Hotel lease. Further, that an expectancy of renewal inhered in that lease. Two questions then arise. Under his contract did he share in that expectancy? And if so, did that expectancy mature into a graft of the original lease? To both questions my answer is " no."

The one complaint made is that Mr. Salmon obtained the new lease without informing Mr. Meinhard of his intention. Nothing else. There is no claim of actual fraud. No claim of misrepresentation to any one. Here was no movable property to be acquired by a new tenant at a sacrifice to its owners. No good will, largely dependent on location, built up by the joint efforts of two men. Here was a refusal of the landlord to renew the Bristol lease on any terms; a proposal made by him, not sought by Mr. Salmon, and a choice by him and by the original lessor of the person with whom they wished to deal shown by the covenants against assignment or underletting, and by their ignorance of the arrangement with Mr. Meinhard.

What then was the scope of the adventure into which the two men entered? It is to be remembered that before their contract was signed Mr. Salmon had obtained the lease of the Bristol property. Very likely the matter had been earlier discussed between them. The $5,000 advance by Mr. Meinhard indicates that fact. But it has been held that the written contract defines their rights and duties.

Having the lease Mr. Salmon assigns no interest in it to Mr. Meinhard. He is to manage the property. It is for him to decide what alterations shall be made and to fix the rents. But for twenty years from May 1, 1902, Salmon is to make all advances from his own funds and Meinhard is to pay him personally on demand one-half of all expenses incurred and all losses sustained " during the full term of said lease," and during the same period Salmon is to pay him a part of the net profits. There was no joint capital provided.

It seems to me that the venture so inaugurated had in view a limited object and was to end at a limited time. There was no intent to expand it into a far greater undertaking lasting for many years. The design was to exploit a particular lease. Doubtless in it Mr. Meinhard had an equitable interest, but in it alone. This interest terminated when the joint adventure terminated. There was no intent that for the benefit of both any advantage should be taken of the chance of renewal — that the adventure should be continued beyond that date. Mr. Salmon has done all he promised to do in return for Mr. Meinhard's undertaking when he distributed profits up to May 1, 1922. Suppose this lease, non-assignable without the consent of the lessor, had contained a renewal option. Could Mr. Meinhard have exercised it? Could he have insisted that Mr. Salmon do so? Had Mr. Salmon done so could he insist that the agreement to share losses still existed or could Mr. Meinhard have claimed that the joint adventure was still to continue for twenty or eighty years? I do not think so. The adventure by its express terms ended on May 1, 1922. The contract by its language and by its whole import excluded the idea that the tenant's expectancy was to subsist for the benefit of the plaintiff. On that date whatever there was left of value in the lease reverted to Mr. Salmon, as it would had the lease been for thirty years instead of twenty. Any equity which Mr. Meinhard possessed was in the particular lease itself, not in any possibility of renewal. There was nothing unfair in Mr. Salmon's conduct.

I might go further were it necessary. Under the circumstances here presented had the lease run to both the parties I doubt whether the taking by one of a renewal without the knowledge of the other would cause interference by a court of equity. An illustration may clarify my thought. A and B enter into a joint venture to resurface a highway between Albany and Schenectady. They rent a parcel of land for the storage of materials. A, unknown to B, agrees with the lessor to rent that parcel and one adjoining it after the venture is finished, for an iron foundry. Is the act unfair? Would any general statements, scattered here and there through opinions dealing with other circumstance, be thought applicable? In other words, the mere fact that the joint ventures rent property together does not call for the strict rule that applies to general partners. Many things may excuse what is there forbidden. Nor here does any possibility of renewal exist as part of the venture. The nature of the undertaking excludes such an idea.

So far I have treated the new lease as if it were a renewal of the old. As already indicated, I do not take that view. Such a renewal could not be obtained. Any expectancy that it might be had vanished. What Mr. Salmon obtained was not a graft springing from the Bristol lease, but something distinct and different — as distinct as if for a building across Fifth avenue. I think also that in the absence of some fraudulent or unfair act the secret purchase of the reversion even by one partner is rightful. Substantially this is such a purchase. Because of the mere label of a transaction we do not place it on one side of the line or the other. Here is involved the possession of a large and most valuable unit of property for eighty years, the destruction of all existing structures and the erection of a new and expensive building covering the whole. No fraud, no deceit, no calculated secrecy is found. Simply that the arrangement was made without the knowledge of Mr. Meinhard. I think this not enough.

The judgment of the courts below should be reversed and a new trial ordered, with costs in all courts to abide the event.

POUND, CRANE and LEHMAN, JJ., concur with CARDOZO, Ch. J., for modification of the judgment appealed from and affirmance as modified; ANDREWS, J., dissents in opinion in which KELLOGG and O'BRIEN, JJ., concur.

Judgment modified, etc.[1]

HARROP *v.* COLE.

COURT OF CHANCERY, NEW JERSEY. 1914.

85 N. J. Eq. 32 [2]

On final hearing on bill, answer and proofs taken in open court.
STEVENSON, V. C.

As to the facts, the weight of evidence and the probabilities are

[1] For comments on the principal case, see 29 Col. L. Rev. 367; 42 Harv. L. Rev. 953; 13 Minn. L. Rev. 711; 38 Yale L. Jour. 782.

[2] The decree was unanimously affirmed by the Court of Errors and Appeals. 86 N. J. Eq. 250.

on the side of complainants. The defendant's story rests upon his uncorroborated testimony, and in many respects his story and his manner of narrating it upon the stand discredit his cause.

I find that the complainants verbally employed the defendant to negotiate on their behalf the purchase of a parcel of land in Passaic county. The defendant thus charged with this business, in which he had the confidence of his employers, violated his duty, purchased the land with his own money and took a deed thereof to himself.

With the view of the evidence which I entertain, the case resolves itself into a well-defined question of law about which there has been a remarkable diversity of opinion expressed in decisions of the courts and in the text-books.

Mr. Perry seems to accept as established law that " parol proof cannot be received to establish a resulting trust in lands purchased by an agent, and paid for by his own funds, no money of the principal being used for the payment." 1 Perry Trusts § 135. Mr. Browne, in his authoritative work on the statute of frauds, appears to favor the contrary view. Browne Fraud. § 96.

In volume 15 of the Am. & Eng. Encycl. L. (2d ed.) (at p. 1187), cases on both sides of this question are cited, and it is stated that " it seems to be held by the weight of authority that a court of equity cannot grant relief " by holding the agent " a constructive trustee."

We have the supreme court of the United States and the English courts, and the courts of several of the states, firmly supporting the rule that the derelict agent can be decreed in equity to hold in trust for his betrayed and defrauded principal. Other courts of various states of high authority have held otherwise.

It is important to note that the whole basis of objection to the granting of relief to the deceived principal rests upon the statute of frauds. The argument, as stated by Mr. Perry, is that " the relation of principal and agent depends upon the agreement existing between them, and the trust in such a case must arise from the agreement and not from the transaction, and where a trust arises from an agreement, it is within the statute of frauds and must be in writing."

I think that this view is entirely erroneous and the trend of the decisions is toward its rejection. A trust which is more correctly classifiable as a constructive trust (1 Pom. Eq. § 155; 1 Perry Trusts § 166) than as a resulting trust (1 Perry Trusts § 135), is established by proof of the betrayal of confidence, of the violation of duties arising out of a fiduciary relation. The fiduciary relation may be established in a large number of ways. It is a mere accident that in this particular case, and in large numbers of others, the fiduciary relation grows out of a verbal promise. As the authorities abundantly show, equity will not tolerate the betrayal of confidence and it makes no difference how this confidence has been obtained.

When one man assumes to act as agent for another, as the representative of another, he necessarily establishes a fiduciary relation between himself and the other person who stands as his principal. This is in the very nature of the transaction because the agent undertakes to act not for his own benefit but for the benefit of his principal, and his principal stays out of his own business and confides in the agent to attend to this business for him. It is the assumption by the agent of his representative status and the confidence necessarily reposed in him by the principal which create the agent's peculiar liabilities and cast special limitations and obligations upon him. The agency may be established by a written contract or a verbal contract, or no contract whatever, the assumption and confidence involving a purely gratuitous service for which the agent is to receive no compensation in any form.

In a large class of cases analogous to the one in hand, equity intervenes where a fiduciary relation is found to exist between contracting parties, and sets aside or modifies the most solemn written contracts, and for that purpose admits parol evidence. 2 Pom. Eq. § 956; 1 Perry Trusts § 210.

In the case of Lillis v. P. Ballantine & Sons, decided by me about three years ago, but not reported, I held that "an obligation and a disqualifying fiduciary relation may be created contemporaneously, and the latter may infect the former precisely as if the fiduciary relation had antedated the legal obligation," citing the remarks of Mr. Justice Pitney in his opinion for the court of errors and appeals in Lynde v. Lynde, 64 N. J. Eq. 756.

It is not worth while, however, in my opinion, for the purposes of this case to spend much time in the examination of the reasoning of judges and text-writers in regard to this much controverted question, because I think the question is settled in New Jersey by the decision of the court of errors and appeals in the case of Rogers v. Genung (1909), 76 N. J. Eq. 306. In this case the court of errors and appeals reviewed the decree advised by Vice-Chancellor Stevens, whose opinion is published in 75 N. J. Eq. 13. The vice-chancellor held in that case that the alleged agent, Genung, who the complainant claimed had undertaken by an oral contract to buy the land in question for him, was already the agent of the owner of the farm and bound as such to get the highest possible price, and was therefore incapacitated to become the agent of or to enter into any confidential relation with a possible purchaser to whose attention he brought the farm, and to whom he offered it for sale. The court of errors and appeals took a different view of the facts, and, notwithstanding that Genung was a real estate agent on whose books the farm in question was listed, and who "offered" it to the complainant for sale, they found that there was nothing in the case upon which to base such an agency on the part of Genung for the owner, Conkling.

As to the law laid down, Vice-Chancellor Stevens, recognizing the conflict of authorities, doubted whether he would be "justified in following the more recent English rule, even if it were considered to be the better," in view of the decisions of this court in Wallace *v.* Brown (Chancellor Williamson, 1855), 10 N. J. Eq. 308, and several more recent cases which he cites.

The court of errors and appeals, however, not being bound by prior decisions of the court of chancery, and having found that Genung, the purchaser, was not disqualified from being employed as agent by the complainant, in unmistakable terms adopted the modern English rule overruling without citing all prior conflicting cases and established a constructive trust in favor of the complainant. . . .

A decree will be advised establishing a constructive trust on behalf of the complainants, and directing the defendants to execute the trust by conveying the land to the defendant upon payment of the price. The rights of the defendant who has purchased a portion of the land will be considered and protected to the extent necessary, and any unconsidered matters will be determined upon settlement of the decree.[1]

BEATTY *v.* GUGGENHEIM EXPLORATION COMPANY, 225 N. Y. 380 (1919): The plaintiff was employed by the defendant, an exploration and mining corporation, under an agreement that he would

[1] Havner Land Co. *v.* MacGregor, 169 Iowa 5; Rush *v.* McPherson, 176 N. C. 562; Kern *v.* Smith, 290 Pa. 566, *accord.* But see *contra,* Bibb *v.* Hunter, 79 Ala. 351 (*semble*); Fischli *v.* Dumaresly, 3 A. K. Marsh. (Ky.) 23; Kimmons *v.* Barnes, 205 Ky. 502; Farnham *v.* Clements, 51 Me. 426; Emerson *v.* Galloupe, 158 Mass. 146.

In the following cases where there was a pre-existing fiduciary relationship a constructive trust was imposed. Dexter *v.* Houston, 20 F.(2d) 647 (partnership or joint adventure); Allen *v.* Jackson, 122 Ill. 567; Kochorimbus *v.* Maggos, 323 Ill. 510; Rolikatis *v.* Lovett, 213 Mass. 545 (attorney); Wakeman *v.* Dodd, 27 N. J. Eq. 564 (business advisor); Rogers *v.* Genung, 76 N. J. Eq. 306 (broker); Abramson *v.* Davis, 135 Atl. 774 (N. J. Eq. 1927) (partner); Miller *v.* Walser, 42 Nev. 497 (joint adventure); Mattikow *v.* Sudarsky, 248 N. Y. 404 (partnership or joint adventure).

See a large collection of cases in 42 A. L. R. 10; 54 A. L. R. 1195. See Brightman, Oral Partnership Agreements Concerning an Interest in Land, 9 Cornell L. Quar. 97. See 23 Col. L. Rev. 378; 14 Mich. L. Rev. 238; 3 Va. L. Rev. 398; 63 U. Pa. L. Rev. 580; 5 L. R. A. (N.S.) 112; Perry, Trusts, sec. 206; Scott, Cases on Trusts, 1 ed., 511.

If a person merely agrees orally to purchase land for another and to resell it to him, he is not chargeable as constructive trustee. McDonald *v.* Conway, 254 Mass. 429.

On the question of imposing a constructive trust upon the purchaser of property who orally promises the owner of the property that he will reconvey it, see Hartzell *v.* Whitmore, 271 Pa. 575, *ante.*

On the question of imposing a constructive trust upon the purchaser of property where he advances the purchase price by way of loan to another, see Herlihy *v.* Coney, 99 Me. 469, *ante.*

On the question of imposing a constructive trust upon the purchaser where he wrongfully uses the money of another in buying the property, see sec. VI, *post.*

not become directly or indirectly interested in, or connected with, any person, partnership or corporation engaged in any similar business. He was sent by the defendant to investigate certain mining claims in Alaska on which the defendant had an option. The plaintiff found certain other claims not included in the option but which appeared to be necessary for the successful operation of those which were included. In partnership with a third person, he bought these claims. The court held that the defendant could hold him as constructive trustee of his interest in the claims so purchased; but that the defendant was barred by its subsequent consent to his keeping the property. Cardozo, J., said (p. 385):

"The plaintiff was sent to the Yukon to investigate mining claims which were the subject of an option. He found certain other claims which were not included in the option, but which he believed to be essential to the successful operation of those that were included. In conjunction with Perry, he purchased rights in the new claims. The two were partners in the venture. Later his employer, appreciating the importance of the claims, determined to buy them for itself. We think it had the right to say to the agent that he must renounce the profits of the transaction and transfer the claims at cost. A different situation would be presented if the claims had no relation to those which the plaintiff was under a duty to investigate. But they had an intimate relation. One could not profitably be operated without the other. Let us suppose that the plaintiff, instead of buying the claims as a partner with Perry, had bought them alone. No one, we think, would say that he could have retained them against his employer, and held out for an extravagant price, as, of course, he could have done if the purchase was not affected by a trust. It is not an answer to say that he was not bound to risk his money as he did, or to go into the enterprise at all (Rose v. Hayden, 35 Kan. 106, 118). He might have kept out of it altogether, but if he went in, he could not withhold from his employer the benefit of the bargain (Trice v. Comstock, 121 Fed. Rep. 620; Felix v. Patrick, 145 U. S. 317, 327; Massie v. Watts, 6 Cranch, 148; Ringo v. Binns, 10 Pet. 269; Gardner v. Ogden, 22 N. Y. 327; Sea Coast R. R. Co. v. Wood, 65 N. J. Eq. 530; Fox v. Mackreth, 1 Wh. & T. Lead. Cases in Eq. 141; Perry on Trusts [6th ed.], sec. 206).

We think, therefore, that aside from the special provisions of this contract, the agent became a trustee at the election of the principal. But the contract reinforces that conclusion. It is true that an agent or a partner who breaks a covenant not to engage in some other business does not, as a matter of course, become chargeable as a trustee for the profits of the forbidden venture (Dean v. MacDowell, L. R. 8 Ch. Div. 345; Trimble v. Goldberg, 1906, A. C. 494, 500; Aas v. Benham, 1891, 2 Ch. Div. 244; Latta v. Kilbourn, 150 U. S. 524, 547, 548). The agent may be discharged; the partnership may be dissolved; there may be an action for damages. But to raise a trust there must be more. It is sometimes said that the profits of the forbidden venture must have been diverted from the business of the principal or the partnership (See cases, *supra*). We think it may fairly be found that there was a diversion of profits here. But the test of diversion is not exhaustive. For most cases it may supply a working rule, but the rule is a phase or illustration of a principle still larger. A constructive trust is the formula through which the conscience of equity finds expression. When property has been acquired in such circumstances that the holder of the legal title may not in good conscience retain the beneficial interest, equity converts him into a trustee (Moore *v.* Crawford, 130 U. S. 122, 128; Pomeroy Eq. Jur. sec. 1053). We think it would be against good conscience for the plaintiff to retain these profits unless his employer has consented. The tie was close between the employer's business and the forbidden venture. The profits which the agent claims have come from the employer's coffers. If the agent must account as a trustee, the price which the employer pays is to that extent diminished. If the agent retains the profit, the price is to that extent increased. Of course it is true that if Perry had made the purchase alone, without the aid of plaintiff, the employer might be no better off. That is true whenever an agent goes into some competing venture. His associates might have succeeded in diverting equal profits without him. The disability is personal to him. Others may divert profits from the business of the principal. He may not. If he does, he must account for them."[1]

BECHER *v.* CONTOURE LABORATORIES.

SUPREME COURT OF THE UNITED STATES. 1929.

279 U. S. 388.

CERTIORARI, 278 U. S. 597, to review a decree of the Circuit Court of Appeals, which affirmed a decree of the District Court refusing a preliminary injunction in a suit for infringement of a patent, and dismissed the bill.

MR. JUSTICE HOLMES delivered the opinion of the Court.

In September, 1927, the respondents brought an action in the Supreme Court of the State of New York in which they obtained a judgment that the defendant, the petitioner, was trustee *ex maleficio* for Oppenheimer of an invention and letters patent issued to the de-

[1] A principal cannot hold his agent as constructive trustee if the agent, before purchasing the property, gave the principal an opportunity to purchase it and the principal declined. Spar Mountain Co. *v.* Schwerin, 305 Ill. 309.

In Pine *v.* White, 175 Mass. 585, the court expressed the opinion that it might be a breach of trust for a trustee of a half interest in land not to buy the other half interest if he had an opportunity to purchase it and had trust money available for the purpose.

fendant; that the defendant deliver to the plaintiffs an assignment of the letters patent and give up instruments similar to the invention; that he be enjoined from using, manufacturing, selling, &c., such instruments, and from transferring any rights under the patent, and that he pay costs. The judgment was based on the facts alleged and found, that Oppenheimer, having made the invention in question, employed Becher as a machinist to construct the invented machine and improvements made by Oppenheimer from time to time, and that Becher agreed to keep secret and confidential the information thus obtained and not to use it for the benefit of himself or of any other than Oppenheimer. It was found further, that while engaged in making instruments for Oppenheimer and after having learned from him all the facts, Becher without the knowledge of the plaintiffs and in violation of his agreement and of the confidential relation existing, applied for and obtained a patent, of which Oppenheimer knew nothing until after it had been issued, and while Becher was still making for him the Oppenheimer machine.

The judgment was entered on July 5, 1928, and at about the same time the present suit was brought in the District Court for the Southern District of New York, in which the parties are reversed. Becher sets up his patent, alleges infringement of it and prays an injunction. He also states the earlier proceedings in the State Court, and, although not in very distinct terms, seems to deny the jurisdiction of that Court inasmuch as the allegations of Oppenheimer if sustained, as they were, would show the Becher patent to be invalid; a question, it is said, for the Patent Office and the Courts of the United States alone. An injunction was asked restraining the defendants from further prosecuting their suit in the State Court. A preliminary injunction was denied by the District Court and on appeal the decree was affirmed, and the appellant's counsel consenting if the Court decided that the State Court had jurisdiction, the bill was dismissed. 29 F.(2d) 31.

It is not denied that the jurisdiction of the Courts of the United States is exclusive in the case of suits arising under the patent laws, but it was held below that the suit in the State Court did not arise under those laws. It is plain that that suit had for its cause of action the breach of a contract or wrongful disregard of confidential relations, both matters independent of the patent law, and that the subject matter of Oppenheimer's claim was an undisclosed invention which did not need a patent to protect it from disclosure by breach of trust. Irving Iron Works *v.* Kerlow Steel Flooring Co., 96 N. J. Eq. 702. Du Pont de Nemours Powder Co. *v.* Masland, 244 U. S. 100. Oppenheimer's right was independent of and prior to any arising out of the patent law, and it seems a strange suggestion that the assertion of that right can be removed from the cognizance of the tribunals established to protect it by its opponent going into the patent office for a later title. It is said that to establish Oppenheimer's claim is to invalidate Becher's patent. But, even if mistakenly, the attempt was not to invalidate that patent but to get an assignment of it, and an assignment was decreed. Suits against one who has received a patent of land to make him a trustee for the plaintiff on the ground of some paramount equity are well known. Again, even if the logical conclusion from the establishing of Oppenheimer's claim is that Becher's patent is void, that is not the effect of the judgment. Establishing a fact and giving a specific effect to it by judgment are quite distinct. A judgment *in rem* binds all the world, but the facts on which it necessarily proceeds are not established against all the world, Manson *v.* Williams, 213 U. S. 453, 455, and conversely establishing the facts is not equivalent to a judgment *in rem*.

That decrees validating or invalidating patents belong to the Courts of the United States does not give sacro-sanctity to facts that may be conclusive upon the question in issue. A fact is not prevented from being proved in any case in which it is material, by the suggestion that if it is true an important patent is void — and, although there is language here and there that seems to suggest it, we can see no ground for giving less effect to proof of such a fact than to any other. A party may go into a suit estopped as to a vital fact by a covenant. We see no sufficient reason for denying that he may be equally estopped by a judgment. See Pratt *v.* Paris Gas Light & Coke Co., 168 U. S. 255. Smith & Egge Manufacturing Co. *v.* Webster, 87 Conn. 74, 85.

Decree affirmed.[1]

ESSEX TRUST CO. *v.* ENWRIGHT.

SUPREME JUDICIAL COURT, MASSACHUSETTS. 1913.

214 Mass. 507.

BILL IN EQUITY, filed in the Superior Court on November 3, 1911, by the trustee under a mortgage made to secure the bonds of the Lynn Publishing Company, a corporation, against Frederick W. Enwright and the Lynn Publishing Company, to enjoin the defendant Enwright, as lessee under a lease from the International Trust Company, from evicting the plaintiff or the Lynn Publishing Company from certain premises on Willow Street in Lynn, where a newspaper called the Lynn Evening News was published by the plaintiff as trustee, and to have the defendant Enwright declared a constructive trustee holding such lease for the benefit of his former employer, the Lynn Publishing Company, and of the plaintiff as mortgagee in possession, and also to have the defendant ordered to assign such lease to the plaintiff.

The defendant Enwright in his answer asked that the bill might

[1] See 16 A. L. R. 1177; 32 A. L. R. 1037; 44 A. L. R. 593.

be dismissed, and also filed a motion to dismiss. Certain holders of the bonds secured by the mortgage made to the plaintiff as trustee filed a motion to be allowed to prosecute the suit in the name of the plaintiff, as trustee, for the benefit of themselves and other bondholders.

The case was heard by *Jenney,* J. He denied the motion to dismiss, and allowed the motion of the bondholders to be permitted to prosecute the suit. On the facts found by him he made an order that the bill should be dismissed with costs, and reported the case for determination by this court as described in the opinion. If the order of the judge was correct, the bill was to be dismissed with costs; otherwise, such decree was to be entered as should be ordered by this court.

LORING, J. The question on which the decision in this case depends is this: In case a reporter on a newspaper in the course or by reason of his employment learns that the premises on which the business of publishing the paper is conducted are of peculiar value to his employer or one carrying on his business, has he the right without his employer's knowledge to take a lease of the premises and hold them as his own to the injury of his employer's property?

The case comes before us on a report without the evidence. The statement in the report of the facts of the case is in one or more material points somewhat meagre.

The material facts stated in the report were in substance as follows: The defendant Enwright, hereinafter called the defendant, was a reporter on a daily newspaper published in Lynn, which was mortgaged to the plaintiff trust company to secure an issue of bonds, the amount of which is not stated. The business of making up and printing the newspaper was carried on in two stories and in the basement of a building in Lynn, of which two stories and basement the Lynn Publishing Company (the mortgagor) was a tenant at will. The printing press of the Publishing Company was " situated in the basement upon a foundation of concrete, embedded in the earth underneath the building, and could not be removed from said basement and set up in some other place in less than two weeks' time, and at a very considerable expense. While the press was being taken down and being set up in another place the paper could not be published unless it made arrangements for its printing from some other press, and it appeared in evidence that no press was in Lynn that could be used for that purpose in connection with the electrotyping plant of the company except after expensive alterations in the electrotyping plant." " Outside of its machinery, type, fixtures, and furniture, it depended for the value of its property on the good will of the business, and upon the ability to get out its paper daily."

On July 1, 1911, the Publishing Company defaulted on the mortgage interest. By the terms of the mortgage the mortgage trustee could not take possession until ninety days after the default. On Tuesday, October 3, 1911, the plaintiff trust company took possession and proceeded to take the necessary steps to foreclose its mortgage by a sale in accordance with its terms. The trust company continued the publication of the paper.

The defendant had been employed as a reporter by the mortgagor for a period not stated. He did not devote his whole time to the business and was paid " at the rate of five to seven dollars a week for such services as he rendered in gathering and reporting news." When the plaintiff trust company took possession on October 3, 1911, it continued to employ the defendant as a reporter. " About " that time the defendant applied to one Porter for a lease of the premises in which the business of publishing was conducted by his employer. Porter told him that he was the lessor of the second story only, and that the International Trust Company was the lessor of the first floor and the basement. Porter refused to give the defendant a lease of the second story, the premises owned by him. Thereupon, on October 4, 1911, the defendant applied to the agent of the trust company for a lease of the first floor and basement, telling the agent " that he represented parties who were going to take over the paper." " A few days later " a written lease from October 2 (October 1 being a Sunday) was delivered to the defendant for a term not stated, and on October 31 the defendant gave the plaintiff notice to quit on the following Friday, which was November 3.

The findings already stated establish the peculiar value which these premises had to the defendant's employer or to any one carrying on the employer's business of publishing this newspaper. And it is evident from the facts found by the judge who heard the case in the Superior Court that the defendant realized that. It is found that " during the summer after the interest had been defaulted, the defendant went to various bondholders and endeavored to buy their bonds," and that " he offered them fifty cents upon the dollar therefor," and that " after obtaining the lease he went to various bondholders and offered them twenty-five cents on the dollar " for the same bonds. It further is found that " he stated to various persons that the person who had secured the lease would be the winner in the long run, and asked some of these persons if they were going to the funeral, meaning the funeral of the paper published by the publishing company."

It is not found directly as a fact, but it is the fair inference to be drawn from the facts found, that the defendant learned in the course or by reason of his employment of the peculiar value which these premises had for his employer. It was found directly (in effect) that knowledge of the fact that his employer was in arrears in the payment of rent came to the defendant by reason of his employment. That fact, however, is a fact of secondary importance.

The doctrine invoked by the plaintiff in this suit had its origin in two decisions by Lord Eldon. In Yovatt *v.* Winyard, 1 Jac. & W. 394, the defendant (formerly employed as a clerk by the plaintiff, who was a veterinary surgeon) was enjoined from using medicines compounded from the plaintiff's recipes which he (the defendant) had surreptitiously copied while in the plaintiff's employ. In Abernethy *v.* Hutchinson, 3 L. J. (O. S.) c. 209, the publication in the Lancet of lectures on surgery delivered by the plaintiff at St. Bartholomew's Hospital, which the defendants had obtained from the students attending the lectures, was enjoined. The ground on which Lord Eldon went in this case was subsequently stated by Turner, V. C., in these words: " I well remember that upon the first argument he refused to grant the injunction on the ground of copyright, Mr. Abernethy not being able to swear that the whole lecture was written; but that afterwards, on a second argument, he granted it on the ground of breach of confidence." See Turner, V. C., in Morison *v.* Moat, 9 Hare, 241, 257.

Since then the doctrine has been applied in England in a number of cases. In Morison *v.* Moat, 9 Hare, 241, the defendant was enjoined from using a secret formula for compounding a medicine which had been disclosed to him, in violation of a contract made with the originator of the formula. In Tuck & Sons *v.* Priester, 19 Q. B. D. 629, the defendant, who had been employed by the plaintiff to print two thousand copies of a picture belonging to him, was enjoined from selling further copies of it which he had taken surreptitiously. In Pollard *v.* Photographic Co., 40 Ch. D. 345, a similar decision was made; in that case the defendant printed for his own use further likenesses of the plaintiff from a negative which he had made when photographing the plaintiff in the ordinary course of his business as a photographer. In Helmore *v.* Smith, 35 Ch. D. 449, a clerk was committed for contempt on its being shown that he had taken a copy of the customers of a business conducted by a receiver appointed by the court and that he had solicited their custom for a competing business which he had set up for himself. A similar decision as to the use of a list of the plaintiff's customers surreptitiously copied by a clerk was made in Robb *v.* Green, [1895] 2 Q. B. 1. In Merryweather *v.* Moore, [1892] 2 Ch. 518, a clerk was enjoined from communicating to a subsequent employer the details of machinery manufactured by his former employer, the plaintiff; and in Lamb *v.* Evans, [1893] 1 Ch. 218, the defendants, who had been employed to secure advertisements for the plaintiff's Trades Directory and who by the terms of their employment furnished at their own expense the blocks and materials necessary for producing the advertisements, were enjoined from using the blocks and materials so obtained in aid of a competing directory. For two other cases where the doctrine was applied see Tipping *v.* Clarke, 2 Hare, 383, 393 and Kirchner *v.* Gruban, [1909] 1 Ch. 413,

422. In the latest of these cases (Kirchner v. Gruban, [1909] 1 Ch. 413, 422), Eve, J., states the doctrine of these cases in these words: "I think it is abundantly clear upon the authority of Robb v. Green, [1895] 2 Q. B. 315, that the real principle upon which the employee is restrained from making use of confidential information which he has gained in the employment of some other person is that there is in the contract of service subsisting between the employer and employee an implied contract on the part of the employee that he will not, after the service is determined, use information which he has gained while the service has been subsisting to the detriment of his former employer."

This doctrine was applied by this court in Peabody v. Norfolk, 98 Mass. 452. In that case the plaintiff, having invented a process of manufacturing gunny cloth from jute butts, had built a factory where gunny cloth had been so manufactured. The defendant Norfolk had been employed by him as an engineer in his factory, and had agreed not to disclose to others the construction of the machinery. On leaving the plaintiff's employ Norfolk imparted the nature of the machinery to one Cook, who knew of Norfolk's agreement. Both were enjoined. The doctrine was recognized by this court in Chadwick v. Covell, 151 Mass. 190, and Covell v. Chadwick, 153 Mass. 263, which had to do with formulas for compounding medicines, and in the recent case of American Stay Co. v. Delaney, 211 Mass. 229.

There are two cases, one in California and the other in Illinois, which have gone as far in the application of this doctrine as we are asked to go in the case at bar. In Gower v. Andrew, 59 Cal. 119, the defendant, a clerk employed by the plaintiffs, who were warehousemen, secured a lease of the warehouse in which the business was conducted, behind his employers' backs by telling the owner of it that the "plaintiffs would probably give up the warehouse," and offering an advance of $50 a month in the rent. The defendant then began soliciting custom for himself as the successor of his employers. On this becoming known he was discharged by his employers and was ordered by the court to assign the lease to the plaintiffs. In Davis v. Hamlin, 108 Ill. 39, Davis, who was the defendant in the court below, was hired by Hamlin, the lessee of one of four important theatres in Chicago, as his business manager. A year and three months before Hamlin's lease expired Davis behind Hamlin's back secured for himself a lease (to begin on the expiration of Hamlin's lease) by giving $4,500 more rent a year. It appeared in evidence that Hamlin had built up a good will in connection with his theatre by ten years' occupancy. Davis was directed to hold the lease which he had secured as trustee for Hamlin.

The defendant has argued that he was not within this rule because the duty of securing a lease was not entrusted by his employer to him. The same contention was the main argument put forward in Davis *v.* Hamlin, and was true of the clerk in Gower *v.* Andrew. The complaint against the defendant is that he has made use of information which has come to him in his employment to the detriment of his employer. In our opinion that is enough to entitle the employer to equitable relief.

We find nothing in the cases cited by the defendant which calls for notice. There is one case not cited by the defendant which requires a word of explanation. We refer to Clark *v.* Delano, 205 Mass. 224. The facts found by the master in that case were as follows: The plaintiff had employed the defendant as one of several brokers to secure a loan of the money necessary to prevent the foreclosure of a mortgage on his (the plaintiff's) land. The defendant was employed before the end of May. A foreclosure sale of the land was advertised for June 26. On June 18 the defendant learned from some one other than the plaintiff of the impending foreclosure sale. On June 18 or 19 he reported to the plaintiff that he had not been able to secure the loan. The plaintiff asked him to continue his efforts, to which the defendant made no answer, but the master found that the plaintiff was justified in believing that he intended to continue them. The plaintiff did not attend the foreclosure sale, relying on a statement by the mortgagee that he supposed that no one would attend and that he, the mortgagee, would have to bid the property in, " in his own interest and that of the plaintiff." The defendant bought the property for himself at the foreclosure sale, having conceived the idea of doing so the day before the sale. It was held that he had a right to do so. Of this case it is to be remarked in the first place that the defendant (the broker) did not forestall his employer by buying behind his back, but bought at a foreclosure sale in no way brought about by him, at which he had to compete with the plaintiff (his former employer) on equal terms. And what is of more importance, the land had no peculiar value to the employer, as the premises in question in the case at bar have to this plaintiff, and as the buildings in question in Gower *v.* Andrew and Davis *v.* Hamlin had to the plaintiffs in those cases. For these two reasons the defendant in Clark *v.* Delano was not taking advantage of information obtained in the course of his employment as to the peculiar value of the property to his employer by securing it for himself behind his employer's back, to his (the employer's) detriment.

The bill, which was originally filed by the trustee named in the mortgage, is now being prosecuted, by leave of court, in its name by the bondholders who bought in the property at the foreclosure sale. The foreclosure sale was had after the hearing in the Superior Court, but before the case was reported to this court. The defendant originally objected to this, but the objection has not been argued on the brief or at the bar, and we treat it as waived.

The plaintiff is entitled to a decree directing the defendant to assign to the plaintiff the lease obtained by him on being paid the amount of the rent, if any, paid by him under it, and to its costs. See American Circular Loom Co. *v.* Wilson, 198 Mass. 182, 206. But the plaintiff is under no obligation to the defendant as to the rent due from the Lynn Publishing Company (the mortgagor) to the International Trust Company and paid by the defendant to it.

A decree for the plaintiff on these terms must be settled in the Superior Court.

So ordered.

SECTION VI.

Where Property is Acquired by One Person by the Wrongful Use of the Property of Another.

SHALER *v.* TROWBRIDGE.

COURT OF ERRORS AND APPEALS, NEW JERSEY. 1877.

28 N. J. Eq. 595.

THIS cause was argued at May Term, 1876, before Hon. Amzi Dodd, a special master, to whom it had been referred by the chancellor. The facts sufficiently appear in his opinion, and in that delivered on the appeal.

VAN SYCKEL, J.[1] In January, 1865, Joseph A. Trowbridge, Brainard Shaler, John Kiersted and Wynkoop Kiersted entered into partnership in the leather business, which was terminated by the death of Trowbridge, December 14, 1869. During its continuance, Trowbridge had charge of the books and finances. The contested question on this appeal is, whether certain real estate and certain policies of life insurance, to which Mary E. Trowbridge held the legal title at her husband's death, should be decreed to be in equity the property of the firm? The evidence shows that Trowbridge alone drew the firm checks, and exclusively managed its money affairs, and that the yearly balance-sheets, made up and presented by him to the firm, were false and fraudulent. Checks of the firm to the amount of $103,155.97 were drawn by him to his own individual use, and paid at the bank, none of which were either included in his yearly balance-sheets, or charged to him on the books of the firm. At the same time the amount drawn by him during the existence of the partnership, and actually charged to his accounts, exceeded what he would have been entitled to, by the articles of copartnership, by more than $15,000; so that, upon an adjustment of the partnership concerns, he will be indebted to the firm in more than $118,000.

[1] The opinion of the special master is omitted.

Out of the moneys drawn upon the uncharged checks, or by the checks themselves in some instances, Trowbridge paid for the real estate and the policies of insurance now in controversy. The policies were issued, in the first place, in favor of Trowbridge himself, and the half-yearly premiums paid by the uncharged checks of the firm to the insurance company's agent. In April, 1868, they were changed, by Trowbridge's request, so as to be payable to his wife, who, after her husband's death, received the several amounts due upon the policies from the insurance companies. Upon this statement of facts, which the case satisfactorily establishes, shall the real estate, and the proceeds of the policies, be declared to be held in trust by the wife as the property of the firm?

This is not a case of resulting trust, where the trust results, or is implied, from the contracts and relations of the parties. It arises, *ex maleficio,* out of the active fraud and dishonest conduct of the partner Trowbridge, and may be termed a constructive trust, which equity will fasten upon the conscience of the offending party, and convert him into a trustee of the legal title, and order him to hold and execute it in such manner as to protect the rights of the defrauded party, and promote the interest and safety of society. It differs from other trusts in that it is not within the intention or contemplation of the parties at the time the contract is made upon which it is construed by the court, but it is thrust upon a party contrary to his intention and against his will. 1 Perry on Trusts, sec. 166.

If a person, occupying a fiduciary capacity, purchases property with fiduciary funds in his hands, and takes the title in his own name, he will, by construction, be charged as a trustee for the person entitled to the beneficial interest in the fund with which such purchase was made. This rule applies to a partner who fraudulently purchases for himself with the partnership funds, and it extends to personal as well as real estate; in every case the equitable ownership rests in the person from whom the consideration moves. Johnson *v.* Dougherty, 3 C. E. Gr. 406; Cutler *v.* Tuttle, 4 C. E. Gr. 558; Dyer *v.* Dyer, 1 Lead. Cas. in Eq. 203; 1 Perry on Trusts, secs. 127–130.

In Taylor *v.* Plumer, 3 M. & S. 575, Lord Ellenborough said that if A is trusted by B with money to purchase a horse for him, and he purchases a carriage with that money, B is entitled to the carriage. That it made no difference, in reason or in law, into what other form, different from the original, the change may have been made, for the product of or substitute for the original thing still follows the nature of the thing itself, as long as it can be ascertained to be such, and the right ceases only when the means of ascertainment fail. This is declared to be the settled rule, in Story's Eq. Juris., secs. 1258, 1259.

So completely are the two things identified, even at law, where the conversion can be clearly traced, that in equity a distinction can never be drawn, between the money misappropriated and the results of its investment, in favor of the fraud-doer.

Nor does it make any difference that the investment turns out to be a profitable one, for, whatever the profit may be, it must belong to the *cestui que trust*. It is a constructive fraud upon the latter to use his property unlawfully and to retain the profit of the misapplication, it being a fundamental principle in regard to a trustee that he shall derive no gain to himself from the employment of the trust fund. 2 Story's Eq. Juris., sec. 1261; McKnight's Ex'rs *v.* Walsh, 9 C. E. Gr. 509.

Much more does public policy require that one who has corruptly thrust himself into the position of a trustee, shall not profit by his fraud. The fact that this property has been passed into the hands of the wife does not prevent the application of these equitable principles. She received it as a gift from her husband, without paying any consideration whatever for it. Where once a fraud has been committed, not only is the person who committed the fraud precluded from deriving any benefit from it, but every innocent person is so, likewise, unless he has, in good faith, acquired a subsequent interest for value; for a third person, by seeking to derive any benefit under such a transaction, or to retain any benefit resulting therefrom, becomes *particeps criminis*, however innocent of the fraud in the beginning. 1 Perry on Trusts, sec. 172, and cases cited.

It is urged that a life policy should be exempt from the equitable rule which applies to other transactions, because it differs in its character from ordinary investments, and is a beneficent provision for the family, which should be favored.

Public policy clearly forbids the adoption of this suggestion; it would invite the commission of the wrong by assuring the wrong-doer that there is one mode in which he could surely profit by his turpitude, in securing a provision for his family. The policy is the thing which the partnership money purchased, and it stands in the place of what was corruptly abstracted. Whether the policy would be productive, when terminated by death, of more or less than the premiums paid upon it, would depend upon the length of the life insured. The fact that it has a contingent value does not distinguish it, in principle, from an investment in the purchase of stock, or of an annuity, and can give no support to the claim of the widow, that nothing should be exacted from her beyond the amount of premiums paid upon it out of the firm funds. If this suit had been prosecuted in the life-time of the husband, and the policy had been disposed of to the company for its surrender value, it would hardly have been insisted that he could claim, in a court of conscience, a right to any excess of the proceeds after refunding to his firm the amount of the premiums. All the premiums were paid with the partnership funds — nothing was paid by the wife. The transfer to her, therefore, cannot change the equities, nor divest the trust.

The inflexible rule, in equity, will be equally violated, whether she takes the value of the policies in excess of the premiums paid, or the appreciation in the real estate.

Trowbridge contributed nothing, in money or otherwise, to the purchase or support of the policies. The entire sum derived from them is the product of the partnership money. He did no act upon which he could have based the slightest claim in equity to be benefited by the transaction. It would be idle to denounce his turpitude, and, at the same time, to reward it by allowing him to transmit its fruits to his family. His wife can derive, through so corrupt a source, no equitable rights to these policies; neither public policy, nor the intrinsic justice of the case, would be promoted by permitting her to do so.

In my opinion, the decree below should be affirmed, and the case remitted, that it may be proceeded in accordingly.

Decree unanimously affirmed.[1]

[1] See the following cases where misappropriated money was used in paying insurance premiums. Vorlander *v.* Keyes, 1 F.(2d) 67 (corporate officer); Lehman *v.* Gunn, 124 Ala. 213 (fraud on creditors); Massachusetts Bonding & Ins. Co. *v.* Josselyn, 224 Mich. 159 (administrator); Holmes *v.* Gilman, 138 N. Y. 369 (partner); Truelsch *v.* Miller, 186 Wis. 239 (employee). See 38 A. L. R. 930.

In Hubbard *v.* Stapp, 32 Ill. App. 541, the court was of the opinion that the claimant was entitled only to a lien for the amount of his money used in paying premiums. In Bennett *v.* Rosborough, 155 Ga. 265, not even a lien was allowed. See 26 A. L. R. 1408.

If the insured pays the premiums out of his general assets while he is insolvent and the transaction is held to be in fraud of creditors, it has been held that the creditors are entitled to an equitable lien upon the policy or its proceeds for the amount of the premiums so paid, but are not entitled to the whole of proceeds. Central Bank *v.* Hume, 128 U. S. 195; Harriman Nat. Bank *v.* Huiet, 244 Fed. 216.

In the following cases it was held that where a person with misappropriated money purchased a homestead or other property exempt from the claims of creditors, he held the property upon a constructive trust for the owner of the money. Shinn *v.* Macpherson, 58 Cal. 596; Pierce *v.* Holzer, 65 Mich. 263; Nebraska Nat. Bank *v.* Johnson, 51 Neb. 546; Preston *v.* Moore, 133 Tenn. 247. See Jones *v.* Carpenter, 90 Fla. 407 (equitable lien for improvements on homestead). See 27 Col. L. Rev. 467.

If misappropriated money is used in making improvements, the owner of the money is entitled only to a lien and not to a *pro rata* share of the property. Jones *v.* Carpenter, 90 Fla. 407; Hardy *v.* Hardy, 149 Ga. 371, 20 Col. L. Rev. 103; American Ry. Express Co. *v.* Houle, 169 Minn. 209; Warsco *v.* Oshkosh Sav. & T. Co., 190 Wis. 87.

Similarly, if misappropriated money is used in discharging an encumbrance, the owner of the money is entitled to a lien but not to a constructive trust. Shinn *v.* Macpherson, 58 Cal. 596. See M'Mahon *v.* Fetherstonhaugh, [1895] 1 I. R. 83, *post*.

The Statute of Frauds does not bar the claim of the *cestui que trust* to land acquired by the misuse of trust funds. Lane *v.* Dighton, 1 Amb. 409, overruling earlier cases which reached the opposite result.

CAMPBELL v. DRAKE.

SUPREME COURT, NORTH CAROLINA. 1844.

4 Ired. Eq. 94.

CAUSE removed from the Court of Equity of Wake county, at the Fall Term, 1845.

The bill states that the plaintiff kept a retail shop in Raleigh, and that a lad, by the name of John Farrow, was his shopkeeper for several years; and that, while in his employment, Farrow abstracted, to a considerable amount, money and goods belonging to the plaintiff, and that with the money of the plaintiff, taken without his knowledge or consent, Farrow purchased a tract of land at the price of $500. The bill states a great number of facts, tending to show that Farrow paid for the land with the effects of the plaintiff, which he dishonestly converted to that purpose. Farrow afterwards died under age, and the land descended to his brothers and sisters; and the plaintiff, having discovered his losses of money and merchandize, and that Farrow had purchased the land as aforesaid, filed this bill against his heirs, and therein insists, that he has a right to consider the purchase as made, and the land held, for the use of the plaintiff, and that Farrow should be declared a trustee for him.

The bill was answered, so as to put in issue the various charges of dishonesty by Farrow, and the fact that the land was paid for with money purloined from the plaintiff: and much evidence was read to those points.

RUFFIN, C. J. The Court, though naturally inclined to every presumption in favor of innocence, and especially of a young person who seems to have been so well thought of while he lived, is satisfied from the proofs, that the plaintiff was much plundered by this youth; and we have no doubt, that every cent of the money with which he paid for the land, he had pilfered from his employer. Nevertheless, we believe the bill cannot be sustained. The object of it is to have the land itself, claiming it as if it had been purchased for the plaintiff by an agent expressly constituted; and it seems to us, thus stated, to be a bill of the first impression. We will not say, if the plaintiff had obtained judgment against the administrator for the money as a debt, that he might not come here to have the land declared liable, as a security, for the money laid out for it. But that is not the object of this suit. It is to get the land, which the plaintiff claims as his; and, upon the same principle, would claim it, if it were worth twenty times his money, which was laid out for it. Now, we know not any precedent of such a bill. It is not at all like the cases of dealings with trust funds by trustees, executors, guardians, factors, and the like; in which the owner of the fund may elect to take either the money or that in which it was invested. For, in all those cases, the legal title, if we may use the expression, of the fund, is in the party thus misapplying it. He has been entrusted with the whole possession of it, and that for the purpose of laying it out for the benefit of the equitable owner; and therefore all the benefit and profit the trustee ought, in the nature of his office, and from his relation to the *cestui que trust,* to account for to that person. But the case of a servant or a shop-keeper is very different. He is not charged with the duty of investing his employer's stock, but merely to buy and sell at the counter. The possession of the goods or money is not in him, but in his master; so entirely so, that he may be convicted of stealing them, in which both a *cepit* and *asportavit* are constituents. This person was in truth guilty of a felony in possessing himself of the plaintiff's effects, for the purpose of laying them out for his own lucre; and that fully rebuts the idea of converting him into a trustee. If that could be done, there would be, at once, an end to punishing thefts by shop men. If, indeed, the plaintiff could actually trace the identical money taken from him, into the hands of a person who got it without paying value, no doubt he could recover it; for his title was not destroyed by the theft. But we do not see how a felon is to be turned into a trustee of property, merely by showing that he bought it with stolen money. If it were so, there would have been many a bill of the kind. But we believe, there never was one before; and therefore, we cannot entertain this. But we think the facts so clearly established, and the demands of justice so strong on the defendants to surrender the land to the plaintiff, or to return him the money that was laid out in it, that we dismiss the bill without costs.

Decree accordingly.

FUR & WOOL TRADING CO., LTD. *v.* FOX, INC.

Court of Appeals, New York. 1927.

245 N. Y. 215.

Appeal, by permission, from a judgment of the Appellate Division of the Supreme Court in the first judicial department, entered February 10, 1927, unanimously affirming a judgment in favor of defendant entered upon an order of Special Term granting a motion by defendant for a dismissal of the amended complaint.

Andrews, J. The complaint alleges that goods belonging to the plaintiff were taken from its possession by force. The defendant receiving them with knowledge of the facts, sold them at a large profit but at a price unknown to the plaintiff. It has refused a demand to account for the sums received. The plaintiff, consequently, brings an action in equity to compel the defendant to disclose what amounts were so received by it, to repay the proceeds of such sale, and it asks for general equitable relief. This it has been held may not be done. The only redress is such as the law may give. Therefore, upon motion the complaint has been dismissed.

Some remedy at law there certainly is. The plaintiff might sue for conversion. If successful, it would, as a general rule, recover a personal judgment for the value of the goods at the time and place of the conversion. Or if the goods had remained in the hands of the wrongdoer, an action in replevin would have afforded a complete remedy for their recovery. Or again if they have been sold there is an action for money had and received, resulting in a personal judgment for the proceeds. If the plaintiff has no information as to this sum it may acquire it should it be necessary to enable it to frame a complaint by an examination of the defendant. (Matter of Erie Malleable Iron Co., 90 Hun, 62.) Even though this be so is the plaintiff entitled to still other relief in excess of what a court of law is competent to give? Or is his case one where under historic rules, equity has been wont to assume jurisdiction?

At the outset we should say that the action may not be sustained as a bill of discovery, brought as such a bill was, not as an end in itself but as an aid to an independent proceeding. A complete remedy of this character being otherwise provided, such an action no longer survives. (Civ. Prac. Act. sec. 345.) But in certain cases equity will entertain a suit for an accounting. This is so where such a relation exists between the parties as under established principles entitles the one to demand it of the other. (Schantz v. Oakman, 163 N. Y. 148; Brown v. Corey, 191 Mass. 189.) A trustee in possession of trust funds may in a proper case be called to account to his *cestui que trust* (Brinckerhoff v. Bostwick, 105 N. Y. 567), and this rule is enforced as well where the trust is implied as where it is express. (Hawley v. Cramer, 4 Cow. 717.)

Clearly a thief, having sold stolen goods may be treated as a trustee of the proceeds and also of any property into which they have been transformed, so long as either may be identified. Under such circumstances broader relief may be obtained in equity than at law. Where necessary, an accounting may be had. A lien may be declared. A surrender of the trust property may be decreed. (Newton v. Porter, 69 N. Y. 133; American S. R. Co. v. Fancher, 145 N. Y. 552; Hammond v. Pennock, 61 N. Y. 145; Jaffe v. Weld, 220 N. Y. 443.) The added reason that the defendant is insolvent is not essential. Such was not found to be the fact either in Newton v. Porter or in Jaffe v. Weld.

Where, however, the specific proceeds, in their original or in their transformed shape may not be traced, then no lien may be obtained. (Matter of Cavin, 105 N. Y. 256; Matter of Hicks, 170 N. Y. 195.) No identification — no lien. The complaint will not be dismissed, however, if ultimately it is determined that such proceeds are not found in possession of the defendant. Because a trustee has mingled them with his general funds the right to a resort to equity is not ended. The same rule exists as to a trustee *ex maleficio.* If equity has properly obtained jurisdiction it may retain it so as to afford proper relief — personal judgment in such a case against the wrongdoer.

At least such jurisdiction is obtained where the trust fund has come into the hands of the trustee, where the *cestui que trust* is ignorant of its amount and of its subsequent fate, and where the trustee refuses to account. Such either by express statement or by fair inference is the complaint we consider. We so held in Lightfoot *v.* Davis (198 N. Y. 261). Bonds are stolen and sold. Years thereafter the estate of the thief was required to account for the proceeds and repay that amount to the true owner from its general assets. The only relief prayed for, we said, was that the administrator " may account and pay over the amount of said bonds and the income thereof if it can be traced, and if it cannot be traced " that the plaintiff have judgment for the sum of $16,000, and we added: " The method by which equity proceeds in all these cases is to turn the wrongdoer into a trustee. If it may do so for the purpose of subjecting identified funds to the claim of the defrauded party, I do not see why it should not pursue the same method wherever it is necessary to protect the rights of the original owner. In the case of an actual trustee, the *cestui que trust* may not only reclaim the trust property if he is able to trace it, but failing to trace it, he is entitled to an accounting and personal judgment against the trustee."

So we decide that the order dismissing the amended complaint was erroneous. The facts alleged entitle the plaintiff to an accounting and to the general equitable relief for which it prays. To that we confine our decision. The judgment of the Appellate Division and that of the Special Term should be reversed and the motion for judgment dismissing the complaint denied, with costs in all courts.

CARDOZO, Ch. J., POUND, CRANE, KELLOGG and O'BRIEN, JJ., concur; LEHMAN, J., dissents.

Judgment accordingly.[1]

---

[1] The principle of following misappropriated property into its product is applicable not only in the case of trustees and other fiduciaries, such as guardians, executors or administrators and partners, but also in the case of non-fiduciaries.

If property is acquired by fraud, the owner of the property may follow it into its product, and is entitled at his option either to an equitable lien upon the product or to a constructive trust. Falk *v.* Hoffman, 233 N. Y. 199; Ames, Cas. Eq. Juris., 44; Ames, Lect. Leg. Hist., 414.

The same result has been reached where property is acquired by duress. In St. Louis & San Francisco Railroad Co. *v.* Spiller, 274 U. S. 304, a railroad obtained money from a shipper by excessive charges. It was held that the shipper was not entitled to priority over other creditors, but only because the money could not be traced.

The owner of a patent or of a trade mark is entitled to recover profits made by an infringer. Hamilton Shoe Co. *v.* Wolf Bros., 240 U. S. 251. In this case Pitney, J., stated that the principle is " analogous to that which

DIXON v. CALDWELL.

SUPREME COURT, OHIO. 1864.

15 Oh. St. 412.

ERROR to the district court of Ross county.

The defendant in error, Caldwell, was the owner of a military bounty land warrant, No. 31,694, for 160 acres, issued to him by the government of the United States, under the act of congress of February 11, 1847; and, shortly after he received the same, it was fraudulently obtained from him, and replaced by a spurious or forged warrant, which, for a long time, he supposed genuine.

Without the knowledge or consent of Caldwell, the genuine warrant was sold and assigned to George Dixon, Jr., the plaintiff in error, by some person representing Caldwell, and who forged his name thereto.

Dixon, being ignorant of the fraudulent manner in which the warrant had been obtained, and alike ignorant of the forged assignment thereof, on the seventh day of February, 1849, purchased the warrant, and paid therefor one hundred and thirty dollars, believing the assignment to be the genuine assignment of Caldwell, and that, by his purchase, he was acquiring full and complete title to the warrant.

Having thus in good faith acquired, as he supposed, the warrant, Dixon, without any notice of the fraudulent manner in which it had been obtained, or of the forgery, located the same upon the land described in the petition, and obtained a patent therefor before the commencement of the original suit.

Upon this state of fact Caldwell sought to charge Dixon, as his

---

charges a trustee with the profits acquired by wrongful use of the property of the *cestui que trust*."

If property is converted, the owner of the property may follow it into its product, and is entitled to charge the converter as constructive trustee of the product. Pioneer Mining Co. v. Tyberg, 215 Fed. 501; Bank v. Waggoner, 185 N. C. 297; Newton v. Porter, 69 N. Y. 133; Lightfoot v. Davis, 198 N. Y. 261; Nebraska Nat. Bank v. Johnson, 51 Neb. 546; O'Neill v. O'Neill, 227 Pa. 334; Preston v. Moore, 133 Tenn. 247. But see *contra*, Campbell v. Drake, 4 Ired. Eq. (N. C.) 94, *ante;* Hart v. Dogge, 27 Neb. 256; Pascoag Bank v. Hunt, 3 Edw. Ch. (N. Y.) 583; Union Bank v. Baker, 27 Tenn. 447. See 37 Yale L. Jour. 654.

The owner of converted property is entitled to an equitable lien upon its product. Humphreys v. Butler, 51 Ark. 351; Harrison v. Tierney, 254 Ill. 271; National Mahaiwe Bank v. Barry, 125 Mass. 20; Edwards v. Culberson, 111 N. C. 342.

In Lightfoot v. Davis, 198 N. Y. 261, it was held that a suit in equity for the amount of the proceeds of stolen bonds could be maintained, although an action for conversion was barred by the Statute of Limitations and although the proceeds of the bonds could not be traced. But see U. S. v. Bitter Root Co., 200 U. S. 451.

trustee, for the land so located; and, in his petition, prayed for a conveyance of the portion of the lands remaining unsold; for an account of the proceeds of the part which had been sold, and for a judgment against Dixon for the amount found, with interest; also for an account of the rents and profits.

In the court of common pleas Dixon was adjudged to be a trustee of the plaintiff for the lands; and the relief prayed for was granted.

This judgment was, on error, affirmed by the district court, and to reverse this judgment of affirmance is the object of the present petition in error.

WHITE, J. The distinction between legal and equitable rights exists in the subjects to which they relate, and is not affected by the form or mode of procedure that may be prescribed for their enforcement. The code abolished the distinction between actions at law and suits in equity, and substituted in their place one form of action; yet, the rights and liabilities of parties, legal and equitable, as distinguished from the mode of procedure, remain the same since, as before, the adoption of the code. Dixon, the defendant below, is the legal owner of the land in controversy, as patentee. This is conceded by Caldwell, the plaintiff below, but, he claims to be the equitable owner, and that Dixon is his trustee, and, as such, in equity, bound to account for the proceeds of the portion of the land sold, and surrender the remainder.

There is no pretense of an express trust; nor is it claimed that the defendant acquired the property in fraud or by other unfair means. The property, therefore, having been fairly acquired, before a constructive trust can be raised in equity, and fastened upon the defendant, so as to convert him into a trustee for the plaintiff, the circumstances of the transaction must appear to be such, that it would be violating some principle of equity, to allow the defendant to retain the legal title to the land for his own benefit.

The controversy here is not solely in regard to the land warrant. The legal title to that was clearly vested in the plaintiff, and for its conversion he has a plain legal remedy against the defendant for its value; and, before it was lost in entering the land, for its recovery in specie.

The question is, whether, in the light of equity, the measure of legal relief is to be regarded as inadequate; and the defendant required, by a court of equity, to surrender the land to which he acquired the legal title in good faith, and, as he supposed, for his own benefit, by the combined use of the warrant and his own means, industry and enterprise.

The defendant claims to be a *bona fide* purchaser of the land in controversy for value, without notice of the plaintiff's rights; and relies for his defense upon the rules of equity for the protection of such purchasers.

The land warrant in question was assignable in law, was in the possession and apparent ownership of the vendor, and the assignment was regular in form. The defect in the vendor's title was not apparent, and there was no reasonable ground for suspicion that the assignment had been forged. The defendant purchased and paid full value for the warrant, and is not chargeable with a want of reasonable diligence in so doing. Having no reason to suspect the existence of the plaintiff's title to the warrant, he was, in equity and good conscience, chargeable with no duty toward him in relation to its future use. If he withheld it from entry he would have been liable to return it to the plaintiff, or pay him its value. The good faith of his purchase would have been no answer to the plaintiff's legal demand. After the location of the warrant, the holder of the legal title thereof acquired an equity in the land upon which the location was made; and before the defendant clothed himself with the legal title, and while the equities were open between the parties, Caldwell's equity, being older in time, would have been better in right. But Dixon, unaffected with fraud or notice, and upon a valuable consideration paid, having obtained the legal title to the land in controversy, brings himself within the protection awarded in equity to the holder of the legal estate.

A court of equity, says Sugden in his Treatise on Vendors, vol. 3, side p. 417, acts upon the conscience, and as it is impossible to attach any demand upon the conscience of a man who has purchased for a valuable consideration, *bona fide*, and without notice of any claim on the estate, such a man is entitled to the peculiar favor and protection of a court of equity.

Where a court of equity cannot deal directly with the thing which is the subject matter in controversy, but has to reach it through the consciences of the parties, its jurisdiction is necessarily limited to enforcing the fulfillment of their equitable obligations, and cannot extend to compelling the relinquishment of any right or the abandonment of any interest which can be retained consistently with equity and good conscience.

This principle applies especially where the aid of a court of chancery is sought to enforce the surrender of an estate in land. As in such case, the court can only act on the land, through the medium of the parties, it must first inquire whether the party against whom its assistance is sought, is conscientiously bound to comply with the demand urged against him, for if he be not, the case will fall without the scope of a jurisdiction which is founded upon the obligations of conscience. . . .

It is not deemed necessary to examine in detail, in this opinion, the authorities relied on by the counsel of the defendant in error. Where the benefit of the rule has been denied, the party was found to be affected with notice; and, as we have already stated, it is indispensable for the party holding the legal title, and seeking protection in equity, to show that he is a purchaser for a valuable consideration; that his purchase was in all respects fair, and free from every kind of fraud; and that at the time of his purchase he was not chargeable with notice of the adverse claim.

The conclusion, therefore, at which we have arrived, is, that Dixon cannot be required to surrender the legal title of the unsold land to the plaintiff below, nor to account for the proceeds of the part sold; and that the court erred, in requiring him to do so. But, as before stated, he is under a clear legal liability for the value of the warrant. The judgment of the district court, and of the court of common pleas, is therefore reversed, and the cause remanded to the common pleas for further proceedings.[1]

BRINKERHOFF, C. J., and SCOTT, DAY, and WELCH, JJ. concurred.

SIEGER v. SIEGER.

SUPREME COURT, MINNESOTA. 1925.

162 Minn. 322.

ACTION in the district court for Hennepin county to obtain title to certain premises. The case was tried before Nye, J., who ordered judgment in favor of plaintiff. Defendant appealed from an order denying her motion for a new trial. Affirmed.

WILSON, C. J.

Plaintiff sues his divorced wife. Prior to the divorce, he, being unable to read or write, intrusted his wife with the purchase of the real estate involved and on which they were then living. He relied upon her, and reposed absolute confidence in her, and believed that she would guard his interests, and that the legal title to the property would be taken in his name as grantee, but contrary thereto and in violation of the trust imposed, she, wrongfully and without his knowledge or consent, procured a deed with her name as grantee

---

[1] See Ames, Following Misappropriated Property into its Product, 19 Harv. L. Rev. 511, 516; Ames, Lect. Leg. Hist. 412, 416.

A *mala fide* transferee from the original wrongdoer is chargeable as a constructive trustee of any profit made by him. U. S. v. Dunn, 268 U. S. 121; Wheeler v. Kirtland, 23 N. J. Eq. 13; Fur & Wool Trading Co. v. Fox, 245 N. Y. 215, *ante*.

If an innocent donee of misappropriated property acquires title to it and gives it away before he has notice of the misappropriation, he is not liable. Blake v. Metzgar, 150 Pa. 291; Bonesteel v. Bonesteel, 30 Wis. 516. It is immaterial that he subsequently reacquires the property after it has passed to a *bona fide* purchaser. Mast v. Henry, 65 Iowa 193.

If an innocent donee of misappropriated property acquires title to it and sells it before he has notice of the misappropriation, he is liable only for the value of the misappropriated property or the amount of the proceeds at his option. Robes v. Bent, Moore K. B. 552; Wheeler v. Kirtland, 23 N. J. Eq. 13 (*semble*); Truesdell v. Bourke, 29 App. Div. 95, aff'd 161 N. Y. 634.

If, however, the donee sells after he has received notice, the claimant has the option of holding him for the value of the property or the proceeds. Standish v. Babcock, 52 N. J. Eq. 628.

and caused the same to be recorded. Plaintiff did not learn of this until 16 months later when he demanded a conveyance to him. She refused.

Plaintiff has been an industrious and frugal man and the defendant a hard-working and provident woman. Except for $525 received by the wife from her mother's estate, the property owned by the parties was largely the product of plaintiff's labor. When this property was acquired for $3,400, the sum of $2,000 received from the sale of other property and belonging to plaintiff was used, and the balance of the purchase price was paid principally out of funds belonging to defendant. The property is now worth $5,000.

The court found that plaintiff was the owner of an undivided two-fifths of the property and that defendant held the title to such interest in trust for plaintiff. Defendant moved for amended findings or for a new trial. The motion was denied and defendant has appealed from the order denying her motion for a new trial.

Our statute, section 8086, G. S. 1923, provides that no trust shall result in favor of a person who pays the consideration when the title is taken in the name of another. Section 8088 provides that the statute shall not extend to cases where the alienee named in a conveyance has taken the same as an absolute conveyance in his own name, without the knowledge or consent of the person paying the consideration, or when such alienee, in violation of some trust, has purchased the lands so conveyed with moneys belonging to another person.

The conduct of defendant as found by the court shows that she obtained the title to this property in bad faith and in taking advantage of a fiduciary relation. She did this in such an unconscientious manner that she should not in equity and good conscience be permitted to keep it. Under such circumstances equity will impress a constructive trust upon it in favor of the husband. Such trusts are those which arise purely by construction in equity and are independent of any actual or presumed intention of the parties. They are known as trusts ex maleficio or ex delicto. They sound in fraud. [Citing cases.]

There is some confusion between resulting and constructive trusts. In the former there is always the element, although it is an implied one, of an intention to create a trust. The latter arises by operation of law without any reference to any actual or supposed intention of creating a trust and frequently directly contrary to such intention. In fact just as in the case at bar the grantee in the deed holds title in hostility to the world but equity in its benevolence forces a trust upon her conscience and compels her to respond to that which is right. It is put against one not assenting. Stone v. Robinson, 118 Ala. 273, 24 South. 984, 45 L. R. A. 66, 76; 1 Pomeroy, Eq. Jur. § 155 (4th ed.); 3 Pomeroy, Eq. Jur. § 1044.

In Shearer v. Barnes, 118 Minn. 179, 136 N. W. 861, the defendant, Barnes, had wrongfully taken $10,000 out of the funds of a corporation of which he was an officer and invested the same in the purchase of realty at a price of $28,000 and took the title thereto in his own name as grantee without the consent or knowledge of the company. It was held that a pro tanto trust arose in favor of the corporation to the extent of its funds $10,000 invested therein. This court in the Barnes case quoted with approval from Primeau v. Granfield, 184 F. 480, to-wit:

" No one disputes that when the trustee makes a separate investment of trust funds, though wrongfully, the beneficiary may follow the money into the res, or may elect to pursue the money as a lien or charge upon the res. The claim is that, when the trustee's money is mixed with that of the beneficiary, he loses the right to follow the res as property, and has the right only to hold it for a charge to the extent of the claim. On principle there can be no excuse for such a rule. There is no reason why, by adding his own funds to the beneficiary's, the trustee should change the beneficiary's rights in the investment, provided there is no doubt what was the proportion of ownership in the funds actually invested."

In Cisewski v. Cisewski, 129 Minn. 284, 152 N. W. 642, a husband and wife were equal owners in common of a fund of $4,337 in custody of the wife. Without the knowledge or consent of the husband, the wife gave the money for real estate causing title to be of record in a daughter's name, the wife holding an unrecorded deed. It was held that such use of the funds was a breach of trust and that the husband had the right to claim his half of the property.

We think the rule should be, both as to constructive trusts and resulting trusts, that a trust exists pro tanto the amount of the funds used when the amount thereof is definite or constitutes an aliquot part of the whole consideration. [Citing cases.] Substance and not form is the important element in equity. The owner of the money that pays for the property should be the owner of the property. Such is the foundation for a resulting trust, and equity should be no less considerate of one whose property has been misappropriated for an investment than for one who intended that the beneficial interest is not to go with the legal title.

Defendant now claims that, because plaintiff did not pay the whole consideration, he cannot establish a trust. She also says that the facts do not show a " violation of some trust " within the meaning of the statute. Our attention is called to Schierloh v. Schierloh, 148 N. Y. 103, 107, 42 N. E. 409, 410, wherein a wife made the claim that, because she had furnished $1,175 of the purchase price of $13,500, the whole estate vested in her when the husband had promised to have deed made to her, but that, notwithstanding such promise he took the deed in his own name without her knowledge or consent. The decision is in support of defendant's contention. However this case uses this language:

"It may be that in cases where an aliquot or some other definite part of the consideration has been advanced, the parties intending that some specific interest shall vest in the person paying it, or in proportion to the sum paid, there might be a resulting trust to that extent."

But the New York court, in a later case of Leary *v.* Corvin, 181 N. Y. 222, 73 N. E. 984, 106 Am. St. 542, 2 Ann. Cas. 664, where a daughter made contribution to the purchase of the property on the faith of an agreement with her father which he violated by failure to carry out his agreement to secure to her the property upon his death, used language more consistent with our views. The daughter was unaware that her father had taken an absolute deed in his own name. The exception in our statute permits the common law to operate. So it did in New York and the court said:

"The plaintiff's rights are to be determined under the common law rule. Now, while the rule is as stated, that a trust results in favor of the person paying the consideration for a conveyance, it is the settled law that to bring the case within the rule the payment must be either of the whole consideration or of some aliquot part thereof, or for the value of some particular estate in the premises conveyed."

We are of the opinion that the Schierloh case is inconsistent with our decisions which we believe are based upon reason and justice.

In Skehill *v.* Abbott, *supra,* the facts are much the same as here with the element of deception a little weaker and the court termed the consequence a resulting trust.

The appellant urges the doctrine that the rule relative to resulting trusts in favor of the person paying the purchase money for property conveyed to another does not apply where the conveyance is made to the wife of the person paying the money, but in such a case it is to be presumed that the conveyance was intended as a gift, settlement or advancement to the wife and not as a resulting trust to the husband. 39 Cyc. 136. This presumption however, is rebuttable and is not conclusive. There is ample evidence to support the trial court. It is enough that the decision of the trial court was not plainly wrong. But in this case the trust was a constructive trust.

Under the facts in this case we hold: First, that there was a violation of a trust within the meaning of the statute, and, secondly, that it is not necessary for the cestui que trust to pay all the consideration but it is sufficient if he pays a definite or aliquot part thereof and then he is entitled to a trust pro tanto. Constructive trusts are created by equity for the purpose of protecting those who are wronged. Equity cannot look with favor upon the suggestion that the wrongdoer may use two per cent of his own money and ninety-eight per cent of money belonging to another and by virtue of this mixture avoid a trust. This would ignore the reason for the trust, namely, the protection of the party wronged.

Affirmed.[1]

JAMES ROSCOE (BOLTON), LIMITED v. WINDER.

HIGH COURT OF JUSTICE, CHANCERY DIVISION. 1914.

[1915] 1 Ch. 62.

THE plaintiff company was in voluntary liquidation and the defendant was the trustee of the property of William Wigham under an administration order in bankruptcy made on July 9, 1913, Wigham having died on June 20, 1913.

By an agreement dated March 13, 1913, Wigham agreed to purchase from the company, for 900*l*., the goodwill of its business, together with certain assets.

Clause 5 of the agreement was as follows: " The vendors shall permit the purchaser to collect, and the purchaser will collect and get in with all reasonable speed, the book debts of the said business owing at the date hereof without remuneration, and will, on or before April 30 next, pay over to the vendors all moneys received by him on account of such book debts up to that date, such amount to be equal to the gross amount of the debts owing on March 1, 1913, as shown by the books of the vendors. Thereafter all debts then outstanding shall belong to the purchaser."

Wigham paid only part of the 900*l*.

The gross amount of book debts owing on March 1, 1913, was

---

[1] Wedderburn *v.* Wedderburn, 4 Myl. & C. 41; Primeau *v.* Granfield, 184 Fed. 480 (reversed on another ground in s. c., 193 Fed. 911); Treacy *v.* Power, 112 Minn. 226; Shearer v. Barnes, 118 Minn. 179; Fant v. Dunbar, 71 Miss. 576; Holmes *v.* Gilman, 138 N. Y. 369, 378 (*semble*); Dayton *v.* Claflin Co., 19 N. Y. App. Div. 120; Watson *v.* Thompson, 12 R. I. 466, *accord*. But see *Re* Hallett's Estate, 13 Ch. D. 696, 709; Bresnihan *v.* Sheehan, 125 Mass. 11.

In the following cases it was held that where a part of the premiums of life insurance policies was paid with misappropriated money, a constructive trust will be imposed *pro rata.* Vorlander *v.* Keyes, 1 F.(2d) 67; Massachusetts Bonding & Ins. Co. *v.* Josselyn, 224 Mich. 159; Dayton *v.* H. B. Claflin Co., 19 N. Y. App. Div. 120; Truelsch *v.* Miller, 186 Wis. 239.

In Bowling *v.* Bank of New Haven, 219 Ky. 731, the court said (p. 738): " The general rule is that, where trust funds have been misappropriated by the trustee and invested in property not permitted by the instrument creating the trust, or have been mingled with funds of the trustee in the purchase of property and the trust fund is traceable as having furnished in part the money with which the investment was made, and the proportion it formed of the whole money so invested is known or ascertainable, the cestui que trust is entitled to elect to take such a proportion of the whole property which the trust money contributed to purchase as the trust money bore to the whole money invested or to take a lien on the property for the amount of the trust fund. The reason for the rule is that the trustee cannot be allowed to make a profit from the use of trust money."

SECT. VI.] JAMES ROSCOE (BOLTON), LIMITED *v.* WINDER 491

623*l*. 8*s*. 5*d*., and Wigham collected and received this amount, namely, 304*l*. 12*s*., before April 30, 1913, and 318*l*. 16*s*. 5*d*. after April 30, but before or on May 19, 1913, and out of this Wigham paid 455*l*. 18*s*. 11*d*. into his own banking account on or before the lastly named date. He then drew on the account for his own purposes and not in payment for the book debts to the company, with the result that on May 21, 1913, the banking account was in credit to the extent of 25*l*. 18*s*. only, and with that exception all moneys previously paid into the account had been drawn out by Wigham. He subsequently paid in and drew out other moneys, including two sums of 118*l*. 3*s*. 5*d*. and 196*l*. 13*s*. 6*d*. (making together 314*l*. 16*s*. 11*d*.) paid out on cheques in favour of his wife, with the result that at the time of his death he had a credit balance at the bank of 358*l*. 5*s*. 5*d*.

The 314*l*. 16*s*. 11*d*. had been paid over by the wife (who made no claim to it) to the defendant, and in the present action the plaintiffs claimed (*inter alia*) a declaration that the plaintiffs were entitled to or alternatively to a lien or charge on the balance of 358*l*. 5*s*. 5*d*. in part payment of or as security for the 455*l*. 18*s*. 11*d*. moneys alleged to have been received by Wigham in trust for the plaintiffs; an order on the defendant to do all acts and things necessary to enable the plaintiffs to be paid the said sums or such part thereof as was required to replace the 455*l*. 18*s*. 11*d*.; and inquiries, accounts, and incidental relief.

The defendant by his defence said that Wigham's banking account was his general banking account into which moneys from many sources were paid by him, and out of which many payments were from time to time made by him; that any moneys received on behalf of Wigham on account of the plaintiffs and paid into the bank had been expended by him, and therefore no part of the credit balance of 358*l*. 5*s*. 5*d*. was money received on account of the plaintiffs, except, perhaps, the 25*l*. 18*s*.; and, while denying liability, the defendant paid into Court the 25*l*. 18*s*., the credit balance in the bank on May 21, 1913.

SARGANT, J. This is an action which raises a point connected with the decision in *In re* Hallett's Estate, 13 Ch. D. 696, and in which the claim of the plaintiffs, if successful, would result, in my opinion, in a very large extension of the doctrine laid down in that case. [His Lordship referred to the agreement and read clause 5 of it, and continued:] That clause is the really material clause for the present purpose. The gross amount of the book debts owing at the date fixed by the agreement was 623*l*. 8*s*. 5*d*., and the debtor in fact collected and received that amount. Part of that amount, 304*l*. 12*s*., was received by him up to April 30, 1913, and the balance, 318*l*. 16*s*. 5*d*., was received by him after April 30, but before or on May 19, a date the importance of which will appear later. Out of the amount so received by the debtor he paid the sum of 455*l*. 18*s*.

11*d*. into his general banking account, and at the date of his death, on June 20, 1913, that account showed a credit balance of 358*l*. 5*s*. 5*d*.

What is now claimed in the present action (because one or two other points have been given up) is a charge upon the 358*l*. 5*s*. 5*d*. remaining to the credit of the debtor's account at the time of his death, for the sum of 455*l*. 18*s*. 11*d*. received by him in respect of these book debts and paid into his banking account. That is the strict legal way of putting the claim, but, of course, practically it amounts of claiming the full sum of 358*l*. 5*s*. 5*d*., since that sum is less than the amount of the charge claimed.

The first point that was taken against the claim was that no trust was created by the agreement as to the book debts to be collected under it. In my opinion, that objection cannot be sustained. It seems to me that the true effect of clause 5 of the agreement is that the purchaser is throughout collecting the book debts on behalf of the vendors, and that he has to pay over the money received on account of the book debts; the language of the clause is express in that respect. No doubt, he has on April 30 to make up to the vendors the full amount of the book debts if he has not by that time received them himself. That is a personal obligation on his part to make up the deficiency, but I do not think that in any way affects his obligation to hand over the actual book debts to the vendors so far as he does in fact receive them. And, incidentally, I think that the concluding words of clause 5, " thereafter all debts then outstanding shall belong to the purchaser," do not mean after April 30, but after the time when the purchaser shall have fulfilled his obligation to make up the deficiency of the book debts collected by him to the full amount. Accordingly, so far as the purchaser did collect these book debts, he did, in my opinion, hold the amount in trust for the vendors.

That being so, we have a case where, as in *In re* Hallett's Estate, 13 Ch. D. 696, the banking account of the debtor comprised not only moneys belonging to himself for his own purposes, but also moneys belonging to him upon trust for some one else, and that being so, and apart from the circumstance I am going to mention, it seems to me clear that the plaintiffs would be entitled to the charge they claim, and to receive the whole balance of 358*l*. 5*s*. 5*d*. standing to the debtor's credit at the time of his death, and that although there had been payments out of the account which, under the rule in Clayton's Case, (1816) 1 Mer. 572, would have been attributable to the earlier payments in.

In re Hallett's Estate, which would but for the circumstance I am going to mention entirely conclude this case, decided two clear points: First, that when a trustee mixes trust moneys with private moneys in one account the *cestuis que trust* have a charge on the aggregate amount for their trust fund; and, secondly, that when payments are made by the trustee out of the general account the payments are not to be appropriated against payments in to that account as in Clayton's Case, because the trustee is presumed to be honest rather than dishonest and to make payments out of his own private moneys and not out of the trust fund that was mingled with his private moneys.

But there is a further circumstance in the present case which seems to me to be conclusive in favour of the defendant as regards the greater part of the balance of 358*l*. 5*s*. 5*d*. It appears that after the payment in by the debtor of a portion of the book debts which he had received the balance at the bank on May 19, 1913, was reduced by his drawings to a sum of 25*l*. 18*s*. only on May 21. So that, although the ultimate balance at the debtor's death was about 358*l*., there had been an intermediate balance of only 25*l*. 18*s*. The result of that seems to me to be that the trust moneys cannot possibly be traced into this common fund, which was standing to the debtor's credit at his death, to an extent of more than 25*l*. 18*s*., because, although *prima facie* under the second rule in *In re* Hallett's Estate, any drawings out by the debtor ought to be attributed to the private moneys which he had at the bank and not to the trust moneys, yet, when the drawings out had reached such an amount that the whole of his private money part had been exhausted, it necessarily followed that the rest of the drawings must have been against trust moneys. There being on May 21, 1913, only 25*l*. 18*s*. in all, standing to the credit of the debtor's account, it is quite clear that on that day he must have denuded his account of all the trust moneys there — the whole 455*l*. 18*s*. 11*d*. — except to the extent of 25*l*. 18*s*.

Practically, what Mr. Martelli and Mr. Hansell have been asking me to do — although I think Mr. Hansell in particular rather disguised the claim by the phraseology he used — is to say that the debtor, by paying further moneys after May 21 into this common account, was impressing upon those further moneys so paid in the like trust or obligation, or charge of the nature of a trust, which had formerly been impressed upon the previous balances to the credit of that account. No doubt, Mr. Hansell did say, "No. I am only asking you to treat the account as a whole, and to consider the balance from time to time standing to the credit of that account as subject to one continual charge or trust." But I think that really is using words which are not appropriate to the facts. You must, for the purpose of tracing, which was the process adopted in *In re* Hallett's Estate, put your finger on some definite fund which either remains in its original state or can be found in another shape. That is tracing, and tracing, by the very facts of this case, seems to be absolutely excluded except as to the 25*l*. 18*s*.

Then, apart from tracing, it seems to me possible to establish this claim against the ultimate balance of 358*l*. 5*s*. 5*d*. only by saying that something was done, with regard to the additional moneys which are needed to make up that balance, by the person to whom those moneys belonged, the debtor, to substitute those moneys for the purpose of, or to impose upon those moneys a trust equivalent to, the trust which rested on the previous balance. Of course, if there was anything like a separate trust account, the payment of the further moneys into that account would, in itself, have been quite a sufficient indication of the intention of the debtor to substitute those additional moneys for the original trust moneys, and accordingly to impose, by way of substitution, the old trusts upon those additional moneys. But, in a case where the account into which the moneys are paid is the general trading account of the debtor on which he has been accustomed to draw both in the ordinary course and in breach of trust when there were trust funds standing to the credit of that account which were convenient for that purpose, I think it is impossible to attribute to him that by the mere payment into the account of further moneys, which to a large extent he subsequently used for purposes of his own, he intended to clothe those moneys with a trust in favour of the plaintiffs.

Certainly, after having heard *In re* Hallett's Estate stated over and over again, I should have thought that the general view of that decision was that it only applied to such an amount of the balance ultimately standing to the credit of the trustee as did not exceed the lowest balance of the account during the intervening period. That view has practically been taken, as far as I can make out, in the cases which have dealt with *In re* Hallett's Estate. *In re* Oatway, [1903] 2 Ch. 356, a decision of Joyce, J., was cited to me in support of the plaintiff's case, but I do not find anything in it to help them. All that Joyce, J., did in that case was to say that, if part of the mixed moneys can be traced into a definite security, that security will not become freed from the charge in favour of the trust, but will, together with any residue of the mixed moneys, remain subject to that charge. I am sure that nothing which he said was intended to mean that the trust was imposed upon any property into which the original fund could not be traced. The head-note to the decision of North, J., in *In re* Stenning, [1895] 2 Ch. 433 (which accurately represents the effect of the case) is stated in such terms as to indicate that the application of the doctrine in *In re* Hallett's Estate, implied that there should be a continuous balance standing to the credit of the account equal to the balance against which the charge is sought to be enforced. And certainly in the recent case of Sinclair *v.* Brougham, [1914] A. C. 398, I can see nothing in any way to impeach the doctrine as to tracing laid down in *In re* Hallett's Estate.

In my opinion, therefore, the only part of the balance of 358*l.* 5*s.* 5*d.* which can be made available by the plaintiffs is the sum of 25*l.* 18*s.*, being the smallest amount to which the balance, to the

SECT. VI.]   *In re* WALTER J. SCHMIDT & CO.   495

credit of the account had fallen between May 19, 1913, and the death of the debtor.[1]

In re WALTER J. SCHMIDT & CO.

DISTRICT COURT, S. D. NEW YORK. 1923.

298 Fed. 314.

IN Bankruptcy. In the matter of Walter J. Schmidt & Co., bankrupts. Claims by one Feuerbach, one Hunsberger, and one Bonynge against funds and the estate considered and determined.

Sur exceptions to a special master's report in bankruptcy. The bankrupts were stockbrokers doing business in New York. The petitioners were their customers, for whom they had bought various

---

[1] Mercantile Trust Co. *v.* St. Louis & S. F. Ry. Co., 99 Fed. 485; *Re* Mulligan, 116 Fed. 715 (*semble*); Bank of British N. A. *v.* Freights, 127 Fed. 859 (affirmed s. c., 137 Fed. 534); American Can Co. *v.* Williams, 178 Fed. 420; *Re* M. E. Dunn & Co., 193 Fed. 212; Powell *v.* Missouri Co., 99 Ark. 553; Woodhouse *v.* Crandall, 197 Ill. 104; Cable *v.* Iowa State Sav. Bank, 197 Iowa 393; Waddell *v.* Waddell, 36 Utah 435; Chase & Baker Co. *v.* Olmsted, 93 Wash. 306; State *v.* Foster, 5 Wyo. 199, *accord*.

If there is always an amount in the fund equal to or greater than the amount of the plaintiff's claim, the plaintiff will be able to get full satisfaction of his claim. *Re* Hallett's Estate, 13 Ch. D. 696, 731; Massey *v.* Fisher, 62 Fed. 958; Hutchinson *v.* Le Roy, 113 Fed. 202; *Re* Royea's Estate, 143 Fed. 182; Smith *v.* Mottley, 150 Fed. 266; Butler *v.* Western German Bank, 159 Fed. 116; *Re* Stewart, 178 Fed. 463; Southern Cotton Oil Co. *v.* Elliotte, 218 Fed. 567; Elizalde *v.* Elizalde, 137 Cal. 634; Whitcomb *v.* Carpenter, 134 Iowa 227; First Nat. Bank *v.* Eastern Trust and Banking Co., 108 Me. 79; Fogg *v.* Tyler, 109 Me. 109; Board of Fire & Water Commissioners *v.* Wilkinson, 119 Mich. 655; Patek *v.* Patek, 166 Mich. 446; Blair *v.* Hill, 50 N. Y. App. Div. 33 (affirmed s. c., 165 N. Y. 672); Widman *v.* Kellogg, 22 N. D. 396; Conneautville Bank's Assigned Estate, 280 Pa. 545; Emigh *v.* Earling, 134 Wis. 565.

If the fund is wholly drawn out and dissipated, the claimant is relegated to a mere personal claim against the wrongdoer. Schuyler *v.* Littlefield, 232 U. S. 707; Beard *v.* Independent District, 88 Fed. 375; Hewitt *v.* Hayes, 205 Mass. 356; *Re* Assignment of Bank of Oregon, 32 Ore. 84.

On the question, however, how far additions by the wrongdoer may be regarded as a restoration of the money withdrawn, see *Ex parte* Kingston, L. R. 6 Ch. App. 632; Cable *v.* Iowa State Sav. Bank, 197 Iowa 393; State Savings Bank *v.* Thompson, 128 Pac. 1120 (Kan. 1913); Supreme Lodge *v.* Liberty Trust Co., 215 Mass. 27; Jeffray *v.* Towar, 63 N. J. Eq. 530, 546; Van Alen *v.* American National Bank, 52 N. Y. 1; Baker *v.* N. Y. Bank, 100 N. Y. 31; United National Bank *v.* Weatherby, 70 N. Y. App. Div. 279; Hungerford *v.* Curtis, 43 R. I. 124, 19 Mich. L. Rev. 231; Garst *v.* Canfield, 44 R. I. 220. Compare Sharp *v.* Jackson, [1899] A. C. 419 (affirming New *v.* Hunting, [1897] 2 Q. B. 19); Taylor *v.* London and County Banking Co., [1901] 2 Ch. 231, 254; *Re* Cozens, [1913] 2 Ch. 478. See *Re* Northrup, 152 Fed. 763. Compare the analogous cases where a broker wrongfully disposes of a customer's stock, such as Gorman *v.* Littlefield, 229 U. S. 19; Duel *v.* Hollins, 241 U. S. 523. See note to People *v.* Meadows, 199 N. Y. 1, *ante*.

See 26 A. L. R. 3; 35 A. L. R. 747; 55 A. L. R. 1275.

securities, which they pledged as collateral to their own loans with banks. In no case had the petitioners paid for the securities in full, and some had signed consents that the brokers might pledge all securities, regardless of the state of the customer's account, unless it were paid in full. The several petitioners make claim against the receiver for interests in various funds in his hands, asserting that they represent the proceeds of their securities. These claims were referred and disposed of by the special master.

LEARNED HAND, District Judge. For various reasons not necessary to state the petitioners Schrader, Bonynge, and Salmond all have claims against the bank deposit in the Lincoln Trust Company, which the receiver recognizes as entitling them collectively to the whole of it as a trust fund. The only question is how it shall be divided between them. The special master upheld the claims of Cole, Bonynge, and Schrader, and divided the fund, under the authority of Empire, etc., Co. v. Carroll County, 194 Fed. 593, 114 C. C. A. 435, on the principle that the petitioner whose money was last deposited should withdraw from the fund first and so on in inverse order of deposit until the same is exhausted. To this Schrader, who comes last, objects, on the ground that the deposit should be ratably divided, and also because the claims of Cole and Bonynge were improperly allowed. Salmond's claim was not passed on, because, under the rule applied, the fund was exhausted before he could withdraw.

(1) The rule adopted by the special master has indeed the support of considerable authority, but none of it is authoritative upon me. Empire, etc., Co. v. Carroll County, 194 Fed. 593, 114 C. C. A. 435; Hewitt v. Hayes, 205 Mass. 356, 365, 91 N. E. 332, 137 Am. St. Rep. 448; Re Stenning [1895] L. R. 2 Ch. Div. 433; Knatchbull v. Hallett, L. R. 13 Ch. Div. 696. It depends upon charging withdrawals from a fund held by two joint cestuis que trustent against the earlier of the two, following or assuming to follow the rule in Clayton's Case, 1 Mer. 572. However, as pointed out by Professor Scott in 27 Harv. Law Rev. 130, note 15, the circumstances are wholly different. The rule in Clayton's Case is to allocate the payments upon an account. Some rule had to be adopted, and though any presumption of intent was a fiction, priority in time was the most natural basis of allocation. It has no relevancy whatever to a case like this. Here two people are jointly interested in a fund held for them by a common trustee. There is no reason in law or justice why his depredations upon the fund should not be borne equally between them. To throw all the loss upon one, through the mere chance of his being earlier in time, is irrational and arbitrary, and is equally a fiction as the rule in Clayton's Case, *supra*. When the law adopts a fiction, it is, or at least it should be, for some purpose of justice. To adopt it here is to apportion a common misfortune through a test which has no relation whatever to the justice of the case.

It does not follow, however, that the claimants should divide the fund in the proportions of their original deposits. An illustration will perhaps be clearest. Suppose three claimants, A., B., and C., for $5,000 each, whose money was deposited at intervals of a month, January, February, and March. Suppose that the fund had been reduced on some day in January to $3,000. A. has lost $2,000, which he cannot throw on B. Hence, when B.'s money is deposited on February 1st, A. and B. will share $8,000 in the proportion of 3 to 5. Suppose that during February the account gets as low as $4,000. A. and B. cannot throw this loss on C., and when C.'s money is deposited they will share the $9,000 in the proportion of 3, 5, and 10. But any subsequent depletion below $9,000 they must bear in that proportion, just as A. and B. bore theirs in February. At least, to me it would be a parody of justice if, out of a remainder, for example, of $7,000, C. should get $5,000, B. $2,000, and A. get nothing at all. Such a result, I submit with the utmost respect, can only come from a mechanical adherence to a rule which has no intelligible relation to the situation.

(2) Next, as to Schrader's challenge of Cole's and Bonynge's claims. Each of these customers had securities in the bankrupts' hands on which there were sums due. The bankrupts had hypothecated these with the bank, so far as appears, quite lawfully. Being desirous of taking them out of the account, each customer asked the amount of his debit balance and paid the balance due. The bankrupts cashed the checks and put the proceeds in the Lincoln Trust Company, where they were at the time of the receivership, or at least some part of them. It is against this fund that the claimants now seek to prove.

The situation is not new in the courts, and the claimants must lose. When the brokers actually received the securities for Cole and Bonynge, they became their property, and the purchase price, for which the brokers had became liable to the sellers, was due from the customers to them. In paying the money, they merely paid that debt to the brokers. If the securities were converted, their sole remedy was to follow the proceeds. In re A. O. Brown, Ex parte First National Bank of Princeton, 175 Fed. 769, 99 C. C. A. 345 (C. C. A. 2). In that case I had decided that the customer might rescind for nonperformance and follow the consideration, but that was reversed. The case is different from In re A. O. Brown & Co., Ex parte Horrocks, 185 Fed. 766, 107 C. C. A. 656; In re A. O. Brown & Co., Ex parte Smart (D. C.) 185 Fed. 972; s. c. (D. C.) 189 Fed. 432, where the question was whether the broker, having executed the order, had ever received the securities.

In re Bolognesi & Co., 254 Fed. 770, 166 C. C. A. 216, and People v. Meadows, 199 N. Y. 1, 92 N. E. 128, are in this class. Why the customer should not have an equal right to rescind, whether the broker had received the stocks or not, was not and is not apparent to me, since delivery is as much a part of his obligation as receiving.

However, A. O. Brown & Co., Ex parte First National Bank, *supra*, is a ruling on that point which I must accept. Under it Cole and Bonynge are confined to the proceeds of the securities.

I have not before me any report upon that subject, and therefore cannot pass upon their rights. The learned master has dealt only with the bank deposit. Hence Schrader and Salmond *et al.* must divide that between them in accordance with the rule laid down at the outset, providing Salmond can make good his claim. Cole and Bonynge may prove against any sum into which they can trace their securities. . . .

SUPPLEMENTAL OPINION

Since filing my opinion of November 12, 1923, counsel have called to my attention the case of *In re* Bolognesi & Co., 254 Fed. 770, 166 C. C. A. 216, to which I referred. The end of that case, which I regret to say I did not observe at the time, distributed the funds in accordance with the rule of Knatchbull *v.* Hallett, L. R. 13 Ch. Div. 696, and Empire, etc., Co. *v.* Carroll County, 194 Fed. 593, 114 C. C. A. 435. Of course, it constitutes authority absolutely binding upon me and I must therefore modify my directions to the referee so as to accord with the law which controls in this circuit, regardless of my own opinion on the question. The referee will therefore in dividing the trust fund follow the principle that the last depositor shall be paid in full and so on until the fund is exhausted. This is the only modification necessary.[1]

In re OATWAY.

HERTSLET *v.* OATWAY.

HIGH COURT OF JUSTICE, CHANCERY DIVISION. 1903.

[1903] 2 Ch. 356.

THIS was a creditor's action for the administration of the estate of Lewis John Oatway, a solicitor, who died insolvent in 1902. The defendant Christiana Mary Oatway was his sole executrix. In the course of the administration a question arose as to the title to a sum

[1] See *Re* Hallett's Estate, 13 Ch. D. 696; Hancock *v.* Smith, 41 Ch. D. 456 (*semble*); *Re* Stenning, [1895] 2 Ch. 433; Mutton *v.* Peat, [1899] 2 Ch. 556, 560 (*semble*); Empire State Surety Co. *v.* Carroll County, 194 Fed. 593, 605; *Re* Bolognesi & Co., 254 Fed. 770; Hewitt *v.* Hayes, 205 Mass. 356. But see *Re* Mulligan, 116 Fed. 715, 719.

In Yesner *v.* Com'r of Banks, 252 Mass. 358; Central Auto-Tire Co. *v.* Com'r of Banks, 252 Mass. 363; and Downing *v.* Cunningham, 256 Mass. 285, in which money obtained from several persons by fraud was deposited in a bank account and it did not appear in what order the deposits were made, it was held that the claimants were entitled to divide *pro rata* what remained in the account. See also Cunningham *v.* Brown, 265 U. S. 1; U. S. Fidelity & G. Co. *v.* Union Bank & T. Co., 228 Fed. 448; *Re* Young, 294 Fed. 1; People *v.* California Safe Dep. & T. Co., 175 Cal. 756.

of 2474*l.* 19*s.*, being the proceeds of sale of 1000 shares in a company called the Oceana Company, which at the date of the testator's death were standing in his name.

The testator and one Maxwell Skipper were co-trustees under the will of Charles Skipper, deceased. In 1899 and 1900 sums amounting to 3000*l.* were advanced in breach of trust out of Charles Skipper's estate to Maxwell Skipper upon the security of a mortgage of an undivided share of certain real estate to which he was entitled under his grandfather's will. In 1901 Maxwell Skipper went abroad, having given to Oatway a power of attorney under which and as mortgagee he on August 15, 1901, sold Maxwell Skipper's reversionary interest for the sum of 7000*l.* This sum Oatway paid into his own banking account, which at that time was in credit to the extent of 77*l.* 13*s.* 4*d.* He did not replace the 3000*l.* which had been advanced to Maxwell Skipper out of Charles Skipper's trust estate.

On August 15, 1901, Maxwell Skipper was indebted to Oatway in the sum of 1779*l.* 7*s.* 1*d.*, and also in a further unascertained amount in respect of costs.

On August 24, 1901, Oatway purchased the Oceana shares for 2137*l.* 12*s.* 3*d.*, which he paid for by a cheque on his banking account. Before the purchase of the shares Oatway had made further payments into the account to the extent of 30*l.* 1*s.* 11*d.*, and had drawn out sums amounting to 510*l.* 8*s.* 6*d.*; so that when he drew the cheque for 2137*l.* 12*s.* 3*d.* in payment for the shares the credit balance of his account was 6635*l.* 6*s.* 4*d.*, which sum included the 3000*l.* belonging to the estate of Charles Skipper.

After paying for the shares, Oatway paid further sums into the account, but his subsequent drawings for his own purposes exhausted the whole amount standing to his credit, and there was nothing to represent the 3000*l.* except the proceeds of the Oceana shares.

This was a summons taken out by Maxwell Skipper, who was also a defendant to the action, asking that the sum of 2474*l.* 19*s.*, being the proceeds of the Oceana shares, might be paid to him either in his personal capacity or as trustee under the will of Charles Skipper.

Austen-Cartmell, for the applicant. Oatway was bound when he received the 7000*l.* to replace the 3000*l.*, which, in breach of trust, had been advanced to Maxwell Skipper out of Charles Skipper's estate. He then had to account to Maxwell Skipper for the balance of the 7000*l.* The whole of the 7000*l.* having disappeared except that which can be traced into the Oceana shares, the proceeds of those shares clearly belong to the applicant either personally or as trustee.

In a case of this sort the second part of the holding in *In re* Hallett's Estate, 13 Ch. D. 696, does not apply. It cannot be said that the shares were bought by Oatway out of his own money, and that therefore he is entitled to hold them as against the beneficiaries under Charles Skipper's will. Where a trustee has mixed trust money with his own and has purchased land or chattels out of the mixed fund, the beneficial owner can follow the trust money and is entitled to a charge on the purchased property: *In re* Hallett's Estate. The applicant does not desire to press his personal claim to the proceeds of the shares, provided that the Skipper trust gets the benefit of them; but he submits that he is entitled to recover against Oatway's estate.

Younger, K. C., and *Ashworth James*, for the plaintiffs, who were beneficiaries under Charles Skipper's will. The proceeds of the Oceana shares clearly belong to the Skipper trust.

Dibdin, K. C., *A. Whitaker*, and *Crossfield*, for the defendant Christiana Mary Oatway. When Oatway bought the shares the balance to his credit at the bank was sufficient to enable him to pay for them apart from the 3000*l.* trust money. The proceeds of the shares belong to Oatway's estate. It was his own money which he drew out to pay for them. He was entitled as against Maxwell Skipper to do that: *In re* Hallett's Estate.

Cur. adv. vult.

JOYCE, J. Oatway was co-trustee with Maxwell Skipper of the will of Charles Skipper, the father of the latter. In breach of trust 3000*l.* was advanced from the trust to Maxwell Skipper upon the security of a mortgage given by him to Oatway alone. Oatway, as mortgagee, and under a power of attorney from Maxwell Skipper, sold the mortgaged property, and as mortgagee received and gave a receipt for the 3000*l.* trust money, part of the proceeds of sale, which amounted to 7000*l.* The rest he received as agent of or on behalf of Maxwell Skipper, from whom he held a power of attorney. Oatway, instead of investing the 3000*l.* upon proper trust securities in the joint names of himself and Maxwell Skipper, the trustees, paid in the whole 7000*l.* on August 15, 1901, to his own banking account, which was then in credit to the amount of 77*l.* 13*s.* 4*d.* Between August 15 and 24 he paid in sums amounting to 30*l.* and drew out 510*l.*, which he paid away to creditors or otherwise applied to his own purposes in such a manner as to be irrecoverable.

On August 24, out of the balance to the credit of the account, Oatway paid 2137*l.* 12*s.* 3*d.* for the purchase of certain shares in the Oceana Company, which remained in his name at the time of his decease, and have since been sold by arrangement. It is the proceeds of these shares which is now in question. The balance to the credit of the account after this payment, with some other sums paid in from time to time by Oatway, was subsequently exhausted by his drawings on his own account.

The balance of the 7000*l.*, after discharging the mortgage, belonged to Maxwell Skipper, but it is alleged that Oatway as a creditor of his had claims thereon to a large amount. Maxwell Skipper, who was himself a party to the original breach of trust, could not under the circumstances, and in fact does not, oppose the claim of the trust to the proceeds of the Oceana shares. For the purposes of this case we may consider Oatway to have been entitled to the balance of the 7000*l*. after discharging the 3000*l*. mortgage.

There is no conflict between different fiduciary owners or sets of *cestuis que trust*. It is a principle settled as far back as the time of the Year Books that, whatever alteration of form any property may undergo, the true owner is entitled to seize it in its new shape if he can prove the identity of the original material: see Blackstone, vol. ii, p. 405, and Lupton *v.* White, (1808) 15 Ves. 432. But this rule is carried no farther than necessity requires, and is applied only to cases where the compound is such as to render it impossible to apportion the respective shares of the parties. Thus, if the quality of the articles that are mixed be uniform, and the original quantities known, as in the case of so many pounds of trust money mixed with so many pounds of the trustee's own money, the person by whose act the confusion took place is still entitled to claim his proper quantity, but subject to the quantity of the other proprietor being first made good out of the whole mass: 2 Stephen's Commentaries (13th ed.), 20. Trust money may be followed into land or any other property in which it has been invested; and when a trustee has, in making any purchase or investment, applied trust money together with his own, the *cestuis que trust* are entitled to a charge on the property purchased for the amount of the trust money laid out in the purchase or investment. Similarly, if money held by any person in a fiduciary capacity be paid into his own banking account, it may be followed by the equitable owner, who, as against the trustee, will have a charge for what belongs to him upon the balance to the credit of the account. If, then, the trustee pays in further sums, and from time to time draws out money by cheques, but leaves a balance to the credit of the account, it is settled that he is not entitled to have the rule in Clayton's Case, (1816) 1 Mer. 572, applied so as to maintain that the sums which have been drawn out and paid away so as to be incapable of being recovered represented *pro tanto* the trust money, and that the balance remaining is not trust money, but represents only his own moneys paid into the account. Brown *v.* Adams, L. R. 4 Ch. 764, to the contrary ought not to be followed since the decision in *In re* Hallett's Estate, 13 Ch. D. 696. It is, in my opinion, equally clear that when any of the money drawn out has been invested, and the investment remains in the name or under the control of the trustee, the rest of the balance having been afterwards dissipated by him, he cannot maintain that the investment which remains represents his own money alone, and that what has been spent and can no longer be traced and recovered was the money belonging to the trust. In other words, when the private money of the trustee and that which he held in a fiduciary capacity have been mixed in the same banking account, from which various payments have from time to time been made, then, in order to determine to whom any remaining balance or any investment that may have been paid for out of the account ought to be deemed to belong, the trustee must be debited with all the sums that have been withdrawn and applied to his own use so as to be no longer recoverable, and the trust money in like manner be debited with any sums taken out and duly invested in the names of the proper trustees. The order of priority in which the various withdrawals and investments may have been respectively made is wholly immaterial. I have been referring, of course, to cases where there is only one fiduciary owner or set of *cestuis que trust* claiming whatever may be left as against the trustee. In the present case there is no balance left. The only investment or property remaining which represents any part of the mixed moneys paid into the banking account is the Oceana shares purchased for 2137l. Upon these, therefore, the trust had a charge for the 3000l. trust money paid into the account. That is to say, those shares and the proceeds thereof belong to the trust.

It was objected that the investment in the Oceana shares was made at a time when Oatway's own share of the balance to the credit of the account (if the whole had been then justly distributed) would have exceeded 2137l., the price of the shares; that he was therefore entitled to withdraw that sum, and might rightly apply it for his own purposes; and that consequently the shares should be held to belong to his estate. To this I answer that he never was entitled to withdraw the 2137l. from the account, or, at all events, that he could not be entitled to take that sum from the account and hold it or the investment made therewith, freed from the charge in favour of the trust, unless or until the trust money paid into the account had been first restored, and the trust fund reinstated by due investment of the money in the joint names of the proper trustees, which never was done.

The investment by Oatway, in his own name, of the 2137l. in Oceana shares no more got rid of the claim or charge of the trust upon the money so invested, than would have been the case if he had drawn a cheque for 2137l. and simply placed and retained the amount in a drawer without further disposing of the money in any way. The proceeds of the Oceana shares must be held to belong to the trust funds under the will of which Oatway and Maxwell Skipper were the trustees.[1]

[1] See Primeau *v.* Granfield, 184 Fed. 480 (reversed on another ground in s. c., 193 Fed. 911); *Re* A. O. Brown & Co., 189 Fed. 432; Brennan *v.* Tillinghast, 201 Fed. 609; City of Lincoln *v.* Morrison, 64 Neb. 822, 831; Lamb *v.* Rooney, 72 Neb. 322. But see Board of Commissioners *v.* Strawn, 157 Fed. 49; *Re* City Bank of Dowagiac, 186 Fed. 413; *Re* Brown, 193 Fed. 24 (affirmed, without mention of this point, *sub nom.* First Nat. Bank *v.* Littlefield, 226 U. S. 110); Empire State Surety Co. *v.* Carroll County, 194 Fed.

M'MAHON v. FETHERSTONHAUGH.

HIGH COURT OF JUSTICE, CHANCERY DIVISION. IRELAND. 1894.

[1895] 1 I. R. 83.

ADJOURNED SUMMONS on behalf of James F. Darcy, that he might be declared owner of so much of the Waterford and Limerick Railway of Ireland Stock, transferred by the Bank of Ireland to the credit of the matter as should be of the value of £433 5s., or that he might be admitted to claim against the assets of the deceased for that amount. The applicant, in an affidavit filed in support of the summons, stated that he had in September, 1892, employed the deceased, who had been a stockbroker, to sell £400 4½ per cent. preference stock of the Waterford and Limerick Railway, and that he afterwards received the deeds of transfer from the deceased, and executed them and returned them to him.

The deceased received from the brokers for the purchaser their cheque on the Bank of Ireland for £433 5s., the amount of the purchase-money of the said shares, which, deducting Mr. Reynold's commission, left £428 17s. payable to Mr. Darcy. This cheque was payable to "Reynolds or bearer," and was lodged on the day it was received, 7th September, 1892, to the credit of his current account with the Bank of Ireland. At the time of lodging the cheque the deceased had two accounts with the Bank, one his current account, on which he had a balance to his credit, the other a loan account, on which he was indebted to the Bank, but which was amply secured. On the 8th Sept. Mr. Reynolds died without having paid to Mr. Darcy the price of the stock sold for him. On the 16th September the Bank appropriated the entire credit balance of deceased, amounting to £818 9s. 4d., towards payment of the amount due to them on the loan account, and discharged the balance due, by sale of some of the securities. The remainder of the securities, consisting of forty-nine shares of the nominal value of £50, representing £2450 Waterford and Limerick Railway Stock was transferred by the Bank, to the credit of the matter. The defendant was the administratrix of the deceased.

593; Covey v. Cannon, 104 Ark. 550; Bright v. King, 20 Ky. Law Rep. 186; Standish v. Babcock, 52 N. J. Eq. 628; Waddell v. Waddell, 36 Utah 435.

In Glidden v. Gutelius, 96 Fla. 834, a trust company mingled funds which it held as administrator with its general funds and purchased securities with the commingled funds and thereafter failed, having on hand less cash than was necessary to satisfy its obligations as fiduciary. It was held that the beneficiaries of the estate were entitled to reach the securities in priority to general creditors.

In City of Lincoln v. Morrison, 64 Neb. 822, a part of the commingled fund was used in buying property which was sold at a profit. The claimant was allowed to reach this profit.

THE VICE-CHANCELLOR [CHATTERTON]. The principles of equity applicable to this case are clear and well established. It appears that Mr. Darcy employed the deceased in this matter to sell certain shares for him, which he accordingly sold, and was paid by the broker for the purchaser. Mr. Reynolds lodged the cheque which he received in payment, together with a small sum of money, to his current account on 7th September. He had at the same time a loan account, on which there was a considerable balance due to the Bank. Mr. Reynolds died on the following day, and the case is not complicated by any drawings against that lodgment. As the tree fell so it lay. There was £818 due to Reynolds by the Bank on his current account, while on his other account, which was a fully secured loan account, there was a balance due to the Bank.

There is as clear proof of identity as could possibly be required, and Mr. Darcy's money is traced into the £818. There is no question as to that. What was the consequence of Reynolds lodging this money in the way he did? The very moment it was lodged it became liable to the Bank's lien. The Bank had a clear right to appropriate this £818 to the debt due to them on the loan account, but the equity which Mr. Darcy had of marshalling against the securities held by the Bank was not thereby disturbed. The Bank have paid themselves out of Mr. Darcy's money, and *pro tanto* released the securities which have been lodged in Court, and the equity which Mr. Darcy had to marshal against those securities could not be disturbed by the action of the Bank in lodging the securities in Court. The rights of the parties are the same as if the securities were still in the hands of the Bank, and I hold that Mr. Darcy is entitled to stand in the place of the Bank as to these remaining securities, and accordingly I must declare that he has a lien on the fund brought in by the Bank of Ireland to the credit of this action for the sum of £428 17s., portion of £818.

The defendant must have her costs in the action, and Mr. Darcy is entitled to his costs with his demand.[1]

SLATER v. ORIENTAL MILLS.

SUPREME COURT, RHODE ISLAND. 1893.

18 R. I. 352.

BILL IN EQUITY to establish a charge upon an assigned estate.

July 12, 1893. STINESS, J. The question, raised by the demurrer to the bill, is whether the Forestdale Manufacturing Company, of which the complainants are stockholders, has a preferred claim upon

[1] *Re* Ennis, 187 Fed. 720; *Re* A. O. Brown & Co., 189 Fed. 432; Red Bud Realty Co. *v.* South, 96 Ark. 281; Ordway Bldg. & Loan Ass'n *v.* Moeck, 106 N. J. Eq. 425 (*semble*); Title Guarantee & Trust Co. *v.* Haven, 196 N. Y. 487; Pittsburgh-Westmoreland Coal Co. *v.* Kerr, 220 N. Y. 137; Buist *v.* Williams, 88 S. C. 252; Oury *v.* Saunders, 77 Tex. 278, *accord.*

the respondent assignee of the Oriental Mills, an insolvent corporation, for funds wrongfully taken from the former company and used to pay liabilities of the latter company, and otherwise, by persons who were officers in control of both companies.

The rule is clear that one has an equitable right to follow and reclaim his property, which has been wrongfully appropriated by another, so long as he can find the property, or its substantial equivalent if its form has been changed, upon the ground that such property, in whatever form, is impressed with a trust in favor of the owner. If the trustee has mingled it with his own, he will be deemed to have used his own, rather than another's, and so to leave the remainder under the trust; and this is a sufficient identification for the owner. But in this case we are asked to go further and to hold that where one's property has been wrongfully applied and dissipated by another a charge remains upon the estate of the latter for the amount thus wrongfully taken, upon the ground that his estate is thereby so much larger and that the trust property is really and clearly there, in a substituted form, although it cannot be directly traced. This view is pressed with much skill and some authority, but we are unable to adopt it.

While one who has been wronged may follow and take his own property, or its visible product, it is quite a different thing to say that he may take the property of somebody else. The general property of an insolvent debtor belongs to his creditors, as much as particular trust property belongs to a *cestui que trust*. Creditors have no right to share in that which is shown not to belong to the debtor, and conversely a claimant has no right to take from creditors that which he cannot show to be equitably his own. But right here comes the argument that it is equitably his own because the debtor has taken the claimant's money and mingled it with his estate, whereby it is swelled just so much. But, as applicable to all cases, the argument is not sound. Where the property or its substantial equivalent remains, we concede its force; but where it is dissipated and gone, the appropriation of some other property in its stead simply takes from creditors that which clearly belongs to them. In the former case, as in Pennell v. Deffell, 4 DeG., M. & G. 372, and *In re* Hallett's estate, Knatchbull v. Hallett, L. R. 13 Ch. Div. 696, the illustration may be used of a debtor mingling trust funds with his own in a chest or bag. Though the particular money cannot be identified, the amount is swelled just so much, and the amount added belongs to the *cestui que trust*. But in the latter case there is no swelling of the estate, for the money is spent and gone; or, as respondent's counsel pertinently suggests, "Knight Bruce's chest, — Jessel's bag, is empty." Shall we therefore order a like amount to be taken out of some other chest or bag, or out of the debtor's general estate? Suppose the general estate consists only of mills and machinery acquired long before the complainant's money was appropriated. Upon what principle could that property be taken to reimburse them? But the complainants say: "Our money has been misappropriated by the debtor without our consent and without our fault; why should we not be reimbursed out of his estate?" Undoubtedly is it right that every one should have his own; but, when a claimant's property cannot be found, this same principle prevents the taking of property which equitably belongs to creditors of the trustee to make it up. The creditors have done no wrongful act, and should not be called upon, in any way, to atone for the misconduct of their debtor. It is an ordinary case of misfortune on the part of claimants, whose confidence in a trustee or agent has been abused.

In examining the question upon authority we think it is equally clear that there can be no equitable relief except in cases where the fund claimed is in some way apparent in the debtor's estate. Of the cases cited by the complainants only four go to the extent of holding that a *cestui que trust* is entitled to a lien for reimbursement on the general estate of the trustee where the trust fund does not, in some form, so appear. These are Davenport Plow Co. *v.* Lamp, 80 Iowa, 722; McLeod *v.* Evans, 66 Wisc. 401; Francis *v.* Evans, 69 Wisc. 115; Bowers *v.* Evans, 71 Wisc. 133. In the first of these cases the court lost sight of the distinction, which we desire to make clear, between funds remaining in the estate, which go to swell the assets, and funds which, having been dissipated or used in the payment of debts, do not remain in the estate, and so do not swell the estate. Upon the former fact, as we have stated above, we concede the right to relief. But the court, in the Iowa case, seems to ignore this very important distinction, and in so doing overthrows the foundation on which its decision is based. For it says: "The creditors, if permitted to enforce their claims as against the trust, would secure the payment of their claims out of trust moneys." Now how can this be so if the trust moneys, or their substantial equivalent, are not there? The court assumes that the payment of debts is the same thing as an increase of assets; or, perhaps, that it works the same result to a creditor by increasing his dividends. But this is not so. How the satisfaction of a debt by incurring another of equal amount either decreases one's liabilities or increases his assets can only be comprehended by the philosophic mind of a Micawber. If a debtor is solvent it is all right either way, because he will have enough to pay everything he owes. But if he is insolvent the injustice of the doctrine of the Iowa court is made almost painfully plain by the following illustration, from the dissenting opinion of Taylor and Cassoday, JJ., in Francis *v.* Evans, *supra*. "Supposing that an insolvent debtor, D., has only $1,000 of property, but is indebted to the amount of $2,000, one-half of which is due to A., and the other half to B. In this condition of things, D.'s property can only pay fifty per cent of his debts. By such distribution, A. and B. would each be equitably entitled to

$500. Now, suppose D., while in that condition, collects $1,000 for F., but instead of remitting to him the money, as he should, he uses it in paying his debt in full to A. By so doing, D. has not increased his assets a penny, nor diminished his aggregate indebtedness a penny. The only difference is that he now owes $1,000 each to B. and F., whereas he previously owed $1,000 each to A. and B. Now, if F. is to have preference over B., then his claim will absorb the entire amount of D.'s property, leaving nothing whatever for B. In other words, the $500 to which B. was equitably entitled from his insolvent debtor, upon a fair distribution of the estate, has, without any fault of his, been paid to another, merely in consequence of the wrongful act of the debtor." It is impossible to state the case more clearly. The illustration demonstrates that the mere fact that a trustee has used the money, does not show that it has gone into his estate. If used to pay debts, he has simply turned it over to a creditor, thereby giving him a preference, while his own estate and indebtedness remain exactly as before; because he owes the same amount to his *cestui que trust* from whom he has taken it. Suppose he had stolen the money and turned it over to somebody from whom it could not be reclaimed. Can anyone say the owner should have an equitable lien upon the thief's insolvent estate in preference to his creditors? They and the owner are equally innocent, and each must bear his own misfortune. There seems to be some confusion also upon the ground that because there might be an equitable lien upon the trustee's property in his own hands, the same lien must follow it into the hands of the assignee, because he has no greater rights than the assignor. The assignee is primarily a trustee for creditors, yet it is indeed true that he has no greater right than the assignor to specific property. But suppose, after a creditor had attached property in possession of a debtor, a complainant should seek an equitable lien upon it for the reason that the debtor had misappropriated property which belonged to the complainant, and of which the attached property was in no way a part. We see no ground upon which he could succeed. When the creditor seeks to establish his lien for his debt he stands equal in equitable right with a claimant who can show no peculiar equitable claim to the property in question. The fact that the *cestui que trust* has not entered into the relation of debtor and creditor with the trustee does not affect the question. So long as he seeks to recover what he can show to be his own, he is in the position of an owner; but when he cannot do this and seeks to recover payment out of the trustee's general estate he is in the position of a creditor. Substantially the same criticisms are applicable to the Wisconsin cases, with the additional remarks that they are decisions of a court nearly evenly divided, and that in our opinion, the better reason and weight of authority are with the dissentient judges.

In support of the views we have expressed it is sufficient to select the following cases: Little *v.* Chadwick, 151 Mass. 109; National Bank *v.* Insurance Company, 104 U. S. 54; Matter of Cavin *v.* Gleason, 105 N. Y. 256; Englar *v.* Offutt, 70 Md. 78; Thompson's Appeal, 22 Pa. St. 16; Commercial National Bank *v.* Armstrong, 39 Federal Reporter, 684. The question whether any of the property of the Forestdale Company has gone into the hands of the assignee, in original or substituted form, whereby the assets are so much larger, is a question of fact. As to the sum of $149.39 on deposit in the Columbian National Bank of Boston, no question being made that it was a part of the funds of the Forestdale Company, it may, according to National Bank *v.* Insurance Company, 104 U. S. 54, be claimed by the owner; but that question cannot be determined in this suit, as the money is not in the hands of the assignee, and the bank is not a party to the suit. As to the $3,103.33 invested in cotton and made into manufactured goods, following the doctrine of the cases cited, the court will attribute ownership in such goods, if any such came to the assignee, to be in the *cestui que trust* to the amount or value disclosed.

This being a question of fact it must stand for hearing, and the demurrer to the bill, upon the points argued, must be overruled.[1]

SPOKANE COUNTY *v.* FIRST NATIONAL BANK.

CIRCUIT COURT OF APPEALS, U. S., NINTH CIRCUIT. 1895.

68 Fed. 979.

APPEAL from the Circuit Court of the United States for the Eastern Division of the District of Washington.

This was a suit by the county of Spokane, Wash., against the First National Bank of Spokane and F. Lewis Clark, its receiver, to

[1] For cases holding that the claimant is entitled to no priority where his money was used in paying the wrongdoer's debts, see *Re* Hallett & Co., [1894] 2 Q. B. 237; City Bank *v.* Blackmore, 75 Fed. 771; American Can Co. *v.* Williams, 178 Fed. 420; Bettendorf Metal Wheel Co. *v.* Mast, 187 Fed. 590; Empire State Surety Co. *v.* Carroll County, 194 Fed. 593; *Re* Larkin & Metcalf, 202 Fed. 572; *Re* Wilson & Co., 252 Fed. 631; *Re* Jarmulowsky, 261 Fed. 779; Farmers' Nat. Bank *v.* Pribble, 15 F.(2d) 175; Smith Reduction Corp. *v.* Williams, 15 F.(2d) 874; Bellevue State Bank *v.* Coffin, 22 Idaho 210; Jones *v.* Chesebrough, 105 Iowa 303; Drovers' Bank *v.* Roller, 85 Md. 495; City of St. Paul *v.* Seymour, 71 Minn. 303; Horigan Realty Co. *v.* Flynn, 213 Mo. App. 591; Matter of Cavin, 105 N. Y. 256; Ferchen *v.* Arndt, 26 Ore. 121; Nonotuck Silk Co. *v.* Flanders, 87 Wis. 237. See 37 Yale L. Jour. 1150.

But see *contra,* State *v.* Bruce, 17 Idaho 1 (but see Bellevue State Bank *v.* Coffin, 22 Idaho 210); Davenport Plow Co. *v.* Lamp, 80 Iowa 722.

In Jones *v.* Chesebrough, 105 Iowa 303, *supra,* the court resented the reference to Micawber in the criticism of Davenport Plow Co. *v.* Lamp in the principal case and stated the Iowa rule as being that a person whose money has been used in paying the wrongdoer's debts is entitled to preference only if those debts would otherwise have been paid with the wrongdoer's other assets.

impress a trust upon assets of the bank in the receiver's hands. The circuit court sustained a demurrer to the bill for want of equity. Complainant appeals. Affirmed.

Before MCKENNA and GILBERT, Circuit Judges, and KNOWLES, District Judge.

GILBERT, Circuit Judge. The county of Spokane brought a suit against the First National Bank of Spokane and its receiver to recover the balance of public funds deposited with said bank by the treasurer and tax collector of said county between the 9th day of January, 1893, and the 26th day of July of the same year, alleging that between said dates there was deposited with said bank by said officer for safe-keeping $81,257.55, all of which had been repaid to the complainant save and except the sum of $11,355.68, "which said sum the said defendant the First National Bank does now wrongfully retain and hold, and has wrongfully retained and held ever since the 26th day of July, 1893." It is further alleged in the bill that on or about the 26th day of July, 1893, the bank became insolvent and suspended payment, and has not since resumed business, and that the receiver, since his appointment as such, has received of the assets of the said bank " sufficient money and funds wherewith to pay and satisfy the said balance deposited and received as aforesaid." A demurrer to the bill for want of equity was sustained by the circuit court, and from that ruling this appeal is taken.

It is contended on behalf of the appellant that the money deposited with the bank by the county treasurer was impressed with the character of a trust fund, and that the trust may be enforced against any assets of the bank in the hands of its receiver. It is not alleged in the bill that any of the money of the complainant, or any assets or property thereby procured, has come into the hands of the receiver. It is true it is averred that the bank still retains $11,355.68 of the complainant's money, but it is not said that any portion of that sum was in the possession of the bank when it closed its doors. We interpret the averments of the bill to mean, as in fact it was conceded upon the argument, that the money which the receiver holds is not that which was turned over to him as such when the bank was closed, but that it is the proceeds of collections by him made since that date. If it had been alleged in the bill that at the time of its failure the bank held a sum of money equal to or less than the amount here sued for, the court might lawfully presume that sum to be of the public funds of Spokane county, since it will be presumed that trust funds have not been wrongfully misappropriated or criminally used by the officers of the bank. But while that presumption would prevail as to money on hand, it would not be extended to other assets, for the officers of the bank had as little right to divert the public funds into investment in other property as they had to appropriate them to their own use. But it is said that the complainant has a lien upon the funds in the hands of the receiver upon the theory that the estate of the bank has received the benefit of the complainant's money, and its present assets are thereby increased. There are some decisions of the courts, particularly in cases of suit to recover public funds, that go to the extent of supporting this doctrine, and while the public benefit to be derived from the application of that rule to cases where school and county funds have been misappropriated by banks appeals strongly to the consideration of the court, we are unable to discover that the power to dispense such relief rests upon any of the established principles which govern the action of courts of equity.

There is no recognized ground upon which equity can pursue a fund and impose upon it the character of a trust, except upon the theory that the money is still the property of the plaintiff. If he is permitted to follow it and recover it, it is because it is his own, whether in the form in which he parted with its possession, or in a substituted form. Under the earlier rule, he was required to identify it as the very property which he had confided to another. The newer and more equitable doctrine permits him to recover it from any one not an innocent purchaser, and in any shape into which it may have been transmuted, provided he can establish the fact that it is his property or the proceeds of his property, or that his property has gone into it and remains in a mass from which it cannot be distinguished. The earlier English doctrine, as declared in the opinion of Lord Ellenborough in Taylor *v.* Plumer, 3 Maule & S. 575, in which were reviewed the prior decisions of the English courts, was to the effect that the owner of property intrusted to another could follow and retake the same from the possession of the holder, whether he were agent, bailee, or trustee, or from others who were in privity with him, so long as they were not *bona fide* purchasers for value, and this irrespective of whether such property remained in its original form or had been changed into some other form, so long as it could be ascertained to be the same property or the proceeds of the same property, but that the right ceased when the means of ascertainment failed, and it was held that such means of ascertainment failed whenever the property was in the form of money, and had been then mixed and confused in a general mass of money of the same description. The more recent doctrine, however, follows the rule announced in *Re* Hallett's Estate (Knatchbull *v.* Hallett) 13 Ch. Div. 696, which is that, if money held by one in a fiduciary character has been paid by him to his account at his banker's, the person for whom he held the money can follow it, and has a charge on the balance in the banker's hands, and that if the depositor has commingled it with his own funds at the bank, and has afterwards drawn out sums upon checks in the ordinary manner, he must be held to have drawn out his own money in preference to the trust money, and that if he destroyed the trust fund "by dissipating it altogether, there remains nothing to be the subject of the trust, but so long as the trust property can be traced and followed into other property into which it has been converted, that remains subject to the trust."

The American courts, while uniformly approving the doctrine of that decision, have exhibited a diversity of holding as to its meaning. Some, as we have shown, have interpreted it to mean that, in a suit brought to pursue trust property and affix upon it the character of a trust, it is only necessary to show that the defendant's estate, although insolvent and in the hands of an assignee or receiver for distribution, has actually received the benefit of the trust fund, and that it makes no difference that the plaintiff is unable to show that his fund, or property which represents it, is then in the estate in any form, or has actually come into the hands of the assignee or receiver. [Citing cases.] Decision in these cases would seem in the main to have been influenced by the consideration that the estate of the insolvent, and thereby the general creditors thereof, must have received the benefit of all trust funds unlawfully used by the insolvent in the course of business or the payment of debts. . . .

We are unable to assent to the proposition that, because a trust fund has been used by the insolvent in the course of his business, the general creditors of the estate are by that amount benefited, and that therefore equitable considerations require that the owner of the trust fund be paid out of the estate to their postponement or exclusion. If the trust fund has been dissipated in the transaction of the business before insolvency, it will be impossible to demonstrate that the estate has been thereby increased or better prepared to meet the demands of creditors, and even if it is proven that the trust fund has been but recently disbursed, and has been used to pay debts that otherwise would be claims against the estate, there would be manifest inequity in requiring that the money so paid out should be refunded out of the assets, for in so doing the general creditors whose demands remain unpaid are in effect contributing to the payment of the creditors whose demands have been extinguished by the trust fund. Both the settled principles of equity and the weight of authority sustain the view that the plaintiff's right to establish his trust and recover his fund must depend upon his ability to prove that his property is in its original or a substituted form in the hands of the defendant. [Citing cases.]

The decree is therefore affirmed, with costs to the appellees.[1]

[1] The decisions show a great divergency on the question how far the claimant, in order to get priority over other creditors, must trace his misappropriated property. In some cases it is held sufficient that the assets of the wrongdoer were originally increased by the misappropriation. In other cases it has been held that it is necessary to show that the increase remained until the assets of the wrongdoer passed into the hands of an officer of the court or until distribution is directed by the court. In others the claimant must point

ROREBECK v. BENEDICT FLOUR & FEED CO.

CIRCUIT COURT OF APPEALS, 8TH CIRCUIT. 1928.

26 F.(2d) 440.

APPEAL from the District Court of the United States for the Northern District of Iowa; George C. Scott, Judge.

Suit by the Benedict Flour & Feed Company against E. F. Rorebeck, receiver of the First National Bank of Forest City, Iowa. From the judgment, both parties appeal. Reversed in part.

Before VAN VALKENBURGH, Circuit Judge, and REEVES and OTIS, District Judges.

OTIS, District Judge. These are cross-appeals from the judgment below in a suit in equity brought by the Benedict Flour & Feed Company, an Iowa corporation, hereinafter designated as the plaintiff, against the First National Bank of Forest City, Iowa, and the receiver of that bank, hereinafter designated as the defendants. The general nature of the plaintiff's claim, as stated in its petition is this:

Through the Fidelity Savings Bank of Marshalltown, Iowa, plaintiff drew three sight drafts on merchants of Forest City, Iowa, which were sent to the defendant bank for collection. The drafts were paid in full by the drawees in the manner following: One, for $1,113.75, drawn on Emil Anderson, was paid by him by check against his account in the defendant bank; another, for $440, drawn on Sam Bloom, was also paid by him by check against his account in the defendant bank; the third, $217.50, drawn on C. M. Larson, was paid by him by check drawn on a bank other than the defendant bank.

On November 4, 1925, the defendant bank reported collection and sent to the forwarding bank drafts for the proper amounts, drawn on the Federal Reserve Bank of Chicago. The Federal Reserve Bank refused to pay these drafts, for the reason that on November 5, 1925, at the end of banking hours on that day, the defendant bank was closed by a government examiner. When closed it had cash on hand in excess of the amount of plaintiff's claim.

The total amount paid by Anderson, Bloom, and Larson to the

---

out the misappropriated property or its product of a specific mass into which it went and which still remains at the time of distribution. The confusion is greatest in the very large class of cases where priority is sought in the distribution of the assets of an insolvent bank. See Bogert, Trusts, 527–535; Ames, Lect. Leg. Hist., 421–24, 19 Harv. L. Rev. 521; Townsend, Constructive Trusts and Bank Collections, 39 Yale L. Jour. 980; Dec. Dig., Banks and Banking, sec. 80; Dec. Dig., Trusts, secs. 351–4, 358; 77 U. Pa. L. Rev. 785; L. R. A. 1916C 21.

defendant bank, less commissions for collection, was $1,769.35. The defendant receiver having refused to pay plaintiff this amount, this suit was brought, on the theory that the amount collected by the defendant bank was a trust fund, and that the plaintiff was entitled to payment in full out of funds in the receiver's hands and before general creditors. The case was tried on an agreed statement of facts. It included, among other matters, the facts alleged by plaintiff as set out above, amplified as follows:

On November 2, 1925, Emil Anderson had to his credit in his checking account in the First National Bank of Forest City, Iowa, more than $1,800. On that day he went to the First National Bank, Forest City, Iowa, and wrote and signed and delivered to said bank his check, drawn on his account therein, for the full amount of the draft No. 1928, to wit, $1,113.75. The First National Bank, Forest City, accepted the check, charged it against Anderson's account on its books, marked same "Paid," and surrendered the draft No. 1928 (also marked "Paid") to Anderson in exchange for this check.

On November 2, 1925, Sam Bloom & Sons had to their credit in their checking account in the First National Bank, Forest City, Iowa, more than $800. On that day a member of this firm went to the said bank, and wrote, signed, and delivered to said bank a check of said firm, drawn upon its said account in said bank for the full amount of draft No. 1929, to wit, $440. Whereupon said bank accepted the check, charged it against Sam Bloom & Sons' account on its books, marked the same "Paid," and surrendered the draft No. 1929 (also marked "Paid") in exchange for this check.

In the afternoon of November 2, 1925, C. M. Larson delivered to the First National Bank, Forest City, Iowa, checks for $217.50, on his checking account in another bank, to wit, the Forest City National Bank, in exchange for which he received draft No. 1920, stamped "Paid." These checks were presented at the close of business of November 2, 1925, by the First National Bank to the Forest City National Bank, together with a number of other checks drawn on the latter bank. The Forest City National Bank then held checks drawn on the First National Bank of a total amount of $2,277.37 in excess of those held by the First National Bank on it. These sets of checks were that evening exchanged or cleared between the banks, and, to make up the deficiency in the clearings against it, the First National Bank gave to the Forest City National Bank a Chicago draft on the Federal Reserve Bank of Chicago, which was duly honored in the sum of $2,277.37. No cash passed between these banks for any of these checks.

Upon the facts thus stated the trial court found that " a trust relation existed between the plaintiff and the defendants, and that the plaintiff is entitled to have its claim established as a preferred claim to the extent of the lowest amount of cash on hand and available for transmission after the completion of the collection and before the closing of the bank; that such an amount was, as shown by the evidence, the sum of $1,275.49 on hand at the close of business November 4, 1925; and that the balance of plaintiff's claim should be established as a general claim in the sum of $445.76." The decree was that " plaintiff have and recover of the defendants the sum of $1,721.25, and that of such amount $1,275.49 be established as a preferred claim against the funds in the hands of the receiver, to be prorated with other preferred claims of the same class, and that the balance in the sum of $445.76 be established as a general claim against all funds available to the payment of general creditors."

Defendants appealed from that part of the decree allowing plaintiff a preference as to a part of its claim, and the plaintiff from that part denying preference as to the remainder.

1. First as to the payments made by Bloom and Anderson, which were by checks drawn upon the defendant bank, and which obviously did not result in any increase in the bank's funds. As to this branch of the case the recent decisions of this court in Larabee Flour Mills v. First National Bank of Henryetta, Okl., and Farmers' National Bank of Burlington, Kan. v. Kansas Flour Mills Co., decided June 12, 1926, and reported as one case in 13 F.(2d) 330, are squarely in point. In a similar state of facts it was there said:

"It is difficult to explain or understand by what equitable right one who has not contributed to the creation of a fund should be given a special and superior interest therein, though some of the state courts seem to so hold. The collecting banks acted as agents (Commercial Bank v. Armstrong, 148 U. S. 50, 13 S. Ct. 533, 37 L. Ed. 363), and had they collected and retained the funds called for by the drafts, as was their duty on account of insolvency, the equities of claimants would be plain; but, instead of doing so, they merely shifted credits on their books and records. No part of the funds in the banks when they failed was placed there by claimants, or by any one for them. In each case the draft was paid by check on the insolvent. No additional funds were brought into the bank by either transaction. If the drafts which they held for collection had been paid in currency or by check on some other bank, the insolvents' assets would have been increased that much, when thereafter their remittance drafts were dishonored; and in that event equity would have regarded the collections as trust funds, followed them into the increased assets, and to the extent of the increase applied them first in discharge of these claims. This is our conception of the rule and the reason for it, applied in the federal courts. It has been repeatedly announced by this court."

It follows, from this case and the numerous supporting authorities therein cited, that the plaintiff is entitled to no preference as to the Bloom and Anderson payments.

2. The Larson payment was to the defendant bank, not as in

the other instances by check on the defendant bank, but by check on another bank, the Forest City National Bank, but in the exchange of checks between that bank and the defendant bank, checks of the two banks were offset, and no cash came into the defendant bank by reason of the Larson check. So that here also the funds of the defendant bank were not augmented by the payment, and plaintiff is entitled to no preference. Larabee Flour Mills v. First National Bank of Henryetta, Okl., *supra;* Mechanics & Metals National Bank of New York v. Buchanan (C. C. A.) 12 F.(2d) 891. The use of the Larson check in the exchange of checks brought about no increase in the assets of the defendant bank, but, as was said in a like situation by this court in Farmers' National Bank v. Pribble (C. C. A.) 15 F.(2d) 175, 177, " the only effect of the use of the draft . . . in the clearance . . . was not in any way to increase the assets of the . . . bank, but possibly, perhaps probably, to diminish its indebtedness or liability by the amount of the draft, and such a reduction of its indebtedness creates no preferential trust in or lien on the assets of the insolvent over the claims of its general creditors."

Our conclusion is that the plaintiff's claim is entitled to no preference, and the judgment below, to the extent that it decrees a preference and assesses the costs of the cause against the defendants, is reversed. Our finding is for the appellant in No. 7660 and for the appellee in No. 7673.[1]

[1] In the following cases it was held that where a bank collected by receiving a check upon itself, or where the bank was the drawee by debiting the account of the drawer, the depositor was not entitled to priority over other creditors on the failure of the bank. Anheuser-Busch Brewing Ass'n v. Clayton, 56 Fed. 759; American Can Co. v. Williams, 178 Fed. 420; Nyssa-Arcadia Drainage Dist. v. First Nat. Bank, 3 F.(2d) 648; Larabee Flour Mills v. First Nat. Bank, 13 F.(2d) 330, 36 Yale L. Jour. 682, 75 U. Pa. L. Rev. 69, *certiorari* denied 273 U. S. 727; United States Nat. Bank v. Glanton, 146 Ga. 786; Union Nat. Bank v. Citizens Bank, 153 Ind. 44; Hecker-Jones-Jewell Milling Co. v. Cosmopolitan Trust Co., 242 Mass. 181; Sherwood v. Milford State Bank, 94 Mich. 78; Sunderlin v. Mecosta County Bank, 116 Mich. 281; *Re* Seven Corners Bank, 58 Minn. 5; Billingsley v. Pollock, 69 Miss. 759; Midland Nat. Bank v. Brightwell, 148 Mo. 358; Corporation Commission v. Bank, 137 N. C. 697; Frank v. Bingham, 58 Hun (N. Y.) 580; Freiberg v. Stoddard, 161 Pa. 259; Commonwealth v. State Bank, 216 Pa. 124; Citizens Bank v. Bradley, 136 S. C. 511; Sayles v. Cox, 95 Tenn. 579; Peters Shoe Co. v. Murray, 31 Tex. Civ. App. 259.

In the following cases, however, it was held that the bank was a trustee, and the depositor was given priority. *Re* City Bank of Dowagiac, 186 Fed. 250; Spokane & Eastern Trust Co. v. U. S. Steel Products Co., 290 Fed. 884; Ellerbe v. Studebaker Corp., 21 F.(2d) 993 (deposit made to meet draft); State Nat. Bank v. First Nat. Bank, 124 Ark. 531; Darragh Co. v. Goodman, 124 Ark. 532; Nat. Life Ins. Co. v. Mather, 118 Ill. App. 491; People v. Iuka State Bank, 229 Ill. App. 4; Messenger v. Carroll Trust & Sav. Bank, 193 Iowa 608; Kansas State Bank v. First Nat. Bank, 62 Kan. 788; Goodyear Tire & Rubber Co. v. Hanover State Bank, 109 Kan. 772; Kesl v. Hanover State Bank, 109 Kan. 776; Bauck v. First State Bank, 178 Minn. 64; Bank of Poplar Bluff v. Millspaugh, 313 Mo. 412; Federal Reserve Bank v. Millspaugh, 314 Mo. 1; Hawaiian Pineapple Co. *v.* Browne, 69 Mont. 140; Arnot *v.* Bingham, 55 Hun (N. Y.) 553.

See 75 U. Pa. L. Rev. 69; 36 Yale L. Jour. 682; 39 Yale L. Jour. 980, 1003; 40 Yale L. Jour. 456; 14 Minn. L. Rev. 407; 37 W. Va. L. Quar. 88; 24 A. L. R. 1152; 42 A. L. R. 754; 47 A. L. R. 761.

In the following cases it was held that where a bank collected by clearing and the balance on the clearing was against the collecting bank, the depositor was not entitled to priority on the failure of the collecting bank. Nyssa-Arcadia Drainage Dist. *v.* First Nat. Bank, 3 F.(2d) 648; Farmers' Nat. Bank *v.* Pribble, 15 F.(2d) 175; First Nat. Bank *v.* Williams, 15 F.(2d) 585; Smith Reduction Corp. *v.* Williams, 15 F.(2d) 874; Dickson *v.* First Nat. Bank, 26 F.(2d) 411; *Re* Seven Corners Bank, 58 Minn. 5. But see *contra*, Kansas State Bank *v.* First State Bank, 62 Kan. 788; Bauck *v.* First State Bank, 178 Minn. 64. See 39 Yale L. Jour. 980, 1004.

The Bank Collection Code adopted in several states gives priority although the proceeds cannot be traced. See 43 Harv. L. Rev. 307.

On the question whether a bank becomes a debtor or an express or constructive trustee, see Chap. I, sec. IV, and particularly Lippitt *v.* Thames Loan & Trust Co., 88 Conn. 185, and Northwest Lumber Co. *v.* Scandinavian Amer. Bank, 130 Wash. 33, *ante.*

For authorities on the general question of the right to follow misappropriated money or other property into its product, see Bogert, Trusts, sec. 124; Perry, Trusts, secs. 835–842; 3 Pomeroy, Eq. Juris., sec. 1051; Ames, Lect. Leg. Hist., 412; Ames, Following Misappropriated Property Into Its Product, 19 Harv. L. Rev. 511; Williston, Right to Follow Trust Property, 2 Harv. L. Rev. 28; Scott, The Right to Follow Money Wrongfully Mingled with Other Money, 27 Harv. L. Rev. 125; Townsend, Constructive Trusts and Bank Collections, 39 Yale L. Jour. 980; Dec. Dig., Trusts, secs. 349–358.

CHAPTER VI.
THE ADMINISTRATION OF TRUSTS.

Section I.
The Nature of the Remedies of the Cestui que Trust against the Trustee.

MEGOD'S CASE.
Queen's Bench. 1585.

4 Leon. 225.

A. enfeoffed B. to the intent that B. should convey the said land to such person as A. should sell it. A. sold it to C., to whom B. refused to convey the land; and thereupon he brought an action upon the case against B. And by Wray, Chief Justice and Gawdy, Justice here is a good consideration, for here is a trust, and that which is a good consideration in the Chancery is in this case sufficient. Shute, Justice was of a contrary opinion, and afterwards judgment was given for the plaintiff.[1]

[1] For cases holding that the *cestui que trust* cannot sue the trustee in an action of special assumpsit, see Ames, 240n.; Scott, Cases on Trusts, 1 ed., 565.

An action of special assumpsit, as well as an action of account, was allowed against a factor or bailiff who had expressly promised to render an account; but such actions were rare because of the competing jurisdictions of equity. See Ames, 240n.

Formerly, when there was no chancery jurisdiction in Massachusetts and Pennsylvania, a *cestui que trust* was allowed to sue the trustee in special assumpsit and recover damages for breach of trust. Newhall v. Wheeler, 7 Mass. 189, 198; Martzell v. Stauffer, 3 Pa. 398. See Fisher, Administration of Equity through Common Law Forms, 2 Sel. Essays in Anglo-Amer. Leg. Hist., 810; Pomeroy, Eq. Juris., secs. 286, 311–321, 338–342.

"Indeed I think it impossible so to define a contract that the definition shall not cover at least three quarters of all the trusts that are created. For my own part I think that we ought to confess that we can not define either agreement or contract without including the great majority of trusts and that the reasons why we still treat the law of trusts as something apart from the law of contract are reasons which can be given only by a historical statement. Trusts fell under the equitable jurisdiction of the Court of Chancery and for that very reason the Courts of Law did not enforce them. Just now and again they threatened to give an action for damages against the defaulting trustee — but they soon abandoned this attempt to invade a province which equity had made its own. Therefore for a very long time to come I think that we shall go on treating the law of trusts as something distinct from the law of contracts — we shall find the former in one set of books, the latter in another set. Only let us see that in the common case a trust originates in what we can not but call an agreement. S transfers land or goods or

SHARINGTON *v.* STROTTON, Plowd. 298 (1565). — *Bromley*, counsel for the defendant, *arguendo*, said (p. 308) : " Then as to the second point, admitting the considerations to be insufficient, or admitting that no considerations had been expressed, yet the covenant of itself, without consideration, is sufficient to raise the uses. And in order to understand this the better, let us see what advantage the party here shall have by the deed, if the deed be not sufficient to raise the uses. And it seems clearly that he shall have none. For he cannot have an action of covenant upon the deed, because there is nothing executory here; for Andrew has covenanted with Edward that he and all persons seized of the land shall from thenceforth stand and be seized to the uses limited. And if they did not stand seized, there is no default in Andrew, but in the law, for he granted that from thenceforth, viz. immediately, he would be seized, and no default can be charged in him if he did not stand seized. Nor can Edward have an action of covenant against him, for an action of covenant shall never be brought, but where it is covenanted that a thing shall be done in time to come, or that it was done in time past; as in the case put in 21 H. 7. where the covenant was that the land shall revert, remain, or descend; or if a man covenants to build a house, or to give a horse or to make such an assurance, or the like, which may be executed and performed afterwards; or where I have done such a thing. But there is no such matter here, for he covenanted and granted presently to stand seized to use, upon which no action of covenant lies. For if I covenant and grant with you, that my white horse shall from henceforth be your horse, you shall not have an action of covenant against me, although I detain the horse, for I have not covenanted to do any thing in time to come, nor that any thing was done in time passed; but the phrase of speech amounts to the effect to vest a present property in you. So here, when he covenanted from thenceforth to be seized to the uses limited, the phrase contains in effect a present actual seizin to use, and if the law be that the uses shall be presently made by it, then is he seized to the uses, and if the law be not so, and will not suffer it, then he is not seized to the uses, and there is no default in him; and from thence it follows, that the covenant and grant and the deed shall be void and of no effect. But here Andrew made the deed, and sealed and delivered it, and it was according to the intent of both the parties, and Andrew could never plead *non est factum*, and then if it be his deed, to make it of no value would be a hard exposition, and inconsistent with the existence of the deed. For a deed is

---

debts to T upon a trust; T promises, expressly or by his conduct, that he will be bound. If you please you can analyse the transaction into a proposal and an acceptance — Will you hold this land, these goods, in trust for my wife and children? Yes, I will." Maitland, Equity, 54. See *ibid.*, 115; 2 Pol. & Mait., Hist. Eng. Law, 2 ed., 232; Pollock, Contracts, 8 ed., 219; 17 Col. L. Rev. 269, 270.

SECT. I.] CLARK'S CASE 519

not a deed but to some end and effect, and to say that it is a deed and of no effect, is a contrariety. And if the uses should not be raised, no other advantage, benefit, or effect, could be made of it here. So that we see no action of covenant shall be maintainable upon the deed, nor any other advantage made of it, if it does not raise the uses." [1]

CLARK'S CASE.

COMMON PLEAS. 1612.

Godbolt 210.

NOTE it was said by Cook, C. J., and agreed by the whole Court, and 41 and 43 E. 3. &c., that if a man deliver money unto I. S. to my use, that I may have an action of Debt, or Account against him for the same, at my election.[2] . . .

[1] "Nor has any case been found in which the feoffor obtained relief against the feoffee to uses on the latter's covenant to perform the use. Such a covenant, it is true, is mentioned in one or two charters of feoffment, but such instances are so rare that the remedy by covenant may fairly be said to have counted for nothing in the development of the doctrine of uses." Ames, Lect. Leg. Hist., 236. See *ibid.*, 148, 241.

Conversely, if the transaction is in the nature of a promise rather than of a transfer, covenant will lie, but no use is raised. Wingfield v. Littleton, 2 Dyer 162. See Sanders, Uses, 96. But words of covenant may be construed as a grant when so intended by the parties. Holms v. Seller, 3 Lev. 305; Rowbotham v. Wilson, 8 H. L. Cas. 348; Barnes v. Alexander, 232 U. S. 117; Bronson v. Coffin, 108 Mass. 175, 180; Hogan v. Barry, 143 Mass. 538.

In Adey v. Arnold, 2 DeG. M. & G. 432, and Holland v. Holland, L. R. 4 Ch. App. 449, it was held that money due from the estate of a trustee for breach of trust was not a specialty debt although the trust instrument was under seal and the trustee signed an acceptance under seal of the trust; in the absence of express covenant to perform the trust. See Frishmuth v. Farmers' Loan & T. Co., 107 Fed. 169 (corporate mortgage). There is authority, however, to the effect that if a trustee covenants to perform the trust he becomes a specialty debtor. See Scott, Cases on Trusts, 1 ed., 568; 39 Cyc. 294.

[2] See Ames, 4n. Formerly debt did not lie in such a case, account being the only available action. Y. B. 6 Hen. VI. fol. 7, pl. 33; Ames, 1.

"The action of account is very analogous to a trust. There is a marked analogy between a receipt of money by B. to the use of C., a bailment of goods to B. for the use of C., and a feoffment of land to B. for the use of C. In the case of goods the title passed, and C. had a legal remedy; in the case of land there was no remedy except in equity; in the case of money the only remedy was account. But the care required is the same in all three cases, — the liability apart from procedure was the same." Ames, Lect. Leg. Hist., 119.

"A trustee is obviously under an obligation to account with his *cestui que trust* for the trust property or its income; but this obligation is merely equitable, and therefore a bill by a *cestui que trust* against his trustee is never a bill for an account in point of jurisdiction." Langdell, Brief Survey, 97. See Cearnes v. Irving, 31 Vt. 604.

FARRINGTON v. LEE.

COMMON PLEAS. 1677.

1 Mod. 268.

THE COURT.[1] Whereas it has been said by Serjeant Newdigate, that the plaintiff here has an election to bring an action of account, or an *indebitatus assumpsit*, that is false; for till the account be stated betwixt them, an action of account lies, and not an action upon the case. When the account is once stated, then an action on the case lies, and not an action of account. And by NORTH, C. J. If upon an *indebitatus assumpsit* matters are offered in evidence that lie in account, I do not allow them to be given in evidence.

DALE v. SOLLET.

KING'S BENCH. 1767.

4 Burr. 2133.

THIS was an action for money had and received to the plaintiff's use: *non assumpsit* was pleaded; and issue joined.

CASE. — The defendant, a ship-broker, was the plaintiff's agent in suing for and recovering a sum of money for damages done to the plaintiff's ship; and did recover and receive 2,000*l.* for the plaintiff's use; and paid him all but 40*l.* which he retained for his labour and service therein; which the witness (Mr. Fuller) swore he thought to be a reasonable allowance. And the jury were of opinion "that the defendant ought to retain 40*l.* as a reasonable allowance." Consequently, the plaintiff was not intitled to recover.

The plaintiff objected, at the trial, "that the defendant could not give evidence in this manner, of this labour and service; but ought to have pleaded it by way of sett-off, or at least have given notice of it as a sett-off."

A verdict was found for the plaintiff; subject to the opinion of this Court: and if the Court should be of opinion against him, then judgment to be entered as upon a nonsuit.

Accordingly, on Tuesday last, (the 10th instant,) *Mr. Dunning* moved on behalf of the defendant, "that judgment might be entered against the plaintiff, as upon a nonsuit:" and had a rule to shew cause.

Sir Fletcher Norton, on behalf of the plaintiff, now shewed cause; and insisted that the defendant ought either to have pleaded it, or given notice of a sett-off: but that he could not take advantage of it in this manner, without either plea or notice.

[1] A part of the case is omitted.

LORD MANSFIELD had no doubt of the defendant's being at liberty to give this evidence.

This is an action for money had and received to the plaintiff's use. The plaintiff can recover no more than he is in conscience and equity entitled to: which can be no more than what remains after deducting all just allowances which the defendant has a right to retain out of the very sum demanded. This is not in the nature of a cross-demand or mutual debt: it is a charge, which makes the sum of money received for the plaintiff's use so much less.

The two other Judges concurred.

PER CUR'. *Judgment for the defendant, as on a nonsuit.*[1]

FLYE v. HALL.

SUPREME JUDICIAL COURT, MASSACHUSETTS. 1916.

224 Mass. 528.

RUGG, C. J. This is an action of tort or contract. The declaration as amended contains three counts, one for the conversion of money, the second for money had and received, and the third on an account annexed, all being for the same cause of action. The first and second counts in substance aver that the plaintiff's intestate during her life handed to the defendant various sums of money to be used for the support of the plaintiff's intestate, the defendant's mother, and that a part only had been used for that purpose.

The defendant demurred to the declaration on various grounds. In support of the demurrer an elaborate and extended argument has been presented. It might have required detailed discussion in days when greater strictness of civil pleading was required. Now it is enough if the substantive facts necessary to constitute a cause of action are stated concisely and with substantial certainty. R. L. c. 173, § 6.

There is no objection to the combination in one declaration of a count for conversion with one for money had and received and

[1] Lord Mansfield's innovation, sanctioning the use of *Indebitatus assumpsit* against a defendant, who is entitled to allowances in the way of commissions and expenses, has been almost everywhere followed. It is impossible for the plaintiff in such a case to prove his allegation that the defendant is indebted to him, as has been pointed out by Professor Langdell in 2 Harvard Law Review, 253–257; but the great convenience of this common count, as compared with the action of account, or a bill in equity, the legitimate substitute therefor, has led the courts to shut their eyes to this objection. Accordingly *Indebitatus assumpsit* has been allowed against a factor, agent for collection, pledgee or mortgagee for surplus proceeds of a sale, trustee of insurance policy for proceeds of policy, and guardian. — AMES.

As to the scope of the action of account and on the question how far debt and *indebitatus assumpsit* have become concurrent with account, see Ames, 1–8; Ames, Lect. Leg. Hist., 116–121; Langdell, Brief Survey, 85–89; 2 Harv. L. Rev. 253–257.

another on an account annexed for the same transaction. Devlin *v.* Houghton, 202 Mass. 75. Brown *v.* Sallinger, 214 Mass. 245, 248. It is not fatal to the maintenance of this form of action that a suit in equity might have been maintained for the termination of a trust and an accounting. Spear *v.* Coggan, 223 Mass. 156. The same facts may be the basis for an action for money had and received. Farrelly *v.* Ladd, 10 Allen, 127. The particulars of the amounts of money placed in the defendant's hands having been set forth in the body of the count, need not have been repeated by items in a bill of particulars.

Details which might be necessary in evidence, such as the date of the intestate's death, the circumstances of the deposit of the money with the defendant, and the precise terms of the arrangement between her and the intestate, need not be pleaded. . . .

Exceptions overruled.[1]

[1] In the following cases an action of *indebitatus assumpsit* or its equivalent was allowed. Allen *v.* Impett, 8 Taunt. 263 (refusal to pay dividends received); Hart *v.* Minors, 2 Cr. & M. 700 (account stated); Roper *v.* Holland, 3 A. & E. 99 (account stated); Topham *v.* Morecraft, 8 E. & B. 972 (account stated); Howard *v.* Brownhill, 23 L. J. Q. B. 23 (account stated); Davis *v.* Dickerson, 137 Ark. 14 (wrongful sale); Daugherty *v.* Daugherty, 116 Iowa 245 (wrongful sale); Nelson *v.* Howard, 5 Md. 327 (account stated); Henchey *v.* Henchey, 167 Mass. 77 (misappropriation of money by trustee); Clifford Banking Co. *v.* Donovan Com. Co., 195 Mo. 262 (donee of trust money); Hanford *v.* Duchastel, 87 N. J. L. 205 (transferee of trust money with notice); Boughton *v.* Flint, 74 N. Y. 476 (account stated); Van Camp *v.* Searle, 147 N. Y. 150 (account stated); Spencer *v.* Clarke, 25 R. I. 163 (account stated). See Ames, 37n.; Langdell, Brief Survey, 86; 2 Harv. L. Rev. 254.

In the following cases it was held that the remedy at law was exclusive: Taylor *v.* Turner, 87 Ill. 296 (factor); Tenn. etc. Co. *v.* Fitzgerald, 140 Ill. App. 430 (factor); Crooker *v.* Rogers, 58 Me. 339 (mortgagee); Frue *v.* Loring, 120 Mass. 507 (trustee); Township *v.* Crane, 80 N. J. Eq. 509 (tax collector); Van Seiver *v.* Churchill, 215 Pa. 53 (trustee); Franks *v.* Craven, 6 W. Va. 185 (transferee of trust property).

In the following cases it was held that the remedy at law was not exclusive: Clews *v.* Jamieson, 182 U. S. 461; Smith *v.* Amer. Nat. Bk., 89 Fed. 832; Dorenkamp *v.* Dorenkamp, 109 Ill. App. 536; Lupton *v.* American Wholesale Corp., 143 Md. 333; Hussong Dyeing Mach. Co. *v.* Morris, 89 Atl. 249 (N. J. Ch. 1913); Bullock *v.* Angleman, 82 N. J. Eq. 23.

"This court will not allow itself to be ousted of any part of its original jurisdiction, because a court of law happens to have fallen in love with the same or a similar jurisdiction, and has attempted (the attempt for the most part is not very successful) to administer such relief as originally was to be had here and here only." Eyre *v.* Everett, 2 Russ. 381, 382, *per* Lord Eldon. See Pomeroy, Eq. Juris., secs. 182, 276–278; 23 Col. L. Rev. 59.

If the trustee is not under an immediate and unconditional duty to pay over money, the beneficiary cannot maintain an action at law against him. Bartlett *v.* Dimond, 14 M. & W. 49; Haynes *v.* Greene, 46 R. I. 32; Scott, Cases on Trusts, 1 ed., 576n.

If a trustee of land in breach of trust gives it away, he is not liable in an action for money had and received. Norton *v.* Ray, 139 Mass. 230.

A trustee who negligently causes damage to the trust property is not liable in an action on the case. Hukill *v.* Page, 6 Biss. (U. S.) 183. See

ANONYMOUS.

COMMON PLEAS. 1464.

Y. B. 4 Edw. IV. f. 8, pl. 9.

IN a writ of trespass *quare vi et armis clausum suum fregit*, &c., *et arbores succidit*, &c., *et herbas conculcavit et consumpsit*, &c.

Catesby. You should have no action, for we say that a long time before the supposed trespass one J. B. was seised of certain land, &c., the place where, &c., in fee, and being so seised enfeoffed the plaintiff thereof in fee, &c., to the use of the defendant, &c., upon confidence, and afterwards the defendant by the sufferance and will of the plaintiff occupied this land and cut trees upon the same, &c., and trampled the grass, which is the same trespass, &c.

Jenney. This is no plea, for there is no certain matter, for such sufferance and will cannot be tried, &c.; and in such case to make a good issue or traversable matter, he should plead a lease by the plaintiff to the defendant to hold at will, which is traversable and may be tried.

Catesby. Why shall he not plead this matter when it follows reason that the defendant enfeoffed the plaintiff to the defendant's use, and so the plaintiff is in reason in this land only to the defendant's use, and the defendant made the feoffment upon trust and confidence, and the plaintiff suffered the defendant to occupy the land, so that in reason the defendant occupied at his will,[1] which proves that the defendant shall therefore have the advantage of pleading the feoffment in trust to justify the occupation, &c.

Bishop *v.* Houghton, 1 E. D. Smith (N. Y.) 566. A trustee who misappropriates trust property is not ordinarily liable in an action of trover or detinue. Redwood *v.* Riddick, 4 Munf. (Va.) 222. The *cestui que trust* cannot recover against the trustee in an action of ejectment. White *v.* Costigan, 138 Cal. 564.

Such actions, however, have been allowed in some cases, at least where the trust is an informal trust. See Doyle *v.* Burns, 123 Iowa 488, 497 (*semble*); Simmons *v.* Barns, 263 Mass. 472; Robinson *v.* Tower, 95 Neb. 198; Jackson *v.* Moore, 94 N. Y. App. Div. 504; Gibson *v.* Gillespie, 291 Pa. 77 (trespass); Royce, Allen & Co. *v.* Oakes, 20 R. I. 252; Snyder *v.* Parmalee, 80 Vt. 496. But *cf.* Royce, Allen & Co. *v.* Oakes, 20 R. I. 418; Larson *v.* Dawson, 24 R. I. 317.

In Holderman *v.* Hood, 70 Kan. 267, and Brys *v.* Pratt, 55 Wash. 122, it was held that, in the case of an informal trust at least, the trustee was liable in an action at law for a fraudulent sale at an inadequate price.

As to the nature of the remedies of the beneficiary, see Bogert, Trusts, 466–70; Perry, Trusts, sec. 843; Dec. Dig., Trusts, sec. 359.

[1] A *cestui que trust* in possession of the land by the permission of the trustee was treated as a tenant at will under Stat. 3 & 4 Wm. IV. c. 27, § 2. Garrard *v.* Tuck, 8 C. B. 231, 251–254 (explaining Doe *v.* Phillips, 10 Q. B. 130). Compare Melling *v.* Leak, 16 C. B. 652. — AMES.

MOYLE, J. This would be a good matter in the chancery, for the defendant there shall plead the intent and purpose upon such feoffment, for by conscience one shall have remedy in the chancery, according to the intent of such a feoffment; but here by the common law in the Common Bench or King's Bench it is different, for the feoffee shall have the land, and the feoffor shall not justify against his own feoffment, whether the feoffment was upon confidence or not.

Catesby. The law of chancery is the common law of the land, and if there the defendant shall have advantage of such a feoffment, why not likewise here?

MOYLE, J. That cannot be in this court as I have told you, for the common law of the land varies in this case from the law of chancery on this point, &c.[1]

BACON, READING ON THE STATUTE OF USES, 7. — But these books are not to be taken generally or grossly; for we see in the same books, when an use is specially alledged, the law taketh knowledge of it; but the sense of it is, that an use is nothing for which remedy is given by the course of the common law, so as the law knoweth it, but protects it not; and therefore when the question cometh, whether it hath any being in nature or conscience, the law accepteth of it; and therefore Littleton's case is good law; that he who hath but forty shillings freehold in use, shall be sworn in an inquest,[2] for it is ruled *secundum dominium naturale*, and not *secundum dominium legitimum, nam natura dominus est, quia fructum ex re percipit.* And some doubt if upon subsidies and taxes *cestuy que use* should be valued as an owner: so likewise if *cestuy que use* had released his use unto the feoffee for six pounds, or contracted with a stranger for the like sum, there is no doubt but it is a good condition or contract whereon to ground an action upon the case; for money for release of a suit in chancery is a good *quid pro quo;* therefore to conclude, though an use be nothing in law to yield remedy by course of law, yet it is somewhat in reputation of law and conscience.

[1] In Weakly *v.* Rogers, 5 East 138n., it was held that the trustee can maintain an action of ejectment against the *cestui que trust.* See Ames, 242.

Today in most jurisdictions the *cestui que trust* may defeat an action of ejectment brought by the trustee by a statutory equitable plea; in a few jurisdictions such a plea has been allowed without the aid of a statute. Cushing *v.* Danforth, 76 Me. 114; Ames, 242, 243.

A trustee of a chattel may recover it from the *cestui que trust,* or damages for its conversion, in an action at law, except in jurisdictions allowing equitable pleas. Langille *v.* Nass, 31 Nova Scotia Rep. 429; Ames, 243.

[2] Co. Litt. 272a, b. See Y. B. 15 Hen VII. fol. 13, pl. 1.

Co. Litt. 272b. — *Nota,* an use is a trust or confidence reposed in some other, which is not issuing out of the land, but as a thing collaterall, annexed in privitie to the estate of the land, and to the person touching the land, *scilicet,* that *cesty que use* shall take the profit, and that the terre-tenant shall make an estate according to his direction. So as *cesty que use* had neither *jus in re,* nor *jus ad rem,* but only a confidence and trust, for which he had no remedie by the common law, but for breach of trust, his remedie was only by *subpoena in chancerie.*

THE EARL OF KILDARE *v.* EUSTACE.

Chancery. 1686.

1 Vern. 405, 419.

The plaintiff's bill was to be relieved touching the trust of certain lands in Ireland. The defendants had appeared and answered the bill, and had not any way objected to the jurisdiction of this court: but the cause coming now to be heard, the Lord Chancellor objected, this court could not hold pleas of land in Ireland.

For the plaintiff it was urged, that he was proper for relief in this court by reason that both plaintiff and defendant were here in England, and that a court of equity does only *agere in personam;* its proceedings are to reform the conscience of the party, and if at any time a court of equity may be said to *agere in rem,* it is only in the case of sequestration, which is for the contempt of the party; and that therefore the defendant being served with a subpœna here, and living in England, this court had proper jurisdiction of the cause, though the land lies in Ireland; and the rather, for that it was never yet pretended that there was any local action in equity: and they instanced for precedents the late cases of the Lord Arglasse and Muschamp, 1 Vern. 75, and Lord Arglasse and Pit, and Archer's Case, (see Barker *v.* Dormer, 1 Show. 192), and insisted that otherwise there would be a failure of justice, for the defendant living here could not be served with process issuing out of the Chancery in Ireland.

But the Lord Chancellor [Jeffreys] overruled the plaintiff's counsel, and said as to the cases of the Lord Arglasse, the fraudulent contracts were made here in England; and as to the present case there would be no failure of justice, for they might have a subpœna out of this court returnable in the Chancery of Ireland; as in his own experience in cases between master and 'prentice in the city of London, he had known subpœnas to have issued out of this court returnable in the Mayor's court in London for persons that lived out of the jurisdiction; and therefore pronounced the rule for the dismissing the bill: but at the importunity of the plaintiff's counsel gave them a week's time to search for precedents.

The Lord Chancellor and the Judges having been attended with precedents, Sir John Holt argued for the plaintiff, as to the preliminary point only (to wit) whether this court had jurisdiction, and might hold plea of the lands in question which lay in Ireland. . . .

The defendant's counsel in a manner waived the preliminary point, and would not enter into the debate whether this court might not decree the trust of lands in Ireland, the trustee living here; but that it was certainly a matter discretionary in the court, whether they would do it or not; and that as this case was circumstanced, they apprehended the court would not interpose. . . .

After long debate, the judges [BEDINGFIELD, C. J. and ATKINS, C. B.] concurring with his Lordship, that the court had a proper jurisdiction in this case, and that the judges in England were proper expositors of the Irish laws, and that by the true construction of this statute the trust was vested in the king, and not the land itself, and the proof being full as to the identity of the person, decreed for the plaintiff, as to one moiety; the trust as to the other moiety being for Sir Morrice Eustace himself, and not for Fitzgerald.[1]

METHODS OF PROTECTING EQUITABLE INTERESTS. 1. A defendant who fails to obey a decree of a court of equity is punishable for contempt. 2 Daniell, Ch. Pl. & Pr., 6 Am. ed., *1042 et seq.

2. By a writ of assistance or by its modern substitute, a writ of possession, a court of equity may put the complainant in possession of the property in dispute. 2 Daniell, *1062. This gives the complainant some relief and may operate indirectly to compel the defendant to convey. Huston, Decrees in Equity, 80. See Schenck v. Conover, 2 Beas. (N. J.) 220.

3. By a writ of sequestration the court may take possession of property of the defendant as a means of compulsion. "This court hath from time to time enlarged its power to make its decrees effectual; it was held all along until King James's time, that the decrees of this court bound only the person, and could not meddle with sequestering of land; neither did the court of exchequer ever do it till of late; but finding their decrees would be useless in many cases where the person was obstinate, it is now the common practice of

---

[1] "The Courts of Equity in England are, and always have been, courts of conscience, operating *in personam* and not *in rem;* and in the exercise of this personal jurisdiction they have always been accustomed to compel the performance of contracts and trusts as to subjects which were not either locally or *ratione domicilii* within their jurisdiction." Per Lord Selborne, in Ewing v. Ewing, 9 App. Cas. 34, 40, 10 App. Cas. 453, s. c. See also Black Point Syndicate v. Eastern Concessions, 79 L. T. 658; Re Clinton, 88 L. T. 17; Gilliland v. Inabnit, 92 Iowa 46. See cases cited Ames, 245n.

For reasons of convenience or of policy, relief as to property outside the jurisdiction may be refused. Ames, Cas. Eq. Juris., 22n.; 20 Harv. L. Rev. 392; 17 Col. L. Rev. 497.

both courts." Lower *v.* Weale, Freem. C. C. 107, 109 (1689). See Swetland *v.* Swetland, 105 N. J. Eq. 608. Personal property may even be sold and the proceeds used to satisfy the complainant's claim. See Hide *v.* Pettit, 1 Chan. Cas. 91, Freem. C. C. 125; Daniell, *1047 *et seq.*

4. A receiver may be appointed to take possession of and manage the trust property. Perry, Trusts, secs. 818–820.

5. By the Judgments Act, 1838 (1 & 2 Vict. c. 110) secs. 18, 19, it was provided that a decree in equity whereby a sum of money shall be payable, shall have the same effect as a judgment at law. 2 Daniell, *1031. There are similar statutes in this country. Huston, 83.

6. Finally there are statutes allowing the court, either directly by its decree or by a conveyance by an officer of the court, to vest title in the complainant or in a new trustee. Felch *v.* Hooper, 119 Mass. 52; Ames, 249n. See Chap. III, sec. II, *ante*. The statutes in some states apply to personalty as well as to land. For a discussion of the nature of such a proceeding, see Amparo Mining Co. *v.* Fidelity T. Co., 74 N. J. Eq. 197, 75 N. J. Eq. 555. See also Cook, The Powers of Courts of Equity, 15 Col. L. Rev. 37, 106, 228; Huston, chap. V.

If the *res*, as well as the trustee, is beyond the jurisdiction, no relief can be given. Ames, 249n.

Although the trustee is subject to the jurisdiction of the court, a decree cannot operate in *rem* when the *res* is outside the jurisdiction. Fall *v.* Eastin, 215 U. S. 1, aff'g Fall *v.* Fall, 75 Neb. 104.

On the question what law governs the creation or administration of trusts, see Beale, Equitable Interests in Foreign Property, 20 Harv. L. Rev. 382; Cavers, Trusts *Inter Vivos* and the Conflict of Laws, 44 Harv. L. Rev. 161.

If a *chose* in action is held in trust and the trustee is outside the jurisdiction but the obligor is within the jurisdiction, it has been held that the *cestui que trust* can maintain a suit directly against the obligor. Ettlinger *v.* Persian Rug & Carpet Co., 142 N. Y. 189. If the trustee is within the jurisdiction he is a necessary party to the suit. See Cope v. Parry, 2 J. & W. 538; Wood *v.* Williams, 4 Madd. 186. But see Head *v.* Lord Teynham, 1 Cox 57. See Bogert, Trusts, 464.

Section II.

Powers and Duties of the Trustee.

SMITH *v.* MOONEY.

Court of Chancery, New Jersey. 1927.
139 Atl. 513.

Suit by Thomas J. Smith, surviving executor of Mary Ann Smith, deceased, against Frederick H. Mooney, for specific performance. Decree for complainant.

Backes, Vice Chancellor. The surviving executor and trustee under the last will and testament of Mary Ann Smith, deceased, entered into a written contract with the defendant to sell him a piece of land belonging to the estate. The bill is filed to compel the defendant to perform his contract, and he is willing to do so, but contends that the complainant cannot give him a marketable title, asserting that the executor has not the power to sell. That depends upon the true construction of the will. The testatrix, after some specific bequests and devises, by the fifth clause of her will, which is too long to set out in full, devised and bequeathed all the rest, residue, and remainder of her property to her executors upon trust to hold the principal of her estate during the lifetime of her six children and upon the death of the survivor to divide it as hereinafter stated. In the meantime the income was to be paid to the children and one Catherine Burke, in equal shares, the children of any deceased child to take the parent's share of the income, with discretionary right in the trustee to withhold the income, or otherwise dispose of it, not now important to state. Upon the death of all the children the will directs that the principal of the estate, and accumulations of income, if any, be divided among the issue of the testatrix's six sons and Catherine Burke. The share to each is given in substantially, if not precisely, the same language as follows:

"One share of the principal of my estate to the children of my son Philip Smith, living at the time herein fixed for *distribution*, to be equally *divided* among them, the issue of any of his deceased children to take the parent's share, in case all his children shall be then dead and the issue of none be then living, then his share to be *divided* equally among my then surviving grandchildren."

The testatrix died possessed of considerable personal property and many houses and vacant lots of land in and about Newark, and, if distribution of the estate were made at this time, some of the pro rata shares would be as low as a one seventy-second of the whole.

There are, it is true, no words expressly authorizing the sale of the real estate, but full effect could not be given to the testatrix's direction to *divide* the estate — the real and personal property as a unit — at the time fixed by her for its *distribution*, unless there was a conversion of the realty. The testatrix obviously contemplated that the division should be in money shares, and to that end that the real estate should be sold. The power of sale in the trustee is clearly implied. This view is supported by the cases in this state construing similar provisions in wills. Executors of Vanness *v.* Jacobus, 17 N. J. Eq. 153; Wurts *v.* Page, 19 N. J. Eq. 366; Haggerty *v.* Lanterman, 30 N. J. Eq. 37; Belcher *v.* Belcher, 38 N. J. Eq. 126; Moore *v.* Wears, 87 N. J. Eq. 459, 100 A. 563.

The complainant can unquestionably convey a marketable title, and a decree that the contract be enforced will be advised.[1]

[1] See Robinson *v.* Robinson, 105 Me. 68; Dreier *v.* Senger, 130 Atl. 5 (N. J. Ch. 1925).

As to the power of the court to authorize a sale, see Colonial Trust Company *v.* Brown, 105 Conn. 261; Suiter *v.* McWard, 328 Ill. 462; Sparrow *v.* Sparrow, 171 Ky. 101; *Re* Abrams' Estate, 114 Wash. 51.

See also Bogert, Trusts, sec. 88; Perry, Trusts, secs. 764–787; Pomeroy, Eq. Juris., sec. 1062; Underhill, Trusts, art. 61; 32 L. R. A. (N. S.) 676; Ann. Cas. 1913C 979; 57 A. L. R. 1118; Dec. Dig., Trusts, secs. 188–204.

In Oak Investment Corp. *v.* Martin, 107 N. J. Eq. 123, it was held that where the trustee was forbidden to sell the trust property for five years a contract to sell made during the five-year period is improper.

As to power to exchange trust property, see 63 A. L. R. 1003.

Power to mortgage. As to the power of a trustee to mortgage or pledge the trust property, see Neill *v.* Neill, [1904] 1 I. R. 513; Fergusson *v.* Fergusson, 148 Ark. 290; McLoughlin *v.* Shaw, 95 Conn. 102; Russell *v.* Russell, 109 Conn. 187; Sharp's G'dn *v.* Sharp's Ex'trx, 217 Ky. 171; Tuttle *v.* First Nat. Bank, 187 Mass. 533; Warren *v.* Pazolt, 203 Mass. 328, 348; Shirkey *v.* Kirby, 110 Va. 455. See Bogert, Trusts, sec. 89; Perry, Trusts, sec. 768; 36 Yale L. Jour. 582; 7 L. R. A. (N. S.) 263; 1 Ann. Cas. 942; 9 Ann. Cas. 643; 63 A. L. R. 795; Dec. Dig., Trusts, sec. 206.

As a general rule a power to sell does not confer power to mortgage. See 10 Ann. Cas. 255; Ann. Cas. 1916C 606.

Power to lease. The trustee normally has power to lease land held in trust. As to the existence and extent of this power, see Russell *v.* Russell, 109 Conn. 187; Marsh *v.* Reed, 184 Ill. 263; *Re* Hubbell Trust, 135 Iowa 637; Marshall's Trustee *v.* Marshall, 225 Ky. 168; Sweeney *v.* Hagerstown Trust Co., 144 Md. 612; St. Louis Union T. Co. *v.* Van Raalte, 214 Mo. App. 172; Raynolds *v.* Browning, King & Co., 217 App. Div. 443, *aff'd mem.* 245 N. Y. 623; Cox *v.* Lumber Co., 175 N. C. 299; Will of Caswell, 197 Wis. 327; 14 Minn. L. Rev. 274; 7 N. C. L. Rev. 94; Bogert, Trusts, sec. 90; Perry, Trusts, sec. 484; 13 L. R. A. (N. S.) 497; 61 A. L. R. 1368; Dec. Dig., Trusts, sec. 205.

In Russell *v.* Russell, 109 Conn. 187, *supra,* Maltbie, J., said (p. 204): "Leases by trustees which will not run beyond the termination of the trust, or if its termination is indefinite in time, beyond its probable duration, are ordinarily within their implied powers, and leases extending beyond those limits may be, if it appears that they are reasonably necessary for the accomplishment of the purposes of the trust or the preservation of the trust property. Unless the necessity to make leases of the latter class is clear, trustees should seek the advice of the Superior Court as to the period they may be made to run."

Power to make repairs and permanent improvements. As to the author-

DOILY v. SHERRATT.

CHANCERY. 1735.

2 Eq. Cas. Abr. 742.

[VERNEY, M. R.] A. by will appoints two trustees, to whom and their heirs, executors and assigns, he devises his real and personal estate on several trusts; and in case one die then the other to execute the same. During their joint lives if one refuse to act, the other cannot act without him, but the trust devolves upon the Court.[1]

WATLING v. WATLING.

CIRCUIT COURT OF APPEALS, U. S., 6TH CIRCUIT. 1928.

27 F.(2d) 193.

Appeals from the District Court of the United States for the Eastern District of Michigan; Charles C. Simons, Judge.

Suit by Lucile Watling against John W. Watling and others. From the decree (15 F.[2d] 719), both parties appeal. Affirmed.

Before DENISON, MOORMAN, and KNAPPEN, Circuit Judges.

MOORMAN, Circuit Judge.[2] John A. Watling died testate in 1919, leaving a wife, Eunice W. Watling, a son, John W. Watling, and a daughter, Lucile Watling. After making some special devises and bequests, his will provided that the residue of his estate should be disposed of as follows: One-third to the son; one-third to John W. Watling and William F. McCorkle, in trust for the testator's wife, with power in the trustees to manage, care for, invest, and reinvest the same, and with directions to pay the income therefrom, after paying the costs incident to the care of the estate, to the beneficiary thereof, in quarterly payments, during her natural life. It further provided that the trust estate thus created should be divided, at the beneficiary's death, into two equal parts, one of which should go to the son, "if then living; if not, to his issue then surviving, if any; if there be none," to become a part of a trust estate created for the daughter, and that the other half should be added to the trust

---

ity of the trustee to make repairs and permanent improvements, see Russell v. Russell, 109 Conn. 187, 14 Minn. L. Rev. 194; Warren v. Pazolt, 203 Mass. 328; Re Miller, 67 N. J. Eq. 431; Bogert, Trusts, sec. 86; Perry, Trusts, secs. 477–477b.

[1] As to the necessity of unanimity, see Swale v. Swale, 22 Beav. 584 (distinguishing between executors and trustees); Wilbur v. Almy, 12 How. (U. S.) 180. See Ames, 512; Bogert, Trusts, sec. 94; Perry, Trusts, secs. 411–413; Dec. Dig., Trusts, sec. 239.

[2] A short concurring opinion by Knappen, J., and a dissenting opinion by Denison, J., are omitted.

estate created for the daughter, if she were then living, and, if not, should go to the son. The remaining one-third was devised to John W. Watling and William F. McCorkle, in trust for the daughter, with the same powers of management and disposition of income as those pertaining to the wife's estate, and with the proviso that at the death of the daughter the trust estate so created should be divided into two equal parts, one of which should go to the son, if living; if not, to his issue then surviving, if any; and, if there be none, to become a part of the trust estate created for the wife, and the other half should be added to the trust estate created for the wife, if she be then living, and, if not, should go to the son.

The concluding paragraph of the will is: "Should my trustees hereinbefore named at any time think it advisable to do so, they may terminate the trust hereinbefore created for the benefit of my wife, and pay over and assign to her the property, or any part thereof, held in trust by them for her benefit, to be hers absolutely and free from any claim upon the part of my said daughter or son, or the issue of my said daughter or son. And I also hereby empower my said trustees, should they in their discretion think it wise to do so, at any time to pay over and transfer to my said daughter the property or any part thereof held by them in trust for the benefit of my said daughter, and, in case they shall do so, she shall take the same for her own absolutely, free and clear of all claims on the part of my said son or my said wife, or the issue of my said son."

John W. Watling was appointed trustee under the will by the probate court of Wayne county, Michigan, but McCorkle formally declined to act as trustee. When the bill was made in 1909, the daughter, Lucile, was confined in a government hospital for the insane as a mentally incompetent person. About a year after her father's death, she was released from the hospital and formally adjudged sane. Her mother died in 1922, and Lucile demanded of her brother, as trustee, about that time, that he turn over to her the estate devised to her in her father's will. This he refused to do, and in June of 1923 he resigned as trustee, and the probate court of Wayne county appointed in his place the Union Trust Company. This suit was brought by Lucile against the trust company to compel it to turn over to her her estate.

The trust company's defense to the suit was that whatever discretion was vested in the trustee under the will to pay over and transfer to the daughter the trust estate was personal to the original trustees and did not pass to it. John W. Watling and his infant children who were made parties defendant to the suit, defended it on that ground, and on the additional ground that the power given the trustees was a power to be exercised only to the extent that it was necessary to use the principal of the estate for the comfortable living of the beneficiary, or, if not so limited, it was a power to be exercised solely and exclusively at the will of the trustee, with which a court of equity could not interfere. The trial court held that the power passed to the successor trustee, and that the will created an active trust as to both capital and income for the benefit of the daughter; that there was annexed to the trust a power, granted to the trustee as donee thereof, and coupled with the trust, to transfer absolutely to the beneficiary all or any of the estate so held for her, at any time during her lifetime, when the trustee, in the exercise of an honest, well-intentioned, proper discretion, should think such transfer to be for her benefit and welfare and to her best interest; but further held that there was nothing in the record to show bad faith on the part of the trustee in failing to exercise the power, and until it appeared that there was bad faith or failure to exercise an honest discretion on the part of the trustee, after being judicially advised of its possession of the power, the court would not undertake to determine whether the property should or should not be turned over to the cestui que trust.

Whether a discretionary power given a trustee is personal to the trustee named or passes to a substituted trustee upon the former's death or resignation depends necessarily upon the intention of the creator of the trust. Where there is a discretionary right to terminate the trust by turning over the entire estate to the beneficiary, it is generally held that the power passes to the successor trustee. Perry on Trusts and Trustees (6th Ed.) § 503. The trial court held that the power passed in this case upon the sustaining authority of Sells *v.* Delgado, 186 Mass. 25, 70 N. E. 1036, Greenwich Trust Co. *v.* Converse, 100 Conn. 15, 122 A. 916, Hicks *v.* Hicks, 84 N. J. Eq. 515, 94 A. 409, and other cases. We think the holding was right.

When the will was made, appellant was ill and confined in a hospital for the insane. In this situation the testator might well have established a fund, and given to the trustees thereof the power to use the income therefrom, and the principal, if necessary, for the daughter's support during her life. With equal consideration for her future, he might have given the trustees the power, should the time come when they thought it wise to do so, to turn over the principal to her. She had been an unusually intelligent young woman, and the testator must have thought it possible, if not probable, that she would eventually recover; otherwise, he would have made no provision by which the trustees might turn over to her her estate. If he had intended, even though she recovered, merely to authorize the use, if necessary, of the corpus of the estate for her living, he could easily have expressed that purpose in unmistakable terms. As against the inferences to be drawn from his failure so to do, reference is made to the provision which he made for his wife, which is said to show identity of purpose with that respecting the daughter; that is, a purpose to insure his daughter's comfort for life by the use, if necessary, of the corpus of her estate, but, if not necessary, by the use of the income therefrom only and the preservation of the corpus for the children of his son. To say that it was the testator's intention, as disclosed in the will, so to restrict the use of the power given his trustees, would be to say that, except in that necessity, there would be no power. This we cannot do. Besides, differences in the circumstances and the business qualifications of the wife and daughter, as shown by the proofs, do not, we think, admit of an inference that it was the intention of the testator to put the same limitations upon the use of the two estates. Moreover, we do not discover in the will any purpose to pass the property ultimately to the children of the son. The son took his share outright, and, if he survives his sister, will also take her share at her death, if in the meantime it is not turned over to her. To provide that his children were to stand in his place, if he should not be living when the daughter died, was merely to say that they should take if the trustees had not exercised the power given them by the will. In this they were given a broad discretion, and we find nothing in the will respecting the son's children or otherwise that restricts the use of this discretion to the living expenses of the daughter.

Neither do we construe the will as granting a power which the trustees were required to exercise if and as soon as the plaintiff was adjudged to be sane or believed to be capable of looking after her estate, nor, similarly, as a power to be exercised solely at the will of the trustee and not subject to control by the courts.

The provision in question did not direct the trustees, should they believe appellant to have recovered and to be capable of looking after her property, to turn it over to her; it merely gave them the power to turn it over, should they in their discretion think it wise. They were given the discretion of exercising the power upon the exercise of their judgment or precedent discretion of finding it wise to do so. This is not, therefore, a case where the power is directed to be exercised upon the happening of some event, or upon the finding by the trustees of the existence of a condition, but is a power conferred with a discretion to exercise it upon the exercise of a precedent discretion. It is perhaps quite true, as appellant contends, that upon the exercise of the precedent discretion in favor of the beneficiary, it would be the duty of the trustee to exercise the power, just as if it were directed to do so, and there would be no further discretion, or rather that evidence showing the dishonest exercise of the precedent discretion would also show dishonest use of the power. Nevertheless there is a discretion in the trustee upon which the use of the power depends, and the duty to use it would not result, in our opinion, from a mere finding that appellant was sane and capable of prudently managing her estate. Other considerations, even in those circumstances, might be sufficiently potent to make the use unwise. The chances of a recurrence of her former illness, the state of her health, with the probable effect thereon of her taking over the management of her affairs, are matters that should also have consideration.

It is, of course, the duty of the trustee to exercise an honest and well-intentioned discretion. Read *v.* Patterson, 44 N. J. Eq. 211, 14 A. 490, 6 Am. St. Rep. 877; Thompson *v.* Denny, 78 Ind. App. 257, 135 N. E. 260; Perry on Trusts and Trustees, § 508. And, if it fails to do so, a court of equity will check it, and, if need be, will exercise the power itself. Keating *v.* Keating, 182 Iowa, 1056, 165 N. W. 74; Bull *v.* Bull, 8 Conn. 47, 20 Am. Dec. 86; Cochran *v.* Paris, 11 Grat. (Va.) 348. But a court ought not to overrule the trustee's discretion, except upon the clearest of proof; that is, proof that it has not exercised a good faith discretion. Morton *v.* Southgate, 28 Me. 41. Such proof does not appear in this case, since it does not appear, as stated by the trial court, that the trustee has considered whether it ought or ought not to pay over the money from any standpoint other than that of its power. It is to be presumed that, being assured of the existence of that power it will exercise an honest discretion. As to what that should lead to we express no opinion.

Decree affirmed.[1]

ANONYMOUS.

3 Swanst. 79n.

SIR J. JEKYLL cited a late case at the Rolls, where one who was trustee for a woman and her children did, with the woman's consent, assign his trust to another who was guilty of a breach of trust, and the first trustee decreed to make satisfaction, because trustees cannot divest themselves of their trust at their pleasure.

[1] *Survival of powers.* See Lane *v.* Debenham, 11 Hare 188; Whitaker *v.* McDowell, 82 Conn. 195; Matter of White, 135 N. Y. Misc. 377. See Ames, 515; Bogert, Trusts, sec. 94; Perry, Trusts, secs. 491–506; Kales, Estates, 2 ed., sec. 626; 1 Tiffany, Real Property, 2 ed., sec. 322; 23 Harv. L. Rev. 59; 16 Ann. Cas. 325; Dec. Dig., Trusts, sec. 243.

As to the effect of a disclaimer by one or more trustees, see 36 A. L. R. 826.

There are statutes in a number of states providing for the survival of powers.

Control of discretionary powers. As to the extent to which the discretion of the trustee may be controlled by the court, see Gisborne *v.* Gisborne, 2 App. Cas. 300; Hooker *v.* Goodwin, 91 Conn. 463; Keating *v.* Keating, 182 Iowa 1056; Elward *v.* Elward, 117 Kan. 458; Williams *v.* Hund, 302 Mo. 451; Viall *v.* R. I. Hospital Trust Co., 45 R. I. 432.

On the power of corporate trustees to exercise discretion, see 11 A. L. R. 300.

See Bogert, Trusts, sec. 96; Perry, Trusts, secs. 510–511*a*; Underhill, Trusts, art. 60; 32 A. L. R. 441 (power to pay principal); 39 A. L. R. 40 (power to make advances); Dec. Dig., Trusts, sec. 177.

GRAHAM v. KING.

SUPREME COURT, MISSOURI. 1872.

50 Mo. 22.

WAGNER, J. The respondents, Graham and wife, executed a deed of trust on a piece of land lying in St. Charles county to secure the payment of a debt, and one of the appellants (King) was made the trustee therein. The deed contained the usual and ordinary provisions, and after default was made in the payment of the debt authorized the "said King as trustee to proceed to sell the property" after having given the requisite notice in some newspaper published in St. Charles county. Payment not being made when the note became due, King advertised the property for sale in the St. Charles *Democrat*, a German newspaper, but the notice was inserted in the English language.[1] . . . At the sale, King, the trustee, was not present, but left the matter in the hands of his son, a minor. It is alleged that the property sold for greatly below its value, and an injunction was asked to restrain the trustee from making a deed to the purchaser at the sale. After hearing the proof the court below decreed a perpetual injunction. . . .

The office and duties of a trustee are matters of personal confidence, and he must exercise a just and fair discretion in doing whatever is right for the best interest of the debtor. He must in person supervise and watch over the sale, and adjourn it if necessary, to prevent a sacrifice of the property, and no one can do it in his stead unless empowered thereto in the instrument conferring the trust. A trustee cannot delegate the trust or power of sale to a third person, and a sale executed by such delegated agent is void. (Perry, Trusts, § 779, and notes.)

Judgment affirmed. The other judges concur.[2]

[1] The court decided that the notice should have been inserted in a newspaper published in the English language.

[2] As to delegation of a power of sale, see Ames, 516.

In general as to the duty of the trustee not to delegate, see *Ex parte* Belchier, Amb. 218; Speight *v.* Gaunt, 22 Ch. D. 727, aff'd 9 App. Cas. 1; Meck *v.* Behrens, 141 Wash. 676. See Ames, 516, 527; Bogert, Trusts, sec. 95; Perry, Trusts, secs. 402–409; 50 A. L. R. 214; Dec. Dig., Trusts, sec. 176.

Under Trustee Act, 1925, 15 Geo. V. c. 19, secs. 23–25, trustees are permitted to employ agents without liability for their defaults if they are employed in good faith; and a trustee intending to remain out of the United Kingdom for more than one month may delegate the execution of the trust to another but subject to liability for his acts.

MORLEY v. MORLEY.

Chancery. 1678.

2 Cas. Ch. 2.

The defendant was trustee for the plaintiff, an infant, and received for him £40 in gold; a servant of the defendant living in the house with him robbed his master of £200 and the £40 out of his house. The robbery, *viz.*, that the defendant was robbed of money was proved; the sum of £40 was proved by only the defendant's oath.

Lord Chancellor [Finch]. He was to keep it but as his own, and allowed it on account; so in case of a factor; so in case of a person robbed, for he cannot possibly have other proof.[1]

[1] *Cf.* Shoemaker *v.* Hinze, 53 Wis. 116, *ante.*

As to the standard of care and skill required of trustees, see Bogert, Trusts, sec. 97; Underhill, Trusts, art. 51; 29 Mich. L. Rev. 125; 3 L. R. A. (n. s.) 415; Dec. Dig., Trusts, sec. 179.

As to the effect of exculpatory provisions as to the liability of the trustee, see Thompson *v.* Hays, 11 F.(2d) 244; Warren *v.* Pazolt, 203 Mass. 328; Tuttle *v.* Gilmore, 36 N. J. Eq. 617. See 29 Mich. L. Rev. 355.

Types of trustees. Mr. Augustine Birrell in his Lectures on the Duties and Liabilities of Trustees, after calling attention to the earlier strictness of courts of equity in applying to trustees a high standard of care and skill, points out the effect of the change in procedure permitting oral testimony. He says: "Now it is all different. The real Trustee, for example, goes into the box — some farmer, it may be, who from a sense of cronyship has consented to act as a Trustee under the will of a neighbour with whom on market days he has often had a friendly glass. There he stands, ignorant for certain, pigheaded very likely, quarrelsome possibly but honest, palpably honest and perspiring. He is charged with losses occasioned by his disregard of the strict language of a will he never understood, or for not having properly controlled the actions of his co-trustee, the principal attorney of his market town. It may be necessary to ruin such a man, to sell his horses and his cows, his gig and his carts, and to drive him from his old home, but it cannot be done without a qualm. Hence has come about that new spirit and temper to which I have ventured to refer at too great length."

In Matter of Clark, 136 N. Y. Misc. 881, Slater, S., said (p. 889): "In trust relations these days, when trust companies have entered the business, much more is expected from a corporate trustee than from the old-fashioned individual executor or trustee. Trust companies seek this character of business, claiming that they are specially qualified and financially responsible. They make a specialty of trust matters and claim to be familiar with the authority of executors and trustees as to trust investments. They have claimed that each estate and trust will receive the personal attention of one trust executive whose life work is the administration of estates and trusts, and decisions with regard to the purchase and sale of securities will be independently arrived at by these officers in consultation with investment experts. The courts, and particularly the Surrogate's Court, vigilantly enforce the highest standard of fidelity of trustees and zealously guard the rights of beneficiaries." See Linnard's Estate, 299 Pa. 32, 39; 30 Col. L. Rev. 1166, 1171.

By Trustee Act, 1925, 15 Geo. V, c. 19, sec. 61, it is provided that where a trustee is liable for a breach of trust but has acted honestly and reasonably

In re THOMSON.

HIGH COURT OF JUSTICE, CHANCERY DIVISION. 1929.

(1929) W. N. 243.[1]

AT THE DATE of his will the testator was carrying on the business of a yacht agent in offices on the first floor of 25, Haymarket. He was assisted in its conduct by the defendant, who was under no obligation which prevented him from quitting the testator's service and carrying on a competing business. By his will made on March 6, 1928, the testator appointed the plaintiffs, his daughter Blanche and A. H. Wyatt, and the defendant executors and trustees thereof, and directed them, or any two of them, to carry on his business, and to pay a certain proportion of the profits to the defendant. An option to purchase the business was given in turn to the defendant and another, which was not exercised, and, in the event of a sale thereof by the trustees otherwise than to either of those persons, the whole of the proceeds were bequeathed to Miss Blanche Thomson.

The testator died on August 1, 1928, and the plaintiffs and the defendant then proceeded to carry on his business in the same offices as the testator had done until February 1, 1929, when, their tenancy of the old offices being about to expire, they removed the business to offices on the second floor, and on February 15 a lease of these offices was granted to the defendant, of which fact the plaintiffs were not aware until March 19. Negotiations had been carried on between the defendant and the plaintiffs with a view to the formation of a private company to take over the testator's business, but the parties failed to agree, and the negotiations were broken off about March 19, 1929, and the defendant then claimed the right to hold the new lease for his own benefit, and, further, a right, while still remaining one of the executors and trustees, to exclude his co-executors and trustees from the new offices and to set up a business of a yacht agent on his own account in competition with the testator's business. Hence the issue of the writ, in which the plaintiffs claimed (1) a declaration that the defendant held the new lease as a trustee for the estate of the testator, and (2) an injunction to restrain him from doing what he was threatening to do. However, since the issue of the writ, namely, on June 21, 1929, the new lease was assigned by the defendant to Miss Blanche Thomson, and the goodwill of the testator's business was assigned to her by the three trustees, with the consequence that it became no

and ought fairly to be excused for the breach of trust or for omitting to obtain the directions of the court, the court may relieve him either wholly or partly from personal liability.

[1] s. c. [1930] 1 Ch. 203.

longer necessary to grant any of the relief claimed, and it was only necessary to determine the question whether the defendant was entitled when the writ was issued to the rights which he claimed was for the purpose of deciding how the costs of the action ought to be borne.

CLAUSON J. said it was plain that the defendant was in the circumstances wrong in claiming to retain the new lease for his own benefit, and that in the face of that claim the plaintiffs were justified in bringing the action. The other part of the case raised a more difficult question. Was the defendant entitled, as he claimed to be, to sever his connection with the testator's business, and, while still remaining a trustee of the will, to set up a similar business in competition with the testator's business. As the defendant himself stated in his defence, the business of a yacht agent was similar to that of a house agent. The greater number of the yachts for the time being on the market got on to the books of all yacht agents, and the agent earned a commission on a sale who was first in securing a purchaser. Therefore every yacht agent carried on a business which was bound to compete with that of every other yacht agent. There could be no question that, as between the defendant and the beneficiaries under the will, there existed a relation of a fiduciary character. Translating the principle laid down by Lord Cranworth L. C. in Aberdeen Railway Co. v. Blakie, (1854) 1 Macq. 461, 471 (which was there applied to the director of a company), to the present case, an executor and trustee having to discharge the duty of carrying on the testator's business to the best advantage of the beneficiaries should not be allowed to enter into engagements in which he had or could have a personal interest conflicting or which possibly might conflict with the interests of those whom he was bound to protect. Having regard to the special nature of the business, it was clear that if the defendant were to do what he claimed a right to do he would be transgressing that principle. In applying it to certain other businesses, there might well be more difficulty. The only order would be that the defendant should pay all the costs of the action.[1]

COLONIAL TRUST COMPANY v. BROWN.

SUPREME COURT, CONNECTICUT. 1926.

105 Conn. 261.

SUIT to determine the construction of the will of Robert K. Brown, late of Waterbury, deceased, brought to the Superior Court in New Haven County and reserved by the court, *Dickenson*, J., upon an agreed statement of facts, for the advice of this court.

[1] As to the trustee's duty of loyalty to the beneficiary, see further Chap. V, sec. V.

Robert K. Brown died in 1916, leaving a will made five months before in which, after making a few small bequests, he gave all his property to the plaintiff in trust, directing it to pay certain annuities, and providing for the distribution of the residue among the heirs of the blood of his father *per stirpes.*

By the fourth article of the will it was provided that " No leases shall be given for a period exceeding one year on any of my property."

By the eleventh article of the will it was provided as follows: " Eleventh. It is my will and I direct said trustee to pay off the incumbrances on my Exchange Place property and West Main and Meadow Streets property so fast as it shall have any unexpended funds in its hands, or to use the funds of said estate as it may deem necessary and proper for the improvement and construction of said Exchange Place and West Main and Meadow Street property; provided, however, that any new buildings placed upon said land shall not exceed three stories in height. The said trustee having full power to use its discretion as to whether it will first remove the said incumbrances on said property, or build upon and improve the same. In the event of damage by fire or other cause to buildings more than three stories high, said buildings shall not be repaired above the third story, but all stories above the third shall be condemned and removed, leaving the buildings three stories in height."

The testator's estate consisted principally of the two pieces of property referred to in the ninth paragraph of his will as the Exchange Place property and the Homestead.

The Exchange Place property was acquired by testator's father in 1848, and at his death in 1881, by the testator. It is located in the heart of the financial and retail business district of Waterbury, is as valuable as any land in the city, and most favorably adapted for buildings containing stores and offices. There is, and for a long time has been, upon it a group of several old buildings. They are costly to maintain, expenditures for this purpose during the last seven years absorbing more than fifty per cent. of the gross rentals. Their condition, arrangement and appearance are such that the lower floors are not desirable for use for retail stores and the upper floors are ill-adapted to commercial or business purposes. So long as the height of buildings upon the property is restricted to three stories, it cannot be improved so as to get the best income return and the restriction is likely to have a more serious effect in the future. Even if the properties were improved, the best income return cannot be secured, so long as leases can be given only for one year, and this restriction, too, is likely to have a more serious effect in the future; it in fact diminishes the ground floor rentals by at least twenty per cent., and about seventy per cent. of the gross income from the property is derived from these rentals. Tenants of the most desirable class cannot be secured for the property, and could not be, even if the properties were improved, unless leases for more than one year could be given. This reacts upon rental values and the character of the business done in the neighborhood and retards the normal development of the property in use and value. At the testator's death the property was assessed for taxation at $418,300, and in 1924, at $746,000, its fair market value being approximately $1,000,000. There is a mortgage upon it which amounted at his death to $181,500, but which has since been reduced by a payment of $6,000.

The Homestead property was in part acquired by the testator from his father in 1876 and in part purchased by him in 1889. The land is occupied by several dwelling-houses, which have been substantially unchanged since the testator acquired them, except that the use of one has had to be abandoned, and by a brick barn, which since the testator's death has been converted into an automobile service station and salesroom. The property cannot be improved, so long as the height of buildings upon it is restricted to three stories, or, if improved, cannot be rented so long as leases upon it are restricted to one year, so as to secure the best income return from it, and the effect of these restrictions is likely to be more serious in the future. This property was assessed for taxation at the testator's death in 1914 at $50,000, and in 1924 at $80,400, its market value now being approximately $100,000.

The effect which would be caused by the restrictions as to height of buildings and length of leases to be given, inserted in the will, was apparent when the testator executed it and thereafter until his death was known to him. The net income received from the two properties for the three years before the date of the will averaged $20,000. Since then, although the annuities provided in the will have been paid, and $6,000 has been applied on the mortgage, there has been an accumulation of excess income to such an extent that, with certain other funds added, the trustee, on December 31st, 1925, held personal property to the amount of $288,469.63.

MALTBIE,[1] J. . . . We are asked to advise whether the provision in the fourth article, restricting leases of the property to one year and forbidding any promises of longer leases, and that in the eleventh article, directing that no new buildings placed upon the Exchange Place property and the Homestead shall exceed three stories in height, are binding upon the trustee. In Holmes *v.* Connecticut Trust & Safe Deposit Co., 92 Conn. 507, 514, 103 Atl. 640, in holding invalid certain conditions attached to the enjoyment of a trust estate by the *cestui que trust*, as fraught with danger to the proper conduct of the marital relationship, we said: " As a general rule, a testator has the right to impose such conditions as

---

[1] The statement of facts is abridged, and a part of the opinion as well as that of Wheeler, C. J., is omitted.

he pleases upon a beneficiary as conditions precedent to the vesting of an estate in him, or to the enjoyment of a trust estate by him as *cestui que trust*. He may not, however, impose one that is uncertain, unlawful or opposed to public policy." So it may be said of the directions and restrictions which a testator may impose upon the management of property which he places in a trust, that they are obligatory upon the trustee unless they are uncertain, unlawful or opposed to public policy. Lewin on Trusts (12th Ed.) 90. In the instant case, the length of time during which the testator directed that the property should remain in the trust and the complete uncertainty as to the individuals to whom it would ultimately go, preclude any thought of an intent on his part to forbid the cumbering of the property by long leases or the burdening of it with large buildings, lest the beneficiaries be embarrassed in the development of it along such lines as they might themselves prefer. The only other purposes which can reasonably be attributed to him is to compel the trustee to follow his own peculiar ideas as to the proper and advantageous way to manage such properties. That the restrictions are opposed to the interests of the beneficiaries of the trust, that they are imprudent and unwise, is made clear by the statement of agreed facts, but that is not all, for their effect is not confined to the beneficiaries. The Exchange Place property is located at a corner of the public square in the very center of the city of Waterbury, in the heart of the financial and retail business district, is as valuable as any land in the city, and is most favorably adapted for a large building containing stores and offices, and the Homestead is located in a region of changing character, so that its most available use cannot now be determined. To impress the restrictions in question upon these properties, as the statement of agreed facts makes clear, makes it impossible to obtain from them proper income return or to secure the most desirable and stable class of tenants, requires for the maintenance of the buildings a proportion of income greatly in excess of that usual in the case of such properties, and will be likely to preclude their proper development and natural use. The effect of such conditions cannot but react disadvantageously upon neighboring properties, and to continue them, as the testator intended, for perhaps seventy-five years or even more, would carry a serious threat against the proper growth and development of the parts of the city in which the lands in question are situated. The restrictions militate too strongly against the interests of the beneficiaries and the public welfare to be sustained, particularly when it is remembered that they are designed to benefit no one, and are harmful to all persons interested, and we hold them invalid as against public policy. Mitchell *v.* Leavitt, 30 Conn. 587, 590; Egerton *v.* Earl Brownlow, 4 H. L. Cas. 1, 143, 148, 150.[1] . . .

[1] The court may direct or permit the trustee to deviate from the terms of

Section III.

The Investment of Trust Funds.

Ex parte CATHORPE.

CHANCERY. 1785.

1 Cox Eq. Cas. 182.

UPON an application to lay out on a mortgage a sum of 3,000*l*. in the hands of the Accountant General, belonging to the lunatic's estate, *Madocks* produced several orders of the same nature, which had been made in this very lunacy. But the LORD CHANCELLOR [THURLOW] said, that although he was perfectly convinced, by what was stated to him, that this security was perfectly good, yet he could not permit such a precedent to be made; and that he was aware that in former times the Court had laid out the money not only of lunatics but of infants in this manner; but in latter times the Court had considered it as improper to invest any part of the lunatic's estate upon a private security, and it would be a dangerous precedent to break in upon that rule; and he therefore directed the money to be laid out in the 3 per cent. Bank annuities.[1]

---

the trust, if it appears to the court that compliance is impossible or illegal or otherwise against public policy or if it appears that owing to circumstances not known to the testator and not anticipated by him compliance would defeat the purposes of the trust. See *Re* New, [1901] 2 Ch. 534; Russell *v.* Russell, 109 Conn. 187, 14 Minn. L. Rev. 194; Johns *v.* Montgomery, 265 Ill. 21; Cary *v.* Cary, 309 Ill. 330; Suiter *v.* McWard, 328 Ill. 462; Stout *v.* Stout, 192 Ky. 504, 31 Yale L. Jour. 559; Davis, petitioner, 14 Allen (Mass.) 24; Pennington *v.* Metropolitan Museum, 65 N. J. Eq. 11; Price *v.* Long, 87 N. J. Eq. 578.

The court will not permit or direct the trustee to deviate from the terms of the trust merely because it appears that such deviation would be advantageous to the beneficiaries. See *Re* Tollemache, [1903] 1 Ch. 457, 955; Johns *v.* Johns, 172 Ill. 472.

See 78 U. Pa. L. Rev. 1000; Ann. Cas. 1916A 999.

As to the power of the court to hasten the enjoyment of the trust fund by decreeing advances to the beneficiary, see 39 A. L. R. 40.

[1] Although in some of the early cases a different view was taken, Lord Thurlow's view came to be generally approved in England. Lewin, Trusts, 402. But in 1859 by Lord St. Leonards' Act, 22 & 23 Vict. c. 35, sec. 32, first mortgages on land in any part of the United Kingdom, as well as stock in the Bank of England or Ireland or East India stock, were authorized. By subsequent statutes the scope of trust investments has been further enlarged. See Trustee Act, 1925, 15 Geo. V. c. 19, secs. 1–11. In the United States investments in first mortgages on real estate have been generally upheld without statutory authorization.

In some jurisdictions it is a breach of trust to invest in second mortgages; but in others although presumptively such investments are improper, they

In re SALMON.
PRIEST v. UPPLEBY.
COURT OF APPEAL. 1889.

42 Ch. D. 351.

COTTON, L. J.[1] This is an appeal by the plaintiff from a decision of Mr. Justice Kekewich dismissing an action brought against Uppleby, a retired trustee of the will of Eliza Salmon, to make him responsible for an improper investment.

There are two questions to be considered. The first is, whether the investment in question was wrongful. It was within the terms of the trust, for it was an investment on mortgage of a freehold estate. In one sense, therefore, it was in accordance with the trusts, and if the trustee took due care as to its sufficiency there would be no breach of trust, and nobody could complain, though it ultimately proved insufficient. The case differs from that of an investment not within the terms of the instrument, which is necessarily a breach of trust, so that if any loss occurs the trustees must be liable for it. The question here is, whether Uppleby took proper care in seeing to the sufficiency of the security.

Now as regards the rule which has been so much discussed, as to the amount which may be lent on a given security, the law is thus summed-up in Learoyd v. Whiteley, 12 App. Cas. 727, 733: "As a general rule the law requires of a trustee no higher degree of diligence in the execution of his office than a man of ordinary prudence would exercise in the management of his own private affairs. Yet he is not allowed the same discretion in investing the moneys of the trust as if he were a person *sui juris* dealing with his own estate. Business men of ordinary prudence may, and frequently do, select investments which are more or less of a speculative character; but it is the duty of a trustee to confine himself to the class of investments which are permitted by the trust, and likewise to avoid all investments of that class which are attended with hazard. So, so long as he acts in the honest observance of

---

are not absolutely prohibited. See Scott, Cases on Trusts, 1 ed., 776; Ames, 485; Bogert, Trusts, 363; Perry, Trusts, secs. 457-8; 44 L. R. A. (N. S.) 911.

Equitable mortgages and leasehold mortgages have generally been held improper. Scott, 777.

As to contributory or participating mortgages, see Webb v. Jonas, 39 Ch. D. 660; *Re* Dive, [1909] 1 Ch. 328; McCullough v. McCullough, 44 N. J. Eq. 313; Doud v. Holmes, 63 N. Y. 635. See Lewin, Trusts, 438. As to trust companies, see Matter of Union Trust Co., 219 N. Y. 514; Matter of Thomson, 135 N. Y. Misc. 62; 24 Yale L. Jour. 286.

[1] Only the opinion of Cotton, L. J., upon the propriety of the investments is given.

these limitations, the general rule already stated will apply. The courts of equity in England have indicated and given effect to certain general principles for the guidance of trustees in lending money upon the security of real estate. Thus it has been laid down that in the case of ordinary agricultural land the margin ought not to be less than one-third of its value; whereas in cases where the subject of the security derives its value from buildings erected upon the land, or its use of trade purposes, the margin ought not to be less than one-half. I do not think these have been laid down as hard and fast limits up to which trustees will be invariably safe, and beyond which they can never be in safety to lend, but as indicating the lowest margins which in ordinary circumstances a careful investor of trust funds ought to accept." These rules are there recognized, though they have been impeached by Mr. Warmington and Mr. Wood. In the present case the value of the property was mainly derived from buildings. I do not think that the valuation of the property has been successively impeached. We must take the property as having been worth 1750*l*. The trustees lent 1300*l*. upon it. Now, we must have regard not only to the value, but to the nature of the property. It consisted of small houses let at weekly rents, and we know the class of tenants likely to be attracted by cottage property in Hull. It was certainly not prudent to lend to this extent upon property the value of which depended on laborers' houses being wanted in that part of Hull. The investment, therefore, was a breach of trust as having been made improvidently.[1] . . .

DICKINSON, Appellant.

Supreme Judicial Court, Massachusetts. 1890.

152 Mass. 184.

Appeal from a decree of the Probate Court, disallowing in part the account of William A. Dickinson as trustee under a deed of trust. Hearing before C. Allen, J., who reported the case for the determination of the full court. . . .

Field, C. J. The general principles which should govern a trustee in making investments, when the creator of the trust has given no specific directions concerning investments, have been repeatedly declared by this court. Harvard College *v.* Amory, 9 Pick. 446; Lovell *v.* Minot, 20 Pick. 116; Brown *v.* French, 125

---

[1] Gilbert *v.* Kolb, 85 Md. 627; Taft *v.* Smith, 186 Mass. 31, *accord.* See Ames, 488n.

For the present English rule, see Trustee Act, 1925, 15 Geo. V. c. 19, sec. 8 (not more than two-thirds of the value as reported by a surveyor or valuer). By similar statutes in the United States the margin is not uncommonly, either by decision or statute, fifty or sixty per cent. of the value of the property. See McKinney, Trust Investments.

Mass. 410; Bowker v. Pierce, 130 Mass. 262; Hunt, appellant, 141 Mass. 515.

The rule in general terms is, that a trustee must in the investment of the trust fund act with good faith and sound discretion, and must, as laid down in Harvard College v. Amory, at page 461, "observe how men of prudence, discretion, and intelligence manage their own affairs, not in regard to speculation, but in regard to the permanent disposition of their funds, considering the probable income, as well as the probable safety of the capital to be invested."

It is said in the opinion in Brown v. French, *ubi supra:* "If a more strict and precise rule should be deemed expedient, it must be enacted by the Legislature. It cannot be introduced by judicial decision without working great hardship and injustice." It is also said, "The question of the lawfulness and fitness of the investment is to be judged as of the time when it was made, and not by subsequent facts which could not then have been anticipated." A trustee in this Commonwealth undoubtedly finds it difficult to make satisfactory investments of trust property. The amount of funds seeking investment is very large; the demand for securities which are as safe as is possible in the affairs of this world is great; and the amount of such securities is small, when compared with the amount of money to be invested. Trusts frequently provide for the payment of income to certain persons during their lives, as well as for the ultimate transfer of the corpus of the trust property to persons ascertained, or to be ascertained, at the termination of the trust; and a trustee must, so far as is reasonably practicable, hold the balance even between the claims of the life tenants and those of the remaindermen. The life tenants desire a large income from the trust property, but they are only entitled to such an income as it can earn when invested in such securities as a prudent man investing his own money, and having regard to the permanent disposition of the fund, would consider safe. A prudent man possessed of considerable wealth, in investing a small part of his property, may wisely enough take risks which a trustee would not be justified in taking. A trustee, whose duty it is to keep the trust fund safely invested in productive property, ought not to hazard the safety of the property under any temptation to make extraordinary profits. Our cases, however, show that trustees in this Commonwealth are permitted to invest portions of trust funds in dividend paying stocks and interest bearing bonds of private business corporations, when the corporations have acquired, by reason of the amount of their property, and the prudent management of their affairs, such a reputation that cautious and intelligent persons commonly invest their own money in such stocks and bonds as permanent investments.

The experience of recent years has, perhaps, taught the whole community that there is a greater uncertainty in the permanent value of railroad properties in the unsettled or newly settled parts of this country than was anticipated nine years ago. Without, however, taking into consideration facts which are now commonly known, and confining ourselves strictly to the evidence in the case, and the considerations which ought to have been present to the mind of the appellant, when in May and August, 1881, he made the investments in the stock of the Union Pacific Railroad Company, we think it appears that he acted in entire good faith, and after careful inquiry of many persons as to the value of the stock and the propriety of the investments. We cannot say that it is shown to our satisfaction that the trustee so far failed to exercise a sound discretion that the investments should be held to be wholly unauthorized. Still, it must have been manifest to any well informed person in the year 1881, that the Union Pacific Railroad ran through a new and comparatively unsettled country; that it had been constructed at great expense, as represented by its stock and bonds, and was heavily indebted; that its continued prosperity depended upon many circumstances which could not be predicted; and that it would be taking a considerable risk to invest any part of a trust fund in the stock of such a road.

In this case the whole trust fund appears, by the first account, to have been $16,260.05. On May 9, 1881, the trustee bought thirty shares of the stock of the Union Pacific Railroad Company at $119 per share, which, with commissions, amounted to $3,573.75. This is an investment of between one fourth and one fifth of the whole trust fund in this stock, and is certainly a large investment relatively to the whole amount of the trust fund to be made in the stock of any one corporation. After this, on August 16, 1881, he purchased twenty shares more at $123 per share, amounting with commissions to $2,475. The last investment, we think, cannot be sustained as made in the exercise of a sound discretion. While we recognize the hardship of compelling a trustee to make good out of his own property a loss occasioned by an investment of trust property which he has made in good faith, and upon the advice of persons whom he thinks to be qualified to give advice, we cannot on the evidence hold that the trustee was justified in investing in such stock as this so large a proportional part of the property.

It appears by the report of the single justice before whom the case was tried, that "the time has now come for a final distribution of said trust fund." It does not appear that, when the first account was allowed, there was any adjudication of the questions now before us, and they are not therefore *res judicata*, and no assent to these investments is shown on the part of the persons now entitled to the trust property. The result is, that this last investment is disallowed, and that the trustee must be charged with the amount of it, to wit: $2,475, and with simple interest thereon from August 16, 1881, and must be credited with any dividends therefrom which he has received and paid over, with simple interest on each, from the time each dividend was received.

The decree of the Probate Court must be modified in accordance with this opinion.

Decree accordingly.[1]

BABBITT *v.* FIDELITY TRUST COMPANY.

COURT OF CHANCERY, NEW JERSEY. 1907.

72 N. J. Eq. 745.

ON THE 19th day of July, 1898, Charles G. Campbell, by appropriate instruments, transferred all of his property of every description to the Fidelity Trust Company, of Newark, as trustee.

The latter on that date executed a declaration of trust with respect to the said property. In said instrument it " declares that it holds the property, real and personal, this day conveyed to it by Charles G. Campbell in trust for the following uses and purposes:

[1] Davis, Appellant, 183 Mass. 499, *accord.*

Massachusetts gives trustees more latitude than is given by the great majority of states. All jurisdictions allow investments in certain public securities, and nearly all allow first mortgages on realty. Many allow investments in bonds of private corporations. A few, like Massachusetts, allow investments in corporate stock. And in Massachusetts, contrary to the great weight of authority (Mattocks *v.* Moulton, 84 Me. 545; Mich. etc. Society *v.* Corning, 164 Mich. 395), an unsecured loan is not necessarily improper. Hunt, Appellant, 141 Mass. 515.

In the absence of authorization in the trust instrument it is in general not permissible to buy land with the trust fund; but where the trustee forecloses a mortgage it may be permissible to buy in the mortgaged property to save the trust fund. *A fortiori* in the absence of authorization a trustee is not justified in engaging in trade or business with the trust fund. Trull *v.* Trull, 13 Allen (Mass.) 407.

Even in states like Massachusetts it is improper for the trustee to purchase speculative securities. It is generally improper to invest in the securities of a new and untried enterprise. As to investments outside the jurisdiction, see Scott, Cases on Trusts, 1 ed., 782.

See Bogert, Trusts, sec. 101; Perry, Trusts, secs. 452–467; 12 A. L. R. 574; 26 A. L. R. 612.

Statutory provisions. In many states the matter of trust investments is regulated by statute. The statutes almost universally permit bonds of the United States and bonds of the state. Most of them permit bonds of other states and a few permit bonds of foreign nations. Many of them permit, subject to certain limitations, bonds of railroad corporations and public utility corporations. A few permit bonds of industrial corporations although in Alabama, Pennsylvania and Wyoming there are constitutional provisions prohibiting investments in stocks or bonds of private corporations. A few statutes allow investment in the stock of banks or trust companies. Participating mortgages are allowed in five states. In several states statutes allow investments in such securities as are legal for savings banks. Real estate mortgages are expressly permitted by statute in most of the states and are probably legal everywhere. For a summary of the statutes of the several states, see Loring, Trustee's Handbook; McKinney, Trust Investments.

(1) To hold and possess or dispose of and convey the same, by proper instruments of conveyance, as in its judgment may be deemed advisable, and to collect the principal of securities and reinvest the same from time to time. (2) To collect the income from the personal property, and the rents, issues and profits, from the real property." . . .

The net income is to be paid monthly, in certain stated amounts, to the settlor, his sisters, his son, Charles B. Campbell; his daughter, Anna D. Graham (since intermarried with Babbitt), and the father of a deceased daughter's children.

Upon the death of Charles G. Campbell certain sums are to be paid to his sisters and the balance is to be divided among his heirs-at-law according to the intestate laws of this state, the personal property according to the statute of distributions, and the real property according to the statute of descent. . . .

Charles G. Campbell died on the 29th day of May, 1905, and left him surviving his daughter, the complainant; Charles B. Campbell, a son, and Robert C. Denny, Walter B. Denny and Julia Denny, children of Jennie B. Denny, deceased, who was the daughter of Charles G. Campbell and the wife of Edward B. Denny. . . .

[The bill in this case is filed by Anna D. Babbitt for the purpose, *inter alia*, of securing an accounting from the trustee.]

GARRISON, V. C. The property which Charles G. Campbell had, and which, on the 19th day of July, 1898, he turned over to the Fidelity Trust Company as trustee, was of varied character and of large value. It consisted of real estate, mortgages, bonds, stocks of companies, furniture, pictures, bric-a-brac, money in bank, and other characters of personal property such as an active business man of large means would possess. . . .

The only remaining question under the exceptions relates to the conduct of the trustee concerning shares of stock of the Prudential Insurance Company. . . .

At the time of the making of the declaration of trust the settlor owned and transferred to the trustee one hundred and sixty-seven and twenty-seven hundredths shares of such stock. This was disposed of by the trustee at the following rate per share of $50 each: February 23d, 1899, sixty shares at $360; February 6th, 1900, thirteen shares at $350; August 20th, 1901, twenty shares at $375; December 7th, 1903, thirty shares at $200; December 23d, 1903, twenty-five shares at $195; January 25th, 1904, nineteen and twenty-seven hundredths shares at $200.

It will be observed that the first three sales averaged about $360 a share, and that these took place prior to the year 1903. The sales made after that date do not average quite $200 per share. The proofs show that down to about November, 1902, the stock of the Prudential Insurance Company was readily salable at about the average figure shown above, namely, $360 per share, and that since that date the latter average has been about the obtained price, namely, $200 per share. . . .

The trust in this case was of a unique character. It was a transfer by a living person of all of his property of every kind and description, including even his household goods and his money in bank. It was, in the broadest sense of the word, a general trust. Under such circumstances I think it the duty of the trustee, so soon as it could do so in the exercise of reasonable diligence and good judgment, to convert the securities which came to it from the settlor into cash and invest the same in securities authorized by law.

It is admitted by all of the counsel in the case that there is no statute law involved, excepting to the extent that the statute points out the investments in which trustees are authorized to place trust moneys, and it is conceded that the stock of the Prudential Insurance Company is not one of those so authorized.

The general principle deducible from the cases and text-books is well stated in 17 Am. & Eng. Encycl. L. 454, as follows:

"While a fiduciary may, as a rule, in the exercise of his discretion, retain such investments as are proper for the fiduciaries to hold, all others he must call in, and invest the proceeds in an authorized manner." Perry Trusts, §§ 460, 461, 465; Ashhurst *v.* Potter, 29 N. J. Eq. (2 Stew.) 625 (Court of Errors and Appeals, 1878).

The trustee in the case at bar seeks to escape the responsibility involved in the application of this principle. In the brief of counsel for the trustee its position is thus stated:

"The rule contended for has undoubted existence, but is not of universal application. It is applicable to trusteeships where the subject of the trust has come to the trustee as a *general* estate or an *aliquot* portion of an estate, but is not applicable where it comes as certain and specific property, unless there be a direction to convert."

It therefore insists —

First. That this was a trust of a specific thing, and that it was entitled to hold that thing, chargeable only with the exercise of reasonable discretion.

Second. That by the declaration of trust it was given discretion with respect to investments, and therefore is not chargeable for anything excepting negligence.

As I have before said, I do not concur at all in the view that this is a trust of a specific thing, or that this is a case to which the authorities relating to duties of trustees under trusts of specific things can be applied. It is true, of course, that a specific thing, or rather a great number of specific things, were by this settlor turned over to this trustee, but the real transaction was a turning over by the settlor of everything that he possessed to the trustee for it to handle and manage under its obligation as trustee, subject to the responsibilities thereof.

I shall not stop to cite or analyze the various cases in which the subject-matter of the trust was held to be specific, but will content myself with saying that in each case, as I have read them, it was clear that the settlor intended that the identical thing transferred should be held by the trustee. There is not the slightest evidence in this case of the settlor's intention that this trustee should hold any specific thing, and it is quite clear, I think, from the circumstances, that there could have been no such intention. Among other property transferred to the trustee were household furniture, pictures, bric-a-brac, and money in banks. Certainly it was not intended that these several species of property were to be held *in specie* by the trustee. Similarly there is nothing to show that any of the transferred property was to be so held. The intention clearly shown was to hand over all of the property owned by the settlor to the trustee for the latter to deal with as trustee, and under such circumstances the law is clear that the trustee can only escape responsibility by converting the unauthorized securities thus transferred to it into authorized securities so soon as it conveniently and reasonably may do so.

In the case in hand it is clearly shown that it could have sold the Prudential stock during the years 1898, 1899, 1900, 1901 and 1902 for at least $360 per share. The income from this stock was very small, being ten per cent. upon $50 par, and therefore about one and one-half per cent. on the market value of the stock. There was therefore no reason, properly viewed by the trustee, to induce it to hold an unauthorized security, paying so little, at a time when the market for its sale was open and a large price could have been obtained for it, and that price could have been invested in authorized securities to yield a rate of interest at least three times greater than that received from the then investment.

With respect to the argument that by the terms of the declaration of trust the trustee was so vested with discretion that it is not chargeable for maintaining unauthorized investments it is necessary to refer to the language of the instrument.

The material part thereof is that in which the trustee declares that it holds the property, real and personal, in trust for the following uses and purposes:

" To hold and possess or dispose of and convey the same, by proper instruments of conveyance, as in its judgment may be deemed advisible, and to collect the principal of securities and reinvest the same from time to time."

From this clause the respective parties draw diametrically opposing meanings. The complainant insists that the meaning of this clause is that the trustee has enjoined upon it the absolute duty of collecting the principal of securities. In other words, it draws from this clause the inference that the settlor intended to direct the trustee to collect the principal of securities, and therefore it has not only the duty cast upon it by law, but also the positive injunction of the settlor with respect thereto.

The trustee, on the other hand, lays great stress upon the presence of the words "as in its judgment may be deemed advisable," and argues that they relate not only to the first part of the sentence concerning conveyances, but also to the last part of the sentence. It therefore repudiates the idea that it was directed to collect the principal of securities, and contends that the whole matter was left to its discretion, and it can only be chargeable if negligent.

The trustee further argues that stocks are not "securities," and therefore, even if it is required to collect the principal of securities, this would not relate to stocks generally.

I do not find it necessary to determine whether this clause should be construed so as to positively require the trustee, by force of its terms, to convert the securities, including the stocks, into money, and reinvest the same in authorized securities, because I think the result of a fair reading of this clause in any legitimate way is not to vest in the trustee any greater or other discretion than is vested in trustees generally.

Differently stated, I think that this clause confides the property to the trustee to be dealt with as its judgment deems advisable, subject to those rules which govern trustees; that its discretion, in other words, was not to do unauthorized things, but to exercise its judgment concerning what authorized things it would do. . . .

I therefore conclude that this trustee is chargeable with the difference between the price at which the seventy-four and twenty-seven hundredths shares were sold in 1903 and 1904, namely, about $200 per share, and $360 per share, which I find to be the price at which it could have been sold at any time within five years after the date of the execution of the declaration of trust.[1] . . .

[1] On the duty of the trustee to convert into authorized investments, see Matter of Hirsch, 166 App. Div. 367, aff'd 188 N. Y. 584; Taylor's Estate, 277 Pa. 518; Will of Leitsch, 185 Wis. 257. See Perry, Trusts, sec. 465; McKinney, Trust Investments, 13; 79 U. Pa. L. Rev. 77; 37 A. L. R. 559; 57 A. L. R. 1118.

By statute in some states a trustee is authorized to retain investments made by the settlor although they are not otherwise proper trust investments.

By the terms of the trust the trustee may be authorized or directed to retain investments. Arnould v. Grinstead, W. N. (1872) 216; Old Colony Trust Co. v. Shaw, 261 Mass. 158; Linnard's Estate, 299 Pa. 32; Scott, Cases on Trusts, 1 ed., 790.

If not authorized by the will, executors or trustees have no authority to continue carrying on a business in which the testator was engaged, except so far as it is necessary to enable them to sell the business as a going concern. Re Evans, 34 Ch. D. 597; Eufaula Nat. Bank v. Manassas, 124 Ala. 379; Campbell v. Faxon, 73 Kan. 675; Donnelly v. Alden, 229 Mass. 109; 40 L. R. A. (N. S.) 201. See Warren, Cas. Wills, 589 et seq.

On the question whether a trustee who is authorized to retain shares of a certain corporation can properly retain shares of another corporation into which the old corporation is merged, see Old Colony Trust Co. v. Shaw, 261

In re ARGUELLO.

SUPREME COURT, CALIFORNIA. 1893.

97 Cal. 196.

BELCHER, C. This is an appeal by the administrator of the estate of the decedent from an order of the Superior Court of San Diego County requiring him to pay to the creditors of the estate whose claims had been duly presented and allowed certain sums of money.

The sum of money in controversy was $4,846.80, which was received by the administrator for and on account of the estate, between July 5, 1891, and October 15, 1891, and deposited by him in the California Savings Bank, in the city of San Diego, in his own name.

The court below found the facts to be as follows: —

"That at the time said funds were deposited by said administrator in said California Savings Bank, said bank was reputed to be and was considered a safe and solvent bank and place of deposit, and was of good credit and standing, and was believed by said administrator to be solvent and safe; that said deposit was made in the individual name" of the administrator, "without any designation or indication of his representative capacity, but said administrator had no other funds or account with said bank, and deposited such with that particular bank for the express purpose of keeping the same separate from, and so that it would not be unnecessarily mingled with, his own property or individual funds."

"That in depositing said funds in said California Savings Bank as aforesaid, said administrator acted in good faith."

"That on the twelfth day of November, 1891, said California Savings Bank became suddenly, unexpectedly, and wholly insolvent, suspended business, and has not been able to pay the amount so deposited by said administrator with it, or any part thereof."

"That said administrator has been guilty of no negligence or want of care in the administration of said estate, except that he

---

Mass. 158; Anderson *v.* Bean, 172 N. E. 647 (Mass. 1930); Mertz *v.* Guaranty Trust Co., 247 N. Y. 137. *Cf.* Buist's Estate, 297 Pa. 537.

Although investments are proper trust investments when made by the trustee or received by him, it may subsequently become his duty to sell them. See Johns *v.* Herbert, 2 App. D. C. 485, 499; State Street Trust Co. *v.* Walker, 259 Mass. 578; Beam *v.* Paterson Safe Dep. & T. Co., 81 N. J. Eq. 195; Matter of Clark, 136 N. Y. Misc. 881, 29 Mich. L. Rev. 125. See 30 Col. L. Rev. 1166.

The trustee is not liable, however, for failure to sell if the failure was not imprudent. *Re* Chapman, [1896] 2 Ch. 763 (and see Trustee Act, 1925, sec. 4); Booker *v.* Pierce, 130 Mass. 262; Green *v.* Crapo, 181 Mass. 55; Beam *v.* Paterson Safe Dep. & T. Co., 83 N. J. Eq. 628; Matter of Weston, 91 N. Y. 502; Matter of Mercantile Trust Co., 156 App. Div. 224, *aff'd* 210 N. Y. 83; Dauler's Estate, 247 Pa. 356; Estate of Allis, 191 Wis. 23.

deposited such funds in the California Savings Bank in his individual name, instead of in his representative capacity, or in the name of the estate."

And as conclusions of law the court found that the administrator was responsible for the money so deposited by him, and that he must pay it over to the creditors of the estate.

The appellant contends that an administrator is only required to act in good faith, and to exercise such skill, prudence, and diligence in managing the affairs of the estate as men ordinarily bestow upon their own affairs; and that when he has, in good faith and with reasonable care, deposited funds of the estate in bank, which have been subsequently lost by the failure of the bank, he will not be held liable for the loss, unless he has wilfully and unnecessarily mingled the trust property with his own, so as to constitute himself in appearance its absolute owner; and hence that, under the facts found in this case, the order of the court was erroneous, and should be reversed.

The question presented has many times been before the courts of England and of this country, and the decisions upon it have been practically unanimous, and to the same effect as the decision of the court below in this case.

The law upon the subject is stated in Perry on Trusts, sec. 443: "A trustee may deposit money temporarily in some responsible bank or banking-house; and if he acted in good faith and with discretion, and deposited the money to a trust account, he will not be liable for its loss, . . . but he will be liable for the money in case of a failure of the bank, or for its depreciation, if he deposits it to his *own credit,* and not to the separate account of the trust estate." And again, in sec. 463: "So if the trustee pays the money into a bank in his own name, and not in the name of the trust, he will be responsible for the money in case of the failure of the bank."

A reference to a few of the numerous cases cited will be sufficient. . . .

But whatever may be the rule elsewhere, the appellant insists that the rule in this state is declared in sec. 2236 of the Civil Code, and that that does not make him liable. The section referred to reads as follows: —

"Sec. 2236. A trustee who wilfully and unnecessarily mingles the trust property with his own, so as to constitute himself in appearance its absolute owner, is liable for its safety in all events."

We do not think this section was intended to change the rule generally prevailing, or to limit liability under it; on the contrary, the section seems to be in entire accord with the general rule, and in effect to declare it in unmistakable terms.

In our opinion the order appealed from should be affirmed.

VANCLIEF, C., and HAYNES., C., concurred.

For the reasons given in the foregoing opinion, the order appealed from is affirmed.[1]

PATERSON, J., GAROUTTE, J., HARRISON, J.

CORNET v. CORNET.
SUPREME COURT, MISSOURI. 1916.
269 Mo. 298.

BROWN, C. . . . During the entire time the defendant acted as trustee of this fund he was the senior member of the firm of Cornet & Zeibig, real estate dealers and loan brokers, and the uninvested funds of this estate were deposited in bank in the general checking account of the firm. The undisputed evidence shows that the credit balance of this account was always in excess of the amount of uninvested funds of the estate. During the last five years of the administration the bank paid the firm two per cent interest on its monthly balances. The plaintiff contends that this amounted to a conversion of the trust fund and that the trustee should be charged compound or at least simple interest at the rate of six per cent per annum on these balances. This contention was disallowed, and the court allowed the interest actually received.

This question should be considered in connection with the finding of the referee, in which, after a careful examination of the evidence, we concur, that the trustee used reasonable care to keep the fund invested, and that it had not been used by the firm for its own profit otherwise than by the payment of interest on bank balances as above stated. We do not see how the trust fund lost anything by this practice. We are satisfied that the trustee was not guilty of the wilful violation of the general rule forbidding the mingling of the trust funds with his own. He was, we believe, simply ignorant that such rule existed. The imposition of a penalty on that account would necessarily be purely punitive, and not in any sense compensatory. This would be no less true because the penalty would inure to the beneficiary. While it would be our duty not only to compel the restoration of anything that might appear to have been lost by this practice but also to protect

[1] Chancellor v. Chancellor, 177 Ala. 44; Allen v. Leach, 7 Del. Ch. 83; Gatewood v. Furlow, 19 Ga. App. 74; Corya v. Corya, 119 Ind. 593; Dirks v. Juel, 59 Neb. 353; O'Connor v. Decker, 95 Wis. 202 ("guar."), *accord.* See Ames, 484n.; Ann. Cas. 1915C 54; 45 L. R. A. (N. S.) 1; 43 A. L. A. 600.

A fortiori the trustee must answer for the solvency of the bank where the trust money is blended with the trustee's individual account. Ames, 484n.

Similarly, it is improper for a trustee to invest trust funds in his individual name. DeJarnette v. DeJarnette, 41 Ala. 708 (mortgage); White v. Sherman, 168 Ill. 589 (stock); Knowlton v. Bradley, 17 N. H. 458 (note); *Re* Hodges' Estate, 66 Vt. 70 (mortgage).

the beneficiary against possible wrong which might have been concealed by it, yet when punishment alone is involved our discretion should be used to avoid unnecessary hardship. The master was correct in his recommendation in this respect and the action of the court in confirming it is approved.[1] . . .

Section IV.

Successive Beneficiaries.

PLYMPTON v. BOSTON DISPENSARY.

Supreme Judicial Court, Massachusetts. 1871.

106 Mass. 544.

Bill in equity filed May 24, 1870, by the trustee under the will of Benjamin Dearborn, for the instructions of the court as to the payment of an assessment made by the city of Boston for betterment of an estate on Avon Place, upon laying out that place as a highway. The case was reserved by the chief justice, upon the bill and answers, for the determination of the full court, and was in substance as follows:

[1] A trustee may properly deposit trust funds for a reasonable time in a reputable bank, taking care to have the credit run to him in his fiduciary capacity. Scott, Cases on Trusts, 1 ed., 784; Ann. Cas. 1915C 50; 45 L. R. A. (n. s.) 1; 43 A. L. R. 600.

He is liable, however, if he does not use reasonable care in selecting the bank. Germania etc. Co. v. Driskell, 66 S. W. 610 (Ky. 1902).

He is liable if he allows the deposit to remain for an unreasonably long time and the bank fails. Cann v. Cann, 33 W. R. 40 (1884); Scott, Cases on Trusts, 1 ed., 784.

If the trustee makes a time deposit it has been held that he is liable if the bank fails. Scott, 784.

It has been held that the trustee is liable if he surrenders control over the deposit, for example by agreeing that checks must be countersigned by his surety. Estate of Wood, 159 Cal. 466; Fidelity & Deposit Co. v. Butler, 130 Ga. 225.

See Perry, Trusts, secs. 443–45; 34 Harv. L. Rev. 467; 21 L. R. A. (n. s.) 399; 36 L. R. A. (n. s.) 252; Ann. Cas. 1915C 50; 43 A. L. R. 600; Dec. Dig., Trusts, sec. 221.

On the question whether a corporate trustee can properly deposit trust money in its own banking department, see Hayward v. Plant, 98 Conn. 374, 390; Tucker v. New Hampshire T. Co., 69 N. H. 187 (deposit in savings department); Herzog v. Title Guarantee & T. Co., 148 App. Div. 234, *aff'd* 210 N. Y. 531; Matter of People's Trust Co., 169 N. Y. App. Div. 699; Reid v. Reid (No. 2), 237 Pa. 176. But see Union Trust Co. v. Preston Nat. Bank, 144 Mich. 106; St. Paul Trust Co. v. Kittson, 62 Minn. 408. See 23 Col. L. Rev. 465; 16 Va. L. Rev. 392. In New York by Banking Law, sec. 188(11), a trustee is required to pay interest at not less than 2% on money received by it as trustee. See Enright v. Sedalia Trust Co., 20 S. W.(2d) 517 (Mo. 1929).

As to a deposit by an individual trustee in a private bank owned by him, see Genesee Wesleyan Seminary v. United States F. & G. Co., 247 N. Y. 52.

Benjamin Dearborn died and his will was admitted to probate in 1838. His wife had two daughters by a former marriage, one of whom had intermarried with his son, John M. Dearborn, and the other died long since. By the will, he devised all his real estate in trust to pay one third of the income (in compliance with a contract of jointure executed in 1830, just before his marriage) to his wife for life, and after her death to her two daughters, or the survivor of them, for life; and the remaining two thirds of the income in ten equal shares, to various persons for life, namely, one share to his wife for life and her daughters or the survivor of them for life, two to John M. Dearborn for life and after his death to his wife, and one to her for life, and the other six shares to different persons for life and after their deaths to the Boston Dispensary, a charitable corporation chartered in 1801; and upon the deaths of all those entitled to share in the income, the whole principal of the trust fund to vest absolutely in the Boston Dispensary. The testator's widow, his son John M., and all the other devisees for life, except the son's wife, died before the bringing of the bill, leaving her entitled, under the will, to nine fifteenths, and the Boston Dispensary to six fifteenths, of the income during her life, and the Boston Dispensary to the whole residue after her death.

The testator directed, as to repairs on any of the buildings belonging to the estate, that whenever the trustee should " decide on the necessity or expediency of paying money for repairs, or for any other purpose which in their opinion may contribute to the value of the estate or the comfort of its tenants, the required sum shall be drawn from the succeeding income of the whole estate."

The will also contained the following provision: " It is my wish that my dwelling-house in Avon Place may continue to be pleasing to my wife as her place of residence, and that its use at a moderate rent may constitute part of the income secured to her by the contract above mentioned [namely, the contract of jointure]; but on this subject I only express a wish without dictating; for it is my desire that her own choice may be the governing principle in selecting a dwelling for herself and family, with full liberty to take a residence in any place she may prefer, either at housekeeping or boarding. Influenced by this desire, I direct that during the time in which my house in Avon Place shall be occupied by my wife or her daughters, or by my son, John M. Dearborn, the rent of said house shall be estimated at twenty dollars per calendar month, being at the rate of two hundred and forty dollars per annum. This sum is less than three and a half per cent. on the value of the estate, if my improvements be added to the first cost."

The bill alleged that the house on Avon Place was occupied, under the provisions of the will, by the testator's widow during her lifetime, and after her death by John M. Dearborn and wife, and since his death by his wife, paying only the rent mentioned in the will;

that she still occupies the house, claiming the right to do so for the same rent; that the yearly rental value long has been much greater than two hundred and forty dollars, and is now more than two thousand dollars; that on September 25, 1868, the city of Boston, acting or claiming to act under authority of law, laid out Avon Place, from Washington Street to Chauncey Street, as a public highway, and on April 5, 1869, made assessments for alleged betterment on said estate and other estates; that the assessment so made on said estate was $1716, for which the city claims, and threatens to enforce, a lien thereon; and that the plaintiff was ignorant whether the amount of such assessment should be paid by him, and, if so, whether, wholly or in part, from the funds in his hands belonging to Mrs. Dearborn, or from those belonging to the Boston Dispensary; and prayed for an injunction against the city, and for instructions in the execution of the trust.

The Boston Dispensary, in its answer, admitted all the material allegations of the bill; and contended that Mrs. Dearborn should pay or contribute to the payment of the assessment for betterment, or the plaintiff should pay or contribute to the payment of the same out of her funds in his hands as trustee. Mrs. Dearborn, in her answer, also admitted all the material allegations, except that she denied that the yearly value of the premises on Avon Place was more than two thousand dollars; and she alleged that by the will she was entitled to occupy the premises only as a residence, and that their value as a dwelling place had been greatly diminished by the act of the city of Boston in extending Avon Place to Chauncey Street and making it a thoroughfare for public travel; and contended that the assessment for betterment should be paid, if at all, by the Boston Dispensary, who upon her death would become the absolute owners of the estate, and that she was entitled to receive nine fifteenths of the income in the hands of the plaintiff, without any deduction therefrom on account of the assessment. The city of Boston filed no answer.

GRAY, J. It is admitted that the assessment for betterment was duly laid by the city upon the estate in Avon Place, and must be paid. The question argued is, how the plaintiff shall charge or apportion the amount upon the interests of the Boston Dispensary and of Mrs. Dearborn in the trust fund in his hands. This question may be most conveniently treated by considering first the general rules of law in like cases, and then how far the application of those rules is affected by the provisions of the will.

As between tenant for life and remainderman, ordinary taxes are to be paid by the tenant for life. Fountaine *v.* Pellet, 1 Ves. Jr. 337. Varney *v.* Stevens, 22 Maine, 331. Cairns *v.* Chabert, 3 Edw. Ch. 312. But when the whole estate is subject to, and benefited by the discharge of, an incumbrance not created by either, equity will apportion it ratably between their different interests. In the case of a mortgage, for instance, the tenant for life is bound to keep down the interest, but not to pay the principal; and upon a discharge of the mortgage by the remainderman, a strict adherence to the rule would require the tenant for life to pay interest on the amount during his life; although, for the convenience of all parties, the value of such an annuity is usually estimated, and paid at once in gross. 4 Kent Com. (6th ed.) 74, 75. Swaine v. Perine, 5 Johns. Ch. 482. Van Vronker v. Eastman, 7 Met. 157. An assessment for betterment, under our statutes, upon the laying out of a highway, is a tax; but it is not an ordinary tax; it is an extraordinary assessment laid on the premises, in view of the permanently increased value of the estate by reason of the public improvement in the vicinity. Harvard College v. Aldermen of Boston, 104 Mass. 470. Codman v. Johnson, Ib. 491. It must therefore be treated, as between tenant for life and remainderman, as an incumbrance on the whole estate, to which the tenant for life must contribute to the extent of interest during his life on the amount paid, and at his death the remainderman bear the charge of the principal. The burden of an assessment for betterment is thus borne by them in the same proportions in which they would have received the benefit of entire damages assessed against the city, in case the estate had been injured, instead of being benefited by the improvement. Gen. Sts. c. 43, § 17. Gibson v. Cooke, 1 Met. 75.

The will of this testator contains no provision as to the payment of taxes, but leaves that to be settled by the general rules of law. The clause as to repairs relates only to expenses voluntarily incurred by the trustees. Mrs. Dearborn is not obliged to occupy the estate on Avon Place, but may do so at her discretion. If she does, the rent, at the moderate rate fixed by the will, is to be computed as part of her share of the income of the trust property, of which that estate forms part. If she does not, the income of this estate, like that of the rest of the trust fund, is to be divided between her and the Boston Dispensary, in the proportion of nine fifteenths to her and six fifteenths to that institution. In the first case, so long as she occupies the house on Avon Place, she is tenant for life; Co. Lit. 42a; and as such must pay the ordinary taxes on the house. In the second case, such taxes would be paid proportionably by her and by the other party entitled to share in the income. The same rule of apportionment must be applied to the payment of interest on the amount paid out of the principal of the trust fund to discharge the assessment for the betterment of the estate in question. So long as she may see fit to occupy it as a dwelling, and thus enjoy the exclusive use of the premises, she must pay the interest. If she should at any time elect to abandon the occupation, the burden of this charge will rest upon her and the Boston Dispensary in the same proportion as the benefit of the income. It would not be equitable to charge her, by reason of her occupation at the time of the assessment, with the present value of an annuity on the amount thereof; because she is not bound by the terms of the will to make her election immediately to occupy the estate throughout her lifetime, and if she should at any time hereafter elect to give up such occupation, she would be chargeable for the rest of her life with only nine fifteenths of the interest.

The result is, that the amount of the assessment for betterment is to be paid out of the principal of the trust fund, and interest thereon is to be charged by the trustees annually to Mrs. Dearborn so long as she shall live in the house; and the interest so charged is to be distributed between her and the Boston Dispensary in proportion to their interests in the income, by allowing her to retain nine fifteenths, and collecting from her and paying to that corporation six fifteenths thereof. If she shall at any time cease to live in the house, the trustees will have no occasion afterwards to keep a separate account of the interest on the sum paid out for the betterment; for that sum, having been paid from the principal of the trust fund, will proportionately diminish the income payable during the rest of her life to her and to the other *cestui que trust*.

Decree accordingly.[1]

NIRDLINGER'S ESTATE.

SUPREME COURT, PENNSYLVANIA. 1927.

290 Pa. 457.

OPINION BY MR. JUSTICE KEPHART, June 25, 1927:

Samuel F. Nirdlinger died leaving a will devising his entire estate in trust. He authorized his trustees either to retain his securities, or sell them and invest the proceeds, without being limited to those regarded as "legal investments." The "rents, issues, income, dividends and revenue" were to be paid by the trustees to designated beneficiaries for life, and, at their death, the corpus was to pass to remaindermen. In September, 1920, the orphans' court authorized the trustees to enter into an agreement with Erlanger and others by which leases of certain theaters were procured. Five corporations were organized for the purpose of operating the theaters. The trustees became owners of one-fifth of the stock in these corporations, their total financial interest, purchase price and loans, being about $21,370. This stock was sold for $170,000, and it is claimed that $40,000 of this sum represented income earned by the theater companies during the life of the agreement, and was distributable as such to the life tenants under the will. The auditing judge held that the

[1] As to the allocation of taxes, carrying charges and other expenses, see Bogert, Trusts, sec. 102; Perry, Trusts, secs. 552–554; Ann. Cas. 1918E 947, 989; 10 L. R. A. (N. S.) 342; 17 A. L. R. 1384; 47 A. L. R. 519; Dec. Dig., Trusts, sec. 274.

income must pass with the corpus, and, unless dividends were in fact declared, the rule should not be otherwise. Exceptions to the adjudication having been dismissed by the court in banc, this appeal by the life tenants followed.

The theory of appellants is, that, since the acts of the parties constituted a joint adventure carried on by five close corporations, the corporate fiction should be disregarded and the increased amount received from the investment divided as profits, or the accumulated earnings should be paid to the life tenants, the original investment not being impaired.

In deciding appellant's case, we determine rights as between life tenant and remainderman where trustees sell shares of stock, receiving a price greater than the value of the stock at the time of testator's death, the increase being due in part to an ascertained accumulated surplus from the earnings of the corporation. It is necessary then to review generally these rights where the subject of the trust consists of shares of corporate stock. We must carefully distinguish between the decided cases wherein these rights as they relate to income or earnings in certain aspects have been considered, and the situations which, it is argued, leave open other aspects of income and earnings in which the relative rights have not been ascertained, and evolve, if possible, from the former, a rule for the latter. For convenience we shall consider the subject under the following general heads: the judicial attitude, (A) where earnings qua earnings come into the hands of the trustee through an actual distribution by the corporation; (B) where the earnings are undistributed by the corporation, but their value is reflected in dollars in the hands of the trustee through a sale of the stock by him; and (C) where earnings have not been distributed by the corporation and the stock is unsold in the trustees's hands. Earnings of a corporation may be divided into gross and net, and the net earnings may again be divided into (1) that portion applicable to a usual or customary dividend at a fixed per cent or sum per share, paid at regular periods, and (2) extraordinary dividends which may assume an unusual form and amount, paid at irregular intervals from accumulated surplus or earnings. Both kinds of dividends must, of course, be declared out of earnings or profits.

(A) Where the corporation distributes its earnings in dividends.

1. It is the general rule as to ordinary dividends, well established in Pennsylvania, that when the trustee receives, after the creation of the trust, money as earnings of the estate or income, its source being an ordinary dividend paid by a corporation, it belongs to the life tenants, regardless of how soon thereafter it is declared. The reason given for this rule is that dividends, unlike interest on bonds, are not earned de die ad diem, and, consequently, are not, in the absence of unusual circumstances, apportionable.

2. When the earnings have been permitted to accumulate by a cor-

poration and their proceeds invested in corporate property, in working capital, or retained as cash or its equivalent, and an extraordinary dividend is declared in stock or cash, the respective rights of life tenants and remaindermen have been variously adjudicated. Three rules prevail — the Massachusetts, Pennsylvania and Kentucky rules.

(a) Under the Massachusetts rule, the rights of the life tenant and the remainderman depend on the substance and intent of the action of the corporation in declaring the dividend: Rand *v.* Hubbell, 115 Mass. 461, 474; Minot *v.* Paine, 99 Mass. 101, 108, 96 Am. Dec. 705. This means, in general, that all cash dividends are awarded to the life tenant, and all stock dividends to the remainderman.

The Massachusetts rule is one of convenience. In Minot *v.* Paine, *supra*, it was said (p. 108) : " A trustee needs some plain principle to guide him; and the *cestui que trust* ought not to be subjected to the expense of going behind the action of the directors, and investigating the concerns of the corporation, especially if it is out of our jurisdiction. A simple rule is to regard cash dividends, however large, as income, and stock dividends, however made, as capital." It is not claimed that the application of this rule will accomplish exact justice in all cases (see Boardman *v.* Boardman, 78 Conn. 451, 62 Atl. 339), and it has been admitted at times it is entirely opposed to the intentions of the testator. See D'Ooge *v.* Leeds, 176 Mass. 558, 560, 57 N. E. 1025. This has led the court to look behind the vote of the directors to discover the substantial purpose of the declaration: Heard *v.* Eldredge, 109 Mass. 258; Leland *v.* Hayden, 102 Mass. 542; Davis *v.* Jackson, 152 Mass. 58, 25 N. E. 21; Lyman *v.* Pratt, 183 Mass. 58, 66 N. E. 423. The present tendency, as indicated by the cases of Gray *v.* Hemenway, 212 Mass. 239, 98 N. E. 789, and Boston Safe Deposit & Trust Co. *v.* Adams, 219 Mass. 175, 106 N. E. 590, seems to lean toward more liberal treatment of the life tenant.

The Massachusetts rule has been applied by the Supreme Court of the United States (Gibbons *v.* Mahon, 136 U. S. 549) and by the highest courts of Connecticut, Georgia (by statute), Illinois, Maine, North Carolina, Rhode Island and West Virginia. See cases collected in 24 A. L. R. 29. The modern English rule is substantially the same: see Bouch *v.* Sproule, 12 App. Cas. 385; *In re* Hopkins, L. R. 18 Eq. 696; Jones *v.* Evans, (1913) 1 Ch. 23.

(b) Under the Pennsylvania or American Rule, adopted in most American jurisdictions, the rights of the life tenant and the remainderman to an extraordinary cash or a stock dividend declared during the life tenancy are determined by a division of the dividend between the claimants so as to preserve intact the book value of the devised property (the corpus) as it existed at testator's death. This was made clear by the decision in Earp's App., 28 Pa. 368, long recognized as a leading authority. The effect of the rule is to give to the life tenant the income which has been earned since the trust came into being, but, at the same time, to preserve the value of the corpus as it was at the date of the death of the testator, or, to use a more convenient term, to preserve the intact value of the estate. This intact value includes the par value of the stock plus any accumulation of income earned before the death of the testator: Earp's App., *supra*. From it must be subtracted capital losses: Dickinson's Est., 285 Pa. 449. In Earp's App., *supra*, we said, " The distribution of it [the stock dividend] among the stockholders in the form of new certificates has no effect whatsoever upon the equitable right to it. It makes no kind of difference whether this fund is secured by 540 or by 1,350 certificates. Its character cannot be changed by the evidences given to secure it. Part of it is *principal* — the rest is ' income,' within the meaning of the will. The principal must remain unimpaired during the lives of the appellants [life tenants], and the ' income ' arising since the death of the testator is to be distributed among them. Standing upon principle and upon the intent of the testator, plainly expressed in his will, we have no difficulty whatever in making this disposition of the fund." In Pritchitt v. Nashville Trust Co., 96 Tenn. 472, 36 S. W. 1064, it was said: " There can be no doubt that reserved and accumulated earnings . . . are corporate property; nevertheless, we are unable to see how that fact determines or affects the question of interest therein as between life tenant and remainderman of shares. Those persons acquire their interest under the will or deed, and not through any action of the corporation."

The rule of apportionment of extraordinary dividends has been consistently followed in Pennsylvania from Earp's App., *supra*, down to Mandeville's Est., 286 Pa. 368. See Smith's Est., 140 Pa. 344; Boyer's App., 224 Pa. 144; Stokes's Est. (No. 1), 240 Pa. 277; Sloan's Est., 258 Pa. 368; Waterman's Est., 279 Pa. 491; Flaccus's Est., 283 Pa. 185; Wittmer's Est., 283 Pa. 311; Harkness's Est., 283 Pa. 464; Dickinson's Est., 285 Pa. 449. It has also been widely adopted in other jurisdictions. See *In re* Gartenlaub's Est., 185 Cal. 375, 197 Pac. 90; Thomas v. Gregg, 78 Md. 545, 28 Atl. 565; Goodwin v. McGaughy, 108 Minn. 248, 122 N. W. 6; Holbrook v. Holbrook, 74 N. H. 201, 66 Atl. 124; Ballantine v. Young, 79 N. J. Eq. 70, 81 Atl. 119; Lang v. Lang's Ex'r, 57 N. J. Eq. 325, 41 Atl. 705; *In re* Osborne, 209 N. Y. 450, 103 N. E. 723; Wallace v. Wallace, 90 S. C. 61, 72 S. E. 553; Cobb v. Fant, 36 S. C. 1, 14 S. E. 959; Pritchitt v. Nashville Trust Co., *supra; In re* Heaton, 89 Vt. 550, 571, 96 Atl. 21; Pabst v. Goodrich, 133 Wis. 69, 113 N. W. 398.

(c) Under the Kentucky rule, a dividend, whether of stock or cash goes to the person entitled to receive the income at the time the dividend is declared, without regard to the time when it was earned: Cox v. Gaulbert's Est., 148 Ky. 409, 147 S. W. 25; Hite v. Hite, 93 Ky. 257, 265, 20 S. W. 778; McLouth v. Hunt, 154 N. Y. 179; 48 N. E. 548. This is another rule of convenience. Since the New York

Court of Appeals in the case of *In re* Osborn, *supra*, decided to abandon this rule (and to follow Pennsylvania), Kentucky is probably the only state adhering to it.

3. There is another situation where a corporation for its own purposes issues new stocks for which rights to subscribe are given shareholders. They are commonly called " rights," and as such have a value. The benefit of these rights, whether sold by the trustee or exercised by taking new stock, is in other states generally awarded to the remaindermen. See DeKoven *v.* Alsop, 205 Ill. 309, 68 N. E. 930; Lauman *v.* Foster, 157 Iowa 275, 135 N. W. 14; Hyde *v.* Holmes, 198 Mass. 287, 84 N. E. 318; Ballantine *v.* Young, 79 N. J. Eq. 70, 81 Atl. 119; Robertson *v.* DeBrulatour, 188 N. Y. 312, 80 N. E. 938; Baker *v.* Thompson, 168 N. Y. Supp. 871, aff'd, 224 N. Y. 591, 120 N. E. 858. In jurisdictions following the Massachusetts rule, this result follows as a logical consequence. In other jurisdictions it would seem the life tenant should receive the benefit of the right so far as it is attributable to earnings that have accumulated during the life interest, provided the intact value of the corpus be maintained. This was the decision in Holbrook *v.* Holbrook, 74 N. H. 201, 66 Atl. 124. As noted, however, in Lauman *v.* Foster, *supra*, the decision in the Holbrook Case is contrary to the great weight of authorities.

There is some conflict in the Pennsylvania cases on this point. See Wiltbank's App., 64 Pa. 256, and Moss's App., 83 Pa. 264, where Wiltbank's App., *supra*, was distinguished upon the ground that the rule there stated applied only where there was an actual profit, whereas in the case then before the court the issue of the new shares reduced the value of the original shares held by the trust estate. See also Biddle's Est., 99 Pa. 278; Eisner's Est., 175 Pa. 143; Veech's Est., 74 Pa. Superior Ct. 373.

In Thompson's Est., 262 Pa. 278, a national bank, incapable of declaring a stock dividend, gave to its stockholders rights to subscribe for new stock, and at the same time declared a dividend exactly equal to the amount of the stock's subscription. The trustee exercised the option, although he did not use the dividend check to pay for the stock, which was claimed by the life tenant. Mr. Justice SIMPSON, in affirming the decree of the court below awarding the stock to the life tenant said that three possible courses were open to the trustee: (1) He could sell the option to subscribe, in which case he would have received more than $20,000 in addition to the cash dividend of $8,000, and the life tenants would have received both cash sums, the remainderman's interest remaining intact; (2) He could refuse to exercise the option which would have probably surcharged him in a sum necessary to make up to the life tenants the amount they would have received from a sale of the option; (3) He could have subscribed for the stock and paid for it exactly with the sum received as a special dividend, which was the course actually pursued. Judge HENDERSON, speaking for the Superior Court, in Veech's Est., *supra*, distinguished Thompson's Estate upon the ground that a dividend was declared by the corporation. This does not seem to be reconcilable with our opinion as written by Mr. Justice SIMPSON.

(B) The question under this division arises where earnings are undistributed and the stock with earnings as value included therein is sold. The corporation has, undivided, an accumulation of earnings, profits or income, called surplus. It is rightfully divisible among the shareholders if the managers of the corporation should choose to distribute it. The trustees, as shareholders, in right of the estate, would be entitled to participate in such distribution. In McKeown's Est., 263 Pa. 78, one phase of accumulated earnings presented itself when the stock of one company was sold by its shareholders to another concern. What actually happened was a sale of stock by the trustee, but we treated it as a distribution by a corporation in the course of liquidation. A part of the proceeds was accumulated earnings; we held it should be distributed as though the company had in fact declared a dividend, and hence was payable to the life tenant, the intact value being unimpaired. The facts in that case, important to the instant case, were substantially as follows: Four thousand shares of stock of the Pure Oil Company at the death of testator had an intact value of $12.22 a share. It was sold for $24.50 a share to an Ohio company, which acquired all Pure Oil Stock. The book value at this time was $15.18, the difference, $2.96, being due to accumulation of earnings. The difference between the selling price and the then book value, $9.32, represented the inherent, intrinsic, or supervalue of the stock, over and above its then book value, and was awarded, without objection, to the corpus of the estate. The life tenant claimed the accumulated profits, or $2.96 per share. The court below refused to allow the claim, and was reversed by this court in an opinion by Mr. Justice SIMPSON. It may be well to state that, in reaching our conclusion in that case, it was necessary to consider generally the respective rights of life tenants and remaindermen in all situations similar to that which we were then called upon to determine, and also the general effect of that decision as bearing upon other similar situations of a slightly different nature emanating through similar channels. To strip that authority of its persuasive effect in other disputes, is to deny the correct and logical foundation on which it is based, as well as its logical sequence. We will not detail the reasoning on which we reached the conclusion that accumulated earnings, not declared by dividends, but realized on a sale, belong to the life tenant, but will state the four primary rules evolved by Mr. Justice SIMPSON from the decided cases. " (1) An ordinary corporate dividend is usually payable in its entirety to the party entitled to the income at the time the dividend was declared. (2) An extraordinary corporate dividend is presumptively payable to the party entitled to the income at the time the dividend was declared; but this presumption must yield to proof of the fact, and if it appears that by such dividend the corporate assets are reduced below their value at the time the trust began, the principal must be made good before anything is awarded to income. (3) If stock is sold which belongs to the principal, ordinarily all the proceeds thereof also belong to the principal. (4) When a corporation is liquidated, those entitled to the income of the trust are to be awarded so much of the sums received for the stock as they show was income accruing after their right to income began, and the balance goes to principal; and this is so although the course pursued takes the form of a sale of the stock." The auditing judge in McKeown's Estate found the sale of the stock by the trustee, including accumulated and undistributed income as part of its value, amounted to a liquidation of the oil company and the distribution by it of the corporate earnings. The instant case, though of slightly different aspect, is governed by the principle controlling the last of these general rules.

Where the trustee in an ordinary business transaction sells stock, the value of which has been enhanced by accumulated surplus and earnings not declared as a dividend by the corporation, what distribution should be made of the accumulated earnings and surplus? Should it go to the life tenant or to the remainderman? Or, in other words, why should the minor liquidation of interest in a corporation by a member thereof in selling his shares of stock therein not be effective as a liquidation which reflects substantially a distribution by the corporation of its accumulated earnings and increment value by reason of that membership? It would seem the reasoning in McKeown's Est., *supra,* and Earp's App., *supra,* answers the general question in the affirmative. Earp's App., *supra,* p. 374, states: " The managers might withhold the distribution of it for a time, for reasons beneficial to the interests of the parties entitled. But they could not, by any form of procedure whatever deprive the owners of it, and give it to others not entitled. The omission to distribute it semiannually, as it accumulated, makes no change in its ownership."

The profits or income of a corporation is earned by the capital stock and may be declared as a dividend by the managers: Struthers *v.* Clark, 30 Pa. 210, 213. The capital stock is evidence of the estate's ownership in the corporation; it is the estate's certificate of membership in the association measured by so many shares. These shares earn for the estate a proportionate share of the income, profit or earnings of the company. When a dividend rate is fixed, so much of these earnings, necessary for payment, are taken from the corporate stock, represented by income, and the balance is carried forward as an accumulation of income, surplus or profits. This accumulation may be retained by the company to enlarge the business or to provide working capital, or as a reserve fund to provide against losses. These may be transferred into capital account, where the evidence may be stock distributed as an extraordinary dividend. Where the earned accumulations remain in the company undisposed of, the shareholders' interest therein and right thereto is undisturbed; no matter what such accumulations may be called by the corporation or what form they may assume, the names do not aid in determining the rights of the life tenant and remaindermen to such income.

The testator gave the income of his estate to the life tenants. "Income" may be defined as a gain which proceeds from labor, business or property of any kind, the profits of commerce or business. It includes the return earned by capital stock. It has a broader meaning than the term "dividend"; it includes profits. We said in Quay's Est., 253 Pa. 80, that profits included not only the accumulations of earnings, but the advances or increment in value. It is not necessary to include the latter in the definition. What the testator did was to give to the life tenant all this income. It included all the earnings which his membership in the company or ownership in stock are responsible for, or would bring about, but not the stock's earning power. That inheres in the stock. Income of the corporation is a product of capital, part of which was furnished and owned by this estate: Com. v. Pitts., Fort Wayne and Chicago Ry. Co., 74 Pa. 83, 90. Therefore every principle of justice demands that the direction of testator be fulfilled, and that life tenants should receive this income. There is not one single element of justice that speaks for the corpus of the estate to take the earnings. The mere fact that it is earned and retained by the company should not prevent the life tenants from ultimately receiving it unless that receipt does harm to the corpus (intact value) of the estate. Where the intact value is in money in the trustee's hands, as here $21,370, with the assumed accumulated surplus, $40,000, and the increment in value, $110,000, also in money, to hold that the corpus should be entitled to all would be to disregard the positive instructions of the testator; the income at least should be given to his life tenant beneficiaries.

The argument most generally advanced is that as the accumulated earnings are definitely ascertained as to time and amount by the corporation the managers alone are responsible for its division among members. They should be permitted freely to discharge that duty to their fellow members by distributing the earnings in a manner and at a time which to them shall be deemed most advantageous for the corporation itself. This overlooks the really important question in this and other cases; it is not the right between the corporation on the one side and the life tenant and remaindermen on the other that we are discussing, but the right as between the latter two; as stated by Mr. Justice SIMPSON in McKeown's Est., *supra*, p. 84: "That is a matter solely between the corporation and the stockholder, and does not necessarily determine the rights of a life tenant and remainderman in an estate owning such stock. If the company declares a dividend, whether of stock or cash, partially out of earnings and partially out of principal, a court of equity, made cognizant of the fact, will apportion the dividend between the life tenant and the remainderman, in such a way as to maintain intact the principal of the estate, only giving the balance to the life tenant. So also, if a corporation sells its capital and accumulated income for a gross sum, a court of equity should distribute that sum according to like equitable principles." We are not interested in the conduct of the affairs of the corporation.

Courts, in determining rights as between life tenants and remaindermen, do not endeavor to control, manage or direct the internal affairs of a company, nor do they attempt to require that money held as surplus for corporate reasons shall be divided among the members in order that any one member shall receive the accumulated earnings. Nothing is done that, in the slightest, involves the financial structure of the company. When a trustee sells the stock of a company and the profit represents an accumulation of earnings or surplus in addition to intact value, he has physical possession of the income apart from any other consideration. The only screen held up to defeat the life tenants is that the corporation did not formally declare it as a dividend, though it has every such quality, except the name, withheld by the company. In such cases, the sale, in substance and effect, amounts to a distribution, as in the case of liquidation of a corporation. The court will disregard the form, and treat it as a distribution of accumulated interest or earnings, keeping in mind always that the intact value of the corpus shall not be in any way depleted. Equity looks through the form and holds to the substance, and will distribute that sum according to equitable principles. In Quay's Est., *supra*, the court went farther than is necessary for us to do, but the case illustrates the judicial leaning toward the rule that accumulated earnings should go to the life tenant and remaindermen in a just proportion as indicated in the distribution of stock dividends. In Peterson's Est., 242 Pa. 330, where there was a distribution of accumulated earnings worth many times more than the intact value at death, we said, (pp. 333–4) : " These earnings were income pure and simple; the fact that they were allowed to accumulate instead of being regularly distributed did not change their character in this regard. Being income, and so far in excess of the reasonable and legitimate requirements of the business of the corporation that its distribution could have been enforced at any time by those entitled to receive it, their permitting it to accumulate was on their part the assertion of ownership. Mrs. Peterson was the undoubted owner in her own right of a share in these accumulations in the proportion that the 250 shares of stock in the trust fund stood to the whole issue of stock. This was hers to do with as she pleased; it was free from any trust; leaving it in the corporation was her own act, and the corporation thereupon became her debtor to that extent." The income was undoubtedly Mrs. Peterson's. When the company distributed it after her death, her husband was entitled to receive it regardless of the form it took.

The question has been before courts of other jurisdictions. In Simpson *v.* Millsaps, 80 Miss. 239, 31 So. 912, a testator directed his trustees to pay to the life tenant the entire net income of his estate and part of the estate was invested in bank stock, the earnings of which were accumulated instead of being distributed. The trustees sold the stock and it was held that the accumulated earnings were the property of the life tenant. In United States Trust Co. *v.* Heye, 224 N. Y. 242, 120 N. E. 645, 648, the New York Court of Appeals, which is committed to the Pennsylvania rule, in discussing situations like this, said: " The fundamental principle involved in these questions is whether there has been a distribution or division of the earnings, profits or accumulations of the corporation. Until there has been such division, the life tenant is not entitled to any increase in the value of the principal of the trust fund, or the capital and assets of the corporation, shares of which constitute the trust fund. *But when there has been a division of the corporate property, no matter what form it may take,* that part thereof which consists of accumulated profits or earnings belongs to the life tenant and that which is capital to the remainderman." In Schaffer's Est., 165 N. Y. Supp. 19, 222 New York 533, 118 N. E. 1076, stock, held by trustees for the benefit of the life tenant and remaindermen, was sold for more than the intact value. During the years the trustees held the stock, the company did not distribute all the profits but retained a portion of the net earnings each year as a surplus or profit. " These profits . . . went to the enhancement of the assets and it is to the retention and investment of this surplus that at least some of the increasing value of the stock is to be attributed." After stating the three rules as to the disposition of dividends, the court said: " These general rules are not questioned by the trustees, but they say that they are inapplicable here because there had been no payment by way of dividend and no liquidation of the company, which still remains a going concern. . . . It is true that there has been no general liquidation of the company but there has been a liquidation so far as concerns one-half of its capital stock. . . . The trustees have at least liquidated — that is to say, have turned into money — their interest in the company which was formerly represented by shares of stock. What does this money in their hands represent? Concededly, it represents in part accumulated profits earned during the lifetime of the trust, . . . Otherwise, . . . the accumulated profits will go to the unlawful increase of the corpus of the estate and the enrichment of the remaindermen at the expense of the life beneficiary." The life tenant had apportioned to him so much of the surplus as was earned during the trust.

In Wallace *v.* Wallace, 90 S. C. 61, 72 S. E. 553, where the trustees sold stock after the death of the life tenant, it was held that accumulated earnings of a corporation should be distributed between the life tenant and remaindermen according to the time such earnings are made and not according to the chance action of corporate officers in withholding or declaring dividends. This, of course, has reference to earnings accumulated during the life tenancy. To the same effect is the Sherman Trust Case, 190 Iowa 1385, 179 N. W. 109, the court there saying, " As between remaindermen and life tenants the question is not what corporation management may do about declaring dividends so far as stockholders are concerned. What these managements may do is corporation law. What the rights of the remaindermen and life tenants are in corporation shares is a question of what it may reasonably be found was the intent of the creator of the trust." As the court intimates, there is not a single disposition which required the income to be subjected to the hard and fast rule of corporation law in the distribution of dividends. On the other hand, the Kentucky court, in Guthrie's Trustee *v.* Aikers, 157 Ky. 149, 163 S. W. 1117, there intimated that they placed it in the power of the corporation " to enhance the interests of the remaindermen, to the injury of the life tenant." But if, on the other hand, the trustee may sell and thus in effect declare a dividend, it would produce the same result as if the corporation did it. Schaeffer's Est., *supra*, is in line with the thought of this opinion, and wherever Connolly's Est. (No. 1), 198 Pa. 137, touches the question, McKeown's App., *supra*, overrules it. In Connolly's Est. (No. 1), *supra*, p. 143, it is stated: " The increase in value of these stocks is no doubt due in part to surplus earnings retained by the corporation . . . also in part to the enhancement of their original value. ' Such enhancement belongs not to the tenant for life but to the remainderman ': Eisner's Est., 175 Pa. 143; and as there is no evidence here from which the proportions of the increase due to the surplus earnings and to the enhancement of the original value of the stock can be found . . . Earp's Appeal should not be followed." The rise in the value of trust investments, where such rise has not been shown by one claiming as a life tenant to be due to undistributed earnings, has always been properly regarded, like the rise in the value of lands held in trust, to be an accretion of the principal, and, therefore, belongs to the remainderman. See Park's Est., 173 Pa. 190.

From what we have said, it follows that where the trustee sells stock which represents in part accumulated earnings sufficiently ear marked that they can be ascertained, the life tenants are entitled to an apportionment of these earnings, not in any manner reducing the intact value of the corpus. This is true regardless of the form, whether in stock after death, as in Peterson's Estate, cash, as in this and McKeown's Estate, or other corporate securities, is immaterial. There is one condition to which this rule is subject, wherein it would seem that part of the earnings should go to the corpus of the estate; this is where the stock is sold when an ordinary dividend is anticipated, but not paid. The fact that the price appears to have been enhanced by reason thereof, or that the price may represent, in part, expected dividends, does not entitle the life tenant to that increase. In McKeown's Est., *supra*, it was held that the seven cents per share was in fact earnings which were to be declared as an ordinary, regular dividend and the sale of the stock by the trustee before they were payable permitted the new holder, the purchaser, to receive the dividend. The vendor was not entitled to it as a current dividend until it was declared, and the increase should be considered as increment.

But it is said that it would be extremely difficult to prove how much of the price realized in fact represented income. This should not be difficult at this time. The United States Government requires a fairly regular set of books to be kept for income return. Therein depreciation, renewals, reserves, replacements, and all the various charges are kept. There is the fixed fact, the amount realized from the sale of the stock. There is the amount set apart as earnings, divided into dividends paid and undivided as surplus which may be found in the " profit and loss " account. This may not be conclusive or the only method, but it is an illustration. However the accounts are kept, it is quite easy to strike a balance; but, even if it is difficult, " the difficulty of proving a fact," as Mr. Justice SIMPSON observes in McKeown's Est., *supra*, " has never been held to deprive one of a right, growing out of such fact, if and when proved; and as to the former it is sufficient to say that in a court of equity, as the orphans' court is within the sphere of its jurisdiction, substance is never sacrificed to form," even though the corporation may be of another state. These difficulties are often present. That much litigation would follow is no objection; there will always be litigation over estates when testators choose to place them in a position for litigation.

Again, it is said innumerable difficulties would beset the trustee in deciding whether or not he should sell or hold the securities in order not to be liable in case of depletion for holding them. Where the authorizing instrument permits the investment in nonlegal securities, it should not be troublesome. The readers' attention is invited to the opinion of the Chief Justice in Taylor's Est., 277 Pa. 518 and to Brown's Est., 287 Pa. 501, wherein these questions are discussed.

(C) This brings us to the last matter which may have any bearing on the question: May the trustee who holds the stock be required to distribute these earnings out of other property of the estate, or may he be required to sell the stock in order to realize the accumulated earnings? As to the first proposition, the answer must, of course, be in the negative. The stock, with its accumulated earnings and intact value and whatever other element of value which may attach to it, is subject to the vicissitudes of corporate life, and as such it must bear its share of whatever comes and goes. Other property of the estate cannot be required to be set apart to pay life tenants the accumulated surplus retained by the corporation. The surplus and all other items of value remain, subject to debts, reverses, losses and decline in value because of business conditions. As long as the stock remains in the hands of the trustee, he is not required to account to life tenants for anything except the dividends received. Therefore, such requirements cannot be considered in the management of the estate; and in this connection we may say the increment of value in the stock itself, or the intrinsic value of the stock, is the property of the remainderman. This refers, in the McKeown's Est., *supra*, to the $9.32 above noted.

As to the right to compel the trustee to sell such stock through petition in the orphans' court, we express no opinion. Generally speaking, it is subject to the same rules that govern any property in the hands of a trustee. Whether it be for the best interest of the estate to make a sale under given circumstances or not, is addressed largely to the discretion of the court below. As to the possible liability of the trustee for failure to make a sale, this, as we suggested above, is determined by the rules in the cases before referred to in this opinion.

In conclusion we may summarize what has been said above. First, an ordinary dividend belongs entirely to the life tenant (McKeen's App., 42 Pa. 479, and see McKeown's Est., 263 Pa. 78, 85). Second, an extraordinary dividend paid out of accumulated earnings, presumptively belongs to the life tenant but, if it be shown that the distribution impairs the intact value of the estate, the court will make an apportionment (Earp's App., 28 Pa. 368). Third, where the corporation gives to the trustee the right to subscribe for new stock, the weight of the authorities in this State would seem to require that it be apportioned (see Wiltbank's App., 64 Pa. 256; Moss's App., 83 Pa. 264; Eisner's Est., 175 Pa. 143; Thompson's Est., 262 Pa. 278. Fourth, where the trustee sells stock and the sale in substance effects a distribution, as in the case of liquidation of the company, the court will disregard the form and treat the sale as a distribution (McKeown's Est., *supra*). Fifth, where the trustee sells stock and receives a price greater than the value of the stock at the time of the death of the testator, or at the time it was acquired, the profit being due to an accumulation of income, the court should apportion the proceeds. Sixth, where the trustee sells stock and receives a price greater than the value of the stock at the time of the death of the testator, or at the time it was acquired, the super value being due to the enhancement or increment of original value through the stock's earning power or what may be termed its " good will " or its intrinsic value, this increased value is part of the corpus and belongs to the remainderman. Seventh, where the stock is held by the trustee, and its value is enhanced by reason of accumulated earnings which have not been declared in dividends, the life tenant is not entitled to payment out of other property of the estate. Eighth, where the trustee sells stock at a profit which is due to enhanced market value, and not to accumulated earnings, the increase must be regarded as a capital gain (Connolly's Est. (No. 1), 198 Pa. 137, 141, 143; and see Neel's Est. (No. 2), 207 Pa. 446; McKeown's Est., 263 Pa. 78).

We have noted in this opinion that the intact value of this present estate was about $20,000. The sale price was $170,000, and it was assumed by Judge GEST and the court in banc that $40,000 of this sum represented accumulated earnings. It was on that basis the case was decided and evidently the court below was impressed with the fact that the accumulated surplus had been sufficiently proven. When we turn to the record we notice the statements of counsel that this was a fact, and appellee did not then controvert it. When the case was argued in this court by appellant, it was on the basis that such income did exist. This conclusion was strenuously resisted by the present appellees here, and, as we read the record, there is nothing which adequately supports a finding of $40,000 surplus. There was undoubtedly considerable confusion as to this primary fact evidenced by the manner in which it and other facts were stated. No doubt the court below felt that the statement of counsel had been accepted by appellees because of their silence. We could not reverse a judgment when the record is in this shape, but we realize that it is not entirely just to appellants who seemed to rely upon the fact that statements of counsel were apparently accepted as proof. The only judgment we can enter here is one of affirmance without prejudice to the right of appellants to ask that the judgment be opened in the court below in order that satisfactory evidence may be procured to prove that the purchase price included $40,000 accumulated earnings.

The judgment is affirmed without prejudice, as last above stated, at the cost of appellants.[1]

[1] See comments to the principal case in 26 Mich. L. Rev. 555; 76 U. Pa. L. Rev. 589. See also Bogert, Trusts, sec. 103; Perry, Trusts, secs. 544 *et seq.*; 24 A. L. R. 9; 42 A. L. R. 448; 50 A. L. R. 375; 56 A. L. R. 1287; 59 A. L. R. 1532.

In New York it is provided by statute (Laws 1926, c. 843) that stock dividends are principal unless otherwise provided by the trust instrument. Pers. Prop. Law, sec. 17a.

As to the rights as between life tenants and remaindermen in the increase in the value of the estate, see 13 A. L. R. 1004; 56 A. L. R. 1315.

EDWARDS v. EDWARDS.

SUPREME JUDICIAL COURT, MASSACHUSETTS. 1903.

183 Mass. 581.

BILL IN EQUITY, filed March 23, 1903, by the trustees under the will of James Edwards, for instructions as to the application of the proceeds of the sale of a certain valuable tract of vacant land on Huntington Avenue in Boston.

The case came on to be heard before *Braley, J.*, who reserved it upon the bill and answer and an agreed statement of facts for the consideration of the full court, such order to be made therein as justice and equity might require.

KNOWLTON, C. J. This is a bill for instructions by trustees appointed under the will of James Edwards. By the will he gave all his property to these trustees, stating the trust as follows: " To invest and reinvest the same at their discretion, in such securities as the laws of this Commonwealth allow savings banks to invest their funds in, and the whole net income therefrom shall be paid to my said wife as long as she shall live, for her own use and disposal, with the exception that I direct that from said income there shall be paid monthly to my son, William Edwards, and his wife, Alice J. Edwards, in equal shares, the sum of one hundred dollars, as long as my said wife shall live." At the death of his wife the trustees are to pay the income to his children and to the wife of one of them, and at the termination of the trust, to pay over the remainder to his grandchildren or to his heirs at law. The value of the personal property that came into the hands of the trustees was nearly $70,000, and the value of the real estate was more than $200,000. Much of the personal property that he left was stock carried by brokers on margins, and the most valuable part of the real estate was unproductive land on Huntington Avenue which was appraised in the executor's inventory, filed November 11, 1896, at $150,000, and in the trustees' inventory, filed December 31, 1898, at $155,000, and was sold by the trustees on September 1, 1899, for $196,500. The question relates to the apportionment of income and principal between the life tenant and the remaindermen, from the proceeds of the sale of the land on Huntington Avenue. It is agreed that the value of this land at the time of the testator's death was the same at which it was appraised in the executor's inventory, and that the trustees used every reasonable effort to sell it, and in view of the improvements in that vicinity, exercised a sound judgment in holding it until the time of the sale. It did not produce sufficient income to pay the taxes and expenses upon it. Under language like that of this will, which gives the trustees all the property, real and personal, and does not indicate an intention that the time for establishing the fund shall be postponed, and which gives to a life tenant the annual income, it is well settled law in this Commonwealth that the income is to be computed from the time of the testator's death. Sargent v. Sargent, 103 Mass. 297, 299. Westcott v. Nickerson, 120 Mass. 410. In the present case the testator obviously intended that the entire property should be converted into one fund, and that the unproductive and speculative investments which he had at the time of his death should be changed without unreasonable delay. Much of the property held on margins was not of such a kind " as the laws of this Commonwealth allow savings banks to invest their funds in," and the land on Huntington Avenue was not in a condition to be held as a permanent investment. It was, therefore, the duty of the trustees to convert this property into an income-producing fund, and this they did according to their best judgment and discretion. The testator is presumed to have expected that some time would be required to accomplish this. At the same time, he is presumed to have intended that the rights of the life tenant to income should be ascertained on the creation of the fund, as if the fund had come into existence immediately after his death. This is in accordance with the rule repeatedly stated by this court. Kinmonth v. Brigham, 5 Allen, 270, 278. Sargent v. Sargent, 103 Mass. 297. Westcott v. Nickerson, 120 Mass. 410. Mudge v. Parker, 139 Mass. 153. The rule is applicable as well when the delay in converting the property is necessary as when it is caused by the voluntary act of default of the trustees. Loring v. Massachusetts Horticultural Society, 171 Mass. 401, 404. In Westcott v. Nickerson, *ubi supra,* Chief Justice Gray says of the property in such cases, " The necessary inference and the established rule are that it must be invested as a permanent fund, and the value thereof fixed at the time when the right of the first taker begins, that is to say, at the death of the testator." In Sargent v. Sargent, *ubi supra,* the same justice says, " The general rule is established, that the tenant for life is entitled to the income of a residue given in trust, from the time of the testator's death."

The question raised by this bill for instructions relates only to the proceeds of the sale of the land on Huntington Avenue. The life tenant, the widow of the testator, is one of the trustees who bring the suit, and in the bill she states her claim as follows: " The widow of the testator, who with the annuitants, is entitled to the income of the trust fund from the time of the testator's death to the filing of this bill, claims that she is entitled to receive a proportionate part of the proceeds of the sale of said Huntington Avenue land, as the income of that part of the trust estate, and contends that all the taxes, assessments and brokers' commissions, which the trustees and executors have paid, and are bound to pay, should be charged to the funds received from said sale, and that the fund should then be so divided as to constitute a fund at the time of the testator's death, which, with interest at a reasonable rate, to wit, four per cent, will produce the amount for which the said estate was sold, less the expenses accruing on the same, and all betterments against said premises which the trustees are bound to pay, and that then she is entitled to said interest or income, and that the fund determined as aforesaid shall form a part of the corpus of the estate." The question arises whether, in apportioning the principal and income, we are to assume that the fund, if established at the time of the testator's death, would have earned income at the rate of six per cent per annum, or only at some lower rate. It was said at the argument, and we suppose it to be a fact of common knowledge, that a fund invested in such securities as savings banks may invest in under our laws, cannot be made to produce an income of nearly so much as six per cent per annum, and the life tenant, in stating her claim, suggests the allowance of "interest at a reasonable rate, to wit, four per cent." In this statement she recognizes the principle that in this case we are not to deal with interest as an allowance made by law to represent damages for the failure to pay money when it is due. We are to deal with the income which could have been obtained by the trustees if the fund had been ready for investment and had been invested immediately after the death of the testator. The failure to invest it then was not the fault of anybody, and we are not called upon to allow interest as interest, but only to ascertain the probable income. Whenever interest is to be allowed for the failure to pay a legacy when it is due, or for any other neglect to pay money, the law knows no other rate than six per cent per annum. Welch *v.* Adams, 152 Mass. 74. Loring *v.* Massachusetts Horticultural Society, 171 Mass. 401. Bartlett, petitioner, 163 Mass. 509, 521. But we are to ascertain as between tenant for life and remainderman, what part of a gross sum now in hand shall be treated as capital and what part as income, and when we are called upon to find out what sum at an earlier date, if invested by trustees, would have been sufficient to produce, with its income, the gross sum now in hand, we must look to the actual income that can be obtained from investments, and not to the rate of interest established by law.

In Westcott *v.* Nickerson, *ubi supra*, it is said that the amount obtained "is to be distributed between the tenant for life and the remainderman, by computing what sum, if received at the death of the testator, adding interest at six per cent with annual rests, would produce the amount afterwards actually received . . . and by investing the original sum, so computed, as principal, and distributing the residue as income." In Kinmonth *v.* Brigham, *ubi supra*, a direction is given in similar language. But in neither of these cases was any consideration given to the possible difference between the income actually obtainable and the rate of interest prescribed by law. The first of these cases was decided in 1876, and the other in November, 1862, and at the time to which the decisions relate there was little if any difference between the usual earnings of capital and the rate of interest established by law. Neither the parties nor the court had any occasion to consider the question now raised.

We are of opinion that the case should be referred to a master to ascertain what sum would have been sufficient if invested by the trustees immediately after the death of the testator, to produce, with the income which they reasonably could have obtained from it, the sum in the hands of the trustees as the net proceeds of the land on Huntington Avenue, after deducting their disbursements on account of the property. That sum is to be held as principal and the remainder is to be paid over as income.

So ordered.[1]

---

[1] By what is called the rule in Howe *v.* Earl of Dartmouth (7 Ves. 137*a*), if there is a bequest of one's personal estate or of the residue thereof to be enjoyed by persons in succession, it is the duty of the trustees to convert so much of the property as is of a wasting or perishable nature or which is unproductive, into permanent approved securities. See Ames, 491.

As to the allocation on sale of unproductive property, see Equitable Trust Co. *v.* Kent, 11 Del. Ch. 334; Lawrence *v.* Littlefield, 215 N. Y. 561; Furniss *v.* Cruikshank, 230 N. Y. 495; Matter of Pinkney, 208 App. Div. 181, *aff'd mem.* 238 N. Y. 602; Matter of Hopkins, 133 N. Y. Misc. 554. But see Matter of Marshall, 136 N. Y. Misc. 116 (small amount of unproductive land).

The same principle is applicable to reversionary interests. Wilkinson *v.* Duncan, 23 Beav. 469; *Re* Earl of Chesterfield's Trusts, 24 Ch. D. 643; *Re* Baker, [1924] 2 Ch. 271.

It is applicable to investments which become unproductive. Greene *v.* Greene, 19 R. I. 619. *Cf.* Hagan *v.* Platt, 48 N. J. Eq. 206; Tuttle's Case, 49 N. J. Eq. 259.

As to the allocation on sale of wasting or hazardous property, see Brown *v.* Gellatly, L. R. 2 Ch. App. 751 (ships); *Re* Wareham, [1912] 2 Ch. 312 (leaseholds); *Re* Evans' Will Trusts, [1921] 2 Ch. 309 (royalties and profits from copyrighted books); Gay *v.* Focke, 291 Fed. 721 (leaseholds); Buckingham *v.* Morrison, 136 Ill. 437, 448 (interest in partnership); Kinmonth *v.* Brigham, 5 Allen (Mass.) 270 (interest in partnership); Westcott *v.* Nickerson, 120 Mass. 410 (interest in partnership); Cairns *v.* Chaubert, 9 Paige (N. Y.) 160 (profits of toll bridge for term of years); Matter of Housman, 4 Dem. Surr. (N. Y.) 404 (furniture in rented house); Matter of James, 146 N. Y. 78 (stock in corporation whose only profits came from sale of land) (*semble*); Matter of Elsner, 210 N. Y. App. Div. 575 (royalties on a book); Matter of Golding, 127 N. Y. Misc. 821 (leaseholds); Matter of Hall, 130 N. Y. Misc. 313 (leaseholds); Estate of Wells, 156 Wis. 294 (stock in lumber and mining corporation).

The life beneficiary is not entitled to compel a sale nor to share in the proceeds of the sale if it is expressly or impliedly provided otherwise by the terms of the trust. Old Colony Trust Co. *v.* Shaw, 261 Mass. 158; Matter of James, 146 N. Y. 78; Frankel *v.* Farmers' L. & T. Co., 152 App. Div. 58, *aff'd mem.* 209 N. Y. 553; Matter of Hall, 127 N. Y. Misc. 238. See Perry, Trusts, sec. 548.

Authority to retain investments unconverted is an indication of the same intention. *Re* Bates, [1907] 1 Ch. 22 (hazardous securities); Gay *v.* Focke,

MATTER OF STEVENS.

COURT OF APPEALS, NEW YORK. 1907.

187 N. Y. 471.

[The testatrix created trusts for her grandchildren, the income to be applied to the use of each grandchild until he should reach the age of thirty when the principal was to be paid to him. In the event of the death of any grandchild without issue before thirty, the fund was to go to the surviving children and grandchildren.] [1]

CULLEN, C. J. . . . The trustees have invested large portions of the fund, which came into their hands on the dissolution of the Brooks Company, in bonds purchased at a premium. The appellant Tyler contended before the surrogate that from the interest collected on those bonds there should be deducted, as it was collected, a sum sufficient to make good at the maturity of the bonds the amount paid as a premium. The surrogate overruled this claim and awarded the whole amount of the interest coupons to the life tenant as income. This disposition was erroneous and is in conflict with the recent decision of this court in New York Life Ins. & Trust Co. v. Baker (165 N. Y. 484). It was there held that where trust funds are invested by the trustee in bonds having a term of years to run and purchased at a premium, such a proportionate deduction should be made from the nominal interest as will, at the maturity of the bonds, make good the premium paid, and thus preserve the principal of the fund intact. It is true that in that case the late chief judge of this court said that the language of the will and the surrounding circumstances might indicate a different intention on the part of the founder of the trusts, in which case the testator's intent would control. Such was the case in Matter of

---

291 Fed. 721 (leaseholds); Buckingham v. Morrison, 136 Ill. 437 (interest in partnership); Green v. Crapo, 181 Mass. 55 (unproductive land); Jordan v. Jordan, 192 Mass. 337 (unproductive land); Old Colony Trust Co. v. Shaw, 261 Mass. 158 (mining shares); Martin v. Kimball, 86 N. J. Eq. 10, 432 (unproductive land); Berger v. Burnett, 97 N. J. Eq. 169 (stock paying no dividend). The result is different, however, if the trustees are given power merely to postpone conversion. Re Beach, [1920] 1 Ch. 40; Re Trollope's Will Trusts, [1927] 1 Ch. 596.

In Creed v. Connelly, 172 N. E. 106 (Mass. 1930), 30 Yale L. Jour. 275, the court held that the absence of a direction or authorization to convert unproductive land indicated an intention that there should be no apportionment.

In the following cases apportionment was denied. Ogden v. Allen, 225 Mass. 595 (sale after death of life beneficiary); Spring v. Hollander, 261 Mass. 373 (successive legal estates).

See Bogert, Trusts, sec. 103; Perry, Trusts, secs. 548–551; Underhill, Trusts, arts. 48, 49.

[1] The dissenting opinion of Edward T. Bartlett, J., is omitted.

Hoyt (160 N. Y. 607), where a testator left as a trust fund for his daughter and only child a comparatively small share of a vast fortune and directed the income to be applied to her use " in the most bounteous and liberal manner." It was held by a divided court that the life tenant should not be charged with any part of the premium paid for the security in which the trust fund was invested. In the earlier case of McLouth v. Hunt (154 N. Y. 179) it was held that the life tenant should not be charged with premium on bonds received in kind from the estate of the testator. But as to investments made by the trustees it was said: " There were $5,000 of the United States bonds purchased by the trustees after the erection of the trusts at the same premium. There may be reasons for charging the life tenants with the premium on these bonds that do not apply to the others. But that item is so insignificant that it does not play any part in the controversy. All questions as to the premiums on these bonds were virtually waived on the argument." While we admit, in accordance with the decision in Matter of Hoyt, that the terms of the will may be such as to take a case without the general rule that the principal of the fund must be preserved intact, we think that to justify such an exception to the rule the intent should be expressed in the very clearest manner. If we are to lay down the doctrine that the question is to be determined on the peculiar facts and language of each particular case, no trustee will know how to safely act, and a question constantly arising in the administration of estates will be involved in great confusion and be the cause of great litigation, the latter often at an expense to the estate greater than the sum involved. Such a result would prove very unfortunate.

The justification for the rule is very apparent. The income on a bond having a term of years to run and purchased at a premium is not the sum paid annually on its interest coupons. The interest on a $1,000 ten-year five per cent bond, bought at 120%, is not fifty dollars, but a part thereof only, and the remainder is a return of the principal. All large investors in bonds, such as banks, trust companies and insurance companies, purchase bonds on the basis of the interest the bonds actually return, not the amount they nominally return. Nor is the premium paid on the bond an outlay for the security of the principal. All government bonds have the same security, the faith of the government; yet they vary in price, a variation caused by the difference in the rate of interest and the time they have to run. It is urged that there is often a speculative change in the market value of a bond, and a bond may be worth more at the termination of the trust than at the time of its purchase. This has no bearing on the case. The life tenant should neither be credited with an appreciation nor charged with a loss in the mere market value of the bond. But apart from any speculative change in the market value, there is from lapse of time an inherent and intrinsic change in the value of the security itself as it approaches maturity. It is this, and this only, with which the life tenant is to be charged. We, therefore, adhere to the rule declared in the Baker case, that in the absence of a clear direction in the will to the contrary, where investments are made by the trustee, the principal must be maintained intact from loss by payment of premium on securities having only a definite term to run, while if the bonds are received from the estate of the testator, then the rule in the McLouth case prevails, and the whole interest should be treated as income. These rules may not work perfect justice in all cases, and we fully appreciate that there may be inconsistencies between them, but it is far better that they should be uniformly adhered to, even at the expense of a particular case, than that the administration of estates should be subjected to constant litigation and disputes. It is also to be said that unless the rule in the Baker case is to be observed, the relative rights of life tenant and remainderman would largely depend on the favor or caprice of the trustee who might either buy a bond bearing a high rate of interest at a great premium and impair the principal, or buy a bond bearing a lower rate of interest substantially at par, and preserve the principal intact.

The order of the Appellate Division and the decree of the surrogate of Chautauqua county should be modified in accordance with this opinion, and for that purpose the proceedings remitted to the surrogate to state the account, with costs to both parties payable out of the estate.

HAIGHT, WILLARD BARTLETT and HISCOCK, JJ., concur with CULLEN, Ch. J.; VANN and WERNER, JJ., concur with EDWARD T. BARTLETT, J.

Ordered accordingly.[1]

[1] By the weight of authority where bonds are purchased by the trustee at a premium the premium must or at least may be amortized. New York Life Ins. Co. v. Edwards, 3 F.(2d) 280; Estate of Gartenlaub, 185 Cal. 648; Curtis v. Osborn, 79 Conn. 555; New England Trust Co. v. Eaton, 140 Mass. 532; Ballantine v. Young, 74 N. J. Eq. 572; New York Life Ins. & T. Co. v. Baker, 165 N. Y. 484; Estate of Allis, 123 Wis. 223. But see *contra*, Meyer v. Simonsen, 5 DeG. & Sm. 723; Hite v. Hite, 93 Ky. 257; Penn-Gaskell's Estate (No. 2), 208 Pa. 346. See 4 A. L. R. 1249; 16 A. L. R. 527.

This principle has been applied even though the bonds are sold at more than they cost. New England Trust Co. v. Eaton, *supra;* Estate of Wells, *supra.*

It has been held that if the bonds were originally received as a part of the trust estate and were selling at a premium at the time when they were received, the trustee ordinarily has no duty to amortize. Connecticut Trust Company's Appeal, 80 Conn. 540; Higgins v. Beck, 116 Me. 127; Hemenway v. Hemenway, 134 Mass. 446; Ballantine v. Young, 74 N. J. Eq. 572; McLouth v. Hunt, 154 N. Y. 179; Robertson v. de Brulatour, 188 N. Y. 301. But see Estate of Wells, 156 Wis. 294.

In Estate of Gartenlaub, 198 Cal. 204, 15 Cal. L. Rev. 66, it was held that the life tenant is not entitled to the increase in value of bonds purchased at

SECTION V.

Liabilities of the Trustee to the Beneficiary.

ROBINSON v. ROBINSON.

CHANCERY. 1851.

1 DeG. M. & G. 247.

LORD CRANWORTH, L. J.[1] . . . In the present case it will be observed the executors had the option of investing the trust money at their discretion on real or government securities, and in such a case Sir J. Leach held, in the case of Marsh v. Hunter, 6 Madd. 295, that trustees, by whose default the money is lost, are chargeable, not with the amount of stock which might have been purchased, but only with the principal money lost, and of course, though the report is not so expressed, with interest thereon.

That decision occurred in 1822. Four years later, namely, in 1826, occurred the case of Hockley v. Bantock, 1 Russ. 141, before Lord Gifford. There the executors had a similar discretion of investing either on real or government securities; and, on a bill seeking to charge them with balances improperly retained in their hands, Lord Gifford directed an inquiry as to the price of 3l. per cents at the several times when the balances ought to have been invested. Such an inquiry would have been improper if the executors could not have been charged with the value of the stock; and the case, therefore, is an authority that, in the opinion of Lord Gifford, they might be so charged. Notwithstanding this last case, however, Sir J. Leach adhered to his own view of the law, and acted on it in an unreported case of Gale v. Pitt at the Rolls on the 10th of May, 1830.

Lord Gifford's authority had been followed by Lord Langdale in several reported cases, to which we were referred in the argument; namely, Watts v. Girdlestone, 6 Beav. 188, Ames v. Parkinson, 7 Beav. 379, and Ouseley v. Anstruther, 10 Beav. 456.

On the other hand Sir James Wigram, in Shepherd v. Mouls, 4 Hare 500, and my learned brother in Rees v. Williams, 1 DeG. & S. 314, have refused to follow the authority of Hockley v. Bantock, and have acted on the earlier case of Marsh v. Hunter. In

---

a discount. See also Wood v. Davis, 168 Ga. 504; Townsend v. U. S. Trust Co., 3 Redf. (N. Y.) 220; 48 A. L. R. 684.

See Edgerton, Premiums and Discounts in Trust Estates, 31 Harv. L. Rev. 447; 5 St. Louis L. Rev. 134; 8 *id.* 1; Bogert, Trusts, 392; Perry, Trusts, 548a, 548b.

[1] The statement of facts and part of the opinion are omitted.

this irreconcilable conflict of authority, it is absolutely necessary for us to look to the principles on which the doctrine rests.

There can be no doubt but that, where trustees improperly retain balances in their hands, or, by want of due care, cause or permit trust money to be lost, they are chargeable with the sums so retained or lost, and with interest on them at 4*l.* per cent.

It may also be true that, where trustees have in their hands money which they are bound to secure permanently for the benefit of their *cestuis que trustent*, then, in the absence of express authority or direction to the contrary, they are generally bound to invest the money in the 3*l.* per cents. This obligation is not the result of any positive law, but has been imposed on trustees by the court as a convenient rule affording security to the *cestuis que trustent*, and presenting no possible difficulty to the trustees.

Suppose, then, that trustees have improperly retained in their hands balances which they ought to have invested in 3*l.* per cents, either by reason of this general rule of the court, or because such a duty was expressly imposed on them by the terms of the trust, or have by neglect allowed such balances to be lost, what, in such a case, is the right of the *cestuis que trustent?*

In all such cases, or at all events in all such cases where there has been an express trust to invest in 3*l.* per cents, the *cestuis que trustent* have the option of charging the trustee either with the principal sum retained and interest, or with the amount of 3*l.* per cents which would have arisen from the investment if properly made. The doctrine of the court where it applies this rule is, that the trustee shall not profit by his own wrong. If he had done what he was bound to do, a certain amount of 3*l.* per cents would have been forthcoming for the *cestuis que trustent*. And therefore if called on to have such 3*l.* per cents forthcoming, he is bound to do so; just as, in ordinary cases, every wrong-doer is bound to put the party injured, so far as the nature of the case allows, in the same situation in which he would have stood if the wrong had not been done. All this is very intelligible.

Again, suppose the trustee has not only improperly retained balances, but has lent or used them in trade. There the *cestui que trust* has the right, if it is for his interest to do so, to charge the trustee not with the sum retained and interest, but with all the profits made in the trade.

The ground on which this right rests is this. The employment in trade is unwarrantable; but if it turns out to have been profitable the *cestui que trust* has a right to follow the money, as it is said, into the trade. In such a case, the trade profits have in fact been produced by the employment of the money of the *cestui que trust;* and it would be manifestly unjust to permit the trustee to rely on his own misconduct in having exposed the funds to the risks of trade, as a reason for retaining the extra profits beyond interest for his own benefit. Even where no such extra profits have been made the *cestui que trust* is in general at liberty to charge his trustee, who has allowed the trust money to be employed in trade, with interest at 5*l.* per cent, that being the ordinary rate of interest paid on capital in trade. This right depends on principles the same, or nearly the same, as those which enable the *cestui que trust* to adopt the investment, and take the profits actually made.

But the grounds on which, in all these cases, the right of election in the *cestui que trust* rests, wholly fail in a case where a trustee, having an option to invest either in 3*l.* per cents, or on real security, neglects his duty and carelessly leaves the trust funds in some other state of investment. In such a case, the *cestui que trust* cannot say to the trustee: If you had done your duty I should now have had a certain sum of 3*l.* per cents, or the trust fund would now consist of a certain amount of 3*l.* per cents. It is obvious that the trustee might have duly discharged his duty, and yet no such result need have ensued.

Where a man is bound by covenants to do one of two things, and does neither, there in an action by the covenantee, the measure of damage is in general the loss arising by reason of the covenantor having failed to do that which is least, not that which is most beneficial to the covenantee; and the same principle may be applied by analogy to the case of a trustee failing to invest in either of two modes equally lawful by the terms of the trust.

It was contended at the bar that, in such a case, the trustee has by his neglect lost his right of electing between the two modes of investment; that he was always bound by the trust to exercise his discretion in the mode most beneficial for the objects of the trust; and that, having omitted to do so at the time when the option was open to him, he can no longer do it when he is called to account for his neglect, and when he can no longer exercise an unbiassed and impartial option. The fallacy of this argument consists in assuming that, in the case supposed, the trustee is called on to exercise any option at all. He is not called on to exercise an option retrospectively; but is made responsible for not having exercised it at the proper time, for not having made one of two several kinds of investment. And a reason for this being in such case chargeable only with the money which should have been invested, and not with the 3*l.* per cents which might have been purchased, is, that there never was any right in the *cestui que trust* to compel the purchase of 3*l.* per cents. The trustee is answerable for not having done what he was bound to do, and the measure of his responsibility should be what the *cestui que trust* must have been entitled to, in whatever mode that duty was performed.

The ground on which Lord Langdale proceeded in the several cases before him appears to have been that when the trustee has failed to discharge his duty in either of the ways which were open to him, the *cestuis que trustent* may then exercise an option which certainly did not belong to them by the terms of the trust: *i.e.*, that if the trustee has failed to exercise his option, then the right of election passes to the *cestuis que trustent*, although not given to them by the instrument creating the trust. But on what foundation does his supposed right of the *cestuis que trustent* to exercise such an option rest? No such right can be derived from the principle that the *cestuis que trustent* are entitled to compel the trustee to do what he was bound to do, for he was not bound to purchase 3*l.* per cents. Nor from the principle that they may follow the trust funds into their actual state of investment, or charge a higher rate of interest in consequence of such investment, for the foundation of the complaint is, that the funds have not been invested at all. The only plausible foundation for the doctrine which occurs to us is this: The trustee was bound to exercise his option not capriciously, but in the mode likely to be most beneficial to the *cestuis que trustent*. And their interests appear in the result to be best served by requiring an investment in 3*l.* per cents. But this reasoning seems founded on a fallacy. The selection of the 3*l.* per cents is thus made to depend not on any option in their favor which the trustee was originally bound to exercise; but on the accident of their subsequent rise in value, a principle of decision from which, with all deference, we differ. If such a principle were to be applied, then, as it was well put at the bar, if in the present case there had been a discretion to invest in railway shares, the *cestuis que trustent* might perhaps now fix on the shares of some particular railway which have risen very highly in value, and say the investment might have been and so ought to have been, on that particular security.

On the whole, therefore, we cannot discover any such right of option as is contended for in the *cestuis que trustent*, not on the ground of their being entitled by the terms of the trust to compel the trustee to make an investment in 3*l.* per cents, for no such obligation was imposed on him; not on the ground of their being entitled to adopt or insist on any actual investment, for no investment was made; not on the ground of any obligation on the part of the trustees to select the 3*l.* per cents as the most beneficial mode of investment, for the advantage of the 3*l.* per cents arises from their accidental and subsequent rise in value, and not from any necessary superiority at the time when the investment ought to have been made.[1] . . .

[1] See Knott *v.* Cottee, 16 Beav. 77. See also 34 L. Quar. Rev. 168.

If the trustee should have invested in particular securities which rise in value he is accountable for the appreciation. Bate *v.* Hooper, 5 DeG. M. & G. 338; Byrchall *v.* Bradford, 6 Madd. 235; Pride *v.* Fooks, 2 Beav. 430; *Re* Lasak, 20 N. Y. Supp. 74.

If a trustee improperly sells the trust securities, and they rise in value he is accountable for the appreciation. See Piety *v.* Stace, 4 Ves. 620, 622.

In re DEARE.

DEARE *v.* DEARE.

HIGH COURT OF JUSTICE, CHANCERY DIVISION. 1895.

11 T. L. R. 183.

THE TRUSTEES of the testatrix to whose estate this summons related retained for many years after her death some London and St. Katharine's Dock stock and some East and West India Dock stock belonging to her. These stocks were not authorized by her will as investments for her trust estate. She died in 1875. By the retention of these stocks a large loss was incurred, the stocks having greatly fallen in value. The trustees also invested other parts of the trust estate in some African securities, which were equally unauthorized. These stocks greatly improved in value, and a considerable profit thus resulted, exceeding, in fact, the loss upon the dock stocks. The Court was asked to allow a set-off of profit

---

A wrongful retention of improper securities makes the trustee liable for principal and interest if the securities fall in value. Villard *v.* Villard, 219 N. Y. 482.

Interest. A trustee who improperly fails to invest the trust fund or improperly invests or converts it, may be charged with the amount of the trust fund and interest. Mades *v.* Miller, 2 App. D. C. 455; Dunscomb *v.* Dunscomb, 1 Johns Ch. (N. Y.) 508. In England the courts have made a distinction between negligence and misconduct, imposing a greater rate of interest in the latter case. In this country, however, in most of the states, no such distinction is made, but the trustee is charged with the legal rate of interest. Ames 496n. But see Backes *v.* Crane, 87 N. J. Eq. 229.

The usual rule is that the trustee is charged with simple and not compound interest, even though he has converted the trust fund and has mingled it with his own funds. Forbes *v.* Ware, 172 Mass. 306; Ames 498n. But see Cal. Civ. Code, sec. 2262; Mont. Civ. Code, sec. 3014; N. Dak. Comp. L., 1913, sec. 6304; S. Dak. Civ. Code, sec. 1640. If however the trustee has used the trust fund in trade, he is usually charged with compound interest, not, according to the modern view, as a punishment for his misconduct but because of the presumption that he has made as much as compound interest. "In some cases it is said that compound interest is imposed as a penalty, but the more correct view seems to be that it is imposed because in the particular case it has been received, or is presumed to have been received, or ought to have been received, or the circumstances were such that the court was unable to determine whether the person charged had or had not received it, and compelled him to account for it in order to make sure that the *cestuis que trust* received all to which they were entitled." Forbes *v.* Ware, 172 Mass. 306, 309. See also Bobb *v.* Bobb, 89 Mo. 411; Ames 498n. Compound interest is also charged against a trustee who fails to comply with a direction to accumulate the interest on the trust fund. See Ames 498n. See also 29 L. R. A. 622.

Profits. If a trustee has in fact made a profit by the use of the trust fund he will be compelled to hold that profit for the *cestui que trust.* Boston etc. Co. *v.* Reed, 23 Colo. 523; Thompson *v.* Knapp, 223 Mass. 277. See Chap. V, sec. VI, *ante.*

against loss to be made. Out of 15 persons interested in the estate nine, who are *sui juris*, were willing that this should be done. The other six had settled their shares, and the trustees of their settlements could not, therefore, consent to relinquish any right which they had as trustees, but could only submit the point to the Court.

MR. JUSTICE NORTH said that the rule was well settled that a trustee could not set off the profit derived from one breach of trust against the loss resulting from another. This rule was clearly stated by Vice-Chancellor Kindersley in "Wiles *v.* Gresham" (2 Drew, 258). The facts of that case were somewhat different from those of the present case, but the principle of the decision had never been impugned, and it would be very wrong to throw any doubt upon it now. The set-off ought to be allowed in the present case, if it were possible to allow it, for the trustees had done nothing dishonest; they had only made a mistake. But the rule was too clearly settled, and, though with reluctance, his Lordship must hold that the trustees were liable to make good the loss. This would not prevent any one of the beneficiaries who was competent and willing to do so from forgoing his claim against the trustees. His Lordship allowed the costs of all parties of the summons to be paid, as between solicitor and client, out of the trust estate.[1]

BAKER *v.* DISBROW.

SUPREME COURT, NEW YORK, GENERAL TERM. 1879.

18 Hun 29.[2]

APPEAL from a decree by the surrogate of the county of Westchester, entered upon the final settlement of the accounts of the respondents, as executors of Philena Disbrow, deceased.[3]

GILBERT, J.: A breach of trust having been shown, the only question before us is in what way the trustees and executors are to be charged. It appears that up to October, 1871, the unauthorized dealings with the trust funds had produced large profits, but that in

[1] To the same effect, see Adye *v.* Feuilleteau, 3 Swanst. 84n.; Wiles *v.* Gresham, 2 Drew. 258, *aff'd* 5 DeG. M. & G. 770. See also *Ex parte* Lewis, 1 Gl. & J. 69; Dimes *v.* Scott, 4 Russ. 195. See Perry, Trusts, sec. 847; Underhill, Trusts, art. 92; Lewin, Trusts, 954.

[2] Affirmed on the opinion of the General Term, 79 N. Y. 631.

[3] For a detailed statement of the facts, see 5 Redf. Surr. 348. The executors with approximately $4300 of trust funds bought a farm which they later exchanged for a house which they sold. A part of the proceeds was invested in land, a part of which they later exchanged for a second farm which was ultimately sold. Up to the time of the exchange for the second farm the trust fund had reached the sum of $13,450. The subsequent transactions diminished it to about $1400. The surrogate held that the executors were not liable for the intermediate profit.

consequence of similar dealings, after that date, all of those profits and some of the principal of the fund had been lost. The trust was " to invest on good bond and mortgage, or in or upon other good and sufficient security." No particular mode of investment, except upon bond and mortgage, was prescribed. The trustees invested in the purchase of real estate. In such a case the rule seems to be that the *cestui que trust* has his election to take the fund and legal interest thereon, or the fund and all the profits that have been made upon the fund. If the *cestui que trust* elects to take the profits he must take them during the whole period, subject to all the losses of the business; he cannot take profits for one period and interest for another. (Hill on Trusts [2d Am. ed.], 534; Perry on Trusts, §§ 470-472, and cases cited; Heathcote *v.* Hulme, 1 J. & W., 122.) The trustee cannot be charged with a greater amount of profits than he has actually received. (Jones *v.* Foxall, 15 Beav., 388-395; Utica Ins. Co. *v.* Lynch, 11 Pai., 523, *et seq.*) The principle is that, in the management of a trust, the trustee may lose but cannot gain. If by any improper use of the fund profits have been realized, they must be accounted for, and if no profits have been made he is to be charged with the fund and interest thereon. The profits which may have accrued at any particular time are a mere accretion to the fund, and the trustee can be charged with them only upon the ground that he has appropriated them to his own use. If upon an accounting, in respect to the fund during the entire period of the trust, it appears that no profits have been made, the trustee is chargeable with interest only. The improper investment is considered as against the trustee himself, as equivalent to no investment. But in favor of the *cestui que trust* it gives an option to claim either the investment made, or the replacement of the original fund, with interest, according as the one or the other may be most for his benefit. (Lane *v.* Dighton, Amb., 409; Marsh *v.* Hunter, 6 Mad., 295; Robinson *v.* Robinson, 1 DeG., M. & G., 256; Docker *v.* Somes, 2 M. & K., 655; *supra,* cases cited.)

The surrogate appears to have been governed by the rule stated, and his decree should be affirmed, with costs to be paid out of the estate.

BARNARD, P. J., and DYKMAN, J., concurred.

Decree of surrogate affirmed, with costs.[1]

[1] See Heathcote *v.* Hulme, 1 J. & W. 122.

CHAPTER VII.
LIABILITIES TO THIRD PERSONS.

TRINITY COLLEGE IN CAMBRIDGE v. BROWNE.

CHANCERY. 1686.

1 Vern. 441.

THE bill was to discover the best beast of *cestui que trust* of a college lease: the defendant demurred, for that the best beast of the *cestui que trust* could not be taken for a heriot: and it also appeared of the plaintiff's own showing that the tenants, who had the estate in law in them, were yet living.

The demurrer was allowed.[1]

LEWIS v. SWITZ.

UNITED STATES CIRCUIT COURT, NEBRASKA. 1896.

74 Fed. 381.

SHIRAS, District Judge. The plaintiff herein, as receiver of the Buffalo National Bank, seeks to recover judgment against the defendant for the amount of an assessment, levied by the comptroller of the currency, upon the shares of stock held in said bank; it being averred in the petition that the defendant is the owner of 50 shares of the capital stock of the bank, of the par value of $100 per share. The defendant, answering said petition, avers, in substance, that he is not in fact the owner of any shares in said bank; that one Hamer was formerly the owner of the shares; that he had become indebted to the bank; that the president of the bank came to defendant, and stated that the only chance the bank had to protect itself from loss by reason of the debt due the bank from Hamer was to purchase the shares of stock and give him credit on the purchase price for the indebtedness due the bank; that he, on behalf of the bank, desired the defendant to take the shares of stock in trust for the bank, and for its benefit; that defendant agreed to

[1] So the trustee, and not the *cestui que trust* of a copyhold, must pay the fine on admission. Earl of Bath v. Abney, 1 Dick. 260, 1 Burr. 206, s. c.; Londesborough v. Foster, 3 B. & S. 805; Hall v. Bromley, 35 Ch. Div. 642, 655, per Lindley, L. J.: "Admittance and the right to admittance depend upon the legal estate, and the lord can look at that only, and has nothing to do with any equitable devolution of title." — AMES.

By Law of Property Act, 1922, sec. 138, manorial incidents, including heriots, were abolished, the abolition to take effect by 1935.

act as trustee in the manner stated, and in pursuance of this arrangement Hamer surrendered the shares held by him, and new certificates therefor were issued in the name of the defendant; that by a written agreement to that effect he (the defendant) holds the shares in fact as a trustee for the bank, and not in his own right, nor for his own benefit. To this answer plaintiff demurs, on the ground that the facts set forth in the answer do not constitute a defense to the action.

The demurrer to the answer admits the fact to be that the defendant is not the actual owner of the shares of stock standing in his name, but that he holds the same as a trustee for the bank. Section 5152 of the Revised Statutes expressly enacts that " persons holding stock as executors, administrators, guardians or trustees, shall not be personally subject to any liabilities as stockholders [but the estates and funds in their hands shall be liable in like manner and to the same extent as the testator, intestate, ward, or person interested in such trust-funds would be, if living and competent to act and hold the stock in his own name.] " If, therefore, when the new certificates of stock were issued to the defendant, it had been made to appear upon the books of the bank that the defendant took the same, not in his own right, but as a trustee, he could not be held personally liable thereon. The averments of the answer show, however, that the character in which the defendant took the stock was not made to appear upon the bank records; but, on the contrary, the certificates were issued to him in his own name, and upon the books of the bank he was carried as the owner, in fact, of the stock. The general rule is well settled that, if a person knowingly permits his name to be entered upon the stock books of a national bank as the owner of stock therein, he cannot be permitted, as against creditors, to show that, in fact, he was not the owner. Thomp. Corp. §§ 3192–3194; Welles v. Larrabee, 36 Fed. 866; Finn v. Brown, 142 U. S. 56, 12 Sup. Ct. 136. The averments in the answer filed in this case show that the defendant consented to the transfer of the shares of stock to himself. He knew that the new certificates were issued in his own name, and he did not cause the books to show that he held the stock, not in his own right, but as a trustee only. Under these circumstances he is liable to creditors, represented by the receiver, for the assessment levied on the stock.

Demurrer sustained.[1]

[1] Baines v. Babcock, 95 Cal. 581, 593; Hurlburt v. Arthur, 140 Cal. 103 (pledgee); Fell v. Securities Co., 100 Atl. 788 (Del. Ch., 1917); Sherwood v. Illinois Trust & Sav. Bank, 195 Ill. 112; Flynn v. Banking & Trust Co., 104 Me. 141, 154 (pledgee); Kerr v. Urie, 86 Md. 72; American Trust Co. v. Jenkins, 193 N. C. 761; Converse v. Paret, 228 Pa. 156; Kirschler v. Wainwright, 255 Pa. 525; Chapman v. Pettus, 269 S. W. 268 (Tex. Civ. App. 1928), *accord.*

In the following cases the registered owner was held not liable where the

LIABILITY FOR TAXES. If the trustee and the beneficiary are domiciled in the same state and the trust property is situated in that state, it depends upon the provisions of the statute imposing a tax whether the tax is payable by the trustee or by the beneficiary. Ordinarily under statutes imposing upon the owner of land a personal liability for taxes, the trustee is liable. Latrobe v. Mayor, etc. of Baltimore, 19 Md. 13; Ames, 279; Ann. Cas. 1917D 948. Similar statutes as to assessments are generally so construed. City of Bangor v. Peirce, 106 Me. 527.

In People v. State Tax Commission, 244 N. Y. 56, it was held that a statute imposing a tax upon the income of trust estates and providing that the tax should be assessed to the estate and payable by the trustee where the distribution of income is in the discretion of the trustee, but that in the absence of such discretion the tax should be assessed to and payable by the beneficiaries, is not unconstitutional as a denial of equal protection of the law.

If the trustee and beneficiary are domiciled in different states, a question of conflict of laws and of constitutional law arises with reference to jurisdiction to impose a tax.[1]

In Maguire v. Trefry, 253 U. S. 12, aff'g Maguire v. Tax Commissioner, 230 Mass. 503, Massachusetts levied an income tax upon a beneficiary, domiciled in Massachusetts, of a testamentary trust created by a testatrix domiciled in Pennsylvania, of which a Pennsylvania trust company was trustee. The trust property consisted of securities which were in the possession of the trustee in Penn-

---

character of his ownership appeared on the books of the company. Pauly v. State Loan & T. Co., 165 U. S. 606 ("A, pledgee," without stating for whom; *semble*, pledgor liable); Lucas v. Coe, 86 Fed. 972 ("A as trustee for B"); Fowler v. Gowing, 165 Fed. 891; McNair v. Darragh, 31 F.(2d) 906 ("A as trustee for B," A's minor child); Andrew v. City-Commercial Sav. Bank, 205 Iowa 42 ("A, trustee" without stating for whom; in fact A was pledgee, word "trustee" held not mere *descriptio personae*); Smathers v. Bank, 155 N. C. 283 ("A, trustee for B, his wife"); trustee held not liable, beneficiary held liable). But see Union Sav. Bank v. Willard, 4 Cal. App. 690; Flynn v. Banking & Trust Co., 104 Me. 141, 154 ("A, trustee," held *descriptio personae*); Commissioner of Banks v. Tremont Trust Co., 259 Mass. 162.

In the following cases it was held that the beneficiary was liable. Ohio Valley Nat. Bank v. Hulitt, 204 U. S. 162 (shares registered in name of agent); Houghton v. Hubbell, 91 Fed. 453 (like preceding case); Fell v. Securities Co., 100 Atl. 788 (Del. Ch. 1917) (*semble*, directors' qualifying shares); Maddison v. Bryan, 31 N. M. 404.

If the trustee purchases the shares in breach of trust and the beneficiary does not affirm the purchase, the trustee and not the beneficiary or the estate is liable for assessments. Brown v. Midland Nat. Bank, 268 S. W. 226 (Tex. Civ. App. 1925).

See Ames 279n.; 1 Cook, Corporations, 7 ed., secs. 245, 246; 6 Fletcher, Corporations, secs. 4110, 4191–2; 30 L. R. A. (N. S.) 1092.

[1] See McCeney v. County Commissioners, 153 Md. 25, 26 Mich. L. Rev. 458; Hutchins v. Commissioner, 172 N. E. 605 (Mass. 1930), 44 Harv. L. Rev. 475; City of St. Albans v. Avery, 95 Vt. 249, 35 Harv. L. Rev. 94.

sylvania. It was held that the imposition of the tax did not violate the Fourteenth Amendment to the Federal Constitution.

In Safe Deposit & Trust Co. v. Virginia, 280 U. S. 83, Virginia levied a tax upon stocks and bonds held in Maryland by a Maryland trust company in trust for beneficiaries domiciled in Virginia under a trust created *inter vivos* by a resident of Virginia. It was held that this was in violation of the Fourteenth Amendment, since the securities had acquired a situs in Maryland and were beyond the jurisdiction of Virginia to tax. Stone and Brandeis, JJ., concurred upon the ground that the statute did not attempt to tax the equitable interest of the beneficiaries. Holmes, J., dissented.[1]

The problems of taxation are usually treated in a separate course.

DANTZLER v. McINNIS.

SUPREME COURT, ALABAMA. 1907.

151 Ala. 293.

McCLELLAN, J. The action is *assumpsit* against appellants by appellee as surviving partner of the late firm of McInnis & Dantzler. Stating the matter with perhaps undeserved favor to appellee, the asserted right to recover arises out of the fact that the appellee's firm, throughout many years, advanced to Susan A. Loper, who was the trustee of or for appellants of certain real estate in Mobile, and charging the same to her individually on their books of account, various sums of money which was sued for and did pay the taxes due on such real estate. It is the positive duty of a trustee to pay the taxes accruing against the *corpus* of the trust estate; and, if without funds of the estate in his hands, he may advance the necessary funds out of his own to pay the taxes, which, when done by him, becomes a charge on the property. — 2 Beach on Trusts, § 510. The rule is settled in this state that a stranger who makes advancements, or extends credit, or renders services, or furnishes necessaries to trustees, though made in execution of the trust, or to enable them to perform their legal duties under the trust, creates only a personal liability against the trustees. The creditors " can look to them (trustees) only for payment and they (trustees) must look for reimbursement, after making the payment, to the trust estate." [Citing cases.] And it is further settled that (unless otherwise provided by section 4183 *et seq.* of the Code of 1896,

[1] For comments on this case, see 30 Col. L. Rev. 539; 43 Harv. L. Rev. 668; 28 Mich. L. Rev. 776; 78 U. Pa. L. Rev. 532; 15 St. Louis L. Rev. 273; 16 Va. L. Rev. 521; 39 Yale L. Jour. 589. *Cf.* 18 Cal. L. Rev. 638; 40 Yale L. Jour. 99.

As to the liability of the settlor to pay an income tax where the trust is revocable, see Corliss v. Bowers, 281 U. S. 376, 15 Minn. L. Rev. 129.

which is unnecessary to be considered) the trust estate can be made liable in equity by subrogation to the trustee's rights only where the trustee is insolvent, as established by the exhaustion of all legal remedies, and on settlement of his administration the estate is indebted to him, and only then when the advancement or property made or furnished by the creditor has inured to the benefit of the trust estate or to the *cestuis que trust*. [Citing cases.] It results from the principle above announced that the *cestui que trust* is not liable directly, even though he and his estate were beneficiaries of the creditor's funds or property. . . .

There being, then, no liability of appellants enforceable against them in this action, the general affirmative charge requested by them should have been given. The judgment will be reversed, and the cause remanded.

Reversed and remanded.[1]

TYSON, C. J., and DOWDELL and ANDERSON, JJ., concur.

[1] Taylor *v.* Davis' Adm'r, 110 U. S. 330 (*semble*); Everett *v.* Drew, 129 Mass. 150 (*cestui que trust* not undisclosed principal); Truesdale *v.* Philadelphia etc. Ins. Co., 63 Minn. 49; Wells-Stone Mercantile Co. *v.* Grover, 7 N. D. 460; Manhattan Oil Co. *v.* Gill, 118 N. Y. App. Div. 17; Hartley *v.* Phillips, 198 Pa. 9; Gates *v.* Avery, 112 Wis. 271, *accord*.

The trustee is personally liable on contracts made by him for the benefit of the trust estate. Allegheny Tank Car Co. *v.* Culbertson, 288 Fed. 406; Bradner Smith & Co. *v.* Williams, 178 Ill. 420; McGovern *v.* Bennett, 146 Mich. 558; Fay *v.* Day, 106 Neb. 370; Blewitt *v.* Olin, 14 Daly (N. Y.) 351; Mitchell *v.* Whitlock, 121 N. C. 166; Fehlinger *v.* Wood, 134 Pa. 517; Connally *v.* Lyons & Co., 82 Tex. 664. See 40 L. R. A. (N. S.) 201. See also note to Philip Carey Co. *v.* Pingree, 223 Mass. 352, *post*. As to the liability of executors and administrations, see Wild *v.* Davenport, 48 N. J. L. 129; Williams, Executors, 10 ed., pp. 1417 *et seq.*; Woerner, Law of Administration, 3 ed., secs. 328, 356.

The creditor cannot, after obtaining a judgment against the trustee personally, thereupon levy on the trust estate. Jennings *v.* Mather, [1902] 1 K. B. 1; Zehnbar *v.* Spillman, 25 Fla. 591; Hussey *v.* Arnold, 185 Mass. 202; Feldman *v.* Preston, 194 Mich. 352 (attachment); Moore *v.* Stemmons, 119 Mo. App. 162; O'Brien *v.* Jackson, 167 N. Y. 31. See Church *v.* Ferril, 48 Ga. 365 (debt improperly incurred).

The trustee's right of reimbursement and exoneration. The trustee is entitled to reimbursement out of the income or *corpus* of the trust estate (enforceable in equity but not at law, Sayles *v.* Blane, 14 Q. B. 205) when he has discharged liabilities properly incurred by him in administering the trust; and he has a lien on the income and *corpus* of the trust estate to secure his right to reimbursement. Williams *v.* Allen, 32 Beav. 650; *Re* Exhall Coal Co., 35 Beav. 449; Dodds *v.* Tuke, 25 Ch. D. 617; Stott *v.* Milne, 25 Ch. D. 710; Governors *v.* Richardson, [1910] 1 K. B. 271; Woodard *v.* Wright, 82 Cal. 202; Perrine *v.* Newell, 49 N. J. Eq. 57; Turton *v.* Grant, 86 N. J. Eq. 191; Livingston *v.* Newkirk, 3 Johns. Ch. (N. Y.) 312; Matter of Ungrich, 201 N. Y. 415. See Pomeroy, Eq. Juris., sec. 1085; Dec. Dig., Trusts, secs. 224, 236, 310.

The trustee who has incurred but not yet discharged a liability in the administration of the trust, is entitled to exoneration from the trust estate. *Re* National Financial Co., L. R. 3 Ch. 791; Hobbs *v.* Wayet, 36 Ch. D. 256. See also *Re* Richardson, [1911] 2 K. B. 705; Buchan *v.* Ayre, [1915] 2 Ch.

MASON v. POMEROY.

SUPREME JUDICIAL COURT, MASSACHUSETTS. 1890.

151 Mass. 164.

C. ALLEN, J. The late Theodore Pomeroy devised his mills and manufacturing property to three trustees, in trust, to continue and carry on his manufacturing business until his son, Theodore L. Pomeroy, should arrive at the age of twenty-one years. They were to provide for the outstanding and current liabilities, and to incur on account of said trust estate, during the continuance of the trust, such further liabilities as a wise and prudent management might require, and when his said son should become twenty-one years of age to convey the property to the testator's two sons, Silas H.

---

474. In *Re* Blundell, 40 Ch. D. 370, Stirling, J., said: "What is the right of indemnity? I apprehend that in equity, at all events, it is not a right of the trustee to be indemnified only after he has made necessary payments . . . but that he is entitled to be indemnified, not merely against the payments actually made, but against his liability. . . . It seems to me, therefore, that a trustee has a right to resort in the first instance to the trust estate to enable him to make the necessary payments to the persons whom he employs to assist him in the administration of the trust estate; that he is not bound in the first instance to pay those persons out of his own pocket, and then recoup himself out of the trust estate, but that he can properly in the first instance resort to the trust estate, and pay those persons whom he has properly employed the proper remuneration out of the trust estate."

In England it has been held that where the creator of the trust is also the *cestui que trust*, the trustee has a right to reimbursement or exoneration from the *cestui que trust* personally. Balsh v. Hyham, 2 P. Wms. 453; Phene v. Gillan, 5 Hare 1; *Ex parte* Chippendale, 4 DeG. M. & G. 19; Cruse v. Paine, L. R. 6 Eq. 641, L. R. 4 Ch. 441; Lacey v. Hill, L. R. 18 Eq. 182. See Fraser v. Murdock, 6 App. Cas. 855. It has been held that he has this right although the *cestui que trust* is not the creator of the trust. Hardoon v. Belilios, [1901] A. C. 118. In this case Lord Lindley said (p. 123): "The plainest principles of justice require that the *cestui que trust* who gets all the benefit of the property should bear its burdens unless he can shew some good reason why his trustee should bear them himself."

If there are several *cestuis que trust* they may be held *pro rata*. Matthews v. Ruggles-Brise, [1911] 1 Ch. 194.

A *cestui que trust* who disclaims or who is not *sui juris* is not personally liable to reimburse the trustee. Hardoon v. Belilios, [1901] A. C. 118, 123 (*semble*).

It has been held that the trustees of an unincorporated club have no right to reimbursement from the members of the club. Wise v. Perpetual Trustee Co., Ltd., [1903] A. C. 139. See Williams, Club Trustees' Right to Indemnity, 19 L. Quar. Rev. 386. See also 3 Col. L. Rev. 407; 17 Harv. L. Rev. 141; 29 *ibid.* 420. *Cf.* Stikeman v. Flack, 175 N. Y. 512, reversing s. c., 58 N. Y. App. Div. 277. The trustees are entitled to reimbursement from the club property. Minnitt v. Lord Talbot, L. R. Ir. 1 Ch. 143. As to the liability of the trustees of a club, see Brown v. Lewis, 12 T. L. R. 455; Samuel Brothers v. Whetherly, [1908] 1 K. B. 184; Nat. Bank of Scotland v. Shaw, [1913] S. C. 133.

and Theodore L., or in case either one of them should decline to continue in business with the other, then to convey the same to the other upon his paying certain sums to the son who should withdraw; with certain other provisions relating to the termination of the trust not necessary to be recited here. The will further provided, that the trustees should be entitled to a fair and reasonable compensation, and that they should not be liable for any loss to the trust estate which did not involve bad faith on their part, and that at the termination of the trust, and before any transfer or conveyance, they should be fully indemnified against any then existing personal liability incurred in the proper execution of the trust.

The three trustees accepted the trust, and carried on the business together till May, 1885, when, in consequence of disagreements which had arisen among them, it was arranged that thenceforth the business should be carried on by Silas H. Pomeroy, one of the trustees; and this was done under the circumstances which are detailed in the master's report. The son, Theodore L., became twenty-one years of age on November 13, 1887, and the time had thus come for the termination of the trust. A large amount of indebtedness was then existing, some of which was incurred by the three trustees while carrying on the business together, and some by Silas H. Pomeroy while carrying on the business alone. A partnership firm belonging to the latter class of creditors brought the present suit in behalf of themselves and of other similar creditors, averring that the trustees refused to pay their said debts, and that neither of them had property open to attachment or execution, and seeking to establish and enforce an equitable right to have their claims paid out of the trust property, and especially to have enforced in their favor the right of the trustees for reimbursement and indemnity out of the trust fund before its distribution.

The principal questions in the case are raised by the two trustees, Atwater and Turnbull, who withdrew from the active management of the business in 1885, and they contend that the creditors whose debts accrued under the joint management are entitled to a priority over the later creditors, and, indeed, that the present bill cannot be maintained at all by the latter. In support of their demurrer, they rely upon the following propositions: 1. That the plaintiffs have no equity, because they do not offer in the bill to make good to the trust fund the losses and defaults occasioned by the acts of the trustee Silas H. Pomeroy, with whom they contracted, and that their right to the trust fund must be limited by his right to indemnity from that fund. 2. That the plaintiffs' sole remedy is at law. 3. That there has been no previous recovery of judgment by the plaintiffs. 4. That there is no community of interest between the plaintiffs, and that one creditor cannot sue in behalf of all.

The most of these objections are answered by a brief consideration of the nature of the bill. It is in its essential character a bill seeking to enforce the proper execution of a trust, which is ready to be terminated, and in which nothing remains to be done but to transfer the trust property in accordance with the equitable rights of the various parties who assert conflicting claims thereto. It is, indeed, difficult to see how this object can be accomplished in any other way than by a suit in equity. The plaintiffs claim equitable rights in the premises. Their position as creditors entitles them to assert such rights, and to seek the determination of the court whether, on the particular facts of the case, their rights should be sustained. That is to say, where trustees who are authorized to carry on a business contract debts, they are not only liable personally for the payment of them, but the creditors may also resort to the trust fund, subject, however, to the rules of equity, as applicable to the facts and circumstances which may exist in any particular case. [Citing cases.] It is indeed contended on the part of the plaintiffs, that their right to resort to the trust property is a primary and original right, which exists independently of any right on the part of the trustee to be indemnified. Wylly *v.* Collins, 9 Ga. 223. The view, however, which has prevailed in England, so far as the question has been discussed, is that the creditors may reach the trust property when the trustees are entitled to be indemnified therefrom, and that the creditors reach it by being substituted for the trustees, and standing in their place. *In re* Johnson, 15 Ch. D. 548. Dowse *v.* Gorton, 40 Ch. D. 536. It is with reference to this doctrine that the defendants contend that the plaintiffs ought to offer in their bill to make good to the trust fund the losses and defaults occasioned by the acts of Silas H. Pomeroy. But this ground is untenable on the demurrer, because, assuming for the present this doctrine to be correct, and taking the plaintiffs' case upon the lowest ground, the bill sets out the right of the trustees to be indemnified against personal liability incurred in the proper execution of the trust, the existence of such liability to the plaintiffs and others, and the equitable right of the plaintiffs and others to have enforced in their favor for the payment of their claims the rights of the trustees for reimbursement and indemnity; and it asserts a right to have their claims paid out of the trust property and estate in full, or, if such property and estate are insufficient, then to have their claims paid in *pro rata* proportions; and prays that the trustees be held and ordered to account for the trust property, and that an account of the creditors may also be taken, and the equitable interest of Silas H. Pomeroy in the trust estate may be sold and disposed of, and the proceeds applied in payment of the plaintiffs and others. There is no occasion for any distinct offer on the part of the plaintiffs to make good any possible losses to the trust estate arising from his misconduct, if any such there were, since they would only succeed to such rights as he might be found to have. There is no suggestion in the bill of any misconduct or default on his part; but if there were, and if the plaintiffs have no higher right than simply to stand in his place, the bill need not contain any such offer to make good losses in order to entitle the plaintiffs to reach whatever upon an account may be found to remain as a fund from which he would be entitled to be indemnified. The result of such an accounting cannot be anticipated on a demurrer. If it should prove finally that there was nothing to which he was entitled, then the plaintiffs would fail on the merits, unless they should succeed in maintaining their case upon some ground independent of being substituted to the equity of the trustee who contracted the debt to them.

It is not necessary that the plaintiffs who institute such a suit should first have recovered judgment on their claims, or even that their claim should be yet due. Whitmore *v.* Oxborrow, 2 Yo. & Col. Ch. 13. 1 Story, Eq. Jur. § 547. And the usual way is for one creditor to sue in behalf of all. Story, Eq. Pl. § 99. Egberts *v.* Wood, 3 Paige, 517, 520. Hallett *v.* Hallett, 2 Paige, 15. Chapman *v.* Banker & Tradesman Publishing Co. 128 Mass. 478. Thompson *v.* Dunn, L. R. 5 Ch. 573.

We can have no doubt, therefore, that the demurrer to the bill should be overruled. . . .

There has been no accounting in which Pomeroy has been found to be in default, as in the case of *In re* Johnson, before cited; and there is nowhere in the master's report any finding that there has been any loss to the trust estate through any fault of his; much less, that there has been any loss which involved bad faith on his part. We are therefore unable to see that he is in any manner indebted to the trust estate, or that there is any equity existing against him to prevent him from being indemnified out of the trust estate for personal liabilities assumed by him in the conduct of the business.

Nor do we see any good reason for giving to the first class of creditors, whose debts accrued while the three trustees were carrying on the business, a priority over the later creditors, whose debts accrued during the management of Pomeroy. . . .

Decree accordingly.[1]

[1] Fairland *v.* Percy, L. R. 3 P. & D. 217; *Re* Pumfrey, 22 Ch. D. 255; Moore *v.* M'Glynn, [1904] 1 I. R. 334; Faulk *v.* Smith, 168 Ga. 448, 28 Mich. L. Rev. 631; King *v.* Stowell, 211 Mass. 246; Laible *v.* Ferry, 32 N. J. Eq. 791; Paul *v.* Wilson, 79 N. J. Eq. 204; Wells-Stone Mercantile Co. *v.* Aultman, Miller & Co., 9 N. D. 520; Ranzau *v.* Davis, 85 Ore. 26; Cater *v.* Eveleigh, 4 Desaus. Eq. (S. C.) 19; Braun *v.* Braun, 14 Manitoba 346, *accord.*

In Strickland *v.* Symons, 26 Ch. D. 245, the court held that the creditor could not reach the trust estate unless the object of the trust was the carrying on of a business. But this seems inconsistent with *Re* Richardson, [1911] 2 K. B. 705. And see *Re* Pumfrey, 22 Ch. D. 255; O'Neill *v.* McGrorty, [1915] 1 I. R. 1.

If the trustee is in default, the creditor's right to reach the trust estate

596   LIABILITIES TO THIRD PERSONS   [CHAP. VII.

In re RAYBOULD.
RAYBOULD *v.* TURNER.

HIGH COURT OF JUSTICE, CHANCERY DIVISION. 1899.

[1900] 1 Ch. 199.

ADJOURNED SUMMONS.

This was an application for payment of a sum of 1092*l.* and costs out of the estate of the above-named testator, Thomas Raybould, which raised the question of the liability of a testator's estate for the tort of a trustee and executor.

---

through the trustee is cut down or extinguished. *Re* Johnson, 15 Ch. D. 548; *Re* Evans, 34 Ch. D. 597; *Re* British Power etc. Co., [1910] 2 Ch. 470; *Re* Morris, 23 L. R. Ir. 333; Hewitt *v.* Phelps, 105 U. S. 393; Wilson *v.* Fridenberg, 21 Fla. 386; King *v.* Stowell, 211 Mass. 246 (*semble*); Clopton *v.* Gholson, 53 Miss. 466; Norton *v.* Phelps, 54 Miss. 467 (*semble*); Wells-Stone Mercantile Co. *v.* Aultman, Miller & Co., 9 N. D. 520 (*semble*).

But if there are two trustees and only one is in default, the creditor may reach the trust estate. *Re* Frith, [1902] 1 Ch. 342.

If the trustee incurs an unauthorized indebtedness, as for example in continuing the testator's business without authority to do so, the creditor cannot hold the trust estate. Farmers' & Traders' Bk. *v.* Fid. & Dep. Co., 108 Ky. 384; Bauerle *v.* Long, 187 Ill. 475; Lucht *v.* Behrens, 28 Oh. St. 231; Tuttle *v.* First Nat. Bk., 187 Mass. 533; Dunham *v.* Blood, 207 Mass. 512; Donelly *v.* Alden, 229 Mass. 109; Laible *v.* Ferry, 32 N. J. Eq. 791; Welsh *v.* Davis, 3 S. C. 110.

If the trustee pays the creditor with trust money, as the creditor knows, he cannot keep the sum so paid if he knows that the trustee acted wrongfully in incurring the debt. Farmers & Traders' Bk. *v.* Fid. & Dep. Co., 108 Ky. 384; Hines *v.* Levers & Sargent Co., 226 Mass. 214.

If the trustee pays the creditor with trust money, as the creditor knows, he need not refund, although on an accounting the trustee is subsequently proved to be in default to the estate, unless at the time of making the payment the trustee was in default to the estate and the creditor knew that he was in default. *Re* Blundell, 40 Ch. D. 370, 44 Ch. D. 1.

To the extent that the trustee has a right against the *cestui que trust* personally for exoneration (Hardoon *v.* Belilios, [1901] A. C. 118), it would seem that the creditor may reach this right by equitable execution. In Poland *v.* Beal, 192 Mass. 559, the *cestuis que trust* expressly promised the trustee to furnish money to pay for certain property which they requested him to purchase for the benefit of the trust estate. It was held that the vendor could maintain a bill in equity against the *cestuis que trust*. See Williston, Contracts for the Benefit of a Third Person, 15 Harv. L. Rev. 767, 775.

In most jurisdictions the creditor cannot avail himself of the trustee's right to exoneration if the trustee is available and solvent. Owen *v.* Delamere, L. R. 15 Eq. 134; Johnson v. Leman, 131 Ill. 609; Stern Bros. *v.* Hampton, 73 Miss. 555. See also Huselton & Co. *v.* Durie, 77 N. J. Eq. 437; Trotter *v.* Lisman, 199 N. Y. 497. But in Massachusetts, where the exhausting of legal remedies is not a condition precedent to equitable execution (Wilson *v.* Martin-Wilson etc. Co., 151 Mass. 515, 517), it is not necessary to show that the trustee is insolvent. See King *v.* Stowell, 211 Mass. 246.

If the trustee is outside the jurisdiction the creditor may reach the trust

In re RAYBOULD

The facts, so far as material for the purposes of this report, were as follows: —

Cornelius Chambers, the surviving trustee and executor of the above-named testator, in 1892 commenced working one of the testator's collieries, and in so doing he let down the surface of the

---

property. Gates *v.* McClenahan, 124 Iowa 593; Norton *v.* Phelps, 54 Miss. 467. See Field *v.* Wilbur, 49 Vt. 157.

The trustee may agree to forego in whole or in part the right to reimbursement or exoneration. Gillan *v.* Morrison, 1 DeG. & Sm. 421. See *Ex parte* Chippendale, 4 DeG. M. & G. 19, 52. His right may be limited to particular parts of the trust property. *Ex parte* Garland, 10 Ves. 110; Burwell *v.* Mandeville's Ex'r, 2 How. (U. S.) 560; Smith *v.* Ayer, 101 U. S. 320; Fridenburg *v.* Wilson, 20 Fla. 359; Wilson *v.* Fridenberg, 21 Fla. 386. *Cf.* M'Neillie *v.* Acton, 4 DeG. M. & G. 744; Lucht *v.* Behrens, 28 Oh. St. 231. Compare the following cases in which it was held not to be so limited: Blodgett *v.* American Nat. Bk., 49 Conn. 8; Moore *v.* McFall, 263 Ill. 596; Willis *v.* Sharp, 113 N. Y. 586; Davis *v.* Christian, 15 Gratt. (Va.) 11. See O'Neill *v* McGrorty, [1915] 1 I. R. 1, 15; Laible *v.* Ferry, 32 N. J. Eq. 791. Where the trustee's right of reimbursement or exoneration is limited to a part of the trust estate, the creditor can reach only that part of the estate. *Ex parte* Richardson, 3 Madd. 138; *Ex parte* Garland, 10 Ves. 110; Cutbush *v.* Cutbush, 1 Beav. 184; Burwell *v.* Mandeville's Ex'r, 2 How. (U. S.) 560; Pitkin *v.* Pitkin, 7 Conn. 307 (*semble*); Wilson *v.* Fridenberg, 21 Fla. 386; Laible *v.* Ferry, 32 N. J. Eq. 791; Willis *v.* Sharp, 113 N. Y. 586 (*semble*); Lucht *v.* Behrens, 28 Oh. St. 231.

Claims of creditors directly against the trust estate. By the weight of authority ordinarily creditors can reach the trust estate only by a proceeding in equity to reach the trustee's right of exoneration. Thus, it has been held that a creditor cannot reach the trust estate by a proceeding at law or in equity against the trustee in his representative capacity. Hampton *v.* Foster, 127 Fed. 468; Odd Fellows Hall Ass'n *v.* McAllister, 153 Mass. 292; United States Trust Co. *v.* Stanton, 139 N. Y. 531; O'Brien *v.* Jackson, 167 N. Y. 31; Mulrein *v.* Smillie, 25 N. Y. App. Div. 135.

The same result has been reached in the case of contracts made by executors. Farhall *v.* Farhall, L. R. 7 Ch. 123; Taylor *v.* Crook, 136 Ala. 354; Austin *v.* Munro, 47 N. Y. 360; Le Baron *v.* Barker, 143 N. Y. App. Div. 492; Decillis *v.* Mascelli, 152 N. Y. App. Div. 304.

The opposite result has been reached in a few states. Askew *v.* Myrick, 54 Ala. 30 (statutory); Wylly *v.* Collins & Co., 9 Ga. 223; Miller *v.* Smyth, 92 Ga. 154; Sanders *v.* Houston, etc. Co., 107 Ga. 49 (statutory); Mathews *v.* Stephenson, 6 Pa. 496; Manderson's Appeal, 113 Pa. 631; Yerkes *v.* Richards, 170 Pa. 346.

In four states it is provided by statute that "A trustee is a general agent for the trust property. . . . His acts, within the scope of his authority, bind the trust property to the same extent as the acts of an agent bind his principal." Cal. Civ. Code, sec. 2267; Mont. Rev. Code, 1921, sec. 7914; N. D. Comp. L., 1913, sec. 6305; S. D. Comp. L., 1929, sec. 1220. There are statutes also in Alabama, Connecticut and Georgia allowing creditors to proceed against the trust estate. Alabama Code, 1928, sec. 10422; Conn. Gen. Stat., 1930, sec. 5640; Ga. Code, 1926, secs. 3786–91.

There is authority to the effect that the creditor can reach the trust estate by a proceeding against the trustee in his representative capacity where the estate is enriched, although the trustee exceeded his authority in incurring the debt. Thomas *v.* Provident Life & T. Co., 138 Fed. 348; Deery *v.* Hamilton, 41 Iowa 16; *Re* Estate of Manning, 134 Iowa 165; De Concillio *v.*

land, and injured the buildings and machinery of an adjoining owner, Messrs. Roberts & Cooper.

In December, 1898, Messrs. Roberts & Cooper recovered judgment against the trustee, in an action in the Queen's Bench Division, for the amount found by a special referee for damages, together with the costs of the action. The special referee had assessed the damages at 1092*l.*, and Messrs. Roberts & Cooper now claimed to be entitled to be paid this amount and the costs directly out of the testator's estate, and took out this summons for the purpose of enforcing this claim. The colliery had been worked for the benefit of the estate; the evidence as to the method of working was conflicting; though the Court ultimately held that the working had been reasonable and not improper, having regard to the engineering advice obtained by the trustee.

BYRNE, J. This is not an easy case, and it is not made easier by the state of the evidence, which is somewhat conflicting.

The first question I have to consider is whether the same principle ought to be applied to the case of a trustee claiming a right to indemnity for liability for damages for a tort, as is applied to the simpler case of claims made against a trustee by ordinary business creditors, where they have been allowed the benefit of his right to indemnity, by proving directly against the assets: the kind of case of which Dowse *v.* Gorton, [1891] A. C. 190, is a recent illustration. It has been argued that there is no authority to justify me in holding that, where damages have been recovered against a trustee in respect of a tort, the person so recovering can avail himself of the trustee's right to indemnity, and so go direct against the trust estate; but the authority of Benett *v.* Wyndham, 4 D. F. & J. 259, goes to shew that if a trustee in the course of the ordinary management of his testator's estate, either by himself or his agent, does some act whereby some third person is injured, and that third person recovers damages against the trustee in an action for tort, the trustee, if he has acted with due diligence and reasonably, is entitled to be indemnified out of his testator's estate. When once a trustee is entitled to be thus indemnified out of his trust estate, I cannot myself see why the person who has recovered judgment against the trustee should not have the benefit of this right to indemnity and go direct against the trust estate or the assets, as the case may be, just as an ordinary creditor of a business carried on

---

Brownrig, 51 N. J. Eq. 532; Stillman *v.* Holmes, 9 Oh. N. P. (N. s.) 193; Field *v.* Wilbur, 49 Vt. 157. But see Hallock *v.* Smith, 50 Conn. 127; Johnson *v.* Leman, 131 Ill. 609; Austin *v.* Parker, 317 Ill. 348; Laible *v.* Ferry, 32 N. J. Eq. 791. For the Scots law, see Menzies, Trustees, 2 ed., 227.

If in the proper administration of the trust the trustee makes a contract to lease or sell trust property, a suit for specific performance can be maintained against the trustee. Judge *v.* Pfaff, 171 Mass. 195; Cormely *v.* Haggerty, 65 N. J. Eq. 596. But *cf.* Jones *v.* Holladay, 2 App. D. C. 279, 289; Givens *v.* Clem, 107 Va. 435.

CHAP. VII.] *In re* RAYBOULD 599

by a trustee or executor has been allowed to do, instead of having to go through the double process of suing the trustee, recovering the damages from him, and leaving the trustee to recoup himself out of the trust estate. I have the parties interested in defending the trust estate before me, and I have also the trustee, and he claims indemnity, and, assuming that a proper case for indemnifying him is made out by the evidence, I think his claim should be allowed.

The next question I have to decide is whether this trustee has worked the colliery in such a way as to be entitled to be indemnified. Having considered all the evidence, I am not prepared to say that the injury done to the applicants' land was occasioned by reckless or improper working, or otherwise than by the ordinary and reasonable management of the colliery; and I therefore come to the conclusion that the trustee is entitled to be indemnified out of the assets against the damages and costs which he has been ordered to pay to Messrs. Roberts & Cooper. It follows, therefore, for the reasons already given, that Messrs. Roberts & Cooper are entitled to stand in the trustee's place for the purpose of obtaining this indemnity direct from this testator's estate. The result, therefore, is that this summons succeeds.[1]

[1] See *Re* Hunter, 151 Fed. 904; Miller *v.* Smythe, 92 Ga. 154.

A trustee is personally liable in tort to third parties for injuries resulting from the condition of the trust premises. Everett *v.* Foley, 132 Ill. App. 438; Wahl *v.* Schmidt, 307 Ill. 331; Louisville Trust Co. *v.* Morgan, 180 Ky. 609; O'Malley *v.* Gerth, 67 N. J. L. 610; Keating *v.* Stevenson, 21 N. Y. App. Div. 604 (*semble*); Boyd *v.* U. S. Mortgage & T. Co., 84 N. Y. App. Div. 466 (*semble*); Trani *v.* Gerard, 181 N. Y. App. Div. 387; Moniot *v.* Jackson, 40 N. Y. Misc. 197 (*semble*); Gillick *v.* Jackson, 40 N. Y. Misc. 627; Prager *v.* Gordon, 78 Pa. Super. Ct. 76. Similarly he is liable for injuries caused by the negligence of himself or of an agent employed by him. Ballou *v.* Farnum, 9 Allen (Mass.) 47; Baker *v.* Tibbetts, 162 Mass. 468; Parmenter *v.* Barstow, 22 R. I. 245 (*semble*); Sprague *v.* Smith, 29 Vt. 421 (*semble*); O'Toole *v.* Faulkner, 29 Wash. 544. See 63 L. R. A. 227; 7 A. L. R. 408; 14 A. L. R. 371; Dec. Dig., Trusts, sec. 235.

As to the trustee's right of reimbursement, see Matter of Lathers, 137 N. Y. Misc. 226; 43 Harv. L. Rev. 1122.

By the weight of authority the trust estate cannot be reached directly by tort creditors by an action against the trustee in his representative capacity. Wahl *v.* Schmidt, 307 Ill. 331; Moniot *v.* Jackson, 40 N. Y. Misc. 197; Norling *v.* Allee, 13 N. Y. Supp. 791, *aff'd* 131 N. Y. 622; Keating *v.* Stevenson, 21 N. Y. App. Div. 604; Boyd *v.* U. S. Mortgage & T. Co., 84 N. Y. App. Div. 466; Parmenter *v.* Barstow, 22 R. I. 245.

In the following cases, however, where the trustee was not personally at fault the opposite result was reached. Ferrier *v.* Trépannier, 24 Can. Sup. Ct. 86; Ireland *v.* Bowman, 130 Ky. 153; Louisville Trust Co. *v.* Morgan, 180 Ky. 609; Prinz *v.* Lucas, 210 Pa. 620; Ewing *v.* Foley, 280 S. W. 499 (Tex. 1926). See Hegstad *v.* Wysiecki, 178 N. Y. App. Div. 733. See 44 A. L. R. 637.

The *cestui que trust* is not personally liable for torts committed by the trustee. Falardeau *v.* Boston Art Ass'n, 182 Mass. 405.

In Birdsong *v.* Jones, 8 S. W.(2d) 98 (Mo. App. 1928), it was held that where the will under which a trust was created provides that all liabilities

600   LIABILITIES TO THIRD PERSONS   [CHAP. VII.

In re RICHARDSON.

Ex parte THE GOVERNORS OF ST. THOMAS'S HOSPITAL.

[1911] 2 K. B. 705.

COURT OF APPEAL. 1911.

BUCKLEY, L. J.[1] In my judgment the appellants succeed, and are entitled to the declaration asked for by their notice of motion by way of appeal. The sum in dispute is 520*l*. The appellants, who are the governors of St. Thomas's Hospital, were freeholders entitled in reversion expectant on certain leases, and the lessee at the relevant time was Richardson, the husband. Richardson was a trustee for Mrs. Richardson, the wife. The leases came to an end in 1908, and there were then sums due for arrears of rent and for repairs enforceable under the covenants contained in the leases. Richardson, the husband, became bankrupt, and under an order of November 18, 1910, made in the bankruptcy, the governors of St. Thomas's Hospital obtained leave to use the name of the trustee in bankruptcy for the purpose of enforcing against the wife the sum which was due in respect of the rent and arrears, upon terms which included a term that if they should recover any sum from her, either in the name of the trustee or in their own names, they should apply to the Court in bankruptcy to determine whether the sum so recovered should be treated as assets divisible amongst creditors, or should be retained by them on account of the debt and costs due to them from the bankrupt. An action was brought in the joint names of the trustee and the governors of St. Thomas's Hospital against the husband and wife. It was discontinued against the husband and prosecuted against the wife and resulted in a compromise order under which the wife paid 520*l*. The question is how that 520*l*. ought to be disposed of. For brevity I am going to call the creditor (the governors of the hospital) A.; the lessee (the husband) who is entitled to be indemnified B.; and the person (the wife) who is liable to give the indemnity C. When B. became bankrupt in 1910, the right of action which B. had against C. was, I think, property which passed to the trustee in bankruptcy. The only way in which you could say it was not, as it seems to me, would be this: that it was a right of action enforceable by B. only for the benefit of A. If it were, it would be trust

---

incurred in the operation of the trust estate, which included a large newspaper business, should be paid by the trustees out of the estate, a person who was injured as a result of the defective condition of the trust premises could maintain a suit against the successor trustees of the estate, although the original trustees were negligent.

[1] The statement of facts and concurring opinions of Cozens-Hardy, M. R., and Fletcher Moulton, L. J., are omitted.

property and would not pass to the trustee. But that is not the right way to regard it. It is a right of action in B.'s trustee enforceable for the benefit of B. because it is a right of action whose use will relieve B. and B.'s estate from a debt which ought not to be borne by B., but ought to be borne by C. That is the first step. I think that the right of action vested in the trustee. Then what was it that vested in the trustee? It was a right to indemnity. Indemnity is not necessarily given by repayment after payment. Indemnity requires that the party to be indemnified shall never be called upon to pay, and, according to my recollection, the judgments which have been pronounced in Courts of Equity upon rights of indemnity have assumed that form. The one that occurs to me is in Cruse *v.* Paine, L. R. 4 Ch. 441. There B. was the legal owner of shares: C. was the *cestui que trust* of the shares: C. had to indemnify B. The decree was this: " Declare that the defendants are bound to procure the release or discharge of the plaintiff's estate from the calls and let the defendants procure such release or discharge accordingly either by payment of the said calls or otherwise and indemnify his (the plaintiff's) estate against all such costs and charges as aforesaid." Let us work this out. If the sum which the trustee recovers in respect of the right of action (which, I agree, is vested in him) is to be applied for the benefit of the creditors generally, what is the result? Let us suppose that the trustee exercises his right of action and recovers judgment against C. for 520*l.*, and C. satisfies the judgment and B.'s trustee receives the 520*l.* Supposing then B.'s trustee having received the 520*l.* applies it with other money in payment of dividends to the creditors, say 10*s.* in the pound to all creditors of B., A. will receive 10*s.* in the pound like every one else. Subsequently further assets come in. A. of course is entitled to a further dividend, and he calls for a further dividend and receives it. B. can get nothing further from C. because C. has paid everything which he is bound to pay. The result therefore is that B. has not been indemnified. He has had the 520*l.*, but owing to the fact that the sum has not reached its proper destination, namely, the pocket of A., B. or his estate is still liable to A. and can make no further claim against C. Effect is therefore not given to an obligation to indemnify if the sum paid by C. is applied, not in discharge of the obligation due to A., but only partially to that and partially to some other purpose.

That ground seems to me sufficient to dispose of this case. This is an obligation to indemnify. How can effect be given to an obligation to indemnify? Only in one of three ways. If B. has paid the money to A., he may get it back from C. and may put it into his pocket. If B. has not paid the money to A., but calls on C. to pay the money to A., then if C. pays the money to A., B. is never out of pocket at all. In either of those cases B. is indemnified. But lastly, if B. has not paid the money to A. but calls upon

C. to pay the money to him, B., in order that he may pay it to A., then B. is not indemnified if the money is paid, not to A. alone, but to A. and others. According to the view put forward by the trustee in this case B. is not indemnified. The two propositions are perfectly consistent the one with the other, namely, (1.) that the right of action is property vested in the trustee and (2.) that it is a right of action which can only be enforced for giving effect to the contract of indemnity. In that way the estate does get the benefit of the right of action which is vested in the trustee. The trustee having recovered from C. pays A., and thus effect is given to the contract for indemnity. I am not aware of any authority directly in point on this case, but all the cases which have been referred to are perfectly consistent with this view, and in the Stock Exchange cases, of which there have been a good many, I think there are indications, if not decisions, that this is the right view. For these reasons I think that the money recovered from the wife — the 520*l*. — is applicable in paying exclusively that debt against which the trustee is entitled to be indemnified, and therefore that the 520*l*. is payable to the governors of St. Thomas's Hospital.

Appeal allowed.[1]

In re OXLEY.
JOHN HORNBY & SONS *v.* OXLEY.
Court of Appeal. 1914.
[1914] 1 Ch. 604.

Cozens-Hardy, M. R.[2] This is an appeal from a decision of Joyce J., and it raises a point which has been presented to us in very able arguments as one of great difficulty. I am, however, bound to say I do not feel pressed with any of the suggested difficulties. The case is one in which a boilermaker made a will and appointed as executors his widow and one of his sons. The widow was the sole residuary legatee. The estate as sworn to by the executors for the purposes of probate was solvent, and I have not heard anything to satisfy me or even to suggest the probability that the estate was not perfectly solvent at the death. The will contained no provision whatever as to carrying on the business. There was no trust to that effect in the will, but the widow, who was obviously dependent upon what she could get from the business for her

[1] See First Nat. Bank *v.* Thompson, 61 N. J. Eq. 188. As to the right of a creditor on a promise made by a third person to the debtor to pay the debt, see Williston, Contracts, sec. 363. Compare also cases involving the rights of a person injured by another who was insured against liability. 6 Cooley, Briefs on Insurance, 5702; 41 A. L. R. 516.

[2] The statement of facts and a part of the opinion, together with concurring opinions of Buckley and Phillimore, L. JJ., are omitted.

maintenance, carried the business on with the aid of the son who was co-executor and three other sons who were employed in the business and who received wages. The result was that the widow received from 3*l.* to 30*s.* a week, which supported and maintained her until the time arrived in the autumn of 1912 when the executors, who had carried on the business under the style of " Executors of Barker Oxley," got into difficulties, and execution was put in. That was followed by bankruptcy proceedings. It was also followed by an action, which is the one before us, commenced by John Hornby & Sons and J. Utley on behalf of themselves and all other the creditors of the testator against the executors. Now what was that action, and what was the decree that was made in it? It was a common administration decree. The only order that was made was for an account of the assets of the testator. I do not read the form because it is a perfectly well known common form. There is nothing whatever in it about assets which were produced by the trading subsequent to the death. It has nothing whatever to do with that, it is simply a proceeding in which admitted creditors say that there are assets of the testator which are still *bona testatoris* in existence and that they must be applied in payment of their debts. But then it is said that the executors carried on the testator's business for three or four years, and that they did it openly; they traded as executors. The creditors must have known and I assume did know, I think it is proved they did know, that the business was being carried on by the executors; and it is said there is something which entitles the executors to have a lien upon all the assets of the testator to indemnify them against the liabilities which they have incurred in carrying on this business; and it is said first of all that Dowse *v.* Gorton, [1891] A. C. 190, decides this in their favour. Now Dowse *v.* Gorton seems to me to be a case which is very strongly against the application and certainly is not in favour of it. Dowse *v.* Gorton was a case where there was a trust to carry on the business; a trust of course which bound the beneficiaries under the will, bound them to give, not a personal indemnity, but an indemnity out of the estate in favour of the trustees who in the due exercise of that trust carried on the business. Then came the further question, were the creditors bound to give the same indemnity? Had they in fact put themselves in the true legal position of being beneficiaries or *cestuis que trust* under the trust contained in the will? It was held there, in circumstances to which I must briefly refer, that they had put themselves into that position, and that they could not in those proceedings and having regard to the view which they themselves had taken in that action be allowed to approbate and to reprobate at the same time. Now the proceedings there which were taken were by originating summons by one of the true creditors of the testator which asked not merely that all the assets of the testator at the date of the testator's death, but that everything which was in existence at the date when the business ceased to be carried on by the executors, should be applied in payment of the debts of the testator, and in priority to any claim for indemnity by the executors — that is to say, those creditors sought to get the benefit of the subsequent trading without any provision for giving indemnity to the persons who had produced those assets. Now anything more unlike than the present case to Dowse *v.* Gorton I cannot imagine. The plaintiffs here have never claimed the subsequent assets, which have nothing to do with them; they have taken simply a common administration decree. But in Dowse *v.* Gorton the House of Lords, following the Court of Appeal, except in one respect, went into considerations which satisfied the noble Lords that there was an actual assent to the executors carrying on this business for the benefit of the creditors, and that being so it was not difficult to arrive at the conclusion which seems to me inevitably to have followed, that the creditor who had given that assent was in precisely the same position as a beneficiary under the will, and just as a beneficiary under the will could not take the subsequent assets without giving effect to the indemnity, so the creditor who deliberately elected to come in could not get the benefit of the subsequent assets without giving effect to the indemnity. That really is I think the substance of Dowse *v.* Gorton. Lord Macnaghten gave a very elaborate and valuable judgment as to the rights of a creditor of a testator in a case like that, and he points out that if the creditor knows of the trading and is minded to do so he can take proceedings against the executors for a breach of trust for endangering the assets in carrying on the business more than may be required for the necessary disposal of the assets of the business. To me it is quite startling to suggest that a creditor of a testator, having a knowledge of that which he might claim to be a breach of trust, is bound by abstaining from taking proceedings to admit that the business was carried on with his assent and that he for all purposes must be deemed to have assented to that breach of trust. Take any other breach of trust than this. A creditor may know that executors have invested 10,000*l.* forming part of the estate in an improper security which has been lost. Is he to be deemed to have acquiesced in that, and to be debarred from claiming to be paid out of the true assets of the testator's estate which are left after the loss by reason of the breach of trust? I think the proposition really scarcely requires to be more than stated. . . .

The appeal will be dismissed with costs.[1]

[1] *Re* Millard, 72 L. T. N. s. 823; Willis *v.* Sharp, 115 N. Y. 396 (*semble*); Morrow *v.* Morrow, 2 Tenn. Ch. 549, *accord. Cf.* Van Allen *v.* Dorough, 15 F.(2d) 940.

But if the business is carried on with the consent of the testator's creditors

PHILIP CAREY COMPANY v. PINGREE.

SUPREME JUDICIAL COURT, MASSACHUSETTS. 1916.

223 Mass. 352.

CARROLL, J. This is an action for work and material. The defendants are trustees of the Melrose Real Estate Trust. They contend that they are not liable, because the work and material were furnished to the trust and the contract was signed by them not, as individuals, but as trustees. At the trial, against the exception of the plaintiff, the defendants introduced evidence of an oral agreement, made before the written contract was signed, by which the plaintiff agreed not to look to the defendants for payment.

The jury found in answer to a question, that there was no such oral agreement, and also found for the plaintiff. The case is here on a report made by the judge at the request of the defendants, which is in substance, that if no error of law appears, judgment is to be entered for the plaintiff.

The defendants attempted to prove that there was this oral agreement, earlier in date than the written. Even if this evidence were admissible, they cannot now complain of any error of law, since the jury found, as a fact, that there was no such agreement.

By adding the word "trustee" to their names, the defendants did not exempt themselves from personal responsibility, nor did they, by such a signature, provide that the plaintiff was to look solely to the trust estate. Carr v. Leahy, 217 Mass. 438.

According to the terms of the report, judgment is to be entered for the plaintiff, for the sum of $725.71 and interest from the date of the verdict.

So ordered.[1]

---

and for their benefit, the new creditors take precedence over the testator's creditors. *Ex parte* Garland, 10 Ves. 110; Dowse v. Gorton, [1891] A. C. 190; *Re* Hodges, [1899] 1 I. R. 480; *Re* Frith, [1902] 1 Ch. 342. See Brooke v. Brooke, [1894] 2 Ch. 600; Healy v. Oliver, [1918] 1 I. R. 366; Braun v. Braun, 14 Manitoba L. Rep. 346. The result is the same even in the absence of consent of the testator's creditors where the business is carried on temporarily until it can be sold as a going concern. Wright v. Beatty, 2 Alberta 89. *Cf.* O'Neill v. McGrorty, [1915] 1 I. R. 1, 15. See Williams, Executors, 10 ed., 1430, 1554, 1634.

[1] Muir v. City of Glasgow Bk., 4 App. Cas. 337, 352 (*semble*; "as trustee disponees"); Duvall v. Craig, 2 Wheat. (U. S.) 45 ("T, trustee for C"); Taylor v. Davis' Adm'x, 110 U. S. 330 ("T, trustee of C"); Hall v. Jameson, 151 Cal. 606 ("T, trustee"); Knipp v. Bagby, 126 Md. 461 ("T, trustee"); Dunham v. Blood, 207 Mass. 512 ("Estate of C by T, trustee"; trustee contracting without authority); Rosenthal v. Schwartz, 214 Mass. 371 ("T, as he is the administrator of the estate of C"); Carr v. Leahy, 217 Mass. 438 ("T, as trustee"); McGovern v. Bennett, 146 Mich. 558 ("C Estate by T, trustee"); Peterson v. Homan, 44 Minn. 166 ("T, trustee for C"; trustee

JESSUP v. SMITH et al., AS TRUSTEES, et al.

COURT OF APPEALS, NEW YORK. 1918.

223 N. Y. 203.

CARDOZO, J. In October, 1913, George W. Smith was one of the trustees under the will of Samuel J. Tilden. Lewis V. F. Randolph was a co-trustee. The two trustees had power to select a third to fill the vacancy created by the death of John Bigelow. They could not agree upon a choice. They differed also in respect of other problems of administration. A deadlock had been reached, which threatened, as the findings state, the orderly and efficient execution of the trust.

Some of the beneficiaries under the will, in union with Mr. Randolph, began a proceeding in the Supreme Court for the removal of Mr. Smith, and for the appointment of Mr. Cornelius B. Tyler as his successor. They alleged that there was lack of harmony between the trustees which was injuring the estate, and they charged Mr. Smith with inefficiency and misconduct. Upon the service of this petition, Mr. Smith retained the present plaintiff, Mr. Jessup. He told Mr. Jessup that he was poor, and unable to pay the fees of counsel, who would have to look to the estate for payment. The finding is that Mr. Jessup " agreed to accept such retainer, and to render his professional services in the premises on the faith of the trust estate and with knowledge of the poverty of the defendant, George W. Smith, as trustee, and his inability personally to pay for such service."

Under that retainer, Mr. Jessup opposed the application for the removal of his client. He made at the same time a cross-application to appoint a third trustee. In all that he did, he was successful. The application to remove was denied. The cross-application was granted. The Hon. Charles F. MacLean, for many years a

---

contracting without authority); Germania Bk. v. Michaud, 62 Minn. 459 (" Estate of C by T, administrator "); Koken Iron Works v. Kinealy, 86 Mo. App. 199 (" T, trustee "); Pumpelly v. Phelps, 40 N. Y. 59 (" T, trustee "); Whalen v. Ruegamer, 123 N. Y. App. Div. 585 (" T, trustee "); Dunlevie v. Spangenberg, 66 N. Y. Misc. 354 (" T, trustee "); Ogden Ry. Co. v. Wright, 31 Ore. 150 (" T, as trustee of C "); McLeod v. Despain, 49 Ore. 536 (" T, trustee "); Roger Williams Nat. Bk. v. Groton Mfg. Co., 16 R. I. 504 (" T, trustee, estate of C "); McDowell v. Reed, 28 S. C. 466 (" T, trustee "); Moss v. Johnson, 36 S. C. 551 (" T, trustee "); Jordan v. Trice, 6 Yerg. (Tenn.) 479 (" T, as trustee "); Warren v. Harrold, 92 Tex. 417 (" T, assignee "); McIntyre v. Williamson, 72 Vt. 183 (" T, trustee "), *accord.*

In Allegheny Tank Car Co. v. Culbertson, 288 Fed. 406, it was held that the trustees were not relieved of liability because of a provision in the declaration of trust which was of record, where the contract did not stipulate against such liability, and the creditor had no actual knowledge of the terms of the trust.

justice of the Supreme Court, was named as the third trustee. On appeal to the Appellate Division the order was affirmed.

The plaintiff then began this action, joining as defendants all persons interested in the estate, and praying that the value of his services be declared a charge upon the trust, which consists of money and securities. The trial judge found that the services had been rendered; found that the opposition to the attempted removal was just and reasonable; found that the value of the services was $1,750; but held that the services were beneficial to Mr. Smith personally, and not to the estate. Judgment was therefore granted dismissing the complaint. At the Appellate Division, the judgment was affirmed by a divided court. The affirmance was put upon the ground that the contract of retainer bound the client personally. (Ferrin v. Myrick, 41 N. Y. 315; Austin v. Munro, 47 N. Y. 360; Parker v. Day, 155 N. Y. 383; O'Brien v. Jackson, 167 N. Y. 31.) The client, it was held, must pay the counsel fees himself, and seek reimbursement from the estate upon the settlement of his accounts.

We reach a different conclusion. Undoubtedly, the general rule is as the Appellate Division has declared it. But there are exceptions as settled as the rule itself. A trustee who pays his own money for services beneficial to the trust, has a lien for reimbursement. But if he is unable or unwilling to incur liability himself, the law does not leave him helpless. In such circumstances, he " has the power, if other funds fail, to create a charge, equivalent to his own lien for reimbursement, in favor of another by whom the services are rendered." (Schoenherr v. Van Meter, 215 N. Y. 548, 552; New v. Nicoll, 73 N. Y. 127, 131; Noyes v. Blakeman, 6 N. Y. 567; Van Slyke v. Bush, 123 N. Y. 47, 51; O'Brien v. Jackson, supra, 36; Clapp v. Clapp, 44 Hun, 451; Randall v. Dusenbury, 7 J. & S. 174; 63 N. Y. 645.) That is exactly what this trustee assumed to do. He was unable to pay; he explained the situation to the plaintiff; he was exonerated from personal liability; and the acceptance of the retainer was, by express agreement, on the credit of the estate.

The question remains whether the services were beneficial in the preservation of the trust. We have no doubt that they were. Mr. Smith had been named in the will as a trustee. He owed a duty to the estate to stand his ground against unjust attack. He resisted an attempt to wrest the administration of the trust from one selected by the testator and to place it in strange hands. He did more. By his cross-application, he procured the appointment of a third trustee, and broke a deadlock which threatened the safety of the estate. Plainly, such services, if paid for by the trustee personally, would justify reimbursement on his accounting before the surrogate. (Matter of Ordway, 196 N. Y. 95, 98; Matter of Higgins, 80 Misc. Rep. 609; Matter of Assignment of Cadwell's Bank, 89 Iowa, 533,

542; Lycan v. Miller, 56 Mo. App. 79.) That must be because they were beneficial to the trust. But reimbursement on an accounting before the surrogate presupposes payment in advance. (Code Civ. Pro., former sections 2729, 2730, 2810: present sections, 2726, 2731, 2732, 2753; Matter of Blair, 49 App. Div. 417; Matter of Spooner, 86 Hun, 9.) There must, therefore, be some other remedy where such payment is impossible. If that were not so, there would be no safety either for an indigent trustee or for the estate committed to his care. The law is too far-sighted to invite such consequences.

The judgment of the Appellate Division and that of the Special Term should be reversed, and the plaintiff should be decreed to have a lien upon the trust estate for $1,750 with interest from June 8, 1915, and costs in all courts. If any further directions become necessary for the enforcement of the lien, they may be made by the Supreme Court on the application of either party.

HISCOCK, Ch. J., CHASE, HOGAN, POUND and ANDREWS, JJ., concur; McLAUGHLIN, J., not sitting.

Judgment accordingly.[1]

---

[1] A trustee who signs "as trustee but not individually," or otherwise indicates an intention not to be personally bound, is not personally liable. Thayer v. Wendell, 1 Gall. (U. S.) 37; Glenn v. Allison, 58 Md. 527; Shoe & Leather Nat. Bk. v. Dix, 123 Mass. 148; Hussey v. Arnold, 185 Mass. 202 (*semble*); King v. Stowell, 211 Mass. 246 ("Estate of X, by T, trustee"); Rand v. Farquhar, 226 Mass. 91; Adams v. Swig, 234 Mass. 584 (National Realty Co. by T, trustee"); Packard v. Kingman, 109 Mich. 497 (*semble*); Brackett v. Ostrander, 126 N. Y. App. Div. 529. It was held otherwise in Watling v. Lewis, [1911] 1 Ch. 414. See also Furnivall v. Coombes, 5 M. & G. 736. But in Re Robinson's Settlement, [1912] 1 Ch. 717, 728, it was said by the Court of Appeal that the trustee is not liable. Cf. Williams v. Hathaway, 6 Ch. D. 544, where there was a limitation on, but not a total exemption from, personal liability.

As to the liability of the trust estate when the trustee has exempted himself from liability, see Gisborn v. Charter Oak Ins. Co., 142 U. S. 326; Noyes v. Blakeman, 6 N. Y. 567; New v. Nicoll, 73 N. Y. 127; O'Brien v. Jackson, 167 N. Y. 31; Fowler v. Mutual Life Ins. Co., 28 Hun (N. Y.) 195; Wadsworth etc. Co. v. Arnold, 24 R. I. 32. See Bushong v. Taylor, 82 Mo. 660. Cf. Bank of Topeka v. Eaton, 100 Fed. 8, aff'd s. c., 107 Fed. 1003. In King v. Stowell, 211 Mass. 246, it was said that the right of the creditor against the trust estate is dependent upon the trustee's right to exoneration. See Clack v. Holland, 19 Beav. 262.

If the trustee properly mortgages or pledges the trust estate, the creditor has a direct right against the estate. Re Bellinger, [1898] 2 Ch. 534; Gilbert v. Penfield, 124 Cal. 234; Townsend v. Wilson, 77 Conn. 411; Iowa L. & T. Co. v. Holderbaum, 86 Iowa 1; Roberts v. Hale, 124 Iowa 296; Warren v. Pazolt, 203 Mass. 328; Packard v. Kingman, 109 Mich. 497. As to the power of a trustee to mortgage or pledge trust property, see note to Smith v. Mooney, 139 Atl. 513, *ante*.

See Brannan, Negotiable Instruments Law, 4 ed., 176, 331; 42 L. R. A. (N. S.) 1, 156; L. R. A. 1915C 1047.

As to an implied warranty by the trustee that he has authority to bind the trust estate, see Equitable Trust Co. v. Taylor, 330 Ill. 42.

On the subject of the present chapter, see Brandeis, Liability of Trust-

RHODE ISLAND HOSPITAL TRUST CO. v. COPELAND.

SUPREME COURT, RHODE ISLAND. 1916.

39 R. I. 193.

VINCENT, J. This is a bill for instructions by the complainant as executor and trustee under the will of William A. Copeland, late of the city of Providence, deceased.

The bill recites that the complainant in its said capacities holds 625 shares of the so-called preferred stock of the Martin-Copeland Company, and that these shares will probably constitute from eighteen to twenty-two per cent. in value of the residuary trust estate. The Martin-Copeland Company is not a corporation, but is organized and exists by virtue of a written agreement, dated August 8, 1912. . . .

William A. Copeland deceased on March 14, 1913, leaving a last will and testament. By this will the complainant was appointed executor and also trustee under certain trusts thereby created. The property thus placed in trust includes the 625 shares in the Martin-Copeland Company. The complainant duly qualified as executor and has now reached the point in its administration of the estate where it is ready to transfer the residue to itself as trustee.

At this juncture the complainant alleges that it has become uncertain as to some questions involving the interpretation of the agreement of August 8, 1912, under which the Martin-Copeland Company was organized, and especially as to the liability of the holders of the so-called preferred stock thereof; the liability of the trustee when it shall come to hold the same under the trusts imposed by the will of William A. Copeland, and as to the proper management and disposition of such stock by the trustee after it shall have been duly transferred to it, and has formulated its request for instructions as follows: " a. Whether under said agreement the persons interested therein, the holders of the so-called preferred stock, are or are not under individual and personal liability for any of the obligations or indebtedness of the said trust or association, and if so whether the general estate of the said William A. Copeland beyond the amount represented by said shares remains and will remain liable until a transfer of said shares.

" b. Whether your orator as executor or trustee can continue to hold said shares of so-called preferred stock without making itself

---

Estates on Contracts Made for Their Benefit, 15 Amer. L. Rev. 449; Stone, Liability of Trust Estates for the Contracts and Torts of the Trustee, 22 Col. L. Rev. 527; Scott, Liabilities Incurred in the Administration of Trusts, 28 Harv. L. Rev. 725.

liable in its own corporate capacity for any obligation or indebtedness of said trust or association.

" c. Your orator is further in doubt whether, even if it will incur no personal liability under said agreement, it is proper for it to continue to hold as trustee all of said shares of stock or any part of them, or whether it ought to convert into cash the whole or some part thereof and reinvest the proceeds in other trust securities." [1]

The first question to be determined is whether those interested in the business of the Martin-Copeland Company, called stockholders, are personally liable to creditors as copartners. In other words, is the Martin-Copeland Company a copartnership and the several holders of shares therein individually liable for its debts or is it a true trust where such holders are only *cestuis que trustent?*

In considering this question we must first look to the terms of the agreement of August 8, 1912. It is entitled " An Agreement and Declaration of Trust." It commences with a declaration of trust and its further provisions embraced in some forty paragraphs may be briefly summarized.

The name of the company is fixed, provision is made for the issue of shares, preferred and common, to be represented by certificates; the trustees are authorized to acquire, hold and dispose of shares in the same manner as though they were not trustees; the shares are made transferable both by act of the party, owner or by operation of law; the shareholders' rights are defined; title to the property is to be in the trustees only; they are given the most ample powers to deal with the property forming the subject-matter of the trust; they are authorized to make by-laws and regulations; to represent the shareholders in legal proceedings; to indemnify themselves or any of them from the trust property for liabilities incurred in the carrying out of the trust; to determine what is income and what is capital for the purposes of the trust.

The number of trustees is fixed at not more than four. They are authorized to appoint officers; the authority of the officers is outlined; provision is made for the appointment of new trustees and for authority to one or more of the trustees to delegate their powers to another of the trustees. They are authorized to call meetings of the common shareholders at any time they see fit and are required to do so on request of the holders of twenty-five per cent. of the common shares outstanding. Provision is made for the warning of meetings of the common shareholders; for the voting at such meetings by proxy and for share votes, forty per cent. of the outstanding common shares being required for a quorum.

The trustees are empowered to fix the compensation of officers and agents; they are especially prohibited from binding the shareholders personally and the latter are not to be liable for any assess-

[1] A part of the opinion on point " c " is omitted. The court refused to decide this point without further information.

ment. The trustees' acts within the powers conferred by the agreement and declaration are done as trustees and not individually and persons contracting with the trustees are required to look to the fund and not to the trustees personally, nor to the stockholders for payment. No bond is required of any trustee and each is liable only for his own wilful breach of trust. Anyone paying money or other property to the trustees is not required to see to the application of the money or property.

The trustees are given power to declare dividends on both classes of shares, but the amount and payment of them is in the sole discretion of the trustees, except that preferred dividends shall be at the rate of six per cent. per annum, and no more, and they have priority over common dividends. They are empowered also to create a reserve or surplus fund.

Provision is made for amending the agreement and declaration on certain conditions and in a certain manner. The trusts may be terminated by two-thirds vote of the common shareholders and they are limited in any event to twenty-one years after the death of certain identified persons. Thereupon the affairs of the trust are to be wound up in a specified manner.

The respondents have in their brief referred to and commented upon some of the earlier English cases in which the sharing of profits was the test applied in determining whether or not a partnership existed. While these cases are interesting and instructive they do not demand any particular notice at this time.

In the year 1860 the case of Cox v. Hickman, 8 H. of L. 268, after having passed through the inferior courts where the old "sharing profit" test had been applied and a partnership found to exist, reached the House of Lords for final decision. The decision was unanimous. Lord Cranworth said in his opinion: "The liability of one partner for the acts of his co-partner is in truth the liability of a principal for the acts of his agent," and Lord Wensleydale said: "The law as to partnership is undoubtedly a branch of the law of principal and agent; and it would tend to simplify and make more easy the solution, the questions which arise on this subject, if this true principle were more constantly kept in view."

Though the case of Cox v. Hickman may have brought into existence the test of principal and agent as embodied in a judicial decision, such test had long before been suggested for we find in Story on Partnership, Section 1 (1841), "Every partner is an agent of the partnership; and his rights, powers, duties, and obligations, are in many respects, governed by the same rules and principles, as those of an agent. A partner, indeed, virtually embraces the character both of principal and of an agent."

In Cox v. Hickman, Smith & Son, ironmongers, etc., were embarrassed. A creditors' meeting was held. The creditors could force bankruptcy and through a trustee take possession of the plant and business. Instead they elected five trustees, who took over the plant and business and ran the same for the creditors with a provision for its being turned back to Smith & Son when the creditors were paid. Two persons named as trustees, the defendants, who were also creditors, refused to act as trustees. A debt was contracted by the acting trustees. It was represented by a promissory note. The note was not paid. Suit was brought against the defendants to charge them as partners because of their signing the deed and agreeing to take the profits of the business as conducted by the acting trustees and upon this point Lord Cranworth said: " I have hitherto considered the case as it would have stood if the creditors had been merely passively assenting parties to the carrying on of the trade, on the terms that the profits should be applied in liquidation of their demands. But I am aware that in this deed special powers are given to the creditors, which, it was said, showed that they had become partners, even if that had not been the consequence of their concurrence in the previous trust. The powers may be described briefly as, first, a power of determining by a majority in value of their body, that the trade should be discontinued, or, if not discontinued, then secondly, a power of making rules and orders as to its conduct and management.

" These powers do not appear to me to alter the case. The creditors might, by process of law, have obtained possession of the whole of the property. By the earlier provisions of the deed, they consented to abandon that right, and to allow the trade to be carried on by the trustees. The effect of these powers is only to qualify their consent. They stipulate for a right to withdraw it altogether; or, if not, then to impose terms as to the mode in which the trust to which they had agreed should be executed; I do not think that this alters the legal condition of the creditors. The trade did not become a trade carried on for them as principals, because they might have insisted on taking possession of the stock, and so compelling the abandonment of the trade, or because they might have prescribed terms on which alone it should be continued. Any trustee might have refused to act, if he considered the terms prescribed by the auditors to be objectionable. Suppose the deed had stipulated, not that the creditors might order the discontinuance of the trade, or impose terms as to its management, but that some third person might do so, if, on inspecting the accounts, he should deem it advisable; it could not be contended that this would make the creditors partners, if they were not so already; and I can see no difference between stipulating for such a power to be reserved to a third person, and reserving it to themselves." . . .

When we examine the agreement of August 8, 1912, under which the Martin-Copeland Company was organized, in the light of the authorities which we have cited, we cannot escape the conclusion that such agreement evidences both in intention and in law a true trust and not a partnership.

It is therefore our decision that under said agreement, the persons interested therein, the holders of the so-called preferred stock are not under individual and personal liability for any of the obligations or indebtedness of the said trust or association; that the estate of William A. Copeland will not be liable for the obligations or indebtedness of said trust or association, beyond the amount represented by the shares belonging thereto, and that the complainant as executor or trustee can continue to hold said shares of so-called preferred stock without making itself liable in its own corporate capacity for any obligation or indebtedness of said trust or association. . . .

The cause is remanded to the Superior Court with our decision certified thereon for further proceedings.[1]

FARRIGAN v. PEVEAR.

SUPREME JUDICIAL COURT, MASSACHUSETTS. 1906.

193 Mass. 147.

TORT for personal injuries sustained while in the employ of the defendants, the first count alleging that the defendants put the plaintiff to work in an unsafe and dangerous place, and that the defendants knew, or in the exercise of reasonable care might have known, that the place was unsafe and dangerous; the second count making the same allegations and describing the place of danger as a

[1] See Smith v. Anderson, 15 Ch. D. 247; Re Siddall, 29 Ch. D. 1; Schumann-Heink v. Folsom, 328 Ill. 321; Mayo v. Moritz, 151 Mass. 481; Williams v. Milton, 215 Mass. 1; Greco v. Hubbard, 252 Mass. 37; Bouchard v. First People's Trust, 253 Mass. 351; Wells-Stone Mercantile Co. v. Grover, 7 N. D. 460, in which it was held that no partnership or agency was created.

But the beneficiaries may retain such a control over the administration of the trust as to make them partners or principals. Hoadley v. County Commissioners, 105 Mass. 519; Whitman v. Porter, 107 Mass. 522; Phillips v. Blatchford, 137 Mass. 510; Ricker v. American L. & T. Co., 140 Mass. 346; Williams v. Boston, 208 Mass. 497; Frost v. Thompson, 219 Mass. 360; Priestley v. Treasurer, 230 Mass. 452. Cf. Re Associated Trust, 222 Fed. 1012.

On the question whether a provision that the trust shall not be terminated except by a vote of a certain fraction of the certificate holders violates the policy of the Rule against Perpetuities, see Howe v. Morse, 174 Mass. 491. And see Hart v. Seymour, 147 Ill. 598; Pulitzer v. Livingston, 89 Me. 359. See Kales, Estates, secs. 658–661. In some states there are statutes limiting the period during which a trust may continue.

The special problems arising with respect to business trusts are not here considered since they are dealt with in other courses such as those on Partnerships or Business Associations. For a discussion of problems relating to business trusts, see Sears, Trust Estates as Business Companies; 9 Fletcher, Corporations, secs. 6057–6115; Dunn, Business Trusts; Crane & Magruder, Cases on Partnership, ch. 11; Magruder, Position of Shareholders in Business Trusts, 23 Col. L. Rev. 423; Hildebrand, The Massachusetts Trust, 59 Am.

pump pit or well hole in an engine room on the defendants' premises, in close proximity to the exhaust pipe from a gasoline engine from which noxious gases escaped into the pit, and alleging that the plaintiff while at work for the defendants entered the pit by direction of the defendants' agents and was injured by the gases; and the third count alleging failure on the part of the defendants to notify the plaintiff of a danger known to them. Writ dated June 16, 1904.

The answer, in addition to a general denial, alleged that the defendants were trustees of a public charitable institution, and that as individuals they had no interest in the premises where the plaintiff was injured.

In the Superior Court the case was tried before *Pierce*, J. The plaintiff in his opening, in answer to a question from the judge as to the special defence set up in the answer, admitted that the defendants were the trustees, and as such the managers and directors of the Stetson Home, an institution, not incorporated, situated in the town of Barre in the county of Worcester, and so called in memory of the mother of one of the defendants, who was himself the founder and chief benefactor of the institution, which was established and is maintained under a perpetual trust solely for the free and gratuitous education and maintenance of deserving and indigent boys, the entire property and income of the institution being held by the trustees in perpetual trust for that purpose, there being no dividend, profit or emolument whatsoever derived therefrom by or for any of the defendants or any other person.

The plaintiff further admitted that none of the defendants was present when the accident occurred or had knowledge of the incidents or conditions attending the time, place or occasion of the alleged injury to the plaintiff, nor did any of the defendants give, or have knowledge of the giving of any orders or directions by the defendants' agents to the plaintiff in the premises, nor have any participation in or knowledge of the work in which the plaintiff alleged that he was engaged at the time of his injury.

The plaintiff further admitted that there was no personal negligence of the defendants or any of them in the premises " attributable as the proximate cause of the plaintiff's alleged injury," and that if there was any negligence in the premises, causing the alleged injury to the plaintiff, it was that of servants and agents of the defendants, as such trustees, acting in the absence of the defendants and without their knowledge or direction.

L. Rev. 17. See also 7 A. L. R. 612; 10 A. L. R. 887; 31 A. L. R. 851; 35 A. L. R. 502; 46 A. L. R. 169; 58 A. L. R. 518.

For a general discussion of problems relating to trusts for unincorporated associations, see 3 Maitland, Collected Papers, 271–284, 321–404; Smith, Law of Associations; Wertheimer, Law of Clubs, 4 ed.; Wrightington, Unincorporated Associations. See also Laski, The Personality of Associations, 29 Harv. L. Rev. 404.

The judge ordered a verdict for the defendants; and the plaintiff alleged exceptions.

BRALEY, J. The Stetson Home, of which the defendants are trustees, was founded and is maintained under a trust created by gift for the sole purpose of affording an education and maintenance for destitute boys, and whatever advantages the institution offers are conferred without compensation. These distinctive features are ample to bring the home, even if unincorporated, within that class of benevolent institutions whose sole purpose is to furnish relief to destitute and deserving people, and therefore constitutes a valid public charity. . . .

Under the authority of McDonald v. Massachusetts General Hospital, 120 Mass. 432, if the home had been incorporated the plaintiff could not have maintained this action against it, for such a corporation was held in that case not to be liable for the negligence of its servants properly selected when acting in the performance of their prescribed duties. See also Benton v. Boston City Hospital, 140 Mass. 13. Among the reasons given for this exemption it has been said, that being a charitable institution rendering services to the public without pecuniary profit, if the property of the charity was depleted by the payment of damages its usefulness might be either impaired or wholly destroyed, the object of the founder or donors defeated, and charitable gifts discouraged; or that if an individual accepts the benefit of a public charity he thereby enters into a relation which exempts his benefactor from liability for the negligence of servants who are employed in its administration, provided due care has been used in their selection. McDonald v. Massachusetts General Hospital, *ubi supra*. Perry v. House of Refuge, 63 Md. 20. Williamson v. Louisville Industrial School of Reform, 95 Ky. 251. Fire Insurance Patrol v. Boyd, 120 Penn. St. 624. Powers v. Massachusetts Homœopathic Hospital, 109 Fed. Rep. 294, 303. But whatever grounds may have been stated in support of these and other decisions which have held public charities exempt from actions caused by the negligence of attendants or servants, such an exemption may well rest upon the application of the rule of law which makes the principal accountable for the acts of his servant or agent. Accordingly the true inquiry is whether this rule applies to the defendants. They are not shown to have selected incompetent servants, and are conceded not only to have been ignorant of the conditions which caused the alleged injury, but to have given to the plaintiff no instructions; nor can there be imputed to them knowledge in fact of any order given by their agents to him.

By the case of Foreman v. Mayor of Canterbury, L. R. 6 Q. B. 214, following the decision in the leading case of Mersey Docks v. Gibbs, L. R. 1 H. L. 93, it was decided that there was no distinction as to liability for the negligence of servants whether they were employed by a corporation established for a public purpose, or by a private person or corporation. This doctrine was approved and followed in the cases of Glavin v. Rhode Island Hospital, 12 R. I. 411, and of Donaldson v. General Public Hospital, 30 N. B. 279, where a public charity was held liable in tort for damages suffered by patients from the negligence of servants, though subsequently, by the Pub. Laws of R. I. (1880) c. 802, such institutions in that State are now exempt from this measure of liability. The plaintiff's argument in effect asks us to follow the last two cases, which have been decided since our former decision in McDonald v. Massachusetts General Hospital, 120 Mass. 432. But in this Commonwealth the rule of liability enunciated by the principal case has not been so broadly applied, and neither cities and towns in the performance of authorized municipal acts independently of certain exceptions defined by our decisions, nor public officers, although liable in damages for personal acts of negligence which cause injury to the persons or property of others when discharging the duties of their office, are held liable for the misfeasance of their servants. Hill v. Boston, 122 Mass. 344. Tindley v. Salem, 137 Mass. 171. Benton v. Boston City Hospital, *ubi supra*. Rome v. Worcester, 188 Mass. 307. Dickinson v. Boston, 188 Mass. 595, 599, and cases cited. Moynihan v. Todd, 188 Mass. 301, 304–306, and cases cited. Haley v. Boston, 191 Mass. 291, 292. See also 2 Dill. Mun. Corp. (4th ed.) § 974. The reason for this rule is, that acting for the benefit of the public solely in representing a public interest, whether by a municipality or by a public officer, does not involve such a private pecuniary interest as lies at the foundation of the doctrine of *respondeat superior*. While such officers may well be held liable for their personal negligence it would be unreasonable and harsh to hold them responsible for the negligence of their servants or agents.

There would seem to be in principle no sound distinction between an action for negligence by which personal injuries have been received, directly instituted against the charity by the person injured, where its corporate form renders such procedure possible or expedient, and the present case. The object of the charity is the same whether administered by trustees elected by a corporation, or selected and appointed under a deed of gift; and even if the terms of the settlement are not referred to in the exceptions, the trust is stated to be perpetual, and if so its provisions can be enforced in equity. Under either form of administration those who administer the trust act essentially in a representative and not in a private capacity, and such trustees are not within the rule which holds the master liable, because, as we have said, where that rule applies the servant is acting, not only under his orders but also for his benefit, and in the furtherance of the master's business. Farwell v. Boston & Worcester Railroad, 4 Met. 49, 55.

In no correct or just sense can it be said that the defendants were conducting a business, or engaged in an enterprise, from which they received or could expect to derive any monetary advantage or private emolument. They were serving without compensation in the supervision of a home for indigent boys, which was established for the purpose of enabling them to become self-supporting and efficient members of society. Their duty to the plaintiff in the exercise of this function did not extend beyond the requirement of using reasonable care to select competent servants, and the demands of substantial justice are met if as charitable trustees they are not charged with the negligence of those so employed. McDonald v. Massachusetts General Hospital, *ubi supra.*

We are not unmindful that the remedy which the plaintiff may have against a fellow servant for the negligence, if any, which caused the accident may be wholly theoretical and of little practical value, yet we deem it to be in accord, not only with our own decisions but with the weight of authority, to decide that the present action cannot be maintained, and that the ruling directing a verdict for the defendants was right. [Citing cases.]

Exceptions overruled.

GEIGER v. SIMPSON METHODIST-EPISCOPAL CHURCH.

SUPREME COURT, MINNESOTA. 1928.

174 Minn. 389.

OLSEN, C.

Plaintiff recovered a verdict for $3,000 against the defendant as damages for personal injury, claimed to have been caused by negligence on the part of defendant's officers and agents. Defendant had duly moved for a directed verdict and thereafter moved for judgment notwithstanding the verdict, which motions were denied. Judgment was entered, and defendant appealed therefrom.

Defendant is a religious society, a church, incorporated under the laws of this state. It is engaged in the usual benevolent, charitable and religious activities of such a society. It does no business for profit. It is governed by a board of trustees, having general charge of its property, and an official board, consisting of the trustees, the pastor, the heads of the various societies and branches within the church, and certain minor officials and members, having general supervision over the activities and policies of the church.

Plaintiff is a member of this church. At the time of the accident he was a minor official and member of its official board and the teacher and leader of a bible class of young people. The members of this class were having a social meeting, in what is referred to as the dining room, in the basement of the church, and plaintiff was with them as their leader. He attempted to turn or move an upright piano in this room for the purpose of playing upon it for this entertainment. While so doing the piano tipped over and fell upon and broke and otherwise injured plaintiff's leg. The piano was one of a number of such instruments kept and used by the church. It had a broken caster under it at one corner. The evidence sustains a finding that this broken caster caused the piano to tip over. There is evidence that the caster had been in that condition ever since the piano came into the church some six years before; that the caretaker of the church had some trouble in moving the piano soon after it was received and discovered that the caster was broken and that the piano, by reason thereof, had a tendency to tip over on being moved; that he reported the defect and condition of the piano to the trustees, who had general charge of repairs; that the condition of this and other pianos was again reported to the trustees some two years before the accident, and repairs thereto considered; that no repairs were made. Plaintiff testified that he had never examined this piano and did not know that it had a broken caster. Plaintiff claims that the defendant's trustees and officers, having charge of the repair and upkeep of its property, were negligent in failing to have the piano repaired by replacing the broken caster after having notice and knowledge of its defective condition, and that defendant is liable for such alleged negligence. . . .

2. It is contended that this defendant is a charitable institution, to be classed as a privately conducted charity, and that at the time of his injury plaintiff was one of its members and engaged in and a beneficiary of its activities as such; that charitable institutions so conducted are not liable to a beneficiary for negligence of its officers and servants.

Religious societies, such as this defendant, may properly be classified as charitable institutions. [Citing cases.]

If charitable institutions are held exempt from liability for negligence of their officers and servants, religious societies of this kind should properly come within the same class and rule.

3. Coming to the specific question of the exemption of charitable organizations or institutions from liability for negligence of their officers and servants, we find a great diversity of reasoning and adjudication in the numerous decisions in various states. One line of cases holds that these organizations are wholly exempt from liability for such negligence. Another line of cases, apparently the greater in number, holds that these organizations are exempt from such liability to persons who are recipients of their charity or service, who are beneficiaries of the work carried on by the organization. Many of these cases hold that the organization is liable to third persons, who are not beneficiaries, and to its own hired servants and employes on the same basis as private individuals and business corporations. Some cases hold that hospitals and colleges are liable to patients or students who pay full consideration for their treatment or tuition. Others hold that the fact that payment is so received does not make them liable. In many cases it is stated

that such institutions may be held liable for failure to exercise proper care in the selection of officers and servants, and may be held liable for negligently employing incompetent officers and servants, when injury results therefrom.

Different courts give different reasons for the exemption from liability. The following reasons have been given: That the funds of such institutions are held in trust for specific charitable purposes and should not be diverted to pay damages for negligence; that the better public policy is to hold them exempt; that they serve the same purpose as governmental agencies and should come under the same rule; that one who accepts benefits by becoming a patient, student or beneficiary of the institution impliedly consents to hold it exempt or to waive any claim for negligence of its servants; that the doctrine of respondeat superior does not apply to them; that their employes are not, in a legal sense, servants of the organization. Other grounds of exemption have been suggested. All of these reasons have been more or less criticized. . . .

There are comparatively few cases holding unqualifiedly that charitable institutions are liable for the negligence of their officers and servants on the same basis as individuals or corporations generally. Glavin v. R. I. Hospital, 12 R. I. 411, 34 Am. R. 675; Tucker v. Mobile Infirmary Assn., 191 Ala. 572, 68 So. 4, L. R. A. 1915D, 1167; Donaldson v. General Public Hospital, 30 N. B. 279. The Rhode Island case is analyzed and limited to some extent by the later case of Basabo v. Salvation Army, 35 R. I. 22, 85 A. 120, 42 L. R. A. (N. S.) 1144, already cited. The Alabama case goes squarely to the question of liability. That court states [191 Ala. 577]:

"It must be conceded at the outset that the great weight of authority in this country, certainly from a numerical standpoint, lies with the defendant in this case."

The negligence there complained of was that of a hospital nurse in her care of a patient. After citing and reviewing numerous cases holding charitable institutions not liable in like cases, that court concludes that if there is to be exemption from liability it is a matter for the legislature, and not for the court, to grant. It quotes with approval [191 Ala. 602] the following statement from the Glavin case, 12 R. I. 411, 435, 34 Am. R. 675:

"Is it not better and safer for the court to follow out the analogies of the law, and then, if the legislature is of opinion that public policy demands a limitation of this liability, it is in its power to interfere and grant an entire or a partial exemption."

The court further states that it is unable to find a sound legal principle upon which exemption from liability may rest. The New Brunswick case was one of negligence on the part of servants or nurses in a charity hospital in failing properly to care for a patient. The court held that unless the legislature, by express enactment or necessary implication, otherwise provided, the hospital was liable. The New Brunswick case calls attention to the fact that the English cases relied upon in some of the early cases in this country have since been practically overruled and cites the later English cases.

The question was considered in this state in the case of McInerny v. St. Luke's Hospital, 122 Minn. 10, 141 N. W. 837, 46 L. R. A. (N. S.) 548. The injury there was to a hired servant of the hospital and was caused by the failure of the hospital to comply with the statutory requirement to guard dangerous machinery. The case is therefore not directly in point on the facts, as liability might well be based on the fact that plaintiff was a hired servant and not a beneficiary, or on the violation of the statute. The court does however consider the general question of nonliability. The reasoning there expressed, in substance that no good can come from permitting one charitable institution, without liability, to negligently so injure its servants or others that the burden of the future care and maintenance of those so injured must necessarily be cast upon other private or public charitable organizations, does apply here. The court states further that no such situation should be created by any arbitrary rule of exemption unless such exemption is granted by the legislature. The case of Mulliner v. Evangelischer Diakonniessenverein, 144 Minn. 392, 175 N. W. 699, establishes the rule of liability in this state. Defendant there was a charitable corporation. The negligence complained of was the failure of nurses and employes properly to care for a patient. The court, after citing numerous cases holding such institutions not liable in such a situation, adopts the rule of liability in this state as being more just to the persons injured and as best serving the charitable purpose of the institution as well. It states that in the opinion of the court public policy does not favor exemption from liability. In the late cases of Towne and Draayom v. St. Luke's Hospital, 172 Minn. 408, 411, 216 N. W. 221, 222, no question of exemption from liability was raised. These institutions are held to come within the workmen's compensation act in this state. Orcutt v. Trustees of Wesley M. E. Church, 170 Minn. 97, 212 N. W. 173.

We find no valid reason for departing from the rule of the Mulliner case. It is a trite saying that charity begins at home. It may reasonably be said that charitable institutions must first fairly compensate those who are injured and damaged by the negligence of their officers and servants in the conduct of the affairs of such institutions before going further afield to dispense charity and do good. Men and corporations alike are required to be just before being charitable. Charitable, benevolent and religious institutions have been and are doing immeasurable service for the physical and moral welfare of humanity. Such institutions are rapidly growing in number, in resources and influence. They should be encouraged, aided and protected in carrying on their work to the full extent that it may

CHAP. VII.] GEIGER v. SIMPSON METHODIST-EPISCOPAL CHURCH 621

be done without injustice to others. They are generally favored by being relieved, partly or wholly, from the burden of taxation. We do not think it would be good public policy to relieve them from liability for torts or negligence. Where innocent persons suffer through their fault, they should not be exempted. That rule, in the long run, will tend to increased efficiency and benefit them and the public as well as persons so injured. It is almost contradictory to hold that an institution organized to dispense charity shall be charitable and extend aid to others, but shall not compensate or aid those injured by it in carrying on its activities.

No question of diversion of trust funds is presented in this case. In any event, that theory has been so weakened and limited by the decisions that it is not likely hereafter to have much practical application or importance.

4. Defendant claims that the court should have held plaintiff guilty of contributory negligence as a matter of law. Upon the record we do not find any error on that issue. It was a question of fact for the jury.

The judgment appealed from is affirmed.[1]

[1] For comments on the principal case, see 62 Amer. L. Rev. 924; 14 Iowa L. Rev. 212; 27 Mich. L. Rev. 228; 2 U. of Cinn. L. Rev. 443; 15 Va. L. Rev. 58.

In Williams' Admrx. v. Church Home, 223 Ky. 355, it was held that a charitable corporation is not liable in tort although it had procured indemnity insurance.

For cases on the tort liability of charitable organizations, see Zollmann, American Law of Charities, ch. 19; Feezer, Tort Liability of Charities, 77 U. Pa. L. Rev. 191; 8 Cornell L. Quar. 146; 11 Cornell L. Quar. 62; 18 Col. L. Rev. 261; 22 Col. L. Rev. 748; 18 Mich. L. Rev. 539; 19 Mich. L. Rev. 395; 7 N. Y. U. L. Q. Rev. 541; 2 So. Cal. L. Rev. 490; 14 A. L. R. 572; 23 A. L. R. 923; 30 A. L. R. 455; 33 A. L. R. 1369; 42 A. L. R. 971; 62 A. L. R. 724.

CHAPTER VIII.

THE TRANSFER OF THE INTEREST OF THE *CESTUI QUE TRUST.*

BACON, READING ON THE STATUTE OF USES, 16. — For the transferring of uses, there is no case in law whereby an action is transferred, but the *subpoena* in case of use was always assignable.[1]

[1] See Doctor & Student, Dialogue II, c. 22 (1523) *ante;* Y. B. 27 Hen. VIII. fol. 8, pl. 22; Hopkins v. Hopkins, West t. Hardw. 606, 621; Gilbert, Uses, 50. By Stat. 1 Rich. III. c. 1 the *cestui que use* was enabled to pass a legal title.

It was formerly held that in the case of an active trust the *cestui que trust* could not assign his interest. Anon., 6 Jenk. Cent. 244, pl. 30 (1576); Earl of Worcester v. Finch, 4 Inst. 85 (1600). But see *contra,* Warmstrey v. Tanfield, 1 Ch. Rep. 29 (1628).

In the absence of a statute or provision of the trust restraining alienation, the beneficiary can transfer his interest. Brown v. Fletcher, 253 Fed. 15, *certiorari* denied 248 U. S. 569; Merchants' Loan & T. Co. v. Patterson, 308 Ill. 519; Fleming v. Casady, 202 Iowa 1094; Cady v. Tuttle, 127 Me. 104; Estes v. Estes, 267 S. W. 709 (Tex. Comm. App. 1924). See Dec. Dig., Trusts, sec. 147.

As to the validity of a provision restraining alienation, see Brandon v. Robinson, 18 Ves. 429, and Broadway Nat. Bank v. Adams, 133 Mass. 170, *post.*

In Farmers' Loan & Trust Co. v. Winthrop, 238 N. Y. 477, the beneficiary of a trust gave a power of attorney to the trustee under another trust previously created by her authorizing him to receive certain securities from the trustee of the estate of which she was beneficiary, intending that he should hold the securities upon the trust theretofore created by her. She died, however, before the securities were received. The court held that the beneficiary had not made an effective assignment of her interest, since there was no expression of a purpose to effectuate a present gift. Compare Smithwick v. Bank of Corning, 95 Ark. 463, *ante.*

In the absence of a statute or provision of the trust restraining alienation, the beneficiary can mortgage or pledge his interest. First Nat. Bank v. Dougan, 250 Fed. 510; Brown v. Ford, 120 Va. 233. See Dec. Dig., Trusts, sec. 147(2).

An assignment by the beneficiary of his interest is not invalid because gratuitous. See Curriden v. Chandler, 79 N. H. 269, *ante.*

The interest of the beneficiary may be of such a personal character that it is not assignable. Thus, the right to occupy a room in a house or to use land for grazing and pasturage cannot be assigned. Davis v. Harrison, 240 Fed. 97 (*semble*); Cashman v. Bangs, 200 Mass. 498.

If the trustee commits a breach of trust and the beneficiary assigns his interest under the trust, the assignee can hold the trustee liable for the breach of trust. Johns v. Herbert, 2 App. D. C. 485, 500. See *Re* Park Gate, etc. Co. 17 Ch. D. 234; McBurney v. Carson, 99 U. S. 567. On the other hand, an assignment of the mere right to sue for breach of trust is champertous. Hill v. Boyle, L. R. 4 Eq. 260.

ANONYMOUS.

———. 1465.

Y. B. 5 Edw. IV. fol. 7, pl. 16.

IF tenant in borough-English enfeoffed one to the use of him and his heirs, the youngest son shall have the subpœna and not the heir general; [1] likewise if a man makes a feoffment in trust of land descended to him on the maternal side and dies without issue, the heir *ex parte materna* shall have the subpœna.[2]

REX *v.* WILLIAMS.

CHANCERY. 1735.

Bunb. 342.

Two joint purchasers of a lease for years assign this lease to a third person (a friend of one of the jointenants, and with the consent of the other) but it was without consideration, and no declaration of trust was given, and so the defendant confessed in his answer; the jointenant who consented to assign died in debt.

[1] Y. B. 21 Ed. IV. fol. 24, pl. 10; Y. B. 27 Hen. VIII. fol. 9, pl. 22; Jones *v.* Reasbie, 2 Roll. Abr. 780, pl. 7; Fawcet *v.* Lowther, 2 Ves. Sen. 300, 304 (*semble*); Banks *v.* Sutton, 2 P. Wms. 700, 713 (*semble*), *accord.* — AMES.

[2] Burgess *v.* Wheate, 1 Eden 177, 186, 216, 256; Langley *v.* Sneyd, 1 S. & S. 45, 55; Nanson *v.* Barnes, L. R. 7 Eq. 250, *accord.*

"If by a custom of a manor land in fee ought to descend to the eldest daughter only, excluding the other daughters, there being no son, and a trust in equity descends to the heir, this shall go to the eldest daughter only, to be relieved upon this in equity according to the custom for the land. P. 10 Car." 2 Roll. Ab. 780 [D] 7.

In Banks *v.* Sutton, 2 P. Wms. 700, Sir J. Jekyll, M. R., said, p. 713: "That trusts and legal estates are to be governed by the same rules, is a maxim that obtains universally; it is so in the rules of descent, as in gavelkind and borough-English lands, there is a *possessio fratris* of a trust as well as of a legal estate; the like rules in limitations, and also of barring entails of trusts, as of legal estates." See to the same effect Freedman's Co. *v.* Earle, 110 U. S. 710, 713. — AMES.

"A. seised in fee of land in burrough-English makes a feoffment to the use of himself and the heirs males of his body, according to the course of the common law; these words, according to the course of the common law, are void; for customs which go with the land, as this is, and gavelkind, and such-like customs which fix and order the descents of inheritances, can be altered only by Parliament." Anon., 5 Jenk. Cent. Cas., 220, pl. 70.

"It is the maxim of this court that trust estates, which are the creatures of equity, shall be governed by the same rules as legal estates, in order to preserve the uniform rule of property; and that the owner of the trust shall have the same power over the trust as he would have if he had the legal estate for the like interest or extent." Hopkins *v.* Hopkins (1739), West t. Hardw. 606, 618, *per* Lord Hardwicke.

Upon the bill and answer the question was, whether this trust shall result for the benefit of the jointenant surviving only as it would at law; or whether the creditors of the jointenant that died should come in for an equal moiety in equity.

Nota, The trustee was made executor to him that died, and was also a creditor of his.

Nota, The two jointenants continued to receive the profits jointly after the assignment.

Upon this state of the case the whole Court were of opinion that though survivorship is looked upon as odious in equity, yet that in this case the trust shall survive for the benefit of the surviving *cestui que trust* only.[1]

KING *v.* THE EXECUTORS OF SIR JOHN DACCOMBE.

EXCHEQUER. 1618.

Cro. Jac. 512.

KING JAMES made a lease to Sir John Daccombe and others, of the provision of wines for his Majesty's house for ten years, in trust for the Earl of Somerset. They made a lease for all the term except one month, rendering nine hundred pounds a year. The Earl of Somerset being afterwards attainted of felony, the question was, whether the trust which was for the said earl was forfeited to the king by this attainder. And it was referred to all the justices of England, by command from the king, to be considered of, and to certify their opinions.

TANFIELD, Chief Baron, now delivered all their opinions to be, that this trust was forfeited to the king, and that the executor shall be compelled in equity to assign the residue of the term and the rent to the king. And he cited a case to be adjudged, 24 Eliz., where one Birket had taken bond in another's name, and was afterwards outlawed, that the king should have this bond; and that in 24 Eliz., one Armstrong, being lessee for years, assigned the lease to another in trust for himself, and being attainted of felony, this trust was forfeited to the king. But he said they all held, and so it was resolved in another case, [Abington's Case, Hard. 490 (cited)] that a trust in a freehold was not forfeited upon attainder of treason. *Note,* This case I had from the report of Humphrey Davenport, who was of counsel in this case.[2]

[1] Aston *v.* Smallman, 2 Vern. 556; York *v.* Stone, 1 Salk. 158, *accord.* See Pomeroy, Eq. Juris., sec. 408.

In *Re* Michell, [1892] 2 Ch. 87, the interest of a *cestui que trust pur autre vie* passed to a special occupant.

[2] See Ames, 353n., 366n.; Taylor *v.* Haygarth, 14 Sim. 8; Talbot *v.* Jevers, [1917] 2 Ch. 363.

ANONYMOUS.

―――. 1465.

Y. B. 5 Edw. IV. fol. 7, pl. 18.

IF there are lord and tenant, and the tenant enfeoffs one without declaring his will and commits a felony, and is attainted, *quære*, who shall have the subpœna, for the lord shall not have it.[1]

CARPENTER *v.* CARPENTER.
WASBORNE *v.* DOWNES.

CHANCERY. 1686.

1 Vern. 440.

IN these cases it was resolved, that where a common recovery is suffered, or a fine levied by *cestui que trust* in tail, it shall have the same effect, and avail as much in this court, and bind the trust in the same manner as the same would the estate in law in case he had the legal estate in him; and as to a fine, it had never been doubted

―――――――――
[1] See the leading case of Burgess *v.* Wheate, 1 W. Bl. 123, 1 Eden 177, in which the court held, Mansfield, C. J., dissenting, that if the *cestui que trust* of land dies without heirs, the trustee may keep the land. See also Taylor *v.* Haygarth, 14 Sim. 8; King's Att'y *v.* Sands, Freem. C. C. 129; Ames, 364n.; Ames, Lect. Leg. Hist., 197; Hardman, The Law of Escheat, 4 L. Quar. Rev. 318, 330–336. By the Intestates Estates Act, 1884 (47 & 48 Vict. c. 71), sec. 4, it was provided that the law of escheat should apply to equitable interests in land.

In dealing with uses and trusts the Chancellor usually did not follow rules founded upon feudal principles. Thus, it was held that such incidents as relief, wardship (Y. B. 27 Hen. VIII. fol. 8, pl. 22), primer seisin (Jenk. C. C. 190), fine on alienation, as well as escheat, were not applicable to equitable interests. Similarly, rules which derived their force from the technical conception of seisin were held inapplicable to equitable interests. Thus, although at law there could be no overlapping of estates or hiatus between estates, yet shifting and springing uses were allowable. So also although a freehold estate in land could not be devised at common law yet uses were devisable. Maitland, Equity, 26–29; 17 Col. L. Rev. 269, 271–273. See Scott, The Trust as an Instrument of Law Reform, 31 Yale L. Jour. 457.

In the United States if the beneficiary dies intestate without heirs or next of kin, his interest passes to the state. Bogert, Trusts, sec. 111; 1 Woerner, Law of Administration, 3 ed., sec. 133.

In some states by statute if the beneficiary has disappeared for a certain period the court may order his interest disposed of as though he died intestate. De Normandie *v.* Zwinge, 255 Mass. 214.

In some states the interest of an alien beneficiary of a trust of land can be seized by the state. See Cockrill *v.* California, 268 U. S. 258; Isaacs *v.* De Hon, 11 F.(2d) 943. See note to Miller *v.* Davis, 50 Mo. 572, *ante*. As to seizure of the interest of an alien enemy under the Trading with the Enemy Act, see Isenberg *v.* Trent Trust Co., 26 F.(2d) 609. See also Public Trustee *v.* Wolf, [1923] A. C. 544. See 43 Harv. L. Rev. 68.

since the case in the Lord Bridgman's time.[1] And it has been held by some, that even a bargain and sale enrolled by *cestui que trust* of an estate tail should bind the issue, in regard that such a trust is not within the statute *de donis*.[2] . . .

BOTTOMLEY *v.* LORD FAIRFAX.
Chancery. 1712.
Prec. Ch. 336.

In this case it was clearly agreed that if a husband before marriage conveys his estate to trustees and their heirs, in such manner as to put the legal estate out of him, tho' the trust be limited to him and his heirs, that of this trust estate the wife, after his death, shall not be endowed, and that this court hath never yet gone so far as to allow her dower in such case.

WATTS *v.* BALL.
Chancery. 1708.
1 P. Wms. 108.

The case in effect was: One seised of lands in fee had two daughters, and devised his lands to trustees in fee, in trust to pay his debts, and to convey the surplus to his daughters equally.

The younger daughter married and died, leaving an infant son and her husband surviving.

The eldest daughter brought a bill for a partition; and the only question was, whether the husband of the younger daughter should have an estate for life conveyed to him, as tenant by the curtesy?

The husband in his answer had sworn that he married the younger

---

[1] Goodrick *v.* Brown, Freem. C. C. 179, 1 Ch. Ca. 49, 1 Eq. Ca. Abr. 255; Washbourn *v.* Downes, 1 Ch. Ca. 213; Hopkins *v.* Hopkins, West t. Hardw. 606, 621 (*semble*); Brydges *v.* Brydges, 3 Ves. Jr. 120, 127; *Re* White, 7 Ch. D. 201, *accord*.

[2] "Feoffment to the use of one in tail is within the statute *de donis conditionalibus*, as in case Morgan *v.* Manxfield, 19 H. 8, fo. 19." Crompton, Courts, 60. "At common law all inheritable estates were in fee simple, and it was the statute *De Donis* that first gave rise to entails and expectant remainders. As this statute was long prior to the introduction of uses, had equity followed the analogy of the common law only, a trust limited to A and the heirs of his body, and in default of issue to B, would have been construed a fee simple conditional, and the remainder over would have been void; but the known legal estates of the day, whether parcel of the common law or ingrafted by statute, were copied without distinction into the system of trusts, and, equitable entails indisputably existing, the question in constant dispute was, by what process they were to be barred." Lewin, Trusts, 680. As to the methods of barring an equitable entail, equity followed as nearly as possible the analogy of the law. *Ibid.* 680–81. See Ames, 322n.

daughter upon a presumption that she was seised in fee of a legal estate in the moiety; that at the time of the marriage she was in the actual receipt of the profits of such moiety; and it was admitted that this trust was not discovered until after the death of the younger daughter, nor until it was agreed that a partition should be made.

Decreed by LORD CHANCELLOR [COWPER], that trust estates were to be governed by the same rules, and were within the same reason, as legal estates; and as the husband should have been tenant by the curtesy, had it been a legal estate, so should he be of this trust estate; and if there were not the same rules of property in all courts, all things would be, as it were, at sea, and under the greatest uncertainty.

His Lordship added, that this being a case of some difficulty, he could have wished it had not come before him as a cause by consent; but his opinion was, that the husband ought to be tenant by the curtesy, and the rather, because it appeared that he upon his marriage did conceive and presume his wife to be seised of a legal estate in the moiety, and had reason to think so, she being in possession thereof.

Wherefore it was decreed that an estate for life in a moiety in severalty should be conveyed by the trustees to the husband, with remainder in fee to his son.

In this cause, *Mr. How* (who was for the husband) cited the case of Sweetapple *v.* Bindon, 2 Vern. 536, where money was devised to be laid out, for the benefit of a *feme sole* in the purchase of lands in fee; the *feme* married, and had issue, and died, the husband surviving; and decreed in equity that though the money was not invested in a purchase during the life of the wife, yet in regard, in this case, if it had been so laid out the husband would have been tenant by the curtesy, and that this was as land in equity, therefore the husband was equally entitled. . . .

D'ARCY *v.* BLAKE.

CHANCERY, IRELAND. 1805.

2 Sch. & Lef. 387.

IN this case it had been referred to the Master to inquire and report whether the defendant Margaret Blake was entitled to dower out of all or any, and which of the estates of her late husband, if not bound by a certain deed in the plaintiff's bill mentioned. It appeared that the estates in question were let at the time of the marriage upon leases for lives, which continued during the coverture. The Master reported that the defendant was not entitled to dower, to which report the defendant excepted.

LORD CHANCELLOR [REDESDALE]. The general principle on which

courts of equity have proceeded in cases of dower is, that dower is to be considered as a mere legal right; and that equity ought not to create the right where it does not subsist at law; that therefore there can be no dower of an equity of redemption reserved upon a mortgage in fee, though there may of an equity of redemption upon a mortgage for a term of years, because in that case the law gives dower subject to the term. A court of equity will assist a widow by putting a term out of her way, where third persons are not interested. But against a purchaser, a court of equity will not give that assistance, as in Lady Radnor *v*. Vandebendy, Prec. Ch. 65. The difficulty in which the courts of equity have been involved, with respect to dower, I apprehend, originally arose thus: They had assumed as a principle in acting upon trusts, to follow the law; and according to this principle, they ought, in all cases where rights attached on legal estates, to have attached the same rights upon trusts; and consequently to have given dower of an equitable estate. It was found, however, that in cases of dower this principle, if pursued to the utmost, would affect the titles to a large proportion of the estates in the country; for that parties had been acting on the footing of dower, upon a contrary principle, and had supposed that by the creation of a trust the right of dower would be prevented from attaching. Many persons had purchased under this idea; and the country would have been thrown into the utmost confusion if courts of equity had followed their general rule with respect to trusts in the cases of dower. But the same objection did not apply to tenancy by the curtesy; for no person would purchase an estate subject to tenancy by the curtesy, without the concurrence of the person in whom that right was vested. This I take to be the true reason of the distinction between dower and tenancy by the curtesy. It was necessary for the security of purchasers, of mortgagees, and of other persons taking the legal estates, to depart from the general principle in case of dower, but it was not necessary in the case of tenancy by the curtesy. Pending the coverture, a woman could not alien without her husband; and therefore nothing she could do could be understood by a purchaser to affect his interest: but where the husband was seised or entitled in his own right, he had full power of disposing, except so far as dower might attach; and the general opinion having long been that dower was a mere legal right, and that as the existence of a trust estate previously created prevented the right of dower attaching at law, it would also prevent the property from all claim of dower in equity; and many titles depending on this opinion, it was found that it would be mischievous in this instance to the general principle that equity should follow the law; and it has been so long and so clearly settled that a woman should not have dower in equity who is not entitled at law, that it would be shaking everything to attempt to disturb the rule. In point of remedy, a woman claiming dower may be assisted in equity: a court of equity will put out of her way a term which prevents her obtaining possession at law; but that is only as against an heir or volunteer, not a purchaser, the heir or volunteer being considered as claiming in no better right than she does. When, therefore, any question of dower has arisen in courts of equity, and doubts have been entertained of the title to dower, the constant practice in England has been to put the widow to bring her writ of dower at law. The courts will assist her in trying her right, and enjoying the benefit of it, if determined at law in her favor, by giving her a discovery of deeds, by ascertaining metes and bounds; and they do not require her to execute the writ with all the formalities necessary at law; and the right being ascertained by judgment at law, will give her possession according to her right; but still they require that the question of her title to dower, if subject to doubt, should be determined at law. What was thrown out by Sir Joseph Jekyll in Banks *v.* Sutton, 2 P. Wms. 700, has been long overruled. See Cox's note (1), 2 P. Wms. 719. The rule of courts of equity, so far as it excludes a widow from dower of an equitable estate against an heir or volunteer, goes perhaps beyond the reason of the rule. But I have called this subject to my recollection a good deal, by looking into the authorities since this case was first mentioned; and the decisions to the full extent are so old, so strong, and so numerous, so generally adopted in every book on the subject, and so considered as settled law, that it would be very wrong to attempt at this time to alter them. Nor do I think that the doubts which have been suggested with respect to an equitable estate can be fairly raised in this case, where the claim is of dower of estates leased for lives before the marriage, and continuing subject to such leases, at the death of the husband. Of those parts of his estate the late husband of the defendant Margaret Blake was not so seised as to entitle her to dower at law; and if equity were strictly to follow the law, she could have no claim in equity for dower of those estates. He had not such seisin as to entitle her to dower; and the exception must be therefore overruled.[1]

[1] In the old law as to uses it was settled that a widow of the beneficiary was not entitled to dower nor a surviving husband to curtesy. In the case of the modern trust, however, it has been held without the aid of statutes that the husband is entitled to curtesy; but in the absence of a statute it has been generally held that the widow of the *cestui que trust* is not entitled to dower. See Ames, 375n., 380n.; Scott, Cases on Trusts, 1 ed., 593. In the United States by statute a wife is generally given dower in her husband's equitable estates in land. In some of the states she is entitled to dower only if the husband was beneficially entitled on his death; in others she is entitled to dower if he was beneficially entitled at any time during coverture. Scott, 593. See 1 Woerner, Law of Administration, 3 ed., sec. 111; Perry, Trusts, sec. 324; Bogert, Trusts, sec. 111; Herriott, Dower in Trust Estates in Wisconsin, 4 Wis. L. Rev. 92.

MELENKY v. MELEN.

Court of Appeals, New York. 1922.

233 N. Y. 19.

APPEAL, by permission, from an order of the Appellate Division of the Supreme Court in the fourth judicial department, entered July 1, 1921, which reversed an order of Special Term sustaining a demurrer to the complaint and overruled said demurrer.

The following question was certified: " Does the complaint herein state facts sufficient to constitute a cause of action? "

CARDOZO, J. The case is here on a demurrer to the complaint.

In December, 1913, Reuben Melenky conveyed land in the city of Rochester to his son Asher P. Melenky, now Asher P. Melen. The deed was made that the son might manage the property in the absence of the father, and was coupled with an oral promise to reconvey upon demand. In August, 1914, the father married again; and the plaintiff is his wife. Before the marriage, he told her that he was the owner of valuable real estate in Rochester. She relied upon his statement in consenting to the marriage. Four years later, the son, when asked to reconvey, made a deed of an estate for life, but refused to reconvey the fee. The father, under pressure of age, infirmity and want, accepted the deed as tendered. The purpose of the son in retaining the fee was to deprive the plaintiff of her dower. She prays that an inchoate right of dower be established and a reconveyance adjudged. Father and son are joined as defendants. The demurrer is by the son.

" A widow shall be endowed with a third part of all the lands whereof her husband was seized of an estate of inheritance, at any time during the marriage " (Real Property Law, section 190; Consol. Laws, ch. 50). The plaintiff's husband is not seized of such an estate, nor has he been since the conveyance. A different question would be here if the trust had been declared in writing. There would be no need, in such circumstances, of the judgment of a court. The beneficial owner (there being none of the four express trusts) would have the legal estate by force of the mandate of the statute (Real Prop. Law, secs. 92, 93; Wright v. Douglass, 7 N. Y. 564; Murray v. Miller, 178 N. Y. 316, 322; Monypeny v. Monypeny, 202 N. Y. 90, 93). This trust, however, was oral. The statute, far from executing it automatically, pronounced it unenforcible in its creation (Real Prop. Law, sec. 242). True, a court of equity, finding an abuse of confidence, might give relief upon the ground of fraud (Wood v. Rabe, 96 N. Y. 414; Goldsmith v. Goldsmith, 145 N. Y. 313, 318; Ahrens v. Jones, 169 N. Y. 555; Leary v. Corvin, 181 N. Y. 222, 228; Reynolds v. Reynolds, 224 N. Y. 429, 433; Ames, Lectures on Legal History, 425, 429). Even then, its jurisdiction would be exerted to undo rather than to enforce, or to enforce only as a substitute for undoing, since justice might fail if remedies were rigid. Until the entry of a decree, the defrauded grantor is not the owner of an estate. He is the owner of an obligation, a chose in action (Wheeler *v.* Reynolds, 66 N. Y. 227, 236; Ames, *supra;* Hohfeld, Fundamental Legal Conceptions, 24, 106, 108; Pound, 33 Harvard L. R. 420; cf. Real Prop. Law, sec. 100; Schenck *v.* Barnes, 156 N. Y. 316, 321). The right which is his during his life may pass upon his death to his heirs or devisees (Williams *v.* Haddock, 145 N. Y. 144), but it is still "a remedial expedient" (Pound, *supra*). Seizin there is none either "in deed" or "in law" (2 Pollock & Maitland, History of English Law, p. 60; Co. Litt. 31a). Reconveyance does not evidence a seizin continuously retained. It reinstates a seizin that would otherwise be lost.

This grantor has not attempted to enforce his chose in action. He has not asked a court of equity to undo the conveyance and reestablish the divested title. He is willing to let the transaction stand, or unwilling, at all events, to take active measures to annul it. We are now asked to say that the wife may reclaim what the husband would abandon. This means, of course, that the chose in action is not solely his, but is hers also, to the extent of the benefit that would come to her if he had chosen to enforce it. We find no adequate basis for such a conclusion either in principle or in precedent. Decisions, hardly to be distinguished, announce a different ruling (Phelps *v.* Phelps, 143 N. Y. 197; Nichols *v.* Park, 78 App. Div. 95; Leonard *v.* Leonard, 181 Mass. 458, 461). Dower attaches, not to choses in action, but to estates. (Seaman *v.* Harmon, 192 Mass. 5). The law will not create the estate in order to subject it to the incident. This is not a case where the *grantee* has abused a confidence reposed in him by the wife. She was not a party to the conveyance, which was made before the marriage. This is not a case where the *grantor* has attempted by a clandestine transfer of the title to modify the incidents of a marriage about to be contracted (Youngs *v.* Carter, 10 Hun, 194; Bookout *v.* Bookout, 150 Ind. 63). The transfer was made to promote his business convenience, when no marriage was in view. He is not subject to the reproach of plotting a fraud upon his wife (Walker *v.* Walker, 66 N. H. 390; Brownell *v.* Briggs, 173 Mass. 529). No such charge, indeed, is made. The most that can be said is that he is unwilling to assume the burden of seeking redress for a fraud which another has practiced upon *him*. In this, we find no breach of duty. The right of election is his, either to submit or to contend. His wife may not elect for him, nor overrule his choice. One might as well say that while he was yet alive, she could compel the specific performance of a contract of purchase which he was willing to forego (Hawley *v.* James, 5 Paige, 318, 452, 453, 454). The wrong to the husband may be the misfortune of the wife. We think it is nothing more.

The order of the Appellate Division should be reversed, and the interlocutory judgment of the Special Term affirmed, with costs in the Appellate Division and in this court, and the question certified answered in the negative.

HISCOCK, Ch. J., HOGAN, POUND, McLAUGHLIN, CRANE and ANDREWS, JJ., concur.

Order reversed, etc.

WITHAM'S CASE.

CHANCERY. 1590.

Fourth Ins. 87.

WITHAM'S CASE in the chancery was, that a term for years was granted to the use of a *feme sole*, she took husband and died; whether the husband should have the use, or the administrators of the *feme*, was referred to the judges; and by them it is resolved, that the administrators should have it, and not the husband, because that this trust of a *feme* was a thing in privity, and in nature of an action, for which no remedy was but by writ of *subpœna*. And so it was resolved by the justices in Waterhouse's Case, Hil. 8 [38?] Eliz. [Cro. El. 466, Poph. 106.] *Eborum*, for the trust runneth in privity in this case, and a husband should not be tenant by the curtesie of an use, nor the lord of the villain should have it at common law.[1]

WIFE'S SEPARATE ESTATE IN EQUITY. By a most remarkable piece of judicial legislation the courts of equity have held that one who gives a woman an equitable interest may prevent her husband from acquiring rights in that interest corresponding to the legal rights which a husband has at common law in property legally owned by his wife. The legal title might be given to a third person or to the husband as trustee or even to the woman herself, in

[1] Co. Litt. 351a; Anon., Jenk. 6 Cent. 245 pl. 30, Dy. 369a, s. c.; Denie's Case, Lane 113, cited; Hunt v. Baker, Freem. Ch. 62, *accord.*

But in Rex v. Holland (1647), Aleyn 15, Witham's case being cited, "Rolle, J., said that it hath been since resolved that the husband shall have it in that case." See in agreement with the opinion of Rolle, J., *Re* Bellamy, 25 Ch. D. 620; Archer v. Lavender, Ir. R. 9 Eq. 220; 1 Preston, Abst., 343; Lewin, Trusts, [12 ed.], 959]. — AMES.

For a brief summary of the effect of marriage at common law upon a wife's legal interests in property, either in freeholds, chattels real, chattels personal or *choses* in action, see Dicey, Law and Opinion, 2 ed., 372n.

As to what constitutes reduction to possession by the husband of the wife's equitable interest in a *chose* in action, see Elwin v. Williams, 13 Sim. 309; Ames, 388n., 389n.

which last case her husband became trustee for her. In order fully to protect her, a provision restraining alienation by her was also upheld. These holdings revolutionized the position of women, at least women of the well-to-do class. See Dicey, Law and Opinion, 2 ed., 371–395. See also Gray, Restraints, secs. 125 *et seq.*

If an equitable fee simple is given to a woman for her separate use and she dies without having alienated her interest, her husband is entitled to curtesy. Appleton v. Rowley, L. R. 8 Eq. 139; Ames, 383n. On the question whether the creator of the separate use may by express provision exclude the husband from curtesy, see Ames, 383n.

On the question whether a separate use arises in the event of a subsequent marriage, see Robbins v. Smith, 72 Oh. St. 1; Ames, 389–391; Gray, Restraints, sec. 274.

The whole subject is today largely regulated by statute. It is generally dealt with in the course on Persons.

BARTHROP v. WEST.

CHANCERY. 1671.

2 Ch. Rep. 62.

THE PLAINTIFF'S suit is to have the benefit and equity of redemption of leases mortgaged, and other trust estates, made liable for the payment of his debt, being on judgment for 2000*l.*, and to have a voluntary deed of trust set aside, as against the plaintiff.

This court decreed the plaintiff to have the equity of redemption to be liable, and as assets to satisfy his said debt of 2000*l.*, and set aside the said voluntary deed of trust, and all trust estate and surplus thereof after preceding debts paid, to be assets in equity for the payment of the plaintiff.

MARSHALL'S TRUSTEE v. RASH.

COURT OF APPEALS, KENTUCKY. 1888.

87 Ky. 116.

JUDGE LEWIS delivered the opinion of the court.

The second clause of the will of J. B. Marshall is as follows: " All the rest and residue of my estate, of every description, including what is left of my tract of land after laying off said fifty acres to Mrs. Hickman, I give and bequeath, subject to the payment of all my just debts, to my two brothers, Wm. J. Marshall and John H. Marshall, to be divided equally between them, but subject to this condition: that my brother John's part is to be held in trust for him by my brother William, who shall manage and control John's part, and pay him only such part of the proceeds and profits as in his discretion the said William may think best, the intention being to invest William with the legal title to John's part, to be held in trust as aforesaid."

It appears that after the death of the testator a division was made of the land by commissioners, and that part held by Wm. J. Marshall in trust separated from the other. And appellees, creditors of John H. Marshall, instituted their several actions, which were consolidated, to subject his interest in the land so allotted, and in all other property held in trust for him under the will. And whether the judgment for sale of the land to satisfy the debts was proper, is the question now before us.

Section 21, article 1, chapter 63, General Statutes, is as follows: "Estates of every kind held or possessed in trust shall be subject to the debts or charges of the person to whose use or for whose benefit they shall be respectively held or possessed, as they would be subject if those persons owned the like interest in the property held or possessed as they own or shall own in the use or trust thereof." That provision has been the law since 1796, and often construed and applied in cases before this court. . . .

Although a discretion may be given to the trustee in the management and control of the estate, and as to the amount of profits therefrom to be paid, and in the manner of paying them to the person for whose use and benefit it is held, the rights of creditors are not thereby impaired. For such discretion is to be reasonably and in good faith exercised for the benefit of the beneficiary of the estate, and incidentally for the protection of his creditors, and is always subject to the control of a court of equity. . . .

By the will of J. B. Marshall, the estate devised is plainly, in the meaning of the statute, to be held in trust for the use and benefit of John Marshall, and cannot be diverted from that object; but the trust may, if necessary, be enforced by a court of equity, at the instance of the beneficiary, and, as a logical result, the estate may be subjected to payment of his debts.

It does not appear that the debts could have all been satisfied in a reasonable time from the rents and profits, and the court did not, therefore, abuse a sound discretion in directing a sale of the land for that purpose.

Judgment affirmed.[1]

[1] In Showalter *v.* G. H. Nunnelley Co., 201 Ky. 595, a creditor of the beneficiary was allowed to reach his beneficial interest. The trustee was a son of the beneficiary and had refused to apply the income to the payment of the beneficiary's debts. The court held that the proper procedure was to appoint a receiver. Clay, J., said (p. 598): "But it is insisted that the court erred in appointing a receiver in the absence of allegation or proof that the income or profits from the farm in question were in danger of being lost, removed or materially injured. On the other hand, the creditors prosecute a cross appeal and insist that the court should have ordered a sale of appellant's interest in the farm for the purpose of satisfying their claims. It does appear that appel-

CHAP. VIII.] REMEDIES OF CREDITORS OF *Cestui que Trust* 635

REMEDIES OF CREDITORS OF CESTUI QUE TRUST. In the United States as in England, in the absence of a statute, creditors of the *cestui que trust* cannot ordinarily reach his interest by execution at law. Gray, Restraints, secs. 171–173. But in the absence of a statute or provision of the trust restraining alienation, his creditors can reach his interest by a proceeding in equity, called a creditor's bill or bill to reach and apply or bill for equitable execution. First National Bank *v.* Dougan, 250 Fed. 510; Coyne *v.* Plume, 90 Conn. 293; Forbes *v.* Snow, 239 Mass. 138, 245 Mass. 85; Capital Trust & Sav. Bank *v.* Knauft, 172 Minn. 83; Flanagan *v.* Olderog, 226 N. W. 316 (Neb. 1929). See 5 Pomeroy, Eq. Juris., sec. 2302; Ann. Cas. 1914B 945, 950; Dec. Dig., Trusts, sec. 151. As a rule the creditor must exhaust his remedies at law before resorting to a bill for equitable execution. Trotter *v.* Lisman, 199 N. Y. 497; 23 L. R. A. (N.S.) 1. In Massachusetts the rule is otherwise. Barry *v.* Abbot, 100 Mass. 396; Wilson *v.* Martin-Wilson etc. Co., 151 Mass. 515, 517.

The Statute of Frauds, 29 Chas. II, c. 3, sec. 10, permitted a creditor by execution at law to reach the interest of the *cestui que trust;* but the statute was applicable only to passive trusts of real estate. Ames, 437n; Glenn, Creditors' Rights and Remedies, sec. 9. See Judgments Act, 1838, 1 & 2 Vict. c. 110, sec. 11.

The provisions of sec. 10 of the Statute of Frauds were adopted in several states. Gray, Restraints, sec. 174. In many states statutes have gone much further than the Statute of Frauds in subjecting equitable interests to execution at law. See Gray, Restraints, sec. 170; Bogert, Trusts, sec. 112; Scott, Cases on Trusts, 1 ed., 598–9; 37 Yale L. Jour. 1165.

In England in the absence of a statute it was held that a creditor cannot by equitable execution reach the interest of the *cestui que trust* in *choses* in action held in trust. Dundas *v.* Dutens, 1 Ves. Jr. 196, 2 B. & B. 233 (cited). By the weight of authority in the United States, however, it is held otherwise. See 5 Pomeroy, Eq. Juris., sec. 2300; Scott, 600. The English rule was a supposed corol-

---

lant had the power to select the trustee, that he selected his own son, that his son refused to pay the debts in question and mortgaged the produce of the farm. Manifestly, if the control of the land were left in his hands, he could manage it in such a way as to defeat the claims of the creditors. Clearly, the creditors were entitled to some relief, and the only relief available was a sale or the appointment of a receiver. As sales of life estates usually result in a sacrifice of the property, and therefore operate to the prejudice of both creditor and debtor, it is the better practice, we think, to appoint a receiver and not order a sale until after the lapse of a reasonable time, during which the efficacy of the receivership may be fully tested, and as the chancellor adopted this plan, which was more favorable to appellant than an immediate sale of his interest in the property, we perceive no reason for reversing the judgment either on the original or cross appeal."

lary of the rule that a creditor could not reach his debtor's legal interests in *choses* in action. The English rule both as to legal and equitable interests was changed by Judgments Act, 1838, 1 & 2 Vict. c. 110, secs. 12, 14.

On the question whether a judgment creates a lien on equitable interests of the judgment debtor, see Atwater *v.* Manchester Sav. Bank, 45 Minn. 341; Cummings *v.* Duncan, 22 N. D. 534; Fridley *v.* Munson, 46 S. D. 532; 2 Freeman, Judgments, 5 ed., sec. 937; Ann. Cas. 1914B 978; L. R. A. 1915B 340; 30 A. L. R. 504; Dec. Dig., Judgment, sec. 780(2); 7 Minn. L. Rev. 420.

The owner of an equitable interest in land may have a homestead therein exempt from the claims of creditors. Radford *v.* Kachman, 27 Oh. App. 86. See Bogert, Trusts, sec. 111.

FOLY'S CASE.
Chancery. 1679.
Freem. C. C. 49.

The executors of Foly preferred a bill against all the creditors, some being by judgment, some by bond, and some by simple contract; the testator having devised lands to the executors for the payment of his debts; and he had in the first place in his will devised an annuity of 50*l. per ann.* to be paid to his wife.

Lord Chancellor [Nottingham] directed, first, that the lands being devised to his executors, it shall be construed that the testator intended they should be paid in the same order as the law directs; that is to say, that the debts should be first paid before this annuity, which was but a legacy, let the wording of the will be how it will; although it devised the lands charged with this annuity for the payment of debts, yet the debts should have the preference; but he held that the debts of all kinds, whether by judgments, bonds, or simple contract, should be satisfied *pari passu,* and if the value of the land fell short, then that they should be satisfied in proportion, only judgments that did affect the land without any such devise were to have the preference; but a debt by a decree in Chancery should be but in equal degree with debts by bond or contract, because that doth not bind the land until sequestration.

But so far as the personal estate did extend, he ordered that the debts should be paid in that order as the law did direct, and there a debt by a decree in Chancery should have the preference of a bond.

Equitable Assets. If a debtor dies leaving equitable interests in property, these interests are liable for the payment of his debts to the same extent as the corresponding legal interests. Creditors who are entitled to priority out of the legal interests are also entitled to priority out of such equitable interests. It was at one time thought that all equitable interests should be applied to the payment of the testator's debts *pro rata.* See Gray *v.* Colvile, 2 Ch. Rep. 143, 1 Vern. 172; Creditors of Cox, 3 P. Wms. 341; Ames, 435n, 438n. But the principle that equity follows the law finally triumphed in the courts and was recognized by the Statute of Frauds, sec. 10.

Quite different however is the principle governing " equitable assets " properly so called. " Ordinarily and strictly, the term, *equitable assets,* applies only to property and funds belonging to the estate of a decedent, which by law are not subject to payment of debts, in the course of administration by the personal representatives, but which the testator has voluntarily charged with the payment of debts generally, or which, being non-existent at law, have been created in equity, under circumstances which fasten upon them such a trust." Freedman's Co. *v.* Earle, 110 U. S. 710, 717. Such assets are applied *pro rata* to the payment of the decedent's debts. See Maitland, Equity, 199–201, quoted Warren, Cas. Wills, 666; Ames, 438n. By Administration of Estates Act, 1925, 15 Geo. V. c. 23, sec. 32, all real and personal property, legal or equitable of a deceased person, is made assets for the payment of debts.

The doctrine of equitable assets is of slight consequence in this country because, in the first place, the testator's lands as well as personalty can be reached by his creditors; and, secondly, priorities among different classes of creditors are largely abolished. See 4 Gray, Cas. Prop., 2 ed., 558.

BRANDON *v.* ROBINSON.

CHANCERY. 1811.

18 Ves. 429.

THE bill stated that Stephen Goom, by his will, dated the 1st of August, 1808, devised and bequeathed to the defendants Robinson and Davies all his real and personal estates upon trust to sell, and to divide or otherwise apply the produce to the use of all and every his child or children, living at his decease, in equal proportions; deducting from the share of Thomas Goom the sum of 500*l.* which had been advanced to him, and from the share of William Goom what should be due from him to the testator at his decease, — the said sums so to be deducted to be divided equally among the other children; and he declared his will, that the said several legacies, shares, and eventual interests of such of the legatees as at the time of his decease should have attained the age of twenty-one should be considered as vested interests; and, if there should be but one survivor, upon trust to pay and transfer the same unto such only survivor, his or her executors, &c., for his or her own use, subject nevertheless to such directions as after mentioned in respect to the shares or interests of such of the said legatees as were females, and also in respect to the share and interest of the said Thomas Goom; and he directed that the eventual share and interest of his said son Thomas Goom, of and in his estate and effects, or the produce thereof, should be laid out in the public funds or in government securities at interest by and in the names of his said trustees, &c., during his life; and that the dividends, interest, and produce thereof, as the same became due and payable, should be paid by them from time to time into his own proper hands, or on his proper order and receipt, subscribed with his own proper hand, to the intent the same should not be grantable, transferable, or otherwise assignable, by way of anticipation of any unreceived payment or payments thereof, or of any part thereof; and that upon his decease the principal of such share, together with the dividends and interest and produce thereof, should be paid and applied by his trustees or executors, their heirs, executors, &c., unto and amongst such person or persons as in a course of administration would become entitled to any personal estate of his said son Thomas Goom, and as if the same had been personal estate belonging to him, and he had died intestate.

The bill further stated, that after the death of the testator his son Thomas Goom, having attained the age of twenty-one, became a bankrupt. The plaintiff was the surviving assignee under the commission; and the bill prayed an execution of the trusts of the will and an account, that the estates may be sold, and the clear residue ascertained, and that the plaintiff may receive the benefit of such part or share thereof, or of the interest therein, as he shall be entitled to as assignee under the commission.

To this bill the defendants, the trustees, put in a general demurrer.

Mr. Leach and *Mr. Roupell*, for the plaintiff, gave up the claim to the principal. . . .

THE LORD CHANCELLOR [ELDON]. There is no doubt that property may be given to a man until he shall become bankrupt. It is equally clear, generally speaking, that if property is given to a man for his life, the donor cannot take away the incidents to a life-estate; and, as I have observed, a disposition to a man until he shall become bankrupt, and after his bankruptcy over, is quite different from an attempt to give to him for his life, with a proviso that he shall not sell or alien it. If that condition is so expressed as to amount to a limitation, reducing the interest short of a life-estate, neither the man nor his assignees can have it beyond the period limited.

In the case of Foley *v.* Burnell, 1 Bro. C. C. 274, this question afforded much argument. A great variety of clauses and means was adopted by Lord Foley with the view of depriving the creditors of his sons of any resort to their property; but it was argued here, and, as I thought, admitted, that if the property was given to the sons, it must remain subject to the incidents of property, and it could not be preserved from the creditors, unless given to some one else.

So the old way of expressing a trust for a married woman was, that the trustees should pay into her proper hands, and upon her own receipt only; yet this court always said she might dispose of that interest, (Pybus v. Smith, 1 Ves. Jr. 189; 3 Bro. C. C. 340. See the notes, 1 Ves. Jr. 194; 5 Ves. 17), and her assignee would take it; as, if there was a contract, entitling the assignee, this court would compel her to give her own receipt, if that was necessary to enable him to receive it. It was not before Miss Watson's Case that these words, " not to be paid by anticipation," &c., were introduced. I believe these were Lord Thurlow's own words, with whom I had much conversation upon it. He did not attempt to take away any power the law gave her, as incident to property, which, being a creature of equity, she could not have at law; but as under the words of the settlement it would have been hers absolutely, so that she could alien, Lord Thurlow endeavored to prevent that by imposing upon the trustees the necessity of paying to her from time to time, and not by anticipation; reasoning thus, that equity, making her the owner of it, and enabling her, as a married woman, to alien, might limit her power over it: but the case of a disposition to a man, who, if he has the property, has the power of aliening, is quite different.

This is a singular trust. If upon these words it can be established that he had no interest, until he tenders himself personally to the trustees to give a receipt, then it was not his property until then; but if personal receipt is in the construction of this court a necessary act, it is very difficult to maintain that if the bankrupt would not give a receipt during his life, and an arrear of interest accrued during his whole life, it would not be assets for his debts. It clearly would be so.

Next, is there in this will enough to show that, as this interest is not assignable by way of anticipation of any unreceived payment, therefore it cannot be assigned and transferred under the commission of bankruptcy? To prevent that it must be given to some one else; and unless it can be established that this by implication amounts to a limitation, giving this interest to the residuary legatee, it is an equitable interest, capable of being parted with. The principal, at the death of the bankrupt, will be under quite different circumstances. The testator had a right to limit his interest to his life; giving the principal to such person as may be his next of kin at his death, to take it as the personal estate, not of the son, but of him the testator, — as if it was the son's personal estate, but as the gift of the testator.

The demurrer must, upon the whole, be overruled.[1]

BROADWAY NATIONAL BANK v. ADAMS.

SUPREME JUDICIAL COURT, MASSACHUSETTS. 1882.

133 Mass. 170.

MORTON, C. J. The object of this bill in equity is to reach and apply in payment of the plaintiff's debt due from the defendant Adams the income of a trust fund created for his benefit by the will of his brother. The eleventh article of the will is as follows: "I give the sum of seventy-five thousand dollars to my said executors and the survivors or survivor of them, in trust to invest the same in such manner as to them may seem prudent, and to pay the net income thereof, semiannually, to my said brother Charles W. Adams, during his natural life, such payments to be made to him personally when convenient, otherwise, upon his order or receipt in writing; in either case free from the interference or control of his creditors, my intention being that the use of said income shall not be anticipated by assignment. At the decease of my said brother Charles, my will is that the net income of said seventy-five thousand dollars shall be paid to his present wife, in case she survives him, for the benefit of herself and all the children of said Charles, in equal proportions, in the manner and upon the conditions the same as herein directed to be paid him during his life, so long as she shall remain single. And my will is, that, after the decease of said Charles and the decease or second marriage of his said wife, the said seventy-five thousand dollars, together with any accrued interest or income thereon which may remain unpaid, as herein above directed, shall be divided equally among all the children of my said brother Charles, by any and all his wives, and the representatives of any deceased child or children by right of representation."

There is no room for doubt as to the intention of the testator. It is clear that, if the trustee was to pay the income to the plaintiff under an order of the court, it would be in direct violation of the intention of the testator and of the provisions of his will. The court will not compel the trustee thus to do what the will forbids him to do, unless the provisions and intention of the testator are unlawful.

The question whether the founder of a trust can secure the in-

[1] In England it is settled law that restraints on the alienation of an equitable as well as a legal interest are invalid. Underhill, Trusts, art. 10.

In England as in the United States, however, a *forfeiture* upon alienation of a life estate, legal or equitable, or of a term for years, created by a third person, is valid. Ames, 395n.; Scott, Cases on Trusts, 1 ed., 609; Gray, Restraints, secs. 73–103.

come of it to the object of his bounty, by providing that it shall not be alienable by him or be subject to be taken by his creditors, has not been directly adjudicated in this Commonwealth. The tendency of our decisions, however, has been in favor of such a power in the founder. Braman *v.* Stiles, 2 Pick. 460. Perkins *v.* Hays, 3 Gray, 405. Russell *v.* Grinnell, 105 Mass. 425. Hall *v.* Williams, 120 Mass. 344. Sparhawk *v.* Cloon, 125 Mass. 263.

It is true that the rule of the common law is, that a man cannot attach to a grant or transfer of property, otherwise absolute, the condition that it shall not be alienated; such condition being repugnant to the nature of the estate granted. Co. Lit. 223*a*. Blackstone Bank *v.* Davis, 21 Pick. 42.

Lord Coke gives as the reason of the rule, that "it is absurd and repugnant to reason that he, that hath no possibility to have the land revert to him, should restrain his feoffee in fee simple of all his power to alien," and that this is "against the height and puritie of a fee simple." By such a condition, the grantor undertakes to deprive the property in the hands of the grantee of one of its legal incidents and attributes, namely, its alienability, which is deemed to be against public policy. But the reasons of the rule do not apply in the case of a transfer of property in trust. By the creation of a trust like the one before us, the trust property passes to the trustee with all its incidents and attributes unimpaired. He takes the whole legal title to the property, with the power of alienation; the *cestui que trust* takes the whole legal title to the accrued income at the moment it is paid over to him. Neither the principal nor the income is at any time inalienable.

The question whether the rule of the common law should be applied to equitable life estates created by will or deed, has been the subject of conflicting adjudications by different courts, as is fully shown in the able and exhaustive arguments of the counsel in this case. As is stated in Sparhawk *v.* Cloon, above cited, from the time of Lord Eldon the rule has prevailed in the English Court of Chancery, to the extent of holding that when the income of a trust estate is given to any person (other than a married woman) for life, the equitable estate for life is alienable by, and liable in equity to the debts of, the *cestui que trust,* and that this quality is so inseparable from the estate that no provision, however express, which does not operate as a cesser or limitation of the estate itself, can protect it from his debts. Brandon *v.* Robinson, 18 Ves. 429. Green *v.* Spicer, 1 Russ. & Myl. 395. Rochford *v.* Hackman, 9 Hare, 475. Trappes *v.* Meredith, L. R. 9 Eq. 229. Snowdon *v.* Dales, 6 Sim. 524. Rippon *v.* Norton, 2 Beav. 63.

The English rule has been adopted in several of the courts of this country. Tillinghast *v.* Bradford, 5 R. I. 205. Heath *v.* Bishop, 4 Rich. Eq. 46. Dick *v.* Pitchford, 1 Dev. & Bat. Eq. 480. Mebane *v.* Mebane, 4 Ired. Eq. 131.

Other courts have rejected it, and have held that the founder of a trust may secure the benefit of it to the object of his bounty, by providing that the income shall not be alienable by anticipation, nor subject to be taken for his debts. Holdship v. Patterson, 7 Watts, 547. Shankland's appeal, 47 Penn. St. 113. Rife v. Geyer, 59 Penn. St. 393. White v. White, 30 Vt. 338. Pope v. Elliott, 8 B. Mon. 56. Nichols v. Eaton, 91 U. S. 716. Hyde v. Woods, 94 U. S. 523.

The precise point involved in the case at bar has not been adjudicated in this Commonwealth; but the decisions of this court which we have before cited recognize the principle, that, if the intention of the founder of a trust, like the one before us, is to give to the equitable life tenant a qualified and limited, and not an absolute, estate in the income, such life tenant cannot alienate it by anticipation, and his creditors cannot reach it at law or in equity. It seems to us that this principle extends to and covers the case at bar. The founder of this trust was the absolute owner of his property. He had the entire right to dispose of it, either by an absolute gift to his brother, or by a gift with such restrictions or limitations, not repugnant to law, as he saw fit to impose. His clear intention, as shown in his will, was not to give his brother an absolute right to the income which might hereafter accrue upon the trust fund, with the power of alienating it in advance, but only the right to receive semiannually the income of the fund, which upon its payment to him, and not before, was to become his absolute property. His intentions ought to be carried out, unless they are against public policy. There is nothing in the nature or tenure of the estate given to the *cestui que trust* which should prevent this. The power of alienating in advance is not a necessary attribute or incident of such an estate or interest, so that the restraint of such alienation would introduce repugnant or inconsistent elements.

We are not able to see that it would violate any principles of sound public policy to permit a testator to give to the object of his bounty such a qualified interest in the income of a trust fund, and thus provide against the improvidence or misfortune of the beneficiary. The only ground upon which it can be held to be against public policy is, that it defrauds the creditors of the beneficiary.

It is argued that investing a man with apparent wealth tends to mislead creditors, and to induce them to give him credit. The answer is, that creditors have no right to rely upon property thus held, and to give him credit upon the basis of an estate which, by the instrument creating it, is declared to be inalienable by him, and not liable for his debts. By the exercise of proper diligence they can ascertain the nature and extent of his estate, especially in this Commonwealth, where all wills and most deeds are spread upon the public records. There is the same danger of their being misled by false appearances, and induced to give credit to the equitable life tenant when the will or deed of trust provides for a cesser or limitation over, in case of an attempted alienation, or of bankruptcy or attachment, and the argument would lead to the conclusion that the English rule is equally in violation of public policy. We do not see why the founder of a trust may not directly provide that his property shall go to his beneficiary with the restriction that it shall not be alienable by anticipation, and that his creditors shall not have the right to attach it in advance, instead of indirectly reaching the same result by a provision for a cesser or a limitation over, or by giving his trustees a discretion as to paying it. He has the entire *jus disponendi*, which imports that he may give it absolutely, or may impose any restrictions or fetters not repugnant to the nature of the estate which he gives. Under our system, creditors may reach all the property of the debtor not exempted by law, but they cannot enlarge the gift of the founder of a trust, and take more than he has given.

The rule of public policy which subjects a debtor's property to the payment of his debts, does not subject the property of a donor to the debts of his beneficiary, and does not give the creditor a right to complain that, in the exercise of his absolute right of disposition, the donor has not seen fit to give the property to the creditor, but has left it out of his reach.

Whether a man can settle his own property in trust for his own benefit, so as to exempt the income from alienation by him or attachment in advance by his creditors, is a different question, which we are not called upon to consider in this case. But we are of opinion that any other person, having the entire right to dispose of his property, may settle it in trust in favor of a beneficiary, and may provide that it shall not be alienated by him by anticipation, and shall not be subject to be seized by his creditors in advance of its payment to him.

It follows that, under the provisions of the will which we are considering, the income of the trust fund created for the benefit of the defendant Adams cannot be reached by attachment, either at law or in equity, before it is paid to him.

Bill dismissed.[1]

[1] A powerful attack upon spendthrift trusts was made by the late Professor John Chipman Gray in his book on Restraints on Alienation. In the preface to the second edition, published in 1895, he said that he believed that "the old doctrine was a wholesome one, fit to produce a manly race, based on sound morality and wise philosophy." He said that the rapid growth of the new doctrine allowing spendthrift trusts was due to the influence of the opinion of Mr. Justice Miller in Nichols v. Eaton, 91 U. S. 716; to the spirit of the times which looked with complacency on the failure to pay debts, both public and private; to the reaction against the "doctrines of *laissez faire,* of sacredness of contract, and of individual liberty, which were prevalent during the greater part of the [nineteenth] century"; to the spirit of paternalism,

STATUTORY RESTRAINTS ON ALIENATION. In several states it is provided with slight variations in the language that " No person beneficially interested in a trust for the receipt of the rents and

"which is the fundamental essence alike of spendthrift trusts and of socialism." He was particularly indignant at decisions to the effect that where the beneficiary of a trust is permitted to retain what is necessary for his support, that support is to be measured by the character of his associates and his individual standard of living; he said that to apply such a doctrine " is to descend to a depth of as shameless snobbishness as any into which the justice of a country was ever plunged." He admitted that except for occasional dissenting opinions he would be " *vox clamantis in deserto*"; and indeed the course of decisions and of statutes since 1895 has amply justified the admission.

It would seem that spendthrift trusts are not permitted in Alabama, Kentucky and Rhode Island. They were rejected in North Carolina and in Virginia until by statute they were allowed to a limited extent. They are permitted either by statute or decision in most of the other states. For a collection of authorities, see Scott, Cases on Trusts, 1 ed., 603, 608; Ames, 400; Perry, Trusts, sec. 386*a*; Pomeroy, Eq. Juris., sec. 989; Kales, Estates, 2 ed., secs. 711 ff.; Davis, Spendthrift Trusts in Life Insurance Policies, 5 B. U. L. Rev. 91; White, Restraints on Alienation, Spendthrift Trusts, and Indestructible Trusts in Ohio, 2 U. Cinn. L. Rev. 333; Horack, Spendthrift Trusts in Iowa, 4 Iowa L. Bull. 139; Clark, Spendthrift Trusts in New York, 9 Bench & Bar (N.S.) 59, 106; 9 Minn. L. Rev. 562; 74 U. Pa. L. Rev. 496; 77 U. Pa. L. Rev. 554; 3 Ann. Cas. 586; 18 Ann. Cas. 218; Ann. Cas. 1918C 965; Dec. Dig., Trusts, secs. 12, 152.

Language necessary. Where spendthrift trusts are allowed, no particular form of words is necessary to create such a trust. Seymour *v.* McAvoy, 121 Cal. 438; Berry *v.* Dunham, 202 Mass. 133; Ewalt *v.* Davenhill, 257 Pa. 385. See Ann. Cas. 1917B 394.

Legal interests. A restraint on the alienation of a legal interest in realty or personalty whether absolute or for life is invalid. Kales, Estates, 2 ed., sec. 730; Scott, 609. But see Hinshaw *v.* Wright, 124 Kan. 792, 13 Cornell L. Quar. 461, 41 Harv. L. Rev. 920.

Equitable interests in fee. There is a conflict of opinion on the question whether a restraint on the alienation of an equitable interest in fee simple or of an absolute equitable interest in personalty is valid. Such a restraint was held invalid in Haley *v.* Palmer, 107 Me. 311; Flanders *v.* Parker, 80 N. H. 566; Ullman *v.* Cameron, 186 N. Y. 339; Bergmann *v.* Lord, 194 N. Y. 70; Spann *v.* Carson, 123 S. C. 371; Morgan's Estate (No. 1), 223 Pa. 228; McCreery *v.* Johnston, 90 W. Va. 80. But see *contra,* Wallace *v.* Foxwell, 250 Ill. 616; Hopkinson *v.* Swaim, 284 Ill. 11; Boston Safe Dep. & T. Co. *v.* Collier, 222 Mass. 394. See 2 A. L. R. 858; 16 A. L. R. 552.

Perpetuities. A restraint on alienation, which is otherwise valid, is invalid if it is to continue beyond the period of perpetuities. Gray, Rule ag. Perp., sec. 121*ii*; Kales, Estates, 2 ed., secs. 658, 661; Kales, Cas. Fut. Int., 981–1019. See Hopkinson *v.* Swaim, 284 Ill. 11.

Trust for the settlor. A man cannot settle property upon trust for himself so as to exclude transferees or creditors. Ames, 400n.; Scott, Cases on Trusts, 1 ed., 608; Griswold, Spendthrift Trusts Created for the Settlor, 44 Harv. L. Rev. 203.

Particular classes of claimants. On the question whether the interest of the beneficiary can be reached by particular classes of claimants, such as his wife or child, or one who has furnished necessaries, see Griswold, Reaching the Interest of the Beneficiary of a Spendthrift Trust, 43 Harv. L. Rev. 64; 41 Harv. L. Rev. 409; 72 U. Pa. L. Rev. 220; 52 A. L. R. 1259. See also 35 A. L. R. 1034.

CHAP. VIII.] STATUTORY RESTRAINTS ON ALIENATION   645

profits of lands, can assign or in any manner dispose of such interest; but the rights and interest of every person for whose benefit a trust for the payment of a sum in gross is created are assignable." There are provisions to this effect in Michigan, Minnesota, Montana, New York and Wisconsin.[1] There is a similar provision in New York as to personal property. Personal Property Law, sec. 15. In Indiana and Kansas there is a similar provision as to trusts of land except that the beneficiary cannot dispose of his interest " unless the right to make disposition thereof be conferred by the instrument creating such trust." [2]

In California it is provided that " The beneficiary of a trust for the receipt of the rents and profits of real property, or for the payment of an annuity out of such rents and profits, may be restrained from disposing of his interest in such trust, during his life or for a term of years, by the instrument creating the trust." Cal. Civ. Code, sec. 867. There are similar provisions in North Dakota, Oklahoma and South Dakota.[3]

In Arizona, Connecticut, North Carolina and Virginia there are statutes which provide that the interest of the beneficiary of a trust may be made inalienable when the terms of the trust are in a prescribed form or when the amount held upon trust does not exceed a stated amount.[4]

Under the Trading with the Enemy Act the interest of the beneficiary of a trust who was an alien enemy could be seized by the Alien Property Custodian, although his interest was exempt from the claims of creditors. 43 Harv. L. Rev. 68.

Accrued income. In states in which spendthrift trusts are valid, creditors of the beneficiary of such a trust cannot reach income which has accrued in the hands of the trustee but has not been paid to the beneficiary. 43 Harv. L. Rev. 83. It has been held that it can be reached, however, after it has been paid to the beneficiary. Kruse v. Baeder, 1 Oh. Dec. 283; 43 Harv. L. Rev. 84.

Contract to assign. In Bixby v. St. Louis Union Trust Co., 22 S. W.(2d) 813 (Mo. 1929), the beneficiary of a spendthrift trust contracted to assign future income under the trust. It was held that the assignee could not reach income which had subsequently accrued and been deposited in escrow with a bank to await the outcome of the suit. The court said that the agreement to assign was void. But compare Shellabarger v. Commissioner, 38 F.(2d) 566.

[1] Mich. Comp. L., 1915, sec. 11583; Minn. Stat. (Mason 1927), sec. 8098; Mont. Rev. Codes, 1921, sec. 6794; N. Y. Real Prop. Law, sec. 103; Wis. Stat., 1929, sec. 231.19.

[2] Ind. Stat. (Burns 1926), sec. 13445; Kan. Rev. Stat. Ann., 1923, sec. 67-404.

[3] N. D. Comp. L., 1913, sec. 5377; Okla. Comp. Stat. Ann., 1921, sec. 8478; S. D. Comp. L., 1929, sec. 384.

[4] Ariz. Rev. Code, 1928, sec. 3647; Conn. Gen. Stat., 1930, sec. 5723 (liable if trustee to pay over income without provision for accumulation or express authorization to withhold income, and income not expressly given for support of beneficiary or his family; if for support of beneficiary or his family creditor can reach surplus); N. C. Code, 1927, sec. 1742 (for relatives where income does not exceed $500); Va. Code, 1930, sec. 5157 (estate not exceeding $100,000 in value).

In Illinois, Michigan, New Jersey and Tennessee there are statutes which provide that creditors may reach the interest of the beneficiary of a trust " except where such trust has been created by or the fund so held in trust has proceeded from some person other than the defendant himself." [1]

In New York it is provided that " the surplus of such rents and profits, beyond the sum necessary for the education and support of the beneficiary shall be liable to the claims of his creditors in the same manner as other personal property, which cannot be reached by execution." Real Property Law, sec. 98, applying also to personal property. There are similar statutes in California, Connecticut, Michigan, Minnesota, Montana, North Dakota, Oklahoma, South Dakota and Wisconsin.[2]

In New York it is elsewhere provided that creditors may reach ten per cent. of the income of any trust when the income exceeds $12 a week. Civ. Prac. Act, sec. 684.

PERABO v. GALLAGHER.

SUPREME JUDICIAL COURT, MASSACHUSETTS. 1922.

241 Mass. 207.

BILL IN EQUITY, filed in the Superior Court on November 29, 1919, to establish a debt for the care and custody of the defendant's son and to reach and apply in payment of the debt the interest of the defendant in a trust fund created by her mother's will, which is described in the opinion.

The suit was referred to a master who filed a report containing findings described in the opinion. The suit was heard upon a motion to confirm the master's report by *Sisk*, J., who allowed the motion by consent and ordered a final decree entered that the defendant pay to the plaintiff the sum of $585.85 with costs in the amount of $23.97 and that in default of such payment within thirty days a special master, thereby appointed, should sell " all the right, title and interest, legal and equitable," which the defendant had in her mother's estate at the time the bill was filed. The defendant appealed.

BRALEY, J. The will of Barbara M. Smith devised and bequeathed to her five daughters, among whom was Anna J. Hergt, now by

[1] Ill. Rev. Stat. (Cahill 1929), c. 22, sec. 49; Mich. Comp. L., 1915, sec. 12302(6); 1 N. J. Comp. Stat., 1910, pp. 435–37 (exemption from the claims of creditors is, however, limited to income less than $4000 per year); Tenn. Ann. Code (Shannon 1918), sec. 6092 (" declared by will duly recorded or deed duly registered ").

[2] Calif. Civ. Code, sec. 859; Conn. Gen. Stat., 1930, sec. 5723; Mich. Comp. L., 1915, sec. 11577; Minn. Stat. (Mason 1927), sec. 8092; Mont. Rev. Codes, 1921, sec. 6788; N. D. Comp. L., 1913, sec. 5369; Okla. Comp. Stat. Ann., 1921, sec. 8470; S. D. Comp. L., 1929, sec. 376; Wis. Stat, 1929, sec. 231.13.

marriage the defendant Anna J. Gallagher, " all the real and personal estate . . . of which I may, at the time of my decease, be seized possessed of, or entitled to, equally, share and share alike to be their absolute property, and free from the control of all persons whomsoever except as hereinafter provided.

" In the event of the death of any of my said daughters prior to my decease, then I give, devise and bequeath to the issue of any such daughter, equally, share and share alike, the share of my estate which the mother of such issue would have received had she survived me; and in the event of any of my daughters dying before me, and leaving no issue, then I give, devise and bequeath the share of my estate which such daughter would have received, had she survived me, to my surviving daughters and to the issue of any deceased daughter equally, share and share alike.

" It is my desire, and I hereby direct that the legacies of my said daughters, Emma Inman and Anna J. Hergt, be held in trust for them for the term of ten (10) years from the date of my decease, and for that purpose I do hereby appoint John F. McDonald of said Boston, trustee for my said daughters, Emma Inman and Anna J. Hergt, to have and to hold all property, both real and personal, which they may be entitled to under the terms of this will for the term of ten (10) years from the date of my decease, or for such further term as may be necessary for him to settle his accounts as such trustee.

" I hereby give unto the said John F. McDonald, trustee, aforesaid, absolute and unqualified charge and control of all the property, both real and personal, which my said daughters, Emma Inman and Anna J. Hergt, shall receive under the terms of this will, to be controlled, managed, sold, invested, or paid over to them in whatever manner, and at whatever times as he shall in his discretion deem most advantageous and beneficial to them."

The master reports that when the bill was filed the defendant trustee had in his possession a fund held for Anna J. Gallagher more than sufficient to satisfy the plaintiff's debt. But the testatrix died on August 31, 1911, and, suit having been brought on November 29, 1919, the question is whether the fund can be reached and applied before the expiration of the period of ten years. The answer depends upon the construction of the will. If the testatrix had expressly said that the income was to be paid to the beneficiary upon her order or receipt in writing free from the interference or control of her creditors and never by way of anticipation or assignment, it could not be levied upon by the plaintiff. Boston Safe Deposit & Trust Co. v. Collier, 222 Mass. 390, and cases there collected and reviewed. But no precise form of words is necessary to create a spendthrift trust. Baker v. Brown, 146 Mass. 369, 371. Slattery v. Wason, 151 Mass. 266. Wemyss v. White, 159 Mass. 484, 485. Huntress v. Allen, 195 Mass. 226. Berry v. Dunham, 202 Mass. 133,

140. The intention of the testatrix which must control is to be ascertained from the wording of the whole paragraph. Nickerson *v.* Van Horn, 181 Mass. 562, 563. It is first stated that the bequest or share is to be the property of the legatee " free from the control of all persons whomsoever except as hereinafter provided," and then follows the provisions that the share is to be held in trust for a period of ten years, during which the trustee is given absolute and unqualified charge and control of all the property which the defendant in common with her sister Emma Inman received " to be controlled, managed, sold, invested, or paid over to them in whatever manner, and at whatever times as he shall in his discretion deem most advantageous and beneficial to them." The testatrix could dispose of her property as she pleased. The decennial limitation before the legatee could come into possession of the *corpus* of the gift was valid, and she could transfer her title to the principal at any time but could not thereby terminate the trust created for her benefit. Cushman *v.* Arnold, 185 Mass. 165, 169. Security Bank of New York *v.* Callahan, 220 Mass. 84, 87. Boston Safe Deposit & Trust Co. *v.* Collier, 222 Mass. 390. Wright *v.* Blinn, 225 Mass. 146.

We are of opinion that the intention of the testatrix to leave the defendant Anna J. Gallagher without any absolute right of alienation of income during the term of the trust is manifest. The defendant trustee had the power to withhold the income in his discretion and apply the whole or such portion as he saw fit for the benefit of Anna J. Hergt, and she has no interest in the income which can be assigned or reached by creditors. Nickerson *v.* Van Horn, *supra.* Berry *v.* Dunham, *supra.* Endicott *v.* University of Virginia, 182 Mass. 156, is plainly distinguishable.

It follows that the decree which provides that if the plaintiff's claim is not satisfied by the defendant within thirty days from the date of entry a special master is to sell " all the right, title and interest, legal and equitable, which the said Anna J. Gallagher had, at the time of the filing the complaint . . ." must be modified by limiting the decree to a sale of her right, title and interest in the principal, and when so modified, it is affirmed, with costs to the defendant of the appeal.

Ordered accordingly.[1]

---

[1] See Vellacott *v.* Murphy, 16 F.(2d) 700 (bankruptcy); Estate of Hall, 248 Pa. 218 (assignment).

Contingent interests. In the following cases it was held that creditors or the trustee in bankruptcy of the *cestui que trust* could not reach his interest because of its contingent character. Suskin & Berry *v.* Rumley, 37 F.(2d) 304 (son's interest contingent on surviving mother, remainder to issue of life tenant living at her death); Smith *v.* Gilbert, 71 Conn. 149 (son's interest contingent on surviving mother); Safe Deposit & Trust Co. *v.* Independent Brewing Ass'n, 127 Md. 463 (wife's interest contingent on surviving husband); Clarke *v.* Fay, 205 Mass. 228 (beneficiary entitled if his father should predecease other beneficiaries and they should die without issue); Mitchell *v.* Choctaw Bank, 107 Miss. 314 (contingent on surviving until all children came

EATON v. BOSTON TRUST COMPANY.

SUPREME COURT OF THE UNITED STATES. 1916.

240 U. S. 427.

THE facts, which involve the construction and application of § 70a (5) of the Bankruptcy Act, and of the rights of the life tenant in a trust fund created under the laws of Massachusetts, are stated in the opinion.

HOLMES, J. This is a bill of instructions, brought by the Trust Company, the principal defendant in error, to ascertain whether a fund bequeathed to it in trust for Mrs. Luke, codefendant in error, passed to her trustee in bankruptcy. The bequest was of seventy-five thousand dollars, " The whole of the net income thereof to be paid my adopted daughter, Fannie Leighton Luke, wife of Otis H. Luke, of said Brookline during her life quarterly in each and every year together with such portion of the principal of said trust fund as shall make the amount to be paid her at least Three Thousand Dollars a year during her life, said income to be free from the interference or control of her creditors." It is established law in Massachusetts that such trusts are valid and effective against creditors, Broadway National Bank v. Adams, 133 Mass., 170, and, subject to what we are about to say, against assignees in insolvency or trustees in bankruptcy. Billings v. Marsh, 153 Mass., 311. Munroe v. Dewey, 176 Mass., 184. The trustee in bankruptcy seeks to avoid the effect of these decisions on the ground that Mrs. Luke's equitable life interest was held by the Supreme Court of the State to be assignable, and that therefore it passed under § 70a (5) of the Bankruptcy Act, vesting in the trustee all property that the bankrupt " could by any means have transferred." The Supreme Judicial Court, however, held that the above cited cases governed and that the property did not pass. 220 Mass., 484.

If it be true without qualification that the bankrupt could have assigned her interest and by so doing could have freed from the trust both the fund and any proceeds received by her, the argument

---

of age); Mitchell v. Gewin, 73 So. 888 (Miss. 1917) (same will); Myer v. Thomson, 35 Hun (N. Y.) 561. See also Hill v. Fulmer, 39 So. 53 (Miss. 1905) (not subject to execution at law).

Creditors were successful in Thompson v. Zurich State Bank, 124 Kan. 425 (contingent on living until brother came of age); Reilly v. Mackenzie, 151 Md. 216 (son's interest contingent on surviving mother); Re Moore, 22 F.(2d) 432 (D. Md. 1927) (same); Clarke v. Fay, 205 Mass. 228 (child's interest contingent on surviving parent). A present interest may be reached by creditors although it is subject to be diminished by a condition subsequent. First Nat. Bank v. Dougan, 250 Fed. 510 (possibility of future children enlarging class).

See 37 Yale L. Jour. 1165; 27 L. R. A. (N. s.) 454; 48 A. L. R. 784.

would be very strong that the statute intended the fund to pass. There would be an analogy at least with the provision giving the trustees all powers that the bankrupt might have exercised for her own benefit, § 70a (3), and there would be difficulty in admitting that a person could have property over which he could exercise all the powers of ownership except to make it liable for his debts. The conclusion that the fund was assignable was based on two cases, and we presume was meant to go no farther than their authority required. The first of these simply held that an executor was not liable on his bond for paying over an annuity to an assignee as it fell due, when the assignor to whom it was bequeathed free from creditors had not attempted to avoid his act. Ames *v.* Clarke, 106 Mass., 573. The other case does not go beyond a dictum that carries the principle no farther. Huntress *v.* Allen, 195 Mass., 226. It is true that where the restriction has been enforced there generally has been a clause against anticipation, but the present decision in following them holds the restricting clause paramount, and therefore we feel warranted in assuming that the power of alienation will not be pressed to a point inconsistent with the dominant intent of the will. Whether if that power were absolute the restriction still should be upheld as in case of a statutory exemption that leaves the bankrupt free to convey his rights it is unnecessary to decide.

The law of Massachusetts treats such restrictions as limiting the character of the equitable property and inherent in it. Dunn *v.* Dobson, 198 Mass., 142, 146. Lathrop *v.* Merrill, 207 Mass., 6, 9. Whatever may have been the criticisms upon the policy and soundness of the doctrine, and whatever may be the power of this court to weigh the reasoning upon which it has been established by the Massachusetts cases, Page *v.* Edmunds, 187 U. S. 596, 602, it has been established too long and is too nearly sanctioned by the decisions of this court to be overthrown here. Nichols *v.* Eaton, 91 U. S. 716. Shelton *v.* King, 229 U. S. 90, 99. The policy of the Bankruptcy Act is to respect state exemptions, and until the Massachusetts decisions shall have gone farther than they yet have we are not prepared to say that the present bequest is not protected by the Massachusetts rule.

Decree affirmed.[1]

HULL *v.* FARMERS' LOAN & TRUST COMPANY.

SUPREME COURT OF THE UNITED STATES. 1917.

245 U. S. 312.

BRANDEIS, J. Charles Palmer, of New York City, by will executed shortly before his death, bequeathed to the Farmers' Loan

[1] But see Hopkinson *v.* Swaim, 284 Ill. 11. *Cf.* Croom *v.* Ocala etc. Co., 62 Fla. 460 (if interest assignable, creditors can reach it). See 43 Harv. L. Rev. 76.

& Trust Company the sum of $50,000, in trust, to pay the income to his son Francis, during his life, with a remainder over to others, subject to the "wish . . . that . . . my said son shall have the principal of said trust fund whenever he shall become financially solvent and able to pay all his just debts and liabilities from resources other than the principal of this trust fund."

Promptly after probate of the will, Francis filed a voluntary petition in bankruptcy, and in due time received his discharge. Then the Trust Company instituted proceedings in the Surrogate Court for a judicial settlement of the estate; and, the court adjudging that Francis had become entitled to the principal of the trust fund (65 Misc. N. Y. 418), it was paid over to him. Later, the trustee in bankruptcy who had not been a party to proceedings in the Surrogate Court, brought suit in the Supreme Court of New York against the Trust Company and Francis to recover the principal. He claimed that the right to it had passed to him under § 70a (5) of the Bankruptcy Act of 1898, c. 541, 30 Stat. 544, and that the whole fund was required to satisfy the balance due on debts proved against the bankrupt estate and the expenses of administration. No claim was asserted against the income of the trust fund. A complaint setting forth these facts was dismissed on demurrer; and the judgment entered by the trial court was affirmed both by the Appellate Division (155 App. Div. 636) and by the Court of Appeals (213 N. Y. 315). The case comes here on writ of error.

Plaintiff asserts that the case presents this federal question: Does a contingent interest in the principal of personal property assignable by the bankrupt prior to the filing of the petition necessarily pass to his trustee in bankruptcy? And, to sustain his claim to recovery, he contends, that under the law of New York (1) the words used by the testator create a trust; (2) vesting in the beneficiary a contingent interest in personal property; (3) which is an expectant estate; (4) assignable by him; and (5) that, in view of the Surrogate's decision and the action thereon, the defendants are estopped from denying that the contingency requiring payment of the principal had arisen. Plaintiff contends also that, under the federal law, (6) this assignable estate in expectancy passed to the trustee when Francis was adjudged bankrupt, and (7) the trustee, as holder of the estate became entitled to the principal when the discharge rendered Francis solvent.

We need not enquire whether the several propositions of state and federal law which underlie this contention are correct. This is not a case where a testator seeks to bequeath property which shall be free from liability for the beneficiary's debts. Ullman *v.* Cameron, 186 N. Y. 339, 345. Here the testator has merely prescribed the condition on which he will make a gift of the principal. Under the law of New York he had the right to provide, in terms, that such payment of the principal should be made, only if and when Francis should have received in bankruptcy a discharge from his debts and that no part of the fund should go to his trustee in bankruptcy. The language used by the testator is broader in scope, but manifests quite as clearly, his intention that the principal shall not be paid over under circumstances which would result in any part of it being applied in satisfying debts previously incurred by Francis. The Bankruptcy Act presents no obstacle to carrying out the testator's intention. Eaton *v.* Boston Safe Deposit and Trust Co., 240 U. S. 427. As the Court of Appeals said: " The nature of the condition itself determines the controversy." The judgment is

Affirmed.[1]

In re BULLOCK.
GOOD *v.* LICKORISH.

CHANCERY. 1891.

60 L. J. Ch. 341.

BY the will and codicil of Edwin Bullock (who died on the 14th of February, 1870), all the real and personal estate of the testator were vested in the plaintiffs Charles Patten Good and Henry Williams, and the testator's widow Mary Bullock, his executors and trustees, in trust for the testator's children, and the issue born in his lifetime of Mary Bullock, as she should by deed or will appoint, and, failing such appointment, and so far as the same should not extend, in trust for those of his six children who should be living at her death, and the issue of such as should be then dead leaving issue.

Mary Bullock, by her will dated the 29th of May, 1883, directed and appointed as follows: —

" My late husband's trustees or trustee shall stand possessed of 15,000*l.*, further part of the said net proceeds, upon trust to invest the same in some or one of the modes of investment by law authorized for the investment of trust funds, and to pay the income of such investments to the said Theodore Walter William Bullock, during his life or until he shall become a bankrupt or a liquidating debtor, or cease to be entitled to receive such income, or any part thereof, for his own personal use or benefit, by any means or for any purpose. And in the event of, and upon the said T. W. W. Bullock becoming a bankrupt or a liquidating debtor, or ceasing to be entitled to receive the said income, or any part thereof, for his own personal use or benefit by any means or for any purpose, to pay to him or apply for his benefit, during the remainder of his life, either the whole, or so much, and so much only of the said income, as my late husband's trustees or trustee shall in their or

[1] See Siemers *v.* Morris, 169 N. Y. App. Div. 411. But see Davidson *v.* Chalmers, 33 Beav. 653; Gray, Restraints, sec. 167*a*. See 43 Harv. L. Rev. 78.

his uncontrolled discretion think fit, and, subject to the aforesaid interest hereinbefore appointed in favor of the said T. W. W. Bullock, my late husband's trustees or trustee shall hold the said 15,000*l*., and the investments and income (including any accumulations of income) thereof, in trust for the child, if only one, or all the children equally if more than one, born in my lifetime, of the said T. W. W. Bullock, and if there be no such child, in trust for the said William Bullock, Mary Holyoake Bullock, Constance Bullock, and Dorothy Marian Good as tenants in common in equal shares."

The testatrix died on the 29th of December, 1886, and her will, and several codicils which did not affect the above appointment, were proved by her executors, the plaintiffs Charles Patten Good and Henry Williams, on the 15th of February, 1887.

The above-named T. W. W. Bullock was a son of the testator and testatrix, and W. Bullock, M. H. Bullock, and C. Bullock, were the children of E. L. Bullock, a son of the testator and testatrix, who died in the lifetime of the latter, and E. M. Good was a child of L. M. Good, a daughter of the testator and testatrix.

The trustees invested the 15,000*l*. in the purchase of 12,011*l*. London and North-Western Railway Company 4 per cent. perpetual debenture stock, the interest on which was payable on the 15th of January and 15th of July, and the interest was paid to T. W. W. Bullock up to and including the 16th of July, 1890.

On the 23rd of August, 1890, the trustees received notice of a memorandum of charge dated the 30th of January, 1889, from T. W. W. Bullock to Lickorish & Bellord, solicitors, on all his interest under the will of the testatrix to secure money of which about 500*l*. was stated to be owing.

On the 23rd of October 1890, a receiving order was made against T. W. W. Bullock, and on the 14th of November, 1890, the trustees received a notice that the official receiver claimed the 12,011*l*. stock as trustee in the bankruptcy of T. W. W. Bullock; he subsequently claimed the proportion of interest due at the date of the receiving order; but the claims of the trustee were afterwards withdrawn. The trustees took out an originating summons, asking (*inter alia*) whether the plaintiffs properly might during the life of T. W. W. Bullock apply the whole, or any, and what part, of the income of the trust fund in providing in such manner as they might from time to time think fit for the past and future lodging, board, clothing, maintenance, and support of T. W. W. Bullock, and the payment of sundry legal expenses incurred by him or on his behalf in and since July, 1890, or how the said income ought to be dealt with by the plaintiffs.

This summons was adjourned into Court.

KEKEWICH, J. At the conclusion of the arguments on this point, I held that the particular assignee represented by Mr. Maidlow was not entitled to any part of the income in which Theodore Walter William Bullock takes an interest under the will. He only claimed that which accrued before notice of his assignment was given to the trustees of the will, and that on the ground that until such notice was given the assignment was not perfect, and Mr. Bullock could not until then be said to have ceased to be entitled to receive the income for his own personal use or benefit. I held that, although for some and important purposes the assignment might fairly be said to be not perfect until notice given, yet, as between assignor and assignee, it was perfect as from its date, and operated a cesser of the assignor's title to receive the income. I advert to this now because, with reference to the point remaining to be decided, it is important to observe that the particular assignee has no interest. It is also important to observe that the general assignee — that is, the trustee in bankruptcy — makes no claim. He has abstained from doing so deliberately, and I have no doubt wisely. He could not, so far as I can see, have put forward any tenable argument in support of a claim if made. The question is therefore raised as between Mr. Bullock and those entitled under the gift over — or rather such of them as claim adversely to him, for they do not all act together or take the same view. Mr. Warmington's argument for them was that the language of the will only empowers the trustees to pay the income to Mr. Bullock or to apply it for his benefit, and that neither of these things can be done. As regards payment, reliance was placed on the decision in *In re* Coleman, Henry *v.* Strong, 39 Ch. D. 443, and my own judgment in *In re* Neil, Hemming *v.* Neil, 62 L. T. Rep. 649, to which, on reflection, I adhere; and it was said that to pay income to Mr. Bullock would be to make a payment in derogation of the overriding title of the trustee in bankruptcy, and therefore a wrongful payment, which would be no discharge to the trustees of the will, and would render them accountable to the trustee in bankruptcy. That argument is, I think, well founded. As regards applications for the benefit of Mr. Bullock, the argument took this form: — It was said that where the Court has upheld a discretionary trust for application, arising on bankruptcy, or the equivalent of bankruptcy, the discretion has been exercisable with reference to wife and children as well as the bankrupt, and the decisions of the Court have proceeded on the impossibility of determining beforehand what, if anything, the trustees would, in the exercise of their discretion, apply for the benefit of the bankrupt as distinguished from the other objects of their power. For this, reference was made to two cases as examples of a class, — Godden *v.* Crowhurst, 10 Sim. 642, and Kearsley *v.* Woodcock, 3 Hare 185. The language of the judgments, and especially that of Vice-Chancellor Shadwell in Godden *v.* Crowhurst, countenances the argument, but the precise point which I have now to consider was not before the Court in either case, and I cannot think that either Judge intended to decide it. I can see no reason on principle for defeating the obvious intention of the testatrix. That obvious intention was to enable the trustees, in the event of Mr. Bullock's bankruptcy, to apply for his benefit the income, or an adequate part of the income, which he thereupon ceased to be entitled to receive. It is clear, and the trustee in bankruptcy has practically admitted, that he can take no interest in income thus applied; and it is difficult to see how those entitled under the gift over can successfully claim as coming to them what, if it does not come to them, would not go to the trustee in bankruptcy. The argument in opposition to their claim is strongly supported by Chambers *v.* Smith, 3 App. Cas. 795. It is a Scotch case, but the Scotch law was expressly stated to be on this point in no way different from that of England. It was there held that trustees possessing a discretionary power, such as the trustees of this will possess, might exercise it in favor of the beneficiaries occupying Mr. Bullock's position, notwithstanding arrestment by judgment creditors. The law is expounded by the several learned Lords who gave their opinions to the House, but it will suffice to refer to those of Lord Chancellor Hatherley and Lord Blackburn. There is a passage in the Lord Chancellor's judgment (p. 804) which seems to me directly applicable to the case in hand. It may be thus applied: Mr. Bullock has no control over the fund when the trustees resolve to exercise their discretionary power. He cannot, and no one claiming through him can, make a claim against the trustees for payment. It would be a sufficient answer to any such claim to say, " We have postponed such payment to you personally, and intend ourselves to apply the money for your behoof." And on page 807 he says, " If I am correct in holding as I do that the trust powers could not be destroyed by the objects of them becoming indebted, which, indeed, seems the time at which the testator would have desired them to be brought into action, then the trustees are not innovating, but only exercising their rights as conferred upon them by their truster at their own discretion." On page 817 Lord Blackburn notices the great and fundamental difference between a gift to one, either direct or through the medium of trustees, who are mere conduit-pipes to convey the gift to the beneficiary, and a gift subject to a power reserved to trustees, to be exercised paramount to the beneficiary and in his despite; and adds, " I think the arrestment fixes the date at which it is to be determined whether the arresters have a right to attach the fund, and anything that is subsequently done by the debtor, or by those who have rights against the debtor, or by those who claim under him, comes too late after that." In other words, the assignment in this case, which is equivalent to the arrestment in the case before the House of Lords, called the discretionary power of the trustees into operation; and it would be a contradiction to hold that the power is inoperative just when it was intended to be exercised. What the trustees, in the exercise of their discretion, do not from time to time think fit to apply for the benefit of Mr. Bullock goes, by the words of the will, to those entitled under the gift over; but they take only this overplus, and cannot claim what the trustees determine to apply. I was asked by the trustees to define the limits within which they may apply the income for Mr. Bullock's benefit. I find it extremely difficult to do this in the abstract, and I am unwilling to fetter the trustees' discretion, which was intended to be, and ought to be construed as, large. I could not refuse to determine any particular question submitted by them to the Court, and if any real difficulty occurs, they would probably be justified in asking the Court's protection. I can say no more at present than that they certainly may, in my opinion, spend the whole or any part of the income in maintenance, using that word in its most general and widest sense; and I doubt whether I was right in saying in the course of the argument that they could not properly pay Mr. Bullock's debts. The discretion is vested in them, and though, as already mentioned, they are entitled to the assistance of the Court if a case of real difficulty occurs, they must exercise it; and so long as they exercise it honestly — that is, as men of ordinary business habits and prudence, and with due regard to all the circumstances of the case — the Court will not interfere with them.[1]

[1] If the trustees are directed to *apply* the whole or a certain amount of the income of a trust fund for the benefit or support of A, although at such times and in such manner as the trustees deem fit, A's assignee, creditor or trustee in bankruptcy may, in jurisdictions following Brandon *v.* Robinson, demand from the trustees the income or such part thereof as the *cestui que trust* was entitled to demand. Green *v.* Spicer, 1 R. & My. 395; Snowdon *v.* Dales, 6 Sim. 524; Younghusband *v.* Gisborne, 1 Coll. 400; Dick *v.* Pitchford, 1 Dev. & B. Eq. (N. C.) 480; Pace *v.* Pace, 73 N. C. 119; Hutchinson *v.* Maxwell, 100 Va. 169. But see *contra,* Godden *v.* Crowhurst, 10 Sim. 642.

If the trustees may in their discretion refuse to pay to A or apply for his benefit any portion of the income, and they do not so pay or apply any part of the income, his assignee, creditor or trustee in bankruptcy cannot demand any part of the income. Twopeny *v.* Payton, 10 Sim. 486; Lord *v.* Bunn, 2 Y. & C. C. C. 98; Holmes *v.* Penney, 3 K. & J. 90; Chambers *v.* Smith, 3 App. Cas. 795; Davidson *v.* Kemper, 79 Ky. 5; Baker *v.* Brown, 146 Mass. 369; Slattery *v.* Wason, 151 Mass. 266; Brown *v.* Lumbert, 221 Mass. 419; Wolfman *v.* Webster, 77 N. H. 24; Keyser *v.* Mitchell, 67 Pa. 473; Stone *v.* Wescott, 18 R. I. 517; Heath *v.* Bishop, 4 Rich. Eq. (S. C.) 46 (*semble*); Staub *v.* Williams, 5 Lea (Tenn.) 458. See also *Re* Landon, 40 L. J. Ch. 370; Train *v.* Clapperton, [1908] A. C. 342.

If the trust is for the support of A and others, for example his wife or his family, in some cases it is held that A cannot insist upon any part of the income nor can his assignee, creditor or trustee in bankruptcy. Holmes *v.* Penney, 3 K. & J. 90; Durant *v.* Hosp. Life Ins. Co., 2 Low. (U. S.) 575; Hill *v.* MacRae, 27 Ala. 175; Bell *v.* Watkins, 82 Ala. 512; Tolland etc. Co. *v.* Underwood, 50 Conn. 493; Damhoff *v.* Shambaugh, 200 Iowa 1155; Nickell *v.* Handly, 10 Gratt. (Va.) 336. But in some cases the beneficial interest has been held to be severable and the assignee, creditor or trustee in

TRUSTEE ACT, 1925, SEC. 33(1).
Stat. 15 Geo. V., ch. 19.

WHERE any income, including an annuity or other periodical income payment, is directed to be held on protective trusts for the benefit of any person (in this section called "the principal beneficiary") for the period of his life or for any less period, then, during that period (in this section called the "trust period") the said income shall, without prejudice to any prior interest, be held on the following trusts, namely: —

(i) Upon trust for the principal beneficiary during the trust period or until he, whether before or after the termination of any prior interest, does or attempts to do or suffers any act or thing, or until any event happens, other than an advance under any statutory or express power, whereby, if the said income were payable during the trust period to the principal beneficiary absolutely during that period, he would be deprived of the right to receive the same or any part thereof, in any of which cases, as well as on the termination of the trust period, whichever first happens, this trust of the said income shall fail or determine;

(ii) If the trust aforesaid fails or determines during the subsistence of the trust period, then, during the residue of that period, the said income shall be held upon trust for the application thereof for the maintenance or support, or otherwise for the benefit, of all or any one or more exclusively of the other or others of the following persons (that is to say) —

    (a) the principal beneficiary and his or her wife or husband, if any, and his or her children or more remote issue, if any; or

---

bankruptcy has been held entitled to the whole income except a proper allowance for the wife or family. Page v. Way, 3 Beav. 20; Kearsley v. Woodcock, 3 Hare 185; Wallace v. Anderson, 16 Beav. 533; Jones v. Reese, 65 Ala. 134. In Honeker Sons v. Duff, 101 Va. 675, it was held that the words "and his family" merely indicated the motive of the testator, and the creditors were allowed to reach the whole income. See Bogert, Trusts, 436; Perry, Trusts, sec. 386b.

If the trustees are directed to pay to A or apply for his benefit so much of the income as in their discretion they think fit, it has been held that they are accountable to A's assignee, creditor or trustee in bankruptcy for payments made to A after notice. Lord v. Bunn, 2 Y. & C. C. C. 98; Re Coleman, 39 Ch. D. 443; Re Neil, 62 L. T. N. s. 649. And A is also accountable for what he has received. Re Ashby, [1892] 1 Q. B. 872. On the question whether they are responsible if income is not paid to A but is applied for his benefit, see Re Coleman, 39 Ch. D. 443. But see Lord v. Bunn, 2 Y. & C. C. C. 98; Gray, Restraints, sec. 167j. See Underhill, Trusts, art. 10.

(b) if there is no wife or husband or issue of the principal beneficiary in existence, the principal beneficiary and the persons who would, if he were actually dead, be entitled to the trust property or the income thereof or to the annuity fund, if any, or arrears of the annuity, as the case may be;

as the trustees in their absolute discretion, without being liable to account for the exercise of such discretion, think fit.[1]

HAMILTON v. DROGO.

COURT OF APPEALS, NEW YORK. 1926.

241 N. Y. 401.

APPEAL from an order of the Appellate Division of the Supreme Court in the first judicial department, entered July 13, 1925, which affirmed an order of Special Term denying a motion for an order directing that an execution issue against the income derived from a trust fund.

The following question was certified: " Can the trust fund created by will of defendant's mother in his favor, held by and in the possession of the United States Trust Company of New York, be reached on execution of a judgment in favor of the plaintiff against the defendant under section 684 of the Civil Practice Act?"

ANDREWS, J. By her will the dowager Duchess of Manchester bequeathed to trustees (now represented by the respondent) over one million dollars in trust, during the life of her son, to apply the annual income " for the maintenance and support or otherwise, for the benefit of all or any one or more exclusively of the other or others of him my said son his wife and children or other issue as my . . . trustees in their sole and uncontrolled discretion without being liable for the exercise of such discretion think fit." There was no attempt to provide for any accumulation of this income. Therefore, as the son in question, the present duke, has both a living wife and living children it became the duty of the trustee, annually or oftener, to exercise the discretion so confided to it, and to distribute the income among some or all of the persons mentioned as possible beneficiaries. Precisely how or when this discretion should be exercised is not material, but having been exercised those or the one to share in the income then to be distributed were or was entitled to receive the allotment made to them or him.

The appellant obtained a judgment in the Supreme Court against the Duke of Manchester. An execution was issued and returned unsatisfied. Thereupon the judgment creditor applied to a justice

[1] See Re Boulton's Settlement Trust, [1928] Ch. 703; Underhill, Trusts, 69.

at Special Term for an order that an execution issue against the income from the trust funds of the defendant in the possession of the respondent as trustee to the amount of ten per cent thereof pursuant to Civil Practice Act, section 684. This section provides that after the entry of judgment and the return of an execution unsatisfied " where any . . . income from trust funds . . . are due and owing to the judgment debtor or shall thereafter become due and owing to him to the amount of twelve dollars or more per week " upon application of the creditor the justice must grant " an order directing that an execution issue against the . . . income from the trust funds . . . of said judgment debtor, and on presentation of such execution . . . to the person or persons . . . from whom such . . . income from trust funds . . . are due and owing or may thereafter become due and owing to the judgment debtor, said execution shall become a lien and a continuing levy upon the . . . income from trust funds . . . due or to become due to said judgment debtor " for a certain percentage thereof. There is no requirement that the income be due at the time the order is made and the execution served. It is enough either that it will become due in the future from the trustee to the *cestui que trust*, or that it may become so due. If ever the day of payment arrives the lien of the execution attaches. The intention of the Legislature was to extend the scope and effect of an execution as it had theretofore existed.

In the present case no income may ever become due to the judgment debtor. We may not interfere with the discretion which the testatrix has vested in the trustee any more than her son may do so. Its judgment is final. But at least annually this judgment must be exercised. And if it is exercised in favor of the duke then there is due him the whole or such part of the income as the trustee may allot to him. After such allotment he may compel its payment. At least for some appreciable time, however brief, the award must precede the delivery of the income he is to receive and during that time the lien of the execution attaches.

The orders appealed from should be reversed, with costs in all courts. An order should be granted directing the issuance of an execution in the form prescribed by Civil Practice Act, section 684, with ten dollars costs. We construe the question certified to mean: May the income of the trust fund held by the respondent, after the whole or any part thereof exceeding twelve dollars per week has been allotted to the Duke of Manchester, be reached on execution; and as so construed we answer it in the affirmative.

HISCOCK, Ch. J., CARDOZO, POUND, MCLAUGHLIN, CRANE and LEHMAN, JJ., concur.

Orders reversed, etc.[1]

---

[1] But see Kiffner v. Kiffner, 185 Iowa 1064. See 26 Col. L. Rev. 776; 43 Harv. L. Rev. 83.

DEARLE v. HALL.

CHANCERY. 1828.

3 Russ. 1, 48.

THE LORD CHANCELLOR [LYNDHURST].[1] The cases of Dearle v. Hall and Loveridge v. Cooper were decided by Sir Thomas Plumer; and from his decree there is in each of them an appeal, which stands for judgment. As the two cases depend on the same principle, though the facts are, to a certain degree, different, the better course will be to dispose of both together; and as Dearle v. Hall was the first of the two which came before the court below, though it was not argued on appeal till after Loveridge v. Cooper had been heard, I shall first direct my attention to the facts on which it depends.

Zachariah Brown was entitled, during his life, to about 93*l.* a year, being the interest arising from a share of the residue of his father's estate, which, in pursuance of the directions in his father's will, had been converted into money, and invested in the names of the executors and trustees. Among those executors and trustees was a solicitor of the name of Unthank, who took the principal share in the management of the trust. Zachariah Brown, being in distress for money, in consideration of a sum of 204*l.*, granted to Dearle, one of the plaintiffs in the suit, an annuity of 37*l.* a year, secured by a deed of covenant and a warrant of attorney of the grantor and a surety; and, by way of collateral security, Brown assigned to Dearle all his interest in the yearly sum of 93*l.*: but neither Dearle nor Brown gave any notice of this assignment to the trustees under the father's will.

Shortly afterwards, a similar transaction took place between Brown and the other plaintiff, Sherring, to whom an annuity of 27*l.* a year was granted. The securities were of a similar description; and, on this occasion, as on the former, no notice was given to the trustees.

These transactions took place in 1808 and 1809. The annuities were regularly paid till June, 1811; and then, for the first time, default was made in payment.

Notwithstanding this circumstance, Brown, in 1812, publicly advertised for sale his interest in the property under his father's will. Hall, attracted by the advertisement, entered, through his solicitor, Mr. Patten, into a treaty of purchase; and it appears from the correspondence between Mr. Patten and Mr. Unthank that the former exercised due caution in the transaction, and made every proper inquiry concerning the nature of Brown's title, the extent of any incumbrances affecting the property, and all other circum-

[1] Only the opinion of the Chancellor is here given.

stances of which it was fit that a purchaser should be apprised. No intimation was given to Hall of the existence of any previous assignment; and, his solicitor being satisfied, he advanced his money for the purchase of Brown's interest, and that interest was regularly assigned to him. Mr. Patten requested Unthank to join in the deed; but Mr. Unthank said, "I do not choose to join in the deed; and it is unnecessary for me to do so, because Z. Brown has an absolute right to this property, and may deal with it as he pleases." The first half-year's interest, subject to some deductions, which the trustees were entitled to make, was duly paid to Hall; and, shortly afterwards, Hall for the first time ascertained that the property had been regularly assigned, in 1808 and 1809, to Dearle and to Sherring.

Sir Thomas Plumer was of opinion that the plaintiffs had no right to the assistance of a court of equity to enforce their claim to the property as against the defendant Hall, and that, having neglected to give the trustees notice of their assignments, and having enabled Z. Brown to commit this fraud, they could not come into this court to avail themselves of the priority of their assignments in point of time, in order to defeat the right of a person who had acted as Hall had acted, and who, if the prior assignments were to prevail against him, would necessarily sustain a great loss. In that opinion I concur.

It was said that there was no authority for the decision of the Master of the Rolls, — no case in point to support it; and certainly it does not appear that the precise question has ever been determined, or that it has been even brought before the court, except, perhaps, so far as it may have been discussed in an unreported case of Wright *v.* Lord Dorchester. But the case is not new in principle. Where personal property is assigned, delivery is necessary to complete the transaction, not as between the vendor and the vendee, but as to third persons, in order that they may not be deceived by apparent possession and ownership remaining in a person, who, in fact, is not the owner. This doctrine is not confined to chattels in possession, but extends to *choses in action*, bonds, &c.; in Ryall *v.* Rowles, 1 Ves. Sen. 348, 1 Atk. 165, it is expressly applied to bonds, simple contract debts, and other *choses in action*. It is true that Ryall *v.* Rowles was a case in bankruptcy; but the Lord Chancellor called to his assistance Lord Chief Justice Lee, Lord Chief Baron Parker, and Mr. Justice Burnett; so that the principle on which the court there acted must be considered as having received most authoritative sanction. These eminent individuals, and particularly the Lord Chief Baron and Mr. Justice Burnett, did not, in the view which they took of the question before them, confine themselves to the case of bankruptcy, but stated grounds of judgment which are of general application. Lord Chief Baron Parker says, that, on the assignment of a bond debt, the bond should be delivered, and notice given to the debtor; and he adds, that, with respect to simple-contract debts, for which no securities are holden, such as book-debts for instance, notice of the assignment should be given to the debtor, in order to take away from the debtor the right of making payment to the assignor, and to take away from the assignor the power and disposition over the thing assigned. 1 Ves. Sen. 367; 2 Atk. 177. In cases like the present, the act of giving the trustee notice is, in a certain degree, taking possession of the fund; it is going as far towards equitable possession as it is possible to go; for, after notice given, the trustee of the fund becomes a trustee for the assignee who has given him notice. It is upon these grounds that I am disposed to come to the same conclusion with the late Master of the Rolls.

I have alluded to a case of Wright *v.* Lord Dorchester, 3 Russ. 49n., which was cited as an authority in support of the opinion of the Master of the Rolls. In that case, a person of the name of Charles Sturt was entitled to the dividends of certain stock, which stood in the names of Lord Dorchester and another trustee. In 1793 Sturt applied to Messrs. Wright & Co., bankers at Norwich, for an advance of money, and, in consideration of the moneys which they advanced to him, granted to them two annuities, and assigned his interest in the stock as a security for the payment. No notice was given by Messrs. Wright & Co. to the trustees. It would appear that Sturt afterwards applied to one of the defendants, Brown, to purchase his life interest in the stock; Brown then made inquiry of the trustees, and they stated that they had no notice of any incumbrance on the fund: upon this B. completed the purchase, and received the dividends for upwards of six years. Messrs. Wright then filed a bill, and obtained an injunction, restraining the transfer of the fund or the payment of the dividends; but, on the answer of Brown, disclosing the facts with respect to his purchase, Lord Eldon dissolved that injunction. At the same time, however, that he dissolved the injunction, he dissolved it only on condition that Brown should give security to refund the money, if, at the hearing, the court should give judgment in favor of any of the other parties. That case was attended also with this particular circumstance, that the party who pledged the fund stated by his answer that, when he executed the security to Wright & Co., he considered that the pledge was meant to extend only to certain real estates. For these reasons I do not rely on the case of Wright *v.* Lord Dorchester as an authority; I rest on the general principle to which I have referred; and, on that principle, I am of opinion that the plaintiffs are not entitled to come into a court of equity for relief against the defendant Hall. The decree must, therefore, be affirmed, and the deposit paid to Hall.

The case of Loveridge *v.* Cooper, though the circumstances are somewhat different, is the same in principle with Dearle v. Hall, and must follow the same decision.[1]

[1] The principal case is followed in a considerable number of states; in other states, however, it is held that the prior assignee prevails over a subsequent assignee without regard to notice to the trustee or obligor. The doctrine of Dearle v. Hall was rejected in Salem Trust Co. v. Manufacturers' Finance Co., 264 U. S. 182.

Where the doctrine of Dearle v. Hall is accepted, it is applied both to successive assignments of legal *choses* in action and to successive assignments of equitable interests in personalty. In Parks v. Innes, 33 Barb. (N. Y.) 37, however, the court applied the doctrine of Dearle v. Hall to successive assignments of equitable interests, although it had been held not applicable to successive assignments of legal *choses* in action.

The doctrine of Dearle v. Hall has been held in England inapplicable to equitable interests in land; but by law of Property Act, 1925, 15 Geo. V. c. 20, sec. 137, the rule is changed. See Lewin, Trusts, 696. In the United States priority as to equitable interests in land is usually governed by recording statutes.

Even under the doctrine of Dearle v. Hall an assignee of an equitable interest or legal *chose* in action prevails over a subsequent attaching or garnishing creditor or trustee in bankruptcy although the assignee has not given notice of the assignment. Williston, Contracts, sec. 434.

If the second assignee of a *chose* in action in the form of a specialty obtains the document containing the obligation, he is preferred. Re Gillespie, 15 Fed. 734; Graham Paper Co. v. Pembroke, 124 Cal. 117 (written evidence); Bridge v. Conn. Mut. Life Ins. Co., 152 Mass. 343; Goodhue v. State Street Trust Co., 267 Mass. 28 (certificate of shares in real estate trust); Washington v. Nat. Bk., 147 Mich. 571; Fisher v. Knox, 13 Pa. 622. See also Uniform Stock Transfer Act. sec. 4. If the specialty is delivered to the first assignee, he will prevail against the second assignee regardless of notice to the obligor. Spencer v. Clarke, 9 Ch. D. 137; West of England Bk. v. Bachelor, 51 L. J. Ch. 199; Société Générale v. Walker, 11 App. Cas. 20 (*semble*); Kamena v. Huelbig, 23 N. J. Eq. 78; Maybin v. Hall, 4 Rich. Eq. (S. C.) 105; Strange v. Houston etc. Co., 53 Tex. 162. See 1 Machen, Corporations, sec. 885. But see *contra*, Fraley's App., 76 Pa. 42; Pratt's App., 77 Pa. 378.

The second assignee is preferred to the first if in good faith he obtains payment of the claim assigned, or if he reduces his claim to a judgment in his own name, or if he effects a novation with the obligor, whereby the obligation in favor of the assignor is superseded by a new one running to himself. Judson v. Corcoran, 17 How. (U. S.) 612; Mercantile etc. Co. v. Corcoran, 1 Gray (Mass.) 75; Bridge v. Conn. Mut. Life Ins. Co., 152 Mass. 343; Rabinowitz v. People's Nat. Bank, 235 Mass. 102; Bentley v. Root, 5 Paige (N. Y.) 632, 640; New York etc. Ry. Co. v. Schuyler, 34 N. Y. 30, 80; Strange v. Houston Co., 53 Tex. 162. See Coffman v. Liggett, 107 Va. 418; Pomeroy, Eq. Juris., sec. 698.

In Kelly v. Selwyn, [1905] 2 Ch. 117, it was held that if the trust *res* is in England and the *cestui que trust* made an assignment in New York (where Dearle v. Hall is not followed) and a later assignment in England, and notice of the second assignment was given to the trustees before notice of the first assignment, the second assignee prevails.

See Williston, Contracts, secs. 435–438; Ames, 326–328; Scott, Cases on Trusts, 1 ed., 622–4; Pomeroy, Eq. Juris., secs. 693–702; 19 Yale L. Jour. 258; 19 Col. L. Rev. 70; 66 L. R. A. 760; 31 A. L. R. 876; Dec. Dig., Assignments, secs. 83–85.

BELKNAP v. BELKNAP.

SUPREME JUDICIAL COURT, MASSACHUSETTS. 1862.

5 Allen 468.

BILL IN EQUITY, praying for the removal of Edward Belknap, as trustee under the will of his father, and that an assignment by him of his interest in the trust fund might be declared void, and for other relief.

At the hearing in this court, before Hoar, J., it appeared that John Belknap died in 1856 . . . and disposed of the residue of his estate as follows: —

"All the rest and residue of my estate, real, personal, and mixed, not herein before devised and bequeathed, I hereby give, devise, and bequeath, in trust, to my sons Edward Belknap and Henry Belknap, and the survivor of them, and the heirs of such survivor, to be held in trust and managed by them for the following purposes, to wit: . . . 3. To divide the remaining income, after the payment above described, into four equal parts, for the use of my four children, Edward, Jane, Henry, and George; the parts for Edward, Henry, and Jane to be paid to them, and that of George to be paid to his mother, for his use under her direction during his minority; after he becomes of age, to be paid to himself." Then followed provisions for the disposition of the estate after the decease of his widow, which are not now material.

By codicils to this will Edward Belknap was left the sole trustee. He accepted the trust in June, 1856, gave a bond according to law, and received a large amount of property, real and personal, and, after the settlement of his second account, absconded, having appropriated to his own use a large portion of the trust estate. On the 2d of April, 1859, being largely indebted to the Union Bank, in New York, for money borrowed, he executed to them an assignment . . . by which he purported to transfer "the share of the estate, both real and personal, of my late father, John Belknap, which by the terms of my said father's will can in any event vest in me, as one of his heirs or devisees, and all my right, title, and interest therein, including any accumulations made, or hereafter to be made of the income of said estate." This assignment was made as additional collateral security, the bank not being satisfied with what they then had. The greater part of that indebtedness is still unpaid. It did not appear whether he was a defaulter to his father's estate at the time of executing the assignment; but it did appear that the officers of the bank had no knowledge or reason to believe that no [a?] default or misapplication of the funds held under the will had then been made.

As against Edward Belknap, the bill was taken for confessed;

and the Union Bank alone opposed the granting of the relief sought for. A receiver was appointed to take charge of the estate, pending the suit; and it appeared by his accounts that the share of the income, and the commissions, to which Edward might have been entitled, if he had not been a defaulter, had been reserved. It was contended, in behalf of Henry Belknap, that this share of the income and the commissions ought to be applied to make up the amount of the principal which has been misapplied by Edward; and other parties contended that the same should be applied first to make up the deficiency in the income.

The case was reserved for the determination of the whole court.

HOAR, J. We shall have no occasion to decide the question which has been argued in this case, whether the assignment by Edward Belknap to the Union Bank was of any validity whatever; because it is very clear, upon principle and authority, that the estate in the hands of the trustee is bound in equity to discharge the legacies to the other *cestuis que trust*, before he or his assigns can claim any part of it, if the estate has been diminished by a violation of his duties as trustee. The equities of those to whom he is bound by his assumption of the trust are prior and superior to any which he can create in the trust fund by contract. As it was held in Fuller *v.* Knight, 6 Beav. 205, a trustee cannot bargain away his power to make good a deficiency in the trust fund, arising from his breach of trust.

The doctrine is very succinctly stated in Morris *v.* Livie, 1 Y. & Coll. 380, of which the marginal note is as follows: " If an executor assigns his reversionary legacy, the assignee takes it subject to the equities which attached to the executor; and therefore if the latter, though subsequently to the assignment, wastes the testator's assets, the assignee cannot receive the legacy till satisfaction has been made for the breach of trust."

That case was very elaborately argued and carefully considered, and seems more directly in point than any other which has been cited. Though not binding upon this court as an authority, we are satisfied that it rests upon sound principles of equity.

A distinction has been strongly pressed by the counsel for the Union Bank, supposed to arise from our statute provisions which require security to be given by executors and trustees for the faithful performance of their trusts. But it is difficult to see any equity which the assignee of a trust fund which is to remain in the hands and under the management of the assignor can have against the sureties on his official bond. The assignor certainly has no claim on the surety to make good to him any loss by his own unfaithfulness. If there were no assignment, equity would obviously require the trustee to pay everything due to others beneficially interested in the fund, if the fund were diminished by his dishonesty, before applying any further part of it to his own use. And there seems to be no good reason why the assignee should be put in a better condition than the assignor. It would be in effect to allow the assignor to take to his own use his share of the trust fund, and by contract with a third party to cast upon his official surety the burden of making it good to a purchaser.

The Union Bank, when they took the assignment, knew that it was of a fund held by Edward Belknap in trust, and which was to continue under his care and management. They took it subject to all the risks of such a condition of things; subject to all equities in favor of the other *cestuis que trust*, arising from the fact that the assignor was trustee; and they acquired no equitable rights against the sureties in the probate bond, because their grantor had none which he could convey.

It does not appear that the defalcation by Edward Belknap is equal to the share of the estate of which he is entitled to the income. If it is not, it is equally for the interest of the bank, and of those who may be entitled to the reversionary interest if he should not survive his mother, that his share of the income should be applied to make good the capital.

The decree will therefore be, that the assignment shall have no force or effect against any persons beneficially interested in the estate, other than Edward Belknap.

The commissions which have been retained as belonging to Edward Belknap are to be applied first to the payment of the charges and expenses of the receiver. If there is any part remaining, it is next to be applied to the costs of the suit; and the remainder, if any, is to be distributed as income.

The income belonging to Edward Belknap must be applied to make good the deficiency in the trust fund which he has caused. He must be removed from the trust, and a new trustee appointed, and the case sent to a master to take an account; and all other questions, including that of the ultimate rights of the Union Bank under the assignment, except so far as already determined, be reserved.[1]

---

[1] Wilkins v. Sibley, 4 Giff. 442; Re Knapman, 18 Ch. D. 300 (*semble*); Doering v. Doering, 42 Ch. D. 203 (subsequently acquired interest); American Surety Co. v. Vinton, 224 Mass. 337; Jenkinson v. N. Y. Finance Co., 79 N. J. Eq. 247, 254 (*semble*); Stanley v. U. S. Nat. Bank, 110 Ore. 648 (*semble*); Hart's Estate (No. 5), 203 Pa. 503 (*semble*), accord. Macpherson's Judicial Factor v. Mackay, [1915] S. C. (Scot.) 1011; Wilkes v. Harper, 2 Barb. Ch. 338, 355, 1 N. Y. 586, *contra*. See also Re Sewell, [1909] 1 Ch. 806; Re Rhodesia Goldfields, [1910] 1 Ch. 239 (breach before assignment); Re Towndrow, [1911] 1 Ch. 662; Re Dacre, [1916] 1 Ch. 344, *aff'g* s. c., [1915] 2 Ch. 480; Cogswell v. Weston, 228 Mass. 219; Raynes v. Raynes, 54 N. H. 201; Matter of Eisner, 129 N. Y. Misc. 106 (trustee-beneficiary misappropriated before assignment but misappropriation not discovered until after assignment). *Cf.* Re Pain, [1919] 1 Ch. 38. See 40 Harv. L. Rev. 123.

CHAPTER IX.
THE PERSONS WHO ARE BOUND BY A TRUST.
NOTE.
———. 1453.

Fitzh. Abr. Subpoena, pl. 19.[1]

IF I enfeoff a man to perform my last will and he enfeoffs another, I cannot have a subpœna against the second because he is a stranger, but I shall have a subpœna against my feoffee and recover in damages for the value of the land. Per *Yelverton* and *Wilby*, clerks of the rolls, who said that if my feoffee in confidence enfeoffed another upon confidence of the same land, that I should have a subpœna against the second, but otherwise when he was enfeoffed *bona fide*, for then I am without remedy, and so it was adjudged in the case of the Cardinal Winchester.

ANONYMOUS.
———. 1465.

Y. B. 5 Ed. IV. fol. 7, pl. 16.[2]

IF J. enfeoffed A. to his use and A. enfeoffed R., although he sold the land to him; if A. gave notice to R. of the intent of the first use, he is bound by writ of subpœna to perform the will, &c.[3]

---

[1] Crompton, Courts, 54, s. c.

[2] Fitzh. Abr. Subpoena, pl. 2, Crompton, Courts, 59, s. c.

[3] "If my trustee conveys the land to a third person who well knows that the trustee holds for my use, I shall have a remedy in the Chancery against both of them: as well against the buyer as against the trustee; for in conscience he buys my land." Y. B. 11 Ed. IV. fol. 8, pl. 13 (1471), translated 3 Maitland, Collected Papers, 345. See Fitzh. Abr. Subpoena, pl. 18 (1492); Bacon, Uses, 15.

In New York it is provided by statute that where a trust of real property is expressed in the instrument creating the estate, every sale, conveyance or other act of the trustee in contravention of the trust shall be absolutely void. Real Property Law, sec. 105. There is similar legislation in California, Indiana, Kansas, Michigan, Montana, North Dakota, Oklahoma, South Dakota and Wisconsin.

ANONYMOUS.

———. 1468.

Y. B. 8 Ed. IV. fol. 6, pl, 1.[1]

AND it was moved whether a subpœna would lie against an executor or heir. And CHOKE, J., said that he had formerly sued a subpœna against the heir of a feoffee, and the matter was long debated. And the opinion of the Chancellor and the justices was that it did not lie against an heir, and so he sued a bill to Parliament.

FAIRFAX. This matter is a good store for discussion when the others come, &c.

ANONYMOUS.

———. 1474.

Fitzh. Abr. Subpoena, pl. 14.

NOTE, that a subpœna lies against the heir of the feoffee who survives. Mich. 14. E. 4.[2]

ANONYMOUS.

COMMON PLEAS. 1522.

Y. B. 14 Hen. VIII. fol. 4, pl. 5.

FITZHERBERT, J. . . . If I enfeoff B. to hold to him his heirs and assigns, my trust and confidence are in him, his heirs and assigns: and this is easily shown, for the heirs will be bound to perform the feoffor's will as much as the father, and the second feoffee as much as the first, if there is no consideration, and so it is if the feoffee suffer a recovery without a consideration. For it shall be intended since he parted with the land without consideration that he parted with it in the most proper way, *i.e.* to hold it as he held. For when an act rests in intendment and is indifferent, the law makes the most favorable presumption, for if I see a priest and a woman together suspiciously, still as long as there is doubt whether he is doing good or evil the former is to be presumed, . . . and so here when he makes a feoffment or grant without any consideration.[3] . . .

---

[1] [Fitzh. Abr. Subpoena, pl. 8, Crompton, Courts, 46], Ellesmere, Office of Chancellor, 86, pl. 26, s. c., to which report the author adds: "Note that it must be intended that the heir had not this land, but that the land was sold before by the feoffee to a stranger; for if the heir had the land, he is liable to the trust as well as the feoffee." See also Cary, 10, 12; Ellesmere, Office of Chancellor, 94, pl. 49. — AMES.

[2] See Y. B. 22 Ed. IV. fol. 6, pl. 18 (1482); Keil. 42, pl. 7 (1501); Keil. 46b, pl. 7 (1502); Y. B. 14 Hen. VIII. fol. 4, pl. 5 (1522); Weston v. Danvers, Toth. 105; Bacon, Uses, Rowe's ed., 23, n. 39; Scott, Cases on Trusts, 1 ed., 629.

[3] In Otis v. Otis, 167 Mass. 245, Holmes, J., said (p. 246): "A person to

CHAP. IX.] NOEL v. JEVON 669

COMPLEAT ATTORNEY, ed. 1656, 310. — And the tenant in dower, and by curtesie, should not be seised to uses in being, for all these wanted privity of estate.[1]

NOEL v. JEVON.

CHANCERY. 1678.

Freem. C. C. 43.

THE bill was to be relieved against the defendant's dower, her husband being only a trustee; and it appearing that the husband was but a trustee, the defendant was barred of her dower, contrary to the opinion of Nash v. Preston, Cro. Car. 191; and so it was said is the constant practice of the court now.[2]

---

whose hands a trust fund comes by conveyance from the original trustee is chargeable as a trustee in his turn, if he takes it without consideration, whether he has notice of the trust or not. This has been settled for three hundred years, since the time of uses."

It is sometimes said that the reason is that the donee is presumed to have notice of the use or trust. Compleat Attorney, 309, 310; Langdell, Summary Eq. Pl., 211. But if an innocent donee of a fractional interest in trust property subsequently purchases in good faith and for value another fractional interest, he takes the latter interest clear of the trust. Giddings v. Eastman, 5 Paige (N. Y.) 561. For a discussion of the reasons for binding a donee, see Ames, Lect. Leg. Hist. 255; 17 Col. L. Rev. 283; *ibid.*, 479.

It is unnecessary to cite cases for the proposition which was stated by the judges in the principal case and from which the courts have never deviated, that a purchaser from a feoffee to uses or trustee who takes the legal title for value and without notice of the uses or trusts, takes it free and clear. See Ames, 286n; Bogert, Trusts, sec. 124; Dec. Dig., Trusts, sec. 357.

Illegal transactions. One who takes trust property in an illegal transaction, although without notice of the trust, takes subject to the trust. Banque Belge v. Hambrouck, [1921] 1 K. B. 321 (illegal co-habitation); Joslyn v. Downing, Hopkins & Co., 150 Fed. 317, 20 Harv. L. Rev. 657 (gambling); Glasgow v. Nicholls, 124 Wash. 281, 127 Wash. 693, 129 Wash. 319 (gambling). See 2 A. L. R. 345; 35 A. L. R. 427.

[1] See Y. B. 14 Hen. VIII. fol. 4, pl. 5; Bro. Abr. Feff. al Uses, pl. 40; Chudleigh's Case, 1 Rep. 114, 122a; Lewin, Trusts, [12 ed., 2, 246, 276]. — AMES.

[2] See Ames, 374; Gilbert, Uses, 18; Lewin, Trusts, 12 ed., 246, 276; Perry, Trusts, sec. 322.

A wife has no homestead interest in land held by her husband as trustee. Osborn v. Strachan, 32 Kan. 52.

A husband is not entitled, in equity at any rate, to curtesy in lands of which his wife was seised merely as trustee. Bennet v. Davis, 2 P. Wms. 316; King v. Bushnell, 121 Ill. 656; Chew v. Commissioners, 5 Rawle (Pa.) 160. See also Welch v. Chandler, 13 B. Mon. (Ky.) 420; Perry, Trusts, sec. 322.

General and special occupant. In Stephens v. Baily, Nels. 106 (1665), it was held that where a tenant *pur autre vie* contracted to convey his interest, but died before making the conveyance, and his heir entered as special occupant, the heir was bound by the contract. See Gell v. Vermedun, Freem. C. C. 199. But see Anon., Freem. C. C. 155. It would seem, however, that an occupant was not bound by a use. Bro. Abr. Feff. al Uses, fol. 338, pl. 10.

ANONYMOUS.

——. 1580.

6 Jenk. Cent. pl. 30.

AT this day, where the tenant of the land is attainted of felony or treason, the use and trust for this land are extinguished; for the king, or the lord to whom the escheat belongs, comes in in the *post* and paramount the trust; and upon a title elder than the use or trust, *viz.* the right of his lordship by escheat for want of a tenant.[1]

Merger of term for years. In Saunders *v.* Bournford, Finch 424 (1679), it was held that where a tenant of a term for a thousand years assigned the term to two trustees, one of whom was the heir of the lessor, although on the death of the lessor there was a merger of a moiety of the term, the trust was not extinguished.

In *Re* Albert Road, [1916] 1 Ch. 289, a corporation which was, in effect, trustee of a leasehold interest, was dissolved, with the result that the lease terminated. It was held that the interest of the *cestui que trust* was not destroyed by merger, but that the reversioner became trustee to the extent of the term, and the court appointed a new trustee and made a vesting order. See also Gilbert, Uses, 16. See Thorn *v.* Newman, 3 Swanst. 603; 3 Preston, Conveyancing, 3 ed., 314–327. The result is different if the reversioner is a purchaser of the term for value and without notice. Wilkes *v.* Spooner, [1911] 2 K. B. 473.

"If a lease be made to a charitable use, and the lessee commits a forfeiture by feoffment etc., if the lessor enter for the forfeiture, he shall be bound by decree, during the years to come of that lease." Duke, Char. Uses, 161 (1676).

Similarly, equity will give relief when a remainderman by fraud induces the tenant for years to surrender his term. Danby *v.* Danby, Finch 220.

Equity protects the trustee as well as the *cestui que trust,* as, for example, where an estate of the trustee held in his own right, is merged in an estate held in trust. 3 Preston, Conveyancing, 3 ed., 326.

[1] *Uses.* The lord taking by escheat on the death of a feoffee to uses without heirs was not bound by the use. Y. B. 14 Hen. VIII. fol. 4, pl. 5; Y. B. 14 Hen. VIII. fol. 24, pl. 2; Bro. Abr. Feff. al Uses, pl. 40; Chudleigh's Case, 1 Rep. 122*a,* 139*b;* [Compleat Attorney, 310. But see Duke, Char. Uses, 161.]

In Chudleigh's Case, 1 Rep. 114, Popham, C. J., said (p. 139*b*): "The reason why the lord by escheat, or the lord of a villain, should not stand seised to an use, is, because the title of the lord is by reason of his elder title, and that grows, either by reason of the seigniory of the land, or of the villain, which title is higher and elder than the use or confidence is; and therefore should not be subject to it."

Trusts of Land. The lord taking by escheat was not at common law bound by a trust. Ellesmere, Office of Chancellor, fol. 93, pl. 48; Peachy *v.* Somerset, 1 Stra. 447, 454; Burgess *v.* Wheate, 1 Ed. 177, 201, 246 (*semble*); King *v.* Mildmay, 5 B. & Ad. 254; Atty. Gen. *v.* Leeds, 2 M. & K. 343; Benzein *v.* Lenoir, 1 Dev. Eq. 225; King *v.* Rhew, 108 N. C. 696, 700. See also Reeve *v.* Atty. Gen., 2 Atk. 223. [And see Hardman, Law of Escheat, 4 L. Quar. Rev. 318, 329.]

The notion that the lord taking by escheat is bound by a trust is countenanced only by the dissenting opinion of Lord Mansfield in Burgess *v.*

POAGE v. BELL.

COURT OF APPEALS, VIRGINIA. 1837.

8 Leigh 604.

[ONE Imboden conveyed certain personal property to trustees in trust to pay his debt to the plaintiff. This is an action of *assumpsit* to recover the proceeds of a wagon and team of horses which the plaintiff claims were included in the conveyance and which he alleges were sold by the defendant with knowledge of the trust deed. The defendant pleaded the general issue. The circuit court held that the action could not be maintained and directed a verdict for the defendant.]

TUCKER, P. In this case we are of opinion that there was no error in the opinion of the court instructing the jury that the action was not maintainable by the plaintiff upon the case made by him, he being only a *cestui que trust*, but was only maintainable in a court of law by the plaintiff's trustee. Though an action has in many cases been entertained at law by a *cestui que trust* against his trustee,

---

Wheate, 1 Ed. 177, 229 (the reasoning in which is fully answered in Lewin, Trusts, 12 ed., 277), by an alleged but improbable dictum of Lord Bridgman in Geary v. Bearcroft, Cart. 57, 67 (see 1 Hargrave's Juris. Exer. 383, 391), and by loose dicta in Eales v. England, Prec. Ch. 200, and White v. Baylor, 10 Ir. Eq. R. 43, 54.

By Intestates Estates Act, 1884, 47 & 48 Vict. c. 71, sec. 6 (following the earlier acts 39 & 40 Geo. III. c. 88, sec. 12 [4 & 5 Will. IV. c. 23], and 13 & 14 Vict. c. 60, secs. 15, 46), the right of the *cestui que trust* is saved, although the legal title escheats by the failure of heirs of the trustee. See *Re* Martinez's Trusts, W. N. (1870), 70. — AMES.

As to the distinction between escheat and forfeiture, see Challis, Real Property, 3 ed., 37. See Pawlett v. Attorney General, Hard. 465 (equity of redemption); Pimbe's Case, Moore 196, *ante*.

Personalty. On the death of a trustee of personalty, intestate and without next of kin, the Crown at common law took the legal title to the trust property as *bona vacantia*. And on the attainder of the trustee of personalty for felony or treason, the Crown likewise took the legal title to the trust property. It seems however that in both these cases the Crown took subject to the trust. Hix v. Attorney General, Hard. 176. But since no bill in equity lies against the sovereign, relief is given only upon petition. Ames, 215. As to the practice on petitions of right, see 144 L. T. 170.

It is now however provided by statute that the Crown shall not take, but a new trustee shall be appointed by the court. 4 & 5 Will. IV. c. 23.

In the United States there is of course no attainder of treason or felony. In those jurisdictions in which on the death of the trustee the trust property vests in new trustees appointed by the court, the fact that the trustee dies intestate and without heirs or next of kin is of course immaterial. When trust property does vest in the state, relief can be obtained only by act of the legislature. See Briggs v. Light-Boats, 11 Allen (Mass.) 157. See also N. J. Sess. Laws, 1912, c. 230.

where the trust is no longer continuing, but is *functus officio*, and a balance is in the trustee's hands, yet we know no case in which an action has been maintained by a *cestui que trust* against a third person, who has either wrongfully converted the property of the trust to his own use, or has received the trust funds without paying them over. Apart from the technical objection that he only can maintain an action at law, who has the legal title, there is the vital objection that the trustee is bound to execute the trust in all regards, and in doing so the rights of other *cestuis que trust* may be involved, who are not and cannot be made parties to the suit. Thus in the case before us, an essential point in the plaintiff's case is the indebtedness of Imboden to him. But how is this matter to be tried, when Imboden is no party? This shows the propriety of confining the *cestui que trust* to a court of equity, (when that jurisdiction is proper for him) where all persons interested may be made parties, and of requiring the action to be brought by the trustee, when the remedy is only at law. . . .

Judgment affirmed.[1]

[1] *Action at law.* The *cestui que trust* merely as such cannot maintain an action at law against a third person for conversion of personalty nor for trespass to land. Ames, 255–256.

A *cestui que trust* in possession may like any other possessor bring possessory actions. Stearns v. Palmer, 10 Met. (Mass.) 32. The *cestui que trust* has also been allowed to maintain an action where the purposes of the trust have been fully performed. Bogert, Trusts, sec. 115.

The *cestui que trust* cannot maintain an action of ejectment against a stranger to recover possession of the trust premises. Langdon v. Sherwood, 124 U. S. 74. In Doe d. Bristow v. Pegge, 1 T. R. 758n. (*a*), the court held that the owner of an estate of inheritance subject to an outstanding term given to trustees upon a trust for purposes not yet accomplished might bring ejectment. The principal opinion was delivered by Lord Mansfield. It has long since been overruled. See Doe v. Staple, 2 T. R. 684; Lewin, Trusts, 12 ed., 871; Ames, 254n. In Pennsylvania where there was formerly no equity jurisdiction, the *cestui que trust* may maintain ejectment against a stranger. Kennedy v. Fury, 1 Dall. 72; Brolaskey v. McClain, 61 Pa. 146.

The trustee of course can maintain an action at law against a third person to recover the trust property or damages for a tort with respect to the property. Ames, 256.

Suit in equity. If the trustee refuses to bring an action against a third person who has taken possession of or injured the trust property, the *cestui que trust* may bring a suit in equity joining the trustee and the third person as defendants. See Chap. I, sec. VIII, *ante.*

Procedure under the codes. It is provided by the codes of procedure that "Every action must be prosecuted in the name of the real party in interest, except that an executor or administrator, a trustee of an express trust, or a person expressly authorized by statute, may sue without joining with him the persons for whose benefit the action is prosecuted." Under this provision, the *cestui que trust* ordinarily cannot maintain an action against a third person for a tort, although if the trustee refuses or neglects to sue he can bring an action joining the trustee and the third person as parties. See Clark, Code Pleading, sec. 27; Bogert, Trusts, sec. 115.

Eminent domain. It has been held that where property held in trust is condemned by a railroad, the trustee, and not the *cestui que trust*, is the proper

LORD COMPTON'S CASE

Common Bench. 1580

3 Leon. 196.[1]

Note, it was holden by Lord Anderson, C. J., in this case, that if *cestui que use* after the Statute 1 Rich. III. leaseth for years, and afterwards the feoffees release to the lessee and his heirs, having notice of the use; that that release is to the first use. But where the feoffees are disseised and they release to the disseisor, although that they [he?] have notice of the use, yet the same is to the use of the disseisor; and no subpœna lieth against the disseisor.[2]

---

party to recover compensation. Davis v. Charles R. etc. R. R. Co., 11 Cush. (Mass.) 506; Packard v. Old Colony R. R. Co., 168 Mass. 92.

If a railroad condemns land subject to a restrictive covenant as to use for residential purposes only, it has been held that the owner of the dominant estate is entitled to compensation. Flynn v. N. Y. etc. Ry. Co., 218 N. Y. 140. But see Doan v. Cleveland etc. Ry. Co., 92 Oh. St. 461. In Flynn v. N. Y. etc. Co., *supra,* the court said (p. 146): "These restrictive covenants create a property right and make direct and compensational the damages which otherwise would be consequential and non-compensational."

[1] 2 Leon. 211 s. c.

[2] See Chudleigh's Case, 1 Rep. 114, 120a; Earl of Worcester v. Finch, 4 Coke Inst. 85; Turner v. Buck, 22 Vin. Abr. 21, pl. 5; Ames, 372; 17 Col. L. Rev. 284–287; *ibid.,* 478–479.

"The reason why a disseisor should not stand seised to an use was, because *cestui que use* had no remedy by the common law for any use, but his remedy was only in chancery; and because the right of a freehold or inheritance could not be determined in chancery, his title should not be drawn into examination there; and for this reason a disseisor shall not be compelled in the chancery to execute an estate to *cestui que use,* but *cestui que use* shall compel his feoffees in the Court of Chancery to enter upon the disseisor, or to recover the land against him at the common law: and then the chancery will compel the feoffees to execute the estate according to the use." Chudleigh's Case, 1 Rep. 114, 139b.

"And if a disseisor, abator, or intrudor, had come to the possession of the land, whereof the use was, albeit he had notice of the use, yet the use was suspended during their possession, and they should not have been seised to the use as the feoffee was, for they come not to the land in the *per* but in the *post.*" Compleat Attorney, 310.

"The disseisee doth release unto the disseisor rendering rent, the render is void, for a rent cannot issue out of a right; so an use cannot be out of a release by the disseisee, for such release to such purpose shall not enure as an entry and feoffment." Read v. Nash, 1 Leon. 147, 148.

"Release of right *in rem* to disseisor extinguishes it — use grafted on right *in rem* disappears also. Today disseisor would be made constructive trustee. But lessee for years had no seisin; therefore grantee of seisin with notice of use took subject to it." Ames, MS. note to Lord Compton's Case.

LEWELLIN v. MACKWORTH.

CHANCERY. 1740.

2 Eq. Cas. Abr. 579.[1]

LORD CHANCELLOR HARDWICKE. The rule in this court, that the Statute of Limitations does not bar a trust estate, holds only as between *cestui que trust* and trustees, not between *cestui que trust* and trustee on one side and strangers on the other, for that would be to make the Statute of no force at all, because there is hardly any estate of consequence without such trust, and so the act would never take place; therefore, where a *cestui que trust* and his trustee are both out of possession for the time limited, the party in possession has a good bar against them both.[2]

WYCH v. EAST INDIA COMPANY.

CHANCERY. 1734.

3 P. Wms. 309.

THE East India Company were bound by contract to make an allowance of two rupees per cent. to the plaintiff's intestate, for which the plaintiff, the administrator *de bonis non* of his father, brought a bill. The intestate, with whom the company made the contract, was then beyond sea, and there died, leaving an infant son of tender years. Upon the death of the intestate, administration was granted to A. until the said son should come to twenty-one, *ad usum et commodum* of the infant, who at that time was about ——— years of age. The administrator in trust for the infant never

---

[1] 2 Atk. 40; 15 Vin. Abr. 125n., s. c.

[2] It is immaterial that the *cestui que trust* is under a disability, or has only a future interest. Hovenden v. Annesley, 2 Sch. & Lef. 607, 629; Meeker v. Olpherts, 100 U. S. 564; Molton v. Henderson, 62 Ala. 426; Cruse v. Kidd, 195 Ala. 92; Patchett v. Pac. etc. Ry. Co., 100 Cal. 505; Hall v. Waterman, 220 Ill. 569; Crook v. Glenn, 30 Md. 55; Nelson v. Ratliff, 72 Miss. 656; Wren v. Dixon, 40 Nev. 170 (*semble*); Kirkman v. Holland, 139 N. C. 185; Cameron v. Hicks, 141 N. C. 21; Young v. McNeil, 78 S. C. 143; Appel v. Childress, 53 Tex. Civ. App. 607, *accord.* See Ames, 271; Huston, Decrees in Equity, 142–144; Wood, Limitations, 4 ed., sec. 208; Perry, Trusts, sec. 858; 2 A. L. R. 41.

On the other hand, if the trustee is under a disability, the Statute of Limitations will not run against the *cestui que trust* even though the latter be *sui juris.* Clayton v. Rose, 87 N. C. 106; Waring v. Cheraw etc. Co., 16 S. C. 416. See also Grimsby v. Hudnell, 76 Ga. 378. So, if a devisee in trust disclaims, so that under a statute the title vests in the Supreme Court, the Statute of Limitations will not begin to run until a new trustee is appointed. Ayer v. Chapman, 146 Ga. 608; Dunning v. Ocean Bank, 6 Lans. 296.

If the owner of land subject to a restrictive covenant is disseised, and the disseisee is barred by the Statute of Limitations, the covenant still binds the land. *Re* Nisbet & Potts' Contract, [1906] 1 Ch. 386, *aff'g* [1905] 1 Ch. 391.

commenced any suit on this contract; but the son within six years after his attaining twenty-one, brought this bill against the company, who pleaded the statute of limitations, viz. that the cause of action did accrue above six years before the suit commenced,

Whereupon it was argued, that as the time did not run against the father, with whom the contract was made, because he was beyond sea, and died there; so after the death of the father the son was an infant, and ought not to be barred or prejudiced by the neglect or default of his trustee, the administrator, during his minority.

LORD CHANCELLOR [TALBOT]. The administrator during the infancy of the plaintiff had a right to sue; and though the *cestui que trust* was an infant, yet he must be bound by the trustee's not suing in time; for I cannot take away the benefit of the statute of limitations from the company, who are in no default, and are entitled to take advantage thereof as well as private persons; since their witnesses may die, or their vouchers be lost. And as to the trust, that is only between the administrator and the infant, and does not affect the company. So where there is an executor in trust for another, and the executor neglects to bring his action within the time prescribed by the statute, the *cestui que trust,* or residuary legatee, will be barred; therefore allow the plea.[1]

WETMORE, AS EXECUTOR, *v.* PORTER.

COURT OF APPEALS, NEW YORK. 1883.

92 N. Y. 76.

APPEAL from judgment of the General Term of the Superior Court of the city of New York, entered upon an order made April 3, 1882,

---

[1] See Mason *v.* Mason, 33 Ga. 435; Ames, 271; Perry, Trusts, sec. 859. See Spickernell *v.* Hotham, Kay 669, *ante.*

Release of obligor. If a *chose* in action is held in trust, a release given by the obligee-trustee to the obligor is a good discharge at common law. If the obligor paid value for the release and had no notice that it was given in breach of trust, the obligor's discharge is effective in equity as well as at law. If, however, the obligor has notice that the release was given in breach of trust, or if he gave no value for the release, the *cestui que trust* will be protected; the release may be set aside in equity, or the courts of law will prevent the defendant from taking advantage of it. See Scott, Cases on Trusts, 1 ed., 646.

As to the effect of a release by the *cestui que trust,* see Supreme Lodge *v.* Rutzler, 87 N. J. Eq. 342, *ante.*

Set-off. If the obligee-trustee sues the obligor, the latter may at common law set off a debt due to him from the plaintiff individually. But equity will prevent the obligor from relying on the set-off if he knew of the rights of the *cestui que trust.* Ames, 270n. See note to Bischoff *v.* Yorkville Bk., 218 N. Y. 106, *post.*

If the obligee-trustee sues the obligor, the latter may not at common law set off a debt due to him from the *cestui que trust.* But such set-off is allowed in equity or by way of equitable defense. Ames, 270n.

which affirmed a judgment in favor of defendant, entered upon an order sustaining a demurrer to plaintiff's complaint herein.

RUGER, Ch. J. The defendant demurred to the complaint upon the grounds:

1st. That there was a defect in the parties defendant, in that the plaintiff should also have been made a defendant.[1] . . .

The complaint sets forth among other things that one Alpheus Fobes died at New York city about the 1st day of July, 1872, having executed a last will and testament, which was admitted to probate by the surrogate of the county of New York, and letters testamentary were duly issued thereon to Abram B. Wetmore as sole executor, who thereafter took the oath of office and duly qualified; that nine $1,000 railroad bonds were of the assets belonging to said estate and were of the value of $12,000; that by an order of the surrogate made on or about the 26th day of May, 1874, the plaintiff was directed to keep the property of the estate, including said bonds, then remaining in his hands invested, and to continue in the discharge of his trust according to the terms of the will; that said bonds came into the custody of the defendant by an arrangement between the plaintiff and defendant (who then knew that the same were trust funds) whereby they were to be used as collateral security at a bank in New York for the firm notes of Porter & Wetmore. That firm consisted of the plaintiff and defendant, who were engaged in carrying on a general commission business for their joint individual benefit. The complaint further alleges that the bonds did not belong to the plaintiff individually, but were owned by the estate, and that plaintiff had long tried to re-obtain possession of them for the purpose of holding them to accomplish the objects of the trust, but that his efforts had been defeated by defendant; that on the 11th day of April, 1881, the bonds were procured to be sold by the defendant, and on the 12th day of April, 1881, and on several occasions previous thereto, the plaintiff demanded the return of the bonds or the payment of the value thereof from the defendant, but that the defendant, admitting that they were in his custody or control, refused to return them or pay their value to the plaintiff. The complaint closed by demanding judgment for the sum of $15,000 with costs. . . .

The General Term, by a memorandum indorsed upon the papers, and which contains the only information we have of the reasons for their decision, seem to have placed it upon the ground that the complaint showed upon its face that there was a defect of parties defendant. In other words, that the plaintiff should have been made a party defendant with Thomas E. Porter in any action to recover the value or possession of the bonds in question. It, therefore, becomes necessary to refer briefly to the additional allegations contained in the complaint.

[1] Only as much of the opinion is given as relates to this ground of demurrer.

It substantially alleges, in addition to what has been recited, that the plaintiff, at the request of the defendant, removed the bonds from the Safe Deposit Company, where the securities of the estate were deposited for safe keeping, and also at defendant's request left them at the Shoe and Leather Bank in New York as security for loans made, and to be made of said bank, by the firm of Porter & Wetmore, to carry on the partnership business, and that the bonds were ordered by defendant on or about the 11th day of April, 1881, to be sold by the Shoe and Leather Bank, and the proceeds applied to pay a firm note of the amount of $10,000, then held by the bank. It was also alleged that Porter was then owing the plaintiff a large sum of money in respect of the firm business, and had sufficient money belonging to the firm to more than pay the amount of the note, at the time of the sale of the bonds.

Upon this state of facts the court below has held upon the strength of the maxim "*Ex turpi causa non oritur actio*," that inasmuch as Abram B. Wetmore in his individual capacity was in collusion with the defendant in despoiling this estate, that he could not in his representative capacity reclaim these bonds from one who had wrongfully come into their possession, and restore them to the trust estate. The court further said that " the remedy of the *cestui que trust* is to have another trustee appointed who shall bring the proper action." In this, we think, it proceeded upon a mistaken view of the rights and duties of the parties. The legal title to these bonds, and the right to their custody, was and remains in the trustee, at least until they reach the possession of some person who has paid full value and is ignorant of their trust character. Whoever receives property knowing that it is the subject of a trust, and has been transferred in violation of the duty or power of the trustee, takes it subject to the right, not only of the *cestui que trust*, but also of the trustee, to reclaim possession of the specific property, or to recover damages for its conversion in case it has been converted. Briggs *v.* Davis, 20 N. Y. 15.

In the case of the Western R. R. Co. *v.* Nolan, 48 N. Y. 517, this court says: " The trustees are the parties in whom the fund is vested, and whose duty it is to maintain and defend it against wrongful attacks or injury tending to impair its safety or amount. The title to the fund being in them, neither the *cestui que trust*, nor the beneficiaries can maintain an action in relation to it as against third parties, except in case the trustees refuse to perform their duty in that respect, and then the trustees should be brought before the court as parties defendant."

It is an alarming proposition to urge against the legal title which a trustee has to trust funds that his recovery of their possession may be defeated by a wrong-doer, upon the allegation that the lawful guardian of the funds colluded with him in obtaining their possession. This action is sought to be maintained by the plaintiff solely in his representative capacity as executor or trustee under the will of Alpheus Fobes. . . .

The twin maxims "*Ex dolo malo non oritur actio*" and "*Ex turpi contractu actio non oritur*" have no application to the cause of action set up in the complaint. It is not founded upon and does not grow out of the illegal or unauthorized dealings between the plaintiff and defendant, but such dealings are invoked by one of the wrongdoers to defeat a party who is asserting a legal right and who in this action appears in a representative character alone. We see no reason why a trustee who has been guilty even of an intentional fault is not entitled to his *locus penitentiæ* and an opportunity to repair the wrong which he may have committed. . . .

The judgment should be reversed and judgment ordered for the plaintiff upon the demurrer, unless the defendant within thirty days pay plaintiff's costs and answers in the action.

All concur.

Judgment accordingly.[1]

PARKER *v.* HALL.

SUPREME COURT, TENNESSEE. 1859.

2 Head 641.

WRIGHT, J. The bill in this case, is filed to recover of the defendant, Jesse D. Hall, a slave, Judy, and her child Henry. . . .

The decision of this case rests upon the following facts, to-wit: In October, 1842, George H. Parker, the father of complainants, George A., Mary and Alvin D. Parker, and of their deceased sister, Malvinia M. Parker, was duly qualified as their guardian in the County Court of Weakley county, in this State; and as such, received into his possession a fund belonging to them.

This fund was derived by them under the will of Alonzo P. Smith, a deceased relation.

On the 6th of May, 1843, the said George H. Parker, the guardian, with a portion of said funds, purchased of C. McAlister, the slave Judy. . . .

The slave Henry is a child of Judy, born after the execution of the bill of sale.

[1] Zimmerman *v.* Kinkle, 108 N. Y. 282; Ludington *v.* Bank, 102 N. Y. App. Div. 251; Mansfield *v.* Wardlow (Tex. Civ. App., 1906), 91 S. W. 859, *accord.* See Ames, 264. So also the co-trustee of the trustee who committed the breach of trust may sue. Clemens *v.* Heckscher, 185 Pa. 476. Or a substituted trustee may sue. Leake *v.* Watson, 58 Conn. 332; Safe D. & T. Co. *v.* Cahn, 102 Md. 530; First Nat. Bk. *v.* Nat. etc. Bk., 156 N. Y. 459, 467.

If the trustee lends trust money in breach of trust, the trustee may recover it. Atwood *v.* Lester, 20 R. I. 660.

If the trustee has erroneously paid the life beneficiary what should have been retained for the remainderman, he may recoup out of the income the amount necessary to restore the capital. Ballantine *v.* Young, 74 N. J. Eq. 572.

Some two years after its date, the said George H. Parker, with his wards and their mother, and said slaves, removed from Obion, to Tipton county, in this State; and on the 26th of May, 1845, while he was yet a stranger in said county, sold and conveyed Judy and Henry to the defendant, Hall. . . .

At the time of these transactions, these wards were infants of tender years, and one of them, viz., Alvin D., a complainant, is yet an infant under twenty-one years of age.

They were all infants under twenty-one, in May, 1845, when their guardian sold Judy and Henry to Hall, and when he took possession of them, and for sometime thereafter.

George H. Parker, the guardian, died soon after the sale to Hall; and since his death, Malvinia M., one of the wards, died; and complainant, Mary A., her mother, is her administratrix.

The defences relied upon, are that of an innocent purchaser for value, without notice and the statute of limitations.

Neither of these defences can be allowed to avail the defendant. If he had not actual, he had constructive notice, which is equally fatal to him. . . .

As to the statute of limitations, it can have no operation in the case. When the cause of action accrued, the owners of these slaves were *all* under the disability of infancy, and *one* of them was still an infant, at the institution of this suit; and upon the principles of Shute *v.* Wade, 5 Yer., 1, all are saved from the bar.

The position, that when the trustee is barred all the beneficiaries are barred, though they may be under disability, has no application here. That doctrine only applies where the trustee could sue, but fails to do so, as where a stranger intrudes himself into the trust estate and holds wrongfully, and *adversely both to the trustee* and *the beneficiaries.* In such a case, if the trustee fail to sue and is barred, the beneficiaries, though infants, &c., are also barred. But here, George H. Parker, the trustee and owner of the legal estate, had estopped himself from suing by his bill of sale. He had turned against his wards, and united with the defendant in a breach of trust. The wrong *was to them, not to him.* He could not sue for, or represent them. In such a case it has been repeatedly held, by this Court, since Herron *v.* Marshall, 5 Hum., 443, that the beneficiaries can alone sue, and if they are under disability when the cause of action accrues, they will not be barred until they are allowed the time given in the statute after the disability is removed.

The record entirely fails to disclose any fraud, or other act on the part of complainant, towards defendant, when he purchased this property which will estop, or repel them from a Court of Equity. 4 Hum., 212; 1 Swan, 437.

The decree of the Chancellor will be reversed, and complainants will have a decree for the slaves Jude and Henry, and increase of Judy, born since the defendant's purchase, with hires and interest;

but if the slaves have been so disposed of that they cannot be had, then a decree will go for their present value, hires and interest. 10 Yer., 217.

Decree reversed.[1]

RINGO *v.* MCFARLAND, 232 Ky. 622 (1930): A county employee embezzled county funds and used them in purchasing and improving certain real estate. He gave a note to his attorneys for $2000, secured by a second mortgage on the real estate, in payment for services to be rendered by them in defending him in the criminal proceedings which were about to be instituted against him. It was held that the county was entitled to an equitable lien upon the real estate, and that the attorneys were not *bona fide* purchasers, since although they took the mortgage in good faith they had not rendered substantial services before they received notice of the equitable lien. DIETZMAN, J., said (p. 628):

"We are next confronted with the question whether or not the appellants are within the rule of a bona fide purchaser for value without notice, for, if they are, then their mortgage lien will be superior to the equitable lien asserted by the county. We accept without question the statement of the appellants that they did not actually know at the time they took their mortgage that Smith had embezzled the funds of the county or that he had used any embezzled funds in the payment for or improvement of his property. They frankly admit that they knew the county was claiming that Smith had embezzled its funds, but they state that they did not know to what extent he had embezzled such funds or that he had used them upon the St. Ann street property. We need not decide whether the facts which they admit knowing put upon them any further inquiry or not, because, under the facts as disclosed by this record, the appellants are not within the rule of bona fide purchasers, even though at the time they took their mortgage they were ignorant of the county's equitable lien. The proof in this case establishes that the note and mortgage were given for services *to be rendered*. They were executed and delivered on Saturday. The appellants admit that at least from the following Monday on,

[1] See Kennedy *v.* Daly, 1 Sch. & Lef. 355, 377; Holloway *v.* Eagle, 135 Ark. 206; Tippin *v.* Coleman, 59 Miss. 641; Elliott *v.* Landis Machine Co., 236 Mo. 546; Case *v.* Goodman, 250 Mo. 112; Case *v.* Sipes, 280 Mo. 110; 11 Col. L. Rev. 686; 12 Harv. L. Rev. 132; Wood, Limitations, 4 ed., sec. 208. But see Johnson *v.* Cook, 122 Ga. 524; Hart *v.* Bank, 105 Kan. 434; Willson *v.* Trust Co., 102 Ky. 522. See Perry, Trusts, sec. 860; Evans, The Colluding and the Mistaken Trustee, 17 Ky. L. Jour. 382; 33 Harv. L. Rev. 738.

If a trustee in good faith paid to the life beneficiary what should have been retained for the remainderman who was an infant, the latter may recover against the trustee or the life beneficiary if the period of the Statute of Limitations has not run since the remainderman reached his majority. Ballantine *v.* Young, 74 N. J. Eq. 572.

they knew the county was claiming an equitable lien and was insisting that this lien was superior to the mortgage lien of the appellants. The record fails to disclose that the appellants performed any substantial service to Smith until after they had discovered and knew of the claim of the county to an equitable lien upon the St. Ann street property."[1]

MANN v. THE SECOND NATIONAL BANK.

SUPREME COURT, KANSAS. 1883.

30 Kan. 412.

BREWER, J. This was an action on a negotiable promissory note. Trial by jury. The court instructed the jury peremptorily to find for the plaintiff, and of this defendants complain. The note was given in payment of a Champion harvester and cord binder. In the sale of this machine a warranty was given, and the defense was a breach of the warranty, and therefore a failure of the consideration. Upon the trial, testimony was offered in support of this defense, and finally it was admitted that the defendants were entitled to a verdict, unless the plaintiff was a purchaser of the note for a good and valuable consideration before maturity, without notice of the failure of the warranty. The note was in form to the order of Amos Whitely, president. It was due January 1, 1882, and was indorsed and transferred to plaintiff, December 14, 1881. The note, though in form to the order of Amos Whitely, was the property of the Champion machine company, was taken by it on the sale of the

[1] In Dixon v. Hill, 5 Mich. 404, Campbell, J., said (p. 408): "Such purchasers [purchasers for a valuable consideration] are protected upon the equitable principle that they should not be deprived of that which they have honestly, and without notice of any fraud, bought and paid for in fair dealing with the person holding the legal title. But the consideration must, in all cases, be actually passed before notice. Unless payment has been actually made in such shape, the authorities are quite clear that the purchase will not be upheld." See also Hardingham v. Nicholls, 3 Atk. 304.

A promise of marriage is held to be a valuable consideration, at least so as to prevent a transfer from being a fraudulent conveyance. Smith v. Allen, 5 Allen (Mass.) 454; Huntress v. Hanley, 195 Mass. 236 (*semble*); De Hierapolis v. Reilly, 44 App. Div. 22, aff'd 168 N. Y. 585. See American Surety Co. v. Conner, 251 N. Y. 1, 42 Harv. L. Rev. 832 (gift in consideration of marriage which was later annulled). But cf. Wilson v. Nolen, 200 Ky. 609 (note in consideration of promise to marry, maker died).

The giving of a negotiable instrument which is subsequently negotiated to a *bona fide* purchaser is value. Davis v. Ward, 109 Cal. 186 (*semble*); Partridge, Wells & Co. v. Chapman, 81 Ill. 137; Freeman v. Deming, 3 Sand. Ch. (N. Y.) 327.

If the purchaser gives his negotiable instrument and it has not been negotiated at the time he receives notice, it is generally held that he is not protected. Davis v. Ward, 109 Cal. 186; Gleaton v. Wright, 149 Ga. 220; Rush v. Mitchell, 71 Iowa 333; Jones v. Glathart, 100 Ill. App. 630, 641; Schwarz v. Munson, 94 N. J. Eq. 754. But see *contra*, Citizens' Bk. v. Shaw, 14 S. D. 197.

machine, in the name of its president, for convenience, and by it, through the indorsement of its president, transferred to the plaintiff. The failure of the warranty was communicated to the general agent of the company at St. Joseph, Missouri, before the note became due, and while it was in the possession of the company. It further appears, that the only officer of the bank who took part in the discount and purchase of this note by the plaintiff, was its cashier, John G. Benalack, who had been cashier since August 15, 1881. Up to a month prior to such time, he had been book-keeper of the Champion company, and knew in a general way that the consideration of notes received by the company was its machines. He had no personal knowledge of the consideration of this note, or the failure of the warranty in the sale of the machine, or of any other matters connected with it. The note was brought to him by the cashier of the Champion company for discount, in the ordinary course of business. After having been discounted, it was held by the bank until sent forward for collection. Suit was commenced March 11, 1882. Amos Whitely, the president of the machine company, who indorsed this note, was a director of the plaintiff bank, and one of the three members constituting its discount committee at the time this note was discounted. The note was never formally presented to the discount committee, but it was discounted by the cashier, under general instructions from the officers to discount any paper offered by certain customers of the bank, included among whom was the Champion machine company. These instructions were given by the president, and perhaps, according to the testimony of the cashier, by Amos Whitely, also. Prior to the first of January, 1882, Amos Whitely was in the habit of visiting the bank once or twice a week, and was as familiar with its business as directors usually are. His connection with the Champion machine company was not only as president, but also as its actual business manager.

Further, at the time of discount no money was paid directly to the machine company, but the amount of the discount, $142.14, was credited to the account of the machine company. At that time, and since, up to the time of the commencement of this action, the machine company carried an average balance of several thousand dollars in the bank.

This, we believe, covers all the material testimony. All bearing upon the indorsement and transfer of the note to plaintiff, and the relations of the Champion machine company to the plaintiff, was in the deposition given by the cashier of the plaintiff. Upon this testimony two important questions arise: First, did the bank take with notice of the defense to the note?[1] second, had it so paid for the note that it could claim the benefits of a *bona fide* purchase for value? . . .

[1] The court was inclined to think that the bank should be held bound by the knowledge of Whitely. The part of the opinion relating to this is omitted.

In reference to [the second] question, it will be observed that the bank in fact paid nothing to the company at the time of the discount. It simply credited the company on its books with the amount of the discount, and thereby enlarged the company's account with the bank. It is not a case in which the company's account was overdrawn, and in which it was indebted to the bank, which indebtedness was reduced by the amount of the discount. On the contrary, the bank owed the company, and it simply, by the discount, increased the amount of this indebtedness, an indebtedness which continued until after suit was brought, and the bank had full notice of the defense. Now conceding that the bank was a *bona fide* holder, that it acquired title, in the first instance, without any notice of any infirmity, to what extent is it protected? The general rule in such cases is, that a *bona fide* holder is protected to the amount he has paid, or lost, by virtue of the discount. In the case of Dresser *v.* The Construction Co., 93 U. S. 92, it was held that a *bona fide* holder of negotiable paper purchased before its maturity, upon an unexecuted contract, on which part payment only had been made when he received notice of fraud and a prohibition to pay, is protected only to the amount paid before the receipt of such notice. In the opinion, which covers simply that point, the authorities are fully cited, and the conclusion reached is the unanimous opinion of the court. In Bank *v.* Valentine, 18 Hun, 417, it is held that the mere discounting of a note, and giving a party credit on the books of the bank for the amount thereof, does not constitute the bank a holder for value. A similar proposition is laid down in Dougherty Bros. & Co. *v.* The Bank, 93 Pa. St. 227.

We do not cite the various cases in support of the general proposition, for they are fully cited and discussed in the opinion of the court in 93 U. S., *supra*. The proposition rests on the plainest principles of justice, and in no manner impairs the desired negotiability and security of commercial paper. Whenever the holder is a *bona fide* holder, he has a right to claim protection, but protection only to the extent he has lost or been injured by the acquisition of the paper. If he has parted with value, either by a cash payment or the cancellation of a debt, or giving time on a debt, or in any other manner, to that extent he has a right to claim protection; but when he has parted with nothing, there is nothing to protect. A mere promise to pay is no payment. He may rightfully say to the party from whom he purchased: " The paper you have given me is valueless, and therefore I am under no obligations to pay;" and if the paper be in fact valueless, payment cannot be compelled. Now the relation of a bank to its depositor is simply that of debtor. The bank owes the depositor so much. If the deposit is valueless its obligation to pay is without consideration, and it may decline to pay. There is nothing in the relation of a bank to its depositor which takes its obligation to its depositor out of the general rule of debtor to creditor. The case of Bank *v.* Crawford, 2 Cin. Superior Court, cited by defendant in error, is a case in which the depositor's account was overdrawn, and the discount therefore was practically the payment of an antecedent debt. In such a case the bank, having taken the paper in payment of an antecedent debt, was entitled to protection to the amount of such debt. Draper *v.* Cowles, 27 Kas. 484.

We therefore think that the bank, having paid nothing at the time of its discount, having simply increased its debt to the depositor, the machine company, and that debt remaining unpaid at the time suit was brought, and it having received actual notice of the infirmity of this paper, cannot claim the protection of a *bona fide* holder for value. . . .

The judgment will therefore be reversed, and the case remanded for a new trial.[1]

All the Justices concurring.

TOURVILLE *v.* NAISH.

Chancery. 1734.

3 P. Wms. 307.

A. purchased an estate, and having paid down part of the purchase money, gave bond for the residue. The plaintiff had an equitable lien on the purchased premises, of which the defendant

[1] If money or negotiable paper is deposited in a bank, it has been held that the bank is not a purchaser for value merely because it credits the depositor with the amount of the deposit. McNight *v.* Parsons, 136 Iowa 390; City Deposit Bank Co. *v.* Green, 130 Iowa 384; Citizens' State Bank *v.* Cowles, 180 N. Y. 346; Manufacturers' Nat. Bank *v.* Newell, 71 Wis. 309; Hodge *v.* Smith, 130 Wis. 326.

The opposite result has been reached in England. Royal Bank *v.* Tottenham, [1894] 2 Q. B. 715; Capital & Counties Bank *v.* Gordon, [1903] A. C. 240. If, however, the bank does not agree to allow the customer to withdraw the deposit, the bank is not a purchaser for value. Underwood, Ltd. *v.* Bank, [1924] 1 K. B. 799.

If payment of the deposit is subsequently made by the bank, it is a purchaser for value. Fox *v.* Bank, 30 Kan. 441; First Nat. Bank *v.* McNairy, 122 Minn. 215; Cunningham *v.* Holmes, 66 Neb. 723; U. S. Nat. Bank *v.* McNair, 114 N. C. 335; Merchants Nat. Bank *v.* Santa Maria Sugar Co., 162 N. Y. App. Div. 248.

If the depositor makes subsequent deposits and withdrawals it has been held that the rule in Clayton's Case, 1 Mer. 572, is applicable, and the withdrawals are to be treated as made in the order in which deposits were made. Merchants Nat. Bank *v.* Santa Maria Sugar Co., 162 N. Y. App. Div. 248, *supra.* But there is a conflict of authority on this point.

For a collection of cases, see Ames, 287; Pomeroy, Eq. Juris., secs. 750, 751; Brannan, Negotiable Instruments Law, 4 ed., 227, 385 *et seq.;* Frye, Crediting an Account as "Value," 2 Wis. L. Rev. 408; 7 Minn. L. Rev. 583; 72 U. Pa. L. Rev. 61; 77 U. Pa. L. Rev. 690; 33 Yale L. Jour. 628; 6 A. L. R. 252; 24 A. L. R. 901; 60 A. L. R. 247.

alleged he had no notice at the time of making his purchase, but was apprised thereof before payment of the money due on the bond. And it was contended, that this notice was not material, since the giving the bond was as payment; and the purchaser, after he had given his bond for payment of the purchase money, is bound in all events to proceed, and cannot plead at law that there is an equitable incumbrance on his purchased premises.

LORD CHANCELLOR [TALBOT]. If the person who has a lien in equity on the premises, gives notice before actual payment of the purchase money, it is sufficient; and though the purchaser has no remedy at law against the payment of the residue, for which he gave his bond, yet he would be entitled to relief in equity, on bringing his bill, and shewing, that though he has given his bond for payment of the residue of his purchase money, yet, now he has notice of an incumbrance, under which circumstances the court would stop payment of the money due on the bond. This the Lord Chancellor declared, though in the principal case there was proof of a notice precedent to the purchase, by a letter read to the purchaser, mentioning the equitable lien on the premises.[1] . . .

HOWELLS v. HETTRICK.

COURT OF APPEALS, NEW YORK. 1899.

160 N. Y. 308.

BARTLETT, J. It is sought in this action to have an assignment to plaintiff's intestate in 1879 of the interest of Margaret W. Hettrick in the estate of the late John H. McCunn adjudged to be a superior lien to a claim made upon the same interest by defendant.

The assignment to plaintiff's intestate was executed and delivered about August 21st, 1879, as collateral security to a debt that is undisputed.

On the 5th of September, 1882, the defendant recovered a judgment against Margaret W. Hettrick for the sum of $2,683.22.

On the 11th of October, 1882, plaintiff's intestate recovered judg-

[1] The weight of authority supports the principal case, but allows the purchaser to retain the title until he is repaid the amount paid by him before notice. Henry v. Phillips, 163 Cal. 135; Gleaton v. Wright, 149 Ga. 220; Schwarz v. Munson, 94 N. J. Eq. 754; Youst v. Martin, 3 S. & R. (Pa.) 423; Ames, 288; Pomeroy, Eq. Juris., sec. 750.

In a few cases it has been held that a purchaser who has paid part of the purchase price may retain the property purchased, subject to a lien in favor of the equitable encumbrancer for the amount of the unpaid purchase money. Citizens' Bk. v. Shaw, 14 S. D. 197; Mitchell v. Dawson, 23 W. Va. 86. See Ames, 288; Pomeroy, Eq. Juris., sec. 750.

Payment part in cash and part in satisfaction of an antecedent debt is value. Curtis v. Leavitt, 15 N. Y. 9, 179 (*semble*); Glidden v. Hunt, 24 Pick. (Mass.) 221; Baggarly v. Gaither, 2 Jones Eq. (N. C.) 80.

See 32 W. Va. L. Quar. 257.

ment against Margaret W. Hettrick for $2,391.25, the amount of his claim against her.

The assignment to plaintiff's intestate was not recorded as a mortgage, but by error was placed in a book of Conveyances.

On the 26th of September, 1882, Margaret W. Hettrick executed and delivered to the defendant a warranty deed which conveyed to him an undivided two seventy-fifths part in fifteen certain parcels of land in the city of New York; this conveyance was duly recorded.

The consideration for the deed was the satisfaction of the judgment recovered by the defendant against Margaret W. Hettrick September 5th, 1882, as aforesaid, which was recorded September 30th, 1882.

The premises, a portion of which was covered by the foregoing deed to defendant, were partitioned, and the sum of two thousand dollars, the share of Margaret W. Hettrick, is now held by the United States Trust Company as the fund involved in this action.

It is conceded that if the defendant took without actual notice of the assignment, and is a *bona fide* purchaser under his deed, that his claim upon the fund is superior to that of the plaintiff under her unrecorded assignment. . . .

The course of the trial below leads strongly to the conclusion that it is highly improbable the defendant, on a new trial, can succeed in showing he did not have actual notice of the plaintiff's assignment, but it is exceedingly doubtful if the record shows that he certainly cannot.

It, therefore, is necessary to consider the sufficiency, in law, of the consideration which the defendant claims supports the conveyance to him, and we will assume for the argument's sake that he took his deed without actual notice of plaintiff's assignment.

The nature of the consideration for this deed rests upon undisputed evidence.

The trial court found that it was the satisfaction of the judgment that defendant recovered against Margaret W. Hettrick September 5th, 1882. The complaint resulting in this judgment shows that the indebtedness was for money loaned and property sold Margaret W. Hettrick years before. It is clear that the judgment represented an antecedent indebtedness of long standing.

In DeLancey *v.* Stearns (66 N. Y., at page 161), Judge Rapallo said: " It has been held in numerous cases that one who, without notice of a prior unrecorded mortgage, takes a conveyance of land in payment of an existing debt or as security therefor, without giving up any security, divesting himself of any rights, or doing any act to his own prejudice on the faith of the title, before he has notice of the mortgage, is not a *bona fide* purchaser."

The surrender by defendant of the right to enforce his judgment just recovered as a consideration for a deed which was the absolute payment of the greater part of his claim, which for years had remained uncollected, was not divesting himself of any right or security to his own prejudice, but was the act of assuming a far more favorable position.

Within all the controlling cases in this state the defendant is not a *bona fide* purchaser, assuming he had no notice of the plaintiff's assignment. (Dickerson *v.* Tillinghast, 4 Paige, 215; Evertson *v.* Evertson, 5 Paige, 644, and cases cited; Weaver *v.* Barden, 49 N. Y. 286, 293; Cary *v.* White, 52 N. Y. 138; Westbrook *v.* Gleason, 79 N. Y. 28, and cases cited; Young *v.* Guy, 87 N. Y. 462.)

The judgment appealed from should be affirmed, with costs.

All concur.

Judgment affirmed.[1]

[1] Except in the case of negotiable instruments or money, it is generally held that one who takes property as security for an antecedent debt is not a purchaser for value. Millard *v.* Green, 94 Conn. 597 (stock); Orthey *v.* Bogan, 226 N. Y. 234 (mortgage). And in the case of payment of an antecedent debt, the weight of authority is to the same effect, although there is considerable authority the other way. Bogert, Trusts, 519; Pomeroy, Eq. Juris., sec. 749; Williston, Sales, sec. 620. See 12 A. L. R. 1048.

By the Uniform Sales Act, sec. 76, it is provided that "'Value' is any consideration sufficient to support a simple contract. An antecedent or pre-existing claim, whether for money or not, constitutes value where goods or documents of title are taken either in satisfaction thereof or as security therefor." See Williston, Sales, sec. 619. See also Uniform Stock Transfer Act, sec. 22.

By the great weight of authority at common law, one who takes either money (Holly *v.* Missionary Society, 180 U. S. 284; Spaulding *v.* Kendrick, 172 Mass. 71; Stephens *v.* Board of Ed., 79 N. Y. 183) or negotiable paper in satisfaction of or as security for an antecedent debt is a purchaser for value. The rule was formerly otherwise in New York and Pennsylvania in the case of taking negotiable paper as security for an antecedent debt. Coddington *v.* Bay, 20 Johns. (N. Y.) 637.

By the Negotiable Instruments Law, sec. 25, it is provided that "an antecedent or pre-existing debt constitutes value." At first the New York courts were inclined to hold that this did not make one who takes negotiable paper as security for an antecedent debt a purchaser for value. But this view was later abandoned. Kelso & Co. *v.* Ellis, 224 N. Y. 528.

As to the effect of the surrender or cancellation of securities held by the creditor, see Franklin Sav. Bank *v.* Taylor, 53 Fed. 854; Richardson *v.* Wren, 11 Ariz. 395; Grand Rapids Nat. Bank *v.* Ford, 143 Mich. 402; Pomeroy, Eq. Juris., sec. 749.

Deposits in bank. By the weight of authority where a trustee or other fiduciary deposits fiduciary funds in a bank, and the bank has no notice of the fiduciary character of the funds, it can set off the pre-existing indebtedness of the fiduciary to it. In some states, however, the bank is protected only if it changes its position in reliance upon the deposit. See 38 Harv. L. Rev. 800; 7 N. C. L. Rev. 55; 13 A. L. R. 324; 31 A. L. R. 756; 50 A. L. R. 632. See note to Evansville Bank *v.* German-American Bank, 155 U. S. 556, *ante*.

On the question of notice, see note to Bischoff *v.* Yorkville Bank, 218 N. Y. 106, *post*.

CHACE v. CHAPIN.

SUPREME JUDICIAL COURT, MASSACHUSETTS. 1881.

130 Mass. 128

COLT, J. This is a bill in equity in which the plaintiff seeks to recover a dividend on certain shares of the capital stock of the Old Colony Railroad Company, now standing in the name of Chapin and Braley, as the assignees in bankruptcy of Samuel A. Chace. He claims to be entitled to the income of this stock for life, by virtue of and in accordance with the terms of a trust created by Mrs. Holmes when she transferred to said Samuel a legal title to the stock.

The defendants deny the existence of the trust; and Chapin and Braley, as assignees in bankruptcy, contend that, as holders for value in good faith and without notice, they are entitled to have the stock discharged of any trust that may have existed while the title was in the bankrupt. . . .

As to the claim of the assignees in bankruptcy, that the trust, if it ever existed, was discharged by the conveyance of Chace to Brayton as trustee, to secure his debts to the Union Mills and others, on the ground that Brayton took as a holder for value without notice, the first answer is, that at common law an assignee under a general assignment for the benefit of creditors takes no better title and no higher rights than the assignor himself had, and is not to be regarded as a purchaser for a valuable consideration without notice. If the assigned estate is subject to a trust, the assignee takes subject to the rights of the equitable owner. *In re* Howe, 1 Paige, 125. Van Heusen *v.* Radcliff, 17 N. Y. 580. Griffin *v.* Marquardt, 17 N. Y. 28.

A further answer to the claim is that the conveyance to Brayton was wholly defeated by the subsequent bankruptcy of Chace. The assignees took, not as purchasers of Brayton's title, but under their rights as assignees in bankruptcy, and subject to all the legal and equitable claims of others. The statute declares that " no property held by the bankrupt in trust shall pass by the assignment." U. S. Rev. Sts. § 5053. " Assignees in bankruptcy do not, like heirs and executors, take the whole legal title in the bankrupt's property. They take such estate only as the bankrupt had a beneficial as well as legal interest in, and which is to be applied to the payment of his debts." Rhoades *v.* Blackiston, 106 Mass. 334. See also Cook *v.* Tullis, 18 Wall. 332; Kelly *v.* Scott, 49 N. Y. 595; *In re* McKay, 1 Lowell, 345.

Decree for the plaintiff.[1]

---

[1] *Assignee for creditors.* By the great weight of authority it is held that an assignee for the benefit of creditors is not a purchaser for value. Martin *v.*

FARMERS SAVINGS BANK v. PUGH.

SUPREME COURT, IOWA. 1927.

204 Iowa 580.

STEVENS, J.— I. This is an action in equity, in the nature of a creditor's bill, to subject real estate to the payment of a judg-

---

Bowen, 51 N. J. Eq. 452; Smith v. Equitable T. Co. (No. 1), 215 Pa. 418; Stainback v. Junk Bros. etc. Co., 98 Tenn. 306; Ames, 393; 2 Pomeroy, Eq. Juris. sec. 749. But see *contra*, Wickham v. Lewis Martin & Co., 13 Gratt. (Va.) 427; Chapman v. Chapman, 91 Va. 397 (*semble*); Gilbert Bros. v. Lawrence Bros., 56 W. Va. 281; Marshall v. McDermitt, 79 W. Va. 245.

Trustee in bankruptcy. A trustee in bankruptcy is not a purchaser for value. Ames, 342. The National Bankruptcy Act (1898), sec. 70*a* (5) provides that there shall pass to the trustee in bankruptcy " property which prior to the filing of the petition he could by any means have transferred or which might have been levied upon and sold under judicial process against him." By the amendment of 1910 to sec. 47*a* (2), it is provided that "such trustee . . . shall be deemed vested with all the rights, remedies and powers of a creditor holding a lien by legal or equitable proceedings."

The trustee in bankruptcy does not even get the legal title to property held by the bankrupt as an express trustee. *Ex parte* Chion, 3 P. Wms. 187n.; *Ex parte* Gennys, Mont. & M. 258; Ames, 392.

Judgment creditor. A judgment creditor is not a purchaser for value. Whitworth v. Gaugain, 3 Hare 416, 1 Phil. 728; Dyson v. Simmons, 48 Md. 207; Harney v. First Nat. Bk., 52 N. J. Eq. 697; Ames, 408–414; Pomeroy, Eq. Juris., sec. 721. In Whitworth v. Gaugain, 3 Hare 416, Wigram, V. C., said: " The most plausible way of stating the case in favor of the judgment creditor is by supposing his right to be founded in contract, and not to be the result of a proceeding *in invitum*; and this, no doubt, may be the truth of the case, when the judgment is voluntarily confessed; and I paid the greatest attention to the arguments of counsel upon that point. But, admitting that view to be correct, how does it alter the case? The question remains, — what was the contract? It was a general contract for a judgment, and the fruits of a judgment; and the original question, therefore, — what right does a judgment confer? — remains wholly untouched by the concession. If a party contracts specifically for a given property, pays the purchase-money, and obtains the legal title, without notice up to the time of obtaining the conveyance, as well as of paying his money, that may give him a right to be preferred to an equitable claim which is prior in point of time. But there is no principle upon which a court of justice can be required to imply that a general contract to give a judgment is a contract to give that which does not belong to the debtor. If the trustee were to confess a judgment, am I to imply that it amounts to a specific contract to give the creditor an interest in that which belongs to the *cestui que trust?* That appears to me to be the true distinction. In one case the party contracts for a specific thing, — in the other he merely takes a judgment, that gives him nothing more than a right to that which belongs to his debtor."

A creditor who attaches or levies execution is not a purchaser for value. Waterman v. Buckingham, 79 Conn. 286; Houghton v. Davenport, 74 Me. 590; Harris v. Gaines, 2 Lea (Tenn.) 12. See Byrne v. McGrath, 130 Cal. 316; Perry, Trusts, sec. 815*b*.

Under the recording statutes of some states, however, a creditor is treated as a purchaser for value. Pomeroy, Eq. Juris., sec. 722.

ment in each of two cases consolidated for trial. The property involved is a tract of 160 acres in Iowa County, to which William Pugh acquired the legal title in 1902, and which, on or about April 4, 1924, he conveyed by warranty deed to his wife and co-appellant, Katherine Pugh. Both deeds were promptly filed for record and recorded in the proper office. Judgment was entered in each of the respective cases on April 15, 1924. They aggregate in amount, with interest and costs, something over $7,000. The purchase price of the land was paid in part with money received by Katherine Pugh from her father, and title, as stated, taken in the name of her husband. There is a divergence of opinion between counsel for the respective parties as to whether the facts and circumstances of this transaction created a resulting trust in the land in favor of the wife. In view of the conclusion reached, we shall assume that appellants' contention at this point is correct, and that William Pugh was possessed only of the legal title to the farm. With this concession to appellants, we pass to a brief statement of the material facts.

The deed conveying the legal title to William Pugh was executed with the knowledge and consent of his wife. Both parties were, apparently, influenced by the advice of their attorney. The wife testified that the reason she permitted title to be taken in the name of her husband was that she thought it would give him a better standing.

The judgment in each of the consolidated cases was based upon the promissory notes of one Gallagher, which William Pugh signed as surety. The first Katherine Pugh knew that her husband had signed the Gallagher notes was when she received a letter from the appellee bank regarding the Gallagher notes. She then demanded that the legal title be conveyed to her.

Appellants do not claim that there was an agreement between them for the repayment of the money of the wife that was invested in the farm. This being true, she did not, at the time of the conveyance, occupy the position of creditor of her husband. The conveyance cannot, therefore, be sustained upon the theory that her husband, in making the conveyance, rightfully preferred her to other creditors. Mahasta County *v.* Whitsel, 133 Iowa 335; Daggett, Bassett & Hill Co. *v.* Bulfer, 82 Iowa 101; Jones *v.* Brandt, 59 Iowa 332; Sims *v.* Moore, 74 Iowa 497; Garr, Scott & Co. *v.* Klein, 93 Iowa 313. Nor was the deed executed for the purpose of placing the legal title in Katherine Pugh a mere voluntary conveyance, without consideration, and fraudulent as to the existing creditors of her husband. She already possessed the beneficial title to the land. The effect was to enable her to show her ownership of record.

II. Appellees alleged, and have at all times claimed, that they extended credit on the Gallagher notes signed by William Pugh as surety, in reliance upon the record title as evidence of the ownership of the property in William Pugh, and in the belief, and without knowledge to the contrary, that he was in fact the true owner thereof. Their main reliance is upon the estoppel thereby suggested. This contention of appellees' constitutes the vital issue in this case.

The general rule, many times repeated in the decisions of this court, that, if the wife permits title to real estate belonging to her to be taken and held in the name of her husband, under such circumstances that she knew, or ought to know, that others dealing with him would reasonably or naturally, in extending credit, rely on his apparent ownership of the real estate, she will be estopped to assert her own claim to the property, as against such creditors, is not controverted by appellants. Their contention is in avoidance of the rule, and is that it is not applicable to obligations of suretyship assumed by the husband. Iseminger v. Criswell, 98 Iowa 382; McCormick H. M. Co. v. Perkins, 135 Iowa 64; Willey v. Hite, 175 Iowa 657; Farmers St. Bank v. Schleisman, 203 Iowa 585.

Actual or intentional fraud on the part of Katherine Pugh cannot, we think, upon the record, be imputed to her. That she was in good faith in permitting the title to be taken in her husband's name, we think perfectly clear. Final decision of the case does not, however, necessarily turn upon the question of her good or bad faith in the transaction, nor is it necessary to the relief sought by appellees that there should have been actual fraud in the execution of the deed by William Pugh to his wife. Much stress is laid by counsel upon the testimony of Katherine Pugh that she permitted or caused title to be taken in the name of her husband for the purpose of giving him a better standing. No contractual right under which the husband might deal with the land as his own in obtaining credit for any and all purposes is to be implied from this testimony. Were it decisive of the questions before us, we would be inclined to hold that it was the intention of the wife to assist her husband to obtain a better standing in the community for the purpose of carrying on the business of operating and managing the farm and of obtaining the necessary credit for that purpose. The inevitable conclusion in this case does not rest upon a limitation to be implied from the testimony of Katherine Pugh as to her purpose in the matter. She permitted the legal title to remain in her husband for more than twenty years. The record of titles in the county recorder's office did not disclose any prior interest in the land until, so far as she was concerned, the deed executed in 1924 was filed for record. During that long period of time, William Pugh had managed the business in his own name, and, so far as the record shows, none of appellees knew anything of the claim now asserted by Mrs. Pugh. Her husband, with her knowledge and consent, was possessed of the indicia of title to the land. Some reliance is placed by appellants upon the record of an affidavit signed and sworn to by Katherine Pugh. The affidavit was executed for the apparent purpose of making a showing of record that a $3,100 mortgage, given by appellants in 1902, at the time of the purchase of the land in question, was executed to secure a note of that sum to Henry Smith, the father of the affiant; that Henry Smith died intestate, February 17, 1907; and that the persons named therein are his sole heirs at law. Constructive notice of this affidavit did not extend beyond the recitals therein and such inquiry as might be suggested thereby. There is nothing in the affidavit from which one having actual knowledge thereof could imply that William Pugh was not the owner of the land, or that it had been purchased with money received from Henry Smith or from his estate. The mortgage described was released of record by appellant and the other heirs at law named in the affidavit. The purpose of the affidavit was to show such matters of record as would make clear the right of the heirs at law of Henry Smith to release the instrument.

Many cases are cited by counsel for appellants, and pressed upon us with vigor. None of the decisions of this court support their contention that Katherine Pugh did not in fact, and was not bound to, anticipate that her husband would become surety of Gallagher or anyone else, or assume obligations inconsistent with her claim that he held title only for the purpose of enabling him to operate and manage the farm and to secure the credit necessary for the purpose. . . .

Equitable estoppel does not arise in such cases merely because the wife knew of the transaction involved and permitted her husband, without protest or notice to the other party, to proceed to his injury, or because she may have had reason to suppose that he would not act to her prejudice. It is the rule in this state that the taking and holding of the title of the wife's property in the name of the husband, the deed being duly recorded, and the exercise of the usual and customary indicia of ownership for a long series of years, together with the acquiescence therein by the wife, estop her, when the claims of creditors who have extended credit to him in reliance thereon are involved, from setting up her own equitable title against them. This is the rule in most jurisdictions. Any other rule would open the way to the husband to perpetrate the grossest fraud upon others.

The decree of the court below, subjecting the property in question to the payment of the judgments of appellees, is affirmed. — *Affirmed.*[1]

EVANS, C. J., and DE GRAFF, KINDIG, and WAGNER, JJ., concur.

[1] In the following cases the creditors of the trustee were protected on the ground of estoppel. Bryant *v.* Klatt, 2 F. (2d) 167, *ante;* Goldberg *v.* Parker, 87 Conn. 99; Smith *v.* Willard, 174 Ill. 538; Bergin *v.* Blackwood, 141 Minn. 325, 328.

In the following cases it was held that the beneficiary was not estopped, and he prevailed over creditors of the trustee. Basak *v.* Damutz, 105 Conn. 378; Liberty Trust Co. *v.* Hayes, 244 Mass. 251; Huot *v.* Reeder Bros. Shoe Co., 140 Mich. 162; Southern Bank *v.* Nichols, 235 Mo. 401; Mayer *v.* Kane, 69 N. J. Eq. 733; McGovern *v.* Knox, 21 Oh. St. 547; Beman Thomas Co. *v.* White, 269 Pa. 261; Burns *v.* Boyne, 294 Pa. 512; Lukens *v.* Wharton Avenue Baptist Church, 296 Pa. 1.

PUGH v. HIGHLEY.

SUPREME COURT, INDIANA. 1899.

152 Ind. 252.

BAKER, J. — Suit to foreclose vendor's lien. Appellees conveyed lands to one Clayborn Highley and took his unsecured note therefor. Afterwards appellant recovered judgment against the grantee and caused execution to issue. The sheriff levied on the lands in question. At the sale, appellant was the purchaser. When the time for redemption expired, she received a sheriff's deed for the lands.

Complaint in two paragraphs. The first is silent concerning notice to appellant of appellees' equity. The second charges that appellant had notice before receiving the sheriff's deed. Appellant's several demurrers for want of facts were overruled. A demurrer was sustained to an answer of appellant's, in which she averred that she bid at the sale, paid the costs, and receipted the sheriff for the full amount of her judgment, without knowledge or notice of appellees' claim. Judgment for appellees after trial on issues completed by answers of general denial and payment and reply denying payment.

The question is: Does a judgment creditor, who in good faith buys at a proper execution sale on his own valid judgment, take the land subject to prior secret equities?

The lien of a judgment attaches only to the actual interest of the debtor in the land. While the judgment remains unexecuted, the lien may be subordinated to any prior equity, though secret; for the creditor pays or surrenders nothing to or for the debtor, and continues to hold against the debtor his full claim, which the court has merely changed from a cause of action into a judgment.

A security for an antecedent debt will be upheld between the parties; but the taker will not be protected against prior secret equities, because he parts with nothing.

But a purchaser who pays the owner the value of the land takes the title clear of equities of which he has no notice.

And a creditor who, without notice, cancels a preëxisting debt in consideration of his debtor's conveying him land, is a good faith purchaser for value. To hold that the debtor may sell his land to a stranger and turn over the purchase price (money, notes, goods, land) to his creditor in satisfaction of the debt, whereby the creditor is free from claimants of secret equities; and to hold that the creditor, if the debtor conveys the land to him in payment of the debt, is liable to be affected by secret equities, — is to approve

---

See Ann. Cas. 1914C 1066; 30 L. R. A. (N. s.) 1; 21 C. J. 1172; Dec. Dig., Estoppel, sec. 74.

the roundabout and involved, and to condemn the straight and simple, method of accomplishing the same result, — using the land to pay the debt.

A good faith purchaser, other than the judgment creditor, at a proper execution sale on a valid judgment, who pays the sheriff the amount of his bid, acquires all the right, title and interest in the land sold (except redemption) that the judgment debtor could have conveyed to him by deed of bargain and sale. As to secret equities, he stands on the same footing with the good faith purchaser for value from the apparent owner of land. In both cases, the purchaser irrevocably parts with his money, relying and having the right to rely on getting not merely what the debtor actually owns, but what from the public records he apparently owns. In either case, — before the debtor himself conveys, or before the sheriff conveys for him, — the holder of the prior secret equity has had it in his power to prevent any one's being misled by the false situation. If either the subsequent purchaser or the holder of the secret equity must suffer or be postponed, it should be the latter, since his initiative made delusion by the debtor's apparent circumstances possible.

What, now, is the position of the judgment creditor who purchases at a proper execution sale on his own valid judgment? (The premises exclude the question of the effect upon the judgment creditor of irregularities in the proceedings.) The authorities holding that he is not a good faith purchaser for value seem to be based upon either or both of two propositions: that he has parted with nothing, — has not changed his position for the worse; and that he will not be permitted to urge a claim that rises higher than the source of his right (by that, meaning the lien of his judgment).

The judgment creditor purchaser has parted with value and has changed his position for the worse. He has paid to the sheriff the amount of his bid in cash, actually or constructively; for, if he merely receipts for payment of his judgment in whole or in part, the transaction in contemplation of law is the same as if he had paid the sheriff in cash and the sheriff had paid him in cash. His payment is just as irrevocable as that of a stranger purchaser. His right to vacate the satisfaction of the judgment is no greater than that of a stranger purchaser. (And under section 765 R. S. 1881, section 777 Burns 1894, section 765 Horner 1897, there can be no right of that kind in the present case, for defects in the proceedings and want of title in the debtor are excluded from the question, by the facts.) If the judgment creditor purchaser does not pay at the time of the sale, he is liable to judgment for the amount of the bid, and damages, interest and costs, like any other purchaser. Section 760 R. S. 1881, section 772 Burns 1894, section 760 Horner 1897.

He has also changed his position for the worse, if he is not to be permitted to hold under the execution sale the same as a stranger purchaser. The debtor may have directed the sheriff to levy upon the very land that was subject to the secret equity. Manifestly the judgment creditor without notice is ethically as innocent in bidding as is the stranger. By the sale, the execution becomes *functus officio* and the judgment creditor has lost the lien of his execution upon the goods and chattels of his debtor. By the sale, the judgment is satisfied *pro tanto* and the judgment creditor has lost the lien of his judgment upon the other lands of his debtor.

But, it is said, he may not urge a claim of higher value than the source of his right, that is, his judgment lien. Why not?

If an innocent stranger pays for a deed, he acquires the apparent title of the grantor and the holder of the secret equity will not be heard to say aught against it. That is, the purchaser gets more than the debtor had. Stronger than the innocent stranger's, however, are the equities of the judgment creditor purchaser without notice. For the holder of the secret equity has less opportunity to protect himself against the stranger than he has against the judgment creditor; since he may have no means of ascertaining, even by the exercise of the highest vigilance, to whom his secret trustee is about to convey, but it is only his own inaction that can prevent his learning of the judgment before sale, — in time to subordinate the lien to his rights. Shall equity offer a premium for sloth? If not, then the judgment creditor purchaser should likewise take more than the debtor had.

If an owner of an antecedent debt cancels in good faith the obligation in consideration of a deed from his debtor, he takes the title free from secret equities. That is, the purchaser gets more than the debtor had. Shall the private, maybe secret, extinguishment of the debt be held of more exalted worth in equity than the law's public and open satisfaction thereof? If not, then the judgment creditor purchaser should likewise take more than the debtor had.

If a stranger without notice buys at execution sale, his purchase cuts off secret claims against the land. That is, the purchaser gets more than the debtor had. The law does not prohibit, but, on the contrary, encourages the judgment creditor to bid; for it is in the interest of the law's execution of the judgment and to the advantage of the debtor that he should compete with the other bidders. If a stranger purchases, the sheriff pays over the money to the judgment creditor who thereby receives satisfaction out of property on which his judgment may not have been actually a lien. Shall equity accredit the circuitous, and discredit the direct, means to the same end? If not, then the judgment creditor purchaser should likewise take more than the debtor had.

It is a misapprehension to say that the rights of a judgment creditor purchaser arise from the judgment lien and therefore continue subject to prior secret equities. His position as purchaser is in no sort of legal privity with his position as judgment creditor. When the sale is made, he ceases to be a judgment creditor. His rights thenceforward are those of a purchaser at execution sale. The contention that the rights of a purchaser at execution sale are one thing if he is a stranger and another if he is the judgment creditor is untenable in reason. . . .

Judgment reversed, with instructions to sustain the demurrer to each paragraph of complaint.[1]

MORE v. MAYHOW.

CHANCERY. 1663.

1 Chan. Cas. 34.

THE PLAINTIFF'S bill was to be relieved upon a trust, and charged the defendant with notice of that trust, and that he had gotten a conveyance of the lands upon which the trust was had; and that at or before his taking the said conveyance, he had notice of the said trust for the plaintiff.

The defendant, by way of answer, denied that he had any notice of the trust, at the time of his purchaser or contract, and pleaded that he was a purchaser for a valuable consideration. It was insisted the plea was not good, because he did not say what the valuable consideration was; for 5s. was a valuable consideration; but yet no equitable consideration.

THE COURT declared that the plea in this case was well enough.

It was further insisted, that the plea was founded upon the answer, *viz.* that the defendant had no notice, &c., and that the point of notice was not well answered in that the defendant denied notice at the time of the purchase only, and the word purchase might be understood when the contract for the purchase was made; and it might be he had not notice then, and might have notice after, before, or at sealing of the conveyance; and if there was any notice before the conveyance to him executed, that should charge the defendant: and that it was so lately decreed in a cause between Sir William Wheeler and —— and Yarraway and Nicholas, by the Lord Chancellor. And so the plea was over-ruled.

[1] Riley v. Martinelli, 97 Cal. 575, 21 L. R. A. 33; Halloway v. Platner, 20 Iowa 121; Gower v. Doheny, 33 Iowa 36; Wood v. Chapin, 13 N. Y. 509, *accord.*

Beidler v. Beidler, 71 Ark. 318; Dickerson v. Tillinghast, 4 Paige (N. Y.) 215; Wright v. Douglass, 10 Barb. (N. Y.) 97; Reed v. Kinnaman, 8 Ired. Eq. (N. C.) 13; Stith v. Lookabill, 76 N. C. 465; Williams v. Hollingsworth, 1 Strob. Eq. (S. C.) 103; Ayres v. Duprey, 27 Tex. 593; Orme v. Roberts, 33 Tex. 768; Main v. Bosworth, 77 Wis. 660, *contra.* See Pomeroy, Eq. Juris., sec. 724.

By the great weight of authority a third person purchasing on execution sale takes free of equities of which he has no notice. Ellis v. Smith, 10 Ga. 253; Den v. Richman, 13 N. J. Eq. 43; Jackson v. Chamberlain, 8 Wend. (N. Y.) 620; Paine v. Moreland, 15 Oh. 435; Ayres v. Duprey, 27 Tex. 593, 605; Ehle v. Brown, 31 Wis. 405. But see *contra,* Banning v. Edes, 6 Minn. 402. See Pomeroy, Eq. Juris., sec. 724.

TOPLAN v. HOOVER.

COURT OF CHANCERY, NEW JERSEY. 1926.

100 N. J. Eq. 466.

ON bill for injunction. On final hearing.

INGERSOLL, V. C.

On September 22d, 1921, George R. Beck and Robert F. Hoover rented of one Rettie M. Goff, a lot of land fronting on the boardwalk in Wildwood. No building was upon this land. It was agreed between them that the premises should not be used for any other purpose than for the business commonly known as "The Automatic Baseball Game," and the party of the second part agreed to erect at (his) own expense a building suitable, &c.

Although it was agreed between the parties to the lease that the building could be removed at the expiration of the lease, this clause was inadvertently not included in the lease.

Through mesne conveyances the fee of the property is now in the complainant, who, upon being advised that the lessee would remove the building at the expiration of the lease, filed this bill and obtained the preliminary restraint.

The complainant contends he is a *bona fide* purchaser for value, without notice of defendant's claim or right. It is admitted that he had notice thereof at the time of the settlement for the purchase of the property and before it had been conveyed to him.

To be a *bona fide* purchaser without notice the purchaser must not only have agreed to purchase without notice, but he must also have actually paid the purchase-money and taken his deed without such notice. Brinton v. Scull, 55 N. J. Eq. 747; Dean v. Anderson, 34 N. J. Eq. 496.

I will advise the dismissal of the bill.[1]

---

[1] A purchaser is not protected from a prior equity if he receives notice of it at any time before the conveyance is executed, even though he may have paid the purchase-money before notice. *Re* Samuel Allen, [1907] 1 Ch. 575; Louisville & Nashville R. R. Co. v. Boykin, 76 Ala. 560; Wenz v. Pastene, 209 Mass. 359; Grimstone v. Carter, 3 Paige (N. Y.) 421. See Ames, 288, 305; Ames, Purchase for Value, 1 Harv. L. Rev. 8, Lect. Leg. Hist. 261; Pomeroy, Eq. Juris., secs. 683, 691, 755; Tiffany, Real Property, 2 ed., sec. 566; 37 Yale L. Jour. 790; 21 Ann. Cas. 463.

The mere fact that the trustee has the *indicia* of title to the trust property is not sufficient to protect a purchaser who pays in reliance thereon but who has not received a conveyance before he has notice of the trust. Cory v. Eyre, 1 DeG. J. & S. 140, 167; Shropshire etc. Canal Co. v. Queen, L. R. 7 H. L. 496, 506; Carritt v. Real & Personal Advance Co., 42 Ch. D. 263; Burgis v. Constantine, [1908] 2 K. B. 484, 496; Hill v. Peters, [1918] 2 Ch. 273, *post.* But see Scott v. Scott, [1924] 1 I. R. 141. — ED.

Estoppel. But if a *cestui que trust,* or equitable mortgagee, or other equitable claimant, by words or conduct encourages the belief that the trustee or mortgagor is the absolute beneficial owner of the property, he will of course

AMES, PURCHASE FOR VALUE WITHOUT NOTICE:[1] An honest purchaser will, furthermore, be protected, although he did not obtain the legal title at the time of his purchase, if he did acquire at that time an irrevocable power of obtaining the legal title upon the performance of some condition, and that too, although, before performance of the condition, he received notice of the prior equitable claim. Thus, if a trustee, in violation of his duty, should sell the trust property to one who had no notice of the trust, and should deliver the deed in escrow, the defrauded *cestui que trust* could not restrain the innocent purchaser from performing the condition, nor could he obtain any relief against him after he had acquired the title. Dodds *v.* Hills, 2 H. & M. 424, 427, per Wood, V. C. On the same principle one who acquired at the time of his purchase an irrevocable power of obtaining the legal title upon the performance of some act by a third party, which that party is in duty bound to perform, will be as fully protected as if he had acquired the title itself at the time of his purchase. Hume *v.* Dixon, 37 Oh. St. 66, is a case in point. The owner of land subject to a vendor's lien sold it to an innocent purchaser; but, under the law of the State, the deed failed to convey the legal title, for the reason that the officer who took the acknowledgment of the deed forgot to sign his name thereto. He subsequently signed the deed, but after the grantee had notice of the lien. The purchaser was protected.[2] Another illustration is furnished by Dodds *v.* Hills,

---

be estopped to assert the trust or mortgage against a subsequent equitable incumbrancer who has acted on the faith of such words or conduct. Waldron *v.* Sloper, 1 Drew. 193; Rice *v.* Rice, 2 Drew. 73; Worthington *v.* German, 16 W. R. 187; Dowle *v.* Saunders, 2 H. & M. 242; Layard *v.* Maud, L. R. 4 Eq. 397; Hunter *v.* Walters, L. R. 7 Ch. Ap. 75; L. R. 11 Eq. 292, s. c.; Bickerton *v.* Walker, 31 Ch. D. 151; Farrand *v.* Yorkshire Co., 40 Ch. D. 182; Stoner *v.* Brown, 18 Ind. 464; Besson *v.* Eveland, 26 N. J. Eq. 468; Wilson *v.* Hicks, 40 Oh. St. 418. See also Union Bank *v.* Kent, 39 Ch. Div. 238; Niven *v.* Belknap, 2 Johns. 573; Leach *v.* Ansbacher, 55 Pa. 85. — AMES.

In Lloyd's Banking Co. *v.* Jones, 29 Ch. D. 221, the owner of land deposited title deeds with a bank as security for future overdrafts. Without having overdrawn his account he conveyed the land to a trustee who gave the bank no notice of the conveyance and carelessly allowed the bank to retain possession of the title deeds. The former owner then overdrew his account. It was held that the trustee was estopped by his negligence and that the equity of the bank was superior to that of the beneficiaries. See Lloyd's Bank *v.* Bullock, [1896] 2 Ch. 192; Walker *v.* Linom, [1907] 2 Ch. 104. But see Capell *v.* Winter, [1907] 2 Ch. 376. In Jenkinson *v.* N. Y. Finance Co., 79 N. J. Eq. 247, 257, it is pointed out that representations by the trustee should not estop the *cestui que trust*.

As to estoppel, see Ballantine, Purchase for Value and Estoppel, 6 Minn. L. Rev. 87; Costigan, Protecting Purchasers for Value, 12 Cal. L. Rev. 356; Williston, Sales, sec. 312; Ewart, Estoppel.

[1] Ames, Lect. Leg. Hist., 257, 1 Harv. L. Rev. 5.
[2] In Duff *v.* Randall, 116 Cal. 226, it was held that a purchaser at an execution sale who received a certificate of sale from the sheriff is protected against a prior unrecorded conveyance of which he had no notice although he received notice before delivery of the sheriff's deed. — ED.

2 H. & M. 424. A trustee of shares in a company wrongfully pledged them, transferred the certificates, and executed a power to the innocent lender to register himself as owner of the shares. The transfer was registered after the lender was informed of the breach of trust. Wood, V. C., refused to deprive the lender of his security. There are similar decisions in Scotland and in this country.[1]

SAUNDERS v. DEHEW.

Chancery. 1692.

2 Vern. 271.[2]

ANNE BAYLY, being possessed of a term for years, makes a voluntary settlement thereof, in trust for herself for life, remainder to her daughter Isabella Barnes for life, remainder to the children of Isabella, by Mr. Barnes, her then husband. Isabella, for 200*l.*, mortgages the lands in question to the plaintiff, who pretends he had no notice of the settlement; Isabella, in the mortgage deed, being called the daughter and heir of John Bayly. The plaintiff hearing of it gets an assignment of the term from the trustees.

Per Cur. Though a purchaser may buy in an incumbrance, or lay hold on any plank to protect himself, yet he shall not protect himself by the taking a conveyance from a trustee after he had notice of the trust, for by taking a conveyance with notice of the trust, he himself becomes the trustee, and must not, to get a plank to save himself, be guilty of a breach of trust. And the plaintiff's bill being brought against the children of Isabella to foreclose them, the court refused so to do, saying, if he might be suffered to protect himself, by thus getting in the legal estate, they would not carry it on by a decree in equity to foreclose. . . .

TABULA IN NAUFRAGIO. If one advances money in order to acquire an interest in property, and is ignorant of an outstanding equitable interest in another, and if he obtains a conveyance which he thinks gives him a legal interest or an equitable interest which would be superior to the outstanding equitable interest, although

[1] Redfearn *v.* Ferrier, 1 Dow. 50; Burns *v.* Lawrie's Trustees (Scotch), 2 D. 1348; Brewster *v.* Sime, 42 Cal. 139; Thompson *v.* Toland, 48 Cal. 112; Winter *v.* Belmont, 53 Cal. 428; Atkinson *v.* Atkinson, 8 All. 15; McNeil *v.* Tenth Bank, 46 N. Y. 325. In Dodds *v.* Hills, it will be noticed, the lender was able to complete his title under the power without further assistance from the delinquent trustee. If the lender required the performance of some further act on the part of the trustee in order to complete his title, and if before such performance he received notice of the trust, the loss would fall upon him; for in the case supposed he could not obtain the title without making himself a party to the continuance of the breach of trust. Ortigosa *v.* Brown (47 L. J. Ch. 168) was decided in favor of a defrauded pledgor upon this distinction.

[2] Freem. C. C. 123, s. c.

in fact he gets only a subsequent equitable interest or no equitable interest at all, and if he subsequently gets a conveyance of the legal title, even *after* he has notice of the outstanding equitable interest, the English courts hold that he takes free and clear of that interest, *provided* the transferor of the legal title was not committing a breach of trust or violating any duty in making the conveyance. The leading case is Marsh *v.* Lee, 1 Ch. Ca. 162, 3 Ch. Rep. 62, 2 Vent. 337, 2 White & Tudor, L. C. Eq., 8 ed., 118. See Bates *v.* Johnson, Johns. 304.

The most common application of the doctrine is in the tacking of mortgages. " A third or subsequent mortgagee who when he lent his money had no notice of the second mortgage becomes entitled by paying off the first mortgage and getting a conveyance of the legal estate, to tack his own debt to the first mortgagee's so that the second mortgagee's right will be postponed to both these debts. This doctrine of tacking was abolished by the Vendor and Purchaser Act, 1874, sec. 7, but in the next year it was restored, for that section was repealed as from its commencement by the Land Transfer Act of 1875." Maitland, Equity, 286, 287. See Willoughby, The Legal Estate, 29–87. It has been abolished except in certain situations by Law of Property Act, 1925, sec. 90.

The doctrine of tacking, which has been severely condemned even in England (Jennings *v.* Jordan, 6 A. C. 714), is rejected in the United States. Ames, 296. Moreover, the registry system would make the doctrine unimportant as far as it concerns land. Osborn *v.* Carr, 12 Conn. 196; Grant *v.* Bissett, 1 Caines Cas. in Error (N. Y.) 112; 1 White & Tudor, L. C. Eq., 3 Am. ed., 602; 4 Kent Com. 178; Jones, Mortgages, 7 ed., secs. 537, 1082. And it would have no application in jurisdictions in which a mortgagee has only a lien.

If the transferor of the legal title committed a breach of trust in making the transfer, the transferee, if he knew of the breach of trust, is not allowed to profit thereby. See Maundrell *v.* Maundrell, 10 Ves. 246; *Ex parte* Knott, 11 Ves. 609; Carter *v.* Carter, 3 K. & J. 617; Pilcher *v.* Rollins, L. R. 7 Ch. App. 259.

If the transferor committed a breach of trust but the transferee did not know of the breach of trust, does he take free and clear of the trust? In Mumford *v.* Stohwasser, L. R. 18 Eq. 556, 562, Jessel, M. R., expressed the opinion that he does not. See Ames, Lect. Leg. Hist. 267. But see *ibid.,* 283.

MERRY v. ABNEY THE FATHER, ABNEY THE SON AND KENDALL.

CHANCERY. 1663.

Freem. C. C. 151.

KENDALL contracted with the plaintiff to sell him certain lands in Leicestershire; after which Abney the father, living near those lands, in the behalf of Abney the son, a merchant in London, purchased those lands of Kendall, and had a conveyance from Kendall to Abney the son and his heirs. The plaintiff's bill was to be relieved from this contract with Kendall, and against the conveyance, and charged notice of this contract to both the Abneys. Abney the son pleaded himself a purchaser *bona fide,* upon a valuable consideration, without notice of Kendall's contract with the plaintiff, and without any trust for his father.

CUR': Notice to the father, who transacted, is notice to the son, and shall affect him; so notice of a dormant incumbrance to one, who purchaseth for another, is notice to the purchaser; and accordingly this case was decreed at the hearing, viz. that they should convey to Merry the plaintiff, it appearing at the hearing, that Abney the father had notice of Merry's contract before he purchased for his son.[1]

SHAW v. SPENCER.

SUPREME JUDICIAL COURT, MASSACHUSETTS. 1868.

100 Mass. 382.

BILL IN EQUITY against Spencer, Vila & Co. and Mellen, Ward & Co., two firms of brokers in Boston, and the Calumet Mining Company, a corporation under the law of Michigan, praying for an injunction to restrain Spencer, Vila & Co. from making any sale or

---

[1] See Wenz v. Pastene, 209 Mass. 359; H. C. Girard Co. v. Lamoureux, 227 Mass. 277; Scott v. Scott, 2 N. Y. App. Div. 240.

But if one purchases property and takes title in the name of another and neither has notice of a prior equity, the prior equity is cut off. See Wilkes v. Bodington, 2 Vern. 599; Willoughby v. Willoughby, 1 T. R. 763; Kenicott v. Supervisors, 16 Wall (U. S.) 452; New Orleans etc. Co. v. Montgomery, 95 U. S. 16; Willis v. Henderson, 5 Ill. 13; Peoria etc. R. R. Co. v. Thompson, 103 Ill. 187; Stokes v. Riley, 121 Ill. 166. See Ames, 286. But *cf.* Paul v. McPherrin, 48 Colo. 522. See Costigan, Protecting Purchasers for Value, 12 Cal. L. Rev. 356, 370; Seavey, Notice Through an Agent, 65 U. Pa. L. Rev. 1, 15.

In Westinghouse Electric & Mfg. Co. v. Brooklyn R. T. Co., 291 Fed. 863, it was held that one who purchased bonds of a corporation took free of prior equitable liens on the mortgaged property of which he had no knowledge, although the trustee under the mortgage had knowledge of these liens. But see Miller v. Rutland etc. R. R. Co., 36 Vt. 452. See 42 Harv. L. Rev. 224.

transfer of two thousand shares of the stock of that company, or of the certificates of the same, and the company from recognizing the validity of any such sale or transfer otherwise than to the plaintiff.

A temporary injunction was granted, and at the hearing, before *Wells*, J., the material facts appeared as follows: On the 28th of February 1867, Spencer, Vila & Co. received from New York United States bonds to the amount of a hundred thousand dollars, with a draft for one hundred and six thousand seven hundred and thirty-five dollars on Mellen, Ward & Co., to whom they were to deliver the bonds on payment of the draft. Charles Mellen applied for and obtained the bonds, promising to return with currency or a cashier's check, which he did not do. Mr. Vila, after calling once or twice unsuccessfully at the office of Mellen, Ward & Co. for the money, at last saw Mellen, who offered his check for the whole amount, which was refused. Mellen then offered a check of Kidder, Peabody & Co. for fifty thousand dollars, and the check of Mellen, Ward & Co. for the balance with collateral security, this latter check to go into the bank the next day. This proposal was accepted, and, just before two o'clock, (the hour of the closing of the Boston banks,) the collateral security was delivered to Spencer, Vila & Co., and the check was deposited. This collateral security consisted of two certificates, for one thousand shares each of stock in the Calumet Mining Company, standing in the name of " E. Carter, trustee," with a transfer in blank on the back of each, subscribed " Edward Carter, trustee," (Carter being a member of the firm of Mellen, Ward & Co.,) and the certificates were expressed to be " transferable only on the books of the company, by the holder thereof in person, or by a conveyance in writing, recorded in said books, and surrender of this certificate," and were dated February 7. The blank transfers were dated February 8. The shares which these certificates represented had been owned by Quincy A. Shaw, and were part of a larger number which he had transferred to certain trustees, including himself and the plaintiff, to secure certain debts, and which these trustees afterwards transferred to the plaintiff. And they had been transferred by the plaintiff into the name of " E. Carter, trustee," as collateral security for certain acceptances made by Quincy A. Shaw on drafts of the Huron Mining Company which had been taken by Mellen, Ward & Co. for negotiation, who gave for them the following receipt:

" Boston, February 8, 1867. Received of S. P. Shaw two certificates of stock in the Calumet Mining Company of Michigan, being for two thousand shares in all, each certificate being of one thousand shares, to be used as collateral for acceptances of Q. A. Shaw of Huron Mining Company drafts, which we bind ourselves to return to said S. P. Shaw whenever said acceptances are paid. Said certificates are in the name of E. Carter, trustee.

Mellen, Ward & Co."

There was nothing on the books of the company to show the arrangement with Carter, or the extent or nature of the trust. On the 28th of February nothing was due to Mellen, Ward & Co. on these acceptances. On March 1, Mellen, Ward & Co. failed; and their check which Mellen gave to Spencer, Vila & Co. was dishonored, and never paid. On that day Mr. Farley, a member of the firm of Spencer, Vila & Co., filled the blanks in the transfers of the certificates with the name of that firm, and presented them to Quincy A. Shaw as transfer agent of the Calumet Mining Company, with a request for the transfer to be made and new certificates to be issued in the name of the firm, which was at first declined by Mr. Q. A. Shaw on the ground that he wished to make some inquiries, and afterwards on the ground that an assessment of five dollars per share which had been made on the capital stock was due and unpaid on the shares in question. The next day Mr. Q. A. Shaw heard that Spencer, Vila & Co. held the stock as security for a debt of Mellen, Ward & Co., and not as collateral for Huron Mining Company paper, and addressed to them the following notice:

"Boston, March 2, 1867. Messrs. Spencer, Vila & Co.: Please to take notice that the certificates of stock of the Calumet Mining Company in your hands, and in the name of E. Carter, trustee, are my property, and that I have never received value thereon. Please hold them subject to my direction. Yours respectfully, Quincy A. Shaw, for self and others, trustees."

During the few days following, Mr. Q. A. Shaw had several conversations with Mr. Vila, in which he proposed to submit the question of the title to the stock to certain arbitrators, which proposition Mr. Vila declined. About this time the plaintiff became president, and Mr. Q. A. Shaw treasurer, of the Calumet Mining Company; and on March 18, at the office of the company, Mr. Vila paid the assessment due on the shares in question, to the treasurer, in the presence of the plaintiff, who made no demand for the stock on that occasion. The next day, Mr. Q. A. Shaw returned the amount of this payment to Spencer, Vila & Co. in a letter subscribed like his former letter above recited, and stating that "the assessment was paid and received by mistake," and that the stock was owned by himself; but they refused to receive the amount thus returned. On March 26, the plaintiff served notice on the firm that the stock was his property, and requested them to deliver to him the certificates with such indorsements as would enable him to obtain it; and on the same day filed this bill.

The defendants offered testimony to show: "1. That it is usual with dealers in the stock market to deliver, by way of sales or pledge, certificates of stock, with a blank transfer upon the back; 2. that it is usual for holders of certificates of stock, transferred in blank, to fill them up by inserting the name of some person as transferee or purchaser; 3. that it is a matter of common occurrence for certificates of stock to be issued in the name of some other person as trustee, when in fact there is not any trust; 4. whether certificates of stock, issued to a designated person as trustee, are constantly bought and sold in the stock market, by a simple indorsement of the certificate by the person named as the holder, without inquiry as to the authority by which, or to the use or purpose for which, the transfer was made." But the judge ruled that, " as to the first two propositions, the facts proposed to be shown were immaterial; and, as to the last two, by the rules of law they were inadmissible."

The defendants alleged exceptions; and the judge reported the case for decision thereon, and for such final decree or other order as in the opinion of the full court should be made.

FOSTER, J. The court have bestowed upon this case a degree of attention commensurate with the importance of the principles on which its decision must depend and the magnitude of the amount involved. One of two innocent parties must bear a heavy loss, caused by the gross fraud of a third person.

Under the circumstances disclosed by the evidence, it was a flagrant breach of trust and a criminal fraud to transfer the certificates of stock to Spencer, Vila & Co. They were the property of the plaintiff, who is entitled to reclaim them from any one but a *bonâ fide* holder for value without notice. Charles Mellen, a member of the firm of Mellen, Ward & Co., as collateral security for a debt due from that firm to Spencer, Vila & Co., handed to them two certificates of stock in the Calumet Mining Company for one thousand shares each, standing in the name of another member of that firm, namely, " E. Carter, trustee," and by him transferred in blank. Spencer, Vila & Co. received the certificates thus indorsed in blank with the name of E. Carter, trustee, for a valuable and adequate consideration without other notice of any defect in title than such as the law may impute from the word " trustee " in the body of the certificates and after the signature of Carter upon the blank transfers.

It is clear that a certificate of stock transferred in blank is not a negotiable instrument.[1] Sewall *v.* Boston Water Power Co., 4 Allen, 282. Each of these certificates is expressed on its face to be " transferable only on the books of the company by the holder hereof in person or by a conveyance in writing recorded in said books, and surrender of this certificate." No commercial usage can give to such an instrument the attributes of negotiability. However many intermediate hands it may pass through, whoever would obtain a new certificate in his own name must fill out the blanks, as they were filled in the present instance, so as to derive title to himself directly from the last recorded stockholder, who is the only recognized and legal owner of the shares.

[1] See, however, the Uniform Stock Transfer Act which was adopted in Massachusetts in 1910. Gen. Stats., 1921, c. 155, secs. 24–44.

It cannot possibly be material whether the manual delivery of the certificates was by Mellen or by Carter himself. Unless the word " trustee " may be regarded as mere *descriptio personæ*, and rejected as a nullity, there was plain and actual notice of the existence of a trust of some description. A trust as to personalty or choses in action need not be expressed in writing, but may be established by parol. And that the mere use of the word " trustee " in the assignment of a mortgage and note imports the existence of a trust, and gives notice thereof to all into whose hands the instrument comes, has been expressly decided by this court. Sturtevant *v.* Jaques, 14 Allen, 523. See also Bancroft *v.* Consen, 13 Allen, 50, and Trull *v.* Trull, Ib. 407. It is insisted on behalf of the defendants, that, even if there was actual notice of the existence of a trust, there was no notice of its character, and that the trust might have been such as to authorize the transfer which was made by Carter. But, in our opinion, the simple answer to this position is, that, where one known to be a trustee is found pledging that which is known to be trust property, to secure a debt due from a firm of which he is a member, the act is one *primâ facie* unauthorized and unlawful, and it is the duty of him who takes such security to ascertain whether the trustee has a right to give it. The appropriation of corporate stock held in trust, as collateral security for the trustee's own debt, or a debt which he owes jointly with others, is a transaction so far beyond the ordinary scope of a trustee's authority and out of the common course of business, as to be in itself a suspicious circumstance, imposing upon the creditor the duty of inquiry. This would hardly be controverted in a case where the stock was held by " A. B., trustee for C. D." But the effect of the word " trustee," alone, is the same. It means trustee for some one whose name is not disclosed; and there is no greater reason for assuming that a trustee is authorized to pledge for his own debt the property of an unnamed *cestui que trust* than the property of one whose name is known. In either case it is highly improbable that the right to do so exists. The apparent difference between the two springs from the erroneous assumption that the word " trustee " alone has no meaning or legal effect.

Inasmuch as such an act of pledging property is *primâ facie* unlawful, there would be little hardship in imposing on the party who takes the security, not only the duty of inquiry, but the burden of ascertaining the actual facts at his peril. Where a partner assumes to give for his own private debt the note of his firm, the creditor who takes it must show that it was given with the assent of the other partners, because it is an apparent misuse of the name of the firm and *primâ facie* evidence of fraud. Eastman *v.* Cooper, 15 Pick. 290. But we need not go to that length in deciding the present case. Notice of the existence of a trust is by all the authorities held to impose the duty of inquiry as to its character and limitations. And whatever is sufficient to put a person of ordinary prudence upon inquiry is constructive notice of everything to which that inquiry might have led.

The objection that in the present case the only persons of whom inquiry could have been made were Mellen and Carter, who committed the breach of trust, is sufficiently answered by the words of Sir John Romilly, master of the rolls, in a recent and leading case. " With respect to the argument that it was unnecessary to make any inquiry, because it must have led to no results," he says: " I think it impossible to admit the validity of this excuse. I concur in the doctrine of Jones *v.* Smith, 1 Hare, 55, that a false answer, or a reasonable answer, given to an inquiry made, may dispense with the necessity of further inquiry; but I think it impossible beforehand to come to the conclusion that a false answer would have been given which would have precluded the necessity of further inquiry. A more dangerous doctrine could not be laid down, nor one involving a more unsatisfactory inquiry, namely, a hypothetical inquiry as to what A. would have said if B. had said something other than what he did say." Jones *v.* Williams, 24 Beav. 62. These remarks also explain the cases, cited by the defendants, of Buttrick *v.* Holden, 13 Met. 355, and Calais Steamboat Co. *v.* Van Pelt, 2 Black, 377. In each of these cases the party did make inquiry, and relied upon the answers received, which were of a character calculated to put him off his guard.

If it be asked of whom the defendants could have inquired as to the meaning of the words " E. Carter, trustee," the nature of the trust thereby indicated, and the existence of the power to pledge for the debts of the firm of Mellen, Ward & Co., which Carter was assuming to exercise, the answer is, that the inquiry could have been made of Mellen, and if he replied that he did not know the nature of the trust, then the duty of the defendants would have been to ask Carter himself for an explanation, which it certainly was in his power to give. It is not to be assumed that false answers would have been made, and the defendants have been thereby deceived and misled. On the contrary, the probabilities are that such an investigation would have led to the discovery of the truth. Or if Spencer, Vila & Co., before taking the stock certificates as collateral security, had been prudent enough to require a transfer to be made to them on the books of the corporation, this step would have brought them into contact with Quincy A. Shaw, and have exposed the whole attempted fraud. Some of the cases say that constructive notice is imputed only on the ground of gross negligence. But, if it be so, a court of equity must hold it to be a want of ordinary prudence, or *crassa negligentia*, to omit all inquiry, where there is actual notice that a trust of some kind exists, and the use proposed to be made of the trust property is *primâ facie* a misappropriation.

The case of Ashton *v.* Atlantic Bank, 3 Allen, 217, is not in conflict with these views. It does not proceed on the ground that there was no duty to inquire, but that upon inquiry and examination of the will creating the trust it would have appeared that the trustee might have the right to use the trust funds as he did. He raised money upon the stocks by a discount of his own note with them as collateral; and the court said that it might have been incident to his duties " to discount the trust funds for the sake of making a permanent investment," or " the purchaser might reasonably assume that the money was wanted to discharge liability incurred under the will. Such a case was well warranted by the will creating the trust." In short, the court came to the conclusion that the act of the trustee was in itself lawful in that particular case, and that his fraud consisted only in the misuse of the money when obtained. If this was true, of course the purchaser was not bound to see to the application of the purchase money.

Hutchins v. State Bank, 12 Met. 421, was the case of a sale of shares of bank stock by an executrix. It is the established rule of equity that " purchases from executors of the personal property of their testator are ordinarily valid, notwithstanding it may be affected with some peculiar trust or equity in the hands of the executor; for the purchaser cannot be presumed to know that the sale may not be required in order to discharge the debts of the testator, to which they are legally liable before all other claims. But if the purchaser knows that the executor is converting the estate into money for an unlawful purpose, the purchase will be set aside." Smith on Eq. tit. 1, c. iv. 10, " Where an executor disposes of or pledges his testator's assets in payment of, or as security for, a debt of his own, the person to whom they are disposed of or pledged will take them subject to the claims of creditors and legatees." Elliot v. Merryman, 1 Lead. Cas. in Eq. 89. Hill v. Simpson, 7 Ves. 152. The same doctrine was held by Chancellor Kent in 1823 in Field v. Schieffelin, 7 Johns. Ch. 150, who, upon a review of all the cases down to the time of that decision, thus sums up the result: " The great difficulty has been to determine how far the purchaser dealt at his peril, when he knew, from the very face of the proceeding, that the executor was applying the assets to his own private purposes as the payment of his own debt. The later and the better doctrine is, that in such a case he does buy at his peril." Chief Justice Gibson, in Petrie v. Clark, 11 S. & R. 377, expressly announces the doctrine " that an executor's applying the assets in payment of his own debt is of itself a circumstance of suspicion, which ought to put the purchasing creditor upon inquiry as to the propriety of the transaction."

The rule was thus laid down in 1861 in the house of lords: " Where an executor parts with any portion of the assets of the testator under such circumstances as that the purchaser must be reasonably taken to know that they were sold not for the benefit of the estate but for the executor's own benefit, the result is, that the purchaser holds the assets as if he were himself in respect of those assets the executor." Walker *v.* Taylor, 4 Law Times, (N. S.) 845. See also 2 Redfield on Wills, *c.* viii. § 32.

The power of disposition over a testator's assets, which an executor has, is as extensive as that of a trustee, and the conversion of the testator's personal estate into money is within the ordinary line of an executor's duty. Consequently the authorities which have been cited as to the liability of those dealing with executors are fully applicable to the case of one who takes trust property from a trustee as security for his private indebtedness.

We proceed to consider the testimony offered by the defendants and excluded by the judge at the hearing.

The fact that it is usual for dealers in stock to take certificates with blank transfers upon them and to fill them up with the names of purchasers, was wholly immaterial. Such a practice, as we have already observed, does not make the shares negotiable, and the purchaser whose name is written into the transfer must always derive his title immediately and solely from the stockholder of record. The point is not made by the plaintiff that a transfer in blank is out of the usual course of business, or a suspicious circumstance; so that evidence of usage was not requisite to repel such an inference.

The fact that it is common to issue certificates of stock in the name of one as trustee, when no trust actually exists, has no legal bearing on the decision of the present case. The rules of law are presumed to be known by all men; and they must govern themselves accordingly. The law holds that the insertion of the word "trustee" after the name of a stockholder does indicate and give notice of a trust. No one is at liberty to disregard such notice and to abstain from inquiry for the reason that a trust is frequently simulated or pretended when it really does not exist. The whole force of this offer of evidence is addressed to the question whether the word "trustee" alone has any significance and does amount to notice of the existence of a trust. But this has been heretofore decided, and is no longer an open question in this Commonwealth. Sturtevant *v.* Jaques, 14 Allen, 523.

The circumstance that stock certificates issued in the name of one as trustee, and by him transferred in blank, are constantly bought and sold in the market without inquiry, is likewise unavailing. A usage to disregard one's legal duty, to be ignorant of a rule of law, and to act as if it did not exist, can have no standing in the courts.

It is to be borne in mind that the question under discussion is not whether one holding stock as trustee may sell it in the market and pass a good title to the purchaser. We do not intimate that this cannot be done. The distinction between a sale and a pledge of trust property is palpable and manifest. Nor is the present question whether a trustee may borrow money on the pledge of stock held in trust. We do not decide that such a transaction may not under some circumstances be sustained. These questions are left to be adjudged when they arise. The point now decided is, that one holding stock as trustee has *primâ facie* no right to pledge it to secure his own debt growing out of an independent transaction; and that whoever takes it as security for such a debt, without inquiry, does so at his peril. All the proffers of evidence taken together fall short of showing any usage to do this; and no evidence of usage could legalize such conduct. Because Spencer, Vila & Co. took these certificates of stock to secure an antecedent debt from Mellen, Ward & Co. to them, with notice that they were held in trust, and made no inquiry as to Carter's authority to use trust property for such a purpose, they cannot retain the security against the equitable owner of the stock, when it appears that Carter in making the pledge was guilty of a fraudulent breach of trust.

The remaining questions relate to the effect of the payment on the 18th of March of the assessment of ten thousand dollars on this stock by Spencer, Vila & Co. to Q. A. Shaw, treasurer and transfer agent, in the presence of S. P. Shaw, the plaintiff. On the 2d of March, Spencer, Vila & Co. had received written notice from Q. A. Shaw that Carter had no right to transfer the stock to them, and that their title to it was contested. By receiving the money, which Spencer, Vila & Co. voluntarily offered to pay, the Messrs. Shaw did not induce them to change their position, or deprive them of any rights. They had taken the stock certificates nineteen days before they made the payment, and, when it was made, they had no reason to believe that either S. P. Shaw or Q. A. Shaw intended to abandon their claim, or to waive any of their rights. Q. A. Shaw could not have done so by any act of his own. S. P. Shaw did no act, and only omitted to object to the payment of the assessment. The payment was evidently the voluntary act of Spencer, Vila & Co. intended to fortify their own position, and to entitle them to a new certificate of the stock if their title should prove good. It was made for their own benefit and protection, and no act or declaration of the Messrs. Shaw deceived or misled, or induced them to make it. A waiver is an intentional relinquishment of a known right. An estoppel of the description relied on in this case can be maintained only on the ground that, by the fault of one party, another has been induced innocently and ignorantly to change his position for the worse, in such a manner that it would operate as a virtual fraud upon him to allow the party by whom he has been misled to assert the right in controversy. These simple definitions of the terms "waiver" and "estoppel" exclude the possibility of applying either doctrine to the effect of the payment of this assessment.

The amount paid, with interest, must be refunded before any decree can be made requiring the defendants to retransfer the certificates to the plaintiff. As the bill contains no special prayer for this relief, and no offer to refund the money, it will require amendment before such a decree can be entered. But the injunction heretofore granted is made perpetual.[1] . . .

WILLYS–OVERLAND, INC. v. BLAKE.

SUPREME COURT, FLORIDA. 1929.

97 Fla. 626.

BUFORD, J. — The appellant procured a judgment against one of the appellees, Erle B. Renwick, and placed execution in the hands of the sheriff for collection. The sheriff levied on certain lands in Pinellas County. The appellees (except Renwick and Booth as sheriff) filed a bill to enjoin the sale of certain lands levied upon claiming that they were the beneficial and equitable owners of an un-

---

[1] For decisions in accordance with the principal case, see 34 Harv. L. Rev. 457.

The same result has been reached where the transferee does not know that the trustee in transferring the property is acting for his own benefit. 34 Harv. L. Rev. 458.

There is some authority to the effect that the word "trustee" standing alone is not enough to put the purchaser upon inquiry. Northwestern etc. Co. v. Atlantic Co., 174 Cal. 308.

If a purchaser uses due care in inquiring as to the extent of the trustee's authority, he is not liable if he purchases in good faith although the trustee in fact exceeded his authority. Grafflin v. Robb, 84 Md. 451; Mercantile Nat. Bk. v. Parsons, 54 Minn. 56.

If the trustee's authority is evidenced by an instrument in writing of which the purchaser knows, or which is recorded, the purchaser has failed to use due care if he has not examined the instrument. Marbury v. Ehlen, 72 Md. 206; Donnelly v. Alden, 229 Mass. 109; Stark v. Olsen, 44 Neb. 646; First Nat. Bk. v. National Broadway Bk., 156 N. Y. 459; Ludington v. Mercantile Nat. Bk., 102 N. Y. App. Div. 251.

On the general question of the liability of one who knowingly deals with a trustee, see Perham v. Kempster, [1907] 1 Ch. 373; Perry, Trusts, secs. 225, 800, 814.

Negotiable instruments. It is held that although the addition of the word "trustee" to the name of the payee of a negotiable instrument does not render the instrument non-negotiable, yet a purchaser of the instrument must make inquiry as to the authority of the trustee to negotiate it. 34 Harv. L. Rev. 460–462.

By the Uniform Fiduciaries Act it is provided that if a negotiable instrument payable or indorsed to a fiduciary as such is indorsed by the fiduciary, the indorsee is not bound to inquire whether the fiduciary is committing a breach of duty and is not liable in the absence of knowledge of the breach or bad faith; but if he knows that the fiduciary is transferring the instrument as security for his personal debt or in a transaction for his personal benefit, he is liable if the fiduciary in fact commits a breach of duty in making the transfer. There are similar provisions in respect to checks drawn by a fiduciary.

divided 11/15 interest in the real estate and that Renwick held the legal title to the said property in trust for said complainants, and that Renwick was also the equitable and beneficial owner of an undivided 2/15 of the real estate. The bill alleged that Renwick was insolvent. The Willys-Overland Company filed its answer incorporating demurrers in the answer. A temporary restraining order was granted. Motion was made to dissolve the restraining order and on the 23rd day of December, 1927, the court made an order denying the motion to dissolve insofar as the same applied to all the property described in the bill of complaint except lot 26 of Florida Heights sub-division and lot 13 of Block A. . . .

[On the 25th day of January, 1928, the Court made a further order modifying the order of December 22, 1927, dissolving the restraining order as to four-fifteenths of the property and affirming it as to the remaining eleven-fifteenths.]

From these orders appeal was taken.

The judgment of Willys-Overland Co., as shown by the answer and exhibits, was obtained on the 14th day of September, 1927.

The lands now involved in this appeal were conveyed by M. P. Lawrence and wife to " Erle B. Renwick, Trustee, with full power to sell, convey, transfer and encumber the within described real estate."

It is alleged in the sworn answer, and not contradicted, that there did not appear of record at the time of the recording of such deed or conveyance a declaration of trust by the grantee so described declaring the purposes of such trust, if any, or that the real estate is held other than for the benefit of the grantee.

The controlling question to be determined by this Court is whether or not the complainants in the court below possessed such rights as may be interposed against the right of judgment creditor to subject the property involved to sale and execution. Under the provisions of Sec. 5666,[1] Comp. Gen. Laws of Fla., 1927, (Sec. 3793, R. G. S.) the conveyance under which Renwick acquired the property involved, vested in him a fee simple estate, with full power and authority to sell, convey and grant both the legal and beneficial interest in the real estate. The terms of the convey-

[1] This section provides as follows: " Every deed or conveyance of real estate heretofore or hereafter made or executed, in which the words ' trustee ' or ' as trustee ' are added to the name of the grantee, and in which no beneficiaries are named nor the nature and purposes of the trust, if any, are set forth, shall grant, and is hereby declared to have granted a fee simple estate with full power and authority in and to the grantee in such deed to sell, convey and grant both the legal and beneficial interest in the real estate conveyed, unless a contrary intention shall appear in the deed or conveyance: Provided, that there shall and did not appear of record at the time of the recording of such deed or conveyance, a declaration of trust by the grantee so described, declaring the purposes of such trust, if any, or that the real estate is held other than for the benefit of the grantee."

ance itself authorized him to encumber the real estate. This conveyance had stood on the public records from 1924 to 1927 and until after the judgment was obtained against Renwick without anything appearing of record, as is alleged in the pleadings, to show that any of the complainants in the court below had, or claimed, any beneficial interest in the property. The answer denies that the judgment creditor had any knowledge of any right or claim of any beneficial interest in the complainants. In Feinberg *v.* Stearns, 56 Fla. 279, 47 So. R. 797, this Court say:

" An execution creditor, equally with a subsequent purchaser, is protected under the statute against unrecorded deeds, and in order to deprive such judgment creditor of the protection of the recording statute it must be shown that he had notice in some recognized way of the rights of the party claiming under the unrecorded deed *at the time of the rendition of his judgment.*"

And in Hunter *v.* State Bank of Florida, 65 Fla. 202, 61 So. R. 497, the Court say:

" The lien of a judgment under the statute of Florida is effective only as to the beneficial interest of the judgment debtor in real estate. But if the record shows a beneficial interest in the judgment debtor and there are no circumstances to rebut such showing, or to put interested parties upon inquiry, when in fact the judgment debtor has no beneficial interest, or only a partial or qualified interest, those who have the beneficial interest not shown of record may be estopped from asserting it against a *bona fide* judgment creditor or subsequent purchaser of the judgment debtor, when the judgment creditor or purchaser at a judgment sale under the judgment, reasonably may have acquired substantial rights on the faith of, or by reason of the record showing an interest in the judgment debtor, when in fact such interest belongs to another."

Both of the cases above referred to were decided by this Court prior to the enactment of Chapter 6925, Acts of 1915, which, as amended, is now referred to as Sec. 5666, Comp. Gen. Laws 1927.

Our conclusion is that the parties to this suit occupy the same legal relation toward one another and their respective rights are the same insofar as the questions raised in this litigation are concerned, as if the word " Trustee " had not appeared in the conveyance from P. M. Lawrence and wife to Renwick. That the inclusion of the word " Trustee " in the conveyance in nowise affected the legal right of the judgment creditor to subject the property included in such conveyance to the satisfaction of his judgment when such judgment was obtained without any other notice, by record or otherwise, of the claims of beneficial interests of third parties in and to such property.

For the reasons stated, the orders appealed from should be reversed and it is so ordered.

Reversed.[1]

TERRELL, C. J., AND ELLIS, WHITFIELD AND STRUM, JJ., concur. BROWN, J., dissents.

BISCHOFF *v.* YORKVILLE BANK.

COURT OF APPEALS, NEW YORK. 1916.

218 N. Y. 106.

COLLIN, J. The plaintiff has recovered a judgment against the defendant for the sum of $13,329.04, apart from the sums of interest and costs. The basic facts as found are: In March, 1908, H. F. W. Poggenburg was appointed and qualified as executor of the will of Josephine F. Schneider, deceased. The plaintiff here became his successor in December, 1914, through his removal. In April, 1908, Poggenburg as executor deposited the moneys of the estate in the Bowery Bank in the city of New York in the name of "Estate of Josephine F. Schneider by H. F. W. Poggenburg, executor." He, as an individual, had at that time a deposit account with the defendant, Yorkville Bank. In April, 1908, he sent by mail to the defendant a check upon the Bowery Bank in the sum of five hundred dollars, payable to the order of the defendant, signed "Estate of Josephine F. Schneider by H. F. W. Poggenburg, executor." The defendant received the check in due course, indorsed and transmitted it through the New York Clearing House to the Bowery Bank, which paid it out of the funds of the estate. The defendant placed the proceeds of it to the credit of Poggenburg in his individual account with the defendant. Between April, 1908, and November, 1911, the defendant received through the mail twenty-nine other checks identical, except as to date and amount, with that described (except that one was payable to the order of Poggenburg and by him indorsed payable to the order of the defendant, which counsel assume and we will assume has the character and effect of the others), and dealt with them as it did with that fully set forth. The findings describe with particularity the manner in which the officers and employees of the defendant, in creating the credits, dealt with the checks. The amounts of the checks aggregated $14,005. Additional moneys from sources other than the estate were deposited by Poggenburg with the defendant and credited to him in his account during the interval involved. In April, 1908, the defendant owned the promissory note of Poggenburg for $1,750, which matured June 3, 1908. On June 3, 1908, Poggenburg paid the defendant

[1] Statutes have been passed in a number of states similar to the Florida statute. See 14 Minn. L. Rev. 76.

from his individual account with it, in which the amount standing to his credit was less than the proceeds of the estate checks theretofore deposited therein, $765 upon the note, including interest, and renewed $1,000 of the loan by a new note maturing September 1, 1908. On September 1, 1908, this note was paid the defendant in the same manner and under the like condition. In February, 1911, the defendant was paid, likewise, $1,000 upon a note of Poggenburg held by it for the sum of $2,000. The decree of the Surrogate's Court of April, 1915, by which Poggenburg was removed as the executor and his accounts as executor were settled, declared that he was liable to the estate for the aggregate sum of the thirty checks with interest. All of the funds so withdrawn by the executor from the Bowery Bank and deposited in and placed by the defendant to his individual credit were checked out by Poggenburg in payment of said notes, or for his personal purposes, except the sum of $675.96. Throughout the transactions the defendant made no inquiry at any source as to the deposits of the checks of the executor or the withdrawals from the individual account with it. The judgment recovered by the plaintiff was for the sum of those funds, less the $675.96, with interest and costs. It was affirmed by the Appellate Division by a divided court. The dissenting justice declared that the recovery should have been only the sums Poggenburg paid the defendant. We have reached a conclusion differing from both.

The transfer of the funds of the estate to and the crediting of them by the defendant to Poggenburg, in his individual account, did not overpass the legal right of the executor or the defendant. The method was unwise and hazardous; it did not, however, in and of itself, constitute a conversion. The title to the funds was in the executor, and he possessed the full control and disposition of them. As executor, however, and not as an individual, and for the purposes of administration, was he thus empowered. For many purposes third persons are entitled to consider an executor the absolute owner of the personal assets in his hands. Although he holds the title to them, he holds it in trust to pay the debts and execute the will of the testator. In equity he is a mere trustee charged with the performance of the will. (Leitch v. Wells, 48 N. Y. 585; Blood v. Kane, 130 N. Y. 514; Smith v. Ayer, 101 U. S. 320; Hartnett v. Wandell, 60 N. Y. 346.) A fiduciary may legally deposit the trust funds in a bank to his individual account and credit. Knowledge on the part of the bank of the nature of the funds received and credited does not affect the character of the act. The bank has the right to presume that the fiduciary will apply the funds to their proper purposes under the trust. There are judicial decisions, in cases in which the fiduciary has converted the funds, which hold the contrary. (United States Fidelity & Guaranty Co. v. People's Bank, 127 Tenn. 720; Bank of Hickory v. McPherson, 102 Miss. 852.) The rule stated by us is, however, established in this and other jurisdictions, as the decisions hereinafter cited will disclose, and accords with reason.

The acts of the executor and the defendant in depositing and crediting in the individual account of Poggenburg the proceeds of the checks did not affect the character of the trust funds. The form of each check, in which the defendant was payee, imported the ownership of the moneys represented in them by the executor, and informed the defendant that Poggenburg was depositing with it moneys which were not his and were the executor's. (Squire v. Ordemann, 194 N. Y. 394; Ward v. City Trust Co., 192 N. Y. 61; Cohnfeld v. Tanenbaum, 176 N. Y. 126.) The defendant knew at all times that the credits created by the deposits of those moneys, through the checks of the executor, were equitably assets of the estate and owned by the executor. Trust funds do not lose their character as such by being deposited in a bank for the individual credit and account of the person who is trustee. It may be stated as a general principle that if money deposited in a bank was held by the depositor in a fiduciary capacity, its character is not changed by being placed to his credit in his individual bank account. (Van Alen v. American Nat. Bank, 52 N. Y. 1; Union Stock Yards Bank v. Gillespie, 137 U. S. 411; National Bank v. Insurance Co., 104 U. S. 54; Roca v. Byrne, 145 N. Y. 182.)

Inasmuch as the defendant knew that the credits to Poggenburg created by the proceeds of the checks were of a fiduciary character and were equitably owned by the executor, it had not the right to participate in a diversion of them from the estate or the proper purposes under the will. Its participation in a diversion of them would result from either (a) acquiring an advantage or benefit directly through or from the diversion, or (b) joining in a diversion, in which it was not interested, with actual notice or knowledge that the diversion was intended or was being executed, and thereby becoming privy to it. (Ward v. City Trust Co., 192 N. Y. 61; Squire v. Ordemann, 194 N. Y. 394; Union Stock Yards Bank v. Gillespie, 137 U. S. 411; National Bank v. Insurance Co., 104 U. S. 54; Allen v. Puritan Trust Co., 211 Mass. 409.) In the case last cited it is stated: "The principle governing the defendant's liability is, that a banker who knows that a fund on deposit with him is a trust fund cannot appropriate that fund for his private benefit, or where charged with notice of the conversion join in assisting others to appropriate it for their private benefit, without being liable to refund the money if the appropriation is a breach of the trust," and numerous decisions are cited. (p. 422.) A bank does not become privy to a misappropriation by merely paying or honoring the checks of a depositor drawn upon his individual account in which there are, in the knowledge of the bank, credits created by deposits of trust funds. The law does not require the bank, under such facts, to assume the hazard of correctly reading in each check the purpose of the drawer, or, being ignorant of the purpose, to dishonor the check. The presumption is, and after the deposits are made remains until annulled by adequate notice or knowledge, that the depositor would preserve or lawfully apply the trust funds. The contract, arising by implication of law, from a general deposit of moneys in a bank is, that the bank will, whenever required, pay the moneys in such sums and to such persons as the depositor shall direct and designate. Although the depositor is drawing checks which the bank may surmise or suspect are for his personal benefit, it is bound to presume, in the absence of adequate notice to the contrary, that they are properly and lawfully drawn. Adequate notice may come from circumstances which reasonably support the sole inference that a misappropriation is intended, as well as directly. (Safe Deposit & Trust Co. *v.* Bank, 194 Pa. St. 334; Batchelder *v.* Central National Bank, 188 Mass. 25; United States Fidelity & Guaranty Co. *v.* Home Bank for Savings, 88 S. E. Rep. 109; Brookhouse *v.* Union Publishing Co., 73 N. H. 368; Freeholders of Essex *v.* Newark National Bank, 48 N. J. Eq. 51; Havana Central R. R. Co. *v.* Knickerbocker Trust Co., 198 N. Y. 422.)

In the present case Poggenburg paid to the defendant, as his creditor, on June 3, 1908, the sum of $765 from his account with the defendant. The finding of the trial court, supported by the evidence, is that the account at that time was constituted wholly from the trust funds. At that time and through the transaction the defendant knew that Poggenburg had appropriated $765 of those funds for his private benefit. The presumption that he would not thus violate his duty and lawful right — that he would apply the moneys to their proper purposes under the will then ceased to exist. There was absolute proof in the possession of the defendant to the contrary. The defendant had no longer the right to assume that in paying the checks of Poggenburg it was paying the executor's moneys to the executor and not to Poggenburg, the individual, or that Poggenburg would use the moneys lawfully. It had knowledge of such facts as would reasonably cause it to think and believe that Poggenburg was using the moneys of the executor for his individual advantage and purposes. Those facts indicated that the payment to it was not an isolated incident; they indicated, rather, that it was within a method or system. Having such knowledge, it was under the duty to make reasonable inquiry and endeavor to prevent a diversion. Having such knowledge, it was charged by the law to take the reasonable steps or action essential to keep it from paying to Poggenburg as his own the moneys which were not his and were the executor's, and was bound by the information which it could have obtained if an inquiry on its part had been pushed until the truth had been ascertained. It did nothing of that sort, and by supinely paying, under the facts here, as found, the subsequent checks of Poggenburg, it became privy to the misapplication. It must now pay the plaintiffs the moneys of the estate which it had and received on and after June 3, 1908. (Allen *v.* Puritan Trust Co., 211 Mass. 409; Duncan *v.* Jaudon, 15 Wall. 165.)

What we have written makes clear, we think, the distinction between the instant case and that of Havana Central Railroad Co. *v.* Knickerbocker Trust Co., **198** N. Y. **422**, upon which the defendant firmly relies.

We do not consider the question, because it is not here, as to whether or not a bank would be protected in honoring a check of a fiduciary depositor, regularly drawn upon his account as such fiduciary, and presented by him, even though it had actual notice that he would misappropriate the proceeds. The decisions are not uniform upon this question. The distinction between that question and the question *sub judice* is substantial. In the one, the bank pays, under its implied contract, the moneys to the rightful owner and the depositor; in the other, it pays the moneys to one who, as it knows, is not the rightful owner, after notice that the payee is converting them.

We have examined the other points of the appellant's brief and find nothing which requires discussion.

The trial court adjudged a recovery of the principal sum of $13,329.04, the aggregate sum of the amounts of the thirty checks, less the sum of $675.96, which was not misappropriated. Poggenburg had deposited with the defendant prior to June 3, 1908, $2,300 of the trust funds. There was to his credit on that date $1,298.65. Prior to that date, therefore, he had misappropriated $1,001.35, to which action the defendant was not privy and for which it was not liable. It follows that the principal sum recovered should have been $12,327.69, and the interest in the sum of $3,000.35, computed as directed in the decision of the trial court.

The judgment should be modified accordingly and as modified affirmed, without costs to either party.

WILLARD BARTLETT, Ch. J., CHASE, CUDDEBACK, CARDOZO, SEABURY and POUND, JJ., concur.

Judgment accordingly.[1]

[1] In the following cases it was held that the bank was not liable for the withdrawal and misappropriation by the depositor. Corporation Agencies, Ltd. *v.* Home Bank of Canada, [1927] A. C. 318; Empire Trust Co. *v.* Cahan, 274 U. S. 473, 16 Cal. L. Rev. 523, 17 *id.* 264, 39 Harv. L. Rev. 646, 41 *id.* 91, 75 U. Pa. L. Rev. 64, 6 Tex. L. Rev. 220, 37 Yale L. Jour. 115; Maryland Casualty Co. *v.* City Nat. Bank, 29 F. (2d) 662; Helena *v.* First Nat. Bank, 173 Ark. 197; Mass. Bonding & Ins. Co. *v.* Standard T. & Sav. Bank, 334 Ill. 494; Eastern Mut. Ins. Co. *v.* Atlantic Nat. Bank, 260 Mass. 485; Rodgers *v.* Bankers Nat. Bank, 179 Minn. 197; Whiting *v.* Hudson Trust Co., 234 N. Y. 294, 23 Col. L. Rev. 596, 670, 36 Harv. L. Rev. 762, 21 Mich. L. Rev. 919, 32 Yale L. Jour. 293, 744.

In several states the matter is regulated by the Uniform Fiduciaries Act, which provides that a depository of fiduciary funds is not bound to inquire into the authority of the fiduciary to make the deposit, even where the

718   WHO ARE BOUND   [CHAP. IX.

APPLICATION OF PURCHASE MONEY. — The payment of the purchase money to a trustee authorized to sell, has always been treated as a valid discharge of the purchaser at law. But there were formerly many instances where the purchaser, who had paid the trustee, continued liable in equity if the money paid was not duly applied for the benefit of the *cestui que trust*. This highly artificial doctrine would seem to be indefensible on any principle. Its inconvenience as a working rule became so intolerable that the whole doctrine has been swept away by statute in England, New York and other jurisdictions. In some of our states the doctrine never obtained a foothold in the equity courts. The old learning on this point may be found in Lewin, Trusts, 535 *et seq.*; 2 Perry, Trusts, secs. 790 *et seq.* — AMES.

By the Uniform Fiduciaries Act, sec. 2, it is provided that, " A person who in good faith pays or transfers to a fiduciary any money or other property which the fiduciary as such is authorized to receive, is not responsible for the proper application thereof by the fiduciary; and any right or title acquired from the fiduciary in consideration of such payment or transfer is not invalid in consequence of a misapplication by the fiduciary."

REGISTRY OF TRANSFER OF SECURITIES HELD BY TRUSTEE. It has been held in a number of cases that where the name of the holder of shares of stock or other corporate securities as registered on the books of the corporation is followed by the word " trustee " or other words indicating a fiduciary character, and the holder transfers

---

deposit is made in his personal account, or to make withdrawals, and is not liable in the absence of actual knowledge that he is committing a breach of his obligation as fiduciary, or of bad faith.

If the bank has notice of the fiduciary character of the deposit, it is not entitled to a lien or right of set off nor can it properly receive payment out of the fund. U. S. *v.* Butterworth-Judson Corp., 267 U. S. 387; Fidelity & Dep. Co. *v.* Highland T. & Sav. Bank, 44 F. (2d) 697; Mass. Bonding & Ins. Co. *v.* Standard T. & Sav. Bank, 334 Ill. 494; Tingley *v.* North Middlesex Sav. Bank, 266 Mass. 337. See Scott, 739; 13 A. L. R. 324; 31 A. L. R. 756; 50 A. L. R. 632.

The bank is liable if it knows or suspects that the fiduciary is using or intends to use the funds in breach of trust. British etc. Co. *v.* Bank, [1919] A. C. 658; Farmers' Bank *v.* U. S. Fidelity & G. Co., 28 F. (2d) 676; Scott, 740.

On the question whether the bank is a purchaser for value, see note to Howells *v.* Hettrick, 160 N. Y. 308, *ante*.

See Scott, Participation in a Breach of Trust, 34 Harv. L. Rev. 454; Merrill, Bankers' Liability for Deposits of Fiduciary to his Personal Account, 40 Harv. L. Rev. 1077; Scott, Cases on Trusts, 1 ed., 739–40. See also McCollom, Banks Receiving Trust Checks, 11 Col. L. Rev. 428; Thulin, Misappropriation of Funds by Fiduciaries: the Bank's Liability, 6 Cal. L. Rev. 169; 17 Cal. L. Rev. 258; 14 Cornell L. Quar. 472; 24 Ill. L. Rev. 607; 13 Minn. L. Rev. 242; 1 Notre Dame Law. 167; 75 U. Pa. L. Rev. 64; 77 U. Pa. L. Rev. 804; 15 Va. L. Rev. 613; 16 Va. L. Rev. 402; 13 Va. L. Reg. (N. s.) 193; 35 Yale L. Jour. 854; 25 A. L. R. 1480; 57 A. L. R. 921; 64 A. L. R. 1404.

the securities in breach of trust, the corporation is liable for participation in the breach of trust if it registers the transfer without making inquiry as to the extent of the powers of the trustee, if such inquiry would have disclosed the breach of trust. This rule has been rejected in England. See 34 Harv. L. Rev. 465; 3 Mass. L. Quar. 284.

The Uniform Fiduciaries Act, sec. 3, provides as follows:

" If a fiduciary in whose name are registered any shares of stock, bonds or other securities of any corporation, public or private, or company or other association, or of any trust, transfers the same, such corporation or company or other association, or any of the managers of the trust, or its or their transfer agent, is not bound to inquire whether the fiduciary is committing a breach of his obligation as fiduciary in making the transfer, or to see to the performance of the fiduciary obligation, and is liable for registering such transfer only where registration of the transfer is made with actual knowledge that the fiduciary is committing a breach of his obligation as fiduciary in making the transfer, or with knowledge of such facts that the action in registering the transfer amounts to bad faith."

BOVEY v. SMITH.

CHANCERY. 1682.

1 Vern. 60.

A TRUSTEE having sold the land to a stranger, that had no notice of the trust, and a fine with proclamations and five years past, the trustee afterwards, for valuable consideration really paid, purchases these lands again of the vendee. And it was decreed by the LORD CHANCELLOR [NOTTINGHAM], with the concurring opinion of the LORD CHIEF JUSTICE NORTH, that the trustee, notwithstanding the fine, proclamations, and nonclaim for five years, should stand seized in trust as at first, as if the land had never been sold, nor any fine levied.[1]

[1] Kennedy v. Daly, 1 Sch. & Lef. 379; Re Stapleford Co., 14 Ch. D. 432, 445 (semble); Independent Coal Co. v. U. S., 274 U. S. 640; Huling v. Abbott, 86 Cal. 423; Bourguin v. Bourguin, 120 Ga. 115 (trustee allowed property to be sold for taxes); Johnson v. Gibson, 116 Ill. 294; Trentman v. Eldridge, 98 Ind. 525, 528; Bailey v. Binney, 61 Me. 361; Frost v. Frost, 63 Me. 399; Williams v. Williams, 118 Mich. 477; McDaniel v. Sprick, 297 Mo. 424; Allison v. Hagan, 12 Nev. 38; Brophy Co. v. Brophy Co., 15 Nev. 101; Schutt v. Large, 6 Barb. (N. Y.) 373; Clark v. McNeal, 114 N. Y. 287; Church v. Ruland, 64 Pa. 432; Armstrong v. Campbell, 3 Yerg. (Tenn.) 201; Yost v. Critcher, 112 Va. 870; Troy Bank v. Wilcox, 24 Wis. 671; Ely v. Wilcox, 26 Wis. 91, accord. See Ames, 287; 1 Ames, Cases on Bills and Notes, 691, 692, n. 3; Perry, Trusts, sec. 830; Pomeroy, Eq. Juris., sec. 754. Compare the cases where a mortgagor acquires an outstanding title. Tully v. Taylor, 84 N. J. Eq. 459, L. R. A. 1918B 731.

EYRE v. BURMESTER.

House of Lords. 1862.

10 H. L. Cas. 90.

The Lord Chancellor [Westbury].[1] My Lords, the facts material for the decision of this appeal are few, and may be shortly stated. In October, 1854, the late Mr. John Sadleir made a mortgage to the appellant, Mr. Eyre, of certain estates in Ireland, to secure the payment by Sadleir to Eyre of considerable sums of money. Afterwards, and in September, 1855, John Sadleir, being very largely indebted to the London and County Joint Stock Bank, conveyed these estates and other large estates in Ireland to the respondents, who represent the bank, to secure such debt and fur-

---

In Independent Coal Co. v. United States, 274 U. S. 640, Stone, J., said (p. 647): "It is ancient and familiar learning that one who fraudulently procures a conveyance may not defeat the defrauded grantor or protect himself from the consequences of his fraud by having the title conveyed to an innocent third person. [Citing cases.] Equity may follow the property until it reaches the hands of an innocent purchaser for value. Even then the wrongdoer may not reacquire it free of the obligation which equity imposes on one who despoils another of his property by fraud or a breach of trust. The obligation *in personam* to make restitution persists and may be enforced by compelling a return of the property itself whenever and however it comes into his hands. [Citing cases.] So also, a purchaser with notice of an outstanding equity, despite a transfer to an innocent purchaser for value, may not on a later repurchase hold free of the equity." — Ed.

Innocent donee. But an innocent grantee of a fraudulent grantor is guilty of no wrong in parting with the property if he is still ignorant of the equity of the defrauded person. Bonesteel v. Bonesteel, 30 Wis. 516; [Holly v. Missionary Society, 180 U. S. 284]. He is bound, it is true, to account to the defrauded person for so much as, but no more than, he has received (Robes v. Bent, Moore K. B. 552), in exchange for the property. But, on the other hand, if he reacquires the property from an innocent purchaser for value, he may keep it. Mast v. Henry, 65 Iowa 193. [See Dixon v. Caldwell, 15 Oh. St. 412, *ante*.] — Ames.

As to change of position as a defence to a quasi-contractual action against an innocent donee, see Woodward, Quasi Contracts, secs. 25–31. See also Holt v. Markham, [1923] 1 K. B. 504, 2 Camb. L. Jour. 95, where in the payment of gratuities by the government to demobilized army officers the defendant having been overpaid by mistake invested the money in a company which failed, and it was held that he was not liable because of his change of position.

Third person. If a purchaser for value without notice of equities conveys to any one else, though a purchaser with notice or a donee, the trust does not revive. East-Greensted's Case, Duke, Charitable Uses, 64; Colefield's Case, *ibid.* 68; Wilkes v. Spooner, [1911] 2 K. B. 473; English v. Lindley, 194 Ill. 181; Farmer v. R. C. Tway Coal Co., 204 Ky. 356; Flannagan v. Keefe, 250 Mass. 118; Ziembinski v. Wasniewski, 95 N. J. Eq. 57; Ames, 286; Perry, Trusts, sec. 830; Pomeroy, Eq. Juris., sec. 754; 63 A. L. R. 1362.

[1] The statement of facts and concurring opinions of Lord Cranworth and Lord Chelmsford are omitted. Lord Kingsdown also concurred.

ther advances then made by the bank to Sadleir. No mention was made by Sadleir to the respondents of the fact of the mortgage to Eyre; but the estates in question were conveyed by Sadleir to them as free from any encumbrance. Before this mortgage to the bank was completed by registration of the deeds in Ireland, the fact of Eyre's mortgage was discovered by the agents of the respondents, who therefore refused to allow the arrangement between Sadleir and themselves to remain unless he obtained a release from Eyre of the estates in question. This Sadleir engaged to do; and he prevailed upon Eyre to execute a deed of reconveyance to Sadleir himself of these estates, in consideration of Eyre's receiving from Sadleir other securities of equal or greater value. The substituted securities consisted chiefly of a large number of shares in the Royal Swedish Railway, and of a promissory note for 12,000*l.*, expressed to be made and signed by Mr. Dargan. But the shares were fictitious, having been fabricated by John Sadleir for the purpose, and the promissory note was a forgery. An actual fraud of a gross and criminal character was therefore committed by Sadleir upon Eyre; and by means of that fraud the release of Eyre's mortgage was obtained.

The release was contained in a deed dated the 5th, but executed on the 13th of October, 1855. By it Mr. Eyre reconveyed, granted, released, and confirmed unto John Sadleir the estates comprised in the mortgage deed of October, 1854. No consideration for this reconveyance is expressed in the deed itself, but the real agreement between the parties is contained in a contemporaneous agreement of the 6th of October, 1855.

After the execution of this deed of reconveyance to John Sadleir no further conveyance was made by Sadleir to the respondents. They were assured of the fact of the reconveyance, and the mortgage was either completed or allowed to continue. The estate so reconveyed by Eyre remained in John Sadleir until he committed suicide in the month of February, 1856. On that event, the fraud of Sadleir was discovered.

These estates have been since sold by an order of the Encumbered Estates Court in Ireland. With respect to the proceeds of that sale, a contest has arisen between Eyre and the London and County Bank; Eyre claims the benefit of his original mortgage, and insists that the reconveyance is void for fraud. The bank directors claim the benefit of the reconveyance as purchasers for valuable consideration, without notice of the fraud committed by Sadleir on Eyre, and on that ground the court below has given judgment in their favor.

A purchaser for valuable consideration without notice will not be deprived by a court of equity of any advantage at law which he has fairly obtained for his protection. But in the present case the estate reconveyed by Eyre, remained in Sadleir, and was never conveyed by Sadleir to the bank. In answer to this objection, the respondents insist on the estoppel created by the previous conveyance. This answer would be good as against Sadleir and all claiming under him. The estoppel created by the antecedent contract and conveyance by Sadleir would bind parties and privies, that is, Sadleir and those claiming under him. But the claim of Eyre is against Sadleir by paramount right, to recover the estate of which Eyre had been deprived by fraud, and Sadleir acquired no interest to feed his prior contract by virtue of that fraudulent transaction.

It is urged by the respondents that the reconveyance when made by Eyre enabled Sadleir to obtain money from the bank, and that the mortgage was completed on the faith of the reconveyance. The evidence does not appear to me to prove either of these positions. But granting that it does, the reconveyance was to Sadleir and was obtained by him by fraud and covin. There was no contract or direct communication between the respondents and Eyre, who acted with perfect *bona fides*. The respondents left Sadleir to obtain the reconveyance, and they can claim the benefit of it only under Sadleir, whose act they must take as it is. If (which is not proved) they had advanced money to Sadleir on the faith of the release and their actual possession of it, but without taking a conveyance, they might have had a lien on the deed itself; but their interest in the estate being equitable only would still, in my opinion, have been subject to the superior equity of Eyre. Whilst the estate remained in Sadleir, so long was it liable to be pursued and recovered by Eyre. But there is no sufficient proof of any such advance by the bank; and the only foundation of the bank's claim is the mortgage by Sadleir prior to the deed of reconveyance. That mortgage and contract would bind any interest subsequently acquired by Sadleir. But under the reconveyance he obtained none; for, as between Sadleir and Eyre, the latter was still the owner, and might at any time during the life of Sadleir, by bill in equity have set aside the release, and obtained a reconveyance of the estate, and an interim injunction to restrain any alienation of it by Sadleir. This equitable title still remains unimpaired, and ought to be preferred to any claim by the bank.

I therefore advise your Lordships that the orders of the court below be reversed, and that it be declared that the claim of the appellant to priority in respect of his mortgage, ought to have been allowed; and that the case be remitted, with that declaration, to the Landed Estates Court. If the appellant has obtained any additional security under the agreement of the 6th October, 1855, not comprised in his original mortgage, that must be given up or accounted for to the bank.[1]

[1] Heath *v.* Crealock, 10 Ch. 22; Kelley *v.* Jenness, 50 Me. 455; Sinclair *v.* Jackson, 8 Cow. (N. Y.) 543, 587; Jackson *v.* Hoffman, 9 Cow. (N. Y.) 271; Burchard *v.* Hubbard, 11 Oh. 316; Buckingham *v.* Hanna, 2 Oh. St. 551; Gregory *v.* Peoples, 80 Va. 355, *accord*. See also Hawkins *v.* Harlan, 68 Cal. 236; Elder *v.* Derby, 98 Ill. 228; Chew *v.* Barnett, 11 S. & R. (Pa.) 389.

LONDON AND COUNTY BANKING COMPANY, LIMITED v. LONDON AND RIVER PLATE BANK, LIMITED.

COURT OF APPEAL. 1888.

21 Q. B. D. 535.

THIS action was brought by the plaintiffs to recover from the defendants 9000*l*. Unified Egyptian Bonds, 2000*l*. Egyptian Preference Government Bonds, 300 shares in the Pennsylvania Railway Company, and 2400*l*. New South Wales Bonds. It came on for trial before Manisty, J., and a special jury, but was referred to a special referee to report, and was reserved for further consideration on his report, with power to draw inferences of fact.

From the report of the referee the following facts are taken: —

The plaintiffs were the London and County Banking Company, Limited, Robert Henry Capps, and John Record; but for the purposes of this report the case may be treated as if Capps were the sole plaintiff.

A person of the name of Warden was secretary and manager of the defendant company, and had access to the securities deposited by customers with them. He had, in 1882, incurred a loss in Stock Exchange speculations conducted for him by John Davis Watters, a stockbroker not a member of the Stock Exchange. The dealings of Watters were necessarily conducted by him through members of the Stock Exchange, of whom Capps was one. Record was Capps' manager. To cover the loss above mentioned, Warden handed to Watters securities belonging to the defendant company. In January, 1883, Watters consulted Warden about a loss of his own, and eventually Warden handed him securities belonging to the bank to cover that loss. From that time forward Warden and Watters were continually engaged in large speculative transactions on the Stock Exchange. Before each fortnightly settling-day Watters used to tell Warden what amount of securities he would require, and whatever he wanted Warden abstracted from the bank and gave to him.

The securities thus abstracted were from time to time wanted by Warden at the bank for various purposes — for example, to cut off coupons. They were in particular wanted by Warden at the beginning of October, 1883, to exhibit them at an audit of stocks and shares on which the bank had advanced money to their customers.

If a mortgage covers after-acquired property, and the mortgagor subsequently acquires property subject to an equity, the mortgagee takes subject to the equity. Bear Lake etc. Co. *v.* Garland, 164 U. S. 1; Williamson *v.* N. J. Southern Ry. Co., 28 N. J. Eq. 277, 29 N. J. Eq. 311; Central T. Co. *v.* West India Imp. Co., 169 N. Y. 314. See Jones, Mortgages, 7 ed., sec. 158.

October 1, 1883, was fixed as the audit-day, and a list was prepared for audit by the transfer clerk. Warden gave Watters a list of the securities which had been abstracted and would be required for the audit, and Watters undertook to redeem them. Among these were securities which had been deposited by Watters with Capps in the course of the business transactions between them, and Watters accordingly applied to Capps for them, and handed him a cheque for 13,000*l.* on his own bankers. Capps thereupon obtained the securities to recover which this action was brought from different banks with which he had deposited them, and handed them to Watters, who passed them on to Warden, by whom they were placed among the securities at the defendant bank, and exhibited to the auditors. Watters, however, failed to redeem all the securities abstracted by Warden, and this led to the discovery of the fraud of Warden, and ultimately both he and Watters were tried and convicted in respect of their dealings with property of the defendants other than the securities in question. Capps and Record received the securities without any knowledge of the fraud of either Warden or Watters, and were holders of them for value. Watters, when he gave the cheque for 13,000*l.* to Capps, had only a small balance at his bank, and he intended to meet the cheque by obtaining from Warden either the same securities or other securities which he expected Warden would be able to abstract from the defendant bank, and hand over to him. The cheque was dishonoured but Watters before the discovery of his being implicated in the fraud had paid Capps two sums, amounting to about 1700*l.*, on account of his indebtedness.

On further consideration, before Manisty, J., questions arose as to the negotiability of the Pennsylvania Railway shares, as to the exact identity of certain of the restored bonds with those stolen from the bank, and as to the right of Capps to disaffirm the transfer of the securities to Watters on the ground that it was procured by fraud, but it is not necessary for the purposes of this report to go into these questions. The learned judge gave judgment for the defendants on the ground that they were holders of the securities for valuable consideration, 20 Q. B. D. 232.

The plaintiffs appealed.

LINDLEY, L. J.[1] My brother Bowen desires me to say that he has read and agrees with the following judgment.

In this case the plaintiffs unquestionably acquired the property in these bonds, and if the plaintiffs had continued to hold them the defendants could not have recovered them even if the defendants had prosecuted Warden, and he had been convicted of stealing the bonds from the defendants. See 24 & 25 Vict. c. 96, s. 100, by which stolen negotiable securities in the hands of a *bonâ fide* holder

---

[1] The concurring opinion of Lord Esher, M. R., is omitted.

for value are made an exception to the general rule which applies to the restoration of stolen property on the conviction of the thief.

But the plaintiffs lost possession of the bonds; the plaintiffs were induced to part with them by a fraud; and the bonds were restored to the possession of the defendants by the thief who had stolen them from the defendants in the first instance. The plaintiffs having thus lost possession of the bonds seek to recover them from the defendants; and the question is whether the plaintiffs are entitled so to do.

It is remarkable that this question should be so free from all direct authority as it in fact is. The question has not apparently ever called for decision before. It is absolutely new and must be decided on principle.

The plaintiffs contend that although the defendants are *bonâ fide* holders of the bonds, yet the defendants are not holders of them for value; that the defendants have not acquired them for value since the plaintiffs were induced by fraud to part with them; and that consequently the property in the bonds which had certainly become vested in the plaintiffs has never been divested from them.

In order to deal with this argument it is necessary to consider the legal effect of the restoration of the bonds to the defendants by Warden, who had previously stolen them from the defendants.

The legal consequences of the theft were: 1, to render Warden liable to conviction for a criminal offence: 2, to render him liable in a civil action to restore the bonds or pay their value to the defendants. In addition to his criminal responsibility he was under a civil obligation to the defendants to restore the bonds or their value to them. The existence of this civil obligation affords in my opinion the clue to the solution of the problem which has to be solved.

When Warden restored the bonds which he had stolen, he was doing no more than he was bound to the defendants to do; he was discharging, or, at all events, partly discharging, his obligation to them, and if the defendants chose to accept the bonds in such discharge his obligation to the defendants would have been extinguished, if not wholly, at least to the extent of the value of the bonds restored. In the case supposed, the defendants clearly would have been *bonâ fide* holders of the bonds for value; the value being the extinction of Warden's obligation to themselves; and in the case supposed, the defendants would have acquired a good title as against the plaintiffs.

But then it is said that the defendants did not in fact accept the bonds when they were restored in discharge of Warden's obligations, inasmuch as the defendants did not know that the bonds ever had been stolen from them, and did not know that Warden was under any obligation in respect of them, and did not know of their restoration by him.

All this is perfectly true, but is not in my opinion decisive against the defendants. Their acceptance of the bonds in discharge of Warden's obligation, which existed in truth although the defendants did not know it, may, and in my opinion ought to be presumed in the absence of evidence to the contrary.

This presumption is, I think, warranted by authority, for although the exact point has not been decided, an analogous point has. It was settled as long ago as the time of Lord Coke that the acceptance of a gift by a donee is to be presumed until his dissent is signified, even though the donee is not aware of the gift (Butler and Baker's Case, 3 Rep. 25 a), and this doctrine has been applied even as against the Crown, and so as to defeat a title accruing to it before actual assent: Smith v. Wheeler, 1 Vent. 128, referred to at length in Small v. Marwood, 9 B. & C. 300, at p. 306, and in Siggers v. Evans, 5 El. & Bl. 367, at p. 382. In the last-mentioned case the presumption was held to apply to a gift of an onerous nature; and in Standing v. Bowring, 31 Ch. D. 282, the presumption was also held to apply to a gift which the donor desired to revoke before the donee knew that it had been made. The presumption of acceptance in such cases is artificial, but is founded on human nature; a man may be fairly presumed to assent to that to which he in all probability would assent if the opportunity of assenting were given him. Taking these decisions and this reasoning as guides, I am of opinion that in the absence of evidence to the contrary the defendants ought in point of law to be presumed to have accepted from Warden the bonds which he handed over to them in discharge of his obligation to them, which obligation existed to his knowledge although not to theirs. It would be contrary to human nature to suppose that the defendants would not have kept the bonds if they had known of their theft from themselves, and of their restoration; and we know as a fact that the defendants have insisted on their right to retain the bonds ever since they discovered the theft.

If the above reasoning be correct it follows that as soon as the bonds were restored the presumption of acceptance arose, subject to be rebutted by evidence of non-acceptance; and there being no evidence of non-acceptance, but on the contrary proof of acceptance at a later date, the presumption ought to prevail. Acceptance of the bonds at the date of their restoration being thus arrived at, satisfaction to some extent, if not in full, of the thief's civil obligation follows, and the defendants' position as *bonâ fide* holders for value becomes unassailable.

It is obvious that this reasoning applies not only to the bonds originally stolen and afterwards restored, but also to the 2000*l.* preference bonds, which though never stolen from the defendants were given to them in substitution for bonds which were. It is not the restoration of the stolen bonds which is the important point: it is the handing over to the defendants of negotiable instruments in performance of a civil obligation which is the turning point of the case. Such a handing over is not a gift; the person to whom they are handed over is not a donee. A person from whom property is stolen has a right to demand restitution from the thief, whether the person robbed knows of the theft or not; and this right and the satisfaction of it by restitution places him in the position of a holder for value, and not in the position of a gratuitous donee. Whether he can retain what he has got as against other persons than the thief depends primarily on the nature of the property handed to him. If such property is a negotiable instrument he can, unless at the time of the handing over he has notice that it belongs to some third party. If the property handed over is not a negotiable instrument other considerations arise; but the present appeal relates only to negotiable securities, and does not involve the necessity of dealing with other kinds of property. I consequently forbear from pursuing this matter further.

My judgment is based upon the ground that on October 1 the defendants became holders for value of the bonds in question within the meaning of the doctrine laid down in Miller v. Race, 1 Sm. L. C. 9th ed. 491, and became such holders *bonâ fide,* and without notice of the plaintiff's title or of any fraud upon them.

This being so, it becomes unnecessary to examine, and I express no opinion upon, the other points alluded to by Manisty, J., and discussed by counsel before us.

Appeal dismissed.[1]

[1] See Thorndike v. Hunt, 3 DeG. & J. 563; Taylor v. Blakelock, 32 Ch. D. 560; Colonial Bank v. Hepworth, 36 Ch. D. 36; State Bank v. U. S., 114 U. S. 401; Bank of Charleston v. Bank of the State, 13 Rich. L. (S. C.) 291. But see Voss v. Chamberlain, 139 Iowa 569; Brown v. Southwestern Farm Mortgage Co., 112 Kan. 192 (no change of position after restitution of stolen bonds). See 36 Harv. L. Rev. 858.

If the purchase price of property is paid and the title is subsequently transferred, it would seem that the purchaser is a purchaser for value, even in jurisdictions in which the surrender of an antecedent debt is not held to be value; and if the purchaser had no notice of a prior equity at the time when the conveyance was made he should take free and clear of the equity. Ratcliffe v. Barnard, 6 Ch. 652; Miller & Co. v. Boykin, 70 Ala. 469; People v. Swift, 96 Cal. 165; Gibson v. Lenhart, 101 Pa. 522. See Osgood v. Thompson Bk., 30 Conn. 27.

But in Barnard v. Campbell, 55 N. Y. 456, 58 N. Y. 73, it was held that where one agreed to sell a number of bags of seed and did not own any seed at the time but later acquired some by fraud and delivered it to the purchaser, the buyer was not allowed to keep although he had no notice of the fraud. It was intimated that the result would have been different if the vendors had had legal title at the time they made the contract to sell. To a similar effect, see Central T. Co. v. West India Imp. Co., 169 N. Y. 314.

See Ames, The Doctrine of Price v. Neal, 4 Harv. L. Rev. 297, Lect. Leg. Hist. 270; Woodward, Quasi Contracts, secs. 72, 75.

NEWELL *v.* HADLEY.

SUPREME JUDICIAL COURT, MASSACHUSETTS. 1910.

206 Mass. 335.

LORING, J.[1] This is a bill in equity brought by the surviving trustee under the will of Andrew H. Newell and the beneficiaries of that trust against the trustees and beneficiaries under the will of James B. Pickett.

In November, 1901, one Charles F. Berry was the active trustee of each of these two trusts. His co-trustee in the Newell trust was Andrew Newell, whose residence was in Australia; and his co-trustee in the Pickett trust was Thomas E. Major, whose residence was in Ohio.

On November 15, 1901, Berry found himself in immediate need of $2,000 to be sent to the west in order to carry through a private speculation of his own. The Pickett trust was in need, but not in immediate need, of money for taxes and mortgage interest due in respect of a building or buildings owned and maintained by that trust. The need of money for taxes and mortgage interest on the part of the Pickett trust came from the fact that Berry had previously stolen money from that trust exceeding in amount the money needed for these purposes.

Under these circumstances Berry, on November 15, took to certain brokers a certificate for fifty-one shares of stock, the property of the Newell trust, and instructed them to sell the shares, and asked for an advance of $11,000 on account. He received from the brokers their check for $11,000, payable to "C. F. Berry, trustee." Berry and Major, trustees of the Pickett trust, had a deposit account with the Old Colony Trust Company, on which checks could be drawn by either trustee. Berry indorsed the check for $11,000 and deposited it to the credit of this account. There was at that time the sum of $1,380.44 to the credit of that account. The deposit of the check for $11,000 seems to have been made after banking hours on the fifteenth, and for that reason was credited on the sixteenth, of November. On the afternoon of the fifteenth Berry drew a check for $2,000 on this account, took it to the trust company and obtained for it two drafts on New York, each for $1,000, which he sent to the west to carry through his personal speculation. Thereafter he drew twenty-one other checks on the account. The last check, for $63, was dated December 16, 1901, and resulted in the account being overdrawn to the amount, as stated in the reservation, of $8.88, but which appears to have been $18.88. Four of the twenty-two checks thus drawn, amounting in the aggregate to

[1] A part of the opinion and a dissenting opinion of Knowlton, C. J., are omitted.

$3,864.85, were used by Berry for his personal expenses; eleven, amounting in the aggregate to $7,903.14, were used by Berry in paying on account of the Pickett trust taxes and mortgage interest due on the buildings of the Pickett trust, wages due to the scrubwomen and elevator boys of these buildings, and bills for lighting, steam heating and insurance on these buildings; six checks, amounting in the aggregate to $568.33, were used in payments to the beneficiaries of the Pickett trust of income due to them; and the last check, for $63, of which $18.88 was an overdraft, was used in paying to Mr. Major, Berry's co-trustee in the Pickett trust, the commissions due to him for services as trustee for that trust. That is to say, on the last check $44.12 was drawn out of the $11,000. Berry testified that he had no personal bank account at that time, and that he deposited the check for $11,000 with the Old Colony Trust Company to the credit of Mr. Major and himself, trustees of the Pickett trust, because that "was the handiest place," by which we understand him to have meant that depositing the check for $11,000 to the credit of the account of Major and himself as trustees of the Pickett trust was the most convenient way for him to cash it. He further testified that when he made this deposit "it did not enter my [his] head" to make the deposit as payment of his debt to that trust. At that time he knew that he was largely in debt to the Pickett trust, and on an examination made during the hearing before the single justice he found that the sum then due from him to the Pickett trust amounted to $11,185.50 gross, or, deducting a sum equal to the usual commissions, to $9,515.50. But he testified that at the time (to wit, on November 15, 1901) he did not know the exact amount of that debt. In March, 1902, Berry was again in debt to the Pickett trust to the amount of $8,042.33. From some source or sources not mentioned in the reservation he paid up this amount on March 26 and rendered an account on March 27, 1902, which was allowed. Berry resigned his position of trustee of the Pickett trust in March, 1903, and was succeeded by the defendant Hadley. [Berry was removed as trustee of the Newell trust by order of the Probate Court on April 8, 1905.]

The plaintiff's first contention is that the defendants are liable for the whole $11,000. In our opinion that is not so. Berry did not in fact intend to make the $11,000 the property of the Pickett trust by borrowing that money in behalf of that trust, or by paying with it his debt to the Pickett trust. All that he intended to do was to put the $11,000 in the name of himself and his co-trustee in the Pickett trust as the "handiest" way of cashing the $11,000 check. The $11,000 while it was on deposit in the Old Colony Trust Company belonged in equity to the Newell trust as the property into which its $11,000 had been converted. The whole $11,000 had been all drawn out by Berry before the defendants or any of them knew anything about it. A defendant is not liable to repay to the owner the amount of a stolen check fraudulently put to his (the defendant's) credit to enable the thief to collect the amount of it when the proceeds have been drawn out by the thief before the defendant knows anything about the matter.

It follows that the defendants are not liable for the $3,864.85 applied by Berry for his own use.

The plaintiffs' second contention is that so far as the $11,000 was applied in discharge of debts owed by the Pickett trust the Newell trust has a right of recovery.

The amount drawn out of this bank account to pay debts owed by the Pickett trust is (as we have said) $7,903.14. But there was the sum of $1,380.44 to the credit of the Pickett trust in this bank account when the $11,000 was deposited. There is a question therefore whether the amount of the plaintiffs' $11,000 used in paying the defendants' debts is $7,903.14 or $7,903.14 less $1,380.44, that is to say $6,522.70. As matter of convenience we will now assume that it is the smaller amount (namely, $6,522.70) and we will deal with that matter later on.

On the footing that the amount paid out for debts is $6,522.70, the amount paid out for mortgage interest and taxes was $6,045.19 and for unsecured debts due from the Pickett trust $477.51.

It was decided in Foote v. Cotting, 195 Mass. 55, that under the circumstances of the case at bar the Newell trust has no remedy at law even for the money belonging to it used in paying taxes on the land of the Pickett trust. But it was suggested in that case, at page 63, that to the extent to which one trust has been benefited through the payment out of its money of the taxes on the land of the other (under circumstances such as those in the case at bar) there might be a remedy in equity on the principle of subrogation, citing Webber Lumber Co. v. Shaw, 189 Mass. 366. For a recent case which lends support to that suggestion, see the first case reported under the title of Title Guarantee & Trust Co. v. Haven, 196 N. Y. 487. It would seem that on this principle the plaintiffs would be entitled to a decree (1) for a charge upon the defendants' land to the amount of the tax paid with their (the plaintiffs') money and (2) for a charge, except as against the mortgagee, upon their (the defendants') land to the amount of the mortgage interest paid with their (the plaintiffs') money. But it is not necessary to pursue this further because we are of opinion that the plaintiffs are entitled to a personal decree against the defendants for simple debts paid with their (the plaintiffs') money, and that they are entitled on the same ground to a personal decree for payments of taxes and mortgage interest made with their money.

It has long been the settled law of England that where the money of A has been used in extinguishing the legal liabilities of B (although no debt or other obligation is created thereby at law), equity will let A enforce against B the obligations of B's creditors paid off by his (A's) money. The principle was applied in Harris *v.* Lee, 1 P. Wms. 482, where a wife borrowed money to pay for necessaries and afterwards the husband died having devised land in trust for the payment of his debts. Although a husband is liable for his wife's debts incurred for necessaries, he is not liable for money borrowed by his wife to be used in paying for necessaries. That was admitted in Harris *v.* Lee, *ubi supra,* and Knox *v.* Bushell, 3 C. B. (N. S.) 334, is a decision to that effect. Not only was that decided in Knox *v.* Bushell, but it was also decided there that in such a case there is no remedy on the common counts or in any other way at law. It was held in Harris *v.* Lee that the plaintiff (whose loan to the wife was void) had a right to be paid the sums which were due to the creditor who had furnished necessaries to the wife and who had been paid out of the money furnished the wife under the void loan. The principle was applied also in case of money borrowed by an infant, which was used to buy necessaries. Marlow *v.* Pitfeild, 1 P. Wms. 558. It was pointed out in Marlow *v.* Pitfeild that there is no liability at law in such a case; and Darby *v.* Boucher, 1 Salk. 279, is a decision to that effect. The most common application of this principle has been where money borrowed by a corporation which had no power to borrow money has been used in paying its debts. *In re* Cork & Youghal Railway, L. R. 4 Ch. 748. Blackburn Building Society *v.* Cunliffe, Brooks & Co., 22 Ch. D. 61. *In re* Wrexham, Mold & Connah's Quay Railway, [1899] 1 Ch. 205; S. C. on appeal, *Ibid.* 440. Lastly, this principle was applied in 1906 in a case where the London agent of ship and insurance brokers carrying on business in Liverpool (who had withdrawn money for his own account without right) without authority borrowed money in behalf of his principals and applied it in payment of the expenses of the principal's London business. Bannatyne *v.* MacIver, [1906] 1 K. B. 103.

The case at bar is a stronger case for the application of this principle than any of these mentioned above in which it has been applied. The plaintiffs' money in the case at bar was stolen from them without fault on their part, not lent by them under an invalid contract. Since Berry had the legal right to the custody of the property in which the plaintiffs had the beneficial interest, the plaintiffs were not at fault in letting it remain in his possession. On the other hand it might well have been held that the persons who lent the money in the English cases *ubi supra* were chargeable with knowledge of the invalidity of the loans. See in that connection Bannatyne *v.* MacIver, [1906] 1 K. B. 103, 109.

There are suggestions in some of these cases that the doctrine on which they rest is that in such cases the lender is subrogated to the rights of the creditors. In others it is suggested that in these cases the true owner of the money is allowed to trace his property into the benefit enuring to the defendant, on the principle on which an owner can in equity trace his property into any form into which it has been wrongfully converted. And in others, that this is an independent ground of equitable relief. It is not necessary to determine whether these principles are not in their essence the same or what is the most accurate way of stating the principle on which these cases rest, for we are of opinion that they were well decided, and that the principle on which they rest is well founded and should be adopted by us.

The question, therefore, on which the case at bar depends is whether the money, with which the debts due from the defendants stated above were paid, was the plaintiffs' money. . . .

We have already held that the $11,000 did not become the money of the defendants when it was deposited by Berry to the credit of the defendants' trustees in the Old Colony Trust Company, without their knowledge, to enable him to complete his theft.

But when Berry drew out $6,522.70 of the $11,000 belonging to the Newell trust on deposit in the Old Colony Trust Company and applied it in payment of debts due from the Pickett trust, either he directly paid the defendants' debts with the plaintiffs' money or he in legal contemplation undertook to pay his debt to the Pickett trust with the plaintiffs' money, and used the money so paid to that trust in paying its debts.

If he is to be considered to have paid the defendants' debts directly with the plaintiffs' money, the case at bar comes within the princple of the English cases referred to above.

And the result is the same if in legal contemplation Berry is to be considered to have undertaken to pay his debt to the defendants with the plaintiffs' money and then to have used that money in paying the defendants' debts. This attempted repayment by Berry of his debt to the Pickett trust did not make the money so paid to them their money. It was the plaintiffs' money in the beginning, it remained the plaintiffs' money while it was on deposit in the Old Colony Trust Company, and it did not cease to be the plaintiffs' money when Berry used it in paying his debt to the trust of which he was one of two trustees, because he and he alone acted for the Pickett trust in receiving the attempted payment.

The general rule is that an assignee of money gets no better title than the assignor of it had. But the assignee does get a better title than his assignor had if he is a purchaser for value in good faith and without notice.

Apart from authority it would be a strange doctrine if it were law that the true owner of money lost his title to it by a thief who stole it undertaking to use it in paying a debt owed by the thief to another, when the thief and no one else received for that other the payment so made. It is not conceivable that such a manipulation by a thief of stolen money should result in the true owner's losing his title and the creditor of the thief getting a better title to the money than the thief had to it. . . .

Adopting the words of this court in Atlantic Cotton Mills v. Indian Orchard Mills, 147 Mass. 268, 274: It is not as if Berry, after stealing $11,185.50, or $9,515.50, from the defendant trust (as he did) had called the innocent trustee or the beneficiaries of that trust " together and informed them of his indebtedness and of his desire to make a payment on account, and had then paid over to them the money [this $6,522.70] as money coming from himself, and they had received it without knowledge or suspicion that it had been stolen, and given him credit for it as part payment." In that case the Pickett trust would have been a purchaser without notice within the doctrine invoked by the defendants in the case at bar.

That is not what took place. When Berry repaid in part the money stolen from the defendants by paying their debts with the $6,522.70 stolen from the plaintiffs, Berry and Berry alone represented the defendants in receiving the $6,522.70. They " must be deemed to have known what he knew; and " they " cannot retain the benefit of his act, without accepting the consequences of his knowledge." The defendants " cannot obtain greater rights from his act than if . . . [they] . . . did the thing itself, knowing what he knew," to quote again from Atlantic Cotton Mills v. Indian Orchard Mills, 147 Mass. 268, 274.

But it is said that when this money was used in paying the defendants' debts there was a transaction in which Berry was not the only person on both sides. It is said that the creditors who were paid were on the other side of the transaction. The creditors who were paid were on the other side of a transaction. But the transaction in which the creditors were on the other side consisted in the payment of the debts owed by the defendants to them. In that transaction the creditors got a good title to the money paid to them by Berry. But they took no part in the transaction by which Berry paid his debt to the defendants with money stolen from the plaintiffs. Berry and Berry alone was on both sides of that transaction.

In this connection it should be pointed out that there were payments made out of this $11,000 to the beneficiaries of the defendant trust and to Berry's co-trustee. In receiving these payments the beneficiaries and the co-trustee did not act through Berry. They acted for themselves. They are *bona fide* purchasers without notice of the money so paid to them, and the plaintiffs have no claim for the $612.45 ($568.33 + $44.12) so paid out.

But the defendants say that there was an accounting later on, and that they became purchasers for value without notice by virtue of that accounting within the doctrine recognized by this court in Alantic Cotton Mills v. Indian Orchard Mills, 147 Mass. 268, 279: " There is another class of cases where the same person has been trustee of two different funds, and has fraudulently transferred securities from one trust fund to the other. But in each case of this class which has been cited, there has been something in the nature of an accounting, and the trust fund which has received and has been entitled to retain the benefit has been partly or wholly represented either by the *cestuis que trust,* or by an innocent trustee representing them. Thorndike *v.* Hunt, 3 De G. & J. 563. Taylor *v.* Blakelock, 32 Ch. D. 560. Case *v.* James, 29 Beav. 512; S. C. on appeal, 3 De G., F. & J. 256."

But that is not so in the case at bar. The last of the $11,000 was drawn out by Berry on December 16, 1901. It was drawn out by the check for $63 which paid the innocent trustee the commissions due to him, and that check (as we have said) was an overdraft to the amount of $18.88. The accounting here relied on by the defendants was three months later, in March, 1902.

The accounting in the case at bar was had not only after the repayment had become complete without anybody (but the thief) knowing of the repayment, but the accounting was had three months after the last penny of the money repaid had been expended without anybody but the thief knowing of the repayment and of the expenditure of the money repaid. There was no fund then in existence of which the defendants could become purchasers for value without notice. How that accounting could be held to make the defendants purchasers without notice of money which had been paid out three months before has not been explained.

Apart from its effect upon the defendants being purchasers for value, the accounting which was had did not affect the rights of the parties. When the accounting was had in the case at bar the fact of the repayment was not stated or known to any one but Berry the thief. What happened was that four months after the repayment was made and three months after the money repaid had been expended, Berry filed an account in which he stated that he had received and properly paid out the income of the trust fund, and that account was assented to by the defendants on the footing that it was a true account. In a case where a thief steals money without his principal's knowledge, repays it with money stolen from some one else without his principal's knowledge, and pays out the other stolen money (so repaid by him) without his principal's knowledge, the rights of the parties are not changed by the fact that after the money so repaid has been paid out, the thief makes up a lying account in which no one of these facts is disclosed and the principal assents to it on the footing that it is a true account. Such an account is a fraud on the principal and can be set aside by him at any time. . . .

We are of opinion therefore that whatever view be taken of the transaction the $6,522.70 used by Berry in paying the defendants' debts was the plaintiffs' money.

The only other ground on which the defendants could be thought to have a better equity than the plaintiffs arises from the fact that the defendant trust had provided Berry with money to pay the debts paid by him with the money of the plaintiffs.

The fact that the defendants had put Berry in funds to pay the debts paid with the plaintiffs' money (in our opinion) does not bar them from the equity to which that gives rise. The first act done by Berry was to steal from the defendants $11,185.50, or $9,515.50, whichever is the true sum (as we have stated above). That made Berry the defendants' debtor for that sum. Then Berry repays to the defendants (Berry and Berry alone accepting the payment in behalf of the defendants) $6,522.70, on account of this debt of $11,185.50, or $9,515.50 owed by him to the defendants. The $6,522.70 so repaid did not become the defendants' money because Berry acted for the defendants in receiving it. Then Berry uses this money so repaid to the defendants in paying the defendants' debts. The money used in paying the defendants' debts was the plaintiffs' money. Berry still owes the defendants the $11,185.50, or $9,519.50. That debt was not in part paid by Berry's manipulation of the $6,522.70. It cannot be that in equity the defendants are to have both their claim against Berry for the $11,185.50, or $9,515.50, and the payment of their debts to the amount of $6,522.70. Since Berry's manipulation of the $6,522.70 did not pay his debt to the defendants (and we have seen that it did not), the fact that the occasion for Berry's stealing $6,522.70 from the plaintiffs and using it in paying the defendants' debts was because he had stolen the funds provided by the defendants to pay these debts, does not affect the plaintiffs' equity growing out of the fact that it was their (the plaintiffs') money which in fact paid the defendants' debts, and that a benefit enures to the defendants from that fact.

As matter of authority the only case on the point that has come to our attention, (Bannatyne *v.* MacIver, [1906] 1 K. B. 103,) is in accord with this view of the law. The suit in Bannatyne *v.* MacIver was on a bill for 350*l.*, the amount of unauthorized borrowing of money made by the defendant's London agent (Hudson by name) at four different times. When the first money was borrowed the London business was short of funds without fault on Hudson's part. But subsequently to the first loan and before the other three had been made, the principals had " sent him [Hudson] considerable sums of money, more than sufficient to cover the liabilities of the branch, and rendering any borrowing by Hudson unnecessary," page 104. The necessity for the money borrowed on the last three occasions came from the fact that Hudson had withdrawn sums which he had no right to withdraw. How much of the 350*l.* constituting the four borrowings was attributable to the first, when Hudson had not wrongfully withdrawn money, and how much of it was attributable to the three other borrowings caused by Hudson's wrongful withdrawals does not appear. It was held that the plaintiff's equity to stand in the shoes of the creditors paid off with their money did not depend upon the state of the account between the defendants and Hudson. Romer, L. J., dealt directly with this part of the case in these words: "It [the state of account between the agent and the principals] might be relevant if the plaintiff were seeking to enforce a different equity, that is, the right to stand in the shoes of the agent as against his principal."

It follows that the defendants have no superior equity with respect to the $6,522.70 used in paying the debts of the defendants, and that the plaintiffs to that extent are entitled to be repaid by the defendants.

This brings us to the question which we referred to in the beginning of this opinion and which we then left undecided, to wit, How much of the $7,903.14, paid in discharge of debts due from the Pickett trust was paid out of the $11,000 stolen from the plaintiffs? The plaintiffs claim that the rule in Clayton's case, 1 Mer. 572, applies; and applying that rule, that the $2,000 drawn by Berry on November 15 for his own use must be applied to the balance on deposit when the $11,000 was deposited, so far as the amount of that balance ($1,380.44) goes, and that $619.56 only of that $2,000 was paid out of the $11,000. In other words, that when Berry took $2,000 out of this account for his own use in the afternoon of November 15, he stole $1,380.44 from the Pickett estate and $619.56 only from the Newell trust. The defendants contend, however, that Berry stole this $2,000 from the Newell trust and that the $1,380.44 on deposit in the Pickett account must be taken to have been applied to the payment of the Pickett trust debts. If the contention of the defendants is right, the sum expended out of the $11,000 in payment of the Pickett trust's debts amounts to $6,522.70, as we have said.

We are of opinion that the contention of the defendants is correct, and that the rule in Clayton's case does not apply. The rule in Clayton's case is that as between two *cestuis que trust* the order of drawings on a bankrupt's bank account is the order of application. But when the fund drawn on is a mixed fund belonging to the defendant and his beneficiary, the order in which the drawings are made is not material, and money which could have been properly drawn out by the bankrupt will be appropriated accordingly. Hewitt v. Hayes, 205 Mass. 356. *In re* Hallett's estate, 13 Ch. D. 696. *In re* Oatway, [1903] 2 Ch. 356. The bank account here in question was not Berry's bank account but the bank account of the Pickett trust, and the $11,000 put into that account was put in there primarily to enable Berry to get a draft for the sum of $2,000 on his own account, and secondarily to pay taxes and mortgage interest amounting to $7,903.14, due from the Pickett trust and then overdue because of prior stealings by him from the Pickett trust. It was Berry's duty to use the $1,380.44, so far as it went, in paying this $7,903.14 due from the Pickett trust for taxes and mortgage interest; and under the rule in Hallett's case he must be taken to have done so without regard to the order in which the checks were drawn.

We are therefore of opinion that the plaintiffs are entitled to recover the several sums making up the amount of $6,522.70, with interest at six per cent from the several dates on which they were respectively used in paying debts due from the defendants.

Decree accordingly.[1]

WHITING v. HUDSON TRUST COMPANY.

COURT OF APPEALS, NEW YORK. 1923.

234 N. Y. 394.

APPEAL from a judgment of the Appellate Division of the Supreme Court in the first judicial department, entered August 2, 1922, modifying and affirming as modified a judgment in favor of plaintiff entered upon a decision of the court on trial at Special Term.

CARDOZO, J. The action is in equity, brought by a surviving executor to follow and reclaim trust moneys converted by a deceased fiduciary.

In September, 1915, John C. R. Eckerson had an account in his own name with the defendant, the Hudson Trust Company. He told Mr. Purdy, one of the defendant's officers, that he wished to open a second account, which for his own bookkeeping reasons was to be kept separate from the first. This account, it was agreed, would be designated " special." A day or so later he opened the new account with a deposit of $7,000. He brought with him a certified check for that amount upon the United States Mortgage and Trust Company. The check was signed " Wm. R. Denham by John C. R. Eckerson, att'y, in fact," and was drawn to the order of " John C. R. Eckerson, Trustee." Some comment was made by Mr. Purdy upon the use of the word " trustee " instead of the word " special." Mr. Eckerson said that he supposed the words to be interchangeable, that in fact there was no trust, and that the deposit was his own. Upon his indorsement of the check, an account described as " special " was opened in the defendant's books. At that time the standing of the depositor with banks and in the business community gen-

---

[1] Bremer v. Williams, 210 Mass. 256; Metropolitan Trust Co. v. Federal Trust Co., 232 Mass. 363, *accord.* See Weston, Money Stolen by a Trustee from One Trust and Used for Another, 25 Harv. L. Rev. 602; Jacob, Problem in Trusts: Newell v. Hadley, 25 Ill. L. Rev. 19; 25 Mich. L. Rev. 436.

On the question of imputing to a principal or *cestui que trust* knowledge of the agent or trustee who has a personal interest in the transaction, see Pomeroy, Eq. Juris., secs. 666–676; Seavey, Notice Through an Agent, 65 U. Pa. L. Rev. 1, 15; 29 L. R. A. (N. S.) 558.

erally was high. His reputation went far to disarm suspicion of wrongdoing.

William R. Denham, the drawer of the check through Eckerson as agent, had signed a power of attorney in April, 1915. The power was a broad one, conferring authority on the agent for and in the name of the principal to make and indorse negotiable paper; to borrow money; to keep one or more banking accounts; and to draw against the accounts and make deposits therein. Mr. Denham was ill when the special account was opened, and died a few days later, September 21, 1915. His will named two executors, Eckerson and the plaintiff. Letters were issued to both, but the plaintiff took little part in the administration of the estate. Securities which had belonged to Mr. Denham were kept in a box of the United States Safe Deposit Company. Eckerson removed them, brought them from time to time to McCurdy, Henderson & Co., stockbrokers, and caused them to be sold. Checks of McCurdy, Henderson & Co., aggregating $18,817.36, drawn to the order of J. C. R. Eckerson and J. C. R. Eckerson, " special," were deposited in the special account in April, 1916. They were for the proceeds of sales. Checks of the same firm, aggregating $22,468.54, drawn to the order of J. C. R. Eckerson, " executor," were deposited in the same account in May, 1916. They were for the proceeds of other sales.

Eckerson at these times was the executor and trustee of another estate, that of Joseph H. Snyder. He kept an account as the representative of that estate with the Hudson Trust Company. A judgment of the Supreme Court made in April, 1916, in an action for an accounting directed distribution of $188,089.35, adjudged to constitute principal, and $52,999.81, income. The assets held by the trustee were not sufficient to permit the payments to be made. His embezzlements had brought about a deficit of $166,166.38. In this emergency, he made good his thefts from one estate, or part of them, by stealing from the other. He drew three checks aggregating $29,195 upon the " special " account, which contained the proceeds of the securities belonging to the estate of Denham. The checks, dated in May, 1916, were to the order of the estate of Joseph H. Snyder, and were placed to the credit of Eckerson, as executor. He distributed the moneys thus obtained among the Snyder legatees.

Eckerson died in October, 1916, and his thefts were then discovered. The surviving executor of the Denham estate now looks for reimbursement both to the Hudson Trust Company and to the estate of Joseph H. Snyder, represented by the defendant Taylor, who on the death of Eckerson was appointed the agent of the Supreme Court to execute the trusts. The Appellate Division has held that in accepting the check for $7,000, which opened the account, and in accepting the three checks for $22,468.54, drawn by McCurdy, Henderson & Co. to the order of " Eckerson, executor," the Hudson Trust Company had constructive notice through the form of the checks that the deposit was a breach of trust. Judgment has gone against the trust company for the total of these items, less, however, the balance remaining in the special account on the death of the depositor. The result is to charge the trust company with liability for $18,448.87 principal, and interest $6,008.88, in all $24,457.75. The Appellate Division has held that the defendant Taylor, as agent or trustee, must refund $29,195, principal, and $9,340.40, interest, in all $38,535.40, moneys withdrawn from the estate of Denham and turned over without right to the trustee of the estate of Snyder. Both the Hudson Trust Company and Taylor appeal.

(1) The liability of the trust company will be the first subject of inquiry.[1] . . .

(2) Our final subject of inquiry is the liability of the defendant Taylor as agent or representative of the Supreme Court in the execution of the trusts created by the will of Snyder.

When Eckerson took the money which he held as executor of one estate, and paid it to himself as the representative of another, he had notice in the act of transfer and acceptance that the money was stolen and ought not to be received. The notice was actual. It was not, as in Henry v. Allen (151 N. Y. 1) and like cases, imputed or constructive. Eckerson, trustee under the Snyder will, was not an agent identified with some one else, a principal, as the result of legal fiction. He was the principal himself. It is only a form of words when we speak of him as the representative of an "estate." The "estate" had no separate existence. It was not a legal person. The only person was the trustee. His acceptance with guilty knowledge charged him as trustee with a duty to restore (Atlantic Cotton Mills v. Indian Orchard Mills, 147 Mass. 268; U. S. v. State Bank, 96 U. S. 30; Newell v. Hadley, 206 Mass. 335, also dissenting opinion in same case at p. 358; cf. Weston, Money Stolen from One Trust for Another, 25 Harv. Law Rev. 602 at p. 610). The trustee of an express trust under our statute (Real Prop. Law, § 100; Consol. Laws, ch. 50) has the whole title and estate. The beneficiary has a chose in action, the right to enforce in equity the performance of the trust (Schenck v. Barnes, 156 N. Y. 316, 321). Money accepted by a trustee with knowledge that its acceptance is a theft never becomes of right a part of the trust estate. The beneficiary will not be heard in equity to insist that it shall be so regarded. The trustee's duty to restore is not ended by his death. It devolves upon the Supreme Court, the successor to the trust (Real Prop. Law, § 111; Consol. Laws, ch. 50; Pers. Prop. Law, § 20; Consol. Laws, ch. 41), and now rests upon the agent by whom the trust is to be executed.

We are reminded that the stolen money after the receipt by the trustee was paid out to legatees, to whom distribution was due under a judgment of the court. The distribution may render it impossible

[1] The court held that the trust company was not liable for participation in the breach of trust. See Bischoff v. Yorkville Bank, 218 N. Y. 106, *ante.*

to identify or earmark the money in the hands of the trustee to-day. The impossibility affects the nature and scope of the relief. It does not involve as a consequence a refusal to give relief at all. The equitable lien is destroyed by the dissipation of the fund (Falk *v.* Hoffman, 233 N. Y. 199; Roca *v.* Byrne, 145 N. Y. 182; Schuyler *v.* Littlefield, 232 U. S. 707). There may still be a personal judgment enforcible against the trust estate, to the extent of the unjust enrichment, out of the assets that remain (Lightfoot *v.* Davis, 198 N. Y. 261, 272, 273). A different question is presented where the attempt is, not merely to establish a debt, but to prefer one creditor over others (Lightfoot *v.* Davis, *supra*, distinguishing Matter of Cavin *v.* Gleason, 105 N. Y. 256, and Matter of Hicks, 170 N. Y. 195). That is not the situation here. If a trustee has two bank accounts and stolen moneys are paid into the first, the beneficiaries are not prejudiced because the trustee in making restitution draws his check upon the second. The unjust enrichment is the same whether the increment if left in one compartment or another. We see no reason why judgment, if kept within these limits, may not run against the wrongdoer as trustee as well as individually. There is little analogy between the situation before us here and cases where the attempt is made to charge a trustee in his representative capacity for goods bought and used for the benefit of the trust. At such times the primary remedy is against the trustee individually if the seller has chosen to make the sale upon his credit (O'Brien *v.* Jackson, 167 N. Y. 31). Even then a secondary remedy may exist by subrogation to the right of the trustee to be indemnified for his expenses out of the assets of the trust (Willis *v.* Sharp, 113 N. Y. 586, 591; Hewitt *v.* Phelps, 105 U. S. 393, 400; Stone, Liability of Trust Assets for the Contracts and Torts of the Trustee, 22 Col. Law Rev. 527; Scott, Liabilities in the Administration of Trusts, 28 Harv. Law Rev. 725, 735). There are cases which hold that this remedy will fail to the extent that the trustee as between himself and his beneficiaries is in arrears in his accounts (Matter of Johnson, L. R. 15 Ch. Div. 548; Matter of Evans, L. R. 34 Ch. Div. 597; Stone, *supra*, p. 528; but cf. Wylly *v.* Collins & Co., 9 Ga. 223). In such circumstances, unjust enrichment, it is thought, does not result, since the seller has himself to blame if he has sold upon the personal credit of the buyer. A larger security might have been attained by stipulating in advance for a charge or lien upon the fund (Jessup *v.* Smith, 223 N. Y. 203). How far the right of recourse in such conditions is affected by the state of the accounts between trustee and beneficiaries, we need not now inquire. We are dealing in the case at hand with a very different situation. The defendant's enrichment is a direct and immediate, not an indirect or collateral, consequence of the act of the trustee. It is an enrichment independent of the volition of the defrauded plaintiff or of those for whom he acts. The fruits of the tort are profits in the coffers of the estate. We cannot characterize enrichment so procured as other than unjust (Stone, *supra*, at pp. 528, 538, 539, 543; Scott, *supra*, at p. 741). The trust is still augmented by assets unconscionably retained.

It is argued that the legatees when they received the stolen money on account of a valid debt became holders for value, and acting without guilty knowledge may retain in good conscience the benefits received. Many cases are cited in support of this conclusion (Stephens *v.* Bd. of Education, Brooklyn, 79 N. Y. 183; Ball *v.* Shepard, 202 N. Y. 247; Pittsburgh-Westmoreland Coal Co. *v.* Kerr, 220 N. Y. 137; Newhall *v.* Wyatt, 139 N. Y. 452; Holly *v.* D. & F. Missionary Society, 92 Fed. Rep. 745; 180 U. S. 284; cf. Edgar *v.* Plomley, 1900 A. C. 431). These cases might be applicable if the plaintiff were suing a legatee, who, by force of the payment so made, would hold the legal title. They do not touch a case where he is suing the trustee. The plaintiff is not holding the legatees accountable for anything. He does not attempt to follow the money into their hands on any theory of constructive notice of the fraud of the trustee. What they have, they may retain, though it prove to be far in excess of what is left in the estate. It is one thing to hold that equity will divest a legal title acquired by legatees without notice of defects. It is another thing to hold that equity will affirmatively intervene to clothe them with a title still retained by the trustee. The fact that the present trustee is a successor is unimportant. The transaction is guilty or innocent according to the presence or absence of notice at the time when payment was accepted. A legatee, if guilty, would charge his executor with liability though the executor were innocent. A trustee, if guilty, charges his successor, who assumes the trust *cum onere*. Nothing to the contrary was held in Case *v.* James (29 Beav. 512; affd., 3 DeG., F & J. 256); Thorndike *v.* Hunt (3 DeG. & J. 563), and Taylor *v.* Blakelock (32 Ch. Div. 560). There the money did not reach the trust at all till it was paid to a new trustee who had no knowledge of its origin. Here the taint attached at the moment of acceptance.

It is argued that the effect of the judgment against the trustee under the Snyder will is to make the remaindermen suffer to a greater extent than the beneficiary of the trust for life or her personal representatives. Equity requires, it is said, that the burden of Eckerson's thefts be distributed proportionately between the life interest and the remainders. This, the brief tells us, has not been done. The life beneficiary or her estate has been paid in full; the judgment must be satisfied, it is said, out of assets that are held for the benefit of the remaindermen.

The point, if it is in the record at all, is not there with the clearness essential to make it the basis of our judgment. We do not know the terms of the will. There is no copy of it in the findings or even in the testimony. Possibly the *cestui que trust* for life had equities superior to those of the remaindermen. We do not even know whether the money that was paid to her was part of the stolen money, or was derived from other sources. A deficit existed, but the estate had not been looted altogether, and its own assets were more than adequate to pay the *cestui que trust* in full. The question is not before us whether if she has in fact been overpaid, a remedy against her or her estate is available hereafter at the suit of the remaindermen for a readjustment of the burden.

The judgment against the Hudson Trust Company, both at the Appellate Division and at the Special Term, should be reversed, except as to the conceded balance of $12,064.44, and the complaint dismissed except as to said balance, with costs in the Appellate Division and in this court. The judgment against the defendant Taylor as the agent of the court to execute the Snyder trusts should be affirmed with costs.

HISCOCK, Ch. J., HOGAN, POUND, MCLAUGHLIN, CRANE and ANDREWS, JJ., concur.

Judgment accordingly.[1]

MURRAY *v.* LYLBURN.

COURT OF CHANCERY, NEW YORK. 1817.

2 Johns. Ch. 441.

IN 1809, a bill was filed against Winter, who held certain lands in Cosby's manor, in trust for P. Heatly and others, in behalf of the *cestui que trusts,* charging him with a fraudulent breach of trust, and an injunction was issued against him, in February, 1810, enjoining from acting as trustee, and from selling any of the trust estate, or assigning the securities or proceeds thereof, &c. (*Vide* vol. 1. p. 26, 60, 77, 566.) Winter, notwithstanding, sold a lot of land, part of the trust estate, in August, 1810, to the defendant, Sprague, in fee, and took his bond and mortgage for the purchase money. Winter, afterwards, assigned the bond and mortgage to Robert Lylburn, deceased, whose executors, Lylburn and Isham, were made defendants. Since the assignment, about 180 dollars, part of the money, had been paid to Winter. Sprague, afterwards, in 1814, released all his interest in the land so purchased by him, to Davis, who is in possession thereof.

The defendants, Lylburn and Isham, denied all knowledge of the sale of the land to Sprague, or of the trust; and, according to their knowledge and belief, all notice to their testator, of the suit against Winter, and of the injunction; and they averred that he took the assignment of the bond and mortgage, *bona fide,* for a value consideration.

The bill was taken *pro confesso,* against Sprague and Davis.

[1] See 23 Col. L. Rev. 596, 670; 36 Harv. L. Rev. 762; 21 Mich. L. Rev. 919; 32 Yale L. Jour. 293, 744.

THE CHANCELLOR [KENT]. The question is, whether the executors of Lylburn are to be held accountable to the *cestui que trusts* (in whose behalf Murray, as receiver, instituted the suit) for the bond and mortgage, in like manner as Winter may be, or would have been, had he not assigned them.

The case states, that the bill has been taken *pro confesso* against Sprague, the purchaser, and against Davis, who holds under him. It also states, that Davis is in possession.

The *cestui que trusts* are not entitled to the land, and also to the purchase money. The two claims, as I observed in the analogous case of Murray *v.* Ballou and Hunt, (1 Johns. Ch. Rep. 581,) are inconsistent with each other. The one sets aside, and the other affirms the sale. If the *cestui que trusts* choose to disregard the alienation made by the trustee, pending the suit against him, (as they may do according to the settled doctrines of the court,) then they have nothing to do with these securities, but are to look solely to the land, taking no notice of the alienation by Winter. They ought to be put to their election. I am inclined to think they may, if they please, affirm the sale, and look to these securities; and if they do, then the bill, as against Sprague and Davis, ought to be dismissed.

It is a general and well-settled principle, that the assignee of a *chose in action* takes it subject to the same equity it was subject to in the hands of the assignor. (2 Vern. 691, 764. 1 P. Wms. 496. 1 Ves. 123. 4 Vesey, jun. 121.) But this rule is generally understood to mean the equity residing in the original obligor or debtor, and not an equity residing in some third person against the assignor. He takes it *subject to all the equity of the obligor,* say the judges in the very elaborately argued case of Norton *v.* Rose, (2 Wash. Rep. 233, 254,) on this very point, touching the rights of the assignee of a bond. The assignee can always go to the debtor, and ascertain what claims he may have against the bond, or other *chose in action,* which he is about purchasing from the obligee; but he may not be able, with the utmost diligence, to ascertain the latent equity of some third person against the obligee. He has not any object to which he can direct his inquiries; and, for this reason, the claim of the assignee, without notice of a *chose* in action, was preferred, in the late case of Redfearn *v.* Ferrier and others, (1 Dow. Rep. 50,) to that of a third party setting up a secret equity against the assignor. Lord Eldon observed, in that case, that if it were not to be so, no assignments could ever be taken with safety. I am not aware that this decision was the introduction of any new principle, in the case of actual *bona fide* purchases or assignments *by contracts;* though Lord Thurlow said, in one case, (1 Vesey, jun. 249,) that the purchaser of a *chose in action* must abide by the case of the person from whom he buys; but he spoke this on a question between the assignee and the debtor. In assignments, by *operation of law*, as to assignees of bankrupts, the case may be different; for such assignments are said to pass the rights of the bankrupt, subject to all equities, and precisely in the same plight and condition as he possessed them. (1 Atk. 162. 9 Vesey, 100.) The ground, however, on which I place the right of the *cestui que trusts*, in this case, to pursue the bond and mortgage in the hands of the assignee of Winter, is the constructive notice to all the world, arising from the bill and supplementary bill, filed in 1809, against Winter, for a breach of trust. The object of that suit was to take the whole subject of the trust out of his hands, together with all the papers and securities relating thereto. If Winter had held a number of mortgages, and other securities, in trust, when the suit was commenced, it cannot be pretended, that he might safely defeat the object of the suit, and elude the justice of the court, by selling these securities. If he possessed cash, as the proceeds of the trust estate, or negotiable paper not due, or perhaps moveable personal property, such as horses, cattle, grain, &c., I am not prepared to say the rule is to be carried so far as to affect such sales. The safety of commercial dealing would require a limitation of the rule; but bonds and mortgages are not the subject of ordinary commerce; and they formed one of the specific subjects of the suit against Winter, and the injunction prohibited the sale and assignment of them as well as of the lands held in trust. If the trustee pending the suit changed the land into personal security, as he did in this case, I see no good reason why the *cestui que trusts* should not be at liberty to affirm the sale, and take the security; and whoever, afterwards, purchased it, was chargeable with notice of the suit. He was dealing with a subject out of the ordinary course of traffic, and always understood to be subject to certain equities; and there can be very little ground for the complaint of hardship in the application to such a case, of the general doctrine of the court. There is no principle better established, nor one founded on more indispensable necessity, than that the purchase of the subject matter in controversy, *pendente lite*, does not vary the rights of the parties in that suit, who are not to receive any prejudice from the alienation. The latent equity here might easily have been discovered by Lylburn, when he purchased, by applying to the records of this court. If the *cestui que trust* be entitled, as between him and his trustee, to take the securities or the land, at his election, it ought not to be in the power of the trustee to defeat that election, by selling the securities. The litigating parties are not to have their rights affected by any alienation during the pendency of the suit. . . .

I shall, accordingly, decree, that the plaintiffs, by their solicitor, signify, by an election in writing, signed by such solicitor, and filed in the register's office, their determination whether to proceed against the defendants, Sprague and Davis, for the land, or against the defendants, Lylburn and Isham, for the bond and mortgage mentioned in the pleadings. That if such election be to proceed against the defendants, Sprague and Davis, then the bill, as against the defendants, Lylburn and Isham, shall, from the time of filing such writing, stand dismissed; and the defendants, S. and D., shall, within thirty days, convey the lot in the pleadings mentioned to the present trustees, &c. and pay the costs of the suit against them; but that if such election be to proceed against the defendants, Lylburn and Isham, then the bill as against the defendants, Sprague and Davis, shall, from the time of filing such writing, stand dismissed, and the said defendants, Lylburn and Isham, shall, within thirty days from the service of a copy of this decree, and of such election, at their own expense, reassign and deliver to the said solicitor, or his order, for the use of the *cestui que trusts*, for whose benefit this suit was instituted, the said bond and mortgage, together with all the right and interest of their testator, at the time of his death, therein, and shall also pay the sum of 157 dollars and five cents, which they have admitted, by their answer, to have been received by their testator, on the bond and mortgage, subsequent to the assignment thereof, together with lawful interest thereon, from the 30th of November, 1811, when it was received; and that if the plaintiffs shall not make and file their election, as aforesaid, within forty days from the date of this decree, then the bill, as to all the defendants, shall be dismissed. . . .

Decree accordingly.[1]

[1] The distinction between "latent" and "patent" equities has been repudiated in New York. Bebee v. State Bank, 1 Johns. 529; Bush v. Lathrop, 22 N. Y. 535, and numerous later New York cases. See also Moore v. Jervis, 2 Coll. 60; Brandon v. Brandon, 7 DeG. M. & G. 365; Cory v. Eyre, 1 DeG. J. & S. 149; Re European Bank, L. R. 5 Ch. App. 358; West v. MacInnes, 23 U. C. Q. B. 357; Cowdrey v. Vandenburgh, 101 U. S. 572; Butcher v. Werksman, 204 Fed. 330; Moore v. Moore, 112 Ind. 149; Ames v. Richardson, 29 Minn. 330; Turner v. Hoyle, 95 Mo. 337; Kernohan v. Durham, 48 Oh. St. 1; Patterson v. Rabb, 38 S. C. 138; Downer v. So. Royalton Bk., 39 Vt. 25.

But in a number of states the rule enunciated by Chancellor Kent is followed. See National Bank v. Texas, 20 Wall (U. S.) 72, 89; Mohr v. Byrne, 135 Cal. 87; Western Bk. v. Maverick Bk., 90 Ga. 339; Silverman v. Bullock, 98 Ill. 11; Crosby v. Tanner, 40 Iowa 136; Newton v. Newton, 46 Minn. 33; Moffett v. Parker, 71 Minn. 139; Hibernian Bk. v. Everman, 52 Miss. 500; Losey v. Hoagland, 11 N. J. Eq. 246; Starr v. Haskins, 26 N. J. Eq. 414; Tate v. Security T. Co., 63 N. J. Eq. 559; Appeal of Mifflin Co. Nat. Bk., 98 Pa. 150; Moore v. Holcombe, 3 Leigh (Va.) 597; Church Bldg. Soc. v. Free Church, 24 Wash. 433.

Even in jurisdictions in which assignees of *choses* in action take subject to latent equities, it is held that the purchaser of shares of stock may take free and clear of the trust although he receives notice before a transfer has been made on the books of the company. Dodds v. Hills, 2 H. & M. 424; Powers v. Pacific Diesel Engine Co., 206 Cal. 334; Dueber Watch Case Mfg. Co. v. Daugherty, 62 Oh. St. 589. See Ames, 299n.; 1 Machen, Corps., sec. 882. By the Uniform Stock Transfer Act, certificates of stock are made negotiable by

FIDELITY MUTUAL LIFE INS. CO. v. CLARK.

SUPREME COURT OF THE UNITED STATES. 1906.

203 U. S. 64.

HOLMES, J. This is a bill in equity, brought in the Circuit Court to enjoin the setting up of a judgment at law recovered in the same Circuit Court upon three policies of life insurance, on the ground that the judgment was obtained by fraud. It also seeks to compel

---

indorsement. In general as to a *chose* in action represented by a non-negotiable specialty, see 30 Harv. L. Rev. 103, 104. As to overdue negotiable paper, see Chafee, Rights in Overdue Paper, 31 Harv. L. Rev. 1104.

In general on the question how far "latent" or "collateral" equities in *choses* in action are cut off by an assignment to a transferee for value and without notice, see 29 Harv. L. Rev. 816; 30 *ibid.* 97, 449; 31 *ibid.* 822; Ames, 309, 310; Ames, Lect. Leg. Hist., 258–260; Perry, Trusts, sec. 831; Williston, Contracts, secs. 438–447; Pomeroy, Eq. Juris., secs. 708–712; 5 C. J. 974.

If an assignee of a *chose* in action procures the assignment by fraud and thereafter assigns his interest to a third person, it has been held that the third person prevails over the original assignor, whether or not the *chose* in action is represented by a specialty. There is, however, a conflict of authority on this. See Taylor v. Gitt, 10 Pa. 428; Williston, Contracts, sec. 438; Pomeroy, Eq. Juris., secs. 707, 710; Ames, 310; Ames, Lect. Leg. Hist., 210; Scott, Cases on Trusts, 1 ed., 753; Dec. Dig., Assignments, sec. 115.

In the Restatement of Contracts of the American Law Institute, sec. 174, it is stated that, "If an assignor's right against the obligor is voidable by some one other than the obligor or is held in trust for such a person, an assignee who purchases the assignment for value in good faith neither knowing nor having reason to know of the right of such person cannot be deprived of the assigned right or its proceeds."

In the Explanatory Notes to this Section it is said: "Whatever may be the merit of Chancellor Kent's reason for the rule he laid down, the decisions based on the rule have commended themselves to the Reporter and his Advisers. There is a growing tendency in the law to deal with transfers of contractual rights according to the same rules as transfers of other kinds of property, and since an innocent purchaser of land or goods from a trustee acting in violation of his trust or from one who obtained the property fraudulently, is preferred to the *cestui que trust* or defrauded party, the tendency justifies similarly preferring an innocent purchaser of a contractual right to one who has previously been deprived of it by fraud and to one for whom the right was held in trust by the assignor. It must be admitted, however, that the weight of authority is at present opposed to that view."

Partial assignments. In Holmes v. Gardner, 50 Oh. St. 167, it was held that a partial assignee of a mortgage note who took for value and without notice that the mortgage was given to defraud creditors, took free of the claims of the creditors.

As to the rights of successive partial assignees of a *chose* in action, see Third Nat. Bk. v. Atlantic City, 126 Fed. 413 (priority according to dates of notice to debtor); Moore's App., 92 Pa. 309 (*pro rata*).

As to the effect of a partial assignment of a *chose* in action followed by a total assignment, see Tourville v. Naish, 3 P. Wms. 307; The Elmbank, 72 Fed. 610; Columbia etc. Co. v. First Nat. Bk., 116 Ky. 364; King Bros. & Co. v. Central etc. Ry. Co., 135 Ga. 225; Pickett v. School Dist., 193 Mo.

the plaintiff in the action at law, and other parties to whom interests in the policies were assigned, to repay the sums which they received upon them. The judgment was rendered in a case which came before this court, and the dramatic circumstances of the alleged death are set forth in the report. Fidelity Mutual Life Association v. Mettler, 185 U. S. 308. The appellant is the plaintiff in error in that case, having changed its name. After the date of the judgment the appellant discovered that Hunter, the party whose life was insured, was alive, and that the recovery was the result of a deliberate plot. Thereupon it forthwith brought this bill. One of the defenses set up and argued below and here was that by the Seventh Amendment to the Constitution no fact tried by a jury shall be otherwise reëxamined in any court of the United States than according to the rules of the common law. On the facts alleged and proved the Circuit Court entered a decree against the plaintiff at law, Mettler, now Smythe, but dismissed the bill as against the assignees of partial interests in the policies. The insurance company appealed to this court.

The material facts are these. By way of a contingent fee for the services in collecting the insurance, Mrs. Mettler assigned to the present defendant Clark and his partners one-third interest in the policies, with an additional sum in case statutory damages and attorney's fees were recovered. This afterwards came to Clark alone. Clark and Mrs. Mettler assigned five hundred dollars each, from their respective interests to the defendant Culberson, as a contingent fee for argument and services in this court. Clark also employed the defendant Spoonts, it would seem on a contingent fee. Finally he mortgaged his right to the Phillips Investment Company. When the judgment was recovered, before execution, the insurance company paid the amount ($24,028.25) into court. Out of this the clerk paid to Mrs. Mettler $11,616; to Clark, $8,346; to Spoonts on Clark's order, $1,500; to Culberson, $1,026, and to the Phillips Investment Company, $1,540.24. It is these sums, other than that paid to Mrs. Mettler, that are in question here.

It will not be necessary to consider the constitutional question under the Seventh Amendment, to which we have referred, or some other questions which were raised, because we are of opinion that the appellees are entitled to keep their money, even if the judgment can be impeached for fraud. They all got the legal title to the money which was paid to them, or, what is the same thing, got the legal title transferred to their order. That being so, the appellant must show some equity before their legal title can be disturbed. It founds its claim to such an equity on the mode in which the judgment which

---

App. 519; Fairbanks v. Sargent, 104 N. Y. 108, 117 N. Y. 320; Gillette v. Murphy, 7 Okla. 91. Cf. Bridge v. Conn. Mut. Life Ins. Co., 152 Mass. 343. See Williston, Contracts, secs. 441–443; 30 Harv. L. Rev. 104–105, 480–484; and see Chap. I, sec. VIII, *ante*.

induced it to part with the title to its money was obtained. But fraud, of course, gives rise only to a personal claim. It goes to the motives, not to the formal constituents of a legal transfer, Rodliff v. Dallinger, 141 Massachusetts, 1, 6, and the rule is familiar that it can affect a title only when the owner takes with notice or without having given value. Fletcher v. Peck, 6 Cranch, 87, 133; 2 Williams, Vendor & Purchaser, 674. See The Eliza Lines, 199 U. S. 119, 131. The question is whether the appellant can make out such a case as that.

It is said that the title of the appellees stands on the judgment, and that if the judgment fails the title fails. But that mode of statement is not sufficiently precise. The judgment hardly can be said to be part of the appellee's title. It simply afforded the appellant a motive for its payment into court. The appellees derive their title immediately from Mrs. Mettler, and remotely from the act of the appellant. They stand exactly as if the appellant had handed over the twenty-four thousand dollars in gold to her and she thereupon had handed their proportion to them. We are putting no emphasis on the fact that the thing transferred was money. The appellees knew from what fund they were paid, from what source it came, and why it was paid to Mrs. Mettler. We are insisting only that the title had passed to them. But we repeat that, as the title had passed, the appellant must find some equity before it can disturb it, and we now add that, as there is no question that the appellees took for value, that is in payment for their services, or, if it be preferred, in performance of Mrs. Mettler's contingent promise, the equity must be founded upon notice.

The notice to be shown is notice of the fact that the judgment which induced the appellant's payment was obtained by fraud. But notice cannot be established by the mere fact that while the appellees held an interest in the policies only they were assignees of choses in action, and took them subject to the equities. That is due to a chose in action not being negotiable. It does not stand on notice. The general proposition was decided in United States v. Detroit Lumber Co., 200 U. S. 321, 333, 334, and United States v. Clark, 200 U. S. 601, 607, 608, and earlier in Judson v. Corcoran, 17 How. 612, 615, and, we have no doubt, is the law of England. Of course the assignee of an ordinary contract can only stand in the shoes of the party with whom the contract was made. In the discussions of the rule which we have seen, we have found no other reason offered, as no other is necessary. But the assumption of the good faith of the assignee occurs in more cases than one.

The principle which we apply is further illustrated by the priority given to the later of two equitable titles, if the legal title be added to it, 2 Pomeroy, Eq. 3d. ed., §§ 727, 768, by the doctrine of tacking, and, in some degree, by the great distinction recognized in other respects between the holder of title under an executed contract and a party to a contract merely executory. See 1 Williams V. & P. 540, and cases cited. We may add further that, even if we were wrong, the equities to which an assignee takes subject are equities existing at the time of the assignment, 1 Williams V. & P. 584, and that the notice with which he is supposed to be charged as an assignee can be of nothing more. Therefore merely as assignees the appellees had not notice of the as yet unaccomplished fraud in obtaining the judgment. The policies were honest contracts and it was an interest in the policies which was assigned, at least to Clark.

The appellant is driven, therefore, to contend, as it did contend at the argument, that notice of the denial that Hunter was dead, in the suit on the policy, was notice of the fraud. But it is admitted that the appellees all acted in good faith; that they believed the plaintiff's case. In such circumstances, even if the answer had gone further, and had charged the plaintiff with all that the present bill charges against her, when a jury had decided that the charges were groundless, a judgment had been entered on the verdict, and the insurance company had accepted the result by paying the money into court without waiting for an execution, it would be impossible to say that the supposed notice was not purged. The appellees were not bound to contemplate future discoveries of what they honestly believed untrue, and a bill to impeach the final act of the law. See Bank of the United States *v.* Bank of Washington, 6 Peters, 8, 19.

Decree affirmed.

MR. JUSTICE HARLAN and MR. JUSTICE WHITE dissent.

MR. JUSTICE MCKENNA took no part in the decision of this case.[1]

PHILLIPS *v.* PHILLIPS.

CHANCERY. 1861.

4 DeG. F. & J. 208.

THE LORD CHANCELLOR [WESTBURY].[2] When I reserved my judgment at the conclusion of the argument in this case, it was rather out of respect to that argument than from a feeling of any difficulty with regard to the question that had been so strenuously contested before me.

[1] Merchants' Ins. Co. *v.* Abbott, 131 Mass. 397, *accord.* See Ames, Lect. Leg. Hist., 277, 278; 4 Harv. L. Rev. 304, 305.

It is, of course, well settled that an assignee of a non-negotiable *chose* in action takes subject to equitable defences of the obligor acquired before notice of the assignment. Pomeroy, Eq. Juris., sec. 704; Williston, Contracts, secs. 432–433; Dec. Dig., Assignments, secs. 99–103. See Chap. I, sec. VIII, *ante.*

The result is different if the obligor has done anything to estop himself from setting up his defence. Pomeroy, Eq. Juris., sec. 704.

[2] The statement of facts is omitted.

The case is a very simple one. The plaintiff claims as the grantee of an annuity granted by a deed dated in the month of February, 1820, to issue out of certain lands in the county of Monmouth, secured by powers of distress and entry. The annuity or rent-charge was not to arise until the death of one Rebecca Phillips, who died in the month of December, 1839, and the first payment of the annuity became due on the 8th of March, 1840.

The case was argued on both sides on the admitted basis that the legal estate was outstanding in certain incumbrancers, and is still outstanding. Subject to the annuity the grantor was entitled in fee-simple in equity. In February, 1821, the grantor intermarried with one Mary Phillips. On the occasion of that marriage, a settlement, dated in February, 1821, was executed, and under this deed the defendants claim; and claim, therefore, as purchasers for a valuable consideration. No payment has ever been made in respect of the annuity.

The bill was filed within twenty years, and seeks the ordinary relief applicable to the case. The defendants by their answer insist that the deed was voluntary, and therefore void under the Statute of Elizabeth, as against them in their character of purchasers for valuable consideration, and they also insist upon the Statute of Limitations. But in the answer the defence of purchase for valuable consideration without notice is not attempted to be raised.

At the hearing, an affidavit of Mary Phillips and another person was produced, denying the fact of notice of the annuity at the time of the grant and at the time of the creation of the marriage settlement, and the contention at the bar was that the defence of purchase for valuable consideration without notice was available for the defendants, under these circumstances, and ought to be allowed as a bar to the claim by the court. The Vice-Chancellor in his judgment refused to admit the defence of purchase for valuable consideration without notice, and I entirely agree with him in the conclusion that such a defence requires to be pleaded by the answer, more especially where an answer has been put in.

But I do not mean to rest my decision upon that particular ground because I have permitted the argument to proceed with reference to the general proposition, which was maintained before me with great energy and learning, viz. that the doctrine of a court of equity was this, that it would give no relief whatever to any claimant against a purchaser for valuable consideration without notice. It was urged upon me that authority to this effect was to be found in some recent decisions of this court, and particularly in the case decided at the Rolls of The Attorney-General *v.* Wilkins, 17 Beav. 285.

I undoubtedly was struck with the novelty and extent of the doctrine that was thus advanced, and in order to deal with the argument it becomes necessary to revert to elementary principles. I take it to be a clear proposition that every conveyance of an equitable interest is an innocent conveyance; that is to say, the grant of a person entitled merely in equity passes only that which he is justly entitled to, and no more. If, therefore, a person seised of an equitable estate (the legal estate being outstanding), makes an assurance by way of mortgage or grants an annuity, and afterwards conveys the whole estate to a purchaser, he can grant to the purchaser that which he has, viz. the estate subject to the mortgage or annuity, and no more. The subsequent grantee takes only that which is left in the grantor. Hence grantees and incumbrancers claiming in equity take and are ranked according to the dates of their securities; and the maxim applies, " *Qui prior est tempore potior est jure.*" The first grantee is *potior;* that is, *potentior.* He has a better and superior — because a prior — equity. The first grantee has a right to be paid first, and it is quite immaterial whether the subsequent incumbrancers at the time when they took their securities and paid their money had notice of the first incumbrance or not. These elementary rules are recognized in the case of Brace *v.* Duchess of Marlborough, 2 P. Wms. 491, and they are further illustrated by the familiar doctrine of the court as to tacking securities. It is well known that if there are three incumbrancers, and the third incumbrancer, at the time of his incumbrance and payment of his money, had no notice of the second incumbrance, then, if the first mortgagee or incumbrancer has the legal estate, and the third pays him off, and takes an assignment of his securities and a conveyance of the legal estate, he is entitled to tack his third mortgage to the first mortgage which he has acquired, and to exclude the intermediate incumbrancer. But this doctrine is limited to the case where the first mortgagee has the legal title; for if the first mortgagee has not the legal title, the third does not by the transfer obtain the legal title, and the third mortgagee by payment off of the first acquires no priority over the second. Now, the defence of a purchaser for valuable consideration is the creature of a court of equity, and it can never be used in a manner at variance with the elementary rules which have already been stated. It seems at first to have been used as a shield against the claim in equity of persons having a legal title. Bassett *v.* Nosworthy, Finch, 102, 2 White & T. L. C. 1, is, if not the earliest, the best early reported case on the subject. There the plaintiff claimed under a legal title, and this circumstance, together with the maxim which I have referred to, probably gave rise to the notion that this defence was good only against the legal title. But there appear to be three cases in which the use of this defence is most familiar: —

First, where an application is made to an auxiliary jurisdiction of the court by the possessor of a legal title, as by an heir-at-law (which was the case in Bassett *v.* Nosworthy), or by a tenant for life for the delivery of title-deeds (which was the case of Wallwyn *v.* Lee, 9 Ves. 24), and the defendant pleads that he is a *bonâ fide* purchaser for valuable consideration without notice. In such a case the defence is good, and the reason given is that as against a purchaser for valuable consideration without notice the court gives no assistance; that is, no assistance to the legal title. But this rule does not apply where the court exercises a legal jurisdiction concurrently with courts of law. Thus it was decided by Lord Thurlow in Williams *v.* Lambe, 3 B. C. C. 264, that the defence could not be pleaded to a bill for dower; and by Sir J. Leach, in Collins *v.* Archer, 1 Russ. & Mylne, 284, that it was no answer to a bill for tithes. In those cases the court of equity was not asked to give the plaintiff any equitable as distinguished from legal relief.

The second class of cases is the ordinary one of several purchasers or incumbrancers each claiming in equity, and one who is later and last in time succeeds in obtaining an outstanding legal estate not held upon existing trusts or a judgment, or any other legal advantage the possession of which may be a protection to himself or an embarrassment to other claimants. He will not be deprived of this advantage by a court of equity. To a bill filed against him for this purpose by a prior purchaser or incumbrancer, the defendant may maintain the plea of purchase for valuable consideration without notice; for the principle is, that a court of equity will not disarm a purchaser, that is, will not take from him the shield of any legal advantage. This is the common doctrine of the *tabula in naufragio*.

Thirdly, where there are circumstances that give rise to an equity as distinguished from an equitable estate, — as, for example, an equity to set aside a deed for fraud, or to correct it for mistake, — and the purchaser under the instrument maintains the plea of purchase for valuable consideration without notice, the court will not interfere.[1]

Now these are the three cases in which the defence in question is most commonly found. None of them involve the case that is now before me.

It was indeed said at the bar that the defendants, being in possession, had a legal advantage in respect of the possession, of which they ought not to be deprived. But that is to confound the subject of adjudication with the means of determining it. The possession is the thing which is the subject of controversy, and is to be awarded by the court to one or to the other. But the subject of controversy, and the means of determining the right to that subject are perfectly different. The argument, in fact, amounts to this: "I ought not to be deprived of possession, because I have possession." The purchaser will not be deprived of anything that gives him a legal right

[1] As to the alleged difference between an equity and an equitable estate, see 1 Harv. L. Rev. 2; Ames, Lect. Leg. Hist., 253.

to the possession, but the possession itself must not be confounded with the right to it.

The case, therefore, that I have to decide is the ordinary case of a person claiming under an innocent equitable conveyance that interest which existed in the grantor at the time when that conveyance was made. But, as I have already said, that interest was diminished by the estate that had been previously granted to the annuitant, and as there was no ground for pretending that the deed creating the annuity was a voluntary deed, so there is no ground whatever for contending that the estate of the person taking under the subsequent marriage settlement is not to be treated by this court, being an equitable estate, as subject to the antecedent annuity, just as effectually as if the annuity itself had been noticed and excepted out of the operation of the subsequent instrument.

I have no difficulty, therefore, in holding that the plea of purchase for valuable consideration is upon principle not at all applicable to the case before me, even if I could take notice of it as having been rightly and regularly raised.

We next come to examine the authorities upon which the defence relies. Now, undoubtedly, I cannot assent to some observations which I find attributed to the Master of the Rolls in the report of the case of The Attorney-General *v.* Wilkins; but to the decision of that case, as explained by his Honor in the subsequent case of Colyer *v.* Finch, 19 Beav. 500, I see no reasonable objection, and the principles that I have here been referring to are fully explained and acted on by the Master of the Rolls in the case of Colyer *v.* Finch. It is impossible, therefore, to suppose that he intended to lay down anything in the case of The Attorney-General *v.* Wilkins, which is at variance with the ordinary rules of the court as I have already explained them, or which could give countenance to the argument that has been raised before me at the bar.

I have consequently no difficulty in holding that the decree of his Honor the Vice-Chancellor is right upon the grounds on which he placed it in the court below, and that also it would have been right if he had considered the grounds which have been urged before me in support of this petition of rehearing. I therefore affirm the decree and dismiss the petition of rehearing; but inasmuch as the plaintiff sues in *formâ pauperis*, of course it must be dismissed without costs.

CAVE *v.* CAVE.

Chancery. 1880.
15 Ch. D. 639.

The plaintiffs were the *cestuis que trust* under the settlement executed on the marriage of Mr. and Mrs. Frederick Cave on the

27th of January, 1863. On the 27th of November, 1867, the defendant Charles Cave was appointed trustee of the settlement, and in the year 1871 he became the sole trustee.

The trust funds, which were at that time in his hands, consisted of 3,600*l*. advanced on mortgage and 276*l*. consols. Out of these sums 1,950*l*. and 702*l*. 17*s*. 6*d*. were improperly invested in the purchase of certain lands at Wandsworth in the following manner: —

Charles Cave, the trustee, received the trust moneys which had been secured on mortgage in 1872, and paid it to an account in the National and Provincial Bank in the joint names of himself and his brother Frederick Cave. A cheque was drawn on this account in June, 1872, by the two in favor of Frederick Cave, and the money was laid out in the purchase of freehold land at Wandsworth. Charles Cave acted in the purchase as trustee of the settlement and also as solicitor of himself and of Frederick Cave, and the conveyance of the property was made to Frederick Cave, and the deeds relating to the property were held by Charles Cave, the trustee of the settlement.

In September, 1872, another cheque was drawn by Charles Cave and Frederick Cave on their banking account in favor of the Accountant-General of the Court of Chancery, and the proceeds were applied in purchasing other land at Wandsworth, and the conveyance of the land was prepared by Charles Cave, and was made to Frederick Cave.

The defendant Philip Chaplin, on the 10th of February, 1873, advanced to Frederick Cave 2,500*l*. on a first mortgage of the land thus improperly purchased, which contained absolute covenants for title by Frederick Cave. Charles Cave acted as the solicitor of Philip Chaplin in relation to the said advance, and stated that the land belonged to one of his brothers, and the question arose whether Philip Chaplin had or had not constructive notice through Charles Cave who so acted as his solicitor, that the said lands had been purchased with and represented the trust moneys subject to the trusts of the settlement.

In October, 1873, the defendant John White advanced 1,800*l*. on the same property without notice of the first mortgage, and on this occasion Charles Cave wrote a letter to Mr. White stating that Frederick Cave had lately bought the freehold house and land at Wandsworth, which had compelled him to withdraw some of his capital from his business.

The other defendants, W. Nichols and Haslam, Appleton, & Company, also advanced money on subsequent mortgages of the same land to Frederick Cave, and in 1874 Philip Chaplin, the first mortgagee, made further advances on the same security.

In 1875 Frederick Cave, who had been in business with George Cave, dissolved partnership upon the terms of his paying to George Cave 5,000*l*., 2,250*l*. of which was secured by a mortgage of the same lands. In this case, however, Mr. Justice Fry was of opinion that George Cave had actual notice of the breach of trust.

In April, 1879, Frederick Cave became a bankrupt, and the plaintiffs claimed to prove against his estate for these breaches of trust, and they also claimed priority over all the liens claimed on the land by the several defendants, on the ground that when they took their charges they had constructive notice of the breach of trust.

The defendants denied that they had notice, and relied especially on the fraud of Charles Cave as a circumstance raising a presumption that he would not have communicated the circumstances of his fraud to the mortgagees.

FRY, J., stated the facts, and continued: —

The question before me concerns the priority of the liens or charges claimed against the Wandsworth property. The plaintiff's right to a charge against the original purchaser of the property, Frederick Cave, is not and could not be in dispute. The question, however, arises between persons who claim subsequently to the original purchase by the trustee, or rather by Frederick Cave, who obtained the money from the trustee.

It appears that after the two conveyances were made to Frederick Cave in June and September, 1872, Frederick Cave, in February, 1873, mortgaged the property to the defendant Philip Chaplin for the sum of 2,500*l.*, and subsequent advances were made by Chaplin which bring the amount in all up to 5,550*l*. With regard to the last of those advances, the sum of 550*l.*, it was subsequent to Mr. White's advance, and it has not been contended that it can have priority over that. Between the plaintiff and Chaplin the course of argument has been this: It has been proved that the same solicitor, Mr. Charles Cave, who was also surviving trustee, acted in the matter of Chaplin's mortgage both for Chaplin and for the mortgagor, Frederick Cave.[1] . . .

The conclusion I arrive at is, that Chaplin has sustained the burden cast upon him of proving that the circumstances are such as repel the construction or imputation to the principal of notice to the agent. Therefore I hold that Mr. Chaplin's mortgage has a priority over the plaintiffs'.

The next question arises between the plaintiffs and White, and also between all the other incumbrancers upon the fund. That question is of this nature: all these incumbrancers allege that they are purchasers for value without notice, and they plead that, being purchasers for value without notice, they have a sufficient and conclusive defence. That defence, as we all know, has been the subject of a great deal of decision, and it is by no means easy to harmonize the authorities and the opinions expressed upon the subject. Criticisms upon old cases lie many strata deep, and eminent

[1] A part of the opinion relating to the question of constructive notice to Chaplin is omitted.

Lord Chancellors have expressed diametrically opposite conclusions upon the same question. The case of Phillips *v.* Phillips, 4 D. F. & J. 208, is the one which has been principally urged before me, and that, as being the decision of a Lord Chancellor, is binding upon me, notwithstanding the subsequent comments upon it of Lord St. Leonards in his writings. That case seems to me to have laid down this principle, that, as between equitable interests, the defence will not prevail where the circumstances are such as to require that this Court should determine the priorities between them. The classes of cases to which that defence will apply are other than that. Lord Westbury in the course of his judgment in that case said this (p. 215): " I take it to be a clear proposition that every conveyance of an equitable interest is an innocent conveyance, that is to say, the grant of a person entitled merely in equity passes only that which he is justly entitled to and no more. If, therefore, a person seised of an equitable interest (the legal estate being outstanding), makes an assurance by way of mortgage, or grants an annuity, and afterwards conveys the whole estate to a purchaser, he can grant to the purchaser that which he has, namely, the estate subject to the mortgage or annuity, and no more. The subsequent grantee takes only that which is left in the grantor. Hence grantees and incumbrancers claiming in equity take and are ranked according to the date of their securities, and the maxim applies, ' *Qui prior est tempore potior est jure.*' The first grantee is *potior* — that is, *potentior*. He has a better and superior — because a prior — equity." His Lordship then proceeded to explain the different classes of cases in which that defence is available, and the one which has been relied upon as bringing the case of the defendants within the decision of Lord Westbury is the third class, which is this, that " where there are circumstances that give rise to an equity as distinguished from an equitable estate — as, for example, an equity to set aside a deed for fraud, or to correct it for mistake — and the purchaser under the instrument maintains the plea of purchase for valuable consideration without notice, the Court will not interfere."

Now the question I have to determine is this, is the right of the parties to follow this money into the land an equitable estate or interest, or is it an equity as distinguished from an equitable estate? The decision of Lord Eldon many years ago appears to me to be perfectly conclusive upon the law. I refer to the case of Lewis *v.* Madocks, 17 Ves. 48, 57, where on further consideration directions had been given for an inquiry as to certain trust moneys which had gone into land, the wife claiming an interest in the land as against the heir; and Lord Eldon said this: " The claim of the wife is put in this way, that personal property bound by the trust or obligation, whatever it is called, of this bond is traced into the purchase of a real estate, which estate must therefore be hers; but I do not know any case in its circumstances sufficiently like this to authorize me to hold that doctrine. I am prepared to say that the personal estate bound by this obligation, and which has been laid out in this real estate, is personal property that may be demanded out of the real estate; that the estate is chargeable with it; but it was not so purchased with it, that the estate should be decreed to belong not to the heir but to the wife." In other words, his Lordship held that the estate descended to the heir subject to the charge. That charge appears to me to be a charge in equity, or, in other words, an equitable estate or interest. Very similar was the question which Vice-Chancellor Kindersley had to determine in the case of Rice *v.* Rice, 2 Drew. 73. He had there to adjudicate between two equities, one arising from the right of an unpaid seller to come upon the land, and the other arising by contract creating an equitable mortgage. It is a very leading and instructive case, in which the Vice-Chancellor considered very fully the application of the maxim, " *Qui prior est tempore potior est jure*," and laid it down thus: " To lay down the rule with perfect accuracy, I think it should be stated in some such form as this. As between persons having only equitable interests, if their equities are in all other respects equal, priority of time gives the better equity, or, ' *Qui prior est tempore potior est jure.*' " He then went on to consider and weigh the two equities set one against the other in that suit, and then he says: " Each of the parties in controversy has nothing but an equitable interest; the plaintiff's interest being a vendor's lien for unpaid purchase-money, and the defendant Ede having an equitable mortgage. Looking at these two species of equitable interests abstractedly and without reference to priority of time, or possession of the title deeds, or any other special circumstances, is there anything in their respective natures or qualities which would lead to the conclusion that in natural justice the one is better or more worthy or more entitled to protection than the other? Each of the two equitable interests arises out of the forbearance by the party of money due to him. There is, however, this difference between them, that the vendor's lien for unpaid purchase-money is a right created by a rule of equity without any special contract; the right of the equitable mortgagee is created by the special contract of the parties. I cannot say that in my opinion this constitutes any sufficient ground of preference, though, if it makes any difference at all, I should say it is rather in favour of the equitable mortgagee, inasmuch as there is no *constat* of the right of the vendor to his lien for unpaid purchase-money until it has been declared by a decree of a Court of Equity, whereas there is a clear *constat* of the equitable mortgagee's title immediately on the contract being made. But I do not see in this any sufficient ground for holding that the equitable mortgagee has the better equity."

In my judgment, the right of a vendor for the unpaid purchase-money is an equitable lien, and the right of the *cestuis que trust*, whose trust money has been invested in the lands, is also an equitable lien. I do not think I can really distinguish this equity from such an equitable lien as the Vice-Chancellor held to be in that case an equitable estate or interest of the same description as the equity of an equitable mortgagee. Therefore, I shall conclude that, within the case of Phillips v. Phillips, the interest of the plaintiff in this case is an equitable interest, and not merely an equity like the equity to set aside a deed, and therefore it must take its priority according to the priority of date.[1]

DUNCAN TOWNSITE COMPANY v. LANE.

SUPREME COURT OF THE UNITED STATES. 1917.

245 U. S. 308.

BRANDEIS, J. This is a petition for a writ of mandamus brought in the Supreme Court of the District of Columbia to compel the Secretary of the Interior to restore the name of Nicholas Alberson, deceased, to the rolls under the Choctaw-Chickasaw Agreement of July 1, 1902 (32 Stat. 641), and to execute and record a patent for land described in an allotment certificate issued in his name by the Dawes Commission.

Under that act only the names of persons alive September 25, 1902, were entitled to entry on the rolls. Alberson had died before that date. The entry of his name and the issue of the certificate were procured by fraud and perjury. These facts, now conceded, were established by the Commission to the Five Civilized Tribes; and the Secretary of the Interior upon recommendation of the Commission removed Alberson's name from the rolls, held the certificates for cancellation and allotted the land to others. Notice of the hearing before the Commission was given to Alberson's administrator and attorney of record, but not to the relator, who had,

[1] Beckett v. Cordley, 1 Bro. C. C. 353; Daubeny v. Cockburn, 1 Mer. 626; Re Vernon, 33 Ch. Div. 402; 32 Ch. D. 165 (*semble*); Carritt v. Real Co., 42 Ch. D. 263; Henry v. Black, 213 Pa. 620, *accord*.

Sturge v. Starr, 2 M. & K. 195; Lane v. Jackson, 20 Beav. 535; Penny v. Watts, 2 DeG. & Sm. 501; Re Ffrench's Est., 21 L. R. Ir. 283; Luckel v. Phillips Petroleum Co., 243 S. W. 1068 (Tex. 1922), 36 Harv. L. Rev. 480, *contra*.

In Cloutte v. Storey, [1911] 1 Ch. 18, a donee of a power of appointment of an equitable interest among a class having appointed fraudulently to a member of the class who sold the equitable interest to a *bona fide* purchaser, it was held that the *bona fide* purchaser does not prevail over the person entitled in default of appointment. See 24 Harv. L. Rev. 490. *Cf.* 12 Col. L. Rev. 156.

In Loring v. Goodhue, 259 Mass. 495, it was held that where an executor transferred a certificate of shares in a business trust to a dealer in order to obtain new certificates, and the dealer took new shares in his own name and wrongfully pledged them with one who had no notice of the wrong, the pledgee prevailed. See also Goodhue v. State Street Trust Co., 267 Mass. 28.

CHAP. IX.]   DUNCAN TOWNSITE COMPANY *v.* LANE   759

under the Oklahoma law, recorded the deed assigning the certificates and was in actual possession of the premises. The certificates had issued on or before April 7, 1906. The notation removing Alberson's name from the rolls was made January 11, 1908. The relator purchased the certificates before January 11, 1908, for value in good faith without knowledge of the fraud or notice of the proceedings for cancellation hereinbefore referred to. The Supreme Court entered judgment for the relator, commanding issue and record of the patent, but making no order in respect to restoring Alberson's name to the rolls. The relator acquiesced in the judgment; but on writ of error sued out by respondent the judgment was reversed by the Court of Appeals (44 App. D. C. 63); and the relator brings the case here on writ of error.

The nature of the Choctaw-Chickasaw Agreement and the rights incident to enrollment and allotment have been frequently considered by this court. Enrollment confers rights which cannot be taken away without notice and opportunity to be heard. Garfield *v.* Goldsby, 211 U. S. 249. Certificates of allotment, like receiver's receipts under the general land laws, entitle the holder to exclusive possession of the premises; Act of July 1, 1902, § 23, 32 Stat. 641–644; United States *v.* Detroit Lumber Co., 200 U. S. 321, 337–8. But enrollment and certificates may be cancelled by the Secretary of the Interior for fraud or mistake, Lowe *v.* Fisher, 223 U. S. 95; because although the equitable title had passed, Michigan Land and Lumber Co. *v.* Rust, 168 U. S. 589, 593, the land remains subject to the supervisory power of the Land Department, Knight *v.* Lane, 228 U. S. 6, until issue of the patent, United States *v.* Wildcat, 244 U. S. 111, unless under the statute the power expires earlier by lapse of time. Ballinger *v.* Frost, 216 U. S. 240. Under § 5 of the Act of April 26, 1906, c. 1876, 34 Stat. 137, the legal title can be conveyed only by a patent duly recorded. Brown *v.* Hitchcock, 173 U. S. 473, 478. The provision in § 23 of the Act of July 1, 1902, that "allotment certificates issued by the Commission to the Five Civilized tribes shall be conclusive evidence of the right of any allottee to the tract of land described therein" has relation to rights between the holder and third parties. The title conferred by the allotment is an equitable one, so that supervisory power remained in the Secretary of the Interior.

We are not required to decide whether (as suggested in Lowe *v.* Fisher, 223 U. S. 95, 107) the power to remove Alberson's name from the rolls had, because of § 2 of the Act of April 26, 1906, expired before the Secretary acted. For the Supreme Court of the District did not order the name restored, and its judgment was acquiesced in by the relator. The claim which the relator makes in this court rests wholly upon the fact that the relator was a *bona fide* purchaser for value. But the doctrine of *bona fide* purchaser for value applies only to purchasers of the legal estate. Hawley *v.*

Diller, 178 U. S. 476, 484. It "is in no respect a rule of property, but a rule of inaction." Pomeroy, Equity Jurisprudence, § 743. It is a shield by which the purchaser of a legal title may protect himself against the holder of an equity, not a sword by which the owner of an equity may overcome the holder of both the legal title and an equity. Boone v. Chiles, 10 Pet. 177, 210.

Mandamus is an extraordinary remedial process which is awarded, not as a matter of right, but in the exercise of a sound judicial discretion. It issues to remedy a wrong, not to promote one; to compel the performance of a duty which ought to be performed, not to direct an act which will work a public or private mischief or will be within the strict letter of the law but in disregard of its spirit. Although classed as a legal remedy, its issuance is largely controlled by equitable principles. The relator having itself only an equity seeks the aid of the court to clothe it with the legal title as against the United States, which now holds both the legal title and the equity to have set aside an allotment certificate secured by fraud. A writ of mandamus will not be granted for such a purpose. See Turner v. Fisher, 222 U. S. 204. The judgment of the Court of Appeals is

Affirmed.[1]

[1] Taylor v. Weston, 77 Cal. 534, *accord.*

If A agrees to sell land to B and B transfers his equitable interest to C, C will of course take subject to A's lien for the purchase price. Polk v. Gallant, 2 Dev. & B. Eq. (N. C.) 395; La Belle Coke Co. v. Smith, 221 Pa. 642; Stoner v. Hanis, 81 Va. 451. *Cf.* Dupont v. Wertheman, 10 Cal. 354.

Under the principles suggested by the principal case and the preceding cases, what would be the result in each of the following situations?

(1) X, the owner of Blackacre, contracts to sell Blackacre to A and subsequently contracts to sell it to B who pays the purchase price without notice of the contract with A. Before X conveys Blackacre to B, B has notice of the contract with A. Who prevails, A or B? Is it material that B obtains a conveyance after he has notice of A's claim? Is it material whether A paid the purchase price or not? Would the result be the same where X declares himself trustee for A and subsequently for B?

(2) A, the owner of Blackacre, contracts to sell Blackacre to X. The contract is procured by the fraud of X. X assigns his interest under the contract to B who pays value and has no notice of the fraud. Who prevails as between A and B? Would the result be different if A had been induced by the fraud of X to declare himself trustee for X who had then assigned his interest under the trust to B?

(3) X is trustee of Blackacre for Y. Y declares himself trustee of his equitable interest for A. Y subsequently conveys his equitable interest to B who pays value and has no notice of the rights of A. Who prevails as between A and B?

(4) X is trustee of Blackacre for A. By fraud Y induces A to assign to him his interest under the trust. Y then assigns his interest to B who pays value and has no notice of the fraud of Y. Who prevails as between A and B?

HILL v. PETERS.

HIGH COURT OF JUSTICE, CHANCERY DIVISION. 1918.

[1918] 2 Ch. 273.

ACTION WITH WITNESSES.

The plaintiffs in this action were R. Middleton Hill and A. Barker Basset, the executors and trustees of the will of Mrs. L. A. Gwyn; and the defendant, Mrs. Mary Jane Peters, was executrix and residuary legatee of her husband, P. H. Peters. The plaintiffs and the defendant respectively claimed to be entitled to a charge upon the same premises, and the question of priority arose.

The facts were not in dispute at the trial, and are taken from the judgment of the Court.

On September 29, 1897, Howell Powell Edwards and John Scott Heron, partners in the late firm of Edwards & Heron, solicitors, purported to advance out of moneys belonging to them on a joint account the sum of 4000*l.* to one Sydney Gotto on the security of his one undivided fifth share in the residuary personal estate of his father expectant on the death of his mother, then and still living. Notice of this mortgage was given to the trustees of the father's will on October 13, 1897. At or about the same time Edwards & Heron were about to complete a sale of property belonging to other clients, Philip Hall Peters (since deceased) and his wife, in respect of which a sum of 4800*l.* would be receivable by them on behalf of Mr. and Mrs. Peters. On October 18, 1897, Edwards wrote on behalf of his firm to Mr. Peters: " I enclose you a note of the securities which we have taken up for 4000*l.* as it would not wait, and which you can have if you like, until you are ready for the money to invest elsewhere." No document was identified as the inclosure, nor was any copy of Mr. Peters' reply to that letter produced; but its purport appeared from a receipt dated October 20, 1897, wherein the firm acknowledged having received from Philip H. Peters and wife the sum of 4800*l.* " for advance to Sydney Gotto 4000*l.* at two months' notice, and to repay trustees 800*l.*" On the same day Edwards & Heron executed a declaration of trust declaring themselves trustees of the Gotto mortgage debt and interest, and the security created by the mortgage of September 29, for Mr. and Mrs. Peters as joint tenants, and covenanted at any time, on request, to repay the 4000*l.* on two months' notice. On January 14, 1907, Edwards & Heron, through the agency and with the assistance of one Ernest Tompkins, raised the sum of 4000*l.* from another client, Mrs. L. A. Gwyn, a widow, on the security of Sydney Gotto's one-fifth, concealing from the mortgagee the existence of the declaration of trust in favour of Mr. and Mrs. Peters, and not disclosing to her the fact that Tompkins had no interest in the property, although posing as the mortgagor, and that his apparent title thereto was founded on a fictitious sale and assignment to one Ponsford, which sale and resale were alleged in paragraphs 3, 4, and 5 of the statement of claim. In February, 1907, Edwards & Heron paid off 2000*l.* to Mr. and Mrs. Peters. Down to that date they paid interest on the 4000*l.* to Mr. and Mrs. Peters, and thereafter, down to the death of Edwards in January, 1917, they paid interest on the 2000*l.* to Mr. Peters, and after his death in February, 1911, to Mrs. Peters. Mrs. Gwyn died in August, 1911. Edwards & Heron paid interest on the 4000*l.* advanced by her to Mrs. Gwyn during her lifetime and, after her death, to the plaintiffs, as her executors, down to the death of Edwards. In 1912 the plaintiffs obtained possession of the mortgage deed of September 29, 1897, of a fictitious and incomplete assurance to Tompkins of November 9, 1906, and of the mortgage to their testatrix. On July 6, 1917, they gave notice of the mortgage to their testatrix to the surviving trustee of Mr. Gotto's will, and in December, 1917, they learnt for the first time of the existence of the declaration of trust in favour of Mr. and Mrs. Peters.

In these circumstances the plaintiffs brought this action against Mrs. Peters, claiming a declaration of priority for the 4000*l.* advance made by their testatrix over the defendant's outstanding 2000*l.* The claim in the writ and statement of claim was based upon the assumption that the sales to and by Ponsford were genuine and real transactions, but, this assumption having been shown to be fallacious, the plaintiffs by their reply alleged that Mr. and Mrs. Peters had enabled Edwards & Heron to deal with the security of September 29, 1917, as absolute owners, (1.) by their conduct in taking a declaration of trust as security for the advance of 4000*l.* instead of an assignment of the mortgage of September 29, 1897; (2.) in permitting Edwards & Heron to retain possession of the mortgage deed; (3.) in omitting to have any notice of the declaration of trust indorsed on the mortgage deed; and (4.) in omitting to give any notice of the declaration of trust or of their interest in the mortgage security to Gotto's trustees.

EVE, J., after stating the facts substantially as set out above, continued: By their reply the plaintiffs have raised an alternative case, and rely upon four grounds as sufficient to displace the priority which the relative dates of the declaration of trust in favour of Mr. and Mrs. Peters and the mortgage to Mrs. Gwyn would confer upon the defendant. The first ground is that Mr. and Mrs. Peters, being absolute owners of the 4000*l.*, ought not to have constituted Edwards & Heron trustees for them of the security, but ought to have taken it in their own names either originally or by assignment and transfer from Edwards & Heron. The second ground is that, having constituted Edwards & Heron trustees of the security, they ought not to have left the security in the possession of the trustees. The third is that, having so left it, they ought to have insisted that there should be indorsed upon the mortgage deed notice of the declaration of trust, or of their interest in the moneys thereby secured. There is another and fourth ground which I will deal with separately, but, so far as the three grounds which I have enumerated are concerned, I do not consider that there is any substance in them.

There is nothing to prevent an individual, if he is so minded, from vesting any item of his property in another person as a trustee, and if he so does, the trustee is the proper custodian of the documents of title and other indicia of ownership. Moreover, the settlor is justified in adopting an attitude consistent with a belief on his part in the honesty of the individual whom he has appointed trustee. He is entitled to act on the footing that he has selected an honest man for the position, and not the less so because the person selected happens to be his own solicitor. Further, it is contrary to well-recognized practice to introduce into the transaction any notice of the existence of the trust by an indorsement on the title deeds or otherwise. If authority is needed for these several propositions, it is to be found in Cory v. Eyre, 1 D. J. & S. 149, 165, *In re* Richards, 45 Ch. D. 589, 594, 595, Shropshire Union Railways and Canal Co. v. Reg., L. R. 7 H. L. 496, 507, 508, Bradley v. Riches, 9 Ch. D. 189, and Carritt v. Real and Personal Advance Co., 42 Ch. D. 263, 269, 270.

The suggestion as to the propriety of indorsing notice on the security in the hands of the trustee was put forward in more than one of these cases, particularly in Bradley v. Riches, and in this connection it is not altogether immaterial to point out that in the mortgage deed of September 29 the mortgagees are recited as making the advance out of moneys belonging to them on a joint account, a statement calculated to some extent to raise a presumption that it was raised out of trust moneys, seeing that there is in fact no reference in the document to the moneys constituting any partnership investment. It may be, therefore, that the plaintiffs' testatrix, had she investigated the matter by independent solicitors, would have been put on inquiry and might then have come to learn the sources from which the moneys were obtained to make the advance. But the matter is not worth pursuing, as I am satisfied that there was no negligence on the part of Mr. and Mrs. Peters in forbearing to have the mortgage deed indorsed, as it is suggested they ought to have done.

The fourth ground upon which the plaintiffs rely is that Mr. and Mrs. Peters ought to have given notice of the declaration of trust, or of their interest in the mortgage security, to the trustees of the will of the elder Mr. Gotto. That ground is based upon the assertion, first, that the transaction between Edwards & Heron and Mr. and Mrs. Peters was in fact an equitable assignment, and not the creation of a trust, and, secondly, upon this wider ground, that, even if the true character of the transaction was the creation of a trust, the title of the defendant and her husband as *cestuis que trust* under the declaration could only be perfected, according to the rule in Dearle *v.* Hall, 3 Russ. 1, by notice to the trustees of the will of the elder Mr. Gotto. No such notice having been given, the plaintiffs claim that their security, of which notice was given on July 6, 1917, although posterior in date, is entitled to priority over the defendant's. In my opinion, the declaration of trust was not an assignment or transfer, but the creation of the relationship of trustee and *cestui que trust* as between Edwards & Heron and Mr. and Mrs. Peters. I see nothing in the deed, or in any of the documents produced, to warrant me in treating the transaction as one of any other character, or having any other effect. The proposition that the beneficiaries' title under the declaration required perfecting by notice is a very startling one, for which no authority has been cited, and which, as Mr. Adams frankly admitted, leads to this result — that whenever the trustees hold a chose in action of this nature as part of the trust estate each of the beneficiaries must give notice of his beneficial interest therein, or run the risk of being deprived thereof by some fraudulent transaction between his trustee and an assignee who does give notice. I cannot see any reason whatever for so extending the doctrine of Dearle *v.* Hall. I respectfully indorse the observations of Lord Macnaghten in Ward *v.* Duncombe, [1893] A. C. 369, as to the undesirability of doing anything to extend that doctrine to cases which are not already covered by it. The principle on which the rule in Dearle *v.* Hall is founded, which regards the giving of notice by the assignee as the nearest approach to the taking of possession, has no application, in my opinion, to the beneficiary who has no right to possession himself, and who can only assert his claim to receive through his trustee.

I confess I could have followed a suggestion that Mr. and Mrs. Peters ought possibly to have given notice to Sydney Gotto, the mortgagor; but this naturally has not been advanced, as the plaintiffs themselves have not given any such notice, and, even had they done so, it would not, in my opinion, have availed to give priority to their subsequent security. I do not think there is any more substance in the point founded on Dearle *v.* Hall, 3 Russ. 1, than in the other three points advanced in the reply.

The position, therefore, can be summed up shortly thus: Edwards & Heron, trustees for the defendant of an equitable interest in personalty, in breach of trust, in fraud of their *cestuis que trust* and for their own purposes, without disclosing the existence of the trust, purported to assign the interest by way of mortgage to the testatrix, and afterwards, in further breach of trust, handed over to her executors the instrument creating the interest. In so doing they have not displaced the defendant's priority: see Cory *v.* Eyre,

1 D. J. & S. 149, already referred to, and *In re* Vernon, Ewens & Co., 32 Ch. D. 165, 33 Ch. D. 402. The defendant has not done, or omitted to do, anything to forfeit that priority, and the *bona fides* of the testatrix which is in no way impugned, does not avail to place her later equity in a superior position to the earlier one of the defendant.

The result is that the action fails and must be dismissed with costs. The defendant is entitled on her counter-claim to a declaration of priority and the delivery up to her of the mortgage of September 29, 1897, and the plaintiffs must pay the costs of the counter-claim.

NEWMAN *v.* NEWMAN.
Chancery. 1885.
28 Ch. D. 674.

In the year 1869 a lease of the New Dynevor Colliery was made to certain persons, one being Michael Lewis Brown, who took three-eighths of the colliery, as to one moiety thereof for himself, and as to the other moiety in trust for Edwin Newman.

In 1871 Brown had made large advances for the colliery and to Edwin Newman, and pressed for payment. By a deed made in July, 1871, after reciting that Edwin Newman had a policy on his life for 3,000*l.*, and had assigned that and also his share in the colliery to his wife's mother, Sophie Storie Armstrong, by way of security for 5,700*l.*, it was witnessed that Mrs. Armstrong and Edwin Newman assigned the policy and Edwin Newman's one moiety of three-eighths of the colliery to Brown by way of security for the repayment to him of 3,180*l.*, and subject thereto for Mrs. Armstrong.

Edwin Newman was dead, and a sum representing the 3,000*l.* due under the policy had been paid into Court. Brown had sold the shares in the colliery, and had a balance of 850*l.* arising from the sale.

This action was brought by Violet Ida Newman, one of the children of Edwin Newman, against Brown and against the administrator of Mrs. Armstrong (who was dead), claiming as against Brown that a certain sum of 5,700*l.* had priority over his charge on the colliery shares and on the policy money; and that he might be declared a trustee of the colliery shares as to the 5,700*l.* The plaintiff's case was as follows: —

By an indenture of settlement dated the 24th of September, 1856, made on the marriage of Edwin Newman with Mrs. Armstrong's daughter, certain funds were assigned to three trustees on the usual trusts for Mrs. Newman, Edwin Newman, and their children, of whom the plaintiff, Violet Ida Newman, was one.

The other trustees died or retired, and in 1866 Mrs. Armstrong was appointed sole trustee. The dealings as to the trust funds between Mrs. Armstrong and Edwin Newman were very complicated and obscure, but it was clear that Edwin Newman had borrowed more than 5,000*l*. of the trust money from Mrs. Armstrong; and, according to the case of the plaintiff, the 5,700*l*. due by Edwin Newman to Mrs. Armstrong, as stated in the mortgage to Brown, was the fund so borrowed and was subject to the trusts of the settlement; and then the shares in the colliery and the policy had been assigned by Edwin Newman to Mrs. Armstrong by way of security for the trust money which had been advanced by her to Edwin Newman.

Brown alleged that he took his charge without any notice whatever of the settlement, and that he thought and still believed that the 5,700*l*. was the money of Mrs. Armstrong. . . .

NORTH, J., after fully stating the complicated facts, and referring to the obscurity of the transactions, continued: —

Now out of that state of facts the questions between the parties arise in this way. First, as regards the shares in the colliery, and, secondly, as regards the policy moneys, which stand in rather different positions.[1] As to the colliery, the question is whether, assuming the 5,700*l*. to have been trust money, Brown's charge is prior or subsequent to the charge of the 5,700*l*. It is quite clear that Brown had no notice whatever of the money being trust money, if in fact it was. [His Lordship then referred to some of the evidence.] Therefore it comes to this. Brown has got the legal estate, and he had it prior to the charge in 1871. He took that security without notice of any prior charge. But then it is said that there was already a charge in favor of Mrs. Armstrong, and that the plaintiff for whom she was trustee and who claims under her has a charge prior to Brown's. Brown's answer to that is: "I have the legal estate; and I had no notice of any trust actual or constructive. There was nothing whatever to put me upon any inquiry. I dealt with persons who represented this property to be their own, and I had no notice of any sort that either of them was a trustee. I have clearly got a good charge and I have the legal estate. I cannot now be told that my interest is to be postponed to the plaintiff's when I had the legal estate and dealt with the only persons I knew or could know." It appears to me that even if the 5,700*l*. is trust money he is entitled to succeed upon that defence.

The cases in which a second equitable incumbrancer without notice has got in the legal estate and has protected himself are very numerous and well-known. But it is said that the present does not come within these cases, because Brown was the trustee of the leasehold interest, and held it in trust for the real owners whoever they

[1] So much of the case as relates to the policy moneys is omitted, as well as the arguments of counsel.

were; and that he cannot be heard to say that his own charge which was subsequent in date ought to have priority over the charges of the persons for whom he is trustee. But he is trustee without any notice whatever of any charge, and he dealt with persons who were treated throughout as the only persons interested in the estate. Is there anything to prevent a trustee from dealing with his only known *cestui que trust,* and then taking advantage of the legal estate which he does not get in afterwards but has already?

There are two cases to which I will refer. One is Phipps *v.* Lovegrove, L. R. 16 Eq. 80. The Lord Justice James, sitting for Vice-Chancellor Wickens, says in his judgment: " The trustees at the request and by the direction of the only *cestuis que trust* of whom they had any notice or knowledge whatever, dealt with the funds; and it appears to me, upon more than one ground, that any person claiming under the same *cestuis que trust* has no right to make any claim against them. It is a rule and principle of this Court, and of every Court, I believe, that where there is a *chose in action,* whether it is a debt or an obligation, or a trust fund, and it is assigned, the person who holds that debt or obligation, or has undertaken to hold the trust fund, has, as against the assignee, exactly the same equities that he would have as against the assignor. Down to the date at which the notice of assignment was given to the trustees, the trustees were at liberty to deal with the fund, and to have equities created in their favor by the *cestuis que trust,* until they received notice that some other person had come in and displaced those equities. An insurance office might lend money upon a policy of insurance to a person who had insured his life, notwithstanding any previous assignment by him of the policy, of which no notice had been given to them. Trustees who have got a legal estate, or an estate of any kind, either money or land, may lend money to the *cestuis que trust,* and get a beneficial interest in the trust property, if they have no notice that there have been any prior incumbrances. They have got the legal estate and they have got the legal right; they have therefore got, in respect of the charge created in their favor, before they have got any notice of anything else, a right to retain that which the law has given them." Now it is admitted that this is quite in point, but it was said that the passage referring to trustees who have got the legal estate is merely an illustration by way of *dictum,* and is not necessary for the decision of the case. To a certain extent that is true, but it is an illustration in point and bears upon what the learned judge decided, and it shows his opinion upon the matter to be that a trustee who had got the legal estate could deal with the *cestui que trust* by buying his interest or making an advance, and could maintain that charge against a prior incumbrancer on the ground that he held the legal estate, provided always that it was without notice.

The case of Browne *v.* Savage, 4 Drew. 635, seems to me very much in point, though it does not refer to the legal estate. There Kindersley, V. C., decided that an assignment by one trustee to another gave that trustee notice, and that at any rate during the life of that trustee the notice so given was all that was necessary, and so it has been held in subsequent cases, of which Willes *v.* Greenhill, 29 Beav. 376, is one. The fact that the trustee to whom the assignment was made gave no notice till afterwards to the third trustee was immaterial. It was held that the trustee was competent to deal with the *cestui que trust*, and to get a good charge in priority to other charges of which he had no notice, though he was trustee of the fund for the owners of it, including persons in favor of whom charges had been made of which notice had not been given.

Some little doubt has been thrown upon that case by the remark of Lord St. Leonards in a note to Vendors and Purchasers (14th ed. p. 379). He says: " There is a mistake in the dates; they do not agree with the priorities ordered." But I have looked very carefully at the case, and it seems to me that the note by Lord St. Leonards is inaccurate, and he seems to have confused the notices, and to have thought that the notice given by the second trustee to the third on the 30th of July, 1858, was the ruling notice, whereas the true ruling notice as regards the mortgage of 1858 by Savage to the second trustee was not of that date, but was the assignment itself, which was dated the 29th of March, 1858. It seems to me that the decision of Kindersley, V. C., was quite accurate, and that the priorities were given according to what he decided to be the right order of the notices. It appears to me, therefore, upon these authorities, that the trustee is entitled to hold the leasehold interest as security for what is due to him in priority to any claim by any *cestui que trust*, even assuming the 5,700*l.* to have been trust money.[1] . . .

[1] In Jenkinson *v.* N. Y. Finance Co., 79 N. J. Eq. 247, it was held that if the *cestui que trust* makes an assignment of his interest and then borrows a part of the trust fund from the trustee who has no notice of the assignment, the assignee takes subject to the trustee's right to deduct the amount loaned. See also *Re* Knapman, 18 Ch. D. 300. *Cf.* Bolton *v.* Curre, [1895] 1 Ch. 544.

Conversely the trustee is safe in paying an assignee of the equitable interest who obtained the assignment by fraud, if the trustee has no notice of the fraud. Lovato *v.* Catron, 20 N. Mex. 168; L. R. A. 1915E 451.

But if the trustee by mistake pays one who has never been authorized by the *cestui que trust* to receive payment, the trustee is liable to the *cestui que trust*. Perry, Trusts, sec. 927.

A trustee paying the assignee of an equitable *chose* in action when he should know of a prior equity, because it appears on the face of the assignment, is liable to the person holding the prior equity. Davis *v.* Hutchings, [1907] 1 Ch. 356.

CHAPTER X.
THE TERMINATION OF A TRUST.

DALY v. FARRELL.

SUPREME JUDICIAL COURT, MASSACHUSETTS. 1925.

252 Mass. 569.

BILL IN EQUITY, filed in the Superior Court on November 8, 1923, seeking an accounting and conveyance in accordance with the provisions of the trust deed described in the opinion.

In her answer, the defendant alleged " that the deed was procured by one Joseph B. Moran through misrepresentation, and that the said Ellen Farrell afterwards disaffirmed the transfer . . . that the said Ellen Farrell disaffirmed the trust deed of August, 1905, and in April, 1912, said Ellen Farrell duly executed a will, bequeathing one thousand dollars to the Complainant, Theresa Daly, and all the rest and residue of her estate to the Respondent, Nellie A. F. Farrell."

The suit was heard by *Morton*, J., a commissioner having been appointed under Equity Rule 35 to take the evidence. Material evidence before the judge is described in the opinion. By his order a final decree directing conveyance to the plaintiffs of property in Boston in accordance with the deed was entered. The defendant appealed.

SANDERSON, J. Ellen Farrell, the mother of the plaintiffs and defendant, executed a deed dated August 14, 1905, conveying to the defendant, as trustee, two parcels of land, one in Cambridge and one in Boston. The terms of the trust as stated in the deed were, in part, to pay to Ellen Farrell during her life the net rents and profits and at her death to convey two fifths of the estate to the defendant, two fifths to the plaintiff Theresa E. Daly, and one fifth to the plaintiff Anna M. Moran; with a provision that $300 should be paid out of the estate to her son John P. Farrell, and $1 to her son James F. Farrell. The grantee was given a power of sale and in October, 1910, sold the Cambridge real estate. It appeared that in 1912 the grantor executed and caused to be recorded in the registry of deeds a paper purporting to revoke the deed of trust to the defendant, and stating that the deed was made to evade the law as to wills. At about the same time she made a will, and she died February 2, 1923.

The plaintiffs bring this bill to compel the defendant to convey to them their respective interests in the remaining real estate, in accordance with the terms of the deed of trust. The defendant alleges in her answer that the deed to her was procured by the misrepresentation of Joseph B. Moran, and that it was afterwards disaffirmed by Ellen Farrell. The judge who heard the case found that there were no misrepresentations made, but that on the contrary the grantor executed the deed in full knowledge and understanding of its contents and that the deed carried out her express intention to protect herself and her daughters from a possible undue generosity on her part to a son; that the deed does not on its face indicate a purpose to evade the testamentary laws of the State, as claimed by the mother in her written disaffirmation, and was not so intended by her; and that the " disaffirmance " without the consent of the beneficiaries, which was not given, was ineffective and the defendant must account for such of the real estate conveyed to her, as was claimed by the plaintiff at the hearing.

A final decree was entered requiring the defendant to execute and deliver to the plaintiffs deeds in accordance with the provisions of the trust deed. The material questions of fact have been decided against the defendant's contention, upon evidence admitted without objection. The deed to the trustee established a valid trust and there was no power of revocation reserved.

Decree affirmed with costs.

AYLSWORTH *v.* WHITCOMB.

SUPREME COURT, RHODE ISLAND. 1879.

12 R. I. 298.

BILL IN EQUITY to terminate a voluntary trust created by the complainant for his own benefit and to obtain a reconveyance of the trust property.

POTTER, J. By deed of trust dated July 31, 1875, the complainant, then just twenty-one years of age, conveyed certain real estate and any balance of personal estate he might have to the respondent, his former guardian, to hold to him his heirs and successors in the trust — in trust to take possession and manage, &c., and once in six months to pay over the income to the complainant or his order, and for his use during life, and on his decease to convey the same to such persons as by will he should appoint, " and in default of such will to my heirs at law, according to the statutes of descent then in force."

The complainant alleges that he made the deed at the urgency of his friends, who expressed a fear that he might waste his property; that he executed it under the impression that it was a temporary provision, and that he could revoke it, and that the trustee also acted upon the same understanding; and the prayer of the bill is that a reconveyance may be ordered. The trustee has answered, admitting that the deed was executed on the belief and understanding by both parties that it was revocable. It further appears that there is no personal estate remaining, and that the real estate was at the date of the deed, and is now, subject to mortgage.

This settlement was a voluntary one without any consideration. It is true the instrument contains no power of revocation, but according to the weight of modern authority, this is only a circumstance to be taken into account and is not decisive, and where a deliberate intent to make it irrevocable does not appear, the absence of the power will be *primâ facie* evidence of mistake. . . .

Decree ordering reconveyance.[1]

In re SELOUS.

THOMSON v. SELOUS.

HIGH COURT OF JUSTICE, CHANCERY DIVISION. 1901.

[1901] 1 Ch. 921.

ORIGINATING SUMMONS. A testator who died on September 24, 1890, bequeathed a leasehold messuage to a trustee in trust for two

[1] As a general rule a trust once completely and validly created, whether by a declaration of trust or by a transfer in trust, cannot be revoked by the settlor unless he has reserved a power of revocation. Brown v. Mercantile Trust Co., 87 Md. 377; Ames, 233; Perry, Trusts, sec. 104; 19 Mich. L. Rev. 420; 38 A. L. R. 941; Dec. Dig., Trusts, sec. 59.

If, however, a power of revocation is omitted by mistake, the settlor may revoke the trust. Atkinson v. Atkinson, 157 Md. 648. By the weight of authority the mere absence of a clause reserving a power of revocation raises no presumption that it was omitted by a mistake. Sands v. Old Colony Trust Co., 195 Mass. 575; Coolidge v. Loring, 235 Mass. 220; 38 A. L. R. 941, 1005.

In England an assignment for the benefit of creditors is revocable until assented to by one or more of the creditors. Granard v. Lauderdale, 3 Sim. 1; Johns v. James, 8 Ch. D. 744; Ellis & Co. v. Cross, [1915] 2 K. B. 654. By the weight of authority the rule is otherwise in the United States. Burrill, Assignments, 6 ed., chap. 27; Perry, Trusts, sec. 593.

As to the distinction between trust and agency, see Sayer v. Wynkoop, 246 N. Y. 54, *ante*.

If the settlor reserves a power of revocation in a particular manner he can revoke only in that manner. Richardson v. Stephenson, 193 Wis. 89, 26 Mich. L. Rev. 586; 38 A. L. R. 941, 961. In Dickerson's Appeal, 115 Pa. 198, it was held that though the settlor reserved a general power of revocation he could not revoke by will. See Kelley v. Snow, 185 Mass. 288; Mayer v. Tucker, 102 N. J. Eq. 524; 38 A. L. R. 941; Dec. Dig., Trusts, sec. 59(4).

The intention to reserve a power of revocation may not be expressed but may appear from the circumstances as in the case of trusts of bank deposits. See 43 Harv. L. Rev. 540. See Chap. II, sec. IV, and particularly Matter of Totten, 179 N. Y. 112, *ante*.

The reservation of a power of revocation does not make a trust testamentary. See Chap. II, sec. IV, and particularly Jones v. Old Colony Trust Co., 251 Mass. 309, *ante*.

Rescission or reformation. A trust can be rescinded or reformed upon the same grounds, such as fraud, duress, undue influence or mistake, as are sufficient grounds for the rescission or reformation of a transfer of property. 38 A. L. R. 941, 974; Dec. Dig., Trusts, secs. 45–50, 56, 57.

of his daughters in equal shares as tenants in common. By an indenture dated June 24, 1895, and made between the trustee of the one part and the daughters of the other part, after reciting the above bequest and reciting that the daughters had requested the trustee to execute such assignment to them of the said messuage as was thereinafter expressed, it was witnessed that the trustee, at the request and by the direction of the daughters, assigned the messuage to the daughters to hold the same unto the daughters as joint tenants for the residue of the lease, the daughters entering into a joint covenant with the trustee to pay the rent and perform the covenants of the lease, and to indemnify the trustee against all claims on account of the same.

One of the daughters having died on September 15, 1900, this summons was issued to determine (*inter alia*) whether an equitable moiety of the leasehold messuage belonged to her estate, or whether the entirety belonged to the surviving daughter.

Jason Smith, for the deceased daughter's executors. The assignment of June 24, 1895, only created a joint tenancy of the legal estate, the daughters holding that estate in trust for themselves as tenants in common. The equitable estate did not merge in the legal estate, as these estates were not coextensive, or commensurate, or of the same quality.

It is a common practice to convey freeholds and leaseholds to partners as joint tenants in trust for themselves as part of their co-partnership estate: 1 Key and Elphinstone's Conveyancing, 6th ed. 405; and it has never been suggested that they become joint tenants in equity. We are therefore entitled to the equitable interest in one moiety of the messuage.

T. T. Methold, for the surviving daughter. Where equitable and legal estates, equal and coextensive, unite in the same person, the former merges: Selby *v.* Alston, 3 Ves. 339; Lee *v.* Lee, 4 Ch. D. 175; *In re* Douglas, 28 Ch. D. 327. The same rule must apply where they unite in two persons, and for the purpose of merger a tenancy in common must be treated as equal and coextensive with a joint tenancy. The surviving daughter is, therefore, entitled to the entirety.

Rayner Goddard and *Bovill*, for other parties to the summons.

FARWELL, J. In my opinion the assignment of June 24, 1895, created a joint tenancy in law and equity. It has been contended that it only created a joint tenancy of the legal estate, and that the equitable tenancy in common remained unaffected, the daughters merely holding the legal estate as joint tenants in trust for themselves as tenants in common. But I do not think that is the true view. The rule in Selby *v.* Alston, namely, that where equitable and legal estates, equal and coextensive, unite in the same person, the former merges, or, in other words, that a person cannot be trustee for himself, applies to a case where such estates unite in two or more persons. The only doubt I felt was whether the advantage of a tenancy in common over a joint tenancy raised any presumption against merger. But the difference in interest between these two estates is so small and shadowy that I do not think it would be sufficient to raise that presumption. I hold that two or more persons cannot be trustees for themselves for an estate coextensive with their legal estate.[1]

[1] Connolly v. Connolly, 1 I. R. Eq. 376 (holding that where one of two equitable joint tenants becomes trustee, the joint tenancy is severed). See Tilton v. Davidson, 98 Me. 55; Cooper v. Cooper, 5 N. J. Eq. 9; Bullis v. Pitman, 90 N. J. Eq. 88; Greene v. Greene, 125 N. Y. 506. But see Harris v. Harris, 205 Pa. 460 (holding that where property was given to four persons upon trust for the four until all should agree upon a division of the property, the trust could only be ended by the consent of all four).

A trust is terminated when the sole beneficiary has the legal title. Langley v. Conlan, 212 Mass. 135; Kronson v. Lipschitz, 68 N. J. Eq. 367; Odom v. Morgan, 177 N. C. 367; Ann. Cas. 1918A 481. This happens where the trustee surrenders the legal title to the *cestui que trust* (Miller v. Simonton, 5 S. C. 20); or where the *cestui que trust* releases to the trustee (Newman v. Newman, 28 Ch. D. 674, *ante*; Owings v. Owings, 3 Ind. 142; Ormsby v. Dumesnil, 91 Ky. 601); or where the trustee and *cestui que trust* convey to a third person. Parker v. Converse, 5 Gray (Mass.) 336.

In Cunningham v. Bright, 228 Mass. 385, it was held that a Massachusetts business trust was extinguished by merger when the trustee acquired the whole beneficial interest. See 29 Yale L. Jour. 97.

But if one of several beneficiaries becomes the legal owner, there will be no merger. Burbach v. Burbach, 217 Ill. 547; Miller v. Rosenberger, 144 Mo. 292. But see Wills v. Cooper, 25 N. J. L. 137 (interest subject to execution). So if a beneficiary for life becomes legal owner there will be no merger. Spengler v. Kuhn, 212 Ill. 186. See Losey v. Stanley, 147 N. Y. 560. But see Weeks v. Frankel, 197 N. Y. 304.

If the beneficiary becomes one of several trustees, there will be no merger. See Story v. Palmer, 46 N. J. Eq. 1 (note); Robertson v. de Brulatour, 188 N. Y. 301; Ann. Cas. 1918A 481.

If a testator devises land to his wife in trust for their son, and dies, and the wife later dies intestate, leaving the son as her sole heir, the trust is extinguished; and if the son later dies intestate his heirs *ex parte materna* are entitled to the land both legally and beneficially. Goodright v. Wells, 2 Doug. 771; Doe v. Putt, 2 Doug. 773 (cited); Wade v. Paget, 1 Bro. C. C. 363, 1 Cox 74 s. c.; Selby v. Alston, 3 Ves. 339; Langley v. Sneyd, 1 S. & S. 45; Creagh v. Blood, 3 Jon. & Lat. 133; *Re* Douglas, 28 Ch. D. 327; Nicholson v. Halsey, 1 John. Ch. (N. Y.) 417; Shepard v. Taylor, 15 R. I. 204; Ames, 448n.; 3 Preston, Conveyancing, 3 ed., 328–341.

Spendthrift trusts. A spendthrift trust is valid although one of the beneficiaries of the trust is one of the trustees. Vellacott v. Murphy, 16 F.(2d) 700; Maryland Grange Agency v. Lee, 72 Md. 161; Cummings v. Corey, 58 Md. 494; Overman's Appeal, 88 Pa. 276; Dunglison's Estate, 201 Pa. 592; Denniston v. Pierce, 260 Pa. 129; Thomas v. House, 145 Va. 742. See note to Broadway Nat. Bank v. Adams, 133 Mass. 170, *ante*.

In Fox's Estate, 264 Pa. 478, property was given to a man upon a spendthrift trust for himself for life with remainder to his children; it was held that a valid spendthrift trust was created.

In Hance's Estate, 69 Pa. Super. Ct. 432, a testator gave property to his two sons as trustees to pay income to themselves during their lives, with spendthrift provisions. It was held that a valid spendthrift trust was created. But see Somers v. O'Brien, 129 Kan. 24.

BROOKS v. DAVIS.

Court of Chancery, New Jersey. 1913.

82 N. J. Eq. 118.

Final hearing on bill to terminate a trust under a will.

Leaming, V. C. The bill discloses that the will of Lenora Flowers directs that her real and personal estate be held in trust by her executor, defendant herein, during the lifetime of Aaron Kraft, grandson of testatrix; that the executor is directed to pay to the grandson $4 per week, during his lifetime, from the income of the property, and to pay to him the entire net income of the property during his lifetime in the event of the decease of his wife; that at his death the entire trust estate is to go to certain designated devisees; that since the decease of testatrix complainant has purchased from the life *cestui que trust* his rights under the will, and has also purchased from the several devisees their several rights, and by virtue of such purchases is now the sole and only person interested in the estate. The bill prays that the trust may be terminated and that an accounting may be had and the entire estate turned over to complainant.

A demurrer has been filed by defendant, and in support of the demurrer, it is claimed that the equitable life estate of Aaron Kraft is not assignable and that this court is without jurisdiction. . . .

It is urged in behalf of demurrant that the provision of the will above quoted creates a spendthrift trust in behalf of Aaron Kraft, and that his rights under such a trust are inalienable.

It is clearly unnecessary to here determine whether, or to what extent, in this state a testator may lawfully exempt an equitable life estate created by his will from voluntary or involuntary alienation by the *cestui que trust*. In Camden Safe Deposit and Trust Co. v. Schellinger, 78 N. J. Eq. (8 Buch.) 138, I had occasion to refer to the conflict between what is known as the English rule and the rule which has been adopted by some of the American states, and to suggest that our court of last resort has not, so far as I am aware, been called upon to determine the rule that controls in this state. . . .

But should the most liberal views in support of the right of restraint against alienation be here adopted it is apparent that the terms of the will annexed to the bill in this case are inadequate to accomplish that result. An examination of the authorities collected in the above citations will disclose that the view is adopted with entire uniformity that to create a restraint against alienation it must clearly appear that such was the intention of the testator or donor. Cases are to be found to the effect that a provision exempting the gift from claims of creditors of the donee or a provision that the gift was for the support of the donee may include by implication a provision against voluntary alienation, but it will be observed that in the will here in question no provision in any way suggests a purpose on the part of testator to restrict the donee's powers over the gift, unless the direction for small weekly payments may be held to indicate that purpose. I think it clear, however, that that circumstance cannot properly be held to justify a provision against alienation to be read into the will.

In the absence of an express or implied provision against alienation the assignment from Aaron Kraft to complainant must, under the averments of the bill, be sustained.

The entire estate having at this time become vested in complainant, there can be no doubt of the jurisdiction of this court to grant the relief sought. Huber v. Donoghue, 49 N. J. Eq. (4 Dick.) 125.

I will advise a decree overruling the demurrer.[1]

[1] It was held in the following cases that where a trust was created for successive beneficiaries and one of them acquired by purchase or inheritance the interest of the others, or where all joined in a demand for the termination of the trust, the court would order a termination of the trust. Tilton v. Davidson, 98 Me. 55; Brillhart v. Mish, 99 Md. 447; Whall v. Converse, 146 Mass. 345; Sears v. Choate, 146 Mass. 395; Simmons v. Northwestern T. Co., 136 Minn. 357; Donaldson v. Allen, 182 Mo. 626; McKiernan v. McKiernan, 74 Atl. 289 (N. J. Eq. 1909); L'Hommedieu v. L'Hommedieu, 98 N. J. Eq. 554; Pedrajas v. Bloomfield Trust Co., 101 N. J. Eq. 803; Stafford's Estate, 258 Pa. 595; Thomas v. Rhode Island Hospital Trust Co., 50 R. I. 369; Thom v. Thom, 95 Va. 413; Ann. Cas. 1915B 723; 2 A. L. R. 579; 37 A. L. R. 1420.

The trust will not be continued merely for the benefit of the trustee. Eakle v. Ingram, 142 Cal. 15; Fox v. Fox, 250 Ill. 384; Slater v. Hurlbut, 146 Mass. 308; Robbins v. Smith, 72 Oh. St. 1, 19 (*semble*); Armistead v. Hartt, 97 Va. 316.

After the lapse of a long interval of time after the fulfillment of the purposes of the trust, a conveyance by the trustee to the *cestui que trust* may be presumed. Miller v. Cramer, 48 S. C. 282; Blake v. O'Neal, 63 W. Va. 483, 494. Compare the English cases of satisfied attendant terms, *e.g.*, Goodtitle v. Jones, 7 T. R. 45.

If the purpose for which a trust is created has been accomplished or has become impossible of accomplishment or if the continuance of the trust is unnecessary to carry out the purpose, the court may order a termination of the trust. See Estate of Cornils, 167 Iowa 196, L. R. A. 1915E 762 (divorce of married beneficiary); McNeer v. Patrick, 93 Neb. 746 (divorce of married beneficiary); Dodson v. Ball, 60 Pa. 492 (death of husband of beneficiary); Nightingale v. Nightingale, 13 R. I. 113 (statute emancipating married women). See 38 A. L. R. 941, 1021; 45 A. L. R. 743; Dec. Dig., Trusts, sec. 61. But see Anderson v. Kemper, 116 Ky. 339 (reformation of inebriate beneficiary, but trust did not refer to inebriation as reason for creation of trust); Carpenter v. Carpenter's Trustee, 119 Ky. 582 (similar case as to paralytic).

If on the termination of the trust the legal title remains in the trustee, the trustee is under a duty to convey it to the person entitled to it. By the terms of the instrument creating the trust, or by the Statute of Uses, the trustee may be divested of the title, or the trustee may have taken only a limited estate which terminates when the purposes of the trust are accomplished. Hinds v. Hinds, 126 Me. 521. See Chap. I, sec. I, and particularly Hooper v. Felgner, 80 Md. 262, *ante*.

MATTER OF LENSMAN.

SURROGATE'S COURT, BRONX COUNTY, NEW YORK. 1930.

137 N. Y. Misc. 77.

APPLICATION by Anna Schatchen for advance payment of part of principal of trust fund in which respondent trustee asks for construction of will.

HENDERSON, S. On this application for a payment of part of the principal of a trust fund, the respondent trustee asks for a construction of the will of the decedent, who died July 7, 1924.

The testator gave one-half of his residuary estate in trust to his trustee to receive and pay the income thereof to his sister, the petitioner, until she attains the age of sixty years or becomes a widow prior to that time. Upon the happening of either event he gives her the remainder thereof. Upon her prior death, he gives such remainder to his brother.

The brother consents to such payment, but the petitioner is only fifty-four years old and is still married.

The trust thus created is one to receive the income, rent, revenue and profit thereof and apply them to the use of another person, and is indestructible. (Pers. Prop. Law, § 15, as amd. by Laws of 1911, chap. 327; Real Prop. Law, § 103.)

The right of the petitioner to receive this income cannot be merged in the remainder, so as to terminate the trust, or so as to permit payment of any part of the principal to her. (Matter of Lee, 114 Misc. 511.)

The purpose of the statute is to permit a testator to provide for the support of an improvident person and to place it beyond the reach of such person to defeat the purpose of the trust by alienating and squandering the principal. (Matter of Wentworth, 230 N. Y. 176, 185.) Coupled with this purpose in the present instance is the manifest intention of the testator that his sister should not control any part of the principal during the lifetime of her husband before she reaches the age specified.

The policy of our courts has been to protect trust estates, to carry out the valid will of the testator, and to resist attempts by improvident beneficiaries to obtain their estates outright. (Matter of Harriman, 124 Misc. 320, 324; affd., 217 App. Div. 733.) To permit the petitioner to take any part of the principal at this time would be directly in contravention of the wishes of the testator as expressed in his will. The application is denied. Settle order accordingly.[1]

---

[1] Although the beneficiary of a spendthrift trust acquires the equitable remainder or obtains the consent of the equitable remainderman to the termination of the trust, he cannot compel a termination of the trust. Bowlin v. Citizens Bank & T. Co., 131 Ark. 97; Mason v. Rhode Island Hospital T.

WELCH v. EPISCOPAL THEOLOGICAL SCHOOL.

SUPREME JUDICIAL COURT, MASSACHUSETTS. 1905.

189 Mass. 108.

MORTON, J. This is a petition by the plaintiffs as trustees under the will and codicil of Benjamin T. Reed praying that the trust may be terminated as to two thirds of the property held by them in trust, and that they may be authorized and directed to convey the same to the Trustees of the Episcopal Theological School who are the ultimate beneficiaries of the whole of the trust property. The said Benjamin T. Reed left a widow, and a son who was his sole heir and next of kin. By a codicil to his will he gave the rest and residue of his estate to trustees in trust first to make up out of the income any deficiency of income from property given in trust for his wife if the same did not amount to $15,000 in any one year, and then to divide the rest of the income into three equal shares, one to be paid to his wife for life, one to the son or the son's wife for life and the other to the theological school. On the decease of the testator's wife two thirds of the income were to be paid to the school and the other third was to be paid to the son and his wife or the survivor of them during their lives. On the decease of the son and his wife leaving children of the son the trustees were to convey one third of the principal to such children, and if the testator's wife should then have deceased, the other two thirds to the school. If the son and his wife should decease leaving no children of the son, and the testator's wife should also have deceased, then the trustees were to convey the residue to the school. At the time of the testator's death the son was married. His wife afterwards died and he married the defendant Martha S. Reed and died without children. A question arose as to whether the present Mrs. Reed was entitled under the codicil as the wife or widow of the son. An agreement of compromise was entered into between the widow of the son and the school in which the school recognized and conceded that she was entitled to the rights of the widow of the son for her life, and she agreed that on the death of the testator's widow the principal of the trust fund should be divided into three equal parts two of which

---

Co., 78 Conn. 81; Dale v. Guaranty Trust Co., 168 N. Y. App. Div. 601; Matter of Perry, 126 N. Y. Misc. 616; Moore's Estate, 198 Pa. 611; Moser's Estate, 270 Pa. 217; Hays's Estate, 288 Pa. 348; Cook's Estate, 6 Pa. D. & C. 260; Winters v. March, 139 Tenn. 496.

In National Shawmut Bank v. Fitzpatrick, 256 Mass. 125, it was held that on the compromise of a contest of a will containing a spendthrift trust the trust can be eliminated. But see Cuthbert v. Chauvet, 136 N. Y. 326. Compare Fisher v. Fisher, 253 N. Y. 260, 69 A. L. R. 918; Schnebly, Extinguishment of Contingent Future Interests by Decree and Without Compensation, 44 Harv. L. Rev. 378.

should be conveyed to the school and the other should continue to be held in trust for her benefit for life and then go to the school. The testator's widow has now deceased and the son's widow and the school and the trustees are all desirous that the trust should be terminated as to the two thirds and the agreement between the son's widow and the school carried out as therein provided.

There is no doubt about the power of this court to terminate a trust in a proper case. Williams v. Thacher, 186 Mass. 293. Matthews v. Thompson, 186 Mass. 14. Sears v. Choate, 146 Mass. 395. There is also no doubt that a trust may be terminated as to certain property and continued as to other property. Williams v. Thacher, 186 Mass. 293, 300. Inches v. Hill, 106 Mass. 575. All that the trustees are required to do in the present case is to hold the property and pay over the income. They are not required to exercise an active discretion as in Danahy v. Noonan, 176 Mass. 467. The scheme of the trust is very different from that in Young v. Snow, 167 Mass. 287, and does not contemplate, as that did, the accumulation of income by the trustees and the expenditure by them of so much of it as might be necessary to keep the estate in repair. The case also differs from Claflin v. Claflin, 149 Mass. 19, and Hoffman v. New England Trust Co., 187 Mass. 205. The school is the equitable owner of the whole trust estate. It is entitled to the present income of two thirds of it. The postponement by the testator of the conveyance to it was for the benefit of his wife and his son's wife. The testator's wife is dead and the son's wife agrees to the conveyance. All parties in interest agree to and desire the termination of the trust as to the two thirds of which the school is entitled to the present income and we see no valid objection to it. The questions raised and the doubts suggested by the guardian *ad litem* as to the possibility of reverter in the heirs of the testator in case the corporation of the trustees of the theological school should be dissolved do not seem to us sufficient to warrant us in denying the prayer of the petition.

Decree for the petitioners.[1]

---

[1] In Goodson v. Ellisson, 3 Russ. 583, however, it was held that the court would not compel the trustee to convey to one of the beneficiaries his share of the trust property, although the other beneficiaries were all *sui juris* and consented. The court said that the trustee could be called upon to convey only by the words and descriptions by which the conveyance was made to him.

Where there are several *cestuis que trust*, the court will not usually order a partition or otherwise terminate a trust, wholly or partially, except in accordance with the terms of the trust, unless all the *cestuis que trust* are *sui juris* and consent. Taylor v. Grange, 13 Ch. D. 223, 15 Ch. D. 165; Biggs v. Peacock, 20 Ch. D. 200, 22 Ch. D. 284; *Re* Tweedie, 27 Ch. D. 315; *Re* Horsnaill, [1909] 1 Ch. 631; Anderson v. Williams, 262 Ill. 308; Olsen v. Youngerman, 136 Iowa 404; Kimball v. Blanchard, 101 Me. 383; Wirth v. Wirth, 183 Mass. 527; Hoffman v. N. E. Trust Co., 187 Mass. 205; Shaller v. Miss. Valley T. Co., 319 Mo. 128 ("each child was to receive one-fifth of the net income from the whole trust — not the income from a fifth of the trust");

STEWART v. HAMILTON.

SUPREME COURT, TENNESSEE. 1924.

151 Tenn. 396.

MR. JUSTICE COOK delivered the opinion of the Court.

The cause is here for review upon *certiorari* to the court of civil appeals. The court reversed the decree of the chancellor and dismissed the amended and supplemental bill through which complainant sought to trench upon an estate devised to A. M. Hagan, trustee, for the benefit of complainant's wards, who are Harriet, Mary, and Margaret Hamilton. Their father, W. D. Hamilton, died September 26, 1919. Their mother died some time before the father.

By item 3 of W. D. Hamilton's will dated April 10, 1918, he appointed A. R. Stewart grandfather of his daughters their guardian. Mr. Stewart assumed the responsibility, took his granddaughters into his home, which was in Nashville at that time, and they have since then been objects of his care. Harriet and Mary, twins, were fourteen, and Margaret was twelve years old when their father died September 26, 1919. Upon his death $2,000, from a policy on the life of W. D. Hamilton went into the hands of A. R. Stewart, guardian.

March 26, 1920, the guardian filed the original bill to trench upon the insurance money for the maintenance of his wards. The bill recites that the guardian had expended $800 for the use of the children. This expenditure was ratified by the court, and by subsequent decrees the insurance money was entirely exhausted. In the fall of 1920 Mr. Stewart moved to Columbia, S. C., carrying his wards with him. The family reside there in a rented house. The young ladies have been attending the public schools of the city.

It appears that for some years the trustee appointed by W. D. Hamilton's will has paid to the guardian the net income from the

---

Zabriskie's Ex'ors *v.* Wetmore, 26 N. J. Eq. 18; Story *v.* Palmer, 46 N. J. Eq. 1; Hill *v.* Hill, 49 Okla. 424; Robbins *v.* Smith, 72 Oh. St. 1; Hutchinson's App., 82 Pa. 509; Twining *v.* Girard etc. T. Co., 14 Phila. (Pa.) 74; Richardson's Est., 16 Phila. 326. See Ann. Cas. 1912C 327.

But if the court is of opinion that the interests of the objecting *cestuis que trust*, or those laboring under a disability, are not prejudiced thereby, a partial termination of the trust may be decreed. Harbin *v.* Masterman, [1896] 1 Ch. 351; Wayman *v.* Follansbee, 253 Ill. 602; Camden Safe Dep. & T. Co. *v.* Guerin, 89 N. J. Eq. 556; Henderson's Estate, 15 Phila. 598; Harlow *v.* Weld, 104 Atl. 832 (R. I. 1918). See Matter of Gallien, 247 N. Y. 195.

An equitable tenant for life cannot insist upon a conveyance by the trustees to him of a legal life estate. Russell *v.* Grinnell, 105 Mass. 425; Cooper *v.* Cooper, 36 N. J. Eq. 121; Moss's Est., 15 Phila. 512. But an equitable tenant in tail may insist upon a conveyance to him of a legal estate tail. Saunders *v.* Nevil, 2 Vern. 428.

estate, which is about $750 a year. According to the report of the master under an order of reference it appears that $190 a month is necessary for the proper maintenance of the three young ladies.

February 3, 1923, the complainant filed an amended and supplemental bill setting forth that he had expended for the use of his wards $2,966.22, in excess of the net income from the trust estate and the $2,000 derived from the life insurance. He prayed a sale of the real estate to reimburse him for the expenditure and to provide additional funds for the maintenance and education of his wards through minority.

The real estate described in the bill, and which complainant would have the court subject to these charges, is that particular property disposed of by the will of W. D. Hamilton in the following manner:

" I hereby nominate and appoint my friend A. M. Hagan, in whom I repose especial trust and confidence, as executor of my estate and testamentary trustee, and I do hereby devise, will and bequeath to him as such executor and testamentary trustee all the property of which I may die possessed, both real, personal and mixed, to be held and disposed of by him as herein set forth."

Item 4 provides:

" I hereby direct and provide that my said estate will remain vested in the said A. M. Hagan, as executor and testamentary trustee, with all the powers above enumerated, until my youngest child living at the time, shall have attained the age of twenty-one years, at which time my estate shall be equally divided by agreement of the children, or failing such agreement, by appropriate proceedings, share and share alike; and in the event that, at such time any one of my children shall have died leaving issue, then its share shall go to said issue."

It is insisted for complainant that a court of chancery in the exercise of its extraordinary powers should do what the trust creator would have done had he foreseen the situation of his beneficiaries at this time, and that the judgment of the court of civil appeals should be reversed and the decree of the chancellor affirmed.

The will of W. D. Hamilton vested title to the property in A. M. Hagan to hold in trust until the youngest daughter attained the age of twenty-one years, then, and then only, it would vest in the three daughters if living, but, if any one of the three shall have died leaving issue, then her share would vest in her issue.

We are constrained to concur in the view expressed by the court of civil appeals that the direction in the will that the estate be vested in A. M. Hagan, testamentary trustee, until the youngest child attained the age of twenty-one is tantamount to a positive inhibition against invasion of the *corpus* of the estate for maintenance of the children. This view is strengthened by the limitation over in the will to the issue of either of the daughters, who may die before the date fixed for the determination of the trust. If one or more of the beneficiaries die before the youngest attains twenty-one, either or both leaving children, such children would take under the will, and not by inheritance from their mother.

Courts cannot sustain the taking of property for the maintenance of a *cestui que trust* whose interest is contingent and may, upon the happening of the contingency, pass to the possession and enjoyment of a child or children not in existence. Such a possibility, though remote, is sufficient to forbid taking the property for the use of those who may never be entitled to it.

In Bennett *v.* Trust Company, 127 Tenn. 126, 153 S. W., 840, 46 L. R. A. (N. S.), 43, Ann. Cas., 1914A, 1045, the potential rights of contingent remaindermen offered no obstruction to an exercise of discretion by the court, acting *in loco parentis*, to provide for the exigency which the trustor could not foresee. In that case the trust fund belonged altogether to the beneficiary, whose right of enjoyment was only postponed until she reached the age of twenty-one years, and the court, in the exercise of its discretionary power, doing what it assumed the trustor would have done in the emergency, merely hastened the enjoyment of the estate under the doctrine of imputed intention. The doctrine of imputed intention concerns only the method of management, and may not be availed of to take away fundamental and substantial rights even of a contingent nature. The necessities of the present cannot be satisfied at the expense of some other object of the trustor's bounty. . . .

The testator's children are not given this property absolutely and in all events, and to grant the relief prayed in the bill would be contrary to the clearly expressed intention of the testator and invade the rights of possible contingent remaindermen.

The decree of the court of civil appeals is in all respects affirmed.[1]

SAUNDERS *v.* VAUTIER.

CHANCERY. 1841.

4 Beav. 115.

THE testator, Richard Wright, by his will, " gave and bequeathed to his executors and trustees thereinafter named all the East India stock which should be standing in his name at the time of his death, upon trust to accumulate the interest and dividends which should accrue due thereon, until Daniel Wright Vautier should attain his age of twenty-five years, and then to pay or transfer the principal of such East India stock, together with such accumulated interest and dividends, unto the said Daniel Wright Vautier, his executors, administrators, and assigns, absolutely." And the testator devised and bequeathed his residuary real and personal estate to the persons in his will named.

[1] See 39 A. L. R. 40.

The sum of 2,000*l*. East India stock was standing in the testator's name, at his death, in 1832. A suit was afterwards instituted for the administration of the testator's estate; and Daniel Wright Vautier being an infant, a reference in the cause was made to the Master, to approve of a sum to be allowed for his maintenance. The Master reported his fortune to consist of the East India stock in question, and reported that 100*l*. a year ought to be allowed for his maintenance out of the dividends thereof.

Sir C. C. Pepys, who was then Master of the Rolls, by an order dated the 25th of July, 1835, confirmed the report, and ordered the payment of 100*l*. a year out of the dividends of the East India stock, for the maintenance of the infant, Daniel Wright Vautier.

Daniel Wright Vautier attained twenty-one in March, 1841, and presented a petition to have a transfer of the fund to him.

Mr. Pemberton argued that the petitioner had a vested interest, and that as the accumulation and postponement of payment was for his benefit alone, he might waive it and call for an immediate transfer of the fund. Josselyn *v.* Josselyn, 9 Sim. 63.

THE MASTER OF THE ROLLS [LORD LANGDALE]. I think that principle has been repeatedly acted upon; and where a legacy is directed to accumulate for a certain period, or where the payment is postponed, the legatee, if he has an absolute indefeasible interest in the legacy, is not bound to wait until the expiration of that period, but may require payment the moment he is competent to give a valid discharge.

Mr. Kindersley, for the residuary legatees, most of whom are infants, was proceeding to argue that the petitioner did not take a vested interest until he attained twenty-five, but the Master of the Rolls observed that the contrary must have been decided or assumed when the order for maintenance had been made by the present Lord Chancellor. He did not, at present, see any reason to doubt the propriety of that order, but the argument must assume it to be erroneous, and call upon him to decide in a different manner, and he thought that it would be inconvenient to argue again, in this court, a point on which the judge of the court of rehearing had, probably, already expressed an opinion.

The cause stood over, with liberty to apply to the Lord Chancellor, when the Lord Chancellor held the legacy vested, and ordered the transfer.[1]

---

[1] For English decisions in accordance with the principal case, see Gray, Rule ag. Perp., sec. 120; Scott, Cases on Trusts, 1 ed., 827. See also *Re* Ussher, [1922] 2 Ch. 321; Woolley *v.* Preston, 82 Ky. 415; Rector *v.* Dalby, 98 Mo. App. 189; Huber *v.* Donoghue, 49 N. J. Eq. 125; Jasper *v.* Maxwell, 1 Dev. Eq. (N. C.) 357; Closset *v.* Burtchaell, 112 Ore. 585; Henderson's Estate, 15 Phila. 598. — ED.

The postponement of the conveyance to the son or other beneficiary may be very easily accomplished even in England. The testator has simply to create a trust for an inconsiderable amount, but attaching to the entire trust

CLAFLIN v. CLAFLIN.

SUPREME JUDICIAL COURT, MASSACHUSETTS. 1889.

149 Mass. 19.

FIELD, J.[1] By the eleventh article of his will as modified by a codicil, Wilbur F. Claflin gave all the residue of his personal estate to trustees, " to sell and dispose of the same, and to pay to my wife, Mary A. Claflin, one third part of the proceeds thereof, and to pay to my son Clarence A. Claflin, one third part of the proceeds thereof, and to pay the remaining one third part thereof to my son Adelbert E. Claflin, in the manner following, viz. ten thousand dollars when he is of the age of twenty-one years, ten thousand dollars when he is of the age of twenty-five years, and the balance when he is of the age of thirty years."

Apparently, Adelbert E. Claflin was not quite twenty-one years old when his father died, but he some time ago reached that age and received ten thousand dollars from the trust. He has not yet reached the age of twenty-five years, and he brings this bill to compel the trustees to pay to him the remainder of the trust fund. His contention is, in effect, that the provisions of the will postponing the payment of the money beyond the time when he is twenty-one years old are void. There is no doubt that his interest in the trust fund is vested and absolute, and that no other person has any interest in it, and the weight of authority is undisputed that the provisions postponing payment to him until some time after he reaches the age of twenty-one years would be treated as void by those courts

---

fund for the benefit of another person, *e.g.*, the trustee himself. The son cannot then as a matter of absolute right call for a conveyance of the legal title, because he is not the sole *cestui que trust*. He must therefore appeal to the discretion of the court, which would not ordinarily defeat, under such circumstances, the reasonable expectations of the testator. Harbin *v.* Masterman, 12 Eq. 559; Talbot *v.* Jevers, 20 Eq. 255; Weatherall *v.* Thornburgh, 8 Ch. D. 261. See also Harbin *v.* Masterman, [1894] 2 Ch. 184, [1895] A. C. 186.

Where property is given to trustees upon trust for the children of a certain woman, and in default of children upon trust for another person, the one entitled upon default of children may compel a conveyance of the property by the trustee as soon as the woman, not having children, has become so old that in the estimation of the court she must continue childless. Forty *v.* Reay, Dart V. & P. (5th ed.) 345; Groves *v.* Groves, 12 W. R. 45; *Re* Widdow's Trusts, L. R. 11 Eq. 408; *Re* Millner's Estate, L. R. 14 Eq. 245; Browne *v.* Taylor, W. N. (1872) 190; Maden *v.* Taylor, 45 L. J. Ch. 569; Archer *v.* Dowsing, W. N. (1879) 43; *Re* Taylor, 29 W. R. 350; Croxton *v.* May, 9 Ch. D. 388; Davidson *v.* Kimpton, 18 Ch. D. 213; Browne *v.* Warnock, L. R. 7 Ir. 3; Mellon's Est., 16 Phila. 323. But see Towle *v.* Delano, 144 Mass. 95; [*Re* Smith, 94 N. J. Eq. 1, 23 Col. L. Rev. 50;] List *v.* Rodney, 83 Pa. 483; Bearden *v.* White (Tenn. Ch.), 42 S. W. 476. — AMES.

[1] Only the opinion of the court is given.

which hold that restrictions against the alienation of absolute interests in the income of trust property are void. There has, indeed, been no decision of this question in England by the House of Lords, and but one by a Lord Chancellor, but there are several decisions to this effect by Masters of the Rolls and by Vice Chancellors. The cases are collected in Gray's Restraints on Alienation, §§ 106–112, and Appendix II. [Cases cited.]

These decisions do not proceed on the ground that it was the intention of the testator that the property should be conveyed to the beneficiary on his reaching the age of twenty-one years, because in each case it was clear that such was not his intention, but on the ground that the direction to withhold the possession of the property from the beneficiary after he reached his majority was inconsistent with the absolute rights of property given him by the will.

This court has ordered trust property to be conveyed by the trustee to the beneficiary when there was a dry trust, or when the purposes of the trust had been accomplished, or when no good reason was shown why the trust should continue, and all the persons interested in it were *sui juris* and desired that it be terminated; but we have found no expression of any opinion in our reports that provisions requiring a trustee to hold and manage the trust property until the beneficiary reached an age beyond that of twenty-one years are necessarily void if the interest of the beneficiary is vested and absolute. See Smith v. Harrington, 4 Allen, 566; Bowditch v. Andrew, 8 Allen, 339; Russell v. Grinnell, 105 Mass. 425; Inches v. Hill, 106 Mass. 575; Sears v. Choate, 146 Mass. 395. This is not a dry trust, and the purposes of the trust have not been accomplished if the intention of the testator is to be carried out.

In Sears v. Choate it is said, " Where property is given to certain persons for their benefit, and in such a manner that no other person has or can have any interest in it, they are in effect the absolute owners of it, and it is reasonable and just that they should have the control and disposal of it unless some good cause appears to the contrary." In that case the plaintiff was the absolute owner of the whole property, subject to an annuity of ten thousand dollars payable to himself. The whole of the principal of the trust fund, and all of the income not expressly made payable to the plaintiff, had become vested in him when he reached the age of twenty-one years, by way of resulting trust, as property undisposed of by the will. Apparently the testator had not contemplated such a result, and had made no provision for it, and the court saw no reason why the trust should not be terminated, and the property conveyed to the plaintiff.

In Inches v. Hill, *ubi supra*, the same person had become owner of the equitable life estate and of the equitable remainder, and " no reason appearing to the contrary," the court decreed a conveyance by the trustees to the owner. See Whall v. Converse, 146 Mass. 345.

In the case at bar nothing has happened which the testator did not anticipate, and for which he has not made provision. It is plainly his will that neither the income nor any part of the principal should now be paid to the plaintiff. It is true that the plaintiff's interest is alienable by him, and can be taken by his creditors to pay his debts, but it does not follow that, because the testator has not imposed all possible restrictions, the restrictions which he has imposed should not be carried into effect.

The decision in Broadway National Bank v. Adams, 133 Mass. 170, rests upon the doctrine that a testator has a right to dispose of his own property with such restrictions and limitations, not repugnant to law, as he sees fit, and that his intentions ought to be carried out unless they contravene some positive rule of law, or are against public policy. The rule contended for by the plaintiff in that case was founded upon the same considerations as that contended for by the plaintiff in this, and the grounds on which this court declined to follow the English rule in that case are applicable to this, and for the reasons there given we are unable to see that the directions of the testator to the trustees, to pay the money to the plaintiff when he reaches the age of twenty-five and thirty years, and not before, are against public policy, or are so far inconsistent with the rights of property given to the plaintiff that they should not be carried into effect. It cannot be said that these restrictions upon the plaintiff's possession and control of the property are altogether useless, for there is not the same danger that he will spend the property while it is in the hands of the trustees as there would be if it were in his own.

In Sanford v. Lackland, 2 Dillon, 6, a beneficiary who would have been entitled to a conveyance of trust property at the age of twenty-six became a bankrupt at the age of twenty-four, and it was held that the trustees should convey his interest immediately to his assignee, as " the strict execution of the trusts in the will have been thus rendered impossible." But whether a creditor, or a grantee of the plaintiff in this case would be entitled to the immediate possession of the property, or would only take the plaintiff's title *sub modo*, need not be decided. The existing situation is one which the testator manifestly had in mind and made provision for; the strict execution of the trust has not become impossible; the restriction upon the plaintiff's possession and control is, we think, one that the testator had a right to make; other provisions for the plaintiff are contained in the will, apparently sufficient for his support, and we see no good reason why the intention of the testator should not be carried out. Russell v. Grinnell, 105 Mass. 425. See Toner v. Collins, 67 Iowa, 369; Rhoads v. Rhoads, 43 Ill. 239; Lent v. Howard, 89 N. Y. 169; Barkley v. Dosser, 15 Lea, 529; Carmichael v. Thompson, 5 Cent. Rep. 500; Lampert v. Haydel, 20 Mo. App. 616.

Decree affirmed.[1]

[1] Shelton v. King, 229 U. S. 90; Estate of Yates, 170 Cal. 254; DeLadson

DELADSON *v.* CRAWFORD, 93 Conn. 402 (1919) : A testatrix bequeathed $1500 in trust to pay the income to her niece for ten years and at the expiration of ten years to pay the principal to her. She created a similar trust of the residue for her husband. The niece sold her entire interest to the husband. Before the expiration of the ten-year period suit was brought by the niece and the husband to compel the trustee to pay over the principal. It was held that the trust should not be terminated. Beach, J., said (p. 406) :

"In the interest of the parties and to avoid further litigation on the subject, we also discuss the questions argued before us. The rule relied on by appellants is stated in Gray on Perpetuities (3d Ed.) § 120. In substance it is that when a person is entitled absolutely to property, a provision postponing its transfer or payment to him is void. That if there is a gift over in case the *cestui que trust* dies before the trust terminates, the trustee retains the property for the possible benefit of the substitutionary donee, but to postpone an absolute gift to A by interposing a trust to pay the income to A for a term of years, is void, ' in pursuance of the general doctrine that it is against public policy to restrain a man in the use or disposition of property in which no one but himself has any interest.'

---

v. Crawford, 93 Conn. 402; Lunt *v.* Lunt, 108 Ill. 307; Wagner *v.* Wagner, 244 Ill. 101; Wallace *v.* Foxwell, 250 Ill. 616; Matter of Hamburger, 185 Wis. 270, *accord.* See Rhoads *v.* Rhoads, 43 Ill. 239; Avery *v.* Avery, 90 Ky. 613; Miller *v.* Miller, 172 Ky. 519; Young *v.* Snow, 167 Mass. 287; Danahy *v.* Noonan, 176 Mass. 467. See also Gray, Rule ag. Perp., c. 4; Kales, Estates, 2 ed., secs. 732 *et seq.;* Pomeroy, Eq. Juris., sec. 991; 24 Harv. L. Rev. 224; 65 U. Pa. L. Rev. 647–650; 9 Minn. L. Rev. 562; 38 Yale L. Jour. 686; 37 A. L. R. 1420.

A provision postponing enjoyment does not prevent alienation. DeLadson *v.* Crawford, 93 Conn. 402, 408; Hall's Estate, 248 Pa. 218. See Bronson *v.* Thompson, 77 Conn. 214. But see 9 Minn. L. Rev. 562, 565.

A postponement of enjoyment, which is otherwise valid, is invalid if it is to be effective for too long a time. See Armstrong *v.* Barber, 239 Ill. 389, 403; Winsor *v.* Mills, 157 Mass. 362, 364; Southard *v.* Southard, 210 Mass. 347; *Re* Shallcross's Estate, 200 Pa. 122. See Gray, Rule ag. Perp., secs. 121*i,* 121*j*; Kales, Estates, 2 ed., secs. 658–661, 737; Whiteside, Restrictions on the Duration of the Business Trust, 9 Cornell L. Quar. 422; 20 Harv. L. Rev. 202; 10 Mich. L. Rev. 31, 37; 9 Minn. L. Rev. 314, 326.

In Howe *v.* Morse, 174 Mass. 491, it was held that a business trust is valid although not otherwise limited in duration, if there is no restraint on the alienation of the beneficial interest, and the trust may be terminated by a three-fourths vote of the beneficiaries.

In jurisdictions in which the doctrine of the principal case is recognized, a direction for an accumulation in the case of a charitable trust is valid, unless for so long a time as to be unreasonable. Brigham *v.* Peter Bent Brigham Hosp., 134 Fed. 513; Girard T. Co. *v.* Russell, 179 Fed. 446; Woodruff *v.* Marsh, 63 Conn. 125; St. Paul's Church *v.* A. G., 164 Mass. 188; Ripley *v.* Brown, 218 Mass. 33; Collector of Taxes *v.* Oldfield, 219 Mass. 374; Oldfield *v.* A. G., 219 Mass. 378; Gray, Rule ag. Perp., 3 ed., sec. 679*a.* In jurisdictions

"It is not easy to find a satisfactory legal basis for this rule in the form in which Professor Gray states it. Lord Eldon's statement of the rule in Brandon v. Robinson, 18 Ves. Jr. 429, 433, that 'if property is given to a man for his life, the donor cannot take away the incidents of a life estate,' is self-explanatory; although the rule is not without exceptions in this State. Clark v. Baker, 91 Conn. 663, 101 Atl. 9, and cases cited on page 666. Most of the English cases to which we have been referred, including Gosling v. Gosling, Johns. Ch. 265, which was especially relied on, exemplify the simpler rule that a testator having once made an absolute gift cannot attach to it repugnant conditions subsequent. When, however, the enjoyment of the principal is given upon the condition precedent of an interposed temporary trust for the payment of income only, the assumption that the donee may disregard the condition and demand an immediate transfer of the legal title, requires explanation.

"The English cases do not supply any satisfactory explanation. The present English rule, that a *cestui que trust* may put an end to an accumulation which is exclusively for his benefit, was first actually applied in Saunders v. Vautier, 4 Beav. 115, although the opinion in that case ignores the intermediate trust and disposes of the question, very briefly, as if the gift had been made directly to the legatee, and then the executor had, nevertheless, been directed

---

in which the doctrine of the principal case is not recognized, a provision for accumulation for charitable purposes is not enforceable. Wharton v. Masterman, [1895] A. C. 186, [1894] 2 Ch. 184. See 41 Harv. L. Rev. 514; 16 Va. L. Rev. 370.

In the case of a spendthrift trust, the beneficiaries cannot compel a termination of the trust. Moore v. Sinnott, 117 Ga. 1010; Bennett v. Bennett, 217 Ill. 434; Wagner v. Wagner, 244 Ill. 101; Anderson v. Williams, 262 Ill. 308; Maher v. Maher, 207 Ky. 360; Kiefaber's Estate, 8 Pa. D. & C. 231; Vines v. Vines, 143 Tenn. 517. See 9 Minn. L. Rev. 562.

Consent of the settlor. If the creator of a trust is the sole beneficiary of the trust, it would seem that he can terminate the trust. Johns v. Birmingham Trust & Sav. Co., 205 Ala. 535; Burton v. Boren, 208 Ill. 440, *ante;* Fidelity & Columbia Trust Co. v. Gwynn, 206 Ky. 823; Riedlin's Gd'n v. Cobb, 222 Ky. 654; Stephens v. Moore, 298 Mo. 215. See Perry, Trusts, secs. 101, 920; 37 Yale L. Jour. 1073; 38 A. L. R. 941, 965.

Similarly, it would seem that where a trust is created *inter vivos* it can be terminated by the consent of the settlor and of all the beneficiaries if they are all *sui juris*. In New York Personal Property Law, sec. 23, it is provided that "Upon the written consent of all the persons beneficially interested in a trust in personal property or any part thereof heretofore or hereafter created, the creator of the trust may revoke the same as to the whole or such part thereof, and thereupon the estate of the trustee shall cease in the whole or such part thereof."

If, however, the settlor is not the sole beneficiary, he cannot require a termination of the trust without the consent of the other beneficiaries; and if some of the beneficiaries are unascertained or not *sui juris* the trust cannot be terminated. Underhill v. U. S. Trust Co., 227 Ky. 444; Sands v. Old Colony Trust Co., 195 Mass. 575. See Whittemore v. Equitable Trust Co., 250 N. Y. 298, *ante*.

to withhold the principal and income until the legatee reached the age of twenty-four years. About fifty years later the same question came for the first time to the House of Lords in Wharton *v.* Masterman, L. R. (1895) App. Cas. 186; and Lord Herschell said (p. 193) : ' The point seems, in the first instance, to have been rather assumed than decided. It was apparently regarded as a necessary consequence of the conclusion that a gift had vested, that the enjoyment of it must be immediate on the beneficiary becoming *sui juris,* and could not be postponed . . . unless the testator had made some other destination of the income during the intervening period. It is needless to inquire whether the courts might have given effect to the intention of the testator in such cases to postpone the enjoyment of his bounty to a time fixed by himself subsequent to the attainment by the objects of his bounty of their majority. The doctrine has been so long settled and so often recognised that it would not be proper now to question it.'

" If this authoritative statement of its origin be accepted, the rule in Saunders *v.* Vautier and Wharton *v.* Masterman, is not based either on public policy or reasoned decision. It is merely a rule which, by repetition, has become a rule of property, but was in the first instance based upon the hasty assumption that the enjoyment of a gift vested in interest could not be postponed at the will of the testator, unless for the benefit of another donee.

" In this country the rule has been more or less widely accepted on the authority of the English cases, without much independent examination of the supposed legal necessity for adopting it. In one or more States it is said that the intervening trust for accumulation or payment of income is defeated by the statute of uses, and in others, including Pennsylvania, that the intervening trust is objectionable because it violates the rule of public policy forbidding restraint on the use or alienation of absolute estates. It is characteristic of the lack of any convincing reason for the doctrine of Saunders *v.* Vautier, that ' the mother of spendthrift trusts ' should resort in support of it to a rule of public policy which applies with much greater force to the Pennsylvania form of spendthrift trusts.

" In fact Professor Gray's rule of public policy has no application whatever to trusts of this kind, for they do not constitute a restraint on the disposition or alienation of the corpus of the fund. The estate of the beneficiary is vested, and it may be assigned, attached, or taken on execution. In this case the record shows that Mary F. Cartwright has sold and assigned her entire interest to Edward S. DeLadson. The fact that the principal is withheld for ten years decreases the present value of the legacy, but it does not restrain the disposition of it by the legatee.

" The other branch of the rule, which declares that it is contrary to public policy to restrain a man ' in the use . . . of property in which no one but himself has any interest,' cannot of course be accepted unless limited to the attempted imposition or continuance of an illegal or unreasonable restraint on the use of property.

"The truth seems to be that the real and only basis of the English rule is, as Lord Herschell suggests, the unconsidered assumption that a gift vested in interest, will also vest in enjoyment whenever the donee is or becomes *sui juris*, unless there is an outstanding present or contingent beneficial interest in another person; and this notwithstanding that the testator has attempted to postpone the complete enjoyment of the gift for a term of years. When the proposition is stated in this way, free from the supposed overpowering authority of a rule of public policy, it is seen to present, in another form, the more familiar question whether by postponing the enjoyment of the principal for a term of years, the testator has attempted to impose an unreasonable or illegal condition on the gift of his bounty. Such conditions may seem under some circumstances to be arbitrary and unnecessary, and yet they may rest upon good reasons known to the testator and not to the court. It is certain that the validity of the conditions cannot depend upon the motive which we may rightly or wrongly attribute to the testator as a supposed reason for imposing them. It must depend on the inherent reasonableness or not of a given condition from a legal standpoint, and looking at it in that way the postponement of the enjoyment of the principal of a trust fund for ten years is not an unreasonable exercise of the undoubted right of the testator to impose conditions on the enjoyment of his bounty.

"Nor is there any good reason for declaring such a condition to be illegal. The objections based on its supposed conflict with the rule of public policy have been examined, and the question remains whether there is any necessary legal inconsistency in a *cestui que trust* as to income, having at the same time a vested right as remainderman to the principal of the gift. There is of course no objection to this during a period of temporary incapacity, such as infancy, coverture, or insanity. And by conferring discretionary powers on the trustee a temporary disqualification from enjoying a gift which is vested in interest may be imposed on one who is *sui juris*, when the testator doubts whether he will use it wisely. We have recently upheld such a trust in Williams *v.* Gardner, 90 Conn. 461, 97 Atl. 854.

"We think it follows that a testator may in such cases attempt to exercise his own discretion by postponing the enjoyment of the principal for a term of years, without explaining to the public his reasons for doing so. This is in accordance with the settled policy of our law of which the most recent expression is as follows: 'As a general rule, a testator has the right to impose such conditions as he pleases upon a beneficiary as conditions precedent to the vesting of an estate in him, or to the enjoyment of a trust estate by him as *cestui que trust*.' Holmes *v.* Connecticut Trust & Safe Deposit Co.,

92 Conn. 507, 514, 103 Atl. 640. Our conclusion is that the conditions which the testatrix has imposed in this will are not unreasonable, illegal, or opposed to any rule of public policy of Connecticut."[1]

In re SMITH.

PUBLIC TRUSTEE v. ASPINALL.

HIGH COURT OF JUSTICE, CHANCERY DIVISION. 1928.

[1928] Ch. 915.

ADJOURNED SUMMONS.

The following statement of the facts is substantially taken from his Lordship's judgment: —

The testator, who died on July 30, 1905, by his will dated March 31, 1905, directed his trustees to stand possessed of one-fourth of his residuary estate upon trust during the life of the defendant Mrs. Aspinall at their absolute discretion and in such manner as they should think fit " to pay or apply the whole or any part of the annual income of such one-fourth and the investments thereof or if they shall think fit from time to time any part of the capital thereof unto or for the maintenance and personal support or benefit of the said Lilian Aspinall or as to the income thereof but not as to the capital for the maintenance education support or benefit of all or any one or more of the children of the said Lilian Aspinall and either themselves so to apply the same or to pay the same for that purpose to any other person or persons without seeing to the application thereof And during the period of twenty-one years from my death if the said Lilian Aspinall shall live so long to accumulate the surplus if any of such income at compound interest by investing the same and the resulting income thereof in any of the investments aforesaid by way of addition to the capital of such fund

---

[1] Professor Kales disagreed with Professor Gray's criticism of Claflin v. Claflin and suggested "that Gray's violent dislike for the rule of Claflin v. Claflin is due to his abhorrence of spendthrift trusts." Professor Kales added "It is conceived that the only connection between the doctrine of spendthrift trusts and the doctrine of Claflin v. Claflin, is that both rest fundamentally upon the rule that a testator or settlor can do what he likes with his property so long as no rule founded on public policy is contravened. Hence, where spendthrift trusts are allowed it may be expected that Claflin v. Claflin will be followed. It is by no means true, however, that, because there is no reason of public policy against such a postponement as was sustained in Claflin v. Claflin, there is none against spendthrift trusts. The writer believes, therefore, that while spendthrift trusts are entitled to all the abhorrence which Gray has given them, yet it does not follow that the postponement clause, limited properly as to the time of its duration, is not entirely harmless and proper." Kales, Estates, 2 ed., sec. 738.

As to the question of the power of an assignee to require an immediate conveyance, see Gray, Restraints, sec. 124; Kales, Estates, 2 ed., sec. 738.

as aforesaid and so as to be subject to the same trusts as are hereby declared concerning the same and during the remainder of the life of the said Lilian Aspinall in case she shall survive the said period of twenty-one years to pay or apply such surplus income (if any) to the person or persons or for the purposes to whom and for which the same would for the time being be payable or applicable if the said Lilian Aspinall were then dead And after the death of the said Lilian Aspinall as regards both capital and income both original and accumulated In trust for the child or children of the said Lilian Aspinall who either before or after her decease shall being a son or sons attain the age of twenty-one years or being a daughter or daughters attain that age or marry and if more than one in equal shares." Mrs. Aspinall has had three children, all of whom attained the age of twenty-one years, and one of whom is now dead. Mrs. Aspinall is of an age when it is quite impossible that she should have any further issue. In those circumstances Mrs. Aspinall, the two surviving children and the legal personal representatives of the child who is dead all joined in executing a mortgage dated April 13, 1923, to the defendants, the Legal and General Assurance Company, which took the form of an assignment to the assurance company of all the interests that Mrs. Aspinall and the three children took under the will in any event.

This summons was taken out by the Public Trustee (who was the sole trustee of the will of the testator) for the determination of the question whether he was bound to pay the whole of the income of the one-fourth share of the testator's residuary estate, which was settled by the will upon trust for the benefit of Mrs. Aspinall and her children, to the defendant society, until the discharge of the mortgage, or whether he was at liberty, in his discretion (notwithstanding the notice dated February 6, 1928, given to him by the solicitors of the defendant society, to pay all income then due or to become due in respect of the share of Mrs. Aspinall under the will direct to the society as mortgagees), to apply all or any part of the income or capital of the share for the maintenance or personal support or benefit of Mrs. Aspinall.

ROMER J. [after stating the facts, continued:] The question I have to determine is whether the Legal and General Assurance Company are now entitled to call upon the trustees to pay the whole of the income to them. It will be observed from what I have said that the whole of this share is now held by the trustees upon trusts under which they are bound to apply the whole income and eventually pay over or apply the whole capital to Mrs. Aspinall and the three children or some or one of them. So far as the income is concerned they are obliged to pay it or apply it for her benefit or to pay it or apply it for the benefit of the children. So far as regards the capital they have a discretion to pay it and to apply it for her benefit and, subject to that, they must hold it upon trust for the children. Mrs. Aspinall, the two surviving children and the representatives of the deceased child are between them entitled to the whole fund. In those circumstances it appears to me, notwithstanding the discretion which is reposed in the trustees, under which discretion they could select one or more of the people I have mentioned as recipients of the income, and might apply part of the capital for the benefit of Mrs. Aspinall and so take it away from the children, that the four of them, if they were all living, could come to the Court and say to the trustees: " Hand over the fund to us." It appears to me that that is in accordance with the decision of the Court of Appeal in a case of *In re* Nelson (now reported [1928] Ch. 920n.) of which a transcript of the judgments has been handed to me, and is in accordance with principle. What is the principle? As I understand it it is this. Where there is a trust under which trustees have a discretion as to applying the whole or part of a fund to or for the benefit of a particular person, that particular person cannot come to the trustees, and demand the fund; for the whole fund has not been given to him but only so much as the trustees think fit to let him have. But when the trustees have no discretion as to the amount of the fund to be applied, the fact that the trustees have a discretion as to the method in which the whole of the fund shall be applied for the benefit of the particular person does not prevent that particular person from coming and saying: " Hand over the fund to me." That appears to be the result of the two cases which were cited to me: Green *v.* Spicer, 1 Russ. & My. 395, and Younghusband *v.* Gisborne, 1 Coll. C. C. 400.

Now this third case arises. What is to happen where the trustees have a discretion whether they will apply the whole or only a portion of the fund for the benefit of one person, but are obliged to apply the rest of the fund, so far as not applied for the benefit of the first named person, to or for the benefit of a second named person? There, two people together are the sole objects of the discretionary trust and, between them, are entitled to have the whole fund applied to them or for their benefit. It has been laid down by the Court of Appeal in the case to which I have referred that, in such a case as that you treat all the people put together just as though they formed one person, for whose benefit the trustees were directed to apply the whole of a particular fund. The case before the Court of Appeal was this: A testator had directed his trustees to stand possessed of one-third of his residuary estate upon trust during the lifetime of the testator's son Arthur Hector Nelson: " to apply the income thereof for the benefit of himself and his wife and child or children or of any of such persons to the exclusion of the others or other of them as my trustees shall think fit." What happened was something very similar to what happened in the case before me. Hector Nelson, his wife and the only existing child of the marriage joined together in asking the trustees to hand over the income to them, and it was held by the Court of Appeal that the trustees were obliged to comply with the request, in other words, to treat all those persons who were the only members of the class for whose benefit the income could be applied as forming together an individual for whose benefit a fund has to be applied by the trustees without any discretion as to the amount so to be applied.

I only want to add this out of respect to Mr. Sanger's argument. Where there is a trust to apply the whole or such part of a fund as trustees think fit to or for the benefit of A., and A. has assigned his interest under the trust, or become bankrupt, although his assignee or his trustee in bankruptcy stand in no better position than he does and cannot demand that the fund shall be handed to them, yet they are in a position to say to A.: "Any money which the trustees do in the exercise of their discretion pay to you, passes by the assignment or under the bankruptcy." But they cannot say that in respect of any money which the trustees have not paid to A. or invested in purchasing goods or other things for A., but which they apply for the benefit of A. in such a way that no money or goods ever gets into the hands of A. That depends on a perfectly different principle which in no way assists Mr. Sanger in his argument in the present case.

There will, consequently, be a declaration that, in the events which have happened, the plaintiff is bound to pay the whole of the income of the one-fourth to the defendant society during the lifetime of Mrs. Aspinall, or until the mortgage is discharged.

STAMBAUGH'S ESTATE.

SUPREME COURT, PENNSYLVANIA. 1890.

135 Pa. 585.

On August 4, 1887, Emily L. Hartman and William H. Gardner, executors of the will of John Wolford, who was trustee of Moses Stambaugh, under the will of Philip Stambaugh, deceased, settled a final account of the administration of the trust by their testator. The accountants charged themselves with a trust fund amounting to $3,394.72, received by their testator from a former trustee, and took credit, inter alia, for the payment of $1,529.50, "being part of the corpus of said fund, to Martin E. Stambaugh, Mary C. Stambaugh, and Sarah E. Black, by and with the consent and agreement in writing of Moses Stambaugh, their father, March 3, 1877, as appears by release recorded in the recorder's office of York county;" the account exhibiting a balance of the trust estate in the hands of the accountants amounting to $1,582.47. On August 29, 1887, the account was confirmed nisi.

On January 11, 1888, the cestui que trust, Moses Stambaugh, and his daughter, Mary C. Stambaugh, now Arnsberger, petitioned the court below for a review of said account. The petitions having been answered by the accountants, the court on June 16, 1888, made an order opening the account and referring all questions of fact and law raised by the petitions and answers to Mr. Nevin M. Wanner, as auditor. Subsequently Frederick Grothe was appointed by the court trustee of Moses Stambaugh, in the place of John Wolford, deceased, and allowed to become a party to the proceedings before the auditor.

On August 5, 1889, the auditor reported in part as follows: . . .

The main contention, however, relates to the credit claimed on the part of the accountants, for the $1,529.50, paid out to the three children of Moses Stambaugh, in March, 1877, the receipt of which they acknowledge in their release of that date, in which they are joined by Moses Stambaugh, the cestui que trust. One of these children, Mary C. Stambaugh, now Mary C. Arnsberger, asks to be relieved from the operation of this instrument because she was a minor at the time when she executed it, which fact she has established to the satisfaction of the auditor. The other two have not appeared, nor has the validity of this release as to them and their interest in the trust fund been impeached. For the purpose of this investigation it therefore stands good as against them, and will prevent their participation hereafter in the trust fund to the extent of the payments already made to them. The auditor is of the opinion, however, that the infancy of the other petitioner, Mary C. Arnsberger, avoids the release as to her, and the trustee should be surcharged with the amount for which she released him, to wit, $509.83.

It was contended by counsel for Moses Stambaugh, that the language of the will of Philip Stambaugh, deceased, created an active trust in the trustee, which he was bound to keep alive, and to administer in the precise form indicated by the testator; that it was in the nature of a spendthrift trust, the cestui que trust having become insolvent and made an assignment for the benefit of his creditors shortly before the will was made; that the trustee had no power, during the lifetime of Moses Stambaugh, to divert the fund, or terminate the trust, by paying over the corpus of the fund, or any portion of it, to the heirs of the cestui que trust, even with his consent; that, having done so without warrant or authority, he should be surcharged with the sum so paid over, in order that the cestui que trust may receive his interest on the entire fund during life, notwithstanding his release for a portion of it, and notwithstanding the fact that the heirs of Moses Stambaugh, who were competent to bind themselves with said release, may not be entitled to receive anything after his death. Accountants' counsel contended, that this was a dry trust, and that under the operation of the rule in Shelley's Case, Moses Stambaugh took an absolute estate in this fund, both principal and interest, so that he could dispose of it; and that the trustee was therefore protected in the payment of the $1,529.50, by the release of the cestui que trust and his children, and entitled to credit for the same in his account.

A careful review of the numerous authorities cited by counsel on this question, leads the auditor to the conclusion that this was an active trust in the eye of the law. It was clearly the purpose of testator to keep the principal fund out of the hands of his son Moses, and to provide him an income for life out of the interest accruing thereon. It is only after the death of Moses that he gives the corpus of the fund to his heirs. . . .

Regarding this, therefore, as an active trust, it was the duty of the trustee to faithfully carry out the provisions of the will, in its administration. The payment of a portion of the trust fund to certain of the heirs of Moses Stambaugh, during his lifetime, was a breach of trust on the part of John Wolford. Is he protected against its consequences by the release which he took from the cestui que trust, and by his concurrence at the time it was done?

It has been held by the English courts that a cestui que trust who concurs in a breach of trust is estopped from proceeding against the trustee: 2 Perry on Trusts, § 849; or, he may by long acquiescence be debarred from relief: 2 Perry on Trusts, § 850. He may release the trustee by a formal release for a breach of trust, which will relieve both the trustee and his sureties: 2 Perry on Trusts, § 851. This is only true, however, where the cestui que trust is sui juris, aware of his legal rights, and not imposed upon by the trustee. The evidence does not show that Moses Stambaugh was ignorant of his rights under the will, or overreached by the trustee in the procurement of this release. He seems to have himself desired the arrangement to be made in the form adopted. He was certainly sui juris at the time, and his long silence and acquiescence, until after the death of his trustee, seems conclusive against him in this matter.

In the opinion of the auditor the trustee is entitled to credit for the sums paid out to Martin E. Stambaugh and Sarah E. Black, to wit, $1,019.67, but not for the amount paid to Mary C. Stambaugh, now Mary C. Arnsberger, to wit $509.83. . . .

OPINION, MR. CHIEF JUSTICE PAXSON:

We are of opinion that the will of Philip Stambaugh created an active trust in favor of his son Moses. The language of this portion of said will is as follows:

"And from the other aforesaid divided share of my estate all the just debts and claims that I have and hold against my son Moses Stambaugh are to be subtracted from the same, and the balance thereof is to be placed in the hands of Henry Shaffer, of Jackson township, whom I hereby appoint trustee for to hold the said sum for my son Moses Stambaugh; the said Henry Shaffer is to pay the interest yearly accruing from the same to my son Moses Stambaugh after deducting taxes and necessary expenses, and after the death of my son Moses Stambaugh I bequeath the principal to the heirs of my son Moses Stambaugh, share and share alike."

We think it manifest from this will that the testator intended (a) to sever the product from the fund producing it, and that he wished the former only to be paid to his son during his life; and (b) after his death the principal to go to his children. By the words "heirs" he evidently meant "children." It was urged, however, that this was a mere dry trust; that there is nothing upon the face of the will to indicate an intent to create a spendthrift trust, and that, as the fund was given to Moses and his heirs, there is no purpose for which the trust should be kept alive, and that it is executed in Moses.[1] . . .

Regarding it, then, as plain that this testator intended to create a spendthrift trust for his son Moses, we have the additional fact that he certainly did create an active trust. The income only was to be paid to his son, "after deducting taxes and necessary expenses." The legal title was in the trustee, and therefore the legal and equitable title could not coalesce under the rule in Shelley's Case. Under such circumstances, it requires neither argument nor authority to show that the trustee had no right to pay over any portion of the corpus of the estate to his cestui que trust. That was not what the testator directed him to do; and, as he procured no order from the court, having jurisdiction of his account, to make such payment, it follows necessarily that such disposition of the trust estate was unlawfully and improvidently made. It was at his own risk, and in direct violation of the trust. The release of the life-tenant does not bind him; the release of the alleged remainder-men does not protect the trustee. Non constat that the releasors will be the remainder-men at the death of Moses Stambaugh. If the trustee suffers by this ruling, it is the result of his own folly. He was entitled to procure competent legal advice, and pay for it out of the trust fund. Moreover, he could have been protected by an application to the court. The law does not deal harshly with trustees. It affords them every facility to ascertain and follow the proper legal path in the administration of their trusts. When they unlawfully part with the trust funds committed to their care, they cannot justly complain if they are held responsible.

It is to be observed that no question arises as to creditors. As between the trustee and his cestui que trust, we must give this will the effect of a spendthrift trust.

The decree is reversed, at the costs of the appellees; and it is ordered that the record be remitted to the court below to have the account restated in accordance with this opinion.[2]

[1] The court held that extrinsic evidence of the intention of the testator to create a spendthrift trust was admissible and sufficient to show that he intended to create a spendthrift trust. This view was repudiated, however, in McCurdy v. Bellefont Trust Co., 292 Pa. 407, 411.

[2] In the following cases it was held that where the trustee of a spendthrift

STOKES v. CHEEK.

CHANCERY. 1860.

28 Beav. 620.

THE testatrix bequeathed an annuity of 30*l.* to William Cheek, an annuity of 30*l.* to Eliza Stokes, and other like annuities, and she authorized her trustees to sell her freeholds, copyholds and leaseholds, and directed them, out of the produce, to purchase government annuities for the respective annuitants. The will contained the following clause: —

" And I declare, that no one of the annuitants hereinbefore named shall be, nor shall the executors or administrators of any of them be, *allowed to accept the value of the annuity* to which he or she, respectively, shall be entitled, in lieu thereof, and that the beneficial life interest of each female annuitant shall be and remain free from the control and engagements of her husband for the time being, and as her separate property."

The estate had been sold, and the cause came on for further consideration. The question was, whether the annuitants were entitled to receive the amount necessary to purchase the annuities, instead of having the annuities purchased for them.

---

trust conveyed the trust property to the beneficiary or to another with his consent he is liable to the beneficiary. Lent *v.* Howard, 89 N. Y. 169, 181; Cuthbert *v.* Chauvet, 136 N. Y. 326 (*semble*); Matter of Wentworth, 230 N. Y. 476, 21 Col. L. Rev. 607, 6 Cornell L. Quar. 343.

In Matter of Wentworth, 230 N. Y. 176, *supra,* in order to free the property from the trust the trustee conveyed it to a third person with the consent of the life tenant and remainderman. It was held that the trustee was liable to the executor of the life tenant. Hiscock, C. J., said (p. 183): " We are all agreed upon what seems to be an obvious view that if the interest of the *cestui que trust* in and under this trust was by statute inalienable, the prohibition of the statute could not be circumvented by any process of estoppel. If the statute prohibited alienation by the *cestui que trust* of his interest by direct conveyance he could not indirectly accomplish such alienation by any consent through estoppel which he might give to a conveyance by the trustee."

There is a conflict of authority on the question whether the trustee is liable where he makes unauthorized advances to the spendthrift *cestui que trust.* See 43 Harv. L. Rev. 70.

If the trust is not a spendthrift trust and the trustee conveys the trust property to the *cestui que trust* who has the entire beneficial interest in the property, there is no one who has any standing to file a bill against the trustee even though the conveyance defeated the intention of the creator of the trust. Shelton *v.* King, 229 U. S. 90, 94 (*semble*); Lemen *v.* McComas, 63 Md. 153; Partridge *v.* Clary, 228 Mass. 290; Rowley *v.* American Trust Co., 144 Va. 375. See Brophy *v.* Lawler, 107 Ill. 284; Ames, 258.

If the settlor is not the sole beneficiary, it is a breach of trust to reconvey the property to him without the consent of the other beneficiaries. Ewing *v.* Warner, 46 Minn. 446 (trust for heirs of settlor). Compare Whittemore *v.* Equitable Trust Co., 250 N. Y. 298, *ante.*

THE MASTER OF THE ROLLS [SIR JOHN ROMILLY]. I have, on several occasions, held, that annuitants are entitled to receive the money necessary to purchase their annuities.

It would be an idle form to direct an annuity to be purchased, which the annuitants might sell immediately afterwards.

The annuitants are entitled to such a sum as would be required to purchase their annuities.[1]

Re PHILBRICK'S SETTLEMENT.

CHANCERY. 1865.

34 L. J. Ch. 368.

BY a deed-poll, dated the 4th of March, 1846, a fund was vested in trustees, upon trust, for the separate use of Hannah Philbrick, a married woman, for her life, and after her death upon such trusts as she should by will appoint.

By her will, dated the 20th of June, 1856, and expressed to be made in pursuance of the power, Hannah Philbrick appointed the fund to various persons, giving a life-interest in part of it to her husband, and appointed two executors. She died in June, 1864, and her executors proved her will.

The trustees of the deed-poll being in doubt whether they ought to hand over the trust-fund to the executors, or to distribute it themselves among the appointees, paid the fund into court under the Trustee Relief Act.

The executors thereupon presented a petition for the payment to them of the fund, to be administered by them in accordance with the appointment contained in the will.

[1] *Re* Browne's Will, 27 Beav. 324; Roper *v.* Roper, 3 Ch. D. 714, 721; *Re* Mabbett, [1891] 1 Ch. 707; Parker *v.* Cobe, 208 Mass. 260; Reid *v.* Browne, 54 N. Y. Misc. 481; Matter of Cole, 174 N. Y. App. Div. 534, *accord.* If the legatee dies before the annuity is purchased, his representatives are entitled to the amount which would have been required to purchase it. Palmer *v.* Craufurd, 3 Swanst. 482; *Re* Brunning, [1909] 1 Ch. 276.

If there is a contingent gift over of the annuity, the annuitant cannot insist on taking the purchase price of the annuity or any part of it. Hatton *v.* May, 3 Ch. D. 148; *Re* Dempster, [1915] 1 Ch. 795. *Cf.* Lejee's Est., 181 Pa. 416.

If the annuity is not to be purchased but simply to be charged on the testator's estate, the annuitant is not entitled to a lump payment of the value of the annuity. Yates *v.* Yates, 28 Beav. 637.

See Gray, Restraints, secs. 83–89.

If a testator devises or bequeaths property and directs that it be sold or converted into other property, the legatee if *sui juris* may elect to take the property in specie. Craig *v.* Leslie, 3 Wheat. (U. S.) 563.

If there are several legatees and all are *sui juris* and consent, the result is the same. Huber *v.* Donoghue, 49 N. J. Eq. 125; Mellen *v.* Mellen, 139 N. Y. 210; Trask *v.* Sturges, 170 N. Y. 482; Nye *v.* Koehne, 22 R. I. 118.

But unless they are all *sui juris* and consent, the directions of the testator must be followed. McDonald *v.* O'Hara, 144 N. Y. 566.

Mr. Baggallay, and *Mr. Hardy,* for the petitioners.

Mr. Charles Hall, for the trustees of the deed-poll, submitted that they were the proper persons to distribute the fund. . . .

THE MASTER OF THE ROLLS [SIR JOHN ROMILLY] said that where the donee of a general power appointed the property to certain persons beneficially, the original trustees were bound to carry the appointment into execution; but if the donee appointed the property to trustees, those trustees were entitled to receive the property to be held upon the trusts declared by the donee; and when a married woman made a will in exercise of a power, and appointed executors, inasmuch as she could only make her will by virtue of the power, and could only have appointed the executors for the purpose of administering the appointed property, she must be considered to have appointed the property to the executors as trustees.

The expression in the judgment in Platt *v.* Routh, that the executor could not have administered any part of the appointed property, only meant that, " but for the will exercising the power," the executor could not have administered.

By the appointment of executors, the duty of administering the fund was, in his Honor's opinion, taken away from the original trustees, and committed to the executors; and the provisions of the 23 Vict. c. 15, rather confirmed this view than otherwise. The fund must, therefore, be paid to the petitioners.[1]

[1] Cooper *v.* Thornton, 3 Bro. C. C. 96, 186; Angier *v.* Stannard, 3 M. & K. 566, 571; Wetherell *v.* Wilson, 1 Keen 80, 86; Poole *v.* Pass, 1 Beav. 600; Hayes *v.* Oatley, L. R. 14 Eq. 1; *Re* Hoskin's Trusts, 5 Ch. D. 229; 6 Ch. D. 281, s. c., *accord.* — AMES.

If a *cestui que trust* devises his interest to a new set of trustees upon a trust which fails, the new set of trustees may require a transfer of the legal estate from the old set of trustees, even though, under the doctrine of Burgess *v.* Wheate, 1 W. Bl. 123, there is no one entitled by way of resulting trust. Onslow *v.* Wallace, 1 Hall & T. 513.

Special power. In Busk *v.* Aldam, L. R. 19 Eq. 16, a testator bequeathed money in trust to pay the income to his daughter for life with power to her to appoint the fund to her children " in such manner " as she should direct, and in default of appointment to her children in equal shares. The daughter appointed the fund among the children, some of whom were infants, and directed that it should be paid and transferred to the trustees of her will. A bill was filed against the trustees of the testator's will by the trustees of the daughter's will to compel payment of the fund to them. A demurrer was sustained. Although the appointment to trustees for the children was a valid exercise of the power, it would violate the intention of the testator, the donor of the power, to compel his trustees to transfer the fund. See *Re* Tyssen, [1894] 1 Ch. 56; *Re* Mackenzie, [1916] 1 Ch. 125. See also Scotney *v.* Lomer, 29 Ch. D. 535, 545, 31 Ch. D. 380, 386.

But if the settlor intended to allow the donee of the power to substitute new trustees, then of course the donee may do so. *Re* Paget, [1898] 1 Ch. 290; *Re* Adams' Trustees, [1907] 1 Ch. 695.

APPENDIX A.

Modern Uses of the Trust Device.[1]

The corporate trustee. " Perhaps the most important American contribution to the development of the idea of the trust has been the creation of corporations specially chartered to act as trustees." Isaacs, Trusteeship in Modern Business, 42 Harv. L. Rev. 1048. The earliest instance of such a corporation seems to have been that of the Farmers' Fire Insurance & Loan Company, chartered in New York in 1822, which was specifically granted trust powers.[2] Since that time there has been a constant development of corporate trusteeship. In recent years the growth of the trust business done by corporate trustees has been very rapid. In 1917 by the Federal Reserve Act, national banks were authorized to act as trustees.[3] On June 30, 1930, it appeared that 2472 of the 7252 national banks in operation on that day had obtained authority to administer trusts and 1829 of them had established trust departments and were administering 79,112 individual trusts with assets aggregating nearly $4,500,000,000, and 11,511 corporate trusts and acting as trustee under securities issued aggregating nearly $12,000,000,000.[4] The trust business of state banks and trust companies has also been rapidly increasing, although similarly exact figures are not available.[5]

On the question of the standard of care required of corporate trustees, see the note to Morley v. Morley, *ante*.[6] As to the propriety of deposits of trust funds by a corporate trustee in its own banking department, see the note to Cornet v. Cornet, *ante*. In some states there are statutes making provisions as to the duties

[1] For a summary of the purposes for which trusts have been employed in the past, see Scott, The Trust as an Instrument of Law Reform, 31 Yale L. Jour. 457.

As to the corresponding civil-law devices, see Lepaulle, Civil Law Substitutes for Trusts, 36 Yale L. Jour. 1126.

[2] Smith, The Development of Trust Companies in the United States. See also 42 Harv. L. Rev. 1048, 1058. Compare Stephenson, English Executor and Trustee Business.

[3] See note to Attorney General v. Landerfield, *ante*.

[4] See the Sixty-Eighth Annual Report of the Comptroller of the Currency.

[5] For an account of the various services performed by trust companies, see Smith, Development of Trust Companies in the United States; Stephenson, English Executor and Trustee Business. See in addition such periodicals as the Journal of the American Bankers Association, Trust Companies, Fiduciary Law Chronicle, Banking Law Journal.

[6] See also Posner, Liability of the Trustee under the Corporate Indenture, 42 Harv. L. Rev. 198; 28 Col. L. Rev. 829.

of corporate trustees with respect to investments and other matters, which are not applicable to individual trustees.

Insurance trusts. In recent years schemes have been developed for combining life insurance and trusts. The insured makes the policies payable to a trust company, or assigns the policies to the trust company, upon trust for his widow and children or other beneficiaries. Sometimes the insured also transfers securities to the trust company in trust with a direction to pay the premiums on the policies out of the income of the securities. A trust of the latter sort is commonly called a " funded " life insurance trust.

Life insurance trusts are sometimes created not to provide for members of the family of the insured but for business purposes; as, for example, to furnish funds for the purchase by the surviving partners of the interest of a partner who dies. Such trusts are commonly called business life insurance trusts.

Although there are few judicial decisions in regard to insurance trusts, the problems which arise are discussed in many recent books and magazines.[1] Among the important legal questions with respect to insurance trusts are the following: whether the trust is a testamentary disposition; to what extent the rule against perpetuities and rules against accumulation are applicable; the extent of the rights of creditors of the settlor and of the beneficiaries; questions of liability for inheritance and income taxes.

To a certain extent insurance companies have issued policies under which they agree to hold the proceeds in trust after the death of the insured. It would seem, however, that since no property is held by the insurance company specifically for the beneficiaries, the company is not strictly a trustee.[2]

The trust as an instrument in avoiding or reducing taxes. To a certain extent the owner of property is enabled by the creation of a trust to avoid or reduce the amount of taxes which would otherwise be payable, either inheritance taxes, income taxes or property taxes.[3] It is impossible to consider the question of the efficacy of the trust device for this purpose without considering the whole subject of taxation, which is beyond the scope of a course on Trusts.

[1] See Horton, Some Legal Aspects of Life Insurance Trusts; Shattuck, The Living Insurance Trust; Scully, Insurance Trusts; Stephenson, Living Trusts; Remsen, The Preparation of Wills and Trusts; Prentice-Hall Trust Service; Commerce Clearing House Trust Service; Bogert, Funded Insurance Trusts and the Rule against Accumulations, 9 Cornell L. Quar. 113; Hanna, Some Legal Aspects of Life Insurance Trusts, 78 U. Pa. L. Rev. 346; Fraser, Personal Life Insurance Trusts in New York, 16 Cornell L. Quar. 19.

[2] But see New York Life Ins. Co. *v.* O'Brien, 22 F.(2d) 1016, 27 F.(2d) 773. See Van Hecke, Insurance Trusts — The Insurer as Trustee, 7 N. C. L. Rev. 21; 77 U. Pa. L. Rev. 430; 36 Yale L. Jour. 376. In a number of states statutes have been enacted allowing restraints upon the alienation of the interest of the beneficiaries. See 23 Ill. L. Rev. 755; 7 N. C. L. Rev. 24.

[3] See Robinson, Saving Taxes in Drafting Wills and Trusts.

The trust in business. Trusts have been employed not only for the purposes of testamentary disposition and family settlements but have been frequently employed as a business device. As Professor Isaacs has said,[1] "trusteeship has become a readily available tool for everyday purposes of organization, financing, risk-shifting, credit operations, settling of disputes, and liquidation of business affairs." He also points out that "modern business has become honey-combed with trusteeship. Next to contract, the universal tool, and incorporation, the standard instrument of organization, it takes its place wherever the relations to be established are too delicate or too novel for these coarser devices."[2]

One of the most striking uses of the trust in business is to be found in the business trust or Massachusetts trust, as it is sometimes called. The question how far such trusts are effective for the desired purpose of securing limited liability without incorporation is so dependent upon the law governing partnerships, corporations and other business associations that it is deemed unwise to take it up in a course on Trusts.[3]

The trust has been frequently employed in real estate transactions as in the case of office buildings, suburban sub-divisions, co-operative apartment houses and the like, where there are difficulties in the way of splitting the legal ownership.[4] The business trust in Massachusetts was originally employed for dealing in land because incorporation for such purposes was not permitted by the legislature.

Trusts have frequently been created for the protection of creditors. Thus, it is not uncommon for a debtor who is pressed for payment by his creditors to make an assignment of his property in trust for them, or he may transfer property in trust to pay or as security for the payment of a particular debt. Corporations in issuing bonds or other obligations commonly transfer their property by deed of trust to trust companies or banks as security. In all these cases, however, the law which governs is so profoundly affected by the law governing credit transactions where the trust is not employed that it is commonly considered in other courses rather than in a course on Trusts.[5]

The trust has been employed with varying success in attempts

[1] 42 Harv. L. Rev. 1048.

[2] 42 Harv. L. Rev. 1060. See also Scott, The Trust as an Instrument of Law Reform, 31 Yale L. Jour. 457.

[3] See Rhode Island Hospital Trust Co. *v.* Copeland, *ante.* See also Warren, Corporate Advantages without Incorporation.

[4] See Bogert, Trusts and Escrows in Credit Conveyancing, 21 Ill. L. Rev. 655. See also Chicago etc. Ry. *v.* Des Moines etc. Ry., 254 U. S. 196 (railroad terminal).

[5] See Perry, Trusts, c. 20; Jones, Mortgages, 8 ed., c. 40; Smith, Development of Trust Companies in the United States, c. 5; Kidd, Trust Deeds and Mortgages in California, 3 Cal. L. Rev. 381; 32 W. Va. L. Rev. 61. See Chap. I, sec. VI, *ante.*

to secure united ownership of property. The use of the trust device in attempting to effect combinations in restraint of trade became so notorious that the term " trust " acquired a stigma otherwise undeserved. Voting trusts,[1] equipment trusts, investment trusts, trust receipts,[2] are other instances of the use of the trust in business. In many of these cases, however, although the trust was the device first employed, it has been superseded by other devices, although often the term " trust " is still retained.

Conclusion. No attempt is here made to summarize the purposes for which the trust can be employed, which are limited only by the imagination of lawyers and men of business and by the policy of the law.

[1] As to the legality of voting trusts, see Cushing, Voting Trusts, 2 ed.; Wormser, The Legality of Corporate Voting Trusts and Pooling Agreements, 18 Col. L. Rev. 123; Smith, Limitations on the Validity of Voting Trusts, 22 Col. L. Rev. 627; Finkelstein, Voting Trust Agreements, 24 Mich. L. Rev. 344; Bergerman, Voting Trusts and Non-Voting Stock, 37 Yale L. Jour. 445; 40 Harv. L. Rev. 106.

[2] As to the nature of trust receipts, see Frederick, The Trust Receipt as Security, 22 Col. L. Rev. 395, 546; Hanna, Trust Receipts, 29 Col. L. Rev. 545; 8 Minn. L. Rev. 144; Williston, Sales, 2 ed., sec. 338a.

APPENDIX B.

Form of Deed of Trust.

[This deed of trust is taken from the record of Bemis *v.* Converse, 246 Mass. 131, except that the original has no punctuation marks.]

THIS INDENTURE made this 18th day of November in the year 1910 between Harry E. Converse of Marion of the first part and Frank B. Bemis of Beverly, Moorfield Storey of Lincoln, and Edward M. Benson of Cambridge, all of Massachusetts (hereinafter called the trustees) of the second part

WITNESSETH

That I, the said Harry E. Converse, hereby convey, assign, transfer and deliver to the said Bemis, Storey and Benson the property enumerated and described in the schedule hereto attached marked " A " and verified by the signatures of the parties hereto; To have and to hold the same to the said Bemis, Storey and Benson and their heirs, successors and assigns upon the trusts hereinafter stated, that is to say

In trust to hold and safely invest the same and pay the net income thereof to me during my natural life, and upon my death

In trust to pay the net income thereof in equal shares to such of my children as shall be living when such income accrues, the issue for the time being in existence of any who may have died to take the share which such deceased child would have taken if living as long as any child of mine shall survive me. Provided however that during the minority of each beneficiary subject to the foregoing provisions the trustees shall pay over to him or her or spend for his or her benefit only such portion of such minor's income as shall in their discretion be reasonably needed for his or her support, maintenance or other proper expenditure, holding the balance of such income and investing it for the benefit of such minor until he or she reaches the age of twenty-one years, and then paying it over to him or her, or if he or she shall die without attaining that age then adding the same to the capital of the share from which it arose.

And upon the death of the last survivor of my children or upon my death if I leave no child surviving me *in trust* to divide the principal fund equally among the issue of my children, it being my will that such issue shall take by right of representation according to the stocks treating my children as the original stocks; Provided however that whenever any child of mine shall reach the age of twenty-five years or shall marry under that age the trustees shall pay over to him or her one-fifth part of that share of the principal trust fund of which such child is entitled to receive the income, and further they shall have power in their discretion to pay over to any child of mine at any time and from time to time after such child shall have reached the age of thirty years such further portion or portions of such share as they shall think wise not exceeding however such an amount as including the said one-fifth shall equal two thirds of the said share.

In case upon my death or upon the death of the last survivor of my children there shall be no issue of mine surviving, in that event *In trust* to divide all the trust property in their hands among the persons who in that event would then have been entitled to receive my personal property under the laws of Massachusetts had I then died domiciled in Massachusetts and intestate, each person to receive such share thereof as he would have received of my personal property in that event under the statutes regulating the distribution of personal estate of intestates.

Whenever by death or otherwise the number of trustees shall be reduced to less than three, the remaining trustees or trustee shall appoint in writing a sufficient number of trustees to make with the remaining trustees or trustee the number of trustees up to two at least; and upon such appointment the trust estate and all the powers of the trustees shall be vested in the new trustee or trustees jointly with such remaining trustees or trustee. But notwithstanding this provision the said remaining trustees or trustee may before such appointment have and exercise all the estate, rights, powers and discretions which would have been had or exercised by all the three trustees had no vacancy occurred.

The trustees for the time being acting hereunder shall render in writing to each of my children semi-annual statements of the income and disbursements received and made in respect of said trust funds.

The trustees shall have power to hold the property invested as they receive it or at their discretion to sell and dispose of the same or any part thereof or any substituted property at any time held under the trusts hereof either by public auction or private contract, upon such terms and at such times as they see fit, and to make all requisite deeds and transfers and to invest the proceeds according to their best judgment, with power to convert real estate into personal and personal into real, and to manage and improve all real estate at any time subject to the trusts herein declared, and to insure against fire or other casualty, and to grant leases and to make allowances to and arrangements with tenants and others and to accept surrenders of leases and tenancies and to make such outlay as the trustees shall consider proper for the benefit of the said real estate; And to exchange any such real estate for other real estate, and to make partition of any real estate, and to give and accept money for equality of exchange or partition and to execute for the said purposes all proper deeds and instruments.

The trustees shall also have full power to let real estate for improvement, and any leases which they may grant shall be valid although the trusts may terminate before the end of the term. Such leases may be given to commence at any time and may contain options of purchase. And the trustees shall have power to build or rebuild any buildings upon property and to improve any estate and for that purpose to mortgage with or without power of sale.

The receipts of the trustees for any money or thing paid, transferred or delivered to them shall be sufficient discharges to the person or persons paying, transferring or delivering the same therefor and from all liability to see to the application thereof; And no purchaser or other person or company shall be obliged to ascertain the occurrence or existence of any event or purpose in or for which a sale is herein authorized or directed.

All rents, dividends, and other payments in the nature of income shall for the purposes of the trust be considered as accruing from day to day like interest on money lent and be apportionable in respect of time accordingly. And the trustees shall have full powers of determining all questions in regard to such apportionment, and all questions whether any moneys or things are to be treated as capital or income, and of determining the mode in which the expenses of management and other expenses incidental to or connected with the execution of the trusts hereof ought to be borne as between capital and income or otherwise, which powers shall include the power of determining in case the trustees shall make any investment in any bond or security for money at a premium whether and to what extent and in what manner any part of the actual income of such bond or security shall be dealt with as capital with a view to prevent the diminution of capital by reason of the payment of such premium; And every such determination whether made upon a question actually raised or implied in the acts or proceedings of the trustees shall be conclusive and binding upon all persons interested.

The trustees shall also have power to pay over the whole income of any securities or other investments which they receive from the trust estate to the persons entitled thereto without setting apart any portion thereof for the purpose of making good any waste in such securities or property. In case any trustee hereunder named after qualifying shall be absent from the Commonwealth of Massachusetts or in any way incapacitated, the other trustees shall have full power to act in all matters respecting the trust during such absence or incapacity.

All income payable to any female under any of the provisions of this indenture and all property coming to any female under any of its provisions shall be to her sole and separate use free from the interference and control of her husband. And the provisions of this indenture are made subject to this provision to wit that neither the income nor any part of the income payable to any child of mine or to any issue of any deceased child of mine under any of the provisions hereof shall be paid by way of anticipation or before the payment thereof be assignable or attachable or trusteeable or in any way or manner liable to be taken for or applied to the payment of any debt, liability or contract of such child or issue.

No trustee under this indenture shall be liable for the defaults of any other trustee thereunder but each only for his own wilful neglect or defaults.

The trustees shall have power at any time or times to allot any part or parts of the trust premises in the actual state of investment thereof for the time being or in money in or towards satisfaction of any share thereof and conclusively to determine in such manner as the trustees shall think fit the value of the trust premises or any part or parts thereof for the purpose of such allotment, and every such allotment shall take effect from such time or times and be made in such manner as the trustees shall think proper and may be made upon the terms of such sum or sums of money as the trustees may think proper being paid for equality.

As it will doubtless be convenient in the administration of the trust property that one trustee should attend to the business details, such as the collection of income, the keeping of the books and the current business of the trust estate, I direct that the trustee who shall be charged by his associates with this work shall be paid a reasonable salary to be fixed by the trustees in addition to his share of the compensation received by the trustees, which salary shall be treated as an expense of the trust.

I, the said Harry E. Converse, shall be at liberty at any time to add any real or personal estate to the trust premises comprised in this indenture; And all such real estate shall be vested in the trustees upon and subject to the like trusts, powers and provisions as if the same were real estate in which they had invested part of the trust premises under the provisions hereinbefore contained; And all such personal estate shall be vested in the trustees upon and subject to the like trusts, powers and provisions as if the same were part of the personal estate comprised in these presents; And a description of all real and personal estate so added or intended to be added to the trust premises shall be inserted in the said schedule with a heading or other statement specifying that the same has been added thereto.

It shall be lawful for the said Harry E. Converse at any time or times during his life by any deed or deeds expressly referring to this power or to this indenture wholly or partially to revoke and make void the trusts, powers and provisions herein contained concerning the trust premises, and to declare such new or other trusts of and concerning the same or any part or parts thereof as he may think fit for the benefit of himself and his executors or administrators or any other person or persons or direct the trustees to transfer the trust premises or any part thereof to such person or persons and in such manner as he shall think fit; And the trustees shall thenceforth stand possessed of or deal with the same accordingly.

And we, Frank B. Bemis, Moorfield Storey and Edward M. Benson, hereby accept the transfer and conveyance of the property enumerated in schedule " A " and agree to hold and deal with the same and any other property which may at any time be added thereto upon the trusts hereinbefore set forth.

In witness whereof we, the said Harry E. Converse, Frank B. Bemis, Moorfield Storey and Edward M. Benson, have hereunto set our hands and seals the day and year first above written.

Harry E. Converse
Frank B. Bemis
Moorfield Storey
Edward M. Benson

APPENDIX C.

Form of Unfunded Life Insurance Trust Agreement.[1]

THIS AGREEMENT, made this the ....
day of ...., 19.... and executed
in duplicate between ....
.... of
...., hereinafter called
Insured, and —— Trust Company, a corporation organized under
the laws of the State of ——, hereinafter called Trustee, Witnesseth
That:

Insurance Policies

Item I. Insured has caused his life to be insured, and said insurance is represented by insurance policies deposited with Trustee as set forth on the sheet attached, marked " A " and made a part of this agreement, which policies are now or hereafter will be made payable to Trustee.

Payment of Premiums

Item II. The duty and responsibility concerning the payment of premiums and assessments and other charges on such policies shall rest solely upon Insured.

Rights Reserved by Insured

Item III. Section 1. This agreement shall be operative only with respect to the net proceeds of such policies as may be due and payable upon the death of Insured; and during his lifetime all rights of every nature accruing solely to Insured are hereby reserved by him to be exercised in accordance with the terms of the respective policies, but if the consent of Trustee as beneficiary is necessary at any time Trustee agrees to give its consent which consent shall bind all the beneficiaries of this trust.

Sec. 2. Insured also reserves the right during his lifetime to withdraw any or all of the policies from the operation of this agreement; to change the beneficiaries under the agreement, their respective shares, and the plan of distribution; to designate Trustee beneficiary in additional policies; and to modify, amend, add to, or revoke this agreement.

[1] This form is used by one of the well-known trust companies.

Duties of Trustees as to Collection of Insurance

Item IV. Section 1. As soon as practicable after the death of Insured, Trustee shall make proper proofs of death and shall collect all moneys due under the policies then within the operation of this agreement.

Sec. 2. Trustee shall not be required to maintain any litigation to enforce the payment of any of the policies unless it is indemnified to its satisfaction against all expense and liability arising from such litigation. If Trustee shall elect to demand indemnity, it shall make such demand in writing upon each of the beneficiaries under this agreement by mailing or delivering the same to his last known address. If satisfactory indemnity is not furnished within thirty days thereafter, Trustee shall assign its rights as beneficiary under the policy in question to the beneficiaries under this agreement and thereupon its liability with respect to such policy shall cease.

Sec. 3. Trustee is authorized to compromise and adjust claims arising out of the insurance policies or any of them, upon such terms and conditions as it may deem just, and the decisions of Trustee shall be binding and conclusive upon all persons interested therein.

Powers of Trustee

Item V. Section 1. Trustee shall receive, hold, manage, convert, sell, assign, alter, reinvest, and otherwise deal with the moneys realized from such policies as it in its discretion shall deem to be for the best interests of the beneficiaries hereunder to the same extent that Insured, himself, might do.

Sec. 2. By way of illustration but not of limitation of Trustee's powers, Insured hereby authorizes Trustee:

(*a*) To acquire by purchase or exchange or otherwise properties belonging to Insured's general estate and hold them as a part of the trust estate so long as to Trustee shall seem advisable;

(*b*) To participate in the liquidation, reorganization, consolidation, or other financial readjustment of any corporation or business in which the trust estate is or shall be financially interested;

(*c*) To determine what expenses and other charges shall be charged against principal and what against income;

(*d*) To invest the trust funds in such properties as it shall deem advisable even though they are not technically recognized as legal investments for fiduciaries in the State of ———;

(*e*) To borrow money for the benefit of the trust estate and, if required to do so, secure the same by collateral or mortgage;

(*f*) To compromise, arbitrate, or otherwise adjust claims in favor of or against the trust estate;

(*g*) To execute and deliver deeds of conveyance, assignments, powers of attorney for the transfer of shares of stock, contracts, bills of sale, notes, and other instruments in writing deemed by Trustee to be required for the administration of this trust;

(*h*) To receive all rents, profits, and income of every nature due the trust estate; and

(*i*) To take up or to sell rights accruing to it through the holding of any securities for account of the trust estate.

Sec. 3. Persons dealing with Trustee are not required to see to the application made by Trustee of the funds or other properties received by Trustee from such persons.

Distribution Provisions

Trustee shall administer this trust estate for the following uses and purposes:

Right of Trustee to Resign

Item VI. Trustee reserves the right to resign this trusteeship during Insured's lifetime by giving him thirty days notice in writing, but after his death only for cause satisfactory to the Court of —— of the State of ——, which court shall have authority, if it deem advisable, to accept the resignation and appoint a successor clothed with all the powers of the original Trustee.

Termination of Trust

Item VII. Unless terminated earlier under the foregoing provisions, each trust herein established shall in any event terminate twenty-one years after the death of the last survivor of the beneficiaries of such trust who shall be living at the date of the execution of this trust agreement; at which time — *i.e.*, of such last mentioned termination — the principal, discharged of all trusts, shall be delivered to the one immediately theretofore entitled to the income and, if there shall be more than one beneficiary of the same trust, each of them shall be entitled to the same proportion of the principal as he had been immediately theretofore entitled to the income. This provision is to be construed as a part of and as a limitation upon the duration of each of the trusts created by this trust agreement.

Provision Against Encumbrancing

Item VIII. Every payment of income and distribution of principal herein provided for shall be made to the one entitled thereto upon his receipt only and free in every way from his debts, engagements, and control; and such income or principal shall not be subject to assignment or attachment or execution or other process of law at the hands of creditors, assignees of creditors, or other persons claiming under them or any of them.

Accrued Income

ITEM IX. Dividends declared but not paid and income accrued but not received at the time of the termination of any estate hereunder shall, when received, belong and be payable to the beneficiary entitled to the next eventual estate.

Successor Trustee

ITEM X. If Trustee shall, during the term of this trust, transfer its trust business to any other corporation authorized to do trust business by merger or consolidation or reorganization or be converted into a national banking association authorized to do trust business, such transferee corporation or such association and its successors shall thereupon without further transfer, substitution, act, or deed become subrogated and succeed as Trustee hereunder, vested with all the trust estate, rights, obligations, powers, discretions, immunities, privileges, and compensations herein conferred upon —— Trust Company. This is supplementary to and not in limitation of any law on the subject that now exists or that may be hereafter enacted.

Inspection of Books and Annual Accounts

ITEM XI. Trustee's books relating to this trust shall be open at all reasonable hours for the inspection of any and all adult beneficiaries and guardians of minor beneficiaries of this trust, and Trustee shall render to each adult beneficiary and guardian of minor beneficiary an annual statement of account showing in detail receipts, disbursements, and distributions of both principal and income of the trust estate.

Construction of Contract

ITEM XII. This trust has been accepted by Trustee in the State of ——, and all questions pertaining to its validity, construction, and administration shall be determined in accordance with the laws of said State.

Compensation of Trustee

ITEM XIII. As compensation for its services Trustee shall retain ...... per cent of the gross income to be taken ...., and .... per cent of the principal at its then market value to be taken at the time of ....

IN WITNESS WHEREOF, Insured has hereunto set his hand and affixed his seal; and Trustee, in acceptance of the trusts herein created, has caused these presents to be signed by one of its Vice-Presidents and attested by its Secretary and has caused its corporate seal to be attached on the date stated above.

.................................(SEAL)
Insured

Witness:
.... —— TRUST COMPANY, *Trustee*
Attest:
.... By ....
     Secretary   *Vice-President*

RECEIPT FOR LIFE INSURANCE POLICIES

Sheet A

—— TRUST COMPANY acknowledges receipt of the following life insurance policies which are to be held in trust for the purposes set forth in the foregoing trust agreement of which this sheet is specifically made a part:

INDEX

ALIENATION. See *Transfer of interest of c.q.t.*
APPLICATION OF PURCHASE-MONEY, 718.
APPOINTMENT OF TRUSTEES, 241–245.
ASSIGNMENT. See *Choses in action; Transfer of interest of c.q.t.*
BAILMENT, trust distinguished, 14, 15.
BANKRUPTCY, of c.q.t., 637–656; of trustee, rights of trustee's private creditors, 688; rights of trust creditors, 600.
BANKS, deposit of money, 46–68; general deposit, 46; deposit by trustee, 46; deposit for special purpose, 49–59; deposit for transmission, 59–68; deposit of commercial paper, 69–83; gift of deposit, 158, 162n.; tentative trusts, 200; mingling by bank, 508–516; deposit of trust funds, 552–555; what is value, 681; notice to bank, 713.
BREACH OF TRUST. See *Liability of trustee to c.q.t.; Purchaser.*
CESTUI QUE TRUST, person not *in esse*, 250; who is c.q.t., 251–258; no definite c.q.t., 258–286; erection of tombstone, 275; masses, 275; animals, 277; slaves, 281; blocking up house, 281; voluntary association, 283–286. See *Charitable trusts.*
CHARITABLE TRUSTS, 287–336; Statute of Charitable Uses, 287; no definite c.q.t., 288–299; restrictions on charitable trusts, 299; poverty, 302; religion, 304; education, 308; public purposes, 310; various "causes," 311; definite c.q.t., 317; cy pres, 318–336; tort liability, 613–621.
CHOSES IN ACTION, trust and assignment, 96–109; remedy of assignee, 96; remedy of c.q.t., 98; payment to trustee, 101; payment to c.q.t., 103; remedy of assignee of part, 104; payment to assignor of part, 107, gratuitous assignment, 152–162; gratuitous partial assignment, 164; successive assignments, 660; Statute of Limitations, 674; assignment of chose in action held in trust, 742; payment to purchaser by obligor having equitable defence, 746. See *Consideration; Purchaser.*
CLASS, power of selection among, 125–128, 132, 268, 339.
CONDITION, trust distinguished, 83–88.
CONSIDERATION, 137–172; bargain and sale, 137–139; covenant to stand seised, 139–141; declaration of trust, 142; executory trust, 144; trust and gift distinguished, 145–151; gift of choses in action, 152–165; extinguishment of chose in action, 163; gift of equitable interest, 163; gratuitous partial assignment, 164; voluntary covenant in trust, 166. See *Choses in action; Purchaser.*
CONSTRUCTIVE TRUSTS. See *Resulting and constructive trusts.*
CONTRACT. See *Debt.*
CONVERSION, breach of trust distinguished, 16–20; duty to convert investments, 547; right of c.q.t. to prevent conversion, 797.
CREATION OF TRUSTS. See *Consideration; Intention; Statute of Frauds; Wills.*
CREDITORS, of c.q.t., 633–659; of trustee, 688–696. See *Liabilities to third persons.*
CURTESY. See *Dower and curtesy.*
DEBT, trust distinguished, 20–83; risk of loss, 21; effect of insolvency, 22; effect of provision for payment of interest, 22, 27; nature of remedies, 24; Statute of Limitations, 27; embezzlement, 30; liability of stock-

broker, 30; contract for benefit of third party, 35–43. See *Banks.*
DISCLAIMER, by trustee, 228, 235–237.
DISSEISIN. See *Purchaser.*
DOWER AND CURTESY, death of c.q.t., 626–632; of trustee, 669.
DUTIES OF TRUSTEE. See *Investment of trust funds; Powers and duties of trustee; Remedies of c.q.t. against trustee.*
EMINENT DOMAIN, 672n.
EQUITABLE CHARGE, trust distinguished, 91–96; Statute of Limitations, 91; liability of devisee, 93; right to transfer land subject to charge, 94.
ESCHEAT, death of c.q.t., 338n., 625; of trustee, 670.
EXECUTORS, trustees distinguished, 110–124; Statute of Limitations, 110–117; action for death by wrongful act, 117; when executorship terminates and trust begins, 110; double commissions, 122; carrying on testator's business, 602.
EXONERATION, of trustee, 591n.
FAILURE, of trustee, 226–235; of trust, 337–356. See *Resulting and constructive trusts; Charitable trusts.*
FOLLOWING TRUST-RES. See *Resulting and constructive trusts.*
FRAUD. See *Resulting and constructive trusts.*
GIFTS. See *Choses in action; Consideration.*
HEIR, of c.q.t., 623; of trustee, 668.
ILLEGAL TRUSTS, 281, 307n., 318, 348, 373n., 390, 414.
INCOME AND PRINCIPAL. See *Life tenant and remainderman.*
INTENTION, language necessary for creation of trust, 125–137.
INVESTMENT OF TRUST FUNDS, 542–555; mortgages, 542; duty of care, 543; corporate stock, 544; distribution of investments, 544; converting investments, 547; deposit of trust funds in banks, 552–555. See *Life tenant and remainderman.*
LIABILITIES TO THIRD PERSONS, 587–621; heriot, 587; assessment on stock, 587; taxes, 589; contracts, 590–595; torts, 596; bankruptcy of trustee, 600; carrying on testator's business, 602; contracts " as trustee," 605–608; business trusts, 609; charitable trusts, 613–621.
LIABILITY OF TRUSTEE TO C.Q.T., 580–586; failure to purchase, 580; set off of losses and gains, 584; intermediate profits, 585. See *Powers and duties of trustee; Investment of trust funds; Remedies of c.q.t. against trustee; Resulting and constructive trusts.*
LIFE TENANT AND REMAINDERMAN, 555–579; allocation of expenses, 555; extraordinary dividends, 559; unproductive property, 573; wasting property, 576n.; bonds purchased at a premium, 577.
MERGER. See *Purchaser; Termination of trusts.*
MORTGAGES, trusts distinguished, 89, 90; power to mortgage, 529n.; investment, 542–544; tacking, 699; mortgage by trustee, 753.
MURDER, of ancestor or testator, 406.
NOTICE, by assignee of chose in action or equitable interest, 660, 761; to purchaser, 696–719.
PAROL EVIDENCE RULE, 173.
PERPETUITY, 275–286, 613n., 644n., 786n.
POSTPONEMENT OF ENJOYMENT. See *Termination of trusts.*
POWERS AND DUTIES OF THE TRUSTEE, 528–541; power of sale, 528; mortgage, 529n.; lease, 529n.; repairs and improvements, 529n.; unanimity, 530; survival of powers, 530; control of discretion, 530; delegation, 534–535; duty of care, 536; competition, 537; deviation from terms of the trust, 538. See *Investment of trust funds.*
PRECATORY TRUSTS, 125–131.
PURCHASER, 667–768; purchaser with notice, 667; heir, 668; donee, 668; tenant in dower and by curtesy, 669; general and special occupant, 669n.; escheat and forfeiture, 670; merger, 670n.; converter, 671; disseisor, 673–674; obligor of chose in action, 674; right of trustee against purchaser with notice, 675–680; ef-

fect of Statute of Limitations, 674, 678; who is purchaser for value, 680–696; promise to pay, 680–684; part payment, 684; antecedent debt, 83n., 685; assignee for creditors, trustee in bankruptcy, 688; estoppel, 689; purchaser on execution sale, 693; purchaser acquiring title after notice, 696–700; purchase in name of another, 701; notice, 701–719; repurchase by trustee, 719; conflicting equities, 720–742; assignment of chose in action held in trust, 742; payment by obligor of chose in action having equitable defence, 746; assignment of equitable interest subject to an equity, 749–765; settlement by trustee with c.q.t., without knowledge of assignment, 765.

REIMBURSEMENT OF TRUSTEE, 591n.

REMEDIES OF C.Q.T. AGAINST TRUSTEE, 517–527; special assumpsit, 517; covenant, 518; account, debt and general assumpsit, 20, 519–522; other actions at law, 521–525; land outside the jurisdiction, 525; methods of protecting equitable interests, 526.

REMOVAL OF TRUSTEE, 246–249.

RESIGNATION OF TRUSTEE, 238.

RESULTING AND CONSTRUCTIVE TRUSTS, 337–516.

(1) Failure of express trust, 125, 258, 268, 337–356; partial failure, 339–348; effect of illegality, 348; ineffectual appointment, 352; consideration paid by trustee, 354.

(2) Trust of surplus, 95, 356–367; resulting trust presumed, 357; presumption rebutted, 360; contributions by several persons, 364–367; parol evidence, 368.

(3) Failure to declare trust, 368–413; resulting use or trust, 368; oral agreement to hold for grantor, 370–375; fraud, 375; confidential relation, 378; purchase on judicial sale, 382; oral agreement to hold for third person, 384–386; fraud in preventing execution of will, 386; oral agreement by devisee to hold for third person, 388–406; illegal secret trust, 390; uncommunicated direction to devisee, 391; name of beneficiary not communicated, 394; existence of trust disclosed in will, 398–406; murder by devisee or heir, 406.

(4) Payment of purchase-money for conveyance to another, 413–439; illegal purpose, 414; purchase in name of child, 415; agreement by grantee to hold for purchaser, 419; statute abolishing r.t., 420; to hold for third person, 423; loan to grantee, 428; loan to purchaser, 430; payment by note, 433; payment of part of purchase-money, 435–439.

(5) Acquisition of property by abuse of fiduciary position, 440–475; purchase of trust property by trustee, 440; incumbrance on trust property, 442; sale to trust estate, 443; commissions, 445; renewal of lease, 447–462; purchase by one for himself of property which he orally agreed to purchase for another, 462; acquisition by employee, 465–475.

(6) Acquisition of property by wrongful use of property of another, 475–516; purchase by fiduciary, 475; purchase by non-fiduciary, 479–482; profit made by innocent purchaser from converter, 483; mingling wrongdoer's own money, 486–516; mingling money of several, 495; subrogation, 503; mingling by banks, 508–516.

REVOCATION. See *Termination of trusts.*

SECRET TRUSTS. See *Resulting and constructive trusts.*

SPENDTHRIFT TRUSTS. See *Transfer of interest of c.q.t.*

STATUTE OF FRAUDS, creation of trusts, 172–190; part performance, 174n.; trusts of personalty, 175–179; effect of subsequent memorandum, 180–187; extinguishment of trusts, 188; resulting and constructive trusts,

368–386, 413–439, 462; sec. 10, rights of creditors of c.q.t., 635. See *Resulting and constructive trusts*.

STATUTE OF LIMITATIONS, trust and debt, 33, 44; trust and equitable charge, 91; trust and executorship, 110–117; adverse possession of trust estate, 674; chose in action held in trust, 44, 674; purchaser from trustee, 678.

SUBJECT-MATTER OF A TRUST, 206–220; necessity of trust-*res*, 206; copyright, 207; trade secret, 208; expectancies, 212–216; non-transferable property, 216–220. See *Chose in action; Debt*.

TAXES, 204, 589.

TENTATIVE TRUST, 200.

TERMINATION OF TRUSTS, 769–801; revocation, 769–771; rescission or reformation, 771n.; merger, 771; power of c.q.t. to terminate the trust in whole or in part, 774–796; hastening enjoyment, 779–790; discretionary trust, 790; spendthrift trust, 793; right of c.q.t. to prevent conversion, 797; trust and subtrust, 798–801.

TRANSFER OF INTEREST OF C.Q.T., 622–666; assignability of use and trust, 622; death of c.q.t., 623–625; who takes as heir, 623; death of joint tenant, 623; attainder of c.q.t. of personalty, 624; of realty, 625; barring equitable entail, 625; dower and curtesy in equitable interests, 626–632; husband's rights during coverture, 632; wife's separate estate, 632; rights of creditors of c.q.t., 633–659; equitable assets, 636; restraints on alienation, spendthrift trusts, 637–652; statutory restraints, 644; discretionary trusts, 652–659; successive assignments of equitable interests, 660; assignment by trustee who has a beneficial interest, 664.

TRANSFER BY TRUSTEE. See *Purchaser*.

TRUSTEE, 221–249; sovereign, 221; alien, 222; corporation, 222; infant, 224; lunatic, 225; married woman, 225; failure of the trustee, 226–235; disclaimer, 228, 235–237; incapacity of trustee of living trust, 231; resignation, 238; death of trustee, 240; appointment, 241–245; removal, 246–249.

USES, origin, 1; Statute of Uses, 1; active trusts, 3–7; term for years, 7, 8; devises to uses, 7n.; use on a use, 8–11; legislation in New York, 12.

VESTING OF THE ESTATE, 242–245, 527.

WILLS, devises to uses, 7n.; what is testamentary disposition, 191–205; inheritance tax, 204; resulting and constructive trusts, 363, 386–406.